The not so Perfect Fairy

This edition published in 2004
by Armadillo Books
an imprint of
Bookmart Limited
Registered Number 2372865
Trading as Bookmart Limited
Blaby Road
Wigston
Leicestershire
LE18 4SE

ISBN 1-84322-396-1

1 3 5 7 9 10 8 6 4 2

Produced for
Bookmart Limited by
Nicola Baxter
PO Box 215
Framingham Earl
Norwich NR14 7UR

Designer: Amanda Hawkes
Production designer: Amy Barton

Printed in China

Starting to read – it's perfect!

The not-so-perfect fairy in this story helps to make
sharing books at home successful and enjoyable.
The book can be used in several ways to help
beginning readers gain confidence.

You could start by reading the illustrated words
at the edge of each lefthand page with your
child. Have fun trying to spot the same words in
the story itself.

All the words on the righthand page have already
been met on the facing page. Help your child to
read these by pointing out words and groups of
words already met.

Finally, all the illustrated words can be found
at the end of the book. Enjoy checking all the
words you can both read!

The ^(not so) Perfect Fairy

Written by Nicola Baxter · Illustrated by Pauline Siewert

ARMADILLO

fairy

granny

suitcase

mother

Little Fairy Fluff is very excited. She is going to stay with her granny.

She packs her suitcase with all the things she needs.

"Now I will pack it again with all the things you **really** need!" says her mother.

Her mother packs the suitcase.

house

stairs

bed

book

Fairy Fluff's mother takes her to Granny's house. It is not far away.

"How lovely to see you!" says Granny.

She takes Fairy Fluff up the stairs.

"This is your bed," she says.

There is a big book on the bed.

"Oh dear," says Granny. "I forgot that was there."

Granny takes the book away.

window

rain

shop

basket

The next day, Granny looks out of the window.

"Look at the rain!" she says. "Oh dear, I must go to the shop. You stay here, Fairy Fluff."

"I will put the breakfast things away for you," says Fairy Fluff.

Granny takes her basket and waves goodbye.

"I will only be a minute," she says.

Fairy Fluff waves out of the window.

plate

milk

chair

shelf

Fairy Fluff tries to tidy up. She is not careful.

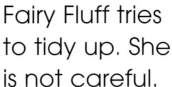

Oh dear! She drops a plate!

Oh dear! She spills the milk!

Oh dear! She knocks over a chair!

Oh dear! Oh dear! Oh dear! Fairy Fluff knocks down a shelf.

"What shall I do now?" says Fairy Fluff. "Look at Granny's house!"

Now Granny's house is not tidy!

wand

Suddenly, Fairy Fluff sees the big book. It is a magic book!

"I could say a spell to tidy everything up," says Fairy Fluff. "I will need my wand."

floor

The wand is in her suitcase. Fairy Fluff is in a hurry.

shoes

clothes

Oh dear! The suitcase falls on the floor! Out fall her shoes and her clothes.

"I will need to hurry to tidy up!"
says Fairy Fluff.

eyes

Fairy Fluff goes downstairs. She chooses a spell. She shuts her eyes. She waves her wand. She says the words in the book.

words

stars

Magic stars appear. But Fairy Fluff has only just learnt to read.

The spell is for a clean, tidy house. Oh no! Fairy Fluff says a spell for a clean, tidy mouse!

mouse

Oh no! Fairy Fluff has a mouse!

rolls

cakes

biscuits

jelly

Just then, Granny comes home. She sees all the mess.

"Oh, Fairy Fluff," she says.

Fairy Fluff is very sorry. Granny smiles. "Never mind. I will say a spell to put everything right."

Soon it is teatime. Granny makes rolls, cakes, biscuits and a jelly!

The house looks lovely again. And the magic book has been hidden safely away!

Everything is all right again.

Picture dictionary

Now you can read these words!

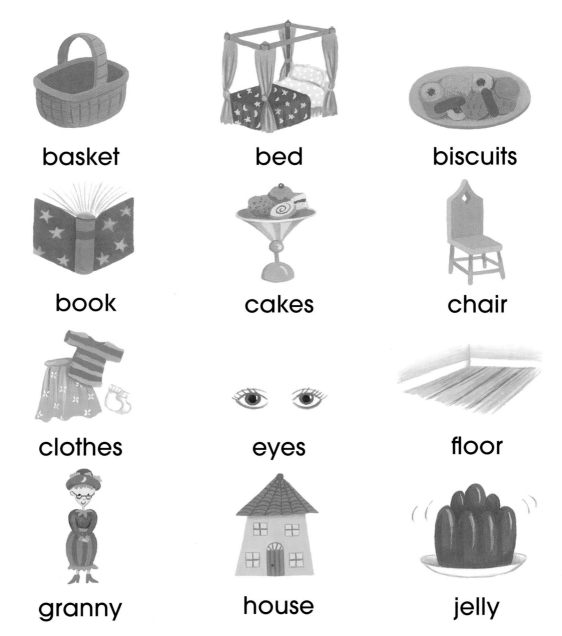

basket

bed

biscuits

book

cakes

chair

clothes

eyes

floor

granny

house

jelly

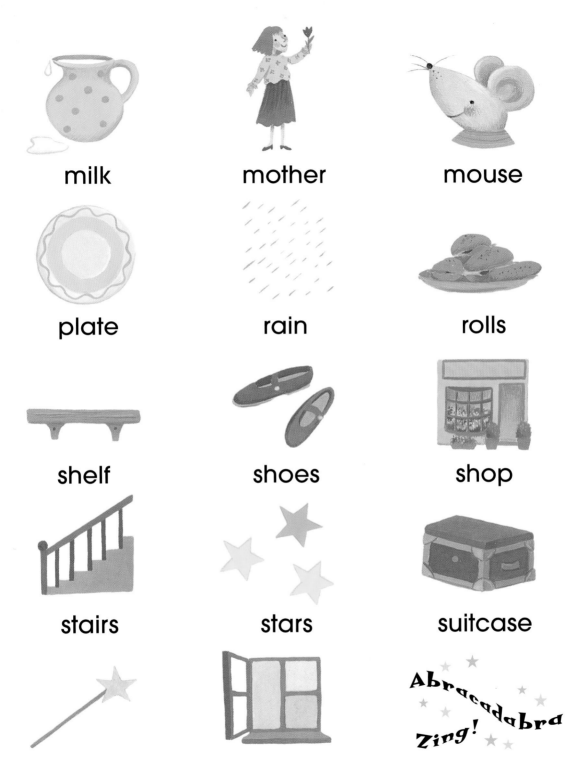

milk

mother

mouse

plate

rain

rolls

shelf

shoes

shop

stairs

stars

suitcase

wand

window

words

online resource centre
www.oxfordtextbooks.co.uk/orc/gillespie_els6e/

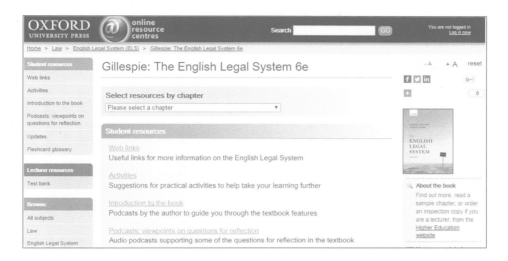

The book is accompanied by an innovative Online Resource Centre offering a range of resources to support teaching and learning:

- Lecturers can track student progress using a **test bank of multiple-choice questions**, offering immediate answers and feedback, which can be loaded on to the university's VLE and customized

- **Regular updates** are an indispensable resource providing easy access to changes and developments in the law that have occurred since publication of the book

- A selection of **annotated web links** facilitate further research in areas of particular interest

- A **glossary** provides a useful one-stop reference point for key words and terms used within the text

- Suggestions for **practical activities** are provided to help take learning further

- **Audio podcasts** by the authors outline opposing viewpoints on controversial topics in this area, encouraging critical thinking and debate

the ENGLISH LEGAL SYSTEM

sixth edition

ALISDAIR A. GILLESPIE

LL.B.(HONS), M.JUR., M.A.(ED), D.LITT.
PROFESSOR OF CRIMINAL LAW AND JUSTICE AND
HEAD OF LAW AT LANCASTER UNIVERSITY

and

SIOBHAN WEARE

LL.B.(HONS), PH.D.
LECTURER IN LAW AT LANCASTER UNIVERSITY

OXFORD
UNIVERSITY PRESS

OXFORD
UNIVERSITY PRESS

Great Clarendon Street, Oxford, OX2 6DP,
United Kingdom

Oxford University Press is a department of the University of Oxford.
It furthers the University's objective of excellence in research, scholarship,
and education by publishing worldwide. Oxford is a registered trade mark of
Oxford University Press in the UK and in certain other countries

Third edition 2011
Fourth edition 2013
Fifth edition 2015
Impression: 1

Published in the United States of America by Oxford University Press
198 Madison Avenue, New York, NY 10016, United States of America

British Library Cataloguing in Publication Data
Data available

Library of Congress Control Number: 2017933148

ISBN 978–0–19–878543–9

Printed in Great Britain by
Bell & Bain Ltd., Glasgow

This book is dedicated to:
Suzanne and Elin
(AAG)
and
James
(SW)

Preface

This book has been written for you, the student. It is likely that you are just starting to learn about law so this text is designed to provide an introduction to the English Legal System that will engage you from the start. It will allow you to understand the key aspects of the English Legal System and help you to question why the law has evolved in this way. Each chapter includes features and questions to help you to reflect upon what you are learning and provides suggested further reading so that you can increase the depth of your understanding by engaging with other sources.

This textbook is only one part of the learning experience; there is also an Online Resource Centre that accompanies this book. Many online resource centres simply act as an 'updating service' whereby anything that happens to arise between editions will feature on a website. That is not the case here. Whilst new developments will, of course, be featured on the Online Resource Centre, the site includes many more resources: there are extra reading resources to take you even further; there are links to many of the specific documents discussed in the book so that, rather than relying on our interpretation of what a document says, you can read it yourself and come to your own understanding of its importance; and there are exercises that will allow you to test and develop your knowledge. Sometimes these are application tests, for example completing forms for litigation so that you can understand how a case progresses. Others are knowledge tests which involve multiple-choice tests, short-answer questions, etc. It is designed to be fully interactive.

The sixth edition has seen modest structural changes. The most notable of these is that the Tribunal System has been brought into Part II alongside discussion of the courts. As will be seen in this book, any gap that exists between the courts and tribunals, and the court judiciary and the tribunal judiciary, is narrowing. Indeed, it is a stated policy of both the Lord Chief Justice and Senior President of Tribunals that there will be a unified judicial system, with work being transferred between them and judiciary sitting where appropriate.

The essential aim of this textbook is to provide you with an introduction to the key concepts of the English Legal System. Each issue is highlighted and discussed in a critical way, allowing the reader to identify the competing arguments and draw their own conclusion.

As usual, thanks are due to a number of people in respect of this book. We acknowledge the assistance of the Crown Prosecution Service, HM Courts and Tribunal Service, and the Ministry of Justice who answered a number of questions in a prompt and efficient manner.

In the first edition of this book Alisdair thanked a number of academics who reviewed each chapter of the book. For subsequent editions they were joined by other academics who provided detailed anonymous reviews of the later editions. These reviews were invaluable, not only because they helped us to check the content and style of the book, but also because they provided assistance in ensuring that the book matched many English Legal System courses. There are now too many academics to name personally but we are extremely grateful to them all and can assure them that we read each review carefully.

Those who have read all editions will know that Alisdair has a tendency to lose editors. He is somewhat careless in this regard and is starting to think that the perpetual loss of editors is OUP giving him a hint! This trend continues and Emily has been replaced with another Emily, Emily Hoyland. The process of writing this book has not been easy and Alisdair, in particular, would like to thank Emily for bearing with him and not getting angry when deadline after deadline was missed.

The fifth edition saw Siobhan Weare being introduced to help Alisdair in the production of that edition. Alisdair is delighted that following this, Siobhan agreed to join the book as co-author. We hope that the introduction of a co-author means that the book has returned to its original aim of being up to date, yet providing critical commentary. Siobhan has entered into this project with enthusiasm and has made significant changes.

The vote to withdraw from the EU features in this book (primarily in Chapter 20, 'The Future') but its consequences are not yet known. The Online Resource Centre will contain our views on what the judgment means but it will not be until the conclusion of the Article 50 negotiations that we will know what impact it will have. Where there has been an impact, however, is in respect of judicial independence. This is discussed in Chapter 9, but the tenor of some of the 'journalism' about this decision has brought ill-informed opinion to the fore, and led to a new low in standards and attacks on the judiciary. It is all too easy to say 'judges have thick skins' but it does have implications for our constitution, and this is discussed in this book.

We hope you find the book interesting. As ever, we are interested in your views on the book and how it could be improved.

AAG and SW
Lancaster
January 2017

New to this Edition

- Comprehensive updating of the key features of the English Legal System.

- Rewritten in-depth analysis of the latest law and guidance in respect of civil litigation and Alternative Dispute Resolution.

- The implications of the vote to leave the European Union are considered in terms of how it is likely to impact upon the English Legal System.

- Full consideration of the future challenges of legal education and continuing professional development.

Outline Contents

Detailed Contents

PART IV The Civil Justice System

Guide to the Book

The English Legal System is enriched with a range of features designed to help support and reinforce your learning. This guided tour shows you how to fully utilize your textbook and get the most out of your study.

Learning outcomes

Each chapter begins with a bulleted outline of the main concepts and ideas you will encounter. These serve as a helpful signpost to what you can expect to learn by reading the chapter.

> **By the end of this chapter you w**
>
> • Understand why the pressure for A
> • Define ADR and explain the three ₁
> • Identify how the courts are able to
> • Appreciate some of the advantage

Examples

Everyday scenarios explain and illustrate how a particular law or legal practice would apply in a real-life situation.

> **Example**
>
> Bernard asked Wreckers Ltd to install a swi
> is not fit for purpose as it leaks, meaning the
> Bernard has been told it will cost £11,000 to
> Realistically Bernard's claim will be for
> £10,000. However, if both Bernard and Wre

Questions for reflection

Why was a particular decision reached in a certain case? Is the law on this point rational and coherent? Is the English Legal System fit for purpose? Questions for reflection encourage you to think about contentious issues and critique the law.

> QUESTION FOR REFLECTION
>
> Should the English Legal System recognize ₁
> Is this not permitting religious law to enter ₁
> However, if arbitration—and indeed most A
> disputes on their own terms, why should it ₁
> dispute according to the religious principles

> LISTEN TO THE PODCAST
>
> For guidance on how to answer this que₅
> to the author's podcast on the Online R
> www.oxfordtextbooks.co.uk/orc/gillesp

Listen to the podcast

Selected questions for reflection are supported by audio podcasts by the authors which appear on the accompanying website. These outline the contrasting viewpoints you may wish to consider and offer advice on how to answer the questions.

Case boxes

Real-life cases demonstrate the way in which legal concepts are used in practice: the facts and decisions are presented to assist you in understanding why the court reached its decision and what the wider implications are.

Case Box *Sweet v Parsley*

The leading case that discusses the absen
was the tenant of a farm but sublet rooms
appellant did not live at the farm. The polic
was charged with the offence of, inter alia, b
ises used for the purpose of smoking cann

 CONCILIATION

Conciliation is often used in industrial disput
and employers disagree over work conditi
to settle disputes before strike action takes
disputes or litigation being brought where
or where the trade union seeks declaration

Key terms and concepts

Some key concepts and important legal terms are highlighted, using both real cases and fictitious examples to illustrate and explain.

Chapter summaries

The central points and concepts from each chapter are distilled into succinct summaries. These help you to reinforce your understanding and can also be used as a revision tool.

 Summary

**This chapter has introduced some of the c
a case proceeds through the small claims c
Court. It has also:**

- Identified that a single set of rules now go

 End-of-chapter questic

1. Should a court discount an award to take a
   kind of investment should they base their
   est rates have been stagnant for the past f

2. Read Penny Darbyshire, *Sitting in Judgmen*

End-of-chapter questions

Problem questions and essay-type questions at the end of each chapter will help to develop your analytical and problem-solving skills.

Further reading

Suggestions for further reading are included at the end of each chapter as a springboard for reliable further study. Each source is accompanied by an explanation of its relevance to your study, guiding you to the key academic literature in the field.

 Further reading

Davies G, 'Civil Justice Reform: Why We Need t
Justice Quarterly 32–51.

**This an excellent article by a former Aust
premises over the place of ADR in civil lit

Table of Cases

Court of Justice of the European Union Cases

European Court of Human Rights Cases

Table of Legislation

xxxiii

XXXV

Table of UK Statutory Instruments

EU Primary Legislation

EU Treaties

EU Secondary Legislation

European Directives

European Framework Decisions

European Regulations

International Instruments

1

The English Legal System

By the end of this chapter you will be able to:

- Define the United Kingdom.
- Identify how many legal systems exist in the United Kingdom.
- Begin to understand the concept of law and how laws differentiate from mere rules.
- Begin to think about 'systems' and understand the key issues within the English Legal System.

Introduction

In this introductory chapter the words 'English', 'Legal', and 'System' will be discussed. These words are often used but it is not always clear why they are used in this phrase and why so many modules now refer to the English Legal System. This chapter will also prepare you for the later chapters as it will help put them into context.

1.1 England

The first word to examine is that of 'England'. The question of identity is something that appears to be raised perpetually in the media and countries are given numerous different wordings. In this country, it is common to refer to living in 'Britain', 'the UK', or the 'United Kingdom'. The country does have a formal legal title, that of the *United Kingdom of Great Britain and Northern Ireland*. The Queen, as sovereign, has many other titles representing many of the dependent territories that exist but the title is as already stated—*United Kingdom of Great Britain and Northern Ireland*. The latest version of the title became relevant in 1920 when Ireland was partitioned and twenty-six counties were given independence, forming the Republic of Ireland.[1] The title also

---

1. It is often erroneously said that the twenty-six counties constitute 'Southern Ireland', presumably as the opposite of 'Northern Ireland'. However, this is both legally incorrect (the formal name of the state is The Republic of Ireland (in English) or Eire (in Gaelic)) and geographically incorrect since the County of Donegal is as northerly as the six counties that constitute Northern Ireland.

demonstrates that 'Britain' or, more correctly, 'Great Britain'[2] is actually the main island grouping of which England is one part.

1.1.1 The constituent parts

The United Kingdom of Great Britain and Northern Ireland consists of four countries (although one was originally a principality). The countries are England, Wales, Scotland, and Northern Ireland. The status of Wales differs from England, Scotland, and Northern Ireland. Traditionally Wales was a principality (a province ruled by a prince) and this is a term that continues to be used by some, not least because the Crown Prince of the United Kingdom is known as the *Prince of Wales* and thus the logic, to some, is that it follows that Wales is a principality. Others disagree and argue that Wales is a country and should be accorded that title. In reality the distinction between principality and country is moot and either title could be used although it would seem that many in Wales itself dislike the term principality. Wales does differ from the other constituent countries in that it has not had its own legal system since the sixteenth century, although this is arguably changing now.

1.1.1.1 England and Wales

Wales does not, as yet, have its own legal system (see, however, the *Government of Wales Act 2006* discussed later—see 'Welsh legislation') and following the *Laws of Wales Act 1535*, Wales in effect became legally 'annexed' by England and ensured that the laws of England would apply in Wales too. This Act was passed by an English-only Parliament but part of its purpose was to ensure that there could be Welsh representation in the (then) English Parliament. A further *Laws of Wales Act* was passed in 1543 and gave further effect to the governance of Wales and the long title of the Act makes express reference to its status as a principality.

The effect of this is that this book, along with every other book on this topic, and most modules, is technically wrong. It is not the *English* Legal System; it is technically the Legal System of *England and Wales*. That this is correct can be seen when one examines the main legal institutions. The senior courts are technically known as the *Superior Courts of England and Wales*.[3] The body for solicitors, known as the Law Society, is actually the *Law Society of England and Wales* and the body for barristers, known as the Bar Council, is actually the *General Council of the Bar for England and Wales*. This extends to judicial offices with the Lord Chief Justice technically being the *Lord Chief Justice for England and Wales*, something perhaps more readily understood with the current holder of the office, Lord Thomas of Cwmgiedd, an obviously Welsh location for his barony.

Welsh legislation

As noted earlier, the *Government of Wales Act 2006* (GoWA 2006) granted Wales a limited form of legislative powers. Initially this was through 'Assembly Powers' which were, in essence, a form of secondary legislation since each power required the approval of the Privy Council[4] but following a referendum in 2011 (which was

---

2. Since the term is derived from Brittany, a French region, what we understand to be Britain is 'Great' (meaning large) Britain.
3. *Constitutional Reform Act 2005*, sch 15.
4. *Government of Wales Act 2006*, s 93.

required under s 103) the Welsh Assembly was permitted the right to pass 'Acts of the Assembly'.[5] These legislative instruments are primary legislation in Wales and, unlike measures, do not require the approval of the Privy Council (although they do, as with UK legislation, require Royal Assent). However, it would be wrong to say that Wales has yet reached the status of either Scotland or Northern Ireland in terms of devolved legislative powers, not least because its legislative competences are somewhat restricted.[6]

A number of Acts of Assembly have been passed, including the *Schools Standards and Organisation (Wales) Act 2013*, the *National Health Service Finance (Wales) Act 2014,* and the *Renting Homes (Wales) Act 2016*. Despite the introduction of these Acts of Assembly, realistically it will be some years before the laws of England and Wales differ dramatically and even then it will not affect the legal system since courts and both civil and criminal procedure are not devolved matters (cf the position in both Scotland and Northern Ireland).

1.1.1.2 Scotland

Scotland is a country and joined the United Kingdom as a result of an Act of Union. The history of England and Scotland is probably well known to most readers and involved numerous battles between the two countries, sometimes with England winning, sometimes with Scotland winning. Indeed some of the battles occurred after the union with perhaps the most notable being the uprising led by 'Bonnie Prince Charlie'[7] who believed that he was the rightful heir to the throne.

Prior to the countries uniting, England and Scotland shared a sovereign, when King James VI of Scotland assumed the throne of England as King James I. This continued even through the 'Glorious Revolution' of 1688 when King William III and Queen Mary II jointly ruled both thrones. The countries were joined by the *Act of Union 1707*. In fact two statutes were passed as both the English and Scottish Parliaments had to pass the Act. The effect of the Act was to extinguish the Parliaments of *both* England and Scotland and create a Parliament of the United Kingdom. This can be contrasted with the position with Wales where Welsh members simply joined the English Parliament. The seat of Parliament was Westminster and this continues to be the case regardless of devolution (see 1.1.2).

Perhaps one of the most important aspects of the Act was the preservation of Scots law. Title 19 of the Act expressly preserved the Scottish Legal System and governed how appointments to the senior judiciary would be made. The principle of a separate legal system has continued throughout and devolution has merely altered the mechanics of this. That is not to say that Westminster does not have power to create Scottish laws since it clearly does—it is the Parliament of the United Kingdom—but there is no *automatic* assumption that laws passed will extend to Scotland (see 1.1.2).

Despite the continuing existence of the *Act of Union*, there has always been a question of whether Scotland should gain independence. Following the formation of the Scottish government after the 2011 parliamentary election, in which the Scottish National Party won a clear majority, an agreement was signed between the Scottish First Minister Alex Salmond and Prime Minister David Cameron on the holding of

---

5. Government of *Wales Act 2006*, s 107.
6. *Government of Wales Act 2006*, s 108.
7. More properly known as Charles Edward Stuart.

a referendum on Scottish independence. In September 2014, the Scottish Referendum took place. The question on the ballot paper was 'Should Scotland be an independent country?' Over 3,500,000 Scots voted in the referendum, with the 'no' vote winning a majority of 55 per cent, with over 2,000,000 votes. Despite the continued union of the United Kingdom, following the vote the Smith Commission was set up to oversee the devolution of additional powers to the Scottish Parliament.

Whilst the Smith Commission was not strongly welcomed by the Scottish National Party, it attracted considerable support from the then three main parties at Westminster at that time.[8] As promised, new legislation was brought before the Houses of Parliament and the *Scotland Act 2016* was given Royal Assent on 23 March 2016. The *Scotland Act 2016* delegates more powers to the Scottish Parliament, including the power to pass laws in areas that were otherwise reserved to Westminster.

At the time of writing, the response to the vote to leave the EU in the UK-wide referendum (see Chapter 20, 'The Future') has led to a further call for an independence referendum. Scotland voted overwhelmingly to stay within the EU and the First Minister has suggested that the 2014 referendum result has been set aside because voters, at that time, voted to remain within a United Kingdom in Europe. Whilst the Scottish Parliament has unveiled a draft Bill for a further referendum, this would not be sufficient as Westminster must give consent for a referendum to be held. Nevertheless, it would be politically difficult for Westminster to refuse if such a Bill were to be passed by the Scottish Parliament.

1.1.1.3 **Northern Ireland**

Northern Ireland is the most recent addition to the United Kingdom, it being created in 1920. Prior to that Ireland was a whole country and it was a member of the United Kingdom as a result of the *Act of Union 1801*. There were many similarities between the *Acts of Union 1707* and *1801* and it was intended that it would be a merger: Ireland did not become part of the United Kingdom of Great Britain but transformed it into a new body, the United Kingdom of Great Britain and Ireland. The merger was political expediency: the two countries had shared the same King since the sixteenth century and there was close cooperation between the Parliaments but it was believed more appropriate to create a single country. Like Scotland, Ireland retained its own legal status and although there were United Kingdom laws (ie laws that applied across the entire United Kingdom) there were also individual Irish laws.

Throughout the nineteenth and twentieth centuries pressure grew for Ireland to have more responsibility for its own actions; a series of 'Home Rule' Bills (in effect devolution) failed but pressure grew for full independence. Eventually the United Kingdom Parliament passed the *Government of Ireland Act 1920* which partitioned Ireland. Twenty-six counties became 'Southern Ireland' and six counties became 'Northern Ireland'. The division was broadly upon religious grounds with Ulster (which included the six counties)[9] being mainly Protestant and the twenty-six counties being mainly Roman Catholic. Of course this is a very crude approximation and there was a significant Protestant population in 'Southern Ireland' and vice versa. However, 'Southern Ireland' never came into existence as a result of the independence

---

8. The general election of 2015 led to the *Scottish National Party* becoming the third-largest party in Westminster. The 'three main parties' prior to 2015 were the Conservatives, Labour, and the Liberal Democrats.

9. Although 'Ulster' is commonly now thought of as being Northern Ireland, it technically includes the counties of Cavan, Donegal, and Monaghan.

movement and the twenty-six counties became an independent Republic, meaning the United Kingdom became the United Kingdom of Great Britain and Northern Ireland. The 1920 Act was repealed by the *Northern Ireland Act 1998* which was part of the devolution process (see 1.1.2) but also in pursuance of the *Good Friday Agreement*, an agreement between the Irish and UK governments to deal with the question of Irish unification.

1.1.2 The United Kingdom

Whilst this book is about the *English Legal System* (but really the Legal System of England and Wales) it is necessary to pause briefly to consider the United Kingdom. The election of a Labour government to the Westminster Parliament in 1997 led to the process of devolution. Theoretically devolution does not affect purely English matters; the law continues to be passed by the Parliament at Westminster. Devolution principally affects Northern Ireland and Scotland and this is outside the scope of this book although it is likely you will discuss them in *Constitutional Law* or similar modules.

Westminster remains the Parliament of the United Kingdom and the devolution instruments expressly preserve the right of Westminster to pass legislation that affects both Scotland and Northern Ireland. This is known as 'extent'. Both prior to and following devolution, the convention is that if an Act of Parliament is silent as to its extent (ie there is not a section within the Act of Parliament that discusses its extent) then it applies only to England and Wales. If the Act is to apply to either Scotland or Northern Ireland then a section within the Act will expressly state this and also the provisions that apply.

⚡ SEXUAL OFFENCES ACT 2003

The Sexual Offences Act 2003 was a major piece of legislation that reformed the criminal law relating to sexual offending. Section 142 states:

142 Extent, saving etc.

   (1) Subject to section 137 and to subsections (2) to (4), this Act extends to England and Wales only.

   (2) The following provisions also extend to Northern Ireland—

      (a) sections 15 to 25, 46 to 54, 57 to 60, 66 to 72, 78 and 79,

      (b) Schedule 2,

      (c) Part 2, and

      (d) sections 138, 141, 143 and this section.

   (3) The following provisions also extend to Scotland—

      (a) Part 2 except sections 93 and 123 to 129 and Schedule 4, and

      (b) sections 138, 141, 143 and this section.

By reading this section (don't worry about the language used within it, this is explained in Chapter 2) it can be seen that the whole of the Act applies to England and Wales but that only certain parts of the Act apply to Northern Ireland (those mentioned in subsection (2)). So, for example, ss 1–5 which are not mentioned would not apply in Northern Ireland and even less of it applies to Scotland (principally only Part 2 of the Act and even then ss 93 and 123–129 do not apply either).

5

1.2 **Legal**

The second word to examine is 'legal' which is the adjective for 'law' but what is 'law'? One of the first things to note is that we talk about a 'body of law' meaning that there is more than one law. Indeed those of you who are studying for a law degree can find that out from your degree title. Most of you will be reading for the degree of LLB(Hons) but do you know what that stands for? It is the abbreviation for *Legum Baccalaureus* which means Bachelor of Laws. Why is it that there are two 'L's? It is because in Latin the abbreviation for a plural is to repeat the first letter (whereas we use 's', ie Law becomes Laws).

1.2.1 **Classifying law**

Before considering what law is (which will require a brief examination of the philosophy of law) it is worth reflecting on the types of law that exist. Law can be classified in various ways and the approach that is taken to the law will be governed by its classification.

1.2.1.1 **Substantive or procedural**

The first division that perhaps has to be discussed is that which exists between substantive and procedural law. It will be seen later that some theorists, most notably Hart, argue that law can be classified into primary and secondary rules. Primary rules are considered to be laws that set out rights, duties, and obligations. Secondary rules determine how the primary rules are to be recognized, interpreted, and applied. Whilst this can be considered relatively simplistic it does assist in our understanding of the distinction between substantive and procedural laws.

What is the first thing you think about when you think of law? There is a reasonably high chance that it will be crime (see 1.2.1.3). This is not uncommon because it is one of the few areas of law that most people know something about but also because it is an interesting area of law and one that the media deal with on a daily basis. The actual crime is *substantive* law, in other words substantive law is that which sets out the rule which must be followed. Where someone is suspected of breaching this substantive law, there has to be an investigation, prosecution, and trial. All of these areas are also governed by laws so that an individual is protected against arbitrary interference by the state. These laws differ from the rule that says a person cannot commit a crime but they are nonetheless laws, and must be followed. These rules are *procedural* law and they set out the framework by which the substantive law will be determined.

Substantive and Procedural Law

Section 1 *Theft Act 1968* states:

(1) A person is guilty of theft if he dishonestly appropriates property belonging to another with the intention of permanently depriving the other of it; and 'thief' and 'steal' shall be construed accordingly.

This is a substantive law. It, in combination with s 7 (which prescribes the punishment for theft), states that a person must not steal.

Section 24 *Police and Criminal Evidence Act 1984* states:

(1) A constable may arrest without a warrant—

    (a) anyone who is about to commit an offence;

    (b) anyone who is in the act of committing an offence;

    (c) anyone whom he has reasonable grounds for suspecting is about to commit an offence;

    (d) anyone whom he has reasonable grounds for suspecting to be committing an offence.

(2) If a constable has reasonable grounds for suspecting that an offence has been committed, he may arrest without a warrant anyone whom he has reasonable grounds to suspect of being guilty of it.

This is procedural law. It sets out the circumstances when a police officer may arrest someone, those being (approximately) that a person has committed, or is about to commit, a breach of the substantive law.

1.2.1.2 Private or public law

The next distinction that needs to be drawn is between private and public law. This is a more subtle distinction as it straddles both substantive and procedural law; ie both substantive and procedural law could be either private or public law. A crude but effective separation is to suggest that private law concerns disputes that exist between citizens, and public law is disputes that exist between the state and the individual. It is perhaps the definition of 'public' that is more relevant since certain disputes between public bodies may actually give rise to private law matters.

7

Example Private and public law

PRIVATE LAW

Rhiannon agrees with Alison to purchase twenty-four bottles of red wine for the price of £150. When Rhiannon comes to collect them, there are only twenty bottles and yet Alison wants the full £150. If not resolved amicably it is quite possible that this dispute will end up before the courts, with Rhiannon suing Alison for breach of contract.

    This is a classic example of private law as it is a dispute between two parties and does not involve the state in its sovereign capacity.[10]

PUBLIC LAW

Jack, a (fictitious) media commentator made derogatory statements about accountants in a newspaper. Sarah runs a campaign group that attempts to raise the profile of accountants. Sarah wishes to lead a march through Jack's home town but the local police force refuses permission.

    This is a good example of public law. Sarah may think that the police force is acting unreasonably and may wish to apply to the courts to challenge this decision. This would be done through the process known as judicial review (considered at 17.3) and is a public law matter because it involves the relationship between a private citizen (Sarah) and the state (the police).

---

10. If the dispute existed between two councils, this would remain a private law matter even though it now involves two public (state) bodies. This is because the dispute is not with the state acting in its capacity as the state, ie the sovereign.

AV Dicey, a nineteenth-century jurist, and someone who is considered to be one of the pre-eminent authorities on constitutional law, stated that there was, in England and Wales, no such thing as 'administrative' law. By this he meant to contrast the position with the continental-based systems (see 1.3) which have always believed that there is a distinction between public and private law matters. Indeed the continental system created separate courts and legal processes to resolve administrative disputes. Dicey argued that this was not the position within England and Wales because everyone was equal under the law, ie the state was bound by the same law as the citizen.

Whilst, during the nineteenth century, this may have been true it is extremely difficult to continue this approach today. The legal system has now created a specific court to deal with administrative law (called the Administrative Court) although it is, theoretically, within the ordinary court system since it merely constitutes part of the Queen's Bench Division of the High Court of Justice. However, there is no doubt that the system has now become a body of law in its own right and there is now an express and specific procedure that governs administrative disputes.[11]

1.2.1.3 Civil or criminal law

It may seem that one of the more obvious distinctions to make is between civil and criminal law but, as we will see, this is not always a simple distinction. The distinction does not, as is sometimes believed, necessarily follow the private and public split.

Civil law is effectively anything that is not criminal. This may appear a trite statement but to an extent it is easier to say this than to suggest that a crime is anything that is not civil. This is because it is generally easier to identify what is criminal rather than civil. The civil law encompasses many different bodies of law mixing both private and public law. Ordinarily criminal matters can be categorized as public law in that the state is becoming involved in its sovereign capacity in relation to a citizen. In criminal matters the state will ordinarily be the prosecutor (for offences that take place in the Crown Court this will normally be through the sovereign (known as Regina when the sovereign is female and Rex when the sovereign is male) and in magistrates' courts ordinarily through the *Director of Public Prosecutions* or *Crown Prosecution Service* (12.1.1)). Whilst many crimes will have a victim, who will almost certainly be a citizen, it is not necessarily a private dispute between citizens. Indeed the state can, if it so wishes, bring a prosecution regardless of the views of the victim (12.4.2). This would make it a public law matter.

However, criminal law can, under certain circumstances, be a private law matter too. Although the state sets out the legal framework and will ordinarily prosecute, there remains in England and Wales the right to undertake a 'private prosecution'. This will be discussed elsewhere (12.1.3) but in essence means that a private citizen acts as the prosecutor and brings court proceedings. Whilst the state can intervene it need not do so, and accordingly in that guise it would appear to be private law (because the state is not present); but the laws are made on the assumption that the state will be the prosecutor so is this not still public law merely instigated privately? This is confusing but does demonstrate an important point: there are no clear answers in law and thus the divisions noted in this chapter will always be somewhat imprecise in practice.

---

11. *Civil Procedure Rules*, pt 54.

What then is a crime? An example was noted earlier (1.2.1.1) and s 1 *Theft Act 1968* appears quite a simple example of a crime. It is a law that prohibits something and carries with it a sanction for breaching the law. The courts have traditionally linked punishment with the idea of a crime[12] but this can in itself cause difficulty. There are many examples of situations where a person may appear to receive a punishment but it would not amount to a crime. A good example would be tax. If you need to complete a self-assessment tax form (to let the government know how much tax you must pay) there is a deadline by which you must submit it. If you miss this deadline then a surcharge (which is sometimes even called a 'fine') is payable. Is this a punishment? The person who receives it probably thinks so but a person surcharged in these circumstances is not considered to have a criminal record or to have committed a crime.

The European Court of Human Rights (ECtHR) has always adopted its own approach of what amounts to a 'crime' when adjudicating upon the *European Convention on Human Rights*.[13] In considering whether a matter is a crime the ECtHR said that domestic labelling (ie whether the state considered it to be a crime) was important but not conclusive. Other factors would include the purpose of any sanction and, in particular, its severity. As a general rule the stricter the 'punishment' the more likely it is that it will be considered a crime.

1.2.2 What is law?

Trying to define what law is, is a question that has taxed jurists and philosophers for centuries and will undoubtedly continue to do so. Some jurists, most notably Hart, never answered the question, appearing to suggest that it was the wrong question[14] and that the more appropriate question would be to consider what distinguishes law from other regulations or what the purpose of law is.

It is beyond the scope of this introductory text to consider this question in detail and you should (eventually) refer to texts on legal theory, philosophy, or jurisprudence to consider (note I am not suggesting you will ever be able to answer) this question. Some of you will have the opportunity to study modules on jurisprudence or legal theory and this will be at the heart of the module.

Law has to be more than just a simple set of rules and regulations. Every society has rules and regulations; most families will have a series of informal rules that must be obeyed. Would anyone categorize these as laws? Every university has a set of rules and some will even refer to the documents holding these rules as statutes. There may be a punishment for breaching some of these rules, but again can it be suggested that a university rule is a law? It is sometimes said that a law must be of general application but this need not be the case. In Chapter 2 the concept of *Private Acts of Parliament* will be discussed and these are of limited application. The simplistic answer is to say that a law is something that is handed down from the state, and that in the United Kingdom it is a rule set out by the Crown to which we, the subjects of the Crown, are bound. Are there limits to law, or where do laws come from, however? It is necessary, at least briefly, to introduce some of the philosophical debates.

12. John Adams and Roger Brownsword, *Understanding Law* (4th edn, Sweet & Maxwell 2006) 147.
13. See, most notably, *Welch v United Kingdom* (1995) 20 EHRR 247.
14. Brian Bix, *Jurisprudence: Theory and Context* (7th edn, Sweet & Maxwell 2015) 6.

1.2.2.1 **Positivism**

One of the more important theories of legal governance is known as positivism. There are a number of positivist theorists but the most important are Bentham and Austin, both nineteenth-century philosophers, and Hart, a twentieth-century jurist. Positivism focuses on what the law *is* rather than what it *should* be. It is often criticized as suggesting that even evil laws are valid and should be followed but this is a misunderstanding of positivism,[15] not least because positivism is not concerned with whether a law should be followed but simply what law is.

Austin believed in the premise of commands. He believed that an action would either be mandated, prohibited, not mandated, or not prohibited.[16] In other words, he believed that there was an imbalance in the state and that the Sovereign Head of State had the power to issue commands that detailed how a citizen could act, and that any other principles (eg commands from God, individual commands of employers etc) were not laws but merely moralistic or private requirements.[17]

Hart disagreed with this contention. He preferred the notion of rules rather than commands as he believed the notion of 'command' was problematic.[18] A significant problem with the idea of commands is that it relies on an unfettered sovereign, ie nobody can command the sovereign. Yet this is not the case in many states where there are limits on what the state can do—sometimes referred to as the 'Rule of Law'. Another key difficulty Hart had with the command theory is that a command requires a sanction, but does every law have a sanction? If one thinks of procedural law especially it is not easy to think of what a sanction would be. Hart argued that the basis of law was rules and that there were two types of rules: primary rules and secondary rules.

⚡ PRIMARY AND SECONDARY RULES

Primary rules are those that apply directly to citizens. They are the rules that provide what our rights, duties, and obligations are.

Secondary rules are those that govern the operation of the primary rules. They put them into effect.

This, to an extent, mirrors the 'substantive' and 'procedural' rules that were discussed earlier. Hart also believed that these rules had to be set within a context of societal norms, ie that it was not just a fear of sanction that led people to follow the rules but the fact that they believed that it was 'normal' to do so.

1.2.2.2 **Natural law**

It has been noted already that a particular criticism of positivism is the belief that moral judgements have little to do with law. Natural-law theorists believe that law is not simply that which our rulers create but that there is a 'higher law' that constrains laws. The concept of natural law dates back millennia, probably first appearing

---

15.   Brian Bix, *Jurisprudence: Theory and Context* (7th edn, Sweet & Maxwell 2015) 34.
16.   James W Harris, *Legal Philosophies* (2nd edn, Butterworths 1997) 29.
17.   James W Harris, *Legal Philosophies* (2nd edn, Butterworths 1997) 31.
18.   Brian Bix, *Jurisprudence: Theory and Context* (7th edn, Sweet & Maxwell 2015) 38.

in ancient Greek philosophies[19] and was certainly strong in the early years of the Christian Church with Aquinas, who later was made a saint, being one of the principal proponents of natural law. The influence of the Church in natural law is perhaps not surprising since to someone of faith, the 'higher' law will be their God.

Aquinas believed that there were four types of law: eternal law, natural law, divine law, and human law.[20] He believed that human law derived from natural law, so that natural law requires a law of murder and accordingly society must create such a law. Aquinas also believed that human law had to be compatible with natural law. For a human law to be valid and enforceable it must be consistent with natural law, that being the requirements of the common good.[21] Where a law is incompatible then Aquinas believed that it was unenforceable and unjust.

A criticism of natural law is that it is not necessarily practicable. Austin, a positivist, suggested that if a crime was punishable by death it meant very little whether it was an unjust law or not since it would, in all probability, be followed leaving the 'criminal' dead but apparently secure in the knowledge that he has become a martyr. The argument of natural lawyers, however, is that it empowers judges not to follow the law. In a common-law-based system (see 1.3.1) it is accepted that judges are the guarantors of law and indeed they can create law. The suggestion is that where a law is incompatible with natural law it should not be followed by judges.

Modern natural-law theorists, most notably Finnis, argue that natural law can be equated with ethical conduct and that it is about the creation of laws that are necessary for man to live ethically.[22] This is an interesting approach and demonstrates one advantage of natural law, that it acts as a valid justification for the creation of many of the most fundamental laws (on murder, theft, marriage, and property), since without these basic laws society could not operate.

Natural law is, to an extent, considered to be the main opponent of positivism and yet there are a number of similarities between them. Both assume the concepts of rules and both accept that a state can produce the rules that surround us. Where the two appear to deviate is that natural law goes beyond positivism and seeks to discuss what the law *should* say. There is constantly a benchmark against which human laws will be measured, that of the 'higher' law.

1.2.2.3 Interpretative/rights theory

One of the more recent philosophical theories on law is referred to as the 'rights thesis' and is propagated by Dworkin, a twentieth-century jurist. Dworkin rejected the principles of positivism because he believed that law was not simply based on a series of rules but on principles, policies, and more general standards.[23] Some of these standards will include morality and it has been suggested that this can be equated, to an extent, with parts of natural law[24] but it is different in that Dworkin did not believe that there is a 'higher' law, merely that the community has institutional morality, ie a common base of principles to which its members adhere.

---

19.   Brian Bix, *Jurisprudence: Theory and Context* (7th edn, Sweet & Maxwell 2015) 70.
20.   Brian Bix, *Jurisprudence: Theory and Context* (7th edn, Sweet & Maxwell 2015) 71.
21.   Brian Bix, *Jurisprudence: Theory and Context* (7th edn, Sweet & Maxwell 2015) 71–2.
22.   Brian Bix, *Jurisprudence: Theory and Context* (7th edn, Sweet & Maxwell 2015) 77.
23.   James Penner and Emmanuel Melissaris, *McCoubrey and White's Textbook on Jurisprudence* (5th edn, OUP 2012) 83.
24.   James Penner and Emmanuel Melissaris, *McCoubrey and White's Textbook on Jurisprudence* (5th edn, OUP 2012) 94.

The centre of Dworkin's criticism is that law is based on the difference between rights (principles) and policy (goals).[25] The importance of policy was that it was a decision for the public good, a decision that influenced the community. This interplays with principles that give rise to individual rights and these may be contrary to the policy goal albeit for appropriate reasons. More than this, however, he argues that judges are obligated to decide matters on the basis of principles (rights) and not policy. This distinction is based on a similar premise to the distinction between politics and the law.

He later sought an interpretative approach to law. This is not interpretation as we understand it (ie reviewing a statute and deciding what it means) but has a more philosophical abstract sense. Dworkin believes that the law is a series of constructive interpretations, that in order for a judge to adjudicate on a problem he must look for a pattern that is discernible in the rights and policies relevant to the issue.[26] This theory of law fits the common-law system (1.3.1) because precedent is an important part of the interpretative approach. The previous decisions of judges help identify a pattern that could lead one to determine what the legal solution to a problem is. Alongside these principles, however, are the moral policies and Dworkin believed that a judge should attempt to make the law as 'good' as it can be, meaning that, where there are different alternatives, the one closest to the moral norm may be best.[27] This is also a response to the argument that positivism neglects amoral laws whereas in the rights-based approach the amoral law is unlikely to ever be the 'best' solution to a given problem and thus the judge will reinterpret the matter.

1.3 System

The final word to examine is that of 'System'. Identifying precisely what a system is can be open to debate but it is probably more than the individual rules or laws and is instead the concept of how law is administered. In the same way that law can be divided into civil and criminal law (1.2.1.3), there are two systems, the criminal justice system and the civil justice system. Thus the system is how the law is to be applied and envelopes some procedural law together with the courts etc.

1.3.1 Common law

The English Legal System is an example of a common-law-based system. This can be contrasted with the other principal system which is sometimes known as the civil system (which can be confusing as it does not mean civil as in the distinction between civil and criminal law) and more readily understood as the continental system. These two legal systems can be found throughout the world and their use reflects the geopolitical influence of Britain, Spain, and France. Accordingly, those areas of the world that were parts of the British Empire (eg the United States of America, Canada, Australia, New Zealand, and certain African states) have all tended to follow the

25. James Penner and Emmanuel Melissaris, *McCoubrey and White's Textbook on Jurisprudence* (5th edn, OUP 2012) 88–94.
26. Brian Bix, *Jurisprudence: Theory and Context* (7th edn, Sweet & Maxwell 2015) 95.
27. Brian Bix, *Jurisprudence: Theory and Context* (7th edn, Sweet & Maxwell 2015) 98.

common-law-based system of law whereas those that formed part of the French and Spanish empires (eg Continental Europe, Latin America, and certain parts of Africa) have adopted the continental approach.

1.3.1.1 **Common-law system**

The principal hallmark of the common-law system is, as its name suggests, the recognition of something called 'common law'. In England and Wales law is not only passed by Parliament (known as statutory law) but also can develop from the previous decisions of courts. It is for this reason that precedent (which is explained in further detail in Chapter 3 but may be summarized here as the basis upon which certain courts set out rulings which they and other courts must follow) is so important to the common-law system.

The origins of the common law are contested. However, there is broad agreement that it emerged following the Norman Conquest and that King Henry II played a pivotal role in its development. Before the Conquest, and indeed for a period afterwards, different areas of England were governed individually by local laws and customs, rather than by a national legal system. Local courts were governed by the King's stewards, with the King himself (perhaps unsurprisingly) presiding over the King's Court (the *Curia Regis)*, which followed him as he travelled around the country. The *Curia Regis* was the origin for the development of the Court of the Exchequer and the Court of Common Pleas, as well as the Court of King's Bench.

When Henry II came to the throne (1154–89) he introduced a series of reforms which sowed the seeds of the common-law system. In 1166 at the Assize of Clarendon, Henry II ordered the non-King's Bench judges to travel around the country's circuits and establish the 'King's peace' by deciding cases. In doing so, rather than applying the piecemeal laws found in local areas, the judges applied the new laws of the state which were 'common' to all. In 1178, he appointed five members of the *Curia Regis* to sit permanently at a court in Westminster 'to hear all the complaints of the realm and to do right'. This court was the origin of the Court of Common Pleas. Eventually the court separated into two, and the Court of the King's Bench emerged, continuing to follow the King around the country. By the 1170s it was also possible to distinguish the work of the Exchequer from that of the rest of the *Curia Regis*, dealing with financial litigation and some matters of equity, eventually leading to the creation of the Court of the Exchequer. Thus, by the thirteenth century three senior courts existed, those of the Common Pleas, the Kings Bench, and the Exchequer. The judicial decisions in these cases produced 'common' law, applicable to all in the country.

The term 'common law' was used to distinguish between law that was decided by the Royal Courts in London and which was applied throughout the kingdom (thus a 'common' approach to the law) and ecclesiastical (Church) law (which remained an important source and application of law until the nineteenth century) and local customary law. Eventually the common law took over the other sources of law, especially as the reporting of decisions became more ordered and it was thus easier to see how judges were applying the law.

The common law remains strong today and, whilst it is comparatively rare for the courts to create a new legal principle, there continues to be a significant amount of law that exists without statutory definition.

⚡ COMMON-LAW CRIME

Perhaps the best example of a common-law crime is that of murder. The crime of murder is not defined in statute.[28] The definition has evolved through the common law with its basis in the definition given by Coke, an eighteenth-century judge. The definition has been amended by statute[29] but its definition continues to be a matter of the common law.

Where there is a 'gap' in the law the superior courts will sometimes continue to rely on their common-law powers. A good example of this is in respect of the protection of the vulnerable (particularly children) where the Family Division of the High Court of Justice claims an 'inherent jurisdiction' which means that it has the power to draw upon the common law to act in the best interests of the vulnerable person.

Common law v equity

Whilst we now refer to the system in England and Wales being a common-law system it is also necessary to refer to the place of equity. Prior to the *Judicature Acts* of 1873 and 1875 equity was considered a parallel system to the common-law courts. It is not true to think of it as being separate to the common law as its jurisdiction was inextricably linked to the common law but the common-law courts were restricted to granting damages and so if somebody could not petition the court, or wished something other than damages, the common-law courts could not assist. There was also a belief that the common-law courts were too mechanistic and that the strict rules of law sometimes created unfairness. People began to petition the King (as Sovereign) for justice and he began to delegate these matters to the Lord Chancellor and eventually created a separate series of courts, the courts of Chancery, to resolve such matters. The courts of Chancery proceeded not on the basis of the strictures of common law but on the principles of justice and they could dispense equitable rather than legal resolutions, something based on fairness, and which incorporated other remedies, including injunctions and the ability to recognize beneficial, and not just legal, interests.

Equity introduced a series of new and innovative resolutions but it became quickly apparent that in many instances a dispute could be resolved either under the common law or equity and the two parallel systems often conflicted. In the *Earl of Oxford's case*[30] the courts were called upon to decide whether common law or equity took priority. It is not necessary to consider the facts of this case in depth and you will probably read about it in *Equity & Trusts* but, in essence, there was an allegation that a judgment of the common-law courts had been obtained by bribery. The Chancery court issued an injunction preventing the common-law order being enforced and this led directly to a conflict between the two jurisdictions. It was ultimately resolved by it being ruled that in a dispute between the common law and equity, equity would prevail.

The *Judicature Acts* of 1873 and 1875 resolved this tension by unifying the jurisdictions and creating one supreme court of judicature (now embodied by the Senior Courts of England & Wales). All courts—not just the courts of Chancery—were able to exercise the equitable remedies and hence now the part of the High Court that is

---

28. Although its punishment now is: see *Murder (Abolition of Death Penalty) Act 1965*.
29. See *Law Reform (Year and a Day Rule) Act 1996*.
30. (1615) 1 Rep Ch 1.

seen as the successor to the common-law courts (the Queen's Bench Division) readily issues equitable remedies such as injunctions or mandatory orders. It is important to note the jurisdictions did not merge and it is possible today to distinguish equity from the common law (and indeed you will do so when you study the module *Equity and Trusts*). Equity is based on a series of principles—known as equitable maxims—which continue to be used and which were considered to encapsulate the inherent fairness of equity.

1.3.1.2 Continental system

The continental system differs from a common-law system in that it is based on the primacy of written laws. Continental systems tend to be codified, meaning that the laws are all set out in a document. This is not only the hallmark of the continental system since in many common-law countries (most notably America) they have a codified criminal law whereby all of the crimes and procedural rules relating to the criminal justice system are set out in one document, commonly referred to as a Penal Code.

The codification system means that judges are not 'creating' new laws or rights but simply interpreting the laws set out by the legislature. Accordingly, if there is a 'gap' in the law then it cannot be filled by the judges. However, of course, in practice the concept of 'interpretation' is almost as fluid as the idea of judicial creations and the fact that many courts will 'follow' the decisions of other judges (even though they arguably do not have a formal system of precedent per se) means that the law will develop in the way that the judges desire.

1.3.2 An adversarial system

The second hallmark of the English Legal System (and indeed all common-law systems) is that it is an adversarial system. This refers to how cases are adjudicated upon and can be distinguished from the inquisitorial system that is frequently found within the continental system.

1.3.2.1 Adversarial approach

The adversarial approach to law is where the adjudication is seen as a contest between two or more sides and it is fought out before a neutral umpire (the judge and/or jury). The judge, whilst able to ask questions, should not seek to become an investigator and should rather concentrate on ensuring that both sides are obeying the procedural rules governing the presentation of their case.[31]

A central plank of the adversarial process is the fact that the parties, not the court, call witnesses. Both parties will gather their evidence, including asking witnesses to give statements. The parties will then decide which witnesses they are going to call to give evidence in court. The opposing party is able to challenge this evidence in two ways. The first is through calling their own witnesses who may provide an alternative viewpoint on the issues. The second, and more combative, method is to allow witnesses to be cross-examined. Cross-examination is where a party directly challenges the witnesses' evidence and puts the contrary case to them.

The other key principle of the adversarial system is that of the importance of orality. In both the criminal and civil systems of justice there is still the assumption that

31. *Jones v National Coal Board* [1957] 2 QB 55.

providing live oral evidence is the best way of arriving at the facts. Indeed in a criminal trial where there is no dispute between the parties as to what the witness will say (ie there will be no cross-examination) then the statement given by that person will be tendered as evidence. The way it is tendered is that it is read out aloud. It is quite possible, or indeed likely, that giving it to the jury to read would be at the very least as effective but the tradition of oral evidence continues.

It will be seen later in this book that changes are being made to the adversarial system in order to take the edge off some of its harshness (see in particular Chapters 17 and 19). However, these are only minor modifications and it is not a shift towards a purely inquisitorial system.

1.3.2.2 Inquisitorial approach

The continental system tends to adopt an inquisitorial approach. In this sense the court becomes the investigator itself. Rather than the judge being a neutral umpire, he is given the authority to seek out the truth by asking questions of the witnesses. The respective lawyers seek to control this questioning by reference to the procedural rules and to this extent it can be argued the roles of counsel and the judiciary are almost mirrored. It has been suggested that one advantage of this model is that it ensures that all relevant witnesses are heard[32] whereas in the adversarial system, if a witness's evidence is not helpful to a side, he or she may not be called.

Consideration was given to whether the English Legal System should move towards an inquisitorial approach but the *Royal Commission on Criminal Justice* argued that this would be a significant cultural shift.[33] Arguably this is correct and it cannot be accidental that common-law systems tend to be adversarial with continental systems being inquisitorial, suggesting that any shift to either model may involve a rethink of the legal system as a whole.

 Summary

In this chapter we have noted that:

- There is a United Kingdom of Great Britain and Northern Ireland. Whilst this is our formal state, it is constituted from four parts; England, Scotland, Wales, and Northern Ireland.

- Historically England annexed the law of Wales and so when we refer to the English Legal System we are actually including Wales too.

- Scotland and Northern Ireland have separate legal systems, these being retained as part of the Acts of Union that created the United Kingdom.

- It is difficult to identify what precisely law is and it is probably a philosophical rather than a practical problem. Law is probably a collection of rules governing rights, duties, and obligations but the extent of these rules and where the authority comes from to use them is more open to debate.

---

32. Michael Zander, *Cases and Materials on the English Legal System* (10th edn, OUP 2007) 375.
33. Michael Zander, *Cases and Materials on the English Legal System* (10th edn, OUP 2007) 377.

- Law can be divided into different classifications including substantive and procedural, public and private, and civil and criminal. These classifications affect how we think about law and what the law does.

- The English Legal System is based on the common law, meaning that judges are able to progress the law themselves. Decisions from previous court hearings still form part of our law.

- The English Legal System is an adversarial system meaning that a case is adjudicated by two competing sides presenting their evidence with a neutral judge or jury deciding which case they prefer.

17

PART I

SOURCES
OF LAW

2

Domestic Sources of Law: Parliamentary Material

By the end of this chapter you will be able to:

- Understand the primary sources of domestic law.
- Differentiate between primary and secondary sources of law.
- Differentiate between primary and secondary legislation.
- Identify, and use, the different approaches to statutory interpretation.

Introduction

You are studying the law but how do you know what the law is? Where do you find law? The skill of being able to find law and the knowledge of knowing how to interpret law are two of the most important abilities of any lawyer. Indeed it is possible to go so far as to say that these are the two most important abilities of a lawyer and of a law student. If you are able to find and interpret law then you can apply those skills to any law—it does not matter whether you have studied the subject or not because all law has the same basic components in it.

Sources of law are an important (and arguably *the* most important) part of legal study since a proper grounding in the subject will allow you to access any substantive legal issue. Chapters 2, 3, and 4 will introduce you to this knowledge but reference should also be made to Legal Skills texts that will help you put this knowledge into practice. This chapter examines parliamentary material, that is to say laws passed by the Houses of Parliament, and Chapter 3 examines material produced by the courts through cases. Chapter 4 will introduce you to international sources of law.

2.1 Domestic law

This chapter discusses the sources of domestic law and we need to be clear at the very beginning of this chapter what that means.

2.1.1 **International relations**

As has already been noted the United Kingdom consists of four countries (England, Scotland, Northern Ireland, and Wales) and there are three legal systems (England and Wales,[1] Scotland, and Northern Ireland) each of which approaches its sources of law in similar (although not exactly the same) ways. However, the United Kingdom is also a signatory to a number of treaties, most notably the *European Convention on Human Rights* (ECHR) and the *Treaty of Rome* (now known by another title: see Chapter 4) which led to the UK joining what was the European Economic Community (EEC) and is now the European Union (EU).

The ECHR is directly relevant because the *Human Rights Act 1998* created a situation where it was deemed that all public bodies would abide by the Convention and provided authorities to the domestic courts to hear challenges to any breach. This chapter will look at how the *Human Rights Act 1998* has altered the way courts approach domestic legislation but will not discuss the sources of the jurisprudence surrounding the ECHR as this will be discussed in Chapter 4 (International Sources of Law). The individual rights established within the ECHR will be examined in Chapter 5 as will some of the effects of the *Human Rights Act 1998*.

The relationship that the United Kingdom has with the EU is more complicated and this too will be examined in Chapter 4. Some EU law becomes directly part of UK domestic law without any domestic proceedings occurring but this is because Parliament has provided for this[2] and it can choose to reverse this decision if it so wishes, and indeed will do when the UK leaves the EU. Accordingly, in this chapter the interface with EU law will not be considered because apart from those situations where a measure is directly applicable into domestic law, any changes are brought about in the same way. Chapter 4 will examine how EU law is created, how decisions are reached as to whether it is directly applicable to individual states, and how that law is implemented.

2.1.2 **Constitution**

This text is not a textbook on the constitution of the United Kingdom and those of you who are studying law as an undergraduate programme will almost certainly study the constitution of the United Kingdom in a specific module, sometimes called *Constitutional Law* and sometimes known as *Public Law*. However, it is necessary to summarize some aspects of the constitutional law so as to understand the sources of domestic law.

Every country must have a constitution which can be defined as a series of legal and non-legal rules that define how a country is governed.[3] However, the term 'constitution' in many countries means a document that enshrines the fundamental rules of governance. Perhaps the most obvious example of this is the Constitution of the United States of America which quite clearly sets out the machinery of governance, expressly creating three instruments of state: the executive (President of the United States of America), the legislature (Congress), and the judiciary (Supreme Court of the United States of America). The American Constitution is not static in that it can be changed (and indeed there are currently twenty-seven amendments, the last having been passed in 1992).[4]

---

1. Although it will be remembered from Chapter 1 that Wales is starting to develop its own system of laws.
2. See *European Communities Act 1972*.
3. Eric Barendt, *An Introduction to Constitutional Law* (OUP 1998) 2.
4. Which protects the 'compensation' (salary) of senators and congressmen.

Most constitutions will enshrine the laws in their constitution, ie they will require a special resolution to amend the instrument. Most democracies will normally operate on a simple majority system to pass legislation but constitutions will require a higher standard to ensure that the constitution, which will normally also prescribe the rights and freedoms of citizens, cannot be abused by rogue governments. In the United States of America any amendment to the Constitution requires Congress to pass an amendment by a two-thirds majority *and* for three-quarters of the individual state legislatures to pass the amendment.

2.1.2.1 Does the United Kingdom have a constitution?

The United Kingdom does not have a written constitution:

> There is no document in the United Kingdom equivalent, say, to the United States Constitution ... Nor, for that matter, is there a set of statutes clearly indicated by their titles as 'Constitutional' or 'Basic' laws.[5]

However, this is no longer strictly true as the *Constitutional Reform Act 2005* obviously contains the word 'constitutional' in it, but the basic point remains intact; within the United Kingdom the legislature rarely expressly refers to pieces of legislation as constituting part of a formal constitution. That is not to say that measures do not exist because quite apart from the 2005 Act, the *Acts of Union 1707* and *1801* which created the United Kingdom (see 1.1.1) must be considered constitutional as must the *European Communities Act 1972* and the *Human Rights Act 1998*. However, the presumption is that so-called 'constitutional' pieces of legislation are no different from any other piece of legislation and could be amended or repealed by a simple majority.

2.1.3 Primary and secondary sources

When locating law it is important to draw a distinction between primary and secondary sources of law. Primary sources of law are authoritative sources of law, ie they are statements of what the law is. Secondary sources are not strictly speaking statements of what the law is but rather interpretations of the law. In other words whilst they are useful in helping us understand the law (including its development) they do not, strictly speaking, say what the law *is*. Whilst you will use secondary sources quite frequently through your law studies you should not misunderstand their place and should cite primary sources where possible (see Figure 2.1).

> **Example** Primary v secondary
>
> The definition of property for the purpose of theft is contained in s 4 *Theft Act 1968*. If you were asked to define property you would refer to that section and not, for example, the pages in your criminal law textbook. However, if you wanted to discuss *why* the definition of property excludes, for example, 'wild flowers' (see s 4(3), TA 1968) then resorting to the primary source will not help. It just tells you what the law is not why that is the case. However, your textbook may explain it as may some academic articles.

5. Eric Barendt, *An Introduction to Constitutional Law* (OUP 1998) 26.

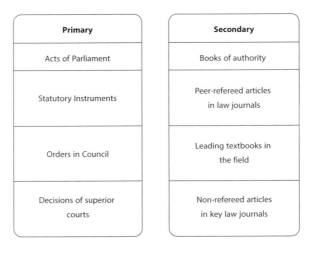

Primary	Secondary
Acts of Parliament	Books of authority
Statutory Instruments	Peer-refereed articles in law journals
Orders in Council	Leading textbooks in the field
Decisions of superior courts	Non-refereed articles in key law journals

Figure 2.1 Primary and secondary sources

Figure 2.1 demonstrates that within each division of sources there are different subcategories and this chapter will discuss which sources should be cited when.

2.1.3.1 Primary sources

It was discussed earlier that there is no enshrined specific constitutional law and thus primary sources of law can be separated into two general parts. The first is legislation, ie measures that come from the legislature (Parliament) and this is known as 'statutory law', and the second is from the decisions of courts and this is what has tended to be referred to as 'common law' but is perhaps more accurately referred to as 'case law' nowadays. The interaction between these forms of law will be discussed in this chapter but statutory law is supreme. The United Kingdom is a monarchy. The formal Head of State is the Queen (which can be contrasted with the President of the United States of America or the President of France) but at the same time we are a democracy and the head of the executive is the prime minister.[6] Sovereign power in the United Kingdom resides in the Queen in Parliament. This means that all legislation requires the approval of the monarch (see 'Royal Assent') but that subject to this Parliament may pass such laws as it wishes. There are different types of democracies but the UK version of parliamentary democracy means that rather than citizens taking votes on issues (known as referendums) the convention is that we elect Members of Parliament who have the right to pass laws subject to their being voted out of office at the next election. There are, of course, exceptions but these are usually provided for by statutory law itself. For example, the *European Union Act 2011* provides that there will be a referendum if certain circumstances apply. However, this is only the case because our representatives decided this. Also, as will be seen, this provision could be repealed if later representatives decided to do so. Whilst politically that might be problematic

---

6. Although interestingly there is no *legal* rule that states that the prime minister is the head of the executive and until comparatively recently, the office did not even necessarily legally exist as it was not mentioned in statutes. It is a *convention* that the prime minister is the head of the executive and this demonstrates the importance of conventions (unwritten rules of custom and practice).

(as it would look as though power was being taken away from the people) as a matter of law it would be unproblematic.

As the Queen in Parliament is supreme then this means that where a statute conflicts with a decision of the court, the statute (legislation) prevails. How (and indeed whether) this happens in practice will be discussed later. However, there are examples of situations where Parliament has passed legislation with the specific intention of overturning a decision of the courts[7] and the courts have had to accept that version of the law.

2.1.3.2 Secondary sources

It can be seen from Figure 2.1 that secondary sources are largely academic material, although other material (for example, government policy papers etc) may also come within this band. The use of the material will be discussed later but it should be noted at the outset that whilst you may use secondary sources frequently in your studies (either to find primary sources or to complete an essay) they are still comparatively rarely mentioned in court. The courts do appear to be citing academic material more often than they ever did and the breadth is increasing: at one point authors would only be cited when they were dead and could not change their mind! Perhaps the growth in academic writings over recent years has led judges to consider that it can be useful to see how others have interpreted the law. However, caution should always be used when citing contemporary academic sources. You should be clear that the academic writing is an opinion on what the law *probably* is. It is not a definitive statement of the law, regardless of how distinguished the person writing it is. This is important to bear in mind when it is a senior judge. Sometimes judges will make speeches or write an article for a learned journal (known as 'extrajudicial' speeches or writing) and this will include statements of what the law may be. However, this remains a secondary rather than primary source because it is their personal view of the issue and not the ruling of a court.

2.2 Statutory law

The first source to discuss is statutory law, that being law passed by Parliament. It was noted earlier that statutory law is a primary source of law but to confuse matters statutory law itself is divided into primary legislation and secondary legislation with primary legislation itself being divided into two! Figure 2.2 may assist.

Figure 2.2 shows that primary legislation is that which is known as an Act of Parliament and that these may exist as either a Public or Private Act. Whilst all forms of parliamentary legislation are statutory, an Act of Parliament is often referred to as a 'statute'. The statutes that you will encounter most of the time are known as Public Acts and these are measures that apply to all of society. Private Acts are those that are limited to a particular company or organization that requires powers beyond those prescribed by the normal law. They tended to be used for the creation of docks, transport links, or other major building programmes.

---

7. For example, the *Sexual Offences Act 2003* states that the test for whether an offender believed a rape complainant was consenting is an objective test whereas the courts had traditionally said that it was a subjective test.

Figure 2.2 Legislation

 PRIVATE ACT

The *University of Wales, Cardiff Act 2004* is a private (sometimes referred to as 'local') Act. Its purpose was to merge the University of Wales Medical School with the University of Wales, Cardiff. Universities can be divided into two groups: those that existed before 1992 and those that gained university status after 1992. The former were generally established by Royal Charter whereas the latter acquired their authority from the *Further and Higher Education Act 1992* and articles of governance approved by the Privy Council. Universities are independent bodies but are limited to the powers set out in either the Royal Charter or the 1992 legislation. In 2004 it was decided that the University of Wales Medical School would be incorporated into the larger University of Wales, Cardiff but neither institution had the power to do this as their status was regulated as already described. They petitioned Parliament and the *University of Wales, Cardiff Act 2004* gave the institutions the power to merge and become a single unit.

The Act thus provided one institution a power that it did not previously have and doing so did not involve it granting any wider power to either that institution or any other institution, the essence of a Private Act.

 PUBLIC ACT

The *Education Act 2005* is a Public Act. Its purpose is to reform the way in which failing schools are identified and required to reform. The Act is of general importance as it applies not to a specific school or authority but to all schools in England.[8] It creates an Inspectorate for Schools in England and provides specific powers and duties for that body.

As the Act provides a general power that applies beyond a single company or authority it is a Public Act and applies as a general law of the land subject to the limitations contained within its drafting.

---

8.   The *Education Act 2005* is also unusual in that it provides a general application for just England rather than England and Wales because education is a devolved matter for Wales (see 1.1.2).

Secondary legislation is slightly easier to define although it is normally referred to as *statutory instruments*. An Act of Parliament will generally provide the general scope of a law and its powers but it will commonly leave some consequential matters out. Such matters could include when a piece of legislation comes into effect (a majority of Acts of Parliament do not come into effect immediately so that preparations can be made for any requisite training or public awareness campaigns) or the precise application of a law (eg what grade a person must be to exercise a power).

The balance between what goes in primary and secondary legislation is a delicate one. Parliament only has a finite amount of time to debate legislation and so if every detail of a law was placed in primary legislation then any changes (eg an organization changes its name) would require another piece of primary legislation to permit this. This would quickly lead to a situation where Parliament would have no time to discuss any other legislation. However, if too much is placed into secondary legislation then Parliament as a whole could lose control of how the law is being implemented because it is far easier for secondary legislation to be passed (see 2.2.1). To put this all into context if we look at the figures for 2015, Parliament passed thirty-seven Public Acts of Parliament while 2,059 pieces of secondary legislation were passed. It is inconceivable that each piece of secondary legislation could have been passed in the same way as primary legislation or had the same level of scrutiny.

⚡ SECONDARY LEGISLATION

Part II *Regulation of Investigatory Powers Act 2000* permits certain public bodies the right to undertake covert surveillance. The Act does not say who these public authorities are or who within the organization may authorize surveillance to be carried out. These details are provided for in the *Regulation of Investigatory Powers (Directed Surveillance and Covert Human Intelligence Sources) Order 2010.*[9] The order lists each organization that may undertake surveillance (eg the police, local authorities, etc) and who within each organization may authorize its use (eg police inspector, director of housing, etc). The advantage of this is that where a new public agency requires the right to conduct surveillance Parliament need only pass a new statutory instrument rather than amend the 2000 Act.

The manner in which legislation is passed, reviewed, and treated depends on whether it is primary or secondary legislation, as will be seen.

2.2.1 Primary legislation

The most important type of legislation is primary legislation. Although noting the existence of Private Acts of Parliament earlier, the remainder of this chapter will focus on Public Acts of Parliament as these are the more important and also the pieces of legislation that you are more likely to encounter.

It was noted that the Queen in Parliament is the sovereign body in this country and in practice this means Parliament through its Acts of Parliament. There are (theoretically) no limits to the power of Parliament and it could legislate to do anything it wishes.

9. SI 2010/521.

> **≡ Example** Smoking in Paris
>
> A common example that is used when discussing the supreme nature of Parliament is that of smoking on the streets of Paris. If Parliament wished to do so it could pass a law that states it is illegal to smoke on the streets of Paris. Could this be enforced? Possibly not but it does not matter because whether a law can be enforced is not relevant to its validity. A statute banning smoking in Paris would be valid and assuming that evidence existed to show that D had smoked in Paris then if D ever set foot in the United Kingdom he could be arrested, tried, and convicted.

The fact that Parliament can legislate for anything has not been compromised by the constitutional changes that have taken place in recent years. It was noted in Chapter 1 that Scotland, Northern Ireland, and (to a much more limited extent) Wales have devolved authority whereby they can create their own law. However, Parliament could as easily choose to withdraw this power and centralize all legislation again. It was noted at the beginning of this chapter that no legislation is enshrined into law (2.1.2) and, accordingly, an Act of Parliament could repeal the devolution legislation. Even without doing this, however, we can see that the UK Parliament remains supreme because the legislation expressly states that the devolution legislation does not preclude the UK Parliament from legislating over devolved areas.[10]

The *Human Rights Act 1998* (HRA 1998) is also compatible with this convention that Parliament can legislate to do anything. Whilst there is a presumption that all legislation will be compatible with the ECHR the statute expressly preserves the power of Parliament to legislate in a way that is *not* compliant with the ECHR.[11] This also serves as an example of the second principal convention that exists on the sovereignty of Parliament which is that Parliament cannot bind its successors. In other words, the current Parliament in any current session may not pass a law that is not subject to repeal. This convention is also likely to ensure that Parliament cannot enshrine legislation as although this would not prevent Parliament from repealing it (enshrining legislation merely raises the threshold for repeal) the setting of a threshold would restrict the competency of Parliament and accordingly all statutes have (theoretically) the same status as each other.

2.2.1.1 Process of creating an Act

We now know what an Act of Parliament is but how is it established? Reference should be made to your constitutional-law/public-law texts which will describe this process in more detail, but it is necessary at least to summarize the parliamentary process in order to understand the impact of statutes.

The general process can be represented in diagrammatic form as shown in Figure 2.3.

For the purposes of Figure 2.3 a Bill has been introduced into the House of Commons but a Bill can begin its parliamentary life in either House. While a Bill is progressing through Parliament it is easy to identify where it originated as the letters '[HL]' are appended to those Bills that start in the House of Lords. Where this happens the boxes in Figure 2.3 listed 'House of Commons' and 'House of Lords' would simply be switched. Each substantive stage will be detailed in brief.

---

10. See, for example, *Scotland Act 1998*, s 28(7).
11. See *Human Rights Act 1998*, s 19(2).

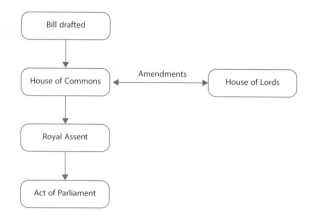

Figure 2.3 The parliamentary process

Table 2.1 The legislative stages

First Reading	Title of the Bill is read out and the Bill is printed.
Second Reading	Debate on the general principles of the Bill. Vote taken on whether to proceed.
Committee Stage	Passes to a Committee of the House.[12]
Report Stage	Amended Bill is reprinted and voted on.
Third Reading	Final amendments and vote. Passed to House of Lords if relevant.

House of Commons

Regardless of whether the House receives the Bill first or second the same format is always adopted (see Table 2.1).

The matter will only not return to the House of Lords if either the Parliament Act is used (see 2.2.1.2) or the two Houses have agreed the content of the Bill following the process described.

House of Lords

The process adopted in the House of Lords is virtually identical but the committee is normally a committee of the whole House and the rules relating to the choice and content of the amendments are not as regulated as they are in the House of Commons. The other significant difference is that by convention a Finance Bill is never defeated in the House and a government Bill that was included in an election manifesto is never defeated at second reading (although it may be later on).

Consideration of amendments

In many cases it is likely that the second House to consider the Bill will produce a slightly different Bill than that which was handed to them not least because members of the second House have had the opportunity to table amendments. Assuming that

---

12.   Where this is a constitutional Bill or part of the Finance Bill ('the budget') then it would normally be a committee of the whole House, otherwise it is more likely that an ad hoc committee of up to 50 MPs is established according to party strength.

this happens then the matter returns to the originating House (so in our example the House of Commons) where that House must consider the amendments. If they do not agree to them (and therefore make further amendments themselves) then the matter returns to the other House and the process is repeated in a 'ping-pong' fashion until one of three things happens:

- the two Houses agree the content of the Bill
- the Houses cannot agree and parliamentary time runs out in which case the Bill is normally lost[13]
- the Parliament Act is invoked (see 2.2.1.2).

Royal Assent

Assuming that the two Houses manage to agree the content of the Bill then the Bill is sent to the Queen for Royal Assent. The date on which the Royal Assent is given is also marked on the Act and it becomes itself part of the Act (see 'Date of Royal assent'). The constitutional position of Royal Assent is often debated but it is usually accepted that the sovereign no longer has power to decline assent.[14]

2.2.1.2 Parliament Act

The normal process by which an Act will be established is as discussed above but an important exception to this is when the Parliament Act is invoked. In fact there are two Parliament Acts, the first is the *Parliament Act 1911* and the second is the *Parliament Act 1949* which amended the 1911 Act. The 1911 Act was created to solve an impasse between the House of Commons and House of Lords whereby government business was being rejected by the upper House. The prime minister of the day, Herbert Asquith, sought to introduce legislation that would limit the right of the House of Lords to reject the wishes of the (democratically elected) House of Commons. If the legislation was not passed then Asquith had gained the support of the king to create sufficient new peers to ensure that the government would have a majority in the upper House, which would have been disastrous in terms of the authority and efficiency of the upper House. With that threat the House of Lords passed the 1911 Act.

The main provisions of the 1911 Act are to be found in ss 1 and 2 of the Act. Section 1 states that the House of Lords may only delay a money Bill for one month and that after this has elapsed the Bill may receive Royal Assent without the authority of the House of Lords. Whether a Bill is a 'money Bill' will depend on whether the Speaker of the House of Commons certifies it as such under s 1(2). The certificate of the Speaker cannot be subject to review by any court of law.[15] This severely restricts the powers of the upper House and was imposed because one of the Bills that was rejected in Asquith's Parliament was the Finance Bill (the government budget).

The second, and more important, part of the 1911 Act is provided for in s 2. This also limits the time in which the upper House can delay a Bill. When it was originally enacted the Bill had to be rejected on the third occasion before s 2 could be used (ie the Bill had

---

13. However, since 1998 the House of Commons can, in certain circumstances, agree that a government Bill can be held over to the next session (see House of Commons Factsheet L1: *Parliamentary Stages of a Government Bill*, 6–7).

14. See for example, Eric Barendt, *An Introduction to Constitutional Law* (OUP 1998) 41.

15. *Parliament Act 1911*, s 4.

failed to gain parliamentary support in at least two successive parliamentary sessions (years)) and the rejection had to be for virtually identical Bills (subject to amendments to reflect the passage of time). If the criterion was met—and the Speaker certified the criterion as being met (s 2(4) with s 4 applying to deny the opportunity to review this certificate)—then after its rejection for the third time the Bill could receive Royal Assent without the House of Lords approving it. The only exceptions to this were money bills (covered by s 1) and any provision that purported to lengthen the duration of Parliament.[16]

The *Parliament Act 1911* has only been used seven times, twice in 1914[17] and four times in the last twenty-five years,[18] but its most controversial use was when it was used to pass the *Parliament Act 1949* which amended the 1911 Act itself. The principal purpose of the 1949 Act was to reduce the threshold in s 2 to one year, meaning that a Bill must merely fail after it has been entered in two consecutive Parliaments and would be passed after the second, rather than third, defeat.

One important point to note about the *Parliament Act 1911* is that it applies only to legislation introduced to the House of Commons. If a Bill introduced into the House of Lords is amended by the House of Commons and the Lords refuse to accede to these amendments over two consecutive years then the Act cannot be invoked.[19]

Validity of the *Parliament Act 1949*

There has for a number of years been a debate over the validity of the *Parliament Act 1949*. The sole purpose of this Act was to amend the 1911 Act and two criticisms have been made of the 1949 Act. The first, as Loveland notes, is that some consider it unconstitutional because the 1911 Act was not designed to limit further the power of the upper House[20] but from a legal standpoint this argument carries little weight due to the competency of Parliament to legislate in any manner. The second argument is that legislation under the 1911 Act is not primary legislation per se but delegated legislation (the delegation being the 1911 Act permitting law to be made in a way contrary to the usual parliamentary process) and that delegated legislation cannot be used to alter primary legislation without express permission to do so.

The debate about the validity of the Act had been played out in the pages of academic books and journals but in 2005 it became a real proposition when it formed the basis of a case before the courts. The *Hunting Act 2004* was arguably one of the most controversial statutes in recent years and it banned certain types of hunting with live animals. The debate in Parliament was acrimonious and the House of Lords refused to pass the legislation. The government used the Parliament Act to force the provision through but the *Countryside Alliance*, an organization created to lobby against the Act, sought to challenge the ruling.

The challenge was rejected by the High Court and the matter proceeded to the Court of Appeal (*R (Jackson and others) v Attorney-General*[21]) who needed to consider the

16. Ensuring that a rogue government could not legislate to continue in power where it had a majority but knew it was unlikely to be re-elected.

17. To legislate for the disestablishment of the Church of Wales (*Welsh Church Act 1914*) and once to legislate for home rule in Ireland (*Home Rule Act 1914*) although this Act was never implemented.

18. To legislate for war crimes (*War Crimes Act 1991*), European parliamentary elections (*European Parliamentary Elections Act 1999*), to legalize certain homosexual acts and to reduce the age of consent for sexual activity (*Sexual Offences (Amendment) Act 2000*), and to ban hunting (*Hunting Act 2004*).

19. Hilaire Barnett, *Constitutional & Administrative Law* (9th edn, Routledge 2011) 354.

20. Ian Loveland, *Constitutional Law, Administrative Law, and Human Rights: A Critical Introduction* (7th edn, OUP 2015) 70.

21. [2005] QB 579.

status of the 1949 Act. The court agreed that legislation under the 1911 Act was delegated legislation rather than true primary legislation. The court argued that this conclusion was inevitable because delegated means the authority arises from another piece of
legislation and this is what happens when the Parliament Act is invoked. The Bill which
is to become an Act can only do so because of the authority vested in the 1911 Act. If the
1911 Act was repealed then a Bill rejected by the House of Lords could not become an
Act of Parliament.[22] However, the court also rejected the suggestion that because it was
delegated legislation it was somehow not as effective as an Act of Parliament and held
that the legitimacy of an Act passed under the Parliament Act was present. In terms of the
1949 Act the court held that although the 1911 Act could not be used to bring further
significant constitutional change (as it did not expressly so provide) the 1949 Act could
not be so categorized. The court also made the important point that the amended Act had
been used three times already without challenge and that the sovereign, Parliament, and
the courts had acted on that Act implicitly acquiescing to the validity of the Act.[23] This
perhaps marks the ultimate conclusion of the courts: if the 1949 Act had been deemed
invalid it would have caused numerous difficulties in its exercise in the past twenty years
and that alone was cause for the courts to be slow to question its validity.

The matter inevitably proceeded to the House of Lords[24] where their Lordships
upheld the decision of the Court of Appeal by dismissing the appeal but reversed the
Court of Appeal on several aspects of its judgment, most notably over whether legislation passed under the Parliament Acts is delegated legislation. Lord Bingham, who gave
the leading speech in the case, stated that the 1911 Act makes clear that the legislation
should be an 'Act of Parliament' and Parliament did not at that time envisage any different status.[25] This, it was submitted, is a crucial point. Constitutionally there has never
been any distinction drawn between the status of Acts of Parliament as distinct from
legislation in general. Acts of Parliament have always been considered to be not only primary sources of law but also primary legislation—and accordingly although the courts
can interpret the provisions (see 2.3) they cannot rule them illegal. The submissions of
the appellants would have created a situation where a distinction was drawn between
Acts of Parliament, which could have undermined the supremacy of Parliament.

Lord Bingham went further and argued that the case being litigated came extremely
close to disrupting the separation of powers, with his Lordship noting that the courts have
consistently stated that they do not have the power to look at the validity of an Act of
Parliament but must merely interpret and implement its provisions.[26] This was not a view
shared by all the Law Lords sitting on the case and Lord Nicholls, for example, argued that
it is not a case of looking at the validity of a properly passed Act but questioning whether
the Act was properly passed.[27] This is probably an important distinction to be drawn as
who else could decide this point? The balance of powers in the state does not provide
Parliament with any power to adjudicate on individual cases but instead leaves that to the
judiciary. Whilst Parliament can overrule a decision of the courts by legislating to overrule
the principle this will ordinarily have no impact on the specific case being litigated. The
only way that the validity of the Parliament Act process could be raised is through the
courts and for this reason a relaxation of the traditional rules would appear appropriate.

22. *R (Jackson and others) v Attorney-General* [2005] QB 579 (QB) 589–93.
23. *R (Jackson and others) v Attorney-General* [2005] QB 579 (QB) 606–7.
24. *R (Jackson and others) v Attorney-General* [2005] 3 WLR 733.
25. *R (Jackson and others) v Attorney-General* [2005] 3 WLR 733, 744.
26. *R (Jackson and others) v Attorney-General* [2005] 3 WLR 733, 746.
27. *R (Jackson and others) v Attorney-General* [2005] 3 WLR 733, 754.

Importantly, the decision in *Jackson* leaves open some questions on the limits of parliamentary accountability to the judiciary, with Cooke (a former Lord of Appeal in Ordinary) suggesting that some judges were prepared to hold that there are certain measures (eg the abolition of judicial review or a similar restriction of judicial access) that could not be passed under the Act.[28] However, it is quite clear from the unanimous decision of the House that legislation passed under the Parliament Acts is not delegated but has exactly the same status as legislation that is passed in the usual way. It is, of course, open to Parliament to repeal the Parliament Acts but unless the repealing Act expressly stated that it was to operate retrospectively the decision of the House of Lords in this case demonstrates that all Acts passed under those instruments are as valid as any other statute.

 QUESTION FOR REFLECTION

Lord Cooke suggests that the *Parliament Act 1949* cannot be used to amend the *Parliament Act 1911* in such a way as to remove the safeguards against a money Bill or the extension of Parliament. Consider the case of *Jackson* (see 'Validity of the *Parliament Act 1949*'), in particular the speech of Lord Bingham. Do you think Lord Cooke is right? If so, does that mean there are no safeguards to prevent a rogue government indefinitely extending the lifetime of Parliament?

 LISTEN TO THE PODCAST

For guidance on how to answer this question and a discussion of the main issues, listen to the author's podcast on the Online Resource Centre: www.oxfordtextbooks.co.uk/orc/gillespie_els6e/

33

2.2.2 **Content of a statute**

Having now discussed what legislation is, what does one look like and what are its contents. If we take, as an example, the *Constitutional Reform Act 2005* (CRA 2005) which we have already used it can be seen that the beginning of the statute will look similar to Figure 2.4.

The relevant aspects to discuss are:

1. Short title
2. Royal Coat of Arms
3. Chapter number
4. Long title
5. Date of Royal Assent
6. Enacting formula
7. Part number and heading
8. Marginal note
9. Section

28. Lord Robin Cooke, 'A Constitutional Retreat' (2006) 122 *Law Quarterly Review* 224, 226.

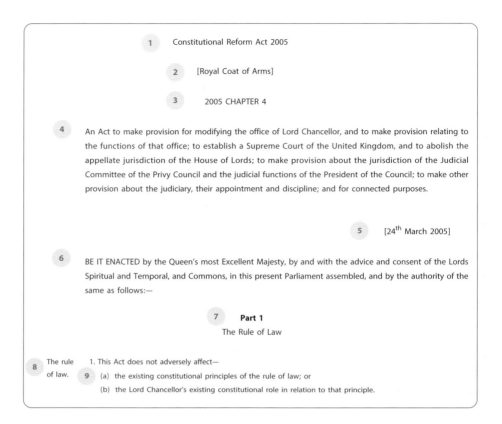

Figure 2.4 An example of a statute

2.2.2.1 Short title

Most statutes will be referred to by their short title, ie in the example earlier the statute will normally be called the *Constitutional Reform Act 2005*. This short title is always displayed at the beginning of the Act but the authority to use a short title must be expressly provided within the statute itself and it will normally come towards the end of the statute. For this statute, s 149 CRA 2005 says: 'This Act may be cited as the Constitutional Reform Act 2005.'

Ordinarily the short title of an Act is uncontroversial but occasionally its use can be misunderstood. Perhaps a classic example of this was in 2008 during the midst of the global financial crisis. An Icelandic bank called *Landsbanki Islands hf* was in financial difficulties and after it went into liquidation the Chancellor of the Exchequer used powers given to him under the *Anti-Terrorism, Crime and Security Act 2001* to seize control of the bank's British assets. This led to the Icelandic government and many global media outlets stating that the British government had used its anti-terrorist legislation against Iceland, the inference being that Iceland was being compared to terrorists. However, the relevant provisions used by the Chancellor were not in the Anti-Terrorism parts of the Act, they were in later sections of the Act. It is easy to see how this could be misrepresented, however, given the short title of the Act. It is perhaps a warning of the political difficulties in putting too much disparate legislation in an Act of Parliament, and also of the requirement to choose short titles with care!

2.2.2.2 **Royal Coat of Arms**

An Act of Parliament is made under the authority of the Queen in Parliament because the United Kingdom is a constitutional monarchy. Accordingly, when any legislation is passed the Royal Coat of Arms is affixed to the statute to act as a seal for the legislation.

2.2.2.3 **Chapter number**

The second official way in which a statute should be cited is in respect of its chapter number. Each Act that is passed by both Houses of Parliament and which receives Royal Assent is assigned a sequential number to identify what order the legislation was passed in any parliamentary session. Modern statutes are governed by the *Parliament Numbering and Citation Act 1962* which provides that the chapter number is assigned by reference to the calendar year. The first statute to be given Royal Assent after 31 December is given the chapter number 1, and each successive piece of legislation is given a sequential number (s 1). Accordingly, in the earlier example, the *Constitutional Reform Act 2005* was the fourth Act to be given Royal Assent in the calendar year 2005.

Prior to the 1962 Act the position was significantly more complicated. Statutes were assigned a chapter number according to the regnal year in which the parliamentary session was begun. The regnal year was the year of the reign of the current monarch. The regnal year starts on the accession to the throne (eg Queen Elizabeth II acceded to the throne on 6 February 1952)[29] and continues until the day before the anniversary of accession (eg the first regnal year of Queen Elizabeth II was 6 February 1952 to 5 February 1953; on 6 February 1953 Her Majesty's second regnal year began). This inevitably meant that there may be an overlap between the regnal years and the parliamentary sessions which typically begin in October or November of each year with the Queen's Speech. The system was extremely confusing because of this overlap and, for example, the twenty-third Act that was passed in the parliamentary session which began in 1961 and lasted to 1962 would be referred to as *10&11 Eliz.2 c.23* which is translated to mean the 23rd Act in the 10th and 11th years of the reign of the Monarch Elizabeth II. This meant that one would need to know the year of accession for all the monarchs in order to identify what year the Act was! Even today in law libraries you will normally find a list of monarchs and their regnal years in order to facilitate paper-based searching of these Acts.[30] Thankfully the 1962 Act simplified this process and most electronic legislative search engines (eg *Westlaw*, *LexisNexis*, etc) use the calendar rather than regnal year for ease of reference.

It has been argued that the only significance of the chapter number is that it allows the courts to identify in which order Parliament is deemed to have acted.[31] If, for example, in the extremely unlikely event that two pieces of legislation are given Royal Assent on the same day but appear to contradict each other, the chapter number identifies which is the later Act and would, therefore, be deemed to have implicitly repealed the earlier legislation.[32]

---

29. Note it is the date of the *accession* (ie assumption) of the throne and not the date of the *coronation*. A monarchy is never without a sovereign and thus as soon as a monarch dies the heir presumptive becomes monarch with this assumption being *confirmed* by coronation but the rule starts at the time of accession. The coronation of Queen Elizabeth II was not until 1953 but she was Queen from 1952.

30. A list can also be found on the Online Resource Centre that accompanies this book.

31. Francis Bennion, *Bennion on Statute Law* (3rd edn, Longman 1990) 128.

32. For more on implicit repeal see Ian Loveland, *Constitutional Law, Administrative Law, and Human Rights: A Critical Introduction* (7th edn, OUP 2015) 31–2. The issue is not necessarily academic discussion. In *R v Richards* [2007] 1 WLR 847 the President of the Queen's Bench Division held the fact that two pieces of legislation were enacted on the same day was evidence that they did not contradict (and thus implicitly repeal) each other (at 853).

2.2.2.4 **Long title**

Although each Act is given a short title by which it will ordinarily be known, there is also a 'long title' to the Act which serves a description of the purposes of the Act. Bennion also notes that procedurally it is important because when a Bill is being debated in the House of Commons (see 2.2.1.1) an amendment can only be tabled to the Act if it is within the scope of the legislation and the long title broadly governs the scope of legislation.[33] Bennion also notes that it should be an aid to construction and this will be considered later (see 2.3.5.1).

2.2.2.5 **Date of Royal Assent**

It was discussed earlier that Royal Assent is the final part of the process required to enact legislation (see 2.2.1.1) and the date on which assent is given is placed on the Act and on all copies of the Act. The sovereign no longer physically signs each Act and the process is now regulated, in part, by the *Royal Assent Act 1967*, s 1(1)(b) of which permits the Speaker of the House of Commons and the Lord Speaker of the House of Lords to notify their House that Royal Assent has been granted.

2.2.2.6 **Enacting formula**

The enacting formula is just a formal wording that demonstrates that the legislation passed the relevant legislative processes. The formula identified in the earlier example is the usual one but where the Parliament Act has been invoked (see 2.2.1.2) the formula changes to:

> Be it enacted by the Queen's most Excellent Majesty, by and with the advice and consent of the Commons, in this present Parliament assembled, in accordance with the provisions of the Parliament Acts 1911 and 1949, and by the authority of the same, as follows—

Obviously it is necessary for this formula to be used as the usual one refers to the advice and consent of the Lords which, of course, did not occur if the Parliament Acts needed to be invoked.

2.2.2.7 **Part number and heading**

The organization of statutory material is important since, especially with long pieces of legislation, it ensures that there is a consistency of approach and permits provisions to be grouped together for interpretation. Where an Act is long it is not uncommon for the Act to be split into Parts. The *Constitutional Reform Act 2005* is divided into seven Parts each dealing with a discrete set of provisions in a broad area. Each Part is usually accompanied by a heading, or more properly referred to as a 'note' and these have the same status as marginal notes (see 'Marginal note').

Where an Act is particularly long or complicated it is possible to further divide the Parts into chapters. For example, the *Constitutional Reform Act 2005* divides Part 4 (judicial appointments and discipline) into four chapters. In this context it is important to note that 'chapter' merely means a subdivision of a Part and is not the same as a chapter number.

---

33. Francis Bennion, *Bennion on Statute Law* (3rd edn, Longman 1990) 42.

2.2.2.8 **Marginal note**

Each section within a statute (see 'Section') is accompanied by a marginal note, which is sometimes also referred to as a side note. In effect it has the appearance of a heading and on electronic versions of statutes it appears alongside the section number with the appearance of a heading; eg s 1, as noted earlier, is presented in electronic versions as:

1. The Rule of Law

   This Act does not adversely affect—

   (a) the existing constitutional principle of the rule of law, or

   (b) the Lord Chancellor's constitutional role in relation to that principle.

However, it is referred to as a marginal note because, as was seen in Figure 2.4, in printed form the notes appear in the margins alongside text. A debate appears to exist as to whether marginal notes are part of the Act or whether they are annotations. This will be discussed in more detail later as it is relevant only to the interpretation of a statute (see 2.3.5.1).

2.2.2.9 **Section**

Each provision within a statute is known as a section. Each section will ordinarily deal with only one topic but it may not be possible to deal with a single topic with only one level of heading within the provision. Accordingly, it is possible to subdivide a section. Four levels are recognized and these are shown in Table 2.2.

Table 2.2 Dividing sections

Level	Name	Appearance
1	Section	1
2	Subsection	(1)
3	Paragraph	(a)
4	Subparagraph	(i)

Example Section 9 *Constitutional Reform Act 2005*

Section 9 states:

(1) The President of the Family Division is Head of Family Justice.

(2) The Lord Chief Justice may appoint a person to be Deputy Head of Family Justice.

(3) The Lord Chief Justice must not appoint a person under subsection (2) unless these conditions are met—

   (a) the Lord Chief Justice has consulted the Lord Chancellor;

   (b) the person to be appointed is an ordinary judge of the Court of Appeal.

(4) A person appointed as Deputy Head of Family Justice holds that office in accordance with the terms of his appointment.

It can be seen that s 9 is broken into four subsections each of which deals with a discrete aspect of the section's provision. Subsection (3) has to be subdivided itself in order to provide for discrete conditions and this division consists of two paragraphs. If either paragraph needed to be divided then this division would be known as subparagraphs and would be represented as (i), (ii), etc.

It is important to note that each level has a distinct appearance. If I wanted to refer to the second paragraph of subsection 3 I would do so by writing s 9(3)(b). Not using the brackets could cause confusion as s 9 3 b might be taken to mean either section 93 or a new section that follows s 93.[34]

The provisions themselves are at the heart of the statute and it is these that the courts need to interpret when adjudicating on cases brought before them.

2.3 Statutory interpretation

It has been noted that statutory law is a primary source of law. It is the statute itself that forms the law and this can cause difficulties. Statutes will invariably use technical language or may leave a degree of uncertainty as to what their meaning is. It is not possible to ask what the meaning of the term is because who would be asked? Parliament sits collectively and passes legislation collectively. It is not possible to ask each Member of Parliament what was meant when they passed the Act. Therefore whilst Parliament sets out the legislation one of the most important roles of the courts is to interpret legislation.

Until comparatively recently it was said that there were defined rules or even 'canons' (a term that suggests something even stricter than rules) of interpretation that governed how courts will interpret legislation. However, it is now recognized that this is not what happens and that interpreting a statute is more complicated. Marshall suggests that there are two approaches to interpretation; the 'purposive approach' and the 'interpretative approach'.[35] However, the former is then immediately cross-referenced to the old 'rules' and the latter is cross-referenced to the approach arising from s 3 *Human Rights Act 1998*. This is therefore perhaps equally unhelpful because if the rules themselves are open to question then consolidating them into an approach is perhaps also unhelpful. The one issue which is undoubtedly correct is in respect of HRA 1998 introducing a new form of interpreting statutes. This will be expanded upon later in the chapter and in Chapter 5 but the approach introduced by that Act differs from the approach of the courts prior to the introduction of that Act.

It has been said that statutory interpretation is unique to common-extract-based jurisdictions because in civil law systems the courts feel they have no need to construe a statute because the text is flexible and more akin to 'living instruments' with the judges having final say over what the law should mean in a particular case.[36]

The concept of statutory interpretation has become increasingly important because, at least in England, the era of 'judge-made law' is probably coming to an end and there is recognition that the legislature creates the law and the role of the courts is to apply it.

---

34. A further explanation of the appearance of provisions is given on the Online Resource Centre accompanying this book.

35. Geoffrey Marshall, 'The Lynchpin of Parliamentary Intention: Lost, Stolen or Strained' [2003] *Public Law* 236, 236.

36. Francis Bennion, *Bennion on Statute Law* (3rd edn, Longman 1990) 83.

That is not to say they are subservient because the courts can impact how the law comes into effect but it does mean that their role is now to interpret rather than create law.

Of course the difficulty with separating out the creation of the law and its interpretation and application is that it will undoubtedly cause tensions. Parliament may believe that it has passed a law that says x and could get frustrated if it perceives the courts as applying it as meaning y. This is perhaps particularly evident in the fields of criminal justice and asylum issues. It is perhaps not surprising that these are the areas of increased tension as they are also the most politically active areas of law with the impression that the electorate is most concerned with these matters. In the early 1990s when John Major was the prime minister and Michael Howard was the Home Secretary this tension began to become somewhat noticeable but in the early 2000s the battle recommenced when David Blunkett was appointed Home Secretary[37] and it is has never eased. The current battle is over judicial review (discussed in Chapter 17) with the current government complaining that judges are frustrating the democratically elected government, yet with the judges saying they are an essential check on executive misuse of power.

⚡ PARLIAMENTARY SOVEREIGNTY: 'GINGER HAIR' TEST

Earlier in this chapter the concept of parliamentary sovereignty was discussed and the ambit of Parliament was discussed in connection with the 'smoking on the streets of Paris' example (see 2.2.1). If Parliament can do what it wishes then does this mean there are no balances and that a corrupt Parliament could use its powers to act in an improper way? Those who argue that the courts are either supreme or, at the very least, a safeguard to an overzealous legislature and executive sometimes point to the 'ginger hair' example.

The essence of this example is that Parliament passes a law that states anyone with ginger hair is to be arrested and sent to gaol. Theoretically Parliament could enact such a law but it is an unjust law and one that is a direct affront to human rights and the right to liberty. Given that the courts will be the ultimate arbitrators of this law it is argued that they could interpret the law so as to make it impossible to implement. For example, if a judge was called upon to rule whether someone had ginger hair, she could adjudicate that the person in fact had red hair or a dark copper colour hair. In this way the courts could act as a 'brake' to Parliament's desire to infringe human rights by ensuring that the law was interpreted in such a way that no injustice is done.

It was noted earlier that traditionally there were thought to be 'rules' that governed how the courts interpreted statutes. It is necessary to know what these rules are because they are discussed a lot but it should be noted once again that these are not formulaic and are not followed rigidly, especially now. Setting aside the HRA 1998 rule the three 'rules' that are commonly referred to are:

- literal rule
- golden rule
- mischief rule.

---

37. See Robert Stevens, *The English Judges: Their Role in the Changing Constitution* (Hart Publishing 2002) 129–36.

2.3.1 **Literal rule**

The literal rule is considered to be the 'normal' rule and it complies with the traditional view of the courts that their role is not to make or subvert the law but rather to apply the law created by Parliament. The essence of the literal rule is that the courts simply look at the words and apply them as they are written with the suggestion that Parliament must have known what they meant.

> ### ▤ **Example** Literal rule
>
> Parliament (hypothetically) creates a law that states:
>
> (1)   A person aged 18 must pay the sum of £150 to the government.
>
> (2)   On receipt of the £150 the government shall grant to the person a certificate.
>
> (3)   No person shall be entitled to drink an alcoholic beverage in a public house without a certificate.
>
> There are a number of parts of this law that may need to be interpreted, including 'aged 18', 'on receipt', 'alcoholic beverage', and 'public house'. The literal approach would simply look towards the ordinary meaning of these words. Accordingly, in subsection (1) it is likely that the courts would hold that a person could not pay £150 until the eighteenth anniversary of their birth, but that they had until the day before the nineteenth anniversary of their birth to pay the £150. A literal interpretation would not suggest that the sum must be paid on the person's eighteenth birthday because it does not literally say that. A literal interpretation of subsection (2) would mean that as soon as the money has been received by the government they should issue a certificate and so, for example, an executive decision taken by the Home Secretary not to issue any certificates until two months after receipt in order to enable people to attend alcohol education programmes could be ruled illegal as it contravened a literal interpretation of the Act. A literal interpretation of subsection (3) would mean that a person could not drink any alcoholic drink in a public house regardless of whether they bought it or indeed knew whether it was alcoholic.

Where the literal interpretation can begin to come unstuck, however, is when grammar is introduced, not least because grammatical rules and styles change over the years.[38] Some have argued that grammar should be ignored but that would be a false premise as punctuation must have been used for a reason. One commentator has suggested that where there are conflicting grammatical meanings the courts must decide between them by looking at the possibilities and the section as a whole,[39] but to remember above all that the purpose of statutory interpretation is to adopt a legal meaning and not necessarily a grammatical meaning.[40]

In deciding the literal meaning of the word the judge will sometimes refer to their own interpretation of the meaning, usually arguing that it is so well known that people know what it means. Alternatively the judge will make reference to a dictionary, usually the *Oxford English Dictionary*, and suggest that this amounts to the literal meaning. The literal rule can sometimes appear harsh with one leading commentator[41]

---

38.   Francis Bennion, *Bennion on Statute Law* (3rd edn, Longman 1990) 130.
39.   Francis Bennion, *Bennion on Statute Law* (3rd edn, Longman 1990) 96–7.
40.   Francis Bennion, *Bennion on Statute Law* (3rd edn, Longman 1990) 88.
41.   Penny Darbyshire, *Darbyshire on the English Legal System* (11th edn, Sweet and Maxwell 2014) 29.

citing the example of *Diane Blood* who was denied the right to conceive by artificial insemination using her late husband's sperm which had been harvested while he was in a coma.[42] The relevant Act (*Human Fertilisation and Embryology Act 1990*) required the consent of the donor before artificial insemination could be undertaken and this was not, of course, possible in these circumstances. Although the courts were deeply sympathetic to the predicament faced by Mrs Blood they said they were forced to rule that the literal language employed by statute was obvious and they were bound to follow the wording of the Act. This also demonstrates the limits of interpretation. Whilst there are other ways of interpreting a statute, the courts cannot interpret the legislation in such a way that contradicts the will of Parliament.

2.3.2 Golden rule

The golden rule picks up from this point. Sometimes following the literal meaning of words could actually contradict what Parliament intended. If that is the case then the courts will need to look at other interpretations and one form of this is the 'golden rule'.

Identifying precisely when the golden rule should apply is not easy. One commentator has suggested that it should be used when Parliament intended its provision to have a wider definition and not one restricted to the literal meaning of its words[43] and this is corroborated by other commentators who note that the rule is traditionally employed when it is decided that a literal interpretation would not encompass the will of Parliament[44] but rather limit it.

However, it has also been suggested that the rule usually applies when it is thought that taking a literal meaning to the phrase in question would lead to an absurdity.[45] This is arguably wider than the suggestion put forward by Bennion in that an absurdity need not be restricted to extent but could be the result of poor drafting.

When can the court adopt the golden rule? Traditionally it has been held that the rule should only be used where the literal rule cannot be used (although this could be because there are a number of different literal interpretations). Where absurdity is the result then the rule is perhaps easier to justify since it can be legitimately argued that it is unlikely that Parliament would intend an absurd situation to arise although that, of course, raises questions as to who decides what is absurd (the answer to which can only be the courts).

The harshness of this can perhaps be illustrated by the example provided in 2.3.1 concerning the *Dianne Blood* litigation. If you read the judgment you cannot but come to the conclusion that all the courts the matter was before had sympathy with Mrs Blood who wished to conceive using her dead husband's harvested sperm. Given that the courts and indeed the parties morally supported her[46] it may be thought that the courts could simply have cast aside the literal meaning of the legislation and adopted a 'fairer' interpretation (such as 'where the person gave consent prior to dying then that

---

42. *R v Human Fertilisation and Embryology Authority, ex p Blood* [1997] 2 WLR 807.
43. Francis Bennion, *Bennion on Statute Law* (3rd edn, Longman 1990) 105.
44. Colin Manchester and David Salter, *Exploring the Law: The Dynamics of Precedent and Statutory Interpretation* (4th edn, Sweet and Maxwell 2011) 47–8.
45. Colin Manchester and David Salter, *Exploring the Law: The Dynamics of Precedent and Statutory Interpretation* (4th edn, Sweet and Maxwell 2011) 47–8.
46. The hospital that in effect refused to undertake the procedure did not do so because it objected in principle to the idea but rather because it believed it had no statutory right to do it and was obliged to reject the approach. This is a common feature in medical cases where there is no 'dispute' as such but doubt exists about the legality of a situation.

consent is effective post mortem'). However, it was not able to do so because there was no uncertainty and certainly no absurdity. The requirement that a person must give active consent to the use of their frozen sperm was a plausible rule and therefore construing the legislation to require that positive consent would not be absurd. The mere fact that Parliament failed to contemplate a situation is not a reason to use the golden rule and all a court can do in these circumstances is bring the matter to the attention of Parliament and suggest that it passes new legislation.

Example Golden rule

Section 57 *Offences Against the Person Act 1861* defines bigamy as:

> Whosoever, being married, shall marry another person during the life of the former husband or wife, whether the second marriage shall have taken place in England or Ireland or elsewhere, shall be guilty [of an offence].

It is not possible to use the literal rule here since the application of that rule would defeat the intention of Parliament. Section 57 says it is illegal to marry another person but as a matter of civil law a second marriage under such circumstances would not be legally valid so the person has not, by law, married. Also, the statute says during the life of the 'former' husband or wife. The purpose of bigamy is to deal with situations where they are still married so 'former' would not apply. If they were the former husband or wife then it would not be bigamy.

The courts, to overcome this obstacle, have used the golden rule so as to construe bigamy as when somebody purports to marry someone else (ie go through a marriage ceremony) whilst already legally married.

 QUESTION FOR REFLECTION

The Online Resource Centre accompanying this book has a summary of the *Diane Blood* litigation. Read this. Do you think that the courts were unduly harsh here? Nobody doubts that the golden rule could have been used to create an exemption where a partner is dead but the question is whether the rule could be used. Instead of looking at absurdity in *the law* (ie on the face of the legislation) could the absurdity not be *in fact* (ie in this case, the fact that it was impossible to gain consent from a dead person)?

 LISTEN TO THE PODCAST

For guidance on how to answer this question and a discussion of the main issues, listen to the author's podcast on the Online Resource Centre:
www.oxfordtextbooks.co.uk/orc/gillespie_els6e/

2.3.3 Mischief rule

The third 'rule' that is most commonly referred to is the mischief rule. This rule differs from the previous two forms of interpretation in that the importance of the words is less significant than the underlying reason of why Parliament legislated.[47] Bennion argues that the rule is historic as it dates back to the time when statutory law did not have a pre-eminent position—ie common law was the more usual and statutory law was only passed when the common law did not cover an issue[48] or, because Parliament disagreed with what the common-law rule and wished to alter it (something it has been noted they have the right to do).

The rule can also be used where Parliament has acted to remedy an apparent defect in a previous statute.[49] Where there is doubt as to the meaning of a word or expression contained in the new statute the courts should start by ascertaining what defect it was that Parliament intended to rectify and construe the statute accordingly.

The mischief rule is sometimes used when a statute is in force for many years. Some statutes will remain current law for decades or even hundreds of years, and will be in continuous use. However, language will frequently move on and therefore the statute may use language that is not readily understood in the context of modern society. The mischief rule permits a court to depart from the literal meaning of a word used at that time and apply the intention of Parliament—to legislate for a particular mischief—in such a way that it can be applied to modern society.

Example Obscenity

An example of the use of the mischief rule can be seen from the case of *R v Stamford*[50] where the appellant had been convicted of sending postal packets containing indecent or obscene material. The relevant statute creating the offence, the *Post Office Act 1953*, did not provide any definition of 'indecent' or 'obscene' and this could be contrasted with the *Obscene Publications Act 1959*, which did. The Court of Appeal was called upon to consider whether it was possible to call expert evidence on what amounted to 'indecent' or 'obscene' material if someone was charged under the 1953 Act. Counsel submitted that they should be able to because expert evidence was permitted under the 1959 Act. In rejecting the submission the court looked to the mischief behind the 1953 and 1959 Acts and decided that the statutes were intended to deal with different mischiefs[51] with the 1953 Act being intended to prevent the misuse of the postal service and the 1959 Act being intended to regulate, inter alia, the publication of obscene material. The court argued that this meant that the test of obscenity under the 1953 Act would be purely objective as it matters not what the addressee thinks of the material as the postal service has been misused irrespective of the intentions of both parties. This could be contrasted with the 1959 Act where it was thought that the views of the likely audience at the publication would be relevant.

The courts needed to use the mischief rule because the literal meaning of 'obscene' would not provide any clue as to the question that was being litigated, ie whether opinion evidence could be admissible. The so-called 'golden rule' would not have helped as there was no absurdity; it was simply not addressed by Parliament, and therefore the most obvious action of the courts would be to consider the mischief behind the prohibition.

47. Colin Manchester and David Salter, *Exploring the Law: The Dynamics of Precedent and Statutory Interpretation* (4th edn, Sweet and Maxwell 2011) 48.
48. Francis Bennion, *Bennion on Statute Law* (3rd edn, Longman 1990) 161.
49. Francis Bennion, *Bennion on Statute Law* (3rd edn, Longman 1990) 163.
50. [1972] 2 QB 391.
51. *R v Stamford* [1972] 2 QB 391, 396–7 (Ashworth J).

2.3.4 **The Human Rights Act 1998**

Regardless of how the courts used to interpret legislation there is no doubt that the *Human Rights Act 1998* fundamentally altered this approach by introducing s 3 of the Act. As will be seen, somewhat ironically, the meaning of s 3 has itself been called into question meaning the courts had to interpret that in order to ascertain how to depart from the customary rules of statutory interpretation.

The HRA 1998 introduces a dilemma to us here as it produces a 'chicken and egg' scenario. Do we look at s 3, HRA 1998 here—alongside the other rules of statutory interpretation—or do we leave it until Chapter 5 when the rest of the HRA 1998 is discussed? Neither solution is perfect. The first four editions of this book adopted the second solution but since the previous edition we have decided to move it to this section. However, a note of caution should be sounded. The powers of the courts under s 3 HRA 1998 exist only as a result of that provision. Therefore they can only be used in connection with cases that raise human rights issues and the powers would (probably) fall away if the HRA 1998 is repealed (which, for example, the Conservative government have pledged to do). Whether that remains the case is the subject of some debate because statutory interpretation is a common-law doctrine and so the courts could decide to retain the powers by introducing a new 'rule' although they could only do so if the repealing legislation did not make clear that the courts could not adopt the approach used in s 3.

The other note of caution that must be sounded is that there is a strong argument for knowing what the purpose of the HRA 1998 is before considering the powers of s 3. Certainly it would be useful to know what human rights means and so you should at least familiar yourself with the outline of the Act before considering this rule. However, it is included here because it allows you to draw a contrast to how statutory interpretation took place before the HRA 1998 was passed.

Section 3(1) states: '[s]o far as it is possible to do so, primary legislation and subordinate legislation must be read and given in a way which is compatible with the Convention rights.' This relatively innocuous statement masks its importance and provides an additional, and extremely powerful, canon to the doctrine of statutory interpretation. Section 3(2) makes it clear that reference to interpreting legislation applies to primary legislation irrespective of whenever it is enacted, meaning that it should apply both to legislation already passed and legislation that will be passed in the future.

It is ordinarily said that Parliament cannot bind its successors but this provision arguably does so, albeit to a limited extent. There is nothing to stop Parliament from repealing s 3 or indeed the whole HRA 1998 itself (discussed at 5.3), although it should presumably be done expressly. However, in the absence of a statement stating that s 3 does not apply then Parliament has decreed that any future piece of legislation can be interpreted in such a way as to make it compatible. In other words the court need not theoretically care whether it was Parliament's intention to act in a way that is incompatible with the Convention so long as it is possible to interpret legislation.

The interaction between ss 3 and 19 is interesting. Whilst s 19 requires a minister to make a statement stating either that legislation is compatible or not compatible with the Convention, nothing within s 19 disapplies the rule in s 3(1). Accordingly, where a minister states, when introducing a Bill, that he believes the provision is not compatible with the ECHR the courts could ignore this and interpret the legislation in such a way as to make it compatible (if it is possible to do so). Of course the easiest way to avoid this issue would be for Parliament to state in that Bill that the provisions of s 3(1) HRA 1998 do not apply (which it could do) but this would raise similar political issues to those discussed in respect of s 19 earlier.

2.3.4.1 So far as it is possible

The key words in s 3(1) are 'so far as it is possible to do so' in that this clearly indicates that Parliament expressly considered that there were limits to the ability of the courts to interpret legislation. It was never the intention of the government to allow the courts to 'strike down' legislation that is incompatible as occurs in some countries (discussed in more depth later). It will be remembered from 2.3.3 that statutory interpretation is ordinarily limited to situations where there is doubt as to the wording of the statute but the same is not true where s 3 is invoked; '... the interpretative obligations under s 3 of the 1998 Act is a strong one. It applies even if there is no ambiguity in the language in the sense of the language being capable of two different meanings.'[52] This is a significant departure from the ordinary rules of statutory interpretation where, it will be remembered, the standard rule is to apply the ordinary definition of words contained in a statute. Section 3 clearly empowers a court to interpret legislation even where Parliament's intentions were clear, if not to do so would result in the provision being incompatible with the ECHR. However, this is subject to the proviso that on occasion it will not be possible to interpret the legislation in this way (as is clear from the use of the words 'so far as it is possible').

The leading case in ascertaining what s 3 means is the case of *R v A*[53] discussed below. As is evident from the wording of Lord Steyn, the House of Lords considered that it had wide discretion to construe statutes and the clear presumption was that s 3 should be used rather than, for example, declaring that the statute was incompatible (through the issuing of a declaration of incompatibility discussed later). This approach, as will be seen, has been followed by subsequent cases and certainly it is clear that the courts view their powers under s 3 as important.

45

Ⅲ\ Case Box *R v A*

The case of *A* concerned the construction of s 41 *Youth Justice and Criminal Evidence Act 1999* which purported to prevent the victim of a sexual offence being questioned about previous sexual history. This provision was widely welcomed at that time and was introduced in the context of a number of cases where rape complainants had been cross-examined as to their complete sexual history, including number of partners and methods used to have sex, in great detail and in public. Parliament believed that such questioning should stop and enacted s 41 to do so.

The appellant A had been charged with the rape of a woman. He sought to question the complainant about consensual sexual intercourse that had taken place between her and the appellant in the weeks preceding the alleged rape. This was quite clearly 'sexual history' and would be excluded by virtue of s 41. However, the House of Lords argued that this evidence was vital in establishing a defence of consent and that excluding the use of what

52. *R v A* [2001] UKHL 25, [2002] 1 AC 45, 67 (Lord Steyn).
53. [2001] UKHL 25, [2002] 1 AC 45.

could be probative evidence would breach Article 6 of the ECHR. Their Lordships therefore unanimously invoked s 3(1) and stated that the exclusion should be subject to an overriding power of the judge to permit such questioning when a failure to do so would amount to a breach of Article 6, the right to a fair trial.

The decision of the House of Lords was unquestionably contrary to the intentions of Parliament and Kavanagh notes that it has been vociferously attacked on that basis.[54] However, Parliament had also made clear that it wished legislation to be interpreted in a way that made it compatible with the Convention and the decision of the House and *R v A* certainly made the provision compatible even though it was contrary to what Parliament had itself intended. Some argue that the House should have made a declaration of incompatibility instead[55] but this would arguably have been contrary to the intention of Parliament expressed in the 1998 Act. It was possible to interpret the legislation and the House did so.

It has been suggested that there are three questions that must be asked by the court when deciding whether to use their powers[56] which are:

- If the HRA 1998 did not exist what would the natural meaning of the legislation be?
- Would the natural meaning of the legislation identified earlier lead to an incompatibility with one or more articles under the ECHR?
- If the answer to the second question is 'yes' then is it possible to read the legislation in such a way as to lead to this incompatibility being resolved?

The second question may seem obvious but it is an important question that must always be answered. Section 3 should be considered as an exception to the ordinary principles of statutory interpretation and one that can only be justified when the HRA 1998 applies. Certainly Lord Woolf has made clear, in his view, that in the absence of a prima facie breach of a Convention right then s 3 can be ignored and the ordinary rules of interpretation apply.[57]

The questions identified by Elliott and Thomas are useful to the extent that they assist us in understanding how the courts approach the use of s 3. Of course what they do not tell us is how far the courts may go when deciding to use their powers. Whilst *R v A* made clear the courts should try to construct the legislation in this way how far can they go?

In *R v Lambert*[58] the House of Lords adopted the approach of re-interpreting legislation even where Parliament had arguably been clear as to what its intention was. *Lambert* concerned a drugs offence under the *Misuse of Drugs Act 1971*. Parliament had purported to reverse the burden of proof once a person was found in possession of a controlled drug, meaning that the defendant needed to prove he was not guilty rather than the prosecution proving he was guilty. This appeared on the face of it to breach Article 6, the presumption of innocence. The House of Lords held that reverse

54.   Aileen Kavanagh, 'Unlocking the Human Rights Act: The "Radical" Approach to Section 3(1) Revisited' (2005) 3 *European Human Rights Law Review*, 259, 268–9.

55.   Aileen Kavanagh, 'Unlocking the Human Rights Act: The "Radical" Approach to Section 3(1) Revisited' (2005) 3 *European Human Rights Law Review*, 259, 273.

56.   Mark Elliott and Robert Thomas, *Public Law* (2nd edn, OUP 2014) 705–6.

57.   *Poplar Housing and Regeneration Community Association Ltd v Donoghue* [2002] QB 48, 71–2.

58.   [2001] UKHL 37, [2001] 3 All ER 577.

burdens were not prima facie a breach of Article 6(1) but drew a distinction between a *legal* burden and an *evidential* burden. The House read the 1971 Act to mean that a defendant had an evidential burden (which would be compatible with the ECHR) even though Parliament almost certainly intended it to be a legal burden. Subsequent legislation has adopted this approach and it is now accepted that where a reverse burden is indicated it is an evidential and not legal burden.

⚡ LEGAL V EVIDENTIAL BURDEN

This is quite a complicated area of the *Law of Evidence* but it is possible to give a brief explanation.

The ordinary rule in criminal cases is that the prosecution must prove every element of the crime. The prosecution prove that D is guilty and it is not for D to prove he is innocent. A legal burden is where the party has to adduce sufficient evidence to satisfy the court that a matter is true. For the prosecution this means proving something beyond all reasonable doubt. Let us assume that D is charged with possessing drugs. The prosecution must prove that D was in possession (meaning custody or control) of a substance and that the substance was illegal.

An evidential burden is where a party (usually the defence) need to adduce some evidence to show *the possibility* that a fact may be true. If an evidential burden did not exist then the prosecution would have to disprove whatever the defence said even if there was no evidence to support the contention. If they could not disprove it beyond reasonable doubt then the defendant would succeed in the contention.

Let us go back to the drugs example. Ordinarily the prosecution would have to prove that the defendant knew that the substance was illegal (the *mens rea*). The *Misuse of Drugs Act 1971* states that if a person is found to have the substance in their factual possession (eg found on their person) then they have to prove that they did not know that the drug was illegal. If this was a legal burden then the defence would need to prove to their standard (preponderance of probabilities) that they did not know the substance was illegal. However, as it is an evidential burden they must simply raise some evidence that shows it is *possible* they did not know (eg it was handed to them by a stranger in a sealed envelope) and it is then for the prosecution to disprove (to the criminal standard) this is correct.

An evidential burden still places some burden on the defence—in that they cannot just say a statement they must adduce some evidence to show it is not just a theoretical possibility—but the main emphasis is still on the prosecution. Accordingly, it does not breach Article 6.

Aside from *A* one of the cases that demonstrates how far the courts are prepared to go to find compatibility is *Ghaidan v Godin-Mendoza*.[59] This was a civil case concerning the possession of a rented flat. The defendant had been in a homosexual relationship with another man who was the protected tenant for a flat. When that man died the landlord began proceedings to evict the defendant. The *Rent Act 1977* gave protection to the spouse of a deceased person but the defendant could not legally be a spouse (this was prior to the recognition of civil partnerships and same-sex marriage). The defendant argued that the 1977 Act was incompatible with Articles 8 and 14 of the ECHR. The wording of the Act (and thus Parliament's intention) was clear but the House of Lords believed (answering the first two questions identified by Elliott and Thomas earlier) that this would lead to an incompatibility with the ECHR. The House considered that the purpose of that part of the Act (protection

59.   [2004] UKHL 30, [2004] 2 AC 557.

of spouses) was to give protection to those in an enduring, stable relationship. That being the case, the House (with Lord Millett dissenting) argued that it was possible to re-interpret the provision of the 1977 Act, using the powers given to them under s 3, to construe it in such a way as to include same-sex partners who were living in a relationship akin to a marriage.

Ghaidan shows how far the courts are prepared to use their powers under s 3. There is no question that the decision the House of Lords reached would not have been possible if the HRA 1998 did not exist. There was no doubt over the wording of the provision of the 1977 Act and so none of the other canons of statutory interpretation could have led to the same result.

2.3.4.2 **Where it is not possible**

The previous section has identified that the courts will go to significant lengths to try and interpret legislation in such a way as to make it compatible with the ECHR but there are limits. It will not always be possible to reach an interpretation. The first limitation is that the courts will not reach an interpretation that is against the intentions of Parliament. For example, in *Lambert*, discussed earlier, the House of Lords limited what Parliament wanted to do (by making it an evidential rather than legal burden) but the essence of the intention remained (ie that the defence must still adduce *some* evidence and not simply sit back and say to the prosecution 'prove it'). Similarly in *Ghaidan* the House of Lords did not prevent the 1977 Act from applying to spouses, they simply extended the protection to include same-sex partners.

Where the only way to make an instrument compatible is to go against the wishes of Parliament then the courts will decline to use s 3 and will instead declare the statute incompatible. A good example of this is *R (Anderson) v Secretary of State for the Home Office*.[60] This case concerned the conditions of prisoners receiving parole. The legislation gave the Home Secretary the ultimate power to decide whether a prisoner should be released and the House of Lords accepted that this contravened Article 6 in that the Home Secretary, as a politician, was involved in what should be a judicial process. However, the House declined to use s 3 as the only way to make it compliant would be to remove reference to the Home Secretary, something that was clearly contrary to the intentions of Parliament (a good summary of the reasoning is provided by Elliott and Thomas).[61] This would not be a case of 'interpreting' legislation but rather re-writing it and so the House, quite correctly, declined to use s 3 and instead made a declaration of incompatibility.

2.3.5 **Aids to interpretation**

The preceding section has considered how the courts approach the issue of interpreting legislation but in order to do this they will sometimes look to other rules that guide how they should act and, in particular, what types of sources they should consider when constructing an Act. The courts normally make reference to the notion of 'aids', ie those 'things' that can assist them in understanding the meaning of legislation. It is generally said that there are two types of aids; intrinsic aids and extrinsic aids, the differences of which are shown in Figure 2.5.

---

60. [2002] UKHL 46, [2003] 1 AC 83.
61. Mark Elliott and Robert Thomas, *Public Law* (2nd edn, OUP 2014) 707–8.

Intrinsic aids
Looking at the content of the statutory material to assist in the interpretation of a provision

Extrinsic aids
Looking at material outside the Act but within the contemplation of the legislature

Figure 2.5 Intrinsic and extrinsic aids

2.3.5.1 **Intrinsic aids**

Intrinsic aids are those contained within the statutory instrument itself. Quite what can be considered to be 'part of a statute' is open to debate. The contents of a statute were discussed earlier and the individual components of legislation may become relevant in deciding how to construe a statute.

A number of issues arise as to what is within the statute however. The two principal issues are the wording of the provisions and the explanatory features of the Act.

Wording of the statute

The first issue to examine is the wording of the Act. An important canon of interpretation is that the Act should be read as a whole[62] which gives rise to three examples, all of which are known by a Latin term notwithstanding the fact that we are trying to remove Latin from the legal language! The common rules are:

- *noscitur a sociis*
- *ejusdem generis*
- *expressio unius exclusio alterius*.

Noscitur a sociis

The first rule is that a statutory provision should be read in conjunction with its neighbouring provisions. Certainly this canon has been employed by the courts on a number of occasions and is a logical step. Given that even the most disparate of Acts will normally be divided into Parts, the neighbouring provisions should assist in ascertaining either the meaning of a word or the mischief behind the Act.

This rule can, in effect, be divided into two aspects. The first of these looks at similar words. A word should have the same meaning throughout an Act[63] although it should be noted that this is only a presumption and accordingly if Parliament expressly wishes to act differently it may do so. A good example of this can be found in the *Sexual Offences Act 2003* where 'sexual' is defined within s 78 but the Act expressly states that a different meaning of the word shall be employed for s 71.

The second aspect to this rule is its logical conclusion: that different words in a statute should normally bear different meanings.[64] Whilst this would appear to be obvious it is not necessarily so and indeed this construction has caused difficulties before.

---

62. Francis Bennion, *Bennion on Statute Law* (3rd edn, Longman 1990) 187.
63. Francis Bennion, *Bennion on Statute Law* (3rd edn, Longman 1990) 188.
64. Francis Bennion, *Bennion on Statute Law* (3rd edn, Longman 1990) 189.

⚡ COMPLICITY

The *Accessories and Abettors Act 1861* is a good illustration of how different words should have different meanings. The provision makes it clear that a person can become an accomplice to the principal offender by acting in one of four ways:

1. aiding
2. abetting
3. counselling
4. procuring.

At first sight it is unclear what the difference is between 'aiding' and 'abetting' or 'abetting' and 'counselling' or even 'counselling' and 'procuring'. Certainly common usage will frequently refer to someone as 'aiding and abetting' and the thesaurus provides 'aid' as the first alternative to 'abet'. In *Attorney-General's Reference (No 1 of 1975)*[65] the Court of Appeal held, however, that each had a different meaning because if it were otherwise then Parliament would not have listed these four separate ways of acting.

This canon can still be controversial, however, and there is sometimes a debate in the courts as to whether different words must necessarily mean anything. A good example of this is the words 'cause' and 'inflict' within the *Offences Against the Person Act 1861*. At first sight they appear to be two different words but they appear in two related sections of the Act (ss 18 and 20 which relate to grievous bodily harm). The difference between the words exercised the courts for many years and in *R v Ireland; R v Burstow*[66] the House of Lords held that for practical purposes there is no longer a distinction between 'cause' and 'inflict'.[67]

Ejusdem generis

This second rule is similar to the first but relates to similar words rather than identical or contrasting words. The expression can be translated into English as 'of the same kind or nature' and it demonstrates the purpose of this rule. The basic principle of the rule is that where words of general meaning are to be found in a provision following words with a specific meaning then the general words are to be read narrowly as though they were linked to the specific words.[68] In other words the general words are considered to be a continuation of any list of words preceding them.

The rule is subject to some restrictions. The first is that all the words must constitute a genus (or 'set' of words) and this genus should be narrower than the literal interpretation of the provision.[69] Bennion provides the following example:

The *Customs Consolidation Act 1876*, s 43 reads: 'The importation of arms, ammunition, gunpowder or any other goods may be prohibited.'[70]

There is no doubt that the words 'or any other goods' are general words and their literal interpretation would encompass virtually any form of trade. However, the *ejusdem*

65. [1975] 2 All ER 684.
66. [1998] AC 147.
67. *R v Ireland; R v Burstow* [1998] AC 147, 160 (Lord Steyn) and 164 (Lord Hope of Craighead).
68. Francis Bennion, *Bennion on Statute Law* (3rd edn, Longman 1990) 196.
69. Francis Bennion, *Bennion on Statute Law* (3rd edn, Longman 1990) 197.
70. Francis Bennion, *Bennion on Statute Law* (3rd edn, Longman 1990) 197.

generis rule would seek to limit the meaning of those general words to a context related to the preceding words, ie the 'any other goods' must be comparable to ammunition, eg gelignite (a high explosive) may come within this provision. Bennion continues by arguing that the 'genus' must also be restricted narrowly:

> The string specified as 'boots, shoes, stockings and other articles' would import the genus 'footwear' rather than the wider category of 'wearing apparel'.[71]

Clearly this is a useful and sensible approach to adopt and does ensure that a provision is no wider than it needs to be.

Expressio unius exclusio alterius

This final rule is related to the *ejusdem generis* rule in that it concerns lists of words but where the rules differ is that the *expressio* rule operates on the premise that in the absence of any general words a list will be exhaustive and accordingly any term not listed within the list will be deemed not to be included within the provision. This principle can be identified from its English translation, 'to list one thing is to exclude another'.

The rule arguably goes further by limiting general words. Bennion's argument is that if a specific word is used to limit a general word (cf the *ejusdem generis* rule where a general word was used to *extend* or *complement* the specific words) then the specific word is taken to mean that it excludes other words that come within that general class.[72] He provides the following example:

> The *Immigration Act 1973*, s 2(3) states that for the purposes of s 2(1) of the Act the word 'parent' includes the *mother* of an illegitimate child. The class to which this extension relates is the *parents* of an illegitimate child.[73]

The logical conclusion of this rule is that the father of an illegitimate child would not be within s 2(1) because the use of the word 'mother' as an express inclusion must be to limit the meaning of the general word 'parent' and accordingly 'father' which is obviously within the general term has been implicitly excluded.

Explanatory issues

Although it will be noted later (see 'Explanatory notes') that some explanatory material is outside of the Act, the statute itself will contain some provisions that explain the significance of the detailed provisions. The two most important features are marginal notes and the long title.

Marginal notes

It was noted that sections will normally be accompanied by something called a 'marginal note' or 'side note'. These are, in effect, descriptions of the section but are they part of the statute and capable of being used as an intrinsic aid? Some commentators argue that the answer is 'no' and they do not form part of the Act and accordingly cannot be used as an intrinsic aid.[74] However, others disagree and argue that they

---

71. Francis Bennion, *Bennion on Statute Law* (3rd edn, Longman 1990) 197.
72. Francis Bennion, *Bennion on Statute Law* (3rd edn, Longman 1990) 202.
73. Francis Bennion, *Bennion on Statute Law* (3rd edn, Longman 1990) 202.
74. Colin Manchester and David Salter, *Exploring the Law: The Dynamics of Precedent and Statutory Interpretation* (4th edn, Sweet and Maxwell 2011) 54–5.

are part of the statute albeit they usually provide only an indication of the provision rather than a necessarily accurate description of the provision.[75] It is submitted that there is no reason why a court could not take account of the marginal note of a provision although caution should be shown because the notes are not debated within Parliament but are placed on the Act by the draftsman.[76] Accordingly, not only is it not necessarily an accurate description of the provision it is the draftsman's deduction of the meaning of the provision.

> ### Case Box *R v Tivnan*
>
> In *R v Tivnan*[77] the Court of Appeal demonstrated that it does occasionally use marginal notes in order to assist in understanding the intentions of Parliament. The appellant had been convicted of drug dealing and a confiscation order had been made against his assets. He claimed that as it could not be proven his assets had been obtained through the proceeds of drug dealing the confiscation order should be quashed. The Court of Appeal considered Parliament's intention was to deprive drug dealers of assets equal to the proceeds obtained by drug dealing not necessarily just those assets that were purchased directly from the proceedings. The court made express reference to the marginal note in seeking the intent.[78]

Long title

The long title of the Act may provide assistance in the construction of a provision. It will be remembered that the long title is part of the preamble to the Act which sets out the purpose of the Act. As the long title is part of, if not the official title for, the Act it would appear appropriate that it should be considered.

> ### Example Animal cruelty
>
> The *Protection of Animals (Amendment) Act 2000* permits a court to make an order, upon the application of a prosecutor, for the care, disposal, or slaughter of animals that have been kept cruelly. In *Cornwall County Council v Baker*[79] the Divisional Court was asked to rule on the meaning of 'animals in question'. The Council had prosecuted the respondent for cruelty to seven farm animals. It also sought an order under the 2000 Act relating to other animals at the farm which were not subject to the prosecution. The magistrates' court refused to make an order in respect of the other animals contending that the 2000 Act applied only to animals subject to proceedings under the 1911 Act. The Divisional Court upheld this ruling on appeal and referred to the long title to demonstrate its purpose.[80]

75. Francis Bennion, *Bennion on Statute Law* (3rd edn, Longman 1990) 128.
76. Francis Bennion, *Bennion on Statute Law* (3rd edn, Longman 1990) 127.
77. [1999] 1 Cr App R(S) 92.
78. [1999] 1 Cr App R(S) 92, 97.
79. [2003] 1 WLR 1813.
80. [2003] 1 WLR 1813, 1819–20 (Toulson J).

2.3.5.2 **Extrinsic aids**

In certain circumstances it may be possible to look outside of the Act for assistance in construing a statutory provision and this is known as using extrinsic aids. There are a number of extrinsic aids that the courts will consider but rules do sometimes exist as to when courts may look outside of the Act for assistance. Broadly speaking, the following aids will be examined:

- explanatory notes accompanying an Act
- parliamentary material
- other statutory provisions
- academic writing
- pre-parliamentary material.

Explanatory notes

Since 1999 all government Bills introduced into Parliament are accompanied by explanatory notes and upon Royal Assent these notes are amended to reflect the agreed wording of the Act.[81] The notes do not form part of the Act and are created by the government department sponsoring the Bill (see *Westminster City Council v National Asylum Support Service*)[82] so they have not been approved within Parliament because while they may be the subject of discussion during the progress of the Bill there is no mechanism for the notes to be amended by Parliament. Further, parliamentary draftsmen have argued that 'explanatory notes are informal in style, are there to improve clarity for the reader, and to this end may be highly discursive'.[83] Clearly, it is contemplated that the reader of a piece of legislation will refer to the notes but does a 'reader' include members of the judiciary? Also, given that the notes are written by draftsmen and not members of the legislature, they arguably suffer from the same problem as marginal notes (discussed earlier).

The courts readily refer to explanatory notes[84] but some question whether they go too far and accord them a 'quasi-legislative' status that it was never intended for them to have. To support this argument reference is made to the comments of Lord Bingham in *Attorney-General's Reference (No 5 of 2002)*[85] where his Lordship argued that the explanatory notes 'strongly supported' his conclusion as to the meaning of the provisions. Given that they are a creature of the executive rather than the legislature it is somewhat surprising that the notes are so readily referred to, especially in light of the rule governing the use of parliamentary material (see 2.3.5.3). However, Lord Steyn in *Westminster City Council v National Asylum Support Service* argued that they were akin to pre-parliamentary material but arguably of more assistance than, for example, White or Green Papers since they reflect the initial wording of the provisions.[86] One concern is that ready use of these notes by the courts could encourage sloppy draftsmanship (on the basis that so

---

81. Roderick Munday, 'Bad Character Rules and Riddles: "Explanatory Notes" and True Meanings of s 103(1) of the Criminal Justice Act 2003' [2005] *Criminal Law Review* 337, 340–1.
82. [2002] 1 WLR 2956, 2958–60 (Lord Steyn).
83. Roderick Munday, 'Bad Character Rules and Riddles: "Explanatory Notes" and True Meanings of s 103(1) of the Criminal Justice Act 2003' [2005] *Criminal Law Review* 337, 341.
84. Roderick Munday, 'Bad Character Rules and Riddles: "Explanatory Notes" and True Meanings of s 103(1) of the Criminal Justice Act 2003' [2005] *Criminal Law Review* 337, 341–2.
85. [2005] 1 AC 167.
86. [2002] 1 WLR 2956, 2960.

long as the notes explain the provision it need not matter whether the provision is tightly defined).[87] The fact that the notes are created by the executive rather than the legislature also creates the possibility that recourse to the notes could give rise to a confusion as to whether a provision reflects the intentions of Parliament or the government with the two not necessarily coinciding. Notwithstanding these points, however, the use of the notes has become an accepted part of statutory construction although more recent decisions of the Supreme Court would appear to suggest that a fundamental review of their use (akin to that undertaken in *Pepper v Hart*;[88] see 2.3.5.3) may soon occur.[89]

Parliamentary material

Parliament is a formal body and is a body of record, ie a number of documents exist governing its proceedings and one possible extrinsic aid may be to use these documents. However, this is one of the more controversial uses of an extrinsic aid and for this reason, and to demonstrate the importance of the general rule, the use of such material is considered in its own section later (see 2.3.5.3).

Other statutory provisions

Whilst some statutes will act as amending or consolidating instruments for existing legislation, a significant amount of legislation is 'new' in that it creates stand-alone laws and procedures. It may be thought therefore that there is little use in examining other pieces of legislation but it is not unusual for similar words to be found in other statutes. Where the mischief is similar between the Acts then comparing or contrasting statutory words could prove useful in helping construct the meaning of the provision under scrutiny.

> ### Case Box *R v Dooley*
>
> In *R v Dooley*[90] the Court of Appeal needed to consider the meaning of the words 'with a view to' which appeared in s 1(1)(c) *Protection of Children Act 1978*. The Act did not define these words but it is a not uncommon phrase to be found within legislation and the court examined how it had been construed in other legislation, including ss 1(2), 20, and 21 *Theft Act 1968* and the *Obscene Publications Act 1964*. The court then argued that applying the same interpretation to the 1978 Act would be logical and it can be seen, therefore, that the other legislation acted as an extrinsic aid.

Perhaps the most common alternative statute to examine is the *Interpretation Act 1978* which, as its short title suggests, was designed to provide assistance in the interpretation of statutes. The 1978 Act is merely the latest reincarnation of the Interpretation Act and it is unlikely to be the last. The Act itself provides a series of common words and the presumption is that if one of these words is used in a statutory provision then it is deemed to have that meaning unless Parliament intended differently, this intention

---

87.   Roderick Munday, 'Bad Character Rules and Riddles: "Explanatory Notes" and True Meanings of s 103(1) of the Criminal Justice Act 2003' [2005] *Criminal Law Review* 337, 347.

88.   [1993] AC 593.

89.   See Roderick Munday, 'Bad Character Rules and Riddles: "Explanatory Notes" and True Meanings of s 103(1) of the Criminal Justice Act 2003' [2005] *Criminal Law Review* 337, 346–9, and 352–4, for a discussion of these issues.

90.   [2005] EWCA Crim 3093.

normally being evidenced expressly. Perhaps the most important interpretative presumptions in the Act are contained within s 6:

In any Act, unless the contrary intention appears—

(a) words importing the masculine gender include the feminine;

(b) words importing the feminine gender include the masculine;

(c) words in the singular include the plural and words in the plural include the singular.

The use of such presumptions is important because otherwise an Act of Parliament could become cluttered and unreadable when a simple provision refers constantly to 'he or she', 'him or her', 'that or those', etc. Where the context clearly means the masculine or feminine gender then obviously the interpretation is so construed as the 1978 Act creates presumptions rather than mandatory rules.

Academic writing

It is often said that the English courts have been somewhat sceptical about the use of academic writings but this is not necessarily the case. Perhaps the most basic example of the use of books as an extrinsic aid is that of the dictionary; it was noted earlier that the usual rule in statutory interpretation is to use the literal meaning of the word and a dictionary is not infrequently consulted to achieve that aim. A dictionary cannot be anything other than an external aid.

The use of academic writing through texts and journals has been slowly developing but was used even in the nineteenth century. However, its use has arguably been growing not least because there is a greater respect between 'academic' and 'practising' lawyers.[91]

The appellate courts are now increasingly turning to the use of academic sources of writing and indeed a failure to do so has led to criticism about the courts taking an unduly lenient approach to construction.[92] That is not to say that academic sources will be automatically consulted and certainly where textbooks are concerned it is not unusual for only the most authoritative to be cited, but where a narrow point of law arises where there has been little case law or what case law there is has been debated amongst eminent academics then the citation of academic writings can be of assistance to the judges although, of course, they are not bound by them.

 ACADEMIC WRITING

BOOKS

In *R v Dooley*,[93] discussed in the previous case study, the Court of Appeal did not just use alternative statutes as an aid but also made reference to Smith and Hogan's *Criminal Law*, undoubtedly the leading criminal law textbook. The arguments made in the text by its editor and author, Professor David Ormerod, were cited by the court as being of assistance.[94]

---

91.   Indeed this 'glasnost' has led to a debate as to whether academics could be appointed direct to the bench (see Chapter 8). Arguably the most famous 'academic' lawyer was Professor Brenda Hoggett QC who moved from academia to the Law Commission. She was then appointed to the High Court bench as Hale J before being promoted to the Court of Appeal, becoming the first female Law Lord in 2004 and is now the Deputy President of the Supreme Court. However, this cannot be said to be a 'pure' academic appointment as she was appointed from the Law Commission rather than from academe.

92.   See for example, commentary by Professor Andrew Ashworth on the Privy Council decision of *Attorney-General for Jersey v Holley* [2005] 2 AC 580 (Andrew Ashworth, 'Commentary on A-G for *Jersey v Holley*' [2005] *Criminal Law Review* 966).

93.   [2005] EWCA Crim 3093.

94.   [2005] EWCA Crim 3093 [14].

ARTICLES

In *R (Purdy) v DPP*[95] the House of Lords became aware of an article by Professor Michael Hirst.[96] Not only did Lord Philips refer to it extensively in his speech but the House also required counsel to supply written submissions on whether they believed the points contained within it were correct.

Pre-parliamentary sources

Legislation does not 'just happen' especially when a Bill is introduced by the government. There will normally be a significant number of documents that were produced and published prior to the Bill being introduced. When the Bill arises out of government policy it is quite likely that a series of official 'papers' may have been published, with a *White Paper* being a statement of the policy with a broad indication as to how the government intends to legislate to tackle the mischief, and a *Green Paper* being a discussion paper issued by the government for assistance in structuring the way in which the mischief should be tackled. The government may also have asked the Law Commission to examine a particular issue and if so the Law Commission will almost certainly have produced a consultation paper and a report to Parliament.[97] In exceptional circumstances where issues of importance need to be examined it is possible that a Royal Commission will be established which will issue a report to Parliament.

Outside of the executive-controlled bodies Parliament itself may have created documents that are relevant to the provision. Both Houses of Parliament create *select committees* that investigate areas of interest to Parliament. Some of these committees are standing committees in that they remain in existence at all times (eg Home Affairs Select Committee, Defence Select Committee) and others will be created for a specific purpose. Committees will produce reports that are publicly available and sometimes these reports will call for legislation to be introduced which the executive may heed.

The use of such material is accepted by the courts but the degree to which it will be useful is perhaps more open to question since it may not reflect the proceedings in Parliament. That said the material will allow the provision to be placed into context and this could assist in its interpretation.

⚡ MODEL CODES

Pre-parliamentary material need not necessarily be accepted, or even debated, by Parliament for it to be used in the construction of a statute. Perhaps the best example of this is *R v G and R*[98] which is an important criminal law case where the House of Lords used its right to depart from its own decisions (see 3.4.3) to overrule *R v Caldwell*[99] which it stated was a 'mistake' even though it had been used for over ten years. Lord Bingham, who gave the leading speech in the House, used the model penal code to construe the meaning of the word 'reckless'. The model penal code was created by the Law Commission and was designed as an exercise to demonstrate how the criminal law could be codified. Parliament has not yet decided that the criminal law should be codified, and indeed the Law Commission has now dropped the proposals believing they

95. [2010] 1 AC 345.
96. [2010] 1 AC 345, 359.
97. Although the executive will refer a matter to the Law Commission the report will always be to Parliament.
98. [2004] 1 AC 1034.
99. [1982] AC 341.

are unlikely to ever be implemented, so the proposals have not been debated by Parliament but this does not stop Lord Bingham from using it as a source of identifying the meaning of 'reckless'.[100]

2.3.5.3 **The rule in *Pepper v Hart***

It has been seen that a basic distinction can be drawn between the legislature and judiciary in that Parliament enacts the law but the courts interpret it. How a court interprets legislation has been discussed and the ability to use extrinsic aids to assist in interpretation has also been identified as a source of help for the judiciary. A logical supposition that could be drawn is that an easy way of interpreting the law would be to examine what was said in Parliament when passing the provision. Debates and written answers in both Houses of Parliament are reported in a series known as *Hansard* and it is published daily both on the Internet and in hard copy.

Where the courts wish to analyse what Parliament's intention is then it may appear sensible to examine *Hansard* to provide clues as to the meaning of the legislation. However, the traditional rule was that it was not permissible to look at parliamentary proceedings to assist in interpretation; in part this was because it was thought that it would lead to unnecessary expense and delays,[101] but it was also because it was thought that it might be a challenge to parliamentary supremacy in that it was thought that the law was that which was passed by Parliament not that which was discussed, ie the wording of Bills changes and only the final Act is law. Looking at the proceedings may lead to the suggestion that the courts were questioning or impeaching the process of Parliament contrary to Article 9 of the *Bill of Rights 1689*.

However, in the landmark case of *Pepper v Hart*[102] the House of Lords, exercising its power to reverse previous decisions of the House (see *Practice Statement (Judicial Precedent)*[103] and see 3.4.3), decided to relax this rule and introduced rules governing when recourse to *Hansard* would be permitted for statutory interpretation. The rule permitted courts to make reference to ministerial statements or the promoter of a Bill so long as three rules were met:

1. The legislation in question was ambiguous, obscure, or led to absurdity.
2. The material relied on consisted of statements by a minister (or the promoter of a Bill).
3. The statements relied on were clear.

It was never thought that this would lead to *Hansard* being referred to frequently, in part because it could be considered an abrogation of the duty of a court to invoke the rule. The clear presumption is that the courts will interpret the law according to the words used (see 2.3.1) and accordingly only where this is not possible will it be possible to consider using the rule. Lord Browne-Wilkinson, who gave the leading speech in the case, stated: 'In many ... cases reference to Parliamentary material will not throw any light on the matter.'[104] This is partly because many provisions of a Bill are not

---

100.   *R v G and R* [2004] 1 AC 1034, 1046, and 1054.
101.   *Beswick v Beswick* [1968] AC 58.
102.   [1993] AC 593.
103.   [1966] 1 WLR 1234.
104.   *Pepper v Hart* [1993] AC 593, 634.

subject to detailed comment or consideration and in part because where the language is obtuse it is unlikely that any ministerial statement will be particularly clear either. Kavanagh argues that restricting an analysis of *Hansard* to the comments of ministers inevitably misrepresents the position and confuses the distinction between the legislature (Parliament) and the executive (government).[105] She argues that Parliament passes legislation even if the majority of legislation is sponsored by the executive as the largest parliamentary party. It does not follow automatically that the language of the legislation will necessarily reflect the executive's desire and most Bills will be full of amendments, and it is always open to Parliament to enforce its powers and pass a Bill different from that required by the executive.

Example Parliament v executive

A good example of where Parliament and the executive may depart from one another is over terrorism legislation. The executive has an interest in obtaining wider powers to deal with terrorists because of the threat that they pose to society at large. Terrorism differs from traditional crimes in the way that it is carried out and most developed countries will have special rules for dealing with terrorism. However, powers can be abused as easily as used and the legislature is therefore careful to ensure that there is a check on any increase in the power of the executive, and indeed this is its very purpose.

In 2005 the Terrorism Bill was being discussed and the government wished to extend the time a terrorist suspect could be held by the police without charge from fourteen days to ninety days. Parliament did not agree and it eventually defeated the government clause proposing this measure, accepting a reduced increase to twenty-eight days. The case for the government was put forward by the Home Secretary and he outlined the reasons why the powers were necessary. If there was any legislative uncertainty as to the meaning of cl 23 of the Bill would recourse to *Pepper v Hart* help? Probably not because the rule permits only statements by ministers to be cited and yet in this case the House of Commons rejected these arguments and put forward its own viewpoint.

The debate on powers may help clarify any uncertainty, and the comments of the backbenchers as to why they would not support ninety days would certainly help a court understand the intention of Parliament in this provision but the rule, as drafted, would be of no assistance—the courts would have to ignore parliamentary debates and reach their own conclusions.

Kavanagh, citing Corry, argues that a further difficulty with the rule is that Parliament is not a bipartisan place. A minister making a statement to either House will not be giving a fully independent rationale comment but will be making the point to support his, and the government's position.[106] Whilst it is true to state that the rules of Parliament make clear that a minister may not mislead either House[107] this is a far step from an independent comment and Kavanagh argues this can be contrasted with

---

105.   Aileen Kavanagh, '*Pepper v Hart* and Matters of Constitutional Principle' (2005) 121 *Law Quarterly Review* 98, 106.

106.   Aileen Kavanagh, '*Pepper v Hart* and Matters of Constitutional Principle' (2005) 121 *Law Quarterly Review* 98, 108.

107.   Malcolm Jack, *Erskine May's Treatise on the Law, Privilege, Procedures and Usage of Parliament* (24th edn, LexisNexis 2011) 429.

a witness who gives testimony in court under oath.[108] Of course others will be sceptical as to whether a witness necessarily gives independent and unbalanced evidence in court but the political nature of Parliament inevitably means that the ministers' statements will be geared towards their desire.

However, the threat to *Pepper v Hart* appears to have retreated for some time as the House of Lords (and now the Supreme Court) showed no desire to widen the scope of its enquiry into parliamentary legislation. Kavanagh notes that when the Court of Appeal sought to widen the scope of the rule in *Wilson v Secretary of State for Trade and Industry*[109] the Speaker of the House of Commons and Clerk to the Houses of Parliament sought the right to make representations to the House as to the application of the rule.[110] Their fear was that a wider treatment of parliamentary legislation could lead to the courts scrutinizing the proceedings of Parliament, something that they are expressly not permitted to do (see Article 9 of the *Bill of Rights 1689*).[111] In *Wilson* the House did not simply prevent the rule in *Pepper v Hart* from being widened but it actually constrained its use by noting that the statement of a minister will not necessarily reflect the intention of Parliament as a whole. The House also stated that it was important to emphasize that any statement was not *law* but an aid to deciding *what* the law was. Accordingly, any statement permitted under the rule of *Pepper v Hart* was simply a tool to help the court decide what the law should be and not a definitive statement of the law. This latter point is to be welcomed and whilst Kavanagh argues that it is a restriction[112] some doubt must exist as to this because it is difficult to believe that Lord Browne-Wilkinson, when formulating the rule, ever intended that a ministerial statement should ever bind a court when deciding the meaning of the law.

So what is the status of *Pepper v Hart*? Kavanagh argues that it has been significantly reduced but in *Jackson v Attorney-General*[113] Lord Nicholls of Birkenhead appeared to disagree:

> In some quarters the *Pepper v Hart* principle is currently under something of a judicial cloud. In part this is due to judicial experience that references to *Hansard* seldom assist …
> It would be unfortunate if *Pepper v Hart* were now to be sidelined. The *Pepper v Hart* ruling is sound in principle, removing as it did a self-created judicial anomaly.[114]

His Lordship argues that the rule continues to be important even if his enthusiasm is tempered by the reminder that the rule is perhaps not as useful as some suggest. Yet Lord Steyn, in the same case, suggests that it may not be as important:

> If it were necessary to do so, I would be inclined to hold that the time has come to rule … that *Pepper v Hart* should be confined to the situation which was before the House in *Pepper v Hart*. That would leave unaffected the use of Hansard material to identify the mischief at which the legislation was directed and its objective setting. But trying to

---

108.   Aileen Kavanagh, '*Pepper v Hart* and Matters of Constitutional Principle' (2005) 121 *Law Quarterly Review* 98, 108.

109.   [2003] 3 WLR 568.

110.   Aileen Kavanagh, '*Pepper v Hart* and Matters of Constitutional Principle' (2005) 121 *Law Quarterly Review* 98, 112.

111.   For more on this see Lord McKay's speech in *Pepper v Hart* [1993] AC 593, 614–16 and Lord Browne-Wilkinson, 621–9, 638–40.

112.   Aileen Kavanagh, '*Pepper v Hart* and Matters of Constitutional Principle' (2005) 121 *Law Quarterly Review* 98, 115.

113.   [2005] UKHL 56.

114.   [2005] UKHL 56 [65].

discover the intentions of the Government from Ministerial statements in Parliament is unacceptable.[115]

Although the ruling in *Pepper v Hart* was about ascertaining the intentions of Parliament and not the government, the difference between what Parliament intends and what the government intends arguably goes to the heart of some of the difficulties that have been raised about this rule. Lord Walker of Gestingthorpe appears to summarize the crux of this area when his Lordship noted that there was a disagreement as to the application of the *Pepper v Hart* principle in the House although his Lordship argued that this need not be resolved in that case[116] and this is probably true with the statements of the other Lords concerning its application being *obiter dicta*.

An interesting question raised by Holland and Webb is whether *Pepper v Hart* applies to criminal cases as strictly.[117] It may seem a strange question but it falls from the particular nature of criminal trials where the liberty of a person (the defendant) is at stake. In *Thet v DPP*[118] Lord Philips, the then Chief Justice, said that he doubted whether the rule in *Pepper v Hart* could apply in criminal cases.[119] The basis of such an approach is that if a criminal statute is ambiguous then the benefit of the doubt should go to the defendant, which is often considered to be a standard legal approach. However, as Holland and Webb point out, the very same judge later used *Pepper v Hart* in a criminal trial irrespective of the fact that the use was to help the prosecution and not the defendant.[120] This perhaps just reinforces how complicated and controversial the rule is.

So what is the status of the rule? Whilst it may have been weakened in some respects it remains an important rule and one that you must try to understand. Courts remain reluctant to admit parliamentary material and certainly will not do so where there is no ambiguity in the statute, perhaps reinforcing the fact that statutory material can only be used where a court needs assistance in understanding what a statute says.

2.3.6 Presumptions

Alongside the rules governing interpretation and the aids used by the courts to identify the correct meaning of words are presumptions that operate in respect of the construction of statutory material. The key presumptions that will be discussed here are:

- against altering the common law
- Crown not bound by Act
- *mens rea* required for criminal offences
- against retrospective approach
- presumption in favour of the defendant.

2.3.6.1 Common law

It has already been noted that until comparatively recently the vast majority of law was judge-made rather than statutory, with Parliament initially simply amending or correcting

---

115. *Jackson v Attorney-General* [2005] UKHL 56 [97].
116. *Jackson v Attorney-General* [2005] UKHL 56 [141].
117. James Holland and Julian Webb, *Learning Legal Rules* (9th edn, OUP 2016) 292.
118. [2007] 1 WLR 2022.
119. *Thet v DPP* [2007] 1 WLR 2022, 2027.
120. See *R v JTB* [2009] 2 WLR 1088.

defects within the common law (see 2.3.3). However, as one would expect, Parliament began to take control of the law and now it is often contended that judges no longer have any right to make law (although as will be seen in Chapter 3 this is contentious). Notwithstanding this, however, there remains a presumption that a statute will not alter the common law unless it was the intention of Parliament to do so. The rationale behind the presumption is that Parliament must know the law before it enacts legislation and accordingly unless it identifies a defect in that law then it is presumed not to be interfering with its course. In *Deeble v Robinson*[121] the Court of Appeal held that only plain words would suffice to interfere with common-law rights, which is taken to mean that the intention of Parliament to interfere with the common-law power should be obvious.

⚡ *DOLI INCAPAX*

Whilst the intention to interfere with the common law need not be express it is not uncommon for Parliament, when wishing to end a common-law rule, to use express blunt terms to do so. A good example of this can be found in the *Crime and Disorder Act 1998* (CDA 1998) where s 34 ended the common-law rule of *doli incapax* (where a child between the ages of ten and fourteen was presumed not to be capable of committing a criminal offence unless evidence was adduced to demonstrate they knew it was legally or morally wrong). Section 34 states:

> The rebuttable presumption of criminal law that a child aged 10 or over is incapable of committing an offence is hereby abolished

which would seem to leave little room for doubt, but see *R v JTB*[122] where the House of Lords had to rule on whether the presumption or the substantive doctrine had been abolished. The House ruled that despite the literal phrasing, the substantive defence, and not just its presumption, was removed by the CDA 1998.

It has been argued that the presumption is extremely controversial[123] and given that Parliament is supreme and can legislate against any matter it does appear strange that there should continue to be a presumption that judge-made law will not normally be affected.

2.3.6.2 **Crown not bound by the statute**

As the United Kingdom is a constitutional monarchy its Head of State is actually the sovereign, currently Her Majesty The Queen Elizabeth II.[124] The term 'the Crown', however, is normally used to denote the machinery of the state through the executive (ie government). Since rules are considered to be binding principles handed down from *ruler* to *subject* the principle has always been that the Crown would not be bound by any law. Note, however, that this does not mean (with the exception of the sovereign) that anyone is personally immune from laws as it is the state rather than an individual who is not subject to laws. The presumption against the Crown not being bound by a statute arises from this doctrine with the principle being that as the Crown is the ruler (the state) it should not be bound unless it expressly says so.

---

121.   [1954] 1 QB 77, 81.
122.   [2009] 1 AC 1310.
123.   Stephen Bailey, Jane Ching, Nick Taylor, and Michael Gunn, *Smith, Bailey and Gunn on the Modern English Legal System* (5th edn, Sweet and Maxwell 2007) 459.
124.   Although in Scotland she is technically the first Queen Elizabeth as the Queen Elizabeth who ruled between 1558 and 1603 was Queen of England but not Queen of Scotland.

An Act of Parliament will now normally state whether it is bound and it has been considered more appropriate for the Act to state expressly whether it is so bound rather than leave it implied which ensures that the courts must construe the appropriate status.

2.3.6.3 *Mens rea*

Many of the important presumptions relate to the criminal law where certainty is to be expected since transgression of the criminal law could lead to the loss of liberty for the transgressor. One of the most important presumptions is that *mens rea* should be implied into statutes unless it was Parliament's intention for there to be none. It is not possible in this text to provide a precise definition of *mens rea* and you should cross-reference to your set text for *Criminal Law* for a fuller definition but suffice it to say that most crimes require two elements; the *actus reus* (the 'conduct' part of a crime) and the *mens rea* (the 'mental requirement' for a crime). It will often be said that *mens rea* can be approximated to 'guilty mind'.

 THEFT

Theft is defined under s 1 *Theft Act 1968* thus: '[a] person is guilty of theft if he dishonestly appropriates property belonging to another with the intention of permanently depriving the other of it.' The *actus reus* of this crime is appropriating property belonging to another. The *mens rea* of the crime is doing so dishonestly and with the intention of permanently depriving the other of the property.

Not every statute will, however, necessarily easily identify a mental requirement and it may appear therefore that only the *actus reus* is required for liability to arise.

> **‖\ Case Box** *Sweet v Parsley*
>
> The leading case that discusses the absence of *mens rea* is *Sweet v Parsley*.[125] The appellant was the tenant of a farm but sublet rooms to other people. At the time of the offence the appellant did not live at the farm. The police found some cannabis resin at the farm and she was charged with the offence of, inter alia, being concerned with the management of premises used for the purpose of smoking cannabis or cannabis resin (s 5(b) *Dangerous Drugs Act 1965*). On the face of the section there was no requirement for *mens rea* and she was convicted by the court as she was concerned with the management of premises—as she was the landlady—at which drugs were found. The House of Lords quashed the conviction and stated that unless Parliament indicated otherwise, *mens rea* should be an essential requirement for any crime. They implied the requirement for knowledge into the criteria.

It is important to note that this is simply a presumption and it can, therefore, be rebutted if it was Parliament's intention to do so. In *B v DPP*[126] and *CPS v K*[127] the House of Lords examined sexual offences against children. Their Lordships argued

---

125.   [1970] AC 132.
126.   [2000] 2 AC 428.
127.   [2002] 1 AC 462.

that indecency with a child and indecent assault (both now repealed) were not crimes of strict liability but they did accept that s 5 *Sexual Offences Act 1956* (now repealed), which created the offence of unlawful sexual intercourse with a girl under 13, was intended to be a crime of strict liability. They reached this conclusion by noting that comparable offences within the same legislation did expressly consider mental requirements and accordingly its absence in s 5 must have been deliberate.[128]

2.3.6.4 Acting retrospectively

The law normally works prospectively—that is to say a law will only change the way we regulate conduct that arises *after* an instrument becomes law. Attempting to regulate conduct that has occurred in the past is known as acting retrospectively and there is a strong presumption that Parliament does not intend to act in this way. Bennion argues that this rule is a matter of fairness since if a person is deemed to know the law (and that well-known saying 'ignorance is no defence to the law' does have a foundation of truth within it) then they should be able to trust the law and act in accordance with their knowledge.[129] If a law were retrospective then it would mean that even if a person knew the law and acted in the way that he knew was lawful, he could later be liable under the law as a result of the retrospective law making his actions culpable.

Where the statute relates to the criminal law then the position becomes more complicated because Article 7 of the ECHR prohibits, inter alia, retrospective crimes and punishment. Accordingly, any statute that purports to do this would be subject not only to the common-law presumption but also to s 3(1) *Human Rights Act 1998* as it would prima facie breach Article 7.

That said it should be emphasized that this is a presumption and Parliament, because it is supreme, can act in a way that is retrospective. Perhaps the most obvious example of this is the *War Damage Act 1965* which was enacted specifically to overturn a decision of the House of Lords in *Burmah Oil Co Ltd v Lord Advocate*.[130] This Act did not just statutorily overrule the decision but was expressly retrospective and ensured that the appellants did not receive that which the House of Lords had held was due to them.

Parliament can expressly choose to act retrospectively and certain retrospective acts will not be considered to harm the principle, most notably purely administrative or procedural changes.[131] It is not uncommon for procedural rules to change and these can come into effect in respect of conduct that occurs prior to the change becoming effective. Non-punitive regulatory conduct can also come within this rule.

⚡ SEXUAL OFFENDING

When the *Sex Offenders Act 1997* came into force, it required sex offenders to be subject to notification requirements through the creation of the Sex Offenders Register. Under ss 1(2) and 1(3) of the Act those who had been convicted of a sexual offence *before* the commencement of the Act were still subject to the notification requirements. In *Ibbotson v UK*,[132] the applicant was serving a sentence for possession of obscene and indecent material when the 1997 Act

128.   *CPS v K* [2002] 1 AC 462, 469–71 (Lord Bingham).
129.   Francis Bennion, *Bennion on Statute Law* (3rd edn, Longman 1990) 151.
130.   [1965] AC 75.
131.   Francis Bennion, *Bennion on Statute Law* (3rd edn, Longman 1990) 152.
132.   (1997) 27 EHRR CD332.

came into force. Due to the retrospective nature of the measures in the Act he was required to register with the police under the notification requirements of the Act. The applicant argued that this retrospectivity violated Article 7 of the European Convention of Human Rights (ECHR) as the requirement to register constituted 'a heavier penalty ... than the one which was applicable at the time the criminal offence was committed'.[133] The Commission rejected this argument, holding that because the Act did not require 'more than mere registration, it [could not] be said that the measures imposed on the applicant amounted to a "penalty" within the meaning of Article 7 of the Convention'.[134] Thus the retrospective nature of the requirements under the Act were not problematic. Whilst the *Sex Offenders Act 1997* has now been repealed, its provisions regarding the registration of sex offenders have been re-enacted and updated within the *Sexual Offences Act 2003*.

2.3.6.5 Presumption in favour of the defence

In the English Legal System—like most developed legal systems—there is, in criminal matters, a presumption of innocence which means that it is not for a defendant to prove that he is innocent but rather for the state to prove that he is guilty. Where the state is not able to demonstrate guilt then the defendant is entitled to an acquittal even if the evidence demonstrates that it is more likely than not that the defendant committed the crime.

The presumption of innocence is taken further and justifies the presumption in favour of the defence. According to this presumption if there are two possible constructions of a statutory provision and one is broadly favourable to the defendant and the other is broadly favourable to the prosecution then this rule states that the construction that favours the defence should be used unless Parliament intends the opposite.

 Summary

In this chapter we have examined the basic concept of domestic sources of law. We have identified that there are two sources of law (primary sources and secondary sources). In particular we have noted that:

- *Primary sources* are considered to be those 'authoritative' sources that are produced by the legal process itself. *Secondary sources* are sources that are produced by others and are, in essence, a commentary on the law.

- Primary sources of law include statutory material and this itself is divided into two types of material: *primary legislation* (Acts of Parliament) and *secondary legislation* (Statutory Instruments, Orders in Council, etc).

- Statutes are Acts of Parliament and are either *Public Acts* (Acts that are of general application) or *Private Acts* (which are limited to a certain body).

133. *European Convention of Human Rights*, Art 7(1).
134. *Ibbotson v UK* (1997) 27 EHRR CD332, 334.

- An Act will normally have to pass both the House of Commons and House of Lords and then receive Royal Assent before it becomes an Act of Parliament. However, subject to limited exceptions, it is possible to use the Parliament Acts, which will allow the House of Commons to override the House of Lords and enact legislation that has passed only one House.

- A statute will ordinarily be broken down into Parts and Chapters but the most important division is in its clauses known as sections. Sections can also be broken down into subsections, paragraphs, and subparagraphs.

- The courts are called upon to interpret legislation and they do this normally by using the *literal* rule where they simply look at the wording of the legislation. Where this leads to an absurdity they can look at either the *golden* or *mischief* rules which allow them to consider what Parliament intended.

- *The Human Rights Act 1998* allows greater interpretation and expressly allows courts to decide whether legislation is compatible with the *European Convention on Human Rights*.

❓ End-of-chapter questions

1. Should the Parliament Acts be used in politically controversial pieces of legislation? The House of Lords is the second chamber of the legislature and thus should it not have the right to block controversial legislation? By allowing the House of Commons to bypass this block does this not mean there is no protection against, for example, a state seeking to diminish human rights?

2. The Supreme Court of the United States of America is allowed to 'strike down' legislation that is incompatible with their Constitution. Should the Supreme Court of the UK be allowed to 'strike down' legislation that is incompatible with the ECHR?

3. Why has the issue of statutory interpretation become increasingly important? What impact has the *Human Rights Act 1998* had on the way that courts interpret legislation?

4. If the intention of Parliament is important in the construction of legislation why shouldn't the courts be allowed to use parliamentary material whenever they wish and in whatever form?

5. Reread the section on the use of explanatory notes ('Explanatory notes') and also read Roderick Munday 'Bad Character Rules and Riddles: Explanatory Notes and the True Meanings of s 103(1) Criminal Justice Act 2003' [2005] *Criminal Law Review* 337, 352–4 and Aileen Kavanagh '*Pepper v Hart* and Matters of Constitutional Principle' (2005) 121 *Law Quarterly Review* 98, 105–8. Is it right that the courts look to statements produced by the government rather than Parliament as a whole when examining parliamentary material? It is used to gauge Parliament's intent and this need not be the government's intent. Should the rule be relaxed?

📃 Further reading

Kavanagh A, 'Unlocking the Human Rights Act: The Radical Approach to Section 3(1) Revisited' [2005] 3 *European Human Rights Law Review* 259–75.

This is an authoritative article where it is suggested that the courts have been reluctant to make the full use of their powers of interpretation.

Marshall G, 'The Lynchpin of Parliamentary Intention: Lost, Stolen or Strained' [2003] *Public Law* 236–48.

This is an article that examines the place of parliamentary intention in the construction of statutes.

For multiple-choice questions, updates to this chapter, and links to useful websites, please visit the **Online Resource Centre** at: **www.oxfordtextbooks.co.uk/orc/gillespie_els6e/**

3

Domestic Sources of Law: Case Law

By the end of this chapter you will be able to:

- Define the principles of *stare decisis*.
- Apply the doctrine of precedent to cases.
- Differentiate between binding, overruling, and distinguishing precedent.

Introduction

The previous chapter introduced the concept of domestic sources of law and it was noted that sources can be divided into primary and secondary sources. Of the primary sources, parliamentary material is supposed to be the most important, with the courts merely implementing the will of Parliament. Often this is expressed as Parliament making the law and the courts applying it but this is not strictly true. It was noted that decisions of the superior courts are a primary source of material in their own right and this is because England and Wales has a common-law-based tradition, ie decisions of the court can amount to law in the same way as statutory law does. It is not just minor matters where the common law becomes involved; quite a significant amount of constitutional law is by convention or through common law, but murder, arguably the most important criminal offence, is a common-law offence. You will not find a statutory definition of murder but it is instead left to the courts to define.

Even where Parliament has passed a law it falls to the courts to decide what this law means and how it will be applied. In the previous chapter it was noted that the courts have created a series of statutory rules to assist them in interpreting the law, but in order to ensure that there is certainty in the law the courts have themselves developed rules on how courts must act when presented with a case. These rules are known as *stare decisis* although the common term of 'precedent' has gained favour. These rules have created a hierarchy of the courts and an understanding of how courts must act when presented with a previous decision.

3.1 Reporting of cases

It has already been noted that the English Legal System is a common-law-based system, which means that historically much of the law was a product of the common law rather than statutes. Even now that statutes are more usual the role of the courts is to interpret the law and many of the common-law rules continue to apply.

At the heart of the common-law system is the system of *stare decisis,* or precedent as it is also known. The term *stare decisis* can be translated as 'let the decision stand' and is designed to bring certainty to the law. The basic proposition of this doctrine is that a case should normally be dealt with in the same way as previous cases were by the courts and that the law can only be changed according to the hierarchy of the courts. How this works in practice will be examined in this chapter but the first issue to consider is how we know what the law is.

One can get the impression that the system of *stare decisis* has a long and distinguished history and to an extent it does. However, until comparatively recently the system was somewhat haphazard because few cases were ever reported. How could the doctrine be applied therefore? A judge who tried a Chancery case in Preston might not be aware of a similar case that was heard in Plymouth three months earlier. If they were decided differently then it would appear that rather than having a consistent approach to law we would have the exact opposite.

The earliest known reports were known as the 'Year Books' and these date back to the thirteenth century (and can still be seen at the Squire Law Library at the University of Cambridge) but very few cases were reported. Those cases that were mentioned tended to be extremely important cases rather than matters that were considered in typical court cases. Also the reports took a considerable time to be reported which did not contribute to a careful analysis of precedent. In the sixteenth century a series of private reports started to be published. These were reports published by individual reporters and normally cited by reference to their name. A principal difficulty with these reports, however, was that there was no sense of order as to what was reported; it tended to depend on the particular idiosyncrasies of the reporters. There was also considerable doubt as to the accuracy of the reporters as there were no rules and regulations that either required a reporter to check the accuracy of reports or indeed specified what qualification the reporters needed to have, if any. That said private reports continue to be available albeit in a changed format (see 3.1.1.2).

Eventually it was decided that if reports were to be produced then it was important that they contributed to, rather than detracted from, the consistency of law. In 1865 the Inns of Court and Law Society, who regulated the legal profession (see Chapter 10), created a new body, the *Council for Law Reporting* and in 1870 it became an incorporated body taking the name, *Incorporated Council of Law Reporting for England and Wales*, the name it continues to be known by today. The patronage of the professions, particularly the Inns of Court where the Masters of the Bench (who are in charge of the Inn) were frequently members of the judiciary (see 10.2.1.2), ensured that the Council succeeded and that its reports became authoritative; indeed even today (as will be seen) reports produced by the Council should be cited in preference to any other series.

If the Year Books and private law reports marked the first age of law reporting and the creation of the *Incorporated Council* marked the second age, we are now in the third age. We now live in the era of the Internet and as you will no doubt be aware a significant number of judgments can now be obtained freely and easily from the Internet. The Law Reports, in all their various guises, never pretend to be able to report every case that occurs in the senior courts but with the Internet this is getting close to being possible. For example, let us look at the Supreme Court. The series *Appeal Cases* did not report every case heard by its predecessor, the House of Lords, but since 14 November 1996 every judgment of the House of Lords (and subsequently the Supreme Court) has appeared on the Internet. To a lesser extent this can also be seen with the Court of Appeal. Whilst not every judgment of the Court of Appeal is reported on the Internet, the majority are, particularly in the Criminal Division where it concerns an appeal against conviction, and certainly considerably more than would have ever been reported in the traditional law reports.

The courts themselves have mixed emotions about the use of ICT to report cases, as on the one hand they have facilitated their use through the provision of neutral citations (see 3.1.2) but on the other hand the courts have argued that it is sometimes possible to refer to too many cases. Perhaps the most notable criticism was given by the Lord Chief Justice in *R v Erskine*.[1] The Lord Chief Justice provided a history of law reporting[2] and emphatically restated a principle first enunciated by Viscount Falkland in 1641: 'if it is not necessary to refer to a previous decision of [the] court, it is necessary not to refer to it.'[3] This has been followed up by the Lord Judge CJ stating that electronic cases should 'not usually be cited unless it contains a relevant statement of legal principle not found in reported authority'.[4]

3.1.1 Printed series

It has been noted that a number of printed series exist. The *Incorporated Council* is responsible for many of these but a number of private reports, normally produced by recognized legal publishers, are also to be found.

3.1.1.1 Incorporated Council

Judgments reported by the *Incorporated Council* should normally be cited in preference to any other series.[5] The reports produced by the Council are fully authorized in that the judges who gave the judgment will check the draft to see whether it is accurate and can indeed change the wording of a judgment they handed down if it clarifies issues. The reports (apart from the *Weekly Law Reports*) also contain the submission of counsel which whilst not forming any part of the judgment can be of assistance when identifying the reasoning of the court.

There are three principal series operated by the *Incorporated Council* which are: the *Law Reports*, the *Weekly Law Reports*, and the *Industrial Cases Reports*, the latter of which is a specialist report. In addition, lesser series are now also produced (eg the *Business Law Reports* and the *Public and Third Sector Law Reports*) but these are of lesser importance. Of the three main series the *Law Reports* are considered to be the definitive reports for the reasons already set out and they are divided into four series, each of which has a different abbreviation and colour (see Table 3.1).

It is important to note that the titles do not necessarily reflect exactly what their contents are. One of the most common mistakes for law students to make is to think

---

1. [2010] 1 WLR 183.
2. *R v Erskine* [2010] 1 WLR 183, 201.
3. *R v Erskine* [2010] 1 WLR 183, 202.
4. *Practice Direction (Citation of Authorities)* [2012] 1 WLR 780.
5. See *Practice Direction (Citation of Authorities)* [2012] 1 WLR 780.

Table 3.1 The Law Reports

Series	Abbreviation	Colour[a]
Appeal Cases	AC	Brown
Queen's[b] Bench Division	QB	Green
Family Division[c]	Fam	Blue
Chancery Division	Ch	Red

a. The reports will either be bound in this colour or will be bound all in beige with the spine including the Division framed by the relevant colour. This tends to be a less popular method of binding now.
b. When the Sovereign is a King then it is automatically the King's Bench Division and the abbreviation KBD is used.
c. Prior to 1972 this series was known as the Probate Division and carried the abbreviation P. In that year, however, the Family Division of the High Court of Justice was established and the series was retitled.

that the *Appeal Cases* series deals with the appellate courts, most notably the Court of Appeal. In fact only matters now heard in either the Supreme Court or Judicial Committee of the Privy Council are reported in that series.[6] A significant proportion, and perhaps even the majority, of cases reported in the *Queen's Bench Division* series are not heard in the Queen's Bench Division of the High Court of Justice but are decisions of the Court of Appeal (Criminal Division), certain decisions of the Court of Appeal (Civil Division), Employment Appeals Tribunal, Consistory Courts,[7] and judgments of the European Court of Justice. Similarly, the Family Division and Chancery Division reports encompass decisions of the Court of Appeal (Civil Division) and European Court of Justice that originated in those Divisions.

The *Weekly Law Reports* are so called because they are generally published weekly but this is not for the fifty-two weeks of the year nor are they produced in the same week as the judgment was handed down (discussed later). There are traditionally three volumes of the *Weekly Law Reports* and it is intended that those reported in volumes 2 and 3 will normally be (eventually) published in the *Law Reports*. That said, it is important to note that this is only an intention and it will not necessarily always occur, in part because by the time a report is produced it may have been considered on appeal.[8] The *Weekly Law Reports* (abbreviated to WLR) are produced much more quickly than the *Law Reports*, in part because they are not checked by judges prior to being published. Accordingly, there may be slight differences between the reports. The speed at which they are produced is also reflected by the fact that the arguments of counsel are not contained in the report either.

3.1.1.2 Other series

A number of other series exist all of which are private reports. In order to have status within the courts the reports must be prepared by a qualified lawyer (see 'Reporters').

6. It previously reported decisions of the House of Lords and the Judicial Committee of the Privy Council.
7. These are ecclesiastical courts and established by the Church of England. Each diocese has a Chancellor who presides over the consistory court. Nowadays the vast majority of cases relate to 'faculties' which are permissions to alter the material content of a church (including its building, windows, or other features that could have a permanent effect on the church).
8. For example, *Davis v Johnson* is reported at [1978] 2 WLR 182 but it has never been reported in *Law Reports* because it was superseded by the House of Lords ruling on that case: see [1979] AC 264.

With the exception of the *All England Law Reports* the series tend to be specialist in terms of reporting a narrow range of cases. The primary reason for this is that it is not easy to compete with the Council, especially given the preferential treatment awarded to it by the courts. Where a practitioner wishes to access specialist material, however, it is unlikely that the general law reports will contain many of the cases as they will not be considered 'important' enough. The principal series are referred to in Table 3.2.

Not every report will necessarily be official in that the judges may not necessarily have the opportunity to review them prior to publication although the better reports do allow this. Also very few of these reports will contain the arguments of counsel, the argument for omitting these being that they do not form part of the judgment.

3.1.1.3 Newspapers and journals

Before leaving the printed series it is worth noting that it is not only specialist publications that report cases but that a limited number of newspaper and journals do so too. *The Times* has long been considered the leading daily newspaper for lawyers in part because it contains law reports usually on an almost daily basis. The reports are highly abridged and would normally only be referred to in court in highly exceptional circumstances (because the case would ordinarily be reported by a series in due course). In contrast to the reporting series already discussed, the words of the judge are not reported verbatim but are simply abridged. The principal advantage of these reports, however, is that the reports are normally produced within days of the judgment being handed down, something that not even the weekly reports can manage.

Legal periodicals also sometimes report cases and perhaps the two most obvious examples of this are the *Solicitors' Journal* and the *New Law Journal*. Both series suffer the same drawbacks as *The Times* in terms of their detail but the speed in which they are reported continues to make them a particularly useful resource.

3.1.1.4 A note on dates

Although all law reports contain a date where the report is carried in print rather than electronically it is likely that there will be a delay between the judgment being handed down and the report being produced. It is a convention that rather than using the date of the judgment the year will normally be taken from the report.

Table 3.2 Common abbreviations for Law Reports

Series	Abbreviation
All England Law Reports	All ER
Criminal Appeal Reports	Cr App R
Criminal Appeal Reports (Sentencing)	Cr App R(S)
European Human Rights Reports	EHRR
Family Court Reports	FCR
Family Law Reports	FLR
Knight's Industrial Reports	KIR
Local Government Law Reports	LGLR

> ## ☰ Example *R v G and R*
>
> The judgment in the leading case of *R v G and R* was handed down by the House of Lords on 16 October 2003. However, it was reported in the *Appeal Cases* series at [2004] 1 AC 1034 and could, therefore, be abbreviated as *R v G and R* (2004).

Of course nothing is simple and some reports are produced earlier than others, most notably the *Weekly Law Reports*. This may mean that there are different years.

> ## ☰ Example More about *R v G and R*
>
> The case of *G and R*, discussed earlier, is also reported at [2003] 3 WLR 1060. However, the year can be taken from whichever series you refer to. It could also, therefore, be referred to as *R v G and R* (2003).

Printed reports do not include every case and occasionally there may be a significant delay in reporting a decision. Where a report is particularly late then it would be wiser not to adopt this convention. Perhaps the classic example of this is *Regal (Hastings) Ltd v Gulliver* where the judgment was handed down on 20 February 1942; it was reported by the *All England Law Reports* at [1942] 1 All ER 378 but the official *Law Reports* did not report the case for another twenty-five years ([1967] 2 AC 134)!

3.1.2 **Internet sources**

The growth in electronic reports led to an increase in the number of unreported cases that were being presented to the courts. Traditionally these were referred to by their case name or the year and 'unreported'. It was difficult for all counsel and the courts to keep track of the cases and clearly as more judgments were becoming available it was preferable for a standardized form to be introduced.

In *Practice Direction (Judgments: Form and Citation)*[9] Lord Woolf CJ issued a direction that transformed the way that judgments were presented. All judgments would now follow a standard pattern with each paragraph being numbered sequentially through the judgment. Also each case would be assigned a neutral citation number so that even unreported cases could be readily indexed, identified, and retrieved. Initially, the practice was restricted solely to the Court of Appeal and Divisional Court of the Queen's Bench Division but it was later extended to the High Court.[10] The House of Lords, Privy Council, and now Supreme Court also follow the system.

The citation has three elements to it: the date, the court code, and the case number. Each number is assigned sequentially by the relevant courts in order of its appearance. The codes are as follows:

---

9. [2001] 1 WLR 194.
10. See *Practice Direction: Supreme Court: Judgments: Neutral Citations* [2002] 1 WLR 346.

Supreme Court	UKSC
House of Lords	UKHL
Privy Council	UKPC
Court of Appeal	
Criminal Division	EWCA Crim
Civil Division	EWCA Civ
High Court of Justice	
Administrative Court[11]	EWHC Admin or EWHC (Admin)
Queen's Bench Division	EWHC (QB)
Chancery Division	EWHC (Ch)
Family Division	EWHC (Fam)
Specialist Courts	
Patents Court	EWHC (Pat)
Commercial Court	EWHC (Comm)
Admiralty Court	EWHC (Admlty)

The code EW stands for England and Wales whereas UK is used for the Supreme Court (which has jurisdiction across the United Kingdom) and the Privy Council. Whilst the Privy Council's cases will now no longer originate in the United Kingdom this convention remains. Rather confusingly there remains some uncertainty where the case number is sometimes to be found. Where the court code does not include parentheses then the number occurs immediately after the code whereas where parentheses are used then the case number is written immediately after the code but before the court code which is placed in parentheses.

Example Neutral citations

The 123rd case in the Court of Appeal (Civil Division) for the year 2003 would be written as:

[2003] EWCA Civ 123

whereas the 45th case to be heard in the Chancery Division of the High Court during the year 2003 would be written as:

[2003] EWHC 45 (Ch).

Neutral citations should usually be used at least once even in reported cases and the (printed) reports should not renumber the paragraphs but use the ones assigned in the judgment. Where a paragraph is being referred to the number is placed in square brackets.

Example Neutral citations—paragraphs

To refer to the 13th paragraph in the (fictional) case of *Smith v Jones*, which has the neutral citation number [2003] EWHC 45 (QB), the following format is used:

[2003] EWHC 45 (QB) at [13].

---

11.   Also known as the Divisional Court of the Queen's Bench Division.

3.1.3 Reporters

So far it has been recognized that cases are often reported but who reports them? The short answer is qualified lawyers. Traditionally cases were reported by barristers and the vast majority of reporters continue to be barristers. In part this was because of the historical divide between the professions (see 10.2.1) with barristers having the exclusive right to litigate in the superior courts. It was thought that as only a barrister could litigate in the superior courts only a barrister would fully understand the procedure and detail of the cases in sufficient detail to report the matter. However, the *Courts and Legal Services Act 1990* ended the Bar's monopoly on accessing the superior courts and s 115 of that Act provides that a law report by a solicitor or other person with a senior courts qualification shall have the same authority as one by a barrister. Accordingly, the position is now that either a solicitor or barrister can act as an official law reporter. It is important to note that the reporter, regardless of which profession he belongs to, must be fully qualified, ie have the right (even if they do not avail themselves of it) to conduct litigation in the higher courts.

3.2 Hierarchy of courts

The system of precedent depends on there being a hierarchy of courts. It is necessary to identify the structure of the courts in order to understand how precedent works. Figure 3.1 sets out a basic understanding of the English Legal System. It can be seen that the Supreme Court is at the very top of the structure and the magistrates' courts are at

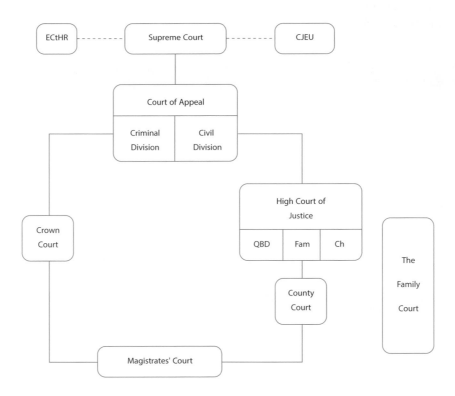

Figure 3.1 The hierarchy of the courts

the bottom. The position of the European Courts (the Court of Justice of the EU (CJEU) and the European Court of Human Rights (ECtHR)) is somewhat complicated and different texts will place them at different levels of the system. In Figure 3.1 it can be seen that the CJEU is parallel to the Supreme Court because although the Court, as will be seen, is bound by the CJEU in certain circumstances this is only because the *European Communities Act 1972* says so and when this is repealed,[12] the Supreme Court will remain as the most senior court in the UK. Placing the CJEU above the system would also misrepresent its role in that the vast majority of English law is not impacted by its decisions. The importance of the CJEU will be discussed later. The ECtHR is linked by a broken line to reflect the fact that technically the ECtHR does not bind any court nor is it reached by an appeal per se (see Chapter 5 for an explanation of this).

The hierarchical principle means that each court will act in accordance with its place in the hierarchy and has responsibilities to those above and below it. When and how the courts can act will be discussed later although it should be noted that the lower courts (ie those below the High Court) do not play any role in *setting* rather than *following* precedent.

3.3 Legal principles

Not every statement of a superior court will necessarily amount to a precedent. Indeed the system of precedent applies only to a narrow part of any case—the legal decision for a case. Harris notes that this is a significant limiting factor as in the vast majority of cases, including appellate cases, there will be no dispute as to the law but rather a dispute as to the facts.[13] In those situations no precedent will arise as decisions of fact do not bind courts.

75

> ### ☰ Example Facts v law
>
> Parliament creates the (fictional) *Motor Vehicle in the Park Act 2015*, which states that a person is guilty of an offence if he drives a vehicle powered by a motor in a public park. Edith is stopped by the police after driving her electrically powered wheelchair through the park.
>
> The district judge trying the case decides that an electric wheelchair is a vehicle powered by a motor and as she drove it in the park convicts her. Edith appeals to the High Court and they decide that permitting wheelchairs to be brought within the legislation would be 'absurd' and contrary to other parliamentary statutes. Applying the 'golden rule' of statutory interpretation (see Chapter 2) they quash the conviction and hold that the purpose of the legislation was to stop motor vehicles (eg cars, vans, etc) driving through the park and that a wheelchair could not be considered a 'motor vehicle' because although it may be driven by a motor it was not a vehicle but a disability aid.
>
> Whether Edith was driving and whether she was in the park are decisions of fact. Whether a wheelchair amounts to a 'vehicle powered by a motor' is a matter of law as it requires the law to be interpreted. In this situation the decision of the High Court that a wheelchair is not a motor vehicle will become a precedent as it is a decision of law.

---

12.   The vote that commits the UK to leaving the EU will mean that the *European Communities Act 1972* will need to be repealed (discussed in Chapters 4 and 20 of this book).

13.   Rupert Cross and JW Harris, *Precedent in English Law* (4th edn, Clarendon Press 1991) 40.

However, in a case many apparent decisions of law may be made but some of them may not be binding as they do not form part of the decision of the case. In the earlier example, the High Court held that the mischief of the Act was to stop cars and vans being driven in the park. This must be a legal rather than factual point but it does not form part of the decision of the case as Edith's case did not involve a car or van; it is an ancillary legal point.

The two types of legal statement identified previously are known as the *ratio decidendi* and *obiter dictum*. The *ratio decidendi* is the legal reasoning for the decision and forms the binding precedent, *obiter dicta* are legal opinions that did not go to the decision but are, in essence, side comments on legal issues.

3.3.1 *Ratio decidendi*

At the heart of precedent is the notion of the *ratio decidendi* as it is this which will form the binding precedent. The term is often shortened to just *ratio* and notwithstanding the fact that there is a retreat from the use of Latin in law the term remains in use.

The *ratio* is sometimes presented as being an easy principle. It is the binding element of the case and it is the reason for this case. Simple. Except it isn't. Judges do not often signpost why they have reached their decision and so there may be several reasons why they have reached their decision. Does that mean that there are multiple *ratios*? Also, who decides what the *ratio* is? Judges do not say 'the *ratio* of this case is …' and it is for the later courts to try and ascertain what it is. Thus it is quite possible that what a later judge declares to be the *ratio* of a case might actually be a different proposition than what the judge giving the initial judgment intended.

Identifying the *ratio* is even more difficult where there is more than one judge pronouncing judgment. Whose judgment forms the *ratio*? It has been suggested that where there are multiple judgments it is possible that there will be no *ratio*[14] although not everyone agrees with this and Harris has suggested that every case must have a *ratio* but it does not follow that there must be only one *ratio*.[15] It is submitted that Harris must be correct since the term *ratio* denotes that there must be a reason for the decision, it is just that identifying precisely what that definition is can be difficult.

The difficulties caused by multiple judgments can perhaps be best illustrated by reference to cases. In *R (on behalf of R) v Durham Constabulary*[16] the issue in question was whether a juvenile offender must consent to being given a formal reprimand or final warning rather than being prosecuted. The decision of the House of Lords that no consent was required was unanimous but Lady Hale disagreed radically with Lord Bingham on the reasons for this. What is the *ratio* of this case? Arguably in this particular case it was the reasoning of Lord Bingham because a clear majority of Law Lords backed his arguments but does this necessarily follow? In this case there were two 'primary' judgments that conflicted on some aspects: what happens if the other judges all agree with the comments of the other judgments even though they say slightly different things (as arguably happened in *R v Ireland; R v Burstow*[17])?

---

14. James Holland and Julian Webb, *Learning Legal Rules* (9th edn, OUP 2016) 192 citing Lord Justice Jacob.
15. Richard Cross and JW Harris, *Precedent in English Law* (4th edn, Clarendon Press 1991) 48.
16. [2005] UKHL 21.
17. [1998] AC 147.

These complications are one reason why in some jurisdictions only a single judgment is given (most notably the US Supreme Court).[18]

So how do we define the *ratio*? Unfortunately there is no easy answer and indeed nobody has suggested a foolproof method. As you read more cases you will start to understand their structure and logic better meaning that it is likely you will identify a possible *ratio* almost subconsciously but proving that it is the *ratio* will be difficult. To an extent it is irrelevant because it is for a court to determine what the *ratio* of a case is and not you (be it now as a student or later as a solicitor or barrister) but it is important that you recognize what *could* amount to a *ratio* so that you can extrapolate how the court will rule. If you can identify a thread as the *ratio* you can then as a lawyer seek to argue that a judge is *bound* to act in a particular way (discussed later) or in an essay you can persuade your tutor the answer is *x* because you can point to the development of the law.

Despite these difficulties some have attempted to show how you can identify a precedent and the two most common theories put forward are those proposed by Wambaugh and by Goodhart.

3.3.1.1 Wambaugh's test

The first possible method of identification is to use the test formulated by Wambaugh. Harris reproduces the earlier text of Cross in considering this work.[19] The test is quite complicated in that it is presented in the negative. It also does not identify the *ratio* but allows a reader to test whether their supposition of what the *ratio* is could be correct. The test, at its most basic level, is that one identifies the supposition of law that the reader believes is a *ratio* and then reverses its meaning.[20] The reader then considers whether the outcome of the case would have been the same. If the answer is 'yes' then the proposition can only be *obiter* and not the *ratio*.

> **Example** Edith
>
> Let us return to the earlier example of Edith. What is the *ratio* of the High Court in that case?
>
> The first possible *ratio* of the case is that only cars and vans are classed as 'motor vehicles'. We reverse the proposition (cars and vans are not classed as motor vehicles) and ask ourselves whether the same decision would have been made in respect of Edith? The answer must be 'yes' because the case did not concern either a car or van and so that proposition will not be the *ratio*.
>
> The second possible *ratio* is that wheelchairs are not motor vehicles. If we reverse our proposition (wheelchairs are motor vehicles) then we need to ask ourselves if the decision would be the same. The answer must be 'no' because the law prohibits the use of motor vehicles so they would have to acquit. Accordingly, the proposition that 'wheelchairs are not motor vehicles' may be the *ratio* of that case.

18. Where the court is divided then there will tend to be a single majority verdict and a separate single dissenting judgment. As a dissenting judgment will not count towards the *ratio*, this means there is no possibility that the judges contradict each other on the *ratio*.
19. Richard Cross and JW Harris, *Precedent in English Law* (4th edn, Clarendon Press 1991) 52–7.
20. Richard Cross and JW Harris, *Precedent in English Law* (4th edn, Clarendon Press 1991) 52.

A difficulty with Wambaugh's test is, however, that it does not work particularly well where there is more than one possible *ratio*. For example, it could be decided that the *ratio* of the example earlier is that a vehicle required for the conveyance of a disabled person is exempt from the legislation. If this proposition was reversed it would not obviously lead to Edith's case being decided differently but is this the *ratio*? Arguably if it does then had Edith not had an electric wheelchair but a quad bike to allow her to move around then are we saying the court would still acquit? It would seem unlikely and yet according to Wambaugh's test is possible. Harris argues that this is a difficulty with the test: it is very good at identifying what *is not* a *ratio* but it is not particularly efficient at identifying what *is* the *ratio* unless there is only a single possible reason[21] and as has been pointed out already this is perhaps unlikely.

3.3.1.2 Goodhart's test

The more authoritative test is that which was put forward by the theorist Goodhart. His test is based on the premise that it is possible to identify the *ratio* by examining the material facts of the case that set the precedent. The logic behind this premise is that all decisions are necessarily based on the analysis of facts and is in line with the comments of Lord Halsbury, the then Lord Chancellor, who has stated that 'a case is only authority for what it actually decides'.[22] Harris, reproducing the work of Cross in commenting on this case, notes that his Lordship was not stating that a case has no binding power beyond its decision but rather was indicating that precedent only applies where the material facts are similar.[23] We will return to this proposition when examining how to escape precedent (3.4.1) but it does validate the premise of Goodhart that an analysis of some facts could reveal the *ratio*.

Not all the facts of a case will be relevant in the search for a *ratio*, indeed a significant proportion of them are unlikely to be critical. Goodhart, therefore, refers to the need to find 'material' facts which are those that go to the central issues of the case. Goodhart himself, however, noted that one particular difficulty with this theory is that it will be for the judge to decide what the material facts are and this may not necessarily be an objective approach to deciding such facts.[24] Whether something is a 'material' fact depends on whether it is essential to the decision of the case.

☰ Example Material facts

The defendant, a 31-year-old female called Sheila, is accused of stabbing the victim, her husband of nine years, in the stomach following an argument. The marriage was a turbulent one with frequent allegations of domestic violence including two where the husband was formally cautioned by the police.

There are a series of facts in this example but the age, name of the accused, and duration of the marriage are unlikely to be material facts in that it would not really matter whether they were present or changed. The sex of the defendant may be a material fact but on the other hand it may not.

---

21. Richard Cross and JW Harris, *Precedent in English Law* (4th edn, Clarendon Press 1991) 56–7.
22. See *Quinn v Leathem* [1901] AC 495, 506.
23. Richard Cross and JW Harris, *Precedent in English Law* (4th edn, Clarendon Press 1991) 57–8.
24. Arthur Goodhart, *Essays in Jurisprudence and the Common Law* (CUP 1931) 11.

> The material facts in this case would appear to be that the defendant stabbed the victim in the stomach, that the defendant and victim were in a relationship (the fact that it was a marriage is probably immaterial), and the allegations (and particularly the proven incidents) of domestic violence.
>
> The material facts are relevant to the decision in the case and therefore go to the *ratio* of the case whereas the immaterial facts are simply irrelevant.

An advantage of Goodhart's theory is that if it were correct then not only would it assist in the identification of a *ratio* but it would also primarily be of assistance in escaping precedent. It will be seen that the most useful tool for a judge or lawyer seeking to escape precedent is the concept of distinguishing (see 3.4.2) and if Goodhart is correct then a case can be distinguished if any of the material facts are not present. This would free the judge to decide the case by doing what she thought most just and not what she believes the higher courts require.

The disadvantage of this approach, however, is that not every case necessarily turns on the material facts of the case. The learned editors of a legal encyclopaedia[25] provide the example of *Donoghue v Stevenson*,[26] arguably one of the most important cases in English law.[27] The material facts of this case were that a third party purchased a drink (ginger ale but the type of drink cannot be considered material) in a dark glass bottle, and the bottle contained (unbeknown to any party in the case until the material time) a decomposed snail. The judgment of the House of Lords arguably had very little to do with any of these material facts and certainly the use of the *ratio* of this case, which became the very foundations upon which the tort of negligence came to be based, have very little to do with the material facts of this case other than the fact that it was a third party that bought the article (and thus it was not a contract case). That being the case then it would suggest that Goodhart's test is not helpful either, meaning we are left with the fact that identifying the *ratio* is very difficult, at least in respect of some cases. The one advantage is that if even the leading theorists and jurists cannot agree how to identify the *ratio* then nobody can expect you to either. Anyone that tells you that they do know how to identify a *ratio* is almost certainly wrong.

Perhaps this demonstrates the fallacy of trying to seek the *ratio*. Bagaric and McConvill have questioned whether the Australian High Court, which operates on almost identical *stare decisis* principles, has caused itself problems by giving separate judgments rather than a single majority and minority judgment but they concluded that, in practice, it made very little difference.[28] This could lend support to the argument that we should not overly worry about what the *ratio* actually is and instead just identify the principal reasons why the judge reached his decision. Once that is understood it is possible to apply the rules of precedent to seek to persuade another judge that they are either bound, or not bound, by one or more of those reasons.

25. See <http://www.ivr-enc.info>.
26. [1932] AC 567.
27. Which is somewhat ironic given that it is actually a Scottish case albeit one heard in the House of Lords!
28. Mirko Bagaric and James McConvill, 'The High Court and the Utility of Multiple Judgments' (2005) 1 *High Court Quarterly Review* 13.

3.3.2 *Obiter dictum*

This second phrase is often shortened to *in obiter* or the *dictum* depending on the preferences of the author although the former is more usual. It is important to note at the outset that a judge will often accidentally create *obiter* statements but in other cases they will wish specifically to raise ancillary issues in this way.[29] One reason for doing this would be to indicate an opinion on how the law should move forward. Accordingly, a judge might say something like, 'whilst I have not been asked to rule on the meaning of [a particular phrase] I would, had I been asked, ruled that it bore the meaning [*x*]'. This can only be *obiter* because it cannot have formed the reason for the decision and so it is *in obiter*.

A difference of opinion appears to exist over whether a judge can ensure that remarks are *only* considered to be *obiter* rather than go to the *ratio* of a case. Lord Devlin in *Behrens v Bertram Mills Ltd*[30] suggested that a judge can, and the principal method of doing so would be to state that the comments are an opinion rather than a cogent statement of the law[31] whereas Megarry J has suggested that a judge has no power to prevent a decision from becoming a precedent, ie part of the *ratio*.[32]

To an extent, Megarry J is correct in that it is for subsequent courts to decide whether they are bound by a decision, but similarly when a court is trying to escape precedent (see 3.4.2) then the motivation for the statement is undoubtedly going to be a factor. One way that a judge may seek to alter a *ratio* to an *obiter* statement would be to state that the reasoning adopted is restricted to the facts of the case. Such a formula is clearly stating that the judge thinks that he foresees no general application of the principle to other cases and it should, therefore, be considered as persuasive rather than binding. But strictly speaking it remains a decision of the later court as to whether they find themselves so bound.

It is also important to note that just because comments are made *in obiter* does not mean that they are unimportant. *Obiter* comments are *persuasive* authority—ie a court should consider them even if they are not strictly bound by them. Where the statement is made by a particularly authoritative body, eg the Supreme Court or Lord Chief Justice, then it is quite possible that the consideration that should be given to these persuasive comments is significant. Indeed it has been stated:

> *Dicta* of the highest degree of persuasiveness may often, for all practical purposes, be indistinguishable from pronouncements which must be treated as *ratio decidendi* ...[33]

A good example of this is presented by Harris[34] when he discusses the well-known case of *Donoghue v Stevenson*.[35] The case was an appeal brought under Scottish law to the House of Lords but the House, as it not infrequently does, suggested that English and Scottish law were the same on this point. The case concerned a person who drank a bottle of ginger beer from a brown bottle and found a decomposed snail at the bottom of the glass. No contract exists between the manufacturer and the consumer (as

---

29. Richard Cross and JW Harris, *Precedent in English Law* (4th edn, Clarendon Press 1991) 42.
30. [1957] 2 QB 1.
31. [1957] 2 QB 1, 25.
32. See *In Re Showerings, Vine Products and Whiteways Ltd* [1968] 1 WLR 1381 and see Richard Cross and JW Harris, *Precedent in English Law* (4th edn, Clarendon Press 1991) 42.
33. Richard Cross and JW Harris, *Precedent in English Law* (4th edn, Clarendon Press 1991) 77.
34. Richard Cross and JW Harris, *Precedent in English Law* (4th edn, Clarendon Press 1991) 43–4.
35. [1932] AC 562 and see Richard Cross and JW Harris, *Precedent in English Law* (4th edn, Clarendon Press 1991) 43–4.

the consumer will purchase the bottle from a shop and not the manufacturer direct) but the House permitted a duty in tort to be established to take reasonable care in the manufacture.

Donoghue v Stevenson is an important case not just for the reasoning in respect of that manufacturer but because of the comments of, in particular Lord Atkin, when he referred to his 'neighbourhood principle', where his Lordship argued that a person owed a duty to a neighbour to take reasonable care. From this statement arguably developed the law of negligence and this comment is still cited today. Yet the comments about neighbours are almost certainly *obiter* because it did not go to the decision of the case. Accordingly, it was not part of the *ratio* but these *obiter* comments have undoubtedly become more important than the *ratio* itself.

3.4 The operation of precedent

Harris argues that '[precedent] creates the expectation that, save for the intervention of the legislature, the law will remain as it is stated to be in the precedent'.[36] However, as will be seen this is not strictly true as the courts do alter precedent through its application. The earlier distinction drawn between *ratio decidendi* and *obiter dictum* is important because it goes to the heart of how precedent operates. Only the *ratio* is applied to precedent as it is this which encapsulates the law and should, according to Harris, continue to be applied. Whilst the *dictum* of a judge is important it does not set out what the law is but rather illustrates potential ways that the law could be applied or developed.

In order to examine how precedent works in practice it is necessary to identify some more of its key terms. These are all discussed in further detail later but are summarized in Table 3.3 for reference.

These terms, or more properly their actions, are the very operation of precedent as they demonstrate how a court should decide cases before it. It is important that the terms are used appropriately. One of the most common mistakes made by students is to use the term 'overrule' when this is not, in fact, what has happened. It is far more common for a precedent to be escaped by either distinguishing or not following it.

Table 3.3 The operation of precedent

Term	Meaning
Binding/bound	A court has to follow the precedent established in an earlier case
Distinguish	The court believes that the case before it is not factually the same as the precedent and accordingly is not bound by it
Not following	Where two or more conflicting precedents are presented the court chooses to follow one and not follow the remainder
Reverse	When an appeal succeeds the decision of the lower court in that case is reversed
Overrule	A higher court (or the Supreme Court) alters a precedent; the original precedent ceases to be good law

36.   Bruce Harris, 'Final Appellate Courts Overruling their own "Wrong" Precedents: The Ongoing Search for Principle' (2002) 118 *Law Quarterly Review* 408, 413.

In neither situation has there been a change of law—the precedent continues to exist and if another case arises then the courts should be bound by it. Where a precedent is overruled, however, then the law changes—the legal principle that was encapsulated by the precedent no longer applies and where another case arises on these issues the courts cannot follow the original precedent any more but must now follow the principle enunciated by the overruling case which becomes, therefore, the new precedent. It is also important to note that not every court has the power to overrule precedents (see 3.4.1) and an extremely common mistake is for a student to say that a court has overruled a precedent when it has no power to do so.

3.4.1 Bound by precedent

If the notion of *stare decisis* is that decisions continue ('let the decision stand') then that means there must be a system of ensuring that judges do not contradict the earlier decisions. This is done by saying that a court is *bound* to follow the previous decision (ie they have to). Obviously if this was strictly enforced then law would never alter and so the system of binding authorities is more complicated as it is necessary to understand which courts are bound and under what circumstances. A higher court, as is seen in Table 3.3, can overrule a lower court and therefore this becomes the new binding process. The question therefore becomes who is bound by whom?

3.4.1.1 Supreme Court

The simplest court to deal with is the Supreme Court. As the highest court in the English Legal System its decisions bind all the courts below it unless they are able to escape the precedent through distinguishing (see 3.4.2).

The House of Lords (which preceded the Supreme Court) decided in 1966 that it did not consider itself bound by its previous decisions.[37] More than this, it has claimed the power to overrule its earlier decisions.[38] What this means will be discussed later but, in essence, 'overruling' means that the earlier precedent ceases to exist and the new decision forms the continuing precedent.

The justification for assuming the power to depart from its own decisions was undoubtedly to help bring clarity to the law since previously the House was either not permitted to depart from its own rulings meaning that no matter how sympathetic they were only legislation could remedy the fault or they would do so by distinguishing previous cases and accordingly leave a number of possible precedents 'active'.

The *Practice Statement* did not give the House of Lords complete freedom and they continued to view decisions as *ordinarily* binding on themselves.[39] The House did, for example, on a number of occasions note that the fact a decision was merely 'wrong' was not enough to justify the use of the statement.[40] Some commentators suggest that distinguishing should be used wherever possible.[41] Harris argues that this is needed to make the law more certain and predictable[42] but given that he expressly

---

37. *Practice Statement (HL: Judicial Precedent)* [1966] 1 WLR 1234.
38. See, for example, *R v G and R* [2004] 1 AC 1034 where the House of Lords expressly overruled the case of *R v Caldwell* [1982] AC 341 ([2004] 1 AC 1034, 1055 (Lord Bingham).
39. Richard Cross and JW Harris, *Precedent in English Law* (4th edn, Clarendon Press 1991) 136.
40. See, for example, *Knuller (Publishing, Printing and Promotions) Ltd v DPP* [1973] AC 435.
41. Bruce Harris, 'Final Appellate Courts Overruling their own "Wrong" Precedents: The Ongoing Search for Principle' (2002) 118 *Law Quarterly Review* 408, 422.
42. Bruce Harris, 'Final Appellate Courts Overruling their own "Wrong" Precedents: The Ongoing Search for Principle' (2002) 118 *Law Quarterly Review* 408, 420–1.

includes precedents that were decided *per incuriam* or are distinguishable because of social movements it is difficult to see why leaving these decisions 'live' would be preferable. It could be argued that simply distinguishing them and labelling them as *per incuriam* etc would be sufficient to inform the lower courts not to follow them. Nevertheless, whilst this may be true, certainty and predictability are not achieved by refusing to tinker with the law unless absolutely necessary, but rather by ending bad decisions. Overruling those types of precedent rather than merely not following them would ensure that no court could resurrect them and would accordingly bring about certainty in the law.

In *Austin v Southwark London Borough Council*[43] the Supreme Court stated that it had assumed the power put forward in the *Practice Statement*. Lord Hope, the Deputy President of the Supreme Court, stated that the Supreme Court had not found it necessary to reissue the statement since it formed part of the ordinary jurisprudence of the court that Parliament had transferred to the Supreme Court.[44] Accordingly, it is clear that the Supreme Court will act in the same way as the House of Lords, ie it will claim the power to depart from its own decisions (or the decisions of the House of Lords) but will do so only when necessary, taking account of the consequences that this can have for the certainty of law. This has been seen in *R v Jogee*,[45] where the Supreme Court departed from the previous decision of the House of Lords in *R v Powell (Anthony); R v English*[46] (as well as disapproving a Privy Council decision[47]) in relation to joint enterprise. In *R v Powell (Anthony); R v English*,[48] the House of Lords held that foresight of an act as a possible incident of the joint enterprise was sufficient to make the secondary party liable. However, in *R v Jogee*, the Supreme Court departed from this, holding that 'foresight was not to be equated with intent to assist' in joint enterprise cases, but rather 'the correct approach is to treat it as *evidence* of intent'.[49]

3.4.1.2 **Court of Appeal**

The Court of Appeal is second in precedence in the English Legal System and is the more usual appellate court (the Supreme Court hearing only a highly limited number of appeals). The simple rule for the Court of Appeal is that it is bound by the Supreme Court and it binds all courts lower than it. Where the complication arises is whether the Court of Appeal is bound by itself.

The leading authority on the matter is *Young v Bristol Aeroplane Co Ltd*[50] where the Court of Appeal stated that it was bound by its own decisions subject to the following exceptions:

1. Where there are two conflicting decisions of the Court of Appeal it may choose which to follow.

2. Where the previous decision of the Court of Appeal, even if not expressly overruled, conflicts with a Supreme Court or House of Lords decision.

3. Where the decision was made *per incuriam*.

---

43. [2011] 1 AC 355.
44. [2011] 1 AC 355, 370.
45. [2016] UKSC 8.
46. [1991] 1 AC 1.
47. *Chan Wing-Siu v The Queen* [1985] AC 168.
48. [1991] 1 AC 1.
49. [2016] UKSC 8 [87] (Lord Hughes and Lord Toulson JJSC).
50. [1944] KB 718.

Others argue that the second ground of *Young* must have been expanded to include the situation where the previous decision of the Court of Appeal conflicts with the European Court of Justice[51] and this is undoubtedly correct. The term *per incuriam* means 'through want of care' and covers those situations where a court neglected to consider an issue that it should have, eg a statutory provision or a binding precedent.

Davis v Johnson

The ruling in *Young v Bristol Aeroplanes* continued for some decades before it came up against Lord Denning MR, who was arguably one of the most influential judges of the past century. Lord Denning had been a Lord of Appeal in Ordinary but had accepted the Master of the Rolls position in part because he believed the Court of Appeal was more influential than the House of Lords due to the number of cases it heard. Lord Denning did not like the fact that the Court of Appeal was bound by itself whereas the House of Lords was not. This dislike culminated in the case of *Davis v Johnson*[52] where Lord Denning empanelled a full Court of Appeal, namely five judges, including Sir George Baker, the President of the Family Division. The case concerned a non-molestation order made under the *Domestic Violence and Matrimonial Proceedings Act 1976*. Previous Court of Appeal decisions, most notably *B v B*,[53] had construed this Act in a way that a majority of the court disagreed with[54] but, according to the rule in *Young v Bristol Aeroplane*, the Court of Appeal should have been bound by that decision. However, a majority of the Court of Appeal held that they could choose not to follow the precedent.[55] Lord Denning sought to argue that the Court of Appeal should have the same right to depart from its own decisions as the House of Lords reserved to itself in the *Practice Direction* of 1966. He based his argument on the fact that the House of Lords may never get an opportunity to reverse a bad law because of the cost of litigation and leave requirements.[56] He also argued that where a ruling was obviously wrong this placed the lower courts in a quandary because an appeal may take a year to be heard by the House but until judgment is handed down by the House the lower courts would be obliged to rule on matters it knows are wrong.[57]

Lord Denning attempted to argue that the doctrine of precedent was not a legal principle but rather a custom of the courts.[58] This would be important because if it was mere custom then courts would have the power to alter the principle whereas, of course, if it was a legal rule then *stare decisis* would bind itself, ie only the House of Lords could rule as to whether the Court of Appeal had the authority to depart from its own judgments. He was joined in this by Sir George Baker P who thought that the decisions could be distinguished but argued that this was itself unsatisfactory because it meant a lower court could still consider them valid precedent when his Lordship believed they were wrong. Sir George Baker suggested that the new exception should be slightly narrower by arguing that a new exception should be granted

---

51. Colin Manchester and David Salter, *Manchester and Salter on Exploring the Law: The Dynamics of Precedent and Statutory Interpretation* (4th edn, Sweet & Maxwell 2011) 18.
52. [1978] 2 WLR 182.
53. [1978] 2 WLR 160.
54. Only one judge, Cumming-Bruce LJ, dissented from this part of the case.
55. Goff LJ joined Cumming-Bruce LJ in dissenting from this decision but he expressly stated that he did so reluctantly as he disagreed with the original precedent.
56. *Davis v Johnson* [1978] 2 WLR 182, 194–5.
57. *Davis v Johnson* [1978] 2 WLR 182, 196.
58. *Davis v Johnson* [1978] 2 WLR 182, 197–8.

where a decision is wrong and appears contrary to the intentions of Parliament.[59] The President appeared to be trying to extend the *per incuriam* rule by stating that it goes against Parliament's will but it cannot come within the rule as of right because the provision was (presumably) brought to the court's attention initially.

The matter proceeded to the House of Lords[60] and their Lordships wasted little time in stating that the Court of Appeal was wrong to believe that it was not bound by itself, with Lord Diplock even suggesting that Lord Denning MR, had 'conducted what may be described ... as a one-man crusade with the object of freeing the Court of Appeal from the shackles ... of *stare decisis*'.[61] His Lordship continued by stating that whilst there was a justification in a final appellate court to have a discretion to right obvious wrongs, there is less justification for this in a lesser court where certainty of law should be a primary consideration[62] before concluding:

> In my opinion, this House should take this occasion to re-affirm expressly, unequivocably [*sic*] and unanimously that the rule laid down in the *Bristol Aeroplane* case ... as to *stare decisis* is still binding on the Court of Appeal.[63]

This invitation was taken up by every other member of the House in their speeches. Lord Salmon tackled the argument of Lord Denning that the costs of litigation and leave requirements may lead to an injustice by commenting that the Court of Appeal itself had the power to grant leave to appeal and could order that the costs are paid by the Exchequer.[64] This is an important point and recognizes the inherent powers of the court. The Court of Appeal did not believe that leave could be granted because leave had been refused in the earlier cases but this misses the point that where the court believes that its earlier decision was wrong this adds weight to that ground of appeal and introduces a public policy argument in favour of leave.

To an extent, Lord Denning did have a point regarding the custom or law issue. When the Court of Appeal created its rules of precedent in *Young v Bristol Aeroplane* it must have done so *in obiter*. The actual dispute that led to the litigation in that case had nothing to do with precedent and the comments on precedent did not go to the heart of the reasons for the decision meaning that it could not form part of the *ratio*. Similarly the House of Lords when rebuking the Court of Appeal in *Davis v Johnson* must also have been speaking *in obiter* as it did not go to the heart of the case. Indeed if one looks solely at the judgment of the courts, the law reports record that the House of Lords *affirmed* the decision of the Court of Appeal even though we are discussing it *reversing* the Court of Appeal in terms of precedent. It has already been noted that *obiter* is not strictly binding so to that extent Lord Denning was probably correct.

However, the House of Lords decision in *Davis v Johnson* was inevitable and would probably have arisen through an appeal in any event where the matter could have been dealt with as a *ratio*. It may have been preferable for the House of Lords to clarify this situation by issuing a Practice Direction but the alternative construction is that this is another example of Harris's comment that some *obiter* comments can be as powerful as a *ratio*. Certainly the decision of the House of Lords in *Davis v Johnson* as to the

59. *Davis v Johnson* [1978] 2 WLR 182, 206.
60. *Davis v Johnson* [1979] AC 264.
61. *Davis v Johnson* [1979] AC 264, 325.
62. *Davis v Johnson* [1979] AC 264, 326.
63. *Davis v Johnson* [1979] AC 264, 328.
64. *Davis v Johnson* [1979] AC 264, 344.

proper function of the Court of Appeal was plain and it did not lead to the Court of Appeal making such a blatant attempt at escaping precedent again.

An emerging exception?

However, some commentators argue that although the Court of Appeal has never expressly challenged the principle in the way that occurred in *Davis v Johnson* they have begun to assert an additional exception to the *Young v Bristol Aeroplane* case, that of declining to follow a case where it was 'manifestly wrong'.[65] The argument stems from the case of *Cave v Robinson Jarvis & Rolf (A Firm)*[66] where counsel argued that the Court of Appeal was not bound by a previous decision of a two-judge bench of the Court of Appeal. It had long since been recognized that the Court of Appeal was not bound to follow a decision made on an interlocutory appeal where the full court argued the case was manifestly wrong.[67] The Court of Appeal declined, in *Cave*, to rule on this proposition principally because it believed there was no longer any difference between two-, three-, and five-judge benches of the court and in part because it was not convinced that the decision was 'manifestly wrong'.

Prime and Scanlan argue, however, that the *obiter* comments made in the case demonstrate that the principle of 'manifestly wrong' is a new exception to *Young v Bristol Aeroplane* and that the court had, albeit *in obiter*, suggested that it had a wider application than merely interlocutory appeals.[68] They also suggested that support for their proposition could be gathered from the case of *Limb v Union Jack Removals Ltd*[69] where Brooke LJ stated, inter alia:

> Any departure from a previous decision of the court is in principle undesirable and should only be considered if the previous decision is manifestly wrong.[70]

The difficulty with this is that it is not certain that Brooke LJ was creating a new exception. This line follows a rehearsal of the reasons when the Court of Appeal may depart from its own decisions and was immediately preceded by this passage:

> The doctrine [of precedent] does not extend to a case where, if different arguments had been placed before the court or if different material had been placed before it, it might have reached a different conclusion.

In this context is would appear that Brooke LJ was arguably developing the *per incuriam* ground. Admittedly, the reference to alternative arguments would widen the doctrine further than it has traditionally been but reference to other material does appear to be in line with that exception. More problematic for Prime and Scanlan is that they argue that a majority in *Cave v Robinson* agreed that a new exception exists but the case does not necessarily say that. Whilst Potter LJ does appear to accept that the rule in *Boys v Chaplin* may still exist he is less than convinced that it has any practical modern use or that it may be analogous to the current 'leave' hearings; Sedley LJ, who Prime and Scanlan argue also approved of such a distinction, is less certain. The

---

65. Terence Prime and Gary Scanlan, '*Stare decisis* and the Court of Appeal: Judicial Confusion and Judicial Reform' (2004) 23 *Civil Justice Quarterly* 212, 220.
66. [2002] 1 WLR 581.
67. *Boys v Chaplin* [1968] 2 QB 1.
68. Terence Prime and Gary Scanlan, '*Stare decisis* and the Court of Appeal: Judicial Confusion and Judicial Reform' (2004) 23 *Civil Justice Quarterly* 212, 220–1.
69. [1998] 1 WLR 1354.
70. [1998] 1 WLR 1354, 1365.

language used by Sedley LJ is not particularly transparent but his Lordship expressly states: 'the solution which this court felt able to adopt in *Boys v Chaplin* would not be adopted in similar circumstances today.'[71] Whilst this does not, of course, say that the exception is closed it does suggest that it is unlikely that it will ever be used.

The position does appear therefore to be somewhat transient although Prime and Scanlan argue that any new exception based on 'manifestly wrong' would be inappropriate.[72] Given the obtuse statements by the Court of Appeal, upon which their hypothesis is based, it would seem more likely that the Court of Appeal is bound by its own decisions subject to the exceptions identified in *Young v Bristol Aeroplanes*.

The Criminal Division

The decision in *Young v Bristol Aeroplanes* was a decision of the Court of Appeal (Civil Division) and accordingly it could be argued that it only bound that Division. However, the Criminal Division has stated that it too is *normally* bound by its own decisions subject to the exceptions set out in *Young*[73] but with an additional exception that arises as a result of the unique cases that the Court of Appeal (Criminal Division) hears. Given that invariably a person who appeals to the Court of Appeal in criminal matters is incarcerated in gaol, the court has, perhaps not unreasonably, taken the approach that where a decision is obviously wrong and would otherwise lead to the appellant remaining in gaol then *stare decisis* should be departed from as even awaiting an expedited Supreme Court ruling would lead to a situation where a person has been deprived of their liberty unnecessarily.

The 'liberty' rule has to be considered exceptional, however, because if there were any area of law where certainty would be desirable it would be the criminal law[74] and the courts appear to have recognized this with Lord Diplock saying:

> [A]lthough the Criminal Division of the Court of Appeal is not so strictly bound by its own decisions as is the Civil Division, its liberty to depart from a precedent which it is convinced is erroneous is restricted to cases where the departure is in favour of the accused.[75]

The latest pronouncement by the Criminal Division was contained in *R v Simpson*[76] where the Court of Appeal (Criminal Division) stated:

> We consider a degree of discretion remains in this court to decide whether a previous decision should be treated as a binding precedent in future or not when there are grounds for saying that the decision is wrong.[77]

Moreover, the court suggested that the 'constitution of the court may be relevant'[78] and Lord Woolf expressly drew attention to the fact that this was a five-judge bench of the court. This appears to contradict earlier decisions and the custom of the Civil Division where it has been held that the number of judges is irrelevant: the authority flows from the court not the numbers. This is certainly the accepted position and the

---

71.   *Cave v Robinson Jarvis and Rolf* [2002] 1 WLR 581, 595.
72.   Terence Prime and Gary Scanlan, '*Stare decisis* and the Court of Appeal: Judicial Confusion and Judicial Reform' (2004) 23 *Civil Justice Quarterly* 212, 222–4.
73.   See the comments of May LJ in *R v Spencer* [1985] QB 771, 779.
74.   Rupert Cross and JW Harris, *Precedent in English Law* (4th edn, Clarendon Press 1991) 117.
75.   *R v Merriman* [1973] AC 584, 605.
76.   [2004] QB 118.
77.   [2004] QB 118 (QB) 131 (Woolf LCJ).
78.   [2004] QB 118 (QB) 131 (Woolf LCJ).

remarks of Lord Woolf bear a striking similarity to the approach of Lord Denning in *Davis v Johnson*.

Arguably *Simpson* concerns the *per incuriam* rule in that it discusses whether all the relevant authority was before the earlier court. To some degree this mirrors the suggestion of Brooke LJ in *Limb v Union Jack Removals Ltd* which suggests that the Court of Appeal is beginning to push the boundaries of precedent once more. The exception of *per incuriam* has previously been restricted to those situations where the court was not referred to relevant statutory material or a binding precedent but both *Limb* and *Simpson* appear to suggest that where alternative arguments could, or rather should, have been submitted this may justify departure from the precedent. *Simpson* is also important because it appears to contradict the approach in *Merriman* in that in this case the decision to depart from precedent was not favourable to the defendant. There is no question that the ruling in *Simpson* was against the interests of defendants and yet the Court of Appeal still departed from precedent.

That said, the limits of *Simpson* should be recognized. In *R v Varma*[79] the Court of Appeal declined to follow *Simpson* when ruling on a matter relating to confiscation orders and their applicability when a defendant has been given a discharge. The facts are not important but the court found itself bound by an earlier decision in *R v Clarke*[80] although this was the only decision that referred to this point (ie there was no conflict of authorities) and the judges of that court had been referred to all the relevant authority. Whilst the Court of Appeal in *Varma* was prepared to concede that *Clarke* may be wrong, it stated that it was bound by it and that *Simpson* did not apply where there was no conflict of interest and where 'it was considered in meticulous detail, and given the closest possible attention'.[81] Whilst *Varma* was reversed in the Supreme Court,[82] it was not reversed in respect of the *Simpson* point and therefore it remains a case of interest on that point.

It appears therefore that, rather than attempt a full-frontal attack on precedent itself, the Court of Appeal has decided to attempt to broaden the recognized exceptions. The easiest exception to broaden is the *per incuriam* rule and both divisions of the court have sought to tackle this. More importantly the Criminal Division has decided to broaden its approach to errors and widen the meaning of injustice to include a guilty person escaping justice rather than just an innocent person wrongly imprisoned. There appears no evidence that the Supreme Court wish to be as rigid as the House of Lords were in *Davis v Johnson*, with the Supreme Court having had sufficient time to comment on this issue if they so wish. It would seem likely that their silence can be taken as affirmation of the minor change brought about by *Simpson*.

⟳ QUESTION FOR REFLECTION

Read *Davis v Johnson* (1978) and also *R v Simpson* (2004). Do you think that the Court of Appeal should be allowed to depart from its own precedent where it believes it is wrong? Few cases reach the Supreme Court (the number of cases has increased in the last few years but there have never been more than seventy-five) and even fewer cases relate to the criminal law. Is it realistic to suggest that only the Supreme Court can correct mistaken precedent?

---

79. [2010] EWCA Crim 1575.
80. [2010] 1 WLR 223.
81. [2010] EWCA Crim 1575 [31].
82. [2012] UKSC 42.

LISTEN TO THE PODCAST

For guidance on how to answer this question and a discussion of the main issues, listen to the author's podcast on the Online Resource Centre:
www.oxfordtextbooks.co.uk/orc/gillespie_els6e/

3.4.1.3 **The High Court**

The High Court of Justice is next in the hierarchy. Whilst there are three principal divisions (Queen's Bench, Family, and Chancery) together with specialist courts (eg Commercial, Admiralty, etc)[83] the other significant court to examine is the Administrative Court, which has a supervisory jurisdiction. Of the three divisions the Family Division also requires special attention when it deals with the welfare of children for public policy reasons akin to the Criminal Division of the High Court.

Non-supervisory jurisdiction

The High Court sits below the Supreme Court and Court of Appeal in the hierarchy and is accordingly bound by their decisions. It binds all lower courts although its principal binding role is in respect of its supervisory jurisdiction (see 'Divisional Court').

When the court is not sitting in its supervisory capacity (ie it is not sitting as either an appellate court or hearing a judicial review case but is rather adjudicating on litigation brought between two parties) then its previous decisions are persuasive but are not binding on itself. That is to say that a judge will normally follow the decision for reasons of consistency but they are able to depart from the decision should they wish to and do not need to find a reason like the Court of Appeal must.[84]

Where children are concerned it is sometimes suggested that the Family Division adopts a more relaxed attitude to the notion of precedent although Wilson J speaking extrajudicially has suggested this is not strictly true.[85] The latitude is said to arise from the fact that s 1(1) *Children Act 1989* states that where a matter relates to the upbringing of a child then the welfare of the child is to be the paramount consideration. In other words nothing is supposed to be more important than the welfare of the child. That does not mean that courts have the right to disregard *stare decisis*, however, something reinforced by Wilson J and evident from cases where matters in the Family Division have been litigated before the appellate courts.[86] However, the welfare principle does allow some leeway in that every case that involves the upbringing of a child will necessarily have individual facts and accordingly it is perhaps easier for the Family Division to distinguish (see 'Divisional Court') precedents than other Divisions may find it. However, where a clear principle of law is enunciated by the appellate courts then the Family Division must follow it.

83. Although these are technically part of the other divisions. For example, the Admiralty Court is part of the Chancery Division and the Technology Court is part of the Queen's Bench Division although they are treated for everyday purposes as separate.
84. See *Police Authority for Huddersfield v Watson* [1947] KB 842.
85. See 'The Misnomer of Family Law', The Atkin Lecture 2002 by Hon Mr Justice Wilson.
86. Perhaps the most notable of these decisions is *Re H (Minors)(Sexual Abuse: Standard of Proof)* [1996] AC 563 where the House of Lords conclusively held that the standard of proof to be used in care proceedings where sexual abuse is alleged was the civil standard but that where a serious allegation was made more evidence would be required to meet this standard. The Family Division has followed this ruling in accordance with *stare decisis*.

Divisional Court

Where the High Court is sitting in a supervisory capacity then matters become more uncertain. The supervisory capacity is ordinarily exercised in the Administrative Court where the challenge is to a public body but all divisions of the High Court exercise supervisory jurisdiction although they would ordinarily do so as a Divisional Court, ie where more than one judge is sitting together. The Administrative Court always used to sit as a Divisional Court but increasingly it is sitting with only a single judge. Even then, however, it is exercising supervisory jurisdiction.

It was always thought that when the High Court is exercising its supervisory jurisdiction then the rules of precedent change and the court is treated in much the same way as the Court of Appeal. The High Court, including a Divisional Court, is quite clearly below the Court of Appeal in hierarchy so it is bound to follow decisions of that court but it was generally thought that it was bound by *its own* decisions unless the exceptions in *Young v Bristol Aeroplanes* apply.[87] However, this has not been conclusively proved and in *R v Greater Manchester Coroner, ex p Tal*[88] the Divisional Court stated that when it was acting in a supervisory role at first instance (rather than when it was acting as an appellate court in, for example, civil or certain criminal cases) it was in no different position than the (ordinary) High Court.

Accordingly, it would now seem that the general rule for the High Court is that whenever it sits as a court of first instance then no binding precedent is set, but when it sits in an appellate capacity binding precedent does apply, something confirmed, albeit probably *in obiter*, by Laws J in *C (A Minor) v DPP*.[89]

3.4.1.4 Family Court

Chapter 6 will discuss the creation of the Family Court. Prior to its creation family matters were heard either by the High Court (Family Division), county court, or Family Proceedings Court (the equivalent of the magistrates' court). However, the Family Court created a court that acts across all levels. So there is 'one court' albeit staffed with judges of different rank.

Section 31C(2) *Matrimonial and Family Proceedings Act 1984* (MFPA 1984) (inserted by the *Crime and Courts Act 2013*) specifically addresses the issue of hierarchy and binding precedent. It states that a decision of a certain category of judge is to be followed by an inferior judge. This can only be considered to be the creation of a binding precedent. The judges who create this precedent are:

- a puisne judge, judge of the Court of Appeal, a Head of Division (including the Lord Chief Justice and Master of the Rolls), Senior President of Tribunals, or a person sitting as a deputy judge of the High Court,
- a former judge of the Court of Appeal, or
- a former judge of the High Court.

In other words, while there is a single Family Court it would seem that the decision of a High Court judge (including a deputy judge) sitting in the Family Court creates a precedent that lower-ranked judges must follow. Interestingly s 31C(2) only talks about

---

87. See *Police Authority for Huddersfield v Watson* (discussed earlier) and *Younghusband v Luftig* [1949] 2 KB 354.
88. [1985] QB 67.
89. [1994] 3 WLR 888, 898.

lesser-ranked judges and therefore presumably the decision of a puisne judge sitting in the Family Court does not bind another puisne judge sitting in the Family Court.

What s 31C does not address is the relationship between the Family Division and the Family Court. Section 31I states that proceedings can be transferred instead to the High Court which would imply that the High Court is superior to the Family Court but it is not clear that it is for the purposes of precedent. Section 31C referred to 'decisions of the Family Court', so what should a circuit judge do when sitting in the Family Court and she is referred by counsel to a decision of the High Court (Family Division)? The Family Court can exercise the powers of the High Court[90] but it is obviously not the High Court. Prudence would indicate that the circuit judge follows the precedent but it is less than clear that he is obliged to do so. It is unlikely that a puisne judge sitting in the Family Court would consider himself bound by a decision of the Family Division (save potentially where it was sitting in its supervisory capacity) but again there is no rule stating that this is the case.

3.4.1.5 Crown Court and inferior courts

It will be seen that the Crown Court is not technically an inferior court[91] but for the purposes of precedent it is de facto an inferior court. No court below the High Court sets a precedent for anyone. Similarly, decisions of each court are not binding on other divisions of that court although it has been said that decisions of a High Court judge sitting in the Crown Court are persuasive despite the fact that Ashworth argues the status of the judge should be irrelevant.[92]

The position of the Crown Court is interesting because it is unquestionably higher than the magistrates' court and indeed appeals take place from the magistrates' court to the Crown Court. However, any decision reached by that court is restricted to the facts and does not set a precedent. It is for this reason that decisions of law are more frequently taken to the Divisional Court, which does bind all magistrates' courts and Crown Courts sitting in its appellate capacity.

3.4.1.6 The Privy Council

The Privy Council is in an unusual position in terms of precedent. Its current jurisdiction does not include English law (as the *Constitutional Reform Act 2005* transferred the last remaining UK jurisdiction of the Council to the Supreme Court) and thus it technically has no place in the English Legal System. It is, however, worth noting its place within precedent, albeit briefly.

Precedent within the Council

The Privy Council has always adopted a relatively lax attitude to precedent in respect of its own decisions, considering them only to be persuasive rather than binding.[93] That said, it is also clear that the Council appreciates that certainty is desirable and will therefore seek to follow its earlier decisions where possible.[94]

90. *Matrimonial and Family Proceedings Act 1984*, s 31E.
91. *Senior Courts Act 1981*, s 45(1).
92. Andrew Ashworth, 'The Binding Effect of Crown Court Decisions' [1980] *Criminal Law Review* 402, 403.
93. Michael Littlewood, 'The Privy Council, the Source of Income and *stare decisis*' (2004) 2 *British Tax Review* 121, 122.
94. Michael Littlewood, 'The Privy Council, the Source of Income and *stare decisis*' (2004) 2 *British Tax Review* 121, 123.

Precedent within the English Legal System

Whilst not strictly speaking part of the English Legal System, the Council is in a peculiar position in that those who sit on the judicial committee are usually Justices of the Supreme Court[95] and accordingly their decisions must, at the very least, be considered highly persuasive.

It has been stated:

> It is possible to refer to cases in which a decision of the Privy Council has not been followed by an English judge of first instance, but it is also possible to point to cases in which a decision of the Privy Council has been persistently preferred to a decision of the Court of Appeal, although the decision of that court has never been overruled.[96]

In other words, Harris is arguing that the Court of Appeal has, in some cases, used a decision of the Privy Council as a method of invoking the *per incuriam* exception in *Young v Bristol Aeroplanes*. This should be relatively uncontroversial as the Privy Council, whilst not strictly part of the English Legal System, is a senior court and its decisions warrant investigation. The Court of Appeal should be able to consider whether the decision reached in that case alters the understanding of the issues they have previously adjudicated.

Where the position becomes more complicated, however, is what happens when a decision of the Privy Council conflicts with a decision of the Supreme Court or House of Lords? Theoretically since the Supreme Court is the most senior domestic court in the English Legal System the Court of Appeal should follow it as precedent but see *R v Mohammed*.[97] The partial defence of provocation[98] entertained the courts for many years prior to its repeal but *R v Smith*[99] appeared to resolve one central part of this partial defence, namely what subjective characteristics could be imputed to the reasonable man used in the test for provocation. The position seemed clear but in *Attorney-General for Jersey v Holley*[100] the Privy Council stated that it thought *Smith* was wrong. Theoretically this was merely persuasive precedent and the Court of Appeal, together with all courts in the English Legal System, would be required to follow *Smith* but the Court of Appeal in *Mohammed* refused to do so and argued that the position in English law was that put forward by the majority in *Holley*.[101] This decision has been followed by other decisions of the Court of Appeal.[102]

It is important to note that this is not a situation where the Court of Appeal has decided that its own decision is *per incuriam* but rather it is making a decision as respects a precedent that it should be bound by, namely the House of Lords decision in *Smith*. It would have been tidier for the court to send the matter to the House of Lords, and it could have done so by granting leave. It is important to note that this was not a case where the liberty of the appellant was at stake (see 3.4.1.2) as the appeal in *Mohammed* was dismissed (as it was in *Shickle*) and thus it would have been tidier to do so. If *stare decisis* is supposed to bring certainty then following the decision of a

---

95. Although it is not restricted to them and certain foreign senior judges and all Lord Justices of Appeal are entitled to sit on the judicial committee.
96. Rupert Cross and JW Harris, *Precedent in English Law* (4th edn, Clarendon Press 1991) 102.
97. [2005] EWCA Crim 1880.
98. *Homicide Act 1957*, s 3. Now repealed by the *Coroners and Justice Act 2009*.
99. [2001] AC 146.
100. [2005] AC 580.
101. [2005] EWCA Crim 1880 [42].
102. See, for example, *R v Shickle* [2005] EWCA Crim 1881.

court outside of the English Legal System is contrary to that principle and if a future comparable situation arises it would be tidier to send the matter to the Supreme Court so that the normal rules of precedent apply.

In *Willers v Gubay*[103] the Supreme Court considered the role of the Privy Council in the system of precedent, and held that it is possible for the Privy Council to depart from a House of Lords or Supreme Court decision:

> There will be appeals to the JCPC where a party wishes to challenge the correctness of an earlier decision of the House of Lords or the Supreme Court, or of the Court of Appeal on a point of English law, and where the JCPC decides that the House of Lords or Supreme Court, or, as the case may be, the Court of Appeal, was wrong. It would plainly be unfortunate in practical terms if, in such circumstances, the JCPC could never effectively decide that courts of England and Wales should follow the JCPC decision rather than the earlier decision of the House of Lords or Supreme Court, or of the Court of Appeal. In my view, the way to reconcile this practical concern with the principled approach identified ... above is to take advantage of the fact that the President of the JCPC is the same person as the President of the Supreme Court, and the fact that panels of the JCPC normally consist of Justices of the Supreme Court.[104]

Where a House of Lords or Supreme Court decision is to be challenged, an appropriate Privy Council can be convened and

> they can, if they think it appropriate, not only decide that the earlier decision of the House of Lords or Supreme Court, or of the Court of Appeal, was wrong, but also can expressly direct that domestic courts should treat the decision of the JCPC as representing the law of England and Wales.[105]

3.4.2 Distinguishing

Whilst a court is bound to follow precedent it is sometimes possible to escape precedent. To an extent this was discussed earlier when it was decided that courts were able to fail to follow a precedent (ie not follow) either because it was decided *per incuriam* or because there were two conflicting decisions. The most usual form of escaping precedent, however, is to distinguish a case. It has already been noted that only the *ratio decidendi* binds a court and this only applies therefore where the facts of a case would lead to the same *ratio* being applied. The concept of distinguishing is where a court argues that the *material* facts of a case are different and accordingly the *ratio* will not apply but rather a different reasoning must be adopted.

Where a judge decides to distinguish a case he should normally explain why the precedent is being distinguished and this reasoning will be subject to criticism by later courts and where the decision is itself appealed it could be reversed by the appellate court.

It can be argued that the concept of distinguishing can be taken further and need not be restricted to factual differences but could also include situations where 'societal factual circumstances have changed since [the precedent] was originally decided'.[106]

---

103. [2016] UKSC 44.
104. [2016] UKSC 44 [19] (Lord Neuberger).
105. [2016] UKSC 44 [21] (Lord Neuberger).
106. Bruce Harris, 'Final Appellate Courts Overruling their own "Wrong" Precedents: The Ongoing Search for Principle' (2002) 118 *Law Quarterly Review* 408, 411.

If this is correct then it would allow courts to develop the law in a way that reacts to society progressing and not require such developments to be constrained by the appellate system.

3.4.3 Overruling

So far the discussion on precedent has concerned situations where a court has either followed precedent or has escaped it. The final issue that needs to be examined is where a precedent ceases to exist because it is overruled. One principal justification for using the power to overrule authority is where the precedent was decided *per incuriam* or its application has left the law unworkable.[107] In both of these situations the court can safely overrule a case knowing that it will bring certainty to the law, something that is supposedly at the heart of *stare decisis*. Similarly, where a decision has created conflicting precedents then simply following one authority may not lead to certainty arising since the absence of overruling the other could mean that a court is still able to 'resurrect' the other potentially increasing uncertainty. It is for this reason that in *Young v Bristol Aeroplanes* it was said that where the Court of Appeal chooses between two conflicting earlier decisions of the court the one it does not follow is overruled.[108] Where a difficulty arises, however, is where the court does not consciously attempt to reconcile all the previous decisions as this could lead to an argument that the judgment was made *per incuriam*. It is therefore incumbent on the court to state expressly that it is choosing between conflicting decisions and stating which case is therefore overruled.

Perhaps the more usual method of overruling is when either a more senior court than that which created the precedent or the Supreme Court overturns the precedent. It is important to note the terminology here. The precedent, ie the case that created the *ratio* that was applied in the case which forms the appeal, is *overruled*. The actual case that is being litigated on appeal will be *reversed*.

The simplest situation is where a more senior court overrules a precedent of a lower court (eg Court of Appeal overruling the High Court, Supreme Court overruling the Court of Appeal). In these situations the court has the right to overrule a case and once this has been done then the case that is being litigated forms the *new* precedent with the old one ceasing to be good law although any *dicta* in the court may continue to be relevant.[109]

> **⬛ Example** Overruling
>
> The (fictional) case of *Smith v Jones* is before the Court of Appeal (Civil Division). The judge at first instance argued that he was bound by the earlier case of *Brown v Bloggs* which was heard by the Divisional Court. The Court of Appeal decides that *Brown v Bloggs* was wrong and that it should no longer be the law. It therefore overrules *Brown v Bloggs* and that case may no longer be cited.

---

107. Bruce Harris, 'Final Appellate Courts Overruling their own "Wrong" Precedents: The Ongoing Search for Principle' (2002) 118 *Law Quarterly Review* 408, 416.
108. [1994] KB 718, 728.
109. Rupert Cross and JW Harris, *Precedent in English Law* (4th edn, Clarendon Press 1991) 128.

A different judge in the High Court is hearing a case that is very similar to *Brown v Bloggs* and *Smith v Jones*. The judge is bound to follow the Court of Appeal decision in *Smith v Jones*, which is now the only precedent available.

A difficulty arises when the superior court does not state that the case is overruled but merely does not follow the lower precedent (which of course they do not need to) or distinguishes it. The higher court may, in *dicta*, cast doubt on it but without overruling it; then presumably it continues to be a precedent. It will be noted that one of the grounds in *Young v Bristol Aeroplanes* was that it was inconsistent with a House of Lords decision and thus it might be that the court could escape the doubted precedent. But this action itself would not overrule the case and it could mean that the position becomes more confused with an additional precedent being created without any being overruled. This can cause difficulty:

> A High Court judge of first instance when confronted with a decision of the Court of Appeal which has not been expressly overruled by a later House of Lords' case may cease to be bound by it because the House of Lords considered that the Court of Appeal misinterpreted the authorities ... The judge is then not obliged to follow the Court of Appeal, but he is not bound to dissent from their conclusion. The previous decision is undermined rather than directly overruled.[110]

If the purpose of *stare decisis* is to introduce certainty into the law then it is obvious that situations such as that described earlier would not be helpful and yet this is a not an uncommon outcome. It is submitted that it is incumbent on the superior courts, particularly the Supreme Court, to take care when they discuss authorities and to use their power to overrule a case where they believe it is necessary—merely doubting its application but leaving it open to be used again is a recipe for confusion in law.

 ## Summary

In this chapter we have examined how the courts use case law. In particular we have noted:

- The courts operate a system of precedent known as *stare decisis* ('let the decision stand').
- The type of precedent set depends on the court sitting, with the most complicated rules arguably occurring in the Court of Appeal. As a general rule of thumb, the court setting the precedent will bind every court below it.
- Only the *ratio decidendi* of a case forms the precedent. Any other aspects of the case are known as the *obiter dicta*.
- Whilst every case must have a *ratio* there need not necessarily be a single *ratio*. Also, identifying the *ratio* can be quite complicated especially where there is more than one judgment.
- Where a superior court changes the ruling of a lower court this is called 'reversing'. A decision is only 'overruled' when the court is saying that the precedent was wrong and should not be followed.

110.   Rupert Cross and JW Harris, *Precedent in English Law* (4th edn, Clarendon Press 1991) 129–30.

- Lower courts are able to 'escape' precedent by 'distinguishing' a case. This is where they accept the validity of the precedent but suggest that it does not apply to the case at hand because there are factual differences between the precedent and the case they are adjudicating.

❓ End-of-chapter questions

1. What do the terms 'binding', 'reversing', 'overruling', and 'distinguishing' mean in relation to precedent?

2. Read *Attorney-General for Jersey v Holley* [2005] UKPC 23, *R v James; R v Karimi* [2006] EWCA Crim 14, and *Willers v Gubay* [2016] UKSC 44. Does this now mean that the Privy Council has become part of the English Legal System for the purposes of *stare decisis*?

3. Consider the following cases and identify their *ratio*:

   (a) *R v G and R* [2003] UKHL 50

   (b) *DPP v Redmond Bates* [2000] HRLR 249

   (c) *Partridge v Crittenden* [1968] 1 WLR 431.

   The Online Resource Centre accompanying this book provides clues and the answers!

4. Read Harris Rupert Cross and JW Harris, *Precedent in English Law* (4th edn, Clarendon Press 1991) 129–30 and Bruce Harris 'Final Appellate Courts Overruling their own "Wrong" Precedents: The Ongoing Search for Principle' (2002) 118 *Law Quarterly Review* 408, 420–2. Are there circumstances when leaving a precedent 'live' by either distinguishing or disapproving of it would be better than formally overruling it? Does that complicate or ease the burden of the lower courts in applying the principle of *stare decisis*?

Further reading

Ashworth A, 'The Binding Effect of Crown Court Decisions' [1980] *Criminal Law Review* 402–3.

This short note discusses whether a judge in the Crown Court sets any precedent for other judges of the Crown Court or magistrates.

Harris B, 'Final Appellate Courts Overruling their own "Wrong" Precedents: The Ongoing Search for Principle' (2002) 118 *Law Quarterly Review* 408–27.

This is an interesting article that examines whether there is any rationale behind the circumstances governing final appeal courts overruling themselves.

Kavanagh A, '*Pepper v Hart* and Matters of Constitutional Principle' (2005) 121 *Law Quarterly Review* 98–122.

This is a wide-ranging but interesting article that examines the role of the courts in precedent and statutory interpretation.

For multiple-choice questions, updates to this chapter, and links to useful websites, please visit the **Online Resource Centre** at: **www.oxfordtextbooks.co.uk/orc/gillespie_els6e/**

4

International Sources of Law

By the end of this chapter you will be able to:

- Identify the key sources of law in international law.
- Differentiate between the European Union and the Council of Europe.
- Understand how EU law has an impact upon domestic law.
- Identify the ways in which international instruments influence the law.

Introduction

So far we have examined how domestic law is created and found. However, modern-day Britain does not exist in isolation and a significant amount of international law has an impact on domestic law. This can perhaps be best demonstrated from our relationship with Europe where two international agreements creating the European Union (EU) and the Council of Europe (CoE) have significant implications for the way in which our domestic law is interpreted and formed. Outside of Europe there are a significant number of international rules that can influence our laws but how does this relate to domestic law? It is important at the outset to note that in this chapter we will not be discussing what international law is as such as this is something that is the topic of significant debate, with some even questioning whether it in fact even exists or whether it is a purely political concept. That debate is best left to options that examine the concept of international law. What nobody can deny, however, is that international law is examined in the domestic context and accordingly we should be aware of how to access this law.

4.1 Identifying the institutions

 A NOTE ON TERMINOLOGY

When one is referring to an individual country that is party to an international agreement then it is normal to refer to the country as being a 'state'. This, of course, does not mean a 'state' in the same sense as in the United States of America or Australia which operate a federal system whereby the country is broken into regions known as states. In this chapter the term 'state' will be used to signify a sovereign jurisdiction, ie an independent country.

To clarify, the United Kingdom (as noted in Chapter 1) is constituted of four countries but it is one 'state'—the UK. France is another 'state' and Germany, which also operates a federal system, is another—each individual region in Germany is not a sovereign jurisdiction in its own right but is subservient to the 'state' of Germany.

This terminology is commonplace in legal texts and so you are likely to encounter it in other books and articles that relate to international law.

International law differs from domestic law in a fundamental way. Apart from very few exceptions (which are normally confined to international criminal law), international law regulates states and not individuals. The basis of international law is that it is an agreement between two or more countries and this law regulates how these countries will act in accordance with those who have signed this agreement and does not impose obligations on individual citizens. That is not to say that international law is irrelevant to individual citizens since frequently the international agreements will require the state to enact domestic legislation to give effect to the agreement and this may impose rules relating to the international agreement. A good example of this is the *European Convention on Human Rights* which exists as an international agreement binding only on the states but which has now been given domestic effect by the *Human Rights Act 1998*.

Where an international agreement has two planes, the domestic plane (ie that which has an impact upon individuals within the domestic country) and the international plane (ie that which governs the agreements between the signatory states), then in order to understand fully the domestic law it will be necessary to access the international law. Even where the instrument exists solely on the international plane it will be seen that domestic courts are increasingly likely to refer to the international instrument to assist in their understanding of the law as they recognize that the state intends their agreements to be in force. For all of these reasons it is necessary to understand where the law is to be found.

That said, however, international law is a complicated subject and not normally one that you will study during the first year of your course and thus the greater part of this chapter will examine the sources of the two international bodies that have most influence on the United Kingdom, ie the EU and the Council of Europe. However, a brief examination of the wider body of international law will be made initially.

At the outset it is vital that you are able to differentiate between the EU and the Council of Europe as they are, contrary to popular belief, completely separate institutions. The EU is the body that many popularly refer to as 'Europe' when they talk about regulation and legal impact. Since 2013 there have been twenty-eight countries within the EU with negotiations ongoing for more to join. The Council of Europe is a much older institution that was set up in the aftermath of the Second World War. Whilst membership of the Council of Europe is a prerequisite for joining the EU, they are separate institutions and some countries belong to the Council of Europe who have no interest in joining the EU (eg Switzerland).

Each of these two European jurisdictions has its own court and you should not, unlike many politicians and journalists, refer to 'the European court' since there are at least two. The *Court of Justice of the EU* is the court for the European Union and has jurisdiction over only EU matters. The *European Court of Human Rights* (ECtHR) is the court for the Council of Europe and has jurisdiction only over the *European Convention on Human Rights*. Confusing the two courts (and indeed institutions) is easily done but it can be a fatal mistake in your studies and is an extremely good way of upsetting your EU lecturer!

4.2 General international sources of law

International law is significantly different from domestic law, not least because there is no machinery of governance. We have already identified in previous chapters that a country will normally have three instruments of state (executive, legislature, and judiciary) and that in common-law systems, such as that operated by England and Wales, the law will normally originate from this machinery. However, in international law there is no hierarchy of states, each nation is sovereign in its own territories, and power is exercised through political and military alliances. Looking at the United Nations it is easy to think that this replicates the machinery of governance but this analogy would be false. The secretary-general does not wield any executive power nor does, for example, the Security Council. The General Assembly (where an ambassador from each signatory nation sits) is not a legislature. The only aspect where there is an element in common is that the United Nations does have its own court, the *International Court of Justice* (ICJ), but it has a limited jurisdiction (see 4.2.2.2). Where does the authority come from?

4.2.1 Finding the law

Before deciding whether an apparent rule is a law, it is first necessary to discover where the law can be found.

4.2.1.1 Conventions and treaties

International law normally arises from conventions and treaties. Fitzmaurice notes that a treaty 'provides a precise method of regulating relations between States'[1] and a simple analogy could be drawn to a contract. Precisely what the difference between a convention and a treaty is, or indeed if such a distinction exists, is not known. One possible way of differentiating between them is that a treaty is normally a bilateral document where there are rights and obligations on both sides (discussed later). This supports the contention of Fitzmaurice. A convention, on the other hand, is often a lateral contract, ie it is one-sided and not infrequently involves a state accepting responsibilities that could be considered to interfere with its sovereignty. A good example of this is the *Vienna Convention on the Law of Treaties*. This is a document that sets out how treaties are to be defined and enforced. There is no bilateral aspect here in that states agree to sign up to the principles contained in the Convention but there is no 'other side' to this contract. The *European Convention on Human Rights* fits this model in the same way since, as will be seen, there is no 'other party' to the agreement to live up to the expectations of the Convention and to contribute to its machinery.

---

1. Malgosia Fitzmaurice, 'The Practical Working of the Law of Treaties' in Malcolm Evans (ed), *International Law* (OUP 2003) 173.

The *Vienna Convention on the Law of Treaties*, as its name suggests, helps provide a definition for treaties and Article 2(2) defines them as:

> [An] international agreement concluded between States in written form and governed by international law, whether embodied in a single instrument or in two or more related instruments and whatever its particular designation.

Fitzmaurice argues that the latter sentence is important because sometimes documents will be called something else but are intended to be treaties[2] and indeed she notes that the term 'convention' is arguably covered by this Article even if it can be distinguished in the way suggested earlier. Malanczuk argues that the ICJ has drawn a distinction, however, by suggesting that conventions are treaties of 'general application'[3] which appears to replicate the distinction drawn earlier although he is clear that international law does not distinguish between them in terms of legal force. He goes on to identify their importance:

> Treaties are the major instrument of cooperation in international relations, and cooperation often involves a change in the relative positions of the states involved ... Treaties, therefore, are often an instrument of change ...[4]

It would appear that treaties are the closest analogy we can draw to primary legislation within the domestic UK law save that they are drawn up by sovereign states rather than any legislature. The distinction between a treaty and convention is then reintroduced by Malanczuk who notes that not every treaty is a law-making treaty as some will just act as a contract and are thus subservient to other treaties.[5] In effect this is demonstrating that some treaties (which could be dubbed conventions) establish the framework of the legal principles, including enforcement action, whilst others seek to use this framework to agree matters between individual states.

4.2.1.2 Custom

In the United Kingdom it has been noted that there is both statutory law and the common law and, to an extent, the same exists for international law. One could easily believe that international law is a relatively modern concept but Neff notes that arguably the concept dates back to the ancient worlds and cites the discovery of a treaty document between Egypt and the Hittite emperor in the thirteenth century BC.[6] In the classical era (seventeenth to nineteenth centuries) when the sea began to be conquered and new lands 'discovered' (colonized) and new geopolitical alliances formed, the use of treaties (and, accordingly, international law) began to increase[7] with this acceleration continuing even now.

However, in these older times not everything was concluded by treaty, not least because there was frequently no shared language, but shared practice was often followed and this has begun to be recognized as international custom.[8] However,

---

2. Malgosia Fitzmaurice, 'The Practical Working of the Law of Treaties' in Malcolm Evans (ed), *International Law* (OUP 2003) 174.
3. Peter Malanczuk, *Akehurst's Modern Introduction to International Law* (7th edn, Routledge 1997) 36.
4. Peter Malanczuk, *Akehurst's Modern Introduction to International Law* (7th edn, Routledge 1997) 37.
5. Peter Malanczuk, *Akehurst's Modern Introduction to International Law* (7th edn, Routledge 1997).
6. Stephen Neff, 'A Short History of International Law' in Malcolm Evans (ed), *International Law* (OUP 2003) 33.
7. Stephen Neff, 'A Short History of International Law' in Malcolm Evans (ed), *International Law* (OUP 2003) 37–41.
8. Peter Malanczuk, *Akehurst's Modern Introduction to International Law* (7th edn, Routledge 1997) 39.

Malanczuk also warns that it is not sufficient for a custom to have existed, it must also be recognized as law which appears to demonstrate that the division between law-making and contract-like treaties appears to be replicated in international custom; that only where a custom creates a law rather than applies the law will it be considered a source. It may appear that custom is akin to the common law in the United Kingdom and whilst historically it may be so (as the common law arguably arose from custom) it is not a true analogy because custom is the practice between the parties (states) and not the decision of any court. A prime example of when custom can give rise to laws is that of the Law of War, often referred to as the Rules of War. Greenwood notes that the idea of a law governing war appears somewhat contradictory,[9] but it is also clear that there are some basic rules within war that have to be obeyed. Some of these are governed by treaty, most notably the *Geneva Convention*, but some are purely based on the custom that has arisen from the conflicts of the past.

4.2.1.3 Court decisions

One of the more problematic sources of law is court decisions. The reason for them being problematic is not that there is any difficulty with the concept of court decisions forming part of the law since this is certainly recognized within common-law jurisdictions, but rather that there is no one single international court. Whilst there is an *International Court of Justice* (ICJ) there is also, amongst others, the *International Criminal Court* (ICC), the *European Court of Human Rights* (ECtHR), and the *European Court of Justice* (ECJ). The jurisdiction of each court is limited to include matters within its competency and indeed to the countries that agreed to abide by the court. A good example of this is the *International Criminal Court*, which the USA refuses to abide by; accordingly the court has no jurisdiction over individual Americans.

Malanczuk notes that the ICJ will normally follow its own decisions[10] and in this way it is similar to the domestic courts in common-law systems which recognize that certainty of law is an important issue that helps progress legal development. However, it is also important to note that there is no suggestion that the international courts are bound by their own decisions and thus it would not be appropriate to argue that *stare decisis* exists at international level in its purest form.

Another difficulty that exists in respect of the use of court decisions as a basis of a source of law is that as the number of international courts and tribunals increases there is a risk that they will examine similar issues but resolve matters differently, potentially leading to conflicting decisions. There is no hierarchy of courts within international law and the ICJ, for example, which is operated by the United Nations, does not have any formal relationship with any other tribunal and so cannot act as the ultimate arbitrator in these matters. Similarly, whilst some courts will examine the decisions of other courts (eg the ECtHR has, on occasions, examined the decisions of other international tribunals), it does so purely on an advisory basis and no court considers itself to be subservient to another tribunal and so it is free to decide cases differently.

Malanczuk makes an interesting point in respect of court decisions when he argues that sometimes decisions of the domestic courts can influence international law.[11] He

---

9. Christopher Greenwood, 'The Law of War' in Malcolm Evans (ed), *International Law* (OUP 2003) 790–1.
10. Peter Malanczuk, *Akehurst's Modern Introduction to International Law* (7th edn, Routledge 1997) 51.
11. Peter Malanczuk, *Akehurst's Modern Introduction to International Law* (7th edn, Routledge 1997) 51.

suggests that this is perhaps most prominent in the field of diplomatic immunity which is one of the central issues of international law. For diplomacy to work properly countries will normally send diplomatic staff (eg ambassadors, consuls, etc) to another country and they will represent the state in that country. The arrangement is normally reciprocal (ie both countries will send and receive diplomats—eg Canada sends diplomatic staff to the United Kingdom and the United Kingdom sends diplomatic staff to Canada) and the diplomats are given immunity from domestic laws. Wickremasinghe argues that the reason for this is that senior diplomats require immunity 'for their protection and facilitation'[12] which she explains as meaning that if a diplomat were liable to arrest then they could not carry out their function and accordingly arbitrarily arresting diplomats would be an easy method to interfere with the diplomatic efforts of a state.

Although a treaty, the *Vienna Convention on Diplomatic Relations*, primarily governs the area, Malanczuk's point was that this does not set out all the circumstances of diplomatic immunity and that domestic courts will often be called upon to rule on the precise application of diplomatic immunity since the immunity will normally arise from an action that occurs in the diplomatic concept. One of the most recent decisions on this area was the *Pinochet* cases where the House of Lords needed to examine whether General Pinochet, the former dictator and ruler of Chile, had diplomatic immunity. A Spanish magistrate had asked for the general to be extradited from London on the basis that an arrest warrant had been issued alleging that he had undertaken war crimes during his reign.[13] One of the issues that needed to be discussed was the limit and proper functioning of diplomatic immunity and some have argued that this analysis is now being used in the international jurisprudence[14] which appears to validate Malanczuk's argument.

4.2.1.4 'Soft law'

The last relevant issue that we need to discuss in this brief overview of international sources of law is the concept of 'soft law'. The term 'soft law' has been adopted to describe issues that are covered by treaties but where there is no serious attempt for the agreement to be legally binding, but nonetheless a country is happy to subscribe to a series of 'goals', 'targets', or 'aims'.[15] If there is no intention to make the agreement legally binding then it cannot be a true source of law but Malanczuk suggests that 'soft law' sometimes evolves into custom if sufficient countries outside of the agreement begin to follow the treaty.[16] That said, it would be a slow and controversial process and it would be preferable for law to develop through true law-making treaties and conventions.

4.2.2 Enforceability

Assuming that there is something called international law and that states can bind themselves, how does one enforce international law? In the domestic context the

12. Chanaka Wickremasinghe, 'Immunities Employed by Officials of States and International Organizations' in Malcolm Evans (ed), *International Law* (OUP 2003) 389.
13. See Lord Millet, 'The Pinochet Case: Some Personal Reflections' in Malcolm Evans (ed), *International Law* (OUP 2003) 8 for a summary of the facts.
14. Dinah Shelton, 'International Law and "Relative Normativity"' in Malcolm Evans (ed), *International Law* (OUP 2003) 156–7.
15. Peter Malanczuk, *Akehurst's Modern Introduction to International Law* (7th edn, Routledge 1997) 54.
16. Peter Malanczuk, *Akehurst's Modern Introduction to International Law* (7th edn, Routledge 1997) 54.

ultimate sanction is imprisonment but this cannot be true in international law, or at least public international law, so how can international disputes be enforced?

The easiest method is where a treaty provides an enforcement action. One particular difficulty in international law is trying to decide what exactly amounts to a breach. Merrills notes that sometimes disagreements at the international level will amount to a dispute of policy rather than legality[17] and accordingly would not be resolved through a legal mechanism.

4.2.2.1 Arbitration

The easiest way in which international disputes are settled is if the treaty that gives rise to the dispute prescribes a particular method of enforceability. Some treaties will do so, eg the ECHR created the ECtHR, but others will leave the matter open. Merrills argues that the oldest method of dispute resolution is arbitration.[18] This remains a popular remedy and exists in domestic disputes too (see 19.3.1.1) and involves taking the dispute to an independent third party (agreed by the parties) who will listen to the submissions for both sides before declaring an outcome. Traditionally arbitration was the resolution of choice for land and territory disputes[19] and has the attraction that it requires no standing commitment, with an arbitrator being selected when a dispute arises.

Arbitration is based on the concept of consent and although both parties must consent to the matter being taken to an arbitrator there is no sanction if the losing party refuses to cede control of the issues.[20] Where a state does refuse to implement the findings of an arbitrator it is likely that discussions as to the law will give way to diplomacy with both countries, and their geopolitical allies, seeking to implement the decision reached.

103

4.2.2.2 International courts

It has been noted already that some international courts have been established and accordingly one method of enforcing a law may be to bring an action against a state in the relevant international court. The jurisdiction and powers of each court are set out in the originating treaty. Some courts have the power to impose real sanctions. For example, the ECJ has the power to fine individual states that breach Convention law. The *Treaty of Rome* (see 'References to the Treaty of Rome') gives the Court that power and if the individual state wishes to continue to be a member of the EU, and purport to uphold its laws, then it must abide by the fine.

The ICJ is a permanent court constituted under the auspices of the United Nations although it is independent from the 'executive' of the United Nations in that although it will 'report' to the General Assembly, its Sixth Committee, and the Security Council, it is not responsible or accountable to anybody for its judgments.[21] There is, therefore, independence of the judiciary even at the international level. The Court is not an appellate or referral court in that it is not open to citizens of a country to refer a matter to

17. John Merrills, 'The Means of Dispute Settlement' in Malcolm Evans (ed), *International Law* (OUP 2003) 530.
18. John Merrills, 'The Means of Dispute Settlement' in Malcolm Evans (ed), *International Law* (OUP 2003) 539.
19. John Merrills, 'The Means of Dispute Settlement' in Malcolm Evans (ed), *International Law* (OUP 2003).
20. John Merrills, 'The Means of Dispute Settlement' in Malcolm Evans (ed), *International Law* (OUP 2003) 541.
21. Rosalyn Higgins, 'Reflections from the International Court' in Malcolm Evans (ed), *International Law* (OUP 2003) 3.

the Court but, rather, it is a means through which individual states can seek to resolve international disputes in a peaceful way after diplomatic means have been exhausted. The Court, unlike most other courts, has no specific jurisdiction but instead has jurisdiction over matters where both parties consent to taking the matter before it.

The Court has fifteen judicial members who are elected by the Security Council and General Assembly and who, at the time of their election, do not represent their country but must act in an independent judicial manner.[22] The judges have diplomatic rank within the United Nations, normally at ambassadorial level, and have the equivalent immunity. However, despite their independent status it is not possible for more than one judge to come from the same country and Thirlway also casts doubt on the independence of their election noting that candidates of the five permanent members of the Security Council tend to be preferred.[23] The term of office of a judge is nine years although it is possible for them to be re-elected by the United Nations.

In domestic courts it would be extraordinary for a person who had a relationship with one of the parties to sit on a matter (see 9.3.3) but in the international context the reverse is true. Where a country brings a matter to the ICJ then they are entitled to appoint an ad hoc judge to the ICJ if one of the judges is not already of that nationality. The argument for this policy at international level is that it is possible for the national judges to explain the legal implications of a particular policy in their own jurisdiction[24] but Thirlway questions the merits of such an approach by noting that whilst permanent judges of the ICJ have not infrequently voted against their own country, no ad hoc judge ever has.[25] It is perhaps understandable that this is the case given the nature of a temporary appointment (and the desire to be nominated for cases again in the future) but the judges are, theoretically, supposed to take the same oath. This perhaps adds weight to the argument that judicial independence can only be secured when tenure is certain (see 9.2.3).

Interestingly Article 38 of the *Permanent Court of International Justice Statute*, which is a statutory instrument issued by the United Nations to give effect to Article 92 of the UN Charter setting up a court, lists the sources of law that are to be considered in disputes and these include international treaties, conventions, custom, general principles of the law, and decisions of tribunals.

Article 60 of the statute states that the judgment of the ICJ is to be final and binding which demonstrates that there is no further judicial appeal from its decision and Article 59 limits the judgment to being binding between the parties and accordingly it can be said that the ICJ does not set precedent per se and that decisions are relevant to future cases but not authoritative. Although the statute refers to matters as being 'binding' this is a relative concept. Article 94(2) of the UN Charter states that where a judgment of the Court is ignored the other party may refer the matter to the Security Council but this is arguably a toothless provision as there is no requirement on the Security Council to act and the actions of the Security Council are political rather than legal. For example, there was widespread debate over whether the decision of the

---

22. Hugh Thirlway, 'The International Court of Justice' in Malcolm Evans (ed), *International Law* (OUP 2003) 362.

23. Hugh Thirlway, 'The International Court of Justice' in Malcolm Evans (ed), *International Law* (OUP 2003) 362.
The five permanent members are China, France, Russia, the United Kingdom, and the United States of America.

24. See David Harris et al, *Law of the European Convention on Human Rights* (Butterworths 1995) 654.

25. Hugh Thirlway, 'The International Court of Justice' in Malcolm Evans (ed), *International Law* (OUP 2003) 563.

United States and the United Kingdom to invade Iraq in 2003 was, in terms of international law, legal. A reference to the Security Council under such circumstances would, however, be pointless as both the United States and United Kingdom have a veto on Security Council resolutions meaning one cannot be passed without their acquiescence. Similarly, the conflict between Israel and the Palestinians would appear to be a classic example of when the ICJ should become involved but any judgment would be academic since both parties have traditional allies in the permanent members of the Security Council meaning any attempt at using the Security Council's powers would be defeated.

4.2.2.3 War

The ultimate sanction for the resolution of any dispute between international states is, of course, war. Some international instruments will seek to 'police' war (eg *Geneva Convention relative to the Treatment of Prisoners of War*) but international law will also sometimes permit, or indeed authorize, the use of military force to enforce a legal right. Perhaps the most commonly used justification is that of self-defence, which Article 51 of the UN Charter expressly retains. However, precisely what amounts to self-defence is, of course, open to debate especially in the post-September 11 era when governments, particularly those of the United States, the United Kingdom, and Australia, have considered self-defence from terrorism acts to be legitimate and have used such a justification for the invasion of Afghanistan. The issue of self-defence is extremely controversial[26] and demonstrates the inevitable paradox that arises from the idea that there can be a legal war.

Theoretically, outside of self-defence there should be no right to recourse to war since Article 2(4) of the UN Charter expressly states that parties will not revert to war when disputes arise, the intention being that recourse would be made to diplomatic means or the use of the ICJ. However, it has been seen that the ICJ does not have any enforcement sanctions available to it and thus the UN Charter contemplates that the UN could authorize the use of military force to uphold international law. The UN Charter provides that the Security Council should monitor acts of aggression and 'threats to peace' and provides that they are able to take action to counter such activities.[27]

105

Example Iraq

The Attorney-General, Lord Goldsmith QC, had to consider, prior to the invasion of Iraq in 2003, whether the United Nations had authorized the use of force. The Attorney-General (controversially) argued that three resolutions of the UN Security Council, taken together, did authorize the use of force (Resolutions 1441, 678, and 687). The argument was controversial because the only resolution that expressly stated that force could be used was Resolution 678, which authorized the use of force to expel Iraq from Kuwait. Resolution 687 suspended Resolution 678 but did not repeal it. The Attorney-General argued that Resolution 1441 lifted the suspension on Resolution 678 but it certainly did not do so expressly. If, however, the

---

26. For an introduction to the arguments see Christine Gray, 'The Use of Force and International Legal Order' in Malcolm Evans (ed), *International Law* (OUP 2003) 599–605.
27. Christine Gray, 'The Use of Force and International Legal Order' in Malcolm Evans (ed), *International Law* (OUP 2003) 607.

Attorney-General was correct then the use of force was legal irrespective of any claim to self-defence.

It had originally been thought that a separate resolution would be required to authorize the use of force and to avoid any uncertainty but the politics of the Security Council became involved again and with the threat of a veto by other permanent members of the Security Council, the United Kingdom and the United States believed it was better to proceed under the ambiguous authority on the basis that they believed it could authorize the use of force whereas a defeated resolution might be taken as reimposing the suspension on Resolution 678 meaning force would not be authorized. This decision continues to be discussed by international lawyers and it demonstrates how contentious international law can be.

Although the UN Charter does, therefore, allow for the use of force it must be recognized that it is a measure of last resort and Article 41 of the Charter states that the Security Council should normally first consider non-military activities such as the use of economic sanctions. This does normally occur and it is noticeable, for example, that sanctions were imposed on Iraq far earlier than military action was ever contemplated.

Where, however, sanctions are not permissible and where the political will exists, Articles 42–49 of the Charter do authorize the use of force. On occasions the force will operate under the UN banner, with perhaps the best-known example of this being the Korean War in which, at least theoretically, each unit operated under UN command. In modern times, however, it is more usual for UN military actions to be under the banner of peacekeeping, occasionally peacemaking, actions with more offensive actions occurring under national or multinational banners but under authority from the United Nations. A good example of this is the first Gulf War—*Operation Desert Storm*—where the action was not undertaken in the name of the United Nations, nor were any units so badged, but instead it occurred under a coalition led by the United States.

There is no doubt that the most recent Iraq campaign has altered the way that the use of legal force is constrained and it has yet to be seen whether the United Nations will continue to have a role in authorizing the use of force or whether individual states will neglect to seek authorization, relying instead on the premise of 'self-defence' or the 'common good'. Where it is the permanent members of the Security Council that operate such a policy (most notably the United States but the United Kingdom traditionally sides with the United States and with the exception of the case of Iraq, France will normally adopt such a posture) then there is very little the United Nations can do to remedy such actions as these states wield a veto in respect of any action and are also the principal contributors to the work of the United Nations.

4.3 European Union

It was noted at the beginning of this chapter that it is important that you should differentiate between the European Union (formerly the European Economic Community (EEC) and then the European Community (EC)) and the Council of Europe (see 4.1). In this section only the EU will be discussed with the Council of Europe being discussed in the next section (4.4).

The decision of the United Kingdom to leave the EU is obviously extremely topical at the time of writing. You may wonder why this section even remains in the book.

The reality is that EU law is going to be within the English Legal System for many years, and this will require an understanding of how EU law works. Also, whenever the UK trades with the EU, it is likely that some, or all, of EU law will apply, again meaning you need to understand this.

At the time this chapter was written, Article 50[28] has not yet been triggered so we do not know what the strategy of either the UK or EU to departure is. However, the Prime Minister has suggested that there will be a 'Great Repeal Bill' which will repeal the *European Communities Act 1972* but, at the same time, transpose EU law into domestic law. Over a period of years—and some would say decades—this law will gradually be changed where it is deemed necessary. This, at the very least, shows why an understanding of EU law is necessary, since to understand these provisions will require an understanding of EU law.

 REFERENCES TO THE TREATY OF ROME

It will be seen that, until the *Lisbon Treaty*, the most important treaty was the *Treaty of Rome*, which was the founding document of the EU and which all states acceding to the EU had to sign. As will be seen, the *Lisbon Treaty* led to the *Treaty of Rome* either being renamed and renumbered or, perhaps more accurately, being replaced. The two new treaties that are relevant to the EU are the *Treaty on the Functioning of the EU* (TFEU) and the *Treaty on the European Union* (TEU). After presenting a brief chronology to understand how *Lisbon* was reached reference will now only be made to these treaties.

107

4.3.1 From EEC to EU

The United Kingdom joined the then European Economic Community on 1 January 1973 but it was not one of the first countries to join the EEC which was established formally in 1957 although its inception would appear to have taken place in the 1950s.[29] The original grouping of states was: France, West Germany, Italy, Belgium, the Netherlands, and Luxembourg. The original intention was simply to form a community governing European steel and coal and so the *European Coal and Steel Community* (ECSC) was formed in 1952. This was then followed by EURATOM, the *European Atomic Energy Community* and then the *European Economic Community*, these being created by the *Treaties of Rome*.

 TREATIES OF ROME

The status of treaties has already been discussed (4.2.1.1). It became commonplace to talk about the *Treaty of Rome*, meaning the treaty that established the EEC, but in fact there were two treaties since one created EURATOM. In essence, however, the principal treaty prior to the *Lisbon Treaty* was the EEC *Treaty of Rome* and all new members of the EEC had to sign the *Treaty of Rome*.

---

28. Article 50 of the *Treaty on the European Union* details the process by which a Member State leaves the European Union.
29. John Fairhurst, *Law of the European Union* (10th edn, Pearson Education 2014) 5.

In 1967 these communities were, in effect, merged (see *Merger Treaty 1965*) and two institutions were created, the *European Commission* and the *Council of the European Communities*. It is essential that the latter is not confused with *the* Council of Europe since they do remain separate and following the *Treaty of Maastricht* it became known as the Council of Ministers or, following the *Treaty of Lisbon*, simply 'the Council'. Although the ministers are in their individual states properly referred to as the executive, within the EU/EEC they are actually, along with the *European Parliament*, the legislature.

The United Kingdom joined the then EEC in 1973 in the second wave of countries to join, the other countries joining at that time being Ireland and Denmark. Joining the Community required, as a result of the legal implications, the passing of domestic legislation (see 4.3.4) and this was provided for by the *European Communities Act 1972*. There are, at the time of writing, currently twenty-eight Member States with Croatia being the most recent to join on 1 July 2013. Turkey, the former Yugoslav Republic of Macedonia, and Serbia are seeking to join within the next few years.

As the Community grew so did its mission and it moved from being a purely economic grouping to much more, with greater harmony in respect of laws and more general cooperation. Successive treaties have then been used to modify the Community and Union and it is certainly clear that the present Union is significantly different from the EEC first created.

4.3.1.1 The road to *Lisbon*

Whilst the *Treaty of Lisbon* is undoubtedly the most important of the subsequent treaties, its predecessors must be placed in context. Perhaps the first treaty of significance was the *Single European Act* (SEA) which should not be confused with domestic definitions of an Act as it is an international treaty. The SEA was signed in 1986 by ministers of the then Member States and the three new Member States that joined later that year. It came into force in 1987 and its primary purpose was to bring about closer cohesion within the European market. In terms of the policy changes, the SEA defined the internal market as being free from all internal constraints in respect of certain fundamental freedoms, this being enforced by the changes to the Commission etc. The Treaty also sought to harmonize certain laws in respect of health and safety etc. It also, importantly, began the trend away from pure economic considerations with the establishment of the framework for a common foreign policy whereby Member States would work together to assist in the security of the Community.

However, the primary mechanism by which the closer cohesion of the Community was progressed under the SEA was to change the European institutions and by granting them extra powers (the argument being that the institutions would be empowered to act against barriers to a Community market).

Perhaps the first major change that was brought about by the SEA was that certain decisions of the Council of Ministers could be taken by majority rather than unanimity. Prior to the SEA all decisions required unanimity across the countries but by the time the Community had reached twelve Member States it had become more difficult to guarantee unanimity and, in effect, this requirement allowed a country to veto a decision irrespective of whether it would be for the greater good of the Community.

⚡ MAJORITY VOTING

When discussing majority voting it is worth noting that it is not necessarily a simple procedure. It may be thought that when there were twelve Member States a majority would be
reached if at least seven states voted for the proposition. However, this was not necessarily true
since each state had a 'weighted' vote, in essence replicating its population and so reflecting
its importance within the EU. For example, under the current system, the United Kingdom
has twenty-nine votes whereas Sweden has ten votes. A majority arises under the total votes
although some votes also require a majority of states to be in favour too. Post *Lisbon* the issue
of majority voting is complicated but this is discussed further later.

The *European Parliament* was also strengthened under the SEA. The Parliament continues to pose an interesting conundrum for Europeans. The Parliament cannot be
easily contrasted with the Westminster Parliament since its powers are shared. For
example, an important feature of the Westminster Parliament's role is to hold the
executive (government) to account. The European Parliament has a similar role but
until the *Treaty of Lisbon* this was primarily the responsibility of the Council of
Ministers. That said, *Lisbon* has potentially placed the Parliament on an equal footing in respect of most matters. The SEA originally created two principal purposes for
Parliament:

- to produce opinions on draft directives and regulations produced by the
  Commission
- to assent to certain treaties concluded by the Commission, most notably any
  treaty that leads to the Community becoming enlarged.

In addition to this it would, of course, undertake debates and motions on aspects
relevant to the EU. The members of the Parliament (known as MEPs—Members of
the European Parliament) are elected in domestic elections and each country sends different numbers of people to the Parliament, again largely according to size. Currently
the United Kingdom sends seventy-three MEPs whereas Estonia sends only six and
Sweden sends twenty.

Maastricht

Prior to *Lisbon* the biggest change to the EEC was brought about by the *Treaty on
the European Union* which was more commonly referred to as the *Maastricht Treaty*
(MT) as a result of it being signed in that city in 1992. Its principal change was to create the European Union, it doing so by stating that the Union consisted of three pillars,
one of which was the European Communities (the others being the Common Foreign
and Security Policy and the Justice and Home Affairs pillars). These pillars have now
been abolished and the various functions subsumed within the Union (considered later
when discussing the *Treaty of Lisbon*).

Apart from this change perhaps the most significant other change brought about
by the MT was the push towards monetary and economic union. This is certainly
the most noticeable change since it led to the establishment of the single European
currency, now known as the Euro, although originally known as the Eurodollar. The
MT sought to bring in a single currency throughout the Union but this was fiercely
rejected by the United Kingdom at the time and was also rejected by Denmark and

109

Sweden (although the latter country is theoretically bound by treaty to join the Euro at some point in the future). Ten of the twelve countries within the European Union at the time of Maastricht did join and it continues to be used within Continental Europe. Whilst there were some tensions surrounding the Euro during the global economic crisis, particularly when it was necessary for countries to produce bail-out packages for countries like Greece and Cyprus, there has been no serious suggestion that the single currency will end. All new countries that join the EU must commit to make the Euro their legal tender at some point but, as Sweden has demonstrated, it is perhaps questionable whether breaching this commitment would lead to any sanction.

The MT also made some changes to the democratic accountability of the EU through changes to the European Parliament but these have been further changed by the *Treaty of Lisbon* and will be discussed at that point and when considering the institutions themselves (see 4.3.2.1).

Amsterdam

Although the MT was the major legislative instrument prior to *Lisbon*, a further treaty was necessary, this being the *Treaty of Amsterdam* (AT) which was concluded in 1997. Realistically this was not a major treaty and its principal cosmetic change was to renumber the *Treaty of Rome* to take account of the changes brought about since its original drafting. Some commentators have argued that the AT did little other than renumber the Treaty[30] and that in essence it was a 'smoke and mirrors' treaty that allowed certain EU countries to work together in a closer way but without the need for all Member States to be involved with ancillary matters.

To an extent, some of the other reforms introduced by the AT were similarly quite cosmetic. The Treaty limited the number of MEPs that could sit in the Parliament (yet Parliament has subsequently increased in numbers) and also defined the powers of the President of the Commission but it was not a wholesale reform of the EU institutions, something that many commentators believed was necessary.[31] The AT also made certain changes to the MT but they are not particularly relevant to the discussion here.

One aspect of interest, however, is the fact that the Treaty made express reference to the *European Convention on Human Rights* which is, of course, run by a separate organization. However, the AT added a provision which allowed the Council to decide to suspend the voting rights of a Member State if it persistently continued to breach the ECHR (Article 7). It will be noted later that there is no direct enforcement action for decisions of the European Court of Human Rights but this provision provided an 'ultimate' sanction for persistent breach by members of the EU.

Treaty of Nice

The last treaty of note before the principal changes brought about by *Lisbon* was the *Treaty of Nice* (TN). This Treaty was concluded in 2000 and its principal purpose was to prepare the Union for expansion. The TN effectively altered the institutions and permitted the Union to increase to twenty-seven Member States.

The interface between the ECHR and the EU returned in the TN, and Article 7—which permits the suspension of a Member State for persistently breaching the

---

30. Nigel Foster, *Foster on EU Law* (6th edn, OUP 2017) ch 1.
31. John Fairhurst, *Law of the European Union* (10th edn, Pearson Education 2014) 17.

ECHR—ceased to require unanimity and thus suspension could occur if four-fifths of the Council vote.[32] Again this is undoubtedly a response to the realities of expansion where there are undoubtedly going to be political groupings established within the Community. If a 'rogue' state could persuade one other country to join them it would have ensured that the Union was paralysed and, accordingly, this measure was perhaps necessary, although whether a four-fifths majority would ever be achieved is perhaps open to debate.

The TN began to put into effect the desire of the EU to concentrate on more than just the EC and other parts of the TN dealt with foreign policy, common defence plans, the European arrest warrant, and closer cooperation.[33] The latter has been particularly controversial in the United Kingdom but it is something that is realistically outside the scope of this chapter, which considers the issue of sources of law.

4.3.1.2 **The Treaty of Lisbon**

After the conclusion of the TN, considerable effort was spent trying to agree a constitution for Europe. This would have codified all of the Treaties but also added to them. As a constitution it required the ratification of all Member States. Voters in both France and the Netherlands rejected the constitution and this led to the suspension of the ratification process.

Following the rejection of the Constitutional Treaty EU leaders attempted to reintroduce certain parts of the Treaty in a new instrument, the *Treaty of Lisbon* (TL). Considerable controversy existed over whether this was, in fact, a distinct treaty or whether it was simply the same treaty but not called a 'constitution'. Countries proceeded to ratify the Treaty and many countries no longer offered their electorate a referendum, arguing that this was no longer necessary. This formed a particular controversy in the United Kingdom since Tony Blair, the then prime minister, stated in the House of Commons that a referendum would be offered in respect of the Constitutional Treaty but Gordon Brown, who later became prime minister, refused to offer a referendum in respect of the TL, arguing the pledge related specifically to the Constitutional Treaty.

Whilst ratification is ordinarily an executive act, s 12 *European Parliamentary Elections Act 2002* states that if a treaty will increase the powers of the European Parliament it requires ratification by the Westminster Parliament and not merely the executive. The government introduced the *European Union (Amendment) Bill* (now Act 2008) providing for ratification. Stuart Wheeler, a prominent Eurosceptic, attempted to judicially review the decision of the government to ratify the TL without a referendum. In *R (on the application of Wheeler) v Office of the Prime Minister*[34] the matter proceeded before the Administrative Court.

The court rejected the application stating that the Treaties were, as a matter of fact, different but also, as a matter of domestic law, the pledge could not give rise to an action in law and that the proceedings were an attempt to usurp the sovereign powers of Parliament. The UK has, therefore, now ratified the TL and, after an initial rejection, Ireland ratified the TL, and with the eventual ratification of the Czech Republic it came into force.

---

32. John Fairhurst, *Law of the European Union* (10th edn, Pearson Education 2014) 22.
33. John Fairhurst, *Law of the European Union* (10th edn, Pearson Education 2014) 23.
34. [2008] EWHC 1409 (Admin).

The TL has made significant changes to the EU. Some of these will be discussed in further depth later (4.3.1.3) when looking at the institutions and laws of the EU. The limitations of this section should be discussed here. The purpose of this chapter is not to provide a commentary on the EU or identify all the structural changes brought about by the Treaty, its purpose is to consider the *sources* of EU law and accordingly this, and the subsequent sections, of the chapter will concentrate only on those aspects that impact on the sources of law.

It has been stated that the TL renumbers (again) the *Treaty of Rome* but more than this it changes its name. Instead of it being the *Treaty establishing the European Community* it becomes the *Treaty on the Functioning of the European Union* (TFEU) (Article 1(11), TL). This is more than merely a semantic change as it does reflect what the *Treaty of Rome* has become. The subsequent changes have, in essence, changed the Treaty into a 'rulebook' for how the EU operates and referring to it as the founding treaty was becoming less tenable. The TL makes clear that the EU is formed on the basis of two treaties of equal status, the *Treaty on the European Union* (TEU) and the *Treaty on the Functioning of the European Union*.[35] It has been remarked that in the absence of a formal constitution (which, as noted earlier, was rejected) the TEU has become the 'repository of the constitutional principles for the European Union'.[36]

At a constitutional level the Treaty created the post of *President of the European Council*. This will be discussed later (4.3.2.2) but it is worth noting that this is a considerable change from the previous system whereby the presidency of the Council would rotate through the Member States every six months. Other executive positions were created including a *High Representative for Foreign Affairs and Security Policy*. The High Representative is a member of the Commission and is also one of the Vice-Presidents.[37] The primary role of the High Representative is to 'conduct the Union's common foreign and security policy'[38] and she also acts as the chair for the Foreign Affairs Council.[39] The High Representative is supported by a secretariat drawn from the civil service of the EU.

One of the more important provisions relates to the competence of the EU. It was noted in the previous section that the MT organized the EU into three pillars. *Lisbon* abolishes these as formal pillars and brings many of the matters into the substantive treaty. Instead of pillars, *Lisbon* refers to the competences of the EU.

4.3.1.3 The EU post *Lisbon*

The revised treaties state that the EU will be based on the issue of competences. Article 4 TEU states that anything that is not within the competences remains with the Member States and thus the Treaty is making clear the extent to which sovereignty is invested within the EU. Article 5 TEU states 'the limits of Union competences are governed by the principle of conferral' making it clear that the EU can only act in situations where the Member States confer sovereignty onto the EU to act in certain areas. This demonstrates the principle of consent: that the EU is established by the Member States joining it and participating in it on the consensual conferral of sovereignty.

---

35. *Treaty on the Functioning of the European Union*, Art 1(2).
36. Paul Craig, 'The Treaty of Lisbon, Process, Architecture and Substance' (2008) 33 *European Law Review* 137, 141.
37. *Treaty on the European Union*, Art 18(4).
38. *Treaty on the European Union*, Art 18(2).
39. *Treaty on the European Union*, Art 18(3).

Allied to this is a new provision contained within the TEU by the TL, Article 50 TEU which states, for the first time, how Member States can withdraw from the EU. Prior to the establishment of Article 50 it was not clear how a Member State would withdraw. It has been suggested that Article 50 reinforces the fact that membership of the EU is voluntary[40] although it is difficult to see how the EU could have prevented a Member State from leaving prior to the establishment of Article 50.

The competences of the EU are divided into three types:

- areas where the EU has exclusive competence[41]
- areas where there are shared competence[42]
- areas where the EU can take action to support, coordinate, or supplement action by Member States.[43]

The differences between these are set out in Article 2 TFEU. Article 2(1) states that where a matter is within the exclusive competence of the EU, 'only the Union may legislate and adopt legally binding acts, the Member States being able to do so themselves only if so empowered by the Union ...'. In other words, Member States surrender the power to legislate in these areas save where permitted to do so by the EU. Article 2(2) states that shared competence means that both the EU and Member States may legislate but that 'Member States shall exercise their competence to the extent that the Union has not exercised its competence'. In other words, Member States may legislate in those areas where the EU has not. Article 2(5) states that where the EU takes action to support, coordinate, or supplement action by Member States it does so 'without thereby superseding their competence in these areas'. In other words, the EU will only support the actions of Member States and their laws will not take precedence over domestic laws in these areas.

In addition to these three competences the EU has competence in respect of economic, employment, and social policy[44] and a common foreign and security policy.[45] The latter, in particular, demonstrates the fact that the pillar structure adopted by the MT has been superseded and that the EU now has general competence in these areas, subject to opt-outs negotiated by various countries.

It has been stated that 'the Treaty of Lisbon distinguishes between the existence of competence ... and the use of such competence, which is determined by subsidiarity and proportionality'.[46] Subsidiarity is explained by Article 5(3) TEU which states that save where a matter is within the exclusive competence of the EU, the EU can only act where it is satisfied that 'the objectives of the proposed action cannot be sufficiently achieved by the Member States... . [but can] be better achieved at Union level'. This is limiting the circumstances under which the EU can act outside of situations where it has exclusive jurisdiction and it is notable that the TL has given additional power to national Parliaments in assessing subsidiarity (see Articles 4 and 6 of Protocol 2 to the TFEU on the application of the principles of subsidiarity and proportionality). National Parliaments will be consulted on draft legislation and where, within

40. G Love, 'Oh Brave New World! Lisbon Enters into Force' (2010) *EU Focus* 1, 14.
41. *Treaty on the Functioning of the European Union*, Art 3.
42. *Treaty on the Functioning of the European Union*, Art 4.
43. *Treaty on the Functioning of the European Union*, Art 6.
44. *Treaty on the Functioning of the European Union*, Art 2(3).
45. *Treaty on the Functioning of the European Union*, Art 2(4).
46. Paul Craig, 'The Treaty of Lisbon, Process, Architecture and Substance' (2008) 33 *European Law Review* 137, 149.

eight weeks of receiving the draft legislation, it believes that it does not comply with the principle of subsidiarity it may notify the Presidents of the European Parliament, Council, and Commission with a reasoned opinion stating why it does not believe that it complies. Such notifications must be taken into account[47] and where at least one-third of all votes allocated to national Parliaments question whether the draft legislation complies with subsidiarity then the relevant institution must formally review the institution.

4.3.2 The institutions

In order to understand how the EU operates it will be necessary to consider its institutions. Article 13 TEU lists the following as institutions of the EU:

- the European Parliament
- the European Council
- the Council
- the European Commission
- the Court of Justice of the European Union
- the European Central Bank
- the Court of Auditors.

It is not necessary to consider all of these institutions since they do not all act as a source of law. For example, the *European Central Bank* will not be considered since although it is, for the first time as a result of the TL, an institution it has limited law-making powers of relevance to the English Legal System. It is also notable that the Bank retains its independence and legal personality.[48] The *Lisbon Treaty* also allows for the creation of a *European Prosecutor's Office*[49] although this has not yet occurred and accordingly it will not be discussed in this book.

4.3.2.1 The European Parliament

The European Parliament is to an extent a relatively recent addition, with the initial legislative consultancy body simply being drawn from representatives of the individual legislatures of the Member States. The *Single European Act* (discussed earlier at 4.3.1.1) attempted to make the legislature more democratic and the European Parliament was, for the first time, composed of representatives elected by direct universal suffrage. Its members, known as Members of the European Parliament (MEPs), hold office for a fixed period of five years although they can be re-elected.

Unlike constituencies in the Westminster Parliament which are based on population, the same is not necessarily true of the European Parliament. Each Member State is allocated a number of seats and this differs according not only to the size of the country but also its importance. The TL has attempted to alter this a little by adjusting the numbers slightly but there continue to be significant differences with, for example, the United Kingdom currently being allocated seventy-three seats (the largest grouping is Germany with ninety-six seats) and, for example, Sweden being allocated

---

47. *Treaty on the Functioning of the European Union*, Protocol 2, Art 7.
48. G Love, 'Oh Brave New World! Lisbon Enters into Force' (2010) *EU Focus* 1, 12.
49. *Treaty on the Functioning of the European Union*, Art 86.

only twenty seats. However, given the variances of population this can mean that the smaller countries do have proportionately better representation than the larger countries but they may have less 'power' than the larger countries. Rather than sitting in national groupings the Parliament divides itself into transnational groupings that reflect the relevant political ethos of the group. Rule 30 of the *European Parliament's Rules for Procedure* dictates when a grouping is recognized. It must currently be a grouping of a minimum of twenty-five MEPs but these must be representatives from at least one-quarter of the Member States (currently six Member States). Thus if thirty MEPs from five Member States wish to form a grouping this would not be formally recognized and would not, for example, receive staffing or resources beyond that given to individual MEPs.

One of the biggest controversies surrounding the European Parliament arises from where it conducts its business. Its 'official' home is Strasbourg but it also sits in Brussels, which is, in essence, the HQ of the EU. This leads to the rather ridiculous situation where meetings are held in two different cities and the MEPs, officials, and resultant paperwork have to shift between the two 'seats'. The expense and inconvenience this involves is frustrating to many and indeed it is believed that a significant number of MEPs would prefer to be based in Brussels where the other institutions are to be found. However, the location can only be changed with the unanimous agreement of the Council of Ministers and this is unlikely to be forthcoming in the immediate future.

The European Parliament cannot be directly compared to a national Parliament since it forms only one part of the legislature (the other being the European Council). Until the TL the powers of the Parliament were somewhat limited but the TL greatly increased the powers of the Parliament, with it being described as an 'institutional winner'.[50] Prior to the TL the European Parliament was to an extent inferior to the European Council but they now act primarily on an equal basis. However, the Parliament does not, unlike the Westminster Parliament, have the right to initiate legislation (this being primarily the preserve of the Commission). Article 225 TEU allows the Parliament, by a simple majority, to request the Commission to submit a proposal for legislation but the Commission need not do so, merely needing to explain to the Parliament why it has failed to do so should it decide not to bring forward any legislation.

Parliament has three principal roles. The first is the participation in the legislative process. The second is its scrutiny of the budget and the third is to supervise the Commission. It also has additional political powers in that it can conduct investigations or hearings into appropriate matters. Its final power is that the Parliament must approve the admission of new Member States.[51]

The Parliament's power to scrutinize legislation is perhaps its most important power. Originally this power was simply to be consulted on legislation and its views could be disregarded. However, the TL has significantly increased the power of the Parliament and it is now involved in the passing of most legislation. The legislative process of the EU is divided into two classes of procedure; the 'ordinary legislative procedure' and the 'special legislative procedure'.

115

50.   Paul Craig, 'The Treaty of Lisbon, Process, Architecture and Substance' (2008) 33 *European Law Review* 137, 156.
51.   *Treaty of the European Union*, Art 49.

Ordinary legislative procedure

This was, until the TL renamed it, known as the co-decision procedure. Its renaming reflects the fact that the TL has expanded the authority of Parliament into almost all areas of competence and that, in essence, the Parliament and European Council are almost on an equal footing. The ordinary procedure is premised on the basis that Commission legislation only becomes law if it and the Council agree. The stages are as follows (see Article 294 TEU):

1. The Commission submits a proposal to the European Parliament and the Council.

First reading

2. The European Parliament adopts its position and communicates this to the Council.

3. If the Council agrees with the position adopted by the Parliament then the relevant act shall be adopted in the wording that corresponds to the position of the European Parliament.

4. If the Council disagrees with the Parliament's position then it adopts its own position, communicates that to Parliament, and states why it adopts the position it does and the Commission indicates what its position is.

Second reading

1. Within three months of receiving a communication from the Council it can:

   (a) approve the position of Council or, if the Parliament fails to adopt a position, it will be deemed to be adopted in the wording of the Council;

   (b) reject the position of the Council by absolute majority (in which case the proposed act is deemed not to have been adopted);

   (c) propose amendments to the Council's position (by absolute majority) in which case the amendment shall be forwarded to the Council and the Commission.

2. Where the Council receives a communication from the Parliament (1(c) above) then acting by a qualified majority (see 'Voting') the Council can:

   (a) approve the amendments made by the Parliament, in which case the legislation is adopted;

   (b) disapprove of the amendments, in which case the matter should be referred to a Conciliation Committee.

Conciliation committee

1. A conciliation committee shall be constituted (including equal numbers of members of the Council and the European Parliament) which shall have the task of reaching an agreement on a joint text within six weeks of it being constituted.

2. The Commission shall participate in the committee (although not be a formal party to it) and shall endeavour to bring the parties together on an agreed text.

3. If, within six weeks of being constituted, the parties do not agree a text then the legislative act is deemed not to be adopted.

Third reading

1. If an agreed text is adopted by the conciliation committee then the Parliament, acting by simple majority, and the Council, acting by a qualified majority, shall each have a period of six weeks to accept the text. If they fail to do so then the measure is deemed to be not adopted.

Whilst this is quite a complicated provision it can be seen that it does give the Parliament power to reject most legislation since there are a number of stages where proposed legislation is considered not to be adopted. This marks a significant difference from the previous position whereby for a significant amount of legislation Parliament could, in essence, merely criticize but not block it. It has been remarked that the co-decision procedure (which, in essence, this is) has broadly worked and allows for a proper balance to be given to state (Council) views and citizens (Parliament).

 ABSOLUTE MAJORITY

Normally when votes (in any institution) are taken a majority is deemed to be where at least one more vote is cast than the opposing votes. For example, if there are one hundred voters all of whom vote then a majority would be fifty-one. However, if nineteen people abstain (ie decide not to vote) or are not present for the vote then a majority would arise with forty-one as the maximum number of opposing votes would be forty.

An absolute majority, however, is where the number is fixed as at least one more vote than the total number of eligible voters. There are currently 750 MEPs all of whom are entitled to a vote. A majority arises when 376 votes are cast on one side (as only a maximum of 374 votes could be cast in opposition). However, this figure remains regardless of how many people actually vote. Accordingly, if 100 MEPs are absent then to carry a resolution, 376 votes still need to be passed even though this equates to 58 per cent of MEPs present voting for the proposition. In essence it is a 'safety net' to ensure that certain powers are exercised only when a true majority of MEPs are in favour of the result.

Special legislative procedure

The second procedure is that known as the 'special legislative procedure'. This procedure is restricted to those areas where the Treaty expressly states that the ordinary procedure is not to be used.[52] In these circumstances it is possible that either the Parliament or the Council will have the right to approve the legislation in consultation with the other (although such consultation is more than a mere formality: consideration should be given to its responses).[53] Where the Council has the right to approve the legislation then the Parliament has no right of veto and can, in essence, merely make comments as to its own views. Few areas continue to adopt the special legislative procedure although the consultation procedure applies to taxation, competition, and the harmonization of legislation not related to the internal market.

---

52. *Treaty on the Functioning of the European Union*, Art 289.
53. *Roquette Frères v Council* [1980] ECR 3333.

QUESTION FOR REFLECTION

A principal aim of the *Lisbon Treaty* was to increase democratic accountability. Does the Parliament realistically have any teeth in legislative scrutiny? It does not have the right to legislate itself and only has the 'nuclear' option of vetoing legislation rather than demanding that individual amendments be accepted. For example, if in a twenty-section regulation it objects to one section of it, does it decide to veto the entire regulation or does it give way on the basis it likes the other nineteen?

Could Parliament's powers be increased to allow amendment of individual sections? What would the implications of this be? How do you think the Council of Ministers would react given that national interest is perhaps easier to control in a Committee of twenty-seven rather than a Parliament of 736.

 LISTEN TO THE PODCAST

For guidance on how to answer this question and a discussion of the main issues, listen to the author's podcast on the Online Resource Centre: www.oxfordtextbooks.co.uk/orc/gillespie_els6e/

Supervision of the executive

Perhaps one of the most important functions of the European Parliament is to assist in holding the European Commission, as the EU's executive, to account. The Commission is not part of the Parliament (and in this way can be distinguished from the Westminster Parliament where the executive and legislature consist of the same people) but will frequently be involved in giving evidence to parliamentary committees considering evidence etc. Thus Parliament can question the Commission and consider the reasoning behind appropriate legislation and, in defined circumstances, veto the legislation.

Article 239 TFEU makes clear that the Commission has a legal responsibility to answer questions put to it by MEPs and this includes written questions. Accordingly, this creates another method by which Parliament may hold the Commission to account not least because most questions and answers will be publicly reported. An important extension of the TL was that approval of the budget is based on the ordinary legislative process[54] and therefore the Parliament now has considerable power over the proposed budget since it has a number of opportunities to reject it.[55]

The European Parliament has the right to approve the appointment of the Commission. The President of the Commission is now elected by the European Parliament[56] although this is slightly limited by Article 17(7) TEU, which states that the European Council, acting by a qualified majority (see 'Voting'), proposes to the Parliament the candidate for President. The Parliament can then approve the appointment by absolute majority and if the candidate fails then the Council must propose a new candidate. Reference to 'new candidate' in Article 17(7) would suggest that it is not open to the European Council to suggest the same person. The Parliament does

54. *Treaty on the Functioning of the European Union*, Art 314.
55. For a further discussion see G Love, 'Oh Brave New World! Lisbon Enters into Force' (2010) *EU Focus* 1, 8.
56. *Treaty of the European Union*, Art 14(1).

not have the right to consider individual commissioners (whose appointment is a matter for the Council: see Article 17(7) TEU) but the Commission as a whole is responsible to Parliament via the power of censure.

The European Parliament has the right to censure the Commission. The arithmetic required for such a censure is slightly complicated. The motion must be passed by a two-thirds majority of those MEPs present in the chamber but they must account for a simple majority of the total number of MEPs. If the motion is carried then the entire Commission must resign.[57]

A simple majority of the total number of MEPs means in essence an absolute majority of MEPs, ie 376. In reality, this means for a motion to be carried it will require a high proportion of the votes cast. For example, if there are only 665 MEPs in the chamber then if 377 voted for the motion of censure (an absolute majority) the motion would fail because the 377 votes only equates to 56 per cent of those present.

In order to pass it would require 441 votes to be cast, 64 votes higher than the absolute majority. This is a safeguard to ensure that any vote of censure is only passed in circumstances when it can be ascertained that Parliament as a whole truly wishes to pass the measure.

Example Edith Cresson

Although the European Parliament has never exercised its powers to dismiss the European Commission it came close to doing so in 1999 and de facto exercised its powers. The European Parliament was angered by the actions of Edith Cresson, a former French prime minister, who was a European commissioner and who had been accused of financial mismanagement and appointing unqualified friends to influential posts.

The European Parliament called on Ms Cresson to resign, something she refused to do. The Parliament had no authority to sack just Ms Cresson and a series of heated discussions and enquiries followed culminating in a vote of censure. Eventually the whole of the EU Commission resigned although the vast majority were automatically reappointed, in part because the Parliament has no power to reject individual commissioners.

Ms Cresson led to further infamy when she became the first commissioner to be stripped of her diplomatic immunity held as a result of being a commissioner. The Commission, on the initiative of Belgium, investigated her for alleged fraud offences although the ECJ ultimately decided not to punish her.

Article 226 TFEU allows the Parliament, where one-quarter of its members so request, to create an ad hoc Committee of Inquiry that will have the power to examine any alleged contraventions or maladministration of Union law save where the matter is currently being examined by a court (so as to ensure that there is no impact on the fairness of such proceedings). However, the Parliament's powers extend only to the publication of a report as to its findings and not any power to order correction. This system is based on the premise that a negative report would be embarrassing although the effectiveness of this strategy could be questioned when one notes the position that exists in respect of the Court of Auditors (discussed later).

---

57. *Treaty on the Functioning of the European Union*, Art 234.

4.3.2.2 **The European Council**

Confusingly, the TEU lists two institutions that sound similar; the *European Council* and *The Council*. 'The Council' is sometimes referred to as the '*Council of the European Union*' although it is notable that Article 13 TEU does not refer to it in this way. 'The Council' will be discussed later (4.3.2.3) but is a member of the legislature and acts in conjunction with the Parliament (discussed earlier). The 'European Council' is different; it is a body that comprises the Heads of State or government of each Member State together with the President of the Council and the President of the Commission.[58] It only became a formal institution as a result of TL; before that it had an unofficial political existence. The President of the European Council is elected separately by the Council itself using qualified majority voting (see 'Voting') and holds office for a term of two and a half years renewable once.[59] The move towards a 'permanent' President of the European Council was a major shift from the previous position where the presidency would rotate between the Member States every six months, with the Head of State or government becoming President. It has been suggested that the permanent presidency will allow an individual to develop a wider vision of the EU.[60]

The European Council must meet twice every six months when convened by its President[61] and its work can be assisted by ministers or commissioners. The European Council is charged with a number of matters but perhaps two of its most important charges are quite generic. The first is: 'The European Council shall provide the Union with the necessary impetus for its development and shall define the general political directions and priorities thereof'[62] and the second is Article 222(4) TFEU which requires the European Council to 'regularly assess the threats facing the Union in order to enable the Union and its Member States to take effective action'. Clearly therefore, the European Council is an important institution not least because it represents the ultimate executive authority for each Member State. It is also clear that the European Council is principally a political body and one that is charged with taking the necessary political steps to facilitate the work. It has no legislative authority.[63]

The European Council will have certain policy matters reserved to it, for example, Article 68 TFEU states: 'The European Council shall define the strategic guidelines for legislative and operational planning within the area of freedom, security and justice.' Also numerous other aspects of the Treaties require matters of dispute to be referred to the European Council. Again, this is a pragmatic decision as it means that where there is dispute between Member States it can be resolved by the heads of government. The Council should ordinarily act by consensus[64] which must mean unanimity. However, there are a number of issues within the Treaty that require decisions to be taken by qualified majority (a system discussed later).

4.3.2.3 **Council**

The second of the two 'Councils' is 'The Council' which is also referred to as either the *Consilium* or the '*Council of the European Union*' and was previously known as

---

58. *Treaty on the European Union*, Art 15(2).
59. *Treaty on the European Union*, Art 15(5).
60. Paul Craig, 'The Treaty of Lisbon, Process, Architecture and Substance' (2008) 33 *European Law Review* 137, 152.
61. *Treaty on the European Union*, Art 15(3).
62. *Treaty on the European Union*, Art 15(1).
63. *Treaty on the European Union*, Art 15(1).
64. *Treaty on the European Union*, Art 15(4).

the 'Council of Ministers' although in the TEU and TFEU it is simply referred to as 'The Council'. Whilst the European Council is a member of the executive and acts on a policy level, the Council is a member of the legislature (sharing legislative power with the European Parliament).[65]

The Council is established by a representative of each Member State who is of ministerial level[66] and so it is a council of ministers. However, it would be wrong to say that there is a single representative since the actual representation will depend on what is being discussed, this compromise being defined as the Council sitting in different 'configurations'. Accordingly, if, for example, the Council is discussing foreign affairs then the minister will be drawn from the foreign office for each state (which may not be the Foreign Secretary but may be a junior minister depending on the importance of the matter) and if it is discussing the agricultural policy then the minister will be drawn from the Department of Environment, Food and Rural Affairs. The Presidency of the Council rotates every six months in the way that the European Council did until a permanent President was appointed.

As noted earlier, the Council operates as the second part of the legislature and ordinarily legislation must be passed by both it and the European Parliament. The method by which legislation is passed was discussed earlier when considering the European Parliament (4.3.2.1) and reference should be made to that.

The Council's own website states that, in addition to its legislative and budgetary competence, it has the following roles:

- to coordinate the broad economic policies of the Member States
- to define and implement the EU's common foreign and security policy (based on the guidance set by the European Council)
- to conclude, on behalf of the Union, international agreements between the EU and other states or organizations
- to coordinate the actions of the Member States and adopt measures in the area of police and judicial cooperation in criminal matters.[67]

Voting

Perhaps the most controversial aspect of the Council is how it votes. The Council would traditionally act on the basis of consensus but increasingly this became untenable since it meant that the smaller states could, in essence, 'veto' policies or legislation even when the measure was necessary for the good of the EU. As the EU expanded this became increasingly problematic and although some decisions were taken by a simple majority this was considered unfair by the larger states who argued that it could mean that a coalition of the smaller states could block initiatives of the larger states. Accordingly, some measures require decisions to be taken by qualified majority, indeed one of the impacts of the TL is that it has widened the number of instances where decisions can be taken by a qualified majority.[68] It was noted that identifying precisely how votes would be calculated was one of the most controversial aspects of the Treaty negotiations.[69]

---

65. *Treaty on the European Union*, Art 16(1).
66. *Treaty on the European Union*, Art 16(2).
67. <http://www.consilium.europa.eu>.
68. See *Treaty on the European Union*, Art 16(3), which states that all decisions shall be taken by qualified majority save where a Treaty says otherwise.
69. Paul Craig, 'The Treaty of Lisbon, Process, Architecture and Substance' (2008) 33 *European Law Review* 137, 154.

Table 4.1 Weighted votes of each Member State

Austria	10	Lithuania	7
Belgium	12	Luxembourg	4
Bulgaria	10	Hungary	12
Czech Republic	12	Malta	3
Denmark	7	Netherlands	14
Germany	29	Poland	27
Estonia	4	Portugal	12
Ireland	7	Romania	14
Greece	12	Slovenia	4
Spain	27	Slovakia	7
France	29	Finland	7
Italy	29	Sweden	10
Cyprus	4	United Kingdom	29
Latvia	4		

Perhaps unsurprisingly the actual voting arrangements are somewhat complicated and are subject to change. The existing arrangement is contained within Protocol 36 of the TFEU. Each Member State is accorded a weighted vote (see Table 4.1). A vote is passed if there are at least 255 weighted votes in favour *and* this accounts for at least two-thirds of the Member States. The total number of weighted votes is 345 meaning that 255 accounts for 74 per cent of the votes cast. The weighting of votes and the requirement for a minimum threshold of population acts as a balance to the power of the large countries who would otherwise be able to push matters through. The actual weighted votes are based on more than just population since, for example, Spain has 27 votes and yet accounts for only 9 per cent of the population whereas Germany has 29 votes and has 16 per cent of the population.

From 1 November 2014 (until 2017) Article 16(4) TEU states that a qualified majority requires two elements:

- 55 per cent of the members of the Council
- that 55 per cent accounts for at least fifteen Member States who account for at least 65 per cent of the population of the Union.

In other words it is not sufficient that fifteen Member States take a vote (fifteen Member States would currently constitute 55 per cent of the members of the Council) since if those fifteen Member States were from the smaller countries then they would not be able to pass the additional test that the majority must account for at least 65 per cent of the EU. This continues to mean that the larger states will be important as smaller states will need to form alliances with the larger states so as to ensure that the measure is passed. However, an additional complication is that Article 16(4) TEU states that a 'blocking minority' must constitute at least four Council members. This latter takes a little explanation. Let us assume that at least 55 per cent of the Council votes for a particular measure and that this 55 per cent comprised twenty-four Member States but that Germany, the United Kingdom, and Spain disagreed with the measure. The combined population of those twenty-four Member States would only amount to 62 per cent and so the measure should fail. However, Article 16(4) TEU requires the minority to account for at least four Council states and thus the 'block' would not be effective and, according to Article 16(4) the measure should be passed irrespective.

The procedure will change after 2017 and there are also some exceptions to this rule contained within Article 238 TFEU.

4.3.2.4 European Commission

The European Commission is arguably the most powerful of the institutions and prior to the recognition of the European Council as an institution it formed the sole executive of the EU (now it forms the executive alongside the European Council and it is arguably the more powerful of the two). The size of the Commission is controversial[70] and currently amounts to one member (commissioners, President, and the High Representative for Foreign Affairs) per country.[71] This position should have ended in 2014 with the Commission then numbering the same as two-thirds of the Member States (currently twenty-eight so it would number nineteen). It was intended that the members would be adopted on 'a strictly equal rotation between the Member States, reflecting the geographical range of all the Member States'.[72] This would have meant countries would, for the first time, lose 'their' commissioner and some doubted whether politically it would ever be possible to move to this new system.[73] In order to ensure that Ireland voted in favour of the ratification of the *Lisbon Treaty* the Council agreed to ensure that representation on the Commission continued to be based on the 'one per member state' basis.[74] It is perhaps somewhat ironic that in order to ensure *Lisbon* passed the Council committed itself to ignoring one of the key changes that the Treaty itself proposed. If the EU continues to expand it will also be interesting to see how an enlarged Commission will cope since there will not be a portfolio for each commissioner (a key reason for reducing the number in the first place). Whether this will lead to 'first-tier' and 'second-tier' commissioners, ie more than one commissioner working on a portfolio, has yet to be announced.

The President of the Commission is now elected by the Council and European Parliament and this was discussed earlier. The President allocates the 'portfolios' of each commissioner[75] although the President is likely to consult national governments as part of their campaign for election. The creation of a President has also transformed the way in which commissioners can be dismissed. Whilst individual commissioners are able to resign it has traditionally been difficult for them to be removed. However, the TL has altered this position to a certain extent and the President of the Commission is now able to ask an individual commissioner to resign.[76] Assuming the President does not do this then the powers of dismissal are limited.

The Court of Justice of the EU has jurisdiction to order the compulsory retirement of a commissioner where he or she 'no longer fulfils the conditions required for the performance

---

70. Paul Craig, 'The Treaty of Lisbon, Process, Architecture and Substance' (2008) 33 *European Law Review* 137, 155.
71. *Treaty on the European Union*, Art 17(4).
72. *Treaty on the European Union*, Art 17(5).
73. John Fairhurst, *Law of the European Union* (10th edn, Pearson Education 2014) 92–3.
74. Margot Horspool, and Matthew Humphreys, *European Union Law (Core Text Series)* (7th edn, OUP 2012) 48.
75. *Treaty on the European Union*, Art 17(6).
76. *Treaty on the European Union*, Art 17(6).

of his duties or if he is guilty of serious misconduct'.[77] This jurisdiction is exercised by the ECJ sitting *en banc* and has never happened. The second method of effective dismissal is where the Commission is required to resign en masse if the European Parliament passes a vote of censure under Article 234 TFEU (see Article 17(8) TEU). The passing of a motion of censure was discussed earlier when considering the European Parliament (4.3.2.1).

Whilst Commission members are drawn from the Member States, Article 17(3) TEU makes clear that they are independent of the Member States and must operate on behalf of the EU and not take instructions from the government or other national body. Their term of office is for five years although they can be reappointed. The primary duties of the Commission are summarized in Article 17(1) TEU:

> The Commission shall promote the general interest of the Union and take appropriate initiatives to that end. It shall ensure the application of the Treaties, and of measures adopted by the institutions pursuant to them. It shall oversee the application of Union law under the control of the Court of Justice of the European Union. It shall execute the budget and manage programmes. It shall exercise coordinating, executive and management functions, as laid down in the Treaties ...

Article 17(2) TEU expressly notes that the ability to initiate legislation is vested solely with the Commission unless the Treaties say otherwise. This is what provides authority for the Commission to be the key instigator of policy and legislative instruments. Arguably this is one of its more important functions and whilst it shares policy with the European Council, a considerable amount of policy remains with the Commission.

An important role of the Commission is to ensure compliance with the Treaties. The Commission is able to take action against Member States where it believes that it is in breach of its applications.[78] It is also able, in some parts of Union law, to take action against individual private companies that act in a way incompatible with the internal market.[79]

Example Microsoft

One of the biggest examples of the Commission taking action against a private body is its action against Microsoft. The Commission considered that Microsoft had been acting in such a way as to abuse its dominant position in the market, particularly in respect of the way that it 'bundled' software on new computers.[80]

The Commission required Microsoft to cease its anti-competitive practices and when it believed that it had failed to do so it issued a fine of €280 million.

4.3.2.5 The Court of Justice of the European Union

The TL has altered the judicial branch of the EU. Prior to the TL there were two courts; the *Court of First Instance* (CFI) and the *European Court of Justice* (ECJ).

---

77. *Treaty on the Functioning of the European Union*, Art 247.
78. *Treaty on the Functioning of the European Union*, Art 258.
79. *Treaty on the Functioning of the European Union*, Arts 101 and 102.
80. For a useful history of this read Simonetta Vezzoso, 'The Incentives Balance Test in the EU Microsoft Case: A Pro-innovation "Economics-Based" Approach' (2006) 27 *European Competition Law Review* 382.

The TL altered this and Article 19(1) TEU creates a new institution, the *Court of Justice of the European Union*, which will be comprised of the *Court of Justice* (what was the ECJ), the *General Court* (what was the CFI), and *specialized courts* which are, in essence, specialist tribunals that deal with matters relating to the Civil Service. All the courts are based in Luxembourg[81] and are thus separate from the political and legislative offices of Brussels and Strasbourg.

The Court of Justice (CJ) is constituted of one judge from each Member State[82] and it is assisted by eight Advocates-General (see later in this section). It is notable that Article 19(2) TEU states that the General Court (GC) shall be constituted of 'at least' one judge per Member State, meaning that in some instances more than one judge can be sent (although currently the number is capped at twenty-eight: see Article 48 of Protocol 3 TFEU). This is in part a reflection on the changing nature of the GC and its increased workload, especially due to the expansion of Member States. Both the judges and Advocates-General (A-G) of the Court of Justice must be qualified for appointment to 'the highest judicial offices in their respective countries'[83] which, in the context of England and Wales, means the same qualification as a puisne judge (discussed in Chapter 8). The judges are appointed for a (renewable) term of six years although their appointment is staggered so that there is a partial replacement every three years (thus ensuring that the CJ does not lose all of its experienced judges at the same time). The judges themselves elect one of their own number as their President. Article 254 TFEU provides comparable requirements for the judges and A-G of the GC. Accordingly, they are appointed for (renewable) terms of six years and must possess the necessary qualification for high judicial office.

⚡ ADVOCATES-GENERAL

Advocates-General have no comparable counterparts within the United Kingdom, with their closest comparison being an *amicus curiae* (friend of the court, ie counsel appointed separate from the parties to put forward a neutral argument or one in the public interest. It is not unusual for the *amicus* to be the Attorney-General.)

Article 252 TFEU makes clear that the role of the Advocate-General is 'to make, in open court, reasoned submissions on cases which … require his involvement'. In other words, the Advocate-General will read the written submissions of both parties and provide an independent viewpoint to the Court of Justice on what it believes the law is.

Although the court is not bound in any way by the opinion of the Advocate-General it normally carries with it significant weight and it will, in fact, frequently be followed[84] and thus the opinion of the Advocate-General can often be an early clue to the parties when identifying how the court is likely to rule.

The appointment of judges and A-G are generally for the Member States but, interestingly, the TL creates a partial appointments commission. Article 255 TFEU creates an ad hoc panel of seven persons 'chosen from among members of the Court of Justice and the General Court, members of national supreme courts and lawyers of recognized

81. *Treaty on the Functioning of the European Union*, Protocol 6.
82. *Treaty on the European Union*, Art 19(2).
83. *Treaty on the Functioning of the European Union*, Art 253.
84. John Fairhurst, *Law of the European Union* (10th edn, Pearson Education 2014) 160.

competence, one of whom shall be proposed by the European Parliament'. The Council is responsible for the creation and operation of this panel and its purpose is to give an 'opinion' on candidates' suitability to perform the duties of Judge and Advocate-General. There is no reference to any power of veto: they may simply discuss their suitability but presumably a negative opinion would be politically embarrassing and thus a Member State may choose to withdraw its candidate although it would seem that it is under no obligation to do so. All judges must swear a judicial oath prior to taking up office.[85]

Court of Justice

The Court of Justice has the power to review decisions of the General Court[86] and, accordingly, it acts as an appellate court to the GC although this power is exercisable only in respect of points of law.

Article 251 TFEU states that the Court of Justice will sit in chambers, a Grand Chamber or, when set out in statute, a full court. Protocol 3 TFEU provides for a 'Statute on the Court of Justice of the European Union', which, in essence, provides further details on how it shall operate. Chambers will ordinarily be divided into divisions of three and five judges[87] and each chamber will elect one of their number as President. A Grand Chamber shall consist of thirteen judges[88] and is presided over by the President of the Court. A matter is heard by a Grand Chamber whenever a Member State or an EU institution so requests it. The full court is heard only when in specific circumstances or where the Court or A-G considers that it raises such a serious point that it should be heard by the full court. Confusingly, whilst the full court should mean that it sits *en banc* (ie all twenty-seven judges) Article 17 of Protocol 3 states that a full court will be quorate with only fifteen judges sitting. The same provision states that a Grand Chamber (which should consist of thirteen judges) is quorate if nine judges sit.

Article 20 of Protocol 3 states that a procedure before the Court of Justice shall consist of two parts: the written part and the oral part. The written procedure involves the usual discovery together with communications from the parties as to the merits of their arguments. The oral procedure involves the reading of documents, the arguments of the lawyers, and any witnesses. Ordinarily the A-G would give a submission as to the law (see earlier in this section) but Article 20 of Protocol 3 allows the Court to rule that no submission is required so long as it hears from the A-G about whether he should make a submission.

Protocol 3 makes a series of references to witnesses and evidence on oath. The broad effect of these rules is that the Court of Justice has the same power of compulsion as a court of a Member State and that a failure to attend is punishable as though it were a failure to attend a court of the Member State. Similar rules apply to testimony and, in particular, false testimony so that false testimony by a British citizen at the Court of Justice in Luxembourg would be punishable as perjury in the courts of England.

General Court

According to Article 256 TFEU the General Court has jurisdiction to determine first-instance actions or proceedings under Articles 263, 265, 268, 270, and 272 unless

---

85. *Treaty on the Functioning of the European Union*, Protocol 3, Art 3.
86. *Treaty on the Functioning of the European Union*, Art 256(1).
87. *Treaty on the Functioning of the European Union*, Protocol 3, Art 16.
88. *Treaty on the Functioning of the European Union*, Protocol 3, Art 16.

they are expressly reserved by Treaty to the Court of Justice. In addition it has jurisdiction to hear appeals against the decisions of the specialized courts. It also has a limited role in respect of preliminary rulings under Article 267[89] although most Article 267 rulings will be heard by the Court of Justice (see the discussion at 4.3.4.3).

Whilst the General Court does have an A-G it is notable that Article 49 of Protocol 3 TFEU states that judges of the General Court can be asked to perform the task of an A-G. The duty of an A-G is the same as with the Court of Justice, ie to provide an independent assessment on the merits of the case. Article 50 of Protocol 3 states that the General Court should sit in chambers of three and five and that each chamber shall elect its own President, but the Article also provides that in some instances it is possible that work of the Court can be exercised by a single judge.

Language

Although it will use any of the official languages of the Court, its official working language for historical reasons is French. That said, where a Member State is a defendant in a case then the proceedings must be heard in that state's official language. As French is the official language, the definitive judgment is produced in French although it will ordinarily be transcribed into the parties' natural language and ordinarily an English version will also be produced.

4.3.2.6 Court of Auditors

The last institution to consider is the Court of Auditors. Since it acts as only a limited source of law it is mentioned here only very briefly. Article 285 TFEU states that it shall be responsible for carrying out the Union's audit and that it shall be comprised of a national from each of the Member States. Article 286 TFEU requires the members to be suitably qualified to perform an external audit and they act for a (renewable) term of six years.[90] They themselves elect a President who holds office for a (renewable) term of three years.

A member of the Court of Auditors can only be removed by the Court of Justice of the European Union when it finds that he no longer meets the requisite conditions or the obligations of his office.[91] In essence this means that the members have independence of office and only where the Court of Justice finds the members have acted in a manner equivalent to corruption can they be removed from office.

The effectiveness of the Court of Auditors has been the subject of some debate. Under Article 287(1) TFEU it has to examine all accounts of the revenue and expenditure of the Union and must provide the European Parliament and Council with a 'statement of assurance as to the reliability of the accounts and the legality and regularity of the underlying transactions'. Prior to 2008 the Court had never certified the accounts as being fair and accurate although the Commission questioned the belief that this meant that, as some sections of the media reported, corruption was rife.[92] Instead the Commission argued it was because the standards were too high in that any qualification, irrespective of how minor this was, meant that the accounts could not be fully certified. In 2008 the Court of Auditors issued an 'unqualified (clean) opinion on the reliability of the 2008 EU accounts'.[93]

---

89. See *Treaty on the Functioning of the European Union*, Art 256(3).
90. *Treaty on the Functioning of the European Union*, Art 286(2).
91. *Treaty on the Functioning of the European Union*, Art 286(6).
92. <http://ec.europa.eu/budget/explained/myths/myths_en.cfm>.
93. Court of Auditors Press Release 2009/11/10. ECA/09/67.

4.3.3 **Sources of EU law**

Now that the institutions have been explained it is necessary to turn our attention to the sources of law. After discussing these sources it will be necessary to consider what impact they have on the law of England and Wales (see 4.3.4). To an extent this section will be considered relatively simple as it is likely that you will receive further instruction on this when you study the law of the EU as a substantive topic on your law degree. Further information on this can also be found in EU textbooks.

The exact number of sources of law is open to debate. One commentator argues that there are three (treaties, legislation, and court decisions)[94] but others have suggested that there could be up to seven different sources.[95] To an extent this difference exists because of the position of the EU law in international law. The argument that there are seven includes the possibility that there are a number of sources of law that are commonly found in other international sources of law, eg 'soft' law etc. For our purposes it is really only necessary to consider the three that are identified by Weatherill.

4.3.3.1 **Treaties**

Arguably the most important source of EU law is the Treaties themselves. An explanation of the Treaties has been given already but it is notable that the TL has created a position whereby the Treaties have now been consolidated into two of relevance, those being the TEU and the TFEU. These Treaties are the most important sources and can be classified as the primary source of law for the EU. This includes the protocols to the Treaty, which include, for example, reference as to how the courts work[96] and what measures countries have opt-outs for.[97]

The TEU and TFEU are automatically binding on all Member States as part of their accession to the EU (save where they have negotiated an opt-out to particular issues: eg the United Kingdom has declined to participate in those areas that relate to freedom, security, and justice: see Protocol 21 TFEU).

Separate to the TEU and TFEU are treaties that are concluded between the EU and another state/organization. This is not a treaty concluded by the individual countries *within* the EU and another country as that would just be an ordinary bilateral treaty. Instead, the EU as a legal entity in its own right has the authority to enter treaties in respect of certain matters and when it does so the Member States are bound to give effect to it as though they had signed it themselves.

Charter of Fundamental Rights

An interesting issue that arises is in respect of the *Charter of Fundamental Rights*. This was originally a stand-alone document agreed in 2000 that was not intended to be legally binding.[98] A declaration annexed to the *Treaty of Nice* announced that there would be a review as to the legal status of the Charter and this has occurred with it becoming fully incorporated into EU law, with Article 6(1) TEU stating: 'The Union recognises the rights, freedoms and principles set out in the Charter of Fundamental Rights of the European Union. ... which shall have the same legal value as the Treaties.'

94. Stephen Weatherill, *Cases and Materials on EU Law* (9th edn, OUP 2010) 27.
95. John Fairhurst, *Law of the European Union* (10th edn, Pearson Education 2014) 56.
96. For example, *Treaty on the Functioning of the European Union*, Protocol 3.
97. For example, *Treaty on the Functioning of the European Union*, Protocols 15–18 and 20–22.
98. John Fairhurst, *Law of the European Union* (10th edn, Pearson Education 2014) 32.

Accordingly, the Charter becomes an essential part of the jurisprudence of EU law, although it should be noted that it remains a separate document, it does not form part of either the TEU or TFEU although it has the same legal status. Whilst it is sometimes said that the UK and Poland are not bound by the Charter this is not strictly true since, as noted earlier, it forms part of the general principles of EU law. Instead the UK has negotiated a 'clarification' of the application of the Charter to it.[99] Article 1 of this Protocol states that it does not extend the ability of the Court of Justice of the EU or any domestic court to decide that the laws or practices of the United Kingdom are inconsistent with the fundamental rights and freedoms and Article 2 states that the Charter applies only to those rights or principles that are recognized by UK law. Quite what the effect of this Protocol is remains questionable. The Charter itself suggests that it does not provide any authority to the ECJ to find that national laws are inconsistent with the rights contained within the Charter. The second Article is also of questionable merit since it, in essence, allows the ECJ to decide what is, or is not, recognized in UK law.[100]

European Convention on Human Rights

Article 6(3) TEU states that the *European Convention on Human Rights* shall constitute general principles of the EU law. It will be seen that signing the ECHR is a prerequisite for membership of the EU but the TEU makes clear that the Convention is part of the ordinary law of the EU meaning that, for example, the Court of Justice could rule on whether the action of an institution is contrary to rights contained within the ECHR.

4.3.3.2 Legislation

The EU produces legislation and it was noted earlier that the Council and Parliament act as the legislatures although only the Commission has the right to initiate legislation. Some students will try to 'map' the legislation of the EU onto the legislation in England and Wales to find comparators but realistically this is impossible to do. EU legislation has its own formulation and it is better not to try to consider it analogous to any other form of legislative act. All EU legislation is delegated to the extent that, as will be seen, the right to enact legislation derives from the Treaties and the legislation cannot be incompatible with the Treaties. The discussion on competences (4.3.1.3) is important here. It will be remembered that the TEU states what the EU has competence over and accordingly if it does not have competence then it may not act and, it follows, may not pass legislation in respect of this.

Article 288 TFEU states that there are three forms of legislation: regulations, directives, and decisions. The effects of these are different and are set out within Article 288:

A regulation shall have general application. It shall be binding in its entirety and directly applicable in all Member States.

A directive shall be binding, as to the result to be achieved, upon each Member State to which it is addressed, but shall leave to the national authorities the choice of forms and methods.

---

99. *Treaty on the Functioning of the European Union*, Protocol 30.
100. For a further discussion see, Paul Craig, 'The Treaty of Lisbon, Process, Architecture and Substance' (2008) 33 *European Law Review* 137, 163.

A decision shall be binding in its entirety. A decision which specifies those to whom it is addressed shall be binding only on them.

In addition to these forms are opinions and recommendations (which may be given by the Council or Commission) but these are not binding and are merely advisory, although they may be taken into account by the Court of Justice of the European Union.

It is not always clear which form of legislation should be used. Sometimes the Treaties themselves will make clear which form to take. For example, Article 46 TFEU governs the freedom of movement for workers and it states that the European Parliament and Council may issue legislation through either regulations or directives. Accordingly, the Parliament and Council can decide which form to pass in respect of a measure relating to Article 46 but could not, for example, issue a decision. Sometimes there is no choice. For example, Article 50 TFEU relates to the freedom of establishment as regards economic activity and it states that the European Parliament and Council may make directives to secure this. Accordingly, a measure designed to support Article 50 could only be legislated by directive. Where the Treaty is silent as to which form of legislation should be used then it is up to the institution sponsoring the legislation to decide which form to adopt.[101] Interestingly, it has been held that it is the substance of the legislation that decides what form it takes and not its label. So, if for example, the Commission issues legislation that it states is a regulation but its substance would appear more akin to a directive then the Court of Justice can alter its status.[102]

All legislation must be 'reasoned', ie the legislation itself must state what the legal basis for the action is. This includes a statement of which Article of a treaty authorizes the legislation to be passed, together with cogent reasons as to why it is being made.[103] This reasoning will include the objectives of the legislation, why it is necessary, who it is addressed to, and what steps must be taken to comply with the legislation. It is possible to use the reasoning as the basis of a judicial review of the legislation.[104] All legislation must be published in the *Official Journal of the EU*[105] and enter into force either on the date specified within the legislation or on the twentieth day following its publication.

Regulations

Regulations are arguably the strictest form of legislation. They are primarily issued by the Commission although they are now ordinarily subject to the ordinary legislative procedure (save where the Treaty states otherwise). Regulations are automatically binding on all Member States and they are of general application, ie they do not provide specific details of legislative purpose.[106] As they are automatically binding on all Member States then the legislatures of the Member States need not take any executive or legislative action in order to ensure compliance: they form part of the law as soon as the regulation comes into force.

---

101. *Treaty on the Functioning of the European Union*, Art 296.
102. See *International Fruit Company v Commission* [1971] ECR 411.
103. *Treaty on the Functioning of the European Union*, Art 296.
104. *Germany v Commission* [1963] ECR 63 and see John Fairhurst, *Law of the European Union* (10th edn, Pearson Education 2014) 147.
105. *Treaty on the Functioning of the European Union*, Art 297(1).
106. Damian Chalmers et al, *European Union Law* (2nd edn, CUP 2010) 133.

A good example of a regulation is Regulation 261/2004. This provided for common rules regarding compensation to be paid to air passengers whose flights were either cancelled or subject to long delays. The airline industry did not welcome this regulation although many passenger groups did. As a regulation it was directly effective and thus created an actionable right. During the summer of 2010 a volcanic explosion in Iceland caused widespread air travel disruption. Certain airlines, especially budget airlines, suggested that they would refuse to pay compensation as required by the Regulation because, in their opinion, it was not fair. The airlines, however, backed down when it was realized that the Regulation was automatically in force and the rights contained within it were legally binding.

Directives

Directives are probably the most frequent form of legislation passed by the EU and this position is likely to increase as, for example, legislation is passed in respect of matters relating to freedom and justice. A directive is only binding on the Member States that are mentioned in the directive although it is possible (and indeed usual) to list all the Member States in the directive. Whilst the directive will say what the purpose of the legislative act is and what the eventual aim is, it will leave the precise details of how this will be achieved to Member States (eg they could use primary or secondary legislation, amend existing or introduce new legislation). A directive will normally state how long (from the date when it comes into force) a Member State has to comply with the directive and a failure to legislate by this date will be actionable by the Commission (discussed earlier).

Example	Data protection

The European Commission issued Directive 95/46/EC which covered the protection of personal data. The UK government was (like those of all Member States) bound to implement this Directive, with the deadline being the end of 1998. The UK government had the choice of enforcement mechanisms and it decided that it would implement the Directive through the use of primary legislation. Accordingly, the Data Protection Act 1998 was passed which met the requirements of the Directive but also dealt with some purely domestic issues too.

Decisions

There used to be two forms of decisions, those which were simply known as decisions (and which survive) and a second form known as a *Framework Decision* which was introduced by the *Treaty of Amsterdam*. These were similar to decisions but were instead collective decisions of the European Council and were designed to harmonize laws. They were primarily used in respect of third pillar business and the abolition of the pillar structure has meant that this form of legislation is no longer required and future work in this area will be undertaken by normal legislative means.

> ### ☰ Example Child protection
>
> The European Union passed a Framework Decision on combating the sexual exploitation of children and child pornography.[107] This was designed to harmonize the laws and to ensure there was a minimum level of protection. The EU had consulted on replacing this Framework Decision with a new Framework Decision but following the *Treaty of Lisbon* such legislation no longer exists and it was replaced by Directive 2012/92/EU on combating the sexual abuse and sexual exploitation of children and child pornography. A directive was chosen on the basis that the EU wishes to set down a threshold for laws but wishes to leave the details to the Member States.[108]

Decisions need not be addressed to Member States but could instead be addressed to a particular institution or body within a Member State. Arguably this is most frequently found in respect of competition matters[109] where the Commission may require an individual body to take particular action so as to ensure that they are not acting in an anti-competitive way. Decisions are generally used where the action sought is administrative or procedural rather that when the object is to harmonize the laws of any country.[110]

4.3.3.3 Decisions of the Court of Justice of the European Union

One of the reasons why some students find EU law complicated is because the approach to case law is different in the EU than that adopted in England and Wales (a point judicially recognized by Lord Denning MR in *Bulmer v Bollinger*[111] which was one of the first cases in the appellate courts of England and Wales to look at EU law). It was noted in Chapter 3 that the system in England and Wales is based on the common-law approach and that *stare decisis* applies. The same approach is not taken by the Court of Justice. There is no 'common law' or residual power: the authority of the Court of Justice is based solely on the Treaties themselves and this is reinforced by the TL which expressly states that in the absence of any competence, the EU has no power to act.[112] That said, the Court has taken account of general principles such as natural justice[113] and, of course, this has been expanded by the TL which has incorporated both the ECHR and *Charter of Human Rights* into the general jurisprudence of the EU. The Court of Justice does not operate a formal system of *stare decisis* although it will, so far as possible, try to act in a way that takes account of its previous decisions.[114]

From a constitutional perspective, the Court of Justice has considerably more powers of review than the courts in England and Wales. This includes not only the right to review any legislation but also the ability to strike down legislation that is incompatible with Community Law.[115] It will be recalled from Chapter 2 that this

---

107. 2004/68/JHA.
108. As this is a matter relating to freedom, justice, and home affairs any directive was not addressed to the UK (which has an opt-out on such matters) but the UK asked to be brought within the directive.
109. PSRF Mathijsen, *A Guide to European Union Law* (8th edn, Thomson Sweet & Maxwell 2004) 29.
110. Damian Chalmers et al, *European Union Law* (2nd edn, CUP 2010) 134.
111. [1974] 3 WLR 202.
112. *Treaty on the European Union*, Art 4.
113. See, for example, *Hauer v Land Rheinland-Pfalz* [1980] 3 CMLR 42.
114. John Fairhurst, *Law of the European Union* (10th edn, Pearson Education 2014) 167.
115. *Treaty on the Functioning of the European Union*, Art 263.

is considerably more power than the courts in England and Wales have, a position that has not changed following the passing of the *Human Rights Act 1998* where a declaration of incompatibility will have no effect on the legal standing of an Act of Parliament (see 5.2.4.2). Indeed, this is often cited as one of the reasons why the UK voted to leave the EU.

Judgments

It is often said that the Court of Justice (including the General Court) will ordinarily give only a single judgment and this can be contrasted with, for example, the Supreme Court of the UK where every judge may speak (although there is an increasing tendency in the Supreme Court to produce a single judgment). However, this is not necessarily correct. Whilst the Court will *ordinarily* give a single judgment and possibly a single dissenting judgment (where it is not a unanimous decision) it is open to judges to produce individual *assenting* and *dissenting* judgments.

Judgments of the Courts are always reserved although the length of delay between the hearing and delivery of judgment will differ between the courts and the type of case, with some being expedited. The official language of the court is French although it is customary to also use English and where a Member State is a party to the proceedings then the language of that state will be used. National modes are used for address and the dress of advocates. Accordingly, where a barrister from England and Wales is speaking in the court, the judges would be referred to as 'My Lords' and the barrister will be fully robed in wig, gown, bands, and collar. All judges of the courts will wear the same dress, which is a judicial robe with a single garment around the neck in place of where judicial bands would be worn by members of the English judiciary.

All judgments of the Courts are published in the *Official Journal* and an official law report series (comparable to *The Law Reports* in England and Wales) is also in existence, the series being known as ECR—*European Court Reports*. All judgments should be published in the official languages of the EU, which can occasionally raise issues about translation. Where there is any doubt then French is considered to be the definitive text and reference will be made to the French text. All judgments can also now be found on the Internet and the Online Resource Centre accompanying this book includes a link to judgments.

Interpretation

It is perhaps necessary briefly to consider how the courts interpret legislation. It was noted in Chapter 2 that England has a series of canons of interpretation (see 2.3) and similar rules apply to the Court of Justice of the EU. It has been suggested that there are four methods of interpretation adopted by the Court of Justice:

- literal
- historical
- contextual
- teleological.[116]

The literal approach is the same as that adopted by domestic courts: the relevant instrument is examined and simply given its ordinary meaning. Of course an interesting

---

116.   John Fairhurst, *Law of the European Union* (10th edn, Pearson Education 2014) 171.

question that arises in Union law is which language should be used when deciding a literal interpretation? The meaning of words does differ amongst languages and the slight differences can be problematic. Unlike with English law there is no presumption that the literal rule is the 'ordinary' rule of statutory interpretation and indeed the Court has, in the past, refused to use the rule even where the wording of the instrument in question was clear.[117] The historical approach has been likened to the mischief rule of interpretation[118] and is rarely used but it does allow the Court to consider the preliminary debates to identify what the purpose of the instrument was.

The more common rules of interpretation are the contextual and teleological rules. Perhaps the classic definition of the contextual approach was given in the case of *CILFIT*,[119] a case that will be examined later. In that case, the ECJ stated:

> … every provision of Community law must be placed in its context and interpreted in the light of the provisions of the Community law as a whole, regard being had to the objectives thereof and to its State of evolution at the date on which the provision in question is to be applied.[120]

This is one of the reasons why legislation must be reasoned as it allows the Court to identify the context of the legislation. However, the latter part of the quote demonstrates that a legislative position need not be fixed and where the legislation is a directive this may be particularly true since there will be a period of time before Member States have actually (lawfully) complied with the directive.

The teleological interpretative method is similar to the contextual approach in that it is based on interpreting the instrument in a way that furthers the aims and objectives of the Union as a whole.[121] Accordingly, the emphasis of the Court is, in many instances, less focused on what the words of the instrument are and more on how the Union's policy can be furthered. This is significantly different from how the English courts would interpret legislation.

↻ QUESTION FOR REFLECTION

Read the *CILFIT* case. At para 18 it was said:

> [I]t must be borne in mind that Community legislation is drafted in several languages and that the different language versions are all equally authentic. An interpretation of a provision of Community law thus involves a comparison of the different language versions.

Is this realistic? How can a lawyer advising a client on a matter of EU law or even a domestic court applying the law (see 4.3.4.1) properly consider multiple sources of law in different languages? Would it not be appropriate to limit the number of languages a document is produced in or even suggest that there is only a single authoritative version? One possible advantage of this is that there would be reduced scope for doubt as to the meaning of a word. A possible disadvantage is that each national court would presumably have to translate this meaning into its own language in any

---

117. *Commission v Council* [1970] ECR 263.
118. John Fairhurst, *Law of the European Union* (10th edn, Pearson Education 2014) 169–70.
119. [1982] ECR 3415.
120. [1982] ECR 3415 [20].
121. John Fairhurst, *Law of the European Union* (10th edn, Pearson Education 2014) 171.

event so that the case can be adjudicated domestically. What further advantages and disadvantages may there be to such a proposal? How can the court deal with conflicts between languages?

4.3.4 Supremacy of EU law

Arguably the most controversial aspect of EU law to some in the United Kingdom is/ was in respect of its supremacy. The notion of supremacy has already been discussed in this book and it was noted in Chapter 2 that Parliament considers itself supreme and can legislate in any way it sees fit. The Treaty, however, makes it clear that Member States are bound by EU law. Declaration 17 of the *Declarations annexed to the final act of the intergovernmental conference which adopted the Treaty of Lisbon* states:

> The Conference recalls that, in accordance with well settled case law of the Court of Justice of the European Union, the Treaties and the law adopted by the Union on the basis of the Treaties have primacy over the law of Member States, under the conditions laid down by the said case law.

This was a political statement agreed by all Member States but the supremacy principle is also contained within the Treaties. It will be remembered that Article 2 TFEU states that where the Union has exclusive competence a Member State shall not legislate in respect of those areas save when permitted by the EU. Also, it will be remembered from earlier that regulations, directives, and decisions are *binding* on Member States (either in general (regulations) or to the Member States that are named). If they are binding then this means that domestic law must be subservient. This is perhaps most notable in respect of regulations which, it will be remembered, are of general effect and have direct effect in law.[122] The ability to make law binding over others must be considered a key factor for supremacy. Of course the counter-argument is that on a purely legal (rather than political) basis, the domestic laws remain supreme because a Member State could, as the UK has now done, choose to withdraw from the European Union. This is undoubtedly true and thus 'ultimate' sovereignty remains with the Member States although only until the Article 50 negotiations are complete will we understand to what extent EU law continues to play a role.

It should be noted that until the time stipulated in Article 50,[123] the United Kingdom continues to be a member of the EU and it remains bound by the Treaties. No matter what certain politicians, political commentators, or newspapers say, until the relevant period is completed, the UK is bound by EU law. How then does EU law take precedence over a Member State?

4.3.4.1 Direct effect

It is important at the outset to differentiate between direct *applicability* and direct *effect*. They are interlinked concepts but are subtly different.

135

---

122. *Treaty on the Functioning of the European Union*, Art 288.
123. Article 50(3) states that the Treaties cease to apply to the withdrawing state when either (a) the withdrawal agreement comes into force (not just agreed), (b) two years have elapsed, or (c) a longer period that is agreed by the European Council and the withdrawing state.

⚡ DIRECT APPLICABILITY/DIRECT EFFECT

The concept of international law has already been discussed and it has been noted that international provisions will not ordinarily become part of domestic law without domestic legislation giving it effect. EU law is, however, different and applies independently and will involve some laws becoming directly applicable in Member States (most notably 'regulations': see Article 288 TFEU), ie it will become part of the domestic laws without the need for individual domestic legislation to be passed each time an EU regulation is passed.

Direct effect is slightly different in that whilst directly applicable laws become automatically part of domestic law, those laws subject to direct effect will be enforceable under the domestic courts but do not automatically form part of domestic law. In other words, the right contained in the EU law is recognized as enforceable in the domestic courts (ie a person can sue to enforce it) but it does not formally become an inherent part of domestic law.

The key to this is the notion of supremacy but what does this mean in terms of its relationship with the United Kingdom? The starting point in understanding direct effect is to examine one of the earliest decisions of the ECJ, that of *van Gend en Loos v Nederlandse Administratie der Belastingen*,[124] which has been described as one of the most important cases the ECJ has adjudicated.[125]

‖‖ Case Box *van Gend en Loos*

In this case, the applicants had attempted to import urea-formaldehyde from Germany into the Netherlands. They were made to pay an import tax which was a direct contravention of the *EC Treaty*.

They petitioned a court in the Netherlands arguing that the tax should be repaid. There was no provision in domestic law for this and the question that arose was whether the applicants could rely on the *EC Treaty* in domestic cases. The matter was referred to the ECJ (see 4.3.4.3) who stated unequivocally that the Treaty was directly effective and thus became automatically enforceable under domestic law in the national courts.

This answered the question for treaties and marked a significant step in the enforcement of Community law. Prior to this decision only the Commission could attempt to enforce Community law and yet this created a situation where the victim would not be recompensed for their breach as it was dealt with at an international level. By providing direct effect it meant that individual citizens—who were supposed to benefit from the creation of the Community (Union)—could now use EU law as part of a domestic action irrespective of whether domestic law had (previously) recognized these issues.

However, because this in effect permits law to be directly imputed there are basic requirements that must be satisfied to ensure that the law is clearly identifiable.[126] The conditions set out by the Court can be summarized as requiring a 'clear, unconditional and negative prohibition which was not dependent upon any further implementing

---

124. [1963] ECR 1.
125. Damian Chalmers et al, *European Union Law* (2nd edn, CUP 2010) 47.
126. John Fairhurst, *Law of the European Union* (10th edn, Pearson Education 2014) 273–4.

measures at either EU or national level'[127] although the requirement that the legislation must create a negative prohibition rather than a positive obligation was later dropped.[128] The basis of the requirements is that it must create identifiable rights that citizens of the EU should have the right to enforce. Thus clarity becomes the most important part of direct effect and they are relatively uncontroversial.

Treaty Articles are, following *van Gend*, classic examples of instruments that are capable of having direct effect but it is important to note that even they must comply with the conditions set out in that case. In *Costa v ENEL*[129] the ECJ held that (the then) Article 97 did not lead to direct effect. This Article allows Member States to take action to prevent the common economic market from being distorted but their action can only take place after consultation with the Commission, thus it could not be said to be 'not dependent upon any further … measures'. Regulations are directly applicable as a result of Article 288 and will ordinarily be directly effective[130] subject to the conditions put forward in the *van Gend* case.

The more problematic form of legislation is that of the directive and it is not clear whether they are directly effective or not. In order to understand the basics of this distinction it is also necessary to distinguish between two types of direct effect, known as vertical direct effect and horizontal direct effect.

VERTICAL AND HORIZONTAL EFFECT

Direct effect is considered to have two planes to it. The first is vertical direct effect and this is where the relevant legislation creates a legal obligation between the individual and the Member State. The second plane is horizontal direct effect and creates a legal obligation between an individual and another individual. A simple explanation of this (which will suffice for now) is to think of import taxes and discrimination. Both are central features of EU law.

VERTICAL EFFECT

Nicola wishes to import some pens from Germany. However, the UK law has (fictitiously) decided that the importation of pens should carry an import tax of 25 per cent, which is contrary to EU law. Amy would take action against the UK government in the domestic courts suggesting that the prohibition of import taxes[131] has vertical effect, ie it binds the government and allows Amy to seek resolution before the domestic courts.

HORIZONTAL EFFECT

Susie is employed by a firm of accountants. She has applied for promotion to partner but been turned down. The post has been given to a less qualified and less experienced man. Amy believes that she has been discriminated against by sex. Amy could take action against her employers arguing that EU law has horizontal effect, ie that it provides rights that would allow Amy to take action against another private body rather than just the state.

Article 288 TFEU states that directives are binding as to the *result* to be achieved but Member States are left with discretion as to how to implement them. Given that this

127. Damian Chalmers et al, *European Union Law* (2nd edn, CUP 2010) 367.
128. Damian Chalmers et al, *European Union Law* (2nd edn, CUP 2010) 270.
129. [1964] ECR 585.
130. John Fairhurst, *Law of the European Union* (10th edn, Pearson Education 2014) 275.
131. *Treaty on the Functioning of the European Union*, Art 28.

means that the implementation of the directive will vary between the Member States it can be questioned whether they could ever meet the test set out in *van Gend* that the legislation will be clear. However, in *van Duyn v Home Office*[132] the ECJ implied that a directive could be directly effective.[133] The ECJ did not go as far as to say that directives *were* directly effective but stated that the *effect* of a measure may be directly effective in terms of providing citizens with a right of redress. Some commentators believe that the case was limited in application because the matter arose as a result of a failure by the United Kingdom to implement a directive.[134] If a directive was neither directly applicable nor effective then this would have meant a citizen could take no action in respect of this but merely wait until the European Commission took enforcement action. The ECJ appears to be adopting a principle of 'estoppel'[135] in that it will not allow non-action to prevent citizens being given the rights the directive was supposed to provide.

It would appear therefore that there was ultimately a recognition that directives could have vertical direct effect if they were sufficiently clear and it was possible to identify what the right provided was, who were entitled to the rights, and who was liable to provide the rights.[136] What of horizontal effect? In *Marshall v Southampton Area Health Authority*[137] the ECJ held that directives were not horizontally directly effective and thus could not be used against a private body. This did cause a number of difficulties in identifying precisely what a public body was and the ECJ accepted that it could not just be domestic classification.[138]

Before ending this brief examination of direct effect, the position of decisions must be noted. These were discussed earlier and they are directly effective in respect of the body they were addressed to[139] so long as they meet the *van Gend* principles. It will be remembered that this could (theoretically) involve an element of horizontal effect in that a decision can be made in respect of either a Member State or a private or public body but it is important to note that it is not possible for a decision to be used against someone other than to whom it is addressed. In those circumstances alternative action would need to be taken.

4.3.4.2 European Communities Act 1972

It has previously been noted that certain EU law will be directly effective but how is that achieved in the United Kingdom? Although the United Kingdom joined the (then) EEC in 1973, it was necessary that the laws of the United Kingdom were prepared for accession and thus the *European Communities Act 1972* (ECA 1972) was passed. This Act was passed in the traditional way by Parliament and it should be noted at the outset that both Houses of Parliament passed the legislation.

Arguably the most important provision within the ECA 1972 is s 2(1) which provides:

> All such rights, powers, liabilities, obligations and restrictions from time to time cre-
> ated or arising under the Treaties, and all such remedies and procedures from time to

---

132.   [1974] ECR 1299.
133.   See, in particular, [1974] ECR 1299 [12] and [13].
134.   John Fairhurst, *Law of the European Union* (10th edn, Pearson Education 2014) 276–7.
135.   John Fairhurst, *Law of the European Union* (10th edn, Pearson Education 2014) 277.
136.   See *Francovich v Republic of Italy* [1991] ECR I-535 and John Fairhurst, *Law of the European Union* (10th edn, Pearson Education 2014) 278.
137.   [1986] ECR 723.
138.   John Fairhurst, *Law of the European Union* (10th edn, Pearson Education 2014) 278–9.
139.   *Treaty on the Functioning of the European Union*, Art 28.

time provided for by or under the Treaties, as in accordance with the Treaties are without further enactment to be given legal effect or used in the United Kingdom shall be recognised and available in law, and be enforced, allowed and followed accordingly.

This is not the most user-friendly provision within a statute but it is possible to identify certain key phrases that demonstrate what the purpose of the Act was. One of the key phrases is 'in accordance with the Treaties' which makes it clear that Parliament is accepting that it is to be bound by the Treaty negotiated by the executive (in this case the *Treaty of Rome* and all subsequent treaties). Its reference to 'all such remedies and procedures' demonstrates that the Act was contemplating a procedural shift: domestic law would have to recognize EU law and the procedures governing its legislation.

Perhaps the most important words are, however, 'without further enactment to be given effect ... in law'. This demonstrates that Parliament was stating unequivocally that not only was the *Treaty of Rome* to be binding on domestic law but that any laws that were made as a result of the Treaty, eg regulations, would automatically apply. This is then followed by s 2(2) which gives effect to legislation that is not automatically applicable (eg directives) and provides that these can be achieved through secondary legislation although there are limits on this in that it is not possible to act retrospectively or to create a term of imprisonment of more than two years. The argument is that such matters would require the full consent of Parliament and should be dealt with purely as an Act of Parliament. Of course this is not the *only* way that EU law can be given effect and it has already been noted that, for example, the *Data Protection Act 1998* was a response to an EC directive and yet took the form of primary rather than secondary legislation.

The source of most controversy in the debate over EU law is as regards supremacy and yet this is something that the 1972 Act expressly refers to:

> Any such provision ... as might be made by Act of Parliament, and any enactment passed or to be passed, other than one contained in this part of the Act shall be construed and have effect subject to the foregoing provisions of this section ...[140]

This clearly refers to s 2 as a whole[141] but the wording of this section is quite important. Section 2(4) is making it absolutely clear that not only does the ECA 1972 alter legislation that has previously been passed (in that it must now be read as though it were compatible with EU law) but that the Act has *prospective* effect in that future legislation must also be construed in a way that is compatible with EU law. The law is quite clear as to this and one commentator has suggested that this will be achieved by 'denying effectiveness to any national legislation passed later which is in conflict [with EU law]'.[142]

It is important to note that the wording of s 2(4) is considerably stricter than the equivalent adopted under the *Human Rights Act 1998* (HRA 1998) (see 5.2.3.2). The HRA 1998 empowers courts to interpret legislation in a way compatible with the Convention 'so far as it is possible to do so' (s 3(1)), ie recognizing that there will be circumstances when this is not possible (and would lead to a declaration of incompatibility: see 5.2.4.2). The ECA 1972 on the other hand states that legislation, including

140. European Communities Act 1972, s 2(4).
141. Nigel Foster, *Foster on EU Law* (2nd edn, OUP 2010) 149.
142. Nigel Foster, *Foster on EU Law* (2nd edn, OUP 2010) 149.

future legislation, 'shall be construed' in a way to give effect to EU law, ie there is no discretion and where there is conflicting wording EU law must take precedence.

Parliament still possesses the ultimate power in that it can (and, at some point will need to) repeal s 2(4) but s 2 would appear to suggest that it is not possible to implicitly repeal s 2(4); merely legislating in a way contrary to s 2(4) (which would ordinarily lead to the repeal of the original legislation) would have to be construed according to s 2(4), ie in a way that does not offend EU law. Ultimately, however, Parliament will repeal s 2, and indeed probably the whole of the 1972 Act, and at that point will no longer be bound by EU law unless the treaty that they agree with the EU as part of the Article 50 process requires any part of EU law to take precedence. Such a treaty would need to have the force of a (domestic) Act of Parliament so parliamentary supremacy is arguably retained in that the UK Parliament could repeal that too, but that would inevitably lead to the termination of the agreement reached as part of Article 50.

Case Box *Thoburn v Sunderland City Council*

The issue of implicit repeal was considered expressly in the case of *Thoburn v Sunderland City Council*.[143] The EU passed two directives (80/181/EEC and 89/617/EEC) which effectively harmonized the system of weights and measurements and required loose goods to be sold in metric rather than imperial measurements. This caused considerable political dispute with many newspapers, particularly the 'right-wing' newspapers, suggesting that it was an inappropriate interference with UK law. The United Kingdom had implemented this measure through the creation of a criminal offence for failing to display metric information.

Thoburn was a market trader who refused either to sell or display anything other than imperial measurements. Sunderland City Council, as the appropriate prosecuting body, prosecuted him under the domestic legislation. Thoburn attempted to argue that as the *Weights and Measures Act 1985* was passed subsequently to the ECA 1972 and was arguably in conflict with s 2 he should not be convicted as s 2 was implicitly repealed by this Act. The High Court rejected this argument holding that implied repeal was not possible.

QUESTION FOR REFLECTION

Foster suggests that there are two possible interpretations of s 2(4). The first is that it is a rule of construction and is, therefore, simply a further rule of statutory interpretation, albeit one stricter than the HRA 1998. The second possibility is that although we traditionally decide that there is no such thing as entrenchment in the United Kingdom, s 2(4) does create an element of entrenchment. This argument is based on the premise that only the express repealing of s 2(4) would permit Parliament to legislate in a way incompatible with EU law and that stating 'This Act of Parliament is not subject to s 2(4)' would not be permissible because this itself would infringe s 2(4).

Having read the previous paragraph do you think that s 2(4) is de facto entrenchment? Now read *Thoburn*.[144] Is EU law entrenched subject to the ultimate power of withdrawing from the European Union?

143. [2002] EWHC Admin 195.
144. [2003] QB 151, 181–5.

LISTEN TO THE PODCAST

For guidance on how to answer this question and a discussion of the main issues, listen to the author's podcast on the Online Resource Centre:
www.oxfordtextbooks.co.uk/orc/gillespie_els6e/

Perhaps the most significant jurisprudence that examined the issue of the supremacy of EU law and the place of s 2 was the *Factortame* litigation which (eventually) resolved the question and held definitively that EU law was supreme.

Case Box *Factortame*

The facts of the *Factortame* litigation need only be summarized as they are complex. The EU has a fishing policy that is designed to control the fishing that is permitted by each Member State. Each state had a quota of fishing rights but foreign fishermen could take advantage of this if they registered themselves in a Member State country. Factortame was a large Spanish fishing firm who registered themselves in England and sought to use the British quota. As a result of protests the UK government passed the *Merchant Shipping Act 1988* which altered the status of shipping registration and would have limited foreign ownership of fish quotas.

Factortame believed that the Act was incompatible with EU rules on the basis that it was discriminating solely on grounds of nationality. It sought to challenge the decision of the government to introduce the Act through judicial review. The matter proceeded to the High Court who referred certain questions to the ECJ (see 4.3.4.3 for details of this procedure) but this would take time. The question arose whether interim relief (ie a temporary injunction pending the conclusion of the litigation) could be given in the meantime. The House of Lords held that under English law it could not (*Factortame v Secretary of State for Transport (No 1)*)[145] but referred a separate question to the ECJ as to whether interim relief should be possible. The ECJ responded that the obligation under the Treaty was for Community law to be given immediate effect (*R v Secretary of State for Transport, ex p Factortame*)[146] meaning that interim relief should be permissible.

The House of Lords, when it received this reply, indicated that as they were so bound s 2 could be used to create an interim relief even though no such domestic remedy existed elsewhere (*R v Secretary of State for Transport, ex p Factortame (No 2)*)[147] and Lord Bridge importantly stated that EU law was supreme and that domestic law would have to be modified to take into account this supremacy. His Lordship also gave short shrift to the argument that this was not known at the time of accession by stating that supremacy had been established by the ECJ before the time the United Kingdom joined the (then) EEC.[148]

An interesting issue arose in 2010 over the compatibility of EU law with domestic law. This time the challenge was not that UK law was not compatible with EU law but rather it was suggested that UK law was void where EU law had not been complied with. In the 1980s the EU passed a directive on technical standards[149] that

145.   [1990] 2 AC 85.
146.   [1990] ECR I-2433.
147.   [1991] 1 All ER 70.
148.   See Nigel Foster, *Foster on EU Law* (2nd edn, OUP 2010) 154.
149.   Directive 83/139/EEC.

required Member States to notify to the European Commission all 'technical regulations' in respect of the sale of certain goods. The United Kingdom had passed the *Video Recordings Act 1984* (VRA 1984) which was designed, in part, to restrict the sale of video recordings unless they had been certified for release. The VRA 1984 was undoubtedly a technical regulation within the meaning of the 1983 Directive. Rather surprisingly it took until 2009 for anyone in government to realize that the Act had never been notified to the EU and, accordingly, the VRA 1984 was technically in breach of the Directive.

Three defendants who had been convicted of various offences under the VRA 1984 sought to argue that their convictions should be quashed since the VRA 1984 was in breach of EU law and should be considered void. In *R v Budmir and Rainbird; Interfact Ltd v Liverpool City Council*[150] the Court of Appeal rejected this contention. The court agreed that the Act was in breach of EU law but it noted that there was nothing within EU law that required the conviction to be quashed in such circumstances. They noted that the defendants had been properly convicted under English law and their conviction should only be quashed where there was an injustice, and no such injustice arose here.

The decision of the Court of Appeal is somewhat complicated[151] but it is perhaps notable that here any breach or incompatibility was simply technical. There was no doubt that the VRA 1984 performed an appropriate function, the only breach of EU law was that the law had not been notified. It is difficult to believe that notification would have made any difference, perhaps something made clear when Parliament repealed the VRA 1984 and enacted the exact same provisions (this time notifying the measure to the EU).[152]

Sovereignty Act

It was reported in late 2010 that the Foreign Secretary of the coalition government was to propose a 'sovereignty Bill' to be placed before Parliament later that year. Whilst no Act was forthcoming, a clause addressing this issue appeared in the *European Union Act 2011* (EUA 2011). Section 18 states:

> Directly applicable or directly effective EU law (that is, the rights, powers, liabilities, obligations, restrictions, remedies and procedures referred to in section 2(1) of the European Communities Act 1972) falls to be recognized and available in law in the United Kingdom only by virtue of that Act or where it is required to be recognized and available in law by virtue of any other Act.

It is not clear what the precise point of this clause is. All it does is state that EU law is only directly applicable or effective because s 2(1) ECA 1972 says so. However, that much is obvious because s 2(1) says that and it is the only provision that permits the legislation to be directly applicable or effective. Unlike with human rights (where there is an argument that the common law would recognize key fundamental rights irrespective of whether the UK withdrew from the ECHR) no one is seriously suggesting that the common law would recognize the supremacy of EU law when the UK withdraws from the EU, since that is the sole basis for its existence. In essence, this

150. [2010] EWCA Crim 1486.
151. For an interesting discussion on its merits see Laura Madhloom, 'Videos and Supremacy of EU Law: Does a Failure to Notify Nullify Domestic Law?' (2010) 74 *Journal of Criminal Law* 496.
152. See *Video Recordings Act 2010*.

clause must be considered to be a political clause that allowed politicians to claim that they were reasserting sovereignty. The reality, of course, is that it did no such thing. Section 18 actually reiterates the fact that the UK has voluntarily surrendered some of its sovereignty albeit with the proviso that it can reclaim that sovereignty at any time by repealing s 2(1) ECA 1972. This is no different to the position created by the passing of s 2(1) and the (eventual) legislation that does repeal the ECA 1972 will be materially different in form.

4.3.4.3 References to the Court of Justice of the EU

It has been seen so far that EU law can be directly applicable and effective; that is to say that some law will slot into domestic law without the Member States having to do anything, and in some other instances the principle will be set out in EU law but domestic law will implement it. In both situations the EU legislation has now become part of domestic law and, through the ECA 1972, it takes precedence over conflicting domestic legislation unless expressly revoked. Accordingly, a person wishing to rely on EU law would bring an action in the domestic courts using domestic procedures as their legal right now exists under domestic law.

What happens where the litigation raises questions as to the interpretation of EU law? Does this remain a matter solely for the domestic courts or is it something that the Court of Justice of the EU should rule upon and, if so, how? Article 267 TFEU states:

> The Court of Justice of the European Union shall have jurisdiction to give preliminary rulings concerning:
>
> (a) the interpretation of the Treaties;
>
> (b) the validity and interpretation of acts of the institutions, bodies, offices or agencies of the Union.

It is notable that the TFEU refers to the 'Court of Justice of the EU' as it will be remembered that this comprises both the *General Court* and the *European Court of Justice* and it is clear that both courts have jurisdiction to give preliminary rulings[153] although only in the circumstances set out in that Article.

Article 267 TFEU states that there are two types of preliminary reference requests: a discretionary system and a mandatory system. The discretionary system is explained as:

> Where such a question is raised before any court or tribunal of a Member State, that court or tribunal may, if it considers that a decision on the question is necessary to enable it to give judgment, request the Court to give a ruling thereon.

Thus *any* court may refer a question to the Court of Justice although the procedures of the domestic courts may limit this to the extent that it is not incompatible with the Treaty. For example, it is unlikely that in England and Wales it would be desirable for a magistrates' court to decide that they should refer a question to the Court of Justice and procedures could be put in place to ensure that, for example, the High Court makes the ultimate decision (this could, for example, be through judicially reviewing a decision to refer or not to refer a question).

153. *Treaty on the Functioning of the European Union*, Art 256.

The mandatory system is explained as:

> Where any such question is raised in a case pending before a court or tribunal of a Member State against whose decisions there is no judicial remedy under national law, that court or tribunal shall bring the matter before the Court.

Thus whilst any court has discretion as to whether to refer a matter to the Court of Justice, a court of final resort would theoretically have no discretion to refer and *shall* refer the matter. Of course this is premised by the first part of Article 267 which is premised on the basis that a question arises. A key issue is under what circumstances a domestic court believes that a question arises and is not, for example, already settled.

Article 267 refers to a preliminary reference procedure because, contrary to what is often said in the media and even some textbooks, it is not possible to 'appeal' to the Court of Justice. Instead the domestic court has to decide whether, and if so to what extent, EU law resolves the dispute before it. This is part of the principle of direct effect: EU law forms part of the national law and thus it is for the national courts, and not the Court of Justice, to resolve this. The preliminary reference procedure, however, recognizes the fact that the Court of Justice is the ultimate arbitrator of EU law and thus where a point of EU law is not settled, the domestic court can seek an opinion of the Court of Justice. Theoretically the Court of Justice does not have the jurisdiction to discuss the compatibility of domestic law with EU law[154] but the obvious solution to this is to ensure that the question is phrased in such a manner that the query is over the application or interpretation of the EU legislation.

In *Irish Creamery Milk Suppliers v Ireland*[155] the (then) ECJ discussed the purpose of the preliminary reference procedure and stated it established 'a framework for close co-operation between the national courts and the Court of Justice based on the assignment to each of different functions'.[156] The different roles can be seen from the fact that the Court of Justice simply answers the questions posed and does not adjudicate on the actual case. The matter is then referred back to the domestic court who must apply the ruling of the Court of Justice to the facts as identified by the national court. The Court of Justice does not make findings of fact; only the domestic courts do this, and accordingly the reference is preliminary to the final adjudication, that being given by the domestic court.

Article 23a of Protocol 3 TFEU states that the rules of procedure can ensure that preliminary references can be sent to the relevant court under an expedited procedure and where the matter relates to the area of freedom, security, and justice that the reference can be sent under an urgent procedure. This is presumably because the latter could involve significant infringements on the liberty of an individual and thus time will be of the essence in deciding on the legality of any instrument or procedure. This is supported by Article 267 TFEU itself which states: 'if such a question is raised in a case pending before a court … with regard to a person in custody, the Court of Justice of the European Union shall act with the minimum of delay.'

Must or should refer?

The Court of Justice has been clear that it is ordinarily for the national court to decide when a preliminary reference should be made[157] although it did suggest that it would

---

154. *Costa v ENEL* [1964] ECR 585.
155. [1981] ECR 735.
156. [1981] ECR 735 [5].
157. *Irish Creamery Milk Suppliers v Ireland* [1981] ECR 735.

be preferable for the factual basis of the case to have been adjudicated so that the questions can be placed into a proper context[158] and in recent years this 'preference' has become more substantial.[159] However, setting aside this issue of timing, it is relatively clear that the Court is comfortable with the idea of the national court deciding whether to refer a matter or not.

Where issues become slightly more complicated is in respect of when a reference *must* be made. The third paragraph of Article 267 states that a reference must be made where there is no appeal against a decision, but what does that mean and does this interfere with the general principle that it is for the domestic courts to interpret legislation? Within England and Wales it may appear obvious that the House of Lords is the court from which there is no appeal but appeal opportunities are restricted from other courts. For example, an appeal from the magistrates' court to the Divisional Court will only be subject to another appeal in extraordinary circumstances (see 16.2.2)—is the Divisional Court required to make a reference?

The position becomes even more complicated when one notes that it may not be possible to identify the last court until it is too late. Foster provides the example of a case litigated in the Court of Appeal and where the Court of Appeal and House of Lords (now Supreme Court) both refuse to give leave to appeal. The Court of Appeal—which was not the lowest court—had *discretion* to refer the matter to the Court of Justice (and let us assume it decided not to) whereas the Supreme Court would *have* to refer it. However, by denying leave the Court of Appeal became the last court but the matter has already been resolved so there is no mechanism for now petitioning the Court of Justice.[160]

Even though Article 267 talks about mandatory referrals this is not strictly correct as there are many instances when a referral need not be made. Perhaps the classic example of this is when the same question has already been adjudicated by the Court of Justice. In those circumstances there is no need to refer the matter again and the final appeal body can just take judicial notice of the original judgment. This was developed into a process known as *acte clair* where national courts would not have to refer where the law is particularly clear.[161] However, could this be abused by the courts?

II\ Case Box *Three Rivers*

In *Three Rivers District Council v Governor of the Bank of England*[162] the House of Lords was called upon to consider the applicability of an EC directive. As the House of Lords is a court from which there is no appeal they should have theoretically referred the matter to the ECJ. However, they did not do so arguing that they were capable of considering Community law with a small risk of them reaching the wrong verdict. No case had previously gone to the ECJ on this exact issue although similar decisions had. The House believed that the disadvantages entailed in a reference were not outweighed by the benefits. Tridimas suggests that this is a liberal interpretation of *acte clair* although he does not expressly suggest that it is wrong.[163]

158. *Irish Creamery Milk Suppliers v Ireland* [1981] ECR 735 [6].
159. See, for example, *Bacardi-Martini SAS, Cellier des Dauphins v Newcastle United* [2003] ECR I-905.
160. For a discussion on this see, John Fairhurst, *Law of the European Union* (10th edn, Pearson Education 2014) 190.
161. Takis Tridimas, 'Knocking on Heaven's Door: Fragmentation, Efficiency and Defiance in the Preliminary Reference Procedure' (2003) 40 *Common Market Law Review* 9, 12.
162. [2000] 2 WLR 1220.
163. Takis Tridimas, 'Knocking on Heaven's Door: Fragmentation, Efficiency and Defiance in the Preliminary Reference Procedure' (2003) 40 *Common Market Law Review* 9, 42.

There must be concern that since it is for the domestic courts to decide whether a reference shall be made, they could simply choose not to refer in cases arguing, like in *Three Rivers*, that the matter was wholly within their competence. This, however, arguably fails to take account of the cooperative procedure that the ECJ sees Article 267 TFEU bringing. There is no identifiable sanction against a court that adopts this approach although presumably the Commission could take action against the Member State arguing that the application of the law by that Member State (through the rulings of the domestic courts) is wrong. Whether such powerful action would be taken over minor issues of Community interpretation is more questionable.

4.4 European Convention on Human Rights

The second European Treaty that is of direct importance to domestic law is the *European Convention on Human Rights* (ECHR). Its importance has grown since 2000 when the *Human Rights Act 1998* came into force and this instrument has already been discussed in Chapters 2 and 3 and we will return to it in Chapter 5. However, in this part of the chapter it is intended to demonstrate where the source of ECHR jurisprudence arises. The use of this law in the domestic context is explained in the other chapters.

4.4.1 Background to the Convention

The ECHR was created in the aftermath of the Second World War and was designed to ensure that some of the atrocities that preceded and occurred during the war could not happen again. That said, it is important to realize that the Convention is not a treaty governing war but rather the treatment of citizens in general. A significant number of the lawyers who drafted the Convention were British and the United Kingdom was the first country to sign the Treaty in 1950.[164] Although the Treaty came into force in 1953 and some countries directly incorporated it into their domestic law, the United Kingdom did not do anything that would lead to it being used by the individual citizen, believing that this was unnecessary as the Treaty simply gave effect to freedoms already secured by the common law. However, in 1966 the United Kingdom accepted the right of individual petition. This allowed UK citizens (and from 1981 citizens of its territories (excluding Hong Kong[165] and the Isle of Man)) to petition the European Commission on Human Rights (ECmHR) alleging a breach of the Convention. Since that time a significant number of cases have been brought and Bingham argued that the high number of cases was one reason to incorporate the Convention into a domestic setting.[166]

The Convention itself consists of sixty-six Articles but of these the most important are Articles 2–18 which create the human rights and fundamental freedoms that citizens of the Council of Europe have as protection. The remaining Articles create the machinery by which the rights and freedoms will be protected. Existing alongside the Convention itself are a number of protocols. The protocols can be divided into two classes. The first are those protocols that amend the Treaty (eg Protocols 3, 5, 8, and 11) and the second

---

164. Lord Bingham, *The Business of Judging: Selected Essays and Speeches* (OUP 2000) 134.
165. This was, of course, prior to Hong Kong being returned to Chinese rule in 1997.
166. Lord Bingham, *The Business of Judging: Selected Essays and Speeches* (OUP 2000) 135–6.

are those that create additional rights and freedoms (eg Protocols 1, 4, 6, 7, and 12). Where the protocols create additional rights then Member States are not obliged to safeguard these rights and freedoms unless they agree to be bound by the protocol or some parts of the protocol.

 PROTOCOLS

Article 1 of Protocol 6 abolishes the death penalty subject to a reservation under Article 2 of the Protocol permitting the penalty to continue in time of war for certain offences. The Protocol was created on 28 June 1983 but the United Kingdom did not ratify this protocol until 1 June 1999 (see s 1(1)(c) HRA 1998 and associated delegated legislation). Protocols 4, 7, and 12 have not been ratified by the United Kingdom and accordingly the additional rights set out in those protocols are not afforded to citizens of the United Kingdom or its territories.

4.4.2 The institutions

When the Treaty was first ratified there were three bodies that were relevant to the Convention:

- Committee of Ministers
- European Commission on Human Rights
- European Court of Human Rights.

Protocol 11 to the Convention altered this to abolish the ECmHR and to remove the judicial function of the Committee of Ministers. The ECtHR is now the pre-eminent body and a Commissioner for Human Rights has been created although the commissioner has, in effect, a political rather than a purely legal function.

4.4.2.1 The Committee of Ministers

The Committee of Ministers was, as its name suggests, a body constituted of relevant domestic ministers of the contracting states. It served as the 'executive' to the Council of Europe and was responsible, therefore, for proposing amendments to the Convention and monitoring that the ECtHR was functioning correctly.[167] (Perhaps its most controversial purpose, however, was that it had the right to adjudicate on disputes that were not referred to the ECtHR.)[168] It has been argued that, in reality, decisions only went to the ministers where it was a minor issue that had already been resolved by the ECtHR in other cases or where the contracting state admitted that there was a breach of the Convention but had indicated that it would not change the domestic provision that infringed the Article.[169] This latter point is an interesting one because although the ECtHR provides declarations of illegality and can order a contracting state to issue compensation[170] its judgments are decisions of an international body and accordingly are not binding on any state. If a state wishes to ignore the law then there is little that can be done about this; unlike the *Treaty of Rome*, the

---

167.   David Harris et al, *Law of the European Convention on Human Rights* (Butterworths 1995) 691.
168.   *European Convention on Human Rights*, Art 32.
169.   David Harris et al, *Law of the European Convention on Human Rights* (Butterworths 1995) 693.
170.   *European Convention on Human Rights*, Art 50.

ECHR does not provide an enforcement mechanism and instead enforcement is left with the Committee of Ministers. This means that a political resolution would need to be sought and, in practice, that has led to some accusations that countries have been able to ignore decisions of the ECtHR although in reality compliance has been 'exemplary'[171] and this is in part because of the diplomacy of the Committee.

Article 32 of the Convention has now been modified to remove reference to the Committee of Ministers and the ECtHR now has jurisdiction over all cases. The Committee continues, however, to supervise the execution of the Court's judgments.

4.4.2.2 The European Commission on Human Rights

It is perhaps understandable that some students get confused between the Council of Europe and the European Union given that both had Commissions and courts. However, the bodies were significantly different from one another with the European Commission on Human Rights (ECmHR) acting as a de facto filter for cases before the ECtHR (before its abolishment).

The Commission was constituted, under Article 20, as including one member from each contracting state, thus mirroring the position in respect of the judges. Article 25 of the Convention stated that all applications had to be referred to the Commission who would then decide whether they were admissible. If the Commission decided that a case was not admissible then the matter could not proceed further. If, however, the Commission considered it admissible then it had to decide whether to refer the case to the Committee of Ministers or, more commonly, the Commission would produce an opinion on the case.

The opinion appeared to be a judgment although it had no legal status and was merely an indication as to what the Commission believed the law to be, including reference to previous decisions of the ECtHR. The Commission would make findings of fact and law, identify whether it thought there was a prima facie breach, and ultimately decide whether it was admissible. The ECtHR was not bound by the opinion and in a number of situations the ECtHR would depart from the Commission; but in the majority of cases the opinion of the ECmHR was a good indication of how the case would progress and there were instances where countries had settled the dispute before it reached the ECtHR as a result of the opinion.

Some argue that the Commission acted as an effective filter for the ECtHR[172] but there was no doubt that it was an extremely costly and time-consuming process. As the Council of Europe increased in size so the number of cases continued to rise and the delay between an application and eventual resolution by the ECtHR grew. It was therefore decided that the ECmHR should be disbanded and a new system of deciding admissibility would be introduced.

4.4.2.3 The European Court of Human Rights

The role of the ECtHR has grown as a result of the abolition of the ECmHR and the reduction of the jurisdiction of the Committee of Ministers. The Court now has responsibility for deciding the admissibility of decisions and then, separately, the resolution of the case. Article 27 states there are three divisions of the Court:

---

171. David Harris et al, *Law of the European Convention on Human Rights* (Butterworths 1995) 702.
172. David Harris et al, *Law of the European Convention on Human Rights* (Butterworths 1995) 574.

- Committees: a panel of three judges
- Chambers: a panel of seven judges
- Grand Chamber: a panel of seventeen judges.

In addition there is the Plenary Court which consists of all judges. The Plenary does not sit judicially but exists to elect the President and Vice-Presidents of the Court together with deciding rules of court etc.[173] More than one type of division outlined earlier can sit and indeed the expectation is that there will normally be more than one Committee and Chamber sitting to increase the number of cases heard. Importantly, Article 27(2) states that whenever the Court is sitting in either a Chamber or Grand Chamber, the defendant Member State must be represented as a judge, either through the ECtHR judge appointed for that Member State or, if that person is unable to sit, an ad hoc judge proposed by the Member State. It may seem unusual for, in effect, the defendant to be represented on the bench but this is a standard feature of international tribunals and is designed to ensure that the judge can guide the other judges through the relevant domestic laws and procedures.

Committees normally sit to consider cases that appear to be manifestly ill-founded and can be withdrawn from the list. Article 28 provides Committees are to rule matters inadmissible where the three judges agree unanimously and expressly states that no right of appeal exists from such a decision. Where no decision is made under Article 28 (ie it is not struck out by the Committee) then the matter proceeds to a Chamber which will then consider the admissibility and merits of the decision.[174] According to Article 29(3) the merits of the case should normally be heard separately from admissibility although this need not occur in exceptional circumstances, eg where there is a particularly pressing need.

Where a matter involves a particularly complicated interpretation of the Convention or where the ECtHR wishes to depart from its previous decisions then Article 30 allows the Chamber to surrender its jurisdiction to the Grand Chamber, thus permitting a much more authoritative analysis of the case to be made. However, this is comparatively rare and the usual expectation is that the matter would be heard by the Chamber.

A decision of a Chamber is normally final but either the applicant or the defending country can petition the Grand Chamber within three months of the judgment of the Chamber.[175] The Grand Chamber shall form a Committee of five judges to consider whether they should entertain this petition, the decision being whether it is a matter of general importance.[176] If they decide to allow the petition then the matter proceeds to the Grand Chamber for a full rehearing. If they refuse the petition then the judgment of the Chamber is automatically final.[177] Decisions of a Grand Chamber are always final[178] and are not subject to any appeal.

4.4.3 Identifying the law

It can be seen from the previous paragraphs that the principal sources of law are the Convention itself and the decisions of the ECtHR. Although the ECmHR has now

---

173. See Art 26.
174. Article 29.
175. Article 43(1).
176. Article 43(2).
177. Article 42.
178. Article 44(1).

been abolished, its decisions remain important as they assist in identifying the boundaries of admissibility. That said it must be remembered that the ECtHR is not bound by the ECmHR and accordingly they amount to a persuasive secondary source of law.

4.4.3.1 **The Convention**

A background to the Convention was provided earlier and an overview of Articles 2–14 is given in the next chapter which details the importance of the HRA 1998. However, it is important to note that the ECtHR has consistently stated that the Convention is not a static document but that it progresses with society:

> That the Convention is a living instrument which must be interpreted in the light of present-day conditions is firmly rooted in the Court's case law … It follows that these provisions cannot be interpreted solely in accordance with the intentions of their authors as expressed more than 40 years ago.[179]

This has implications for the way in which the Convention is to be interpreted. It follows, for example, that a literal interpretation (see 2.3.1) will not be adopted as the meanings of words rarely change. Instead the ECtHR considers the Convention to safeguard society and the passage demonstrates that as society grows and develops the rights of an individual will also adapt.

Example Transsexuals

One of the most obvious examples of the Convention acting as a living instrument can be seen from the treatment of transsexuals. In *Rees v United Kingdom*[180] the ECmHR rejected the suggestion that a ban on transsexuals marrying was an infringement of Article 12 (the right to marry) and this was later confirmed by *Cossey v United Kingdom*.[181] Yet in *Goodwin v United Kingdom*[182] the ECtHR changed its mind and held that a bar was a breach of Article 12 and argued that society had moved on since the earlier stages and that it was no longer appropriate to keep an absolute bar.

The rejection of a literal approach can also be seen from the manner in which the ECtHR approaches its use in the context of the wider international law. In *Fogarty v United Kingdom*[183] the ECtHR said:

> The Convention … cannot be interpreted in a vacuum. The Court must be mindful of the Convention's special character as a human rights treaty, and it must also take the relevant rules of international law into account. The Convention should, so far as possible, be interpreted in harmony with other rules of international law … [184]

This reinforces the fact that the Convention is a set of *minimum* safeguards and that where other international instruments discuss the concept of rights, eg the *United*

179. *Loizidou v Turkey* (1995) 20 EHRR 99, 133.
180. A 106 (1986).
181. A 184 (1990).
182. [2002] IRLR 664.
183. (2002) 34 EHRR 12.
184. (2002) 34 EHRR 12, 314.

Nations Convention on the Rights of the Child, then the ECtHR will try so far as possible to construe the ECHR to take account of these instruments.

European or domestic context?

At the time of writing there are forty-seven countries that are signatories to the ECHR and each has its own legal system. It has been seen in Chapter 2 that language is important when construing instruments and the question must arise therefore whether the Convention is construed in a pan-European way or in respect of each signatory's construction.

The answer to this question is not particularly clear as sometimes the ECtHR will arrive at an autonomous meaning and at other times it will permit the individual signatories some latitude. Some commentators argue that an autonomous meaning is only given to words where there is the capacity for misunderstanding as a result of the way in which words are interpreted.[185]

> **Example** Autonomous meaning
>
> It may be thought that we understand what the term 'criminal charge' means (see Article 6(1)). However, not every country may necessarily have a clear divide between criminal and civil law. Indeed in England and Wales this issue could still raise a problem. We may think of a matter being of a criminal nature where a penalty is imposed but this need not be the case because of regulatory frameworks. A good example of this is tax. If a person is obliged to complete a self-assessment as part of their tax affairs there is a deadline by which the forms must be received by the Inland Revenue. If a person does not meet that deadline then a £100 fine is imposed. Is this a criminal penalty or a regulatory penalty? Certainly someone so fined would not have to declare it as a 'criminal conviction' in any job application so does that mean it is not a criminal charge?

Providing autonomous meanings to words should provide a level of consistency across jurisdictions, including in domestic settings. Of course the position is not immediately clear as questions will arise as to whether a domestic instrument necessarily equates to the autonomous meaning but it does mean that a contracting state could not circumvent human rights by using words that appear to take a matter outside the remit of the Convention.

However, it could also be argued that the Council of Europe is certainly not one homogeneous body and that society in each country could be different to another, especially as the bulk of the ECtHR's work is now in respect of emerging democracies.[186] The ECtHR has recognized this and in respect of certain convention rights will allow domestic institutions latitude in respect of the way that rights and freedoms are secured, this latitude being known as the doctrine of the margin of appreciation.

This doctrine, which first appeared in the leading case of *Handyside v United Kingdom*,[187] recognizes the fact that the domestic institutions (courts and executive)

---

185.   David Harris et al, *Law of the European Convention on Human Rights* (2nd edn, OUP 2009) 16.
186.   Lord Woolf, *Review of the Working Methods of the European Court of Human Rights* (Council of Europe 2005) 9.
187.   (1979) 1 EHRR 737.

are best placed to understand the requirements of society and accordingly the ECtHR will sometimes defer to their finding that a measure is necessary for the protection of society.[188] Loveland expands on this point and notes that a justification for its use is that the ECtHR is not an appellate court per se in that it is not involved with resolving individual cases (as appellate courts are) but rather it has a supervisory role whereby it ensures that national institutions give effect to the rights and freedoms of the Convention.[189] This supervisory role can be seen from the fact that although the ECtHR is happy to extend a margin of appreciation in respect of some matters, it will decline to do so in others and even where the margin is extended it reserves the right to supervise the margin of appreciation (see *Handyside*).

Positive or negative rights

Another feature of the Convention that must be understood is that although many of the Articles are framed in the negative—ie institutions shall not do something—the ECtHR has stated that many of the Articles also have positive obligations. A positive obligation in this sense means that not only must a state not infringe the relevant Article, it must put in place a framework by which a person's right is protected, including preventing other people (including private citizens) from infringing their rights.

:≡ **Example** Rape

In *MC v Bulgaria*[190] the ECtHR held that there was a positive obligation under Article 3 of the Convention to ensure that domestic laws protected women from rape and that such acts were investigated and prosecuted properly. This case followed the earlier decision of *X and Y v Netherlands*[191] which held that Articles 3 and 8 had positive obligations in respect of ensuring that the criminal law protected the vulnerable from sexual offences.

4.4.3.2 The European Court of Human Rights

The second source of law for ECHR matters is, of course, the ECtHR and it has already been noted that this is an important source as the manner in which they interpret the Convention can lead to an extension of rights. For example the plain words of Article 3—'No one shall be subjected to torture or to inhuman or degrading treatment or punishment'—would ordinarily lead one to believe that this was a negative obligation, ie the state should not torture or subject someone to inhumane or degrading treatment. However, the ECtHR has made clear that Article 3 also contains positive obligations and so the impact of Article 3 is significantly wider. Arguably, therefore, whereas in the United Kingdom the judiciary is a secondary source in terms of its relationship to Acts of Parliament the same cannot be said for the ECtHR where its decisions are arguably as important as the Convention itself.

188.　David Harris et al, *Law of the European Convention on Human Rights* (2nd edn, OUP 2009) 11–14.
189.　Ian Loveland, *Constitutional Law, Administrative Law and Human Rights: A Critical Introduction* (7th edn, OUP 2015) 593–4.
190.　(2005) 40 EHRR 20.
191.　(1986) 8 EHRR 235.

Article 45 of the Convention states that the ECtHR must give reasons for its judgments and Article 45(2) expressly provides for the right to give a dissenting or partly dissenting judgment. Reference to 'decisions' includes admissibility decisions and normally, therefore, each case will contain at least two decisions; the first will be given when admissibility is decided and the second, usually much later, is when the merits of the case are given—the judgment. Admissibility decisions are an important source of law as the reasons given for non-admissibility will frequently identify common legal principles and the limits of the Convention Articles.

When giving judgment, the ECtHR, like the Supreme Court of the United States of America, will normally only give a single judgment and, where it is not unanimous, normally a single dissenting judgment.[192] This position can be contrasted with the UK Supreme Court or English appellate courts where it is arguably more common for each judge to give a judgment. There are good reasons for giving a single judgment especially where it involves a Grand Chamber, not least efficiency and time, but the disadvantage is that sometimes it is not always clear precisely what the Court means whereas with individual judgments it is possibly easier to identify the reasons.

Another feature of judgments of the ECtHR is that they will rarely contain the equivalent of *obiter dicta* and certainly not *per curiam* comments. The ECtHR limits its jurisdiction upon applications to real problems and will not answer hypothetical questions except when requested to do so by the Committee of Ministers under Article 47 although it has never been called upon to do so.

Precedent

The ECtHR has, over the past fifty years, decided on a large number of cases and the question then arises as to how the court considers its past decisions. In Chapter 2 it was noted that the courts in England and Wales adopt the doctrine of *stare decisis* believing that certainty and predictability of the law is important. In *Goodwin v United Kingdom*[193] the ECtHR discussed the issue of precedent:

> While the Court is not formally bound to follow its previous judgments, it is in the interests of legal certainty, foreseeability and equality before the law that it should not depart, without good reason, from precedents laid down in previous cases ...[194]

Thus the ECtHR considers precedent a desirable object but it does not feel itself to be formally bound by itself. It may seem that this is comparable to the Supreme Court (see 3.2) but arguably the position is slightly different since the Supreme Court starts with the proposition that it *is* bound but that in exceptional circumstances it can depart from or overrule its own decisions. The ECtHR differs in that it does not have this initial presumption but rather just thinks it is desirable to follow previous cases. In part this rule is necessary because of its belief that the Convention is a 'living instrument'. It was noted that some believe that rigid adherence to the doctrine of precedent can restrain the development of law and the ECtHR clearly believes that this would be a mistake in this field. However, the importance of not departing from previous decisions too easily can be found in the fact that a significant departure is one reason for a case being referred from a Chamber to the Grand Chamber (see 4.4.2.3).

---

192.   Although it is perhaps increasingly common to see individual dissenting judgments, in part because sometimes the dissenters disagree with one another.
193.   [2002] IRLR 664.
194.   [2002] IRLR 664 [74].

Summary

In this chapter we have examined the sources of international law that may have an impact on the English Legal System. In particular we have noted:

- International law ordinarily governs states not individuals.

- The primary sources of international law are conventions and treaties. Treaties are agreements between two or more countries and conventions are international documents where countries agree to be bound by a system of rules or goals.

- International law also relies on custom, that is to say informal rules that have been commonly agreed over a period of time.

- A particular problem with international law is its enforceability. Sometimes the treaty will state how the law will be enforced. The United Nations may become involved to assist in implementing it.

- The United Kingdom joined the (then) EEC in 1972. As part of the conditions for joining the UK agreed that EEC (now EU) law would become automatically part of the law of the United Kingdom.

- The principal treaties governing the EU are the *Treaty on European Union* and the *Treaty on the Functioning of European Union* and disputes are adjudicated by the European Court of Justice.

- The EU has its own executive which is divided between two bodies, the *Commission* and the *European Council*.

- The *Council* and *European Parliament* constitute the legislature of the EU. The powers of the Parliament have been strengthened by the *Treaty of Lisbon* and Parliament now has broadly the same powers as the Council.

- Legislation can be proposed by either the Council or the *European Parliament* or by the *European Commission* itself. Only the *European Commission* can initiate legislation.

- After *Lisbon*, the judiciary is represented in the *Court of Justice of the European Union* which is divided into two standing courts (the *European Court of Justice* and the *General Court*) and specialist courts. Each court currently consists of one judge from each Member State and a President of each court is elected by its judiciary. Both courts ordinarily sit in divisions known as chambers.

- The *European Convention on Human Rights* was written in the aftermath of the Second World War. It is controlled by the *Council of Europe* and is enforced by the *European Court of Human Rights*.

- Any country that wishes to join the *European Union* must first join the *Council of Europe* but the Council also includes countries who have no desire to join the EU.

- The Convention is considered to be a 'living instrument' meaning that it changes with society.

- There is no sanction for failing to implement a decision of the *European Court of Human Rights* but most countries will voluntarily adhere to its decisions in order to discharge their international obligations.

End-of-chapter questions

1. A potential difficulty when considering vertical effect is deciding what amounts to a public body. In some countries the energy supplier will be public (ie state-owned) and in other countries (eg

the United Kingdom) it will be a private body. However, do they do anything different and should they be treated any differently in terms of EU law?

2. Read William Wade, 'Sovereignty: Revolution or Evolution' (1996) 112 *Law Quarterly Review* 568 and John Eekalaar, 'The Death of Parliamentary Sovereignty: A Comment' (1997) 113 *Law Quarterly Review* 185. In the first article Professor Wade argues that the decision in *Factortame* has effectively abrogated parliamentary sovereignty. Professor Eekalaar disagrees. Do you think the position is as simple as Wade suggests or can there be a 'temporary' ceding of sovereignty but with the ultimate right to act in the national interest?

3. Read Marie-Aude Beernaert, 'Protocol 14 and New Strasbourg Procedures: Towards Greater Efficiency? And at What Price?' [2004] 5 *European Human Rights Law Review* 544. Does the increasing number of states joining the Council of Europe mean that the European Court of Human Rights will effectively concentrate on the new 'emerging democracies' rather than developing human rights in the original Member States? Is there not a danger, therefore, that citizens in the United Kingdom and other states will not have adequate protection for a breach of their rights?

 # Further reading

Read the text of the Attorney-General's advice on the legality of the invasion of Iraq. A copy can be found at (2005) 54 *International and Comparative Law Quarterly* 767–78.

The Attorney-General considers many aspects of the applicability of international law to English law and also potential remedies that may be used against the government if it had been proven to be illegal.

Boyron B, 'In the Name of European Law: The Metric Martyrs Case' (2002) 27 *European Law Review* 771–9.

This article considers the implication of the judgment in *Thoburn v Sunderland City Council* (2002) and considers the place of European sovereignty in England and Wales.

Craig P, 'The Treaty of Lisbon, Process, Architecture and Substance' (2008) 33 *European Law Review* 137–66.

This article provides a very readable and comprehensive analysis of the principal changes brought about by the *Treaty of Lisbon*.

For multiple-choice questions, updates to this chapter, and links to useful websites, please visit the **Online Resource Centre** at: **www.oxfordtextbooks.co.uk/orc/gillespie_els6e/**

Further reading

5

Human Rights Act 1998

By the end of this chapter you will be able to:

- Identify the principal Articles of the ECHR.
- Discuss which bodies are bound by the HRA 1998.
- Assess how the HRA 1998 has been used in domestic contexts.
- Understand the HRA 1998's impact on the domestic legal system.

Introduction

In 1997 a Labour government was elected to power in the United Kingdom under the leadership of Tony Blair. One of the manifesto commitments of that administration was to incorporate the *European Convention on Human Rights* (ECHR) into domestic (UK) law. It was seen in the previous chapter that the Convention had been drafted in the aftermath of the Second World War but that the United Kingdom had traditionally decided that there was no need to incorporate it into domestic law arguing that its protections were all to be found in the common law.

By the 1990s there was a growing recognition that this was not true and Labour, who traditionally had been against incorporation, decided that the Convention should be given domestic force. The *Human Rights Act 1998* (HRA 1998) is one of the most important pieces of legislation to have been passed in recent years but its impact was arguably overstated at the time.

This chapter will examine the HRA 1998 and discuss some of the important issues that arise from its use. An overview of the relevant Convention Articles will also be given.

The HRA 1998 itself is a short piece of legislation containing only twenty-two sections but this disguises its importance. In Chapter 2 the changes the Act has made to statutory interpretation were considered and it has been seen that there was a definite change of mindset when human rights issues were involved. However, it is important that we recall that the HRA 1998 does not completely rewrite statutory interpretation and that it only applies where the normal rules of interpretation would lead to a conflict with the ECHR (see 2.3.4).

5.1 **The decision to incorporate**

Bingham, speaking extrajudicially at the time he was Master of the Rolls, stated:

> I would suggest that the ability of English judges to protect human rights in this country and reconcile conflicting rights … is inhibited by the failure of successive governments over many years to incorporate into United Kingdom law the European Convention on Human Rights and Fundamental Freedoms.[1]

This was not a universally popular opinion but by the time the speech was given a significant debate had arisen as to the need to incorporate the ECHR into domestic law. There had been three attempts to incorporate the Convention into domestic law; once in 1987 by Sir Edward Gardiner QC, a conservative MP, and twice in 1994 and 1996 by Lord Lester of Herne Hill QC, a Liberal Democrat peer.[2] The attempts had been resisted because it was thought that the rights were to be found already in domestic law through the common law. Since 1966 UK citizens had the right to petition the European Court of Human Rights (ECtHR) where they believed the state had breached their rights[3] but the decision of the Court was theoretically unenforceable although successive governments had voluntarily acceded to judgments even when they disagreed with them.[4] By the 1990s there was 'an ever-lengthening list of occasions … [when] the Commission or the Court have found the United Kingdom to be in breach of its obligations',[5] which appeared to contradict the traditional opinion that the domestic courts were equally able to give force to the Convention rights.

A matter is only admissible before the ECtHR where domestic remedies have been exhausted (Article 35(1)) so where the ECtHR had ruled against the United Kingdom these matters had already been adjudicated on domestically without any such finding. This caused difficulties as the ECtHR is swamped with work, meaning the delay between petition and hearing can be significant.

The new Labour government argued that it would be more appropriate to allow the Convention to be litigated domestically and issued a White Paper (*Rights Brought Home*) setting out its proposals. The long title of the Act is: 'an Act to give further effect to rights and freedoms guaranteed under the European Convention on Human Rights' and it does not therefore make reference to either incorporation or domestic authority. The Lord Chancellor argued that this phraseology was correct because the Convention was already being complied with and the Bill (now Act) was simply extending this compliance,[6] and another commentator argues that the true position of the HRA can be described thus:

> The Human Rights Act 1998 maintains the dualist distinction between the United Kingdom's obligations in international law and the provisions of domestic law. The United Kingdom's international obligations under the European Convention are not

---

1. Lord Bingham of Cornhill, *The Business of Judging: Selected Essays and Speeches* (OUP 2000) 131.
2. *Rights Brought Home: The Human Rights Bill*, October 1997 (Cmnd 3782) para 1.5.
3. Bingham (2000) notes that the decision to grant a right of petition to the ECtHR was extremely controversial at the time (p 134).
4. *Rights Brought Home: The Human Rights Bill*, October 1997 (Cmnd 3782) para 1.10.
5. Lord Bingham of Cornhill *The Business of Judging: Selected Essays and Speeches* (OUP 2000) 135.
6. Jonathan Cooper, 'Parliamentary Debates on the Human Rights Bill' [1998] *European Human Rights Law Review* 1–4 at 4.

directly applicable in domestic law. Instead, the Human Rights Act 1998, s 1 and s 2, makes a list of 'Convention rights' ... available as rights before the domestic courts.[7]

It is for this reason that the term 'incorporation' would be inappropriate not least because the Convention has not become a full part of the English Legal System. The HRA 1998, as will be seen, only directly applies in respect of actions against the state and not against private disputes although it may exist through 'horizontal effect'[8] because courts are classed as public bodies.[9] Dwyer argues that the HRA 1998 is designed to establish this domestic framework and not to minimize the international obligations of the United Kingdom which can only be regulated by treaty. Fredman suggests that its summary could be:

> [The Act] simply ... empower[s] United Kingdom judges to adjudicate in an area that was formerly the exclusive preserve of the European Court of Human Rights.[10]

Other commentators agree, noting that nothing in the HRA 1998 stops someone from petitioning the ECtHR save that, since the Court itself requires domestic options to have been exhausted, petitioners will have to try domestic proceedings first.[11] It is quite possible that this could have a beneficial impact on the Court itself and Bingham, when arguing for a scheme similar to that created by the HRA 1998, suggested that a full reasoned examination at domestic level could help influence law at the ECtHR.[12]

5.2 The basic framework

It has been remarked that the HRA 1998 is quite a short Act and its key parts are in a small number of sections. Perhaps the most important is that of s 6 which places an obligation on public authorities to act in a way compatible with the ECHR, s 7 which proscribes how it can be used to obtain a remedy in the courts, and ss 2–4 which detail how the Act is to be applied and how legislation can be construed before the courts.

5.2.1 Duty to act compatibly

Arguably the cornerstone of the Act is s 6(1) of the Act which states:

> It is unlawful for a public authority to act in a way which is incompatible with a Convention right.

This recognizes the issue about vertical effect discussed earlier, that at its heart the HRA 1998 is concerned with the relationship between the citizen and the state. It is for that reason that the Act (subject to the discussion on horizontal effect set out later) applies only to public authorities.

---

7. DM Dwyer, 'Rights Brought Home' (2005) 121 *Law Quarterly Review* 359–64, 362–3.
8. Horizontal effect in this context means the adjudication between two private parties as distinct from the 'vertical effect' of adjudicating between the state and private citizen.
9. For a summary of the arguments surrounding 'horizontal effect' see William Wade 'Human Rights and the Judiciary' [1998] 5 *European Human Rights Law Review* 524–5 and Deryck Beyleveld and Shaun Pattinson, 'Horizontal Applicability and Horizontal Effect' (2002) 118 *Law Quarterly Review* 623–46.
10. Sandra Fredman, 'Bringing Rights Home' (1998) 114 *Law Quarterly Review* 538–43, 538.
11. David Feldman, 'Remedies for Violations of Convention Rights under the Human Rights Act' [1998] 6 *European Human Rights Law Review* 691–711, 709–11.
12. Lord Bingham of Cornhill, *The Business of Judging: Selected Essays and Speeches* (OUP 2000) 137, 140.

Of course this immediately begs the question who is a 'public authority' and the HRA 1998 itself is only partially helpful in this regard. Section 6(3) states:

'public authority' includes—

(a) a court or tribunal, and

(b) any person certain whose functions are functions of a public nature,

but does not include either House of Parliament or a person exercising functions in connection with proceedings in Parliament.

Thus it is clear that courts and tribunals are expressly public authorities and that Parliament is exempt. Prior to 2009, when the Supreme Court was established, the highest court in the land was the House of Lords but s 6 expressly dealt with this apparent contradiction by stating that when it sat in its judicial capacity the House of Lords was a public authority.[13]

Why is Parliament exempt? The government and Parliament were obviously concerned that the HRA 1998 could be used to allow the courts to interfere with the parliamentary process. Traditionally it is said that the *Bill of Rights* ensures that the proceedings of Parliament are exempt from judicial scrutiny (the limits of this were discussed in *R v Chaytor*[14] which concerned the criminal prosecution of Members of Parliament who fraudulently claimed expenses). If Parliament was considered to be a public authority then the courts would be able to hold Parliament to account for why it did something and, perhaps more importantly, why it did not do something, which would undermine the principle that Parliament is supreme within the United Kingdom. Whilst it will be seen that there is some question whether the courts are able to interfere with parliamentary supremacy through the interpretation clauses within ss 2–3 of the Act, classifying Parliament as a public body bound to act in a way compatible with the Convention would be an express limitation on parliamentary supremacy.

Interestingly the Act does introduce an element of parliamentary adherence to human rights in that s 19 HRA 1998 states that a minister, when introducing an Act to Parliament, must make a statement that it is compatible with the ECHR. Section 19(1)(b) expressly reserves the right of the government to make clear that it does not believe the legislative instrument is compatible with the ECHR but nevertheless wishes to continue with the legislation. Quite when such a statement would be made is open to question since it would arguably be electoral suicide to state that the government was introducing legislation that it believed was incompatible with its human rights obligations (as distinct from merely stating that it believes that the current interpretations are wrong) and it would be difficult to see how, for example, such legislation could be defended before the European Court of Human Rights.

Section 19 is, to an extent, largely cursory since there is no real enforcement mechanism. Since Parliament is exempt from being a public body as a result of s 6 there is little that a person can do if they believe that the minister is wrong when they make the claim under s 19, indeed the courts have noted that they would be unable to entertain any challenge without infringing the *Bill of Rights*.[15]

159

13. *Human Rights Act 1998*, s 6(4).
14. [2010] UKSC 52.
15. See something suggested (it is submitted correctly) by counsel in *R (Huitson) v Revenue and Customs Commissioners* [2011] QB 174, 176.

5.2.1.1 **Who is a public authority?**

It will be remembered that s 6 provides only a partial definition. Whilst it expressly includes the courts and expressly excludes Parliament it leaves the status of other bodies vague. It will be remembered that the wording is that it must be a 'person certain' (which simply means a legal entity) 'whose functions are functions of a public nature'; but what does this mean? Section 6(5) adds to the uncertainty by stating that a legal entity is not a public authority if 'the nature of the Act is private'.

At the time of the passage of the Bill there was a belief that this language created two tiers of public bodies; those that are obviously public and those which are *capable* of being a public body but which would require further analysis. In *Aston Cantlow and Wilmcote with Billesley Parochial Church Council v Wallbank*[16] the House of Lords accepted that this duality of public bodies was correct and noted that their constitutional significance was less significant than what their functions are. A Parochial Church Council is a legal entity of a parish of the Church of England—an established (ie state) church—and yet the House of Lords held that it was not necessarily a public body for the purposes of the HRA 1998.

The first group of public bodies, which have now been labelled 'core public authorities', are the least problematic and are those that will be inherently a public authority. Classic examples of this would be the police, Fire and Rescue Service, government departments etc (it will be remembered that whilst Parliament is exempt, the government is separate from Parliament and government departments are inherently public).

The second group, sometimes known as hybrid public authorities, are arguably the more complicated because they are only bound by the HRA 1998 when they exercise public functions and not when they exercise private functions. There are a wide range of bodies that could be considered to be a hybrid body. Perhaps the classic example would be that of a private company who runs a prison. Clearly private security firms are not ordinarily public bodies but when they are running a prison they are exercising a public function since the detention of prisoners lawfully sentenced to imprisonment (or a suspect remanded in custody) by a court is certainly a public function.

In *Aston Cantlow* the test of a 'public function' was to assess the status of what the entity was trying to do and, for example, to consider factors such as whether it was 'in possession of special powers, democratic accountability, public funding in whole or in part, an obligation to act only in the public interest, and [has] a statutory constitution'.[17] In the context of that case the Parochial Church Council (PCC) was trying to exercise a 'rectorial property' charge on the lands of the respondent. This is a special type of property interest that could have meant that the owners of a farm were liable for the full cost of repairing the chancel of the local parish church (something that was commonplace centuries ago). The court considered that the essence of what the PCC was trying to do was to enforce a civil debt and therefore this was not a public matter and so in this instance the PCC was not acting as a public body and was therefore not bound by the HRA 1998 (which could have been relevant since arguably the enforcement of the civil charge may have been incompatible with Article 1 of the First Protocol to the ECHR which concerns property rights).

This test was refined by the House of Lords in *YL v Birmingham City Council*.[18] The matter at dispute here was the costs and provision of residential care for the

---

16. [2004] 1 AC 546.
17. [2004] 1 AC 546, 554.
18. [2008] 1 AC 95.

elderly. This was a statutory duty (*National Assistance Act 1948*) and the Council met this, in part, by contracting out some services to private providers. YL was an 84-year-old woman who suffered from Alzheimer's disease. The relatives of YL were, it was alleged, disruptive to the private provider of the residential care and the provider sought to cancel the contract, meaning that YL would be evicted. YL (suing by means of representatives) sought to argue that this would be a breach of the ECHR (Article 8). The question was whether the care home, when cancelling the contract, was acting as a public body.

Applying *Aston Cantlow* it may seem that the answer was 'yes' because although termination of a contract is private, the essence of what they were trying to do was to no longer provide residential care for YL and, as this was a statutory responsibility, it would seem to be of a public nature. However, by a majority of 3:2 the House of Lords held that they were not a public authority. The reasoning of the majority was quite technical, with them drawing a distinction between the provision of a service and the statutory duty to make arrangements to provide accommodation. Thus the House believed that whilst the council was under a duty the care home provider was not exercising a public function—that function being making arrangements—but was instead exercising a private function through the provision of a contractual relationship. In terms of the narrow reading of this decision the government enacted legislation to statutorily overrule the decision in respect of making the provision of accommodation a public function[19] but the reasoning of the case remains. The consequences of this are quite significant in that it is not unusual for public authorities to contract out some of the provision of services and the implications of *YL* are that this may mean that the person delivering the service is not a public body even if the provision of the service is a public function. That said, it will depend on the nature of the contract and what the relevant duties are.[20]

The narrow approach adopted by the House of Lords has not been welcomed and it is noticeable that the Parliamentary Joint Committee on Human Rights has questioned whether such a narrow approach is appropriate.[21] That said, it would be difficult to reverse *YL* without amending the HRA 1998 itself, something that would be politically problematic particularly during the current Conservative government where the very existence of the HRA 1998 itself is subject to debate (see 5.3). It is more likely that the courts will consider the need to soften the approach of *YL* and consider the inherent nature of the contractual arrangement (something that appears evident from *London and Quadrant Housing*).

That said, the courts remain wedded to the principles of both *Aston Cantlow* and *YL*. In *TH v Chapter of Worcester Cathedral and the Bishop of Worcester and Worcestershire County Council*[22] the High Court applied these decisions to a case involving a bell ringer of Worcester Cathedral. Safeguarding concerns had been raised involving TH and the Chapter[23] decided to withdraw permission to ring the bells of the Cathedral. TH sought to challenge this, inter alia, on the grounds that it interfered with his rights under Article 8 ECHR.[24] Coulson J held that neither the Chapter nor

---

19.   See *Health and Social Care Act 2008*, s 145.
20.   For an illustration of this see *R (Weaver) v London and Quadrant Housing Trust* [2009] EWCA Civ 587.
21.   See the report of the Committee on the *Health and Social Care Bill* (HC 46 HL 303 2007–08).
22.   [2016] EWHC 1117 (Admin).
23.   The chapter consists of a group of clerics (the Cathedral Dean and residentiary Canons) and certain lay-persons. They are charged with the administration of the Cathedral on behalf of the Bishop.
24.   Right to respect for private and family life, home, and correspondence (see 5.4.7).

the Bishop sitting in his corporate capacity[25] was a hybrid public authority. He notes that neither act on behalf of the public, neither exercised any governmental function, have no statutory power in respect of safeguarding or were subsidized by public funds. Neither were democratically accountable[26] nor is the UK accountable to the ECtHR for their actions.[27]

The decision is a useful read for students wishing a summary on how the courts should approach what is, or is not, a public authority for the purposes of the HRA 1998.

An interesting distinction between core and hybrid public authorities is whether they themselves can use the HRA 1998. According to Lord Nicholls in *Aston Cantlow* core public authorities will not be able to use the HRA 1998[28] whereas hybrid public authorities may be able to do so.[29] The logic behind this distinction refers back to the vertical nature of the protection of human rights within the ECHR and the HRA 1998. It will be remembered that the purpose of the HRA 1998 is to facilitate the actions of a citizen calling the state to account for breaches of their human rights. As a core public authority is, in essence, an instrument of the state then it cannot, in essence, sue itself for breaches of human rights. A hybrid public authority, when acting in its private capacity, could bring an action because when it is acting in its private, rather than public, role it is not an instrument of the state but is instead a private legal entity that may seek to hold the state to account for its human rights obligations.

5.2.1.2 **Horizontal effect**

It has been seen that the HRA 1998 theoretically only applies to public bodies but on occasion there will be circumstances when the Act may be said to have horizontal effect, ie it would seem to apply even in circumstances where it involves no obvious public authority.

Example Horizontal effect

Amy is suing Mandy, her neighbour, for playing her music too loud and is asking the court to restrict the ability of Mandy to play loud noise. This would seem to be a classic private dispute, neither Amy nor Mandy are public bodies. The right to freely enjoy one's private life is contained within Article 8 and being subject to unreasonable loud music would certainly constitute interference. The court is expressly a public body by virtue of s 6(3) and so Amy could argue that because Article 8 includes positive obligations the court must protect her Article 8 rights. Thus even though the dispute is between two private citizens, the HRA 1998 and ECHR can become engaged because the court should act in a compatible way.

Horizontal effect can be quite controversial since, in essence, it rests on the basis that the courts, as a public authority, could bring Convention rights into any matter. Elliott

---

25.   Diocesan bishops of the Church of England hold both a spiritual office (the bishopric) and a secular office, the latter is designed to allow for diocesan property and businesses to be held by the corporate body of the Bishop's office rather than the bishop in a personal capacity.

26.   Bishops are appointed by the Queen as Head of the Church of England and chapter members are appointed by the Church of England.

27.   [2016] EWHC 1117 (Admin) [67].

28.   [2004] 1 AC 546, 554.

29.   [2004] 1 AC 546, 555.

and Thomas note that the concept of horizontal effect, if it exists, is open to significant doubt as to its impact ranging from denying its very existence (vertical effect only) through to providing full horizontal effect through requiring *all* cases to be decided compatibly even if this means that the courts have to adopt a new cause of action because of a gap in domestic law

Phillipson makes an important point in this regard. He notes that some rights within the ECHR have no obvious impact on disputes between private parties (for example, Article 6) but that others will be of more importance (for example, Article 8). He argues that although all rights are probably *capable* of horizontal effect they do not *in fact* all have this effect.[30] This is partly because the HRA 1998 was not intended to incorporate the ECHR but rather to give it 'greater effect' by permitting their use in the domestic courts. Whilst some matters will require the courts to act in a compatible way on other occasions it will not be necessary because domestic law suffices or human rights are not engaged. That said, this should only be done in a way that will not usurp the rights of Parliament who remain supreme. This could mean implementing horizontal effect where it is possible to do so either by interpreting legislation or developing the common law but will not do so by inventing new laws or processes.

The leading case on the development of horizontal effect is *Campbell v Mirror Group Newspapers Ltd*.[31] This case involved a report in the *Daily Mirror* newspaper which had reported that Naomi Campbell, a well-known supermodel, was attending meetings of Narcotics Anonymous. The story included details of when the meetings were, what was said, and photographs of her leaving the meetings. Traditionally English law did not recognize a tort of privacy but Article 8 of the ECHR recognized the protection of, inter alia, respect for private life and so the question arose as to what the courts should do. The newspaper publishers could not be said to be a public body, either core or hybrid, and thus it became clear that this would be one of the more important tests of whether the HRA 1998 had horizontal effect. If the HRA 1998 did apply then the circumstances of the case would be interesting as there was the direct clash between fundamental human rights; private life on the one hand (Campbell) and the freedom of expression (newspaper) on the other.

In the event the House of Lords arguably sidestepped the issue by deciding that it was not necessary to expressly consider the applicability of the HRA 1998 due to the fact that an alternative cause of action, confidence, was recognized by English law. That said, the tort of confidence that was applied would, prior to *Campbell*, not have covered the circumstances of that case and so there was a development of that law. Why did the law develop? The House, particularly Lord Hoffman, believed that the HRA 1998 empowers the courts to develop the underlying common law in such a way as to include the values of human rights and thus whilst the *ratio* of *Campbell* does not tell us how the courts will interpret horizontal effect the reality of the case is that it is recognition that the courts will take account of human rights principles even in private cases where the rights arguments are important and real. To this extent it is perhaps notable that Article 8 is commonly considered to have a positive element to it—the state must not only ensure that it does not interfere with the right but also should seek to protect it—and this may make it easier for horizontal effect to be developed.

30. Gavin Phillipson, 'The Human Rights Act 1998, "Horizontal Effect" and the Common Law: A Bang or a Whimper?' (1999) 62 *Modern Law Review* 824–9, 837.
31. [2004] 2 AC 457.

5.2.1.3 **Acting in a way incompatible**

Section 6(1) talks about 'acting' incompatibly but s 6(6) makes clear that a failure to act is also actionable unless the failure is in respect of parliamentary material (s 6(a)–(b)). The latter provision was required because although s 6(3) exempts Parliament from the provisions of the Act, without s 6(a)–(b) it would have been possible to bring an action against the relevant government minister alleging that he *should* have brought legislation before Parliament or exercised authority delegated to him by Parliament.

The inclusion of omissions is important because, as will be seen, a number of Articles in the ECHR include positive obligations—ie a duty is imposed on the state to secure the Convention by not merely refraining from interfering with the right itself but also to provide assistance to ensure that the right is not interfered with by others.

The requirement in s 6(1) is that the public body must not act (or fail to act) in a way that is incompatible with the Convention. This simply means that it must act in accordance with the Convention and ensure, where relevant, that it respects a person's rights and freedoms including facilitating this where a positive duty is imposed. The courts must decide whether an action is incompatible and it will be seen later that the HRA 1998 empowers the courts in the way that it interprets legislation and ECHR jurisprudence.

5.2.2 **Litigating the Act**

It has been noted that public authorities must act in a way compatible with the ECHR but how is the Act used before the courts? To answer this question it is necessary to consider who is allowed to bring an action and how this action is brought or defended.

5.2.2.1 **Victim**

In order for a person to bring an action under the HRA 1998 they must be considered a 'victim' (s 7(1) HRA 1998). Victim is then defined by s 7(7) as a person who is considered a victim for the purposes of Article 34 of the ECHR. Article 34, however, does not provide much more clarity, simply stating: '[t]he court may receive applications from any person, non-governmental organisation or group of individuals claiming to be the victim of a violation ...' It is interesting that the HRA 1998 should link to Article 34 since it has been said that Article 34 itself is an autonomous concept that the ECtHR considers independently of any domestic law considerations

The key consideration under Article 34 is that a person must be directly or indirectly affected by the issue they are complaining of. This can potentially be quite wide. For example, in *Open Door and Dublin Well Women v Ireland*,[32] a case that concerned the provision of advice in respect of abortions, the ECtHR appeared to accept that any woman of child-bearing age was potentially a victim.[33] However, what is clear is that there must be some tangible link to the issue and where there is the mere potential that the applicant could be a victim then there is a requirement to produce reasonable and convincing evidence of the potential harm, with mere conjecture being unacceptable.[34] This makes the position of campaign groups more difficult since it has been noted that 'organisations will not be able to claim to be a victim of measures

---

32. (1992) 15 EHRR 44.
33. David Harris et al, *Law of the European Convention on Human Rights* (3rd edn, OUP 2014) 791.
34. David Harris et al, *Law of the European Convention on Human Rights* (3rd edn, OUP 2014) 792.

which affect the rights of their members'[35] although of course this restriction can be circumvented by having one of their members bring the action.

It is clear that the HRA 1998 test is more restrictive than the test of standing that ordinarily applies to, for example, judicial review which is not based on being a victim but only being 'sufficiently interested'.[36] Potentially this can cause difficulties where an action is alleging either breach of domestic law or human rights although it is likely that careful drafting can ensure that the issues are appropriately apportioned, even if it is through relying on the development of common law rather than human rights itself.

It is not clear why the government sought to link the status of victims with Article 34 as no clear rationale was put forward. Some believe, however, that the issue is really something of a distraction since if a victim cannot be found then it probably suggests that the issue is completely hypothetical and the courts should not be troubled by it.[37] Certainly this suggestion may account for why the rule was introduced since at the time of its introduction there was concern in some quarters that the courts would be 'clogged up' with challenges under the HRA 1998, including vexatious ones. In fact, this did not materialize, a point that was made by Lord Irvine, the then Lord Chancellor.[38]

Case Box *R (Al-Skeini) v Ministry of Defence*

It may seem that a victim for the purposes of the HRA 1998 would be a UK citizen or resident but in *R (Al-Skeini) v Ministry of Defence*[39] the House of Lords held that this was not the case. This was a case that arose as a result of military action in Iraq. Several relatives of those who were killed by UK troops petitioned the English courts under the HRA 1998. The House of Lords held that whilst ordinarily the actions of soldiers in places of conflict would be outside of the jurisdiction of the English courts, this was not always the case. One death occurred while the person was within the custody and control of UK forces on a British Army base. The House of Lords held that in these circumstances it could be said that the HRA 1998 should be applied because the prisoner was within the jurisdiction of a UK public body (the military). The decision was extremely controversial, and somewhat misunderstood, because there was a belief by some that human rights have no place on a battlefield. However, this perhaps misses the point that the House of Lords ruled on that point and declared many of the applications inadmissible. What made this case justiciable was the fact that the claimant was brought onto a sovereign base, into the care and custody of British troops. It does show that a 'victim' of a public authority can, in certain circumstances, be someone who resides abroad.

5.2.2.2 Sword

Assuming that a person can be considered to be a victim then they can litigate the Act. Section 7 permits action to be used in two ways; as a sword,[40] ie by using the Act to

35. David Harris et al, *Law of the European Convention on Human Rights* (3rd edn, OUP 2014) 795.
36. See *Senior Courts Act 1981*, s 31.
37. Jonathan Cooper, 'Parliamentary Debates on the Human Rights Bill' [1998] *European Human Rights Law Review* 1–4 at 2.
38. Lord Irvine of Lairg, 'The Impact of the Human Rights Act: Parliament, the Courts and the Executive' [2003] *Public Law* 308–25, 312–13.
39. [2006] UKHL 26.
40. *Human Rights Act 1998*, s 7(1)(a).

initiate civil proceedings against a public body, or as a shield,[41] ie by using the Act to defend action brought against it by the state (be that civil or criminal).

Of the two forms of litigation the use of the sword is perhaps more usual, not least because it includes the possibility of bringing action in anticipation of a breach (s 7(1) expressly makes reference to the fact that a public authority proposes to act in an unlawful way).

> ### Example Anticipated action
>
> Robert is organizing a protest march against capitalism. The police do not wish the route of the march to proceed through the city centre. They plan to use their powers to order the route to be re-routed through outlying areas.
>
> Prima facie this is a breach of Articles 10 (freedom of expression) and 11 (freedom of assembly) and Robert, as a direct victim, could bring an action against the police before the march takes place alleging the actions of the police, a public authority, will interfere with his rights.

The HRA 1998 does not itself create any new form of litigation but instead states it can be used as a basis of action under existing procedures. The HRA 1998 expressly refers to judicial review[42] and it is likely that this will be one of the more usual forms of litigating the Act. The issue of judicial review is discussed in Chapter 17 but it could also be for other forms of action, most notably tort.

Ordinarily actions under the HRA 1998 must be instigated within one year of the alleged breach occurring[43] although the courts have discretion to vary this where they believe it is fair to do so.

5.2.2.3 Shield

The second way that the HRA 1998 can be litigated is as a shield, ie by raising human rights issues as a defence to an action brought against an individual. This could cover a variety of different types of situations. For example, in the civil sphere this may relate to a person raising human rights issues where a local authority seeks to bring an action for breach of planning rules etc. There is no limitation on the use of s 7 as a shield and it could also be used in criminal trials where a person may wish to suggest that a prosecution amounts to a breach of his human rights. The most likely argument in such circumstances would be to raise procedural issues and allege that they have breached Article 6 (right to fair trial) but may also include arguments that some laws are too vague and thus amount to a breach of Article 7[44] or that a sentence imposed on him is greater than that which was prescribed at the time he committed an offence.[45]

41. *Human Rights Act 1998*, s 7(1)(b).
42. *Human Rights Act 1998*, s 7(3)(4).
43. *Human Rights Act 1998*, s 7(5).
44. David Harris et al, *Law of the European Convention on Human Rights* (3rd edn, OUP 2014) 334–5 who discuss the extent to which the ECtHR are prepared to become involved in such arguments.
45. David Harris et al, *Law of the European Convention on Human Rights* (3rd edn, OUP 2014) 337 although it should be noted that this applies only to penalties and thus where an ancillary matter is attached that is not punitive then Article 7 will not apply; see, most notably, *Adamson v UK* (1999) 28 EHRR CD 209.

5.2.3 Interpreting legislation and the Convention

The HRA 1998 places the compatibility of UK laws with the ECHR at the heart of the legislation. It provides specific powers to the courts in how it construes English laws and also how it considers the ECHR when considering the compatibility or otherwise of domestic law. Arguably these are the most important provisions within the Act since, as will be seen, it provides the courts with the ability to go beyond that which ordinary principles of statutory interpretation may require of them.

There are two sections that deal with interpretation in the HRA 1998. Section 2 relates to how the domestic courts should interpret the ECHR itself and s 3 relates to how the courts should interpret domestic legislation so as to make it compliant with the ECHR. There is an obvious interaction between the two sections but of the two s 3 has proven to be the more important.

5.2.3.1 Interpreting legislation

Section 3 of the HRA 1998, it will be remembered from Chapter 2, allows the courts to interpret legislation in a way that is compatible with the ECHR (see 2.3.4). It will be remembered that there are limits to what the courts can do and it does not provide any power to 'strike down' legislation but it certainly allows the courts to go much further than they could under the traditional rules of statutory interpretation.

5.2.3.2 Interpreting the Convention

It has been seen that at the heart of the power under s 3 is the fact that the domestic courts must consider whether they believe legislation is compatible with the ECHR. The HRA 1998 prescribes how the courts should do this in terms of them considering not only the ECHR itself but also the jurisprudence of the ECtHR. This is necessary because, as it will be remembered from Chapter 4, international law does not easily divide into 'primary' and 'secondary' sources and so the decisions of the ECtHR are extremely important in ascertaining what the Convention means, not least because the ECHR has been described as a 'living instrument', ie subject to evolution.[46]

Section 2(1) of the HRA 1998 states that a court 'must take account of', inter alia, a judgment of the ECtHR or the European Commission on Human Rights. The wording is interesting because although it is mandatory ('must') the decision is not to bind the courts but merely to 'take account of' the decisions. It has been noted that the effect of this is that the statute does not instruct courts on how the authorities should be treated by the courts, nor what weight should be given to them.[47]

The general approach by the courts has been to operate on the basis that whilst they are not bound by the ECtHR the courts will mirror the decisions of the ECtHR (ie follow them) if there is clear and consistent authority.[48] The justification for this approach differs but in *R (Anderson) v Secretary of State for the Home Department*[49] Lord Bingham stated that 'the House will not without good reason depart from the principles laid down in a carefully considered judgment of the court sitting as a Grand

46. See *Marckx v Belgium* (1979–80) 2 EHRR 330.
47. Philip Sales, 'Strasbourg Jurisprudence and the Human Rights Act: A Response to Lord Irvine' [2012] *Public Law* 253–67, 257.
48. Philip Sales, 'Strasbourg Jurisprudence and the Human Rights Act: A Response to Lord Irvine' [2012] *Public Law* 253–67, 255–7.
49. [2002] UKHL 46.

Chamber'.[50] This perhaps recognizes that the ECtHR has had the best opportunity of considering the issues before the Court, including the fact that some aspects of the ECHR are considered to have an autonomous meaning, ie one that is considered purely in the context of the ECHR and not by reference to national definitions.[51] However, some have been critical of this rule as it arguably means that decisions of the ECtHR are treated in the same way the Supreme Court treats its own decisions, ie they will ordinarily follow them but exceptionally may depart from them.[52] Certainly this would be beyond that which was ever contemplated by Parliament when the Bill was being passed (where, for example, the government specifically rejected an amendment that would have made the UK courts bound by the ECtHR[53]) but perhaps this is reading too much into what the mirror principle means and it is difficult to understand what else the courts can do in the face of clear rulings from the ECtHR as to do otherwise would arguably mean the UK breaches international law.

Whilst the courts will ordinarily follow Strasbourg they do reserve the right not to do so and one particular exception is where they believe that the ECtHR has not fully understood the subtleties of domestic law. The most notable example of this was *R v Horncastle*.[54] This was an evidence case before the Supreme Court. The appellant had been convicted of causing grievous bodily harm with intent[55] and whilst the victim had given a statement to the police, the victim had (for unconnected reasons) died before the matter came to trial. The statement was read out in court and, whilst there was other evidence, the Court of Appeal (Criminal Division) had ruled that it was 'to a decisive degree' the basis upon which the appellant had been convicted.

The appellant sought to argue that the admission of the statement breached Article 6 of the ECHR as he was unable to cross-examine the victim: the jury therefore only heard one side of the story. Reliance was placed on *Al-Khawaja and Tahery v United Kingdom*[56] where the ECtHR had held that where a statement of a person not able to be cross-examined was 'the sole, or at least, the decisive basis' for a conviction then Article 6 was breached.

The Supreme Court refused to follow the decision of *Al-Khawaja*, in part because Article 43 of the ECHR allows a party to a decision to petition that the matter is heard by the Grand Chamber of the ECtHR (discussed in Chapter 4). This had happened in this case although the matter had not, at that time, been heard. The Supreme Court held that whilst s 2(1) meant that ordinarily a decision would be followed, the Supreme Court reserved the right to rule that certain decisions of the ECtHR did not sufficiently appreciate or accommodate particular aspects of the UK domestic process. In such circumstances it could refuse to follow the Strasbourg court.

Some scholars place emphasis on the fact that because it is possible to disagree with the ECtHR this means that a 'dialogue' exists between the domestic courts and Strasbourg.[57] The genesis of this idea can be traced back to the consultation paper proposing the HRA 1998 with it expressly stating that 'judges will be able to contribute

---

50.   [2002] UKHL 46 [26].
51.   David Harris et al, *Law of the European Convention on Human Rights* (3rd edn, OUP 2014) 16.
52.   Aileen Kavanagh, *Constitutional Review under the UK Human Rights Act* (CUP 2009) 148.
53.   Francesca Klug, 'Follow or Lead? The Human Rights Act and the European Court of Human Rights' [2010] 6 *European Human Rights Law Review* 621–30, 623.
54.   [2010] 2 WLR 47.
55.   Contrary to *Offences Against the Person Act 1861*, s 18.
56.   (2009) 49 EHRR 1.
57.   See, for example, Philip Sales, 'Strasbourg Jurisprudence and the Human Rights Act: A Response to Lord Irvine' [2012] *Public Law* 253–67, 264–6.

to this dynamic and evolving interpretation of the Convention'. However, the logic of this contribution is somewhat dubious, not least because there is not a formal system of reviewing cases to the court (cf the position with the Court of Justice of the EU). Where the individual loses before the domestic courts he can petition the ECtHR which, if it takes the case, can review the logic of the domestic courts' approach to the Convention, but where the individual succeeds and it is the public body that disagrees with the view of the court then there is no recourse to the ECtHR. Given the inherent delays of the Court (discussed in Chapter 4) it must also be questioned whether there is any true discussion since by the time the matter is re-litigated it is quite possible the position has moved on in both domestic and international law.

Some commentators have noted that a difficulty of not generally following the rulings of Strasbourg would be that it could make the law less certain. The rationale behind such a suggestion is that not only would lawyers, advising their clients, have to understand how the ECtHR interprets particular sections of the Convention they would also have to identify the separate domestic interpretation and attempt to reconcile the two.[58] If true, this would certainly seem to be contrary to the general purpose of the law in England and Wales. It will be remembered from Chapter 3 that *stare decisis* was initiated, in part, because there was a belief that certainty of the law was desirable. It would be regrettable if an interpretation of s 2 was to make the law uncertain.

⚡ PRECEDENT V SECTION 2

It has been noted that s 2 requires the courts to take account of ECHR issues and there has been some discussion as to what this means in terms of precedent. How has this resolved itself in practice? In *Kay v Lambeth London Borough Council*[59] the House of Lords stated that the rules of precedent should be followed and that where a binding precedent is incompatible with a decision of the ECtHR the matter should be sent to appeal, even invoking the 'leap-frog' procedure that allows decisions of the High Court to be appealed to the Supreme Court where a matter is of public importance.

An example of this in practice can be found in *R (on behalf of Purdy) v DPP*[60] where the Divisional Court was asked to rule on an assisted suicide issue. The claimant suggested that the DPP should have to publish a specific policy in respect of when he would prosecute people for assisted suicide. This raised a similar (but sufficiently distinct) point from the 'Diane Pretty' litigation. An issue arose as to whether Article 8(1) was engaged. The House of Lords had held in the *Pretty* case that it was not[61] but Diane Pretty had then taken the matter to the ECtHR who held that it had invoked Article 8 (although deciding it was a justifiable interference).[62]

The Divisional Court had to decide whether it was bound by the House of Lords decision in *Pretty* or whether it could follow the ECtHR (which s 2 would seem to imply). They held that the ruling in *Kay* was clear and that they were bound by the House of Lords and that only the House (now Supreme Court) could alter this precedent.[63] The decision in *R v Horncastle*[64] would

---

58. Philip Sales, 'Strasbourg Jurisprudence and the Human Rights Act: A Response to Lord Irvine' [2012] *Public Law* 253–67, 260.
59. [2006] 2 AC 465.
60. [2008] EWHC 2565.
61. *R (on behalf of Pretty) v DPP* [2002] 1 AC 800.
62. *Pretty v United Kingdom* (2002) 35 EHRR 1.
63. [2008] EWHC 2565 [46].
64. [2010] 2 WLR 47.

lend support to this argument as the Supreme Court was, in that case, expressly stating that it had the right to depart from Strasbourg and that other courts must follow the ruling of the Supreme Court.

Margin of appreciation

Whilst the ECtHR will sometimes seek to find a uniform approach to the ECHR it will sometimes recognize that it is not best placed to decide how some matters should be applied and will leave this adjudication to the signatory state. When the ECtHR decides that the state is best placed to decide how to implement a particular issue this is known as the doctrine of the margin of appreciation.[65] The doctrine applies because the essence of the Convention is that the signatory states are responsible for the protection of human rights and the Court has a supervisory role, meaning that it checks that states are adhering to their obligations, taking account of the individual circumstances of countries.[66]

The doctrine was first identified in *Handyside v United Kingdom*[67] which concerned an obscenity trial. The ECtHR held that deciding how to protect morals was primarily a matter for signatory states as each state has different moral standards reflecting the different make-up of society and liberal tendencies. That said, the Court was also clear that any margin of appreciation was subject to its scrutiny, ie it reserves the right to consider whether a state has exercised its discretion in an improper way.

Does the doctrine apply to the HRA 1998? Lord Hope in *R v DPP, ex p Kebilene*[68] thought it did not as it was a matter of international law whereby an international court showed deference to a state in terms of its individual society[69] but Lord Irvine, the then Lord Chancellor, has argued that the courts have adopted their own version of this test.[70] He argues that this version is where the courts defer to Parliament and the executive over some issues surrounding society on the basis that certain areas are political rather than purely legal.[71] It has been said that this deference began with judicial review[72] and has become an established part of HRA 1998 actions with the concept being that the courts will defer to the executive where there is a 'fair balance' between the interests of society as a whole and the individual's human rights.[73] However, Leigh argues that it should be restricted solely to qualified rights (ie Articles 8–11) and not to absolute rights, for example Articles 2 and 3.

Others disagree with this proposition and suggest that there is no reason why deference should not occur in absolute rights too.[74] This argument is based on the premise that there is no such thing as a 'qualified' right and that Articles 8–11 are erroneously so

65. David Harris et al, *Law of the European Convention on Human Rights* (3rd edn, OUP 2014) 11.
66. David Harris et al, *Law of the European Convention on Human Rights* (3rd edn, OUP 2014) 13.
67. (1979) 1 EHRR 737.
68. [2000] 2 AC 326.
69. [2000] 2 AC 326, 380.
70. Lord Irvine of Lairg, 'The Impact of the Human Rights Act: Parliament, the Courts and the Executive' [2003] *Public Law* 308–25, 315.
71. Lord Irvine of Lairg, 'The Impact of the Human Rights Act: Parliament, the Courts and the Executive' [2003] *Public Law* 308–25, 315.
72. Ian Leigh, 'Taking Rights Proportionately: Judicial Review, the Human Rights Act and Strasbourg' [2002] *Public Law* 265–87, 266.
73. Ian Leigh, 'Taking Rights Proportionately: Judicial Review, the Human Rights Act and Strasbourg' [2002] *Public Law* 265–87, 276.
74. Simon Atrill, 'Keeping the Executive in the Picture: A Reply to Professor Leigh' [2003] *Public Law* 41–51, 44.

called because, in essence, the first part of each Article provides only a prima facie right or freedom and it is only when the derogation (the second paragraph of each Article) is applied that it can be decided whether the right applies or not. Accordingly, Atrill argues that all rights are unqualified and that there is no difference between the Articles themselves. Certainly it is true to say that the rights and freedoms traditionally labelled as qualified are not subservient to the absolute rights, with the ECtHR itself arguing that Article 10 (freedom of expression) is an essential foundation for democracy[75] which suggests that it recognizes this as one of the more important rights. However, this would also be slightly misleading in that the ECtHR itself has adopted a strict interpretation to Articles 2 and 3 with any margin of appreciation being highly restricted. That said, it is clear that the ECtHR has applied the margin to Articles 5 and 6, which whilst not absolute are not ordinarily classified as qualified,[76] and so there is no reason why any domestic application should be restricted to Articles 8–11.

Atrill argues that the domestic equivalent to a margin of appreciation—judicial deference—is required for all rights and that not doing so would restrict the development of rights.[77] Lord Irvine appears to believe the correct approach is somewhere between these two polarized opinions. He recognizes that there is a need for the courts to hold the executive and legislature to account and that proportionality (see 'Necessity and proportionality') is a powerful tool in checking the validity and extent of any deference[78] but he also argues that there are some situations where the courts need to defer to the executive and legislature, as bodies with democratic authority.

Necessity and proportionality

Central to many of the Convention rights, but in particular the qualified rights under Articles 8–11, are the concepts of necessity and proportionality. Arguably this is a little simplistic as proportionality is referred to in many Convention Articles, particularly Article 6 (right to a fair trial), and necessity is also a flexible concept. Some argue that necessity is part of proportionality as at its simplest it can be argued that necessity means that just because a public body has the right to do something does not mean that it should. A public authority should only interfere with someone's rights when it has to, not just when it wants to: in other words it is when it *has* to—not when it would be *merely convenient* to do so.

In *Soering v United Kingdom*[79] the ECtHR explained the principle of proportionality:

> [I]nherent in the whole of the Convention is a search for a fair balance between the demands of the general public interest of the community and the requirements of the protection of the individual's fundamental rights.[80]

Thus proportionality is remembering that although a person has a right, this right must be kept in the context of society's rights and should not create a position whereby it causes undue problems for society. In respect of the qualified rights (see 5.4.1.1) proportionality will often mean that the extent of a right should be limited so as to ensure that the public are not unduly constrained. Arguably proportionality has two

75. See, for example, *Hertel v Switzerland* (1999) 28 EHRR 534.
76. David Harris et al, *Law of the European Convention on Human Rights* (3rd edn, OUP 2014) 12.
77. Simon Atrill, 'Keeping the Executive in the Picture: A Reply to Professor Leigh' [2003] *Public Law* 41–51, 51.
78. Lord Irvine of Lairg, 'The Impact of the Human Rights Act: Parliament, the Courts and the Executive' [2003] *Public Law* 308–25, 316.
79. (1989) 11 EHRR 439.
80. (1989) 11 EHRR 439, 469.

dimensions to it. The first is whether a right should be interfered with (and this will incorporate the idea of necessity) and the second is how far the interference should go. It is, in particular, this latter dimension that is particularly relevant to the qualified rights.

☰ Example Proportionality

In Northern Ireland there is a 'Parades Commission' that seeks to adjudicate on disputes arising from marches that occur each year in the Province. The marches are normally undertaken by Protestant organizations (eg the Orange Order) and commemorate historic battles. The battles were part of a series of campaigns between Protestant and Catholic monarchs that sought control of Europe, the United Kingdom, and Ireland. Many marches throughout the island of Ireland take place peacefully but the march in Belfast has often been controversial and has, on a number of occasions, led to violence between Republican and Loyalist factions hiding under the cloak of Protestant and Catholic allegiances.

Articles 10 and 11 provide the right to freedom of expression and freedom of assembly and, taken together, could provide a right to march. However, both are qualified rights and the state (through the Parades Commission in this instance) can interfere with the rights so long as it is for a legitimate aim and proportionate.

In recent years the Parades Commission has banned the march from passing through Catholic areas of Belfast City and instead re-routed it through Protestant areas. Although this is highly controversial to the Orange Order (who claim the right to walk down the Queen's Highway) the decision is arguably proportionate as it seeks a balance between the right of people to march (and indeed the parades and marches do occur) but also between the wider members of certain sections of society who consider the marches offensive. Finding the balance is not easy and it is this tension which the ECtHR was considering (albeit in a different context) in *Soering* and its later pronouncements on proportionality.

When considering whether a public body acted appropriately, the concept of proportionality was alien to the English courts. The traditional view taken was that the courts would only interfere when a decision was illegal, procedurally improper, or irrational (see, for example, *Associated Provincial Picture Houses Ltd v Wednesbury Corporation*[81]). However, proportionality arguably differs considerably from these traditional grounds as the latter examined whether a decision was wrong and yet proportionality is suggesting that there are competing rights. In *R (on behalf of Daly) v Secretary of State for the Home Department*[82] Lord Steyn summarized what he believed were three differences:

> First, the doctrine of proportionality may require the reviewing court to assess the balance which the decision maker has struck, not merely whether it is within the range of rational or reasonable decisions. Secondly, the proportionality test may go further than the traditional grounds of review inasmuch as it may require attention to be directed to the relative weight accorded to interests and considerations. Thirdly, even the heightened scrutiny test ... is not necessarily appropriate to the protection of human rights.[83]

---

81.   [1948] 1 KB 223.
82.   [2001] 2 AC 532.
83.   [2001] 2 AC 532, 547.

His Lordship certainly believed that the intensity of the review of a decision-making process under proportionality is greater than in traditional reviews presumably because of the balance required: ie the courts must look at the rights of both the claimant and society in deciding where the balance is to be struck and not just at whether the decision was wrong. However, it should be remembered that this only applied where a Convention right is in issue; if the matter is purely one of domestic law then the traditional grounds of review continue to be used.

5.2.4 Remedies

It will be remembered that s 7 allows a person to use the HRA 1998 as either a 'sword' or a 'shield' in terms of litigation. Assuming that the courts, when interpreting legislation, conclude that the victim has had their rights infringed (or, if it is anticipatory action, will have their rights infringed) what remedies are available?

To some degree the simple answer is the reference within s 8(1) which states:

> [A court] may grant such relief or remedy, or make such order, within its powers as it considers just and appropriate.

However, this disguises some of the intricacies involved in the discussion of remedies and a number of issues need to be discussed.

5.2.4.1 Article 13: The missing Article

Article 13 of the Convention provides that everyone whose rights are breached under the Convention has the right to an effective remedy. However, Article 13 has, controversially, not been included within the HRA 1998. In part, this is because the government argued that the HRA 1998 itself was the realization of Article 13 and that, whereas before a remedy could only be obtained by petitioning the ECtHR itself, the HRA 1998 allows for domestic remedies. Given that the HRA 1998 does not create any new procedures it was also thought that a remedy will always be granted but this misses the point that damages and relief are often discretionary.

Where the omission of Article 13 may have some relevance is in respect of delayed trials. It will be seen that Article 6 provides, inter alia, that a person will be brought to trial quickly. The ECtHR has held that remedying a breach for Article 6 in these circumstances through the provision of compensation is unlikely to suffice by itself and that it would be more appropriate to provide a solution, ie expediting the trial. Whilst the criminal justice system has suffered considerable delays in recent years it is perhaps questionable whether the delays will be sufficient to lead to a breach of Article 6, as longer periods than are usual in the UK have been upheld by the ECtHR. That said, if such a breach were to be found then in the absence of Article 13 it could be questioned whether the court has sufficient powers to act. It is submitted that the generic wording of s 8 means that a remedy could be granted since the *Criminal Procedure Rules* provide for sanctions to quicken trials and also, where appropriate, the ability to stay proceedings for lack of care. Thus the absence of Article 13 is unlikely to prove too problematic.

5.2.4.2 Declarations of incompatibility

Some courts, most notably the Supreme Court of the United States of America, have the power to 'strike down' legislation, ie declare that it is no longer in force. As noted already the courts in England and Wales do not have this power and the government was very careful, when introducing the HRA 1998, to ensure that this power was not given to the courts.

The previous section identified that the courts have express power to interpret legislation, so far as is possible, in such a way as to ensure compatibility. However, it was also seen that there are limits to the power of the courts under s 3 and sometimes a court will face the conclusion that legislation is incompatible and cannot be interpreted in such a way as to make it compatible. In those circumstances the court is able to make a declaration of incompatibility under s 4 HRA 1998.

One of the first points to note about declarations of incompatibility is that it is discretionary. The wording of s 4(2) is very clear that the court *may* make a declaration and thus even if it believes that legislation is incompatible with the ECHR it could decide that it is not necessary to make a declaration and could instead simply make a ruling that the legislation is incompatible and not, for example, trigger some of the ancillary issues related to a s 4 declaration. It will be seen that the effects of a s 4 declaration can be quite significant and it is for this reason that only certain powers have the right to make a declaration of incompatibility under s 4. Whilst any court can exercise the interpretation clause within s 3, of the English courts only the Supreme Court, Court of Appeal, and High Court can make a declaration.[84] The exception to this is the Court of Protection, which is a relatively new statutory court, but this court may only make a declaration where it is being presided over by the President of the Family Division (who is also the President of the Court of Protection), Chancellor of the High Court (who is its Vice-President), or a puisne judge.[85]

A declaration of incompatibility is an unusual remedy in that it does not have any impact on the matter before the court. This is clear from s 4(6) which states:

A declaration of [incompatibility]—

(a) does not affect the validity, continuing operation or enforcement of the provision in respect of which it is given, and

(b) is not binding on the parties to the proceedings in which it is made.

The effect of this section is twofold. The first is that when deciding the matter in front of it, the court has to ignore the fact that the law is incompatible and proceed on the basis that the law is valid. It is for this reason that the courts have sometimes suggested that a declaration of incompatibility should be a remedy of last resort, with strong preference being given to the use of their interpretative powers under s 3.[86] This would be preferred because, where interpretation is permissible, it would at least mean that the courts could solve the issue that led to the breach of human rights. The second effect of course is that subsequent cases must also be dealt with by applying the law *as is* and not take account of the fact that there is a recognized breach of human rights.

Of course where the court is recognizing a breach of human rights but is not providing a remedy this would appear to be a breach of Article 13 and this is perhaps an additional reason why the government wished to exclude Article 13 from the HRA 1998. It does, however, leave the government in a difficult position since if the claimant takes the matter to the ECtHR then it is highly likely that it would also find a

84. *Human Rights Act 1998*, s 4(5).
85. *Human Rights Act 1998*, s 4(5)(f).
86. See *Ghaidan v Godin-Mendoza* [2004] UKHL 30, [2004] 2 AC 557, 576.

breach (although they are not bound to follow the domestic court) and, having ruled that there is a breach, could award damages as a remedy.

What is the point of a s 4 declaration if it does not affect the issue that is being litigated? The answer lies in the fact that it empowers the government, if it so wishes, to rectify the breach without the need to introduce primary legislation. Section 10 empowers, but does not require, the government to amend primary legislation to make it compatible with the ECHR through the use of secondary legislation, a so-called 'Henry VIII' order. The power can only be exercised if a court has made a declaration under s 4 and there has been no appeal, the time for an appeal has lapsed, or all parties to the dispute state in writing they will not appeal.[87] If the test is met and the minister believes that there are 'compelling reasons' for amending the legislation then the amendment may be by order. The principal advantage of this is speed. It will be remembered from Chapter 2 that primary legislation can take a considerable period of time to progress through Parliament, especially where it is controversial or where there are pressures on parliamentary time. A statutory instrument takes considerably less time and thus the legislation and, presumably the incompatibility, can be undertaken quickly. Whilst legislation is not ordinarily retrospective it does mean that any future challenges would be dealt with under (what would be hoped to be compatible) legislation rather than the text that has been ruled incompatible.

 REMEDIAL CORRECTIONS

In *R (on the application of H) v Mental Health Review Tribunal (North and East London Region)*[88] the Court of Appeal made the first declaration of incompatibility when it held that s 73 *Mental Health Act 1983* was incompatible with Article 5 (right to liberty) of the ECHR. Section 73 stated that where a person had been detained under the Mental Health Act then the burden of showing that the detention was no longer justified was on the patient rather than on the health authority. The government sought to use its powers under s 8 and the *Mental Health Act 1983 (Remedial) Order 2001*[89] was made which amended s 73 to place the burden on the authority.

Of course whilst secondary legislation is quicker it does mean that there is less parliamentary scrutiny which potentially means the government could alter primary legislation without the full consent of the Houses of Parliament (although from Chapter 3 it will be remembered that there are ways of objecting to secondary legislation). It appears that remedial orders are relatively unusual and that it is more common for Parliament to pass primary legislation to amend the offending legislation, presumably in part because of the transparency concerns noted earlier.

5.2.4.3 Remedies against judicial acts

Where the allegation is that a court (which is expressly a public authority by virtue of s 6(3)(a)) has acted contrary to the Convention then the only remedy that lies is a right of appeal or judicial review.[90] This is to ensure that people do not re-litigate their

---

87. *Human Rights Act 1998*, s 10(1)(a).
88. [2002] QB 1.
89. SI 2001/3712.
90. *Human Rights Act 1998*, s 9.

disputes by suing individual judges when they believe that the judgment of the court has infringed their Convention rights. This is a necessary step and has led to little dispute.

Judicial immunity (see 9.2.4) is also expressly contained in the Act when it states that damages may not be awarded when a judicial act has been undertaken in good faith.[91] The only exception to this rule is in respect of Article 5 of the ECHR (right to liberty). Article 5(5) expressly states that where a person has been detained unlawfully by the state they have an automatic right to compensation. Section 9(3) HRA 1998 makes clear, therefore, that the rule against damages does not extend to breaches of Article 5 although the government (via the appropriate minister) must be made a party to the proceedings when any court believes that it will be necessary to award damages under that section.[92]

5.2.4.4 Civil remedies

Assuming that a declaration of incompatibility is not required, what remedies are available when a court adjudicates? Section 8 does not limit the type of remedies available in civil matters and accordingly the full range of remedies are available to the court (discussed more extensively in Chapter 18). The actual remedy will depend on what action was being brought. Where, for example, it was anticipatory action then it is likely that the remedy sought will be an injunction preventing the breach from occurring. Where the action is because there is a belief that human rights already have been breached then it is likely that damages may be sought. That said, it is likely that in some instances a simple declaration would suffice—ie a statement by the judge that rights have been, or will be, infringed. Let us return to our earlier example of Robert (see 'Sword'). It will be remembered that the police wished to re-route his march. It is quite possible that Robert may seek an order quashing the decision of the police to re-route the march but it is also possible that a simple declaration by the judge that the actions would be illegal would suffice, with the police agreeing to respect the ruling.

Damages are perhaps the best-known form of civil remedy and the HRA 1998 does place some limitations on how these operate. The first rule is that only a court or tribunal that has the power to order damages may do so.[93] That may seem obvious, but not every court has the right to make damages, the most notable one being the Crown Court. The effect of s 8(2) would be to prevent the Crown Court, when making a finding that a person's human rights were infringed, ordering compensation (although the defendant could then initiate action in the civil courts which may be difficult to rebut).

The second issue in respect of damages is that the court can only award them if, after considering the other relief that it may order, it is satisfied that it is 'necessary to provide just satisfaction' in the case.[94] When deciding whether to award damages and, if so their quantum, the court must 'take into account the principles applied by the [ECtHR] in relation to the award of compensation under Article 41'.[95] This is an important principle as the ECtHR has adopted particular approaches to the granting of damages, including the fact that sometimes it will decline to provide any compensation beyond legal costs. This is because it sometimes believes, particularly

---

91. *Human Rights Act 1998*, s 9(3).
92. *Human Rights Act 1998*, s 9(4).
93. *Human Rights Act 1998*, s 8(2).
94. *Human Rights Act 1998*, s 8(3).
95. *Human Rights Act 1998*, s 8(4).

in procedural matters, that the mere finding that a person's rights have been infringed will amount to 'just satisfaction'. The ECtHR has also, on occasion, refused to grant compensation on the grounds of public policy although it does so only rarely, but this is something that the domestic courts should take into account.

≡ Example Denying compensation

A significant case where the ECtHR refused to order compensation was *McCann v United Kingdom*.[96] This was one of the most controversial cases before the ECtHR. Three terrorists were shot dead in Gibraltar by members of the Special Air Service. The soldiers believed that the suspects were carrying a remote detonator that would allow them to set off a large explosive device. In fact, there was neither a detonator nor a bomb, as the suspects were on a reconnaissance exercise. In a controversial judgment the ECtHR held that the actual shootings did not breach Article 2 but the circumstances leading up to it did breach Article 2. The Court (in a 10:9 majority decision) believed that there was insufficient planning to identify whether it was possible to arrest the suspects, ie in essence suggesting the plan was always to shoot dead the soldiers. Whilst the ECtHR found a breach of Article 2 it refused to award compensation to the relatives of the dead, in part because it was acknowledged that the three were intending to plant a bomb that was likely to cause death, injury, and significant damage.

Where damages are linked to financial loss the ECtHR will require proof that 'there is a causal link between the violation and any financial loss alleged'[97] and mere speculation will not suffice. As an example of circumstances when they will not find this link, it has been noted that loss of earnings from being imprisoned will not be compensated where a person succeeds in showing a breach of Article 6, the right to a fair trial.[98] Presumably the logic behind this is that it is not the unfair trial that caused the person to be imprisoned, it was the conduct that led to him being charged with an offence in the first place that was the cause (on that basis, where a person is imprisoned for a retrospective law that contravenes Article 7 of the ECHR it is possible that compensation would be awarded).

5.2.4.5 Remedies in criminal cases

It was noted earlier (5.2.2.3) that it is possible to use the HRA 1998 in criminal proceedings. Where a person is charged with a criminal offence what is the remedy for a breach of a Convention right? The HRA 1998 makes clear that it is possible to rely on the Convention as a defence and accordingly it may be possible, in extreme situations, to argue that a defendant should not be convicted as a result of the breach of the Convention but these will be relatively rare examples. More likely is that a serious breach of the Convention could lead to a successful argument that prosecuting the defendant would amount to an abuse of process and, accordingly, the prosecution should be halted. The House of Lords accepted that this could be the case, albeit *in obiter* and *per curiam* in the conjoined cases of *Attorney-General's Reference (No 3*

---

96. (2005) 42 EHRR 849.
97. David Harris et al, *Law of the European Convention on Human Rights* (3rd edn, OUP 2014) 859.
98. David Harris et al, *Law of the European Convention on Human Rights* (3rd edn, OUP 2014) 859.

of 2000); R v Looseley[99] where they accepted that the abuse-of-process doctrine was compatible with the ECHR. However, in a later decision the House stated quite clearly that it would be exceptional for breaches to halt criminal proceedings.

In *Attorney-General's Reference (No 2 of 2001)*[100] the House of Lords was called upon to consider the appropriate remedy in situations where there had been excessive delay in prosecuting defendants and bringing them before the courts for trial. Article 6(1) states a defendant has the right to a trial 'within a reasonable time' and the judge at first instance had stayed the trial arguing this was the appropriate remedy. The Attorney-General referred the matter to the appellate courts[101] and it eventually reached the House of Lords.

The House agreed that undue delay could breach Article 6(1) and argued that the 'clock' will normally start when a person is charged or summonsed before the court although this was not always the case as excessive delay between a formal interview and a charge may also be relevant. However, the House was dismissive of the idea that the only 'effective remedy' for undue delay is a stay of proceedings. Lord Bingham argued that remedies such as an acceleration of the timetable, the granting of bail, or even financial compensation might suffice.[102] His Lordship suggested that a stay should only be granted if the delay was so long that it would no longer be possible to guarantee a fair trial. The rationale behind this is that of proportionality: society has the right to expect protection from those who commit crimes and that where it is possible to do so fairly then a trial should continue. Lord Nicholls went further and argued that a stay would not be an effective remedy because it was against the wrong breach. His Lordship argued that normally the breach is not holding a trial after an excessive delay but rather not holding a trial in sufficient time. If, as the House believed, it is the latter then the trial is not unfair even if there has been a breach of Article 6. If the trial is not unfair then it cannot be an effective remedy to stay the trial. The House was leaving open the possibility that there could be circumstances in which holding a trial after excessive delay would be unfair (but that it is likely to be as a result of other factors, eg witness availability etc) and in those circumstances the effective remedy *may* be the stay of a trial.

It would seem therefore that the opportunities to use the HRA 1998 as a defence in criminal trials are now somewhat restricted although it has been suggested that this is not yet settled law and that the ECtHR itself has been taking a stricter line on procedural defects in trials, especially improper delay.[103] Ashworth appears to be arguing, therefore, that the ECtHR may suggest that delay may by itself lead to an unfair trial which would, following Lord Nicholls' argument, lead to the only effective remedy being a stay. It is notable that in the *Attorney-General's Reference* Lord Hope gave a strong dissenting judgment where he argued that it is not possible to detach the timing of the trial from the fairness of its execution[104] and that any delay that takes place after undue delay is necessarily a breach of the right to a fair trial. Lord Hope was alone in his views but if Ashworth is correct his analysis may find favour in the

99. [2001] 1 WLR 2060.
100. [2004] 2 AC 72.
101. An *Attorney-General's Reference* in this context is a hypothetical appeal whereby the appellate courts are asked a point of law that arises from an acquittal. It proceeds as though it were an appeal but the decision of the appellate courts does not alter the acquittal, it simply forms a precedent for future cases (see 16.4.1).
102. [2004] 2 AC 72, 89.
103. Andrew Ashworth, 'Delay in Criminal Proceedings: Unreasonable Delay (AG Ref (No 2 of 2001))' [2004] *Criminal Law Review* 574–6, 576.
104. [2004] 2 AC 72, 110.

ECtHR. Given that Article 13 is not within the HRA 1998 it is conceivable to see that a person convicted after undue delay but within Lord Bingham's reasoning could petition the ECtHR alleging a breach of Article 6 *and* a breach of Article 13. The ECtHR has no power to quash convictions but it could, presumably, state whether it thought that financial compensation or the granting of bail is an 'effective remedy' for the purposes of Article 6. Whether a domestic court would then follow that decision is perhaps more moot.

⟳ QUESTION FOR REFLECTION

What do you think the remedy should be where a person on trial claims that his human rights have been breached? Does it matter what right is claimed to be breached (eg substantive (such as a complaint that he was beaten in custody) or procedural (eg that he has been subject to unfair questioning))? A difficulty with human rights arguments is that just because a person's rights have been infringed does not mean that he did not commit the crime. Can it ever be justified to quash a conviction, or order a person's acquittal, because a suspect's human rights have been infringed?

5.3 The future of the Human Rights Act 1998

The HRA 1998 came into full force in 2000 and thus has been in effect for over a decade. Yet since the decision to introduce the legislation was first announced in 1997 it has been one of the most controversial pieces of legislation. The Conservative party have been very clear in their dislike of the legislation and much of the media, particularly those that are considered to be to the right of the political spectrum, share the desire to repeal the Act.

The dislike of the Act is nothing new and, speaking sometime after the commencement of the Act, Lord Irvine of Lairg, the then Lord Chancellor, stated:

> One commentator asked recently why the Human Rights Act is still disliked. It is a good question.[105]

If anything, the Act has become more controversial since that statement was made. The press, particularly the right-wing press, have a dislike of the Act which, in some publications, borders on hatred. Like health and safety legislation the press gleefully report stories of 'human rights violations' which generally are false, misinformation, or the product of a non-lawyer suggesting something that the legislation never contemplated. Health and Safety has been the bogeyman for several years (with (erroneous) stories of, for example, banning conker matches at school being prevalent) but human rights is catching up fast in terms of implausible stories.

The Conservative party, which did not vote against the HRA 1998 when introduced into Parliament, has picked up on this zeal and has latterly called for its repeal. In the 2005 general election campaign Michael Howard, the then leader, called for its repeal and this call was repeated in 2010 with the forming of the coalition government.

---

105.   Lord Irvine of Lairg, 'The Impact of the Human Rights Act: Parliament, the Courts and the Executive' [2003] *Public Law* 308–25, 324.

The presence of the Liberal Democrats in the coalition prevented the Conservative party from repealing the Act but it is clear that both the Conservative front and back benches desire change and the 2015 election saw the Conservative party again promise to replace the Act. It is an interesting change from the position in 1998 where there was some ambivalence and even in 2005 the whole of the front bench was not signed up to repeal, with Dominic Grieve MP, the then shadow Attorney-General (and who subsequently became Attorney-General in the coalition government) stating:

> The Human Rights Act has many benefits which it has conferred ... I don't think the ... Act has anything to do with fuelling a compensation culture at all.[106]

The suggestion that the HRA 1998 has fuelled the so-called compensation culture is one of the most prominent attacks against the Act although the reality is that claims-management firms (that are frequently managed by non-lawyers) are more likely to be responsible. Certainly by the time of the next general election Grieve had a change of heart (or was more politically on message) and campaigned for the repeal of the Act and the introduction, in its place, of a British Bill of Rights. Grieve, without any apparent irony, argued that the British courts were 'going further than Strasbourg and [showed] "a marked deference to Strasbourg"'. A principal source of irritation to Grieve was apparently the way that the courts had approached s 2 and he proposed rewording it to allow for UK-specific traditions whilst 'acknowledging the relevance of Strasbourg Court decisions'.[107] Quite how this will differ from s 2 is not explained. It is difficult to see why the courts, who have in essence had a free hand on how to interpret s 2 (as the statute is silent as to its meaning), would alter their approach.

Much of the criticism appears to be piggybacked onto the general Euroscepticism. The media, and indeed many MPs, fail to distinguish between the UK and the EU and thus the ECHR and the HRA 1998 are caught up in the ideology of reacting against 'Europe telling us what to do'. The fact that the ECHR is significantly older than the EU passes many by. A more interesting criticism is that the ECtHR is interfering in issues that were never contemplated at the time the Convention was written. This is arguably a stronger line of attack. There is no question that the ECHR, when drafted, was written to encapsulate a series of minimum standards of *fundamental* human rights. The ECtHR has undoubtedly broadened the scope of this instrument beyond that which the drafters would have contemplated, particularly in respect of social justice where issues such as same-sex rights and immigration matters have become increasingly important. That said, the ECtHR has been clear for some time that the Convention, unlike for example the US Constitution, is considered to be a 'living instrument'. US Constitutional interpretation is frequently based on ascertaining what the 'founding fathers' intended. The ECHR is not and arguably was never intended to be. There is no doubt that rights under the ECHR have shifted dramatically since the 1950s, most notably in respect of same-sex relationships. In earlier decisions of the ECtHR the court adopted a highly sceptical approach yet recently it has adopted an extremely liberal approach. The answer would seem to lie in the fact that society has progressed significantly. In the twenty-first century society expects that people are treated differently and this is particularly true of issues of sexuality where the

---

106. *The Times*, 30 March 2005, news (p 28).
107. Francesca Klug, 'Follow or Lead? The Human Rights Act and the European Court of Human Rights' [2010] 6 *European Human Rights Law Review* 621–30, 627.

expectation is now that gay, lesbian, and bisexual persons should enjoy the same rights as heterosexuals. This is an example of a seismic shift and when coupled with other social changes, most notably in the way that states deal with, for example, immigration, surveillance, or pre-trial detention, undoubtedly causes tension.

A popular attack on the HRA 1998 is that it has politicized judges. The issue of judicial independence will be considered elsewhere in this book (see Chapter 9) but it is clear that there is an argument that relations between the judiciary and government have suffered in recent years, although interestingly perhaps less so in the coalition period. During the New Labour governments attacks on the judiciary were not uncommon and much of this was based on the belief that the HRA 1998 had permitted judges to interfere in areas that were best left to either Parliament or the executive (government).

The question that is not easily answered is whether repealing the HRA 1998 would make any difference. Is it likely that the genie could be placed back in the bottle? Arguably judges have become more active in recent years although there is a debate as to what extent this is the fault of the HRA 1998 and not, for example, the common-law development of judicial review (although it must be conceded that the HRA 1998 has probably encouraged judges to become more active in the field of judicial review). If the HRA 1998 was abolished is it likely that the courts would simply stop holding the government to account or believe that the government has the right to act in a way that is incompatible with human rights? It is difficult to believe that this would ever be the case. Whilst the HRA 1998 can, of course, be repealed it is not clear that the judges would not just rely on the common law to fill the gap, at least in terms of fundamental rights.

The Conservative party has suggested replacing the HRA 1998 with a British Bill of Rights. In October 2014, the party published a strategy paper 'Protecting Human Rights in the UK', setting out their plan to repeal the HRA 1998 and replace it with a *British Bill of Rights and Responsibilities*. Their proposed reforms would put the text of the ECHR into statute whilst further clarifying the Convention rights to ensure that there is recognition that along with rights there are responsibilities. Although the Convention rights will still be used, the Conservative party is proposing to 'break the formal link between Britain and the ECHR', thus altering the relationship between domestic courts and the ECtHR. It is important to note, however, that the Conservative party is not proposing an automatic withdrawal from the Convention. Instead they are suggesting that they will work with the Council of Europe when passing the proposed *British Bill of Rights and Responsibilities* to reach agreement on the way in which the Convention rights will be enshrined in this Bill. It is only in the event that agreement cannot be reached that the Conservative party suggests that the UK would be forced to withdraw from the ECHR. Such a withdrawal from the ECHR would have wide-reaching international implications including withdrawal from both the Council of Europe and the EU. However, without formally withdrawing from the ECHR it is difficult to believe that the courts would simply 'turn back the clock' and act in the way they did before the HRA 1998 was passed. Indeed, arguably the HRA 1998 simply accelerated a trend that was already beginning and so turning the clock back fully would not happen.

David Cameron was relatively lukewarm on the need to withdraw from the ECtHR and the preparation for the 'British Bill of Rights' seemed to be kicked into the long grass. However, his successor as Prime Minister—Theresa May—has long been a critic of the ECtHR, in part because she saw it as thwarting some of her work as Home Secretary.

The vote to withdraw from the EU has undoubtedly meant that the government has little time to work out how to withdraw from the ECHR. Trying to withdraw from both institutions at the same time would take more resource than the government has. However, the Eurosceptic ascendancy has certainly led to renewed calls to withdraw from the ECHR and it will be interesting to see what the 2020 manifesto contains. That said, it is notable that many Conservative MPs do not wish to see withdrawal from the ECHR and therefore it may be (politically) more challenging than withdrawing from the EU.

5.4 The Convention Articles

In this section a very brief examination will be made of the key Convention rights. Not all rights will be discussed here but rather the ones you are most likely to read about. This section is designed to help you understand the basic principle of the Convention rights and how it may be used in practice.

5.4.1 General issues

Before considering the principal Convention rights there are two issues that must be briefly considered. The first relates to the difference between 'absolute' and 'qualified' rights and the other relates to 'positive' and 'negative' obligations.

5.4.1.1 Absolute and qualified rights

It is sometimes said that Articles can be divided into absolute and qualified rights, the latter being Articles that can be interfered with under certain circumstances. The ECtHR itself uses this language when referring to Articles 8–11, each of which is in two parts. The first part sets out what the right or freedom is, and the second part sets out the circumstances under which the state can interfere with this right.

However, some have suggested that this is too basic an analysis[108] and that all rights are subject to some qualifications. Certainly, as will be seen, there is an argument that this may be true. Article 2, the right to life, is often referred to as an 'absolute' right and yet on the face of the Article it states there are circumstances under which the state can kill and not infringe this right. Is this not a qualification? Similarly, other Articles do not appear to contain any qualification, eg Article 6 (right to fair trial), and yet the ECtHR has stated that this is not an absolute right.[109] That said, this is perhaps merely a recognition that there is no 'binary divide' between absolute and qualified rights but that each exists alongside other laws.

The term 'qualified right' will continue to be used in this text especially in relation to Articles 8–11 as this is the wording used by the Strasbourg authorities. This will be discussed further later.

---

108.   See, for example, Simon Atrill, 'Keeping the Executive in the Picture: A Reply to Professor Leigh' [2003] *Public Law* 41–51, 44.

109.   See, for example, *Condron v United Kingdom* (2001) 31 EHRR 1.

5.4.1.2 Positive and negative obligations

Article 1 of the ECHR requires states to 'secure to everyone in their jurisdiction the rights and freedoms [of the Convention]' and this has been construed to mean that some Articles will have a positive obligation on the state to secure the right. A negative obligation is quite standard and merely means that the state (in our case the United Kingdom) must not infringe the rights under the Convention. For example, therefore, this means that the state must not use torture on someone. However, certain Articles (most notably Articles 2, 3, and 8) also place a positive obligation on the state to *protect* a citizen from receiving such treatment.[110] Thus a state will not only be liable for actually infringing a right but also for allowing a private citizen to be harmed by another. That said, the positive obligation is not absolute and merely requires the state to take reasonable action and this includes, for example, ensuring that there are effective laws protecting an individual.[111] To this extent it can be said that there is a limited 'horizontal effect' to the ECHR and, therefore, the HRA 1998.

5.4.2 Article 2: The right to life

The first substantive right to consider is Article 2, which states:

1. Everyone's right to life shall be protected by law. No one shall be deprived of his life intentionally save in the execution of a sentence of a court following his conviction for a crime for which this penalty is provided by law.

2. Deprivation of life shall not be regarded as inflicted in contravention of this article when it results from the use of force which is no more than absolutely necessary:

   a. in defence of any person from unlawful violence;

   b. in order to effect a lawful arrest or to prevent escape of a person lawfully detained;

   c. in action lawfully taken for the purpose of quelling a riot or insurrection.

In England and Wales Article 2(1) could, in fact, be shortened by the deletion of the second sentence (beginning 'No one shall ...') because the United Kingdom has also signed the Sixth Protocol to the Convention which abolishes the death penalty[112] although theoretically it may be introduced to a limited extent in time of war.[113] Whether this means anything in practice is perhaps open to question since the last time the United Kingdom formally declared war was in the Second World War (all other military actions since then have been 'conflicts' not 'war', the latter bearing a particular definition in international law).

5.4.2.1 Positive obligation

Article 2 is a classic example of where a positive obligation arises. Not only does Article 2 prevent the state from killing someone, it has been held that 'everyone's right to life shall be protected by law' means that there is a positive obligation on the state to safeguard those who live within their jurisdiction.[114] This has been explained as

---

110.   See, for example, *Osman v United Kingdom* (2000) 29 EHRR 245.
111.   See, for example, *X and Y v Netherlands* (1986) 8 EHRR 235.
112.   Article 1 of the Sixth Protocol.
113.   Article 2 of the Sixth Protocol.
114.   *LCB v United Kingdom* (1999) 27 EHRR 212.

putting in place a legal framework that deters the commission of homicides but also a law enforcement mechanism to investigate and prosecute homicides.

The obligation to protect life does not mean that euthanasia must be criminalized[115] and this would seem to apply to both active and passive forms of euthanasia[116] and certainly some signatory states, most notably Switzerland, famously have euthanasia laws. What is clear, however, is that there is no right to die implicit within Article 2. Thus where a state does not permit euthanasia, Article 2 cannot be pleaded in an attempt to force the state to permit the ending of a life.

Perhaps the issue that has developed most significantly in recent years relates to the prevention of death. It was noted above that Article 2 includes a positive obligation and this has extended to situations where the state knows, or should know, that a danger exists.[117] The ECtHR has indicated, in particular, that this duty exists where a person is in the detention of the state.[118] The duty has also been considered to apply not only to homicides but also to suicides[119] and thus where the state is aware that a prisoner may commit suicide then they should take preventative measures. One of the more controversial aspects of this positive duty is that it also applies to the level of planning that can be expected from law enforcement operations, in particular there should be careful consideration of the circumstances when lethal force may arise (which, of course, is expressly contemplated by Article 2(2)) and a plan formulated that minimizes those circumstances.[120]

There is also a procedural aspect to Article 2 and it has been held that there should be an independent and effective investigation into any death that has been inflicted by the state or, where the state has breached the duty discussed earlier.[121] This procedural requirement has become increasingly important in recent years with cases discussing whether investigations into shootings by police officers conducted by the Independent Police Complaints Commission satisfy the requirements of Article 2.[122]

5.4.2.2 Use of lethal force

In terms of the circumstances under which lethal force can be contemplated, ie those set out in Article 2(2), it is unlikely that this will cause too many difficulties in the domestic context and it is very similar to domestic law under s 3 *Criminal Law Act 1967* although there is a subtle difference of wording between s 3 and Article 2(2)(a).

5.4.3 Article 3: Prohibition of torture

Article 3 is the shortest of all the Convention articles:

No one shall be subjected to torture or inhuman or degrading treatment or punishment.

This is another absolute right and one that contains a positive obligation on states, ie not only must it not subject somebody to torture, inhuman, or degrading treatment,

---

115.   *Widmer v Switzerland* App No 20527/92 (1993).
116.   See the discussion in *Pretty v United Kingdom* (2002) 35 EHRR 1.
117.   See, most notably, *Osman v United Kingdom* (2000) 29 EHRR 245.
118.   See, for example, *Edwards v UK* (2002) 35 EHRR 487 where a prisoner was killed by another prisoner in circumstances where an attack was possible.
119.   *Keenan v United Kingdom* (2001) 33 EHRR 38.
120.   *McCann v United Kingdom* (1996) 21 EHRR 97.
121.   See, for example, *Jordan v United Kingdom* (2003) 37 EHRR 2.
122.   See, for example, *Saunders and another v IPCC and others* [2008] EWHC 2372 (Admin) which raised questions about the practice of allowing police officers to confer before making their statements.

it must protect the person suffering this from others. Some uncertainty arose as to what the difference in wording was but in *Ireland v United Kingdom*[123] the ECtHR defined the terms. The case followed accusations of mistreatment by the security force in Northern Ireland of suspected terrorists. The Court found that whilst no suspect had been tortured, they had suffered inhuman and degrading treatment, the Court believing that torture involved 'deliberate inhuman treatment causing very serious and cruel suffering' (p 80).

In order for a treatment or punishment to amount to either degrading or inhuman treatment it must pass a minimum threshold of severity[124] since not every type of shameful treatment will amount to a breach of Article 3. That said, this is not to say that it is not actionable since it is possible action could be brought under the right to personal integrity under Article 8 (see 5.4.7). One of the principal battlegrounds in relation to Article 3 is the concept of corporal punishment, with the European Court reaching different conclusions as to its compatibility with Article 3.[125]

Outside of corporal punishment it has been suggested that a respective imbalance in power may lead to the threshold being passed, and accordingly abuse that takes place by law enforcement agencies while a suspect is within their custody is likely to constitute a breach of Article 3.[126]

Sexual assault will almost certainly pass the threshold for Article 3, not least because of the psychological issues that arise in respect of any sexual assault. This is most relevant in the context of the positive obligation placed on states and means that they must have appropriate and effective laws in place to criminalize sexual assaults and ensure they are appropriately investigated.[127] In the (hopefully exceptional) circumstances where a prisoner is sexually assaulted by a state agent this will almost automatically lead to a breach of Article 3.[128]

5.4.4 Article 5: Right to liberty

Article 5 is an important Article within the ECHR as it governs protection from, inter alia, arbitrary arrest. Its form is as follows:

1. Everyone has the right to liberty and security of person. No one shall be deprived of his liberty save in the following cases and in accordance with a procedure prescribed by law:

    (a) the lawful detention of a person after conviction by a competent court;

    (b) the lawful arrest or detention of a person for non-compliance with the lawful order of a court or in order to secure the fulfilment of any obligation prescribed by law;

    (c) the lawful arrest or detention of a person effected for the purpose of bringing him before the competent legal authority on reasonable suspicion of having committed an offence or when it is reasonably considered necessary to prevent his committing an offence or fleeing after having done so;

123. (1979–80) 2 EHRR 25.
124. See *Costello-Roberts v United Kingdom* (1995) 19 EHRR 112.
125. See *Costello-Roberts v United Kingdom* (1995); cf *A v United Kingdom* (1999) 27 EHRR 611.
126. See, for example, *Selmouni v France* (2000) 29 EHRR 403.
127. See *X and Y v Netherlands* (1986) 8 EHRR 235.
128. *Aydin v Turkey* (1998) 25 EHRR 251.

(d) the detention of a minor by lawful order for the purpose of educational supervision or his lawful detention for the purpose of bringing him before the competent legal authority;

(e) the lawful detention of persons for the prevention of the spreading of infectious diseases, of persons of unsound mind, alcoholics or drug addicts or vagrants;

(f) the lawful arrest or detention of a person to prevent his effecting an unauthorised entry into the country or of a person against whom action is being taken with a view to deportation or extradition.

2. Everyone who is arrested shall be informed promptly, in a language which he understands, of the reasons for his arrest and of any charge against him.

3. Everyone arrested or detained in accordance with the provisions of paragraph 1.c of this article shall be brought promptly before a judge or other officer authorised by law to exercise judicial power and shall be entitled to trial within a reasonable time or to release pending trial. Release may be conditioned by guarantees to appear for trial.

4. Everyone who is deprived of his liberty by arrest or detention shall be entitled to take proceedings by which the lawfulness of his detention shall be decided speedily by a court and his release ordered if the detention is not lawful.

5. Everyone who has been the victim of arrest or detention in contravention of the provisions of this article shall have an enforceable right to compensation.

It can be seen that this is a very long article and accordingly only certain parts of the article will be considered. If you study *Civil Liberties*, *Human Rights*, or some *Public Law* modules then you are likely to spend considerable time examining this article because it is a crucial feature of the relationship between the state and the citizen in terms of restricting liberty.

Article 5 provides the circumstances in which a person can be deprived of liberty. It is sometimes said that it provides protection from arbitrary arrest but this is not necessarily true since Article 5 will be engaged only if the arrest leads to a person's liberty being removed, although this could include being prevented from leaving the scene of arrest. Also, Article 5 does not necessarily provide administrative safeguards after arrest as certain aspects (eg police interviews) are to be found in other Convention Articles (eg Article 6).

That said, arrest is arguably the most important frequently used part of Article 5, and Article 5(1)(c) provides that this may be lawful but only where a person is brought before 'the competent legal authority'. It is not immediately clear from the face of Article 5 what this means but in England and Wales the first person a suspect will face is a custody sergeant, a police officer, who will decide whether to authorize his detention.[129] An inspector will then decide whether to continue detention after nine hours[130] and finally a superintendent can take the decision to extend the time, for certain offences, to thirty-six hours in exceptional circumstances.[131] After this time has elapsed the police have two options open to them. They either release the offender or they bring the offender before a magistrate. It is clear that this is the competent authority to whom Article 5(1)(c) refers. Article 5(2) and 5(3) then provide additional

129. *Police and Criminal Evidence Act 1984*, s 37.
130. *Police and Criminal Evidence Act 1984*, s 40.
131. *Police and Criminal Evidence Act 1984*, s 42.

safeguards such as knowing why a person has been arrested and that he should be brought before a judge, which would appear to be an overlap with Article 5(1)(c) but it is clear that the primary purpose of Article 5(3) is dealing with securing liberty rather than the purpose of the arrest. Article 5(3) therefore provides that a person should either be brought before a court or granted bail. It is important to note, however, that it is possible for bail to be subject to conditions. In the early days of the HRA 1998 this had caused some difficulties with some lawyers suggesting that conditional bail was an infringement of human rights but this was quite clearly a misreading of the legal position.[132]

An important aspect of Article 5 is to provide a mechanism for securing liberty. This is to be found in Article 5(4)–(5). This provides that everyone shall have the right to petition a court to question the appropriateness of any detention and that where any detention is found to be unlawful there should be an automatic right to compensation. To an extent this may be thought comparable to the procedure known as habeas corpus but it is an important safeguard.

5.4.5 Article 6: Right to a fair trial

One of the most important rights in the Convention and certainly one of the most quoted is Article 6 of the ECHR. This provides:

1. In the determination of his civil rights and obligations or of any criminal charge against him, everyone is entitled to a fair and public hearing within a reasonable time by an independent and impartial tribunal established by law. Judgment shall be pronounced publicly but the press and public may be excluded from all or part of the trial in the interests of morals, public order or national security in a democratic society, where the interests of juveniles or the protection of the private life of the parties so require, or to the extent strictly necessary in the opinion of the court in special circumstances where publicity would prejudice the interests of justice.

2. Everyone charged with a criminal offence shall be presumed innocent until proved guilty according to law.

3. Everyone charged with a criminal offence has the following minimum rights:

    (a) to be informed promptly, in a language which he understands and in detail, of the nature and cause of the accusation against him;

    (b) to have adequate time and facilities for the preparation of his defence;

    (c) to defend himself in person or through legal assistance of his own choosing or, if he has not sufficient means to pay for legal assistance, to be given it free when the interests of justice so require;

    (d) to examine or have examined witnesses against him and to obtain the attendance and examination of witnesses on his behalf under the same conditions as witnesses against him;

    (e) to have the free assistance of an interpreter if he cannot understand or speak the language used in court.

Entire books have been produced on Article 6 and this discussion will be brief and only consider some of the core elements of the Article. However, this is an issue that

---

132.   Alisdair Gillespie 'Curfew and Bail' (2001) 151 *New Law Journal* 465–6.

you will return to throughout your legal studies as the concept of a fair trial goes to the very heart of due process in the law.

The key words of the Article are actually its marginal note, and the ECtHR will frequently consider everything holistically and balance matters against the 'right to a fair trial' rather than focus on the individual rights. It should be noted that Article 6 applies to both civil and criminal matters although from the wording it is clear that most guarantees exist in respect of criminal trials. It is also important to note that 'in the determination of his civil rights and obligations' does not mean every civil matter will come within Article 6 and issues such as the treatment of state employees have been considered to be outside the scope of Article 6.[133]

In terms of its application to criminal law it can probably be said that the most important aspects of the Article are the 'independent and impartial tribunal',[134] the presumption of innocence,[135] the ability to defend oneself in court,[136] and an implicit doctrine known as the 'equality of arms'.

5.4.5.1 Independent and impartial tribunal

It may be thought that in a system of justice this would not be overly problematic but Article 6 has had a significant impact on how decisions relating to individuals are adjudicated. However, this has been an area of fruitful litigation for some time. Article 6 has had significant impact on how judges are appointed, particularly part-time judges, something most notable in the decision *McGonnell v United Kingdom*.[137] In Scotland the judicial system was placed under severe pressure when it was decided that part-time judges were not independent or impartial because of the manner in which they were appointed,[138] something that although not directly applicable to England led to the Lord Chancellor deciding that he would alter the way in which Recorders were appointed (see Chapter 9).

The same argument led to fundamental changes in the way that courts martial (ie judicial tribunals set up to adjudicate the law relating to serving members of HM Forces) were administered. The ECtHR has long had difficulties with the system of courts martial, not least because the judge and jury used to be all members of the armed services.[139] Eventually civilian judges were introduced to solve this problem[140] but it eventually culminated in new legislation being required to administer service justice.[141]

The most controversial application of this doctrine was, however, undoubtedly in relation to how those convicted of murder were sentenced. There is only one sentence that can be imposed for the crime of murder; that of life imprisonment (adult defendant) or detention for life (young offender). However, the Home Secretary decided how long a person should stay in prison by having the final say over the tariff.

---

133. See, for example, *Lombardo v Italy* (1996) 21 EHRR 188.
134. *European Convention on Human Rights*, Art 6(1).
135. *European Convention on Human Rights*, Art 6(2).
136. *European Convention on Human Rights*, Art 6(3)(b)–(d).
137. (2000) 30 EHRR 289.
138. *Davidson v Scottish Ministers (No 2)* [2004] UKHL 34.
139. *Morris v United Kingdom* (2002) 34 EHRR 52.
140. *Cooper v United Kingdom* (2004) 39 EHRR 8.
141. *Armed Forces Act 2006*.

TARIFF

Although a person is sentenced to life imprisonment it is extremely rare for a person to spend the rest of their life in prison. There is a system of early release which allows prisoners to be released 'on licence' (ie to be on good behaviour). Where a life sentence has been imposed then the minimum period before which a person can be considered for release is known as the tariff. After this period has expired the Parole Board will decide whether a person should be released or not.

The first case to call into question the appropriateness of a politician having this power was that of *T v United Kingdom; V v United Kingdom*.[142] This was the case concerning the killers of Jamie Bulger. 'T' and 'V' were boys aged ten years when they abducted and killed Jamie Bulger, a two-year-old boy. The crime was controversial for a whole series of reasons but one important aspect of the case was that the ECtHR held that it was wrong for a politician to decide how long the boys should spend in prison, suggesting that this should be a judicial and not political function. This eventually culminated in *R (on the application of Anderson) v Secretary of State for the Home Office*[143] in which the House of Lords held that the Home Secretary should not have any say in the setting of *any* tariff, including those for adult offenders. The decision was hugely controversial with the then current and previous Home Secretaries arguing that it should not be a purely judicial factor as society (through the political process) should also have the right to a say in how long its worst prisoners spend in gaol. However, ultimately the rule of law prevailed and the *Criminal Justice Act 2003* gave ultimate responsibility for the setting of tariffs to the judiciary.

5.4.5.2 **Presumption of innocence**

The presumption of innocence has always featured as an inherent part of the English Legal System but Article 6(2) expressly makes reference to this. However, the ECtHR is prepared to go much further than this and have held that the presumption of innocence applies even where Article 6(2) does not. Article 6(2) relates to a 'criminal charge' and thus where a person is no longer charged (because, for example, he has been convicted of the offence) then Article 6(2) would not apply. This was relevant in *Philips v United Kingdom*[144] which concerned a confiscation order made after a person had been convicted of trafficking drugs. Article 6(2) could not apply because he was no longer the subject of a criminal charge but the ECtHR held that the 'right to a fair trial' within Article 6(1) also included the presumption of innocence.

The main source of conflict in relation to Article 6(2) in the UK context has been in respect of the privilege against self-incrimination and the so-called 'right to silence'. At one point, suspects who were interviewed by the police were able to remain silent when questioned and nothing could be drawn from that silence. However, the *Criminal Justice and Public Order Act 1994* introduced the system of adverse inferences, meaning that where a person remains silent but then testifies at court with a statement that seeks to indicate why they did not commit the offence, the jury can take into account the fact that the person remained silent at the time of questioning. In *Murray v United*

---

142. (2000) 30 EHRR 121.
143. [2003] 1 AC 837.
144. [2001] Crim LR 817.

Kingdom[145] and *Condron v United Kingdom*[146] the ECtHR held that this did not amount to an infringement of the presumption of innocence under either Article 6(1) or Article 6(2).

Another source of controversy is domestic laws that seek to reverse the burden of proof. This was discussed earlier in the context of drugs[147] but deserves brief attention here. One of the most prominent cases dealing with this point is *Salabiaku v France*[148] which concerned French legislation about the smuggling of prohibited drugs. The legislation stated that someone who was in actual possession of goods while entering the country was presumed to be smuggling them unless they could prove to the contrary. This was challenged but the ECtHR held that it did not infringe Article 6(2) because the prosecution still had to prove key elements (most notably, possession of the goods, that the goods were illegal, and that the person brought them into the country) and thus the majority of the offence still needs to be proved, it was simply a presumption that could be rebutted by adducing evidence.

5.4.5.3 The right to defend oneself

Article 6(3) provides a series of steps that are designed to allow a person to defend himself when accused of committing a crime. However, in certain offences, most notably sex offences, a tension exists between allowing a person to present a rigorous defence and also ensuring that the victim of a crime is not put through unnecessary distress. This tension has already been examined earlier in this book in the context of statutory interpretation[149] and it will also be examined in later chapters when we look at the course of a criminal trial where this specific issue has been discussed extensively by the courts.

The right to defend oneself is either in person or through the provision of a lawyer. A person should ordinarily be allowed to attend proceedings against him but it is clear that legal representation should ordinarily be permitted. In *Campbell and Fell v United Kingdom*[150] the ECtHR declared there was a breach of Article 6(3) when prisoners, who refused to attend a prison disciplinary panel, were also not permitted to send lawyers in their place. Article 6(3)(c) also encapsulates a right to legal aid, although only where a person lacks 'sufficient means' (which is not defined). The second qualification to this is that it must 'be in the interests of justice to do so' which implies that not all cases will require legally aided representation, and certainly it has been held that where the maximum sentence for an offence was a modest fine legal aid was not necessary.[151] In *Granger v United Kingdom*[152] the ECtHR found a breach where an appeal was more complicated than was initially thought. Presumably the complexity meant that it was unreasonable to expect a layperson (the appellant) to be capable of arguing the appeal without expert legal assistance.

145. (1996) 22 EHRR 29.
146. (2001) 31 EHRR 1.
147. *R v Lambert* [2001] UKHL 37.
148. (1991) 13 EHRR 379.
149. See *R v A (No 2)* [2002] 1 AC 45 and see 2.3.4.
150. (1985) 7 EHRR 165.
151. *Gutfreund v France* (2006) 42 EHRR 48.
152. (1990) 12 EHRR 469.

5.4.5.4 **Equality of arms**

One of the central features of Article 6(1) is that the ECtHR has held that there must be an 'equality of arms'[153] (and this applies to both civil and criminal cases). Put simply it means that the parties should be given reasonable opportunity to present their case in circumstances that do not put them at an obvious disadvantage to their opponent. The principal effect of this is to ensure, so far as possible, the neutrality of procedural issues and the opportunities of sides to adduce expert evidence, particularly in rebuttal.

5.4.6 **Article 7: No punishment without law**

Article 7 of the ECHR is particularly important within the criminal context. It provides:

1. No one shall be held guilty of any criminal offence on account of any act or omission which did not constitute a criminal offence under national or international law at the time when it was committed. Nor shall a heavier penalty be imposed than the one that was applicable at the time the criminal offence was committed.

2. This article shall not prejudice the trial and punishment of any person for any act or omission which, at the time when it was committed, was criminal according to the general principles of law recognised by civilised nations.

Whilst there are many issues enveloped within Article 7, the most important is that criminal offences should not be retrospective. It has already been noted that whilst Parliament is competent to legislate as it sees fit, there is a convention that it will not create retrospective criminal offences (see 2.3.6.4). This rule undoubtedly pre-dates Article 7 but following the introduction of the HRA 1998 it continues to be an extremely important principle by which Parliament must be guided.

Although Article 7 prevents retrospective punishment it is important to note that the Article does not prevent the interpretation of the law evolving through time. Perhaps the most important example of this is in respect of marital rape.

Example Marital rape

Historically the law had taken the approach that a man could not be guilty of raping his wife. This approach was based on the fact that the contract of marriage included the right to conjugal relations. The rule was widely condemned and eventually in *R v R*[154] the House of Lords held that the rule no longer had any role in modern society.

This ruling led to the appellant's conviction for rape being upheld along with his custodial sentence. He petitioned the ECtHR arguing that this ruling contravened Article 7. His argument was that at the time of the rape the law had recognized a marital exemption and that the House of Lords decision had therefore turned a lawful act into an unlawful act retrospectively. In *SW v United Kingdom*[155] the ECtHR dismissed this argument suggesting that all the House of Lords had done was evolved the law and made it applicable to contemporary society. They also held that this evolution was predictable and thus was not retrospective.

---

153.   See, most notably, *Neumeister v Austria* (1979–80) 1 EHRR 91.
154.   [1992] 1 AC 599.
155.   (1996) 21 EHRR 363.

An important restriction of Article 7 is that it applies only to criminal penalties. This has caused some debate where governments seek to introduce preventative measures on certain offenders. Perhaps the classic example of this in the context of the UK was the introduction of sex offender notification requirements (aka 'sex offender register'). In 1997 the UK government introduced a system whereby those who were cautioned or convicted of certain offences were required to notify their name and address to the police and also to notify any changes, including being away from their house for a specified period of time.[156] The Act applied to all those cautioned and convicted on the date it came into force but it also applied to those who had been convicted prior to the date it came into force and had not yet been released. In *Ibbotson v United Kingdom*[157] the ECmHR (which was still in existence at the time) declared the application inadmissible holding that the scheme was not a punishment within the meaning of Article 7.[158]

A second use of Article 7 tends to focus on the 'quality of the law'. It has been held that a law is required to be accessible to allow a person to appreciate that they are transgressing the law. Article 7 is taken to mean that a law should be defined with such precision that a person can identify whether they are committing a criminal act.[159] Some crimes in England and Wales remain creatures of the common law, ie they are not set out anywhere in statute and only exist through the definitions established by the courts. It has been argued before that such crimes may fall foul of Article 7 although the courts remain sceptical of this argument and rarely entertain such applications.[160]

5.4.7 Article 8: Right to respect for private life

Alongside Article 6, Article 8 is one of the more popular rights that is litigated under the Convention. It provides:

1. Everyone has the right to respect for his private and family life, his home and his correspondence.

2. There shall be no interference by a public authority with the exercise of this right except such as is in accordance with the law and is necessary in a democratic society in the interests of national security, public safety or the economic well-being of the country, for the prevention of disorder or crime, for the protection of health or morals, or for the protection of the rights and freedoms of others.

This is the first of the 'qualified rights' and it can be seen immediately that the qualification is contained in Article 8(2). Article 8(1) sets out the right, and Article 8(2) states the circumstances under which the right can be infringed.

As with Article 6, entire books have been produced just on the meaning of Article 8 and this is another right that you will come across throughout your legal studies, including in modules such as *Land Law, Equity and Trusts, Medical Law*, etc.

5.4.7.1 Not just private life

Article 8 is often referred to as the right to respect for private life yet Article 8(1) makes clear that a person has the right to respect for:

156. *Sex Offenders Act 1997* now contained within *Sexual Offences Act 2003*, pt 2.
157. (1999) 27 EHRR CD 332.
158. Something confirmed by the ECtHR in *Adamson v United Kingdom* (1999) 28 EHRR CD 209.
159. See, for example, *R v Rimmington* [2005] UKHL 63 (relating to the offence of public nuisance).
160. An interesting example of this can be seen in *R v Norman* [2016] EWCA Crim 1564 [47]–[49].

- private life
- family life
- home
- correspondence.

Not infrequently these will be subsumed within the concept of 'private life' but it is important to note that this need not be the case and, for example, correspondence can be a significant issue for prisoners. The ECtHR has held that it is not appropriate for prisoners' correspondence to be routinely intercepted[161] although it does accept that where there is a pressing need to do so, this can be justified (ie it will allow Article 8(2) to apply) although the limits of such interference will be strictly considered.[162]

The ECtHR has consistently stated that the purpose of Article 8 is to protect an individual from arbitrary interference with a person's rights by the state[163] and this takes on a series of forms. Perhaps one of the most significant in recent years has been in regulating surveillance. The United Kingdom traditionally operated on the basis that because the law did not state that public authorities could not put somebody under surveillance, they were free to do so[164] whereas the ECtHR argues the opposite is true under the Convention. Accordingly a legal basis must exist under which Article 8 can be interfered with[165] and this law must be readily accessible with appropriate legal (rather than administrative) safeguards against abuse of authorities.[166] Within the context of surveillance this led to the enactment of the *Regulation of Investigatory Powers Act 2000*.

5.4.7.2 **Positive obligation**

Article 8, like Articles 2 and 3, contains both a positive and a negative obligation. This means that the state should not only ensure that they do not infringe Article 8 themselves but also ensure that they protect individuals from having their Article 8 rights infringed by others. A good example of this can be seen from *Moreno Gomez v Spain*[167] where the ECtHR considered that the positive obligation meant that the impact of noise and smells must be considered when deciding whether to grant a licence to a night club within a residential area.

More significantly, the positive obligation also gives rise to the right to physical integrity and accordingly treatment that is below the minimum threshold for Article 3 (see 5.2.3.2) may come within Article 8.[168] In *Pretty v United Kingdom*[169] the ECtHR confirmed that 'private life' is a broad concept that cannot be precisely defined but that it covered, in essence, the respect for human dignity. The ECtHR conceded that whilst no right to suicide could be included within Article 2, it may be possible to infer a limited right under Article 8 but it also held that a blanket ban on assisted suicide could be justified under Article 8(2).

---

161.   *Valasinas v Lithuania* App No 44558/98.
162.   *Foxley v United Kingdom* (2001) 31 EHRR 25.
163.   See, for example, *Glaser v United Kingdom* (2001) 33 EHRR 1 [63].
164.   See, for example, *Malone v Commissioner of Police for the Metropolis (No 2)* [1979] Ch 44.
165.   *Malone v United Kingdom* (1985) 7 EHRR 14.
166.   *Govell v United Kingdom* (1997) 23 EHRR CD101.
167.   (2005) 41 EHRR 40.
168.   See *X and Y v Netherlands* (1986) 8 EHRR 235.
169.   (2002) 35 EHRR 1.

5.4.8 Article 10: Freedom of expression

Although Article 10 is a qualified right it has been said that freedom of expression is the bedrock upon which a democracy is built[170] and it is accordingly one of the most important Convention Articles. It provides:

1. Everyone has the right to freedom of expression. This right shall include freedom to hold opinions and to receive and impart information and ideas without interference by public authority and regardless of frontiers. This article shall not prevent States from requiring the licensing of broadcasting, television or cinema enterprises.

2. The exercise of these freedoms, since it carries with it duties and responsibilities, may be subject to such formalities, conditions, restrictions or penalties as are prescribed by law and are necessary in a democratic society, in the interests of national security, territorial integrity or public safety, for the prevention of disorder or crime, for the protection of health or morals, for the protection of the reputation or rights of others, for preventing the disclosure of information received in confidence, or for maintaining the authority and impartiality of the judiciary.

Article 10 is, in essence, the Convention equivalent of the right to free speech although it has a much wider remit than this. Together with Article 11 (see 5.4.9) it is the primary right to allow protests. This is another Article that you will encounter throughout your legal study and particularly in modules such as *Public Law*, *Constitutional Law*, or *Civil Liberties*.

The classic case examining Article 10 was *Sunday Times v United Kingdom*[171] which was also known as the 'Spycatcher case'. The ECtHR made clear that Article 10 should be interfered with only when strictly necessary to do so and that where the press were concerned the proportionality was raised further because the press acts as the 'public's watchdog'.[172] This is undoubtedly recognition of the fact that totalitarian states will frequently control the press and that one of the easiest ways of controlling the public is to place restrictions on the press.

194

⦂ Example Spycatcher

In 1985 a former member of MI5 (now the Security Services) sought to publish a memoir of his time within MI5. This was unprecedented as it provided operational details of his work within what was, at that time, still a secret service (indeed MI5 was not officially recognized until the enactment of the Security Service Act 1989). This included allegations that MI5 had bugged embassies, and also allegations that it and its sister service MI6 (now the Secret Intelligence Service) planned assassinations.

The book was immediately banned in the United Kingdom although ultimately certain newspapers, most notably *The Sunday Times*, tried to serialize the book. Injunctions were taken out restraining publication and when these were breached contempt of court proceedings were initiated. *The Sunday Times*, and others, alleged that this was a breach of Article 10 of the ECHR, something that the ECtHR ultimately agreed with.

---

170. *Bowman v United Kingdom* (1998) 26 EHRR 1.
171. (1992) 14 EHRR 229.
172. (1992) 14 EHRR 229 [50].

The book received official clearance in 1988 when it was accepted that it had been serialized and published so widely around the world that it was illogical to ban sale in the United Kingdom especially since many copies had legitimately been imported from abroad.

However, Article 10 should not be considered merely a tool of the press and it is extremely important within the context of personal protests. Perhaps one of the most important statements came in the case of *Redmond-Bate v DPP*[173] in which Sedley LJ said:

Free speech includes not only the inoffensive but the irritating, the contentious and the eccentric, the heretical, the unwelcome and the provocative provided it does not tend to provoke violence. Freedom only to speak inoffensively is not worth having.[174]

This is an important point and one undoubtedly within the spirit of Article 10. That said, however, it is also important to note that Article 10 is not absolute. Sedley LJ expressly considered that speech that tended to provoke violence would fall outside of his scope and Article 10(2) expressly considers qualifications in other situations. Perhaps the most controversial is 'morals' since this can be used to disguise a multitude of possibilities.

The leading case on the use of 'morals' as a qualification is *Handyside v United Kingdom*[175] where the ECtHR stated that it was not possible to identify a single moral basis across all contracting states.[176] Accordingly the Court would extend a 'margin of appreciation' to the individual states meaning that they would enjoy discretion to decide the moral standpoint of their society. However, the Court was also clear that the ECtHR had a supervisory role in ensuring that the application of this margin together with any restrictions placed on expression by the contracting states were strictly necessary. In the context of morals this must also take into account that society evolves and that something which may infringe society's standards at one point in time may not do so later.

5.4.9 Article 11: Freedom of assembly

Article 11 is another key provision within the Convention and can be considered a fundamental principle of democracy. Alongside Article 10 it governs the right to protest but it also has a wider remit. The provisions of Article 11 are:

1. Everyone has the right to freedom of peaceful assembly and to freedom of association with others, including the right to form and to join trade unions for the protection of his interests.

2. No restrictions shall be placed on the exercise of these rights other than such as are prescribed by law and are necessary in a democratic society in the interests of national security or public safety, for the prevention of disorder or crime, for the protection of health or morals or for the protection of the rights and freedoms of others. This article shall not prevent the imposition of lawful restrictions on the exercise of these rights by members of the armed forces, of the police or of the administration of the State.

173. [2000] HRLR 249.
174. [2000] HRLR 249, 260.
175. (1979–80) 1 EHRR 737.
176. (1979–80) 1 EHRR 737 [48].

195

It can be seen that Article 11 is concerned with the right to be associated with others, either by assembly (eg a demonstration) or to join organizations and unions. However, it is important to note that this is a qualified right and that the right to join is not universal. The final sentence makes clear that Article 11 may not extend to agents of the executive, particularly in respect of the police and armed forces. Given the nature of these agencies it is understandable that restrictions may need to be put in place to ensure the smooth operation of these important bodies. In the United Kingdom this exception has been used with the police and members of HM Forces being denied the right to join a union. As regards the police there are other bodies that fulfil some of the responsibilities of unions (the Police Federation for officers up to and including the rank of chief inspector, the Superintendents' Association for officers of the rank of superintendent and chief superintendent, and the Association of Chief Police Officers for those of chief officer rank) but their responsibilities are curtailed and the police are not allowed to strike. This rule has also been used to justify restrictions on political activity for certain posts within local authorities.[177]

However, perhaps the more usual manner of engaging Article 11 is in respect of peaceful assembly. It can be seen from the very wording of Article 11(1) that the right only exists to peaceful protest and it follows therefore that where violence is likely then interferences may be possible. That said, issues of proportionality and necessity arise and, if at all possible, the state should try to minimize disruption rather than prevent assembly as a whole.

> ### Example Parades Commission
>
> We have already discussed the issue of the Parades Commission in Northern Ireland (see 'Necessity and proportionality') but this is also a classic example of the balance to be drawn under Article 11. The parades undertaken by Loyalist members of the Northern Ireland community are extremely controversial especially when routed through or near to Nationalist areas of the Province. There has been a long history of violence breaking out on such parades. However, the Parades Commission does not find it necessary to ban such assemblies but rather it exercises its powers to re-route the parades in order to minimize violence.[178]

5.4.10 Article 17

An important but often neglected Article within the Convention is Article 17 which prohibits abuse of the Convention itself. Article 17 is not an independent Article, in that it cannot be the sole subject of litigation but is instead used in combination with other Articles. It is particularly of importance to Articles 10 and 11. Article 17 provides:

> Nothing in this Convention may be interpreted as implying for any State, group or person any right to engage in any activity or perform any act aimed at the destruction of any of the rights and freedoms set forth herein or at their limitation to a greater extent than is provided for in the Convention.

177. See *Ahmed and others v United Kingdom* (2000) 29 EHRR 1.
178. See *Re Tweed's Application for Judicial Review* [2001] NI 165.

The essence of this right is that one cannot rely on the Convention in order to undermine the rights of others. The classic example of this would be in respect of Articles 10 and 11 where someone may wish to join a racist organization that has as its purpose the undermining of the rights of others due solely to their colour. The Convention will not allow such matters because the right claimed is an affront to the rights and freedoms contained within the Convention.

Case Box *Glimmerveen and Hagenback v Netherlands*

In *Glimmerveen and Hagenback v Netherlands*[179] the applicants had been convicted under Dutch law of distributing leaflets that were racist in character and called for the creation of a white state. The European Commission on Human Rights said: 'the general purpose of Article 17 is to prevent totalitarian groups from exploiting in their own interests the principles enunciated by the Convention.'[180] It dismissed the applicants' contention that Article 10 protected their right to distribute the leaflets on the basis that they were seeking to use Article 10 in such a way as to undermine the rights and freedoms of others and thus Article 17 applied.

It is right that the ECHR contains such a provision although it is important that those who interpret the Convention do not abuse the power given to them under Article 17 since the rights under Articles 10–11 do include the right to be unpopular and offensive. However, where the rights claimed seek to undermine the rights of others it is quite clear that this should be stopped.

197

Summary

The *Human Rights Act 1998* is an extremely important instrument and it is one that you will encounter throughout your law studies and your career. In this chapter we have noted:

- Public bodies have a duty to act compatibly with the Convention. This is a *civil* and not *criminal* duty.
- Defining a public authority is not easy although all courts and tribunals are automatically covered.
- Public authorities tend to be divided into 'pure' public bodies (eg the police, prison service, local authorities etc) and 'hybrid' public authorities (eg universities).
- The courts are given a wide discretion in interpreting the legislation to ensure that it is compliant with the Convention and they may also interpret the legislation itself.
- The definition of a victim in the *Human Rights Act 1998* is more restricted than, for example, judicial review procedures but this is in line with the ECHR itself.
- Article 13 (right to an effective remedy) is not contained within the HRA 1998. There are competing arguments as to whether the HRA 1998 is itself a response to Article 13 or whether this means rights in the UK are not as protected.

179.   (1982) 4 EHRR 260.
180.   (1982) 4 EHRR 260, 267.

- Certain rights contain a *positive obligation* on the state. This means that not only must the state ensure that it does not breach the right, it must also ensure that it can protect its citizens from others infringing their right. The most obvious example of this is Article 2 where a state must protect its citizens where there is a known risk of harm.

? End-of-chapter questions

1. To what extent do you think it is possible to repeal the *Human Rights Act 1998*?

2. Should the *Human Rights Act 1998* be fully incorporated, ie apply both vertically and horizontally? What do you think the implications of extending the Act horizontally would be?

3. Read the box at 5.2.3.2 concerning precedent and s 2. Is the decision in *Kay* not in direct contravention of s 2 HRA 1998? Was it not Parliament's intention that the courts follow decisions of the ECtHR and does this not mean that a court of first instance, when faced with such a precedent, will be acting incompatibly with the ECHR, thus breaching it?

4. Read Chapter 16 on criminal appeals. If a court, including the ECtHR, considers that a trial is unfair should the conviction be quashed? Read *R v Rowe, Davis and Johnson (No 3)* [2001] 1 Cr App R 8.

Further reading

Dwyer DM, 'Rights Brought Home' (2005) 121 *Law Quarterly Review* 359–64.
   This is a useful article which looks at how the HRA 1998 has been implemented.

Klug F and Starmer K, 'Standing Back from the Human Rights Act: How Effective is it Five Years on?' [2005] *Public Law* 716–28.
   This is a very good article, co-authored by the (now) Director of Public Prosecutions, which examines how the Act has been used in practice.

Fredman S, 'From Deference to Democracy: The Role of Equality under the Human Rights Act 1998' (2006) 122 *Law Quarterly Review* 53–81.
   This is a good article which includes a useful examination of the margin of appreciation.

Sales P, 'Strasbourg Jurisprudence and the Human Rights Act: A Response to Lord Irvine' [2012] *Public Law* 253–67.
   This is an excellent article that dissects the approach adopted to s 2 HRA 1998.

For multiple-choice questions, updates to this chapter, and links to useful websites, please visit the **Online Resource Centre** at: **www.oxfordtextbooks.co.uk/orc/gillespie_els6e/**

PART II

THE COURTS AND THE PRACTITIONERS

6

The Structure of the Courts

By the end of this chapter you will be able to:

- Identify how the courts in England and Wales are organized and funded.
- Identify the principal courts in England and Wales.
- Discuss the types of cases heard in each court.
- Understand what the other courts do.

Introduction

Of all the institutions within the English Legal System, the courts are perhaps the most recognizable. Most people are aware of what a court is but they perhaps do not know that there are several different types of courts nor fully understand what each does.

This chapter will consider how the modern court structure is organized and what each court does. It will not consider the historical development of the courts but those wishing to understand the evolution of the courts should consult the further reading identified at the end of the chapter.

The tribunals are not dealt with in this chapter (instead being discussed in the next chapter) for ease of understanding. However, it is important to note at the outset that there are increasing links between the courts and tribunals. Indeed, there are perhaps more similarities than differences in their roles, how they are run, and certainly in how they are staffed (discussed in Chapter 8).

6.1 The organization of the courts

The first issue to examine is how courts are organized. As will be seen later, there are many different types of court and this raises questions as to how they can be classified and how their day-to-day business is organized.

6.1.1 **Classifying the courts**

The first issue to examine is how courts are classified. The variety of courts have led some to question whether the courts can be grouped together but, as will be seen, this is not necessarily the easiest thing to do.

6.1.1.1 **Civil/Criminal**

It may be thought that the easiest way of classifying the courts would be to designate whether they are civil or criminal. In principle this would seem appropriate since it is recognized that there is a civil justice system and a criminal justice system.

The difficulty is that whilst it is easy to designate the Crown Court as a criminal court and the Family Court as a civil court it is less easy to categorize any other court. The magistrates' court (see 6.2.1), for example, deals with the vast majority of criminal cases but it also has a civil jurisdiction and so it cannot be said to be a purely criminal court. The High Court of Justice (see 6.2.5) is predominantly a civil court but it also has a limited criminal jurisdiction. The Court of Appeal (see 6.2.6) is divided into two divisions, the civil division and the criminal division, so that is relatively easy but the Supreme Court (see 6.2.7) has jurisdiction over both civil and criminal matters in England and Wales.

It can be seen therefore that classifying courts as either civil or criminal courts is impracticable.

6.1.1.2 **Original or appellate jurisdiction**

Another potential classification system is to examine whether courts have original jurisdiction, ie they hear matters of first instance (eg trials) or whether they hear appeals from other courts.

As an abstract idea, this, as with the civil/criminal distinction, seems logical but the existing court structure immediately poses challenges. For example, whilst the magistrates' court and county court only possess original jurisdiction, the Crown Court exercises both an original and appellate jurisdiction. The same is true of the Family Court and the High Court and this is without even considering whether judicial review is original or appellate jurisdiction (something complicated by the fact that certain courts and tribunals may be subject to judicial review).

Accordingly, it can be seen that this categorization does not assist either.

6.1.1.3 **Superior and inferior courts**

One of the most traditional forms of classifying the courts is to examine whether they are superior or inferior courts.

Ascertaining what the superior courts are is not always easy. The starting point is that those labelled a superior court within s 1 *Senior Courts Act 1981* (SCA 1981) are. The courts listed are the *Crown Court, High Court of Justice*, and *Court of Appeal*.

However, other courts are known to be superior courts. For example, the Employment Appeals Tribunal which, as its name suggests, is technically a tribunal is, in fact, a superior court. It is so designated by statute.[1] The Courts-Martial Appeal Court is considered to be a superior court[2] so could it be argued that the superior

---

1. *Employment Tribunals Act 1996*, s 20(3).
2. *Courts-Martial (Appeals) Act 1968*, s 1(2).

courts are only those that are so designated by statute? Certainly now the Supreme Court is in being then this may be true (as s 40(1) *Constitutional Reform Act 2005* (CRA 2005) states that the Supreme Court is a superior court of record) but it was certainly not true historically since the House of Lords was a superior court and yet this arose not through statute but through the fact that it was an intrinsic part of Parliament.

What of inferior courts? Statute rarely states that they are inferior so perhaps the solution is that where a statute does not state that a court is superior then it should be treated as inferior. Unfortunately this does not appear to be a safe proposition as historically some courts were treated as being superior in the absence of statute (for example, the Central Criminal Court prior to the establishment of the Crown Court).

In *R v Cripps, ex parte Muldoon and others*[3] it was said:

> It is necessary to look at the relevant functions of the tribunal in question including its constitution, jurisdiction and powers and its relationship with the High Court in order to decide whether the tribunal should properly be regarded as inferior ... [4]

The meaning of its relationship with the High Court is taken to be that where the High Court is able to act in a reviewing capacity over the tribunal, ie it is subject to judicial review, then the court is an inferior court. However, this does not always work since, for example, the Crown Court may sometimes be subject to judicial review (where the matter does not concern its jurisdiction over indictable offences) and yet it has been seen that, by statute, it is a superior court.

6.1.1.4 A need for classification?

It can be seen that it is not easy to identify a classification for the courts. In practice it is rarely necessary to clarify the courts and instead a distinction is drawn between the types of justice. Some would argue that there are three types of justice systems; criminal, civil, and family, but in reality the distinction is between two: civil and criminal. Accordingly, it can be said that the need for classification, at least in practice, is perhaps questionable.

6.1.2 HM Courts and Tribunal Service

Setting aside the classification of the courts, how are they organized in practice? The main courts of England and Wales (ie the magistrates' court, county court, Family Court, Crown Court, High Court, and Court of Appeal) are operated by Her Majesty's Court and Tribunals Service, an executive agency of the Ministry of Justice. The Supreme Court is not operated by HM Courts and Tribunal Service (HMCTS) but is responsible for its own administration (through its Chief Executive) this status reflecting the fact that it is a court of the United Kingdom and not just of England and Wales and also because historically the House of Lords (its predecessor) was administered separately.

Prior to 2011 the courts were administered by HM Court Service (HMCS), a body created in 2005 when the previous Court Service was combined with the administration of the magistrates' courts (which had previously been a complicated administration based

---

3. [1983] 3 WLR 465.
4. [1983] 3 WLR 465, 87 (Robert Goff LJ).

on localities). In 2011 it was decided to merge HMCS with the Tribunal Service which administers the separate body of tribunals, in part to save costs. However, it should be noted that some tribunals are devolved (ie are specific to either Scotland or Northern Ireland) and they remain administered locally. The Lord Chancellor, as Minister of Justice, is politically responsible for the functioning of the service although it is headed by a chief executive, a senior civil servant. HMCTS is also overseen by an executive board which includes four executive members (ie senior members of HMCS including the Chief Executive), three judicial members (ordinarily a member of the senior judiciary, a senior tribunal judge, and a district judge representing magistrates' courts), three non-executive members (usually including a lawyer), and a Ministry of Justice representative member. The board is overseen by an independent chairman. The *Courts Act 2003* (CA 2003) provides that the Lord Chancellor has responsibility for appointing court officers and staff responsible for serving the courts, and HMCTS exercises this power on his behalf.

Historically (the then) HMCS was organized into forty-two areas corresponding to the previous geographical areas used by the criminal justice areas, but this ultimately changed and it is now organized into eight regional areas (seven geographical and one specifically dedicated to the Royal Courts of Justice). Each area has its own director who is responsible to the chief executive and the executive board. HMCS itself employs the staff that service the courts, including the administrative staff, the clerks to the courts (or legal advisers), ushers etc. It does not employ members of the judiciary as they are office holders who, depending on their rank, are appointed either by the Lord Chancellor himself or by the Queen (discussed in Chapter 8).

6.1.2.1 Judicial administration

Whilst HMCTS have responsibility for the administration of the courts they do so alongside the judiciary.

The courts in England and Wales are divided into six circuits and each is assigned at least two presiding judges[5] (the South-Eastern circuit, which is one of the busiest, currently has four). The presiding judges are puisne judges (meaning judges of the High Court: see 8.1.2.3) and while presiders they have responsibility for the administration of justice on the circuit. A Lord Justice of Appeal (Court of Appeal judge: see 8.1.2.2) is appointed as the senior presiding judge[6] who coordinates the work of the presiding judges (currently the post is held by Lord Justice Fulford).

Having at least two presiding judges for each circuit means that ordinarily one judge will always be on circuit (at least during the legal year). This means that they are in a better position to oversee matters. In the early days it has been said:

> In broad principle the Presiding judges were responsible for the judicial or operational side of the circuit, while the circuit administrator was responsible for the administrative support. But in practice the two overlapped ...[7]

This overlap continued and by 2008 it was being suggested that their administrative responsibilities were becoming almost overwhelming. The principal responsibility of the presiding judge is to assign judges to the relevant cases. It will be seen in Chapter 8

---

5. *Courts and Legal Services Act 1990*, s 72(1).
6. *Courts and Legal Services Act 1990*, s 72(2).
7. Robin Dunn, *Sword and Wig: Memoirs of a Lord Justice* (Quiller Press 1993) 217.

that only certain judges are entitled to sit on certain cases. However, even where a judge is entitled to sit on a case, the presiding judge has to identify who is the most appropriate. *The Telegraph* reported that while trying a serious murder, Mr Justice Gibbs (then presiding judge of the Midlands circuit), had to respond in a single week to twenty letters and seventy circuit-connected emails together with various telephone calls and that this, together with the other commitments being a presider brings, led to him working seventy hours per week while on circuit.

6.1.3 The Supreme Court

It was noted earlier that HMCTS does not administer the Supreme Court.

Section 48 CRA 2005 states that the Supreme Court will have a chief executive. They are appointed by the President of the Court.[8] Section 49 permits the President of the Supreme Court to appoint staff to service the court, although the chief executive will decide the number and type of staff. Presumably the President will also be involved in such discussions although it is notable that s 49 does not require this. The Supreme Court would seem to have a larger staff than when it was the House of Lords although this is, in part, because much of the administration of the judicial committees was subsumed within the wider House of Lords administration.

6.1.4 Funding

It will be remembered that HMCTS is an executive agency of the Ministry of Justice. Accordingly, the funding for the courts—except for the salary of the judiciary—comes from the departmental budget of the Ministry of Justice. Prior to the creation of the Ministry, in 2007, the money came from the Lord Chancellor's Department.

The creation of the Ministry of Justice led to considerable tension between the judiciary and executive. It will be seen in Chapter 8 that changes to the office of the Lord Chancellor also led to concerns and it would have been thought that the government would have attempted to resolve these issues by being careful to keep the judiciary informed of planned changes to the organization of the courts. However, following a series of political difficulties for the Home Office it was decided to separate some parts of the functions of the Home Office and to combine them with the powers of the Lord Chancellor's Department to create the Ministry of Justice. In an extrajudicial speech, the then Lord Chief Justice commented:

> The first I or the then Lord Chancellor, Lord Falconer, learnt of the creation of the Ministry of Justice was when we were reading our Sunday Telegraphs on the 21 of January 2007. Once again the government had not consulted on a key constitutional change ... No guarantees of the protection of the independence of the judiciary were given. There was no promise to protect the administration of justice within the new Department.

The concern of the judiciary was focused on a number of issues but one of the most important was whether the budgets of the court were separate.

One department was to uphold the rule of law and the independence of the judiciary and yet the same department would also have responsibility for criminal justice. That department would have one pot of money from which to fund the court system

8. *Constitutional Reform Act 2005*, s 48(2).

and the prisons. The judiciary was concerned that the department would rob Peter to pay Paul—Peter being the judges and Paul being the prisons. Would the department be able to prioritize the administration of justice while dealing with criminal justice policy?

Since the administration of government is a matter of prerogative not statute, no legislative measure was required to establish the Ministry of Justice. This, in turn, meant there were few opportunities to address concerns. The judiciary wished the budget of HMCTS to be 'ring-fenced', ie it could only be used for the administration of the courts and not used when other aspects of the Ministry's budget were under strain. The government refused this request and the dispute between the judiciary and executive became public.

Eventually a pragmatic solution was created. This was twofold. The first was the establishment of an executive council (now the Board of HMCTS: see 6.1.2) which includes representatives of the judiciary. The second was the establishment of a formal *Framework Document* which was published by the Ministry of Justice in April 2008. This document was designed to recognize that the administration of justice requires cooperation between the executive and the judiciary and, in particular, a commitment to the independence of the judiciary. In 2011 this document was revised to take into account the inclusion of the Tribunal Service into the new agency. Most recently it was updated in 2014 to take into account additions to the executive board (discussed at 6.1.2), introduced to secure additional expertise and experience.

A key part of the *Framework Document* is that all staff 'have joint responsibility to the Lord Chancellor and the Lord Chief Justice for the effective, efficient and speedy operation of the courts and tribunals',[9] which reinforces the fact that HMCTS is truly a partnership between the executive and the judiciary.

It has been stated earlier that the budget for HMCTS is not formally 'ring-fenced' but the document sets out how the judiciary is involved in the setting of the budget. The Lord Chancellor will hold discussions with the Treasury in the same way that any departmental Secretary of State will. The Lord Chancellor must inform the Lord Chief Justice about these discussions[10] and the Lord Chief Justice shall have the right to write to the Lord Chancellor setting out the views of the judiciary and, if he does so, this will be forwarded to the Chief Secretary to the Treasury.[11] This is an interesting provision as it would, of course, provide the Lord Chancellor with detailed support since the document would invariably form part of the public record and thus a government would be careful to take note of the contents.

Once the Lord Chancellor has been given his allocation by the Treasury he will then set the budget for HMCTS and in doing so will have regard to his statutory and other duties to ensure the efficient and effective support of the courts. Where the Lord Chief Justice has concerns about what the budget is then he has the right to make representations to the Lord Chancellor and, if he so wishes, to Parliament. This is, in effect, a 'nuclear option' in that it would demonstrate a breakdown in the trust between the government and judiciary and it would be likely to create a political storm. Whilst this

9. HM Courts and Tribunals Service, *Framework Document* (HMCTS 2014) 5.
10. HM Courts and Tribunals Service, *Framework Document* (HMCTS 2014) 11.
11. HM Courts and Tribunals Service, *Framework Document* (HMCTS 2014) 11.
Note that the Chief Secretary to the Treasury is the second-highest political minister in the Treasury (the Chancellor of the Exchequer being the first). The Chief Secretary is of cabinet rank and it is his job to lead the budgetary negotiations with each government department.

is not as effective as a ring-fence it does act as an effective tool of pressure as both the government and judiciary would wish to avoid such public disagreement and the inevitable political consequences that would arise from that.

 QUESTION FOR REFLECTION

Were the judges right to be concerned that the budgets for the courts are not 'ring-fenced'? If the prison population continues to rise then pressures on the budget will increase. It is theoretically possible that pressure could then be placed on the judges to sentence offenders in a particular way, potentially compromising their judicial independence.

Do you think a framework document is sufficient or should there be a statutory rule stating that the budget for HMCS should be set annually and kept 'ring-fenced'?

6.2 Key courts

So far this chapter has discussed how courts are classified, organized, and funded, but what are the courts in the English Legal System? A number of courts exist and so if a detailed discussion of all these were to take place then this chapter would be extremely long! Instead a summary will be given of the key courts that feature commonly within the English Legal System and later (6.4) a brief outline of some other common courts will be made.

The courts that will be considered in this part are:

- magistrates' court
- county court
- Crown Court
- Family Court
- High Court of Justice
- Court of Appeal
- Supreme Court.

Figure 6.1 shows the approximate structure of the English Legal System. It will be seen that the precise placing of the courts is a matter of debate and also alters depending on the type of work that the court is undertaking.

6.2.1 Magistrates' court

The first court to note is the magistrates' court. This is the lowest of the courts that we are concerned with. Magistrates' courts are local courts. Before the implementation of the CA 2003, the courts were divided into local petty sessional areas and run by local *Magistrates' Courts Committees*. Now, however, they are subsumed within HMCTS and whilst they continue to sit in local locations, their organization and management is undertaken by the local area and regional offices of the Court Service.

Magistrates' courts primarily have a criminal jurisdiction and indeed the vast majority of criminal cases heard in England and Wales take place in the magistrates' court. It will be seen later in this book that criminal matters can be divided into

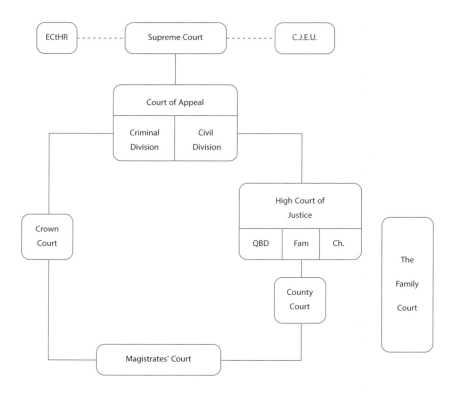

Figure 6.1 The hierarchy of the courts

summary matters, indictable matters, and those that can be tried either summarily or on indictment (see 12.6.1). Summary trials take place in the magistrates' court before either a district judge (magistrates' court) (see 13.1.2) or a bench of lay magistrates (see 13.1.1). The punishment an offender can receive in the magistrates' court is currently limited to six months' imprisonment for a single offence although, at a time yet to be announced, their powers will be increased to imposing twelve months' custody.

A separate criminal jurisdiction that exists in the magistrates' court is in respect of adolescent crime. Here the court is known as the 'youth court' and whilst they are frequently located in the same building, matters are heard in specific courtrooms that are laid out in a less formal manner and a separate entrance from the adult magistrates' court must be maintained. The youth court has jurisdiction over all but the most serious of adolescent crime, even where an offence is theoretically triable only on indictment for adult offenders. Separate punishments also exist for youth crime, with the overall aim to be preventing reoffending rather than punishing transgressions of the law.

The magistrates' court also has a limited civil jurisdiction. Its largest role was historically in relation to family law matters, however, with the introduction of the Family Court (see 6.2.4) the magistrates' court no longer deals with such cases. The majority of the courts' civil jurisdiction relates to the recovery of certain debts (including, for example, the supply of services such as gas and electricity) and the licensing of gambling institutions.

6.2.2 **County court**

The second court to examine is the county court. Like the magistrates' court, this is an inferior court (see 6.1.1.3). The county court is a purely civil court and its jurisdiction is set out in statute. The original jurisdiction was set out in the *County Courts Act 1846* but such courts had a very limited jurisdiction and the modern version of the courts was established by the *County Courts Act 1984*.

As an inferior court created by statute, the county courts have limited jurisdiction. If a statutory provision does not grant it jurisdiction to deal with the matter, then a judge of the county court has no right to adjudicate on the matter. In April 2014, with the introduction of the *Crime and Courts Act 2013*, the 173 county courts were replaced by one single county court.[12] The court may sit anywhere in England and Wales, and will, despite the seemingly radical change, largely continue to sit in the current county court buildings, which have been rebranded as 'county court hearing centres'. These court buildings are distributed across the country, with the distribution taking account of population areas.

As noted earlier, the county court has an exclusively civil jurisdiction. Many of the matters relate to types of actions that could also be heard in the High Court but which are considered less serious because either the nature of the claim or the amount of compensation sought is reduced. In terms of general civil jurisdiction the county court deals with matters such as breach of contract, claims in tort (negligence, nuisance etc), personal injury, certain disputes as to land, and even some admiralty claims.

Historically, the county court also had a family jurisdiction, with the vast majority of divorce cases being dealt with by the county court, However, with the introduction of the Family Court (see 6.2.4), any claims or proceedings in relation to family matters must now be heard there. The county court has exclusive jurisdiction over small claims. It is common to hear of the 'small claims court', a title that has quasi-recognition within HMCTS. In fact it is an informal part of the county court and proceedings are instituted within the county court.

The county court originally had its own procedural rules (known as the *County Court Rules* printed in a green volume so colloquially known as 'the Green book') but following a series of reviews it was decided that a single set of procedural rules should exist for the county court, High Court, and Court of Appeal (Civil Division). These rules, known as the *Civil Procedure Rules*, were introduced by the *Civil Procedure Act 1997* and the rules continue to be updated.

6.2.3 **The Crown Court**

The Crown Court is the first superior court that is to be considered (see 6.1.1.3). It is a court of both original and appellate jurisdictions; in other words, some trials at first instance take place but it also hears certain appeals. It is often said that it has an exclusively criminal jurisdiction but that is not quite true in that it has a limited civil jurisdiction in its appellate capacity.

The Crown Court is a relatively modern invention although it is a development from the system of assize courts (which were presided over by puisne judges sent on circuit) and quarter sessions which were locally based criminal courts. The fusion retains some elements of the assize system in that today puisne judges will preside in

---

12. *Crime and Courts Act 2013*, s 17(1).

the Crown Court while sitting on the circuit they are assigned to. The Crown Court came into being through the *Courts Act 1971* although its jurisdiction is now based on the SCA 1981.

6.2.3.1 Trials of first instance

The principal work of the Crown Court is to deal with trials that take place on indictment, ie involving a trial. The work of the Crown Court in this capacity is discussed in Part 3 of the book. The Crown Court can currently sit at seventy-seven Crown Court centres across England and Wales although the most famous remains the *Central Criminal Court*, also known as the 'Old Bailey'. Theoretically each Crown Court centre has the same jurisdiction but, in practice, the Crown Court is divided into different types of court centre. The allocation is by tier and there are three tiers:

Tier One: These are courts where High Court judges will regularly visit and preside and at which circuit judges and recorders will also sit for the full range of Crown Court business. These are also courts where High Court judges will preside over civil High Court business.

Tier Two: Tier-two courts are, in effect, the same as tier-one courts except there is no civil work undertaken.

Tier Three: These are courts where a High Court judge would not normally preside and where cases are heard by circuit judges and recorders.

Circuit judges and recorders deal with Crown Court criminal business in all three of the tiers.

A contested trial will take place before a judge and jury. The process of the trial is discussed in Chapter 15.

6.2.3.2 Appeals

The Crown Court also has an appellate jurisdiction. It may hear appeals from the magistrates' court. This type of appeal is discussed at 16.2.1. Whilst the appeal will ordinarily be for criminal matters, the Crown Court does have a limited civil appeal over some civil orders such as the *Anti-Social Behaviour Order*, *Sexual Offences Prevention Order*, and *Foreign Travel Order*. These are imposed by the magistrates' court sitting in their civil capacity but they are quasi-criminal orders in that they prohibit an offender from doing something contained in the order, and breach of an order amounts to a criminal offence.

6.2.4 The Family Court

The Family Court came into existence on 22 April 2014 by s 17(3) *Crime and Courts Act 2013* as a result of the recommendations made by *The Family Justice Review* report. With the introduction of the Family Court, the separate family divisions in the magistrates' and county courts cease to exist, and instead applications for family proceedings are now made directly to the Family Court. The Family Court has jurisdiction over all family proceedings, with the exceptions of cases involving jurisdiction in wardship (this is a type of court order giving custody of a minor to the court) and international jurisdiction cases, where the case will be heard exclusively in the Family Division of the High Court. It should be noted that the jurisdiction of the Family

Division of the High Court (see 6.2.5.3) remains largely unaffected by the creation of the Family Court.

The Family Court deals with any family matters which arise and are in dispute. These can include the more commonly known matters of adoption, marriage and divorce, and domestic violence. The court can also hear cases specifically involving children. These types of cases fall into two categories; public law and private law. Public law cases are brought by local authorities and may involve proceedings concerning supervision orders, which place the child concerned under the supervision of their local authority. Private law cases are brought by individuals, usually the child's parents or relatives, and may concern issues such as parental responsibility agreements and child arrangement orders.

The Family Court is a national court and therefore can technically sit in any court building in England and Wales. However, in practice hearings tend to be held in county or magistrates' court buildings. The Family Court comprises judges from all levels of the family judiciary, including lay magistrates. Including different levels of the judiciary within the court allows for cases to be allocated by 'gate-keepers' to the appropriate judge depending on the type of proceedings and their complexity.[13] The 'gate-keeping and allocation team' for the local Family Court consists of a justice's clerk and a district judge. Allocating appropriate cases to specific judges aims to ensure that the same judge deals with the case throughout proceedings in the court, therefore streamlining the court process for those involved.

Alongside the creation of the Family Court, numerous Family Justice System reforms were also introduced in April 2014 in the *Children and Families Act 2014*, with the aim of improving the overall functioning of the family courts system. For example, under s 14 of the Act, a time limit of twenty-six weeks has been introduced for completing care and supervision cases to ensure speedier outcomes in finding permanent placements for vulnerable children. Moreover, under s 10 *Children and Families Act 2014*, there is now a legal requirement for separating couples to attend 'family mediation information and assessment meetings' to consider the alternatives to initiating court proceedings when trying to resolve issues associated with finances and their children. There are exceptions to this requirement, for example in cases involving domestic violence or where the court needs to make an urgent order. However, in the majority of cases a 'mediation information and assessment meeting' is required.

6.2.4.1 Appeals

Appeals can be heard within the Family Court. As noted previously, the court includes judges from all levels of the family judiciary, and cases will be allocated to judges depending upon the type of proceedings and the cases' complexity. Appeals can therefore be made from a case heard by a 'lower-level' judge to a more senior member of the family judiciary within the Family Court. Practice Direction 30a (which supplements the Family Practice Directions Part 30) sets out the available routes of appeal. For example, a case decided by a bench of two or three lay magistrates can be appealed to a judge of circuit level sitting within the Family Court. Appeals can also be made outside of the Family Court to the Family Division of the High Court and to the Court of Appeal.

---

13.   See *The Family Court (Composition and Distribution of Business) Rules 2014*, SI 2014/3297, sch 1 'Allocation'.

6.2.5 **High Court of Justice**

The High Court of Justice (or High Court as it is invariably known) is probably the most important court in the English Legal System. It has unlimited jurisdiction in civil matters which means that in the absence of a statutory or common-law rule prohibiting a judge sitting on such a case, the High Court has jurisdiction over the dispute. Whilst it is primarily a court of civil jurisdiction, it does have an important appellate and reviewing jurisdiction in respect of criminal matters.

The High Court is based in the Royal Courts of Justice in the Strand although it also sits in twenty-seven first-tier Crown Court centres (see 6.2.3.1) outside of London. Each circuit has at least one court exercising High Court jurisdiction.

The High Court is divided into three divisions, into which all business of the court will be assigned. The three divisions are the Queen's Bench Division (King's Bench Division when the monarch is a King), Chancery Division, and the Family Division.[14] In 1988 the judiciary suggested that the divisions should be abolished and in the mid-1990s a further proposal was brought forward to reformulate the divisions by, for example, merging the Chancery and Queen's Bench Divisions. In his interim report on *Access to Justice*, Lord Woolf rejected this argument[15] believing that the specialist jurisdiction of the Chancery Division would be lost in a merger and he noted that, for example, there are only a small number of Chancery puisne judges (at the time of writing there are only eighteen judges (including the Chancellor) out of a total of 106 puisne judges) and they work closely together as a team. Lord Woolf, in his final report, did not recommend any changes to the divisional structure and so it continues to consist of three divisions.

6.2.5.1 **Queen's Bench Division**

The largest of the three divisions is the Queen's Bench Division (it currently being staffed by 73 out of 106 puisne judges and with Lord Justices of Appeal sitting in the Administrative Court where required). The principal work of the division can be divided into three distinct areas although, as will be seen, other specialist work also occurs within the division.

General work

The Queen's Bench Division deals with much of the high-value civil work assigned to the High Court. All civil work that falls outside of the Chancery Division or Family Division is heard in the Queen's Bench Division and this includes, for example, most claims from contract, personal injury claims, and libel actions. As will be seen from Chapter 18, much of the classes of work this division hears could also be heard in the county court but the High Court is selected where a matter is particularly complicated or where the amount of compensation sought is high.

Appellate work

The Queen's Bench Division has an appellate jurisdiction. Under the procedure for civil appeals (see Chapter 18) an appeal is ordinarily to the next level of judge. So where a person wishes to appeal against a procedural matter in the county court this

14. *Senior Courts Act 1981*, s 5.
15. Lord Woolf, *Access to Justice: Interim Report to the Lord Chancellor* (HMSO 1995) ch 12, para 17.

will ordinarily be heard by a High Court judge and it will normally be a judge of this division.

The Queen's Bench Division also has a criminal appellate jurisdiction. It is possible to appeal against a finding of magistrates by way of case stated (see 16.2.2). Such an appeal is brought before this division.

Supervisory jurisdiction

The High Court has always had an important supervisory jurisdiction. This is where it exercises the power of review over inferior courts, tribunals, and some public bodies. It is now commonly referred to as 'judicial review' and it is a jurisdiction that has developed extensively over the past few decades yet can be extremely controversial, especially when it involves the court overturning decisions of ministers. This jurisdiction is discussed at 17.3.

The supervisory jurisdiction is exercised by the 'Administrative Court'. Unlike certain 'courts' within the Queen's Bench Division, this is an administrative title that has no statutory force. It is, therefore, technically just a panel of the Queen's Bench Division although the Civil Procedure Rules set out a separate body of rules for this work.[16]

The Administrative Court is headed by a 'lead judge' (currently Mr Justice Cranston) who works with the appropriate administrative staff to administer the working of the court. Other judges of the High Court are designated by the Lord Chief Justice to hear matters in the Administrative Court. Where the judges are not already assigned to the Queen's Bench Division they are considered to be additional temporary judges of that division when hearing the matter.

Specialist jurisdictions

The Admiralty Court and Commercial Court both exist within the Queen's Bench Division. These are statutory courts[17] and deal with specific types of jurisdiction. The Admiralty Court, as its name suggests, exercises particular claims in relation to maritime law, for example, claims relating to salvage or disputes as to the carriage of goods. The Commercial Court is a very specialist jurisdiction and relates to international business law and banking law. The court also has a role in arbitration (a concept discussed in Chapter 19).

The final specialist court is the Technology and Construction Court. Like the Administrative Court, this is not a statutory court but rather an administrative title. The work of the court is set out in Part 60 of the *Civil Procedure Rules* and its work will cover, for example, disputes as to the supply and installation of computer systems, or disputes in relation to construction or engineering projects. Its work requires specialist judges and outside of London it is not unusual for specially trained circuit judges to sit temporarily as acting judges of the High Court.

6.2.5.2 Chancery Division

The Chancery Division is a specialist division of the High Court and considers work relating to, for example, trusts, wills, companies, certain land claims, and certain claims relating to tax. Its work is technical and the judges of this division are

---

16. *Civil Procedure Rules*, pt 54.
17. *Senior Courts Act 1981*, s 6.

supplemented by masters of the Chancery Division. Masters hold a judicial office similar to that of the district judge (see 8.1.3.3) but exercise jurisdiction in the High Court. Whilst the masters cannot hear full trials, they dispose of much of the procedural matters and frequently their involvement will lead to the case being settled before the matter proceeds to trial.

Within the Chancery Division exist three specialist courts. The first is the Patents Court.[18] This court deals with disputes relating to copyright, patents, and intellectual property disputes. The work is very specialist and the judges who sit on these matters are normally given specific training and it is not uncommon for circuit judges to act as an additional judge of the High Court when hearing these matters.

The second court is the Bankruptcy Court. As with the Administrative Court within the Queen's Bench Division, this is an administrative title for convenience. The court, as its name suggests, deals with disputes relating to bankruptcy and insolvency.

The third and final court is the Intellectual Property Enterprise Court (IPEC) which became a specialist court within the Chancery division in October 2013. The court, as its name suggests, deals with disputes relating to intellectual property between small and medium-sized enterprises, typically in relation to patents, copyright, and trade-marks.

6.2.5.3 Family Division

The Family Division is the newest of the three divisions. Prior to 1971 the third division was the Probate, Divorce, and Admiralty Division. The probate function was transferred to the Chancery Division and the admiralty work was assigned to the Queen's Bench Division. Wardship—the state's care of children who cannot care for themselves—was exercised by the Queen's Bench Division but this was transferred to the new Family Division.

The Family Division, as its name suggests, deals with most matters relating to divorce, family disputes, and children. Complicated public childcare matters are heard in this division as well as complicated or high-value matters relating to private disputes.

There are currently twenty judges of the division (including its president) but their work is supplemented by specialist district judges who will be responsible for a considerable amount of the work of the division, including some contested trials. In addition, outside of London it is not unusual for a specialist circuit judge to sit as an acting judge of the Family Division, especially where matters are urgent.

Whilst all divisions will have a judge 'on call' the work of this division often means that the court will 'sit' at unusual times. There is always at least one judge who can be contacted at any time, day or night, and hearings can be heard over the telephone. This may occur, for example, where there is a dispute as to whether a child should have urgent medical treatment, or where somebody is seeking to remove a child from the jurisdiction.

6.2.5.4 Divisional Courts

A Divisional Court is when two or more judges sit in the High Court together to hear the same case.[19] This will ordinarily happen in their appellate or reviewing capacity.

---

18. *Senior Courts Act 1981*, s 6.
19. *Senior Courts Act 1981*, s 66.

Whilst a Divisional Court can be created in any of the three divisions of the High Court, most Divisional Courts have been of the Queen's Bench Division, especially when it is exercising its powers of judicial review. However, since the establishment of the Administrative Court it is more common for judges to sit individually to hear some matters. Where this happens, it is not technically a Divisional Court but simply a hearing of the Queen's Bench Division (within the courtesy-titled 'Administrative Court').

6.2.6 The Court of Appeal

The modern Court of Appeal came into existence in 1966 fusing the previously separate Court of Appeal and Court of Criminal Appeal into a single court consisting of two divisions: the Criminal Division and the Civil Division. The Criminal Division is presided over by the Lord Chief Justice and the Civil Division is presided over by the Master of the Rolls. The Lord Chief Justice, as head of the judiciary, can (and has) appointed judges of the Court of Appeal as vice-president of either or both divisions.[20] The judges of the Court of Appeal can sit in either division and in both divisions (but most frequently in the Criminal Division). Puisne and even certain circuit judges can sit in the court as additional judges.

The Court of Appeal can sit in panels and in both divisions it is common for a single judge (in the Criminal Division this will normally be a puisne judge) to consider whether leave to appeal should be given and within the Criminal Division to hear applications for bail. The Criminal Division ordinarily sits in panels of three, and it must sit in an uneven number of no less than three judges when determining appeals against conviction[21] and certain other appellate decisions. When it sits in panels of two judges (eg for sentences against appeal) if the judges are divided then it must relist the matter for a hearing before three judges.[22] The Civil Division can theoretically dispose of an appeal by a single judge[23] but ordinarily it will sit with at least two judges. As with the Criminal Division, if an even number of judges sit and they are divided as to the outcome, the case should be relisted before a panel of the court consisting of an uneven number of judges.[24]

The Court of Appeal ordinarily sits in the Royal Courts of Justice in London and any number of courts can sit at the same time so long as they are properly constituted. In recent years the Court of Appeal has sat in locations outside of London. This originated with the Civil Division but it has included the Criminal Division and the court has sat in a number of locations, including Cardiff, Manchester, and Newcastle-upon-Tyne. Recently the Criminal Division has also begun using live video-links to allow an appellant to see (and participate) in an appeal hearing whilst saving the costs of transporting the prisoner to London.

6.2.7 The Supreme Court

The Supreme Court is the newest court within the English Legal System although, as noted already, it is a UK court as its jurisdiction is not restricted to English cases. The Court was established by Part 3 CRA 2005 and it came into being in October 2009 (at the start of

20. *Senior Courts Act 1981*, s 3.
21. *Senior Courts Act 1981*, s 55.
22. *Senior Courts Act 1981*, s 55(5).
23. *Senior Courts Act 1981*, s 54(2).
24. *Senior Courts Act 1981*, s 54(5).

the legal year). Its jurisdiction, broadly speaking, includes that which the House of Lords exercised but it also assumed responsibility for devolution issues that were previously within the jurisdiction of the Judicial Committee of the Privy Council (6.4.1).

The Supreme Court was created as part of wider constitutional changes, and an attempt to lead to the separation of powers in respect of the legislature and judiciary. As part of this process, the Lord Chancellor had his judicial functions removed (see Chapter 8) and it was decided to remove the judiciary from the legislature. Members of the judiciary have been debarred from being a member of the House of Commons for some time, but a number of judges, most notably the Lords of Appeal in Ordinary, were entitled to sit in the House of Lords and participate both in its judicial and legislative capacity. The CRA 2005 altered this by stating that peers who serve as a judge may not sit in the House of Lords during their employment,[25] although they will be free to sit when they have retired.

Whilst the government was clear that the primary reason for the establishment of the Supreme Court was the separation of powers,[26] it was suggested that an additional reason was the fact that the work of the Law Lords could not be adequately supported because of the lack of space available in Westminster.[27] This was perhaps a slightly unconvincing reason since there is no reason why a separate annexe could not have been created to provide additional support and space. For example, MPs were given an annexe across from the Palace of Westminster (known as Portcullis House) and a similar arrangement could have been established.

Although the separation of the legislature and judiciary was generally welcomed, the Law Lords themselves were divided as to whether the changes were needed or desirable, with some arguing that their presence in the House of Lords was 'of benefit to the Law Lords, to the House and to others including litigants'.[28] That said, the argument that the Law Lords could intervene in debates to ensure that errors of law were corrected during the parliamentary process was arguably overstated since in 2000 the Law Lords committed themselves to being bound by two principles:

1. that the Law Lords were supposed to be impartial and accordingly in matters of party-political controversy they would not normally speak;

2. participating in Parliamentary proceedings may debar them from sitting as judge when a matter relating to the legislation appears before the Appellate Committee.[29]

However, it was only a convention and there were some interventions. For example, Lord Woolf (the then Lord Chief Justice) and Lord Steyn (a then Law Lord) both criticized elements of the (then) *Asylum and Immigration Bill* as it was passing through Parliament, and at the time this was one of the most politically sensitive and partisan pieces of legislation.[30]

The Law Lords made other contributions to the House. It was reported that twelve places on House of Lords scrutiny committees were taken by serving Law Lords and

25. *Constitutional Reform Act 2005*, s 137.
26. Department for Constitutional Affairs, *Constitutional Reform: A Supreme Court for the United Kingdom* (HMSO 2003) 10.
27. Department for Constitutional Affairs, *Constitutional Reform: A Supreme Court for the United Kingdom* (HMSO 2003) 12.
28. Law Lords, *Law Lords' Response to the Government Consultation on a Supreme Court* (House of Lords 2003) para 2.
29. Hansard, HL Deb, vol 614, col 419, 22 June 2000.
30. David Windlesham, 'The Constitutional Reform Act 2005: The Politics of Constitutional Reform: Part 2' [2006] *Public Law* 35, 40–1.

that one Law Lord had served as the chairman on nine committees.[31] Whilst there may therefore have been a benefit in using the Law Lords for the purpose of scrutinizing legislation it could be questioned whether this was an appropriate use of the most senior judges' time. There are others with legal qualifications in the House, including retired Law Lords, and surely they are as able to identify potential flaws.

The Supreme Court hears only a small number of appeals. In 2015/16 the court received 230 permissions to appeal (it refused 126) and it heard 92 appeals.[32] This can be contrasted with the Court of Appeal. During 2014/15 in the Criminal Division alone a total of 6,036 applications were made and approximately 4,460 applications were considered. For a matter to be heard by the Supreme Court it must involve a point of public importance and the court is slow to allow leave, so as to ensure that it is not overwhelmed by cases. The Court of Appeal (and, to a lesser extent, the High Court) are also now very slow to grant leave to the Supreme Court, arguing that it is for that court to decide which cases it will hear.

The Supreme Court, like its predecessor the House of Lords, does not (unlike the Supreme Court of the USA) usually sit *en banc*, ie together. Instead panels of the court are established, with each panel being a minimum of three justices.[33] Ordinarily leave is dealt with by a panel of three justices and ordinarily this will be dealt with on paper without an oral hearing,[34] although the justices could refer the matter for an oral hearing,[35] again usually heard by a panel of three justices. Substantive appeals are usually heard by five justices although it can sit in larger panels (so long as there is an odd number of justices)[36] and it has done so on a number of occasions, including constitutions of seven[37] and nine.[38] Criteria used when deciding whether to sit in panels of more than five have now been published on the Supreme Court website and are put forward as:

- if the court is being asked to depart, or may decide to depart from, a previous decision
- a case of high constitutional importance
- a case of great public importance
- a case where a conflict arises between decisions in the House of Lords, Judicial Committee of the Privy Council, and/or the Supreme Court has to be reconciled
- a case raising an important point in relation to the *European Convention on Human Rights*.

In *R (on the application of Miller) v Secretary of State for Exiting the European Union*,[39] which was the so-called 'Brexit' case, the Supreme Court did, for the first-time, sit *en banc* with all eleven justices sitting together.[40] They did this because of the constitutional importance of the case. Whether it was wise to do so, however, is

---

31. David Windlesham, 'The Constitutional Reform Act 2005: Ministers, Judges and Constitutional Change: Part 1' [2005] *Public Law* 806, 813.
32. The Supreme Court, *Annual Report and Accounts 2015–2016* (Supreme Court 2016) <https://www.supremecourt.uk/docs/annual-report-2015-16.pdf> 20–1.
33. *Constitutional Reform Act 2005*, s 42(1)(b).
34. *Supreme Court Rules 2009*, SI 2009/1603, r 16(1).
35. *Supreme Court Rules 2009*, SI 2009/1603, r 16(2)(c).
36. *Constitutional Reform Act 2005*, s 42(1)(a).
37. *Re S-B (Children)* [2009] UKSC 17.
38. *Norris v Government of United States of America* [2010] UKSC 9.
39. [2017] UKSC 5.
40. Whilst there should be twelve justices, no replacement has yet been appointed for Lord Toulson who retired in July 2016.

perhaps open to question. The *Pinochet* case[41] set the precedent that decisions of the House of Lords/Supreme Court can be challenged. The rehearing of *Pinochet* was by judges who were not involved in the original decision. If the Supreme Court sits *en banc*, how would this occur? Whilst there is provision for acting justices[42] it would seem slightly odd if a Supreme Court case could be re-heard before judges who had never formed part of the court.

6.2.7.1 The House of Lords

Prior to the establishment of the Supreme Court the highest court was the House of Lords. Traditionally judicial matters were heard in the chamber of the House and any peer could participate, but during the nineteenth century it became clear that a more professional approach should be taken and life barons were created as Lords of Appeal in Ordinary, commonly known as the 'Law Lords'.

The modern House of Lords organized itself into an appellate committee to determine substantive appeals.[43] The appellate committee had to be distinguished from the appeals committee, which was a committee of three Law Lords that decided on applications for leave.

6.3 The 'European Courts'

The structure diagram (Figure 6.1) shows that next to the Supreme Court are two European Courts; the European Court of Justice (which has jurisdiction over matters relating to the European Union) and the European Court of Human Rights (whose primary function is to rule on matters relating to the *European Convention on Human Rights*). Both of these are important courts in their own rights and whilst one will often hear people refer to 'appealing to Europe' this is not technically correct since neither court operates as an appellate court as such.

The detail of these courts and their interrelationship with the English Legal System was discussed earlier in the book (see 4.3.4.3 and 4.4.3.2) and rather than duplicate material, readers should cross-refer to these sections for a discussion of these institutions.

6.4 Other courts

Section 6.2 discussed the key common courts within the English Legal System. Among the other courts three deserve a brief discussion, those are the:

- Judicial Committee of the Privy Council
- Court of Protection
- Coroners' Courts.

The discussion of these courts will be much briefer but will allow the reader to understand the broad jurisdiction of each court.

---

41. *R v Bow Street Metropolitan Stipendiary Magistrate, ex p Pinochet Ugarte (No 2)* [2000] 1 AC 119.
42. *Constitutional Reform Act 2005*, ss 38 and 39.
43. *Appellate Jurisdiction Act 1876*, s 5.

6.4.1 Judicial Committee of the Privy Council

The Judicial Committee of the Privy Council was established by the *Judicial Committee Act 1833* (JCA 1833) although the Privy Council itself is an ancient advisory body to the monarch. Prior to 1833 the Privy Council heard appellate matters and legal petitions from the colonies but it was Privy Councillors rather than judges who resolved the matter. By 1833 this was considered inappropriate and the Act of that year stated that judicial matters were to be heard by the Judicial Committee which would consist of senior judicial officers of the United Kingdom and Commonwealth countries (colonies at that time).

Whilst Court of Appeal judges are appointed to the Privy Council upon appointment (see 8.1.2.2) the modern Privy Council ordinarily takes the form of five Justices of the Supreme Court sitting, thus continuing the traditional staffing that saw it having the reputation as being the House of Lords in all but name. That was never quite true since, for example, other judicial officers sit, including a number of Commonwealth judges, but it is more common for the Justices of the Supreme Court to sit.

The current jurisdiction of the Judicial Committee can be summarized as follows:

- *Appeals to the Queen in Council.* A number of Commonwealth countries and British overseas territories continue to have the Privy Council as their head. Under this jurisdiction the Judicial Committee is technically tendering advice to the monarch and their judgment is then given legal standing by an Order in Council.

- *Appeals to the Head of State.* The Kingdom of Brunei allows an appeal against civil matters to proceed to the Privy Council. By agreement between the UK monarch and the sultan of Brunei the Privy Council tenders advice to the sultan rather than the Queen.

- *Appeals to the Judicial Committee.* Certain republics within the Commonwealth continue to allow appeals to the Privy Council even though the Queen is no longer Head of State. Under this jurisdiction the judgment of the Privy Council is final rather than it being merely advice to the monarch.

- *Domestic jurisdiction.* Appeals from the Channel Islands are heard by the Privy Council as are appeals from certain disciplinary bodies and ecclesiastical courts. Where the High Court sits as a 'prize court' an appeal lies to the Privy Council rather than through domestic avenues of appeal. Prior to the establishment of the Supreme Court devolution issues (discussed in Chapter 1) were also heard by the Privy Council but they are now heard by the Supreme Court.[44]

In addition, the Queen can refer any matter of law to the Privy Council for its advice.[45]

Regardless of which jurisdiction is being exercised only a single judgment is given (in contrast to, for example, the Supreme Court, Court of Appeal, and Divisional Courts where additional assenting and dissenting judgments are presented).

6.4.2 Court of Protection

The *Mental Capacity Act 2005* (MCA 2005) created the Court of Protection as a superior court (see 6.1.1.3) in its own right.[46] Prior to this, issues concerning those

---

44. *Constitutional Reform Act 2005*, sch 9, pt 2.
45. *Judicial Committee Act 1833*, s 4.
46. *Mental Capacity Act 2005*, s 45.

adults who were considered to be unable to act for themselves were dealt with either by the High Court of Justice, usually the Chancery Division or the Family Division. The statute expressly states:

> The court may sit at any place in England and Wales, on any day and at any time.[47]

The implications of this are that the court can sit outside of a formal courtroom and can deal with urgent matters. It will be seen in Chapter 8 that a High Court judge has an inherent power to sit anywhere at any time (see 8.1.2) but this provision is ensuring that there is no doubt that a judge, of whatever rank, has this power when sitting in the Court of Protection.

The court must have a president and vice-president[48] and the President of the Family Division is the president of that court and the Chancellor of the High Court (head of the Chancery Division) is the vice-president. Judges of the High Court, circuit court, and district judges can be designated by either the Lord Chief Justice or the president of the court (if the Lord Chief Justice so delegates) to sit in the Court of Protection. A circuit judge or district judge must be nominated by the Lord Chief Justice (in consultation with the Lord Chancellor) to be the senior judge of the Court of Protection[49] who is, in essence, in day-to-day administrative charge of the court.

The jurisdiction of the court concerns the mental capacity of adults and the court can determine whether a person has appropriate mental capacity and, if not, make declarations as to their finances or welfare along with adjudicating on disputes relating to lasting or enduring powers of attorney, including their discharge. Powers of attorney are where a competent adult is assigned to make decisions as to the welfare of the person lacking capacity.[50]

6.4.3 Coroners' courts

Coroners' courts are one of the most ancient forms of court within England and Wales, with the office of coroner dating back to medieval times. The modern coronial system investigates unnatural and violent deaths or those who die in custody together with a specialist jurisdiction relating to treasure trove (a rather complicated provision but, at its simplest, it is gold, silver, or coins from the same find, that are over 300 years old discovered buried). The coronial system was subject to major changes with the introduction of Part 1 *Coroners and Justice Act 2009* (CJA) on 25 July 2013. This section of the chapter will consider the new system.

As with other aspects of the English Legal System (most notably the system of tribunals, discussed in Chapter 7), the changes to the coronial system were designed, in part, to strengthen their accountability and to reform the offices. Traditionally a coroner did not need to be a lawyer and could instead be a medical practitioner (although under s 2(1) *Coroners Act 1988* such persons needed to obtain a specific legal qualification). However, with the introduction of the CJA 2009, coroners must now be judicial appointments (and satisfy the judicial eligibility condition on a five-year period).[51]

Coroners have traditionally been employed by local authorities and this link survives the CJA 2009 reforms. England and Wales has been divided into coronial areas, each of

47. *Mental Capacity Act 2005*, s 45(3).
48. *Mental Capacity Act 2004*, s 46(3).
49. *Mental Capacity Act 2004*, s 46(4).
50. See *Mental Capacity Act 2005*, pt 1.
51. See *Coroners and Justice Act 2009*, sch 3, para 3.

which equates either to a local authority or a combination of local authority borders.[52] Each coronial area has a senior coroner who is the principal coroner and who is assisted by area and assistant coroners.[53] Coroners will have the equivalent status to an inferior judge in that they hold office for good behaviour but can be removed administratively by the Lord Chancellor with the consent of the Lord Chief Justice.[54]

Coroners' courts differ from the rest of the English Legal System in one very important respect; they are inquisitorial rather than adversarial (see 1.3.2.1). Accordingly, there are no 'sides' to a coroners' court and this can mean that there is difficulty in a family of the bereaved securing legal aid for representation before the coroners' courts. This matter was litigated in *R (on the application of Main) v Minister for Legal Aid*.[55] The applicant lost her mother and sister after a railway accident. She claimed for legal aid to provide representation at the inquest and whilst the Legal Services Commission recommended that representation be given, the Lord Chancellor (as minister responsible for legal aid) refused to allow representation. The Court of Appeal, upholding this decision, stated that the coroner was able to identify the issues without representation from the family and placed strength on the fact that the coronial system was inquisitorial rather than adversarial.

 QUESTION FOR REFLECTION

The decision in *Main* was that the Lord Chancellor could not be compelled to grant legal aid for representation in an inquest. Had the family been able to fund counsel privately then representation would have been permitted. Does this not show a flaw in the coronial system? Does it mean that justice can be 'bought'?

Why do you think the family wanted their own representative? Was the Court of Appeal right to think that a coroner can identify matters without representation from the family?

221

 LISTEN TO THE PODCAST

For guidance on how to answer this question and a discussion of the main issues, listen to the author's podcast on the Online Resource Centre: www.oxfordtextbooks.co.uk/orc/gillespie_els6e/

Coroners' courts are inferior courts and are thus susceptible to judicial review, something that has been exercised a number of times.[56] The jurisdiction of a coronial court is now set out clearly in statute. In respect of deaths, a coroner must investigate where:

- the deceased died a violent or unnatural death
- the cause of death is unknown, or
- the deceased died while in custody or otherwise in state detention.[57]

---

52. *Coroners and Justice Act 2009*, sch 2.
53. *Coroners and Justice Act 2009*, sch 3.
54. *Coroners and Justice Act 2009*, sch 3, pt 4.
55. [2007] EWCA Civ 1147.
56. See, most notably, *R (on the application of Paul) v Deputy Coroner of the Queen's Household and Assistant Deputy Coroner for Surrey* [2007] 2 All ER 509 and *R (on the application of Al-Fayed) v Assistant Deputy Coroner of Inner West London* [2008] EWHC 713 (Admin).
57. *Coroners and Justice Act 2009*, s 1(2).

The purpose of the investigation is:

- to ascertain who the deceased was
- how, when, and where the deceased came by his death
- the particulars (if any) required to be registered concerning the death.[58]

Interestingly s 5(2) continues by stating that the second element will also require ascertaining in what circumstances the deceased came by his death where this is necessary to prevent a breach of the *Human Rights Act 1998*. This, it is submitted, is a reference to the jurisprudence that has been established under Article 2 (discussed in Chapter 5 where it was seen that there are positive obligations in respect of the investigation of any death).

The issue of when a jury should be established has long proven controversial (and was one of the principal reasons for litigation in the inquest relating to Diana, Princess of Wales: see *R (on the application of Paul) v Deputy Coroner of the Queen's Household and Assistant Deputy Coroner for Surrey*:[59] note the office of the Coroner of the Queen's Household was abolished by s 46 CJA 2009). Statute has now clarified this and stated that a jury should not normally hear an inquest[60] save where the coroner has reason to suspect:

- the deceased died while in the custody of the state and the death was violent, unnatural, or unknown
- the death resulted from an act or omission by a police officer or a member of the armed services police in the purported execution of their duty
- the death was caused by a notifiable accident, poisoning, or disease, or
- the senior coroner believes that there is sufficient reason for doing so.[61]

Where a jury is empanelled then it is a jury of seven to eleven persons,[62] the exact number being for the senior coroner. A decision of the jury need not be unanimous, but only where only one or two jurors disagree and the jury has had sufficient time to attempt to reach a verdict.[63] The CJA 2009 has also strengthened the rules relating to jury service, including providing for criminal penalties for those who act inappropriately in respect of being summoned to attend as a juror.[64]

The coronial system, whilst locally based, will be under the administration of a Chief Coroner and Deputy Chief Coroner. The Chief Coroner is appointed by the Lord Chief Justice and must either be a puisne or circuit judge.[65] In August 2016 it was announced that HHJ Mark Lucraft QC was appointed Chief Coroner, with the appointment being effective in October 2016. The Lord Chief Justice may also appoint as many persons as he deems appropriate to be a Deputy Chief Coroner and these persons must be puisne or circuit judges or a senior coroner.[66]

58. *Coroners and Justice Act 2009*, s 5(1).
59. [2007] 2 All ER 509.
60. *Coroners and Justice Act 2009*, s 7(1).
61. *Coroners and Justice Act 2009*, s 7(2)–(3).
62. *Coroners and Justice Act 2009*, s 8(1).
63. *Coroners and Justice Act 2009*, s 9.
64. *Coroners and Justice Act 2009*, sch 6.
65. *Coroners and Justice Act 2009*, sch 8, para 1.
66. *Coroners and Justice Act 2009*, sch 8, para 2.

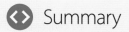 Summary

In this chapter we have noted:

- Classifying the courts is not a simple process since many of the courts have both a civil and a criminal jurisdiction.
- The courts in England and Wales (ie excluding the Supreme Court which is a UK court) are now administered by a single agency, HMCTS.
- The courts of original jurisdiction (ie which hear trials of first instance) are the magistrates' court, county court, Crown Court, and High Court.
- The Crown Court and High Court have both an original and appellate jurisdiction.
- All family-related matters are now heard in the Family Court.
- The High Court is divided into three divisions (Queen's Bench Division, Chancery Division, and Family Division) and when two or more judges sit together in the High Court it is known as a Divisional Court.

End-of-chapter questions

1. Given that the county court and High Court have similar jurisdiction is there any point in keeping them as separate courts? Would it not be appropriate for there to be just one court—a civil court—which could be staffed by different judges? Are there any advantages or disadvantages to this approach?

2. A single Family Court has now been established. What are the advantages of this new court? Are there any disadvantages?

3. Why do we need so many appeal courts? In Chapter 16 it will be noted that it is possible to appeal from the Crown Court to the Court of Appeal and then to the Supreme Court. Is there any need for there to be two appeal courts—should the Court of Appeal not be the final appellate court? In Scotland there is no right of appeal in criminal matters to the Supreme Court, the final appellate court being the Inner House of the Court of Session.

Further reading

Lord Mance, 'Constitutional Reform, the Supreme Court and the Law Lords' (2006) 25 *Civil Justice Quarterly* 155–65.

This is an interesting article written by a Lord of Appeal in Ordinary discussing the work of the House of Lords and the changes a Supreme Court may (or may not) bring.

Robins J, 'Strength in Unity' (2005) 102 *Law Society Gazette* 18–19.

Discusses the possible advantages of creating a single family court.

Samuels A, 'A Unified Civil Court' (2006) 25 *Civil Justice Quarterly* 250–60.

This article discusses whether it would be appropriate to introduce a unified civil court to streamline civil proceedings.

You may also find it interesting to read the annual reports of the Court of Appeal (each Division produces a separate report and they are housed on the judiciary website). A link to the publications can be found on the **Online Resource Centre** at: **www.oxfordtextbooks.co.uk/orc/gillespie_els6e/**

For multiple-choice questions, updates to this chapter, and links to useful websites, please visit the **Online Resource Centre** at: **www.oxfordtextbooks.co.uk/orc/gillespie_els6e/**

7

The Structure of the Tribunals

By the end of this chapter you will be able to:

- Identify the type of disputes that are heard by tribunals.
- Discuss the accountability of tribunals.
- Understand how a matter is heard by the Employment Tribunal.
- Understand how a matter is heard by the Investigatory Powers Tribunal.
- Understand the relationship between the courts and tribunals.

Introduction

Not every dispute will necessarily be dealt with before a court; some disputes will be settled before they reach court. Other cases will never proceed before a court but will instead be heard by a different body. The second part of this chapter will look at the tribunal system, which sits 'parallel' to the courts (see Figure 7.1). The system of tribunals has been created to deal with specific statutory issues. They are administrative rather than purely legal bodies and the rules will often vary between tribunals.

7.1 The tribunal system

The then Senior President of Tribunals, Carnwath LJ, has commented:

> There is no doubt ... that tribunals represent one of the most important pillars of the system of justice in this country ... It is fair to say that more people bring a case before a tribunal than go to any other part of the justice system.[1]

This is a worthy point and demonstrates the importance of a 'parallel' system of justice that exists alongside the courts. Tribunals are administrative bodies that are created by statute to resolve certain disputes. Historically dozens of tribunals have been

---

1. Trevor Buck, 'Precedent in Tribunals and the Development of Principles' (2006) 25 *Civil Justice Quarterly* 458, 459.

created by statute although in recent years this has been reduced to a core number of tribunals that undoubtedly regularly exercise judicial authority. The use of tribunals became quite widespread in the latter half of the twentieth century where it was considered that their use would be preferable to allowing courts to settle administrative disputes. In part, this response was also to minimize pressure on the judicial process by diverting these disputes from the courts.

Whilst tribunals are not strictly courts, they must adhere to the general principles of due process (and a failure to do so will be corrected readily by review either by judicial review or appeal). A key finding of the *Franks Report*, the report of a committee that was set up to examine how tribunals worked, was:

> In the field of tribunals openness appears to us to require the publicity of proceedings and knowledge of the essential reasoning underlying the decisions; fairness to require the adoption of a clear procedure which enables parties to know their rights, to present their case fully and to know the case which they have to meet ... [2]

This is probably the distillation of the minimum requirements of due process but is probably not directly comparable to the judicial system. Since the *Franks Report* the number of tribunals has increased and their importance within the English Legal System has grown. After the *Woolf Report* into civil litigation it was thought that a review of tribunal justice would also be needed, in part to identify whether a separate system of dispute resolution was required alongside a reformed court system. Assuming that such a system was necessary (and the abolition of tribunals was never seriously on the agenda) then their status and effectiveness needed to be discussed in a way similar to the *Woolf* reforms. Together with the *Auld Report* into the criminal justice system this meant that there were, in effect, three reports that covered the entire justice system.

The task of examining the tribunals was given to Sir Andrew Leggatt, a former Lord Justice of Appeal, and he reported in 2001. Leggatt argued that tribunal justice carries with it two advantages: the first is that it consists of a mixture of legal and expert assistance, and the second is that their preparation and hearings should be simpler and more informal than courts.[3] However, he also found that the development of tribunals was ad hoc rather than systematic and that this had created a situation where there was no consistent application of justice within the tribunal system.[4] He recommended that this should change and, as will be seen, it has. The tribunal system is undoubtedly now a parallel system of justice that sits alongside the courts. Recent administrative changes have brought the two systems closer together but they remain distinct, at least in title.

7.2 Structure of tribunals

The *Tribunals, Courts and Enforcement Act 2007* (TCEA 2007) transformed the structure of the tribunals. The Act created a new unified structure, creating two tribunals, known as the 'First-Tier Tribunal' and the 'Upper Tribunal'.

---

2. Oliver Franks, *Report of the Committee on Administrative Tribunals and Enquiries* (Cmnd 218, HMSO, 1957) 10.
3. Andrew Leggatt, *Tribunals for Users: One System, One Service* (HMSO 2001) para 1.2.
4. Andrew Leggatt, *Tribunals for Users: One System, One Service* (HMSO 2001) para 1.3.

7.2.1 **First-Tier Tribunal**

The First-Tier Tribunal consists of seven chambers, known as:

- Social Entitlement Chamber
- Health, Education and Social Care Chamber
- Taxation Chamber
- General Regulatory Chamber
- Immigration and Asylum Chamber
- War Pensions and Armed Forces Compensation Chamber
- Property Chamber.

Each of these chambers comprises similar jurisdictions and involves multiple tribunals and panels. For example, the jurisdictions of the *Health, Education and Social Care Chamber* include mental health, special educational needs and disability, care standard and primary health lists.

Individual tribunals have varying jurisdiction, for example the *Immigration and Asylum Tribunal* has UK-wide jurisdiction, whereas the *Environment Tribunal* is confined to England and Wales only. The First-Tier Tribunal is, in essence, the equivalent of a first-instance jurisdiction even though this jurisdiction may include an appeal from an administrative judgment (eg Criminal Injuries Compensation).

7.2.2 **Upper Tribunal**

The Upper Tribunal consists of four chambers: the *Administrative Appeals Chamber*, *Tax and Chancery Chamber*, *Lands Chamber*, and *Immigration and Asylum Chamber*. The Upper Tribunal largely deals with appeals from the First-Tier Tribunal. As shown in Figure 7.1 the First-Tier Tribunals have a specific appeal route they follow to the Upper Tribunal. For example, the *War Pensions and Armed Forces Compensation Chamber*, the *Social Entitlement Chamber*, the *Health, Education and Social Care Chamber*, and the *General Regulatory Chamber* all appeal to the *Administrative Appeals Chamber*. This ensures that there is one clear system of appeal for the First-Tier Tribunals.

Some complicated first-instance matters on, for example, tax and land can also form part of the work of the Upper Tribunal. Like the High Court, the Upper Tribunal is a superior court of record.

7.2.3 **Appeals**

As noted in above in 7.2.2, appeals from the First-Tier Tribunals proceed to the Upper Tribunal.[5] Further appeals from the Upper Tribunal proceed to the Court of Appeal (Civil Division).[6] A further appeal is only permitted on matters of law and only with leave to appeal from either the Upper Tribunal or the Court of Appeal (Civil Division).[7]

---

5. *Tribunal, Courts and Enforcement Act 2007*, s 11.
6. *Tribunal, Courts and Enforcement Act 2007*, s 13.
7. *Tribunal, Courts and Enforcement Act 2007*, s 13(3).

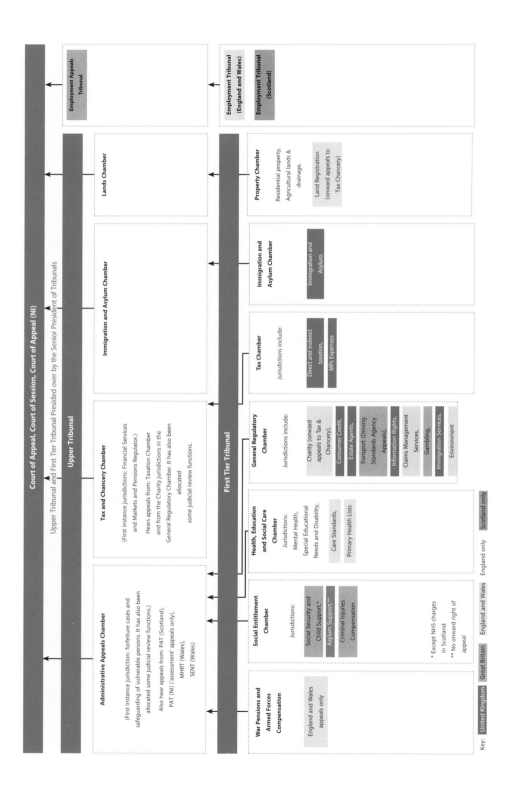

Figure 7.1 The court and judicial structure

Reproduced with permission from HM Courts and Judiciary website

7.2.3.1 Judicial review of tribunals

The TCEA 2007 left unanswered an interesting question over the judicial review of tribunals. Before the reforms of the TCEA 2007, most tribunals were ordinarily considered to be inferior bodies and thus subject to the judicial review of the High Court. However, with the revised tribunal structure (ie the creation of the first tier and upper tier), the First-Tier Tribunal remains an inferior body but the TCEA 2007 purports to transfer the judicial review jurisdiction over this tribunal from the High Court to the Upper Tribunal.[8] Therefore the High Court should decline jurisdiction and instead leave this to the Upper Tribunal (in part based on the rule that judicial review by the High Court should only be permitted where no alternative remedy exists).

What of the Upper Tribunal? It is clear that the Upper Tribunal is a superior court of record[9] but this is not conclusive by itself since, of course, the Crown Court is also a superior court and it is reviewable for matters other than trials on indictment. The answer to the question is to be found in the decision of the Court of Appeal (Civil Division) in *R (on the application of C) v Upper Tribunal*.[10] The Court of Appeal held that the Upper Tribunal is subject to judicial review because it does not have the same status as the High Court, not least because its jurisdiction is based on statute rather than the inherent jurisdiction to resolve matters. The Court of Appeal also noted that the belief that a superior court of record could not be reviewed has never been clarified by the English courts and is not recognized by the Scottish courts (which may be relevant as the First-Tier and Upper Tribunals are UK bodies, not simply bodies of England and Wales). The court preferred to reason that as Parliament is aware of the High Court's power to judicially review, it would have used express words to divest the Upper Tribunal from this power had it so intended, and in the absence of such language, the tribunal is theoretically at least reviewable.

However, the court noted that the fact that it can be reviewed as a matter of law does not mean that it will be in practice or identify what it may be reviewed for. The court noted that judicial review related to various grounds, some of which were controlled by discretion, but that it would be a dereliction of the High Court's duty to let a court or tribunal act in excess of its authority or where it had denied a party a fair hearing.[11] However, in terms of other matters of judicial review (eg procedural impropriety etc) the court noted that Parliament had created the tribunal system to be an independent and self-sufficient system that should correct its own errors of adjudication.

Accordingly, the Court of Appeal held that the Upper Tribunal is amenable to judicial review by the High Court where it purports to exercise jurisdiction it has not been given by Parliament or where it denies the right to a fair trial through, for example, allowing someone to sit as judge who should not. At one level this decision could be considered to be a reasonable compromise in that such challenges will be rarely brought: and the Court of Appeal is stating that where the judicial review is in respect of their adjudication then a review will not be heard and the ordinary appellate rules should apply. On another level, however, this can be said to be a fudge. A right of appeal exists from the Upper Tribunal to the Court of Appeal (Civil Division) on matters of law.[12] The jurisdiction of the tribunal and the right to a fair trial are both

---

8.   *Tribunal, Courts and Enforcement Act 2007*, s 15.
9.   *Tribunal, Courts and Enforcement Act 2007*, s 3(5).
10.   [2010] EWCA Civ 859.
11.   [2010] EWCA Civ 859 [26].
12.   *Tribunal, Courts and Enforcement Act 2007*, s 13.

matters of law and so it must be questioned whether it is truly necessary for the High Court to claim the right to judicially review the tribunal rather than, for example, allowing the Court of Appeal to correct such an error. It may have perhaps been simpler to do this but the courts are slow to limit their own jurisdiction.

7.3 Other tribunals

The First-Tier Tribunal and Upper Tribunal are not the only tribunals in existence. Other tribunals also exist outside the system, most notably the *Employment (and Employment Appeal) Tribunals*. These tribunals are within the *Tribunal Service* but do not feature in the revised 'First Tier–Upper Tier' structure. The Employment (and Appeal) Tribunals are more difficult to locate within the structure, not least because the EAT is considered to be a superior court of record (discussed in more detail below and at 7.5.2). The *Investigatory Powers Tribunal* also sits outside the system. Both of the tribunals are considered in more detail in what follows.

7.3.1 Employment Tribunals

The Employment Tribunals are one of the more well-known tribunals. Their jurisdiction is set out, inter alia, in the *Employment Tribunals Act 1996,* and covers over seventy different types of dispute between employers and employees in relation to employment rights. These include, for example, unfair dismissal and discrimination claims.

In the same way that both civil and criminal courts have rules governing their procedure, so does the Employment Tribunal, these being contained within Sch 1 of the *Employment Tribunals (Constitution and Rules of Procedure) Regulations 2013.*[13] Reference must be made to these rules in order to progress a case, although the tribunal does produce a series of guides to progressing a case.

Once a claim to the employment tribunal has been made, but before the tribunal hearing itself takes place, there will be a preliminary hearing[14] which will ordinarily decide whether there is a prima facie case. This will involve a person demonstrating that they have, for example, suffered unfair treatment or discrimination. Types of evidence that could be adduced at this stage include witnesses, witness statements, and documentary evidence, such as contracts of employment or pay slips. This will be a hearing that usually takes place in private. If the judge decides there is a prima facie case then a date and time is normally set for the final hearing.

The final hearing usually takes place in public.[15] The tribunal is not bound by rules of evidence[16] which theoretically means that any evidence that is relevant can be heard. This can be contrasted with the traditional position in the courts where the probity of evidence was considered to be a relevant factor. Traditionally, hearsay (which for our purposes can be summarized as second-hand evidence) was not permitted by the courts although in recent years this has changed.[17]

---

13. SI 2013/1237.

14. *Employment Tribunals (Constitution and Rules of Procedure) Regulations 2013*, regs 53–56.

15. Subject to the exclusions noted in the *Employment Tribunals (Constitution and Rules of Procedure) Regulations 2013*, SI 2013/1237, sch 1, para 59.

16. *Employment Tribunals (Constitution and Rules of Procedure) Regulations 2013*, reg 41.

17. See *Civil Evidence Act 1995* and *Criminal Justice Act 2003.*

As discussed in 8.1.3.4, similarly to other tribunals, the Employment Tribunal panel constitutes a judge and lay members. Those who sit as lay members of the Employment Tribunals represents employers and employees, and one from each should normally sit.[18]

Once a judgment has been handed down by the tribunal a party can apply to the tribunal, within fourteen days of the original decision being sent to them, to reconsider the judgment.[19] An explanation for why the party wants the decision to be reconsidered must be provided, detailing reasons to justify the reconsideration, for example, the emergence of new evidence. The tribunal can also reconsider cases on its own initiative and this may happen where, for example, a request has come from the Employment Appeal Tribunal.[20] If the tribunal reconsiders its own decision it will either be confirmed, varied, or revoked.[21]

If a party believes that a *legal* mistake was made in their case then they can apply to the *Employment Appeal Tribunal* (EAT). Indeed, the role of the EAT is to rule on the lawfulness of decisions made by the Employment Tribunals.[22] Any party wishing to appeal a point of law in their case must do so within forty-two days of the date that the written reasons for the tribunal panel's decision was sent out to them.[23] If a case is heard by the EAT then, unlike many other appeal tribunals which consist of a judge sitting alone (as the matter under consideration is one of law), lay members consider to sit alongside the presiding judge.

7.3.2 Investigatory Powers Tribunal

Unlike the Employment Tribunals, and indeed many other tribunals, the Investigatory Powers Tribunal (IPT) is not open to the public. Indeed, it is perhaps one of the most restrictive tribunals due to the nature of the work it deals with. The IPT was created by Part IV *Regulation of Investigatory Powers Act (RIPA) 2000*, a statute which (as its name suggests) regulates the use of covert investigation powers by the state. The tribunal has been described as:

> being different from all others in that its concern is with security. For this reason it must remain separate from the rest and ought not to have any relationship with other tribunals.[24]

Although Leggatt is correct to argue that its work relates to security it is less clear as to what this means exactly. There are currently over forty bodies that are authorized to use some or all of the powers within RIPA 2000 (see, for example, the *Regulation of Investigatory Powers (Directed Surveillance and Covert Human Intelligence Sources) Order 2003* (SI 2010/521)) and whilst some undoubtedly deal with security matters (eg GCHQ, the Security Services (MI5), and the Secret Intelligence Service (MI6)) others may appear less important (eg the Food Standards Agency or the Gaming Board for Great Britain).

---

18. *Employment Tribunals (Constitution and Rules of Procedure) Regulations 2013*, SI 2013/1237, reg 8.
19. *Employment Tribunals (Constitution and Rules of Procedure) Regulations 2013*, SI 2013/1237, sch 1, para 70.
20. *Employment Tribunals (Constitution and Rules of Procedure) Regulations 2013*, SI 2013/1237, sch 1, para 70.
21. *Employment Tribunals (Constitution and Rules of Procedure) Regulations 2013*, SI 2013/1237, sch 1, para 70.
22. See, for example, *Jafri v Lincoln College* [2014] EWCA Civ 449.
23. *Employment Appeal Tribunal Rules 1993*.
24. Andrew Leggatt, *Tribunals for Users: One System, One Service* (HMSO 2001) para 3.11.

The powers that are available to these bodies are extremely sensitive and are outside the scope of this book and their use of the powers can be very controversial. The detailed use of the powers will frequently be kept secret, even during a criminal trial, through a process known as *public interest immunity* (PII).[25] Whilst the Act provides for the regulation of these powers through a body known as the *Office of the Surveillance Commissioners*, this body does not examine individual complaints but focuses on whether the powers are, in general, being used appropriately. The use of covert surveillance against a person is a prima facie breach of Article 8 of the ECHR in that it is an interference with a person's private life (see, for example, *Malone v United Kingdom*[26]). If used appropriately this will not matter as it is justified under Article 8(2), but how can this be tested?

It has been noted already that courts, both civil and criminal, are prima facie public bodies and should sit in public and provide for a public pronouncement of the decision. The powers available under RIPA 2000 are so sensitive that the government would not wish them to be discussed in public because it could assist those that they could be used against (ie criminals could use the knowledge to develop anti-surveillance techniques). The HRA 1998 requires that someone who believes the powers are being used against them inappropriately should have the right to take action against authorities[27] and the IPT is this action. Section 65(2) RIPA 2000 states that an action can *only* be brought in the IPT. In *R (on the application of A) v B*[28] the Supreme Court upheld this provision of RIPA 2000 and rejected an argument that the HRA 1998 required that there should be access to the ordinary courts. The Supreme Court held that the IPT had been given exclusive jurisdiction by Parliament and that the courts had no jurisdiction to hear matters within s 65 RIPA even where they did not relate to the regulation of investigatory powers.

The rules of the tribunal are loosely set out in secondary legislation (*Investigatory Powers Tribunal Rules 2000*)[29] but RIPA 2000 itself states that the tribunal shall decide its own procedure in respect of complaints.[30] It is taken to mean that the tribunal can, therefore, issue its own rules but also that it may alter them depending on the circumstances. This rule is subject to the rules set out in the statutory instrument but the tribunal, as the sole arbitrator of claims under HRA 1998, has used its authority to strike down at least one section of the rules (that which requires it to sit in secrecy; see later in this section). Accordingly, the position appears to be that where the rules are incompatible with the ECHR the tribunal reserves the right to be the ultimate arbitrator of its own procedure, in part because of the fact that decisions of the tribunal are not ordinarily the subject of an appeal.

Unlike a traditional matter, the adjudication of a matter raised in the IPT could lead to an investigation. Members of the tribunal are empowered to require the Intelligence or Security Services Commissioners to assist them[31] or to require any public authority to disclose to it such documents and information as it requires.[32] It can be seen, therefore, that the adjudication appears to take the form of an inquisitorial hearing rather

25. Andrew Ashworth and Mike Redmayne, *The Criminal Process* (4th edn, OUP 2010).
26. (1985) 7 EHRR 14.
27. *Human Rights Act 1998*, s 7.
28. [2009] UKSC 12.
29. SI 2000/2665.
30. *Regulation of Investigatory Powers Act 2000*, s 68(1).
31. *Investigatory Powers Tribunal Rules 2000*, SI 2000/2665, r 5(1)(b).
32. *Investigatory Powers Tribunal Rules 2000*, SI 2000/2665, r 5(1)(c).

than a simple adjudication. This is taken further by the fact that there is no disclosure of documents; indeed the statutory rules make it clear that the general rule is that the claimant will *not* be given any details of information provided by the state bodies.[33]

The IPT does not, unlike most other tribunals, have to hold a hearing, the rules making clear that any hearings are purely discretionary,[34] although there may be concerns as to whether this is necessarily compatible with the ECHR since Article 6 is generally taken to mean that there is a right to access a court (or tribunal) where a civil right or obligation is in dispute. As has been noted, covert surveillance is a prima facie breach of Article 8 and thus it is a matter of civil rights or obligation. Accordingly, a person should ordinarily have a right to judicial adjudication although it is less clear whether this right requires an actual hearing or whether it is merely a judicial determination of the issues which could, for example, mean the matter being disposed of by an examination of the relevant papers.

Even if hearings do take place, however, they are unlikely to take the format of the traditional adversarial approach with both sides being in the same room hearing and challenging all the evidence. Rule 9(4) states that it is possible to hold separate hearings for the different sides and at least one commentator has suggested that this will be the normal position.[35] Again this must raise questions over its compatibility with Article 6 of the ECHR since this places significant restrictions on the ability of a person to conduct their case.

Assuming that hearings are held, the statutory rules are quite clear about their nature:

> The Tribunal's proceedings, including any oral hearings, shall be conducted in private.[36]

In other words all matters relating to the tribunal are held in secret with members of the public and press excluded. Again this raises questions about compliance with basic freedoms under both domestic and ECHR jurisprudence where the traditional rule is that hearings are in public. There has always been the opportunity for courts to sit in camera (meaning in secret) where it is necessary to protect information in the interests of security or other public interest matters but this has always been the exception to the rule. The rules purport to state that tribunal activities can *never* be in public and the tribunal has decided that this is incompatible with basic rights and overturned this rule.[37]

It can be seen, therefore, that the IPT operates in a significantly different way from both ordinary tribunals and the courts. Certainly it makes a clear contrast from courts where there are more rigid and formalistic approaches to the adjudication of matters and where the adversarial model of justice remains important. This distinction continues when it relates to evidence. Like the Employment Tribunal the IPT has wide powers over evidence but its rule is formulated slightly differently:

> The Tribunal may receive evidence in any form, and may receive evidence that would not be admissible in a court of law.[38]

233

---

33.   *Investigatory Powers Tribunal Rules 2000*, SI 2000/2665, r 6 and *Regulation of Investigatory Powers Act 2000*, s 69(6).
34.   *Investigatory Powers Tribunal Rules 2000*, SI 2000/2665, r 9(2).
35.   Helen Fenwick, 'Covert Surveillance under the Regulation of Investigatory Powers Act 2000, Part II' (2001) 65 *Journal of Criminal Law* 521.
36.   *Investigatory Powers Tribunal Rules 2000*, SI 2000/2665, r 9(6).
37.   Grania Langdon-Down, 'A Fair Hearing' (2003) 100 *Law Society Gazette* 21, 22.
38.   *Investigatory Powers Tribunal Rules 2000*, SI 2000/2665, r 11(1).

Arguably this is very similar to the form of words adopted for the Employment Tribunals but it is expressed in a stronger way, making clear that there is no doubt that the IPT can receive inadmissible evidence. This can be contrasted immediately with both civil and criminal courts where certain evidence, particularly in respect of covert surveillance, would ordinarily not be admissible in evidence. This would appear to support the earlier argument that the IPT adopts an inquisitorial rather than adversarial system when deciding whether a person's rights have been infringed.

Example Inadmissible evidence—telephone taps

The use of 'telephone taps' (more properly known as an interception of communication) has always been controversial within the English Legal System. Section 17 RIPA 2000 makes clear that the product of an intercept (ie the actual conversation) is not admissible in evidence. Let us take an example.

The police suspect Mandy is involved in the importation of a large quantity of illegal drugs. In order to find out where the drugs originate, they place an intercept onto Mandy's telephone. They hear Mandy talking to Alan and she is heard agreeing to buy 20 kilos of heroin to be imported into Whitby docks.

For whatever reason the drugs do not appear in Whitby. Technically speaking the conversation between Mandy and Alan amounts to a criminal offence (a conspiracy) but since s 17 RIPA 2000 applies, the police cannot adduce the transcript of the telephone conversation and so it is unlikely that any conspiracy could be proven.

Since the IPT can receive any evidence, however, including inadmissible evidence, they could ask for transcripts. Let us assume that Mandy has complained to the IPT that she believes her telephone has been tapped and that the police have been listening to conversations with her lawyer, thus breaching legal professional privilege. Not only can the IPT ask the police whether they have intercepted any conversations but it could demand the transcripts which would allow it to decide whether legal professional privilege has been breached.

The secrecy of the IPT invariably leads to questions being raised as to whether it is a fair system, especially since it rejects many of the adversarial principles that are so coveted in other aspects of the judicial system. The fact that a person is not necessarily able to be involved with the full case nor able to see the evidence on which the state relies must certainly raise questions as to fairness even if these are unproven. These questions are perhaps given more weight when an analysis is made of the statistics.

During 2015 there were 251 complaints made to the IPT of which only 8 (4 per cent) were upheld; 101 (47 per cent) were ruled as 'frivolous or vexatious'.[39] Complaints can be heard in open court, however, once again due to the nature of the IPT's work, the vast majority of cases are heard behind closed doors. 2015 saw 27 per cent of complaints that were not deemed as being out of jurisdiction, out of time, dismissed for administrative reasons or frivolous or vexatious, being heard in open court.[40] Whilst

---

39.   The Investigatory Powers Tribunal, *Volume of Complaints* (IPT 2015) <http://www.ipt-uk.com/content.asp?id=30>.

40.   The Investigatory Powers Tribunal, *Volume of Complaints* (IPT, 2015) <http://www.ipt-uk.com/content.asp?id=30>.

this is higher than in previous years it is still a small proportion of the cases being heard by the IPT.

7.4 Administration of tribunals

The vast majority of tribunals are administered by HM Courts and Tribunals Service (discussed at Chapter 6.1.2) including the Employment Tribunal and EAT. However, there are certain tribunals that are administered differently. For example, School Exclusion Panels are administered by local authorities.

The TCEA 2007 created the Tribunal Procedure Committee,[41] which produces and keeps under review the *Tribunal Procedure Rules*. These Rules are, in essence, the equivalent of the *Civil Procedure Rules* and the *Criminal Procedure Rules* used in the court system. As with the *Civil Procedure Rules*, *Criminal Procedure Rules*, and *Family Procedure Rules* they are based in statutory instruments but are updated frequently. The Tribunal Procedure Committee includes nominees of the Senior President of the Tribunals, the Lord Chancellor, and the Lord Chief Justice.

7.4.1 Judicial administration

The role of Senior President of the Tribunals was created under the *Tribunals, Courts and Enforcement Act 2007*.[42] Lord Justice Ryder is the current holder of the post. The responsibilities of the Senior President include coordinating the work of the tribunals and, in particular, representing the views of the tribunal judiciary.[43] In order to discharge this duty the Senior President has the statutory power to lay written representations before Parliament,[44] and he does not need permission of, for example, the Lord Chief Justice to do so.

7.5 Court or tribunals or courts and tribunals?

Having considered both courts (in Chapter 6) and tribunals, the key question in this area that needs to be answered is what, if anything, is the difference between a court and a tribunal. The answer is not easy, and is arguably getting harder each year. The judiciary—in this context meaning both the courts judiciary and the tribunals judiciary—are determined to bring the two systems of justice closer together. The *Senior President* and the *Lord Chief Justice* are committed to having a single judiciary, capable of sitting in either courts or tribunals.[45] Indeed the Senior President now has his private office in the same wing as the Lord Chief Justice, to send a signal that they are working together in this revolution.

Despite the closeness between the courts and tribunals (something which is set to continue in development, see 20.4.1), there are areas within which some have argued there are differences between the courts and tribunals. We will consider three of these areas next, namely, jurisdiction, precedent, and representation.

41. *Tribunals, Courts and Enforcement Act 2007*, sch 5.
42. *Tribunals, Courts and Enforcement Act 2007*, s 2.
43. *Tribunals, Courts and Enforcement Act 2007*, sch 1, pt 4.
44. *Tribunals, Courts and Enforcement Act 2007*, sch 1, pt 4.
45. See 20.4.1.

7.5.1 **Jurisdiction**

Some argue that the difference between the courts and tribunals is as regards their jurisdiction. There are two parts to this argument. The first is that a court will ordinarily have general rather than specific jurisdiction, ie its work will not be limited to one small aspect of the law, whereas tribunals are created by statute to examine certain specific areas (eg the *Employment Tribunal* which examines employment issues, the *Special Educational Needs and Disability Tribunal* (now within the *Health, Education & Social Care Chamber of the First-Tier Tribunal*) which allows parents and children to ensure that their educational needs are appropriately resourced by the appropriate authorities). As a rule of thumb this can be quite a useful test but it is often said that it is flawed because specialist courts do exist, most notably the Bankruptcy Court (which deals with bankruptcies), the Commercial Court (which deals with high-value commercial transactions between companies, often relating to trade marks), and the Admiralty Court (which deals with disputes relating to shipping). However, it could be argued that this does not contradict the point which is made because technically these 'courts' are not individual courts but rather groupings within the Queen's Bench Division of the High Court of Justice (see 6.2.5). Accordingly, the overarching body—the High Court—does still have general jurisdiction.

The second aspect to the argument about jurisdiction concerns not just the area of law but also the type of decision reached. It is sometimes said that tribunals are there to ensure that administrative actions have been taken correctly. Whilst this is undoubtedly true for some tribunals (eg the *Land Tribunal* (subsumed within the Upper Tribunal) which examines questions about compensation arising from the compulsory acquisition of land by government), it becomes less clear for other tribunals (eg the *Employment Tribunals*). Also, it cannot be determinative since the High Court has a reviewing jurisdiction through the doctrine of judicial review and one of the three grounds for invoking this procedure is procedural impropriety, ie not following the correct administration.[46]

It can be seen therefore that it is not simple to identify what the difference between a court and tribunal is. At one point it was thought that perceptions may be the difference: ie the executive views tribunals as administrative bodies although the judiciary views them as judicial or quasi-judicial bodies.[47] Leggatt suggested that there were three tests to decide whether a matter should be heard by a tribunal or court:

1. **Participation.** Tribunals are considered to be inclusive and are designed, so far as possible, to be dealt with without the need for a lawyer.

2. **Special expertise.** Where a matter is outside the knowledge of the tribunal of fact a court will ordinarily permit the parties to adduce expert evidence by calling witnesses. Tribunals, however, will ordinarily consist of a legally qualified chair with experts sitting alongside them.

3. **Specialist administrative expertise.** Tribunals specialize in dealing with the combination of law and administration that relates to administrative or regulatory bodies. The absence of this would ordinarily leave judicial review as the only option.[48]

---

46.   See *Council of Civil Service Unions v Minister for the Civil Service* [1985] AC 374.
47.   Oliver Franks, *Report of the Committee on Administrative Tribunals and Enquiries* (Cmnd 218, HMSO, 1957) 9.
48.   Andrew Leggatt, *Tribunals for Users: One System, One Service* (HMSO 2001) paras 1.11–1.13.

However, it is not clear that this necessarily helps because many of these factors can be applied to both. For example, the absence of representation (which is discussed later at 7.5.3) is also a feature of the small claims court although this is perhaps not as significant since the small claims court is perhaps not representative of a 'court' and indeed the scheme is often considered closer to arbitration than litigation. However, Leggatt was not necessarily suggesting that these factors will only be found in a court but that it makes it more likely that a matter will be heard in a tribunal.

To an extent it can be argued that the distinction between tribunals and courts is not particularly relevant. Modern tribunals are bound by the HRA 1998 in the same way as are courts[49] and the disputes heard by tribunals will almost certainly be considered a 'right or obligation' within the meaning of Article 6(1) of the ECHR. On that basis it could be legitimately questioned whether there is any significant disadvantage that arises from a matter being heard by a tribunal rather than a court. Two further issues that tend to give concern are issues of precedent and representation.

7.5.2 Precedent

The importance of precedent to the English Legal System has been noted already (see, most notably, Chapter 3) but what is the position with tribunals setting precedent? It has been suggested that this can be a way in which they differ from the courts:

> [A] tribunal is ... in a radically different position from a court of law. Its duty is to reach the right decision in the circumstances of the moment, any discretion must be genuinely exercised, and there must be no blind following of its previous decisions.[50]

Before examining what this means it is necessary to pause to consider whether this is 'radically different' from courts of law. Decisions of the county court do not set precedent nor, it will be remembered, do decisions of the High Court when it is sitting as a court of first instance (see 3.2). However, it is clear that the courts need to follow the precedent of higher courts and also will normally be slow to depart from their own decisions even when technically not bound by them.

However, the point made by Wade and Forsyth is that a tribunal is (supposedly) concentrating on the individual facts of the case at hand rather than adopting a consistent approach to principles. However, is this necessarily either correct or appropriate? It has been suggested that whilst this was true historically the modern role of tribunals requires them to interpret legislation in a similar way to the courts.[51] Accordingly, it can be questioned whether it would not be more appropriate for their interpretations to be consistent? It will be remembered from Chapter 3 that the principle of *stare decisis* is considered to be a fundamental principle of English justice and so the abandonment of this policy at tribunal level could be construed as a lowering of fairness.

In fact it would be naive to suggest that there is no precedent within the tribunal system. Certain tribunals publish their decisions and allow them to be cited (the most obvious example being the EAT). Also, most tribunals are inferior bodies (the principal exceptions being the EAT, IPT, and the Immigration Tribunal) and may (unless

49. *Human Rights Act 1998*, s 6(3)(a) states that a 'public authority' includes a 'court or tribunal'.
50. William Wade and Christopher Forsyth, *Administrative Law* (11th edn, OUP 2014) 778.
51. Trevor Buck, 'Precedent in Tribunals and the Development of Principles' (2006) 25 *Civil Justice Quarterly* 458, 465.

prohibited by statute) be the subject of judicial review. If they are subject to judicial review then they are required to follow the rulings of the High Court (now Upper Tribunal in some cases—see 7.2.3.1) and thus a rudimentary form of *stare decisis* is created.

Even where a tribunal is not subject to judicial review it is possible that rudimentary precedent will be created. It had been customary to differentiate between First- and Second-Tier Tribunals and it has been suggested that precedent replicates the appellate structure and the relationship between the tribunals,[52] and this has now been formalized by the TCEA 2007 reforms.

⚡ FIRST- AND SECOND-TIER TRIBUNALS

It is customary to refer to 'first-tier' and 'second-tier' tribunals. In essence first-tier tribunals are those tribunals that exercise original jurisdiction, ie they make findings of fact and provide an appropriate relief or declaration. Examples of this would include the Employment Tribunal and now the First-Tier Tribunal itself.

Second-tier tribunals are appellate tribunals and are more concerned with ensuring that a person who believes a decision made by a first-tier tribunal has been wrongly made has a means of redress. Perhaps the classic example of this is the EAT. Leggatt proposed a single second-tier tribunal be created to hear appeals from most first-tier tribunals[53] but he did accept that a small number of tribunals would be excepted from this regime and appeals would proceed direct to the courts[54] and that as a consequence alternative appeals, including judicial review, should no longer be permitted.[55] As noted earlier, this is the position that has now largely been created (see 7.2.3) although certain first- and second-tier tribunals exist outside of this structure.

Leggatt considered how precedent should work following his reforms. He suggested that first-tier tribunals should not set precedent,[56] ie a first-tier tribunal would not be bound by the previous decision of a first-tier tribunal. This would appear somewhat logical and comparable to first-instance decisions of courts. However, Leggatt also ruled out decisions of second-tier tribunals automatically creating precedent[57] because he believed that it would be a barrier to access since users of tribunals would be required to be familiar with decisions of the second-tier tribunal. However, others suggest that precedent in tribunals could actually assist tribunal users, not least by efficiently clarifying and developing the law[58] and ensuring that someone seeking advice is able properly to predict the law. The compromise suggested by Leggatt is that some decisions will set a precedent but others will not.[59] The tribunal itself would select which decisions would become precedents and these would be published.

This suggestion can be immediately contrasted with the position in the courts where it has been held that it is *not* for a judge passing judgment to decide what does,

---

52. Trevor Buck, 'Precedent in Tribunals and the Development of Principles' (2006) 25 *Civil Justice Quarterly* 458, 466.
53. Andrew Leggatt, *Tribunals for Users: One System, One Service* (HMSO 2001) para 6.10.
54. Andrew Leggatt, *Tribunals for Users: One System, One Service* (HMSO 2001) para 6.14.
55. Andrew Leggatt, *Tribunals for Users: One System, One Service* (HMSO 2001) para 6.30.
56. Andrew Leggatt, *Tribunals for Users: One System, One Service* (HMSO 2001) para 6.19.
57. Andrew Leggatt, *Tribunals for Users: One System, One Service* (HMSO 2001) para 6.24.
58. Trevor Buck, 'Precedent in Tribunals and the Development of Principles' (2006) 25 *Civil Justice Quarterly* 458, 465.
59. Andrew Leggatt, *Tribunals for Users: One System, One Service* (HMSO 2001) para 6.26.

or does not, create precedent (see 3.3.2). Also, it is not immediately clear how this system will assist users of tribunals as they must become familiar with certain precedents. Presumably, however, since there will be a small number of binding precedents, these could be accompanied by summaries prepared and publicized on, for example, tribunal websites.

 QUESTION FOR REFLECTION

If tribunals adjudicate on questions of law (including the application of a statutory provision) rather than just examine whether an administrative process has been followed, should the system of *stare decisis* not apply in the same way as it does in the court system? One of the reasons why it does not appear to be followed literally is the informal nature of tribunals[60] but is this a valid excuse? Should a person seeking justice before a tribunal not expect a consistent approach to be taken as to the law?

 LISTEN TO THE PODCAST

For guidance on how to answer this question and a discussion of the main issues, listen to the author's podcast on the Online Resource Centre:
www.oxfordtextbooks.co.uk/orc/gillespie_els6e/

7.5.3 Representation

It has been seen that in both the civil and criminal justice system it is not strictly necessary to employ a lawyer to represent oneself in court. However, with the exception of certain proceedings in the magistrates' court (eg guilty pleas to driving offences) or small claims court, it is probably more desirable if lawyers are engaged, but what is the position with tribunals?

A principal advantage of the tribunal system is said to be that they are informal and user-friendly.[61] All of the tribunals try to make themselves accessible to those that need to access them. This includes the provision of step-by-step instructions on how to access the service.[62]

An example of accessibility is the fact that there are extremely wide rights of audience in most tribunals. Not only can the applicant act as a litigant in person during a tribunal but he has the choice to engage a lawyer (unless specifically prohibited by statute) or take any other person as representative.[63] A difficulty with engaging a lawyer is the fact that legal aid is not generally available for tribunals, and where a tribunal does not specifically permit a lawyer to be engaged it is unlikely that the rules of the tribunal will permit the fees to be reclaimed by the successful party. Where legal aid has failed many bodies have stepped in. Those who belong to a trade union will normally be given representation, with most unions employing workers who specialize in tribunal litigation.

---

60. Andrew Leggatt, *Tribunals for Users: One System, One Service* (HMSO 2001) para 6.24.
61. Mark Elliott and Robert Thomas, *Public Law* (2nd edn, OUP 2014) 623.
62. The Online Resource Centre that accompanies this book provides links to the principal tribunal websites which will allow you to access the materials available and understand how to initiate proceedings.
63. *Employment Tribunal Act 1996*, s 6.

The Citizens Advice Bureau (CAB), an independent charity, has also begun to adopt a representation service for those areas of work within its expertise (usually employment, rent, and social welfare). Even universities have entered this sector with some under-graduate law programmes including a 'law clinic' whereby undergraduates, under the supervision of staff (who frequently hold professional practice certificates), undertake legal work in the community including providing representation before clinics.

If representation is permitted by others then this does raise the question whether tribunals are litigant-friendly. It is one thing suggesting that a lawyer does not need to be engaged, but if a representative (eg a union official or CAB worker) is useful then does this not mean that legal representation would be useful? There is evidence to suggest that representation was beneficial to those using tribunals[64] and yet despite this there is strong resistance to the use of representation in tribunals. Some argue that engaging a lawyer would simply add to costs, delay, and complexity.[65] Why is it that the lack of legal representation is considered to be an advantage? Is it truly an advantage or is this a justification that is used to disguise the fact that it would be expensive for lawyers to be used in all tribunals?

It is difficult to argue against the suggestion that representation is helpful because the representative is almost certainly familiar with the tribunal process and will therefore be able to structure the submissions in an effective way that demonstrates the claim made. A litigant in person is unlikely to have legal training and yet is being asked to put forward an argument based, in part at least, on law, something they are unlikely to know anything about. It has been noted that the right to representation, including legal representation, has not traditionally been considered a principle of natural justice[66] but the decision of the European Court of Human Rights in *Steel and Morris v United Kingdom*,[67] which suggested that Article 6 could require legal assistance to be provided where lack of it would lead to an inequality of arms, does take a further step towards identifying a right to legal representation. Whilst it may be thought that an inequality of arms may not exist within a tribunal system of justice it is conceivable to identify circumstances. A spin on the facts of *Steel and Morris* is possible whereby a private individual is seeking to refer a large multinational corporation to an employment tribunal. Other examples may include situations where it is a private individual against the state where one party (the state) can afford to engage leading counsel whereas the individual litigant may not. However, the counter-argument is that the decision in *Steel and Morris* was based, in part, on the fact that High Court proceedings are inherently formal and technical. Since tribunal proceed-ings are not then it could be argued that the same level of representation is not required.

In this era of restricted public legal funding (discussed in Chapter 11) it is perhaps unrealistic to expect an absolute right to legal representation. The current system relies on specialized laypersons stepping into the breach but is this appropriate? In a now rather dated report, Bell noted that there was a perception that tribunal justice did not consider that lawyers needed to be engaged but thought that tribunals should be more inclusive.[68] To some degree this has been taken on board by the tribunals through the provision of guidance to bringing a case, but can a litigant in person ever be considered comparable to a professional representative? It has been suggested that a fundamental

---

64. Andrew Leggatt, *Tribunals for Users: One System, One Service* (HMSO 2001) para 4.21.
65. Andrew Leggatt, *Tribunals for Users: One System, One Service* (HMSO 2001) para 4.21.
66. William Wade and Christopher Forsyth, *Administrative Law* (11th edn, OUP 2014) 782.
67. (2005) 41 EHRR 22.
68. Kathleen Bell, *Research Study on Supplementary Benefit Appeal Tribunals* (HMSO 1975) 19.

principle of tribunal justice is that tribunals are adversarial[69] but it is not clear why this is the case. It is suggested that deviating from the adversarial process means that favouritism could be shown but this does not automatically follow. An inquisitor can remain independent and it has been noted elsewhere that there is a tendency in the civil litigation system to move away from strict adversarial approaches.

Is the solution therefore not to adopt a more inquisitorial system? In that way the emphasis is placed on the tribunals and not the litigants but this may not necessarily be welcome as it could lead to more focus on the constitution of the tribunal, including a consideration as to whether all members (including lay members) should be better rewarded as they will need to alter their approach to a case. The conundrum as to rights of audience looks as though it will continue for some time yet.

 QUESTION FOR REFLECTION

Tribunals are, potentially, dealing with extremely important issues, including the integrity of litigants (in, for example, employment disputes or disputes before the *Care Standards Tribunal* (now *Health, Education and Social Care* Chamber of the First-Tier Tribunal) which decides, inter alia, upon the suitability of teachers to work with vulnerable members of society) and certain disputes will concern significant sums of money. Is it right, therefore, that the engagement of a lawyer should be exceptional in such cases?

What advantages and disadvantages are there to the routine appointment of lawyers (including state-funded lawyers where appropriate)?

 LISTEN TO THE PODCAST

For guidance on how to answer this question and a discussion of the main issues, listen to the author's podcast on the Online Resource Centre: www.oxfordtextbooks.co.uk/orc/gillespie_els6e/

 Summary

This chapter has examined the jurisdiction of tribunals and noted their increasing role within the justice system. In particular it has:

- Noted that tribunals have existed for many years but traditionally operated as an oversight system for administrative issues.
- Identified the fact that in recent years the number of tribunals has increased and their work has included questions of law and not just administrative propriety.
- Considered the work specifically of the *Employment Tribunals* and the *Investigatory Powers Tribunal.*
- Discussed whether tribunals are separate from the judicial system or whether there is an argument that they should be recognized as courts.

69. William Wade and Christopher Forsyth, *Administrative Law* (11th edn, OUP 2014) 775.

- Identified that tribunals see themselves as being more informal adjudicating bodies where traditional rules of evidence do not necessarily apply.
- Considered whether litigants in a tribunal should be represented.

 # End-of-chapter questions

1. Read Chapter 4 of the *Leggatt Report* (available online). Do you think tribunals are truly accessible to ordinary members of the public or do you still require the services of someone who knows the law and procedure? Is there any way of making them truly accessible and would this be desirable?

2. Read *Ewing v Security Service*[70] where the High Court decided that the IPT bore many of the characteristics of a court. Also read Helen Fenwick, 'Covert Surveillance under the Regulation of Investigatory Powers Act 2000, Part II' (2001) 65 *Journal of Criminal Law* 521. Is the IPT really a tribunal or is it a court? What, if any, are the differences and do you believe that the tribunal can properly be said to safeguard a citizen's human rights?

Further reading

Bradley A, 'The Tribunals Maze' [2002] *Public Law* 200–2.

This short article considers the proposals in the *Leggatt Report* to consolidate the tribunals into one service with a smaller number of tribunals.

Buck T, 'Precedent in Tribunals and the Development of Principles' (2006) 25 *Civil Justice Quarterly* 458–84.

This is an interesting piece that considers whether precedent exists within tribunals, whether precedent should exist in tribunals, and, if so, how it would operate.

Burton M, 'The Employment Appeal Tribunal: October 2002–July 2005' (2005) 34 *Industrial Law Journal* 273–83.

This article is written by Burton J, the then President of the Employment Appeal Tribunal, and considers the significant changes that have occurred to the tribunal over a three-year period.

Carnwath LJ, 'Tribunal Justice: A New Start' [2009] *Public Law* 48–69.

This article was written by the (then) Senior President of Tribunals and set out the major changes brought about by the TCEA 2007 and discussed how tribunal justice would operate.

For multiple-choice questions, updates to this chapter, and links to useful websites, please visit the **Online Resource Centre** at: **www.oxfordtextbooks.co.uk/orc/gillespie_els6e/**

70.   [2003] EWHC 2051.

8

Staffing and Appointments to the Courts and Tribunals

By the end of this chapter you will be able to:

- Identify the key judicial offices, their ranks, and styles.
- Understand how judges are appointed and assess the recent changes.
- Understand the staffing of the tribunal system.
- Assess the differences and similarities between the court judiciary and the tribunal judiciary.

Introduction

At the heart of the English Legal System is the judiciary, a body of persons often caricatured in the media as doddery old men who are bordering on senile. The truth, however, is that both the full-time and part-time judiciary in England and Wales are extremely professional persons who have come from the very best of the Bar and solicitors. That is not to say that controversy does not surround the judiciary and, in particular, the way that they operate and are appointed to their office. Whilst the courts judiciary is well known, the tribunals judiciary is perhaps less so, and therefore both will be considered in this chapter.

8.1 The judicial office

As will be seen, there are different types of judges within the English Legal System and these differences are echoed in how they are styled and referred to, something that will be explored in what follows.

The position of a judge is not one that is taken by employment but it is, rather, an office that the holder possesses during his tenure. It is not the place of this chapter to discuss the differences between an office holder and an employee save to say that it normally means an office holder cannot use employment legislation as regards the performance and termination of their office, and the manner in which a person is accountable for disciplinary issues would also differ.

The style, number, and type of judges have differed over the centuries but the modern English Legal System now has a relatively fixed hierarchy of judicial appointments, both full- and part-time. This chapter will not focus on the magistracy as they do not, strictly speaking, hold a judicial office, the office of justice of the peace being a distinct but related office. The appointment of the magistracy is discussed elsewhere (Chapter 13) and in order to allow a proper contrast to be drawn, the position of the district judge (magistrates' court) is also considered in that chapter. It should be noted, however, that the district judge (magistrates' court) is a judicial officer and is appointed in the same way as an inferior judge (see 13.1.2.1).

The modern judiciary has been divided into six pay grades (although there is some subdivision) and this illustrates their relevant place within the hierarchy. Table 8.1 lists the key judicial appointments in each grade. It also, out of simplicity, states where each judge will ordinarily sit and how they are referred to in court.

This grading of judge looks quite complicated but, as will be seen both in this chapter and in Chapter 20 (The Future), it is key to the way that the judiciary are now deployed. As has been noted already, the court judiciary and tribunal judiciary are being brought closer together and the eventual aim is that a judge of a particular grade will be able to sit in any tribunal that she or he is equivalent to, or authorized to sit in. Some of the particularities of this will be discussed in this chapter.

Broadly speaking, the judiciary can be divided into three categories:

1. **Senior Judiciary**. These are the most senior roles, carrying with them judicial leadership functions.

2. **Superior Judiciary**. These are judges who sit, as of right, in the higher courts (High Court of Justice and above).

3. **Inferior Judiciary**. This is all other judges.

8.1.1 Senior judiciary

The senior judiciary are those that are listed as 'senior judges' in statute.[1] However, to this the Senior President of Tribunals should also be added although his office has not yet been added to the statutory list. It is clear from Table 8.1 that the Senior President now ranks with the Heads of Division (see later) and indeed, under statute, the Senior President technically ranks alongside the Lord Chief Justice in terms of judiciary leadership[2] (the Lord Chief Justice being responsible for the court judiciary and the Senior President being responsible for the tribunal judiciary).

The senior judiciary for our purposes[3] are therefore:

- Lord Chief Justice of England and Wales (who is also *President of the Courts of England & Wales*)

- Master of the Rolls (who is also the *Head of Civil Justice*)

- President of the Supreme Court

---

1. *Constitutional Reform Act 2005*, s 60.
2. *Tribunals, Courts and Enforcement Act 2007*, s 2 and sch 1.
3. The senior judiciary in Scotland and Northern Ireland have not been included in the list.

Table 8.1 Judicial appointments

Grade	Judicial Title	Ordinarily sit in …	Referred to in court as …
1	Lord Chief Justice	Court of Appeal; High Court of Justice	My Lord/My Lady
1.1	Master of the Rolls	Court of Appeal	My Lord/My Lady
	President of the Supreme Court	Supreme Court	My Lord/My Lady
2	Chancellor of the High Court	High Court of Justice; Court of Appeal	My Lord/My Lady
	President of the Family Division	High Court of Justice; Court of Appeal	My Lord/My Lady
	President of the Queen's Bench Division	High Court of Justice; Court of Appeal	My Lord/My Lady
	Senior President of Tribunals	Court of Appeal; High Court; Upper Tribunal	My Lord (in courts); Sir (in Tribunals)
	Justices of the Supreme Court	Supreme Court	My Lord/My Lady
3	Lords (or Ladies) Justice of Appeal	Court of Appeal	My Lord/My Lady
4	Puisne judge	High Court of Justice	My Lord/My Lady
5	Circuit judges at the Old Bailey	Crown Court	My Lord/My Lady[4]
	Vice-President of the Upper Tribunal	Upper Tribunal	Sir or Madam
	Presidents of the First-Instance Tribunal Chambers	First-instance tribunal	Sir or Madam
	Senior Circuit judges	Crown Court; county court	Your Honour
	Senior district judge (chief magistrate)	Magistrates' court	Sir or Madam
6.1	Circuit judges	Crown Court; county court	Your Honour
	Deputy Chamber Presidents of the First-Tier Tribunal	First-Tier Tribunal	Your Honour
	Upper Tribunal judges	Upper Tribunal	Sir or Madam
6.2	Deputy senior district judge (magistrates' court)	Magistrates' court	Sir or Madam
	Immigration judges	Upper Tribunal; First-Tier Tribunal	Sir or Madam
7	District judges	County court; High Court of Justice	Sir or Madam
	District judges (magistrates' court)	Magistrates' court	Sir or Madam
	First-Tier Tribunal judges.	First-Tier Tribunal.	Sir or Madam

4.   Whilst circuit judges are ordinarily referred to as 'Your Honour', all circuit judges in the Old Bailey are, for historical reasons, called 'My Lord' or 'My Lady'.

- Supreme Court Justices
- President of the Family Division (who is also the Head of Family Justice)
- Chancellor of the High Court
- President of the Queen's Bench Division
- Senior President of Tribunals.

8.1.1.1 Lord Chief Justice

The Lord Chief Justice has always been the most senior professional judge but, following the changes to the role of the Lord Chancellor, he became the head of the judiciary with the title *President of the Courts of England and Wales*.[5] As President of the courts, he can sit in any of the courts as of right, although traditionally he restricts himself to the Court of Appeal, High Court of Justice, and Crown Courts. The Supreme Court is not one of 'his' courts because it is a UK court but the Lord Chief Justice is entitled to sit in the Supreme Court as an additional member if requested by the President of the Supreme Court.[6] This has happened relatively rarely since the Supreme Court has come into existence, although that might be because the Supreme Court currently has a 'criminal judge' in its ranks.[7]

The Lord Chief Justice was, by tradition, given a peerage upon appointment but following the constitutional reforms to the House of Lords and the removal of the professional judges from the House of Lords it was thought unlikely that this position would continue, in part because by statute, the title remains 'Lord Chief Justice' regardless of whether the holder was a peer or not.[8] However, when the current Lord Chief Justice, Lord Thomas of Cwmgiedd, was announced, he was to the surprise of many given a life peerage even though he is debarred from sitting in the House of Lords. This perhaps demonstrates that despite the recent changes the Queen believes her Lord Chief Justice should remain a peer.

The Lord Chief Justice was traditionally the head of criminal justice and the CRA 2005 makes him titular *Head of Criminal Justice*.[9] The Act does, however, provide for a deputy head in order to allow the Lord Chief Justice to delegate some of the administrative authority and this person will be someone who is a Lord Justice of Appeal.[10] Currently it is Lady Justice Hallett, who is also the Vice-President of the Court of Appeal (Criminal Division).

8.1.1.2 Master of the Rolls

The Master of the Rolls, along with the President of the Supreme Court, ranks joint second to the Lord Chief Justice in precedence and is traditionally the head of the Court of Appeal (Civil Division) and, following the *Courts Act 2003* (CA 2003), was created the *Head of Civil Justice*.[11] The 'Rolls' in his title reflects the fact that

---

5. *Constitutional Reform Act 2005*, s 7(1).
6. *Constitutional Reform Act 2005*, s 38(1).
7. Lord Hughes, who was previously Vice-President of the Court of Appeal (Criminal Division) and had been tipped as a future Lord Chief Justice by some.
8. A comparison could perhaps be drawn to Northern Ireland where the Lord Chief Justice is so called but is actually a knight (the current holder being Sir Declan Morgan). It is also notable that the title remains Lord Chief Justice even if a female holds it, so it would become 'Lady X, Lord Chief Justice of England & Wales'.
9. *Constitutional Reform Act 2005*, s 8.
10. *Constitutional Reform Act 2005*, s 8(4)(b).
11. *Courts Act 2003*, s 62(1).

historically the Master of the Rolls was the clerk responsible for maintaining the rolls and records of the Chancery Court. This responsibility was later transferred to the Public Records Office under ministerial responsibility but the ancient title remains.

The CA 2003 permits a Deputy Head of Civil Justice to be created in order to assist the Master of the Rolls in his work (currently it is Lord Justice Briggs).

8.1.1.3 President of the Supreme Court.

Historically the House of Lords, the predecessor to the Supreme Court, did not have a dedicated president: the judge who had served the longest was considered the 'senior' and thus administratively responsible for the allocation of judges to individual cases.

This changed on 6 June 2000 when Lord Bingham was 'promoted' to the House of Lords to become Senior Law Lord (the promotion carrying with it a pay cut). It was said at the time that creating a Senior Law Lord would bring a more professional management approach to the judicial committee with someone being designated as its head. This was important in the preparatory work for its transformation into the Supreme Court.

The CRA 2005 formalized this approach and created a *President of the Supreme Court*[12] (currently Lord Neuberger) and a deputy (currently Lady Hale). The President and Deputy President have administrative responsibilities over, for example, the judicial operation of the Supreme Court, and the President superintends the Chief Executive for the administrative operation of the Supreme Court.[13] The President also has the power to issue rules and practice directions[14] and these regulate the proceedings of the Supreme Court. The President and Deputy President are responsible for allocating the justices to each case but there is no requirement that they preside over every case and indeed there are a number of occasions when they do not sit, even where the court constitutes a bench of seven (eg *R v Rollins*).[15]

The appointment of Lord Neuberger in 2012 is interesting because Lord Neuberger was a member of the House of Lords but volunteered to return to the English Court of Appeal to preside over its civil division as Master of the Rolls (interestingly replacing the then Master of the Rolls who became Lord Clarke, a Justice of the Supreme Court). At the time, Lord Neuberger referred to the Supreme Court as being formed 'as a result of what appears to have been a last-minute decision over a glass of whisky'.[16] That said, the fact that he now presides over it suggests that his objection was not one that prevented him serving in the court.

It should be noted that the President of the Supreme Court, together with the Justices of the Supreme Court, are not judges of England and Wales, as the Supreme Court has UK jurisdiction. However, they are included here for completeness.

8.1.1.4 Heads of Division

In Chapter 3 it was noted that the High Court is divided into three divisions (Queen's Bench, Family, and Chancery). Each division has a Head of Division although prior to the 2005 Act only the *President of the Family Division* was a Head of Division as

12. *Constitutional Reform Act 2005*, s 23(5).
13. *Constitutional Reform Act 2005*, s 48.
14. *Constitutional Reform Act 2005*, s 45.
15. [2010] UKSC 39.
16. Joshua Rozenburg, 'Fear over UK Supreme Court Impact' BBC Online, 8 September 2009.

of right. The President of the Family Division is now also the Head of Family Justice. A Deputy (who must be a Lord Justice of Appeal) can also be created.

The 2005 Act created the new offices of the *President of the Queen's Bench Division* and the *Chancellor of the High Court*. Prior to the 2005 Act the Lord Chief Justice was President of the Queen's Bench Division but this new office recognizes the fact that, now the Lord Chief Justice is the head of the judiciary, a new Head of Division is required to oversee the work. Judge LJ (as he then was), who previously held the honorific title of *Deputy Chief Justice* (which was neither a statutory office nor remunerated differently to a Lord Justice) became the first holder of this post (in 2008 he was subsequently promoted to be Lord Chief Justice). The Lord Chancellor was also the president of the Chancery Division but there existed a *Vice-Chancellor* who was a de facto Head of Division. The 2005 Act has renamed this office the *Chancellor of the High Court* to reflect the fact that the Lord Chancellor no longer has any judicial responsibilities.

8.1.1.5 Senior President of Tribunals

A Senior President of Tribunals is created by s 2 *Tribunals, Courts and Enforcement Act 2007* (TCEA 2007). Originally the Senior President was to be appointed by the Lord Chief Justice but the statute now requires that appointment is made by the Queen on advice of the Lord Chancellor.[17] The *Constitutional Reform Act 2005* (CRA 2005) has now been amended and the Senior President is a post that the *Judicial Appointments Commission* should now fill.[18] The fact that the Senior President is a UK post is reflected by the fact that the Commission must consult the Lord Chief Justice of England and Wales, Lord President of the Court of Session (Scotland), and the Lord Chief Justice of Northern Ireland.[19]

The first Senior President was (the then) Carnwath LJ who had been the Senior President (designate) for several years while the legislation was being drafted, ie he existed in 'shadow' form in that he had no formal statutory role but assumed a de facto role that was extremely important in the transition of tribunal justice to a parallel system of court justice. The expertise that he brought and the ability to undertake this complex role (even in times when there was no statutory role) was rewarded by his being appointed to the Supreme Court. Lord Carnwath (as he now is) has been an important figure within the Supreme Court since he will be a voice of experience when tribunal matters reach the Supreme Court (as they will almost certainly do).

When Lord Carnwath was appointed to the Supreme Court there was a delay in appointing his successor and there was some talk about whether the role would be filled or subsumed within, as for example, the role of the Lord Chief Justice. However, ultimately Sullivan LJ was appointed to the post although following his appointment he styled himself as Sir Jeremy Sullivan, Senior President of Tribunals, presumably partly because he had responsibility for the tribunals in devolved countries and so the style 'Lord Justice' would be inappropriate. The same approach has been adopted by Sir Ernest Ryder, who is also a Lord Justice of Appeal. When sitting in the Court of Appeal, he is known as Lord Justice Ryder, but when sitting in the tribunals he is known as Sir Ernest Ryder.

---

17. *Tribunals, Courts and Enforcement Act 2007*, s 2(1).
18. *Constitutional Reform Act 2005*, s 75B.
19. *Constitutional Reform Act 2005*, s 75B(3).

The responsibilities of the Senior President include coordinating the work of tribunals and, in particular, representing the views of the tribunal judiciary.[20] In order to discharge this duty the Senior President has the statutory power to lay written representations before Parliament[21] and he does not need the permission of, for example, the Lord Chief Justice to do so. It has been noted that this gives the Senior President proper power as President in his own right and not as a delegate of the Lord Chief Justice.[22]

It is no accident that all of the Senior Presidents have been Lord Justices of Appeal given that the head of the EAT and *Asylum and Immigration Tribunal* are both puisne judges. Whilst the Presidents continue to have leadership within their own tribunals the post of Senior President is obviously central to their coordination and the unification of tribunal justice (and its integration into the wider judiciary).

8.1.2 Superior judiciary

Those judges who are considered to be superior judges are:

- Justices of the Supreme Court
- Lord Justices of Appeal
- puisne judges.

These are judges who sit, as of right, in the higher courts—the High Court and above. Superior judges have unlimited jurisdiction in that their jurisdiction is not limited specifically by statute. In practice this means that they can use something called the *inherent jurisdiction*, ie the common-law powers, and unless a rule of law or statute limits the jurisdiction of the courts in a particular way the judges have the right to act as they deem fit.

249

☰ **Example** Unlimited authority

A simple, but perhaps illustrative, example of the difference in authority can be seen by where a judge sits. An inferior judge can only sit in a designated court—ie one that has been approved by the Ministry of Justice as a court. However, in *St Edmundsbury & Ipswich Board of Finance v Clark*[23] Megarry J decided that he had an inherent power to sit anywhere.[24] The use of the inherent power was permitted because the judicial authority for a superior judge arises from his office whereas the judicial authority for an inferior judge arises from the court. The judge therefore sat in Iken village hall to hear the evidence of a witness. The judge also, as a safeguard, asked the Lord Chancellor to designate the town as a place where the High Court could sit[25] but Megarry J was adamant that this was merely a 'fail-safe' procedure and through the use of the inherent jurisdiction he could sit anywhere.

---

20. *Tribunals, Courts and Enforcement Act 2007*, sch1, pt 4.
21. *Tribunals, Courts and Enforcement Act 2007*, sch1, pt 4.
22. Sir Robert Carnwath, *Administrative Justice and Tribunals Council: Getting There at Last!* (2007). Available at: <http://ajtc.justice.gov.uk/adjust/articles/speech_carnwath.htm>.
23. [1973] Ch 323.
24. [1973] Ch 323, 327.
25. [1973] Ch 323, 328.

8.1.2.1 Justices of the Supreme Court

The ordinary judges of the Supreme Court are referred to as the *Justices of the Supreme Court*[26] and their number is currently fixed at twelve[27] which was the same number as the Law Lords. That said, the *Crime and Courts Act 2013* altered this to a reference for the equivalent of twelve full-time judges. This was part of a wider process of permitting part-time judicial appointments, including potentially by job-share (discussed at 8.4.2.2).

The first justices of the Supreme Court were the existing Law Lords at the time of its creation.[28] At the time the court was created Lord Scott was due to retire and Lord Clarke, the then Master of the Rolls, became the first Justice of the Supreme Court to be appointed direct to the Supreme Court. Law Lords were peers and thus upon their appointment they became Lord or Lady [*n*]. Lord Clarke had been given a peerage prior to his appointment and thus all the original justices were peers. The first appointment not to be appointed a peer was Sir John Dyson, and for a few months he sat as Sir John Dyson JSC. This was the subject of some criticism, the argument being that differentiating between titles could lead to a perception that the non-ennobled justice was somehow less worthy than the others.[29] Eventually the Queen gave her consent to adopt the procedure traditionally used in Scotland for their senior judges, where they were given the honorific title 'Lord' or 'Lady' but without formally being made a peer. Sir John Dyson promptly became Lord Dyson and the same procedure has been adopted for each of the new justices.

Additional judges

The fact that there are only twelve justices can cause difficulties in terms of the workload of the court, especially where there are vacancies. For much of the year 2011–12 the Supreme Court operated with only ten justices due to the vacancy caused by the retirement of Lord Collins not being filled for several months until Lord Sumption assumed office and also because of the illness and death of Lord Rodger. The CRA allows for the President to ask for 'additional judges' to work in the Supreme Court, of which there are two classes:[30]

- a person who holds 'office as a senior territorial judge' (which is defined as a judge of the Court of Appeal in England (which, of course, will include the Heads of Division and the Lord Chief Justice)) or the equivalent in Scotland and Northern Ireland;[31] and

- a member of the supplementary panel under s 39 (ie a former justice of the Supreme Court (or senior territorial judge)) who has retired but is not yet 75 but only if he is appointed to the Panel by the President.[32]

Lords of Appeal in Ordinary

Whilst they no longer exist, it is of historical interest to note that the judges of the House of Lords were known as the Lords of Appeal in Ordinary, although they are

---

26. *Constitutional Reform Act 2005*, s 23(6).
27. *Constitutional Reform Act 2005*, s 23(2).
28. *Constitutional Reform Act 2005*, s 24.
29. Phillip Morgan, 'Don't Let Politicians Dangle Baubles in Front of Judges' *The Times* (24 June 2010).
30. *Constitutional Reform Act 2005*, s 38(1).
31. *Constitutional Reform Act 2005*, s 38(8).
32. *Constitutional Reform Act 2005*, s 38(4).

often referred to as the Law Lords. The 'in ordinary' meant they were remunerated for their work. Each judge was granted a life peerage upon appointment, becoming *Baron* or *Baroness X*. Technically any judge who held, or had held, a high judicial office within the meaning of the *Appellate Jurisdiction Act 1876* and who was also a peer could sit in the House of Lords. This included retired Law Lords, the current and retired Lord Chief Justices, and certain Masters of the Rolls.

8.1.2.2 Lord Justices of Appeal

The ordinary judges of the Court of Appeal are known as Lords or Lady Justices of Appeal.[33] Prior to the 2003 Act the statutory title for a judge of the Court of Appeal was Lord Justice of Appeal.[34] This meant that when Dame Elizabeth Butler-Sloss became the first female member of the Court of Appeal she was officially known as Her Ladyship, Lord Justice Butler-Sloss LJ. Some time after her appointment, the Lord Chancellor and Lord Chief Justice issued a practice direction[35] which stated that for informal purposes she was to be known as Lady Justice Butler-Sloss but it took until 2003 before the feminine alternative was formally permitted.

Upon appointment to the Court of Appeal a person is sworn in as a member of the Privy Council and is thus entitled to the prefix 'Rt Hon' but in court is styled *Lord/ Lady Justice X*.

8.1.2.3 Puisne judges

Puisne judges (pronounced 'puny') is the formal name given to the ordinary judges of the High Court although in practice they tend to be referred to as 'High Court judges'. The term 'puisne' means lower rank and means that they are the lowest rank of the superior court judges. That said, all puisne judges rank above the inferior judges.

Puisne judges are given the honorific title 'Honourable' while they hold that rank and are referred to as Mr or Mrs Justice X—the full title, therefore, being the *Honourable Mr(s) Justice X*. Upon appointment they are also knighted or made Dames, something that happens in a private audience with the Queen rather than at a traditional investiture.[36]

8.1.3 Inferior judiciary

The inferior judges are so called because they do not exercise unlimited jurisdiction but instead their powers are defined by statute. Accordingly, if the statute does not prescribe any authority then they may not exercise any jurisdiction. For our purposes, the inferior judges that we will consider are:

- Circuit judges
- Recorders
- District judges and district judge (magistrates' court)
- Tribunal judiciary.

33. *Courts Act 2003*, s 63.
34. *Supreme Court Act 1981*, s 2(3).
35. *Practice Note (Mode of Address: Lord Justice Butler-Sloss)* [1994] 1 FLR 866.
36. Robin Dunn, *Sword and Wig: Memoirs of a Lord Justice* (Quiller Press 1993) 184. As there is no female equivalent to a Knight Bachelor, female puisne judges are awarded the DBE (Dame of the British Empire), meaning that they 'rank' their male counterparts in terms of etiquette.

Of these, most attention in this chapter will be focused on circuit judges since, as will be seen, these are the most directly comparable to puisne judges. Circuit and puisne judges are the two grades of judge who primarily undertake first-instance trials in the court. Their status is, however, markedly different.

8.1.3.1 Circuit judges

The office of circuit judge is relatively modern, being created by s 16 *Courts Act 1971* although prior to this, other judicial appointments did exist, including the county court judge although this was a civil judge. The office of circuit judge now spans both civil and criminal work and a judge can expect to sit on both types of work. When a judge is appointed he is assigned to one of the six circuits and he will, especially when quite junior, spend time sitting at the various courts within the circuit. As a judge becomes more senior it is more likely that he will sit primarily in one or two courts although they can, at any time, be asked to sit in other courts within the circuit where it is necessary to do so.

Each court centre has a resident judge, who is in administrative control of the criminal list and that judge will normally be the senior judge of that centre. Some resident judges (in the largest court centres) are paid extra for this role and are designated as senior circuit judges: the other resident judges are not paid extra and the role tends to rotate according to seniority. The resident judge has recently been joined by the designated judges who have similar responsibility for the civil work. There are two types of designated judge: the designated family and designated civil judges. Along with the administrative responsibilities, the designated judges will frequently hear High Court-level work. As with resident judges, at the major court centres the designated judges will be paid as senior circuit judges.

Some circuit judges also bear the title *recorder*. This can be a source of confusion for law students as a recorder can be either one of the most junior judicial roles or the title given to the most senior circuit judges, and it is best not to confuse the two! Where it is the senior circuit judge, the term is honorary recorder and it is an office that has existed for many years although traditionally only three full-time posts existed: those of London, Manchester, and Liverpool. These recorderships are substantive posts (ie the posts are specifically advertised as such) and they are automatically senior circuit judges.[37] In the passing of the CA 1971 Parliament had specifically retained the power of local authorities to grant an honorary recordership of the borough.[38] Theoretically this power was vested in the local authority (because the holder of the office becomes a borough dignity, second only in precedence to the lord mayor) but in practice it is made in consultation with the senior presiding judge. No increase in pay is given to the (local) honorary recorders but those appointed have all tended to be the senior judge in the larger court centres (eg Middlesbrough, Bristol, Plymouth) and so were all paid as senior resident judges in any event. The local honorary recorder is not, however, a substantive post and it lapses upon the retirement of the resident judge, when the judge moves to another circuit, or if it was for a determinate period of time. It is for the local authority to decide if, and when, it should be granted again. In recent years the Lord Chief Justice has encouraged the appointment of honorary recorders and their numbers do seem to have expanded.

---

37. Historically the recorders of London, Liverpool, and Manchester were knighted on appointment although this appears to have lapsed as neither the recorder of Liverpool nor Manchester are currently knights.
38. *Courts Act 1971*, s 54.

All circuit judges are styled *His (or Her) Honour Judge X* and upon retirement are entitled to the honorific His or Her Honour. Honorary recorders who are also senior circuit judges wear a different robe (it is red) and are referred to as 'My Lord' or 'My Lady' in court (although ordinarily only when in the town they are recorder of). Upon retirement they keep only the honorific His or Her Honour as with all circuit judges.

8.1.3.2 Recorders

The second type of recorder is the more common and is a part-time judicial role held by practising lawyers. The modern office, like the circuit judge, is relatively modern and was created by s 21 CA 1971 although part-time roles previously existed,[39] including those bearing the title recorder and assistant recorder. A recorder can be appointed to hear either civil or criminal cases but they are restricted to circuit-bench work. Thus, their jurisdiction is broadly similar to that of circuit judges, however, they will usually handle the less complex cases that come before the court.

A recorder is styled as *Mr or Mrs Recorder X* when in court but is given no style or title when they are not sitting as recorders. They are referred to in court as 'Your Honour' since they are sitting as de facto circuit judges. They may continue in private practice. Recorders are expected to sit for thirty days a year.

8.1.3.3 District judges

The most junior judicial rank in the courts is that of the district judge. It is important at the outset to distinguish the district judge from the district judges (magistrates' court) with the former acting solely as a civil judge. Part-time district judges are also permitted and those appointed are known as deputy district judges.

The district judge deals with the majority of cases in the county court so will normally hear procedural and interlocutory matters but they also hear nearly all of the claims heard in the small claims court and some divorce matters.

District judges are styled *District Judge X* for the duration of their appointment and are not given any honorific. They are referred to as 'Sir' or 'Madam' in court.

8.1.3.4 The tribunal judiciary

There are arguably three levels of judiciary in the tribunals:

- Chamber Presidents
- Upper Tribunal judges
- First-Tier Tribunal judges.

Upper Tribunal and First-Tier tribunal judges are relatively straightforward in terms of where they sit. Technically there is no difference between them in terms of their status as inferior judges. Whilst there is a (not insignificant) pay differential, an analogy could be drawn between a circuit judge and a district judge. Both are inferior judges, it is just the type of work that they do that will differ. The same is true of these judges.

One issue to note is that some tribunals, unlike courts, will sit as a mixed bench, that is to say a mixture of judicial and lay (non-judicial) staff. The latter are ordinarily experts in their respective fields (eg accountants, medical practitioners, surveyors,

---

39.   These tended to be criminal-only appointments and were deputy judges of the assizes or Deputy Chairman of the Quarter Sessions.

or those who have specialist knowledge of disability, discrimination, or the military). The legally qualified member will preside and they are the only members of the panel who are given the honorific 'Judge'.[40] The other members of the tribunals are known as 'members' and are not technically part of the judiciary.

How the tribunals operate and what they do is considered in Chapter 7.

8.2 Judicial dress

One of the more distinctive elements of the English court system is the dress worn in courts. The dress of lawyers is discussed elsewhere (Chapter 10) but what of the judiciary? Traditionally the court judiciary, particularly puisne judges, had a wide range of judicial robes to wear but recently there has been a simplified system of robes.

Leaving aside the formal state robes a judge possesses (which are really only used for the ceremony at the start of each legal year) what is the working dress of the judiciary? The simplest of them all are the Justices of the Supreme Court. The justices do not sit in robes although they do have ceremonial robes that were newly created for the court. The robes are only worn at the opening of the court and at other ceremonial occasions. The Justices of the Supreme Court are following the tradition set by the House of Lords where no robes were worn, in part because the appellate and appeals committees were, in essence, comparable to other committees where no robes are worn.

Judges of the Court of Appeal used to sit in the Court of Appeal wearing a black silk robe (similar to that worn by Queen's Counsel) and a judicial wig. Following the *Practice Direction (Court Dress) (No 5) and Amendment No 20 to the Consolidated Criminal Practice Direction (Court Dress)*[41] judges in the Civil Division of the Court of Appeal will now wear a new civil gown (discussed later) and no wig. The practice direction states that there is no change in the Criminal Division[42] so wigs and the black silk gown are worn. It will be interesting to see how long it will be until the new robe is worn in the Criminal Division too.

Puisne judges' dress now differs according to their work. In civil matters, the new civil gown will be worn but the President of the Family Division and President of the Court of Protection (the same person) has stated that no gown should ordinarily be worn in those proceedings save when they are in open court, something that rarely happens.[43] Puisne judges in criminal matters wear the 'winter' robe, which consists of a red robe, black scarf girdle, and a scarlet casting-hood or tippet (sash) worn with a judicial wig.

Circuit judges have a violet robe. Even for civil cases they will not wear the new civil robe because during the consultation they indicated a preference to retain their robe. Quite why this was permitted is open to question since it would have made more sense for a single civil robe to be used rather than accede to the sartorial preferences of the circuit bench. However, wigs and collars will no longer be worn and, as noted earlier, no robe is to be worn in family matters. When sitting on criminal business, a circuit judge wears the lilac robe, a judicial wig, and a red tippet over their left shoulder.

40. As with district judges they gain no additional styling (cf His or Her Honour for circuit judges and the honorific 'Honourable' and knight/damehood for puisne judges). Thus when they retire they return to Mr or Mrs X.
41. [2008] 1 WLR 1700.
42. [2008] 1 WLR 1700 [5].
43. *Practice Note (Family Proceedings: Court Dress)* [2008] 1 WLR 1701.

District judges will ordinarily not sit in robes but when they sit in open court in the civil courts they will wear the new civil robe and no wig. District judges (magistrates' court) will not wear a robe while in the magistrates' court but if they sit in the Crown Court they will wear a black silk gown and judicial wig.

For completeness it should be noted that recorders, as part-time members of the judiciary, wear the practitioner's robe of a barrister (silk if they are Queen's Counsel otherwise a stuff gown) and a practitioner's wig (when sitting in criminal matters) or no wig (when sitting on civil matters). They wear these robes even when the recorder is a solicitor.[44]

Tribunal judiciary do not wear any robes when they sit in tribunals. Where they sit in court, then they will wear their judicial robe if they hold a substantive judicial appointment[45] or, if they do not, then they would wear the same robes as a recorder.

8.2.1 Civil robe

The civil robe is a simple black robe that is worn without wig, band, wing collar, or a collarette. The 'rank' of the judge is set out on colour tabs worn at the neck of the gown as follows:

- Court of Appeal (inc Heads of Division)—gold
- High Court—red
- District judges—blue.

Members of the High Court Masters Group (which are analogous to district judges but for High Court civil work) wear pink tabs.

8.3 Judicial appointments

The process of choosing judges has been the source of some debate for many years and has recently changed to reflect the constitutional changes of the late 1990s and early 2000s. Traditionally judicial appointments, particular of superior judges, were clouded in mystery and secrecy with 'secret soundings' being normal. Lord Elwyn-Jones, the former Lord Chancellor, explained the process:

> When a vacancy had to be filled, the heads of the Divisions … were invited into my office to consider likely names. Usually we agreed as to the one most meriting appointment. Occasionally two names were equally supported. Then the choice was left to me.[46]

When the Lord Chancellor had decided on the appropriate person he would invite them in for a chat and ask whether they would accept a seat on the bench. It was comparatively rare for a person to refuse an appointment[47] although some did, either because they did not wish to cease to be an advocate or because they did not want the inevitable drop in pay.

The traditional system of appointing judges was increasingly said to be untenable, not least because of concerns that the 'old boys' network' was creating a non-diverse and non-representative judiciary. In recent years two significant changes occurred. The first was the

---

44. It will be seen in Chapter 10 that it is discretionary for a solicitor to wear a wig.
45. Some chamber presidents are circuit judges and therefore they would wear the appropriate robe.
46. Frederick Elwyn-Jones, *In My Times: An Autobiography* (Weidenfeld & Nicolson 1983) 265.
47. David Pannick, *Judges* (OUP 1987) 9.

introduction of advertising for inferior judges, this being extended in 1998 to include the first advertisement for a High Court judge[48] and ultimately now for all posts. Whilst a useful first step, this was, at least initially, used only to create a 'long list' of suitable people from whom the Lord Chancellor could select a judge. Additionally, the Lord Chancellor retained the right to invite someone who had not applied to take up a judgeship. The second important step towards accountability was the appointment of the Commissioners for Judicial Appointments who had the responsibility for auditing the appointment process. The Commissioners were independent of the government and published annual reports on the appointment process, the most critical of which was probably their first annual report[49] although the 2003 review of the High Court competition[50] is also critical and specifically stated that the idea of having a mix of invitations and advertisements was unfair.[51]

Eventually the government published a consultation paper on the appointment of the judiciary, something that one commentator described as both 'logical and disappointing'.[52] Stevens argues that it is logical because the pressure for the reform of the judiciary has been building for a considerable time, and disappointing because, in his opinion, it led to a fudge whereby the integrity of the system is not as guaranteed as in other states, most notably through a lack of majority of laypersons. The CRA 2005 placed judicial appointments onto a statutory basis. Two schemes apply for constitutional reasons. The first applies to members of the Supreme Court and the second applies to all other judicial appointments.[53] The systems are actually comparable but the principal distinction is that the former is an ad hoc commission that is constituted when a member needs to be nominated whereas the latter is a permanent body.

What follows applies equally to the court and tribunal judiciary. As already noted, the tribunal judiciary (other than the Senior President of Tribunals) are inferior judges[54] and therefore they are appointed in the same way as other inferior judges. Members of tribunals are not considered here as they are not members of the judiciary.

8.3.1 Judicial Appointments Commission

Focusing on the appointments in England and Wales, the CRA 2005 created the *Judicial Appointments Commission* (JAC) which, unlike the first commission, has a role in the appointing of persons instead of just auditing the process. The *Crime and Courts Act 2013* (CCA 2013) made significant changes to the CRA 2005, principally removing all the procedural detail from statute into statutory instruments, where it is easier to change. Three regulations have been made under the 2013 Act:

- *Judicial Appointments Commission Regulations 2013*,[55] which set out the details of the Commission and how they work

- *Judicial Appointments Regulations 2013*,[56] which set out how judicial appointments will operate in practice

---

48. The advertisement was placed on 24 February.
49. CJA, *Annual Report 2003* (Commission for Judicial Appointments 2003).
50. CJA, *Annual Report 2004* (Commission for Judicial Appointments 2004).
51. CJA, *Annual Report 2004* (Commission for Judicial Appointments 2004) 23–7.
52. Robert Stevens, 'Reform in Haste and Repent at Leisure: Iolanthe, the Lord High Executioner and Brave New World' (2004) 24 *Legal Studies* 1, 22.
53. For clarity this does not include appointments to the magistracy since these are not technically a judicial appointment. The appointment of magistrates is discussed at 13.1.1.1.
54. It has been mooted that there is no reason why judges of the Employment Appeal Tribunal should principally be court judges, and they could be appointed tribunal judges in their own right. As EAT judges include puisne judges, there is no reason why a superior (tribunal) judge could not be appointed as a tribunal judge.
55. SI 2013/2191.
56. SI 2013/2192.

- *Supreme Court (Judicial Appointments) Regulations 2013,*[57] which, as their name suggests, govern how justices of the Supreme Court are selected.

The JAC itself consists of fifteen members, including the chair.[58] The remaining fourteen members are allocated accordingly:

- seven judicial members
- five lay members
- two practising or employed lawyers.[59]

There are quite detailed rules on how these posts are to be filled, particularly the judicial members. Table 8.2 sets out who the members are. The chair must always be non-legally qualified[60] and thus there is a majority of non-judicial members within the JAC although not a majority of lay members.[61] The JAC's independence is also shown by the fact that the Commissioners may not be civil servants,[62] this being considered an important feature of judicial independence.

Table 8.2 Judicial Appointments Commission members

Commissioner Type	Description
Judicial Commissioners	1 Lord Justice of Appeal
	1 puisne judge
	1 senior tribunal office-holder[63]
	1 circuit judge
	1 district judge of a county court, district judge (magistrates' court) or Master of the High Court of Justice
	1 first-instance tribunal judge[64]
	1 non-legally qualified judicial member
Lawyer Commissioners	2 lawyers, meaning a barrister, solicitor, or fellow of CILEX, but they may not hold the same qualification[65]
Lay members	5 who have never held judicial office, never been an employment tribunal member, or have never practised or been employed as a lawyer

57. SI 2013/2193.
58. *Judicial Appointments Commission Regulations 2013*, reg 3.
59. *Judicial Appointments Commission Regulations 2013*, reg 4.
60. *Constitutional Reform Act 2005*, sch 12.
61. There will be six lay (non-legal) members compared to nine judicial or lawyer appointments.
62. *Constitutional Reform Act 2005*, sch 12.
63. This means a judge of the Upper Tribunal, a chamber president of the first-instance or Upper Tribunal, or president of the Employment Tribunals in either England or Scotland (*Judicial Appointments Commission Regulations 2013*, reg 5).
64. This means a judge of the First-Tier Tribunal, regional employment judge, or an employment judge (*Judicial Appointments Regulations 2013*, reg 4(3)).
65. *Judicial Appointments Commission Regulations 2013*, reg 4(4)(5). Thus there could be a solicitor and barrister, or solicitor and CILEX, or barrister and CILEX etc but not two barristers or two solicitors.

Commissioners are recommended by the Lord Chancellor after an appointments process,[66] although that does not apply to the Lord Justice of Appeal, puisne judge Commissioners, and the senior tribunal Commissioner. For the former, the Judges' Council appoints these,[67] and for the latter the Tribunal Judges' Council chooses.[68] Commissioners are to be appointed for not more than five years at a time and may not serve as a Commissioner for a period of ten years or more, consecutively or otherwise.[69] Those Commissioners who do not hold judicial office are remunerated, the others are not.

The principal work of the JAC is, of course, the appointment of the judiciary and the mechanisms by which this should occur. The *Judicial Appointments Regulations 2013*[70] set out five different forms of selection procedures:

- Selection of the Lord Chief Justice
- Selection of the Heads of Division
- Selection of the Senior President of Tribunals
- Selection of Lord Justices of Appeal
- Selection of puisne judges and all other judicial appointments.

The subsequent sections of this chapter will consider the manner of appointment, albeit briefly.

8.3.2 Selection of the Lord Chief Justice

The first selection process is to select the Lord Chief Justice. A panel to appoint the LCJ must consist of five members,[71] who shall be:

1. The chair of the Commission[72]
2. The most senior England and Wales Supreme Court judge (or their nominee)[73]
3. A lay member of the Commission selected by the chair
4. A member of the Commission selected by the chair after consultation with the Lord Chief Justice
5. An England and Wales Supreme Court, Head of Division, or Lord Justice of Appeal chosen by the Lord Chief Justice.

Where there is no Lord Chief Justice (the appointments panel should begin before an LCJ retires, so realistically this means where the LCJ has died or is incapacitated), then the Supreme Court judge mentioned in #2 exercises those functions for the establishment of the panel.

---

66.   *Judicial Appointments Commission Regulations 2013*, reg 9.
67.   *Judicial Appointments Commission Regulations 2013*, reg 10. The 'Judges' Council' is not a statutory body and instead is a body that is constituted by the Lord Chief Justice. It consists of the senior judges and those selected to represent certain constituencies. The current list of members is available on the Online Resource Centre.
68.   *Judicial Appointments Commission Regulations 2013*, reg 11. The Tribunal Judges' Council is, as its name suggests, the equivalent for the tribunal judiciary and it is empanelled under the authority of the Senior President of Tribunals.
69.   *Judicial Appointments Commission Regulations 2013*, reg 17.
70.   SI 2013/2192.
71.   *Judicial Appointments Commission Regulations 2013*, reg 5(1).
72.   Where the chair is vacant or the post-holder is incapacitated or unavailable the chair will be selected by the five lay members.
73.   *Judicial Appointments Commission Regulations 2013*, reg 5(5). This is the most senior justice (by appointment) of the Supreme Court who, before appointment, was a member of the English judiciary.

The language of the third person is interesting. It does not say that it must be a judicial member of the Commission, merely a member. However, by saying that the Lord Chief Justice must be consulted (although it does not say that the LCJ has any sort of veto), it is perhaps suggesting it should be a judicial appointee.

When choosing any of the members, the person making the choice must have regard to the 'desirability' of the panel to include 'both women and men' and 'members drawn from a range of different racial groups'.[74] It may seem extraordinary to consider this only 'desirable' but it is perhaps a reflection of the judiciary. As at least two, and probably three, members will be from the senior judiciary, it may not be possible to always choose a female or someone who has black or minority ethnicity. That said, this makes the initial appointment of the Commissioners even more important.

Where any of the members would otherwise apply for the position of Lord Chief Justice (and it is quite possible that a Supreme Court judge, Head of Division, or Lord Justice of Appeal may choose to do so) then they must obviously stand down, although it is likely that, save for the Supreme Court judge, they would be chosen in the first place as they would have discussed this with the current Lord Chief Justice informally.

The selection panel shall determine how the process will take place,[75] meaning that they will decide whether the post is advertised, for how long, what sort of exercise will be required etc. They will then select a single preferred candidate and forward this to the Lord Chancellor.[76] There are then three stages:

Stage One. Where a person has been selected for appointment as Lord Chief Justice

Stage Two. Where a person has been selected following a rejection or reconsideration

Stage Three. Where a person has been selected following a rejection or reconsideration at stage two.[77]

At stage one, the Lord Chancellor has three options:

1. Accept the selection
2. Reject the selection
3. Require the selection to reconsider its decision.[78]

A rejection is an outright refusal to accept that person. The Lord Chancellor may only do this where she believes 'the person selected is not suitable for the office concerned'.[79] Written reasons must be provided to the panel for doing this.[80] It does not say whether the applicant will be told the reason for that rejection and it does raise an interesting question about whether the decision is challengeable. It would certainly be (politically) difficult to judicially review the decision, but it is probably susceptible to review even if it is highly unlikely a candidate will do so.

The power to order the panel to reconsider can only be given if 'there is not enough evidence that the person is suitable for the Office of Lord Chief Justice', or 'there is evidence that the person is not the best candidate on merit'.[81] Again, this would seem

---

74. *Judicial Appointments Regulations 2013*, reg 5(15).
75. *Constitutional Reform Act 2005*, s 70(2).
76. *Judicial Appointments Regulations 2013*, reg 7.
77. *Judicial Appointments Regulations 2013*, reg 8(1).
78. *Judicial Appointments Regulations 2013*, reg 8(2).
79. *Judicial Appointments Regulations 2013*, reg 9(1).
80. *Judicial Appointments Regulations 2013*, reg 9(3).
81. *Judicial Appointments Regulations 2013*, reg 2(2).

to be more of a figleaf then anything else, because who would determine whether the Lord Chancellor is right or wrong? Would a prospective candidate for the office of Lord Chief Justice really pursue legal action to establish their right to become the President of the Court? Could such a person be tenable as LCJ?

At stage two, the Lord Chancellor has the same three options, but they can only reject the selection if it was made following a reconsideration at stage one, and they can only ask the panel to reconsider if the candidate was rejected at stage one.[82] This is a slightly convoluted way of saying the following:

> If at stage one, the panel were asked to reconsider, then the Lord Chancellor can either only accept the new recommendation or reject it. She cannot ask the panel to reconsider.

At stage three the Lord Chancellor must accept the recommendation, unless she decides to appoint a person who was previously selected but not put forward again, following reconsideration.[83] This would be extremely rare but an example would be:

> Somebody LJ and Anybody LJ apply to become Lord Chief Justice. The selection panel prefer Somebody LJ and they nominate him at stage one. The Lord Chancellor asks them to reconsider. They do so, but decide that they will still nominate Somebody LJ.
>
> At stage two, the Lord Chancellor again asks them to reconsider. This time, they decide that Anybody LJ is to be preferred.
>
> At stage three, the Lord Chancellor decides that actually Somebody LJ was better and appoints him.

It would be extremely inglorious for this to happen and it would be interesting to know what the Judicial Appointments Commission would make of it. Nothing requires the procedure to be secret and it is likely therefore that if the JAC were annoyed that the Lord Chancellor had rejected their selection, they could presumably say so publicly. Whilst, to the best of our knowledge, no senior judge has been rejected by the Lord Chancellor, in 2010 it was reported that the then Lord Chancellor (Rt Hon Jack Straw MP), asked the JAC to reconsider their proposal in respect of a Head of Division. They nominated the same person again, and he decided not to reject them.

8.3.3 Selection of a Head of Division

The selection of a Head of Division operates on a very similar basis, but the selection panel differs. It again consists of five persons but this time it is:[84]

1. The Lord Chief Justice or his nominee
2. The most senior England and Wales Supreme Court judge or their nominee
3. Chairman of the JAC, or their nominee (who must be a lay commissioner)[85]
4. A lay member of the JAC designated by the person appointed as #3
5. A person designated by the Lord Chief Justice, in consultation with the Chair of the Commission, who must be a judicial Commissioner.[86]

82. *Judicial Appointments Regulations 2013*, reg 8(2).
83. *Judicial Appointments Regulations 2013*, reg 8(5).
84. *Judicial Appointments Regulations 2013*, reg 11.
85. *Judicial Appointments Regulations 2013*, reg 11(11).
86. *Judicial Appointments Regulations 2013*, reg 11(12).

Where it is a nominee for #1 or #2, the nominee must be an England and Wales Supreme Court judge, Head of Division, or Lord Justice of Appeal.[87] This time, it is the Lord Chief Justice who will preside over the panel,[88] which does leave open the question as to why there is a chair of the JAC if they will not actually chair appointment panels.

When the panel reports, the Lord Chancellor has the same three options as she did under the Lord Chief Justice appointment.[89]

8.3.4 Senior President of Tribunals

The appointment of the Senior President of Tribunals is very similar to the previous one, but the panel this time is as follows:

1. The Lord Chief Justice or the Lord Chief Justice's nominee
2. A person designated by the Lord Chief Justice
3. Chairman of the JAC
4. A lay member of the JAC designated by the Chair of the JAC
5. A judicial member of the JAC[90] appointed by the Lord Chief Justice

The rules for who is the person appointed as #2 are somewhat more complicated. They must be:

(a) a person who has held but does not currently hold the office of Senior President of Tribunals

(b) a person who holds, or who has held, office as Chamber President of a chamber of the First-Tier or Upper Tribunal

(c) a person who has been a judge of the Employment Appeals Tribunal

(d) a person who has been the President of Employment Tribunals in either England or Scotland

(e) a person who holds, who has held, 'an office that, in the opinion of the Lord Chief Justice, is such that a holder of it would acquire knowledge or experience of tribunals broadly similar to those above'.[91]

Why this is interesting is because the Senior President of Tribunals is a UK office and yet the members of the panel will generally come from the English jurisdiction. By statute, the Senior President of Tribunals does not need to be an English judge,[92] although all three Senior Presidents have been Lord Justices of Appeal. The Lord Chief Justice is required to consult the Lord President of the Court of Session and the Lord Chief Justice of Northern Ireland[93] (who are his equivalents) but there is nothing that provides them with a veto.

261

87. *Judicial Appointments Regulations 2013*, reg 11(10).
88. *Judicial Appointments Regulations 2013*, reg 11(14).
89. *Judicial Appointments Regulations 2013*, reg 14.
90. Or its equivalent in Scotland or Northern Ireland: see *Judicial Appointments Regulations 2013*, reg 17(11).
91. *Judicial Appointments Regulations 2013*, reg 17(8).
92. *Tribunals, Courts and Enforcement Act 2007*, sch 1, pt 1(2)(b).
93. *Judicial Appointments Regulations 2013*, reg 17(9).

The same three options are open to the Lord Chancellor,[94] and it is notable that nothing appears to require the Lord Chancellor to consult his equivalents in Scotland or Northern Ireland, even though the judiciary is a devolved matter.

8.3.5 Lord Justice of Appeal

The same process is adopted, with the panel being:

1. The Lord Chief Justice or nominee
2. A person designated by the Lord Chief Justice
3. The Chairman of the JAC or a lay member of the JAC
4. A lay member of the JAC chosen by the Chair of the JAC
5. A person nominated by the Lord Chief Justice, in consultation with the Chair of the JAC.

The person chosen as #2 must be a Head of Division or Lord Justice of Appeal.[95] The following can be a person under #5:

(a) England and Wales Supreme Court judge

(b) Head of Division

(c) Senior President of Tribunals

(d) Puisne judge of the High Court

(e) a judge holding an office under Sch 14, *Constitutional Reform Act 2005* (the principal court judiciary ranks)

(f) a member of the Commission who is not a Lord Justice of Appeal.[96]

Technically (f) means that it could be a lay member of the Commission but the preceding provisions make it more likely that it will be a judge. It is not clear why it does not have to be a judicial or lay commissioner of the JAC rather than more broad membership.

Once again, the Lord Chancellor has all three options.[97]

8.3.6 All other judicial appointments

The CRA 2005, as amended by the CCA 2013, creates a single scheme for all judicial appointments for or below the grade of puisne judges (although this does not change the distinction between superior and inferior judges). The process differs in that there is no statutory panel but, rather, it is for the JAC to decide how it will fill the vacancies and, presumably, constitute panels from the members within the JAC. The JAC reports back to the Lord Chief Justice who can accept or reject their selection or require the JAC to reconsider the selection.[98] An additional option also arises where the JAC decide that none of the applicants was suitable for appointment and decline to make a recommendation.[99] When this happens the Lord Chief Justice can

---

94. *Judicial Appointments Regulations 2013*, reg 20.
95. *Judicial Appointments Regulations 2013*, reg 23(8).
96. *Judicial Appointments Regulations 2013*, reg 23(10).
97. *Judicial Appointments Regulations 2013*, reg 26.
98. *Judicial Appointments Regulations 2013*, reg 32.
99. *Judicial Appointments Regulations 2013*, reg 35(1).

ask the JAC to reconsider that decision.[100] In the Annual Report for 2015–16 the JAC reported that during that year the JAC recommended an individual for judicial office (they do not say what level) but the Lord Chancellor rejected the individual due to lack of particular experience required for the office.[101] This demonstrates that although the JAC is independent of the government it cannot be said that all judicial appointments are since the Lord Chancellor, who is a senior government minister, has the power to reject the recommendation.

It is worth noting that the JAC must now establish a pool of persons who can be designated as deputy High Court judges or who are circuit judges asked to sit as High Court judges.[102] Traditionally the Lord Chief Justice could simply appoint someone as a 'section 9 judge' but now they must have been approved by the JAC to form a pool of judges who may be so authorized.[103]

8.3.7 Appointment to the Supreme Court

Appointments to the Supreme Court have to be kept separate because it is a court of the United Kingdom and not England and Wales and the Acts of Union creating the United Kingdom guaranteed that the legal systems of Scotland and Northern Ireland would be preserved as sovereign systems in their own right, so the United Kingdom court cannot be under the direction of English procedures. As appointments are rare—there being only twelve justices in total—there is not a permanent commission but instead the Lord Chancellor must convene an ad hoc commission whenever she is notified that there will soon be a vacancy.[104]

The criteria for appointment to the Supreme Court mirror that of the House of Lords and is either holding high judicial office for a period of at least two years or having higher rights of audience for fifteen years.[105] Whilst the criteria expressly con-template someone other than a judge being appointed (by reference to the rights of audience) this had not happened in the House of Lords in over sixty years[106] and many thought that only judges of the Court of Appeal (and their equivalent in Scotland and Northern Ireland) would be appointed. In 2010 it was reported that Jonathan Sumption QC (as he then was) had been asked to apply to become a Justice of the Supreme Court. Sumption was considered to be one of the finest members of the Bar and whilst he had sat as both a recorder and a deputy High Court judge he had never sat in a full-time judicial role. It was reported at the time that judges reacted angrily to his appointment[107] and ultimately he withdrew from the process, with Sir John Dyson being appointed. However, in 2011 he re-applied to become a Justice of the Supreme Court and this time was successful. Controversy was again raised over his appointment not least because he was given permission to continue acting as a QC in an extremely lucrative case he was acting on. In 2012 he was sworn in as a Justice of the Supreme Court and assumed the honorific title Lord Sumption. In December 2011, in preparation for his appointment, he was sworn in as a member of the Privy

263

100. *Judicial Appointments Regulations 2013*, reg 35(2).
101. JAC, *Annual Report and Accounts 2015–16* (Judicial Appointments Commission 2016) 14.
102. *Senior Courts Act 1981*, s 9.
103. *Judicial Appointments Regulations 2013*, pt 8.
104. *Constitutional Reform Act 2005*, s 26(5).
105. *Constitutional Reform Act 2005*, s 25(1).
106. Lords Reid and Radcliffe were appointed Lords of Appeal in Ordinary direct from the Bar in 1948 and 1949 respectively (Lord Reid from the Scottish Bar).
107. Frances Gibb, 'Supreme Ambition, Jealousy and Outrage' *The Times* (4 February 2010).

Council (so that he can sit in its Judicial Committee) but interestingly because he has never been a puisne judge he is the only Justice of the Supreme Court who does not also hold a knighthood.

The appointment of Lord Sumption has certainly been extremely controversial but it does perhaps show that even the ad hoc appointment commissions that are empanelled to fill vacancies for the Supreme Court are willing to ignore convention if they believe it is helpful in finding the best candidate.

By convention two members of the Supreme Court are from Scotland and one from Northern Ireland. The CRA 2005 does not enshrine this convention into the statute although s 27(8) hints at it by stating:

> In making the selections for the appointment of judges of the Court the commission must ensure that between them the judges will have knowledge of, and experience in, the law of each part of the United Kingdom.

It is regrettable that this language should be employed as it would have been better to use precise language requiring a judge from each of the legal systems within the United Kingdom but perhaps this phrase is sufficient to ensure the convention remains. An interesting issue will be whether a Welsh judge will be appointed in the future. It will be remembered from Chapter 1 that traditionally Wales was part of the English Legal System but it is now starting to diverge in small areas. At the moment there is no need for a Welsh judge as the differences in law are minor but if Wales is given further, more radical, powers then perhaps the time will come when an ad hoc commission has to consider the necessity of having an expert in Welsh law in the court.

The prime minister recommends to the Queen who will be appointed to the Supreme Court[108] but the Lord Chancellor will provide only one name to the prime minister for recommendation and the prime minister may not decline the name[109] which is significantly different from the previous position where prime ministers had the ultimate patronage. Lord Hailsham, Conservative Lord Chancellor between 1970 and 1974 and again between 1979 and 1987, makes clear in his autobiography that Mrs Thatcher, the then prime minister, ensured she was involved in the discussions and that a list of possible names was submitted although he is careful to note that she did not appoint anyone that was not on the list.[110]

The CRA 2005 expressly states that the ad hoc commission must determine the selection process to be applied[111] and this must include, for example, whether it is necessary in order to comply with the convention noted earlier that the competition is restricted to judges from a particular jurisdiction. So far, the selection process has included advertising the positions and this is true of the latest selection exercise in which vacancies were advertised for three Supreme Court justices, to replace Lord Hope as Deputy President of the Supreme Court, Lord Dyson, and Lord Walker. Their replacement appointments were Lord Hodge, Hughes, and Toulson LJJ. Whatever process is adopted the statute makes clear that as part of any process, the Lord Chancellor must consult with the following:

- the First Minister in Scotland
- the Lord President of the Court of Session

108. *Constitutional Reform Act 2005*, s 26(2).
109. *Constitutional Reform Act 2005*, s 26(3).
110. Lord Hailsham, *A Sparrow's Flight* (Collins 1990) 427.
111. *Constitutional Reform Act 2005*, s 27(1).

- the Lord Chief Justice of Northern Ireland
- the First Minister for Wales
- the Lord Chief Justice of England and Wales
- the Northern Ireland Judicial Appointments Commission.[112]

A panel, similar to that used for senior judicial appointments in England and Wales, is created, the members being:

- at least one judge of the Supreme Court (normally the President of the Court)
- a senior judge from anywhere in the United Kingdom who is not a Justice of the Supreme Court (nominated by the President of the Supreme Court)
- one member of each of the JAC for England and Wales, Scotland, and Northern Ireland (at least two of whom must be non-legally qualified).[113]

Under changes introduced by the CCA 2013, where the post of President is vacant then the outgoing President cannot be a member of the panel.[114] Similarly, if the post of Deputy President is vacant, then the outgoing Deputy President cannot sit on the panel.[115] The panel is chaired by the most senior judge on the panel, normally the President.

Although there is a requirement that the judicial appointments commission for each jurisdiction within the United Kingdom is represented the statute does not state, at least expressly, that it must be their lay chair, rather it specifies that two of the three representatives from the JACs must be non-legally qualified.

When the ad hoc commission has nominated a person then the Lord Chancellor has the same three options open to him as exist for judicial appointments in England and Wales and eventually, therefore, a nominee will be recommended to the Queen for appointment to the Supreme Court via the prime minister.

The President and Deputy President of the Court are selected by the same process and this would appear to suggest therefore that the tradition of seniority by appointment ended by the appointment of Lord Bingham is unlikely to return as the JAC could decide to appoint someone from outside the Supreme Court to either position.

8.3.8 Judicial appointments? The solution?

The JAC is certainly a marked contrast to the way in which judges have traditionally been appointed but is this the way forward and will it lead to perceived improvements? Not everyone was supportive of the idea of a commission, including those senior judges who believed that the wider constitutional reform process (including the creation of the Supreme Court) was correct. It has been noted that both Lord Bingham and Lord Woolf have argued that one person is better placed to decide on the suitability of a candidate than a committee which, Lord Woolf argues, could lead to a system of 'Buggins' turn next'.[116]

---

112. *Constitutional Reform Act 2005*, s 27A(3).
   It is not known why, in Northern Ireland, the discussion should not be devolved to the First Minister in the same way it is with Scotland.
113. *Supreme Court (Judicial Appointments) Regulations 2013*, reg 11.
114. *Constitutional Reform Act 2005*, s 27(1C).
115. *Constitutional Reform Act*, s 27(ID).
116. Robert Stevens, 'Reform in Haste and Repent at Leisure: Iolanthe, the Lord High Executioner and Brave New World' (2004) 24 *Legal Studies* 1, 23.

An independent appointments commission should, at least, remove the potential for bias or partisan politics to play a role. Even in most recent times there have been allegations that judicial appointments have been made not on the basis of merit but on connections to the government.

> **Example** President of the Family Division
>
> When Lord Falconer, the then Lord Chancellor, appointed Potter LJ to the position of President of the Family Division in 2005 the media instantly referred to him as a 'crony' because he was the pupil-master to both Lord Falconer and Lord Goldsmith, the Attorney-General. Did that mean the appointment was wrong? The professionals working in the Family Division (ie solicitors and barristers) were surprised as custom appeared to indicate the President would come from within the division whereas Potter LJ was a Chancery Division judge,[117] but others believed that it was a welcome appointment as it was thought that the Family Division was becoming a little too inward-looking and needed an outside manager to ensure efficiency and a fresh look at the issues.[118]

However, others would suggest that Lord Chancellors have proven themselves to be extremely robust when making appointments that may appear controversial. Perhaps the classic example of Lord Chancellors ignoring political issues occurred in 1979 when Lord Hailsham decided to recommend to the Queen that Elizabeth Butler-Sloss, then a registrar of the Principal Registry of the Family Division (which is comparable to, but slightly higher than, a district judge), be elevated to the High Court bench. Civil servants were concerned because she was the sister of the Attorney-General[119] but such concerns were brushed aside as it would be 'wrong in principle to discriminate against her'.[120] Butler-Sloss became one of the most popular and respected judges on the bench, including being made the first Lady Justice of Appeal and first female Head of Division (she became the President of the Family Division).

The Lord Chancellor has not, of course, been removed from the decision-making process, as she still has the power to accept, reject, or ask for reconsideration of recommendations for judicial appointments, and some may have concerns as to whether this underpins the integrity of the appointment system. It has been noted already that a Lord Chancellor chose to exercise that right to question the selection of an individual and some may see this as undermining the judicial appointments process. A former Permanent Secretary of the Lord Chancellor's Department disagrees, however, and he states that the appointment of the judiciary is an executive act and should therefore be undertaken by a minister accountable to Parliament.[121] It was unclear how this accountability would arise but in 2010, when the then Lord Chancellor asked the JAC to reconsider the appointment of Wall LJ as President of the Family Division, it was stated that if he had rejected the nomination he would have had to publicly

---

117. See, for example, Grania Langdon-Down, 'A Fair Hearing' (2003) 100 *Law Society Gazette* 21, 22.
118. Philip Hoult, 'Press Round-up: "Crony" Controversy as Potter Becomes Family President' (2005) 102 *Law Society Gazette* 10.
119. Geoffrey Lewis, *Lord Hailsham: A Life* (Pimlico 1997) 268.
120. Geoffrey Lewis, *Lord Hailsham: A Life* (Pimlico 1997) 269.
121. Thomas Legg, 'Brave New World: The New Supreme Court and Judicial Appointments' (2004) 24 *Legal Studies* 45, 52–3.

state the reasons why. This has been clarified with the introduction of the JAR 2013, which make clear that 'the Lord Chancellor must give the selection panel reasons in writing for rejecting or requiring reconsideration of a selection'.[122] The constitution of the JAC has also led to some concern. The Commission for Judicial Appointments strongly argued that lay members should constitute a majority of people appointed to the JAC.[123] This is now reflected in the amendments made to the CRA 2005 by the CCA 2013 which states in Sch 12 (para 3A): 'the number of commissioners who are holders of judicial office must be less than the number of Commissioners (including the chairman) who are not holders of judicial office.'

 QUESTION FOR REFLECTION

Read CJA (2004) para 3.4 where it is argued that lay members should form a majority of the panel and contrast this with Thomas Legg, 'Brave New World: The New Supreme Court and Judicial Appointments' (2004) 24 *Legal Studies* 45, 53 who suggests the opposite and is of the opinion that a judge should be a chair. Why do you think there need to be lay members on a panel that is deciding whether to appoint (or promote) members of the judiciary? Will lay members understand the subtleties of the judicial office? Who should chair the panels?

8.4 Diversity

Perhaps one of the key areas of controversy of the judiciary is their diversity. A long-held criticism of the judiciary is that they are all from the same mould: white, male, middle-class, privately educated Oxbridge graduates. This position is perhaps exemplified by the current senior judiciary. The five most senior judges (the Lord Chief Justice and the four Heads of Division) list their educational backgrounds. All were educated at either the University of Oxford or the University of Cambridge. Three of the five list their school education and were privately educated. All five are white and male. Admittedly, one point to note is that the second most senior judge in the country—the Master of the Rolls—is gay. Not that long ago it would have been thought unlikely that this could be the case.

Speaking in 1992, Lord Taylor the then Lord Chief Justice said:

> The present imbalance between male and female, white and black in the judiciary is obvious ... I have no doubt that the balance will be redressed in the next few years ... Within five years I would expect to see a substantial number of appointments from both these groups. This is not just a pious hope. It will be monitored.[124]

Twenty years later, Lord Judge LCJ stated:

> I am extremely concerned and unhappy about the proportion of women and people from different minorities who are not represented on the Bench, and, as I repeat, I spend a lot of my time as Lord Chief Justice trying to address that problem.[125]

---

122.   *Judicial Appointments Regulations 2013*, regs 9(3), 15(3), and 27(3).
123.   CJA, *Annual Report 2004* (Commission for Judicial Appointments 2004) para 3.4.
124.   Lord Taylor, 'The Judiciary in the Nineties' (Richard Dimbleby Lecture 1992).
125.   Lord Judge LCJ, *Lord Chief Justice's Press Conference* (HMCTS 2012) <http://www.judiciary.gov.uk/announcements/lcj-press-conference-2012/>, 10.

This could only be an acknowledgment that little had changed in the twenty years between Chief Justice speeches. It is four years since Lord Judge gave his comments—and nearly twenty-five years since the comments of Lord Taylor—and yet very little has changed.

8.4.1 Current statistical position

What is the position as regards diversity at the time of writing?

8.4.1.1 Gender

The number of female students entering university to read law has been increasing since 1970 and since 1988 there have actually been more female entrants than male and since 1992 there have been marginally more newly qualified female solicitors than male solicitors.[126] The last census reported that there was a population in England and Wales of just over 52 million people, of which approximately 26.7 million (51 per cent) are female and approximately 25.3 million (49 per cent) are male. It can be seen, therefore, that in society in general, in law schools, and among newly qualified lawyers there are slightly more females than males.

However, if the judicial statistics are examined it can be seen that the position in terms of gender is extremely poor. There is (as at 1 April 2016) currently no female Head of Division and there has only ever been one (Lady Justice Butler-Sloss was President of the Family Division between 1995 and 2005). Of the twelve Justices of the Supreme Court only one (8.3 per cent) is female. Lady Hale was appointed a Lord of Appeal in Ordinary in 2005 and prior to that there had been no female Law Lords. There are eight (21 per cent) Lady Justices of Appeal, admittedly a higher percentage than previously. There are twenty-two (21 per cent) female puisne judges. This means that, of the senior judiciary as a whole, there are thirty (20 per cent) female judges.

Of the more junior ranks of the judiciary the position is marginally better. There are 160 (26 per cent) female circuit judges (a significant increase in the past two years), and 197 (35 per cent) district judges and district judges (magistrates' court) (the most junior branch of the full-time court judiciary). Of the part-time judiciary, there are 203 (20 per cent) recorders (ie part-time judges of the circuit bench), and 262 (36 per cent) deputy district judges and deputy district judges (magistrates' court) (ie part-time district judges).

Overall this means that only 28 per cent of the judiciary are female. Admittedly there has been an increase in recent years but it is still less than half of the representation of women in society. Why is this? The usual reason was that put forward by Lord MacKay, the then Lord Chancellor:

> As more women progress through the profession, it is to be expected that the numbers of women within the judiciary will increase.[127]

However, this misses the point that women have been members of the profession for a considerable period of time and defies the statistics previously discussed. It has been noted that historically the judiciary have been recruited from the Bar and females have, despite their representation more generally, suffered, in the words of one

126.   Ericka Rackley, 'Representations of the (Woman) Judge: Hercules, the Little Mermaid and the Vain and Naked Emperor' (2002) 22 *Legal Studies* 602, 605.
127.   Clare McGlynn, 'Women, Representation and the Legal Academy' (1999) 19 *Legal Studies* 68, 89.

commentator, 'institutional discrimination' at the Bar.[128] The latest figures from 2015 show that women account for 35.9 per cent of barristers currently in practice (the traditional route for members of the judiciary).

There does not appear to be much evidence for the idea that the numbers will eventually increase (in line with the optimism of Lords Taylor and MacKay). There is an expectation that full-time members of the judiciary will be drawn from part-time members of the judiciary yet it was seen that the representation of women in the part-time judiciary is still below that which can be legitimately expected.

Lord Judge, the former Lord Chief Justice, whilst acknowledging the problem, attempted to argue that this is a problem that is not restricted to the law:

> [W]e are turning a tanker around, and it takes time, 11 per cent of the Queen's Counsel in this country are women. That means 89 per cent are men. Solicitors who are partners in solicitors' firms, who are women, amount to 25 per cent—that is 75 per cent men. It would be surprising if you had a Bench which was not inevitably affected by those sort of statistics when you are choosing lawyers to become judges…. What is our society like in relation to the opportunities given to women and the appointments given to women? … how many editors of national newspapers are female? … how many directors of large companies are female? In that sense the judicial system … is … reflective of society.[129]

This is an argument that has been reiterated more recently by Lord Sumption:

> One has to look at the totality of these problems and not simply at one of them. The lack of diversity is a significant problem, but it isn't the only one. It takes time. You've got to be patient. The change in the status and achievements of women in our society, not just in the law but generally, is an enormous cultural change that has happened over the last 50 years or so. It has to happen naturally. It will happen naturally. But in the history of a society like ours, 50 years is a very short time.[130]

As has been seen this is a common argument that is employed to justify the absence of females in the higher judiciary. Whilst there may be something to be said for the 'tanker' argument, there have been high numbers of very good barristers over the past several decades and it seems incredible that of the top 161 judges in the country (ie the senior judiciary) only thirty-one females were found to be good enough to be a member of the senior judiciary, and of the most senior judges (Supreme Court, Court of Appeal, and Heads of Division) there should only be nine out of fifty-five. These figures suggest it is much more than the turning around of a tanker.

8.4.1.2 Ethnicity

The position in respect of ethnic representation is even worse. The last census suggests that approximately 7.9 per cent of the population consider themselves to be a member of the ethnic minorities. However, the latest judicial statistics demonstrate that no Head of Division belongs to an ethnic minority nor are there any Justices of the Supreme Court or Lord Justices of Appeal. There are now five (4.7 per cent) puisne

269

128. Clare McGlynn, 'Women, Representation and the Legal Academy' (1999) 19 *Legal Studies* 68, 89.
129. Lord Judge LCJ, *Lord Chief Justice's Press Conference* (HMCTS 2012) <http://www.judiciary.gov.uk/announcements/lcj-press-conference-2012/>, 9.
130. Peter Walker, 'Don't Rush Gender Equality in UK Judiciary, Says Supreme Court Judge' (*The Guardian*, 2015) <https://www.theguardian.com/law/2015/sep/22/gender-equality-warning-uk-legal-profession-supreme-court-judge-jonathan-sumption>.

judges. This means that of the senior judiciary as a whole there are only five minority ethnic judges which accounts for 3.1 per cent of the senior judiciary.

Of the junior judicial ranks, there are twenty-three (3.7 per cent) circuit judges who belong to an ethnic minority. This is an increase from two years ago, when there were fourteen circuit judges belonging to an ethnic minority. There are forty-one (7.3 per cent) district judges and district judges (magistrates' court). Of the part-time judiciary, there are sixty-two (5.9 per cent) recorders (a reduction from the previous edition) and forty-one (5.6 per cent) deputy district and deputy district (magistrates' courts) judges. As a whole, only 5 per cent of the judiciary would consider themselves as belonging to a member of the ethnic minorities, an increase from 4.7 per cent in 2015. It is clear that despite the increase in overall numbers the stereotype of a middle-class, white, male judge still exists and the latest statistics suggest that this stereotype has a factual basis behind it.

8.4.1.3 Diversity in the tribunals

What of the tribunal judiciary? Can it be said that these are more diverse? Historically the answer appeared to be 'no' but what of modern times? The position appears to compare favourably to the court judiciary. According to the latest statistics, of the 1,894 judges in the tribunals, 45 per cent were female.[131] The statistics suggest that 10 per cent of tribunal judiciary are of black or minority ethnicity,[132] although a 'health warning' needs to be given to that, as it is of *known* ethnicity. Seven per cent of tribunal judges do not declare their ethnicity and it is likely that these will be primarily white who do not see the point of ethnicity monitoring.

It would also appear that the Bar does not have the same grip on the tribunal judiciary. Sixty-five per cent of the judiciary come from professions outside the Bar,[133] and whilst they note that the proportion reduces towards the senior grades, it remains in excess of 40 per cent for the higher levels of the tribunal judiciary, which compares favourably with the court judiciary.

Happily, the data that accompanies the statistical bulletin allows us to delve deeper into the issue of gender and ethnicity. It will be remembered from Table 8.1, presented at the very beginning of the chapter, that the judiciary are broken down into grades. This allows us to compare their equivalences more easily. Table 8.3 summarizes the equivalences between tribunal and court judiciary.[134]

Table 8.3 Equivalences between tribunal and court judiciary

Salary Scale	Tribunal Judge	Court equivalent
5	Chamber Presidents	Senior circuit judge
6.1	Upper Tribunal judge	Circuit judge
7	First-Tier Tribunal judge	District judge
7	Employment judge	District judge

131. *Judicial Diversity Statistics 2016* (Judicial Office: London 2016) 12.
132. *Judicial Diversity Statistics 2016* (Judicial Office: London 2016) 12.
133. *Judicial Diversity Statistics 2016* (Judicial Office: London 2016) 13.
134. The total number of judges differs between Tables 8.1, 8.2, and 8.3 because it depends on the information that is contained within the statistics.

Table 8.4 Gender in the court and tribunal judiciary

	Courts			Tribunals		
Grade	Total number	Female	Male	Total number	Female	Male
Circuit judge[135]	626	160	466	93	32	61
District judge[136]	563	197	366	1749	798	951

<https://www.judiciary.gov.uk/publications/judicial-statistics-2016/> Diversity Statistics 2016 Tables, Table 1.1 and 2.3.

Table 8.5 Ethnicity in the court and tribunal judiciary

	Courts				Tribunals			
Grade	Total number	White	BME	Not Known[137]	Total number	White	BME	Not known
Circuit judge[138]	626	537	23	66	93	78	11	4
District judge[139]	563	474	41	48	1749	1461	162	126

<https://www.judiciary.gov.uk/publications/judicial-statistics-2016/> Diversity Statistics 2016 Tables, Table 1.1 and 2.3.

Tables 8.4 and 8.5 then present a comparison between the courts and tribunal judiciary.

Thus, if we compare gender, it can be seen that 25.6 per cent of the circuit-judge level court judiciary are female, compared to 34.4 per cent of the tribunal judiciary. At district-judge level, 35 per cent of the court judiciary are female compared to 45.6 per cent of the tribunal judiciary. In both cases therefore there is a statistically significant difference in gender balance. Whether this is reflected in the type of role, or the fact that there is a broader range of professions (including those who come from CILEX) is perhaps more open to question.

If we look at ethnicity, at circuit-level appointments, of those who have declared an ethnicity, 4.1 per cent of court judiciary are of black or minority ethnicity, compared to 12.3 per cent of the tribunal judiciary. At district-judge level, the position is that 8 per cent of the court judiciary are black or minority ethnic, compared to 10 per cent of the tribunal judiciary. That said, these figures should be treated with caution since if reported BME figures are taken into account in the total (rather than reported) figures, the proportions are as shown in Table 8.6.

Regardless of this, however, it can be seen that the tribunal judiciary do appear more representative than the court judiciary. Of course, knowing this and knowing *why* this is, are two very different issues. However, it does suggest that there is something to work with here. If the idea of an integrated judiciary (discussed in

271

135.   This includes senior circuit judges since, by statute, they remain circuit judges, it is just that they are paid more.
136.   This includes district judge (magistrates' court).
137.   Not known, ie the judge has not declared their ethnicity.
138.   This includes senior circuit judges since, by statute, they remain circuit judges, it is just that they are paid more.
139.   This includes district judge (magistrates' court).

Table 8.6 Percentages of black or minority ethnicity judges in the courts and tribunal judiciary

Grade	Courts	Tribunals
Circuit-judge level	3.7%	11.8%
District-judge level	7.2%	9.2%

<https://www.judiciary.gov.uk/publications/judicial-statistics-2016/> Tables 2.3 and 1.1.

Chapter 20) is to progress, then this means judicial promotion within the bands. If the tribunal judiciary could be promoted, then it could have a positive effect on judicial diversity.

8.4.2 Extending diversity

Despite these figures it can be seen that the professions and senior members of the judiciary argue that they are trying to make the judiciary more diverse. The question is perhaps whether these are mere words or whether there is a true move towards the diversification of the judiciary.

Perhaps the first point of note is that whilst recent statutory reforms have allowed feminine judicial titles to be used (eg Lady Justice of Appeal instead of Lord Justice of Appeal and even provision for a Lady Chief Justice)[140] the title of the Law Lords was not changed and thus Lady Hale states that when she was introduced to the House of Lords by letters patent she was introduced as a Lord of Appeal in Ordinary.[141] At a simplistic level this can be dismissed as irrelevant, with everyone knowing that Lady Hale is female, but it does demonstrate what could be perceived as an inherent male bias within the judiciary and prior to appointment she noted that such matters were 'trivial but ... annoying manifestations of the assumption that this is a male profession which women are allowed to join provided that they pretend to be men'.[142]

When thinking about this whole area, one commentator asks quite a pertinent question: '*Why* [sic] should we want a more representative judiciary? Is it simply that there *ought* to be more women judges ...?'[143] Presumably this could be extended further, ie to ask why we should want more female judges and members of the ethnic minorities. It could be argued that we expect our judiciary to be representative of society but is that really what is desired? It is unlikely that in terms of socio-economic factors there would be a desire or expectation for representation and surely the public would wish the best members of the legal profession to become its judges—so why diversity? It has to be something more than just 'to make up the numbers'[144] but Hale,

---

140. See *Courts Act 2003*, s 64(2).
141. Baroness Hale of Richmond, 'The House of Lords and Women's Rights or Am I Really a Law Lord' (2005) 25 *Legal Studies* 72 and see *Appellate Jurisdiction Act 1876*, s 6.
142. Brenda Hale, 'Equality and the Judiciary: Why Should We Want More Women Judges?' [2001] *Public Law* 489, 497.
143. Ericka Rackley, 'Representations of the (Woman) Judge: Hercules, the Little Mermaid and the Vain and Naked Emperor' (2002) 22 *Legal Studies* 602, 609.
144. Ericka Rackley, 'Representations of the (Woman) Judge: Hercules, the Little Mermaid and the Vain and Naked Emperor' (2002) 22 *Legal Studies* 602, 610.

speaking extrajudicially, argues that it is about 'individuals and their rights',[145] ie the right to progress within a profession and not to be discriminated against.

 QUESTION FOR REFLECTION

Do you think the judiciary should be diverse? What about representative? What does judicial representation actually mean? Think about *why* you want a more representative judiciary; what are the advantages that this would bring to the justice system?

It could be suggested that it is a matter of public confidence. How can a white male bastion inspire confidence in the justice system? Whilst one should be wary of looking to the media where attacks are often intemperate, inappropriate, and frequently completely wrong, it is not difficult to think that the judiciary currently make themselves difficult to defend against accusations that they do not know the 'real world'. If they cannot even recognize a multicultural society how can they possibly adjudicate on such matters?

8.4.2.1 Appointment on merit

One commentator notes that the current system of diversity and appointment has been summarized accurately by Lord Lloyd of Berwick, a Lord of Appeal in Ordinary:

> I would like, obviously, the judiciary to be as diverse as we can get it. But that must not interfere with the fundamental principle that we have got to choose the best man for the job.[146]

One cannot help but focus on the last words of this quote. Although, as has been noted, the convention within law is to refer to the masculine and indeed this book follows the convention because to use 'he or she' or the even worse '(s)he' is awkward prose, one cannot help but think that there are times when the inclusion of the words 'or woman' or the substitution of 'person' would be appropriate. Arguably the quote of Lord Lloyd is such an example.

The justification for the slow progress of diversity is that only the best are appointed to be judges and that any move towards positive assistance would be contrary to this rule and could even dilute the quality of judges. Deciding who the 'best' candidate is can always be difficult because if one gets the best schooling and education it can be easy to be the 'best' especially if those choosing you meet the same profile, but what does that mean here?

In a review of the appointments system, it was noted that whilst there is almost unanimity in accepting that judges should be appointed on merit, interestingly there was no clear consensus on what 'merit' actually means.[147] However, the report differentiated between two types of merit, namely 'maximal merit' where only one candidate is judged suitable for appointment as he is the best person available[148] or 'minimal

273

---

145. Brenda Hale, 'Equality and the Judiciary: Why Should We Want More Women Judges?' [2001] *Public Law* 489.

146. Kate Malleson, 'Rethinking the Merit Principle in Judicial Selection' (2006) 33 *Journal of Law and Society* 126.

147. Thomas Legg, 'Brave New World: The New Supreme Court and Judicial Appointments' (2004) 24 *Legal Studies* 45, 49.

148. Thomas Legg, 'Brave New World: The New Supreme Court and Judicial Appointments' (2004) 24 *Legal Studies* 45, 50.

merit' where the selected panel identifies a number of people who are qualified for the appointment and then a person is chosen from that pool on the basis of policy decisions.[149] The implication of this argument is that the latter approach is an inferior way of appointing members of the judiciary even though it can be justified on policy grounds, not least the fact that a more diverse judiciary may assist in securing public confidence.

However, is it this simple? Part of the difficulty of locating the maximal best candidate is the advantages that arise from the status quo. There has, for several years now, been considerable debate as to whether those educated in the public schools were being over-represented at the very best universities, particularly Oxbridge. Those who qualified at Oxbridge were certainly well represented in the major law firms and at the Bar. Did it mean that those who were educated at public schools were more intelligent than those at state schools or could it reflect the fact that public schools, because of their teaching patterns and staff/student ratios, are better able to devote more time and attention to their students thus allowing students to demonstrate their full potential? If it is the latter, as many believe, then simply selecting the maximal merit candidate each time will mean that the cycle could become self-sustaining with those who had the best opportunities becoming the best candidates. The minimal merit scheme (although we dislike the term) has the advantage of setting out the competencies of the judges allowing a broad analysis to be made of their qualities and then deciding how someone fits into the wider considerations. This is not the same as positive discrimination and is no different to many companies who will state that they 'particularly welcome applicants from the ethnic minorities'. This is not watering down quality but ensuring that all applicants have the same opportunities.

Malleson, probably the most authoritative commentator on the area, argues that there need not be a binary system where it is either the maximal or minimal system but rather that the maximal system could be altered through the provision of a 'tie-breaker' system.[150] The basis of this argument is that there will not necessarily be 'one' candidate that appears best but there may be a number of applicants who are equally qualified. In those circumstances it is suggested that there should be a 'tie-break' feature whereby those who come from an under-represented group should be given the position.[151] This is arguably distinct from the 'minimal' system in that the minimal system looks solely at the criteria and ranks the person thereafter whereas the 'tie-break' system is a derivative of the maximal system because it looks at persons but where there is difficulty in deciding between two or more persons, the 'tie-break' is under-representation.

The CCA 2013 introduced provisions in relation to increasing diversity in the judiciary, which are somewhat reflective of Malleson's tie-break principle. Schedule 13, Part Two of the Act has amended the previous provisions found in the CRA 2005 on judicial appointments being solely on merit. Instead it allows that where two persons being considered for judicial appointment are of equal merit, the commission can prefer one over the other in order to increase diversity within the judiciary. Moreover,

---

149. Thomas Legg, 'Brave New World: The New Supreme Court and Judicial Appointments' (2004) 24 *Legal Studies* 45, 51.
150. Kate Malleson, 'Rethinking the Merit Principle in Judicial Selection' (2006) 33 *Journal of Law and Society* 126, 129.
151. Kate Malleson, 'Rethinking the Merit Principle in Judicial Selection' (2006) 33 *Journal of Law and Society* 126, 129.

the Act makes specific reference to the fact that the Lord Chancellor and Lord Chief Justice '[m]ust take such steps as that office-holder considers appropriate for the purpose of encouraging judicial diversity'.[152]

 QUESTION FOR REFLECTION

What do you think of the reforms introduced by the CCA 2013? Are they a sufficient compromise between the need to appoint judges by merit but also to create a 'level playing field' upon which under-represented groups of society can compete for judicial appointments?

8.4.2.2 Family-friendly policies

With the introduction of the CCA 2013, there has been an additional focus on introducing family-friendly policies within the judiciary. It will be seen that it is unusual for a circuit judge to be promoted to the High Court bench or beyond (9.2.3) and therefore if women are to become members of the senior judiciary they will ordinarily begin their full-time career as a puisne judge. The difficulty with the role of a puisne judge is that judges in the Queen's Bench and Family Divisions (and to a lesser extent the Chancery Division) will spend a considerable time 'on circuit', ie sitting away from their home. Life on circuit is not, as the media sometimes presents it, a luxurious exercise since QBD judges will normally act as the 'single judge' during that time and thus work on papers. High Court judges also hold an important social rank and thus there is a considerable amount of entertaining that must be done in the evening, together with work on papers etc.

Until recently a judge 'on circuit' was *required* to stay in judge's lodgings even if his home was within commutable distance. Other circuits will (not infrequently) be a significant distance away from their home so that the judge will spent four to six weeks away from home three, and possibly four, times a year.[153] This can hardly be described as 'family friendly' and is undoubtedly a disincentive to both male and female judges but, arguably, a greater disincentive to female judges who do not wish to be away from what might be young members of a family.[154] McGlynn, citing Sandra O'Connor—the first woman to be appointed to the US Supreme Court—noted that a significant issue may be that a woman may wish to have a child and that the judicial structure should be able to take this into account.[155] This should not just be in respect of a 'pregnant judge' but should also take account of the fact that if a female lawyer takes time out to raise a family this should not prejudice an application for a judgeship later.

In an attempt to combat some of these issues the CCA 2013 has introduced flexible working for judges sitting in the High Court or above, as well as extending the opportunity to work part time to those judges working in both the High Court and the Court of Appeal. Opportunities to work flexibly will be made clear during each JAC selection process. Finally, the Act has introduced a system of 'deployment of the

152. *Constitutional Reform Act 2005*, s 137A.
153. Rt Hon Lord Justice Auld, *A Review of the Criminal Courts of England and Wales* (HMSO 2001) 238.
154. Kate Malleson, 'Rethinking the Merit Principle in Judicial Selection' (2006) 33 *Journal of Law and Society* 126, 131.
155. Clare McGlynn, 'Judging Women Differently: Gender, the Judiciary and Reform' in Susan Millns and Noel Whitty (eds), *Feminist Perspectives on Public Law* (Cavendish Publishing 1990) 97–9.

judiciary',[156] whereby judges can move more easily and flexibly between working in courts of equal or lower status. It is hoped that this will help with career development.

Family-friendly policies are commonplace in society and it is clear that such policies are beginning to be adopted within the judicial system. This is as big an issue as the diversity of the profession since a more diverse application system will only be achieved if people apply for judicial appointments. If they believe the conditions of the post are not suited to their lifestyle they will simply not apply for them regardless of how open the system becomes.

 QUESTION FOR REFLECTION

What do you think of the introduction of 'family-friendly' policies within the judiciary? Do these policies go far enough, or is more needed to allow judges, particularly puisne judges, to provide for 'family time' around their judicial commitments?

8.4.3 The Bar's grip

A particular difficulty in diversification is the fact that there is an undisputed link between the Bar and the Bench and arguably this creates a situation whereby significant numbers of persons are not considered. The reforms of the *Courts and Legal Services Act 1990* (CSLA 1990)[157] altered the Bar's exclusive privilege of putting forward candidates for the senior judiciary but doubts continue to exist as to whether the gap has truly narrowed. The first solicitor to be appointed to the High Court bench was Sachs J although he was appointed via the circuit bench (to which solicitors had been appointed for some time). The first solicitor to be appointed direct from practice was Lawrence (now Lord) Collins who went on to become the first ever solicitor-appointee of the Court of Appeal (2007) and House of Lords (2009) and then subsequently a Justice of the Supreme Court on its creation. However, the third appointment, (Sir) Henry Hodge, was a circuit judge prior to appointment as was the latest appointment, (Sir) Gary Hickinbottom (now Hickinbottom J) who was appointed back in 2009 and who remains the only current puisne judge to be a former solicitor. However, in one pleasing sign, it was announced in 2016 that Hickinbottom J has been 'screened' to become a Lord Justice of Appeal, and will take up his position sometime in 2017 when a vacancy arises.

One reason why the grip has not yet been broken is that the primary criterion for a judgeship was 'visibility' meaning appearing or at least interacting with senior members of the judiciary frequently.[158] The Bar, as will be seen in Chapter 10, traditionally had exclusive rights of audience in the higher courts and even today barristers continue to undertake the bulk of the work there. In addition to this, the Inns of Court are vital and again this lends assistance to the Bar. The Inns are governed by Masters of the Bench who are ordinarily either senior members of the judiciary or Queen's Counsel. A prospective puisne judge who is also a barrister will almost certainly be trying to ingratiate himself with his Inn by undertaking extra work etc which brings

---

156.   *Crime and Courts Act 2013*, sch 14.
157.   See s 71.
158.   Brenda Hale, 'Equality and the Judiciary: Why Should We Want More Women Judges?' [2001] *Public Law* 489, 492.

him to the attention of the senior members of the profession, an advantage that solicitors simply do not have.

The creation of the JAC does not appear to have eased this position and indeed it is arguably worse—as noted earlier the last solicitor to be appointed to the puisne bench was back in 2009 but the only solicitor to be appointed directly to the puisne bench was Lawrence (now Lord) Collins (the others being circuit judges first). It is difficult to believe that there are no solicitors who deserve appointment to the High Court bench. The relative rarity of promotion from circuit to puisne bench does seem to ensure that the Bar continues to dominate judicial appointments especially when, as it will be remembered, most Court of Appeal and Supreme Court appointments come from the High Court and Court of Appeal respectively.

In their annual report for 2010–11 the JAC noted that far from improving the position in respect of solicitors the converse appears to be true. They note that of circuit bench appointments, twenty-two were appointed before the creation of the JAC and only eleven afterwards.[159] That said, the pre-existence figures were over a longer period of time (eight years rather than four) but it must still be a cause of concern. The JAC does not appear to know why this is the case although they do at least see it as an issue that needs examining and have agreed an approach with the Law Society to increase applications.[160] The latest figures available do not appear to indicate any real progress. In 2014–15 the JAC conducted twenty-two legal selection exercises. Of the recommended candidates only 27 per cent were solicitors,[161] suggesting that there were also fewer applications by solicitors.

The difficulty with the approach of deciding to work with the Law Society to encourage applications is that this only works if (a) there is an identifiable shortage of applications, (b) it is known why there is a shortage of applications, and (c) the JAC are confident that there is no inherent flaw in the process of appointment.

Certainly the latest statistical evidence would suggest that there is a shortage of applications—but the more important reason is why they are not applying. Is it because they do not understand they can apply or is it because the low appointment rate means they do not believe there is any point? If the latter then there is considerable work to be done, including identifying whether the actual process remains appropriate. Whilst there is now a degree of independence through the JAC it does not necessarily follow that the process is automatically fair. If there is a flaw in the appointments process—because, for example, 'visibility' remains a key issue—then consideration needs to be given as to whether this requirement remains appropriate. Of course one argument is that it is only comparatively recently that there has been a greater number of solicitor advocates and this therefore may eventually follow through into judicial appointments but it is far from clear that there has been a systematic analysis of whether advocacy is necessarily the correct benchmark for appointment to the bench.

8.4.3.1 Other professions

The then Labour government suggested that restricting the judiciary to the two principal professions was not appropriate and in 2005 proposed that legal executives should be eligible to become members of the judiciary,[162] albeit in the more junior positions,

---

159. JAC, *Annual Report 2010–11* (Judicial Appointments Commission 2011) 18.
160. JAC, *Annual Report 2010–11* (Judicial Appointments Commission 2011) 18.
161. JAC, *Annual Report and Accounts 2015–16* (Judicial Appointments Commission 2016) 16.
162. 'Judges to Come from Wider Pool of Applicants' DCA Press Release 181/05.

eg deputy or full district judges. However, such a system would potentially provide access to other benches since appointment as a district judge can (eventually) act as a 'threshold' for appointment for the Circuit Bench.

The judiciary were not happy with the proposal but Fennell, a legal correspondent for *The Times*, argued the concerns were misplaced, stating: 'I imagine that the proposal to allow legal executives to become judges should do a lot to enhance the quality of common sense on the bench',[163] although his point then becomes confused as the basis of his premise is that the Chartered Institute of Legal Executives (CILEX) provides the opportunity to become qualified as a solicitor. This, as we shall see, is perfectly true (see 10.7.1.3) but theoretically such persons are not disqualified from judicial appointments since when they are made solicitors they will have a general qualification (and thus the most junior positions will be available after a number of years) and if the higher advocacy examinations were taken then all appointments would be open.

The government argued that allowing CILEX members to access judicial appointments would bring more diversity to the bench but there are significant numbers of solicitors and barristers who are from diverse social, ethnic, and sexual backgrounds and it is difficult to see why the judicial members could not be drawn from these ranks. Further, is the quest for diversity or representation? The Law Society and Bar Council have both argued that judicial appointments should reflect society rather than represent it; by this they mean that class, gender, ethnicity, religion, and sexual orientation should not be a bar to any appointment and that a diverse bench would enhance merit and the judiciary but that appointments should not be made on a quota basis.[164]

The government progressed with the proposals and in 2010 the very first CILEX appointment was made.[165] Ian Ashley-Smith, a CILEX Fellow, was appointed to the position of Deputy District Judge (Civil) and sits in Kent.[166] In September 2013, the second appointment of a CILEX Fellow was made, with Simon Lindsey being appointed Deputy District Judge on the South Eastern Circuit. This certainly marks a considerable milestone in the recognition of CILEX as the 'third profession' (discussed further in Chapter 10 (10.7.1)) and it is likely that further appointments at this level will be made in subsequent years. If one looks to tribunals, it would seem that there is a greater use of CILEX Fellows as judges. This may because of the nature of tribunal work (which tends to be specialist, as can CILEX practitioners). However, being a tribunal judge provides judicial experience which can make a person eligible for more senior judicial positions, including the circuit bench.

8.5 Judicial training

When judges are appointed should they be trained? It may seem a peculiar question to ask yet traditionally training was not offered and a lack of experience was certainly no barrier to appointment:

Lord Devlin recalled that when he was appointed to the High Court in 1948, 'I had never exercised any criminal jurisdiction and not since my early days at the Bar had

163. 'Wider Bench', *The Times*, 19 July 2005, Law Supplement.
164. Catherine Baksi, 'World at their Feet' (2005) 102 *Law Society Gazette* 26.
165. JAC, *Annual Report 2010–11* (Judicial Appointments Commission 2011) 16.
166. JAC, *Annual Report 2010–11* (Judicial Appointments Commission 2011) 29.

I appeared in a criminal court ... Two days after I had been sworn in, I was trying crime at Newcastle Assizes.'[167]

Dunn notes that when he was appointed it was a case of speaking to other members of the judiciary to understand the principles of giving judgment and discovering the usual awards for compensation etc.[168] The Lord Chief Justice began to operate 'sentencing conferences' for members of the circuit judiciary and this was eventually extended by the President of the Family Division to include training on family work.

The ad hoc approach of judicial training needed reform, however, and in 1979 the *Judicial Studies Board* (JSB) was created to have an oversight of judicial training, and it has been suggested that it 'discharge[d] an ever more important function' and as it was operated by the judges (as its successor the *Judicial College* is) it contributed to judicial independence.[169] The JSB was originally restricted to criminal law but its successor now applies to all types of law and all levels of the judiciary.

On 1 April 2011 the JSB ceased to exist and the Judicial College took over. This is not a physical college but rather a virtual one—whilst it will be seen that lectures and seminars do take place it is not in a central location but rather occurs in multiple locations and, increasingly, online. The Judicial College also assumed responsibility for the training of the tribunal judiciary and also for legal advisers to the magistrates.

The Judicial College is governed by a Board whose president is a Court of Appeal judge, currently Lady Justice Rafferty. Its other members are:

- a member of the courts judiciary
- a member of the tribunal judiciary
- a representative with responsibility for magistrates and legal advisers
- the Director of Training for the courts judiciary
- the Director of Training for the tribunal judiciary
- the Executive Director of the Judicial College.

In addition to the Board the Judicial College has a series of committees, these being:

- Tribunals Committee—as its name suggests it has responsibility for the training programmes specifically tailored towards the tribunal judiciary
- Courts Committee—which sets out plans for the training for all levels of the courts judiciary
- Diversity & Development Committee
- Wales Training Committee—a recently established committee that is tasked to consider whether specialist training is required as a result of devolution in Wales
- International Committee—the Judicial College is asked to participate in a number of international events, including hosting visiting judges, and this committee considers these issues.

---

167.   David Pannick, *Judges* (OUP 1987) 69.
168.   Robin Dunn, *Sword and Wig: Memoirs of a Lord Justice* (Quiller Press 1993) 181–3.
169.   Thomas Bingham, *The Business of Judging: Selected Essays and Speeches* (OUP 2000) 67.

The actual training is more complicated and broken down into a series of different types of training, the principal groups being:

- civil
- criminal
- cross jurisdictional (this is primarily skills-based training and seeks to tackle those aspects of judging that are common to all jurisdictions)
- family
- magistrates
- tribunals
- senior judiciary (this now includes puisne and Court of Appeal judges although this is still at their own discretion whereas for the inferior judiciary it remains mandatory).

The actual training that is undertaken by judges will differ depending on level and appointment. Upon initial appointment there is often a requirement that a judge attends a residential induction programme of training that will cover many of the basics of the judicial role. The Judicial College produces a 'prospectus' that lists all the training that is available to judges and allows them to pick the courses that they feel are most relevant to them. The 2014–15 prospectus lists twenty-one national seminars across all areas of work.[170] The actual training requirement is relatively minimal. For full-time members of the judiciary below puisne rank the requirement is only for one national seminar a year.[171] For part-time members of the judiciary it does not appear that they are able to even attend a seminar once a year. However, that is subject to two qualifications; the first is that this relates only to national training and so further training also occurs and second, the College's use of 'seminar' does not equate to what a university student would understand as it may include a series of modules within the seminar, often requiring a residential stay (see, for example, the 'Civil Law Seminar' which is constituted of fifteen distinct modules).[172]

Alongside the national seminars is further training. Some of this will be at a more local level. Each circuit will usually organize a series of training events for the judiciary and there are also e-resources on the judicial portal of the Judicial College, which includes updating services (so-called e-letters).[173]

Judicial training has progressed considerably since the times discussed at the start of this section. The Director of Studies of the College, writing in the final annual report of the Judicial Studies Board, notes that the JSB was called 'studies' not 'training' because there was a belief that judges would reject the suggestion that they required training[174] and yet the modern Judicial College is based on the premise that there is an acceptance that training is an essential part of the life of a judge. Some of the training courses—for example the serious sexual offences seminar—is an essential part of authorizing a judge to sit on certain cases. It is this which allows a judge to be 'ticketed' to hear rape and serious sexual offences. There are other examples, including the

170. JC, *Courts Judiciary Prospectus of Education* (Judicial College 2015) 18.
171. JC, *Courts Judiciary Prospectus of Education* (Judicial College 2015) 10.
172. JC, *Courts Judiciary Prospectus of Education* (Judicial College 2015) 21.
173. JC, *Courts Judiciary Prospectus of Education* (Judicial College 2012) 61.
174. JSB, *Annual Report 2010/11* (Judicial Studies Board 2011) 11.

fact that a seminar has been created specifically for those puisne judges who have been appointed to hear matters in the Administrative Court.

However, there remains some concern that there is perhaps more to do. At the very beginning of the section it was stated that a newly appointed judge was just thrown in at the deep end. It may be thought this is no longer true but even in modern times it is can still happen as noted in the comments of a senior judge presented by Darbyshire:

> I gave a party at my old chambers to say goodbye and I asked some friends who came from outside of the law. One said … 'Well I imagine you go off now for three months' training?' I said, 'As a matter of fact you don't'. He said, 'When do you start sitting?' I said 'Tomorrow morning at half past ten'. He said, 'Well I imagine then that they are giving you a case of the kind you used to do at the Bar because you know all about them'. I muttered that they don't and that I was doing an asylum case … He said 'How many of those have you done before?' I said 'None'.[175]

Darbyshire does not state how old that story is although in the context of the book it seems recent. Full-time judges will, of course, initially sit as part-time judges, but there is still the problem that their appointment and training will rarely coincide on the basis that judges do not retire, nor are they appointed, at specific points in the year. They are appointed throughout the year and it would not be very efficient to have individual training programmes for each judge. Perhaps surprisingly there is no requirement for the induction to have occurred before the judge starts sitting and this means situations like Darbyshire's can still occur.

Some have suggested that judges should attend a 'judicial college' for a period of up to two months, with lectures and seminars being supplemented with mock trials.[176] Pannick rejects the idea that because a judge comes from practice there is an inherent ability to cope with the work of a judge, pointing out that the differences between practice and the bench are significant. The cost of doing so would be high and in addition the scheduling of appointments would also have to be centralized so that there was a 'start date' for judicial appointments to allow this to occur. Realistically it is difficult to see how this would happen.

The training for the senior judiciary is also an issue where there is perhaps less certainty. It is clear that there have been considerable advances in the training of puisne judges, including building in protected time for studies when first appointed[177] but the review of training for the senior judiciary continues to be put back each year.[178] It is essential that the training of puisne judges continues to be developed as they are doing some of the most difficult and sensitive work of the judiciary as a whole. Darbyshire reported that a number of her interviewees who held posts within the senior judiciary did think that there was the need for reform[179] and some believed that the lack of training did impact their effectiveness. We have even less detail on the training for the Lord Justices of Appeal and the Heads of Division. In 2010 Tomlinson LJ was entrusted with the task of identifying the training and support needs of those judges[180] but we are not told what, if anything, has been done about that. There are seminars

---

175. Penny Darbyshire, *Sitting in Judgment: The Working Lives of Judges* (Hart Publishing 2011) 111–12.
176. David Pannick, *Judges* (OUP 1987) 71.
177. JSB, *Annual Report 2009/10* (Judicial Studies Board 2010) 36.
178. JSB, *Annual Report 2010/11* (Judicial Studies Board 2011) 36.
179. Penny Darbyshire, *Sitting in Judgment: The Working Lives of Judges* (Hart Publishing 2011) 112.
180. JSB, *Annual Report 2010/11* (Judicial Studies Board 2011) 36.

that take place after court in the Royal Courts of Justice[181] and this will no doubt include a number of events that could be suitably badged as 'continuing professional development' but it is important that the training needs of all members of the judiciary are considered and that they have a formal plan for their training.

The Judicial College is part of the judiciary of England and Wales and therefore it does not formally have a role for Justices of the Supreme Court. The Supreme Court website does not include any formal reference to training for the justices and yet presumably there is recognition that training is valuable for them too. It would be sensible for the court to consider disclosing what training is offered for the justices so that there can be full confidence in the work that they undertake.

 QUESTION FOR REFLECTION

Pannick has suggested that those wishing to be judges should be 'trained' before becoming full members of the judiciary. Do you think this is now unnecessary since full-time judicial appointments will ordinarily come from the part-time judiciary?

8.6 Judicial salaries

Judicial salaries will be considered in the next chapter in the context of judicial independence (9.2.2), as the paying of salaries raises an interesting constitutional question regarding how independent the judiciary are from the state. However, in this section the more mundane aspect of the amount judges are paid will be discussed.

It will be remembered that the judiciary are separated into grades (Table 8.1) and this is reflected in their pay (see Table 8.7).

It will be remembered that many judicial jobs are also part-time. This most notably includes recorders and deputy district judges, but can also include counsel acting

Table 8.7 The current salary grades of the judiciary

Judicial Grade	£
1	249,583
1.1	222,862
2	215,256
3	204,695
4	179,768
5	144,172
6.1	133,506
6.2	125,689
7	107,100

181. JSB, *Annual Report 2010/11* (Judicial Studies Board 2011) 36.

Table 8.8 Daily fees for part-time judiciary

Description	£
Retired Supreme Court judge	978.25
Retired Lord Justice of Appeal[183]	930.43
Retired High Court judges	856.04
Deputy High Court judge[184]	856.04
Recorder[185]	635.74
Deputy circuit judge[186]	635.74
Deputy district judge, including district judge (magistrates' court)	498.14

as a deputy High Court judge, and retired judges who continue to act until they are unable to do so for statutory reasons.[182] A fixed daily fee is given for these, as set out in Table 8.8.

At first sight, the salaries look high when compared to 'ordinary' salaries but these are the brightest and most senior people in their profession. A comparison can be drawn to 'flag rank'[187] in the military who receive comparable pay. However, if one were to compare them to the salaries of the chief executives of FTSE100 companies it would look extremely modest.[188] The same could be true of commerce, where high salaries are paid. If we look to the professions, it has already been noted that high salaries can be commanded by the very best practitioners. It is those that we should target to become judges, meaning that for many a significant pay cut is taken to become a judge.

8.7 Sharing the judiciary

Traditionally, apart from the *Employment Appeals Tribunal*, where puisne and circuit judges would regularly sit, there was no overlap between the court judiciary and tribunal judiciary. They were considered to be distinct personnel and there was no cross-over. Indeed, tribunal judges were not given the title 'judge' and were considered more akin to civil servants than judges.

However, the *Tribunals, Courts and Enforcement Act 2007* brought about changes and the belief that the tribunal judiciary were part of the judicial system. Along with creating the Senior President of Tribunals as a judicial post, the Act permitted an English judge[189] to sit in a tribunal, with the agreement of the Lord

---

182. A judge who has retired may continue to sit until the age of 75, see for example *Constitutional Reform Act 2005*, s 39(2)(c).
183. When sitting in the Court of Appeal. When sitting in the High Court, they receive the retired High Court fee.
184. This is a practitioner sitting as a High Court judge.
185. A practitioner sitting at circuit level.
186. A retired judge sitting at circuit level.
187. ie Rear Admiral/Major General/Air Vice-Marshal and above.
188. Where an average salary of around £5m per annum can be expected.
189. ie Lord Justice of Appeal or below.

283

Chief Justice and Senior President of Tribunals.[200] This meant that some of the more complicated tribunal work began to be heard by judges, bringing greater certainty to the process.

There was then a desire for tribunal judiciary to be able to sit in the courts too. There was recognition that the tribunal judiciary have extensive judicial experience and would be suitable for sitting on cases within the courts too. Given that there is chronic delay in both the civil and criminal justice systems, permitting judges to sit in tribunals and tribunal judiciary to sit in the courts would mean that resources could be deployed more easily. Ultimately this has happened, with the *Crime and Courts Act 2013* stating:

> The Lord Chief Justice's deployment responsibility includes (so far as it would not otherwise do so, and subject to having regard to the responsibilities of the Senior President of Tribunals) responsibility for the maintenance of appropriate arrangements for—
>
> (a) the deployment to tribunals of judiciary deployable to tribunals, and
>
> (b) the deployment to courts in England and Wales of judiciary deployable to such courts.[201]

This has been followed by further statutory amendments that allow chamber presidents, judges of the Upper Tribunal, and presidents of the employment tribunals to act as High Court judges when required.[202] Similarly, judges of the First-Tier and Upper Tribunals have the right to sit in the Crown and County Courts when requested by the Lord Chief Justice with the consent of the Senior President of Tribunals. This has the potential to increase the number of judges who can sit in those courts, something that could be important in the county court where there is concern at the number of circuit judges dealing with civil matters.[203]

Another advantage of the courts and tribunal judiciary being able to sit in either jurisdiction is that it is even possible for them to sit concurrently. This is something that the Senior President of Tribunals has flagged as a potential solution to inefficiencies within the justice system.[204] Certain property disputes require adjudication between two different locations. Certain issues are matters reserved to the county court and yet others are reserved to the tribunals. A pilot is currently ongoing where appropriately qualified judges sit concurrently in both the tribunal *and* the county court, so that the issues are resolved in one hearing. This saves considerable costs and is of greater benefit to the parties who only need to attend once. There are a number of areas where allowing business to be dealt with by a judge sitting as a both a tribunal and court would make sense.

In Chapter 20 a potential shift towards a unified judiciary will be considered. This could ultimately lead to judges being of particular grades rather than titles, although that would be a significant shift from the current position.

---

200.   *Tribunals, Courts and Enforcement Act 2007*, s 6.
201.   *Crime and Courts Act 2013*, s 21.
202.   *Senior Courts Act 1981*, s 9(1) as amended. Note that the judges, including tribunal judges, must have been approved by the JAC to sit as s 9 judges.
203.   See Rt Hon Lord Justice Briggs, *Civil Courts Structure Review: Final Report* (HM Judiciary: London 2016) 87–90. This is partly because the circuit judges are needed to sit in the Crown Court and the Family Court, meaning that civil work is often left to other judges.
204.   See Sir Ernest Ryder 'The Context of Change' Speech to Lancaster University Law School, 4 November 2016. Available at: <http://www.lancaster.ac.uk/law/blogs/staff/lord-justice-ryder-extract-school-lecture/>.

◆ Summary

This chapter has introduced the judiciary and the concept of the judicial office. In particular it has:

- Identified that there are different levels of judges, with the senior judiciary comprising the Lord Chief Justice, Master of the Rolls, and the Heads of Division.
- Noted that the Lord Chief Justice is the Head of the Court Judiciary but that the Senior President of Tribunals heads the tribunal judiciary.
- Identified how the tribunal judiciary are beginning to be integrated into the court judiciary and how judges can now sit interchangeably in the courts or tribunals.
- Identified that superior judges (puisne judges and above) have unlimited authority whereas the inferior judiciary are limited to the jurisdiction provided by statute.
- Considered how appointments to the judiciary are made and discussed how to make the judiciary more diverse.

❓ End-of-chapter questions

1. Why do we need different levels of first-instance judiciary? Is it now not time to abolish the difference between puisne, circuit, and district judge (and their tribunal equivalents)?

2. How can we boost the number of women and judges from black and other minority ethnicities? Has the JAC actually made any difference in terms of progressing this? How much longer should we wait?

3. Should the Lord Chancellor be able to veto the appointment of a judge? Why have a judicial appointments commission if their decisions can be set aside on a ministerial whim?

285

☰ Further reading

Barmes L and Malleson K, 'The Legal Profession as a Gatekeeper to the Judiciary: Design Faults in Measures to Enhance Diversity' (2011) 74 *Modern Law Review* 245–71.

This is an article that considers the gate-keeping role played by the legal profession in the judicial appointments process and suggests that it is a barrier to widening diversity in the judiciary.

Bingham T, 'Judicial Independence' in *The Business of Judging* (OUP 2000).

This is an essay written by Lord Bingham who discusses the concept of judicial independence and places it in the context of the modern judiciary.

Hale B, 'Equality and the Judiciary: Why Should We Want More Women Judges?' [2001] *Public Law* 489.

This remains one of the most important pieces on why greater diversity is required. It is written by Lady Hale, the only female Supreme Court judge to be appointed.

Lord Chancellor, Lord Chief Justice, and Senior President of Tribunals, *Transforming our Justice System* (Ministry of Justice 2016).

> A policy statement by the current Lord Chief Justice and Senior President of Tribunals that discusses how the justice system must transform to stay relevant. Within this plan there is considerable attention paid to ensuring the right judge hears the right case, and discusses ways in which the judiciary may change.

For multiple-choice questions, updates to this chapter, and links to useful websites, please visit the **Online Resource Centre** at: **www.oxfordtextbooks.co.uk/orc/gillespie_els6e/**

9

Judicial Independence

By the end of this chapter you will be able to:

- Assess the independence of the judiciary
- Understand how independence of the judiciary is secured
- Understand issues around judicial ethics
- Consider restrictions on practice.

Introduction

Judicial independence is an important concept that is often discussed and yet there is very little literature that attempts to provide a definition.[1] It is frequently suggested that the classic definition is that judges should be independent from the executive but this is not possible in the most literal sense:

> Judges sit in courts provided by the state, they have offices provided, heated and lighted by the state, they have clerks paid by the state, they use books and computers mostly provided by the state, they are themselves paid by the state.[2]

This is an astute point and demonstrates that full independence is neither practicable nor particularly desirable but what does independence mean and why should judges be independent?

Before considering these questions and others in detail, it is important to recognize that when discussing judicial independence, what is being referred to is the independence of *both* the courts and tribunal judiciary. Indeed, s 1 of the *Tribunals, Courts and Enforcement Act 2007* amended the *Constitutional Reform Act 2005*, to ensure that the guarantee of judicial independence contained therein also applies to the tribunal judiciary.

---

1. Robert Stevens, *The Independence of the Judiciary: View from the Lord Chancellor's Office* (Clarendon Press 2003) 3.
2. Thomas Bingham, *The Business of Judging: Selected Essays and Speeches* (OUP 2000) 57–8.

9.1 Independent from whom?

The first issue to examine is who judges should be independent from. The law dictionary defines judicial independence as:

> The practice in the UK whereby judges are freed from outside pressures …[3].

The notion of 'outside pressure' is significantly wider than simple independence from the executive although the definition continues by stating:

> [It is] secured by, eg the charging of judges' salaries on the Consolidated Fund, separation of judiciary from Parliament, security of tenure of office, judicial immunity.

This demonstrates that independence will ordinarily mean independence from the other arms of the state (executive and legislature) but that it need not be restricted to this, and the opening sentence of the definition—'outside pressures'—does suggest that it could be wider than this.

9.1.1 Independence from the state

It was noted earlier that complete independence from the state would be extremely difficult because the operation of the judiciary is a state responsibility, hence the reason it is considered to be one of the three arms.

9.1.1.1 Legislature

The *Constitutional Reform Act 2005* (CRA 2005) made a number of significant changes to the judiciary and one of these changes was to remove all full-time members of the judiciary from the legislature. Under s 137 CRA 2005 a full-time member of the judiciary may not sit in either House of Parliament. This is a direct contrast to the old system whereby the Law Lords, Lord Chief Justice, and (quite frequently) the Master of the Rolls were members of the House of Lords. Certainly the rule demonstrates independence from the legislature in so far as they are no longer members of both the judiciary and Parliament.

Judicial independence from the legislature is also provided for in parliamentary rules. A good example of this is *Erskine May* (which sets out the rules and protocols of Parliament), which states that a Member of Parliament should not criticize a judge by name in Parliament.[4] Interestingly, of course, this does not stop a Member from criticizing a judge *outside* Parliament and it will be seen that this has happened on a number of occasions. However, if it is outside Parliament then it could be suggested that this was not the *legislature* but merely someone who is a member of the legislature criticizing a judge.

9.1.1.2 Executive

The principal challenge for judicial independence is normally its relationship with the executive. Lord Bingham has already noted that pragmatically there will always be a degree of interrelationship between the executive and the judiciary but the nature of

---

3. Leslie Curzon and Paul Richards, *The Longman Dictionary of Law* (7th edn, Pearson 2007) 327.
4. Malcolm Jack et al, *Erskine May: Parliamentary Practice* (24th revised edn, Butterworths 2011) 443–4.

the interaction is crucial to independence. Until 2005 the principal link between the executive and the judiciary was through the Lord Chancellor.

Lord Chancellor

The Lord Chancellor (more formally the Lord High Chancellor of Great Britain) was historically an extremely important person. It is a historic office whose primary role was as Keeper of the Great Seal (the stamp by which formal documents were sealed by the monarch) but who was often the key counsellor to the monarch. Even in its more modern guise the office was important, and in social precedence is outranked only by members of the Royal Family and the Archbishop of Canterbury. Until 2005 the Lord Chancellor was also paid more than the prime minister although the last holder of the office prior to the 2005 reforms—Lord Falconer QC—voluntarily relinquished some of that pay.

The Lord Chancellor was anathema to the separation of powers. This was the doctrine first put forward by Montesquieu, an eighteenth-century jurist, who stated that man could only be free where the three elements of the state (executive, judiciary, and legislature) were separate. In its modern guise (but before the 2005 reforms) the Lord Chancellor was primarily a member of the executive. He ran his own department (what was known as the *Lord Chancellor's Department* but which then subsequently became the *Department for Constitutional Affairs* and then the *Ministry of Justice*) and was a member of the Cabinet. The Lord Chancellor was a political appointee and he had to resign when required to do so by the prime minister (including during reshuffles) or when the results of a General Election led to a new government being formed.

The Lord Chancellor, like all members of the UK executive, was a member of the legislature but he held a key role in that he presided over the deliberations of the House of Lords. Arguably this was less important than, for example, the Speaker of the House of Commons since the Lords traditionally regulates itself, but he was at least in name the presiding member. Finally, the Lord Chancellor was also a member of the judiciary since he was titular head of the judiciary and, as a member of the House of Lords, could sit (and would preside) in the appellate committee of the House of Lords.[5]

Although there was no doubt about the individual integrity of any modern Lord Chancellor[6] the fact that the Lord Chancellor was both a member of the government and a judge was considered inappropriate by many. The Labour government sought to amend this initially by abolishing the office of Lord Chancellor. The initial attempts were sloppy and created a political and constitutional storm when the prime minister did not apparently tell either the Queen or the Lord Chief Justice that he was going to abolish this most historic of offices. In the end it was decided abolishment was too difficult because of the thousands of references that were made to the office in legislation. Instead the office was reformed.

Section 7 CRA 2005 appoints the Lord Chief Justice as the head of the judiciary and, with the removal of the judges from the legislature, this meant that the Lord Chancellor was no longer a judge. Schedule 6 CRA 2005, as amended by the CCA 2013, also makes provision for the House of Lords to elect a 'Lords Speaker' and so he ceased to be the presiding officer of the Lords.

---

5. Lord Falconer was the only modern Lord Chancellor not to sit on cases but this was because, by the time he was appointed, it had been decided to reform the office of Lord Chancellor.

6. Thomas Bingham, *The Business of Judging: Selected Essays and Speeches* (OUP 2000) 229.

Under the CRA reforms the post of Lord Chancellor remains but it no longer needs to be a peer; as with all other members of the Cabinet he can be a member of either House and simply bears the honorific title 'Lord Chancellor'. In fact after Lord Falconer the subsequent Lord Chancellors[7] have belonged to the Commons. Indeed there is no requirement for the Lord Chancellor to be a lawyer[8] and in the 2012 government reshuffle the first non-lawyer, Rt Hon Chris Grayling MP, was appointed to the office. There was some controversy over the appointment because the CRA 2005 requires that the Lord Chancellor be 'experienced' and Downing Street refused to divulge how this statutory criterion was met, although the statute does permit experience to be gathered not only through the legal professions but also through being a minister, member of either House of Parliament, or 'any other experience the prime minister considers relevant'.

Whilst the office of Lord Chancellor has therefore been significantly reformed, she still does have (political) responsibility for the judiciary through being the Secretary of State for Justice. The Lord Chancellor also has particular responsibility for securing judicial independence, as evidenced by the oath that she must take:

> I [name] do solemnly swear that in the office of Lord High Chancellor of Great Britain I will respect the rule of law, defend the independence of the judiciary and discharge my duty to ensure the provision of resources for the efficient and effective support of the courts for which I am responsible.[9]

The oath reinforces the fact that the Lord Chancellor should remain the voice in government that upholds the independence of the judiciary (this is discussed in more detail below at 9.2.1).

Some have commented that the old system may have meant that the judges had a stronger voice since the Lord Chancellor was a key figure in that he had no 'political ambition'[10] and yet was a political heavyweight that commanded respect around the cabinet table. At that time the Lord Chancellor was not responsible for penal policy (it was the responsibility of the Home Secretary) but as Secretary of State for Justice that is no longer true and there may be concerns that the statements of the Lord Chancellor are seen to be less the cautions of one of the most senior office holders in the land and more, nowadays, the complaints of a cabinet minister who fears colleagues are treading on his territory, ie the ordinary political turf-war of cabinet government. So far, however, there has been no indication that the independence of the judiciary is under threat and the reforms do make the office look more suitable for the twenty-first century as it removes, at the very least, the appearance of executive control. That said, the appointment of the first 'lay' Lord Chancellor did lead some to suggest that the judicial functions should be transferred to the President of the Supreme Court, leaving the Secretary of State for Justice as a pure politician.

Securing independence from the executive

Independence from the executive will include reference to their work. Lord MacKay, a former Lord Chancellor, noted that judges required administrative freedom and

---

7. At the time of writing those being the Rt Hon Jack Straw MP, the Rt Hon Kenneth Clarke, the Rt Hon Chris Grayling, the Rt Hon Michael Gove, and the Rt Hon Elizabeth Truss.

8. *Constitutional Reform Act 2005*, s 2.

9. *Promissory Oaths Act 1868*, s 6A.

10. Robert Stevens, 'Reform in Haste and Repent at Leisure: Iolanthe, the Lord High Executioner and Brave New World' (2004) 24 *Legal Studies* 1, 9.

control, most notably in the selection of cases and listing of matters.[11] In essence this protects against the 'Judge Deed' type situation where there is a perception that the government 'picks' the judge that will sit on a case. Although much of the listing is dealt with by court administrative staff, who are employed for HM Courts and Tribunal Service (part of the executive), they may only do so in conjunction with the judiciary since the resident judge and presiding judge provide guidance on how cases are assigned to judges. It will also be remembered from the previous chapter that court staff owe a joint duty to the Lord Chancellor (representing the executive) and the Lord Chief Justice (representing the judiciary). Were there to be anything untoward there is also the ultimate sanction in that a judge (usually the resident or presiding judge as senior judge in a particular court) can transfer a matter from one list to another or reserve the case for himself. In this way it would suggest that it is possible to demonstrate independence over cases.

Political attacks

What of attacks from the executive? It was noted earlier that Members of Parliament may not criticize a judge by name in Parliament, and in the United Kingdom ministers are drawn from members of either House. The executive should not ordinarily criticize the personal decisions of a judge and yet this has happened on a few occasions. One judge has argued that the relationship between the executive and the judiciary was 'fraught and imbalanced'[12] although the then Lord Chief Justice, Lord Woolf, argued that the relationship was 'based on a satisfactory working relationship ... probably, it is much better than ever before'.[13] That is not to say there have not been tensions, however, in part demonstrated by the fact that Lord Woolf had postponed his retirement because he believed there was a danger that judicial independence might be undermined.

Occasionally highly personalized attacks are made in contravention of the principles enshrined earlier. Perhaps the most notable of these in recent years was the campaign by David Blunkett when he was Home Secretary. In interviews he suggested 'it was time for judges to learn their place'.[14] This comment followed the judgment of Collins J in respect of the treatment of asylum seekers,[15] which the Home Secretary saw as undermining his campaign to regulate illegal immigration. In an interview with the BBC he named Collins J as being responsible for undermining Parliament and suggested that he would continue to do so.[16] In fact, despite the highly personalized comments and briefings by the government against the judge, the Court of Appeal largely upheld the ruling[17] and yet this latter ruling did not meet with any criticism.[18]

Did the criticisms of the Home Secretary undermine judicial independence? It could be argued that they did in that they could be viewed as an attempt to put pressure on the judiciary to rule a particular way. However, the counter-argument is that the Home Secretary was a litigant and was, in effect, suggesting unease at a particular

---

11.   Thomas Bingham, *The Business of Judging: Selected Essays and Speeches* (2000 OUP) 56.
12.   Harold Wilson, 'The County Court Judge in Limbo' (1994) 144 *New Law Journal* 1453, 1454.
13.   Lord Woolf, *The Needs of a 21st Century Judge* (Judicial Studies Board 2001) 5.
14.   Anthony Bradley, 'Judicial Independence under Attack' [2003] *Public Law* 397, 402.
15.   *R (on behalf of Q) v Secretary of State for the Home Department* [2003] EWHC 195.
16.   Anthony Bradley, 'Judicial Independence under Attack' [2003] *Public Law* 397, 400.
17.   *R (on behalf of Q) v Secretary of State for the Home Department* [2003] EWCA Civ 364.
18.   Anthony Bradley, 'Judicial Independence under Attack' [2003] *Public Law* 397, 405.

decision, albeit in intemperate terms. When the appellate courts ruled (in effect terminating further legal resolution) the government accepted the matter.

In recent years the personalized attacks on the judiciary appeared to have been reduced somewhat. However, this changed in 2016 following the UK's decision to leave the EU (discussed in more detail in Chapter 20) when Lady Hale came under attack from several MPs for commenting on the Brexit process during a speech to students in Kuala Lumpur. Jacob Rees-Mogg MP commented: 'Lady Hale's speculation on a comprehensive replacement for the 1972 European Communities Act is a remarkable one for someone who is about to judge the case. It is not an idea that was mentioned in the High Court judgement so it is surprising for a Supreme Court judge to freelance in this way.'[19] Iain Duncan Smith MP accused Lady Hale of 'always [having] been opposed to Britain leaving the EU'.[20] Such criticism was particularly controversial due to her being one of the justices due to hear the government's appeal in the Supreme Court.

 QUESTION FOR REFLECTION

Should the government be able to criticize members of the judiciary? Does it matter which member of the government it is? For example, if the Lord Chancellor or prime minister were to criticize a judge *by name* would that be more serious than a Secretary of State doing so?

 LISTEN TO THE PODCAST

For guidance on how to answer this question and a discussion of the main issues, listen to the author's podcast on the Online Resource Centre: www.oxfordtextbooks.co.uk/orc/gillespie_els6e/

9.1.2 Independence from the media

Judicial independence need not necessarily be restricted to the state and it has been noted that:

> One of the most dramatic changes that has taken place over the past thirty years or so has been the increasing freedom felt by newspapers, in particular, to attack judges with a vigour ... that was formerly quite unknown.[21]

In the twenty-two years since this was written the position has arguably become even more vociferous especially by the tabloids, with the *Sun*, supposedly the most popular newspaper in the country, consistently referring to Lord Woolf, the then Lord Chief Justice, in derogatory terms and in September 2004 asking readers to sign a petition requiring him to be sacked[22] and even sending 'removal men' to the Royal Courts of Justice and his

19. Jonathan Brady, 'Labour Defends Supreme Court Judge After Tory MPs Attack Her Over Possible Brexit Delay' *The Huffington Post* (2016) <http://www.huffingtonpost.co.uk/entry/supreme-court-lady-hale-brexit-article-50-comprehensive-legislation_uk_582c2d33e4b0311a3da243e1>.

20. Jonathan Brady, 'Labour Defends Supreme Court Judge After Tory MPs Attack Her Over Possible Brexit Delay' *The Huffington Post* (2016) <http://www.huffingtonpost.co.uk/entry/supreme-court-lady-hale-brexit-article-50-comprehensive-legislation_uk_582c2d33e4b0311a3da243e1>.

21. Derek Oulton, 'Independence of the Judiciary: A Review' (1994) 21 *Journal of Law and Society* 567, 569.

22. 'The *Sun* Calls on Lord Chief Justice to Quit' *Sun* (22 September 2004).

private residence.[23] This was followed in 2006 with a campaign to 'out' judges that the *Sun* believed had imposed unduly lenient sentences. The names of the judges were given together with derogatory comments made about the sentences that they had passed.

It is not just the criminal justice system that has incurred the wrath of the media. Perhaps the most notable attack by the media in recent times has been in relation to the judiciary's involvement following the UK's decision to leave the EU (commonly referred to as Brexit). Following the High Court's judgment that Parliament needed to be consulted before Article 50 could be triggered and that this was not something that could be done through the Prime Minister's exercise of prerogative powers, many branches of the media launched serious attacks on the judiciary. Newspaper headlines included; 'Enemies of the people' (*Daily Mail*), 'The judges versus the people' (*Daily Telegraph*), and 'Who do EU think you are?' (*Sun*). In particular, the three High Court judges who ruled on the Article 50 case came in for individual criticism. The *Daily Mail* published an article on its website singling each of the judges out: 'The judges who blocked Brexit: One founded a EUROPEAN law group, another charged the taxpayer millions for advice and the third is an openly gay ex-Olympic fencer.' Such an attack was unprecedented, and the *Mail* eventually had to change their headline due to the widespread criticism they received.

The response of the legal profession was swift, with many taking to Twitter and other social media platforms to criticize the media's response, demonstrate their support for the judiciary, and highlight the importance of judicial independence. Public statements were also made from numerous high-ranking QCs, with chairwoman of the Bar Council Chantal-Aimée Doerries QC saying: 'Publicly criticising individual members of the judiciary over a particular judgment or suggesting that they are motivated by their individual views, political or otherwise, is wrong, and serves only to undermine their vital role in the administration of justice. It also does no favours to our global reputation.'[24] It is certainly arguable that the extremely vocal response from the professions and legal experts was not only due to the media's attacks, but also due to the perceived failures of the Lord Chancellor, Liz Truss, to adequately deal with the issue in a timely and appropriate manner (discussed in more detail at 9.2.1).

The scale of the media attack was such that it wasn't just the legal profession who responded, but also politicians from all parties, well-known public figures, and many members of the public. What was perhaps most interesting, however, was the lack of immediate response from many key members of the executive including the Prime Minister and the Lord Chancellor (discussed at 9.2.1).

As for the response from members of the judiciary themselves, this was muted, particularly from the senior judiciary. This was perhaps unsurprising given the fact that leave to appeal to the Supreme Court was granted and the government immediately declared their intention to do so. Indeed, in the Lord Chief Justice's Annual Press Conference in November 2016 following the backlash, but before the hearing of the case in the Supreme Court, he declined to be drawn on the issue in any significant detail. He simply said:

> I think that our independence is paramount. We are an attractive jurisdiction because everyone knows, not only are the judges the best or amongst the best in the world but

293

23. *Sun* (23 September 2004).
24. Will Worley, 'Liz Truss Breaks her Silence but Fails to Condemn Backlash over Brexit Ruling' *The Independent* (2016) <http://www.independent.co.uk/news/uk/home-news/bar-council-liz-truss-brexit-ruling-decision-serious-unjustified-attacks-judiciary-judges-high-court-a7399356.html>.

that we are totally uninfluenced by external events. If and insofar as we need to do things to strengthen that, this is something to which I would like to discuss but it is very difficult for me to discuss that now in the present context, i.e. anything I say in relation to that will be interpreted by one person or by another as some comment on the existing case in relation to Article 50 and what people have said about it and I take the very firm view that it is better to wait until this is over.[25]

The limited response from the judiciary to the media attacks raise ongoing questions about what the response should be to such events. Some judges have, when the media comment has been particularly unpleasant, resorted to the laws relating to defamation and some judges have even suggested that derogatory press comments could amount to contempt of court.[26] This argument would only work with superior courts but even then it would be a complete overreaction and Lord Bingham has stated that the contempt laws should ordinarily have no place in such battles.[27] Indeed His Lordship suggests that judges should be 'thick-skinned' enough to ignore press comments. The response to the Paul Dacre attack led Pannick to question who should respond to attacks. He suggested that it should not be for the Lord Chancellor[28] since although he is protected with upholding judicial independence, this is primarily in respect of attacks by the executive and indeed it could compromise independence if the executive responds on behalf of the judiciary. The answer is perhaps not easy and Lord Bingham's suggestion to leave well alone appears to be the default position.

⟳ QUESTION FOR REFLECTION

Do you believe that judges should have a remedy against the media if they make unjustified personal attacks? Should the press not have the right to comment on the administration of justice? Read Article 10 of the ECHR (see 5.4.8). Does this have any impact on your answer?

9.1.3 Independence from each other

Perhaps one of the most unusual examples of judicial independence relates to the judges themselves. The courts in England and Wales adopt a hierarchical structure and it has been noted already that there are different ranks within the judiciary. This means that, potentially, there may be situations where a judge tries to interfere with another. The Courts and Tribunals Judiciary, when discussing judicial independence, notes this possibility:

> It is vitally important in a democracy that individual judges and the judiciary as a whole are impartial and independent of all external pressures and of each other …[29]

Obviously judicial independence from each other does not extend to ignoring the principles of *stare decisis* as this would cause confusion and end certainty within the

---

25. Judicial Press Office, 'Press Conference held by The Lord Chief Justice of England and Wales' (Judicial Press Office 2016) <https://www.judiciary.gov.uk/wp-content/uploads/2016/11/lcj-annual-press-conference-2016-transcript-1.pdfpdf-1.pdf> 1–2.

26. Robin Dunn, *Sword and Wig: Memoirs of a Lord Justice* (Quiller Press 1993) 182.

27. Thomas Bingham, *The Business of Judging: Selected Essays and Speeches* (OUP 2000) 61.

28. David Pannick, 'Should Judges Respond to Criticism?' *The Times* (27 November 2008).

29. Courts and Tribunals Judiciary, 'Independence' (HMCTS) <https://www.judiciary.gov.uk/about-the-judiciary/the-judiciary-the-government-and-the-constitution/jud-acc-ind/independence/>.

English Legal System. It will also be seen that the hierarchical structure has led to quasi-disciplinary measures being adopted by the higher courts, but the principle is just as important. Traditionally this approach has led to judges adopting an extremely independent system whereby they act in isolation and rarely look at each other's work (although they may discuss cases during lunch or after sitting with other judges as any visitor to the judge's dining room can attest) but Lord Woolf, the then Lord Chief Justice, suggested that perhaps judges should look at each other's performance on the bench,[30] although he rejects the idea of it becoming even a peer-review appraisal system[31] and expressly states the principle of annual reflections would not compromise the independence of the judiciary.[32] So far this scheme has been resisted by the court judiciary, although appraisals do occur in the Tribunal Service. It will be interesting to note whether the court judiciary will follow suit in due course.

9.2 Securing independence

If judicial independence exists how is it secured? The CRA 2005 attempts to encapsulate the protection in statute but other factors are equally important. Some forms have already been discussed but the key issues of securing independence would include salary, tenure (including promotion and discipline), and immunity.

9.2.1 Statutory independence

It has been noted that the judiciary were keen to ensure that with the abolition of the Lord Chancellor there would be provision to guarantee the independence of the judiciary. It was seen earlier that one of the principal responsibilities of the Lord Chancellor was to act as a 'buffer' between the executive and the judiciary.[33] Arguably the Lord Chancellor may still have this responsibility since his oath says, inter alia, 'I will … defend the independence of the judiciary'. In addition to this the CRA 2005 places a statutory duty on the government:

> The Lord Chancellor, other ministers of the Crown and all with responsibility for matters relating to the judiciary or otherwise to the administration of justice must uphold the continued independence of the judiciary.[34]

This includes:

(a) the need to defend that independence;

(b) the need for the judiciary to have support necessary to enable them to exercise their functions;

(c) the need for the public interest in regard to matters relating to the judiciary or otherwise to the administration of justice to be properly represented in decisions affecting those matters.[35]

30. Lord Woolf, *The Needs of a 21st Century Judge* (Judicial Studies Board 2001) 7.
31. Lord Woolf, *The Needs of a 21st Century Judge* (Judicial Studies Board 2001) 8.
32. Lord Woolf, *The Needs of a 21st Century Judge* (Judicial Studies Board 2001) 7.
33. See 9.4.1.1 and see Lord Elwyn-Jones, *In My Times: An Autobiography* (Weidenfeld & Nicolson 1983) 267.
34. *Constitutional Reform Act 2005*, s 3(1).
35. *Constitutional Reform Act 2005*, s 3(6).

These duties are imposed primarily on the Lord Chancellor. Yet how will this be achieved?

The current Lord Chancellor, Liz Truss, has been accused of failing to uphold the independence of the judiciary following her response, or lack thereof, to the unprecedented media attacks on the judiciary (discussed in more detail at 9.1.2) following the High Court decision in relation to triggering Article 50. Truss initially stayed silent in the wake of the attacks and was urged by the Bar Council to speak out 'as a matter of urgency', with them noting that they regretted 'the lack of public statement by the Lord Chancellor condemning these attacks'.[36] On Twitter the hashtag #wheresliztruss was widely used by legal commentators. When she did issue a statement, however, she was widely criticized for merely affirming the independence of the judiciary and failing to specifically address the attacks that were made. She said:

> The independence of the judiciary is the foundation upon which our rule of law is built and our judiciary is rightly respected the world over for its independence and impartiality.

It's also worth noting here that whilst upholding judicial independence is primarily the job of the Lord Chancellor, it is also the responsibility of 'other ministers of the Crown', including the Prime Minister. Despite this, Theresa May's response to the media attacks on the judiciary was similarly limited. She commented: 'I believe in and value the independence of our judiciary. I also value the freedom of our press. I think these both underpin our democracy and they are important.' By highlighting the importance of press freedom when discussing judicial independence, it is certainly questionable whether, similarly to Liz Truss, Theresa May fulfilled her duty.

The ability of the Lord Chancellor to more effectively intercede in media attacks is perhaps demonstrated by other examples. In 2006 there was considerable controversy over the sentence imposed in relation to Craig Sweeney, a convicted paedophile who abducted and sexually abused a very young girl. The media were very critical of what they saw as an extremely lenient sentence and John Reid, the Home Secretary, also criticized the sentence making comments that were probably comparable to those of David Blunkett.[37] The Lord Chancellor publicly stated that it was not the fault of the judge that the sentence was wrong but the legal framework. However, Vera Baird QC, a junior minister in the Department for Constitutional Affairs, criticized the judge by name on BBC Radio 4 suggesting that the judge had personally got the matter wrong.[38] Interestingly, there was then a public exchange of letters between the Lord Chancellor and the junior minister whereby Vera Baird formally withdrew her remarks. This was followed by further public confirmation by the Lord Chancellor that the judge had not erred, even though this implicitly criticized the Home Secretary for making his comments. The media were very much against this sentence and thus the easy political decision would have been either to stay silent or to support the Home Secretary but Lord Falconer did not do this and, in effect, met his statutory obligations.

When appointed, some questioned whether the first 'lay' Lord Chancellor (ie the first non-lawyer to be appointed Lord Chancellor), Chris Grayling MP, necessarily

36.   Bar Council, 'Bar Council Calls on Lord Chancellor to Condemn Attacks on Judiciary' (The Bar Council 2016) <http://www.barcouncil.org.uk/media-centre/news-and-press-releases/2016/november/bar-council-calls-on-lord-chancellor-to-condemn-attacks-on-judiciary/>.
37.   Alisdair Gillespie, 'Sentencing: The Spider's Web' (2006) 156 *New Law Journal* 1153.
38.   Alisdair Gillespie, 'Sentencing: The Spider's Web' (2006) 156 *New Law Journal* 1153, 1154.

appreciated this part of the role. Certainly, without a legal background it is perhaps easier to concentrate on the role of Secretary of State for Justice, a purely political post, rather than being the Lord Chancellor and many of the apolitical aspects that this brings. When he was appointed much was written about him coming from the 'right' of the Tory party (although many believed that this was an oversimplification) and that he would bring a 'tougher' stance to punishment than his predecessor, the perceived liberal conservative, Kenneth Clarke. The reality of course is that in times of financial constraints the punishment of offenders is as much dictated by the Treasury (through the funding of the Prison Service) as it is by the Secretary of State for Justice. However, this does set up the interesting question of whether the Secretary of State for Justice would wish to attack judges for 'soft' sentencing since, when wearing his other 'hat' as Lord Chancellor, he must protect the judiciary from inappropriate political attacks.

When Chris Grayling was first appointed there was a belief that the roles of Secretary of State for Justice and Lord Chancellor should be separated once more, with the title Lord Chancellor being given to a judge (probably the President of the Supreme Court). Whilst this may be attractive in some respects, it does have some disadvantages. The first is that the role of Lord Chancellor has always been political, though the political extent of the post has differed with holders of the office, and the second is that it would almost certainly mean that there would no longer be a senior member of the government who would be responsible for defending the judiciary. Whilst the CRA 2005 could be amended to ensure the Secretary of State for Justice was responsible for securing the independence of the judiciary it is open to question whether a purely political Secretary of State would consider this a primary function of his office.

⟳ QUESTION FOR REFLECTION

It was noted earlier (9.1.1.2) that the Lord Chancellor need not, following the CRA 2005, be legally qualified. Could someone without a background in the law safeguard the independence of the judiciary?

9.2.2 Salary

At first sight judges would appear to be very well paid, with the Lord Chief Justice receiving £129,583 and a circuit judge receiving £133,506 (as of April 2016) but this should be placed into context when many practitioners will earn several times this.[39] Yet salary is important, as has been noted by Lord Bingham:

> There is of course, a close connection between judicial salaries and judicial independence ... if a judge's salary is dependent on the whim of the government, the judge will not have the independence we desire in our judiciary.[40]

In recognition of this, in England and Wales where there has been concern about the salary levels of the judiciary it has been suggested that the government has listened to

---

39. For an interesting analysis on this see Hazel Genn, *The Attractiveness of Senior Judicial Appointments to Highly Qualified Practitioners* (UCL 2009) and also see Penny Darbyshire, *Sitting in Judgment: The Working Lives of Judges* (Hart Publishing 2011), who recounts that a puisne judge initially turned down the appointment because he decided that he could not afford it.

40. Thomas Bingham, *The Business of Judging: Selected Essays and Speeches* (2000 OUP) 65.

the judges and acted accordingly.[41] Indeed, the Ministry of Justice broadly followed the recommendations in the 2016 report from the Review Body on Senior Salaries (which makes recommendations as to the salaries for Senior Civil Servants, the judiciary, and senior public figures), giving an average 1 per cent pay increase to members of the judiciary. Somewhat controversially, this increase was not given to all members of the judiciary, with High Court judges receiving a 3 per cent increase in salary, compared to a 0.55% increase given to lower ranked members of the judiciary.

The current position as regards judicial salaries is that they are undoubtedly less than an applicant for a judgeship earns in practice,[42] but that there are alternative benefits. The judges are paid out of the consolidated fund[43] which means that there is no parliamentary debate on their salaries. The government continue, however, to influence the salary levels because although the *Review Body on Senior Salaries* (SSRB), an independent body, recommends the salary levels, it is for the government of the day to decide whether they will accept the recommendations or not. The decision as to whether to accept the recommendation is reported to Parliament who are entitled to question the relevant ministers as to the reasons for this. In 2005 the SSRB published a consultation paper on whether the judicial salaries bands were correct and how they should be 'pegged' to comparable posts.[44] Ultimately they decided not to 'peg' salaries but they did undertake a comprehensive review of judicial salaries, partly because of the changes of duties and responsibilities brought about by the *Constitutional Reform Act 2005* (CRA 2005).[45] A revised system was recommended, including shifting some categories of judges into a high pay-band, and this was accepted and implemented by the government.[46]

9.2.3 Tenure, promotion, and discipline

Three directly related issues that could conceivably interfere with judicial independence are the tenure of judges, any promotion they receive, and how they are disciplined. In order to discuss these issues it is necessary to distinguish once again between superior judges and inferior judges as the manner in which they are treated is significantly different. The position of judges of the Supreme Court, although obviously superior judges, will also be considered separately because of the changes introduced by the CRA 2005.

9.2.3.1 Superior judges

Superior judges enjoy significantly stronger protections than members of the inferior judiciary. Puisne judges and Lord Justices of Appeal hold office until retirement age (currently 70)[47] 'during good behaviour, subject to a power of removal by Her Majesty on an address presented to her by both Houses of Parliament'.[48] In other words, subject to an additional power of removal through disability, a superior judge may only be removed if both Houses of Parliament pass a resolution

---

41. David Pannick, *Judges* (OUP 1987) 13–14.
42. For an analysis see Hazel Genn, *The Attractiveness of Senior Judicial Appointments to Highly Qualified Practitioners* (UCL 2009).
43. *Senior Courts Act 1981*, s 12.
44. Review Body on Senior Salaries, *Annual Report 2005* (HMSO 2005).
45. Review Body on Senior Salaries, *Annual Report 2006* (HMSO 2006).
46. Review Body on Senior Salaries, *Annual Report 2007* (HMSO 2007).
47. *Senior Courts Act 1981*, s 11(2).
48. *Senior Courts Act 1981*, s 11(3).

requiring them to go. Only one judge has ever been removed in this way, in 1830,[49] and it would be extremely rare for anyone to achieve this 'distinction', not least because most judges would probably prefer to resign rather than be subjected to such an approach.

Where a superior judge is incapacitated by illness or disability then the SCA 1981 provides that the Lord Chancellor may remove him.[50] To ensure that this power cannot be abused, subsection (9) requires judicial consent to this procedure. Where the incapacitated judge is a Head of Division then at least two other Heads of Division must agree; where it is a Lord Justice of Appeal the Master of the Rolls must agree; and where it is a puisne judge the appropriate Head of Division must agree. Given that all of the judges who must agree with this are superior judges holding similar security of tenure, it should ensure that the measure can never be used by a Lord Chancellor in an inappropriate manner.

The CRA 2005 has, however, provided additional disciplinary procedures that may be exercised by the Lord Chief Justice, as head of the judiciary. These powers apply to all levels of judges and are considered in further detail later.

Promotion for the superior judge is a controversial area. Lord Denning once wrote that a judge when appointed had nothing to gain from promotion and did not seek it[51] and at the time this was probably true because there were so few posts in the Court of Appeal. However, this may no longer necessarily be true and Bingham concedes that there may have been a concern that some judges would tailor their judgments in such a way as to gain judicial advancement although he states that he cannot think of any examples of this and it would amount to a violation of the judicial oath.[52] It is certainly not possible to identify any candidates where it might be thought that their decisions had denied advancement, although some may argue that it is possible to identify the opposite, where judges who may have appeared controversial have gained advancement. The changes made by the CRA 2005 have essentially meant that such tailoring would not bring any advantages since appointment to the High Court, Court of Appeal, and Supreme Court will be made by independent appointment commissions. The appointment of Sir Nicholas Wall as the President of the Family Division (discussed at 8.3.8) perhaps illustrates this. There were some who argued that the Lord Chancellor did not want Wall LJ appointed because of his pronouncements but the independent appointments commission led to this issue being resolved in a fair and transparent way.

9.2.3.2 Inferior judges

The security of tenure for a circuit judge is significantly different from that of a superior judge. Circuit judges must retire at the age of 70 but they are also subject to removal by the Lord Chancellor 'on the ground of incapacity or misbehaviour' and with the agreement of the Lord Chief Justice.[53] The CRA 2005 states that where this is to be undertaken then 'prescribed procedures'[54] must be followed which suggests that there will now be a statutory scheme that will lead to dismissal.

49. David Pannick, *Judges* (OUP 1987) 90.
50. *Senior Courts Act 1981*, s 11(8).
51. Lord Denning, *The Road to Justice* (Stevens & Sons 1995) 17.
52. Thomas Bingham, *The Business of Judging: Selected Essays and Speeches* (OUP 2000) 60.
53. *Courts Act 1971*, s 17(4).
54. *Constitutional Reform Act 2005*, s 108(1).

In recent times only one circuit judge has been removed by the Lord Chancellor, and Hailsham, the Lord Chancellor who was responsible for the dismissal,[55] makes it clear in his autobiography that he would have preferred the judge to resign but, at that time, a pension would not be payable to someone who resigns whereas a part pension would be paid to someone who was dismissed.[56] That said, there have been two occasions when dismissal could have occurred. One case arose under the 'old' system and one under the 'new' system of judicial discipline. The difference between the cases is perhaps instructive.

The first of these cases was when senior judges asked the then Lord Chancellor to remove a judge.[57] Lord Hailsham does not mention the judge by name but Judge James Pickles names himself in his own autobiography.[58] Judge Pickles was perhaps one of the most controversial judges in modern times and, by his own admission, was something of a maverick. Hailsham describes him as:

> [an] obscure and absurd judge whose only real claim to fame was the number of times when his behaviour had been criticized and his judgements [sic] reversed by the Court of Appeal ...[59]

Part of the controversy of Pickles was his unconventional views of sex crimes, something that led to him being denied the right to sit on such cases. In his own autobiography he discusses the dress of women and says:

> If [a woman] seems to want sex but does not, a man who tries to grab it from her cannot be excused but she must share the blame.[60]

Sadly such pronouncements were also uttered on the bench and he appeared to ignore sentencing precedents, passing sentences that were frequently anomalous and led to him being criticized in the Court of Appeal, most notably in *R v Scott*.[61] Judge Pickles reacted to these developments by discussing matters with the press and, rather famously, provided an interview on television where he referred to the Lord Chief Justice as 'an ancient dinosaur living in the wrong age'.[62] Lord Hailsham declined to dismiss him because he felt it was unfair that he acted as prosecutor, judge, jury, and executioner.[63] Later when Lord MacKay informed Judge Pickles that he was contemplating dismissing him, Pickles used this argument as a defence to the charges.[64] In the end, the position led to a public letter of rebuke by the Lord Chancellor and Pickles eventually retired.

The second case was more recent. His Honour Judge Gerald Price QC was a circuit judge assigned to the Welsh circuit. He was the subject of a tabloid investigation where he was accused of having an affair with a male sex worker. His conduct was

---

55.   More junior judges have been dismissed. For example, in 2015 it was reported that two district judges, a deputy district judge, and a recorder were dismissed as a result of viewing pornography on judicial computers. The district judges were full-time appointees and were dismissed under the same procedure. These have not been discussed, however, because this section is comparing the position of the two principal first-instance judges, ie the circuit judge and pusine judge.

56.   Lord Hailsham, *A Sparrow's Flight* (Collins 1990) 429.

57.   Lord Hailsham, *A Sparrow's Flight* (Collins 1990) 430.

58.   James Pickles, *Judge for Yourself* (Coronet 1992) 175–96.

59.   Lord Hailsham, *A Sparrow's Flight* (Collins 1990) 430.

60.   James Pickles, *Judge for Yourself* (Coronet 1992) 138.

61.   [1990] Crim LR 440.

62.   James Pickles, *Judge for Yourself* (Coronet 1992) 180.

63.   Lord Hailsham, *A Sparrow's Flight* (Collins 1990) 430.

64.   James Pickles, *Judge for Yourself* (Coronet 1992) 185–95.

investigated by the *Office of Judicial Complaints* and the Lord Chancellor and Lord Chief Justice had decided that he should be removed from office although he resigned before the disciplinary process could be completed.

The cases of Judges Pickles and Price demonstrate a difference between the way in which inferior and superior judges can be dismissed. For example, it would be extremely difficult to administratively control the type of cases a puisne judge can sit on (as there is no requirement of 'ticketing') although the Lord Chief Justice could re-assign the judge to a different division of the High Court. A puisne judge accused of the same conduct as Judge Price would have required an address of both Houses of Parliament to dismiss. One circuit judge has publicly suggested that it is inappropriate for the distinction to remain, not least because circuit judges spend a not inconsiderable period of their time doing High Court work.[65] The reception to the call has not been unanimous with Lord Bingham suggesting that the risk of inappropriate dismissal is theoretical and with little practical consequence.[66]

 QUESTION FOR REFLECTION

It has been suggested by Wilson that judges of all ranks should receive the same security of tenure. Is there any justification for allowing more junior judges to be dismissed by the executive, even where it is supported by the senior judiciary? If not, how does one deal with a problem like Judge Pickles or Judge Price? Had either judge been a puisne judge could either the judiciary or executive have done anything about him?

🔊 LISTEN TO THE PODCAST

For guidance on how to answer this question and a discussion of the main issues, listen to the author's podcast on the Online Resource Centre:
www.oxfordtextbooks.co.uk/orc/gillespie_els6e/

Promotion for the circuit bench has traditionally been extremely limited. It has already been noted that some may be eligible to become a senior circuit judge through the assumption of administrative responsibility for which they are remunerated, but access to the senior judiciary is normally denied to them. Some circuit judges are appointed to the High Court bench but as has been noted already this is quite rare. Given that the statutory qualification for a puisne judge is appointment as a circuit judge[67] it may have been thought that this would lead to an increase in appointments but this does not appear to have been reflected. Of the current puisne bench only thirteen have been promoted from the circuit bench and none have been promoted in the last seven years. Darbyshire, in her book on the lives of judges, recognizes this issue and states that a problem is that few circuit judges wish promotion beyond the circuit bench.[68] This is partly because some do not believe they are 'clever' enough to be a High Court judge (which seems unlikely in many instances) but also because many

---

65. Harold Wilson, 'The County Court Judge in Limbo' (1994) 144 *New Law Journal* 1454.
    Note that some work can be released to a circuit judge and in other cases a circuit judge can sit as a High Court judge (s 9 SCA 1981) and while doing so he has all the powers of a puisne judge.
66. Thomas Bingham, *The Business of Judging: Selected Essays and Speeches* (OUP 2000) 59.
67. *Senior Courts Act 1981*, s 10(3)(c).
68. Penny Darbyshire, *Sitting in Judgment: The Working Lives of Judges* (Hart Publishing 2011) 415–17.

perceive their job to be better since they are not required to stay away from home or sit regularly in the Court of Appeal. They believe, quite rightly according to the research conducted by Darbyshire, that High Court judges frequently work longer hours and many circuit judges prefer the life that they have.

It would seem therefore that whilst denying inferior judges promotion would appear unfair in theory, the reality is that the majority do not seem interested in pursuing that option. It should be noted that of those few circuit judges who have been promoted to the High Court bench only a few have progressed to becoming a Lord Justice of Appeal and so any promotion would seem to be rather limited.

9.2.3.3 Extending disciplinary measures

Judge Pickles, in his autobiography, states:

> It is absurd that the Lord Chancellor has no effective control except the power to remove circuit (not High Court) judges for 'misbehaviour' ...[69]

This, of course, misses the point that the presiding judge and Lord Chief Justice had the power to make directions restricting the types of cases a judge could hear (used against Pickles) but there is some truth to this point, that the only disciplinary measure was dismissal. The CRA 2005 provides a solution to this although the power now rests with the Lord Chief Justice as head of the judiciary. The provisions do not differentiate between inferior and superior judges and empower the Lord Chief Justice, after following due process, to issue 'formal advice, or a formal warning or reprimand'.[70] It is not clear what the effects of such measures are but, presumably, they could be used in conjunction with directions to ensure that judges are limited to the types of work that they carry out if this is appropriate.

> **Example** Lord Justice Thorpe
>
> Judges are, of course, expected to uphold the law and the new powers available to the Lord Chief Justice have been used when a judge has transgressed the law. A notable recent example was when the Lord Chief Justice issued Thorpe LJ with a reprimand after he received a driving ban after accruing twelve penalty points for driving offences. An interesting nugget that arose from the case is that Thorpe LJ also runs a farm complete with an eighty-strong herd of cattle!

The Act also gives the Lord Chief Justice the power to suspend someone from being a judge where a judge is subject to criminal proceedings, serving a sentence, or where the action that led to the criminal proceedings taking place is being used to begin dismissal proceedings.[71] The Lord Chief Justice may also suspend someone who has been convicted of an offence, but where it has been decided not to dismiss the person, if the Lord Chief Justice believes it is necessary to do so in order to maintain the confidence of the judiciary[72] or where a judge is being investigated for misbehaviour other than a criminal offence.[73]

69. James Pickles, *Judge for Yourself* (Coronet 1992) 196.
70. *Constitutional Reform Act 2005*, s 108(3).
71. *Constitutional Reform Act 2005*, s 108(4).
72. *Constitutional Reform Act 2005*, s 108(5).
73. *Constitutional Reform Act 2005*, s 108(6), (7).

Whilst sometimes the reprimands can be as a result of extrajudicial behaviour it is clear that the power of reprimand exists where a judge, in exercising his judicial functions, does something notably wrong. Perhaps the most striking example is that of Peter Smith J, a puisne judge of the Chancery Division. The judge acted in an unprofessional way towards a barrister who had suggested he should recuse himself from a case concerning a legal firm where the judge had attempted to seek employment.[74] The Court of Appeal, in determining the appeal, issued an informal rebuke, but Peter Smith J then issued a somewhat bizarre and argumentative public statement challenging many of the issues. The matter was referred to the Office of Judicial Complaints (as it was called then, now the Judicial Conduct Investigations Office) who decided that his behaviour did amount to misconduct and he was formally reprimanded by the Lord Chief Justice.

Although Peter Smith J is probably the most high-profile judge to have been disciplined, the annual report for the Judicial Conduct Investigations Office (JCIO) 2015–16 notes that across the court judiciary, forty-three were subjected to some form of disciplinary action, including sixteen who were removed from their post.[75] Thirty of those subjected to some form of disciplinary action were magistrates, including fifteen who were removed from office.[76]

9.2.4 Judicial immunity

In Chapter 10 it will be noted that advocates have lost their immunity for negligence but the judiciary have traditionally been immune from actions arising out of their judicial actions. Immunity apparently dates back to the seventeenth century and acts as a privilege to any words that a judge utters within a case.[77] However, there continues to be a distinction between inferior and superior judges in that the latter have immunity from all actions even when acting outside their jurisdiction so long as the words or actions were done in good faith whereas an inferior judge's immunity is restricted to actions within their jurisdiction.

The argument advanced for judicial immunity is that it protects judges from vexatious litigants and an attempt to try and re-litigate each matter, and it has been suggested that in order for the immunity system to work properly the privilege must be absolute: including acts where a judge acts negligently or inappropriately.[78] The same reasons were advanced in support of the immunity of advocates (see 10.8.1.4) and yet this has been ended so why should judges continue to have absolute immunity? At least one commentator believes they should not and that it would not contravene the independence of the judiciary to allow judges to be sued for misconduct in their office.[79] However, it seems unlikely that the judges themselves would ever end their own immunity (through the appellate courts so ruling), nor is it likely that Parliament would do so either; indeed s 9 *Human Rights Act 1998* expressly preserves judicial immunity.

---

74. The full details are set out by the Court of Appeal in *Howell and others v Millais and others* [2007] EWCA Civ 720.

75. Judicial Conduct Investigations Office, *Annual Report 2015–16* (JCIO 2016) 15.

76. Judicial Conduct Investigations Office, *Annual Report 2015–16* (JCIO 2016) 15.

77. David Pannick, *Judges* (OUP 1987) 95.

78. David Pannick, *Judges* (OUP 1987) 98.

79. David Pannick, *Judges* (OUP 1987) 99.

9.3 Judicial ethics

Sir Thomas Bingham (as he then was) wrote extrajudicially:

> Judicial ethics ... appears to have been largely neglected in this country in recent years.[80]

This is a fair comment but indeed the position is arguably replicated by the whole legal profession, which barely touches upon ethics from education through to practice.[81] Yet ethics are an essential part of the administration of justice and, although a significant amount of attention is placed on the ethics of the legal profession, this applies equally to judges.

The ethics of judicial office are arguably based on the judicial office which requires the judge to try cases 'without fear or favour, affection or ill-will'. Certain aspects of this will be discussed elsewhere in this book, most notably in relation to the conduct of judges within a trial, but the issue that should be discussed here is the idea implicit within the oath, that a judge should not be biased or compromised.

9.3.1 Financial issues

If judges are to try cases 'without fear or favour' then their financial interests may well become relevant. It has been noted earlier that their salary tends to be less than that which they received in practice and accordingly it is likely that they may be in possession of various investments. It is clear, however, that judges must ensure that their investments do not conflict with their role as a judge. It has been suggested that whilst a judge could, theoretically, be a 'name' for Lloyds of London,[82] if they sat in the Commercial Court (which principally deals with high-value commercial transactions such as insurance claims) then they would ordinarily relinquish this[83] to save an appearance of bias (see 9.3.3). Many Lord Justices of Appeal will similarly relinquish their status since the Court of Appeal (Civil Division) will not infrequently deal with such matters.

Judges, especially members of the senior judiciary, are frequently asked to undertake extrajudicial work. What should the position be in terms of remunerating such work? If, for example, a judge is asked to provide an after-dinner speech, can he ask for money?

The rules are not set down but it is implicit within the judicial oath and office that a judge will not bring the office of judge into disrepute. Commanding significant fees for outside work would almost certainly do so. It has been suggested:

> [I]t would [not] be generally regarded as improper for a judge to accept a modest honorarium for a lecture or address which he had given, although most would perhaps

80. Thomas Bingham, 'Judicial Ethics' in Ross Cranston (ed), *Legal Ethics and Professional Responsibility* (Clarendon Press 1995) 35.
81. See, for example, Andrew Boon, *The Ethics and Conduct of Lawyers in England and Wales* (3rd edn, Hart Publishing 2014) 171.
82. Lloyds of London is one of the principal insurance markets in the world. It is not an insurance company but rather facilitates its members (known as 'names') to underwrite insurance policies. If nothing happens then the 'names' can achieve significant gains; if there are many disasters they can lose a lot of money. In the early 1990s there was considerable controversy when a number of 'names' faced bankruptcy as a result of many natural disasters.
83. Thomas Bingham, 'Judicial Ethics' in Ross Cranston (ed) *Legal Ethics and Professional Responsibility* (Clarendon Press 1995) 41.

decline or ask that the sum be paid to charity: a gift of wine or a book a judge might, properly in my view, accept, but the identity of the donor and the value of the gift would plainly affect his decision.[84]

Most members of the judiciary would probably agree with this statement and from the occasions when I have organized for a judge to speak at functions this does appear to be the rule, with judges simply accepting the offer of a dinner and specifically rejecting any suggestion of an honorarium.

9.3.2 Politics

By convention judges must be apolitical, and the Lords of Appeal in Ordinary and other senior members of the judiciary when they were entitled to sit in the House of Lords sat on the cross-benches of the House of Lords, ie they were 'independent' members. Whilst there were a number of judges who were appointed from the ranks of Members of Parliament[85] this 'tradition' appeared to have happily faded out in recent years, but in 2007 (Sir) Ross Cranston, a former Labour party MP and former Solicitor-General, was appointed a puisne judge. That said, his appointment was not the source of any political controversy. The establishment of the independent JAC should prevent any future appearance of political bias. A judge should not become involved in any party political issue once appointed and should ordinarily resign from any political party they may belong to. In July 2008 Cranston J recused himself from a case in the High Court because it raised issues about hunting and he had, while an MP, made comments about hunting when the *Hunting Act 2004* was proceeding through Parliament. His Lordship (correctly) considered that it would be inappropriate for him to preside (in part, because it was thought there was a risk of the appearance of bias, see 9.3.3).

305

 RETIRED JUDGES

Whilst there is no rule to suggest that retired judges cannot become political it appears customary for retired Law Lords to sit on the cross-benches whereas retired Lord Chancellors (as political appointees) will ordinarily continue to sit with their party. It appears the same rule applies to retired judges who succeed to peerages. A good example of this is Baroness Butler-Sloss who was elevated to a life peerage in 2006 after retiring in 2005 from her position as President of the Family Division. Baroness Butler-Sloss sits on the cross-benches.

9.3.3 Appearance of bias

Perhaps the most important aspect of judicial ethics is in respect of bias or, perhaps more correctly, the appearance of bias (as it is difficult to know whether a judge has truly been biased).[86] The issue of bias is undoubtedly central to the judicial oath and it is also one of the areas where there has, in recent years, been considerable debate.

84. Thomas Bingham, 'Judicial Ethics' in Ross Cranston (ed) *Legal Ethics and Professional Responsibility* (Clarendon Press 1995) 41.
85. John Griffith, *Politics of the Judiciary* (5th edn, Harper Collins 1997) 16.
86. See *Locabail (UK) Ltd v Bayfield Properties Ltd* [2000] QB 451, 472.

It has been suggested that disqualification for bias can be divided into two forms: automatic disqualification and disqualification for apprehended bias.[87] Automatic disqualification will normally follow when a judge has an interest in the case that creates a situation where the judge appears to be sitting in his own cause. Apprehended bias exists where there is some other reason to believe that there is a 'real danger' that the judge will not consider the matter independently.

9.3.3.1 Automatic disqualification

A judge should never judge his own cause, in other words if the judge has an interest in a case then he should not sit as judge. In *Locabail* it was held that a *de minimis* principle existed within this rule meaning that minor or inconsequential interests could be ignored.[88]

> **Example** Rental income
>
> The case of *Locabail* was actually a series of conjoined appeals and one of the appeals was known as *R v Bristol Betting and Gaming Licensing Committee, ex p O'Callaghan*. The facts of this case are not strictly relevant and can be summarized by stating that the appellant had attempted to judicially review the Committee's decision to grant an extended gaming licence to a branch of Corals, a national bookmakers' firm. The judge in the case was the then Dyson J. It transpired that the family of Dyson J owned a property investment company and that some of their property was rented to branches of Corals. The actual amount disputed was calculated at £5,000 and the Court of Appeal dismissed the suggestion that if a national company the size of Corals was ordered to pay £5,000 it might jeopardize its ability to pay rent on one of its shops—in effect the only interest that Dyson J could have had. This was clearly within the *de minimis* principle and the appeal was dismissed.[89]

Precisely what is significant would depend on each individual case but the benchmark is ensuring that the law is not brought into disrepute. *De minimis*, when translated, means 'minimal things' and thus it is not 'small' or 'reasonable' but 'minimal', meaning, in effect, that anything not trivial would lead to automatic disqualification.

The concept of 'cause' had been restricted in effect to pecuniary or proprietary interests[90] but this was to change in the most dramatic way.

Pinochet

In the late 1990s significant controversy existed over the case of Senator Pinochet, the former dictator of Chile. Senator Pinochet had been visiting the United Kingdom for many years for treatment but he was considered a 'war criminal' by many and a Spanish judge had issued an extradition warrant for his arrest. As a result of bilateral EU extradition treaties, extradition had to be contemplated and a stipendiary magistrate issued two provisional arrest warrants, both of which were executed.

87. Abimbola Olowofoyeku, 'The *nemo judex* Rule: The Case against Automatic Disqualification' [2000] *Public Law* 456.
88. *Locabail (UK) Ltd v Bayfield Properties Ltd* [2000] QB 451, 473.
89. *Locabail (UK) Ltd v Bayfield Properties Ltd* [2000] QB 451, 498–500.
90. Timothy Jones, 'Judicial Bias and Disqualification in the Pinochet Case' [1999] *Public Law* 391, 395.

Senator Pinochet claimed diplomatic immunity and sought to judicially review the decisions claiming both warrants should be quashed. The Divisional Court held that both warrants should be quashed but stayed this until an appeal was heard by the House of Lords (the quashing order needed to be stayed otherwise Senator Pinochet could have left the country which would have rendered any appeal moot). Before the matter reached the House of Lords the campaigning group *Amnesty International* sought, and received, leave to intervene in the proceedings (meaning they could make representations as an 'interested party'). The House of Lords ruled by a majority of 3:2 that the appeal should be granted[91] and thus the arrest warrant was upheld.

However, shortly after the hearing, Senator Pinochet's solicitors were contacted with the allegation that Lord Hoffmann, one of the Law Lords who heard the case and who had voted with the majority, was a director of the charitable arm of *Amnesty International*. The legal team for Senator Pinochet petitioned the House of Lords to overturn the decision arguing that it was procedurally flawed since Lord Hoffmann was party to the proceedings and therefore was automatically excluded from the case.

The House of Lords had never been asked to overturn one of its previous decisions in this way before, but held unanimously that it did have jurisdiction to do so.[92] Further, the House held that the decision did have to be set aside because Lord Hoffmann was automatically disqualified from sitting in judgment on the case because one of the parties to the case (albeit simply as an intervener) was *Amnesty International*. There was no suggestion that there was any financial or proprietary interest in this case; Lord Hoffmann was not paid for his role as director and chair of the charity but it was stated that he did have an interest. The organization *Amnesty International* is unincorporated but the activities of its headquarters are divided into two companies; the first is an ordinary limited company which deals with the non-charitable aims of the organization, and the second was the charitable company that Lord Hoffmann chaired.

The charitable arm of *Amnesty International* had provided funding for a report into the activities of the Chilean government which had concluded that breaches of human rights had occurred and that nobody had ever been held to account for these. Whilst it was *Amnesty International* that intervened (and Lord Hoffmann was not a member of *Amnesty International*) the House of Lords held that though it was not possible to say that Lord Hoffmann was a party to the proceedings—in that *Amnesty International* and the charitable organization were theoretically separate entities—the charitable arm did have an interest in the outcome because its founding documents stated it was, inter alia, incorporated to 'procure the abolition of torture'.[93] Given that it had an interest in the proceedings it then followed that Lord Hoffmann, as one of its directors, also had an interest in the matter and so should have been automatically disqualified.

The decision was unanimous and there were some concerns as to its effect. Lord Hutton had said that the links between Lord Hoffmann and *Amnesty International* were 'so strong that public confidence in the integrity of the administration of justice

307

---

91. *R v Bow Street Metropolitan Stipendiary Magistrate, ex p Pinochet (No 1)* [2000] 1 AC 61.
92. *R v Bow Street Metropolitan Stipendiary Magistrate and others, ex p Pinochet (No 2)* [2000] 1 AC 119.
93. *R v Bow Street Metropolitan Stipendiary Magistrate and others, ex p Pinochet (No 2)* [2000] 1 AC 119, 135.

would be shaken if his decision was allowed to stand'[94] which is a damning indictment of the position. Lord Irvine, the then Lord Chancellor, reportedly argued that it had undermined justice[95] and it was reported that some members of the judiciary believed Lord Hoffmann should have resigned.

The decision of the House of Lords was largely welcomed but at least one commentator has noted that the decision has led to a 'growth industry' of lawyers attempting to find interests that debar a judge from sitting.[96] The vast majority of these challenges are doomed to fail, however, since the House of Lords was quite clear as to why Lord Hoffmann should have disclosed his interest. The facts of that case were unusual in that *Amnesty International* had intervened in the case: had the charity not intervened then the issue would not have arisen.

9.3.3.2 Apprehended bias

The other significant manner in which a judge can be asked to stand down is in respect of apprehended bias. This remains an ethical issue not least because it is apprehended bias—ie there is some factor that makes people believe that there could be the appearance of bias rather than the fact that the judge is *actually* biased.

Precisely what would meet this criterion will differ according to different sets of facts but in *Locabail* the Court of Appeal was quite clear about what would *not* ordinarily give the appearance of bias, including 'religion, ethnic or national origin, gender, age, class, means or sexual orientation'[97] and this has to be right. Perhaps more controversially they stated: 'the judge's social or educational or service or employment background or history ... membership of sporting or charitable bodies'[98] would not lead to the appearance of bias. This may, at first sight, appear to be surprising because it would be relatively easy to think of situations when these factors could lead to the suggestion of bias.

The House of Lords considered similar issues in *Helow v Secretary of State for the Home Department*.[99] This was a Scottish case where the appellant, a Palestinian, had sought leave to remain in the United Kingdom but her application was rejected, and subsequent appeals had been denied and she was to be deported. She complained that Lady Cosgrove, a member of the Court of Session (in this context this is roughly the equivalent of the High Court) who had adjudicated on the final appeal was a member of the *International Association of Jewish Lawyers and Jurists* and had been the founder member of the Scottish branch of this organization.

The appellant sought to argue that the association had a strong commitment to causes and beliefs at odds with the appellant, and she specifically contended that the organization was anti-Palestinian. To support this she adduced speeches by the president of the Association.

The House of Lords rejected her appeal stating that mere membership of the organization was insufficient to show the appearance of bias, and that some stronger

94. *R v Bow Street Metropolitan Stipendiary Magistrate and others, ex p Pinochet (No 2)* [2000] 1 AC 119, 146.
95. Timothy Jones, 'Judicial Bias and Disqualification in the Pinochet Case' [1999] *Public Law* 391, 398.
96. Fred Phillips, *Ethics of the Legal Profession* (Cavendish Publishing 2004) 113.
97. *Locabail (UK) Ltd v Bayfield Properties Ltd* [2000] QB 451, 480.
98. *Locabail (UK) Ltd v Bayfield Properties Ltd* [2000] QB 451, 480.
99. [2008] UKHL 62.

connection would need to be shown, for example a link between the president and the judge. This is certainly consistent with *Locabail* but this decision, and the comments from *Locabail* identified earlier, need to be put into context, in that on the vast majority of occasions where they would be relevant it would not be through the appearance of bias but because of an automatic disqualification. This would apply equally to the employment context. If a judge had worked for a considerable period of time in a firm that was party to the proceedings, then it is likely that this would be covered by automatic disqualification and not appearance of bias.

The test for disqualification for appearance of bias is whether there is a 'real danger of bias'[100] and this should be considered through the eyes of a 'fair-minded and informed observer'. In essence this means questioning whether a reasonable person would perceive the risk of bias. If they do then the judge should step down.

Case Box *AWG Group Ltd v Morrison*

A good example of this test can be seen from the case of *AWG Group Ltd v Morrison*.[101] The judge assigned to the case was looking through the papers when he saw that he recognized one of the directors to be called as a witness. This was someone well known to him and the judge would not have wanted to preside over a case which necessitated him deciding whether the witness was telling the truth or not. The response of the respondents to this dilemma was to remove the director from the list of witnesses and replace him with another director.

The Court of Appeal held that this was not an appropriate response. If there was the appearance of bias then the judge was disqualified from trying the case; a discretionary case-management decision could not remedy this appearance of bias. The director the judge knew was involved in the case even if he was not (now) giving evidence and a reasonable person would perceive a real risk of bias in such a situation.

Solicitors

Where life becomes slightly more interesting is in respect of part-time judges. The rule as to automatic disqualification applies to all judges. Barristers are, as will be seen, technically self-employed and thus are, or should be, aware of those for whom they are currently acting. It is irrelevant whether another barrister within a particular set of chambers is appearing before the judge because as self-employed persons they are not in partnership so the judge is not acting as one of the parties. In *Locabail* it was noted that the position for solicitors is different. A partner in a solicitor's firm is legally responsible for the professional acts of all other partners and employees.[102] Accordingly it would, in the opinion of the Court of Appeal, be inappropriate for a part-time judge to sit on a case where his firm has an interest. This will be relatively easy when the representative of one of the parties is the judge's firm but what about the position whereby the firm used to act for a party? The solution, according to the Court of Appeal, is that the solicitor who is sitting

---

100. *Helow v Secretary of State for the Home Department* [2008] UKHL 62 [14].
101. [2006] EWCA Civ 6.
102. *Locabail (UK) Ltd v Bayfield Properties Ltd* [2000] QB 451, 478.

part-time as a member of the judiciary should, when invited to sit on a case, under-take a careful conflict check to ensure that the firm has never acted for either party in the past.[103]

 QUESTION FOR REFLECTION

The House of Lords were undoubtedly correct to state that apparent bias can undermine the integrity of the justice system but is it realistic to expect a solicitor to check all clients in order to decide whether they can sit on a case? To take an example, Allen & Overy are one of the largest legal firms to be based in the United Kingdom. They operate worldwide and have over 5,200 staff including 530 partners. How easy would it be for a solicitor to check that no work had been undertaken? Or should firms who allow their staff to sit as judges have sufficient systems in place to ensure that there can be no conflict of interest?

9.4 Restrictions on practice

Where a person is elevated to a full-time judicial position then they must cease to practise,[104] something that is quite reasonable as it ensures that there is no conflict of interest. Is the decision to become a judge irrevocable, however? Those who are elevated to the bench will normally consider it to be their last employment with the intention of serving until retirement. However, this need not be the case and in 1970 a puisne judge, Mr Justice Fisher, decided to resign from the bench and work in the city instead. This decision was greeted with outrage[105] as the expectation of the public was that judges would accept a judgeship and sit for the duration of their appointment.

Fisher J did not return to practice but is it possible? It has always been assumed that it is not possible[106] but very recently this assumption has been challenged by the resignation of a puisne judge (Laddie J) and the retirement of a circuit judge (HHJ Cook).[107] Both indicated that they wished to be involved with practice, with HHJ Cook joining a solicitors' firm as a partner and Laddie J joining a solicitors' firm as a senior consultant. HHJ Cook was reported to have commented that whilst the Bar traditionally refused to allow a former judge to return to practice, the Law Society had no such ethic[108] which demonstrates an interesting division between the professions.

Should judges be permitted to return to practice? It is widely reported that the senior judiciary do not believe that it should be possible, with the suggestion that it undermines the appearance of judicial impartiality and, potentially, their independence. However, one argument is that the previous rules have never been more than conventions[109] and questions whether some practitioners may be more ready to join

---

103.   *Locabail (UK) Ltd v Bayfield Properties Ltd* [2000] QB 451, 479.
104.   *Courts and Legal Services Act 1990*, s 75.
105.   David Pannick, *Judges* (OUP 1987) 7.
106.   David Pannick, *Judges* (OUP 1987) 7.
107.   *The Times* (28 June 2005) Law Supplement.
108.   'Lord Chancellor Reviews Ban on Judges Returning to Practice Law' *The Times* (23 June 2005).
109.   David Pannick, 'Judges Must be Able to Take up any Position Once They're off the Bench' *The Times* (12 July 2005).

the bench if they believe it is possible eventually to return, but this misses the point that they could accept a part-time judicial appointment such as recorder or deputy High Court judge.

 ## Summary

This chapter has discussed the independence of the judiciary. In particular it has:

- Noted that a fundamental constitutional principle is that judges are independent.
- Explored the difficulties around securing the independence of the judiciary, in particular, the role of salaries, tenure, promotion, and discipline.
- Acknowledged the differences between the security of tenure for superior and inferior judges.
- Considered the role of judicial ethics in relation to being a judge as well as the part that ethics play in securing judicial independence.
- Noted that where a person is elevated to a full-time judicial position, then they must cease to practise.

❓ End-of-chapter questions

311

1. Why is securing the independence of the judiciary so important?
2. Who are the judiciary independent from?
3. How is judicial independence secured? Do you think that this is sufficient?
4. Read David Pannick, 'Judges Must be Able to Take up any Position Once They're off the Bench' *The Times* 12 July 2005, and compare and contrast Thomas Bingham, 'Judicial Ethics' in Ross Cranston (ed), *Legal Ethics and Professional Responsibility* (Clarendon Press 1995) 50–1. Given the importance of judicial independence (see 9.3) is there not a danger that by allowing judges to move between practice and the bench a judge may be influenced by an advocate appearing before him to whom he may wish later to apply for a job?

 ## Further reading

Bingham T, 'Judicial Independence' in *The Business of Judging* (OUP 2000).
   This is an essay written by Lord Bingham who discusses the concept of judicial independence and places it in the context of the modern judiciary.
Pannick D, 'Judges Must be Able to Take up any Position Once They're off the Bench' *The Times* 12 July 2005.
   This is an opinion piece by David Pannick on judicial restrictions on practice.

Lord Thomas LCJ, 'Judicial Independence in a Changing Constitutional Landscape' available at <https://www.judiciary.gov.uk/wp-content/uploads/2015/09/speech-lcj-judicial-independence-in-a-changing-constitutional-landscape2.pdf>.

Lord Thomas LCJ gave a speech to the Commonwealth Magistrates' and Judges' Association on the subject of judicial independence and the position of the judiciary in the United Kingdom.

For multiple-choice questions, updates to this chapter, and links to useful websites, please visit the **Online Resource Centre** at: **www.oxfordtextbooks.co.uk/orc/gillespie_els6e/**

10

The Legal Professions

By the end of this chapter you will be able to:

- Identify the various branches of the legal profession.
- Understand the differences between the two principal professions.
- Discuss whether the professions should fuse into a single profession.
- Understand how a person qualifies as a member of the professions.
- Identify ethical issues relating to the practice of law.

Introduction

Many of you will start your studies in law with the intention of becoming a lawyer although by the end of their studies only approximately 50 per cent of law students actually seek a position as a member of the legal professions. In this chapter we will discuss what the legal professions are, what they do, and how it is possible for someone to qualify as a member of the professions. The chapter will also examine the rules governing practice as a member of the professions and, in particular, the issue of ethical behaviour.

10.1 Defining the professions

The term 'lawyer' has become an almost standard term that is heard in daily use and the *Oxford English Dictionary* defines it as 'a member of the legal profession' but this masks the point that there is no single legal profession but instead there are two principal professions and some secondary ones. It is for this reason that most law dictionaries will not define 'lawyer' because it is a colloquialism that is used as shorthand but does not describe anyone in particular, as nobody in the United Kingdom is a 'lawyer' per se but has a more specific title.

It is often said that England and Wales is one of three countries to continue to have separate legal professions[1] with the vast majority of countries having a single profession but this is not necessarily correct in that a distinction must be drawn between qualified members of the legal profession and non-qualified members of the profession.

---

1. The others being Scotland and the Republic of Ireland, both of which obviously have strong links to the English Legal System.

In England and Wales there are commonly thought to be two branches of the qualified legal profession: barristers and solicitors. In other countries, for example the United States of America, there is one, commonly known as an attorney. However, other people will consider themselves to be a 'lawyer' and in other jurisdictions, and increasingly within England and Wales, they are an important part of a functioning legal system. In England and Wales the two principal professions are joined by two other types of 'lawyer', those being legal executives and increasingly 'paralegals' (who may also be known by other terms, for example, fee-earners etc), a species of lawyer that has been largely imported from America. These lawyers and certainly the Chartered Institute of Legal Executives (CILEX) which governs legal executives view themselves as a branch of the legal profession and CILEX has, in recent years, managed to make a legitimate claim to be considered as the third branch.

The main focus of this chapter will be on solicitors and barristers, as these remain the principal branches of the profession and the ones most people are familiar with. However, towards the middle of this chapter the other two branches, and in particular CILEX, will be discussed briefly.

10.2 Barristers

The first group to examine are barristers, who are also referred to as 'counsel' and are frequently thought to be the specialist advocates although, as will be seen, this is not necessarily accurate.

 'COUNSEL'

Barristers, especially those who practise as advocates, are often referred to as 'counsel' and may sometimes style themselves as 'of counsel', eg Martin Squires of counsel. When a solicitor instructs a barrister, he will usually summarize the case and the action requested by preparing a document known as 'instructions to counsel' which is also called a 'brief to counsel'. Precisely why barristers are also called counsel is lost in the mists of time but it is important to recognize their dual title.

10.2.1 History of the Bar

Barristers collectively are known as 'the Bar' for reasons that will become clear later. The profession is the older branch, with the term barrister existing as far back as the thirteenth century and until recently they had the sole rights of audience in the higher courts. Whilst there is in existence the Bar Council (more properly known as the General Council of the Bar for England and Wales) which acts as the 'trade body' of barristers, their responsibility is to their Inns of Court, to which all members must belong.

 RIGHTS OF AUDIENCE

'Rights of audience' is a specific legal term. A person does not automatically have the right to appear in the courts and perform advocacy, the rules on when a person may do so differ depending on the profession, the court, and the type of case. The ability to act as an advocate in a court is known as 'rights of audience' and so if one is said to have rights of audience in the High Court, it means that the person can appear in the High Court as an advocate and represent his or her client.

10.2.1.1 Inns of Court

There are now four Inns of Court, all of which are honourable and learned societies, which is why barristers are referred to as *learned* whereas solicitors are not. The Inns are Middle Temple, Inner Temple, Gray's Inn, and Lincoln's Inn. Traditionally each Inn was slightly different and the choice of Inn to some degree was a conscious choice for a barrister's career. Lincoln's Inn was primarily considered to be a Chancery-based Inn, ie its members would specialize in Chancery matters and to an extent this has remained, although its members are certainly more general practitioners now. Gray's Inn traditionally had a provincial focus, again something that has been retained to an extent with many members of the North-Eastern Circuit belonging to this Inn but realistically the modern Inns no longer act as specialists and the choice of an Inn is now one of pure personal preference rather than any career choice.

Traditionally the Inns of Court were responsible for the training of barristers and all education took place within their own Inn. From the mid-nineteenth century, however, the four Inns decided that it would be best to cooperate in the education of barristers and they established the Council of Legal Education and the Inns of Court School of Law which took over the education of student members of the Inns. However, the importance of the Inns to education remains and even today a student member of an Inn is (theoretically) restricted to his own Inn and may only use its facilities until he has become a barrister at which point the facilities of all four Inns become available. The *Bar Standards Board* has taken over as the main body with the day-to-day responsibility of regulating barristers but the Inns of Court continue to have the sole right to call members to the Bar and they execute any punishment arising out of disciplinary hearings, including the ultimate sanction of removing a barrister.

In recent years there has been some discussion as to the purpose of the Inns with one eminent QC describing them as 'self-perpetuating geriatric oligarchies'[2] and another describes them as a glorified private club (something that Dunn, a former Court of Appeal judge, agrees with[3]). However, others disagree and Robins reports the words of a junior barrister who joined the Inn during his vocational training year and says, '[my time] made me feel included in the inn [*sic*] and the workings of the inn, and it gave me a sense of professional history'.[4]

10.2.1.2 Masters of the Bench

The Inns of Court are presided over by a series of senior members of the Inns known collectively as the 'Masters of the Bench' and colloquially referred to as 'benchers'. Most members are elected by benchers of the Inn, although some are, by tradition, ex officio benchers, most notably the senior judiciary. All High Court judges are automatically made a bencher if they have not already been elected (and Rothwell notes

---

2. Jon Robins, 'Inn a Time Warp?' (2005) 102 *Law Society Gazette* 19.
3. Robin Dunn, *Sword and Wig: Memoirs of a Lord Justice* (Quiller Press 1993) 186.
4. Jon Robins, 'Inn a Time Warp?' (2005) 102 *Law Society Gazette* 19, 21.

that this applies to High Court judges who used to be solicitors[5]). Clementi has questioned whether it is correct for members of the judiciary to take an active role in the running of the Inns[6] although he did not take his questioning to the extent of recommending any substantive change and any change would undoubtedly be resisted by the judiciary who consider their membership of the Inns as advantageous, particularly to student members who will come into contact with members of the judiciary at an early stage of their careers and in a friendly place.

⚡ MASTERS OF THE BENCH

Regardless of what title a Master of the Bench holds (eg a judicial office such as Lord Justice of Appeal, Mr Justice, etc) when they are performing their role as a Master of the Bench they are referred to as 'Master [n]' and referred to simply as 'master' (even if they are female). This can cause some confusion to junior members who, for example, see one of their Masters sitting in the Supreme Court (where he will be referred to as 'My Lord') and in the evening be calling him 'Master'. The purpose of the rule is to ensure that all realize that they are all members of the same Inn and, therefore, part of the same community.

The head of the Inn is the Master Treasurer and he is appointed for a one-year term. Whilst it is not a full-time position, it is not far from it and the person appointed will normally undertake less professional work (even judicial work if they are a judge when appointed) during their year of office. The person who is in day-to-day control of the Inns is the Under Treasurer (sometimes called Sub-Treasurer) who is not usually legally qualified but is experienced in senior management and will lead the team of employees of the Inns. A crude, but somewhat accurate, analogy to explain the relationship between the Master Treasurer and Under Treasurer is that between the chairman (Master Treasurer) and chief executive or director of operations (Under Treasurer) of a company, thus reinforcing that the post of Master Treasurer is not a ceremonial one, but one that carries with it executive responsibilities.[7]

10.2.1.3 The 'Bar'

When a person becomes a barrister he is said to have been called to the Bar. This term is another that has historical significance. Before the Inns of Court School of Law was established, the training of barristers took place in the Inn and by members of the Inn. The students and instructors (senior members of the Inn) would sit in the centre of the room set out like a courtroom. The students would sit in the middle of the court, within the bar, and when they were called to 'the utter bar' which means 'outer' they left the middle of the court and took their places outside the bar signifying they were no longer students. When a barrister is called they become a junior barrister and they remain a junior for the rest of their careers unless they opt to 'take silk' and become a Queen's Counsel (QC). This process is discussed later but is mentioned here because when a member of the Inn is appointed a QC they are called 'into' the Bar (as distinct from 'to the Bar').

---

5. Rachel Rothwell, 'The Inn Crowd' (2005) 102 *Law Society Gazette* 22, 23.
6. David Clementi, *Review of the Regulatory Framework for Legal Services in England and Wales* (HMSO 2004) 31.
7. Robin Dunn, *Sword and Wig: Memoirs of a Lord Justice* (Quiller Press 1993) 186–8.

> ⚡ SITTING IN COURT
>
> In many of the old courts the status of a barrister will be reflected in where they sit. In the older and more important courts the first row of the advocates' benches will be separated from the rest by a gate or bar. Only those who have been called into the bar, ie QCs, may sit in that row of benches, with junior barristers having to sit in the row behind. In more modern courts where no gate exists barristers will sit in any row except when a junior barrister is being 'led' by a QC in which case the junior will ordinarily sit behind the QC.

It had been planned that in 2008 the system of calling people to the Bar would change with the introduction of deferred call. In essence this would have meant that a person would not be called to the Bar nor entitled to refer to himself as a 'barrister' until after the completion of pupillage. This would have been a major difference from the current position where anyone who meets the criteria set down by the Inns can be called. However, following consultation, the *Bar Standards Board* in 2007 announced that it was abandoning the proposal to defer call believing that it would cause confusion.

10.2.2 Education and training

The way that barristers were historically trained has been discussed but how are they trained now? Training prior to full qualification is divided into three parts:

- academic stage
- vocational stage
- pupillage.

Once qualified, a practising barrister also has a responsibility to undertake continuing professional development, ie to maintain their training throughout their career. It should be noted here that there are proposed changes to the current education and training system undertaken by barristers, in particular removal of the vocational stage of training for barristers (discussed in more detail at 20.3.) However, these changes have not yet been approved and indeed in many ways are controversial and therefore we will continue to consider the system as it currently stands.

10.2.2.1 Academic stage

The academic stage for those who wish to become solicitors or barristers is currently the same although it is likely that in the next year or so, the position will (once again) differ between solicitors and barristers.

Currently, the length of time it takes depends on the educational background of the candidates. Direct entry to the Bar is only available to graduates but it remains the case that for both solicitors and barristers there is no requirement for them to complete a law degree. If, however, the candidate is not a law graduate then they can undertake a conversion course known as the Graduate Diploma in Law (GDL). Some universities also allow graduate entry to a law degree which is a 'fast-track' law degree on the basis that it is not necessary to develop undergraduate learning techniques as the entrant is already a graduate, which means that the programmes can focus purely on the law. Typically these programmes will last two, rather than three, years.

During the academic stage, regardless of which route is taken, the candidate must, as a minimum, receive education in the following:[8]

- Constitutional Law
- Contract Law
- Criminal Law
- Equity
- Law of the EU
- Land Law
- Law of Tort.

It is also expected that students will receive a good understanding of how to research law and acquire the general skills required to study law. The GDL programme will normally focus solely on these exemption subjects whereas a law degree will generally allow the student to undertake a series of optional subjects which provide a slightly wider grounding in law.

The minimum requirement for acceptance onto the vocational stage for the Bar is a lower-second-class honours degree.

10.2.2.2 Vocational stage

After the completion of the academic stage a candidate must choose which branch of the profession he wishes to pursue. This is not an irrevocable decision as it is possible to change between the professions; in recent years the number of barristers qualifying as solicitors has increased whereas traditionally it was more common for the transfer to be in the opposite direction.

The vocational stage of training is now called the Bar Professional Training Course (BPTC). Prior to the academic year 2010–11 the course was known as the Bar Vocational Course (BVC) (and before that the 'Bar Finals'). Until comparatively recently a student who wished to study for the Bar had to study at the Inns of Court School of Law in London. This had a number of advantages, not least the proximity to the Inns of Courts, but it was thought that the monopoly was bad for student access so, following the lead of the Law Society, the Bar Council allowed universities to offer the course and currently eight institutions do so, with the Inns of Court School of Law itself being taken over by City University, London and the title eventually passing away. Before being able to enrol on the BPTC, candidates need to pass the Bar Course Aptitude Test (BCAT). The BCAT was introduced in November 2013 in response to recommendations made by the *Bar Vocational Course Review Group* and aims to ensure that those embarking on the BPTC have the aptitude to successfully complete this stage of their training.

Technically when one is called to the Bar, it is to the degree of the Bar and this is recognized as a postgraduate-level course. However, the BPTC is primarily vocational in nature, although academic knowledge is required of the rules of litigation, evidence, and ethics. The major focus of the course is the application of legal knowledge to situations and a number of practical training exercises are used which take the form of 'mock' briefs where the student is expected to undertake work that is likely to occur

---

8. Note that some of the names may change between institutions.

in the early years of practice. The course remains a foundation of skills, however, since pupillage is considered to be the appropriate place for the completion of the acquisition of practical skills. In comparison to the Legal Practice Course (see 10.3.1.1) the BPTC concentrates more on advocacy, drafting legal documents, and legal research. Advocacy remains one of the most important skills of a barrister and this is accordingly an important acquisition. The importance of ethics is also highlighted in the course and indeed ethics is a strand that flows throughout the course and it is possible for a student to fail the entire BPTC if they act in an unethical manner.

Students on the BPTC may have an opportunity to begin actual casework during their course. Some institutions have developed law clinics whereby the students work on live cases (under the supervision of academics who are professionally qualified) as part of their curriculum.

10.2.2.3 Pupillage

Perhaps the most important part of the training for becoming a barrister is pupillage. It is perhaps the most difficult to secure as Mason notes that there are over three times the number of would-be pupils as there are pupillages.[9] Indeed the most recent detailed statistics released by the *Bar Standards Board* show that in 2013–14, 1,565 students enrolled for the BPTC, yet over the same time period only 397 BPTC graduates secured first-six pupillages.[10] Although the pupil will have been called to the Bar, during pupillage he will refer to himself as a 'pupil barrister'. Pupillage will normally last for twelve months but exceptionally it is possible that it could last up to eighteen months. Pupillage is broken into six-month blocks referred to as the first six and second six (and exceptionally a third six) and although some chambers will offer twelve-month pupillages these are, in fact, two separate six-month arrangements.

The *Bar Standards Board* refers to pupillage as:

> ... the final stage of the route to qualification at the Bar, in which the pupil gains practical training under the supervision of an experienced barrister.

It is, therefore, the first time when the responsibility for the training passes from universities to the practitioners. A barrister of at least ten years' experience can apply to become a pupil-master, ie someone who is entitled to train pupils and accordingly it can be seen that it is very much practitioner-led. Not every barrister of at least ten years' call can act as a pupil-master and sets of chambers must first register with the *Bar Standards Board* as a 'Pupillage Training Organisation' (PTO). Once appointed a PTO chambers will have to adhere to rules on pupillage (including funding, discussed later) set out by the BSB.

In the first six months the pupil barrister is restricted as to what he can do, and realistically this work amounts to a 'shadowing' operation in which the pupil will observe the work of the master. That said, behind the scenes the pupil will begin to develop many of the 'unseen' skills of a barrister; although Pannick argues that traditionally this part of the pupillage was considered a waste of time[11] the modern position is different. Although a first-six pupil will not be allowed to perform advocacy or meet with a client alone, he will begin to work on paperwork relating to legal cases, including

---

9. D Mason, 'A Ticking Time Bomb?' (2004) 154 *New Law Journal* 1601.
10. Bar Standards Board, 'Data Spreadsheet 2010–2015' (BSB 2015) <https://www.barstandardsboard.org.uk/media-centre/research-and-statistics/statistics/pupillage-statistics/>.
11. David Pannick, *Advocates* (OUP 1992) 208–9.

claim forms, defences, and particulars of claim. All of this documentary work will, of course, be under the supervision of, and probably corrected by, the pupil-master but these are the first steps into practice.

In the second six months a pupil barrister gains limited rights of audience and the ability to undertake legal work, albeit under the (loose) supervision of his master. A pupil in the second six months may well begin to undertake advocacy work, probably in the magistrates' court (crime) and county courts (civil) and is entitled to meet clients in the same way as fully qualified barristers will. It should be emphasized, of course, that the pupil is not yet fully qualified and he can anticipate a lot of questioning from his master as to how he intends to undertake the advocacy etc.

Traditionally pupils were never paid and indeed in historical times (until the early to mid-twentieth century) it was expected that pupils would pay barristers for acting as their masters. In modern times it has been recognized that this is unacceptable and the Bar Council has now stipulated that pupillages, subject to a small number of limited exceptions, must be remunerated. Given the headlines in the tabloid newspapers that scream of 'fat cat' lawyers it might be expected that a pupil's award would be substantial, but in fact the current minimum is £1,000 per month although travelling costs and training courses must also be met by chambers. In the second six months of pupillage it is possible that this £1,000 per month can be by 'guaranteed earnings', ie allowing the pupil to earn money from cases, but with the proviso that chambers must make up the difference if the actual receipted earnings are less than £1,000 per month. Whilst it is true to say that some chambers offer in excess of this amount (the current highest award is by Atkin Chambers who offer £72,500 for a twelve-month pupillage) a significant number are set at this modest level and there may be limited opportunity to earn additional money.

Ⅲ\ Case Box *Iteshi v General Council of the Bar* [2012] All ER (D) 241 (Mar)

In 2011 a Nigerian law graduate began proceedings against the Bar Council in the Employment Tribunals alleging that the rule requiring pupillages to be funded amounted to indirect discrimination. Iteshi, who had made repeated applications for pupillage, argued that since the rule requiring funding was introduced the number of black African pupils had dropped in number. The Tribunal ruled that no application could be made under s 12 *Race Relations Act 1976* in that the rule was not imposed on the claimant but rather on chambers. They further ruled that there was no evidence that the rule discriminated in that there was no statistical evidence to demonstrate a fall in numbers or that the rule adversely affected black applicants. These findings were subsequently upheld by the Employment Appeals Tribunal who noted, in passing, that the representation of black and ethnic minority pupils had increased in recent years.

Status of pupillage?

An interesting issue that arose when awards became compulsory was what the employment status of a pupil barrister is. It will be seen that fully qualified barristers are actually independent practitioners and accordingly are self-employed. A pupil barrister, however, is not entitled to practise without limitations and is under the supervision of his pupil-master so does this change their status? The matter was put to the test in *Edmonds v Lawson and others*[12] where the claimant attempted to sue the respondents (who were the head of chambers and her two pupil-masters) claiming that pupillage was either employment or apprenticeship and, accordingly, she was entitled to the statutory minimum wage. The litigation was unusual in that it was completely friendly—it was a test case that was brought not only with the consent of the Bar Council, but actively encouraged by it; both sets of counsel who appeared in the case were actually instructed by the Bar Council themselves.[13]

The Court of Appeal accepted that the offer, and acceptance, of a pupillage does amount to a legal contract. However, it rejected the idea that it was either a contract of employment or a contract for apprenticeship. Their reasoning for this was that the binding duties of a pupil do not include anything that would not be conducive to the pupil's own education whereas an employee or apprentice must do anything that can be reasonably asked of them.[14] The court also noted that in the second six months of pupillage, the pupil barrister is able to earn money in their own right and that this method of earning money is no different to the way that full practising barristers earn remuneration.[15] Accordingly, no contract of employment or apprenticeship existed and thus the provisions of the *National Minimum Wage Act 1999* did not apply. It is clear, therefore, that a pupil barrister must, like those barristers who practise independently, be regarded as being self-employed.

 QUESTION FOR REFLECTION

Consider *Edmonds v Lawson*:[16] is the decision of the Court of Appeal not simply wrong? Why should a pupil barrister not be entitled to the national minimum wage? Is there really any distinction between a pupil and an employee?

321

 LISTEN TO THE PODCAST

For guidance on how to answer this question and a discussion of the main issues, listen to the author's podcast on the Online Resource Centre:
www.oxfordtextbooks.co.uk/orc/gillespie_els6e/

10.2.2.4 Continuing professional development

The requirements for continuing professional development (CPD) changed quite significantly for barristers on 1 January 2017. The new system is arguably more flexible than the previous system, and is designed to encourage staff to think about their professional development rather than think about how many 'points' they need.

Two programmes have been established; the new practitioner programme (NPP) and the established practitioner programme (EPP). The NPP applies for the first three years of practice, after which the EPP takes over.

---

12. [2000] QB 501.
13. *Edmonds v Lawson and others* [2000] QB 501, 507.
14. *Edmonds v Lawson and others* [2000] QB 501, 517–18.
15. *Edmonds v Lawson and others* [2000] QB 501, 518.
16. [2000] QB 501.

New practitioner programme

The key rules for the NPP are:

- A practitioner must complete not less than 45 hours of CPD within the first three calendar years.
- At least nine of those hours must relate to advocacy.
- At least three of those hours must relate to ethics.
- If not already studied, the Forensic Accounting course must be completed (and which does not count towards the 45 hours).

Advocacy training and ethics courses are offered either on the circuits or, more frequently, by the Inns of Court themselves. One of the consequences of CPD training has been the resurgence of education within the Inns. It was noted earlier that the Inns used to be responsible for educating the Bar, but it passed that control over to the Inns of Court School of Law and then ultimately universities. However, CPD allows the Inns to resume their educational programmes and the Inns take this very seriously, usually ensuring that Masters of the Bench are involved in the oversight of the programme and much of its delivery.

The remaining hours can be spent on CPD courses that the barrister believes are most appropriate to them. They no longer have to submit an annual record of their CPD activity, but they do have a record card that must be kept up to date and must be supplied to the BSB when required. Breach of the requirement would amount to professional misconduct and could be sanctioned by the BSB.

Whilst detailed guidance has not yet been produced, there will presumably be a check that the 45 hours have been completed. Realistically, this is likely to require the submission of the record cards to the BSB at the time they have completed three years.

Established practitioner programme

The EPP is considerably different from the previous rules. Until January 2017, barristers had to complete a minimum of twelve hours of accredited CPD provision per year. This could include attendance at physical events or the completion of online training courses.

Under the new EPP there is no minimum number of hours that must be attained, and instead the programme is designed to facilitate barristers becoming reflective practitioners, capable of identifying their own development needs. There are four stages to the EPP:

1. **Review.** This is where a practitioner plans their activities for the current year, identifying what their needs are and identifying potential courses to assist them. This must be done expressly, ie in their record card they must set themselves learning objectives and identify the learning outcomes that will arise from this. Examples of the types of courses to be undertaken must also be given.

2. **Record.** Whenever a barrister undertakes CPD activity they should record it on their CPD plan.

3. **Reflect.** At the end of the year, the barrister must reflect on their CPD activities for the year. This would include them assessing whether they met their objectives, plugged any need that they may have had, what further issues may have been identified, and what they would do differently next year.

4. **Report.** When a barrister renews their practising certificate, they must certify that they have met their CPD activities. They no longer need to submit their CPD records, and instead these will be the subject of 'spot inspections' by the BSB.

CPD is defined as 'work undertaken over and above your normal commitments as a barrister'[17] which is a fairly woolly statement but it is designed to allow practitioners to develop their skills, knowledge, and professional standards. Whilst not prescribing this, the BSB suggests that barristers should consider five areas of practice:

- Legal knowledge and skills
- Advocacy
- Practice management
- Working with clients and others
- Ethics, professionalism, and judgement.[18]

CPD should be used by barristers to help them develop their career. 'Legal knowledge' CPD would allow barristers to consider new areas of practice that they would seek to work on. 'Practice management' could include the ability to perform direct access work, but it could also allow a barrister to consider development needs that would allow them to take up leadership roles in chambers. CPD could be used by senior barristers to consider what they need to do in order to take silk (ie become a QC) or take a judgeship, including a recordership. Indeed, the latter is likely to be important since, as was noted in Chapter 8, the judicial appointments process is now skills-based and therefore CPD should assist in demonstrating this.

The second principal change is that CPD courses are no longer 'accredited'. Under the previous rules, it was necessary for the BSB to approve the content as being appropriate for the course. Now, however, it will be for barristers to decide whether they constitute professional development. This could include, for example, listening to a podcast or viewing a streamed lecture; attending a lecture or attending a course; giving a lecture or completing a workbook. The flexibility of the new scheme means that CPD activities could be broadly defined.

It could be argued that the new process lets barristers off the hook and encourages laziness. The BSB argues that it will not, and that it is about recognizing that 'one size does not fit all'. That is probably correct. Barristers have different needs, depending on their practice and also depending on their aspirations. When deciding what constitutes 'non-compliance', the BSB suggests the following as *examples*:

- CPD activities that are obviously not relevant to your practice or proposed area of practice.
- Completing a minimal amount of CPD over a number of years, with no justification of this in your learning objectives.
- Completing exactly the same CPD activities over a number of years with no adequate justification (eg attending the same 'Introduction to Advocacy' course).
- Disregarding the CPD process.[19]

323

17. *Continuing Professional Development: Guidance for Barristers* (BSB 2016). Available online at: <https://www.barstandardsboard.org.uk/media/1800835/cpd_guidance_for_barristers.pdf>.
18. *CPD Guidance*, 8.
19. *CPD Guidance*, 23.

The success of this programme will depend on its scrutiny. If the BSB does a reasonable number of spot-checks and does take CPD lapses seriously, including through considering it professional misconduct, then the new process could be very beneficial. Under the old rules, it was sometimes the case that barristers would attend courses just because they needed the hours. This new scheme at least allows people to focus on their practice and development. However, this takes persistence and dedication. Becoming a reflective practitioner is not easy and it is easy to 'go through the motions'. The BSB must be alert to this.

10.2.3 Practice

Once a barrister has fully qualified how do they practise? The rules differ between those who serve as employed barristers and those who act in private practice.

10.2.3.1 Private practice

Perhaps the recognizable type of barrister is that in independent (private) practice.

Chambers

After pupillage it is necessary for a person to find a place from where he can practise, known as a tenancy. Barristers are all self-employed and until 2010 they were not allowed to establish a legal partnership with each other but instead they joined together in loose associations known as chambers (also known as 'sets') in order to pool resources (something that continues to be the norm subject to the rules relating to Legal Disciplinary Practices discussed later).

Each barrister (known as a tenant within chambers) will pay rent and a proportion of their income to cover the expenses of chambers. Chambers itself will employ some staff; some will include administrative assistants, but the most important of the employees are the clerks. The clerk to a barrister is an unusual position and has often been likened to the 'pimp' of a barrister. It is not possible for individual barristers to tout for business and, accordingly, the clerk is responsible, in part, for bringing work into the set. Many briefs will be for specific barristers but some will be chambers briefs where a firm of solicitors is happy to deal with anyone within the set and it will then be for the clerk to decide who gets the brief. Where a trial overruns and this prevents a barrister from starting another case the clerk will also redistribute the work. Traditionally a clerk was given a percentage of the brief fee but in modern times it is now more likely that clerks will be on a salary with bonuses paid depending on performance. The attraction this brings is that clerks will concentrate on all barristers whereby when it was a percentage system there was always the risk that the clerk would concentrate on the more experienced practitioners for whom he could attract a higher fee. Chambers normally has a team of clerks, with one being the senior clerk who has ultimate responsibility for supervising the rest and the general operation of clerking. Increasingly in modern times the senior clerk is being called the 'practice manager' or even 'chambers manager'. Good clerks are extremely useful to chambers and there is a strong market in poaching the best. The very best senior clerks can expect high six-figure salaries and the vast majority of senior clerks will earn significant salaries, quite frequently more than what many of the barristers within their chambers will earn.

Once a person is of at least three years' call he is entitled to work without being a member of chambers, ie from home if he so wishes, or he can establish chambers himself.[20] There does appear to be an increase in the number of sole practitioners and some clever clerks have created schemes whereby they will perform an agency-type clerking service for these persons. Acting as a sole practitioner does bring the advantages of more control over work and is undoubtedly cheaper (no chambers expenses, rent, etc) but there is the difficulty that if a sole practitioner's source of work is not strong it is unlikely that they would pick up briefs from others within a set when they become available because of overrunning trials etc.

Court work

The stereotypical view of a barrister is that they spend most of their time in court, in part because once they are qualified a barrister has rights of audience in every court. However, this general impression is not strictly accurate. Whilst it is true to say that barristers specialize in litigation and advocacy it does not mean that all their time will be spent in court, indeed this depends on their area of practice. Whilst criminal and family practitioners will spend the majority of their time in court, other practitioners will not and for those with a primarily civil practice, especially Chancery matters, court is the measure of last resort and they will feel that they have almost failed if it gets to court (because of the costs of litigation) in that most matters can be settled before trial.

It is, however, true to say that advocacy is the most important tool of a barrister but it need not be restricted to oral advocacy and a considerable amount of written documentation will be prepared by barristers. One of the most important aspects of the work of a barrister is the provision of counsel's opinion. This normally takes place at the beginning of litigation and it is the time when a barrister will assess the likely success of any litigation, and identify the key evidential difficulties. The preparation of counsel's opinion will normally require the barrister to undertake research on a specialist area and then to present this advice to the solicitor and those instructing them. If, after considering the advice of counsel, it is decided to proceed with litigation it is likely that the barrister will also be involved in the drafting of the various documents that are needed for litigation, including the claim form, particulars of claim, defences, and questions between all the parties. All of these are specialist skills and training is developed during the Bar Professional Training Course.

When a barrister does appear in open court he appears in the full rig that the public know so well. Except for tribunals and the magistrates' courts where no robes are worn, all barristers will ordinarily wear a gown, wig, and bands. The robes of QCs will be discussed later, but junior barristers wear a stuff gown, bands (which are the white tails that are worn around the neck—ladies have a wrap-around version which includes a collar whereas male barristers' shirts have detachable collars and they replace the normal collar with a winged one), and the infamous wig. There has been a debate for many years as to whether this costume should remain and in 2003 the government issued a consultation paper which suggested a number of options, the simplest of these being that advocates (of all grades) should only wear a gown.

Despite the fact that civil judges have now abandoned their wigs (see 8.2) proceedings in open court will ordinarily see the barrister fully wigged and gowned although

20. BSB, *The Bar Standards Board Handbook* (2nd edn, Bar Standards Board 2015) 96 rS20.

where a judge sits without robes counsel will ordinarily not wear robes either. The Supreme Court has also recently decided that counsel need not robe although all parties must be in agreement.[21]

The retention of wigs and gowns was considered an important matter for the Bar when consulted although this was perhaps more relevant in criminal matters where it has been suggested that they provide a degree of authority and anonymity (Megarry J in *St Edmundsbury & Ipswich Board of Finance v Clark* made *obiter* comments that discussed the merits of judicial and advocates robes[22]) although the degree of safety this brings is perhaps slightly questionable. In any event it must be seriously questioned whether advocates will continue to wear wigs in civil matters now that judges do not. It would seem inevitable that a practice direction will ultimately follow that counsel follow the lead of the judiciary and abandon wigs, at least for civil matters.

The 'cab rank rule'

Solicitors, to an extent, have the right to pick and choose their clients (although it will be seen later that they tend not to exercise this right). Barristers in independent practice, on the other hand, are bound by their Code of Conduct to adopt something which is called the 'cab rank rule' which is described as:

> If you receive instructions from a professional client, and you are:
>
> 1. a self-employed barrister; or
> 2. an authorized individual working with a Bar Standards Board authorized body; or
> 3. a Bar Standards Board authorized body and the instructions seek the services of a named authorized individual working for you,
>
> and the *instructions* are appropriate taking into account the experience, seniority and/or field of practice of yourself or (as appropriate) of the named *authorized individual* you must ... accept the *instructions* addressed specifically to you, irrespective of:
>
> a. the identity of the client;
> b. the nature of the case to which the instructions relate;
> c. whether the client is paying privately or is publicly funded; and
> d. any belief or opinion which you may have formed as to the character, reputation, cause, conduct, guilt or innocence of the client.[23]

Pannick quotes Lord Irvine QC (later a Lord Chancellor) who describes the rule as:

> ... the duty to appear for the Yorkshire Ripper or any other defendant against whom there may be a hostile climate of public opinion. In civil cases, it is also his duty to appear not only for a particular interest group with which he might prefer to identify but for every interest group ...[24]

---

21. The Supreme Court of the UK, *Practice Direction 6* (UKSC) <https://www.supremecourt.uk/procedures/practice-direction-06.html> 6.6.8.
22. [1973] Ch 323, 333.
23. Bar Standards Board, *The Bar Standards Board Handbook* (2nd edn, BSB April 2015) 44 (rule rC29).
24. David Pannick, *Advocates* (OUP 1992) 136.

In other words personal preference cannot decide what case a barrister takes. A criminal practitioner cannot, for example, decide that he will only defend cases and will never accept a prosecution brief as this would breach the cab rank rule. Similarly, a barrister could not decide that he will refuse to take briefs from companies that trade with a particular country because such personal ethics infringe the rule.

☰ Example Cab rank rule

Arthur Hoskins has been charged with two counts of robbery. The Crown Prosecution Service approaches the clerk to Rhiannon Holloway, a barrister who practises in criminal law. The cab rank rule states that if it is possible for Rhiannon to do this case (ie there is no conflict of interest and she is available during the likely time that this will come to court) then she must accept the brief. Rhiannon could not reject the brief in the knowledge that the defence solicitors, who regularly instruct her and other members of the set, may well approach her and she could get more money acting as the defence. The prosecution came first and therefore that brief has to be taken.

The rule is not universally approved of. Some have argued that it is a restriction on freedom and that it cannot be justified, but Pannick states: 'any lawyer who does not understand [the purpose of the rule] really has no business being an advocate'.[25] The basis for this statement is Pannick's belief that to remove the rule would be to prejudice the impartiality of the advocate and would cause people no longer to understand that an advocate's arguments are not necessarily his own belief but rather the instructions of his lay client.[26] Whether society fully understands this distinction is perhaps somewhat questionable but the essence of the point is almost certainly true and it undoubtedly makes it easier for an advocate to perform his duty without needing to like or approve of his client.

327

🔄 QUESTION FOR REFLECTION

It is arguable that the cab rank rule is archaic; do you agree? If yes, how would people who are suspected of the most serious crimes (eg child abuse or murder) ever be represented? Read 10.9.2.1 which discusses how a lawyer should deal with defending someone they believe guilty. Is there not a danger that by abandoning the cab rank rule the jury will become superfluous with defence counsel deciding whether someone suspected of committing a serious crime is guilty or not? (On this point see *Ridehalgh v Horsefield and another*.)[27]

 LISTEN TO THE PODCAST

For guidance on how to answer this question and a discussion of the main issues, listen to the author's podcast on the Online Resource Centre:
www.oxfordtextbooks.co.uk/orc/gillespie_els6e/

---

25. David Pannick, *Advocates* (OUP 1992) 145.
26. David Pannick, *Advocates* (OUP 1992) 140.
27. [1994] Ch 205, 234.

Is the rule enforced? The *Bar Standards Board* does attempt to uphold it and breach of this rule is considered to be a serious disciplinary offence but Pannick noted that, even in the early 1990s, there was concern that the rule was being avoided through, for example, instructing the barrister's clerk to pretend that the barrister is already committed and a suggestion that a barrister would only act for certain parties (eg trades unions) or would never defend a rapist.[28] Clementi, when discussing the merits of the rule, notes that one submission by a barrister stated:

> [A]ny reasonably successful barrister will be able credibly to assert that his current professional and private commitments preclude him or her taking on a case that is unattractive to him or her—until the next interesting case comes along which they would rather do.[29]

It would appear that the rule can be obscured but whether this should justify the end of the rule is perhaps more questionable. Whilst some believe it is a restriction on practice, to others it is an inherent protection to the vulnerable that no matter how unpopular they are, or how abhorrent an allegation against them is, they can ensure that they are provided with access to the law.

The barrister's client

Using the earlier example, let us assume that the Crown Prosecution Service (CPS) did not brief Miss Holloway first; the solicitors for Mr Hoskins offered the brief to Miss Holloway first and this was accepted. Who is the client of the barrister? It may be thought that given Mr Hoskins is the person who has been charged with the crime and who will ultimately appear in court it will be him but this would be wrong. In fact the client of the barrister is ordinarily the solicitor, and the relationship that exists in respect of this case is between solicitor and barrister not between Mr Hoskins and Miss Holloway. The ultimate client, Mr Hoskins, will be referred to as the 'lay client'.

This 'third party' approach historically caused difficulty in terms of payment. Historically a barrister was not able to sue a solicitor for fees because it was considered that the relationship between solicitor and barrister was not a contractual one[30] and this led to a position whereby barristers incurred a significant amount of 'aged debt', ie debt where a solicitor refused to pay for the barrister's service or held on to the money for a longer period of time (thus recouping the interest). There were undoubtedly tensions that existed between the professions on the subject of late or delayed paying,[31] with solicitors frequently (and perhaps from their point of view somewhat understandably) using a finite amount of money to pay their expenses first and then paying the remainder to the barrister even if this was less than the agreed fee. However, in 2004 the Bar Council changed its position from presuming that the relationship between solicitor and barrister was *not* contractual to presuming it *was* contractual and accordingly the position is now that a barrister can sue a solicitor for reduced or non-payment of fees.

---

28.   David Pannick, *Advocates* (OUP 1992) 144.
29.   David Clementi, *Review of the Regulatory Framework for Legal Services in England and Wales* (HMSO 2004) 131.
30.   See, for example, *Kennedy v Broun* (1863) 143 ER 268.
31.   See Lord Hailsham, *A Sparrow's Flight* (Collins 1990) 440–1.

Direct access

The other historical feature of the third-party rule was that a lay client could *only* access the services of a barrister via a solicitor, and indeed at one point a barrister was never allowed to meet with the lay client without the solicitor being present. Increasingly this rule has been reduced, partly in response to solicitors increasingly exercising rights of audience, but also because there is recognition that requiring two lawyers is unnecessary. The initial approach was through BarDirect which allowed a limited category of persons to approach a barrister but this has now been significantly changed and its latest guise, *Public Access*, widens the range of persons who are able to instruct a barrister direct although it does not apply in respect of some forms of work, most notably criminal trials.

Not all barristers will accept work through *Public Access* and those who do wish to do so will need to be of three years' call (although the *Bar Standards Board* intends to remove this restriction) and have received appropriate training on conducting such work. This will include, for example, work on dealing with lay clients, money-laundering regulations, and appropriate insurance cover. *Public Access* does not take away the duties under the *Code of Conduct* and, in particular, the fact that a barrister should not accept work that could lead to him being professionally embarrassed because, for example, he has no knowledge of that area.[32] A barrister who decides that it is in the interests of justice for his lay client to have a solicitor must not act and instead advise his client of that conclusion.

Whilst there are undoubtedly challenges with *Public Access* it is clear that many of the skills of a barrister, particularly in respect of negotiation, arbitration, and the provision of detailed advice, are likely to be welcome by many and it is this type of work that will primarily be undertaken through *Public Access*.

One of the significant changes that arises with *Public Access* is that the cab rank rule is suspended;[33] a barrister is not required to accept instructions from a member of the public and can, in essence, pick and choose which cases they are prepared to accept direct instructions for. This is perhaps partly because the barrister will have to consider how he will maintain a relationship with the client and may therefore prefer to accept instructions from only certain types of individuals (eg law centres, professional firms (architects, surveyors etc)) rather than everyone.

Public Access does not broaden the type of work that a barrister can do. There remain general restrictions on the type of work that a barrister can conduct and it is important to note that public access is simply a different way of gaining access to a barrister rather than widening the range of activities.[34]

Rather ironically the Law Society has reacted badly to the establishment of *Public Access*.[35] The Law Society has, for many years, campaigned (successfully) for solicitors to be able to exercise the rights of audience in the higher courts so it seems slightly disingenuous to insist that barristers wishing to conduct work must be instructed by a solicitor.

32. Bar Standards Board, *The Bar Standards Board Handbook* (2nd edn, BSB, April 2015) 38 (rule c21).
33. Bar Standards Board, *The Bar Standards Board Handbook* (2nd edn, BSB April 2015) 12.
34. Bar Standards Board, *The Public Access Scheme: Guidance for Barristers* (BSB 2016) <https://www.barstandardsboard.org.uk/media/1725710/the_public_access_scheme_guidance_for_barristers__january_2016_.pdf> 5.
35. Catherine Baksi, 'Law Society Slams Barristers' Public Access Plan' *Law Society Gazette* (14 March 2012).

10.2.3.2 Employed practice

Whilst the majority of barristers will remain in independent practice a significant number of barristers are now employed. The numbers have increased in recent years because of a change in the rights of audience such barristers have. Traditionally only barristers in independent practice had unlimited rights of audience and a barrister who became employed lost their rights of audience in the higher courts and was restricted to those courts that solicitors could appear in. Until comparatively recently this caused problems for agencies such as the CPS where even the Director of Public Prosecutions (DPP), usually a senior barrister, would lose his rights of audience upon taking up his employment. It also meant that those agencies who did seek barristers, eg the CPS, Government Legal Service, could not attract the best barristers because the loss of the rights of audience meant their opportunities were somewhat reduced.

The CLSA 1990 reforms, together with the Bar Council relaxing its Code of Conduct does, however, now mean that the opportunities for barristers in employed practice are quite good. Access to the higher courts is now possible and this means that some companies are creating in-house legal services sections that include barristers. The employed Bar can be quite attractive to barristers, especially newly qualified barristers, because there are not the problems that arise out of self-employment in that an employed barrister will get paid leave, capped working hours, and a regular salary.

Historically the limitations and prohibitions of practising barristers forming partnerships applied to the employed Bar too, and thus barristers working in-house could not own shares in the practice (effectively barring them from being a partner). The *Legal Services Act 2007* (LSA 2007) reforms have relaxed this and as from 2010 it has been possible for barristers to own shares in *Legal Disciplinary Practices*, meaning for example they could be an equity partner in a solicitor-led legal practice. Legal Disciplinary Practices are discussed more extensively later.

10.3 Solicitors

The second principal branch of the legal profession is solicitors who are regulated by the *Law Society for England and Wales*, often referred to as the *Law Society*.

Solicitors are, compared to barristers, relatively modern creatures. Until the mid-nineteenth century, non-barristers were split into different types of lawyers, including attorneys, proctors, and solicitors, the latter being principally Chancery specialists. In 1831 an amalgamating body was granted its Royal Charter under the name of the *Society of Attorneys, Solicitors, Proctors and others not being Barristers, practising in the Courts of Law and Equity of the United Kingdom*, a name which hardly trips off the tongue! In 1903 the name was (thankfully) changed to the *Law Society* and at around that time the term 'solicitor' replaced the other forms of address as the accepted title for this branch of the profession.

The Law Society is governed by an elected president, vice-president, and Council. The day-to-day operation of the Law Society is the responsibility of the chief executive who is a non-legally qualified person who is responsible for the general operations of the organization. The chief executive is, as one might expect, assisted by a number of non-legally qualified staff who undertake administrative responsibility for the work of the society.

When contrasting solicitors and the Bar, people are often tempted to make the analogy that solicitors are the equivalent of GPs, with barristers being akin to consultants. The nature of this analogy is supposed to demonstrate that barristers are more likely to specialize than solicitors but it contains two critical flaws. The first is that consultants tend to be considered a promoted post whereas a would-be lawyer makes the decision as to which branch to enter before commencing training. The second flaw is that it is not actually true to suggest that solicitors do not specialize. Whilst those within a small high-street firm may undertake a variety of work there is still the ability to undertake a degree of specialism with one solicitor perhaps focusing on crime and another on family etc. Within large firms there is arguably even more scope to specialize with many firms being dedicated to one form of work, most usually company or commercial law, and specialisms existing within that field. More than this, however, solicitors are entitled to be employed by other firms and most medium-sized companies will have a legal department, and this allows specialisms through, for example, employment law. Solicitors are also employed by the Crown and this allows for specialist areas to be created; can it be said that a solicitor employed by the CPS is any less specialist in crime than a barrister in a set of chambers dedicated to criminal work?

10.3.1 Education and training

There are now four stages to qualifying as a solicitor:

- academic stage
- vocational stage
- training contract
- Professional Skills Course.

There is also an expectation to undertake CPD; indeed the Law Society introduced compulsory CPD attendance before the Bar Council did. The academic stage is exactly the same as for those wishing to join the Bar, the decision being made at the end of the degree, CPE, or GDL. Similar to the training reforms mentioned in relation to barristers, reforms have also been suggested to the training and education requirements for solicitors (discussed in more detail at 20.3). The reforms suggested by the *Solicitors Regulation Authority* (SRA) are more extensive than those suggested for barristers, and include no longer requiring solicitors to have a degree. As these proposals are yet to be accepted we will continue to consider the current education and training required for solicitors here.

10.3.1.1 Vocational training

Everyone who wishes to qualify as a solicitor, including those who wish to qualify via the CILEX route (see 10.7.1), must currently undertake a vocational training course known as the Legal Practice Course (LPC). There has, for some time, been a debate as to what the status of the LPC is, with many believing that it is at undergraduate rather than postgraduate level but this is somewhat irrelevant and, indeed, the Law Society sets out minimum standards and many universities will now offer a postgraduate qualification to those students who successfully complete the course.

Like the Bar, the Law Society used to have its own training provider, the *College of Law*, but this was granted its independence significantly before the Inns of Court

School of Law. The Law Society also opened up the provision of LPC courses significantly earlier than the Bar and there are currently thirty institutions at which the LPC can be studied, and given that that the College of Law (now the 'University of Law') and BPP have a number of sites, this leads to over forty locations where the course can be completed.

The modern LPC has many similarities to the BPTC in that there are a lot of practical exercises involved in the scheme and whilst there is a core of subjects that must be studied by all students, including conveyancing, accountancy, etc there is also the opportunity to study a series of electives, helping to demonstrate to potential employers the type of work the applicant is interested in. A considerable period of time is spent on preparing the student for the type of work and forms that they are likely to encounter in their early years of practice and thus the preparation of court forms and instructions to counsel follow, together with advocacy skills since it is a myth to say that solicitors do not perform advocacy—many do although it tends to be restricted to the more junior courts (albeit those where the bulk of the work is heard, eg magistrates' courts).

As with the BPTC, some institutions have established legal clinics where students can begin to work directly with the public during their vocational training stage. Gaining such experience at an early stage can be a valuable way of learning the skills necessary to complete the LPC together with the opportunity to meet relevant people who could assist in identifying a training contract.

10.3.1.2 Training contract

The third stage of qualification is the training contract and, as with the vocational stage, unless someone is qualifying via the CILEX route then the training contract must be completed. The training contract is similar to the pupillage stage for barristers in that it is 'hands-on' and is the first opportunity where pure practitioners are involved in the training rather than those who are also academics. The training contract lasts two years and could involve working in more than one body as some firms do form loose partnerships that give a wider experience to the trainees. It is also worth noting that whilst competition for training contracts is intense, especially in the larger city firms, it is not quite as competitive as that for pupillage.

Unlike the position that currently exists for barristers, a person is not entitled to call themselves a 'solicitor' until they have signed the Roll of Solicitors and this will only take place where all the requisite stages have been completed. A person undertaking a training contract will be referred to as a 'trainee solicitor' but they must not hold themselves out as a full solicitor.

The training contract must involve the trainee experiencing at least three types of law (eg personal injury, family law, crime, etc) although some firms will provide a broader base and others will provide different experiences between a particular broad specialism (eg litigation, company formations, etc). The trainee must be quite closely supervised and unlike at the Bar where there is normally a single person for each part of the pupillage (eg first six months, second six months) a trainee solicitor may, and probably will, be under the supervision of a team.

Trainee solicitors are paid throughout their training contract and this has been the norm for many years, certainly long before the Bar decided that it was necessary. The minimum starting salary of a trainee solicitor is set by the Law Society. Historically it was set at £18,590 pa for those employed within Greater London and £16,650 pa for those outside London. In 2012, however, the SRA voted to abolish the minimum training salary and instead from 1 August 2014, trainees could be paid the national minimum wage (currently £6.70 an hour for those under 25 years old, and £7.20 for those 25 and over). However, the Law Society recommends, as a matter of good practice, that trainee solicitors are paid £20,276 in London and £18,183 elsewhere. Certainly it would seem to be impossible to pay trainees a wage lower than the minimum wage since, unlike pupil barristers, trainee solicitors are certainly employees. The argument behind relaxing the minimum salary is that in tough economic climates firms are unable to provide the salary. It has to be questioned how realistic this is. The difference in wage between the national minimum wage and the old Law Society minimum wage is approximately £4,000. The majority of the costs of a training contract are almost certainly in the training provision rather than the salary. The *Young Lawyers Division*, an association for junior lawyers, notes that the new scheme is based on an hourly rate but it is highly unlikely that a trainee will work only 35 hours a week. Is it realistic that a firm will pay the hourly rate or, as they do now, pay a salary and expect employees to work such hours as are necessary? If the latter, then the change is arguably more exploitative. The counter-argument of course is that even the national minimum wage (which, based on a thirty-five-hour week will be over £12,000 pa) compares favourably with what pupil barristers are paid.

Throughout the training contract a trainee solicitor will be completing a portfolio-type document that demonstrates the skills and experiences of their practice. Those responsible for supervising the trainee solicitors must ensure that this is kept up to date and is an accurate record of what happens.

10.3.1.3 Professional Skills Course

The final, and most recently introduced, part of the training to become qualified as a solicitor is completing the Professional Skills Course. This course must be completed by all would-be solicitors regardless of what route they take to qualification. The course is the equivalent of twelve full-time days, although it can be done either in a block or part-time, and takes place at the same time as the training contract and it is the employer, not the trainee, who pays for the costs of the course. There are three core modules on the course:

- advocacy and communication skills
- financial and business skills
- client care and professional standards.

Other modules designed to examine specific areas of law or practice can also be undertaken. The course is designed to allow a trainee solicitor to receive further vocational training (akin to the LPC) while at the same time being linked to the practice that they are experiencing through the training contract.

10.3.1.4 Admission to the Rolls

A person formally becomes a solicitor when they are admitted to the Rolls. A practising certificate must be obtained from the Law Society, for which a fee must be paid (currently £100). The admission can take place either in the person's absence or at a ceremony that takes place twice a month. This used to be before the Master of the

Rolls, who was responsible for admission to the Rolls, but the *Solicitors Regulation Authority* has now assumed this responsibility.

10.3.2 **Practice**

Some aspects of the solicitors' practice have already been discussed and it has been noted that they have a more flexible practice than barristers, there being those who practise in a law firm and those who are employed in a non-law firm to undertake legal services. Like at the Bar, it is not possible for a newly qualified solicitor to set up immediately as a sole practitioner; this is a protection on the basis that newly qualified solicitors still require an element of training and development. It would be naive to suggest that a person at the end of their training contract is fully able to undertake all aspects of legal work.

Before starting a practice (be that as a sole practitioner or in a partnership) there must be at least one person who is entitled to supervise others, and the Law Society define this as being someone who has held a practising certificate for at least three of the last ten years, and who has completed management CPD.

Promotion for a solicitor can arise in a number of ways. Because solicitors have always been able to form partnerships (and indeed frequently do so) the promotion path normally involves someone progressing to a partnership, even though in major firms the partnership may still involve a salary rather than equity share (and so is arguably not a true legal form of partnership).

10.3.2.1 **Rights of audience**

When a solicitor first qualifies he has very limited rights of audience, generally restricted to the junior courts and tribunals. A solicitor's rights of audience encompass all matters in the magistrates' court and county court. Within the Crown Court a solicitor may only appear for preliminary matters following a transfer for trial (see 12.6) or for appeals against the decisions of magistrates where their firm was involved at first instance. In the High Court a solicitor has no automatic rights of audience in open court but can be heard in chambers although this would normally be for preliminary matters.

A solicitor can, however, gain higher rights of audience by taking additional training.

10.3.2.2 **Solicitor–advocates**

Historically the Bar had exclusive rights to the higher courts (defined as the Crown Court, High Court (in open session), the Divisional Courts, Court of Appeal, and House of Lords) but in recent times this caused considerable disquiet from solicitors and certain governmental bodies. It was argued that denying higher rights of audience to solicitors raised costs for a litigant because he needed to brief both a solicitor and a barrister even if the matter was relatively simple.

The then government decided in the late 1980s that it was necessary to break the traditional monopolies held by the professions and the *Courts and Legal Services Act 1990* permitted, for the first time, solicitors to appear in the higher courts. However, the statutory authority was only the first step and it was necessary, before any solicitor–advocates were created, for the Law Society and senior members of the judiciary to agree on a system of authorizing such advocates. It took until 1994 for the agreement to be reached and the first solicitor–advocates to be appointed.

Qualifying

Until 2011 it was necessary for a person seeking to qualify as a solicitor–advocate to have been in practice for at least three years but the *SRA Higher Rights of Audience Regulations 2011* have abolished this requirement and a person can seek to qualify with higher rights as soon as they qualify as a solicitor. There also used to be a requirement that a practitioner could show that he had undertaken *actual* advocacy in the courts (for example, magistrates' court or county court) but this has now also been removed and a person must simply take a specific course offered by the SRA.

There are now two types of licence that can be sought:

- civil proceedings (ie a solicitor–advocate would be able to appear in the higher courts for civil matters but not the Crown Court)
- criminal proceedings (ie a solicitor–advocate could appear in the Crown Court and higher courts for criminal matters but not for civil matters with the exception of the Crown Court where all business is licensed).

It may seem strange to have different types of licence but it makes sense given the type of practice that solicitors may have. A solicitor who is employed by the CPS will not appear in civil matters so why should they need to learn the civil litigation rules etc? Similarly, a solicitor who works for a commercial law firm will never undertake criminal work so why should they learn the specific rules of evidence and court rules governing criminal trials? A person can, of course, seek to hold both licences in which case he will be able to exercise higher rights of audience in respect of both civil and criminal matters. It used to be possible to seek a combined licence but a person must now ask for both licences and undertake the relevant assessments for each.

A solicitor who does qualify to exercise higher rights of audience must undertake additional CPD for the first five years of holding the rights. This CPD must relate specifically to the exercise of higher rights.

Court work and dress

Once the higher rights of audience have been granted a solicitor–advocate is entitled to serve in all higher courts relevant to their licence, including the Supreme Court. A solicitor–advocate is entitled to appear in all matters that counsel can and may appear as though counsel. A solicitor–advocate remains subject to the Law Society's regulations, including further regulations on the conduct of litigation, and does not become subject to the Bar Council's regulations. Their regulator remains the SRA which has developed particular competences for higher-rights work.

Traditionally a solicitor–advocate was not able to wear the wig and simply wore the gown and bands but eventually the judiciary brought about equality and in *Practice Direction (Court Dress)(No 4)*[36] it was stated that solicitor–advocates may (which implies that, unlike counsel they do not have to) wear wigs.

Perceptions of solicitor–advocates

The exercise of higher rights of audience by solicitors is still relatively recent and there continues to be something of a problem in perception of the quality of advocacy. This

36. [2008] 1 WLR 357.

335

is in part because the Bar, and therefore by extension the judiciary (who, it will be recalled, are inevitably drawn from the Bar) are always sceptical about those who exercise advocacy and are not in independent practice. The quality of advocacy, for example, by the Crown Prosecution Service has been questioned for years and the same appears true of solicitor–advocates. Darbyshire, in her study on the working lives of judges, shows that some judges do not appear to believe the quality of advocacy is the same.[37] Moreover, research conducted by the *Bar Standards Board* in 2012 found that over three-quarters of responding practitioners felt that the standards of criminal advocacy had declined over the past five years, partly due to the increased involvement of solicitor–advocates.[38]

To an extent this can be seen to be 'double-counting' since, for example, in the criminal courts the CPS has encouraged its own solicitors to seek higher rights. Whilst it is clear that the criticism is levelled it is perhaps more difficult to know whether it is fair. There is no transparent system of fairly assessing the competencies of advocates and whilst it is undoubtedly true that some solicitor–advocates will be poor the same is true of barristers; there are a number of barristers who are not any good either. It is not something that will be easily resolved but it is clear that solicitor–advocates are here to stay and the relaxation of, for example, the three-year qualification suggests the Law Society are keen to increase the number of solicitor–advocates.

10.4 Queen's Counsel

The highest branch of advocates in England and Wales are called Queen's Counsel (QC).[39] Traditionally this was restricted solely to barristers but in 1996 the system was changed and solicitors were entitled to become QCs, although before 2006 only twelve solicitors had ever been given this distinction, and the vast majority of applicants continue to be barristers. Indeed in the 2015–16 competition only nine solicitors applied, three of which were appointed. Since 2008 only twenty solicitors have been appointed a QC. The process of becoming a QC is known as 'taking silk', the name coming from the fact that the court dress of a QC is a silk rather than stuff robe, worn over a court coat (a long, formal frock coat that is worn instead of a suit jacket). The robe and process has also led to QCs being called 'silks'.

10.4.1 Appointment

The appointment process for QCs has proven to be very controversial and it was suspended from 2003 till 2005 while a new process was established. Before the new system, the Lord Chancellor (as chief legal adviser and representative of the Queen) had absolute control over who was allowed to take silk and this undoubtedly led to a number of silks being created for political reasons.[40] A junior barrister would apply to the Lord Chancellor for silk and would nominate two friendly judges for their application and the Lord Chancellor would then confidentially ask senior judges and barristers

---

37. Penny Darbyshire *Sitting in Judgment: The Working Lives of Judges* (Hart Publishing 2011) 206.
38. Bar Standards Board, *Perceptions of Criminal Advocacy* (BSB 2012) <https://www.barstandardsboard. org.uk/media/1402386/orc_international_-_perceptions_of_advocacy_report.pdf> 3.
39. When the Sovereign is a King then an order of the Privy Council translates all QCs into KCs (King's Counsel).
40. Lord Hailsham, *A Sparrow's Flight* (Collins 1990) 386.

what they thought of the candidate (this being later extended to include major law firms). The Lord Chancellor could also take into account any other issues he believed were relevant[41] and thus the process was far from transparent. Unsurprisingly, in 2002 Sir Colin Campbell, the Commissioner for Judicial Appointments, suggested that the system was deficient and this led to the suspension of the scheme.

The new scheme begins with an application form which includes the provision of a 'self-assessment' scheme where a person is asked to evaluate themselves against a series of competencies. An application can be made by either a barrister or a solicitor–advocate and the same system applies to both. The application forms are then sifted and those who pass the sift stage are sent to the senior judiciary to assess whether there are any issues of integrity. On the application form the candidate must list twelve important cases involving a matter of substance (ie a trial rather than preliminary matter) that they have dealt with in the past two years. The candidate identifies one judge from that list who would provide a reference and the selection committee chooses three others from the list provided. All four judges are approached to provide a commentary on the competence of the applicant. In addition to this, six practitioners (normally already QCs) must be listed and four of these will be approached by the panel for a reference. Those who are considered suitable after this stage will be interviewed by a panel nine strong. The panel will be chaired by a distinguished lay (ie non-lawyer) person; the remaining eight will consist of:

- three lay members
- one senior retired judge
- two senior barristers
- two senior solicitors.

The names of those candidates who are selected by the panel are then passed to the Lord Chancellor and then to the Queen where the letters patent appointing the person a QC will be made. Traditionally new QCs were announced on Maundy Thursday but this practice appears to have (regrettably) failed to survive the new arrangements with the first silks appointed under the new scheme being appointed in July 2006 and the 2016 competition being announced in January.

It has to be accepted that this new process bears little resemblance to the old system and is certainly more transparent. Indeed it could actually be argued that it is too transparent and that the Bar Council and Law Society may have created a beast that is too burdensome. In 2003, the final year operated under the old scheme, 394 applicants applied for silk[42] and by 2016 this had fallen to 237 applicants although this continues to be a significant number. Each applicant must nominate at least eighteen assessors ('referees'), comprising at least eight judicial, six practitioner, and four client assessors. This is a considerable burden on the judiciary when, as it has been seen, judges are already subject to significant administrative burdens. The Judicial Appointments Commissioners were already concerned at the bureaucracy involved in the old system and whether this could lead to references being missed or mislaid[43] and this new scheme does not appear to resolve these issues. The cost of the process must also be of concern.

41. See, for example, the description of the process put forward by Dame Elizabeth Lane, *Hear the Other Side* (Butterworths 1985) 100–1.

42. Commission for Judicial Appointments, *Commissioners for Judicial Appointments Audit Report 2003* (HMSO 2003).

43. Commission for Judicial Appointments, *Commissioners for Judicial Appointments Audit Report 2003* (HMSO 2003) Annex c, para 3.7.

Previously the Department for Constitutional Affairs (DCA) administered the process but it is accepted that this was wrong and it is now administered by an independent body created by the professions. The suggestion was that it should be self-funding yet the appointment commissioners have previously argued that the scheme is not sustainable.[44] Indeed they argued that not accounting for consultees' time, the cost per applicant was £1,150 and yet now a panel interview will be undertaken. The panel members are paid and this inevitably increases the costs. Self-funding has been introduced and the current fee is £2,160 (£1,800 plus VAT) with an additional fee of £3,600 (£3,000 plus VAT) being payable for successful applicants. In 2016 the number of applicants was 237 with 107 (45 per cent) of applications being successful.

10.4.2 Practice

A person who is appointed QC will see a dramatic shift in their practice with the real possibility that their fees will rise because silks are paid more than juniors. However, it is a gamble because a silk should only undertake work that is suitable for them and thus it is possible that someone may have a thriving junior practice but a less stable practice as a silk actually earning less money.[45]

A silk is sometimes also known as a 'leader' because in many cases the QC will appear with other counsel to conduct the litigation, and the QC, as the senior advocate, would normally lead this team (although there is no longer a rule that states a QC must appear with a junior barrister). Unlike in America where huge teams of lawyers are engaged, it is more normal in England and Wales for a team to involve two, and sometimes three, advocates led by one silk. The junior barristers on the team will normally have been involved in the case before the silk is appointed and will conduct much of the preliminary work. However, the junior barristers will also normally be involved in the litigation, not only in reading the papers and deciding on tactics but also normally conducting the examination of more junior witnesses.

When a QC appears in court, he should wear a silk robe over a court jacket (a long formal buttoned jacket that is worn instead of a suit jacket) and a wig. A solicitor who is appointed QC was entitled to wear a wig even before the changes made to the court working dress for solicitor–advocates. Upon being appointed a silk, the QC will purchase a full-bottomed wig (similar to the ones judges possess) but these are never worn in court.

An interesting issue arose during the Lord Chief Justice's annual press conference in 2012 which impacts on the practice of QCs. The Lord Chief Justice was asked a question about the deployment of QCs in cases and, in particular, about a perceived criticism he made about the CPS not engaging leading counsel in a complicated loss of control case (although the official transcript of the case merely records the Lord Chief Justice stating that the trial judge 'did not have the advantage of the careful and detailed submissions made to us by leading counsel').[46] The Lord Chief Justice in the press conference said:

> In our adversarial system high quality advocacy on both sides is more likely to produce a just result ... [W]here there is a new bit of law which is difficult ... it is sensible for a

44. Commission for Judicial Appointments, *Commissioners for Judicial Appointments Audit Report 2003* (HMSO 2003) paras 3.2–3.4.
45. See the cautions of Elwyn-Jones on this matter; Lord Elwyn-Jones, *In My Times: An Autobiography* (Weidenfeld & Nicolson 1983) 153.
46. *R v Clinton* [2012] EWCA Crim 2, [2012] 3 WLR 515, 536.

top-flight lawyer to be appointed to deal with the case. Now, it may be … when the law has settled down and we all know what Parliament actually meant by the statute, that it is not necessary. But where you have new criminal justice provisions which do change the law, or appear to change the law, generally speaking you get a better answer if you have a good quality advice.[47]

This is an interesting comment as it shows that the Lord Chief Justice believes that QCs are important in the development of the law. Judges do not know all the law, they are guided by advocates who put their views on the law. The judge will then read the appropriate authorities and make a ruling. The Lord Chief Justice is clearly stating that where legislation is complicated it is important that the best advocates, QCs, are used even if this may appear to bring additional expense to a trial or in cases where a silk would not ordinarily be used (such as a voluntary manslaughter trial where senior junior counsel may be commonly used).

10.5 Fusion

The preceding sections of this chapter should have demonstrated that traditionally the two sides of the profession (barristers and solicitors) were quite separate and that each performed a specific task. The reforms introduced by the CLSA 1990, and subsequent statutes, such as the *Legal Services Act 2007* (LSA 2007) (see 10.5.3), have meant that the distinction between the branches is no longer quite the same as it once was. England and Wales is one of three jurisdictions to retain a two-branch profession, and in Scotland it is more usual for a person to become a solicitor first before applying to join the *Faculty of Advocates* (as the Scottish Bar is known) although this is no longer essential and it is theoretically possible to qualify direct from university. The system in Ireland is roughly the same as in England and Wales but with barristers having slightly more freedom. In most other jurisdictions, including in common-law jurisdictions[48] there is no formal distinction between advocates and non-advocates and increasingly the question has been asked whether the professions in England and Wales should fuse.

10.5.1 Advantages of fusion

There are undoubtedly some advantages to a fused profession, both from the point of view of the individual lawyer and the general public. The usual arguments advanced include:

- common training programme
- costs
- efficiency.

10.5.1.1 Common training

Although the academic stage for both professions is now the same, the vocational and professional training requirements do differ in both content and time. This, in effect,

---

47. Judge, *Lord Chief Justice's Press Conference* (MOJ 2012) <http://www.judiciary.gov.uk/announcements/lcj-press-conference-2012/> 16–17.

48. This is the expression normally given to those countries whose legal system is historically based on UK principles. It generally includes former and current colonial or Commonwealth countries.

means that someone who wishes to become either a solicitor or barrister must decide early in their career which path to follow. The decision is not irrevocable as it is possible to transfer between the professions but recognizing that one has proceeded down the wrong track could lead to disenchantment and, at the very least, a considerable amount of wasted time. One of the more common forms of fusion that is discussed is that everyone would start as a solicitor and only the best would be given advocacy rights in the higher courts after career development. This would ensure that everyone had the same starting point; it would, however, mean that people who were interested in advocacy might have to wait several years before demonstrating their aptitude. An advantage of fusion to the would-be lawyer is that it is likely to ensure that everyone would have employment rights and a minimum level of salary.

10.5.1.2 Costs

Except for those few situations when either a solicitor–advocate is engaged or where a person contacts a barrister direct, a person wishing to litigate in the higher courts will often have to engage both a solicitor and barrister and, therefore, there is a suggestion that costs would be reduced as only one lawyer would be required rather than two.

However, whilst the argument probably has an element of truth to it, the position is not necessarily as simple as many may think. Whilst there will be a degree of overlap between the work of the solicitor and barrister much of the work is separate and thus even if a single lawyer is engaged then it is likely that much of the work will still be done and payment required for it. It also does not naturally follow that only a single lawyer will work on the case and many large firms currently have litigation departments where a case will be passed and the lawyer working in the litigation department may have a higher rate than the other. Finally, in respect of some simple work it is quite possible that costs could rise. In preparatory or simple matters (eg plea and directions hearings, guilty pleas, etc) an advocate may only be required for an hour, or even less. A barrister will undertake the work for a set fee and hope that he can pick up more than one on a day. A solicitor on the other hand will probably only have the one case and will charge by the hour. If, therefore, the case is listed first this may mean that the costs are less but if the solicitor has to wait at court all day until his case is heard the client will undoubtedly be charged not only for the time when the solicitor was actually advocating but also the time spent waiting, this would be quite costly.

10.5.1.3 Efficiency

Closely related to the issue of costs is efficiency. Where more than one lawyer is involved in a case there is likely to be scope for inefficiencies to be created, especially where they are in different locations. A solicitor and a barrister may have very different diary commitments and thus finding a time when both are available for consultations etc could take longer than for a single practitioner. However, this difficulty is eased by the fact that barristers are now able to see lay clients with a representative from the solicitor's firm rather than the solicitor themselves, or indeed in certain circumstances to see the lay client alone. Where paper and documentation is being sent between individuals there is also the scope for it to be lost etc. Against this argument, however, there is the rather obvious argument that large companies are quite inefficient themselves and having a single firm acting is no guarantee that paperwork will not go missing etc.

10.5.2 Disadvantages of fusion

Not everyone is in favour of fusion and there are a number of reasons why fusion should not occur, the most notable being:

- loss of specialist expertise
- reduction in the standard of advocacy
- loss of the 'cab rank rule'
- loss of professional detachment.

10.5.2.1 Expertise/advocacy

The most common argument against the fusion of the professions is the belief that it could lead to a loss of specialist expertise, particularly the art of advocacy. It has been noted already that a barrister is more likely to specialize in a particular area of the law and it may be thought that fusing the professions may lead to a loss of such expertise. To a degree it could be argued that this would not happen because if the demand for work exists then the same number of experts are going to be required but if, as would seem likely, most would be employed by firms there is likely to be pressure on people to have a wider form of expertise and instead of being briefed nationally it is quite possible that people would try to find more local contacts, perhaps localizing expertise.

The other argument is that the expertise of the art of advocacy itself could be damaged. Certainly in 1977 the *Royal Commission on Legal Services* argued that fusion could lead to a reduction in the standard of advocacy. It could be argued that, following the right of solicitors to gain higher rights of audience, and indeed the ability of solicitor–advocates to take silk, that this is no longer strictly true. However, there are a relatively small number of solicitor–advocates and compared to the Bar they arguably undertake less advocacy work than some barristers, especially in respect of common-law and criminal litigation. Firms may create specialist advocacy departments whose members concentrate on advocacy but it is also quite likely that the fused lawyer would be required to do a lot of other work and thus spend more time out of court than they currently do, perhaps leading to a reduction in their skills.

10.5.2.2 Cab rank rule

The cab rank rule was set out earlier in this chapter (see 10.2.3.1) and it is considered to be an important rule in the provision of legal services. Alongside ensuring that a person can be provided with legal services regardless of their character or the allegations made against them (which is not necessarily a difficulty since although in general solicitors are not bound by the rule it is difficult to identify a person who has been denied access to legal advice because members of that profession, quite rightly, note that even those who society may find repugnant are able to access impartial legal advice) the rule is supposed also to protect someone from being held to ransom in terms of fees. The clerk and those instructing the barrister will agree an appropriate fee and then that case must be dealt with by the barrister and not returned if a more lucrative case arises later.

The cab rank rule is often cited as an argument against fusion, in part because the solicitors' code of practice does not include an ethic for its solicitors requiring them to uphold the principle and so it is arguably for the individual conscience of a solicitor whether to accept instructions. It has been seen that with direct access the Bar has relaxed the cab rank rule and the same exists for those who operate within *Legal Disciplinary Practices* (LDPs) or *Alternative Business Structures* (ABSs) (both discussed later) because the rules under which these operate are set by the *Solicitors Regulation Authority* (SRA).

However, the rule is not completely abolished in that the underlining principle remains. Section 17(3)(c) CLSA 1990 (now repealed) required the regulatory body to establish rules guaranteeing a modified version of the cab rank rule (most notably, the right to an advocate regardless of the advocate's personal opinion on the client or the client's business etc). The Law Society has, in its rules governing solicitor–advocates, included a provision satisfying s 17(3)(c) and so there is no reason why a fused profession would not continue to abide by s 17(3)(c) and thus maintain a (modified) version of the cab rank rule.

10.5.2.3 Professional detachment

It is often said that a barrister tends to be more remote than a solicitor when it comes to dealing with the lay client, but many barristers, particularly those with a criminal practice, may contest this especially in relation to the longer trials. It is also somewhat naive to suggest that because solicitors are with the lay client longer than a barrister they will somehow lose the professionalism that is inherent within the legal profession.

Perhaps the more significant issue, however, is the loss of the 'second opinion' that is currently undertaken. When a solicitor briefs a barrister on a particular case he will inevitably ask counsel's opinion on the matter. It is quite possible that the barrister will identify something that the solicitor has not or disagree with him over the chances of successful litigation. Where the barrister is a specialist advocate this latter possibility becomes slightly more important. If, in a fused profession, a single lawyer were to follow the case from start to finish then it is possible that this would end.

This problem would only exist in the completely fused model whereas others have suggested that an alternative model would be for everyone to enter the profession as a solicitor and for those with an interest in advocacy to become a barrister when their career has progressed. Arguably this could solve many of the previously outlined difficulties.

10.5.3 The beginnings of fusion?

Whilst fusion has been discussed for several years the LSA 2007 has arguably created a position where the beginnings of fusion can be seen, although it has much wider implications, including in the ways that lawyers operate in partnership with non-lawyers.

The LSA 2007 defines 'reserved legal activities' and 'legal activities' and these are crucial to its later provisions. A reserved legal activity is:

(a) the exercise of a right of audience

(b) the conduct of litigation

(c) reserved instrument activities

(d) probate activities

(e) notarial activities

(f) the administration of oaths.[49]

---

49. *Legal Services Act 2007*, s 12(1).

These are, in essence, the type of activities that were historically reserved to the solicitors and barristers. A 'legal activity' is defined as:

(a) a reserved legal activity, and

(b) anything which constitutes one or both of the following:

  (i) the provision of legal advice or assistance in connection with the application of the law or the resolution of legal disputes,

  (ii) the provision of representation in connection with any matter concerning the application of law or the resolution of legal disputes.[50]

This is obviously much wider and must, for example, include the provision of certain advice by the Citizens Advice Bureau and a considerable amount of the advice and representation that takes place in tribunals (see Chapter 7). A person may only carry out a reserved legal activity if he is authorized to do so[51] and it is an offence to do so without authority[52] or to pretend to be so authorized.[53]

This is largely uncontroversial and, in essence, is simply the codification and clarification of existing rules. However, the LSA 2007 goes much further by altering the very structure of the legal profession. It did this initially by establishing Legal Disciplinary Practices (LDPs) but, from late 2011, through the establishment of Alternative Business Structures (ABSs), which are also sometimes known by the moniker 'Tesco Law' (for reasons discussed later). At the heart of both structures is the idea that non-solicitors can share in the equity of a firm or even own and run a firm in which solicitors are employed.

10.5.3.1 Legal Disciplinary Practices

Completely changing the professions was considered too far in one step and so the LSA 2007 created an 'interim' step which is that known as a Legal Disciplinary Practice (LDP). These came into effect in 2009 and marked the shift away from the beginnings of the traditional legal professions. Until the SRA 2007 reforms, solicitor firms could only be owned and run by qualified solicitors. Accordingly, whilst solicitor firms, including large firms, could employ barristers and legal executives, these could never be permitted to hold equity in the firm or be in charge of the firm. This limited the opportunities for these employees since the traditional path of promotion in solicitor firms is to partnership, where the rewards of the business are shared out amongst the equity holders.

The LSA 2007 does not, strictly speaking, create an LDP but rather it allowed for the creation of such structure by amending legislation, most notably the *Solicitors Act 1974* (SA 1974) and *Administration of Justice Act 1985* (AJA 1985) to permit (principally) the *Solicitors Regulation Authority* to recognize LDPs.

Technically an LDP owes its statutory foundations to s 9A AJA 1985 which does not specifically refer to an LDP but rather to a 'legal services' body. According to the Act a legal services body is a body corporate or unincorporated that meets the 'management and control condition' and the 'relevant lawyer condition'.[54]

---

50. *Legal Services Act 2007*, s 12(3).
51. *Legal Services Act 2007*, s 13.
52. *Legal Services Act 2007*, s 14: the offence is punishable by a maximum sentence of two years' imprisonment.
53. *Legal Services Act 2007*, s 17.
54. *Administration of Justice Act 1985*, s 9A(1).

The management and control condition requires:

(a) at least 75 per cent of the body's managers to be legally qualified;

(b) the proportion of shares in the body held by persons who are legally qualified to be at least 75 per cent;

(c) legally qualified persons must have 75 per cent of the voting rights of the body;

(d) all the persons with an interest in the body who are not legally qualified are managers of the body; and

(e) all the managers of the body who are not legally qualified are individuals approved by the SRA as suitable.[55]

The requirement is therefore in essence that those who are legally qualified must account for 75 per cent of those who exercise management of the company (in essence meaning those who hold equity in the firm) although from September 2011, when Alternative Business Structures were authorized, all firms that involve a non-lawyer as a manager must now seek to establish themselves as an ABS. That said, where all managers are lawyers (but not necessarily solicitors, so for example legal executives or barristers) then the firm could continue to be an LDP. At least one of the managers must be a solicitor or a registered European lawyer.[56]

The LDP was a major change and it could have led to radical changes in the way that solicitors interacted with legal executives and barristers. By allowing, for example, barristers to become equity partners it could have led to firms having 'in-house' advocacy departments that were all manned by barristers. However, it would seem that the uptake of LDPs has been somewhat modest. Whilst few LDPs were created, this was perhaps because they were an interim step and people were waiting for Alternative Business Structures, which allowed greater flexibility.

Since 2012 it has not been possible to create an LDP and existing LDPs must transfer to ABSs.

10.5.3.2 Alternative Business Structures

The aim of the LSA 2007 was always to go beyond the creation of LDPs and to permit radical restructuring of the legal profession. The aim was to allow for firms that were not owned by lawyers to be allowed to offer legal services and the moniker 'Tesco Law' was coined to demonstrate the type of organizations that may adopt this structure. Why Tesco? It was simply the recognition that Tesco, and other major-brand supermarkets, have diversified in recent years to provide lots of services other than the sale of goods. The most notable examples are banking and insurance services which most major supermarket chains now provide. The LSA 2007 was expected to lead to situations where they may decide to undertake certain forms of legal services (eg will-drafting, simple divorces, personal injury claims etc).

Alternative Business Structures (ABSs) mark a significant progression from LDPs in that whilst an LDP, as already noted, has limitations as to who may own and manage the firm because, since September 2011, where a non-lawyer is a manager they must now become an ABS. LDPs are also restricted in the work they do (they must be primarily a legal firm), but ABSs are not so restricted. This means, for example, that

55. *Administration of Justice Act 1985*, s 9A(2).
56. *Administration of Justice Act 1985*, s 9A(4).

non-lawyers can own and/or manage firms that undertake reserved legal activities and ABSs can offer alternative work, for example, financial advice. The reserved legal activity can only be undertaken by an appropriate legally qualified person but there are no restrictions as to who can own or manage the firm. Many firms already have 'in-house lawyers' or legal services departments but an ABS differs dramatically from this concept since an in-house lawyer only offers legal advice to his employers: an ABS will be able to offer legal services to the public. A lot of attention in relation to ABSs has focused on the large-scale firms (Tesco et al) but not all ABSs will follow this model and they could, of course, be on a smaller scale. For example, a firm of accountants and lawyers could combine to provide a niche firm. Under existing laws this is not possible because the non-lawyers could not be equity owners but an ABS will permit this.

Even before ABSs came into existence some large brands were already purporting to offer legal services, albeit through (discreetly) subcontracting to legal firms.

The first major brand to become an ABS was not, in fact, Tesco (who rather ironically initially indicated that they were unsure that they would wish to enter the legal services marketplace) but rather the Co-operative. In 2006 the *Co-operative Legal Services* was established and in 2011 became one of the first companies to apply to become an ABS. The advantage this brought was that the venture could be brought closer into the Co-operative group allowing it access to the financial muscle that a large commercial organization brings. However, it is worth noting that in January 2016, *Co-operative Legal Services* only posted an underlying operating profit of £700,000, following a £5 million loss the previous year and a loss of £9.1 million the year before that. Whether, therefore, the rewards of deregulation can be reaped is perhaps open to question.

The take-up of ABSs has been somewhat slow, perhaps unsurprisingly given the conservative nature of the legal profession. As already noted, the Co-operative were the first major 'brand' to decide that it would engage. Other firms have used the ABS structure as a way of seeking a method of raising private finance in all, or part, of the business. Irwin Mitchell, one of the largest firms in the UK, became one of the first firms to do this in respect of certain aspects of their work, with the intention of using the new structure as a way of seeking private equity capital, in essence, seeking investors to turn parts of their firm into a profit-making business. Not all ABSs have adopted this approach though. One firm, Mulderrigs, a two-partner law firm, became an ABS to allow the spouse of one of the partners to inherit a stake in the firm upon his death (the wife had been crucial in the establishment of the firm but, under traditional rules, could not be an equity partner), again demonstrating that ABSs transform the nature of a firm into a company or business where shares are property.

As of 2015, it was estimated that there were only approximately 500 ABSs that had approval,[57] although that did include a number of large names. It is thought that ABSs will continue to increase, as people realize that it is possible to offer legal services within a group that specializes in something else (eg estate agents offering conveyancing services) or while securing private capital. The Bar has begun to see the advantage of ABSs and the BSB was granted approval from the Legal Services Board in 2016 to approve ABSs.[58] When fully implemented, this could see chambers changing

---

57. Catherine Baksi, *Reaping the Benefits of an Alternative Business Structure* (Raconteur, 2015) <http://raconteur.net/business/reaping-the-benefits-of-an-alternative-business-structure>.

58. Bar Standards Board, *Bar Regulator Receives Approval to License Alternative Business Structures* (BSB, 2016) <https://www.barstandardsboard.org.uk/media-centre/press-releases-and-news/bar-regulator-receives-approval-to-license-alternative-business-structures/>.

so that tenants take an equity share in the 'firm', with the senior clerk/chambers chief executive also being an equity partner. It would also allow them to merge with ADR providers etc.

Commercial v legal duties

Some have questioned whether the creation of ABSs could lead to a situation where the professional ethics of lawyers are endangered. As ABSs can be owned and managed by non-lawyers it could mean that lawyers are placed under commercial pressure to do something that is not in the best interests of their client.[59] For example, in civil matters there may be tension between accepting an offer to settle and the commercial benefit that continued litigation may bring. Whilst this is not restricted to ABSs the argument has always been before that since each member of the firm owed a personal duty under the codes of conduct such pressures may be minimized whereas under an ABS only the lawyers will be the subject of a personal duty, the non-legal staff will not.

ABSs are subject to a corporate regulatory framework. Whilst each individual lawyer has responsibilities to their professional body, the ABS itself is subject to regulation by the SRA. The SRA has a specialist unit which will examine the regulation of ABSs and it is notable that the SRA Principles, set out in the SRA Handbook, apply to all persons and firms that are supervised by the SRA (including ABSs) and this expressly includes the protection of integrity, independence, acting in the best interests of the client, and the adherence to compliance regulations.

 QUESTION FOR REFLECTION

Whilst there are currently only a small number of ABSs it is likely that their number will increase in future years. Are there dangers in permitting non-lawyers to be employed by large commercial organizations? Does the work of law neatly fit into, for example, the retail or financial advice sectors? Are there different types of legal work that may be better suited to an ABS than others?

 LISTEN TO THE PODCAST

For guidance on how to answer this question and a discussion of the main issues, listen to the author's podcast on the Online Resource Centre:
www.oxfordtextbooks.co.uk/orc/gillespie_els6e/

10.6 Diversity in the professions

The legal profession is considered to be quite a conservative profession and suffers from a stereotypical view of its members. Many believe that its members are white, middle-class, Oxbridge-educated persons (normally male) and that success within the profession is based on who one knows rather than aptitude. This would be a largely inaccurate reflection but, sadly, one with a degree of truth within it.

---

59.   Harry McVea, 'Legal Disciplinary Practices: Who Needs Them?' (2004) 31 *Journal of Law and Society* 563, 567–71.

In terms of gender, changes are occurring. In 2014 64.8 per cent of students accepted to study on law degrees at university were women.[60] Progress is being made within the professions too, with the pace increasing. In 1992 26.3 per cent of solicitors were female and by 2015 (the latest year for which statistics are available) this had risen to 48.8 per cent of those solicitors who have a practising certificate,[61] which suggests that females are beginning to develop near-parity with men. The position at the Bar differs although the Bar Council continues to actively encourage women to gain access to all positions within the Bar. The position based on the most recent data from 2015 is that women account for 35.6 per cent of practising barristers, slightly more than in 2014 when the figure was 35.2 per cent. These figures compare unfavourably with solicitors and demonstrate that the Bar still has some work to do in order to demonstrate that they are 'female friendly'.

There is some concern that these statistics obscure a glass ceiling, with one commentator noting that the vast majority of partners in solicitors' firms continue to be men, including those who are recently appointed.[62] It is difficult to know how true this remains because although the Law Society states how many women partners there are (8,098) they do not state how many partners there are overall and how many of those described as partners do not hold an equity stake. Commentators have also suggested that there has been 'institutional discrimination' at the Bar.[63] Certainly this would seem to be supported by the applications for QC. In the 2015–16 competition only forty-eight (20 per cent) applications were made by women, although this was a slight increase from the 2014–15 competition where forty-three (19 per cent) applications were made by women. Of those that did apply twenty-five (52 per cent) were appointed but this was a reduction from the previous competition where 58 per cent of applicants were appointed.

What these statistics do mask is the question of whether women are to be found in higher numbers outside of private practice, for example in public-sector employment, where employment conditions are normally better in terms of maternity leave, career breaks, etc. This is potentially a factor with many private practice firms not even allowing part-time work.[64]

Another failure of the statistics is that they do not appear to focus particularly well on the social backgrounds of lawyers (as distinct from judges) although a considerable amount of work has been undertaken at the academic stage which appears to demonstrate that those from the 'new' university sector,[65] whose student members tend to be from more diverse socio-economic backgrounds than the 'traditional' universities, are gaining employment,[66] but more has to be done to examine whether they are managing to progress to all levels. However, the high costs of training to be a lawyer must be considered a barrier to access and it has been questioned how

347

---

60.   The Law Society, 'Entry Trends' (Law Society) <http://www.lawsociety.org.uk/Law-careers/Becoming-a-solicitor/Entry-trends/>.

61.   The Law Society, 'Trends in the Solicitors' Profession: Annual Statistics Report 2015' (Law Society, April 2016) <http://www.lawsociety.org.uk/support-services/research-trends/annual-statistics-report-2015/>.

62.   Richard Abel, *English Lawyers between Market and State: The Politics of Professionalism* (OUP 2003) 134.

63.   Clare McGlynn, 'Women, Representation and the Legal Academy' (1999) 19 *Legal Studies* 68, 89.

64.   Richard Abel, *English Lawyers between Market and State* (OUP 2003) 129.

65.   That is to say, those institutions that were formerly known as polytechnics and which were given university status in 1992.

66.   See Mike Cuthbert, *Law Student 2000* (2003) <http://www.ukcle.ac.uk/directions/previous/issue7/cuthbert.html> although questions have been raised as to whether this is necessarily correct in terms of the Bar, see D Mason, 'A Ticking Time Bomb?' (2004) 154 *New Law Journal* 1601.

realistic it is to suggest that vocational training is anything other than the preserve of the middle classes.[67]

The position as to the representation of the ethnic minorities shows some optimism in recent years. In 1992 only 2 per cent of solicitors were from the ethnic minorities whereas by 2015 this had risen to 13.9 per cent of all solicitors with practising certificates which is a significant jump. The position at the Bar is approximately the same with 11.9 per cent of those practising in 2015 identifying themselves as belonging to an ethnic minority. Again this is an increase from recent years and demonstrates that some progress is being made and it certainly compares favourably with, for example, the judiciary where it will be remembered that the position is not representative. For completeness, the position with QCs should be noted. In respect of the latest competition (2015–16) only thirty-two (13.5 per cent) of the applicants identified themselves as coming from an ethnic minority background. Of these, nine (28 per cent) were appointed.[68] This perhaps demonstrates that a glass ceiling exists although the Bar will argue that it will take time for the increased numbers of ethnic minority barristers to reach the point at which they could make a credible application for silk.

It is suggested that the two principal disadvantages for ethnic minority students are finance and contacts. Finance is always a thorny issue but it is frequently stated that those from the ethnic minorities are often less affluent than those from non-ethnic minority backgrounds. Lammy notes that the professions have attempted to use their funds to create scholarships, with the Law Society (then) providing £150,000 but he states:

> I have to say, as a minister, that £150,000 when students have debts of £35,000 to £40,000 is not going to reach the sorts of numbers we need.[69]

Whilst this is undoubtedly correct it does perhaps miss the point that the debts are accrued because of the government's policy of introducing tuition fees for higher education courses and replacing university grants with loans. In the 1960s and 1970s it was possible to get a grant from some local education authorities to study for the equivalent of the LPC or BPTC and yet now just the fees for these courses can be in excess of £10,000. This is undoubtedly causing difficulties in terms of encouraging access to the legal profession, and this is likely to become worse with students now incurring between £14,000 and £16,000 of debts per annum during the academic stage.[70] The common response to this of course is that lawyers can expect high salaries but it has been noted in this chapter already that a barrister will start on a minimum of £10,000 and a solicitor on the national minimum wage whereas the starting salary for a trainee (graduate) manager at McDonalds restaurants is between £21,500 and £24,500 plus private healthcare benefits.

The second issue raised by Lammy is contacts. Whilst the era of the 'old boys' club' is probably gone, it is still necessary to maintain contacts in order to progress within the profession and he notes that without the contacts it is difficult to get work experience and then the necessary pupillage or training contracts. The position is, according

67. Richard Abel, *English Lawyers between Market and State* (OUP 2003) 121.
68. Bar Standards Board, 'Queens Counsel Statistics—Data Spreadsheet 2010–2015' (Bar Standards Board 2015) <https://www.barstandardsboard.org.uk/media-centre/research-and-statistics/statistics/queen's-counsel-statistics/>.
69. David Lammy *Speech to the Black Solicitors' Network* (Department for Constitutional Affairs 2004).
70. Tuition fees of £9,000 then maintenance loans of either £5,500 (outside London) or £7,675 (inside London).

to Lammy, particularly severe within the major city firms where he alleges black and ethnic minority members are under-represented at management level. The response to this has come from the ethnic minorities themselves through the formation of official associations, most notably the *Black Solicitors' Network*. The position is arguably no better at the Bar where few Masters of the Bench are members of ethnic minorities and where the criteria for appointment as a Master of the Bench continue to relate to factors that are more likely to favour white, middle-class members than members of the ethnic minorities.

10.7 Other legal professions

It was noted earlier that, although it is often considered that the legal profession is divided into two branches, there is an argument that two further branches are developing and these will be discussed briefly.

10.7.1 Legal executives

In January 2012 the (then) Institute of Legal Executives was awarded a Royal Charter and became known as the Chartered Institute of Legal Executives (CILEX). Traditionally legal executives were considered to be assistants to solicitors but increasingly they have become recognized as a profession in their own right, something that the award of a Royal Charter perhaps recognizes.

The beginning of the change of status to legal executives was arguably the CLSA 1990 reforms which provided legal executives with limited rights of audience and allowed them to undertake some litigation work in their own right. There are approximately 22,000 legal executives but more will be in training to become a legal executive. There are a number of different stages to qualifying as a member of CILEX and only when a person has become a Fellow of the Institute can they truly refer to themselves as a 'legal executive', although before then they can refer to themselves as a member of CILEX.

10.7.1.1 Training

Unlike solicitors and barristers, legal executives need not be graduates when they commence their training and indeed the minimum academic qualifications are merely GCSEs. However more recently, a graduate entry scheme has begun and, as with the other principal branches, where a person is a graduate in law an exemption from the academic stage can be granted. It is fair to say, however, that the vast majority of entrants to CILEX continue to be non-law graduates. An attraction of becoming a legal executive is that, unlike for solicitors and barristers, all the training can take place alongside work. Accordingly, instead of accruing debts by attending university, a prospective legal executive will be paid from the moment that he starts with a firm.

To become a qualified Chartered Legal Executive (also known as a Fellow of CILEX) it is necessary to complete both the academic and work-related qualifications. The academic stage is either a specialist fast-track academic qualification for graduates or alternatively the completion of two diplomas. The first is a level 3 *Professional Diploma in Law and Practice* and the second is a level 6 *Higher Diploma in Law and Practice*. The level 3 diploma will ordinarily take two years (one year of which a person will be working) and the level 6 diploma a further two years (both of which take place while working).

The work-related qualification is that a person has to have five years' relevant work under the supervision of a solicitor. Where a person proceeds through the diploma route this will mean that they have only a further two years' work (as they will have undertaken three while studying) whereas a graduate may not have any (unless they have worked, for example, as a paralegal). This does mean that a graduate is arguably worse off than a non-graduate in that they will qualify more slowly since the full five years is required.

Like members of the other branches of the legal profession, a legal executive is expected to continue to develop his education and training through CPD.

10.7.1.2 Practice

Whilst both barristers and solicitors will frequently specialize, they need not and a number remain as general practitioners who will undertake a variety of work. Legal executives, on the other hand, will tend to specialize in an area and remain in that area of work. Legal executives will tend to practise only in civil law although there is no reason why they could not, for example, also qualify as accredited police-station representatives but their practice will tend to be civil-orientated. Legal executives will choose their specialism while training and in order to get the qualifying employment experience required to become a Fellow, they will focus on that area. That said, although they tend to specialize, it can be in a reasonably broad way and could encompass subject headings (eg family law, company law, etc).

A significant part of their work will be assisting a solicitor, and it is worth noting that legal executives do not have independent practising rights; that is to say, they must be supervised by solicitors and cannot create a firm that exists solely of legal executives although following the reforms of the LSA 2007 it is now possible for a legal executive to own shares in a practice (and indeed this has been one of the main reasons why some firms have begun *Legal Disciplinary Practices*). Much of the work of a legal executive will be quite similar to the provision of legal advice by solicitors and will frequently involve dealing with clients direct. Following the reforms of the CLSA 1990 legal executives are now entitled to have limited rights of audience[71] which are generally procedural matters not in open court in the magistrates' and county courts.

It is now possible for a Fellow to seek to become an advocate. This requires additional training and CPD requirements. A Fellow must undertake specialist training to gain one of three certificates (although there is no reason why a person cannot hold more than one certificate at the same time). The certificates are in civil proceedings (providing rights of audience in open court in the county court (except in family proceedings) and magistrates' court or in tribunals or coroners' courts), family proceedings (providing rights of audience in all matters in the county court and the family proceedings court (magistrates' court) or in coroners' courts), or criminal proceedings (all work within the magistrates' court (including the youth court), the Crown Court for an appeal against a decision of the magistrates' court and rights to appear in chambers in the Crown Court or High Court for bail, as well as in coroners' courts).

---

71. The rights of audience available to legal executives are set out in *Legal Services Act 2007*, sch 3, para 1(7).

These rights of audience are comparable to the rights of audience a solicitor has upon qualification (but not comparable to the higher rights that they can accrue by becoming a solicitor–advocate).

10.7.1.3 Qualifying as a solicitor

Although CILEX is keen on its standing as a profession in its own right, a significant incentive for those who join CILEX is that it is also a path to becoming a solicitor. The normal route for qualifying as a solicitor is to study law at undergraduate or graduate level, then undertake a vocational training course and finally undertake a training contract. However, the Law Society will also allow CILEX Fellows to qualify as a solicitor once they have the requisite experience and have passed the conversion course. Once qualified, a CILEX Fellow need not undertake a training contract because the minimum of five years' experience that has been undertaken to become a Fellow acts as the equivalent of a training contract.

The advantages of a CILEX Fellow converting include less restriction on their practice, including the ability to become sole practitioners or to set up their own practices, and also to study for wider rights of audience in the higher courts. It is not known precisely how many CILEX Fellows convert to solicitors, and there are some anecdotal comments about how well their future careers compare to traditionally qualified solicitors, but within a small to medium-sized firm it would be an attractive method of qualifying, not least because of the fact that from the very earliest stage the legal executive will have been earning money.

10.7.2 Paralegals

One of the more recent developments of the legal profession is the so-called 'paralegal'. This was originally an American term, but has become an established part of the English legal framework. Traditionally the paralegal was a euphemism for someone who would photocopy documents and prepare extremely basic documentation but over recent years there has been an expansion in the number of non-qualified people who assist in the execution of legal work.

Within the United States a paralegal is a separate profession in its own right (although it bears some similarity to our legal executives) but in the United Kingdom this has not yet taken place. That said some bodies are trying to create a fourth branch to the profession, with a company creating a national association to provide training for paralegals and CILEX now also operating. The emphasis on this group is on those who have no formal legal education and, to an extent, it can be seen that this is attempting to compete with legal executives, but whereas the latter have statutory recognition, paralegals currently have none and so it has to be questioned why someone would wish to progress through this route.

The more usual type of paralegal within England and Wales is someone who does have a legal background. A person in this group will normally become a paralegal at one of two points in their life. The first is after the completion of their law honours degree and before going on to do either the LPC or BPTC, and the second point is after completing the LPC or BPTC but where they have not secured a training contract or pupillage. For those in this group, it is likely that the post of paralegal will be viewed as a temporary one, with the intention of using it as a stepping stone to a position as a solicitor or barrister. The logic behind this is sound in that as a paralegal one will be meeting members of the profession every day, and where the post sought is in a firm of solicitors it is quite possible that the company that hires the person as a paralegal may, when they recruit a trainee solicitor, look favourably upon someone who has proven themselves already.

Since there is no single definition of a paralegal it is not really possible to say what their duties would be, they will inevitably differ between the firms and organizations that use them. The common theme is that in private practice they will normally act as 'fee earners', that is to say they will conduct a limited caseload for which the company will be able to bill the client. Precisely what work is undertaken will depend on the qualifications and experience of the paralegal but it is likely to include document preparation (witness statements, claim forms, defences, etc) and may even include limited advocacy work in tribunals and non-contested issues.

Paralegals are not restricted to the private sector although they may not be known by this title within the public sector. However, if one were to consider the work of case-workers within, for example, the CPS and the *Criminal Cases Review Commission* it could be argued that these are undertaking comparable work. Caseworkers will undertake much administrative and quasi-legal work on a live case and will often help instruct counsel, attend court, and provide summaries of evidence etc. The work is vital to the smooth operation of these organizations and can provide an interesting career for those who have not sought to become professionally qualified or who have not been able to access the relevant training elements to qualify.

10.8 Complaints and discipline

Lawyers, like any profession, will include a mixture of people, including some who undertake their work inappropriately. The professions must have a system in place that allows for investigations to be undertaken in respect of malpractice.

10.8.1 Codes of conduct

Both barristers and solicitors are bound by (separate) codes of conduct. It has been suggested that one of the purpose of Codes is they 'educate both legal neophytes and qualified lawyers as to how they should behave'[72] although they also act as a statement of standards that the professional bodies indicate to the wider community they will adhere to. They are a relatively recent invention[73] in part because prior to this it was thought that the professions should be able to regulate themselves in looser forms; the difficulty this brings, of course, is a complete lack of transparency and accountability.

The Codes operated by the Law Society (set out in conjunction with the SRA) and Bar Council (set out in conjunction with the BSB) are significantly different, although this is in part because of the nature of the professions. Since barristers cannot form partnerships there is no need for detailed description of the circumstances of when partnerships may be formed and how (were they to join an LDP or ABS then the regulations of both structures are discussed under the SRA rules and barristers would have to adhere to that aspect while also maintaining the standards set out by the BSB for barristers). Barristers will not ordinarily 'hold' money for a lay client, this is done by

72. Donald Nicolson and Julian Webb, *Professional Legal Ethics* (OUP 1999) 96.
73. Donald Nicolson and Julian Webb, *Professional Legal Ethics* (OUP 1999) 98.

the solicitor, and accordingly there was traditionally no need for significant sections of rules that relate to the transparency of lay funds but this has changed slightly by the rules relating to direct access and now separate rules and training exist for those barristers who accept direct access. However, this need not explain all issues and it can be questioned whether the two Codes take a different approach, with the Bar Code taking a 'purposive' approach which seeks to set out the parameters within which a barrister shall practise and the Law Society taking a 'literal' or 'prescriptive' approach whereby the Code operates as a series of specific rules governing the practice of law.

10.8.1.1 Barristers

Discipline is, strictly speaking, a matter for the Inn of Court that a barrister belongs to but all four Inns have established common procedures to ensure that complaints and action are dealt with appropriately. Until comparatively recently, the Bar Council dealt with matters of discipline through its *Professional Conduct and Complaints Committee* but recently this was replaced by the *Bar Standards Board* (BSB).

The BSB is an arm's-length organization of the Bar. Whilst it is funded by the Bar Council and half of the board is from the Bar (although its chair and seven other members are lay members), it is considered to be independent from the Bar Council and no member of the BSB is part of the Bar Council.

In October 2010 the *Legal Ombudsman* (see 'Office of Legal Complaints and the Legal Ombudsman') came into effect and now lay complaints (ie those from a lay client) will be made to that organization which includes the right to order compensation. The *Legal Ombudsman* does not have jurisdiction to consider allegations of professional misconduct and such matters continue to be within the jurisdiction of the BSB. If the BSB believes that a barrister has breached the Code of Conduct then the matter is sent to the Professional Conduct Committee (PCC), which used to be referred to as the Complaints Committee. After an initial investigation the matter may, if it is not dealt with administratively, be passed to the Committee who will adjudicate on the matter.

The PCC includes both barristers and lay members. They have the following options open to them:

- dismiss the complaint (but they may only do so if the majority of lay members present agree)
- dismiss the complaint but require the barrister to apologize in writing to the complainant
- dismiss the complaint but advise the barrister as to his future conduct
- decide that no further action should be taken on the complaint
- direct that a formal written warning or financial penalty be imposed
- refer the matter for resolution by the consent procedure or a Disciplinary Tribunal.

The consent procedure is a less formal way of resolving complaints that the PCC decides has substance to them. It is the equivalent of a 'summary procedure' and should apply where there is no substantial dispute of facts and where it is unlikely that any sanction would include suspension from practice or disbarment. As the name suggests, the barrister who is the subject of the action must consent to the matter being dealt with under the procedure and if this is not forthcoming then the matter proceeds to the Disciplinary Tribunal. The sanctions that can be imposed on the procedure include a fine of up to £50,000, requirement to complete additional CPD, reprimands, or advice.

The Disciplinary Tribunal is reserved for the most serious matters. A tribunal will consist of either three or five persons with the former not being able to suspend a barrister for more than three months or disbar a barrister. If, when hearing a matter, a three-person tribunal decides that its powers are not sufficient then it can require the matter to proceed to a five-person panel.

A three-person panel will ordinarily consist of a QC as chair, a lay member, and a barrister. Where the person subject to action is himself a QC then a judge may be appointed to chair the tribunal. A five-person panel will ordinarily consist of a judge, two barristers (who could include a QC), and two lay members.

The panels usually proceed as though it is a criminal trial (ie the 'prosecution' go first, evidence is tendered and resisted etc). The proceedings take place in open and any findings are listed on the website of the BSB.

10.8.1.2 Solicitors

Traditionally the Law Society regulates the activities of all solicitors, including solicitor–advocates, although solicitors are technically officers of the senior courts (something that barristers are not) and so the court theoretically has the power to regulate solicitors' conduct too although it would be rare for it to do this except through, for example, wasted costs orders (which can also be imposed against barristers).

The Law Society, like the Bar Council, has created an arm's-length organization for its regulation, known as the *Solicitors Regulation Authority* (SRA). The SRA, like the BSB, created an independent system for dealing with complaints from the general public which was known as the *Legal Complaints Service* (LCS). From October 2010 the *Legal Ombudsman* assumed direct responsibility for complaints received from members of the public.

Where there has been professional misconduct by a solicitor then this remains a matter for the SRA, and this will include matters relating to, for example, CPD or the misappropriation of client funds.

Adjudicating on disciplinary matters relating to solicitors is the responsibility of the *Solicitors Disciplinary Tribunal* (SDT). This is a statutory tribunal established under s 46 *Solicitors' Act 1974*. The members of the tribunal are appointed by the Master of the Rolls[74] and include solicitors and laypersons (who may not be barristers or solicitors). One of the solicitor members shall be elected by the members of the tribunal to be President and will serve as President for three years although this is renewable once. Two vice-presidents (one lay member and one solicitor member) shall also be elected, again for a single renewable term of three years.[75]

The tribunal sits in divisions of three; two solicitors (one of which will chair) and one lay member. The tribunal is formal and takes the format of a court trial. Ordinarily the SRA will 'prosecute' the matter and it is empowered, in very serious

---

74. It has been noted already that the Master of the Rolls traditionally had responsibility for the management of the Rolls of Solicitors and whilst this obligation has been transferred to the SRA the Master of the Rolls continues to exercise certain administrative regulatory functions.

75. *Solicitors (Disciplinary Proceedings) Rules 2007*, SI 2007/3588, r 3.

matters, to instruct counsel where appropriate. The tribunal has significant sanctions including:

- striking a solicitor from the Roll
- suspending a solicitor from practising
- reprimanding a solicitor
- fining a solicitor[76]
- excluding a person from legal aid work
- banning the person from working as a solicitor.

The tribunal will also consider requests from solicitors suspended (or struck) from the Roll to resume practice.

An appeal from decisions of the tribunal exists to the High Court[77] although certain administrative matters can be dealt with by the Master of the Rolls. Where the High Court hears the matter it may 'make such order on an appeal … as it may think fit'.[78]

10.8.1.3 Independent oversight

Although both the Bar and Law Society have attempted to show independence through the creation of arm's-length regulatory bodies, there has long been concern about the regulation of lawyers. In 2003 the Lord Chancellor created a review of the regulation of the legal profession and chose Sir David Clementi as its chair, the report being delivered in 2004. Whilst Clementi was broadly sympathetic to some parts of the regulatory systems he did believe it was necessary to increase the accountability of the professional bodies, especially in connection with the complaints procedures.

The government responded in the LSA 2007, which has transformed the oversight of the professions. The Act has two principal issues of relevance here. The first is the creation of an *Office for Legal Complaints* (OLC)[79] and the second is the establishment of the *Legal Services Board* (LSB).[80]

The LSB has a statutory responsibility, inter alia, to ensure standards of regulation, training, and education. Whilst therefore the LSB does not replace either the BSB or SRA it holds these bodies to account on matters such as educational requirements (including both the academic and vocational stages), continuing professional development, and the regulation of lawyers. A body can only act as a regulator for legal services if it is approved by the LSB. Whilst the SRA and BSB are the most obvious regulators other bodies do have approval too, including CILEX (through the ILEX Professional Standards Board), the *Council for Licensed Conveyancers*, and the *Chartered Institute of Patent Attorneys* amongst others. The breadth of regulators perhaps reinforces the fact that the term 'lawyer' is not restricted to solicitors and barristers and the concept of the legal profession within England and Wales is more complicated than many may think.

Along with approving the regulators the LSB has considerable control over how the regulatory bodies discharge their functions. Under the LSA 2007 the regulators must

---

76. Any fine is payable to HM Treasury not to the Law Society.
77. *Solicitors Act 1974*, s 49.
78. *Solicitors Act 1974*, s 49(4).
79. *Legal Services Act 2007*, s 114.
80. *Legal Services Act 2007*, s 2.

consult the LSB before they change any of their rules of professional conduct, and the LSB must give consent to any regulatory changes. This ensures that the bodies are accountable for all aspects of the regulatory process, ensuring that the process is fair, transparent, and accountable to both the professions and service users.

The LSB is chaired by a layperson and consists of the chair, the chief executive, and between seven and ten persons appointed by the Lord Chancellor (there are currently seven members excluding the chair) although this is now also done in consultation with the Lord Chief Justice. A majority of the LSB must be lay[81] meaning not qualified as lawyers.

The LSB must create a 'consumer panel'[82] which includes representation from those who seek the work of lawyers. The panel cannot include a member of the LSB (other than who is appointed to chair the panel, who will be a member of the LSB), a member of the OLC, a lawyer, or member of a regulator of lawyers. The panel will provide advice to the LSB as to the functioning of the provision of legal advice and, presumably, issues such as whether regulation is working.

Office of Legal Complaints and the Legal Ombudsman

As noted earlier, the LSB is responsible for the creation of the *Office of Legal Complaints* (OLC). This consists of a chair and between six and eight members appointed by the LSB with the approval of the Lord Chancellor. The majority of the members must be lay (meaning a non-lawyer). Whilst an ombudsman may sit on the board of the OLC[83] they cannot constitute a majority nor can an ombudsman be chair. These provisions are to ensure that the OLC is both lay-led and is constituted in a way that can hold the ombudsman to account.

The primary responsibility of OLC is to create the *Legal Ombudsman*.[84] Whilst the term appears in the singular the reality is that there is more than one ombudsman, the most senior being known as the *Chief Ombudsman*. The Ombudsman has assumed responsibility for all complaints from service users about the work of lawyers. Thus the BSB and SRA are no longer empowered to examine complaints from members of the public who have engaged a lawyer and who are dissatisfied with their service. The Ombudsman is designed to be fully independent from the professions in order to provide reassurance to the public that any complaint will be treated fairly.

Once a complaint has been registered it will be considered and an analysis made of whether, for example, it meets the criteria of the scheme.[85] One of the more important aspects of the scheme is that the initial complaints should be directed to the lawyer first. With barristers it is likely that this is simply registering a complaint with the barrister himself but with solicitors the SRA requires each firm to have a complaints procedure and this must be complied with.

One of the more controversial aspects (at least from the perspective of the lawyers) is that each complaint leads to a 'case fee' which is paid not by the complainant but by the lawyer. That said, the fee is not charged where the complaint is not upheld *and* the Ombudsman accepts that the lawyer took all reasonable steps to resolve the complaint under their own procedure. The fee is currently charged as a 'flat rate' and is £400 per

81.   *Legal Services Act 2007*, sch 1, para 2.
82.   *Legal Services Act 2007*, s 8.
83.   *Legal Services Act 2007*, sch 15.
84.   *Legal Services Act 2007*, s 115.
85.   The website of the Legal Ombudsman produces guidance to the rules of complaints. A link to these can be found on the Online Resource Centre.

case. The complainant does not pay any fee for making a complaint and so it could be thought that they are free to dispute any degree of service, including fees, just to be a nuisance but the protection that the lawyer has, of course, is that so long as the guidance is complied with then the complaint will be dismissed and no fee paid.

The Ombudsman states that they do not 'take sides' and their initial approach is to deal with the matter informally at first (which would not attract a case fee). If this is not possible then they will proceed to conduct an investigation. Their approach is to consider all the evidence submitted by both the complainant and lawyer and decide whether the standard of service has been appropriate and whether a legal wrong has been committed, for example, a breach of confidence etc.

The principal powers of the Ombudsman are to require a lawyer to tender an apology, pay compensation, or rectify a mistake that has been made. Where they believe that action by a court is required to resolve a complaint then the Ombudsman has the power to refer a matter to a relevant court. This may be required, for example, where an improper charge has been placed on property. Where the Ombudsman orders an apology or compensation to be paid then the lawyer is under a professional obligation to comply with the order of the Ombudsman and failure to do so will amount to professional misconduct.

It is quite possible that during the investigation the Ombudsman considers that the complaint raises issues of professional misconduct. Whilst the Ombudsman cannot deal with such matters it can pass the case to the regulators to action on their behalf. Where the matter raises issues of both misconduct and inappropriate service then both matters can proceed independently.

10.8.1.4 Immunity

Those of you who are also studying the *Law of Tort* at the same time as the module you are currently on will be familiar with the idea of negligence. For those of you who are not currently studying Tort, the law recognizes that where someone holds themselves out as a professional in an area of service, they should be accountable if they fail to meet a basic standard of care in the discharge of their duties, known as being negligent.[86] Should an advocate be liable in law for the negligent handling of cases?

Traditionally the answer was 'no'—a lay client could not sue an advocate on the basis that they lost a case because of their advocate's negligence,[87] but eventually this immunity began to become restricted solely to negligence in court or litigation papers[88] and where a lawyer gave advice negligently an action could arise. There were a number of reasons why this was so, perhaps the most commonly cited being that it could lead to re-litigation. If a person charged with a crime is convicted then the way to challenge this decision is by way of an appeal. If, the argument went, an advocate could be sued for negligence then when the appeals were exhausted a person would have nothing to lose by suing his advocate for negligence. If he won this action then would this grant him the right to another appeal?

In *Hall v Simons*[89] the House of Lords was called to re-examine whether there was a justification for advocates to have an absolute exemption from negligence and they decided there was not. The House carefully considered every possible reason

---

86. See, for example, *Hedley Byrne & Co v Heller & Partners* [1964] AC 465.
87. See, for example, *Rondel v Worsley* [1969] 1 AC 191.
88. *Saif Ali v Sydney Smith Mitchell & Co* [1980] AC 198 comprehensively discussed the immunity.
89. [2002] 1 AC 615.

why the immunity should remain and decided each was unconvincing and that it was against public policy to exempt one profession from litigation when others, arguably with a higher stake for public policy exemptions (eg doctors), have no exemption. The House did not believe that their decision would 'open the floodgates' as they pointed out that the rules of civil litigation permit a judge to strike out vexatious proceedings at an early stage.[90] The House also argued that criminal practitioners would have an additional protection in that using civil negligence laws to challenge convictions would almost certainly be viewed as an abuse of process by the courts and the action quickly stayed.[91]

The decision in *Hall v Simons* was eminently sensible: it is difficult to justify granting immunity to one profession when real harm could be caused by the negligent actions of an advocate. There is not one standard of negligence and since the case there have been few cases alleging negligence perhaps demonstrating that the fears of the profession were unfounded.

10.9 Legal ethics

The issue of discipline was discussed earlier and it was suggested that the Codes governing the professions in effect set out the standards by which a barrister or solicitor should conduct himself. A central part of this conduct can be summed up as ethics and yet it is comparatively rare for students to be introduced to legal ethics during an undergraduate course.[92] However, it is important that you are able to understand some of the ethical issues that lawyers encounter.

10.9.1 Responsibility to clients

Some of the more significant ethical issues relate to what a lawyer can, and cannot, do in respect of their clients (normally meaning their 'lay client' when it is a barrister). Complete books have been written about the issue of ethics but in this section some of the main ethical duties that arise will be discussed.

10.9.1.1 Providing advice not seeking control

Lawyers provide advice but one of the questions that arises is how far they may go in terms of encouraging people to act on that advice. In the criminal context this will ordinarily take place in relation to a 'plea bargain' (discussed in more depth in Chapter 12). However, the concept is wider than this and needs to be outlined here.

A lawyer is supposed to serve his client's best interests but also allow the client to act autonomously so that they are making decisions on the basis of advice. However, concern has been raised as to whether the actions of lawyers seek to push this envelope and actually control or manipulate the decisions of the clients.[93] Perhaps one of the classic examples of this is where a lawyer 'misleads clients in personal injury matters by playing down expectations as to likely compensation so as to encourage

90. *Hall v Simons* [2002] 1 AC 615, 681–3 (Lord Steyn).
91. *Hall v Simons* [2002] 1 AC 615, 679–81.
92. Andrew Boon, *The Ethics and Conduct of Lawyers in England and Wales* (3rd edn, Hart Publishing 2014) 178.
93. Donald Nicolson and Julian Webb, *Professional Legal Ethics* (OUP 1999) 123.

earlier settlement'.[94] It has been remarked that the advantage of this is that there can be a high turnover of work through the processing of more cases.[95] However, it could equally work in reverse whereby for a high-value claim it may be in the interests of a lawyer to raise expectations so that early settlement offers are rejected, thus prolonging the litigation and increasing the costs.

It is essential that lawyers simply set out the legal position and put forward options to the client, but ultimately it must be for the client to decide which option to take. The possible tactics are for the lawyer to explain but it is important that a client is not 'bounced' into accepting something that he does not wish to do. This is particularly true in respect of plea bargains where there is evidence to suggest that some people will feel pressurized by the lawyer to plead guilty even though they believe they are innocent.[96] This simply cannot be justified and it is a particular duty of a judge to ensure that any guilty plea is being tendered correctly and not simply for the sake of convenience.[97]

10.9.1.2 Client confidentiality

One of the most important ethical issues is that of client confidentiality. Yet interestingly it is a duty that could involve a lawyer in other ethical difficulties, for example when a client plans to commit a crime.[98] The justification for the rule is that a person must be entitled to engage a lawyer to seek advice without worrying whether he will inadvertently disclose something that would undermine his own case.[99]

Some have, however, criticized the rule in that whilst it does protect both the individual and lawyer it does nothing to assist third parties or society who may be affected by that individual's actions.[100] Indeed the rule could even cause significant harm to society or an individual since client confidentiality will not be waived even where to do so would protect an innocent person from going to prison.[101]

> **Example** Client confidentiality
>
> Wendy has been accused of the murder of Vanessa. Trevor has been accused of theft but when talking to his counsel, John, he indicates that he was the person who actually killed Vanessa not Wendy. John is bound by client confidentiality and cannot tell anyone what Trevor has said even though Wendy may be sentenced to life imprisonment as a result of this.

The only exceptions to this rule are where someone is at risk of serious harm or where a lawyer is being used to facilitate a crime[102] but the circumstances surrounding these exceptions are somewhat confused, not least because the suggestion is that it is only against *serious* harm, so what happens where less serious harm is to be inflicted? Also, what does

94. Donald Nicolson and Julian Webb, *Professional Legal Ethics* (OUP 1999) 137.
95. Andrew Boon, *The Ethics and Conduct of Lawyers in England and Wales* (3rd edn, Hart Publishing 2014) 376.
96. Fred Phillips, *Ethics of the Legal Profession* (Cavendish Publishing, 2004) 145–6.
97. Phillip Otton, 'The Role of the Judge in Criminal Cases' in Mike McConville and Geoffrey Wilson (eds) *The Handbook of the Criminal Justice Process* (OUP 2002) 326.
98. Donald Nicolson and Julian Webb, *Professional Legal Ethics* (OUP 1999) 248.
99. Donald Nicolson and Julian Webb, *Professional Legal Ethics* (OUP 1999) 249.
100. Donald Nicolson and Julian Webb, *Professional Legal Ethics* (OUP 1999) 253.
101. Donald Nicolson and Julian Webb, *Professional Legal Ethics* (OUP 1999) 254.
102. Andrew Boon, *The Ethics and Conduct of Lawyers in England and Wales* (3rd edn, Hart Publishing 2014) ch 10.

facilitate a crime mean? It appears to include crimes in the future[103] so that, at least, a person cannot go to a lawyer and ask for advice on how to commit 'the perfect murder'.

Money laundering

In recent years some of the most controversial aspects of the rule governing client confidentiality are in respect of money laundering which is described as:

> the process by which 'dirty money'—the proceeds of crime—is changed so that the money appears 'to originate from a legitimate source'.

Solicitors are arguably a target for such behaviour since they hold money for clients and can make transactions on behalf of their clients (including investments, property deals, etc). In recent years the government has attempted to ensure that the proceeds of crime are recovered and this culminated in the *Proceeds of Crime Act 2002* (PoCA 2002) which has led to a statutory exception to the rule of confidentiality.

The Act creates a positive duty on persons to report money laundering, including 'reasonable suspicions'[104] and the fact that it was given in confidential situations is no defence. Further offences are created to deal with situations where, for example, a solicitor tips off his client that money recovery procedures have begun[105] or where a person becomes involved in a transaction that he knows, or suspects, to involve money laundering.[106] It has been suggested that all solicitors must be fully familiar with the money laundering regulations.[107] However, recent decisions have cast doubt on this, with the suggestion that legal professional privilege may 'trump' PoCA 2002.

Legal professional privilege is something that you will study in more depth during a course on *Evidence* but is an offshoot of the confidentiality regime. In essence, anything said to a lawyer in contemplation of, or during, judicial proceedings is privileged—ie it may not be disclosed and is not admissible in court.

II\ Case Box *Bowman v Fels*

The principal decision in this area is *Bowman v Fels*.[108] This was a family case. The solicitors acting for one party received documents that made them believe that repairs to the matrimonial property had been included (illegally) in the business accounts of that party. This could amount to money laundering (although not exactly the typical scenario) and the solicitors believed that they needed to make a disclosure to comply with PoCA 2002 and prevent them from committing an offence.

The Court of Appeal decided that if something arose in the course of ordinary proceedings then there would be no duty to disclose this to the authorities as it would be privileged information. The Court suggested that privilege would override PoCA 2002 except when the solicitor was deliberately trying to act dishonestly, ie by facilitating money laundering with the knowledge that he was so doing.

---

103.   Andrew Boon, *The Ethics and Conduct of Lawyers in England and Wales* (3rd edn, Hart Publishing 2014) ch 10.
104.   *Proceeds of Crime Act 2002*, s 330.
105.   *Proceeds of Crime Act 2002*, s 333A.
106.   *Proceeds of Crime Act 2002*, s 328.
107.   Fred Phillips, *Ethics of the Legal Profession* (Cavendish Publishing 2004) 79.
108.   [2005] EWCA Civ 226.

It is easy to overestimate the importance of *Bowman v Fels*. Although it is an important case[109] it does not state that lawyers are exempt from PoCA 2002 but only decides that if they become suspicious of activity *during the course* of litigation then they do not need to report the matter. Accordingly, if the suspicions arise outside of litigation or if it is more than suspicion—ie direct knowledge—then presumably the matter must be reported.

10.9.1.3 Conflicts of interest

Another significant ethical issue that arises in respect of lawyers is that there must not be a conflict of interest when representing a party. To an extent this has been discussed already in respect of part-time judges who sit on cases where a client of the firm is a party to the proceedings (see 9.3.3). A similar position arises in respect of representing clients, ie a firm should not represent more than one person in the same or similar proceedings. However, there are multitude of different guises to this head of ethics including, perhaps most notably, where the proposed transaction or litigation has an impact on the lawyer's personal interests.[110]

 PERSONAL CONFLICTS

There are numerous examples of when there may be a personal conflict with the solicitor. Perhaps the classic example is where a client wishes to make a will but wishes to leave a substantial amount of money to the solicitor. It would not be appropriate in those circumstances for the solicitor to act unless the client took further independent legal advice. Arguably this could also apply where, for example, the interest is personal but slightly detached. For example, if the solicitor is the treasurer of a local charity and the client wished to leave a substantial amount of money to that charity, there would still almost certainly be a personal conflict of interest.

Perhaps the most common (potential) conflict of interest is that which arises between clients. The rule appears quite clear here: if a dispute arises between two people who are clients of the lawyer then he must not act for either.[111] This rule is not a personal one and so it does not just apply to the individual solicitor dealing with the matter but the whole firm. Accordingly, this does mean that where a firm is engaged by a party they must undertake a careful check of existing clients to ensure that they will not create a conflict of interest.

 QUESTION FOR REFLECTION

Is it realistic to suggest that a large firm will have no conflicts of interest? For example, if a firm has offices across the United Kingdom is it a conflict of interest if their Birmingham office takes a client who is in conflict with a client serviced by the Exeter office? However, is geography a sufficient 'wall' in the era of the Internet and global communication systems?

---

109.   See Michael Pace, 'Litigation and Money Laundering after *Bowman v Fels*' (2005) 4 *Journal of Personal Injury Law* 345.
110.   Fred Phillips, *Ethics of the Legal Profession* (Cavendish Publishing 2004) 294 provides a useful summary of possible conflicts of interest.
111.   Andrew Boon, *The Ethics and Conduct of Lawyers in England and Wales* (3rd edn, Hart Publishing 2014) 379.

There is an exception to the rule[112] and this is where a lawyer does not have any 'confidential information' in respect of the other party. In those circumstances it is possible to act although it may be unwise to do so. However, some argue that this is not sufficient protection and that the mere fact that they used to be a client should prevent the law firm acting for the new client.[113] This is justified on the basis that although there may be no confidential information in existence, the solicitor may have knowledge of their anxiety or how they react to stress etc which could provide a tactical advantage. Similar issues were raised in *Re Z*.[114] A husband and wife were involved in high-value divorce proceedings that had taken over a decade because of reconciliations. The wife was being represented by Mr A from F & Co, the senior partner of which was Mrs F, who used to represent the husband when she worked with the firm G & Co.

The husband sought an injunction preventing F & Co from representing the wife. The High Court applied the ruling of the House of Lords in *Prince Jefri Bolkiah v KPMG*[115] which had said that an injunction can be granted where the claimant can show a real risk that confidential information could be disclosed, however slight that risk is, unless the respondent solicitors can show that they have taken steps to remove the risk. The High Court in *Halewood International Limited v Addleshaw Booth & Co*[116] ruled that confidential information may continue in memories and that whilst a person may not recollect something, this may alter as circumstances change and memories are prompted.

Brodey J ruled in *Re Z* that because Mrs F had acted for the husband for over a year it is likely that she would continue to be aware of some of the circumstances and possibly also the manner in which he conducted himself and business, which could be relevant. Whilst F & Co had undertaken to ensure Mrs F was not involved in the case, the fact that she was the 'hands-on' senior partner of a small firm meant that there was a real risk that confidentiality could be breached. This case perhaps demonstrates how seriously the courts take potential breaches of confidentiality.

10.9.2 Practical ethical issues

Alongside the particular relationship with a client other ethical issues arise in respect of those who seek to practise law. Two of the more commonly raised ethical issues will be discussed in this area: defending the guilty (which is inevitably linked to the 'cab rank rule') and whether those who have been convicted of crimes should be allowed to become lawyers.

10.9.2.1 Defending the guilty

If you qualify as a lawyer then when you attend dinner parties and other social functions you will probably stop telling people that you are a solicitor or a barrister and start to make up another profession because one question is asked above all others: 'How can you represent somebody you know is guilty?'

---

112.   Andrew Boon, *The Ethics and Conduct of Lawyers in England and Wales* (3rd edn, Hart Publishing 2014) 379.

113.   Andrew Boon, *The Ethics and Conduct of Lawyers in England and Wales* (3rd edn, Hart Publishing 2014).

114.   [2009] EWHC 3621 (Fam).

115.   [1988] 2 AC 222.

116.   [2000] Lloyds LR 298.

Suspected guilt

The answer to this question depends on whether a lawyer suspects that the client is guilty or whether he has been told by the client that he is guilty. Initially let us concentrate on the first possibility. The answer to the question in this case is quite complicated and an entire book could be produced discussing the answer. The brief answer, however, is part practical and part philosophical.

The philosophical answer can be simplified to asking the question, who says a person is guilty? The law provides for three mechanisms by which a person is to be found guilty (depending on the court):

- the client pleads guilty
- at summary level, either a majority decision of three justices of the peace or a single district judge (magistrates' court) must declare guilt
- at Crown Court level, at least ten members of the public sitting as jurors must declare guilt.

If for the moment we leave aside the first method and assume the client is saying that he is not guilty but the lawyer believes that he is, then in either situation is it open to a single lawyer to decide guilt or innocence? The state has set down the rules by which a person is to be tried and someone who agrees to work in the legal system must adhere to this principle. If it were to be otherwise then why have a trial? If the lawyer is to decide guilt or innocence then we could save a lot of taxpayers' money by having all cases brought before lawyers who could dispense summary justice on their beliefs. The system would break down and thus it must remain with the duly constituted tribunals of fact. This simple philosophical argument can be easy when one is discussing the theft of a bar of chocolate or a basic assault case but what about cases of child abuse, rape, or murder? Arguably the rule applies even more to these cases as due process is most important in the worst cases. A barrister does not have to like his client but by entering criminal practice he is saying that he is prepared to conduct criminal litigation and unless he withdraws from private practice then this means both prosecuting and defending cases. If someone does not believe that they can defend a rapist then they should not work in independent practice.

Client confirms guilt

What happens in the alternative scenario, where a person tells his lawyer that he is guilty? The Code of Conduct for barristers states that one of the most important principles for a barrister is the duty not to mislead the court[117] and this means that a barrister may not suggest in court that his client is not guilty if he has been *told* by his client that he is guilty. Does this mean that a guilty person cannot be represented? It cannot mean this since where a person intends to plead guilty he still has the right to make representations to the court, and he is able to engage a lawyer to do this on his behalf. Can a guilty person ever legitimately plead 'not guilty'? The answer, perhaps surprisingly, is 'yes' and *Written Standards of Work* exist for this.

In England and Wales the law states that a person is to be found guilty by the courts only where the prosecution can prove beyond all reasonable doubt that the accused

117.   Bar Standards Board, *The Bar Standards Board Handbook* (2nd edn, BSB April 2015) 23 (rule rC3).

committed the crime. Accordingly, it has been decided that it is possible for a barrister to 'test' the prosecution evidence of a guilty client to see whether this threshold has been passed.

The position is normally, therefore, that a lawyer can act for the defendant up until the point of the close of the prosecution case but cannot put forward a defence case as this would tend to suggest that a person is not guilty which would be misleading the court.[118]

10.9.2.2 Criminals as lawyers

Whilst it may seem a strange issue to discuss, can a person who has been convicted of a crime become a member of the professions? The answer is yes although they have additional hurdles.

In order to gain entrance to the Law Society or Inns of Court a student must demonstrate that they are of good character. Both professions define this in a subjective way, ie they will look at individual applicants rather than create an overarching rule that would apply regardless of the specifics of a case. It is important to note that it is not only criminal convictions that could affect the ability of a person to join the professions but also disciplinary and other matters. For example, findings of plagiarism and examination irregularities at undergraduate level are considered to be extremely serious and have stopped people from joining the professions.

Both professions will call applicants who are not of good standing before special committees. For the Law Society this is likely to include a member of the Council and members of the profession whereas for the Bar Council it is likely that the Masters of the Bench of the Inn that the applicant is applying to will hear the matter. The circumstances of the reasons for the bad character will be discussed together with any relevant information on rehabilitation etc. The decision whether to admit will be based purely on whether the panel believes that it would cause professional embarrassment to the profession if such a person is admitted.

> **Example** Louise Woodward
>
> Perhaps the most infamous example of this rule is that of Louise Woodward who was convicted in America of the manslaughter of a child while acting as an au pair after her A levels. Upon returning to the United Kingdom she read for a law degree and, upon its completion, applied to the Law Society for permission to join them as a student lawyer and begin studying the LPC. Her application was considered by a special panel of lawyers and they allowed her to commence studies and a firm of solicitors in Manchester (who did not undertake criminal work) provided her with a training contract. Many people felt uncomfortable about this decision, not least because there was doubt as to whether other people convicted of homicide would be allowed in. The Law Society itself said that it was a unique case and at the time of the trial there was a perception in the United Kingdom that she had been treated unfairly in America (although little authority was adduced for this) and this may have swayed its decision.

118. It should be noted that the Law Society maintains similar rules—see the *Solicitors Regulation Authority Handbook*, ch 5.

QUESTION FOR REFLECTION

Do you think there are any crimes that should lead to a person not being fit to practise as a lawyer? How do you think the general public would react to a lawyer who has a history of fraudulent or violent offending? Do you think that Louise Woodward should have been able to practise as a lawyer? Imagine that the crime had taken place in this country: would the parents of the child believe that the law was being brought into disrepute?

 LISTEN TO THE PODCAST

For guidance on how to answer this question and a discussion of the main issues, listen to the author's podcast on the Online Resource Centre: www.oxfordtextbooks.co.uk/orc/gillespie_els6e/

 Summary

This chapter has examined the legal profession and identified who is entitled to practise law in England and Wales. In particular it has noted:

- There are two principal branches to the legal profession in England and Wales. The first branch consists of barristers and they continue to have automatic higher rights of audience. The second branch consists of solicitors who are now entitled to receive higher rights of audience.

- Barristers tend to practise independently but they form loose associations known as chambers where they will share clerks and administrative staff. Chambers will also have a 'head of chambers' who chairs policy discussions.

- Whilst traditionally barristers were not legally able to form partnerships they may now own shares in an LDP or ABS.

- Solicitors are allowed to form partnerships and it is unusual for them to practise independently.

- There are three stages to qualifying as a member of either profession. The first is the academic stage and involves passing either a qualifying law degree or the Graduate Diploma in Law. The second stage is vocational education and is either the Bar Professional Training Course (for barristers) or Legal Practice Course (for solicitors). The final stage is work-based training and consists of either pupillage (for barristers) or a training contract (for solicitors).

- Existing alongside these principal branches are other forms of lawyers. The Chartered Institute of Legal Executives is probably the next biggest branch. Legal executives work under the supervision of solicitors and can eventually qualify as solicitors themselves. Increasingly they are being recognized as a profession in their own right, including being given access to (junior) judicial roles.

- Concern continues to exist over the diversity of the legal professions and the position in respect of the representation of ethnic minority judges appears to be decreasing.

- A number of ethical challenges exist to the work of the professions and the traditional regulatory role of the professions is being challenged. In recent years, independent oversight of the regulatory process has been introduced to create public confidence in the system.

End-of-chapter questions

1. David Pannick, *Advocates* (OUP 1992) states: 'any lawyer who does not understand [the purpose of the cab rank rule] really has no business being an advocate' (p 145) yet others disagree and David Clementi, *Review of the Regulatory Framework for Legal Services in England and Wales* (HMSO 2004) appears to question whether the rule has any modern application (pp 130–2). Should the cab rank rule be abolished?

2. Jon Robins, 'Inn a Time Warp?' (2005) 102 *Law Society Gazette* 19 reports that the Law Society are pleased with the new process of appointing QCs with the suggestion that it could lead to more solicitors being awarded this distinction. In the same article, however, Andrew Dismore MP refers to QCs as 'a price-fixing cartel to defraud the public'. Should we have a system of QCs and if so, should it apply to all lawyers or only to advocates?

3. Read A Myers and L Flannery 'Wannabe Barristers?' (2004) 154 *New Law Journal* 1698 (at pp 1698–9) where two solicitor–advocates are interviewed about their job. One suggestion put to them is that they should become barristers. Is this not the crux of the matter? Why should solicitors be given higher rights of audience when they are not constrained by the regulations governing barristers (eg prohibition of partnerships, cab rank rule etc)? If we are going to allow solicitors to have higher rights of audience then should the distinction in dress and mode of address be removed?

4. Stephen Irwin QC, the chair of the Bar Council during 2004, argued that Clementi was wrong to suggest that a central regulatory system was required saying: 'the Bar regulates itself very successfully and very cheaply because we have high degree of commitment from barristers who are pretty tough on their own colleagues.' Why should lawyers be investigated or regulated by outside bodies rather than their own internal systems?

Further reading

Nicolson D, 'Demography, Discrimination and Diversity: A New Dawn for the British Legal Profession?' (2005) 12 *International Journal of the Legal Profession* 201–28.

This article discusses whether enough is being done to make the legal professions more diverse.

Robins J, 'Inn a Time Warp?' (2005) 102 *Law Society Gazette* 19–20.

This article questions the relevancy of the Inns of Court in the modern legal practice and questions whether they hold the profession back as 'gentlemen's clubs'.

Webb J, 'Legal Disciplinary Practices: An Ethical Problem in the Making?' (2005) 8 *Legal Ethics* 185–94.

This article considers whether the disciplinary changes proposed by the Clementi report will in fact raise greater ethical dilemmas.

For multiple-choice questions, updates to this chapter, and links to useful websites, please visit the **Online Resource Centre** at: **www.oxfordtextbooks.co.uk/orc/gillespie_els6e/**

11

Access to the Law

By the end of this chapter you will be able to:

- Identify the background to legal aid.
- Understand some of the controversies that exist over state funding of legal action.
- Identify how state funding is provided.
- Consider the merits of 'conditional fees' and assess whether they are an alternative to state funding.

Introduction

Litigation is expensive and is becoming more expensive. This applies equally to both civil and criminal trials. This chapter will consider how people can gain access to justice. In this context, this means considering how a person who cannot afford to instruct a lawyer privately can gain access to the law. Traditionally this has meant 'legal aid', is a relatively modern concept in English law. However, legal aid is one of the most politically controversial schemes in the English Legal System and is now heavily curtailed. It is also the arena of a hostile fight between politicians and lawyers, with the former suggesting that 'lazy fat-cat lawyers' milk the state dry with excessive fees and the latter accusing the government of ensuring only the rich can litigate. Alternatives to legal aid have had to be developed, but as will be seen, these tend to rely on the goodwill of the professions.

11.1 Background to legal aid

Legal aid is a comparatively modern concept within the English Legal System and in effect traces its history to the Second World War. But it has expanded to the point where it is considered to be an everyday feature of the legal process. Since the 1980s, however, it has become an incredibly political 'hot potato' with Conservative, Labour, and coalition governments suggesting that 'fat cat' lawyers have abused the system although at least one commentator argues that the latest attacks are arguably just more noticeable since legal aid has always had a troubled existence.[1] It has been suggested that the principal justification for legal aid is that failing to assist the poorest in society accessing the law is a 'significant denial of justice'.[2] This is a particularly strong argument since it is frequently the very poor who are most in need of the law's protection as they can be readily exploited by those who know they are unable to take action. Within the sphere of employment law this was one of the reasons why unions became important since they would assist with legal proceedings to enforce conditions of employment. A similar rationale lies behind the national minimum wage (see the *National Minimum Wage Act 1999*) and here the state, through HM Revenue and Customs, acts on behalf of the low-waged to ensure that they are given an appropriate wage.

It has been suggested that there have been three stages of legal aid in this country[3] although since 2013 a fourth must now probably be added. The first stage was when it was funded directly by the state and administered by the Law Society. This period lasted forty years (1949–1989). The second stage was when the Legal Aid Board (LAB) took over the administration of the scheme from the Law Society, in part because there were concerns at solicitors being responsible for their own payment. This also marked the beginning of the principal political controversy surrounding this area. This second phase is said to have lasted from 1989 to 1999 but realistically it was not until 2000 when the third phase began. The third phase was the creation of the *Legal Services Commission* (LSC) created by the *Access to Justice Act 1999* with a remit to revolutionize the legal aid scheme. The fourth, and current phase, has been introduced by the *Legal Aid, Sentencing and Punishment of Offenders Act 2012* (LASPOA) which has abolished the LSC and brought legal aid back under the direct control of the Ministry of Justice.

A common aspect within all the phases of the legal aid scheme has been the concept of means-testing. Since legal aid is considered to be a solution for those who cannot access lawyers it was considered appropriate that it should be restricted to those who could prove they were of low income. This was particularly true in respect of representation at court but was also supposed to happen at the pre-trial hearings. However, there has, for many years, been suspicion about how high-profile figures have managed to obtain legal aid, including key businessmen who lived in houses worth millions. Some have suspected that it is possible to 'hide' money by ensuring that income and assets are held elsewhere.

Linked to the concept of means was the recovery of legal aid. As will be seen later in this book, the general rule in civil litigation is that the 'loser pays' all the costs. Accordingly, if a person who is legally aided wins then the costs of the litigation should be claimed against the opposing side meaning that the legal aid budget does not suffer. However, there are many exceptions to the 'loser pays' principle (see 15.1.3.1) and the legal aid provisions did allow for legal fees to be recovered from any awards that were made to the claimant.

Perhaps the biggest change from the initial legal aid scheme and the current one is that of budgets. Theoretically, throughout all stages of legal aid there has been a budget set but until the most recent set of reforms there was no upper limit on the

1. John Flood and Avis Whyte, 'What's Wrong with Legal Aid? Lessons from outside the UK' (2006) 25 *Civil Justice Quarterly* 80.
2. Michael Zander, *Cases and Materials on the English Legal System* (10th edn, OUP 2007) 585.
3. Michael Zander, *Cases and Materials on the English Legal System* (10th edn, OUP 2007) 586.

expenditure set, ie it did not matter if the budget was overspent, often by significant amounts. This led to enormous pressures on the system and transformed the way the practices operated. One commentator noted that the greatest growth was in the period 1975–1984 where the Bar's legal aid earnings rose threefold and accounted for half of the Bar's income.[4] The rise for solicitors was even more pronounced, rising from £40 million in 1975 to £280 million in 1984, a sevenfold increase.[5]

The then Conservative government was determined to cut back on legal aid and commented that although it was an important feature of the legal system it 'could not be a blank cheque from the taxpayer'.[6] One of the strongest criticisms was that it encouraged cases to be dragged out since lawyers were paid by the hour. However, the profession's response to this was that this was also true with private cases but they were a professional body and accordingly would not prolong matters that were not justified. However, at the very least the *perception* that this could happen was present and the media appeared to be largely on the government's side, the popular belief being that lawyers are overpaid.[7]

The Conservative government argued that it was necessary to centralize the legal aid system, in part to recognize that it was not just private law firms that provide advice but that other bodies (eg Citizens Advice Bureaux, Law Centres, etc) also provided assistance and were supported by the state. The government wished to rationalize this system[8] but also ensure that there was a control mechanism on spending. It proposed the creation of the LSC and suggested that it would be operationally independent although funded by the government. The LSC would have the power to decide what areas of law to fund and there was an intention that not every area of law would continue to be funded.

Ultimately the Conservative reforms were left unfinished and the incoming Labour government had to decide what to do. In opposition, the Labour party had been strongly opposed to many of the Conservative measures, arguing that limiting legal aid could be considered a barrier to access,[9] but this position altered dramatically after it was elected and at least one commentator has suggested that the Labour government has effectively ended 'legal aid as we know it'[10] which, whilst dramatic, is undoubtedly correct.

The reality of the system was that legal aid continued to place increased pressure on the government's budget and that it was unsustainable for this to increase whilst the government sought to limit funding on other aspects of the state. The professions reacted badly to the proposals of the government and it culminated in a heated debate between the professions and the government. Perhaps the most notable aspect of the debate was when the government produced a list of the top earners from legal aid which was condemned by the professions as an attempt at humiliating them.[11] However, the government argument was that it demonstrated a problem with the legal aid scheme, that a judge would receive a salary of only £100,000 per year but some lawyers earned £1 million per year from legal aid. However, at the junior end of

4. Richard Abel, *English Lawyers between Market and State* (OUP 2003) 241.
5. Richard Abel, *English Lawyers between Market and State* (OUP 2003) 241.
6. Richard Abel, *English Lawyers between Market and State* (OUP 2003) 244.
7. Richard Abel, *English Lawyers between Market and State* (OUP 2003) 244–5.
8. Michael Zander, *Cases and Materials on the English Legal System* (10th edn, OUP 2007) 586.
9. Richard Abel, *English Lawyers between Market and State* (OUP 2003) 293.
10. Richard Abel, *English Lawyers between Market and State* (OUP 2003) ch 8.
11. Richard Abel, *English Lawyers between Market and State* (OUP 2003) 304, 310.

the profession the position was significantly different with small rewards being given.[12] Nonetheless, the media debate inevitably focused on the 'high end' of the profession since it was easy to portray lawyers as 'fat cats'. This ultimately turned the tide of the discussion and led to the government winning the battle for legal aid.

In the end the budget continued to grow and controversy existed over the types of persons and cases that provided for legal aid. Ironically, given they were responsible for the creation of the LSC, the Conservative-led coalition government abolished it and decided to centralize legal aid within the Ministry. This gives the Lord Chancellor more direct control over the budget and how it is to be spent.

11.1.1 Reviews of legal aid

Continued pressure on the legal aid budget led to a major review of legal aid conducted by Lord Carter in 2005. A further review (the Magee Review) was held in 2009 and this was read in conjunction with the report of Jackson LJ on costs in civil litigation. Many of the recommendations of these reviews have been brought forward in LASPOA 2012.

Carter believed that a more market-orientated approach to legal aid should be developed and certainly this was something that quickly took hold. The primary response was to ensure that a smaller number of firms held a larger proportion of the work, these contracts being awarded through a competitive bid process whereby (generally) the lowest bid won the contract (subject to certain quality thresholds and performance indicators). The reforms were extremely controversial since it meant that many firms did not hold a contract for legal aid work meaning that a person could not necessarily have their lawyer of choice.

Another key change was the manner in which legal aid was paid to lawyers. Traditionally legal aid was similar to ordinary payments of fees, ie a lawyer was paid depending on how much work he undertook. Carter recommended a move away from negotiated fees to standardized graduated fees.[13] This means that a lawyer would be given a set fee for a set classification of work. It was designed to promote efficiency but, of course, some critics noted that no two law cases are the same and this may mean that lawyers would have less time to spend on complex matters. A safeguard against lawyers cutting corners was the introduction of a peer-review scheme to assess the quality of service provided by firms.

A unique problem within criminal law is that known as Very High Costs Cases (VHCC) which were the small number of complex criminal cases that would cost the most in terms of legal aid (murder, fraud etc). Carter believed that this accounted for a disproportionately high part of the legal aid budget[14] and that tendering could be used to try and reduce costs. The initial approach by the *Legal Services Commission* was to attempt to limit the pay of counsel conducting VHCC work. The rates of the Bar would have been cut dramatically but the response was one of intransigence, with many silks and senior juniors refusing to undertake legal aid work. They could do this without breaching the 'cab rank rule' because the process of tendering meant that lawyers, including advocates, would have to 'sign up' to the scheme in order to receive

12. Richard Abel, *English Lawyers between Market and State* (OUP 2003) 304.
13. Lord Carter, *Legal Aid: A Market-based Approach to Reform* (Department for Constitutional Affairs 2006) 4.
14. Lord Carter, *Legal Aid: A Market-based Approach to Reform* (Department for Constitutional Affairs 2006) 4.

work. Thus by not signing up to the scheme they were never put in the position of refusing a case since it could not have been offered to them in the first place.

The stand-off led to some heated words and potential injustices. In the autumn of 2008 it was reported that the trial of the persons accused of the murder of the school-boy Rhys Jones might have had to be postponed because there was no agreement as to fees. In the event the LSC backed down and provided an exemption from the scheme. A compromise was reached in 2010 when a panel-based system was rejected for individual contracts but with fixed fees being paid for much of the work. The fees were also a reduction in what had previously been paid but not to the extent that was first proved. That said, VHCC continues to be extremely controversial and it is likely to prove so under the new scheme.

Civil legal aid was similarly problematic and there was thought to be a case for reducing the type of cases that would be funded by civil legal aid. Carter appeared to believe that, subject to certain exemptions, the civil legal aid budget should not be fixed but would rather be whatever was left of the overall budget after criminal legal aid had been paid. There was concern that the tendering process adopted for legal aid work could lead to communities being without any legal representation services and he suggested that firms could form alliances with community organizations to overcome this.[15]

The Magee review differed in some respects from Carter, most notably in recommending that there should be separate budgets for civil and legal aid[16] which would have, in effect, led to more protection for civil legal aid than was envisaged by Carter. One of the principal recommendations made by Magee was acted upon quickly when the administration of legal aid was removed from the LSC, a non-departmental public body, and brought back within the Ministry of Justice. Magee suggested that social welfare law could be removed from legal aid funding and replaced by providing additional assistance to community organizations, including the Citizens Advice Bureaux, to permit social advice to be provided in a more efficient manner. Whether this has happened is more questionable. Whilst there has undoubtedly been a greater expectation that social welfare advice should be provided by the CAB there was a question of whether the budget was similarly carried over. Many CABs had legal-aid contracts but the ending of legal aid for certain types of advice (discussed later) meant that they lost a substantial amount of income. Ultimately the government had to step in because they realized that CABs are essential to the functioning of advice and large grants were ultimately made to individual bureaux.

11.2 Legal aid today

This section of the book will consider how the latest guise of legal aid—that in force following the passing of LASPOA 2012—operates.

11.2.1 Administration of legal aid

Legal aid is now administered by an executive agency of the Ministry of Justice, which is known as the *Legal Aid Agency*.[17] As an executive agency, it is run from within the

---

15. Lord Carter, *Legal Aid: A Market-based Approach to Reform* (Department for Constitutional Affairs 2006) 4.
16. Ian Magee, *Review of Legal Aid Delivery and Governance* (HMSO 2009) 72.
17. *Legal Aid, Sentencing and Punishment of Offenders Act 2012*, s 38.

Ministry of Justice, unlike its immediate predecessor who was a non-departmental public body.[18] The Secretary of State for Justice (who is also Lord Chancellor) is placed under a statutory duty to 'secure legal aid',[19] which disguises the fact that the principal aim of the LASPOA 2012 was to tighten, once again, the availability of legal aid.

The day-to-day responsibility for administering legal aid is passed to a senior civil servant who is known as the 'Director of Legal Aid Casework'.[20] As will be seen the Director has responsibility for making decisions in respect of individual cases. In order to protect the independence of the legal process the Act specifically provides that whilst, as would be expected, the Director can be directed as to how to carry out his functions[21] which, in essence, means detailing how the legal aid scheme will be carried out, the Lord Chancellor is expressly prevented from making directions in respect of an individual case[22] and 'must ensure that the Director acts independently of the Lord Chancellor' when making such decisions.[23] The latter phrasing is quite interesting because it is potentially wider than not making directions. It is difficult to believe that when the Secretary of State for Justice, a senior governmental minister, makes his views known, a civil servant may not be influenced by that, but the phrasing of s 4(4)(b)—to ensure that independence is maintained—would arguably cover such situations meaning the Lord Chancellor may have to be extremely careful about making comments in respect of an individual case.

The Lord Chancellor is empowered to set quality standards for those who wish to provide legal aid services,[24] including by creating a system of accreditation.[25] This is not surprising as in recent years there has been an increased tendency to ensure that legal aid work was of a particular standard. Under the AJA 1999 reforms the LSC had contracted with certain firms and would only do so where they had been awarded a 'quality mark'. The loss of a quality mark could have had serious repercussions for a provider, including the loss of services.

The Director of Legal Aid Casework must ensure that an annual report on legal aid is produced[26] and the Lord Chancellor must ensure that this is laid before Parliament and published. Whilst this is statutory recognition of the need to be transparent about the legal aid budget and how it has been administered, it does not differ dramatically from what happened under the LSC as the LSC and its daughter agencies (the *Community Legal Service* and *Criminal Defence Service*) all provided annual reports.

11.2.2 Civil legal aid

Perhaps the greatest changes brought about by LASPOA 2012 relate to civil legal aid. Traditionally an exclusionary system has been adopted, ie legal aid was available for any form of action unless legislation provided otherwise.[27] LASPOA 2012 expressly reverses this, however, and adopts an inclusionary rule, ie that legal aid is only available

---

18. Known as the *Legal Services Commission* (see Administration of Justice Act 1999 for details of its creation and operation).
19. *Legal Aid, Sentencing and Punishment of Offenders Act 2012*, s 1.
20. *Legal Aid, Sentencing and Punishment of Offenders Act 2012*, s 4(1).
21. *Legal Aid, Sentencing and Punishment of Offenders Act 2012*, s 4(3).
22. *Legal Aid, Sentencing and Punishment of Offenders Act 2012*, s 4(4)(a).
23. *Legal Aid, Sentencing and Punishment of Offenders Act 2012*, s 4(4)(b).
24. *Legal Aid, Sentencing and Punishment of Offenders Act 2012*, s 3(1).
25. *Legal Aid, Sentencing and Punishment of Offenders Act 2012*, s 3(2).
26. *Legal Aid, Sentencing and Punishment of Offenders Act 2012*, s 7.
27. Anthony Edwards, 'Legal Aid, Sentencing and Punishment of Offenders Act 2012—the Financial Procedural and Practical Implications' [2012] *Criminal Law Review* 584, 585.

if legislation states that it is available.[28] The types of actions are set out in Part 1 of Sch 1 and Part 2 includes an exclusionary rule in that it includes types of actions where legal aid will not be permitted. It may seem unusual to have an exclusionary rule if an inclusionary approach is being adopted but this is partly explained by s 10 which allows the Director of Legal Aid to permit legal aid where a matter falls outside of Part 1 of Sch 1 if it is required in exceptional circumstances.

The extent to which exceptional cases have been accepted has been the subject of some controversy. In *R (on the application of Gudanaviciene and others) v Director of Legal Aid Coursework and the Lord Chancellor*[29] the Court of Appeal held that guidance issued on how s 10 should operate was incompatible with the ECHR because it was overly restrictive. The guidance suggested s 10 should only be used where a failure to offer legal aid would make 'the claim practically impossible or lead to an obvious unfairness in proceedings. This is a very high threshold.'[30] The Court of Appeal found that this was not correct and that there were broader considerations that needed to be taken into account when making the decision, although the likelihood of a decision to deny legal aid leading to a breach of Article 6 was one factor.

The guidance was revised although it continues to be controversial. In *Director of Legal Aid Casework and the Lord Chancellor v IS*[31] the revised guidance returned to the Court of Appeal (Civil Division) after the High Court had struck it down as, once again, carrying too high a risk that breaches of the ECHR could be caused by refusing legal aid.

Particular criticisms this time around included the fact that the form that was required to be completed to apply for s 10 consideration was so detailed and complicated that a litigant in person could not complete it, with only specialist lawyers being able to understand it. Further, no funding was provided to complete the form (save where it was successful), meaning few specialist law firms would risk spending the time to complete the form. The form was also alleged to pre-judge the outcome as there was a clear steer that the presumption was that no representation would be offered.[32]

This time, however, the Court of Appeal upheld the guidance. Whilst they were not enthusiastic in supporting the guidance, they felt it could no longer be considered to be incompatible with the ECHR. Burnett LJ noted that the trial judge had held the low success rate demonstrated the incompatibility, but suggested that in reality the success rate had increased since *Gudanaviciene* and that it was not possible to suggest what a success rate for exceptional cases should be.[33]

However, the limits of *IS* should be understood. The Court of Appeal was not prepared to strike down the guidance under which s 10 operates, but the court was similarly certain that individual decisions not to provide legal aid could be incompatible with s 10. Thus, the Director of Legal Aid Casework will need to consider carefully whether a case is sufficiently exceptional to justify legal aid.

Section 8(1) of the Act sets out what civil legal aid means and this has a broad definition:

(a) providing advice as to how the law operates,

(b) providing advice and assistance in legal proceedings,

---

28. *Legal Aid, Sentencing and Punishment of Offenders Act 2012*, s 9(1)(a).
29. [2014] EWCA Civ 1622.
30. [2014] EWCA Civ 1622 [15].
31. [2016] EWCA Civ 464.
32. [2016] EWCA Civ 464 [20].
33. [2016] EWCA Civ 464 [85].

(c) providing other advice and assistance to the prevention of disputes about legal rights or duties or the settlement or other resolution of disputes, and

(d) providing advice and assistance in relation to the enforcement of decisions in legal proceedings or other decisions by which legal disputes are settled.

This will cover most forms of legal advice but it is interesting to note that the statute expressly makes reference to the prevention of 'disputes' and their settlement. This must be statutory recognition that legal aid can be used to facilitate Alternative Dispute Resolutions (discussed in Chapter 19). Providing legal aid in these circumstances could mean that individuals are, in essence, funnelled towards ADR since it may be that legal aid for a particular matter will not be available for litigation but only for ADR or only permitted once ADR has been attempted. If this does occur then this is something that should be welcomed since, as will be seen from Chapter 19, ADR brings many advantages but it is not always chosen by litigants.

11.2.2.1 Schedule 1

It is not possible in a book such as this to detail what is in Sch 1 since the schedule itself takes up over fifty pages in the printed Act of Parliament. It is, however, possible to summarize some of the key points from within it. Broadly speaking the schedule continues legal aid in respect of serious events relating to the state. Thus legal aid continues for public childcare proceedings, vulnerable children and adults, and in respect of challenging certain benefits. Protection from domestic violence is also contained within the schedule but general family proceedings (divorce etc) is not covered. This has led some to question whether there will be an increase in claims of domestic violence (so that fees are paid) although the proof required for this perhaps makes it slightly less likely. Where legal aid is available is in respect of mediation for family disputes and this echoes the point made earlier that it would seem that the government may be using LASPOA (2012) to promote ADR.

Actions against the state as a public body are also found within the schedule. Importantly judicial review is contained within Sch 1 and this means that individuals will still be able to challenge the decisions of public authorities that they believe will adversely affect them. Similar protection is afforded by permitting legal aid for the writ of habeas corpus, which is a specialist order sought from the High Court declaring that a person is being held by the state illegally and should be freed. Legal aid will also be permitted where an action is being brought that alleges the abuse of a position of trust by a public authority or where it is believed that a public authority will be in breach of the *European Convention on Human Rights* (ECHR) (ie actions under the *Human Rights Act 1998* (HRA 1998)). Controversially legal aid will continue to be available for certain actions relating to clinical negligence. It will be seen later that ordinarily damages for injury and death are excluded and the cost of paying damages by the NHS has been controversial for some time but Parliament maintained that where there is clear clinical negligence that leads to severe neurological injury to an infant then legal aid should be permitted. Legal aid will also be permitted in respect of certain immigration and asylum matters, albeit with restrictions in terms of what can be claimed and how many proceedings can be initiated. Provision is also made in respect of those who are at risk of losing their home.

As noted earlier, Part 2 of Sch 1 discusses general circumstances when legal aid will not be permitted. There are sometimes exceptions to this rule (most notably where injury has been caused by the state or to comply with the ECHR) but the exceptions are quite broad. The key exceptions are civil litigation in respect of injury or death or many actions in tort (including negligence, assault, trespass), damage to property, defamation, conveyancing, and matters dealing with wills and trusts. It may seem surprising that legal aid will not be included for many actions relating to injury to the person but the position of the government is that this is the type of case that should now be dealt with by alternative funding models (discussed later). However, as will be seen, changes to funding may mean that someone who does not have the means to pay for litigation will be worse off in terms of overall damages than someone who does have the means to litigate. The implications of this will be discussed later.

11.2.2.2 Qualifying for legal aid

Just because legal aid is available does not mean that a person will necessarily be eligible for it. In recent years the rules governing who is eligible for legal aid have been increasingly tightened and LASPOA 2012 continues this.

Section 11(1) sets out the framework and states that the Director of Legal Aid (or, more realistically, those who are employed to act on his behalf) must decide on the eligibility of legal aid taking account of the financial resources condition (s 11(1)(a) reading across to s 21) and also 'criteria set out in regulations' which, at the time of writing, have not yet been formulated. The context of the regulations is, however, set out in s 11(3) and includes, for example, cost–benefit, the availability of resources, the nature and seriousness of the issue being litigated, the likelihood of alternative sources of funding being available, the conduct of the would-be litigants, and the public interest.

The essence of the s 11 requirement is that the mere fact that a matter is contained within Part 1 of Sch 1 does not mean that a person will necessarily receive legal aid. This is not a new threshold as the AJA 1999 system included a 'merits test' which was very similar to the factors proposed here. Of course until the regulations are published it will not be possible to know whether the criteria will be any more strict than under the old scheme but it is important to note that it was never a mere filter and many applications were turned down for failing to meet the merits test.

11.2.2.3 Providing legal services

When legal aid first came into being almost every lawyer would have been involved in the scheme but increasingly there have been attempts to centralize services. The AJA 1999 reforms led to contracts with the LSC meaning that firms would have to 'bid' for work and could only take a fixed quota of cases. LASPOA 2012 reforms continue this trend.

Section 27(3) makes it clear that the duty to provide legal aid does not include the duty to ensure that the services are provided by the person selected by the individual. That, in combination with the general power of the Lord Chancellor to make contracts, almost certainly means the continuing of the policy that legal aid will only be available through firms that have been selected.

Section 27(1) states that the Lord Chancellor's duty under s 1 does not include a duty to ensure that the services are those chosen by the applicant. The extent of this is explained by subsection (2) which states that the duty could be discharged by arranging for 'the services to be provided by telephone or other electronic means'. In other words legal advice need not always be face-to-face and may include, for example, a person ringing a telephone helpline or consulting a website. To an extent this is not new as the *Community Legal Service* operated both a website and telephone system that allowed certain people to ask legal questions. In many situations it will not be necessary to see a lawyer face-to-face and so this may be a sensible approach. However, there are also dangers to its use. For example, there will be many instances where face-to-face contact is required or where it is better for the individual (particularly when they are, for example, vulnerable). Also, where telephone or Internet-based services are used it is perhaps easier to use non-legally qualified persons to provide the advice. Again, in uncomplicated matters this may not be overly problematic but in specialist cases it is essential that a person has contact with a qualified lawyer.

11.2.3 Criminal legal aid

The duty under s 1 LASPOA 2012 is in respect of both criminal and civil aid. Criminal legal aid has been very contentious for a number of years. Over recent years both the government and media have been very vocal over the perceived failings of criminal legal aid where, in particular, it looks as though very rich people have been granted legal aid. These questions were raised in particular during the trials of former parliamentarians who were charged with fraud in respect of their parliamentary expenses and also, in 2012, the trial of Asil Nadir, a former businessman who was accused of a multi-million-pound fraud.

A complication with criminal legal aid is the dual role of the state. The then Lord Chancellor, Lord Irvine, commented that criminal legal aid was the classic example of 'demand-led' costs, but it has been pointed out that this neglects the fact that it is the state itself that creates the demand as it is the state, and not private citizens, who decide whether to prosecute an offender.

11.2.3.1 Advice and assistance for people in custody

The first time a person may require legal aid is when they are arrested by the police and taken into custody for questioning. Currently there is an absolute right to receive free legal advice in these circumstances but s 13(1) LASPOA 2012 suggests that it could become discretionary in that it states advice will be offered if 'the Director has determined that the individual qualifies for such advice and assistance in accordance with this Part'. That said, s 58 *Police and Criminal Evidence Act 1984* permits free legal advice and thus LASPOA 2012 cannot be intended to remove that restriction. Certainly an attempt by the government to introduce means-testing at this stage was defeated by Parliament and is not contained within LASPOA 2012.[34]

Section 13(3) states that the Director can decide how assistance is to be granted and, as with civil legal aid, this will almost certainly mean that some forms of advice will be by telephone rather than in person. This already happens but it is controversial since many would argue that a person should always be able to meet a lawyer, particularly where it is likely that they are to be interviewed.

---

34. Anthony Edwards, 'Legal Aid, Sentencing and Punishment of Offenders Act 2012—the Financial Procedural and Practical Implications' [2012] *Criminal Law Review* 584, 586.

11.2.3.2 **Criminal proceedings**

Section 14 defines criminal proceedings and it is given a broad definition so as to include, amongst other types, criminal trials, sentencing hearings, extradition hearings, and certain appeals. Section 15 permits the Lord Chancellor to provide, by regulations, the provision of advice and assistance in connection with criminal proceedings. It is anticipated that the regulations will permit the 'duty solicitor' scheme to continue in magistrates' courts[35] in part because the regulations must permit legal aid where it is in the public interest.[36]

This is then taken further by s 16 which permits legal aid to be granted for representation in criminal proceedings. Representation is to include situations such as bail proceedings, resisting appeals, and the actual trials. Section 17 sets out the criteria by which a person is qualified to receive representation although, as with much of the Act, most of the detail will be put forward in regulations.

Unlike in civil legal aid there is no merits test, not least because this would be contrary to the presumption of innocence, but there is a financial eligibility test and an 'interests of justice' test.[37] The interests of justice test is defined in s 17(2) as taking into account—

(a) whether the individual would be likely to lose his liberty or livelihood or suffer serious damage to his reputation if he were to lose,

(b) whether the proceedings involve consideration of a substantial question of law,

(c) whether the individual may be unable to understand the proceedings or to state his or her own case,

(d) whether the proceedings may involve the tracing, interviewing or expert cross-examination of witnesses on behalf of the individuals, and

(e) whether it is in the interests of another person that the individual be represented.

Example Substantial questions of law

Factor (b) is quite important because it will sometimes be the case that what appears to be a simple case is actually more complicated because of issues that have not been raised before. A good example of this is in respect of the parliamentary expenses claim. In *R v Chaytor*[38] three former Members of Parliament sought to argue that they could not be tried for fraud in respect of their parliamentary expenses because to do so would have breached the *Bill of Rights* which excludes court action from the proceedings of Parliament. This was an important issue that had not been raised before and eventually reached the Supreme Court. The Supreme Court accepted that it was an important point but ultimately ruled that privilege did not apply. Leaving aside privilege the facts of the cases were relatively simple but it was in the interests of justice for this matter to be considered by the courts, including the Supreme Court, before being tried.

35. Anthony Edwards, 'Legal Aid, Sentencing and Punishment of Offenders Act 2012—the Financial Procedural and Practical Implications' [2012] *Criminal Law Review* 584, 586.
36. *Legal Aid, Sentencing and Punishment of Offenders Act 2012*, s 15(3).
37. *Legal Aid, Sentencing and Punishment of Offenders Act 2012*, s 17(1).
38. [2010] UKSC 52, [2011] 2 AC 684.

The decision to grant legal aid can either be made by the Director of Legal Aid or a court. The Act reverses the position under the AJA 1999 in that under the previous system the default position was (theoretically) that the court made the determination whereas now the default position is that the Director will make the decision. That said, this is not as radical a change as might be expected since the reality was that the power of the court to make a determination as to the availability of legal aid was steadily reduced. Section 19 provides the court with the power to determine the availability of legal aid.

Contributions

The most controversial aspect of criminal legal aid in recent years has been the fact that some people have had to contribute to the costs of their defence. Section 23 LASPOA 2012 preserves this. The essence of the scheme is that persons who are considered to have the means to pay will be asked to make a contribution to their defence costs upfront.

The threshold for contributions is quite low in that where a person has a disposable income in excess of £3,398 (which is, effectively, £280 per month) then a contribution would be expected. The rate of contribution is 90 per cent of disposable income each month up to a maximum of five months (although if a payment was missed then an additional payment could be demanded). There is also a cap beyond which persons would not be expected to pay but which was complicated to work out and varied between each offence. For example, the maximum cap is £6,731 for burglary and £185,806 for a case of murder. Contributions are extremely controversial since, of course, a person is presumed innocent until proven guilty and taking, in effect, 90 per cent of their disposable income would mean that potentially they could suffer real hardship during the progress of a trial.

Recouping defence costs

Where a person is acquitted then the rule, prior to LASPOA 2012, was that they would receive not only their contributions but could also apply to the court for their legal fees to be paid. The argument behind the state paying the fees for an acquitted offender is that the state had accused them of a crime which they did not commit. If a person is innocent they should not be forced to pay to defend themselves although the court can, if it believes it appropriate to do so, decline to order the costs to be paid.

The government has, for some time, been concerned at the cost of refunding fees for an acquitted person. Through the *Costs in Criminal Cases (General) (Amendment) Regulations 2009*[39] the government attempted to reduce payments by no longer refunding the expenses incurred by defendants but rather paying according to fixed fees. This was challenged by the Law Society (see R *(on the application of the Law Society) v Lord Chancellor)*[40] who successfully argued that these changes could only be brought about by primary, and not secondary, legislation. LASPOA 2012 provides this statutory authority.[41] One of the implications of this is that where defence costs are recoverable then it is highly likely that the rates that will be paid will not be those which the defendant paid but whatever legal aid rates are. Thus a person who pays for private representation in the magistrates' court (or

39. SI 2009/2720.
40. [2010] EWHC 1406 (Admin), [2011] 1 WLR 234.
41. *Legal Aid, Sentencing and Punishment of Offenders Act 2012*, s 62.

Crown Court on an appeal from the magistrates' court) will only receive a proportion of the fees that they have spent.

Paying a lower level than a defendant has paid is controversial in that it goes against the principle of being able to choose one's legal representative which has traditionally been considered an important part of the legal system. However, it will be remembered that LASPOA 2012 does not guarantee that approach when it comes to legal aid and therefore this change could be considered consistent with that. The main source of controversy with LASPOA 2012 is the manner in which it deals with legal aid in the Crown Court.

It is clear that all defendants who are charged on indictment are eligible for legal aid although, as noted earlier, they may be liable for contributions depending on their means. Historically a person would choose a lawyer and either make an application for legal aid or pay for the matter privately and seek an order for the recovery of defence costs if acquitted. This has changed. A person must either choose to accept legal aid or will not be permitted to recoup the costs of their defence, even at the legal aid rate. This is because LASPOA 2012 amends the *Prosecution of Offences Act 1985* (PoOA 1985) in such a way as to permit legal costs to be recovered only in certain proceedings.[42] Rather surprisingly a trial at the Crown Court is not prescribed[43] and so whilst a recovery of defence costs order may be made, this cannot include payment for legal costs.

This change of rules places the defendant in the Crown Court in quite an invidious position. It will be remembered from earlier that not every lawyer will necessarily be able to offer criminal legal aid as the work is likely to be contracted. Thus a person can only choose a contracted lawyer (or have a lawyer chosen for them) and if their lawyer of choice (who, for example, may be an expert in the offence they have been charged with) is not contracted then they must pay the costs privately and not be reimbursed for these legal costs even if they are acquitted. The costs of a Crown Court trial can be very significant and few people, it is submitted, are likely to be able to afford them. It is questionable whether the very best lawyers will wish to seek legal aid work which potentially undermines the quality of advocacy. Certainly Edwards, a leading solicitor, has argued that the changes 'will represent the end of the proud boast of early legal aid lawyers that they would offer the same quality of service to publicly financed clients as they offer to private services'.[44]

⟳ QUESTION FOR REFLECTION

Does it matter that a person is not able to pick their own lawyer? Surely if there are minimum quality standards for work (see s 3 LASPOA 2012) then it does not matter who undertakes the work as a defendant is able to be reassured that their interests will be protected during a trial?

Recouping costs from the defendant

It has been shown that an acquitted defendant will be able to recover some of their costs (save for when they are being tried in the Crown Court) but what of the convicted

---

42. *Prosecution of Offences Act 1985*, s 16A.
43. *Prosecution of Offences Act 1985*, s 16A(3).
44. Anthony Edwards, 'Legal Aid, Sentencing and Punishment of Offenders Act 2012—the Financial Procedural and Practical Implications' [2012] *Criminal Law Review* 584.

defendant? Should they have to pay either the prosecution costs or indeed their own legal-aid defence costs?

Section 18 *Prosecution of Offences Act 1985* permits a court to make an order against the defendant to pay for the prosecution costs. It is common in summary trials for an order as to costs be made, especially in respect of driving cases. It is perhaps less common in the Crown Court, in part because where an offender is sentenced to imprisonment it is likely that the result of this is that the offender will lose his livelihood. The general rule is that costs should only be ordered when a person has the means to pay for them[45] and this is an important issue; it is not supposed to be an additional punishment but rather a reimbursement of costs (or partial costs) where it is deemed the offender is of sufficient means.

Of more relevance is perhaps the issue of whether an offender must repay their legal aid. The purpose of legal aid is to allow a person to be represented in the Crown Court so that they can challenge the case against them, including (where they are pleading guilty) the basis upon which the Crown is basing their case or to put forward mitigation. It is an essential part of the equality of arms and ensures that everyone is able to be represented at court when it is in the interests of justice to do so (a right guaranteed under Article 6(3)(c)). However, where a person has been convicted and has been proven to have breached society's rules then the question arises whether they should be asked to repay, should they be able to do so, some or all of the money that they were given by the state to defend themselves.

The general rule is that a person who has been convicted of an offence will ordinarily be asked to repay their legal aid costs.[46] The clear presumption is that a person in the Crown Court will be asked to repay some or all of the costs although only where the offender is not in receipt of certain benefits and has:

- capital of at least £3,000
- equity in the defendant's principal residence over £100,000, or
- a gross national income over £22,235.[47]

It is for the court to decide how much of the costs should be recovered and this includes the possibility of providing partial payment.[48]

This position is expressly preserved by LAPSOA 2012[49] and it is likely that the same position will be adopted, ie there will be a minimum threshold and a court will make the ultimate determination. Interestingly the (then) Lord Chief Justice, in his annual press conference, specifically referred to criminal legal aid as follows:

> I do not mind [apparently wealthy people] receiving legal aid. What I mind about is them keeping the assets afterwards, and not having their assets used to pay for their legal aid. ... if, after the trial is over, it emerges that the defendant is absolutely stashed with cash, then I would expect the cost of his defence to be paid out of his stashes of cash, save to the extent that they are the proceeds of crime, in which case they should be confiscated.

It is a widely held belief that the recovery of defence costs is likely to be a future priority.

---

45. *R v Maher* [1983] QB 784.
46. See *Criminal Defence Service (Recovery of Defence Costs Order) Regulations 2001*, SI 2001/856, reg 3 as amended.
47. *Criminal Defence Service (Recovery of Defence Costs Order) Regulations 2001*, SI 2001/856, reg 4(3).
48. *Criminal Defence Service (Recovery of Defence Costs Order) Regulations 2001*, SI 2001/856, reg 5.
49. Section 22.

11.3 Legal aid and human rights

The status of legal aid has proven somewhat controversial over the years and perhaps the most interesting question that should be asked is whether it is a right or whether it is a discretionary measure from the state. Should it also differ depending on whether the matter is civil or criminal?

11.3.1 A human right?

It may appear at first sight to seem extraordinary to suggest that legal aid could be considered a human right since we have an understanding in our minds as to what such concepts could be, but there is at least an arguable case that in some situations a right could exist.

Article 6(3) of the ECHR states:

Everyone charged with a criminal offence has the following minimum rights:

(c) to defend himself in person or through legal assistance of his own choosing or, if he has not sufficient means to pay for legal assistance, to be given it free when the interests of justice so require ...

Clearly therefore at least in terms of criminal charges a person does have the right to legal aid albeit in limited circumstances. The first limitation is that the Article is premised as inherently based on means—'if he has not sufficient means to pay for legal assistance'—and, accordingly, if a person can pay for representation then clearly they should. The second limitation is that it is not expressed as an absolute right—'when the interests of justice so require'—although where guilt is contested or where the sentence could lead to a person being sent to gaol it would appear likely that the interests of justice would so require it. Perhaps the most interesting potential qualification is in respect of the choice of adviser.

The first sentence of Article 6(3)(c) is relatively clear and uncontroversial. If a person is able to pay for representation then they should have the right to choose their representative. The second part of the sentence becomes less clear. It could be construed that Article 6(3)(c) is stating that if a person cannot afford legal advice then assistance should be provided to him, ie a solicitor is assigned to him. The second way of construing the sentence is to suggest that it is an extension of the previous words. Accordingly, a person should have the right to choose an adviser and if he cannot afford to pay that adviser then the state should pay for the assistance. It would be extremely controversial to suggest that the second possible reading is correct and the courts have certainly taken the line that the former is more likely to be correct.[50]

Article 6(3) expressly relates to criminal proceedings and there is no comparable right for civil proceedings so it would appear at first sight that there is no right to legal aid for civil law actions. However, in *Steel and Morris v United Kingdom*,[51] the European Court of Human Rights suggested that the right could be based under Article 6(1), the right to a fair trial.

---

50. See, for example, *R v De Oliveira* [1997] Crim LR 600.
51. (2005) 41 EHRR 22.

Case Box *Steel and Morris v United Kingdom*: The 'McLibel' case

Steel and Morris v United Kingdom marked the end of one of the most interesting legal campaigns to have been fought in recent times. Steel and Morris were two environmental campaigners who handed out leaflets outside a McDonalds restaurant which made various claims about the nutrition of McDonalds burgers and the way in which the company performed its operations.

McDonalds decided to sue Steel and Morris for libel. They were represented by a high-profile legal team led by Richard Rampton QC whereas Steel and Morris could not afford representation. Legal aid was not available for defamation actions (either as a defendant or claimant) and thus they had to represent themselves. The trial judge (Bell J) assisted them in some of the technical rules relating to the litigation but they were otherwise responsible for their own litigation. By popular assent it was considered that Steel and Morris performed extremely well in court and possibly even better than some lawyers!

However, the absence of funding did cause significant problems. The cost of transcribing each day's proceedings was £750 which they could not afford. Initially McDonalds provided the transcripts to the respondents without charge but this was withdrawn because Steel and Morris refused to provide an undertaking that they would only use it for the purposes of court proceedings and not for publicity etc. There were over 20,000 documents produced and many of the factual and legal issues were extremely complicated. It was suggested that without proper assistance they could not adequately prepare their defence.

The litigation undertaken before the domestic courts was extremely complicated and indeed at the time this was one of the longest cases that had taken place before the courts (although this may in part be as a result of only one side having legal representation) but the quantity of written materials produced together with the number of ancillary proceedings and witnesses examined meant that realistically both Steel and Morris were at a disadvantage compared to McDonalds in the exercise of the litigation. The ECtHR stated that a fundamental part of Article 6(1) is the right to equality of arms; in other words in order for both sides to receive a fair trial they should ordinarily be in roughly the same position in terms of access to the law. The ECtHR stated that during this litigation, because legal aid was not permitted, there was an inequality of arms and that this was caused, at least in part, by the state, thus creating a breach of Article 6.

Whilst this is clearly an extremely significant case in that the ECtHR has, for the first time, accepted that granting legal aid for civil cases may be a human right, it is crucial not to overstate the importance of the case. The ECtHR did not rule expressly that Steel and Morris *had* to be given legal aid; what the Court stated was that the blanket denial of legal aid by the government meant that there was *inevitably* an inequality of arms and thus the state had failed in its obligations to allow a fair trial to occur. This is something subtly different to stating that legal aid should have been given. It has been suggested that the test for inequality is 'whether or not the [party] suffered a substantial disadvantage compared to his adversary'[52] and this must mean taking account of all factors in the case including the parties themselves.

52. Shirley Shipman, '*Steel and Morris v United Kingdom*: Legal Aid in the European Court of Human Rights' (2006) 25 *Civil Justice Quarterly* 5, 12.

QUESTION FOR REFLECTION

Is there a justification for denying legal aid from a class of civil actions? The ECtHR implied that Steel and Morris should have received legal aid, but why should the state fund an action that was based on their own personal thoughts and actions? However, if no legal aid is given does this mean campaigns etc become the preserve of the rich or those well versed in legal matters?

11.3.2 Fair trial through free representation

Perhaps the second element of any 'rights-based' argument in respect of legal aid is to consider whether a person receives a fair trial while on legal aid. To an extent this was considered in respect of the *McLibel* litigation discussed earlier, but it is of crucial importance in criminal proceedings. If the state is to pay a fixed amount or even employ lawyers to represent the defendant then it is essential that this does not interfere with the right to a fair trial.

It has been noted that research from jurisdictions outside the United Kingdom has suggested that publicly paid defenders sometimes pressure their clients to plead guilty in order to maximize the number of fixed-paid clients they can process.[53] Interestingly, research conducted in Scotland suggested that whilst solicitors would strongly contest any allegation of pressure, they suggested that they were more likely to be 'realistic' with their clients because they did not, unlike for privately paid clients, depend on prolonging cases.[54] Certainly their evidence suggested that state-funded solicitors would 'settle' a case earlier in the process, usually through tendering a plea of guilty.[55] What is less known, however, is which of the two possible explanations stated earlier is correct.

Interestingly the same research demonstrated that clients were less likely to have confidence in 'salaried' public defenders than private practitioners[56] although it is not clear why this is. It is possible that it is because they view the fact that the state pays them as potentially objectionable and this does raise questions as to whether they are being open to them. In Chapter 13 it will be seen that many have suspicions about lay magistrates because there is a belief that they become over-accustomed to the court staff and lawyers and perhaps a similar argument is raised against public defenders, with there being some concern as to whether they are properly distant from the judiciary, justices, and prosecutors. This theory is perhaps substantiated slightly from the finding that the principal reason for disliking state defenders was the absence of choice; that a defendant could not choose a solicitor but one was found for them.[57] Perhaps the reason they thought this is because of the suspicion that a state employee would not do all they could for them.

---

53.   Cyrus Tata et al, 'Does Mode of Delivery Make a Difference to Criminal Case Outcomes and Client Satisfaction? The Public Defence Solicitor Experiment' [2004] *Criminal Law Review* 120, 126.
54.   Cyrus Tata et al, 'Does Mode of Delivery Make a Difference to Criminal Case Outcomes and Client Satisfaction? The Public Defence Solicitor Experiment' [2004] *Criminal Law Review* 120, 126.
55.   Cyrus Tata et al, 'Does Mode of Delivery Make a Difference to Criminal Case Outcomes and Client Satisfaction? The Public Defence Solicitor Experiment' [2004] *Criminal Law Review* 120, 127.
56.   Cyrus Tata et al, 'Does Mode of Delivery Make a Difference to Criminal Case Outcomes and Client Satisfaction? The Public Defence Solicitor Experiment' [2004] *Criminal Law Review* 120, 132.
57.   Cyrus Tata et al, 'Does Mode of Delivery Make a Difference to Criminal Case Outcomes and Client Satisfaction? The Public Defence Solicitor Experiment' [2004] *Criminal Law Review* 120, 133.

One question that has not been answered is how clients react to their state-appointed solicitor in terms of openness. If a client has no confidence in his solicitor then it is less likely that the latter will be open with the client and this may inhibit a fair trial. It is unlikely that the courts would entertain such a challenge especially since the professional bodies would regulate state-funded defenders in the same way as private-sector defenders.

 QUESTION FOR REFLECTION

Should the fact that a lawyer within the public defender service is bound by the same code of conduct as a private-sector lawyer mean that doubts as to their independence are no longer justified?

11.4 Alternative funding arrangements

With legal aid being so heavily restricted what are the alternative sources of funding that a person can use to fund litigation? It will be remembered that legal aid is now generally not permitted in respect of injuries and most torts and thus alternative sources of funding are important. Setting aside the fact that some will be able to pay for the litigation costs privately there are three key methods that will be discussed; conditional fee arrangements, law centres, and *pro bono* arrangements. There are other types of funding arrangements of course. One of the most common relates to motor insurance. Many people, when taking out their car insurance, will pay extra for legal services. This means that if they are involved in an accident the costs of litigation are paid by the insurance company.

11.4.1 Conditional fee arrangements

Conditional fee arrangements (CFAs) are often considered to be a very modern concept and although it is true to state that the AJA 1999 reforms made their use more common, they were first permitted by reforms introduced in the *Courts and Legal Services Act 1990* (CLSA 1990). The AJA 1999, however, made them attractive to lawyers and litigants alike by allowing the conditional fee to be recovered from the losing party. Whilst this has now changed, they continue to be an important source of funding for legal services.

At the heart of a CFA is the notion of 'no win, no fee' arrangements. Ironically this scheme has been enthusiastically supported by professions outside the law, most notably 'claim management companies' who are often insurance-type bodies seeking easy-to-handle personal injury claims. It is more often the actions of these bodies (who use slogans such as 'Where there's blame, there's a claim') that lead to the belief that the United Kingdom has developed a 'compensation culture' with litigation becoming the standard response to any unpleasant incident.

A CFA is where a lawyer (or lawyers—some barristers will take CFA cases) agrees to undertake litigation on a contingency basis. Whilst it is often said that this is 'no win, no fee' it is not always this simple given the nature of the fees.

NO WIN, NO (OR SOME) FEE

A sues B for negligence on a contingency fee basis. A loses. B is allowed to claim the costs of defending the action from A. Whilst A's lawyer will not charge A for his fees, A is still liable for the fees of B. Most CFAs will require A to take out insurance that will pay out if A loses and A will therefore be responsible for the costs of that insurance. Some firms will waive that insurance but many will not.

In addition to this, the successful lawyer was able to levy a 'success fee' which was designed to incentivize lawyers to take on cases where there is a risk of losing. In essence, the lawyer is gambling that the case is strong enough to recoup their costs, and to justify that gamble, they would get an additional payment. However, if they lose, then the lawyer would receive no fee: the insurance would simply pay the costs of the successful party (since costs are ordinarily paid by the losing party).[58]

The AJA 1999 reforms attempted to make CFAs more attractive, with the intention of persuading more people to use this form of litigation rather than trying to use legal aid and indeed the existence of CFAs was used to justify the withdrawal of legal aid from most forms of actions in tort. The principal reforms were to allow the success fee and the costs of the insurance policy from the losing litigant, in essence meaning that the successful litigant recovered all of their damages.

> **Example** Successful litigant
>
> Vanessa sues Lowprices Ltd, her local supermarket, because she slipped on a spill that they negligently failed to clean up. Vanessa suffers a broken arm and collarbone. Vanessa approaches Sue, Grabbit & Run, a local solicitors firm, who agree to take the matter on a contingency fee. Vanessa has to pay £20 per month insurance (for the twenty months the matter lasted for) and the costs of litigating amounted to £6,300. Sue, Grabbit & Run agreed a 100 per cent success fee. Vanessa is awarded £4,000 compensation.
>
> As Lowprices Ltd lost they are liable to pay both the compensation and the costs.
> The amount of money that Lowprices Ltd must pay is as follows:
> Compensation £4,000
> Vanessa's legal fees £6,300
> Insurance premiums £400
> Success fee £6,300
> Total £17,000
> In addition Lowprices Ltd will have to pay their own legal fees.

It is easy to see why CFAs were attractive to litigants since, if successful, the litigant was awarded all their compensation and it cost them nothing. If they did not succeed then the costs of litigating would be quite small, either the cost of the insurance premiums or (in some cases) nothing at all. However, this raised questions about the fairness of litigation and whether this had led to the compensation culture. The fact that a person had nothing to lose meant, to an extent, that people would willingly litigate in

---

58.   Discussed further at 15.3.

circumstances where they otherwise would not. More than this, claims management firms would use the cost of litigation as a way of encouraging a claimant to settle irrespective of the merits of the claim. Let us use as an example the case in the previous example box. Lowprices was not a large multinational company but was instead a corner shop. Whilst the shop may (and should) have public liability insurance, they may not have, in which case the costs of litigation may be borne by the owner. Even if they are insured the excess may be high and the shop owner may be worried that their premiums would rise to an unaffordable level after a claim. For that reason the owner may be more willing to settle even if they believe they are not at fault.

Most of the challenges to CFAs were based on the fact that a success fee could be charged. One of the first legal challenges to this was *King v Telegraph Group Ltd*[59] where the Court of Appeal was asked to declare that permitting a 100 per cent success fee was unfair and, in the context of defamation claims, a breach of Article 10 of the ECHR (on the basis that it could cause media outlets to be more careful about what they write because of the threat of expensive litigation). The court rejected these arguments but noted that there was the potential for unfairness. However, they ruled that Parliament had provided for these schemes and the court must acquiesce to their use when mandated by Parliament. The courts were not enthusiastic, however, and in *Campbell v Mirror Group Newspapers (Costs)*[60] the House of Lords warned that CFAs can have a chilling effect on litigation, recognizing that it meant litigation could become a weapon to frighten a defendant into settling inappropriately.[61]

The courts did have the power to mitigate the potential unfairness primarily through the use of a costs cap. This is a rule whereby the costs payable by the losing side are limited to a prescribed sum, in essence limiting the amount of 'success fee'. In *Henry v BBC (Costs Capping)*[62] the Court of Appeal recognized that CFAs could create a situation where the matters were so unequal between the parties that it would be unreasonable to allow the uplift and thus a cap could be imposed (although in that case no cap was imposed because any cap must be prospective and not retrospective). However, the courts were slow to exercise this power, in part because Parliament was clear that CFAs, including a 100 per cent success fee (the level having been set by Parliament), could be used.

11.4.1.1 CFAs and public authorities

Perhaps the more notable criticism is in respect of actions against public authorities, particularly the state. In late 2010 the Metropolitan Police Commissioner wrote to the Home Secretary to complain about the manner in which compensation is awarded for police misconduct. The reaction to this was extremely negative, with it being presented that the police were seeking to avoid responsibility for their errors, but at least some part of their point must be true. The costs of claims against the police may be inflated as a result of conditional fee arrangements. Where, therefore, the police decide to defend a claim or refuse to settle for what the claimant considers reasonable, there is a risk that the police will end up paying the costs of defending the litigation, plus the costs incurred and an additional uplift.

---

59. [2005] 1 WLR 2282.
60. [2005] UKHL 61.
61. [2005] UKHL 61 [31].
62. [2006] 1 All ER 154.

To one extent this is uncontroversial: the claimant's lawyers have taken the risk that the litigation may not succeed and thus they should perhaps be entitled to receive a reward for taking that risk (not least because if this was not the case then a lawyer would only take cases that are absolutely guaranteed success: under the present scheme there are at least some cases that they will lose and thus not be paid for their work). There is also the argument that the police, or other public body, should accept liability when they have done something wrong. However, this neglects two principal facts. The first is that sometimes it will be open to debate as to whether a fault exists (and indeed what level of compensation should be awarded) and secondly the fact that public bodies only have finite resources. If, for example, the police or another public body has to pay out up to 100 per cent of the legal fees as an 'uplift' then this could have had a significant impact on front-line public services.

11.4.1.2 **Variable CFAs**

An interesting situation arose in respect of CFAs in *Gloucestershire County Council v Evans*.[63] Whilst the standard CFA is premised on the basis that you do not pay anything if you lose, there is nothing within the statute which required that. In this case Gloucestershire County Council reached an agreement with solicitors governing the fees that they would charge in respect of litigation. The basic hourly charge was £145 per hour and a success fee of 100 per cent would be payable if the Council won. However, if they lost then they would only charge the Council £95 per hour. Thus instead of this CFA being a 'no win, no fee' it became a 'no win, lesser fee' arrangement.

The Council won their claim and the losing party appealed against the order of the costs judge that they were liable for the success fee arguing that, in essence, the basic fee was £95 per hour and the successful party was therefore trying to recover a success fee well in excess of 100 per cent, something prohibited by the CLSA 1990. The Court of Appeal rejected this and stated that the provisions of the Act were clear. A success fee was payable on the costs incurred by the winning party. The agreement clearly stated that these fees would be £145 and thus a 100 per cent uplift was permitted. If the solicitors were prepared to accept a lesser amount when they lost (but not the 'no fee' that ordinarily would be given) then this was a matter for them. To an extent this may seem a surprising decision since it would appear to alter the risk/benefit ratio at the heart of CFAs. The solicitors were taking the risk that they would recover a lower fee than their standard charge but this is arguably a lower risk than not being paid at all. Whilst the use of the standard charge for the uplift was undoubtedly correct it must be questioned whether it was fair or reasonable to charge the maximum possible uplift (100 per cent) as the success fee. Where the risk is reduced then it would seem appropriate that the uplift is similarly reduced.

11.4.1.3 **CFAs and the LASPOA 2012**

Jackson LJ was asked to prepare a report on the costs of litigation and one of the issues that he was asked to look at was the CFA scheme and whether it leads to injustices. The Labour government had previously attempted to reduce the 'success fee' from 100 per cent to 10 per cent but had dropped the proposal after concerns that it would lead to lawyers simply refusing to take cases.

---

63.   [2008] EWCA Civ 21.

Jackson LJ's report led to the suggestion that there should be a marked shift in the CFA scheme.[64] He agreed that the CFA scheme could be problematic and he recommended that allowing for the insurance premiums and success fee to be claimed from the loser is inappropriate. He preferred the system whereby the costs are recovered from the compensation awarded although he recommended that this should be subject to a cap, the cap being 25 per cent.

These plans have been taken forward by LASPOA 2012 and, in effect, merge CFAs with damages-based agreements, something that was previously only permitted in employment law. Section 44 continues to authorize CFAs but only if they are made in such a way that complies with conditions, some of which are contained in the statute and others in regulations to be made under the Act. The most significant condition is that any success fee must be expressed as a percentage of damages and will be subject to a limit set by regulations.[65] For personal injury cases this cap has been set at 25 per cent[66] and for all other types of litigation it remains at 100 per cent.[67] The major change, in line with the Jackson review, is the revised s 58(6) which will state:

A costs order made in proceedings may not include provisions requiring the payment by one party of all or part of a success fee payable by another party under a conditional fee arrangement.

This then becomes a direct reversal of the previous system and means that it is not possible to recover the additional costs from the losing side but instead they will now come from the damages received. Of course it should be noted that this is restricted to the success fee—the actual fees of the litigation will continue to be recovered from the losing side but it is the extra element that can no longer be claimed.

It will be remembered (see earlier) that the changes could be considered to make litigation fairer but does this create a situation whereby a person of modest means will now be treated in a less favourable way than someone who can afford litigation?

Example CFAs and means

Yvonne and Rachael are walking along a road when a car, travelling too fast, skids on ice and careers into them. Both Yvonne and Rachael suffer personal injuries, both receiving a broken leg and spinal injuries. Both issue proceedings against Kenneth, the driver of the car. Rachael has private means and she can afford to engage a solicitor by herself. Yvonne enters into a CFA with a solicitors' firm. The judge at court awards both £20,000 compensation and awards costs against Kenneth. Rachael will receive the full £20,000 whereas Yvonne will only receive £15,000 as the remaining £5,000 will be the success fee (that being 25 per cent of the compensation).

In this example the two claimants have been injured in exactly the same way but they will get two very different awards. Of course the argument for Rachael getting a

64. Lord Justice Jackson, *Review of Civil Litigation Costs: Final Report* (HMSO 2010).
65. *Court and Legal Services Act 1990*, s 58(4B).
66. *The Conditional Fee Agreements Order 2013*, SI 2013/689, reg 5(1)(a).
67. *The Conditional Fee Agreements Order 2013*, SI 2013/689, reg 5(1)(b).

higher award is that she has risked her own money in litigation—if she had lost then she would have had to pay not only her own legal fees but also the fees of the opposing side. Of course whether this can be justified in situations where liability is obvious is perhaps more open to question.

The second principal change relates to the costs of insurance (known as 'after-the-event insurance'). As was noted earlier, most CFAs required a litigant to take out insurance to cover the cost of legal fees in the event of losing. The premiums charged for this insurance will no longer be recoverable.[68] The sole exception to this is where insurance is taken out to cover the costs of preparing expert evidence for clinical negligence claims.[69] The costs of expert reports in clinical insurance claims can be extremely expensive and yet are an essential feature of proving a claim. It is for this reason that they continue to be used.

 QUESTION FOR REFLECTION

Re-read the section on CFAs. Do you think that the new system is fairer? Is it right that someone who has no private means will receive less money than someone who does?

11.4.2 Insurance

It is now possible for insurance to cover the costs of litigation. By insurance, what is meant is 'before the event' insurance (as distinct from 'after the event' insurance required for CFAs). A before the event insurance is a policy that a person takes out, believing that they may need to litigate in the future.

Before the event policies have been common for some time in respect of insurance policies, without people necessarily understanding what these are. If you seek to insure a car or house, you are invariably now offered the opportunity to have 'legal protection'. This is, in fact, a before the event insurance policy. They will pay a set amount of money to litigate (subject to conditions). Those policies attached to a car insurance will normally relate to the recovery of the car, personal injury compensation etc. Those policies relating to home insurance will normally be wider and include employment-law assistance, personal injury claims etc. There is anecdotal evidence that few people realize that they have these policies and therefore pay for legal advice in circumstances when they need not.

It is also possible to purchase bespoke before the event policies. This may include, for example, a policy that will cover family disputes (an area that most home insurance policies will not cover), landlord insurance, house purchase insurance, and even business protection for small business holders.

Before the event insurance policies will normally have conditions placed on them in terms of when the claim can proceed. An insurance company is unlikely to fund a hopeless case, but the threshold is often lower than that which may trigger a CFA. The principal advantage of them is that there is no success fee or other insurance company. If a person wins the litigation then the claimant can receive 100 per cent of the compensation (unlike the position now with CFAs).

---

68. *Legal Aid, Sentencing and Punishment of Offenders Act 2012*, s 46.
69. *Courts and Legal Services Act 1990*, s 58C(2).

Another disadvantage is that frequently the policy will say which solicitor firm has to be used, so you do not get to choose your own lawyer as you would with private work. However, it is often possible to negotiate this in the event of a claim, and some firms will allow you to choose a firm if that firm agrees the rate of pay. In any event, under legal aid it is not possible to choose a firm, as only some firms hold legal aid certificates, and so it is often an inconvenience that is worth it to receive free legal services.

11.4.3 Law centres

Law centres are perhaps closer to legal aid than CFAs in that they are still based on the premise of free legal assistance. Law centres became established in the late 1960s with the first such centre being opened in North Kensington, London. Law centres were considered to be part of social responsibility changes and provided fully qualified lawyers to provide free legal assistance to those within the community. By the end of the 1970s some thirty law centres had been established and by the 1980s there was a further increase to approximately fifty-five. However, since the 1980s there has been no further increase, in part because of different governmental priorities over social responsibility and also because of changes to the legal aid budget.

Law centres are independent and are often managed locally by elected boards of management. As independent charitable-sector bodies, seeking funding has always been difficult; although legal aid (now the CLS) will pay a proportion of the fees, other sources of income are required. Although some local authorities will contribute this will frequently be insufficient and law centres have to try to raise funds themselves.

Ordinarily the work of law centres will be the provision of advice although they will undertake limited advocacy work, most notably in respect of tribunals where it has been more difficult to obtain representation (see 7.5.1 for a further discussion on this). Another significant difference between law centres and legal aid is that there is no means-testing for users for initial advice, they would provide advice to anyone. However, where the advice went beyond initial advice then the ordinary rules of legal aid would apply.

11.4.4 Citizens Advice Bureaux

Whilst the number of law centres has started to recede, the Citizens Advice Bureau has continued to offer advice. The Citizens Advice Bureau (CAB) is a national network of individual bureaux. Each is affiliated to the national CAB but they are managed and run locally. The CAB has, for several decades, provided advice on common issues such as employment and consumer advice. As with law centres the initial advice is often free and non-means-tested.

Many CABs bid for legal aid contracts so that they could do casework in several types of law, including employment and family law. This has led some bureaux to employ solicitors alongside caseworkers so that they can also undertake representation. The changes to legal aid meant that many of these contracts were terminated, in part because legal aid for their work was withdrawn. The government, when discussing the withdrawal of legal aid, justified restricting legal advice by saying that the CAB was available to help which perhaps showed that they did not understand the funding arrangements of the CAB.

The government eventually realized that some form of governmental assistance was required by the CAB, and a charity grant was given to them.[70] However, it does not replace the funding they used to receive, and the amount of legal work that they can undertake is now generally reduced. Most CABs now tend to offer advice rather than provide the full legal service that they did when they held legal aid funding certificates.

The gradual reduction in other grants (CABs tended to receive money from local authorities, something increasingly difficult in times when local authorities are having their spending squeezed) has meant that a number of bureaux have had to close. This further reduces the likelihood that a person can find free legal advice.

11.4.5 *Pro bono*

The final form of funding to consider, albeit briefly, is where work is undertaken *pro bono*, in other words for free. The professions have seen *pro bono* work as part of a social responsibility programme and in recent years it has been encouraged by both professions and large City firms. Some will argue that it is a convenient public-relations exercise to avoid criticism of large fees but it is quite clear that it does assist many individuals who would otherwise want for advice and/or representation.

One of the earliest *pro bono* units was that operated by the Bar Council and this was later joined by the Inns of Court School of Law (now City Law School) Free Representation Unit (FRU). The FRU was an interesting development in that it used trainee barristers to present cases and provide advice, although they were supported by both Inns of Court School of Law staff and practising members of the Bar.

The model has rolled out and many universities now operate 'Law Clinics' whereby students, usually under the supervision of a qualified lawyer, provide legal advice to members of the public. The models of law clinics differ depending on the institution, with some providing a 'full service' (ie advice and representation) and others offering more limited services (either advice or representation, or support in litigating) but they all tend to coalesce around the idea of providing free legal services to the community.

The pedagogic benefits of this are well known.[71] So-called 'clinical learning' is extremely useful, with participating students getting experience of working with real-life examples. Real-life problems rarely involve topics that are to be found within the pages of textbooks and thus students must understand how the law operates, how to research precedents and applications. They must then be able to communicate what are often extremely complicated provisions into language that the client can understand. This is excellent experience for the student as it allows them to see beyond the confines of individual modules as most solutions are not to be found in a single 'class' of law (eg *Contract Law*, *Law of Torts*, etc).

Law clinics also help the community. They usually provide legal advice that is free for the local community, albeit generally in a more restricted way as it will be tied to teaching periods. This provides an additional safety net for the loss of legal aid.

As already noted, the professions themselves will also usually have a strong *pro bono* commitment, with individual barristers and solicitors' firms often acting in deserving cases on a *pro bono* basis. Some law clinics have established links with

---

70.   This was recommended by the Magee Report 2009. See Ian Magee, *Review of Legal Aid Delivery and Governance* (HMSO 2009).

71.   See, for example, Richard Wilson, 'Training for Justice: The Global Reach of Clinical Legal Education' (2004) 22 *Pennsylvania State International Law Review* 421–32.

practitioners so that the clinic acts almost as a filter, ensuring that those truly needing help can gain a full service.

The government sees *pro bono* as a positive element and so it is. However, its limits must be understood. It is easy to think of *pro bono* as 'putting something back into the community' but in reality it is working for free. There will be a limit as to how much free work can be given and there has been talk about ensuring better co-ordination of *pro bono* activities. Few professions offer as much *pro bono* work as the legal profession, and yet it rarely impacts upon how they are perceived. The characterization of 'fat cat' lawyers remains strong, even though the reduction in legal aid means that for many barristers and solicitors, their earnings can be below those in comparable professions.

Summary

This chapter has examined the funding of legal services, with particular emphasis on whether the state should fund services. In particular it has:

- Noted that legal aid first started just after the Second World War.
- Identified that the legal aid budget continued to rise until it became politically problematic.
- Noted that legal aid has become an increasingly political issue with many politicians believing that public money should not be spent on lawyers.
- Identified the latest changes to legal aid, including the fact that legal aid is withdrawn from significant forms of civil litigation.
- Noted the significant changes to criminal legal aid, including the ending of the idea of a person choosing his own lawyer and being able to recoup private funds spent on successfully defending oneself before the Crown Court.
- Charted the growth of conditional fee arrangements (CFAs) and noted how the latest changes will ensure that a successful litigant will no longer be able to claim a success fee from the losing party.
- Identified how non-legal organizations also operate in the provision of legal advice.

❓ End-of-chapter questions

1. Read Cyrus Tata et al, 'Does Mode of Delivery Make a Difference to Criminal Case Outcomes and Client Satisfaction? The Public Defence Solicitor Experiment' [2004] *Criminal Law Review* 120, particularly pp 132–3. Their empirical research has suggested that defendants prefer the freedom to choose a solicitor and not have one chosen for them. Do you think a person should have the right to choose their legal representative even if they are not paying for the service?

2. If a person is acquitted of an offence why should he not receive all of his defence costs? He has been proven to be not guilty so should he be penalized for selecting his own lawyer of choice and paying privately?

3. Will the fact that the 'success fee' in conditional fee arrangement cases is now limited to a percentage of damages make it more difficult to find a solicitor who is prepared to take the risk of working for free?

4. Flood and Whyte ask: '[o]ne of the questions that emerges ... is about the status of legal aid as a right, is it one? Or is it something—a boon or a gift—to be given or withdrawn at the whim of the state?' (John Flood and Avis Whyte, 'What's Wrong with Legal Aid? Lessons from Outside the UK' (2006) 25 *Civil Justice Quarterly* 80, 81). Do you believe that legal aid should be considered a right? Do you think it depends on the nature of the case? For example, where the state is involved (eg crime, judicial review, or public care proceedings) should legal aid be given automatically since to do otherwise may limit the right of a citizen to hold the state to account?

 Further reading

Cape E, 'The Rise (and Fall?) of a Criminal Defence Profession' [2004] *Criminal Law Review* 401–16.
  Whilst now old, this is an interesting article that charts the history of legal aid in the criminal justice system over forty years.

Edwards A, 'Legal Aid, Sentencing and Punishment of Offenders Act 2012—the Financial Procedural and Practical Implications' [2012] *Criminal Law Review* 584–91.
  This is a very useful summary of the changes brought about by LASPOA 2012.

Maclean M and Eekelaar J, 'Legal Representation in Family Matters and the Reform of Legal Aid: A Research Note on Current Practice' [2012] *Child and Family Law Quarterly* 223–33.
  This is a very good article that examines the changes LASPOA 2012 will bring to family legal aid.

Shipman S, 'Steel and Morris v United Kingdom: Legal aid in the European Court of Human Rights' (2006) 25 *Civil Justice Quarterly* 5–19.
  This is an interesting article that critiques the case of *Steel and Morris v United Kingdom* and suggests that the ECtHR has raised many questions that it has so far failed to answer.

For multiple-choice questions, updates to this chapter, and links to useful websites, please visit the **Online Resource Centre** at: **www.oxfordtextbooks.co.uk/orc/gillespie_els6e/**

PART III

THE CRIMINAL JUSTICE SYSTEM

12

Bringing a Prosecution

By the end of this chapter you will be able to:

- Understand the different stages in the prosecution process, and identify who completes the steps.
- Identify alternatives to prosecution.
- Identify how prosecutorial decisions may be challenged.
- Understand how a case is assigned to an appropriate court and how it is transferred.

Introduction

This chapter is the first of a number of chapters that will examine the criminal justice system, and it examines preliminary issues, ie some of the issues that take place before the trial begins. The next chapter will consider lay justice and, in particular, it will consider the differences between a summary trial and a Crown Court trial. Subsequent chapters will then identify who features in the courts, how a trial proceeds, and then what appeals are possible.

It should be noted that this examination will not start at the very beginning of the process, the investigation of crime, as this is ordinarily covered in other subjects (eg *Public Law*, *Constitutional Law*, or *Civil Liberties*). The starting point for this examination will be that the crime has been investigated and the police believe that there is sufficient evidence to suggest that their suspect is the person who committed the crime.

In this chapter there will be an examination of some of the issues that must occur before a trial takes place. Three of the main controversial aspects of the pre-trial criminal process will be examined: the decision to prosecute, bail, and transfer for trial.

12.1 Prosecuting agencies

Although this chapter will be focusing on the principal prosecuting agency, the Crown Prosecution Service (CPS), this is not the only body that is allowed to prosecute and it will be necessary to examine some of the other agencies before continuing the analysis of how prosecutions occur.

12.1.1 **The Crown Prosecution Service**

The CPS is the principal prosecuting agency in England and Wales. It is a relatively modern creature, having been created by the *Prosecution of Offences Act 1985* (PoOA 1985) but it became 'live' in 1986, although its professional head, the Director of Public Prosecutions (DPP) is a historic office.[1] Before the establishment of the CPS the police would act as both the investigators and prosecutors of crime. There was considerable disquiet over whether the police were capable of exercising this role appropriately,[2] with the belief that they were prosecuting too many weak cases which had consequences for wasting time, costs, and placing victims and defendants in undue distress.[3]

The Royal Commission on Criminal Justice argued that a central prosecuting authority should be created and this eventually led to the PoOA 1985 and the establishment of the CPS. At the time this was extremely controversial, with the police, in particular, being against the establishment of an independent prosecutor since they believed that prosecuting lawyers were 'theirs' and they should instruct them.[4] However, the Act rejected such an approach and the premise of the system is that the CPS independently examines the action of the police and decides whether the full engagement of the law is required. The level of independence the CPS has from the police has been questioned over the years[5] and although recent reforms could, as it will be seen later, arguably strengthen this independence the contrary could be true since CPS lawyers are sometimes located within police stations, potentially weakening their professional independence.[6]

The Royal Commission believed that a series of local prosecutors should be created, each accountable to the same political authority as the police. However, this was ultimately rejected and the CPS became a national organization under the governance of the DPP. However, recent years have seen this altering, in part because there was a belief that there was insufficient correlation between the CPS and police areas. There was also concern that the national agency was overly bureaucratic and did not properly represent a professional prosecuting agency. Eventually a formal review of the CPS was undertaken, this being chaired by Sir Ian Glidewell, a former Lord Justice of Appeal. His report was damning of the CPS and he found that it had not achieved the goals set out upon its creation.[7] He argued that the CPS was too centralized and focused on administration. The then DPP, Dame Barbara Mills QC, was blamed for many of these problems although it would perhaps be fairer to argue that they were institutional failings. In any event the DPP (as professional head) had to take responsibility and she resigned from the post of DPP shortly after the report was released which allowed reforms of its structure to be made.

The structure of the CPS has altered significantly over the years. Until recently, the CPS was organized into forty-two areas which mapped onto the forty-three

---

1. David Calvert-Smith and Stephen O'Doherty 'Legislative Technique and Human Rights: A Response' [2003] *Criminal Law Review*, 384.
2. Gavin Dingwall and Christopher Harding, *Diversion in the Criminal Process* (Sweet & Maxwell 1998) ch 2.
3. Andrew Ashworth and Mike Redmayne, *The Criminal Process* (4th edn, OUP 2010) 195.
4. Andrew Sanders, 'Prosecution Systems' in Mike McConville and Geoffrey Wilson (eds), *The Handbook of the Criminal Justice System* (OUP 2002) 156.
5. Michael Zander, *Cases and Materials on the English Legal System* (10th edn, OUP 2007) 245–6.
6. Michael Zander, *Cases and Materials on the English Legal System* (10th edn, OUP 2007) 264; cf Sir Iain Glidewell *The Review of the Crown Prosecution Service* (HMSO 1998) 32.
7. Michael Zander, *Cases and Materials on the English Legal System* (10th edn, OUP 2007) 247.

police forces in England and Wales (London has two police forces—the City of London Police and the Metropolitan Police—whereas it only had one CPS area). However, recently this has been reduced and there are now thirteen areas, straddling police force areas. Each CPS area is headed by a Chief Crown Prosecutor (CCP). Sir David Calvert QC (as he then was),[8] a former DPP, argued that each CCP would become a 'mini DPP' meaning that they would hold delegated authority from the DPP and would be responsible for making decisions for their area. Sitting alongside the DPP (although in reality slightly below since the PoOA 1985 is clear that the DPP is the head of the CPS (s 1(1)(a) PoOA 1985)) is a chief executive. Sir Ian Glidewell recommended this approach and it allows the DPP to concentrate most of his effort on his legal responsibilities. A parallel approach occurs in the CPS with each area having its own area business manager who acts as a local chief executive, ie assisting the CCP with the administrative responsibilities. With the advancement of statutory charging (see 12.2.1) the local areas have also been joined by a 'virtual area' known as *CPS Direct*. This is a division of the CPS which offers out-of-hours support to the police. CPS Direct has its own CCP and business manager but its jurisdiction is not territorial but temporal (ie CPS Direct offers services when the main area offices are closed). A fifteenth CPS area, 'Proceeds of Crime' (CPSPOC) was launched in June 2014, comprising three central units based in CPS Headquarters in London and nine regional teams. CPSPOC recovers assets and criminal profits from any criminal activity but in particular serious organized crime and serious economic crime.

January 2010 marked another milestone in the history of the CPS when the *Revenue and Customs Prosecutions Office* (RCPO) came within the CPS. The RCPO was a relatively new organization (it being established by the *Commissioners for Revenue and Customs Act 2005*) which had been set up because of concerns that HM Revenue & Customs, who originally prosecuted in their own name, were not effective.[9] This followed a series of high-profile errors in prosecution[10] and independence from the investigative side along the model of the CPS was introduced by the 2005 Act. However, to save money it was decided to merge the RCPO and CPS and as of January 2010 the RCPO is now a division of the CPS ('Revenue and Customs Division') and the DPP is responsible for their work.

The establishment of the CPS has in effect led to a division in the responsibility for the prosecution of crime. The police (and now Customs) now have responsibility only for the investigation of the crime and indeed no longer have the power to decide whether someone should be prosecuted (see 12.2). This was not always the case and for many years there was an 'uneasy relationship' between the police and CPS where the latter did not have the responsibility in deciding the charges but acted only as a 'reversing authority' whereby it could challenge a decision to instigate proceedings but not a decision to decline to instigate proceedings.[11] This has now been resolved and the CPS now has responsibility for the disposal of offenders.

8. Sir David Calvert QC was the first modern DPP to be elevated to the High Court bench shortly after standing down from the post of DPP.
9. Robin White, 'Investigators and Prosecutors or, Desperately Seeking Scotland: Re-formulation of the "Philips Principle"' (2006) 69 *Modern Law Review* 143, 160.
10. Robin White, 'Investigators and Prosecutors or, Desperately Seeking Scotland: Re-formulation of the "Philips Principle"' (2006) 69 *Modern Law Review* 143, 162–3.
11. Andrew Sanders, 'Prosecution Systems' in Mike McConville and Geoffrey Wilson (eds), *The Handbook of the Criminal Justice System* (OUP 2002) 158.

How has this change altered the independence argument? Auld, in his review, appeared to suggest that the CPS should become involved at a much earlier stage and that it should adopt a more proactive approach to the pre-trial investigation of crime.[12] The question that this raises, of course, is whether becoming involved in pre-trial matters will necessarily prejudice its independence. It is certainly known that the CPS will become involved from the very early stages of crime and where there is a particularly large or complicated crime it would not be unusual for the CPS to work alongside the police in the preparation of the case, including advising on the appropriate type of evidence to be gathered. It has been suggested that the division of responsibility has 'now been dismantled'[13] although the reason for this is apparently a belief that the investigation and prosecution of offences will become fairer and easier.

 QUESTION FOR REFLECTION

What do you think the role of a prosecuting agency should be? Should prosecutors, who are familiar with the intricacies of evidential rules, be involved in the investigation of crime? Indeed could it not be argued that the lawyer should have overall responsibility for the investigation of serious crimes? What would the implications of such an approach be?

 LISTEN TO THE PODCAST

For guidance on how to answer this question and a discussion of the main issues, listen to the author's podcast on the Online Resource Centre: www.oxfordtextbooks.co.uk/orc/gillespie_els6e/

12.1.2 Other state-funded prosecuting agencies

It has been suggested that up to 20 per cent of crime is prosecuted by agencies other than the CPS[14] and these can be very diverse with state agencies including the Health and Safety Commission, Pollution Inspectorate, Post Office, and local authorities who have responsibility for licensing and Trading Standards.[15]

It has been suggested that these prosecuting authorities tend to use prosecutions in a different way to the police, in that a prosecution becomes a measure of last resort.[16] This argument is based on the premise that the police will ordinarily act on the assumption that their purpose is to establish whether a crime has taken place and, if so, there is an expectation that a prosecution will be brought. This need not occur (see 12.2) but it is certainly a presumption. With the exception of the Serious Fraud Office (SFO) this is perhaps less true of the other state prosecuting agencies. For many of these agencies a prosecution is used only where a matter is so serious that it is the only form of disposal or where other forms of disposal have not succeeded. Other

12. Rt Hon Lord Justice Auld, *A Review of the Criminal Courts of England and Wales* (HMSO 2001) 399.
13. Andrew Ashworth and Mike Redmayne, *The Criminal Process* (4th edn, OUP 2010).
14. Andrew Sanders, 'Prosecution Systems' in Mike McConville and Geoffrey Wilson (eds), *The Handbook of the Criminal Justice System* (OUP 2002) 159.
15. See Andrew Ashworth and Mike Redmayne, *The Criminal Process* (4th edn, OUP 2010) 178.
16. Fiona Cownie, Anthony Bradney, and Mandy Burton, *English Legal System in Context* (6th edn, OUP 2013) 304.

(principally administrative) mechanisms tend to be put in place by these bodies in the hope of avoiding prosecutions.

Whether this system is necessarily comparable is perhaps more questionable. It will be seen that the CPS has a non-prosecutorial disposal system (see 12.3.3) and this will not infrequently involve minor crimes. However, the crimes prosecuted by many of the alternative state prosecution bodies are not as serious so it is perhaps easier to justify such avoidance.

12.1.2.1 Serious crimes

Where matters become more complicated, however, is in respect of serious crimes. The Serious Fraud Office (SFO) deals with crimes that involve multi-million-pound crimes and yet its success rate has been seriously questionable.[17] The SFO has, as its name suggests, a remit in respect of serious or complex fraud cases (s 1(3) *Criminal Justice Act 1987* (CJA 1987)) and it remains separate from the DPP with its own director accountable to the Attorney-General. The SFO retains a joined-up investigatory and prosecutory system whereby the director of the SFO is empowered to investigate serious frauds and prosecute them where she finds it necessary to do so (s 1(5) CJA 1987). The SFO has a small team of investigators itself but may require the police to assist them. A lawyer heads each investigation and is in charge of the investigation although the practicalities of this will almost certainly be delegated to senior operational investigators. Once the evidence is gathered the lawyer will then decide whether to prosecute the matter.

The integrated process of investigation and prosecution is to be found in regulatory matters[18] (see 13.1.2.2) but the SFO is not a regulator, it deals with major crime. However, it was argued that creating small multidisciplinary teams headed by a lawyer would ensure that the evidence gathered would be appropriate for prosecution. The success of the SFO has been somewhat questionable and this has led some to question whether the fact that there is not an independent oversight of the evidence is perhaps leading to weaker cases being prosecuted.

The SFO remains the only 'serious crime' body to continue with the integrated approach. In 2005 the *Serious and Organised Crime Agency* (SOCA) was created. It was popularly dubbed Britain's answer to the Federal Bureau of Investigation (FBI) in that it has a national remit but such comparisons are false. Whereas the FBI deals with Federal matters (ie a separate system of law that coexists with state laws), SOCA did not have a different jurisdictional basis but rather a territorial one: it was allowed to work across force boundaries but only in respect of serious crime. Its agents were not sworn constables although police officers can be seconded and many of its early members were not police officers but civil investigators. In October 2013 with the passing of *The Crime and Courts Act 2013* SOCA was replaced by the 'National Crime Agency' (NCA) (again accompanied by newspaper headlines that said this will be the UK version of the FBI). The major difference between SOCA and the NCA is that the NCA has a larger range of responsibilities including being responsible for tackling serious and organized crime, fighting cyber-crime, and protecting children from sexual abuse and exploitation.

17. Robin White, 'Investigators and Prosecutors or, Desperately Seeking Scotland: Re-formulation of the "Philips Principle"' (2006) 69 *Modern Law Review* 143, 160.

18. See Robin White, 'Investigators and Prosecutors or, Desperately Seeking Scotland: Re-formulation of the "Philips Principle"' (2006) 69 *Modern Law Review* 143, 160.

The relationship between investigators and prosecutors would be crucial. Early indications appeared to suggest that an integrated approach would be taken since it was stated that there needed to be a different approach to prosecution of serious crime[19] but in the end the integrated model was rejected on the basis that the prosecutors and investigators needed independence.[20] It can be legitimately questioned why the same conclusion cannot be drawn in respect of the SFO.

12.1.2.2 Less serious crime

It is not just serious crime that is prosecuted by agencies other than the CPS, indeed this probably accounts for very few of these 'outside' prosecutions. The more likely agencies are those that deal with minor crime or regulatory functions. Classic examples of these bodies are the Health and Safety Executive and most notably local authorities. When one thinks about law enforcement, local authorities are often neglected and yet they are an important part of the process with powers ranging over issues such as trading standards, health and safety, and regulatory compliance. Most local authorities will have a legal department and this department will handle the prosecutions on behalf of the authorities. The departments will also, however, deal with many other aspects including public childcare law, education law, electoral law, etc.

Members of a local authority legal team are unquestionably employees of the local authority and are certainly subordinate to the chief executive, even in larger organizations where the head of legal services may command an important position within the organization. Is there any independence in prosecutions here? It could be argued that there is internal independence in that the legal team will not normally have line-management responsibility for the operational teams in trading standards etc but ultimately there is no independence since all departments are accountable to the chief executive.

QUESTION FOR REFLECTION

Revisit your previous answer relating to the independence of prosecutors (12.1.1). Do you think it makes any difference that some prosecutors will not be operationally independent from the investigators? Do you think it is easier to justify when the prosecutions are regulatory and used as a matter of last resort?

An interesting question arose in 2010 about what happens where a body does not have any statutory authority to prosecute. The *Financial Services Authority* (FSA) regulates the financial industry in the UK and it has express power to prosecute offences under ss 401–402 *Financial Services and Markets Act 2000*. However, it has recently purported to be able to prosecute for offences relating to money laundering even though it has no express power to do so. In *R v Rollins*[21] the appellant, who was being prosecuted for money laundering, argued that in the absence of any power to do so the FSA lacked competence. The Supreme Court ruled that the FSA, as a person in being (a registered company has a legal personality), has the right to bring a private prosecution

---

19. Robin White, 'Investigators and Prosecutors or, Desperately Seeking Scotland: Re-formulation of the "Philips Principle" ' (2006) 69 *Modern Law Review* 143, 177.

20. Robin White, 'Investigators and Prosecutors or, Desperately Seeking Scotland: Re-formulation of the "Philips Principle" ' (2006) 69 *Modern Law Review* 143, 178.

21. [2010] UKSC 39.

(see 12.1.3) for any offence not reserved to a particular prosecutor. Accordingly, the FSA did not need any express statutory power to prosecute.

12.1.3 Private prosecutions

Although we think of the state as being responsible for prosecutions this is not always the case and indeed English criminal law is founded on the basis that private citizens (and indeed anyone the law considers to have a legal personality: see the discussion about the FSA earlier) may launch a prosecution. The creation of the 'principal' national prosecuting agency did not alter this principle and s 6(1) PoOA 1985 expressly reserves the power of a private citizen to bring a private prosecution subject to the caveat that the DPP may take over any prosecution.[22]

In *Gouriet v Union of Post Office Workers*[23] Lord Diplock argued that the private prosecution was an important constitutional safeguard 'against capricious, corrupt, or biased failure or refusal of those authorities to prosecute offenders'.[24]

However, this statement was given before the establishment of PoOA 1985 and although the power of private prosecution was retained by that Act it could be argued that the independent examination of evidence means it is less appropriate for the action to continue.

The retention of private prosecutions remains controversial and in *Jones v Whalley*[25] Lord Bingham, the then Senior Law Lord, described its retention as 'anomalous';[26] part of this controversy is over the fact that a person may be privately prosecuted after being told that the state will not prosecute him. However, it now appears that this depends on what the offender has been told. In *Jones v Whalley* the respondent (Whalley) assaulted the appellant (Jones). The police were informed and they issued a caution (see 12.3.3.1) which included a statement to the effect that by accepting a caution no court action would be taken against him. The respondent sought to start a private prosecution at the magistrates' court and the appellant argued that this was an abuse of process and so should be stopped. The justices accepted this but the Divisional Court overturned the decision holding that the right to private prosecution should not be impugned. The House of Lords, however, reversed that decision and decided that the proceedings *would* be an abuse of process and may not occur.

The House of Lords accepted that the police were wrong to give the assurance they provided but argued that this was sufficient to justify a stay for abuse. Lord Bingham even went so far as to state:

> A crime is an offence against the good order of the state. It is for the state by its appropriate agencies to investigate alleged crimes and decide whether offenders should be prosecuted.[27]

The House declined to consider whether the provision of a caution will always amount to an abuse of process but stated that in this case it was because the police had misled the defendant by failing to mention the possibility of a private prosecution. The House argued that the solution to this problem would be for the respondent to judicially

---

22. *Prosecution of Offences Act 1985*, s 6(2).
23. [1978] AC 435.
24. *Gouriet v Union of Post Office Workers* [1978] AC 435, 477.
25. [2006] UKHL 41.
26. *Jones v Whalley* [2006] UKHL 41 [15].
27. *Jones v Whalley* [2006] UKHL 41 [16].

review the decision to impose a caution on the basis that its wording was flawed. It will be seen later in this chapter, and indeed in this book, that judicial review is not an easy, cheap, or quick remedy and this suggestion by the House of Lords is somewhat unhelpful. The House clearly found private prosecutions distasteful but the House lacked the courage to decide one way or the other whether they should be permitted to continue. Given that Parliament stated that private prosecutions should continue to exist, it is difficult to see how this ruling can be considered compliant with Parliament's intention since the private individual has little or no control over the actions of the police and CPS.

It was noted that the DPP has the right to take over prosecutions and it is submitted that there are two reasons for doing so. The first is, rather obviously, to prosecute the offender rather than require the private individual to do so. If this occurs then the matter ceases to be a private prosecution and it becomes a state prosecution in the ordinary way. The second and more common reason is to discontinue a prosecution. Once the DPP has taken over the prosecution then he can discontinue any action, meaning the proceedings would stop.[28] In *R v DPP ex p Duckenfield*[29] the Divisional Court held that when deciding whether to exercise his powers to take over a private prosecution, the DPP did not need to refer to the Code for Crown Prosecutors, in part because it would be unusual for a private prosecution to take place where both tests are satisfied (as under those circumstances the CPS would ordinarily prosecute). The decision of the Divisional Court appears contrary to that expressed by Auld who suggested that private prosecutions should adhere to both prosecution tests[30] but if this were the case then for what reason would the DPP not take over a prosecution? Indeed it could be argued that if both tests were satisfied then it would be unreasonable of the DPP not to do so and that a judicial review could succeed.

Example Stephen Lawrence

In 1993 Stephen Lawrence, a black teenager, was murdered by a white gang in a racist killing. The police investigation of the crime was handled extremely badly with allegations that the Metropolitan Police Service was 'institutionally racist'. Five suspects were identified but the CPS eventually had to drop any planned prosecutions as a result of a lack of evidence. The Lawrence family decided to launch a private prosecution but in 1996 this collapsed because the evidence (gathered by the police) was insufficient and key parts of it were ruled inadmissible.

In 1998 after further evidence came to light a senior CPS lawyer suggested that the private prosecution had 'wrecked' any chance of bringing the killers to trial (at the time the relaxation of 'double jeopardy' had not occurred (see 16.4.3)). However, that has not proven to be true since Gary Dobson, one of those acquitted, had his acquittal quashed by the Court of Appeal (see *R v Dobson*).[31] He, and another person, David Norris, were convicted in January 2012 of the murder of Stephen Lawrence.

28. *Prosecution of Offences Act 1985*, s 23.
29. [2000] 1 WLR 55.
30. Rt Hon Lord Justice Auld, *A Review of the Criminal Courts of England and Wales* (HMSO 2001) 415.
31. [2011] EWCA Crim 1255, [2011] 1 WLR 3230.

QUESTION FOR REFLECTION

Do you think it is right to allow private prosecutions to occur? Lord Bingham clearly believes that they are anomalous and that it is a public law matter. Consider the arguments for and against abolishing the right (eg if we take the Lawrence example, what other solution did the Lawrence family have?).

 LISTEN TO THE PODCAST

For guidance on how to answer this question and a discussion of the main issues, listen to the author's podcast on the Online Resource Centre: www.oxfordtextbooks.co.uk/orc/gillespie_els6e/

12.2 Decision to prosecute

For the remainder of this chapter, our examination will concentrate on the CPS. The first issue to examine is how the decision to prosecute is made. This is not a decision that should be taken lightly. It is always likely to cause distress to the suspect and possibly other people connected with the suspect (eg partner, children, etc). With some crimes (eg violence, dishonesty, or sexual offences) it can cause a stigma to be attached to the suspect irrespective of whether the matter is even proven. Prosecuting someone will also incur expense, both by the state as prosecutor and the person who has to defend himself. A trial can also be difficult for both witnesses and the victim who are cross-examined over their evidence and it is incumbent on the prosecuting authorities, therefore, to ensure that only those cases where there is a likelihood of success are instigated.

12.2.1 Charging

When the CPS was created the initial decision. as to whether a suspect should be the subject of a prosecution, was made by the police through a process known as 'charging'.

There were suggestions that the charging system was inconsistent with some people being charged regardless of the strength of the evidence whilst others against whom there was strong evidence would be released or cautioned.[32] Indeed there has been some concern over whether ethnicity and socio-economic factors influenced these decisions.[33]

Some argued that one reason for this is that the decision whether to charge and indeed what to charge rested with the custody sergeant and he would be heavily influenced by the arresting officer or officer in charge of the case, especially where that person was senior in rank to him.[34] There were also suggestions that policies and practices

405

---

32. Andrew Sanders, 'Prosecution Systems' in Mike McConville and Geoffrey Wilson (eds), *The Handbook of the Criminal Justice System* (OUP 2002) 154.
33. See, for example, Andrew Rutherford, 'Race and Criminal Justice' (2001) 151 *New Law Journal* 117, and, Andrew Ashworth and Mike Redmayne, *The Criminal Process* (4th edn, OUP 2010) 185–6.
34. Andrew Sanders, 'Prosecution Systems' in Mike McConville and Geoffrey Wilson (eds), *The Handbook of the Criminal Justice System* (OUP 2002) 154.

differed over different types of offences and this all led to a position whereby it was thought that the CPS were being called upon to review prosecutions that were too weak even at the investigation stage let alone the prosecutorial stage.

Auld believed that the disparity between charging and review was stark, leading to a waste of resources in reviewing inappropriate cases[35] and he recommended that the CPS and police agree from an early stage what the charge should be.

The eventual response to Auld was the creation of a scheme known as 'statutory charging' which was rolled out as a pilot in 2002, this pilot being extended in 2004 and subsequently extending across all CPS areas with statutory authority under Part 4 of the *Criminal Justice Act 2003* (CJA 2003). This provided for a phased approach but the CPS quickly ensured that all areas were covered by the scheme.[36]

The essence of the statutory charging scheme is that the CPS and not the police have responsibility in deciding whether an offender should be charged. The police lose their discretion as to whether someone should be prosecuted although some have suggested that they have a residual power to impose simple cautions without reference to the CPS.[37]

12.2.1.1 Action by the police

Section 37 *Police and Criminal Evidence Act 1984* (PACE 1984) now states that where someone is being investigated by the police after arrest they may take one of four actions:

1. to release the suspect without charge and on bail for the purpose of enabling the CPS to decide whether to prosecute

2. to release the suspect on bail but not for the purpose of enabling the CPS to decide whether to prosecute (ie to permit further investigations to be made etc)

3. to release the suspect without charge and without bail

4. to charge the suspect.

The custody sergeant has the sole responsibility in deciding which option to take[38] which may lead some to question whether anything has changed from the previous system, especially since they retain the ultimate discretion under option 3. If the police decide not to refer a matter to the CPS then no review by the CPS can take place[39] although it is perhaps more unlikely that they would do this where there is evidence that needs to be considered.

It should be noticed that there is a difference between options 1 and 4. The former allows the police to bail a person while the CPS considers whether to charge somebody, and after that consideration the person may (if the CPS so direct) be charged. After charge the police sergeant will decide whether to grant bail or remand the person in custody until the next available sitting of a magistrates' court (see 12.6.2). However, a case does not need to be delayed to consider a charge and where the matter

---

35. Rt Hon Lord Justice Auld, *A Review of the Criminal Courts of England and Wales* (HMSO 2001) 399.
36. CPS, *Annual Report and Resource Accounts 2005–06* (Crown Prosecution Service 2006) 18.
37. Ian Brownlee 'The Statutory Charging Scheme in England and Wales: Towards a Unified Prosecution System' [2004] *Criminal Law Review* 896.
38. *Police and Criminal Evidence Act 1984*, s 36(7A).
39. Ian Brownlee, 'The Statutory Charging Scheme in England and Wales: Towards a Unified Prosecution System' [2004] *Criminal Law Review* 896, 900.

is particularly serious it is likely that the suspect will be charged at the expiry of the detention period following arrest.

The CPS has reacted to these changes in a 'twin-track' approach. The first is that there is a duty prosecutor who will ordinarily be available within designated police stations during normal working hours. This means that the investigating officers can have immediate discussions with a prosecution lawyer as to the strength of the case and the appropriate charges to be made. The second approach exists outside working hours and is the creation of CPS Direct, a system of 'on-call' prosecutors who work outside of normal working hours. These prosecutors, who do not work within a geographical context, can provide advice from local CPS offices as well as their homes as the CPS has invested in placing specialist communication equipment in the homes of Crown prosecutors.[40] This allows the prosecutor to review the evidence in a timely manner and ensure that the charges are accurate.

12.2.1.2 CPS options

Section 37B PACE 1984 sets out the responsibilities of the CPS when a case is referred to it. The first decision that must be taken is whether there is sufficient evidence to justify a prosecution. If there is sufficient evidence then the prosecutor must consider whether to charge him with a particular offence or whether the matter could be dealt with by a caution.[41] This latter part of the test is interesting since it means, for the first time, that considering the applicability of a caution is mandatory whereas it was previously discretionary.

The question that this raises of course is what does 'sufficient evidence' mean? The issue of 'sufficient evidence' has been perhaps the most debated and controversial issue since the inception of the CPS. The PoOA 1985, PACE 1984, and CJA 2003 are silent as to what this means but the Code for Crown Prosecutors (CCP)[42] makes it clear that there are in fact two possibilities.[43] Where the intention is to hold the defendant in custody after charge (ie effectively where the advice is 'immediate') then the 'threshold test' applies, whereas in all other circumstances (ie where the case has been referred to the CPS while the offender is still on bail) the 'full code' test is adopted.

When the 'threshold test' is used the full prosecution tests will be considered at a later stage: the threshold test is simply an interim stage.

Threshold test

The threshold test is in two parts and is based on the evidence currently available.[44] The first part of the test is whether the prosecutor is satisfied that 'there is at least a reasonable suspicion that the person to be charged has committed the offence'.[45] The second part of the test is whether the prosecutor believes 'that there are reasonable grounds for believing that the continuing investigation will provide further evidence … so that all the evidence taken together is capable of establishing a realistic prospect of conviction'.[46]

40. CPS, *Annual Report and Accounts 2003–04* (Crown Prosecution Service 2004) 15.
41. *Police and Criminal Evidence Act 1984*, s 73B(3).
42. The Code for Crown Prosecutors is issued under the authority of s 10 PoOA 1985 and details the rules and regulations that supposedly govern the prosecution process.
43. Code for Crown Prosecutors, para 3.4.
44. Code for Crown Prosecutors, paras 5.2 and 5.4.
45. Code for Crown Prosecutors, para 5.5.
46. Code for Crown Prosecutors, para 5.8.

It is worth noting that the test is framed on 'reasonable suspicion' which is similar to that required by a police officer to arrest[47] so it is undoubtedly a low threshold and, as has been noted by others, paradoxically lower than that required where the suspect's liberty is not at stake.[48] However, the argument is that this is necessary given the tight timescales and in any event there must be an agreed date by which the full tests will be considered.

12.2.1.3 **The prosecution tests**

The CCP provides that there are two 'full' tests that must be satisfied before any prosecution may be started: the evidential test and the public-interest test.[49] Both of these are somewhat controversial and there have been doubts raised as to whether this is actually anything more than a paper exercise[50] with the real analysis being made by reference to confidential prosecution manuals.

Evidential test

The first test that must be satisfied is the evidential test. It was noted a few paragraphs earlier that where the lower 'threshold test' was used at the time of charging, this test must be considered. Where the decision to charge has not yet been made then this will be the first test to use when deciding whether to charge a person with a criminal offence. The CCP defines the evidential test as:

> Prosecutors must be satisfied that there is sufficient evidence to provide a realistic prospect of conviction against each suspect on each charge. They must consider what the defence case may be, and how it is likely to affect the prospects of conviction. A case which does not pass the evidential test must not proceed, no matter how serious or sensitive it may be.[51]

The most obvious question that this raises is what is the meaning of 'realistic prospect of conviction'? This is an important issue and it is one that is inextricably linked to the standard of proof in a criminal trial. In order to provide that there is a realistic prospect of a conviction then it must be more likely than not that the evidence supports a prosecution. However, debates arise as to what this means in practice.

QUESTION FOR REFLECTION

Consider the meaning of 'realistic prospect of conviction'. What do you think it means?

If it means that it is more likely than not that the evidence supports a prosecution then does this mean that if there is a 51 per cent chance that the suspect committed the crime the test is satisfied? Or do you think it means that if there is a 51 per cent chance that the evidence gathered is likely to lead to a prosecution that the test is satisfied. Is there any difference between these two statements?

---

47. *Police and Criminal Evidence Act 1984*, s 24(1).
48. Ian Brownlee, 'The Statutory Charging Scheme in England and Wales: Towards a Unified Prosecution System' [2004] *Criminal Law Review* 896, 902.
49. Code for Crown Prosecutors, para 4.1.
50. Allan Hoyano, 'A Study of the Impact of the Revised Code for Crown Prosecutors' [1997] *Criminal Law Review* 556.
51. Code for Crown Prosecutors, para 4.4.

This conundrum has been at the heart of some of the criticism of the CPS particularly by the police where they believe that the CPS is sometimes too cautious in its application and does not let the courts decide on weak cases. In part this was based on the premise that it is thought that the police would use the 'prima facie test' (ie is there evidence that would make the case at least arguable?).[52] The argument for the CPS test is that a prosecution is an expensive and emotionally challenging business and one that should not be engaged without a realistic prospect of success. What is clear is that the CPS prosecutors must examine all the evidence and make judgements as to whether it is likely to be admissible and what weight is likely to be given to the evidence by the tribunal of fact, ie its reliability.[53] The CPS must also consider the evidence the defendant may adduce.

The CCP makes clear the importance of this test. If there is insufficient evidence then a person should not be charged, or if charged then the prosecution should be halted.[54] Indeed this principle is so strong that the matter will be kept under review throughout the history of the case and if at any stage, including at court, it is believed that the evidential test is no longer satisfied then the case will be halted.

Public-interest test

The second test is whether it is in the public interest for a person to be charged or prosecuted. Statute makes it expressly clear that the CPS may decide not to charge someone notwithstanding the fact that there is sufficient evidence to show that he may be guilty.[55] This is a welcome reinforcement to the principle contained in the CCP.[56]

In other words, just because someone has committed a crime does not necessarily mean that they should be prosecuted. There could be any number of reasons why a decision is taken not to prosecute even where there is clear evidence to suggest that the law has been broken. The CCP provides a list of factors that make it more or less likely that a prosecution will take place[57] and the public-interest test requires prosecutors to take these into account.

Prosecution policies

The CCP is the overarching prosecution policy but it does not specifically state the circumstances when a person will be prosecuted for a particular crime. This became relevant in the context of those people suffering from permanent debilitating illnesses who wished to commit suicide (which is not illegal) but could not without assistance (which is illegal).

The first case of note was *R (Pretty) v Director of Public Prosecutions*[58] where the House of Lords were asked to rule on a case where a woman wanted her husband to assist her in suicide. Diane Pretty suffered from advanced motor neurone disease and could not therefore take an overdose herself. She wished to die but needed her husband to feed her enough pills to make her die, which would amount to a criminal offence under s 2 *Suicide Act 1961*. A prosecution under s 2 can only be brought if the DPP gives his permission[59] and thus the applicant asked for an assurance that he would not

---

52. Andrew Ashworth and Mike Redmayne, *The Criminal Process* (4th edn, OUP 2010) 200.
53. Code for Crown Prosecutors, para 4.6.
54. Code for Crown Prosecutors, para 4.6.
55. See *Police and Criminal Evidence Act 1984*, s 37B(5)(b).
56. See para 4.8.
57. See Code for Crown Prosecutors, para 4.12ff.
58. [2002] 1 AC 800.
59. *Suicide Act 1961*, s 2(4).

409

be prosecuted. The DPP refused to give this assurance and the applicant (Mrs Pretty) applied for judicial review of that decision.

The main decision of the House was based on the *European Convention on Human Rights* (ECHR) where it held that the Convention did not provide a right to die (something that was implicitly upheld by the European Court of Human Rights when it declined an application by Mrs Pretty: *Pretty v United Kingdom*[60]) but of more interest was the court's observations about the DPP's power. The House held that the DPP had no right to confer immunity on an individual person[61] although Lord Bingham suggested that he might be able to produce a policy document explaining the circumstances under which someone would not be prosecuted for a crime although it was conceded that it may be an unwise action.[62] Such policies exist in a number of offences (published on the CPS website) but there had been no indication that such policies were required and Lord Bingham did not appear to be going so far as to require them.

The ruling was controversial and at least one academic has suggested that it created an inappropriate state of affairs whereby a person would not know the circumstances in which their planned actions will be culpable.[63] The matter inevitably returned to the courts and was the subject of the last-ever judgment of the House of Lords.

Debbie Purdy suffered from primary progressive multiple sclerosis and was wheelchair bound and incapable of doing the most basic tasks herself. She had no wish to live in what she believed to be an undignified manner and so, at a time of her choosing, she wanted to be able to travel to another country and commit suicide. In order to do so she would have needed assistance to travel and she was concerned that if her husband had assisted her abroad he would be guilty of the offence under s 2 *Suicide Act 1961*.

Debbie Purdy did not seek to persuade the DPP to provide her husband with immunity (as Diane Pretty had done) but instead focused on the suggestion by Lord Bingham that additional guidance was required. She argued that the DPP should be required to produce guidance indicating the factors that would be considered when deciding to prosecute. The matter proceeded through the courts and in *R (on the application of Purdy) v Director of Public Prosecutions*[64] the House of Lords held that the DPP did have a legal obligation to publish advice which indicated the circumstances which would lead them to decide whether to prosecute or not. The House ruled that Article 8 of the ECHR required the law to be clear and accessible and that this required advice on the particular circumstances.

The ruling was important not only for the particular circumstances relating to Debbie Purdy's case but also because it showed that the statutory code (the CCP) is not sufficient by itself to show how prosecutorial discretion will be exercised. It also undoubtedly means that the individual offence policies produced (which are published on the CPS website) must be taken into account.[65]

---

60. (2002) 35 EHRR 1.
61. *Pretty v United Kingdom* (2002) 35 EHRR 1 [39] (Lord Bingham).
62. *Pretty v United Kingdom* (2002) 35 EHRR 1 [39].
63. Richard Tur, 'Legislative Technique and Human Rights: The Sad Case of Assisted Suicide' [2003] *Criminal Law Review* 3, 10.
64. [2009] UKHL 45.
65. Debbie Purdy's health deteriorated significantly and she was unable to go through with her plan to travel abroad to die with the assistance of an assisted-suicide organization. She died in November 2014 in a hospice.

12.3 Selecting the charges

Assuming that the prosecution tests have been satisfied then the next step is to decide what a person should be charged with. In many cases this may appear simple but need not be because the criminal law is complicated and there are many overlapping offences.

12.3.1 Principles

The CCP details how the CPS should approach the issue of charging. They should:

- reflect the seriousness and extent of the offending supported by the evidence
- give the court adequate powers to sentence and impose appropriate post-conviction orders
- enable the case to be presented in a clear and simple way.[66]

These steps may seem relatively ordinary but history suggests that in many cases there has been over-charging (see 12.3.2). The conduct element of many crimes will cover many different offences and these guidelines are supposed to ensure that the charge is reflective of the conduct and consequences.

Example Wounding

The *Offences Against the Person Act 1861* (OAPA 1861) provides for a number of non-fatal offences ranging from assault occasioning actual bodily harm (ABH: s 47) to wounding or causing grievous bodily harm with intent (GBH: s 18). Existing alongside this is the crime of common assault (s 39 *Criminal Justice Act 1988* (CJA 1988)). Each has its own definition and sentence. As you will find out in your Criminal Law module, the definition of a wound is simply any cut that penetrates all layers of the skin.[67] Consider the following case:

Jordan was holding some paper when David came over and ripped it from his grasp. This action caused a paper cut to Jordan's finger.

What should the correct charge be? According to *Moriarty v Brookes* David has caused a wound to Jordan and so is theoretically liable for the offence of unlawful wounding contrary to s 20 OAPA 1861. This is punishable by a maximum sentence of five years' imprisonment and usually tried in the Crown Court (although it may also be tried in the magistrates' court).

Charging s 20 would be a gross overreaction to a simple paper cut, however. If any charge had to be laid (and that is itself open to question) then it would likely be one of common assault, which is a summary-only offence triable in the magistrates' court.

The second factor listed earlier is, however, extremely significant. It is important to note that the court must have sufficient powers available to it when dealing with an offence.

---

66. Code for Crown Prosecutors, para 6.1.
67. *Moriarty v Brookes* (1834) 6 C & P 684.

12.3.2 **Over-charging**

A common criticism of the CPS by the police was that the CPS would 'downgrade' charges.[68] In other words, the police would opt for one charge but the CPS would either reduce the charge to a lesser offence or accept a plea of guilty to a lesser charge. Sir Ian Glidewell, in a review of the CPS, was asked specifically to consider whether the CPS was systematically downgrading charges.

The conclusion of Glidewell was that there was no evidence to suggest downgrading although he suspected that it might be occurring.[69] However, this was contested by a report of Her Majesty's Inspectorate of the CPS who, when considering crimes of domestic violence, found that the police were systematically over-charging offenders but was critical of the CPS for not always taking prompt action to remedy this situation.[70] It would seem therefore that the criticism was actually a mirror of what the true position was: far from the CPS systematically downgrading charges inappropriately it was the correction of an initial mistake by the police.

The changes to charging brought about by statutory charging should mean that this does not occur since the CPS will be the one deciding the charges from the outset. This should mean that there are fewer pleas of guilty to an alternative charge although at the time of writing there is no evidence to suggest whether this has occurred.

12.3.3 **Diversion**

Whilst outside the scope of this book it is quite possible that the CPS may decide to divert a person away from the criminal justice system. Diversion works on the premise that although there is sufficient evidence to show that a crime has taken place and that it is in the public interest for formal action to be taken, the offender need not be prosecuted but could be given non-judicial action. The three principal types of diversion are:

- simple cautions
- conditional cautions
- final warnings and reprimands.

Alongside these formal forms of diversion there exists the inherent power to take informal diversionary action, ie to warn a person as to their conduct but this would ordinarily take place prior to the CPS involvement. Diversion is controversial with Lord Judge CJ, in his first press briefing in 2009, suggesting that a failure to prosecute individuals could undermine public confidence in the criminal justice system. The DPP agreed and was reported to have said in 2009 he wanted only minor offences to be dealt with by a caution or diversionary scheme but statistics continue to show that this is not always the case and cautions have been imposed for serious offences, including rape and robbery.

12.3.3.1 **Simple cautions**

Simple cautions were, in effect, the original diversion and it is where the police in effect give a formal warning for an offence. A caution forms part of an offender's

---

68.   Andrew Ashworth and Mike Redmayne, *The Criminal Process* (4th edn, OUP 2010) 210.
69.   Ian Glidewell, *The Review of the Crown Prosecution Service* (HMSO 1998) 84.
70.   HM Crown Prosecution Service Inspectorate, *Violence at Home: A Joint Inspection of the Investigation and Prosecution of Cases Involving Domestic Violence* (HMCPSI 2004) 96.

criminal record and can be discussed in court,[71] although it does not have the status of a conviction.

A simple (as distinct from conditional) caution does not have any statutory authority. In essence its status derives in part from the statement of Lord Shawcross (see 12.2.1.3) and through non-statutory guidance. The latest guidance is found in the Ministry of Justice *Simple Caution for Adult Offenders* Guidance which states that a simple caution can only be made where there is sufficient evidence to pass the 'evidential' prosecution test (see 12.2.1.3), where there has been a clear and reliable admission of guilt by the defendant, and it is in the public interest for a caution to be given. Given that there is no statutory basis for a caution it could be questioned why a caution should be recorded on the Police National Computer as a disposal. In part this is, presumably, because a person must admit guilt before a caution can be administered and in this way they are accepting the fact that they did break the law.

A particular difficulty with cautions is that their ancillary effect can be not insignificant. In early 2006 there was significant controversy when it was identified that some of those who had been cautioned for a sex offence were teaching in schools.[72] It was considered that this was inappropriate, presumably because of their admission of guilt. Similarly, if a person accepts a caution for a prescribed sexual offence they are liable to comply with the sex offender notification regime (most commonly referred to as the 'sex offenders register') for a period of five years (see s 82(1) *Sexual Offences Act 2003*). Given that the evidence is not tested by a court it could be questioned whether this is appropriate. The argument in favour of simple cautions is that one can only be imposed if a person consents, but research suggests that such consent will not always be free[73] and could, in fact, result from the person seeking to avoid the publicity of a trial irrespective of its outcome.[74]

12.3.3.2 Conditional cautions

Conditional cautions were introduced by the CJA 2003 of which s 22 permits a prosecutor to order a conditional caution to be imposed. Whilst the term 'conditional caution' is used it is submitted that the scheme has more in common with a community sentence order than a simple caution. In essence it is a caution that can contain requirements on it. The requirements are such that 'facilitate the rehabilitation of the offender' or ensure that he 'makes reparation for the offence'[75] and this potentially could include a wide range of powers although the central ethos is that the conditions must be rehabilitative or reparative rather than punitive.

A conditional caution can only be imposed if five conditions found in s 23 are satisfied:

- there is evidence to show the offender committed the offence
- the prosecutor is satisfied that the evidential test is satisfied and that a conditional caution is appropriate (this would seem to imply the public-interest test)
- the offender admits that he committed the offence

71. Ministry of Justice, *Simple Cautions for Adult Offenders* (MOJ 2015) [13].
72. Alisdair Gillespie, 'Caution Ahead: Teachers, Vetting and the Law' (2006) 18 *Education and the Law* 19.
73. Keith Soothill, 'A Cautionary Tale: The Sex Offenders Act 1997, the Police and Cautions' [1997] *Criminal Law Review* 482, 484.
74. Alisdair Gillespie, 'Caution Ahead: Teachers, Vetting and the Law' (2006) 18 *Education and the Law* 19, 23.
75. *Criminal Justice Act 2003*, s 22(3).

- the offender is warned that breach of the conditions could lead to him being prosecuted
- the offender signs a document that contains an admission, his consent to the caution and a list of the conditions.

As noted in the previous paragraph, the 'sting' in a conditional caution is that if the conditions are breached then the person may be prosecuted for the original offence.[76] This can be contrasted with a simple caution, where there is no penalty for reoffending.

Conditional cautions are undoubtedly controversial since they are bordering on amounting to a punishment (although it is likely that the government will argue that they do not amount to a punishment because of their rehabilitative purpose).[77] The principal difficulty with the scheme is that it is administrative. Although a prosecutor must be assured that there is sufficient evidence, no court has tested the evidence or the reliability of the confession. On that basis can it really be justified to impose potentially onerous conditions on an offender?

That said, it is clear that the government believes conditional cautions are an important disposition for offenders, particularly where the conduct is relatively minor. It is notable that the *Criminal Justice and Immigration Act 2008* (CJIA 2008) has introduced a system of conditional cautions (based heavily on the adult system) for adolescents called Youth Conditional Cautions. The system of youth cautions (see 12.3.3.3) continues to exist but the Youth Conditional Caution, with its ability to control behaviour, is now also an option for prosecutors.

12.3.3.3 Youth cautions

The *Legal Aid, Sentencing and Punishment of Offenders Act 2012* (LAPSOA 2012) repealed and replaced the final warnings and reprimand system which existed under the *Crime and Disorder Act 1998*. A youth caution, as with an adult caution, is allowed even if a person has been cautioned or convicted of an offence before. It is given if that is the most appropriate disposal. A youth caution will only be permitted when the police are satisfied that there is sufficient evidence to charge D with an offence, that D admits to the police that he committed the offence, and that the police do not believe that a prosecution or conditional caution is the appropriate response.[78]

A youth caution given to someone under the age of 17 must be given in the presence of an appropriate adult,[79] defined as either their parent or guardian, a social worker, or any responsible person over 18 years of age who is not a police officer or employed by the police.[80] If the young person is in the care of the local authority or a voluntary organization, then a person representing that authority or organization can also be considered an appropriate adult for the purposes of the Act.[81]

A person who receives a youth caution should be referred as soon as is practicable to a Youth Offending Team (YOT).[82] This allows the YOT to have a complete record of

---

76. *Criminal Justice Act 2003*, s 24.
77. See *Welch v United Kingdom* (1995) 20 EHRR 247; *Ibbotson v United Kingdom* (1999) 27 EHRR CD 332.
78. *Crime and Disorder Act 1998*, s 66ZA(1).
79. *Crime and Disorder Act 1998*, s 66ZA(2).
80. *Crime and Disorder Act 1998*, s 66ZA(7).
81. *Crime and Disorder Act 1998*, s 66ZA(7).
82. *Crime and Disorder Act 1998*, s 66ZB(1).

the young person's offending behaviour, as well as considering whether a rehabilitative programme is necessary, potentially including counselling, treatment, or mediation.[83]

Unlike adult cautions and conditional cautions, a juvenile does not need to consent to being disposed of by a youth caution (although the youth caution must be given in the presence of an appropriate adult). This lack of a requirement of consent reflects the decision in an extremely controversial case where the House of Lords ruled that there was no requirement for a child to consent in the context of the previous system of final warnings and reprimands.[84]

This decision can be criticized for effectively denying due process to a juvenile.[85] Despite what the House of Lords said, the consequences (of what was a warning, now a youth caution) are probably punitive and yet there is no judicial oversight of the requirement to impose a reprimand or warning (now replaced by youth cautions). This cannot be correct yet the European Court of Human Rights rejected an application to challenge the decision[86] stating that because the police were expressly not prosecuting him, it was not the determination of a criminal charge and thus outside the remit of Article 6. It is unfortunate that the ECtHR ruled this way as it raises questions as to whether adolescent offenders—who may be the most in need of protection—are not protected by judicial or legal oversight. Indeed, one of the main concerns with the introduction of youth cautions under LAPSOA 2012 is that there is no requirement of consent combined with the requirement that the young person admits to committing the offence which could lead to young people suffering an injustice as a result.

12.4 Challenging the decision

Eventually a decision will be made as to whether to prosecute an offender and it would be extremely naive to suggest that this decision would be welcomed by all parties. Many people will seek to disagree with this decision but what, if anything, can be done about it? There are, it is submitted, two classes of people who are most likely to be able to justify a challenge: those being the accused and the victim (including the dependants of a murder victim).

12.4.1 The accused

The person most likely to seek to challenge a decision to prosecute is arguably the accused. Should a defendant be permitted to challenge a decision to prosecute? The argument against permitting a challenge is that if the defendant believes that the prosecution is wrong then he can plead not guilty and let the matter proceed to trial. However, is it that simple? Lord Shawcross, it was noted earlier, suggested that not every crime should be prosecuted and accordingly perhaps the decision to prosecute should be open to challenge.

There are a number of reasons why challenges may be brought but they are all likely to revolve around the issues of fairness. Perhaps the most common reason for challenging a decision is that the CPS has made a procedural fault in its decision to prosecute.

---

83. Michael Zander, *Cases and Materials on the English Legal System* (10th edn, OUP 2007) 256.
84. *R v Durham Constabulary and another, ex p R* [2005] 1 WLR 1184.
85. Alisdair Gillespie, 'Reprimanding Juveniles and the Right to Due Process' (2005) 68 *Modern Law Review* 1006.
86. App No 33506/5.

An example of this would be that some offences require the permission of the Attorney-General or DPP before they can be commenced. If the CPS has failed to obtain the necessary permission then this must mean that the decision is automatically flawed.

Another possible reason for challenging a decision to prosecute may be to argue that the criminal offence itself is contrary to established legal principles or prosecuting a person for that offence is unlawful. If the offence is flawed then it would be perfectly reasonable to argue that a person should not be prosecuted for breaching it. Post-2000 the most likely form of argument under this head would be that either an offence or the prosecution would breach the ECHR.[87] Such challenges are permitted by virtue of s 7 *Human Rights Act 1998* (see 5.2.2.2).

A third common reason for challenging a decision is that the prosecution is simply unfair. A good example of this would be where the defendant argues that he has been tricked into committing the crime by law enforcement agents. This is commonly referred to as 'entrapment'. However, it is a long-standing rule of English law that entrapment is no defence[88] and thus a defendant could not plead not guilty in court and then ask the tribunal of fact to acquit him on the basis of entrapment. Is it fair, however, for a person to be tricked into committing a crime? It could be argued that it is not and that it would not be in the public interest to prosecute someone under those circumstances. A decision to prosecute under these circumstances could be challenged.

It has been suggested that the number of judicial reviews of prosecutorial decisions has risen in recent years[89] and whilst this is probably true the courts do appear to draw a distinction between the types of challenges.

12.4.1.1 Decisions to prosecute

In *R v DPP, ex p Kebilene*[90] the House of Lords was asked to consider, inter alia, whether it was possible to judicially review the decision of the DPP to give consent to a prosecution. The case concerned a particular terrorist offence which required the DPP's consent before a prosecution could be commenced. Lord Hope argued that judicial review of the DPP's consent should not be permitted, not least because the only remedy would be for the court to ask him to reconsider his position as a court could not order the DPP to give consent.[91] Lord Steyn went further and suggested that a decision to prosecute should not be subject to judicial review, in part because alternative remedies exist.[92] This principle was strongly reaffirmed in the more recent case of *R (Pepushi) v Crown Prosecution Service*[93] in which Thomas LJ said:

> [W]e wish to make it clear ... that applications in respect of pending prosecutions that seek to challenge the decision to prosecute should not be made to this court.[94]

The reasoning of his Lordship was that of Lord Steyn, that alternatives to judicial review exist, but what are these alternatives? The most obvious is to plead not guilty and be the subject of a trial. Where the criticism is based on a flaw in the offence rather

87. See, for example, *R v Dehal* [2005] EWHC 2154 (Admin).
88. See *R v Sang* [1980] AC 402 and in particular *R v Looseley; Attorney-General's Reference (No 3 of 2000)* [2001] 1 WLR 2060.
89. Andrew Sanders, 'Prosecution Systems' in Mike McConville and Geoffrey Wilson (eds), *The Handbook of the Criminal Justice System* (OUP 2002) 163.
90. [2000] 2 AC 326.
91. *R v DPP, ex p Kebilene* [2000] 2 AC 326, 375–6 (Lord Hope).
92. *R v DPP, ex p Kebilene* [2000] 2 AC 326, 370–1.
93. [2004] EWHC 798 (Admin).
94. *R (Pepushi) v Crown Prosecution Service* [2004] EWHC 798 (Admin) [49].

than the fact that the defendant did not commit the *actus reus* this would be unlikely to succeed. However, there is the alternative of asking the judge to rule whether the offence is known to the law or if a prosecution is an abuse of process.

The concept of 'abuse of process' is one that has been refined over the years, and is a doctrine that has been developed through the inherent jurisdiction of the courts. The doctrine is based on the fact that proceedings ought to be fair to the defendant and where there are material irregularities that make the process unfair then the trial should be halted irrespective of whether a person actually committed a crime.

 QUESTION FOR REFLECTION

Let us assume that David has been accused of possession of a class A drug with intent to supply. This is a very serious offence and one that would carry a substantial term of imprisonment if he were to be convicted. If the drugs were to reach the streets then a number of people could become addicted to the drugs. David accuses Elaine, a Detective Constable in Anytown Police, of coercing him to get the drugs. He claims Elaine told him where to buy drugs and to whom he could sell them. Should David be able to argue that he should not be prosecuted for this crime? What are the arguments for and against requiring David to stand trial? Would it make any difference to your argument if he had previously been convicted of a drug-dealing offence?

 LISTEN TO THE PODCAST

For guidance on how to answer this question and a discussion of the main issues, listen to the author's podcast on the Online Resource Centre: www.oxfordtextbooks.co.uk/orc/gillespie_els6e/

12.4.1.2 Decision not to prosecute

Although it might seem extraordinary, there may be circumstances when a suspect may wish to challenge a decision not to prosecute him, ie he wants the prosecution to go ahead in order to 'clear his name'. There have been reported instances of this but it is submitted unlikely that the courts would entertain such an application. The overriding principle is that a person is innocent until proved guilty and accordingly the courts would almost certainly view the position as being that the suspect has nothing to 'clear'. Where someone is alleging that he is guilty then alternative remedies would exist for this, eg an action for defamation of character.

12.4.2 Victims

The suspect is not the only person who may wish to challenge a decision to prosecute; it is quite possible that a victim would also wish to do so, yet it has been stated:

> The main group concerned with non-prosecution decisions are victims. Their 'stake' in official prosecutions is not formally recognised by the common law.[95]

---

95. Andrew Sanders, 'Prosecution Systems' in Mike McConville and Geoffrey Wilson (eds), *The Handbook of the Criminal Justice System* (OUP 2002) 161.

The place of victims within the criminal justice system has always been controversial and will probably remain so. One of the tensions that exist between the police and the CPS is that the former perceive themselves as assisting the victim whereas the latter cannot. Indeed the Code for Crown Prosecutors makes this quite clear:

> … the prosecution service does not act for victims or their families in the same way as solicitors act for their clients, and prosecutors must form an overall view of the public interest.[96]

Historically the victim is just one character within the case. Whilst there may be an increasing recognition of victims and the pressures that a criminal case can place upon them they remain semi-detached from the process, since in England and Wales, unlike in other jurisdictions, the victim does not have any formal prosecuting role.[97]

However, it would be naive to suggest that victims have no place within the proceedings or influence in its decisions and the Code continues:

> In deciding whether a prosecution is required in the public interest, prosecutors should take into account any views expressed by the victim regarding the impact the offence has had.[98]

This suggests that victims have a say but not a veto in decisions. However, some have argued that this is not necessarily reflective of the position and that the particular views of an individual victim should not be taken into account when deciding whether to bring a prosecution as it is purely a matter of the public interest.[99]

Example Domestic violence

Perhaps the classic example of a situation where the victim's wishes may be controversial is that of domestic violence. It is not uncommon for victims of domestic violence to retract an allegation made against their partner.[100] If this happens, should a prosecution be stopped? Domestic violence is a particularly brutal form of assault because of the psychological abuse it entails. Society should try to stamp out such violence and thus there is a significant public interest in a prosecution proceeding. There is also evidence to suggest that a victim of such violence suffers cognitive distortions as a result of their treatment and thus a withdrawal of complaint need not be in the best interests of the victim or indeed their true wishes. Alternatively, however, if a prosecution does go ahead there may be difficulties in establishing the evidence (will the victim testify?) and it could in fact cause the victim hardship. The victim may need to leave the house (and possibly her children) or if the man is the main earner then the victim may be placed in a position where she has no money.

How should the wishes and interests of the victim of domestic violence be balanced?

12.4.2.1 Decision not to prosecute

The most likely challenge that would be brought by a victim would be against a decision not to prosecute. The House of Lords in *Kebilene*[101] (see 12.4.1.1) was careful

---

96. Code for Crown Prosecutors, para 4.12(c).
97. Alisdair Gillespie, 'Child Abuse Prosecutions and the Human Rights Act 1998' (1998) 150 *New Law Journal* 620.
98. Code for Crown Prosecutors, para 4.12(c).
99. Andrew Ashworth and Mike Redmayne, *The Criminal Process* (4th edn, OUP 2010) 218.
100. Andrew Ashworth and Mike Redmayne, *The Criminal Process* (4th edn, OUP 2010) 178.
101. *R v DPP, ex p Kebilene* [2000] 2 AC 326.

to ensure that they limited their denial of judicial review to decisions to prosecute. Lord Steyn expressly stated that a judicial review of a decision not to prosecute is possible.[102] His Lordship noted that the main justification for permitting a review of a decision not to prosecute is the absence of any alternative options. Strictly speaking this is not technically true since private prosecutions exist (see 12.1.3) but this is not a particularly realistic alternative, something noted by the Court of Appeal:

> ... only the most sardonic could regard the launching of a private prosecution (a process which, incidentally is become regarded with increasing disfavour in this country) as being equally convenient, beneficial and appropriate [as judicial review].[103]

In *R v DPP, ex p C*[104] the Court of Appeal was asked to consider the principles under which judicial review could begin and Kennedy LJ stated:

> [Judicial review can occur] if and only if it is demonstrated to us that the Director of Public Prosecutions acting through the Crown Prosecution Service arrived at the decision not to prosecute:
>
> (1) because of some unlawful policy ...
>
> (2) because the Director of Public Prosecutions failed to act in accordance with his or her own settled policy as set out in the Code; or
>
> (3) because the decision was perverse. It was a decision at which no reasonable prosecutor could have arrived.[105]

In essence this statement reflects the traditional grounds of judicial review but the one that may be of most interest is ground 2 which refers to the Code. The CCP has been discussed previously but there is considerable doubt as to how it is used:

> Most prosecutors regard the Code as a very basic document to which they saw no need to refer on a regular or even occasional basis ... The Code is a Noddy's guide to the principles on which the CPS operates.[106]

Their argument is that prosecutors will ordinarily make a reference to the individual prosecution policies that will detail individual factors to be taken into account.

However, even if the Code is rarely used this should not detract from the second point since the Code does represent the minimum statement of policy in relation to prosecutions. Accordingly, if a case fails to adhere to the Code, regardless of whether the Code was actually examined, then a judicial review could arise.

Permitting a judicial review to be brought is only one part of the story, however. Whilst there are a number of remedies open to the High Court when disposing of a judicial review, no court has stated that it has the right to order the CPS (or more realistically the DPP) to prosecute but has instead limited itself to quashing the decision of the DPP not to prosecute. In *ex p C* it was made clear by Kennedy LJ that this did not mean that a prosecution must occur because it remained at the discretion of the DPP, and simply entailed the DPP reconsidering the decision albeit this time in the correct way.[107]

102. *R v DPP, ex p Kebilene* [2000] 2 AC 326, 369.
103. *R v Metropolitan Police Commissioner, ex p Blackburn* [1968] 1 All ER 763, 777 (Edmund Davies LJ).
104. [1995] 1 Cr App R 136.
105. *R v DPP, ex p C* [1995] 1 Cr App R 136, 141.
106. Allan Hoyano, 'A Study of the Impact of the Revised Code for Crown Prosecutors' [1997] *Criminal Law Review* 556, 558.
107. *R v DPP, ex p C* [1995] 1 Cr App R 136, 144.

In the case of *R v Christopher Kinnick*,[108] the Court of Appeal held that victims have a right to seek a review of a CPS decision not to prosecute and that they should not have to seek recourse to judicial review (discussed earlier) in such circumstances. In response to this judgment the CPS set out the *Victims' Right to Review Scheme* which came into effect in June 2013. Under the scheme victims can seek review where the CPS make a 'qualifying decision' that is, that the CPS decides: 'not to bring proceedings; decides to discontinue ... all proceedings, offers no evidence in all proceedings ... or decides to leave all charges in the proceedings to "lie on file" '.[109]

Under the scheme victims will be notified of the CPS decision not to proceed and will be informed as to whether they are able to exercise the right to review. If the victim decides that they would like a review to take place, they should notify the CPS of their request for review within five working days of receiving the notification regarding the halt of proceedings.[110]

Once the CPS have received the request for review they will carry out a 'local resolution', which involves the local CPS office or CPS Direct looking again at the decision and deciding whether it was correct. If it is felt that the original decision was incorrect and proceedings should and indeed can be recommenced, the CPS will notify the victim. If they determine that the original decision was in fact correct the victim will be provided with additional information regarding the decision and will be informed of their option to contact the Appeals and Review Unit or the Chief Crown Prosecutor for an 'independent review'. The 'local resolution' process is normally completed within ten working days of the review request being received by the CPS.[111] If the victim requests an 'independent review' a new reviewing prosecutor will reconsider the evidence and the public interest,[112] with the outcome being communicated to the victim within thirty working days of the review request.

When deciding whether to overturn a decision to end proceedings or not to prosecute, the CPS must be satisfied: 'that the earlier decision was wrong in applying the evidential or public interest stages of the Full Code Test (as set out in the Code for Crown Prosecutors); and that for the maintenance of public confidence the decision must be reversed.'[113]

In *S v CPS*[114] a suspect chose to judicially review a decision to prosecute him, which occurred due to a successful right of review of a decision not to prosecute. The suspect alleged that the policy was unlawful and that the decision to overturn the appeal was irrational. The latter point was rejected for reasons that do not concern us (as they were fact-specific) but it is worth noting that Leveson P comprehensively rejected the suggestion that the right of review policy was unlawful, stating the 'Guidance is a lawful policy in its entirety'.[115]

In *L v DPP*[116] it was stated unequivocally that a judicial review of a decision not to prosecute cannot be brought without first challenging the decision through the right of review.[117] This is arguably just an ordinary principle of judicial review—that a person

108.   [2011] EWCA Crim 1608.
109.   CPS, *Victims' Right to Review Guidance* (Crown Prosecution Service 2014) 3.
110.   CPS, *Victims' Right to Review Guidance* (Crown Prosecution Service 2014) 5.
111.   CPS, *Victims' Right to Review Guidance* (Crown Prosecution Service 2014) 6–7.
112.   CPS, *Victims' Right to Review Guidance* (Crown Prosecution Service 2014) 7.
113.   CPS, *Victims' Right to Review Guidance* (Crown Prosecution Service 2014) 8.
114.   [2015] EWHC 2868 (Admin).
115.   [2015] EWHC 2868 (Admin) [17].
116.   [2013] EWHC 1752 (Admin).
117.   [2013] EWHC 1752 (Admin) [12].

must first exhaust all other remedies—but it is also clear that this case, in combination with *S v CPS*, shows that the courts strongly support the right of review process.

The second point that was stated in *L v DPP* is perhaps as important. Thomas P stated:

> [I]f there has been a review in accordance with this procedure, then it seems to me, that the prospects of success [in bringing a judicial review] will...be very small.[118]

Again, this can only be the courts demonstrating that they will interfere with a prosecutorial discretion in extreme situations. Realistically it will be very difficult to show that a decision is irrational, meaning that the claimant will need to show that the reviewing prosecutor did not follow an established policy or otherwise acted unlawfully. This is a difficult hurdle, given that reviews take place before senior prosecutors.

12.4.2.2 Decision to prosecute

It may seem extraordinary but there may actually be circumstances when a victim may wish to challenge a decision to prosecute. Perhaps the most obvious example of this would be when it is believed that a prosecution is not in their interests and a good example of this could be in cases involving children:

> It may well be safe to assume that it is in the public interest that child abusers should be prosecuted ... Yet, in many cases, once the child's protection has been assured, there may well be a conflict between the public interest in pursuing a prosecution and the child's best interests in having the case dealt with in a manner which causes the least stress and disruption.[119]

This is an interesting issue as it demonstrates that there could be tension between the public interest and the victim. The principal issue will always be the strength of the public interest:

> [A] decision not to prosecute may indicate to the abuser that, so far as the community is concerned, he did not commit the offence.[120]

In other words, whilst prosecuting may not be in the interests of the victim and could even be contrary to the best interests (and/or wishes) of the victim, not prosecuting may cause more harm to the public interest. What should be the position here? Some have suggested that the law should accept a challenge to a decision to prosecute as this would require the judges to consider the rights of each individual victim[121] but others argue that society would probably prefer the prosecution to continue.

12.5 Immunity

There has, over many years, been a debate as to how persons who assist the prosecution are treated by prosecutors. As a minimum it would normally lead to a reduction in their sentence[122] but there has always been doubt as to whether prosecutors

---

118.   [2013] EWHC 1752 (Admin) [13].
119.   Catherine Cobley, *Child Abuse and the Law* (Cavendish Publishing 1995) 160.
120.   Jane Fortin, *Children's Rights and the Developing Law* (3rd edn, OUP 2009) 656.
121.   Alisdair Gillespie, 'Child Abuse Prosecutions and the Human Rights Act 1998' (1998) 150 *New Law Journal* 620.
122.   See, for example, *R v A (Informer: Reduction in Sentence)* [1999] 1 Cr App R(S) 52.

had given de facto immunity to someone cooperating by testifying. In essence such an approach could probably have been justified on the basis of the public-interest test: that it is in the public interest to encourage people to inform against serious crime and that this may have overridden the competing interest that someone who has committed a (minor) crime should be prosecuted.

No formal basis existed for deciding immunity—it was simply a matter of prosecutorial discretion—but this has now changed with the passing of the *Serious Organised Crime and Police Act 2005* which permits immunity to be granted. Section 71 permits, inter alia, specified prosecutors to grant total immunity for any offence other than an offence under s 188 *Enterprise Act 2002* (which deals with cartels and which is subject to immunity provisions within the 2002 Act). Immunity is conferred by a notice and this allows the prosecutor to set out the limits of the immunity (presumably the obligations of the subject) and if these are breached then the immunity may be lifted.[123]

12.6 Transferring the matter to court

Once the decision has been made to prosecute an offender how does the case arrive in court? There are two courts of first instance that hear criminal matters; the magistrates' court and the Crown Court. Chapter 15 considers the competing interests involved in a trial in the magistrates' court and a trial in the Crown Court, including reasons why a person may choose each. However, in this section of the chapter the actual process of making the decision will be discussed.

12.6.1 Classification of offences

All criminal offences can be classified in one of three ways:

- summary-only matters
- those triable only on indictment
- either-way offences.

Summary matters are those that are heard only in the magistrates' court. Offences triable only on indictment are those that are heard only in the Crown Court and either-way offences are, as their name suggests, heard in either court. Identifying what classification an offence is can be quite simple. Common-law offences are triable only on indictment unless the alternative is stated.

⚡ COMMON-LAW CRIMES

The offences of assault and battery are defined in the common law but s 39 CJA 1988 prescribes their mode of trial as summary only. Murder, on the other hand, is a common-law crime and one that has not been prescribed and accordingly it is triable only on indictment.

The vast majority of crimes are, however, created by statute and the Act will ordinarily state what the classification is.

---

123. *Serious Organised Crime and Police Act 2005*, s 71(3).

⚡ CLASSIFICATION OF OFFENCES

The following are examples of how to discover the classification of offences.

SUMMARY-ONLY OFFENCES

(4) A person guilty of an offence under this section is liable on summary conviction to a fine not exceeding level 5 on the standard scale.

TRIABLE ONLY ON INDICTMENT

(4) A person guilty of an offence under this section is liable, on conviction on indictment, to imprisonment for a term not exceeding 10 years.

TRIABLE EITHER WAY

(4) A person guilty of an offence under this section is liable—

  (a) on summary conviction, to imprisonment for a term not exceeding 12 months or to a fine not exceeding the statutory maximum or both.

  (b) on conviction on indictment, to imprisonment for a term not exceeding 10 years.

Unfortunately this rule does not apply to all historic crimes. A classic example of this is theft where s 7 *Theft Act 1968* gives the penalties for those convicted of theft. The section states:

A person guilty of theft shall on conviction on indictment be liable for imprisonment for a term not exceeding seven years.

This would appear to create an offence triable only on indictment and yet theft is, in fact, triable either way. The reason for this change was that the *Criminal Law Act 1977* (CLA 1977) downgraded many indictable-only offences to permit a more balanced approach to be taken to the court system. Some offences became summary-only but many became triable either way. Schedule 1 *Magistrates' Court Act 1980* (MCA 1980) produces a consolidated list of offences that have been re-categorized and accordingly where an offence is contained in a statute prior to this it is wise to check Sch 1 to assess how it is to be tried.

12.6.1.1 Summary matters

Approximately 97 per cent of all crime is tried summarily[124] and the bulk of this work is summary-only offences. An offence can only be triable summarily if the statute expressly states so, and the CJA 2003 has increased the maximum punishment the magistrates' court can pass to twelve months' imprisonment (s 154) (although this is not yet in force). Whether this means that there may be further 'reordering' of offences is more questionable but this increase in penalty probably has more impact on either-way offences.

 Traditionally a magistrates' court only had jurisdiction to deal with summary matters that took place within its own county[125] but s 44 of the *Courts Act 2003* (CA 2003) extended its jurisdiction and it can now hear summary matters irrespective

124. Penny Darbyshire, 'An Essay on the Importance and Neglect of the Magistracy' [1997] *Criminal Law Review* 627.

125. *Magistrates' Courts Act 1980*, s 2(1).

of wherever the crime took place. This brings summary-only offences into line with either-way offences where magistrates' courts always had the power to try crimes regardless of where they had taken place. This could be advantageous when a crime takes place in one county and ends in another.

12.6.1.2 Indictable-only offences

Indictable-only offences were relatively few in number but the *Sexual Offences Act 2003* has increased their number considerably. However, it is still true to state that offences that can only be tried on indictment are comparatively uncommon and are normally reserved to the most serious offences. As noted earlier, common-law crimes are indictable only although the number of common-law crimes has decreased since the certainty of statutory law is to be preferred.

> **Example** Conspiracy
>
> Section 1 *Criminal Law Act 1977* repealed, in part, the common-law crime of conspiracy and replaced it with a statutory crime of conspiracy which is triable only on indictment. The offence is committed when two or more persons agree to commit a criminal offence, including a summary-only offence. Accordingly, as a quirk of the mode-of-trial proceedings a conspiracy to commit a summary offence is triable only on indictment whereas if the offence were actually to be completed it would be triable only summarily. The punishment for the conspiracy is the maximum that could be passed for the substantive offence.

12.6.1.3 Either-way offences

The largest grouping of criminal offences are those triable either way and most new offences appear to come within these offences. This category of offences has caused the most debate over the years and two particular offences appear to be at the heart of this debate: theft and criminal damage.

Theft

In 1977 consideration was given as to whether the theft of a small amount of money or goods of low monetary value should be classified as a summary-only matter. The argument was that the low monetary value meant that the offence was quite trivial and should, therefore, be disposed of summarily. This proposal was fiercely contested, however, since theft is a crime of dishonesty and accordingly a finding of theft is a finding that a person has acted dishonestly.

QUESTION FOR REFLECTION

Why would a conviction for theft be considered any more serious than, for example, a crime of violence? Yet common assault is triable only summarily. What reasons are there for resisting the reduction to summary-only status? (For example, think about the occupation of the offender: would it make any difference if it was a police officer who was charged with the theft of a bar of chocolate rather than a cleaner?)

In the 1990s when mode-of-trial decisions were the subject of some debate in Parliament (see 12.6.2.2) the issue was revisited but the position remained (and still remains) the same: theft is an either-way offence.

Criminal damage

At the same time as theft was being debated, an argument arose whether modest criminal damage should be reclassified as a summary matter. The argument differed slightly, in that criminal damage is not a crime of dishonesty and accordingly fewer objections were raised. The CLA 1977 did lead to a partition in the way criminal damage is tried. The modern distinction is that if the damage is to goods of a value of less than £5,000 then the offence is triable only summarily.[126] Where the damage is for more than £5,000 then the offence is triable either way and can, therefore, be tried summarily or on indictment.

When criminal damage was reclassified the sentencing powers of the magistrates' court were also restricted so that damage to property of less than £5,000 is punishable by a maximum of three months' imprisonment rather than the usual maximum for summary matters.[127]

12.6.2 Transferring the matter

Now that classification has been discussed, how is a case transferred to the correct court? The principal distinction is, in effect, between either-way offences and the others.

12.6.2.1 Non-either-way offences

Trial on indictment gets its name because the accused is asked to plead to an indictment, ie a formal document that lists the charges for which the person is to be tried. The equivalent document for a summary trial is called the 'information'. Where a person has been charged by the police the charge sheet will be sent to the magistrates' court. Where the offender is not arrested and charged (as not everyone will necessarily be arrested, the classic example of this perhaps being speeding offences or a failure to pay a TV licence) then a form listing the charges is prepared by the prosecutor and this is laid before the magistrates' court.

The information must be listed within six months of the crime being committed.[128] If the information is out of time then ordinarily no action can be taken against the person. This, however, only applies to summary-only offences and not to either-way offences.

Once the information has been laid before the court, a summons will be delivered to the defendant and this is the court to which he will appear. The course of a summary trial is discussed in the next chapter.

Indictable-only matters

The pre-trial procedure for those crimes that are triable only on indictment is now simple. Historically, persons were sent to the Crown Court from the magistrates'

425

126. *Magistrates' Courts Act 1980*, s 22; in *R (Abbott) v Colchester Magistrates' Court* [2001] EWHC Admin 136 the Divisional Court held that this meant the value of the damage and not the value of any compensation claimed.
127. *Criminal Justice Act 2003*, s 154.
128. *Magistrates' Courts Act 1980*, s 127.

court by way of committal. This required the magistrates to decide whether there was a case to answer. The original form of committal was that all the evidence was heard and it became, in essence, a 'mini trial'. Eventually this was changed to permit 'paper' committals where only documentary evidence was required. The principal advantage of this was a reduction in time and costs but it also meant that the defendant did not have to disclose his or her defence until the time of trial, something that could be tactically advantageous.

⟳ QUESTION FOR REFLECTION

Why would not disclosing the full defence evidence be advantageous to the defendant?

The *Crime and Disorder Act 1998* (CDA 1998) introduced a new 'fast-track' approach to transferring cases to the Crown Court, often referred to as 'Narey transfers' since the initial idea arose from the Narey Report on delays within the criminal justice system.[129] Section 51 of the 1998 Act ensures that where an offender is charged with an indictable-only offence this matter is sent directly to the Crown Court and there is no requirement, or indeed power, for magistrates to review the case save for issues of bail etc. Where the offender has been charged with either-way offences and summary-only offences at the same time as indictable-only offences then, so long as the charges are 'related' (meaning 'it arises out of circumstances which are the same or connected with those giving rise to the indictable only offence'[130]) then they may also proceed directly to the Crown Court.

Committal was, in essence, the opportunity for the defendant to challenge the prosecution case and argue that there was insufficient evidence to convict (although data suggests that only approximately 0.2 per cent of cases are dismissed at committal stage[131]). In order to permit a challenge to be brought under the new scheme the statute permits a defendant to make an application to a Crown Court judge for the matter to be dismissed for lack of evidence.[132] If the judge, after reviewing the evidence before the court, does not believe that there is sufficient evidence for a jury properly to convict the defendant then the matter must be dismissed.[133]

12.6.2.2 Either-way offences

It has been stated that the debate as to who decides the venue of the trial has been one of the most contested issues within the criminal justice system.[134] During the period 1998–2000 there was a concerted effort by the newly elected Labour government to abolish the defendant's de facto veto. It is important, when considering this debate, to ensure that the language is correct. Whilst many will talk about the right of a defendant to elect his or her trial venue, this is not strictly true. A defendant could elect trial on indictment and veto a summary trial but could only ask for a matter to be tried summarily. If the magistrates disagreed with his request and thought that a trial on indictment would be more suitable then the defendant had no veto.

---

129. Martin Narey, *Review of Delay in the Criminal Justice System* (Home Office 1997) ch 6.
130. *Crime and Disorder Act 1998*, s 51(2).
131. CPS, *Annual Report and Accounts 2014–15* (Crown Prosecution Service 2015) 68.
132. *Crime and Disorder Act 1998*, sch 3, para 2.
133. *Crime and Disorder Act 1998*, sch 3, para 2(2).
134. Andrew Ashworth and Mike Redmayne, *The Criminal Process* (4th edn, OUP 2010) 328–30.

The debate was long and became quite intemperate at times but ended with the government conceding that the defendant's veto should not be removed. Why did this debate arise? The Home Office, in 1999, argued that during 1998 some 18,500 cases were sent to the Crown Court and that 75 per cent of offenders pleaded guilty at Crown Court. The implication was, therefore, that this was wasting Crown Court time since if defendants were to plead guilty then they could have done so at magistrates' court level. However, it has been suggested that these figures were slightly misrepresentative in that the 75 per cent included those who were sent to the Crown Court on matters that were triable only on indictment and where the magistrates had decided that the case was too serious for the offence to be heard as a summary matter.[135] The then Attorney-General appeared to recognize this when, in the House of Lords debate, he argued that 60 per cent of those who elect trial in the Crown Court pleaded guilty,[136] although these figures continued to be controversial.

The principal justification for attempting change was undoubtedly costs. There is a significant difference between the costs of a summary trial and a trial on indictment, in part because there are a greater number of lawyers and a professional judge together with a jury. Whilst members of a jury are not paid, they do receive expenses, but it appears that they add to the length of the trial, with jury trials taking significantly longer than those in magistrates' courts. The government estimated in 1999 that the changes to mode of trial would have saved it approximately £100 million per year.[137]

Despite these perceived advantages, the attempts were rejected after two separate government Bills were introduced to bring about this change. In part it can be explained by comments of the then Lord Chief Justice, Lord Taylor, who stated: 'in our culture and perception trial by jury is a fundamental right.'[138] Whilst this may be true it is slightly less obvious than it may seem. Many at the time argued that trial by jury was a historic right, even tracing it back to the Magna Carta; however, this is simply not true. The Magna Carta did provide for trial by one's peers—it meant just that a peer (Lord) could be tried by other peers (Lords) and it did not apply to the ordinary citizens. However, Lord Taylor was almost certainly correct when he argued that in recent times the choice has taken on the mantle of a right.

QUESTION FOR REFLECTION

Why should the right to a jury trial be considered a fundamental right? If anything other than a jury trial is not as 'fair', why do we allow other courts to hear matters?

The *Criminal Justice and Public Order Act 1994* (CJPOA 1994) heavily altered the mode-of-trial position but left the right of veto intact. The principal changes were to allow for a smoother transfer to the Crown Court where both parties wished the matter to proceed there, and also for the defendant to provide an early indication as to how he was likely to plead before the decision as to mode of trial was taken.

An illustration of the complexity of this issue is the fact that the first edition of this book was written with the expectation that amendments put forward by the CJA 2003

---

135. Satnam Choongh, 'Defendant's Right to Elect Jury Trial Under Threat—Again' [1998] *Justice of the Peace* 936.
136. Lord Williams of Mostyn, *Hansard*, HL Deb, col 1292 (20 January 2000).
137. Explanatory notes to the Mode of Trial (no 1) Bill 1999, para 15.
138. Andrew Ashworth, 'Plea, Venue and Discontinuance' [1993] *Criminal Law Review* 830, 832.

would be shortly in force. In fact this has proven to be wrong and indeed governments of all political persuasions have postponed their introduction and indeed the CJIA 2008 reversed one principal change contained within the CJA 2003.

It will be necessary briefly to summarize the current position and identify what changes may (in the fullness of time) occur. The 'plea before venue' system introduced by the CJPOA 1994 remains in force. In essence this requires that the charge is put to the defendant in words of ordinary language and he is asked to indicate how, if the matter proceeds to trial, he is likely to plead.[139] The defendant should be warned that if he indicates that he would plead guilty then the matter will proceed at summary level but that the court can commit him to the Crown Court for sentence where it believes its powers are inadequate. If he does indicate that he would plead guilty then this is then taken to be his plea and the court proceeds to a sentencing hearing.

If the defendant indicates that he is likely to plead not guilty then the matter proceeds as a mode of trial. The magistrates ask the prosecution and defence for their views on whether a summary trial or trial on indictment would be most suited. The court must take into account the nature of the case, whether the circumstances appear to make the offence serious, whether the powers of punishment following a summary trial would be adequate, and any other circumstance the court feels relevant.[140] When the allocation guidelines are produced (mentioned later) the court will have to take these into account as an 'other circumstance'.

If the magistrates believe that the matter should be tried on indictment then the matter proceeds to committal. Where, however, the magistrates believe that the matter is suited to summary trial then they must explain this to the defendant, explain (once again) that he could be committed to the Crown Court for sentence if the court finds the matter serious, and then ask whether he consents to be tried summarily.[141] If he does not consent to a summary trial then the matter is sent for committal whereas if he does consent, the matter is heard as a summary trial.

Schedule 3 CJA 2003 has introduced a number of significant changes to the process. One of the most notable is that it allows a single lay magistrate to decide mode of trial rather than the current bench of three. Another key change is that the prosecution is able to adduce previous convictions at the mode-of-trial hearing[142]—historically the magistrates were not told this. The essence of the change is to allow the court, at the earliest stage, to identify whether its powers of sentencing would be adequate. To counter any unfairness, it had originally been intended to restrict the ability of the magistrates to commit the defendant to the Crown Court after conviction at summary trial except where it was thought he was dangerous. However, the CJIA 2008 has reversed this change and magistrates are able to commit a defendant where they believe the matter is so serious that the Crown Court's sentencing powers should be available.

The other significant change is to permit the defendant to ask for an indication of sentence when asked to indicate his intended plea.[143] An indication of sentence will allow a court (although it will not have to do so)[144] to inform the defendant of the type

---

139. *Magistrates' Courts Act 1980*, s 17A.
140. *Magistrates' Courts Act 1980*, s 19(3).
141. *Magistrates' Courts Act 1980*, s 20.
142. *Criminal Justice Act 2003*, sch 3, para 5.
143. *Criminal Justice Act 2003*, sch 3, para 6.
144. *Criminal Justice Act 2003*, sch 3, para 6.

of sentence that is likely to be imposed if they try the matter summarily (eg custodial, non-custodial, financial penalty, etc).

 QUESTION FOR REFLECTION

Should a court be able to give an indication of sentence? Why would a court decide not to grant an indication?

The changes introduced by the (amended) CJA 2003 are undoubtedly an attempt to simplify the procedure and bring about a more sensible approach to elections. Permitting the magistrates to know the previous convictions of the defendant is a welcome step and one that is probably overdue. There existed a debate over the appropriateness of permitting a defendant's previous convictions to be known by the tribunal of fact, but it did not necessarily follow that the magistrates deciding mode of trial would also try the defendant. Previous convictions do influence a sentence and for this reason it would have been preferable for this change to have occurred sooner. However, it is perhaps more difficult to justify the CJIA 2008 amendment to still permit committal for sentence. If the magistrates are now to know the offender's previous convictions then they should be able to determine whether the case (taken at its highest, ie if what the prosecution say can be proven) is too serious for them. If it is then it should go to the Crown Court. If it is not then it should be dealt with at summary level, including sentence.

12.7 The plea

Before a trial can start the defendant must first have the accusations put to him and be asked to plead to each charge. Whilst it may be thought that this is a relatively simple exercise there are, in fact, four pleas: guilty, not guilty, *autrefois convict*, and *autrefois acquit*. In addition to these it is also possible to provide a conditional plea by pleading guilty to an alternative charge. If a defendant refuses to tender a plea then this is recorded as being a plea of 'not guilty' because all defendants are innocent until proven guilty.

12.7.1 *Autrefois*

There are two forms of autrefois and these are summarized here:

Autrefois acquit—previously been acquitted of the charges.

Autrefois convict—previously been convicted of the charges.

The logic behind *autrefois* is that a person should only be tried for the same facts once and, accordingly, if a defendant has been previously convicted or acquitted then the prosecution should not proceed. In recent years there has been a change from this position as a result of two statutory amendments. The first was the abolition of the year and a day rule in homicide cases[145] which abolished the common-law rule that for a person to be convicted of murder the death must occur within a year and a day

145. *Law Reform (Year and a Day Rule) Act 1996.*

of the actions of the defendant. The change to this rule means that it may be possible that a person could be tried for a non-fatal offence but then to be later tried for a fatal offence following the death of the victim.

> ### ☰ **Example** Keith Stephenson
>
> Keith Stephenson was originally charged with grievous bodily harm when he attacked his victim in a public park. He was sentenced for that crime. Three years later his victim died as a result of an epileptic fit brought on by the original injury. The Attorney-General consented to a manslaughter charge being brought and, in April 2005, Stephenson pleaded guilty to this charge in the Crown Court in Newcastle.

The second, and perhaps more significant, change to this rule is that introduced by CJA 2003 which amends the rule of double jeopardy, the rule that states a person should not be tried for the same offence twice. Part 10 CJA 2003 permits those who have been acquitted of certain serious offences to be retried but only if the Court of Appeal (Criminal Division) allows this. This rule is explored in more depth in Chapter 16 (see 16.4.3) but it is important to note that the rule has not been abolished completely. Unless the Court of Appeal quashes the acquittal (according to the rules set out in Part 10 CJA 2003) then the principle of *autrefois acquit* still applies.

12.7.2 **Plea bargaining**

Otton suggests that there are four forms of plea bargaining:

- an agreement between the judge and accused that if the accused pleads guilty to an offence the sentence will take a particular form
- an agreement between the accused and the prosecutor that if the accused pleads guilty to some offences the prosecution will leave the other offences off the indictment and/or ask the judge for a lighter sentence
- an agreement between the prosecution and defence that they will accept a plea of guilty to a lesser offence than the offence charged
- an agreement that the accused will plead guilty to some of the counts upon the indictment but not to others and the prosecution will not seek a trial for the remaining counts.[146]

The first two of these examples are, theoretically, illegal under English law whereas the latter two are accepted parts of the criminal justice system. The position has become slightly more complicated by the *Serious Organised Crime and Police Act 2005* (SOCPA 2005) which attempts to regulate certain arrangements between the prosecutors and defence. The position in England and Wales can be contrasted with the position in other jurisdictions, most notably the United States of America, where all four forms of plea bargaining identified earlier are commonplace.[147]

---

146. Philip Otton, 'The Role of the Judge in Criminal Cases' in Mike McConville and Geoffrey Wilson (eds), *The Handbook of the Criminal Justice Process* (OUP 2002) 326.
147. Mike McConville, 'Plea Bargaining' in Mike McConville and Geoffrey Wilson (eds), *The Handbook of the Criminal Justice Process* (OUP 2002) 353.

The most common form in England and Wales is the reduction in charge, in part because so many acts can be covered by different offences. Perhaps the most usual are those shown in Table 12.1. Otton argues that it is important that the judge is involved in this process although concern has been raised as to whether this invariably happens. A judge has the power to reject a plea bargain and perhaps one of the most famous examples of this is when the judge refused to accept a plea of manslaughter in respect of Peter Sutcliffe, the so-called 'Yorkshire Ripper'. The Attorney-General of the day, leading for the prosecution, had been prepared to accept this plea but the judge's veto meant that the matter proceeded to trial. Sutcliffe was convicted of murder by the jury. In the majority of situations, however, it is more likely that the judge will approve the bargain because it will save on costs and, in certain cases, prevent vulnerable witnesses from the need to testify.[148]

The position in England and Wales is governed by a series of rules put forward in the case of *R v Turner*[149] and the essence of the rules is that any discussion between counsel and the judge should be given in open court and no undue pressure must be placed on the defendant to plead guilty. However, this no longer means that a person should not necessarily be told the likely type of sentence (ie non-custodial or custodial) if they were to plead guilty to an offence (*R v Goodyear*[150]) but it is at the discretion of the judge to decide whether to provide an indication.

It is perhaps this latter point that is the most difficult in the area of plea bargaining. There are undoubted cost benefits in trials resulting in guilty pleas but a person should only plead guilty when they are and should not be influenced by the threat of a loss of liberty if they do not do so. However, research appears to suggest that quite often defendants will consider themselves to be under significant pressure, including from their own lawyers.[151] Indeed some commentators argue that there is a cultural belief that this is an acceptable way of dealing with a criminal case.[152] This belief appears to be borne out by other commentators with Darbyshire, for example, noting that the Northern Circuit has a reputation for 'endemic plea negotiations'.[153]

The more difficult spin on this therefore is whether an innocent person is forced to plead guilty because of this pressure or incentive. There appears to be almost unanimous support by commentators that some innocent people will succumb to the pressure,[154] but there is some dispute as to the role of defence counsel. It has been seen that some believe that counsel actively encourage such deals whereas others argue that it raises an interesting ethical problem for defence counsel if he suspects his client is innocent but nonetheless decides to tender a plea in the hope of getting a reduced sentence.[155]

148.   Philip Otton, 'The Role of the Judge in Criminal Cases' in Mike McConville and Geoffrey Wilson (eds), *The Handbook of the Criminal Justice Process* (OUP 2002) 326.
149.   [1970] 2 QB 321.
150.   [2005] EWCA Crim 888.
151.   Mike McConville, 'Plea Bargaining' in Mike McConville and Geoffrey Wilson (eds), *The Handbook of the Criminal Justice Process* (OUP 2002) 369.
152.   Andrew Ashworth and Mike Redmayne, *The Criminal Process* (4th edn, OUP 2010) 299.
153.   Penny Darbyshire, *Sitting in Judgment: The Working Lives of Judges* (Hart Publishing 2011) 208.
154.   Andrew Ashworth and Mike Redmayne, *The Criminal Process* (4th edn, OUP 2010) 311; Mike McConville 'Plea Bargaining' in Mike McConville and Geoffrey Wilson (eds), *The Handbook of the Criminal Justice Process* (OUP 2002) 369; Mike McConville, 'Plea Bargaining: Ethics and Politics' in Sean Doran and John D Jackson (eds), *The Judicial Role in Criminal Proceedings* (Hart Publishing 2000) 71.
155.   Mike McConville, 'Plea Bargaining: Ethics and Politics' in Sean Doran and John D Jackson (eds), *The Judicial Role in Criminal Proceedings* (Hart Publishing 2000) 72; but cf Meredith Blake and Andrew Ashworth, 'Some Ethical Issues in Prosecuting and Defending Criminal Cases' [1998] *Criminal Law Review* 16, 25 who note that the American Bar Association goes as far as to say that 'reasonable persuasion' may be used to induce a defendant to plead guilty if it is in his best interests.

Table 12.1 Alternative charges

Murder	Manslaughter
Grievous bodily harm with intent	Grievous bodily harm
Actual bodily harm	Common assault
Burglary	Theft
Robbery	Theft and separate common assault offence

Plea bargaining, although never referred to as that in court, appears to be here to stay and indeed it even seems to be becoming more formalized. Recent legislation has confirmed in statute the principle that cooperation between defendants and prosecutors should lead to a reduction in sentence[156] and this is undoubtedly, perhaps for the first time, the introduction of the second tier of Otton's plea bargaining being introduced into the English Legal System. That said the limits of this section should be appreciated. In *R v Dougall*[157] the Lord Chief Justice noted that it is not open to prosecutors and defence to agree what the sentence of a court would be.[158] Whilst s 73 will allow prosecutors to state the extent to which a person has cooperated in the investigation it remains a matter solely for the judge what the sentence, and indeed type of sentence, would be. In *Dougall* the Director of the SFO purported to tell the court not to sentence the offender to a term of imprisonment and the Court of Appeal was adamant that this was inappropriate and an interference with the powers of a judge.

The CJA 2003 has formalized the previous common-law rule that a person who pleads guilty should receive a reduction in sentence,[159] with the Sentencing Council stating that this should be up to one-third for an early plea, although the discount will drop dramatically as the case progresses. For example, where a person pleads guilty at the beginning of the trial, they will ordinarily only receive a 10 per cent discount.[160] Some, as noted earlier, do question whether this places a degree of pressure on an offender to plead guilty even where they believe they are innocent.

12.7.2.1 *Newton* hearings

Another possible form of plea may be where a defendant agrees to plead guilty to the charge but challenges the prosecution facts presented. This could be significant because with some offences the factual basis for the conviction may have an impact on the sentence (eg in an assault case stamping on the head of the victim would be significantly more serious than punching someone). What happens in these situations? In *R v Newton*[161] the Court of Appeal stated there are three potential options:

* accept the defence version of the facts and proceed to sentence on that basis

* decide that the plea is actually one of not guilty and, accordingly, proceed to trial

* the judge could hear evidence to decide the factual basis of the plea and sentence accordingly.

---

156. *Serious Organised Crime and Police Act 2005*, s 73.
157. [2010] EWCA Crim 1048.
158. *R v Dougall* [2010] EWCA Crim 1048 [19].
159. *Criminal Justice Act 2003*, s 144.
160. See, for example, *R v Samuriwo* [2016] EWCA Crim 1948. The Sentencing Council is proposing to re-issue their guideline on guilty pleas in Spring 2017. This is likely to lead to clearer guidance on how the plea scales from one-third to zero discount.
161. (1982) 77 Cr App R 13.

The final stage of this is known as a *Newton* hearing and, if it occurs in the Crown Court, involves the judge sitting as the tribunal of fact and determining the factual basis upon which to sentence (in the magistrates' court the magistrates sit as normal). This demonstrates the point made earlier that judges in the Crown Court can act as tribunals of fact. There is no need to empanel a jury because guilt is not in issue but clearly the facts do need to be ascertained. A *Newton* hearing could potentially involve a full trial with the prosecution and defence providing witnesses to this fact and so the decisions of fact are not trivial.

Example *Newton* hearing

Gary is accused of actual bodily harm (s 47 *Offences Against the Person Act 1861*). The prosecution allege that he got into a fight with the victim and after punching him in the head several times, caused the victim to fall to the floor and then stamped on his head three times causing severe internal bruising.

Gary admits to the assault but denies stamping on the victim's head saying that after he punched him he fell onto the pavement and hit his head. Stamping on someone is a serious aggravating factor and therefore the sentence that Gary would receive for an actual bodily harm without stamping would be substantially different from one where he was found to have stamped on the victim. Accordingly, the judge or prosecution may ask for a *Newton* hearing to ascertain the true position.

It should be noted that the second option presented earlier—empanelling a jury (in the Crown Court)—is used where the plea actually amounts to the tendering of a defence or the suggestion that the charge is (legally) wrong. Under those circumstances it is only fair that the matter is considered to be a not guilty plea so that the prosecution version can be properly tested.

433

Example A (partial) defence

Gail is accused of wounding with intent contrary to s 18 *Offences Against the Person Act 1861*. She admits that she did stab the victim but says it was not deliberate. In those circumstances Gail is actually saying that she is not guilty of an offence under s 18 but is guilty of an offence contrary to s 20. If the prosecution fail to accept this alternative plea then a jury should be empanelled to try her for the s 18 offence.

12.7.3 Tendering the plea in the Crown Court

One procedural point to note arises in respect of the Crown Court. It will be remembered from 12.7 earlier that where a person is charged with an either-way offence he will be asked to indicate how he intends to plead. Of course this is technically only an intention but should (theoretically) mean that a matter is only sent to the Crown Court where the defendant intends to plead not guilty (unless the magistrates decline jurisdiction). Despite this, it has been noted already that a majority of defendants in the Crown Court will plead guilty (although, of course, this will include those who have been accused of an indictable-only offence and those where the magistrates decline jurisdiction).

One reason for late guilty pleas is that the prosecution must undertake full disclosure for Crown Court trials and thus it is possible that at magistrates' court level the defence did not believe the prosecution case to be as strong but once receiving the full details of the prosecution case through disclosure it may become apparent that it would be difficult to fight the case and accordingly they plead guilty. There is now an incentive to encourage early guilty pleas (ie in either-way offences in the magistrates' court) which is by providing a discount of up to one-third from the sentence imposed.[162] Where the plea is left to the last minute then a discount of only 10 per cent can be expected.[163]

The defendant will be asked to plead at the time of his arraignment. This is the time when the charges that he has to answer are formally put to him through the clerk of the court reading aloud the indictment. The arraignment is also the time at

---

IN THE CROWN COURT AT ANYTOWN　　　　　　No 0432101/A

INDICTMENT

The Queen

v

PAUL JONES

PAUL JONES is charged as follows:

Count 1　　　　　　　　　　Statement of Offence

Theft contrary to s.1 of the Theft Act 1968

Particulars of Offence

PAUL JONES, on the 2nd day of February 2010, did steal a pen belonging to GILLIAN FOXGROVE.

Count 2　　　　　　　　　　Statement of Offence

Burglary contrary to s.9(1)(b) of the Theft Act 1968

Particulars of Offence

PAUL JONES, on the 5th day of February 2010, having entered as a trespasser a building, being a dwelling known as 11, Acacia Avenue, stole therein a ruby necklace.

Figure 12.1 An example of a typical indictment

---

162. Sentencing Guidelines Council, *Reduction in Sentence for Guilty Plea Definitive Guideline (Revised 2007)* (Sentencing Guidelines Council 2007) 5.

163. Sentencing Guidelines Council, *Reduction in Sentence for Guilty Plea Definitive Guideline (Revised 2007)* (Sentencing Guidelines Council 2007) 5.

which the trial on indictment is deemed to begin and after this point any decisions of a judge sitting in the Crown Court are not liable to judicial review but only to a formal appeal.[164]

The indictment is the formal document that lists the particulars of each offence the defendant is charged with. There are two parts to an indictment: the statement and the particulars. The former is the offence which the defendant is charged with and the latter provides an extremely brief summary of when the law was breached. Each offence is known as a 'count' and a typical indictment will be like that which is displayed in Figure 12.1. Each count of the indictment is read to the defendant by the clerk of the court and a plea must be made against all those offences unless they are 'alternative counts', ie those which are expressly alternative offences (one a 'major' and one a 'minor' offence, in which case a plea of guilty to the 'major' offence will mean that there is no point in pleading to the 'minor' offence). A typical indictment is shown in Figure 12.1.

 ## Summary

In this chapter we have examined three of the main aspects of the pre-trial criminal justice system. In particular we have identified that:

- A prosecution begins at the earliest stage through a defendant being charged by the police but under the authority of the Crown Prosecution Service (CPS). The CPS, if it has not already done so, must then review the decision to prosecute and, in particular, this requires the CPS to have reference to two prosecution tests (evidential and public-interest tests). If the decision to prosecute is made then the appropriate forms are laid before the court and transfer or mode of trial takes place.

- A prosecution need not take place and if an offender admits his guilt it is possible that diversion from prosecution may occur. The most notable formal diversionary procedures are cautions and conditional cautions (for adults) and youth cautions (for children).

- A decision not to prosecute can be challenged by way of judicial review in the courts. The courts are less sure about permitting a decision to prosecute to be subject to judicial review because they argue that this is a matter for the trial judge to resolve.

- A decision not to prosecute can also be challenged by the *Victims' Right to Review Scheme*. It will not be possible to judicially review a decision not to prosecute an offender without first exercising this right of review.

- Crimes are divided into three categories: summary, indictable-only, and either-way. There are two courts where criminal matters are heard (magistrates' court and the Crown Court) and the categorization of offences has an impact on where the matter should be heard. The most controversial category is the either-way offence where currently the defendant has a veto over a trial being heard in the magistrates' court. Where a matter is to be heard in the Crown Court, the case now proceeds directly there without the magistrates considering the strength of prosecution evidence.

---

164.   See *Senior Courts Act 1981*, s 29(3) as interpreted by *R v Maidstone Crown Court, ex p Clark* [1995] 1 WLR 831.

End-of-chapter questions

1. Juveniles are, potentially, more vulnerable than adults so is it correct that they can be dealt with in a way that is arguably less transparent than adults?

2. Read Gillespie (1998). If there is evidence to demonstrate that prosecuting a parent for neglect or physical abuse could damage the best interests of the child should the prosecution go ahead?

3. Why should the defendant be allowed to veto summary trial? Does this not suggest there are doubts as to the fairness of proceedings in the magistrates' court (if we are saying that a defendant can choose to be tried elsewhere)? If so, why have summary trial for any matters?

4. Should it be possible to bring a judicial review against a decision not to prosecute? Now there is the right to review a prosecution then surely that means a victim has had two opportunities to make representations and permitting judicial review simply means that the limited resources of the CPS are reduced and a suspect is caused distress and anxiety by having their decision as to charge being delayed even further.

Further reading

Ashworth A and Strange M 'Criminal Law and Human Rights' [2004] 2 *European Human Rights Law Review* 121–40.

This is a comprehensive article that examines many of the key issues relating to how human rights legislation has impacted upon the criminal justice system.

Cammiss S, 'I Will in a Moment Give you the Full History' [2006] *Criminal Law Review* 38–51.

This is an interesting empirical study that discusses the decision-making process in mode of trial decisions.

Gillespie A, 'Child Abuse Prosecutions and the Human Rights Act 1998' (1998) 150 *New Law Journal* 620–1.

This article considers whether prosecution rights of review necessarily assist the victim of a crime. It considers whether for a certain class of victims (victims of child sex offences) there is an argument that it may not be in their best interests for a prosecution to be brought. It considers whether a victim can demand a prosecution is *not* brought rather than *is* brought.

Hoyano A, 'A Study of the Impact of the Revised Code for Crown Prosecutors' [1997] *Criminal Law Review* 556–64.

This is an interesting article that discusses whether the Code for Crown Prosecutors is followed in practice.

For multiple-choice questions, updates to this chapter, and links to useful websites, please visit the **Online Resource Centre** at: www.oxfordtextbooks.co.uk/orc/gillespie_els6e/

13

Lay Justice

By the end of this chapter you will be able to:

- Identify how magistrates are appointed and what the difference is between a lay magistrate and a district judge (magistrates' court).
- Understand how decisions of fact and law are taken in the magistrates' court.
- Understand who is eligible to serve on a jury.
- Identify how a jury is called to sit on a case.
- Identify the relative advantages and disadvantages of the involvement of laypersons in the criminal justice system.

Introduction

It will be remembered from Part II of this book that there are two criminal courts of first instance; the magistrates' court and the Crown Court. Chapter 12 discussed how a person would choose between the two courts but this chapter will discuss some of the issues that may influence the decision to select the court.

This chapter focuses on lay justice. The use of laypersons is widespread in criminal trials in England and Wales. Summary trials (ie those that take place in the magistrates' court) ordinarily take place before three lay justices of the peace (although, as will be seen, it could be before a single judge) and whilst Crown Court trials take place before a judge, those who are responsible for making decisions of fact are the jury, twelve laypersons chosen for that case. This chapter presents the different types of lay justice that exist and compares the two forms of lay involvement.

13.1 Magistrates

Whilst in Chapter 9 we discussed the judiciary it did not cover all judicial posts as it did not discuss the magistracy. The office of magistrate is an ancient one that dates back to their use by the Sovereign to keep order. It is now a judicial role although, as will be seen, not usually a full-time role.

For the purposes of this chapter it is necessary to distinguish between lay magistrates and district judges (magistrates' court), the latter of whom are technically members of the judiciary. This section will detail both types of magistrate, discuss the merits of each, and then consider whether either should be preferred.

13.1.1 Lay magistrates

The first type of magistrate to discuss is the lay magistrate, also known as a Justice of the Peace (JP), an ancient office that indicated a person was assigned the role of the keeping the King's Peace over a defined area. The office has changed significantly over the years and now, rather than being directly responsible for the arrest of persons and the investigation of crime, modern magistrates keep the peace by sitting in judgment on those who are brought before them.

It is necessary to distinguish between two types of magistrate. The first is the lay magistrate who is unpaid and, as will be seen, not legally qualified. The second group used to be known as stipendiary magistrates but are now more properly known as district judges (magistrates' court) which will be discussed later. Lay magistrates are the biggest of the 'judicial' groupings. On 1 April 2016 there were 17,552 magistrates, a number which has been in decline since 2012. The reduction is partly because there has, in common with other branches of the court service, been a reduction in the number of magistrates' courts and, therefore, magistrates. There has also been a reduction in recruitment, combined with the resignation or retirement of approximately 2,000 magistrates a year.

Apart from certain preliminary matters, lay magistrates do not sit alone and they are therefore assigned to a local justice area which is often known as a 'bench'. Each year they elect a lay magistrate as the Chairman of the bench[1] who is responsible for keeping the magistrates on their bench up to date with criminal justice reforms and dealing with pastoral issues. This is an unpaid administrative role that involves the person being the leader and representative of the bench. It also involves the chair (and nominated deputies) convening the training and ensuring that, in conjunction with the clerk to the justices (see 14.1.2), the operation of the bench runs smoothly.

The organization of magistrates' courts used to be rather complicated with benches being accountable to Magistrates' Courts Committees (MCCs) but from April 2005 the system was simplified when magistrates' courts were brought into (the now) HM Courts and Tribunal Service.

13.1.1.1 Appointment

As might be imagined from the term, lay magistrates are not legally qualified although, interestingly, neither is legal qualification a barrier to appointment and there have, in the past, been lawyers and legal academics who have sat as lay magistrates. However, the vast majority of lay magistrates have no legal knowledge other than that gained through their training. Lay magistrates are also so styled because, unlike their professional brethren (discussed later), they are unpaid. Lay magistrates are volunteers although they are eligible for expenses[2] to cover loss of wages (although this amount is 'capped', meaning some justices will actually sit at a loss), travelling expenses etc.

To be appointed a lay magistrate, a person must either reside in the petty sessional area that they wish to sit in, or live within fifteen miles of this area. This is, in part,

---

1. *Courts Act 2003*, s 17.
2. *Courts Act 2003*, s 15.

because it has always been thought that a significant advantage of the magistracy is that they know the local area. That said, whilst magistrates were traditionally not allowed to sit outside of their petty sessional area, this is no longer true and there is now a mechanism that permits magistrates to sit in other areas.[3] This change was recommended as it was believed it could be useful for justices to assist neighbouring benches to tackle any delay that might accrue because of a reduction (temporary or otherwise) in the number of justices sitting in that area.[4] To an extent it can be argued that this is not dissimilar to the way that circuit judges can be moved around a circuit, although on a much smaller scale. That said, it does appear to conflict with the idea of the magistracy bringing local representation.

The maximum age for appointment to a magistrate is 65 on the basis that they must retire at the age of 70 and accordingly the Lord Chancellor will not appoint someone over 65 since by the time the training programme has been completed effectively there will be little time left for the justice to sit. The minimum age for appointment is 18 although the Lord Chancellor used to state that it would be exceptional for a person to be appointed under the age of 27. However, the Lord Chancellor has withdrawn this comment and there has been a concerted effort by the government to appoint younger magistrates. The rule was effectively relaxed in 2003.[5] In 2015 Alex Hyne became the youngest person to be appointed to the magistracy at age 18.

 QUESTION FOR REFLECTION

Is it realistic to suggest that a magistrate can be appointed at the age of 18? Would they command the required respect of defendants, lawyers, and fellow magistrates?

 LISTEN TO THE PODCAST

For guidance on how to answer this question and a discussion of the main issues, listen to the author's podcast on the Online Resource Centre:
www.oxfordtextbooks.co.uk/orc/gillespie_els6e/

Certain persons are automatically disqualified from being a magistrate, the most notable being those listed in Table 13.1.

There is also, of course, the proviso that individuals may not be suitable depending on their own circumstances. The Ministry of Justice has listed the qualities of a magistrate:

- good character
- maturity and sound temperament
- understanding and communication
- sound judgement
- social awareness
- commitment and reliability.

3. *Courts Act 2003*, s 10.
4. Lord Justice Auld, *A Review of the Criminal Courts of England and Wales* (HMSO 2001) 100.
5. 'Younger Magistrates Wanted', DCA Press Release, 27 October 2003.

Table 13.1 Automatic disqualification

Serving or recently retired police officers (including Special Constables)	Bailiffs
Traffic wardens or civilian employees of police forces	An undischarged bankrupt
Prison Service employee (and spouses/partners)	Anyone who has, or whose partner has, been convicted of a serious offence or number of minor offences
Spouses, partners, or close family relative of the above if they work in same local justice area.	Store detective
Those whose work on community activities that make being appointed a magistrate inappropriate (eg CPS, Probation Service etc)	National Crime Agency employee

13.1.1.2 Diversity

Successive governments have attempted to broaden the magistracy because there continues to be a perception that the magistracy, like most of the judiciary, is a bastion of the white, middle-class male. Actually, as will be seen, this is no longer true and lay magistrates are amongst the more representative members of the judiciary. Traditionally perceptions persisted because of media caricatures but it is now possible to rebut some of these perceptions through the use of published statistics.

The *Judicial Diversity Statistics 2016* show that there are more female lay magistrates (9,299) than male magistrates (8,253), something that has been the case since 2008.

What of ethnicity? The latest judicial statistics suggest that the magistracy are more representative than other sectors of the judiciary. Eleven per cent of the lay magistracy consider themselves to be a member of the ethnic minorities, which roughly equates to the percentage of people who identify themselves as a member of the ethnic minority in the general population. This is significantly better than any other group within the judiciary (discussed in Chapter 9) although it does not, of course, mean that recruitment campaigns to increase ethnic minority representations can end since it should not just be a question about getting fair representation but ensuring that members of the ethnic minorities are an accepted part of the judicial system.

Whilst sex and race appear to contradict the traditional stereotypes of the magistracy other data are perhaps less helpful. Recent data show that only four per cent of magistrates would class themselves as having a disability although it is difficult to identify an agreed definition of disability to gain comparable statistics from, for example, the national census. That said, less than five per cent does appear quite low and is probably unrepresentative of the general population.

Age is particularly relevant. The latest judicial statistics show that over eighty per cent of the magistracy are above the age of 50, with less than one per cent below the age of 30. This is perhaps one of the greater challenges and arguably should be less problematic than with members of the judiciary. Whilst judges will be somewhat older by the time they are appointed because they have had to prove themselves as a member of the legal professions first (discussed in Chapter 9) the same is not necessarily true of lay magistrates. It will be recalled earlier that the Lord Chancellor has recently appointed teenagers to the magistracy. Whilst there may be some eyebrows raised by such appointments it is clear that a magistracy where over eighty per cent are above the age of 50 does not assist in rebutting the prejudice that magistrates are all old.

 QUESTION FOR REFLECTION

Were you surprised by the figures on representation in the judiciary given earlier? Before reading this page what were your perceptions on how diverse the magistracy were? Do you think it matters whether the magistracy are diverse or not?

Apart from ethnicity and race the other factor that is often a talking point is their socio-economic backgrounds. Certainly Auld accepted, without adducing any modern evidence to support this, that magistrates were not necessarily representative but that this did not prevent them from discharging their duties.[6] Identifying the socio-economic background of the magistracy is not easy since the government does not apparently collate such information.[7] However, in a recent report published by *Transform Justice* it was suggested that 'magistrates are still disproportionately middle class, with over half in manager, senior official or in professional occupations ... and only 1.5% in sales or customer services ...'[8] Collating more detailed data in this area is certainly a way of tackling diversity (including correcting misperceptions), as seen in the context of ethnic minority diversity, and it may be advisable for the same to occur in relation to socio-economic backgrounds.

Another possible reason for the socio-economic background of magistrates is that they tend to be appointed from professional backgrounds,[9] in part because of the sitting requirements. Unlike with jury service there is no obligation to let an employee have time off to sit as a magistrate although there are benefits in doing so. Public bodies will consider it a civil obligation and will normally therefore give the time off without a requirement for leave. The same could be true of medium- to large-scale professional firms but how easy would it be for a builder or decorator to take a day off?

 QUESTION FOR REFLECTION

Should it matter what the background to the magistracy is? Would it not be better to concentrate on whether the candidate is capable of judging evidence dispassionately or do you think that representation is important?

13.1.1.3 Training

One of the significant changes in recent years has been the training that lay magistrates undertake. As noted earlier, they are not normally legally qualified but, although they are assisted by a legal adviser, they do form the tribunal of both fact and law in summary trials, ie they do decide on legal points. Also, criminal justice policy is one

---

6. Lord Justice Auld, *A Review of the Criminal Courts of England and Wales* (HMSO 2001) 98.
7. *Hansard*, HC WA, vol 434, col 638W (9 June 2005).
8. Transform Justice, *Magistrates: Representatives of the People?* (Transform Justice 2014) 11.
9. Penny Darbyshire, 'Magistrates' in Mike McConville and Geoffrey Wilson (eds), *The Handbook of the Criminal Justice Process* (OUP 2002) 296.

of the faster-moving areas of political controversy and most governments will introduce changes to criminal process or sentencing regularly. Lay justices need to understand their powers and duties, along with having a basic familiarity over some of what they hear.

Training is now overseen by the Judicial College (discussed at 8.5) although much of it is undertaken locally. According to the Magistrates Association, the main associative body for lay magistrates, training is split into initial training (undertaken during the first year) and continuing training (which, as its name suggests, continues while a magistrate continues to sit).

The initial training consists of five phases:

1. **Initial basic training**. This takes place before a new magistrate will sit in court. This will involve the basic training about the role of a magistrate, conduct of trials etc.

2. **Mentoring**. Each new magistrate will be assigned an experienced magistrate who will act as their mentor and guide them through the training process. The new magistrate will undertake six formal mentored sittings during the first year or so where the mentor will discuss issues that arise.

3. **Core training**. To ensure that magistrates are aware of all aspects of the criminal justice system they will visit penal establishments, police stations etc. They will also be given an individualized work plan that will discuss the training that they are required to undertake.

4. **Consolidation training**. This takes place at the end of the first year and builds upon the sittings that the magistrate has undertaken and also the various training courses that the magistrate has attended.

5. **First appraisal**. The new magistrate will, sometime after the first year, be given a formal appraisal where a more experienced (and specially trained) magistrate will sit in court and observe how the magistrate acts, follows procedures etc.

Continuing training is required for all magistrates. Every three years a magistrate will be given a formal appraisal which is designed to ensure that the magistrate continues to meet the competencies required of their role. If a magistrate does not meet this then remedial training may be given. As legislation is passed or key decisions made then they will be given update training. Increasingly this may be by e-learning or will take place in small groups led, for example, by the justices' clerk or a senior legal adviser.

Specific training is also required to do more than the 'basic' work. Thus, for example, if a magistrate wishes to sit in the youth court they will need to undertake specialist training and appraisals. Similarly, a person who wishes to sit as chair of a panel will also need further training and assessment.

13.1.1.4 Duties

Magistrates must sit for a minimum of twenty-six sessions each year, each session normally lasting a half-day, although it is not uncommon for magistrates to combine their sittings into a full day. Where the magistrates sit in the family proceedings court or youth court then there is normally an expectation that they will sit more often. The Magistrates Association states that the average magistrate sits for thirty-five sittings per year (seventeen and a half days) and the ordinary maximum is seventy sessions (although some believe that this is occasionally broken).[10] The average of thirty-five is a reduction from research published in 2000 where it was found that the average was forty-one sittings.[11] No reason has been given for this reduction but, even with the overall reduction in numbers of magistrates, it does not appear that there is any significant delay in the magistrates' court which suggests that the reduction in sittings is perhaps a result of demand.

As will be seen in Chapter 15 lay magistrates will ordinarily sit in panels of three, and will always do so during trials (which will be discussed at 15.1.1). However, a single lay justice does also have some powers. Broadly speaking these are pre-trial matters, including the issuing of a summons or arrest warrant, certain matters relating to bail, including extending bail, the power to dismiss information where no evidence has been offered, the power to seek reports relating to sentencing, the granting of legal aid and some case-management rulings, including setting a timetable, and the service of documents and even ascertaining how the offender wishes to plead. Moreover, with the introduction of the *Criminal Justice and Courts Act 2015* (CJCA 2015), single magistrates can now conduct proceedings 'on the papers' against adults.[12] They are only able to try a written charge in relation to an adult who has been charged with a summary offence that is not punishable with imprisonment. The term 'trial by single justice on the papers' essentially refers to cases where everything is conducted in writing and there is no attendance of a prosecution or defence and thus the case does not need to be heard in a courtroom. The types of cases that would be tried in this way include driving without insurance and TV licence evasion, with the aim of dealing with such cases, where uncontested and straightforward, in a more timely and proportionate manner.

13.1.2 District judge (magistrates' court)

The second type of magistrate is a very different creature. Now known as a district judge (magistrates' court) (DJMC) they used to be known as a 'stipendiary magistrate'. As their old name suggests, DJMCs are paid a salary (unlike lay magistrates). They are technically members of the judiciary and have similar terms of service to the other members of judiciary.

Historically the only area of the country where stipendiary magistrates have been used for a considerable period of time was Inner London. The *Middlesex Justices Act 1792* created stipendiary posts and it was not until the 1940s that lay magistrates (who had been principally dealing with quasi-administrative matters such as licensing etc) became more involved with some of the London courts. According to the most recent statistics there are 132 DJMCs and 101 deputy DJMCs (a part-time appointment akin to a recorder in the Crown Court). Under s 23 CA 2003 there is provision to create the senior district judge (chief magistrate) and a deputy. The Act is silent as to what responsibility the holders of these offices have but the website of HM Courts and Tribunals Service states that the chief magistrate will hear the most sensitive cases in the magistrates' court, provide pastoral support for other DJMCs, and liaise with the senior judiciary on matters relating to DJMCs. The current senior district judge (chief magistrate) is District Judge Emma Arbuthnot and she is based in Marylebone magistrates' court.

---

10. Penny Darbyshire, *Sitting in Judgment: The Working Lives of Judges* (Hart Publishing 2011) 411.
11. Rod Morgan and Neil Russell, *The Judiciary in the Magistrates' Courts* (Home Office 2000) 13, 18.
12. *Magistrates' Courts Act 1980*, s 16A as amended by *Criminal Justice and Courts Act 2015*, s 48.

13.1.2.1 **Appointment**

As noted earlier, the DJMC is a judicial post and in order to be appointed as either a DJMC or deputy DJMC a person must 'satisfy the judicial appointment eligibility condition on a five-year basis'.[13] This, in effect, means a solicitor (with rights of audience) or a barrister who has been qualified for five years. Realistically, however, a person would have to be qualified for a longer period than this to be appointed.

The actual appointment of DJMCs and deputy DJMCs is handled by the Judicial Appointments Commission (discussed at 8.3.1) and the same process that is discussed for circuit judges and recorders applies equally to DJMCs. Before being appointed a DJMC it is expected that a person will have served as a deputy DJMC first. The expectation for deputies is that they will sit for a minimum of fifteen days per year although it is possible that they will sit for more. A deputy will be superintended by a full DJMC but it is quite possible that they will be sitting in different petty sessional areas and thus the deputy may be the senior judge in a petty sessional area. A DJMC is currently paid £107,100.[14] Deputy DJMCs are paid a daily rate which is currently £498.

Unlike circuit judges and above, a DJMC is not accorded any honorific title and so they remain simply Mr, Mrs, or Ms [name]. This is true of even the senior district judge (chief magistrate) who is given no special styling. DJMCs do not normally wear robes in court. They will be referred to as 'Sir' or 'Madam'.

13.1.2.2 **Diversity**

It was noted earlier that the lay magistracy is diverse, at least in terms of sex and race, and certainly more diverse than the judiciary. What is the position of DJMCs? A key difference, of course, is that DJMCs are drawn from lawyers and, as has been noted already, lawyers are not necessarily representative of society as a whole.

The latest statistics posted on the judiciary website show that there are forty-four (33 per cent) female DJMCs and thirty-one (31 per cent) female deputy DJMCs. Certainly this is not as representative as the lay magistracy where, as was seen earlier, there are actually more female magistrates than male, but it compares favourably with the mainstream judiciary (discussed in Chapter 9). If this is compared to the circuit bench, for example, only twenty-six per cent of judges are female and the position is even lower for the senior judiciary (19.3 per cent).

In terms of race, 106 (80 per cent) full-time DJMCs are white which would, at first sight, appear to suggest that there is some (albeit limited) diversity but twenty DJMCs are of 'unknown' ethnicity (usually because the post-holder has refused to complete a statistical form) which would account for a further fifty per cent of posts. Of those that do declare an ethnicity only five per cent declare themselves as being from an ethnic minority background. In terms of deputy DJMCs the position is slightly better. Sixty-four deputy DJMCs (63 per cent) are white although thirty-one (30.7 per cent) do not declare their ethnicity. Of those who do declare ethnicity, 5.9 per cent declare themselves as being from an ethnic minority background.

It would seem therefore that DJMCs (including deputies) are not representative of society as a whole but how do they compare with other members of the judiciary? It will be remembered from Chapter 9 that the latest statistics suggest that of the full-time circuit

---

13.   *Courts Act 2003*, s 22.
14.   And is classified as a group 7 appointment. The deputy senior district judge (magistrates' court) is a group 6.2 appointment and is paid £125,689 and the senior district judge (magistrates' court) is a group 5 appointment and paid £144,142.

bench only 3.7 per cent declare themselves as coming from an ethnic minority, with an even lower proportion being found in the senior judiciary (3.1 per cent). Accordingly, it can be argued that DJMCs are more representative than the mainstream judiciary and the slightly higher percentage of deputy DJMCs may suggest that the position could improve.

The latest figures also show the professional backgrounds of DJMCs and deputy DJMCs. Unlike in the mainstream judiciary (discussed in Chapter 9) there are more former solicitors who are DJMCs (eighty-seven or 65 per cent) and deputy DJMCs (sixty-six or 65 per cent) than barristers. It is not clear why this should be the case although it could partly be the belief of barristers that they stand a higher chance than solicitors of gaining a circuit-bench appointment. It may also be about perceptions of status. It has been noted that DJMCs believe that they are the 'forgotten judiciary'[15] and that they have little to do with the ordinary judiciary.

13.1.2.3 Duties

Unlike lay magistrates, DJMCs will ordinarily sit alone and when they do so they have the same powers as the bench of three lay magistrates. If they do sit with lay magistrates (which is rare) then they would automatically become the chair and the lay magistrates would sit as wingers. That said, they would each have only one vote and it would be perfectly possible for the lay magistrates to outvote the DJMC.

DJMCs and deputy DJMCs have, since 2000, been able to sit nationally and, unlike lay magistrates, they tend to sit outside their 'base' court more frequently. This is particularly important because district judges will frequently sit on complicated or lengthy trials, in part because they can sit alone.[16] One of the difficulties traditionally with lay magistrate trials is that the justices will only sit in a half-day block which means they can only conduct short cases. Where a trial is likely to take longer than this then a district judge can hear the case as he will sit either permanently or, where he is a deputy, in a block of time. This type of case may not arise in one single petty sessional area so a national jurisdiction allows the district judges to try matters in other areas in a way analogous to how circuit judges move around the circuit.

There has undoubtedly been tension between lay magistrates and DJMCs and stories abound about how DJMCs have been shunned by members of the lay magistracy.[17] Auld, who identified a similar trend, believed that there was a belief in the lay magistracy that there was somehow a national policy to replace lay magistrates with DJMCs[18] although he rejected this belief. Certainly given the number of lay magistrates that exist it would seem highly unlikely that such a policy could ever succeed, not least because of the cost. Increasingly the DJMCs have tried to 'build bridges' with the lay magistrates and this has included, for example, inviting lay justices to talk with them and to observe them in court.[19]

13.1.3 Lay magistrates or DJMCs?

It has already been noted that there is tension between lay magistrates and DJMCs but which should be used and why? It has been noted that lay magistrates do not appear to always trust DJMCs and believe that they are trying to replace them which seems

15. Penny Darbyshire, *Sitting in Judgment: The Working Lives of Judges* (Hart Publishing 2011) 168.
16. *Courts Act 2003*, s 26.
17. See Penny Darbyshire, *Sitting in Judgment: The Working Lives of Judges* (Hart Publishing 2011) 166, who presents some examples.
18. Lord Justice Auld, *A Review of the Criminal Courts of England and Wales* (HMSO 2001) 98.
19. Penny Darbyshire, *Sitting in Judgment: The Working Lives of Judges* (Hart Publishing 2011) 166.

somewhat unrealistic. Perhaps the greater fear, however, is that some lay magistrates are concerned that if DJMCs are appointed to their courts they will lose the 'interesting' work.[20] Certainly if 'interesting' is classified as the more serious crimes then it is quite likely that this will be true. It has been noted that DJMCs can sit for longer periods of time, including consecutive days, and thus the more serious trials, which are probably lengthier, will take place before DJMCs.

13.1.3.1 Representative

It is clear from the preceding analysis that DJMCs are less representative than lay magistrates but does this matter? Certainly there is some evidence that people believe it can matter. The skills research showed that '[m]agistrates were perceived to come from a wider cross section of society than DJs'[21] and that they were perceived to be more 'in touch' and 'down to earth' which could have an impact on the confidence that people have in the magistracy.

What do we mean by representative though? It will be remembered that whilst statistics clearly demonstrate that they are representative in terms of sex and race, it is less clear that they are representative in other ways, particularly social demographics. Arguably this is even more true of those who sit in family and youth matters where the minimum number of sittings is greater, meaning that unless an employer gives them the time off as a public duty (which tends to occur only in the public sector and professional backgrounds) there is less likelihood of people wishing to undertake these duties as it would require them using their annual leave allowance.[22] There is also concern about age. Whilst it was noted earlier that some very young magistrates have been appointed (which potentially raises issues as to their life experience) the majority of lay justices are over 50 and less than one per cent are younger than 30.

The idea of magistrates being local officers of justice has always been considered an important factor and certainly there is some evidence that this means they can represent local issues.[23] The same research suggested that the link to localities was welcomed by many respondents. However, is this necessarily true or important anymore? Robson, herself a magistrate, has argued that the concept of locality is being eroded. 'Even before the [court closures], courts have been serving wider areas so that although the personnel may seem more representative of the population at large it may no longer have many local ties.'[24] Certainly over recent years there has been a push towards closing small, local courts and merging them into larger courts that cover a wider regional area. Whilst the magistrates are still appointed through a link to their community, at these larger courts they will sit on cases from all over the area, not just the cases from their own locality. Accordingly, can it be said that they are representative of the locality and, in any event, is that always a good thing? Whilst there have

---

20. Penny Darbyshire, *Sitting in Judgment: The Working Lives of Judges* (Hart Publishing 2011) 166.
21. Ipsos Mori, *The Strengths and Skills of the Judiciary in the Magistrates' Courts* (Ministry of Justice 2011) 18.
22. Ipsos Mori, *The Strengths and Skills of the Judiciary in the Magistrates' Courts* (Ministry of Justice 2011) 19.
23. Ipsos Mori, *The Strengths and Skills of the Judiciary in the Magistrates' Courts* (Ministry of Justice 2011) 17.
24. Glenna Robson, 'No Further Forward?' (2012) 176 *Criminal Law & Justice Weekly* 39, 40.

been some community justice initiatives it must be questioned whether we want local variances when it relates to crimes actually being dealt with at court.

13.1.3.2 Efficiency

The manner in which DJMCs hear cases will often differ dramatically from how lay magistrates hear cases. As practitioners of law they are familiar with many of the aspects and arguments that are likely to be raised, including legal issues. Whereas a lay bench would have to confer about decisions and also receive advice from their legal adviser on any legal issues that were raised, including any submission of no case to answer (discussed at 15.2) a DJMC is able to just deal with the matter alone.

An effect of this is that trials are conducted considerably faster than in a trial presided over by lay magistrates.[25] It may be thought that the trials take place more quickly because they are more prepared to accept the arguments of the prosecution (discussed at 13.1.3) but when Darbyshire undertook shadowing of a DJMC she found that it was often the prosecution who were at the wrong end of judicial wrath for inappropriate preparation[26] and that this was, in part, to demonstrate their independence.

An interesting comment that arose out of the research of Darbyshire was that some DJMCs considered their role to be inquisitorial rather than adversarial.[27] It will be remembered from Chapter 1 that the English Legal System tends to operate on the basis of the adversarial principle save for very few exceptions. The criminal justice system is supposed to be the paradigm of the adversarial system and it is perhaps surprising therefore that such comments are made. However, DJMCs do appear to be more interventionist than lay magistrates are or indeed what a circuit judge would be (for fear of prejudicing a jury).

The skills research showed that DJMCs will ordinarily deal with matters in a pro-active way: 'A number of professional users and court staff also noted that district judges were more proficient case managers as they got to the heart of the issue and moved cases on more efficiently than magistrates.'[28] This can be an important point and links to the 'inquisitorial' point made earlier. As a legally qualified professional, with the powers of both the tribunal of fact and law, it is likely that a DJMC can identify what the key issues are that will lead to him deciding guilt or innocence and direct attention to these points, removing some of the superfluous statements or evidence that will not greatly assist (for example, opening speeches). Careful and rigorous case management is now a requirement of the *Criminal Procedure Rules*[29] and where cases are longer and more complex then this may be a significant reason for allowing a DJMC to deal with the matter.

An interesting question is whether DJMCs need legal advisers. It will be seen from Chapter 15 that legal advisers can play an important role in a summary trial where a matter is heard before a lay bench (15.1.2). As DJMCs are legally qualified then there is a question of whether they need a legal adviser (for example, recorders and circuit judges do not have a legal adviser although the court clerks will ordinarily be legally qualified). Certainly there is clear evidence that even when they are in court with a

---

25. Penny Darbyshire, *Sitting in Judgment: The Working Lives of Judges* (Hart Publishing 2011) 162, and Rod Morgan and Neil Russell, *The Judiciary in the Magistrates' Courts* (Home Office 2000).
26. Penny Darbyshire, *Sitting in Judgment: The Working Lives of Judges* (Hart Publishing 2011) 163.
27. Penny Darbyshire, *Sitting in Judgment: The Working Lives of Judges* (Hart Publishing 2011) 163.
28. Ipsos Mori, *The Strengths and Skills of the Judiciary in the Magistrates' Courts* (Ministry of Justice 2011) 21.
29. Ministry of Justice, *Criminal Procedure Rules* (as amended April and October 2016) r 3.2.

DJMC they tend to act very passively[30] which suggests that there is little need for them to sit in court with a DJMC and it may be that it would be preferable for them to be deployed to courts that are presided over by a lay bench.

13.1.3.3 Case-hardened?

Padfield argues that district judges are more likely to become 'case-hardened' (meaning they become less convinced by arguments since they see the same excuses being used in each case) and 'judicially burnt out' than lay magistrates[31] although no conclusive evidence is shown for this. There has always been some concern as to whether magistrates become 'case-hardened' and thus less inclined to acquit a suspect. Certainly it was found that district judges were more likely to remand a person into custody rather than provide bail[32] and significantly more likely to impose a harsher punishment.[33] However, this by itself does not necessarily mean that district judges are more 'case-hardened' because these judges tend to get the more serious and complicated cases and this may explain the distinction. Morgan and Russell were unable to compare a trial by a lay bench with a trial by a district judge because the number of trials observed was so low that any comparison would be meaningless.[34]

Darbyshire, in her impressive anthropological study on judges, sat with three DJMCs and whilst it would be unwise to draw empirical conclusions from this study, it was clear that she did not necessarily find evidence of case-hardening. It is particularly noticeable that one of the DJMCs—Portia—sitting in the youth court was prepared to give the prosecution a hard time and was regularly exasperated by their preparation and presentation.[35] That said, it was also clear that matters were dealt with very briskly. On the first day that Darbyshire sat with Portia in the youth court she dealt with three cases in under fifteen minutes,[36] although it would seem that they were guilty pleas. However, it was also clear that she was concerned that defendants were given an opportunity. Darbyshire recounts a story of a 15-year-old boy who was charged, inter alia, with driving with excess alcohol and who 'wanted to get it over with'. The DJMC persuaded the mother not to allow him to make a plea straight away but instead to talk to the duty solicitor first as 'these cases can be complex and I don't know how a 15-year-old can be confident he can understand the technicalities'.[37] A case-hardened judge may not have done so since a 15-year-old cannot legally drive in any event.

The speed at which DJMCs handle cases and the fact that they are significantly more interventionist than lay magistrates may lead to the appearance that DJMCs are case-hardened, but without being able to properly account for the differences in conviction rates (including the possibility that lay magistrates may improperly acquit) it is difficult to know whether case-hardening does, in fact, exist.

13.1.3.4 Tinkers, tailors, and judges?

One interesting issue of note is that there is suspicion of the lay magistracy by the judiciary, including (but not restricted to) DJMCs. Darbyshire notes that the DJMCs

30. Penny Darbyshire, *Sitting in Judgment: The Working Lives of Judges* (Hart Publishing 2011) 167.
31. Nicola Padfield and Jonathan Reed, *Text and Materials on the Criminal Justice Process* (5th edn, LexisNexis 2016) 277.
32. Rod Morgan and Neil Russell, *The Judiciary in the Magistrates' Courts* (Home Office 2000) 50.
33. Rod Morgan and Neil Russell, *The Judiciary in the Magistrates' Courts* (Home Office 2000) 52.
34. Rod Morgan and Neil Russell, *The Judiciary in the Magistrates' Courts* (Home Office 2000) 52.
35. Penny Darbyshire, *Sitting in Judgment: The Working Lives of Judges* (Hart Publishing 2011) 161.
36. Penny Darbyshire, *Sitting in Judgment: The Working Lives of Judges* (Hart Publishing 2011) 155–6.
37. Penny Darbyshire, *Sitting in Judgment: The Working Lives of Judges* (Hart Publishing 2011) 156.

are contemptuous of lay magistrates[38] and that the feeling was shared by many judges who considered them to be 'biased towards authority—the police and social workers'.[39] Of course it is difficult to prove such assertions, not least because there are so many reasons why the conviction and acquittal rates may be different. Certainly, however, it is clear that DJMCs convict a higher proportion of defendants but lay magistrates convict a higher proportion of defendants than juries (discussed later). Whether that tells us anything is another question though since it is impossible to know how many convicted people are innocent or guilty people acquitted. However, research does appear to suggest that some lay justices do appear to set the criminal standard of proof too low[40] and that this is one reason why there are concerns within the professional judiciary about the quality of the lay magistracy.

It was noted earlier that some people believe that DJMCs may get case-hardened and the speed at which they deliberate on cases may raise questions as to whether justice is too summary. Some have suggested that the ideal solution would be to merge the current position, ie make the magistrates' court a 'mini Crown Court' with a DJMC presiding over the court alongside two lay justices.[41] Under such an approach the tribunal of law would be the DJMC and the lay justices would have to take the law from him but the tribunal of fact would be the three judges collectively (this model currently occurs in appeals from the magistrates' court to the Crown Court, see 16.2.1). Some wonder whether, however, such an approach could lead to the DJMC dominating the court, and the lay justices feeling that they must follow the lead of the DJMC.

Liberty suggested an alternative whereby the tribunal would be a DJMC and three lay justices, the DJMC being the tribunal of law and the lay justices being the tribunal of fact.[42] This would, in effect, create a true 'mini Crown Court' albeit with justices of the peace rather than jurors. The immediate difficulty with this is that lay magistrates sit for half-days and thus complicated or longer trials would not be able to cope with this system. The solution that Liberty proposes is that lay magistrates sit in blocks of time[43] but this itself carries with it disadvantages, not least the fact that it may put off more employers from releasing their staff, thus potentially increasing the reliance on magistrates drawn from the public sector.

Nothing came of the suggestion of a hybrid court and DJMCs continue to primarily sit alone. Auld argued that this was the preference of both the lay magistracy and the district judges[44] with the former liking the ability to chair their own courts[45] and the latter not seeing any real purpose in using lay magistrates. An issue that has never been truly resolved is that there is no clear guidance as to when a district judge should be used and when a case should be heard by a lay bench. It has been noted that the suggestion has always been that a district judge should be used for the more serious and complicated cases but lay magistrates may well be unhappy with this as it creates a de facto second class of summary trials, ie those presided over by magistrates.

38. Penny Darbyshire, *Sitting in Judgment: The Working Lives of Judges* (Hart Publishing 2011) 166, 172.
39. Penny Darbyshire, *Sitting in Judgment: The Working Lives of Judges* (Hart Publishing 2011) 411.
40. Penny Darbyshire, 'An Essay on the Importance and Neglect of the Magistracy' [1997] *Criminal Law Review* 627.
41. See Liberty, *Magistrates' Courts and Public Confidence* (The Civil Liberties Trust 2002) who believed strongly that a mixed bench could bring much-needed certainty to the bench.
42. Liberty, *Magistrates' Courts and Public Confidence* (The Civil Liberties Trust 2002) 10–13.
43. Liberty, *Magistrates' Courts and Public Confidence* (The Civil Liberties Trust 2002) 12.
44. Lord Justice Auld, *A Review of the Criminal Courts of England and Wales* (HMSO 2001) 102.
45. Obtainable from the Judicial Communications Office.

The use of district judges is likely to continue, not least because of their efficiency as discussed earlier. This can only be taken so far though. Morgan and Russell argue that one district judge could replace thirty lay magistrates,[46] but the expense of that would be enormous (24,000 lay justices, on that formula, would be replaced by 800 DJMCs, each on over £100,000 per year) and so it is simply not realistic. The skills research suggested that it was more complicated than Morgan and Russell suggested it was and that efficiency of a DJMC did not always compensate for the extra expense[47] although it was true when they were dealing with the more complex 'either-way' offences.

However, irrespective of the costs, successive governments have reaffirmed their commitment to the lay magistracy, as have senior members of the judiciary, and it is likely that district judges will, therefore, continue to act alongside, rather than replace, lay justices.

13.2 Juries

The second form of lay justice is that of the jury. Although 95 per cent of all criminal cases take place in the magistrates' court it is probably the jury that is most recognizable as a feature of lay justice.

The jury has undoubtedly an important status within the criminal justice system with Lord Devlin, a one-time Lord of Appeal in Ordinary, commenting that it is 'the lamp that shows freedom lives'[48] a statement approved of by Lord Taylor, a previous Lord Chief Justice, who said: 'in our culture and perception trial by jury is a fundamental right.'[49] Both are therefore of the opinion that juries demonstrate democracy in action, something that the House of Lords affirmed:

> The institution of jury trial, with all its imperfections, is still trusted by the public as a method of determining the guilt of persons charged with criminal offences.[50]

What is interesting from this quotation is that there is recognition that trial by jury is arguably not a perfect way of dealing with trials, indeed it can be argued that it is quite flawed. If you ever speak to a lawyer or judge who specializes in criminal law you will always find that they have at least one story to tell about a jury who managed to reach the wrong verdict or who approached their task in an unprofessional manner etc. Yet these same practitioners will almost certainly state that the jury system retains their confidence.[51]

Juries are often quoted as being a historic guarantee of the rights of the common man to sit in judgement on his fellow citizen; however, this is not strictly true and until 1972 property was a primary factor in the eligibility of people to serve on a jury, meaning that juries tended to be men of a certain economic status.[52] However, the use of lay members is often cited as being an important part of the democratization of the justice system[53] and the fact that a jury consists of twelve members is often cited as being reason to ensure that the decision is fair as the prejudices or lack of interest

46. Rod Morgan and Neil Russell, *The Judiciary in the Magistrates' Courts* (Home Office 2000) 85.
47. Ipsos Mori, *The Strengths and Skills of the Judiciary in the Magistrates' Courts* (Ministry of Justice 2011) 48.
48. Patrick Devlin, *Trial by Jury* (Stevens & Sons, 1956) 164.
49. Andrew Ashworth and Mike Redmayne, *The Criminal Process* (4th edn, OUP 2010).
50. *R v Smith (No 2)* [2005] UKHL 12 [7] (Lord Carswell).
51. Lord Justice Auld, *A Review of the Criminal Courts of England and Wales* (HMSO 2001) 135.
52. Michael Zander, *Cases and Materials on the English Legal System* (10th edn, OUP 2007) 486.
53. See, in particular, Patrick Devlin, *Trial by Jury* (Stevens & Sons, 1956).

shown by an individual juror can be counterbalanced by the others. However, this point is somewhat weakened when one examines the rules as to majority verdicts (see 15.6.2.6) and does not take account of the strength of character of some individuals.

13.2.1 Eligibility for jury service

Those who are prima facie eligible for jury service are:

- registered on the electoral roll and between the ages of 18 and 75;
- ordinarily resident in the United Kingdom, Channel Islands, or Isle of Man for the last five years; and
- not disqualified from jury service.[54]

These criteria mask a more significant change which is that previously a wider range of persons were either able to ask for excusal or were disqualified from sitting as a juror. Those who were eligible for excusal (and thus it was a matter for them as to whether to seek an excusal) included those between the ages of 65 and 70, Members of Parliament, members of the medical profession, and members of HM Forces.[55] However, the new scheme removes this excusal system other than for members of HM Forces where their commanding officer certifies that it would be 'prejudicial to the efficiency of the service' for them to serve, although even then normally a deferral rather than full excusal should be permitted.[56]

What the Act does not do, of course, is to tackle the issue of under-representation identified by Auld. It is accepted that the turnout for elections is very low, especially amongst the younger members of society and the ethnic minorities. Given their apathy towards voting it is not unreasonable to assume that they have neglected to register themselves with the appropriate authorities. The suggestion of Auld to use alternative methods of identifying those eligible to serve was worthy of more consideration and its rejection should be reviewed by Parliament.

451

⟳ QUESTION FOR REFLECTION

Do you agree that alternative databases should be used to widen the jury pool? What databases do you think should be used? How important is it that the potential pool contains representatives of as many sections of society as possible?

◀)) LISTEN TO THE PODCAST

For guidance on how to answer this question and a discussion of the main issues, listen to the author's podcast on the Online Resource Centre: www.oxfordtextbooks.co.uk/orc/gillespie_els6e/

13.2.1.1 Disqualification

Alongside the changes to the excusal from jury service, the range of those who are disqualified from serving was dramatically altered by the *Criminal Justice Act 2003*

---

54. *Juries Act 1974*, s 1.
55. *Juries Act 1974*, s 9(1) and sch 1, pt III, as originally enacted.
56. *Juries Act 1974*, ss 9(2) and 9A.

Table 13.2 Disqualification from jury service

Subject to provisions within the Mental Health Act 1983 and Mental Capacity Act 2005	Disqualified for duration of being subject to provisions
Life imprisonment (or equivalent)	Disqualified for life
Imprisonment for public protection	Disqualified for life
Imprisonment for a term of five years or more	Disqualified for life
Any term of imprisonment (including suspended)	Disqualification for ten years
Community sentence	Disqualification for ten years

(CJA 2003). Previously those whose occupation, or whose spouse's occupation, was allied to the criminal justice system (eg judiciary, lawyers, police, etc) were disqualified from sitting on a jury, as were members of the clergy. Auld had argued that this was a historical irrelevancy and he spent a considerable time noting that in the United States of America it was not uncommon for members of the legal profession, including members of the judiciary, to be called to serve.[57] This proposal caused much controversy but it was accepted by the government and the list of people who are disqualified (ie may not sit on a jury regardless of whether they wish to or not) is now restricted to those who are subject to certain provisions within the Mental Health Act 1983 or Mental Capacity Act 2005 and those convicted of a crime and may be summarized as shown in Table 13.2.

Nobody is now automatically excused as a result of their occupation and since the CJA 2003 has come into force two Lord Justices of Appeal, Dyson LJ (as he then was) and Tuckey LJ, have served on a jury along with numerous other judges and lawyers. Whether this is correct remains a topic of heated debate. Auld clearly wished to widen the pool of available juries but the use of judges, particularly senior judges, does appear slightly at odds with the overriding principle of the review which was to quicken up the criminal justice system. Jury trials are longer than summary trials and although a juror will often sit for only a two-week period, that is two weeks when a court, including the Court of Appeal (which suffers from delays), will be without a judge; is this necessarily in the best interests of the criminal justice system?

More serious, however, is the issue of bias. It was noted in Chapter 9 that the issue of perceived bias is something that needs to be guarded against (9.3.3) and this must be true of juries too. Whilst it may be unproblematic if a judge—who is supposed to be impartial—sits, what signal does it send if a police officer or prosecutor sits on a jury? The matter inevitably led to litigation. The first, and most important, case is *R v Abdroikov*.[58] Abdroikov and two other appellants (from different trials) appealed to the House of Lords complaining about the composition of the juries hearing their trials. In *Abdroikov*, the foreperson of the jury was a serving police officer, and in another appellant's case a member of the jury was employed by the CPS although the juror did not know anyone connected to the case.

The House of Lords noted that the law had changed and it was quite clear that the range of people entitled to sit on the case had been widened but Baroness Hale

---

57. Lord Justice Auld, *A Review of the Criminal Courts of England and Wales* (HMSO 2001) 140–1, 146–9.
58. [2007] 1 WLR 2679.

makes the pertinent point that just because a person can be summoned for jury service does not mean that they should sit on the case they have been summoned for.[59] Her Ladyship noted that whether they can sit depends on whether it would render the trial unsafe.

In respect of the police officer sitting, the House noted that there was no real dispute between the evidence of the police and defendant and there was no link between the station in which the police officer was based and the police witnesses in the trial. The House concluded there was no risk of prejudice. However, it reached a different conclusion in respect of the CPS employee. Lord Bingham noted that it was doubtful it was ever intended for a crown prosecutor to sit on a jury brought by their agency since that would appear to have the appearance of bias because a juror is employed by the prosecutor.

This ruling was explained by the Court of Appeal in *R v Khan*[60] which concerned similar issues. The court in that case indicated that the mere fact that a police officer works in the same locality as a witness does not provide evidence of bias, nor does the fact that he works on similar types of cases. The court also noted that the limitation on CPS employees sitting on juries was limited to those trials where the CPS was the prosecutor. Where an alternative prosecuting agency brought the prosecution (in this case the Department of Trade and Industry) then being the employee of a prosecution service would not show bias.

🔄 QUESTION FOR REFLECTION

Do you think the House of Lords and Court of Appeal were right to say there is no appearance of bias where a police officer on a jury is in the same police force as a police witness? Is there realistically any difference between this and the CPS employee? Should police officers only be permitted to sit on jury cases which involve police witnesses from outside their police area (eg a Warwickshire police officer could sit on a case involving Leicestershire police but not Warwickshire police)? Could that cause any practical difficulties?

🔊 LISTEN TO THE PODCAST

For guidance on how to answer this question and a discussion of the main issues, listen to the author's podcast on the Online Resource Centre: www.oxfordtextbooks.co.uk/orc/gillespie_els6e/

Bias is not restricted to those who come within the criminal justice system. What happens where someone has made public statements in respect of law and justice issues? Does this raise the possibility of bias? In *R v Cornwall*[61] a juror was a well-known columnist for the *Sun* who had made a series of pronouncements about knife crime, drugs, and immigration. The appellant was a drug dealer who was accused of stabbing a person to death. The Court of Appeal rejected an argument that the juror was biased and noted that there was no evidence that he had not tried the case in accordance with his oath. The court noted that a jury may well have people with strong views on the

---

59. [2007] 1 WLR 2679, 2696–7.
60. [2008] 2 Cr App R 13.
61. [2009] EWCA Crim 2458.

criminal justice system but that will be one person amongst twelve. The court accepted that public pronouncements could lead to an allegation of bias but they would need to relate specifically to issues before the jury and in this particular case they did not and there was no risk that an independent observer would consider the juror to be biased.

13.2.1.2 **Disability**

It will be seen from Chapter 14 that a judge may ask a person to stand down if they are disabled but what are the rules regarding the use of disabled jurors? Section 9B *Juries Act 1974* (JA 1974) states that there is a clear presumption in favour of disabled jurors being able to sit but that where a judge is of the opinion that the person could not, as a result of his disability, act 'effectively' as a juror he should be stood down. In *Re Osman*[62] His Honour Judge Verney, the Recorder of London, stood down a juror who was profoundly deaf and who could only follow the proceedings if a sign-language interpreter was used. The principal reason for this ruling was that the interpreter would have to attend the jury room and would, therefore, become a thirteenth person when only twelve are permitted.[63] The fact that the interpreter would not be expressing personal opinions was not considered sufficient safeguard. This case was followed in 1999 when a Mr McWhinney was called to the jury. Mr McWhinney was also profoundly deaf and required the services of an interpreter and he was similarly stood down.[64]

These cases were controversial and there was a commitment to review the matter[65] but no change in the law has yet occurred. Indeed, in 2000 the then Lord Chancellor, Lord Irvine, argued that he saw no reason why a deaf person should not serve on a jury[66] but he left open the argument as to the effect of a thirteenth person being in the jury room.

Where a third person is not needed then there is no significant objection and it is notable that, for example, there have been cases where a blind juror has sat, although there may be objections if evidence at a trial is particularly focused on visual evidence. Where it is not (and a significant proportion of trials will not require visual evidence to be shown, as distinct from it merely assisting a jury) then there is no reason why a blind person should not sit. Indeed, it is submitted that it is a matter of disgrace that the de facto presumption against deaf jurors still appears to be in existence. There is no reason why a qualified interpreter could not be appointed by the judge and such interpreters be given training as to the limits of their duties (ie not to enter into personal discussions within a jury room). There are currently approximately 11 million people in the UK who are deaf or hard of hearing although only approximately 900,000 of them are severely or profoundly deaf. However, in an era where we are trying to expand jury service it is nonsensical not to permit deaf people to sit on a jury.

⊙ QUESTION FOR REFLECTION

Do you agree that deaf and blind jurors should be able to sit on juries? Are there any reasons why they should not be permitted? Are these reasons that would stop a juror sitting in a particular case or such that it justifies a blanket ban?

---

62.   [1996] 1 Cr App R 126.
63.   *Re Osman* [1996] 1 Cr App R 126, 128.
64.   Amir Majid, 'Jury Still out on Deaf Jurors' (2004) 154 *New Law Journal* 278.
65.   Amir Majid, 'Jury Still out on Deaf Jurors' (2004) 154 *New Law Journal* 278, 279, and Lord Justice Auld, *A Review of the Criminal Courts of England and Wales* (HMSO 2001) 153.
66.   Lord Justice Auld, *A Review of the Criminal Courts of England and Wales* (HMSO 2001) 153.

13.2.1.3 Enforcing jury service

Jury service is a civic responsibility and accordingly when a potential juror is summoned to court he is expected to attend. However, Auld noted that 15 per cent of jurors refused to answer the jury summons. It is a criminal offence to fail to answer a jury summons, theoretically as contempt of court but more frequently as a summary-only offence punishable by a fine.[67] However, Auld noted that it was comparatively rare for courts actually to pursue those who neglect a jury summons, and accordingly this had created a position whereby significant numbers failed to meet their civic duty. Arguably the position may be somewhat better now since a central jury-summoning bureau has been established so instead of individual courts being responsible for deciding the eligibility or otherwise of jurors a central bureau does this. Accordingly, if courts make the appropriate returns to this system they could be charged with pursuing those who neglect their service.

However, some disagree with this policy, and Auld himself noted that the difficulty with enforcement is that it could clog up courts with a relatively trivial matter. Auld suggested the imposition of a fixed penalty notice[68] although that does raise the question why it is that Auld believes that someone who fails to respond to a jury summons would respond to a fixed penalty notice; presumably a significant proportion would fail to pay the ticket necessitating enforcement proceedings at this stage. However, Auld is undoubtedly correct in deciding that something has to be done since the jury system is based upon the premise that citizens will do their part and accordingly those who neglect this duty should be held to account.

13.2.2 Diversity

455

Juries should ordinarily be randomly selected[69] and so it may seem unusual to talk about diversity but there have been, for some years, questions about how diverse juries are. The two principal questions that arise in respect of diversity are in respect of race and also in terms of the professional background of juries.

13.2.2.1 Race

A particular concern over the years has been whether juries are diverse in terms of racial composition. There has, to an extent, been a belief that juries are predominantly white and do not reflect the diversity of the UK. A leading study published in 2007 noted, however, that there was no evidence of this and they noted that apart from two courts (out of eighty-four) there were no statistical anomalies between the jurors summoned and the ethnic minority population of the relevant catchment area[70] and that indeed in some courts ethnic minority jurors were over-represented. That said, one troubling result of the survey was that ethnic minority jurors were more likely to seek to avoid jury duty[71] and it has been speculated that this may be because there is a lower confidence in the justice system. It is certainly regrettable that there is a desire to avoid jury service and it would be extremely problematic if this was as a result of a loss of confidence since ethnic minority jurors are necessary in order to provide confidence in the justice system.

---

67. *Juries Act 1974*, s 20.
68. Lord Justice Auld, *A Review of the Criminal Courts of England and Wales* (HMSO 2001) 145.
69. *Juries Act 1974*, s 11.
70. Cheryl Thomas, *Diversity and Fairness in the Jury System* (Ministry of Justice 2007) 57.
71. Cheryl Thomas, *Diversity and Fairness in the Jury System* (Ministry of Justice 2007) 131.

Being called to jury service does not necessarily mean that there will be appropriate representation on each jury since jurors are brought within a 'pool' of jurors from which the trial jury are selected (see 13.2.2.2). The research demonstrated that there was more sporadic diversity in respect of each individual jury[72] and this echoes concerns that have been raised previously about whether juries should be empanelled in respect of a particular racial composition. One interesting finding was that, at least anecdotal evidence suggested that one reason for this is that the final 'draw' is made in open court and that clerks may 'avoid cards where a juror's name is difficult to pronounce'.[73] It was difficult to confirm this finding[74] although it certainly was not disproved. If this is true, it is certainly an issue that should not occur. The most obvious solution is to 'number' the jury-in-waiting rather than 'name' them so that the position becomes less subject to decisions being made on the ease of pronunciation.

The issue of whether there should be a particular racial bias has been discussed on a number of occasions. The first was *R v Danvers*[75] where the Court of Appeal found that a court had no power to order the empanelment of a jury in a way that provided specific representation on the basis of ethnicity. This rule was challenged under human rights legislation in *R v Smith*[76] where the defendant was one of three men convicted in respect of charges relating to, inter alia, grievous bodily harm with intent (contrary to s 18 *Offences Against the Person Act 1861*). Much of the evidence in the case related to witness testimony and the appellant sought to argue that there were racial dimensions to the case, including the fact that all the jury were white.[77] Whilst the defendant had not asked for a multiracial jury at the time of trial he sought to argue that his being tried by an all-white jury in a case that contained racial elements and where the defendant felt he had been racially abused breached Article 6 ECHR.[78] The Court of Appeal specifically rejected this argument stating that they were not convinced that there was any residual unfairness in being tried by a randomly called all-white jury[79] and that a properly directed jury would be able to try the offender in a fair manner.

Interestingly, whilst they said that nothing in their judgment should be taken as meaning that alternative methods should be required, they did specifically say of this case that '[i]t was not a case where a consideration of the evidence required knowledge of the traditions or social circumstances of a particular racial group'[80] which does beg the question whether if that was required a different result would have been achieved. Whether, if such circumstances exist, this is a requirement for a jury of a particular ethnic mix or a requirement for expert evidence on cultural factors is perhaps another question.

The courts place great emphasis on the random nature of a jury and where this randomness is missing then they will intervene.[81] However, others have disputed the idea of randomness in all respects and have suggested that there should be racial profiling, at least in part.

72. Cheryl Thomas, *Diversity and Fairness in the Jury System* (Ministry of Justice 2007) 147.
73. Cheryl Thomas, *Diversity and Fairness in the Jury System* (Ministry of Justice 2007) 151.
74. Cheryl Thomas, *Diversity and Fairness in the Jury System* (Ministry of Justice 2007) 152.
75. [1982] Crim LR 680.
76. [2003] 1 WLR 2229.
77. *R v Smith* [2003] 1 WLR 2229, 2233.
78. *R v Smith* [2003] 1 WLR 2229, 2234.
79. *R v Smith* [2003] 1 WLR 2229, 2239.
80. *R v Smith* [2003] 1 WLR 2229, 2239.
81. See, for example, the Privy Council case of *Rojas v Berllaque* [2004] 1 WLR 201 where the fact that juries were inevitably all male because of the nature of how juries were called was considered to be inappropriate.

Perhaps the most notable recent call to alter the empanelment of a jury was made by Auld who recommended that a jury should, where race is a factor, be empanelled on a random basis but if, after nine persons have been empanelled, the jury is all-white then the remaining three spaces should be filled by members of an ethnic minority.[82] Part of the justification for this was that Auld LJ believed that research indicated that 'white juries are, or are perceived to be, less fair to black than to white people'.[83] However, in Thomas' 2010 study involving case simulation and jurors, she found that 'all-White juries did not discriminate against BME defendants [with] no tendency for all-White juries to convict a Black or Asian defendant more than a White defendant'.[84] Of course Auld referred not only to actual unfairness but perceptions of unfairness too although it is difficult to see how this perception will be solved by requiring a minimum number of ethnic minorities to be included within a jury because it could be argued that this shows white jurors cannot be trusted by themselves to pass a fair judgment.

There were practical problems with Auld's recommendation (including how one identifies that a correct number of people are summoned for the jury pool—it is not a case of having three members of the ethnic minority per jury since the randomness could, for example, lead to a jury with many more members) but also the point about whether this assists. Auld's report treats all ethnic minorities the same—they are just 'not white'. There is no indication or evidence that a person belonging to a particular ethnic minority is going to be more (or indeed less) reassured by the presence of other members of ethnic minorities of ethnicities different from his own. It may well be that this is not true and it will inevitably lead to questions about whether juries must belong to particular ethnicities, and whether certain ethnicities should not sit on juries because of perceived biases against each other's ethnicities.

QUESTION FOR REFLECTION

Should juries be empanelled in such a way that each panel is representative of the diversity in the particular catchment area of a court? If a defendant is a member of an ethnic minority should a jury always include a member with an ethnic minority background and, if so, should it be of the same ethnicity as the defendant?

13.2.2.2 Social demographics

The second area of concern about diversity has always traditionally been the perception that 'intelligent' or professional jurors escape jury service and that juries 'are made up of the unemployed and retired'.[85] Interestingly the research conducted by Thomas did not show this and indeed suggested that the opposite may even be true. Thomas found that employed jurors were, if anything, over-represented on juries[86] and that when occupation was taken into account the largest group of employed persons were professionals.[87] It would seem therefore that the perceived concern is therefore simply not true.

---

82. Lord Justice Auld, *A Review of the Criminal Courts of England and Wales* (HMSO 2001) 159.
83. Lord Justice Auld, *A Review of the Criminal Courts of England and Wales* (HMSO 2001) 158.
84. Cheryl Thomas, *Are Juries Fair?* (Ministry of Justice 2010) ii.
85. Cheryl Thomas, *Diversity and Fairness in the Jury System* (Ministry of Justice 2007) 134.
86. Cheryl Thomas, *Diversity and Fairness in the Jury System* (Ministry of Justice 2007) 134.
87. Cheryl Thomas, *Diversity and Fairness in the Jury System* (Ministry of Justice 2007) 137.

An interesting question, however, is how pleased we should be about this and whether jury service can actually cause the public difficulties. It will be remembered that the CJA 2003 reforms widened eligibility and were coupled with a stricter approach to granting exemptions from jury service. Some have questioned the desirability of this, with Parliament and the media being quite exercised by health practitioners and, to a lesser extent, the judiciary. For example, reference has been made to the fact that a senior consultant had to cancel 300 patient appointments to undertake jury service and a sole-practitioner GP had to close her surgery for weeks to accommodate jury service.[88] When judges have been called to serve on juries questions have been raised about whether that has meant further delays in the court system because the judge (who could preside on trials) is serving on a jury.

It is relatively easy to see the logic in arguing that some people may be exempted. The doctor would seem to be a classic example but then who else? Presumably the same can be said of dentists, but what of nurses and other medical practitioners? What of the emergency services? Leaving aside the police (who have been discussed already) there is the Fire and Rescue Service, paramedics, and even the RNLI. Each of these may be impacted if a member has to take a significant period of time off work. The difficulty with exemptions is that it is possible to identify a category of persons who will always be able to claim that they will be materially affected by jury service or that it will have an impact on others. If exemptions are given then it could quickly develop to the situation before where there were real doubts about how diverse the juries were in terms of socio-economic disparity.

13.3 Summary trials or trials on indictment?

Perhaps the key question that arises in respect of lay justice is whether a defendant should be tried summarily (at the magistrates' court) or on indictment (at the Crown Court). It has been seen that a summary trial will not necessarily involve lay justice since it may be conducted by a district judge (magistrates' court) but in the majority of situations this decision will be between what role laypersons play in the trial: as the tribunal of both fact and law (summary trial) or simply the tribunal of fact (trial on indictment).

The process of sending a case to the correct court was discussed in the previous chapter (12.2) but it is worth remembering that the decision as to whether matters should be dealt with at summary level or in the Crown Court is one of the most contested and controversial issues of the criminal justice system. This is partly because there is a belief that the right to jury trial can be traced back to the Magna Carta although that claim is slightly disingenuous in that the Magna Carta was not designed for the common man but for nobles, and the trial by peers was arguably as much about trial by combat or for the nobility to be tried by themselves as anything else. However, irrespective of its origins it is clear that the right to jury trial as we now understand it has existed for several centuries and, as noted earlier, it is considered by many the ultimate safeguard.

Yet the reality is that juries are rarely used in the context of overall crime. It has already been noted that 95 per cent of cases are tried in the magistrates' court where no jury sits. Of those matters that do reach the Crown Court, juries are used in about

---

88. S Broadridge, 'Recent Developments Concerning Juries' House of Commons Library Paper, 2009 SN/HA/2867, 3–4.

1.5 per cent of cases. Of course these bare statistics mask the fact that juries are used in the most serious of cases (such as homicide and serious sexual offences) but it shows that the place of juries in the criminal justice system is not necessarily as it is perceived by the public at large although, of course, the place of lay justice is significant.

Jury trials are expensive and they are usually slower than a trial in the magistrates' court, especially one conducted by a DJMC. The costs are higher because of the greater number of people involved in a case (discussed at 12.6.2.2) and the fact that many of those are paid. Whilst jurors are not paid, they can receive expenses and (a capped) contribution to financial loss. In 1999 the government argued that they could save some £100 million per year if they restricted the number of people who proceeded to the Crown Court.[89]

The debate surrounding the decision as to which court a matter should be tried in has rarely been about whether jury trials should be abolished, or even whether further offences should be listed as triable only in the magistrates' courts, but rather who should decide what court an offender is tried in. There are three categories of offences; those triable only summarily (which are heard in the magistrates' court), those triable only on indictment (which are tried in the Crown Court), and those triable either-way (which can be tried in either the magistrates' court or Crown Court). The mechanics of this decision were considered in Chapter 12 but it will be remembered that the defendant, charged with an either-way offence, has a veto over being tried in the magistrates' court. He cannot demand to be tried in the magistrates' court (although he can request this the magistrates do not need to accede to this submission) but he can demand to be tried in the Crown Court.

Successive governments have attempted to keep more cases within the magistrates' court[90] and the usual rationale has always been considerations of cost and delay rather than any reasoned discussion about justice requirements. Three of the most important reviews into the criminal justice system (the Royal Commission on Criminal Justice (1993), Narey Report on Delays (1997), and Auld Report (2001)) have all recommended that the right of a defendant to veto a summary trial should be altered by allowing the court, rather than the defendant, to decide where the trial will take place.

Perhaps the most significant attempt to introduce this change took place around the turn of the millennium when the New Labour government sought to introduce legislation to remove the veto. The Bills led to an outcry with the (inevitable) suggestion that the government was seeking to remove jury trial which was not strictly true, although it would have led to the removal of the right to demand a jury trial in respect of either-way matters. Whilst made before these attempts, the comments of the then Lord Chief Justice, Lord Taylor, summarize the approach of the judiciary: 'in our culture and perception trial by jury is a fundamental right.'[91] Of course this is simply not true since summary justice has existed for centuries but the perception of the right exists and public pressure, together with a rebellious House of Lords, meant that two separate Bills failed.

It can be argued whether this was more about posturing than any identifiable problem. Whilst a defendant can veto a summary trial it has been shown that defendants are increasingly less likely to be responsible for the trial venue.[92] In 2003–4 73 per

---

89. Explanatory notes to the *Mode of Trial (No 1) Bill 1999*, para 15.
90. Steven Cammiss, 'I Will in a Moment Give you the Full History' [2006] *Criminal Law Review* 38, 39.
91. Andrew Ashworth, 'Plea, Venue and Discontinuance' [1993] *Criminal Law Review* 830, 832.
92. Steven Cammiss, 'I Will in a Moment Give you the Full History' [2006] *Criminal Law Review* 38, 40.

cent of relevant cases arrived at the Crown Court because the magistrates declined jurisdiction;[93] in 2012 this statistic reached 88 per cent.[94] However, the latest 2015–16 data shows this has decreased slightly to reach 78.5 per cent.[95] This suggests that abolishing the veto would not make a significant difference.

More interesting is to know why the magistrates send matters to the Crown Court. The usual reason given is that their powers would be insufficient to deal with an offender. Magistrates are currently only able to sentence an offender to a maximum of six months' imprisonment (whilst the *Criminal Justice Act 2003* provided for the power to allow this to be raised to twelve months' imprisonment this has never come into force) and so if they feel that a higher sentence is likely to be required then they should pass the matter to the Crown Court. That said, there is clear evidence that a substantial number of defendants then receive a sentence that is well within the powers of a magistrate[96] and perhaps this means that more training needs to be provided on likely sentences. Of course the discrepancy in sentences could be as a result of evidence that is only adduced during the trial but, when deciding the mode of trial, the magistrates should consider whether, if the prosecution evidence is all accepted, the sentence is outside of their powers. If it is not then perhaps the presumption should be that magistrates should accept jurisdiction unless other reasons can be advanced.

 Summary

This chapter has considered the issue of use of laypersons within the criminal justice system. In particular we have noted that:

- The main judges in the magistrates' court are known as lay justices or justices of the peace.

- A lay justice is not legally qualified and sits in a voluntary capacity.

- There are a number of paid, professional magistrates known as district judges (magistrates' court) or deputy district judges if they sit part-time.

- Lay magistrates sit in benches of three whereas district judges will normally sit alone.

- Although not qualified, lay magistrates remain responsible for decisions of both fact and law. They are assisted with the law by a legal adviser who is superintended by the clerk to the justices.

- Juries are responsible for decisions of fact in the Crown Court but they are not responsible for decisions of law.

- The *Criminal Justice Act 2003* widened the eligibility for jurors and the presumption is that most people are now eligible for jury service.

- Refusing a jury summons is a criminal offence.

- It is not permitted to artificially create a racially mixed jury.

---

93. Steven Cammiss, 'I Will in a Moment Give you the Full History' [2006] *Criminal Law Review* 38, 40.
94. CPS, *Annual Report and Accounts 2011–12* (Crown Prosecution Service 2012).
95. CPS, *Annual Report and Accounts 2015–16* (Crown Prosecution Service 2016) 64.
96. Steven Cammiss, 'I Will in a Moment Give you the Full History' [2006] *Criminal Law Review* 38, 41.

End-of-chapter questions

1. Read Liberty, *Magistrates' Courts and Public Confidence* (The Civil Liberties Trust 2002) and Penny Darbyshire, 'Magistrates' in Mike McConville and Geoffrey Wilson (eds), *The Handbook of the Criminal Justice Process* (OUP 2002) 292–4. Why do you think we continue with the idea of lay benches? Would it not be advisable for at least one justice to be a district judge (magistrates' court)? Can a trial before lay justices properly be called fair?

2. How representative should a bench of magistrates be? If the defendant is a member of the ethnic minorities should the bench also contain a member who identifies himself as coming from an ethnic minority?

3. Do you think it is right that police and prison officers are allowed to serve on a jury? Can they be truly considered independent?

4. Is it not a waste of resources to have a judge sitting as a juror? By taking the judge away from his court for two weeks it could prevent several trials from being heard. Is it not more sensible to restrict judges to judging?

 # Further reading

Auld LJ, *A Review of the Criminal Courts of England and Wales* (HMSO, 2001) ch 5.
  This is the chapter of the Auld report that discusses the use of juries and their constitution.

Darbyshire P, *Sitting in Judgment: The Working Lives of Judges* (Hart Publishing 2011) ch 8.
  This presents the working lives of district judges (magistrates' court) in a very informative and user-friendly way.

Davis G and Vennard J, 'Racism in Court: The Experiences of Ethnic Minority Magistrates' (2006) 45 *Howard Journal of Criminal Justice* 485–501.
  This is an interesting study that interviews magistrates who come from an ethnic minority background and assesses how they are treated by fellow magistrates and those within the system.

Doran S, 'Trial by Jury' in Mike McConville and Geoffrey Wilson (eds), *The Handbook of the Criminal Justice Process* (OUP 2002).
  This is an intelligent essay that highlights some of the controversies of a trial on indictment, including issues relating to the jury.

Grove T, *A Magistrate's Tale* (Bloomsbury, 2002).
  Ordinarily I would be loath to recommend an entire book but this is a fascinating insight of the author's selection to be a member of the magistracy and his initial period of sitting. You should also consider reading *A Juryman's Tale* which has long since been considered essential reading by the Judicial College and depicts life serving on a jury. Both are entertaining reads written by a journalist.

461

For multiple-choice questions, updates to this chapter, and links to useful websites, please visit the **Online Resource Centre** at: **www.oxfordtextbooks.co.uk/orc/gillespie_els6e/**

14

Those in Court

By the end of this chapter you will be able to:

- Identify who sits in each type of trial.
- Identify who presides in each trial.
- Understand the role of the principal actors in the trials.
- Understand why each person is required and whether there are circumstances when someone (eg lawyers or the defendant) do not need to be present.

Introduction

Chapter 12 left at the point where a trial was about to start, either in the magistrates' court or the Crown Court. Before examining the trial process (which will occur in Chapter 15) it is first necessary to consider who will be present during the trial. Presenting these people will allow you to understand what role each has during the trial and will allow you to more readily understand how the trial process takes place.

14.1 Summary trials in the magistrates' court

The first court to examine is the magistrates' court. Whilst the precise number and types of people will vary depending on the nature of the trial, and in particular, the seriousness of the offence, a number of core people will ordinarily always be present such as:

- magistrates
- lawyers
- court clerk
- the defendant
- witnesses
- probation officers.

It is not necessary to consider all of these people but the main people will be explored so that their role and purpose can be more readily understood.

14.1.1 **Magistrates**

A summary trial is one that takes place within the magistrates' court (or youth court when the defendant is under the age of 18: see 15.7) and so the most obvious starting point is the magistrates. It will be remembered from Chapter 13 that there are two types of magistrate that may sit in the magistrates' court; lay justices of the peace (who are not legally qualified and will ordinarily sit in panels of three) and district judges (magistrates' court) who used to be known as 'stipendary magistrates' and who will ordinarily sit alone. It will be remembered that a district judge (magistrates' court) is technically a member of the judiciary and is therefore legally qualified.

The appointment of both lay justices and district judges (magistrates' court) was considered previously in this book. How does one decide whether lay magistrates or a district judge will preside? The answer is not necessarily easy. Some courts have a tradition of using stipendiary magistrates (now district judges (magistrates' court)), particularly in inner London, and so a trial that is held there will ordinarily be heard by a district judge. The lay magistracy remains the more common panel and these will be found in the vast majority of courts. As lay magistrates are often employed they can ordinarily only sit for a finite period of time. Indeed it will be remembered from Chapter 13 that the minimum requirement is 26 half-days. Whilst many will sit for a full day, not all will. Where, therefore, a trial will take longer than one day it is quite possible that the court may decide that it is more appropriate for the matter to be heard by a district judge.

District judges will ordinarily also be used where the case is likely to raise significant points of law. Some quite technical laws are triable only summarily, particularly certain environmental offences, where the powers of the magistrates' court are beyond that which they can ordinarily impose. Some of these technical offences will raise issues of law that are better decided by a district judge. Similarly, in an ordinary trial it is possible that some of the evidence will be the subject of legal challenge (because, for example, it raises issues such as hearsay or has been illegally obtained). Even though lay magistrates are not legally qualified they are not prevented from making decisions of law, indeed they do so routinely, and are advised on the law by their clerk but where it is particularly complex it may be advisable to use a district judge, who is legally qualified and able to make the decision without advice.

Chapter 13 rehearsed the competing arguments for the use of lay magistrates or district judges and this will not be rehearsed here. The magistrates or district judge are in charge of the court and are ordinarily accorded the respect that would be due to a judge. They hear the evidence, rule on submissions, decide guilt or innocence, and impose sentence. Where a panel of three lay justices sits it is ordinarily only the chairman (who will sit in the middle of the panel) who will speak; the other lay justices will present their questions through the chair. That said, it should be remembered that the magistrates are in charge of proceedings and local courts do sometimes differ: do not be surprised if you go into a court and see one of the other magistrates speaking.

⚡ CHAIR AND WINGERS

It will be remembered from Chapter 13 that one lay magistrate holds the office of 'chairman of the bench' which carries with it certain administrative responsibilities. Every time the court sits, however, there must be a chair of that court. Chairs are experienced magistrates who have sat for a number of years and who have received additional training. The remaining justices are known as 'wingers' because they sit on either 'wing' of the chair. Ordinarily they will not speak in a public court but instead pass their questions via the chair. However, they remain an important part of the panel and they have an equal vote when making rulings on submissions and deciding issues of law.

14.1.2 Justices' clerk/legal advisers

One of the most important positions in the magistrates' court is that of the justices' clerk, increasingly being called a legal adviser. The position of the clerk is particularly important where lay magistrates sit in judgment. Yet despite its importance it has been suggested that it is a role that is largely hidden from the consciousness of those who use the court[1]—in other words, those who are not aware of the duties and responsibility of the clerk would not realize the importance of the role.

Their importance is perhaps best summed up by Leveson LJ, the (then) Senior Presiding Judge for England and Wales, who stated:

> The Justices' Clerk occupies a unique position within Her Majesty's Courts Service in that, although a civil servant and subject to the management of the Area Director for administrative purposes, he/she has complete independence from direction (other than by the High Court), both when undertaking a judicial function and when giving legal advice to magistrates.[2]

This passage highlights not only their unusual status but also reinforces the fact that they have both a judicial and an advisory function, something that has become increasingly common in recent years. The reference to independence is one that is enshrined within statute[3] and ensures that, whilst technically civil servants, they act independently when exercising judicial functions or providing legal advice to the justices.

Before examining the duties and responsibilities of the clerk it is important to differentiate between the various terms. Local justice areas will have at least one justices' clerk and that is the person who is appointed to that area by the Lord Chancellor after consultation with the Lord Chief Justice.[4] The justices' clerk can be appointed to more than one local justice area[5] and this is likely in more rural areas. The clerk is, in effect, responsible for servicing numerous benches within the local justice area.[6] They are assisted in their function by deputies or assistant clerks who are more properly known as 'assistant to a justices' clerk'[7] and also by legal advisers, a new creature that has no formal statutory footing (discussed later).

14.1.2.1 Appointment

As noted earlier there is a formal role called the justices' clerk but separate to this there is now the legal adviser to the magistrates.

---

1. Penny Darbyshire, *The Magistrates' Clerk* (Barry Rose 1984) 1.
2. Brian Leveson, *Role of the Justices' Clerk and Legal Advisor* (Judiciary 2007) 1.
3. *Courts Act 2003*, s 29(1).
4. *Courts Act 2003*, s 27.
5. *Courts Act 2003*, s 27(3).
6. Penny Darbyshire, 'Raising Concerns about Justices' Clerks' in Sean Doran and John Jackson (eds), *The Judicial Role in Criminal Proceedings* (Hart Publishing 2000) 183.
7. *Courts Act 2003*, s 27(7).

Court clerk

Section 27 CA 2003 sets out the appointment criteria for a justices' clerk. Under s 27(2) the criteria are that a person has a five-year magistrates' qualification, is a barrister or solicitor who has served for not less than five years as an assistant to a justices' clerk, or has previously been a justices' clerk. Reference to 'magistrates' court qualification' to be a clerk means that it could be wider than just being a solicitor or barrister. 'Magistrates' court qualification' is defined under s 71(3)(f), *Courts and Legal Services Act 1990* as having 'a right of audience in relation to all proceedings in the magistrates' courts'. It will be remembered from Chapter 10 that legal executives can now exercise rights of audience in the magistrates' court although they will only hold rights of audience in relation to *all* proceedings when they hold the qualification for criminal, civil, and family matters (discussed at 10.7.1.2).

Legal advisers

Section 2(1) CA 2003 provides the Lord Chancellor with the power to appoint 'such officers and other staff as appear to him appropriate for the purpose of discharging his duty in relation to the courts'. This power applies to all civil servants and includes the provision of legal advisers since, as noted earlier, a clerk or assistant clerk can only be appointed if that person has a five-year qualification.

Since clerks and assistant clerks can be appointed to more than one local justice area[8] it is clear that there is a need for more legal advisers than there are clerks. The clerk has specific statutory responsibilities whereas the legal advisers will assist the clerk in his work but will also primarily provide legal advice to individual benches of magistrates. As all advisers must be legally qualified there are two ways of being appointed a legal adviser. The first is where a person is qualified as a solicitor or barrister, ie they have completed all stages of their training including their training contract or pupillage (where they have five years' post-qualification experience then they are eligible to be appointed a clerk or assistant clerk as noted earlier). Where a person in these circumstances is appointed then they become a 'legal adviser in training' and they begin to work as a legal adviser while studying a specialist course with the Judicial College (lasting two years). A legal adviser in training may act as a legal adviser to a bench but their work will be closely supervised by a more experienced adviser and/or the clerk himself.

The second method of entry is to apply to become a trainee legal adviser. Persons who have completed the academic and vocational stages of qualifying to be a lawyer (10.3.1) are eligible to be appointed as a trainee legal adviser and their training takes the form of a training contract or pupillage together with completing the two-year Judicial College course. A person who completes the relevant training course will not only become a legal adviser but will also become a fully qualified solicitor or barrister and thus eligible to enter private practice should they leave the court service.

14.1.2.2 Function

It will be remembered from the earlier quote from Leveson LJ that justices' clerks have two principal functions; the provision of advice to the magistracy and exercising judicial functions. The latter has increased significantly in recent years although it has been the subject of some controversy. Under s 28 CA 2003 rules may provide

---

8. *Courts Act 2003*, s 27(3)(a).

for anything to be done by a single lay justice to be done instead by a justices' clerk or assistant clerk. It should be noted that the power is expressly delegated to a clerk although rule 3 of the *Justices' Clerk Rules 2005*[9] provides that this can also include an assistant clerk when he has been authorized to do so by the clerk. However, it will be remembered that clerk and assistant clerk have a specific statutory definition and accordingly a legal adviser who is not designated a clerk or assistant clerk cannot exercise these functions.

The *Justices' Clerks Rules 2005* (as amended) provide the functions that can be exercised and they include a number of functions that would ordinarily be considered clearly judicial, including the issuing of an arrest warrant[10] and the discharging of an accused where the prosecution offers no evidence.[11] There are also functions relating to costs, bail, and the transfer for trial of an accused. Permitting justices' clerks to exercise these functions is somewhat controversial since, unlike lay magistrates and district judges (magistrates' court) they have not been appointed to a judicial role, their primary function is administrative and advisory. That said, they are now legally qualified and so it was suggested that it may be more efficient to use them to undertake certain pre-trial matters, allowing magistrates to concentrate on their core function, that of hearing cases. Certainly the issue of delay has long been a cause of concern to the criminal justice system and using justices' clerks may help minimize this delay by allowing them to quickly deal with administrative matters and allowing magistrates to spend their time hearing trials.

Example Justices' clerk: the 'judicial' role

Paragraph 15 of Schedule 1 to the *Justices' Clerks Rules 2005*[12] prescribes that a justices' clerk may fix or set aside a date of trial, time, and place for the trial of information. Paragraph 14 allows a justices' clerk to receive a plea. These powers may mean that where, for whatever reason, justices are not available progress can be made through lists by the justices' clerk exercising judicial powers to receive a plea and, if the plea is 'not guilty', setting down the date of trial and the location where the trial will take place.

The statement of Leveson LJ, noted earlier, makes clear that when exercising a judicial function the justices' clerks must act in a judicial manner and adhere to the ordinary principles of judicial ethics.[13]

The remainder of this section will consider their 'normal' function of advising the (lay) magistrates. For the purposes of this section it does not matter whether the person is the clerk, an assistant clerk, or a 'legal adviser' as their role and function remains the same. The duty of a clerk to advise the justices on matters of law is a statutory function[14] and it arises because magistrates, including lay magistrates, are responsible for decisions of both fact and law. In the Crown Court, as will be seen, this is split between the judge and jury, with the judge being the sole arbitrator of the law.

9.   SI 2005/545.
10. *Justices' Clerks Rules 2005*, SI 2005/545, sch 1, para 3.
11. *Justices' Clerks Rules 2005*, SI 2005/545, sch 1, para 5.
12. SI 2005/545.
13. Lord Justice Leveson, *Role of the Justices' Clerk and Legal Advisor* (Judiciary 2007) 2–4.
14. *Courts Act 2003*, s 28(4).

> **≡ Example** Fact vs law
>
> Suzy is charged with criminal damage contrary to s 1 *Criminal Damage Act 1971*. The damage is spray-painting pink paint onto a tank destined for service in Afghanistan. The estimate of the damage is £450 (the cost of removing the paint) hence it is a summary-only matter.
>
> Suzy does not deny that she was responsible for the damage to the tank but she argues that it was justified because the war in Afghanistan is illegal. If the defence is to be effective then two decisions must be made. First, there is a matter of law as to whether this justification is capable of amounting to a defence to a criminal charge. Second, if it can amount in law to a defence, does it, as a matter of fact, arise here?
>
> In a trial on indictment the first decision would be made by the judge, and the second decision would be a matter solely for the jury. In a summary trial both matters are decisions for the justices.

It has been suggested that mixing law and fact in this way is 'peculiar' since although the justices are entrusted with the decisions of law, lay justices rely wholly on their (subordinate) adviser as to what the law is. This leads to the position where:

> legal argument takes place in court, the argument [being] addressed to the justices who may hardly follow a word of it; in reality, however, it is intended for the ears of the clerk. Rulings ... are supposed to be made by the justices ... in practice, however, the decisions must be taken by the clerk ... [15]

Whilst made over sixty years ago that argument still holds good today: a lawyer is not really explaining the finer points of law to the lay magistrates but rather to the legal adviser (the same is not true, of course, where it is a district judge (magistrates' court)). Theoretically a justice need not follow the advice of their adviser as it is merely advice but failing to follow the advice can have consequences (see 14.1.2.3) not least where it leads to the court acting in a way contrary to the law as in such cases it is likely that either the prosecution or defendant would appeal by way of case stated (discussed in 16.2.2). Realistically this means that the magistrates will ordinarily follow the legal advice they are given.

It could be argued that the requirement to follow the advice is an argument for creating a hybrid court whereby lay magistrates sit only with a district judge (magistrates' court) but as it was seen in Chapter 13 this proposition was rejected. Similarly an attempt by clerks, at the time of the Narey Review of delays in the criminal justice system, to be 're-badged' as district judges and to chair panels was opposed by lay magistrates and ultimately rejected by the government, perhaps fearful as to whether sufficient lay magistrates would sit under any new regime.

14.1.2.3 Provision of advice

It will be remembered that it was said that a statutory duty of the justices' clerk is to provide advice to the magistrates and this responsibility continues even when he is not 'personally attending on them'[16] meaning that the justices' clerk must ensure there is sufficient cover to provide advice, including through the use of a legal adviser.[17]

---

15. Glanville Williams, *The Proof of Guilt* (Stevens 1955) 290.
16. *Courts Act 2003*, s 28(4).
17. Ministry of Justice, *Consolidated Practice Direction* (Ministry of Justice 2013) V.55.1(c).

Where a clerk is sitting in court, the statute makes clear that they can be proactive:

> The powers of a justices' clerk include, at any time when he thinks he should do so, bringing to the attention of any or all of the justices of the peace to whom he is clerk any point of law ... that is or may be involved in any question so arising.[18]

In other words, the clerk does not have to wait until the justices ask for advice but can, if he so wishes, provide advice whenever he believes it is necessary to do so. The *Consolidated Practice Direction* makes clear that this can include interrupting lawyers and asking questions of witnesses and the parties so as to clarify the issues involved in the case[19] and, in particular, it makes clear that they have the responsibility for ensuring that the proceedings of the trial are fair, something that is an inherent part of the rule of law. Of course the right to ask questions of the parties and witnesses raises again the issue of who is truly in control of proceedings, the magistrates or the court clerk? Theoretically it is the magistrates who are in control but if the clerk can intervene where they believe it is necessary to do so then it could be argued that they are truly in control.

Status of the advice

As magistrates are responsible for matters of both law and fact it is has been noted that technically advice is just that, advice, and the ultimate decision rests with the magistrates. That said, in *Jones v Nicks*[20] the Divisional Court, with the then Lord Chief Justice presiding, argued that if the justices rejected the advice they could be personally liable for any costs incurred during an appeal by way of case stated. The argument is presumably that ignoring the advice is unreasonable and not something that justices should ordinarily do.

However, blindly following advice appears equally wrong. In *R v Lincoln Justices, ex parte Count*[21] the Divisional Court warned that where a decision was perverse then costs may be incurred by the magistrates even when they followed the advice of their clerk. Admittedly this was an unusual case in that the court held that the magistrates should have known the advice they received was obviously wrong, but it does set a precedent and ascertaining where the line is may not always be simple.

The key to understanding this issue is perhaps considering what the advice is. If a clerk is setting out the legal framework and stating the principles of law that the justices must apply then this would be advice that they should follow. However, where the clerk goes beyond this and suggests to the justices how the law should be applied, or what the obvious conclusion to their advice is, then this encroaches on the judicial function of the magistrates and should be ignored.

14.1.2.4 Assisting the unrepresented defendant

The *Criminal Procedure Rules* have made explicit the fact that one of the duties of the legal adviser is to 'assist an unrepresented defendant'.[22] This has traditionally been an important role of the legal adviser/clerk and one that is not replicated in the Crown Court. Not every defendant will be represented by a lawyer (14.1.3) and out of fairness

---

18. *Courts Act 2003*, s 28(5).
19. Ministry of Justice, *Consolidated Practice Direction* (Ministry of Justice 2013) V.55.5.
20. [1977] RTR 72.
21. [1995] COD 351.
22. *Criminal Procedure Rules 2015* (as amended October 2016) r 9.4(3)(a).

it has traditionally been accepted that the legal adviser can, and should, assist the defendant. In part this is because where only lay justices sit (and it should be noted that rule 9.4 contains a presumption that it will not apply where a district judge sits)[23] and the defendant is not legally represented then there is a risk that the justices will only get a one-sided view of the facts because a defendant may not appreciate how to cross-examine a witness. This role is reinforced by the fact the rules also require the adviser to '... ask any questions required by the Rules in this Part'[24] which suggests that the adviser can ask questions of witnesses to clarify the points of the defence. Clearly the adviser does not act as counsel for the defendant and should remain impartial but it is an important safeguard to ensure that the unrepresented defendant receives a fair trial.

14.1.3 Lawyers

To some it may appear obvious that lawyers would be involved in a summary trial but this is not necessarily the case and some trials could theoretically take place without a lawyer being present.

14.1.3.1 Rights of audience

The magistrates' court is the lowest court in the English Legal System and the rights of audience are wide. The general rule is that all solicitors and barristers have rights of audience for summary trials as of right and this was the position prior to the extension of rights under the *Access to Justice Act 1999*.

14.1.3.2 Lay prosecutors

Section 53 of the *Crime and Disorder Act 1998* inserted a provision within the *Prosecution of Offences Act 1985* (PoOA 1985)[25] to permit non-legal staff to be designated as 'associate prosecutors' (formerly they were called 'designated caseworkers' but have since been renamed 'associate prosecutors'). Those so designated were able to exercise the powers of a crown prosecutor for matters relating to, inter alia, bail and the conduct of criminal proceedings in magistrates' courts other than trials, including sentencing matters following a guilty plea.[26]

The use of lay prosecutors is undoubtedly controversial but it could be argued that it is beneficial to allow lawyers to concentrate on those matters where liability is to be contested or where difficult issues of law arise. Given the CPS will only employ a finite number of lawyers there may be some logic to this argument but the concern must be that instead of using associate prosecutors to plug any gap caused by a shortage of lawyers they are being used to reduce the number of lawyers required, ie it is justice on the cheap. Associate prosecutors are given additional training (undertaken by CILEX) but this is not the same as being legally qualified and there is no requirement, for example, for them to qualify as a legal executive. It is perhaps regrettable that the CPS has introduced a fourth category of lawyers without considering whether it would have been better for associate prosecutors to become a legal executive. Indeed, arguably that is one of the reasons why legal executives exist and this procedure should have been used.

---

23. *Criminal Procedure Rules 2015* (as amended October 2016) r 9.4(1)(b)(i).
24. *Criminal Procedure Rules 2015* (as amended October 2016) r 9.4(2)(b).
25. *Prosecution of Offences Act 1985*, s 7A.
26. *Prosecution of Offences Act 1985*, s 7A(2).

There is no doubt that associate prosecutors undertake a significant part of the work of the CPS. In 2003–4 there were 254 designated caseworkers (the title used prior to them being (administratively) labelled 'associate prosecutors') but by 2012 this number had risen to 434.[27] In 2004 a review was launched into their use[28] (CPS) and this led to further changes to the PoOA 1985 by the *Criminal Justice and Immigration Act 2008* (CJIA 2008) which widened the scope of their use. The revised s 7A states that those designated by the DPP may act in the following matters:

- applications for, or relating to, bail in criminal proceedings
- the conduct of trial in the magistrates' courts other than trials of offences triable either-way or offences which are punishable with imprisonment in the case of persons aged 21 or over
- the conduct of applications or other proceedings relating to preventative civil orders
- the conduct of proceedings (other than criminal proceedings) assigned to the Director of Public Prosecutions.

When associate prosecutors were first authorized there was a restriction on them dealing with matters that were triable only on indictment, ie the most serious offences, but the CJIA 2008 reforms abolished this[29] meaning that theoretically an associate prosecutor could deal, for example, with bail matters relating to the most serious offences, including murder.

The extension of these powers is significant. Perhaps the most notable change is that associate prosecutors can now undertake trials so long as they are not an either-way offence or imprisonable. There are a number of offences that are non-imprisonable including many common offences, for example speeding and careless or inconsiderate driving. As legal aid may now not cover non-imprisonable matters (discussed in Chapter 11) extending rights of audience to associate prosecutors in these cases means that potentially neither side will be represented by a legally qualified individual and the magistrates will be reliant on their legal adviser to ensure that the law is adhered to. It is submitted that there is a danger in this approach. Even a matter as simple as a speeding offence can raise issues of law, including the admissibility of evidence and the appropriateness of defences.

It must be seriously questioned whether it is right for the state to prosecute matters without a lawyer being present to ensure that all legal aspects have been followed. There was a danger under the old regime that a person could plead guilty to a crime not known to law (because, for example, the particular factual circumstances of the case mean that they cannot, in law, be guilty) but at least there was the protection that it was likely the case had been reviewed by a lawyer. By extending associate prosecutors' rights of audience to trials the danger of a miscarriage of justice is increased. The guilt or innocence of a person is not something that should be treated as a trivial matter even where there is no risk of liberty. A conviction can have social consequences, including the loss of employment, and a contested trial should, it is submitted, only occur where the prosecution are represented by a legally qualified individual. To do otherwise is trivializing justice.

---

27. Freedom of Information Request, June 2012.
28. CPS, *Annual Report and Accounts 2003–04* (Crown Prosecution Service 2004) 22.
29. *Criminal Justice and Immigration Act 2008*, s 55(4).

14.1.4 **The defendant**

It may seem obvious that the defendant will be in court but this is not necessarily true in a summary trial.

14.1.4.1 **Pleading guilty by post**

Section 308 of the *Criminal Justice Act 2003* (CJA 2003) permits a defendant to plead guilty by post to any summary-only offence irrespective of what penalty can be imposed on them. It is important to note that the provision applies only to summary-only offences and not, for example, either-way offences. When a summons issued in a summary-only offence is posted the defendant is given a brief summary of the prosecution facts and details of the postal procedure.[30]

If the defendant chooses to plead guilty then the prosecution are not allowed to expand on the facts given in the statement,[31] this being a protection to ensure that the prosecution do not seek to allege a more serious version of events (potentially leading to a greater sanction) than that which the defendant has accepted. The defendant has the right to put forward written representations in reply to the accusation and this will be considered to be his plea of mitigation (ie the reasons he wishes the court to take into account when deciding sentence).

🔄 QUESTION FOR REFLECTION

Why should a person be permitted to plead guilty by post? If a person is summoned to court should they not attend? What reasons might there be for permitting a person to plead guilty by post?

A person cannot be sentenced to prison in his absence under this procedure and accordingly if the magistrates are minded to impose a custodial sentence they must adjourn the matter and summon the defendant to court. In reality the system tends to be used only for minor offences and therefore this issue rarely arises (where there is a risk of imprisonment it is likely that the defendant would wish to be legally represented in any event).

14.1.4.2 **Defendant in person**

The defendant may wish to represent himself in court and in common with other trials this is to be permitted. There is no rule in the magistrates' court that requires an offender to be represented legally and the court cannot order representation in the absence of a request by the defendant. A defendant can be accompanied by someone who is not legally qualified. These have, in the past, been referred to as a 'McKenzie friend'[32] although the Court of Appeal has disapproved of this term as it suggests a special class of person when, in fact, any person has the right to lay assistance and it does not matter what their qualifications are.[33] Ordinarily such a person cannot act

---

30.   *Magistrates' Court Act 1980*, s 12.
31.   *Magistrates' Court Act 1980*, s 12(8).
32.   *McKenzie v McKenzie* [1970] 3 WLR 472.
33.   *R v Leicester City Justices, ex parte Barrow* [1991] 3 WLR 368 and see Philip Thomas, 'From McKenzie's Friend to Leicester Assistant: The Impact of the Poll Tax' [1992] *Public Law* 208, for a critique of the case.

on behalf of the defendant (that is to say, speak) but rather assists in the preparation of the case and makes suggestions as to the questioning of witnesses etc.[34]

 QUESTION FOR REFLECTION

If the prosecution are allowed to be represented by non-legally qualified persons in contested trials (see the discussion of 'associate prosecutors' at 14.1.3.2) why should the defendant be restricted in who can present on his behalf? With legal aid being restricted does this mean that a shy, nervous defendant may be at a disadvantage? If so, does that make the trial unfair? What are the dangers in allowing anyone to appear for a defendant, however?

14.1.4.3 The missing defendant

What happens where a defendant is summoned to appear but does not attend (or does not use the plea by post scheme)? Traditionally the magistrates had discretion to decide how to proceed in such matters but amendments contained within the CJIA 2008 have fettered this. The first step was to adjourn the proceedings and attempt to secure the attendance of the defendant at the next hearing. The usual method of securing attendance would be to issue a warrant of arrest for the offender. If the offender was already on bail then this would be by way of an arrest warrant[35] but if he was not then the arrest warrant could only be issued if the justices are satisfied that the summons was served appropriately or that the non-appearance arises from a previous adjournment where the accused was present.[36]

Before the CJIA 2008 the magistrates had discretion to try an offender in his absence[37] although they had to be sure that the summons and/or the date of any adjourned hearing had been properly served on the defendant. The CJIA 2008 amended s 11 to state that, when dealing with an adult, the court 'shall proceed in his absence unless it appears to the court to be contrary to the interests of justice to do so'.[38] Section 11(2A) states that where the court believes that there is an acceptable reason for the defendant not appearing then it should not proceed in his absence.

Even under the new system the magistrates will ordinarily adjourn the hearing once, usually also issuing a warrant of arrest. A new date will be decided and if the defendant fails to turn up again (and it is quite possible that he will not as it is unlikely that in many summary-only matters the defendant would be remanded in custody prior to the trial) then they may consider a trial in his absence.

If the magistrates do decide to proceed with a trial in his absence then a not guilty verdict is formally recorded and the prosecution case then proceeds as set out in 15.1. This is not a mere formality: the prosecution are required to satisfy the burden of proof and if, at the conclusion of the prosecution case, the court is not satisfied to the appropriate standard that the prosecution have shown guilt then the bench must acquit the defendant.

---

34. It should be noted that in February 2016 the Lord Chief Justice issued a consultation on reforming the courts' approach to McKenzie friends.
35. *Bail Act 1976*, s 7.
36. *Bail Act 1976*, s 13.
37. *Magistrates' Court Act 1980*, s 11.
38. *Magistrates' Court Act 1980*, s 11(1)(b) as amended.

Where a person is sentenced to prison in his absence then he must first be brought before the court.[39] Presumably this is to provide an opportunity for him to explain himself and, as importantly, for the court to explain to the offender why they viewed the matter as one requiring him to be imprisoned. The court will also explain the duration of any sentence, including arrangements for release on licence.

⟳ QUESTION FOR REFLECTION

In *Lala v Netherlands*[40] the European Court of Human Rights held that it was 'of utmost importance' that a defendant should be present at his trial. Do you think it can ever be fair to try a defendant in his absence? (You may find it useful to read *R v Jones*.[41])

14.2 Trials on indictment in the Crown Court

The previous section identified who should be present during a summary trial and this section will now detail those who should be present in the Crown Court during a trial on indictment. The key players will be:

- the judge
- the jury
- lawyers
- court clerk
- stenographer
- the usher(s)
- the defendant
- witnesses.

As with the previous section it is not necessary to consider each of these people but an examination should be made of some.

14.2.1 The judge

Perhaps the key difference between a summary trial and trial on indictment is the presence of a judge and jury. The judge has ultimate responsibility for the proceedings and has sole responsibility for the law. Unlike with magistrates where there was a question over whether they, or their clerk, were ultimately in control of proceedings, no doubt exists in the Crown Court: the judge is in charge. The judge is always a legally qualified paid person and the following judges are entitled to sit in the Crown Court:

- any judge of the High Court
- any circuit judge (including deputy circuit judges)[42]

---

39. *Magistrates' Court Act 1980*, s 11(3).
40. (1994) 18 EHRR 586.
41. [2002] UKHL 5.
42. These are persons who retired as a Lord Justice of Appeal, puisne judge, or circuit judge but who are still under the age of 75 (s 24 *Courts Act 1971*).

- a recorder
- a district judge (magistrates' court).[43]

In addition to these judges the Lord Chief Justice, as the President of the Courts of England and Wales, has the inherent right to sit in the Crown Court.[44] Recent Lord Chief Justices have tended to exercise this right albeit only occasionally and even then they have tended to sit on sentencing matters rather than trials. In the past the Lord Chief Justice would invariably sit on the most serious trials but this has not occurred for many years. Other members of the judiciary are permitted to sit in the Crown Court but only if invited to do so by the Lord Chief Justice[45] and if they are not so invited then they have no jurisdiction to act in the Crown Court regardless of the seniority of their office.[46]

14.2.1.1 Allocation of the judge

In the review of the criminal justice system it was said:

> One of the greatest ills of the system is its lack of flexibility in the matching of judges, courts and cases.[47]

The decision as to how a judge is appointed to a particular case is relatively complicated and arguably a matter of chance in the majority of cases, but with some there is a defined procedure that must be followed. Not every judge is permitted to hear every case and, for example, in cases of murder and sexual offences a judge below the rank of puisne judge must receive additional training before he can hear such cases. This system is known as 'ticketing' and is designed to ensure that only experienced judges hear sensitive cases.[48] It had been suggested that the system of ticketing should be removed[49] but as yet this does not appear to have been acted upon, not least because there is a danger that removing the ticketing system could undermine the confidence of the public in the judicial system.

Example His Honour Judge Pickles QC

One of the most controversial judges in modern times was HHJ Pickles QC who was a circuit judge who attracted significant controversy, particularly in respect of sex crimes (see 9.2.3). Following a series of incidents, including a rebuke in *R v Scott*[50] Pickles was informed that he would no longer be sitting on further sex offence cases. In effect his 'ticket' was removed.

Criminal matters on indictment are divided into three classes (see Table 14.1) and the *Consolidated Practice Direction* then sets out which type of judge can hear what type of case (see Table 14.2).

---

43. District judges (magistrates' court) sit as recorders when in the Crown Court (s 65 *Courts Act 1971*).
44. *Constitutional Reform Act 2005*, s 7.
45. *Senior Courts Act 1981*, s 9(1).
46. *R v Lord Chancellor, ex parte Maxwell* [1997] 1 WLR 104.
47. Lord Justice Auld, *A Review of the Criminal Courts of England and Wales* (HMSO 2001) 226.
48. Ministry of Justice, *Consolidated Practice Direction* (Ministry of Justice 2013) IV. 33.
49. Lord Justice Auld, *A Review of the Criminal Courts of England and Wales* (HMSO 2001) 237.
50. [1990] Crim LR 440.

Table 14.1 Classification of offences

Class 1	(A) Murder, attempted murder, manslaughter, infanticide, child destruction, abortion, assisting a suicide.
	(B) Genocide, torture, and offences under the *War Crimes Act 1991*, terrorism offences, piracy, treason, an offence under the *Official Secrets Acts*.
	(C) Prison mutiny, riot in the course of serious civil disturbance, serious gang related crime, complex sexual offences cases, cases involving people trafficking.
	(D) Causing death by dangerous, careless, disqualified, or uninsured driving, cases resulting in a fatality or permanent serious disability.
Class 2	(A) Arson with intent to endanger life, cases involving explosives or firearms, kidnapping or false imprisonment, cases in which the defendant is a police officer, member of the legal profession or public figure, cases where the complainant or an important witness is a public figure, child cruelty.
	(B) Any sexual offence (other than those in class 1C), some kidnapping or false imprisonment cases.
	(C) Serious and complex fraud, money laundering, bribery, corruption cases, complex cases in which the defendant is a corporation, where the defendant is a corporation with a turnover in excess of £1bn.
Class 3	All other offences not listed in classes 1 or 2.

Table 14.2 Allocation of judiciary

Class 1	(1) a High Court judge, or
	(2) a circuit judge … provided (a) that in all cases save attempted murder, such judge is authorized by the Lord Chief Justice to try murder cases, and (b) the presiding judge has released the case for trial by such a judge.
Class 2	(1) a High Court judge, or
	(2) a circuit judge … or recorder, provided that in all cases the judge is authorized to try class 2 cases by the Lord Chief Justice and the case has been assigned to the judge by or under the direction of either the presiding judge or resident judge in accordance with guidance given by the presiding judges.
Class 3	Cases in class 3 may be tried by a High Court judge, or in accordance with guidance given by the presiding judges, a circuit judge … or a recorder. A case in class 3 shall not be listed for trial by a High Court judge except with the consent of a presiding judge.

It should be noted that the release in class 1 is specific—ie the presiding judge (unless he designates this responsibility to a senior circuit judge) shall examine each case and state that it can be released to a particular judge. The release in class 2 is more general and is a statement that particular crimes could be released to particular types of judges (eg senior circuit judges, resident judges, deputy circuit judges, recorders etc). The role of the presiding judge is, therefore, an important one but also a time-consuming one. It is an onerous job and perhaps this is why it is held only for a short time.

QUESTION FOR REFLECTION

Why should there be such a complex way of allocating judges to cases? If a person is appointable as a judge then why should he not be able to sit on any crime? If a judge has particular expertise in a particular area in practice should he not be able to sit on those trials without added experience? Are there any safeguards in allocating trials in this way?

Whilst a different judge may be responsible for the pre-trial arrangements, once a judge has begun to hear a case then it is not possible to change the judge and if, for some reason, the judge must retire from the case (eg sickness etc) then the trial ends and it must begin again.

14.2.1.2 Responsibilities of the judge

It was seen earlier that magistrates have responsibility for both fact and law (see 14.1.2.2). It is often said that in the Crown Court this responsibility is divided between judge and jury but in fact that is an oversimplistic distinction because there are numerous situations when a judge will have to make findings of fact.[51] Examples of where decisions of fact will need to be made include preliminary matters, admissibility decisions, and where a guilty plea is tendered the judge may actually become the sole tribunal of fact (in a procedure known as a *Newton* hearing; see 14.2.2.1).

Although a civil case, the leading statement of what the responsibilities of a judge in an adversarial trial are was set out by Lord Denning MR:

> [He] is to hearken the evidence, only himself asking questions of witnesses when it is necessary to clear up any point that has been overlooked or left obscure, to see that the advocates behave themselves seemly and keep to the rules laid down by law.[52]

And his Lordship warns that the principal danger for a judge is dropping 'the mantles of a judge and assum[ing] the robes of an advocate'; in other words the judge has to rise above the cut and thrust of advocacy and assure that the rules are followed. The role of a judge is often given a sporting analogy:

> The judge is not an advocate. Under the English and Welsh system of criminal trials he is much more like the umpire at a cricket match. He is certainly not the bowler, whose business it is to get the batsman out.[53]

Perhaps the most important duty of a judge is to control proceedings. The judge has ultimate responsibility for proceedings including the order of witnesses and evidence that may be adduced.[54] The *Criminal Procedure and Investigations Act 1996* (CPIA 1996) marked a significant change in the way judges controlled proceedings through the provision of formalized pre-trial hearings.[55] These hearings are known as Plea and Directions Hearings (PDH).

---

51. Sean Doran, 'The Necessarily Expanding Role of the Criminal Trial Judge' in Sean Doran and John Jackson (eds) *The Judicial Role in Criminal Proceedings* (Hart Publishing 2000) 5.
52. *Jones v National Coal Board* [1957] 2 QB 55, 65.
53. *R v Gunning* [1994] 98 Cr App R 303, 306 (Cumming-Bruce LJ).
54. Philip Otton, 'The Role of the Judge in Criminal Cases' in Mike McConville and Geoffrey Wilson (eds), *The Handbook of the Criminal Justice Process* (OUP 2002).
55. Jenny McEwan, 'Co-operative Justice and the Adversarial Criminal Trial: Lessons from the Woolf Report' in Sean Doran and John Jackson (eds), *The Judicial Role in Criminal Proceedings* (Hart Publishing 2000) 172.

If controlling the proceedings is the most important duty, perhaps the least well-known duty of a judge is to halt a case where it is no longer appropriate for it to continue. Although the Crown Court is often thought to be a 'jury court' only about 1 per cent of defendants dealt with through the criminal justice system will actually be placed in the hands of a jury.[56] This may seem surprising but it is indicative of the system: 97 per cent of defendants are dealt with summarily. Of the 3 per cent who will go to Crown Court, a significant number will plead guilty and others will be acquitted without the jury deliberating. Up to two-thirds of those ultimately acquitted in the Crown Court are actually acquitted on the direction of the judge[57] meaning that the jury have no option but to acquit and do not retire to consider their verdict.

Why should a judge intervene? If a defendant pleads not guilty then is it not for the jury to decide guilt or innocence? The answer lies in the fact that a conviction is both a matter of law and fact. In its most understandable guise it is a matter of fact: the jury decide that a person has in fact done the crime that he was accused of. It is also a matter of law, however, in that a person can only be convicted if there is proof beyond all reasonable doubt that he committed the offence. Whilst it will normally be for the jury to decide whether that proof exists, there may be circumstances when a judge concludes that there is insufficient evidence to go before a jury and that it is simply not possible for them to convict. In those circumstances there is no point in asking the jury to deliberate because, as a matter of law, their decision can only be not guilty. Under those circumstances the judge would step in and direct a jury to acquit. The mechanics of this are that the judge will choose a person as the foreperson (usually it is the person in the front row of the jury box sitting closest to the judge) and tell the foreperson that as a matter of law they can only acquit the person. He will then require the foreperson to say that the jury find them 'not guilty'. It could be argued that this last bit is an unnecessary piece of stage management: if the jury cannot convict then the judge should be able to acquit the defendant but the law requires that in the Crown Court a jury must deliver the verdict once a trial has begun so this unnecessary farce is played out.

14.2.2 The jury

Along with the bewigged judge the most recognizable feature of the Crown Court is the presence of the jury. The jury has undoubtedly an important status within the criminal justice system with Lord Devlin, a one-time Lord of Appeal in Ordinary, commenting that it is 'the lamp that shows freedom lives',[58] a statement approved of by a previous Lord Chief Justice, Lord Taylor, who stated: 'in our culture and perception trial by jury is a fundamental right.'[59]

The advantages and disadvantages of the jury were considered in Chapter 13 and readers should return to that chapter to familiarize themselves with the reasons why the jury continues to exist and in what form it exists.

14.2.2.1 Trial by judge alone

Although it may seem that the jury is synonymous with the Crown Court it is possible for a judge to hear a trial alone and without a jury. In this situation the judge is both

56. Andrew Sanders and Richard Young, *Criminal Justice* (4th edn, Butterworths 2010).
57. Andrew Sanders and Richard Young, *Criminal Justice* (4th edn, Butterworths 2010).
58. Patrick Devlin, *Trial by Jury* (Stevens & Sons 1956) 164.
59. Andrew Ashworth and Mike Redmayne, *The Criminal Process* (4th edn, OUP 2010).

the tribunal of fact and law and the position is perhaps somewhat analogous to that of a district judge (magistrates' court) sitting on a summary trial.

In England and Wales such trials are extremely controversial and rare but in other jurisdictions within the United Kingdom it is not that unusual. During the period when Northern Ireland was subject to what is commonly referred to as 'the Troubles' there was a real risk of jury tampering and thus the 'Diplock courts' were born in Northern Ireland. The courts were so named after Lord Diplock, the former Law Lord, who had recommended that trial by jury was suspended for certain terrorist-related trials. In Scotland there has long been a tradition of a Sheriff (the equivalent of a circuit judge) sitting by himself to try a number of offences, including those punishable by imprisonment.

The CJA 2003 allowed for the possibility of trial by judge alone. It should be noted that in this context a trial means the hearing that leads to a decision on the guilt or innocence of the defendant. There are other occasions when a judge may sit alone, most notably when ruling on the admissibility of evidence (which could lead to a *voir dire* (a so-called 'trial within a trial')) or a *Newton* hearing (where the judge decides the factual basis upon which a person should be sentenced: discussed at 14.2.1.2). The power is set out in s 44 CJA 2003 and applies where the judge concludes that there 'is a real and present danger that jury tampering [will] take place' and that despite alternative arrangements being put in place (including the possibility of police protection for jurors) it is in the interests of justice to hold a trial by judge alone. The first approval for a trial to take place by judge alone was given in *R v T*[60] which concerned the trial of a number of defendants for an alleged large-scale robbery that took place at Heathrow Airport. After several previous cases collapsed, the Court of Appeal agreed that there was a real risk of jury tampering and that those risks could not be adequately minimized by the police. The trial began in January 2010 and led to the conviction of four men. The trial was extremely controversial with many lawyers arguing that trial by jury was an inherent human right (but see *R v Twomey*[61] where the one of the four defendants appealed on the basis that it was a breach of human rights but where the court dismissed the appeal).

It had been thought that *T* would lead to a number of judge-alone trials but the Court of Appeal has shown that it is willing to approve such trials only where a trial by jury is unfeasible. In *R v J*[62] the Court of Appeal quashed the decision of a judge to order trial by judge alone where it believed that preventative measures could be taken. The court emphasized that trial by judge alone was a last resort and the strong presumption is that a jury should hear a matter. The court noted that a trial could take place and if jury tampering occurred then the judge could always discharge the jury and hear the remainder of the matter alone[63] although such a course of action is likely to be extremely controversial, not least because counsel will have prepared the case on a very different basis.

14.2.2.2 Empanelling the jury

Jurors are rarely summoned for a single trial but instead form part of a general jury pool that attends court on a specific date. The actual process is that the

60. [2009] EWCA Crim 1035.
61. [2011] EWCA Crim 8.
62. [2010] EWCA Crim 1755.
63. *Criminal Justice Act 2003*, s 46.

court service, on behalf of the court, issues a jury summons, ie a legal summons addressed to an individual requiring them to attend court. Jury service is considered a civil responsibility and thus the expectation is that jurors should attend when summoned. Auld, in his review of the criminal justice system, found that 15 per cent of jurors refused to answer the jury summons[64] and this amounts to a criminal offence if done without a valid excuse. It is most likely to be charged as a summary-only specific offence, punishable by a fine.[65] That said, Auld noted that it was comparatively rare for courts to actually pursue those who ignore a jury summons and this led to the position whereby significant numbers of people failed to meet their civil duty. Arguably the position should now be better since there is a central jury-summoning bureau that is now responsible for all summonses and it also has responsibility for deciding whether an excuse is justifiable, meaning that there is a consistent approach.

A difficulty with enforcing jury service by criminal sanction is, of course, that it could clog up the courts with enforcement proceedings. Auld suggested that non-compliance could be dealt with by a fixed penalty notice[66] although this has two principal difficulties. The first is that it is not clear why a person who has failed to respond to a summons would choose to respond to a fixed penalty notice (although at least that could arguably be enforced by non-judicial means) and second, it creates the position whereby the wealthy could avoid jury service by simply choosing to pay a fixed penalty fee. Since it has been noted that the constitution of juries is somewhat debatable (see 13.2.2) this may not assist in widening the participation of jurors.

Employers

Some jurors may wish to attend jury service but are prevented by their employers, or are reluctant to attend jury service fearing how it may impact their jobs. An employer is legally obliged to release an employee for jury service and a refusal to do so amounts to contempt of court for which the employer could be fined or even imprisoned. An employee has the right not to be subjected to any detrimental treatment as a result of being on a jury[67] and a person who is dismissed for serving as a juror will be considered to have been dismissed unfairly.[68]

An employer does not need to pay an employee who is serving as a juror. This potentially can cause financial hardship (which may be considered a reason for excusal) since whilst a juror is paid expenses, they are subject to fixed limits. Financial loss (which includes loss of earnings, child-minding fees etc) is limited to £64.95 per day for the first ten days of a jury trial so long as at least four hours per day have been spent on jury service (otherwise it is one-half the rate) and then it is raised to £129.91 per day for trials that last over ten days and up to 200 days and then £228.06 per day for trials that last over 201 days. The ordinary payment of £64.95 equates to just over £320 per week, leading to a 'salary' of £16,887. Many employees will receive significantly more than this as salary and it should be remembered that this allowance includes payment for childcare, something that is likely to take up most, if not all, of this allowance. Where an employer does not pay an employee for undertaking jury service this, in

64. Lord Justice Auld, *A Review of the Criminal Courts of England and Wales* (HMSO 2001) 145.
65. *Juries Act 1974*, s 20.
66. Lord Justice Auld, *A Review of the Criminal Courts of England and Wales* (HMSO 2001) 145.
67. *Employment Rights Act 1996*, s 43M.
68. *Employment Rights Act 1996*, s 98B.

effect, means that a person could lose quite significant sums of money for serving on a jury and it is perhaps not surprising therefore that some seek to avoid service.

Vetting

In Chapter 13 it was noted that some jurors are disqualified, either temporarily or permanently, if they have been convicted of a criminal offence (13.2.1.1). It is perhaps not surprising that potential jurors are now routinely matched against the Police National Computer (PNC) to ensure that the members called are not so disqualified.[69] This is uncontroversial and indeed sensible but it may be a surprise to know that certain trials involve a more detailed vetting, including consulting police intelligence and sometimes the Security Service.[70]

This practice has a long history although the first identifiable case of jury vetting took place in relation to a trial under the Official Secrets Act where the prosecution had vetted 'for loyalty' the jury pool but had not removed three potential jurors, two of whom had signed the Act in question and one of whom (who became the foreperson of the jury) was a former member of the Special Air Service (SAS).[71] The result of this disclosure was significant criticism and the Attorney-General agreed to produce guidelines that would limit when any vetting could occur.[72]

The guidelines make clear that vetting should only occur where the trial concerns a matter of public interest or in a terrorist case. The vetting takes place only with the authorization of the Attorney-General[73] and is designed to allow the prosecution to exercise their power of 'stand by' (see 'Challenging a juror'), the cause presumably being something in the juror's background that is a cause for concern.

A particular difficulty with this whole exercise is that although the guidelines are published they are not particularly clear and are open to interpretation in a way that would allow the state to 'rig' a jury if they so wished. It has been noted that the guidelines do not place an obligation on the prosecution to 'stand by' a juror who would be biased against the defendant and yet the defendant would have no real way of knowing that they were.[74] It also goes against the rule that a jury should be drawn randomly and that the specific characteristics of jurors should not ordinarily be taken into account.[75]

Article 6 of the ECHR is commonly said to have an 'equality of arms' dimension to it, that is to say that both parties should be operating at roughly the same strength. Whilst it is never possible to obtain absolute parity (in either direction) the rule is based on the fact that one side should not be able to abuse its own position to the detriment of the opposing party. The system of jury vetting would appear to be a classic example of an inequality-of-arms position since the defence do not have the resources or contacts to be able to vet potential jurors. The complete absence of independence

---

69.　See <http://www.cps.gov.uk/legal/h_to_k/jury_vetting/> which sets out the current policy.

70.　See *Practice Note (Juries: Right to Stand By: Jury Checks)* (1989) 88 Cr App R 123, discussed in Sean Doran, 'Trial by Jury' in Mike McConville and Geoffrey Wilson (eds), *The Handbook of the Criminal Justice Process* (OUP 2002) 389.

71.　Andrew Sanders and Richard Young, *Criminal Justice* (4th edn, Butterworths 2010) 558.

72.　The guidelines are to be found at (1989) 88 Cr App R 123. Before this, the guidelines were not public and were instead dealt with by virtue of a Home Office Circular and communicated to chief constables and certain other officials (see *R v Mason* [1981] QB 881, 885).

73.　It is not possible to delegate this power (other than to the Solicitor-General) and thus one of HM Law Officers must personally authorize the vetting.

74.　Andrew Sanders and Richard Young, *Criminal Justice* (4th edn, Butterworths 2010) 558.

75.　Sean Doran, 'Trial by Jury' in Mike McConville and Geoffrey Wilson (eds), *The Handbook of the Criminal Justice Process* (OUP 2002) 390.

and the inevitable security that accompanies the vetting system also lead to the conclusion that there is no transparency within the process. It is difficult to see how this would not amount to a breach of Article 6 but perhaps its limited scope may save it. The European Court of Human Rights (ECtHR) has stated before that Article 6 is not an absolute right and that issues of national security may mean that some aspects of a fair trial may need to be balanced against important state interests.

For the moment the position of vetting appears settled but this is, in part, because the defence will not always know when jury vetting has taken place. Challenges for cause can be made at any stage and could theoretically be made to the judge without the defence knowing (on the basis that their objection might lead to the jurors never being included in the 'jury in waiting'). This makes the possibility of challenging the regime somewhat difficult.

14.2.2.3 The trial jury

As noted earlier, jurors are summoned into a general pool from which the usher will bring twenty into a court and they become known as the 'jury in waiting'. The potential jurors will normally be told the name of the defendant and asked if they know him. If they do then they will leave the court and return to the jury pool to be used by an alternative court. The names of the individual potential jurors are on cards and handed to the clerk. The clerk of the court then shuffles the cards and calls twelve names out. In *R v Comerford*[76] the Court of Appeal upheld a policy adopted by the judge of assigning numbers to jurors instead of calling their names out. However, in that case there was a real risk of jury intimidation and accordingly it was accepted as an exception to the general rule.

Where a trial is going to be lengthy or complicated the *Consolidated Practice Direction* states that judges should ask the jury whether they have any personal commitments that may affect their service.[77] This is purely discretionary and the judge can decide not to waive the summons. In certain traumatic cases jurors have been excused because it may have been difficult for them to concentrate on the case but this is again highly exceptional because arguably the more traumatic a case is, the more important an independent jury is.

Challenging a juror

In the United States empanelling a jury can take a considerable period of time because both parties have the right to object to a juror. In Northern Ireland the right to peremptorily challenge a juror (ie to object to a juror without having to give any reason) still exists but in England and Wales this right was abolished in 1988.[78] That is not to say that there is no opportunity to challenge a juror but the defence can now only challenge for cause although the prosecution have the additional ground of asking a juror to 'stand by'.

Challenges for cause exist for both parties and the challenge is made by counsel (or the defendant himself if unrepresented) who says 'Challenge' immediately before the juror takes the oath. The party who makes the challenge has the burden of proving, on the balance of probabilities, the unsuitability of the juror. The

---

76. [1998] 1 Cr App R 235.
77. Ministry of Justice, *Consolidated Practice Direction* (Ministry of Justice 2013) IV, 42.2.
78. *Criminal Justice Act 1988*, s 118.

normal reason is bias but there must be proof of the appearance of bias, something that is not easy when, as Doran notes, it is not possible to ask questions of jurors in the way that is common in America.[79] It is relatively uncommon for challenges to be made.

The other possible method of objecting to a jury is when the prosecution use their power of asking a juror to stand by. Theoretically this just means that the person does not automatically become a member of the jury and returns to the jury in waiting. If enough potential jurors were unable to be sworn in then this could mean that the person stood by could be sworn in but this would be highly unlikely and, in fact, it would mean that the person is not used. Indeed it has been stated that:

> The guidelines [of the Attorney-General] restrict the exercise of the right of stand by to two situations; first, where a juror is clearly unsuitable and the defence agrees that the juror should be excluded, for example where it becomes apparent that a juror selected to try a complex case is in fact illiterate; secondly, where jury checks reveal information justifying the exercise of the right to stand by.[80]

The first ground is relatively uncontroversial but the second undoubtedly remains controversial. That said, the concept of jury vetting (see 'Vetting') appears to be something that is here to stay.

The judge also has an inherent power to stand down a juror and the usual reason for this use would be when the judge realizes that the person is not sufficiently literate to serve on the jury[81] or where disability or infirmity may make the person unsuitable to sit as a juror.

Disabled jurors

The previous sentence noted that a judge may ask a person to stand down if they are disabled but what are the rules regarding the use of disabled jurors? Section 9B JA 1974 states that there is a clear presumption in favour of disabled jurors being able to sit but that where a judge is of the opinion that the person could not, as a result of his disability, act 'effectively' as a juror he should be stood down (for a discussion on the eligibility of disabled jurors see 13.2.1.2).

14.2.2.4 Taking the oath

A juror in waiting becomes a juror when he is selected and takes the oath. The *Consolidated Practice Direction* states that the person taking the oath must say:

> I swear [by Almighty God] that I will faithfully try the defendant and give a true verdict according to the evidence.[82]

Where the person does not wish to swear an oath then they may affirm instead, the wording being:

> I do solemnly, sincerely and truly declare and affirm that I will faithfully try the defendant and give a true verdict according to the evidence.

---

79. Sean Doran, 'Trial by Jury' in Mike McConville and Geoffrey Wilson (eds), *The Handbook of the Criminal Justice Process* (OUP 2002) 388.
80. Sean Doran, 'Trial by Jury' in Mike McConville and Geoffrey Wilson (eds), *The Handbook of the Criminal Justice Process* (OUP 2002) 388.
81. John Sprack, *A Practical Approach to Criminal Procedure* (15th edn, OUP 2015) 258, 18.35.
82. Ministry of Justice, *Consolidated Practice Direction* (Ministry of Justice 2013) IV, 42.4.

At this point the person is a juror and he will take his seat in the jury box. When all twelve jurors have been sworn in then the jury is complete.

14.2.2.5 Judicial Direction on behaviour

The *Consolidated Practice Direction* states that a judge must now direct the jury about their behaviour and expectations:

> Judges should take the opportunity, when warning the jury of the importance of not discussing the case with anyone outside the jury, to add a further warning ... The effect of the further warning should be that it is the duty of jurors to bring to the judge's attention, promptly, any behaviour among the jurors or by others affecting the jurors, that causes concern ...[83]

The reason for this is that there have been a number of situations when jurors have acted in a way that could prejudice the trial and/or the rights of the defendant. Indeed, under ss 20E–20G *Juries Act 1974* it is not an offence to disclose information about jury deliberations where jury impropriety is suspected or occurs during the trial. This may include, for example, racist comments being made in the jury room or ignoring the judge's direction not to discuss the case outside of the courtroom or bringing external material into court.

In recent years there have been a number of issues of misbehaviour by the jury. This will be discussed later in the chapter (14.2.2.6 on improper deliberations by a jury) but it is worth noting that the Internet has caused new opportunities for jurors to act improperly and judges must now warn jurors specifically about the use of the Internet.[84] Depending on the misconduct of the juror it may lead to their discharge (14.2.2.6) or it could lead to criminal proceedings being taken against them.

Example Joanne Fraill

One of the more unusual examples of juror misconduct relates to Joanna Fraill. She was a juror who heard a complicated trial involving eight defendants. After deliberating the jury brought in partial verdicts in relation to some defendants, including acquitting one female defendant of all counts.

That evening Fraill sought out the female defendant on Facebook and began to have conversations with her about the trial, including information concerning how the jury were voting. This was capable of amounting to contempt of court (s 8 *Contempt of Court Act 1981*)[85] but was also completely against directions the judge had given about the use of the Internet in a trial.

The judge ultimately discovered the contact because the female defendant, worried that she was in more trouble, informed her solicitor and barrister who, in turn, told the judge.

Fraill was separated from the other jurors and then discharged. However, the judge decided that her conduct was so serious that he had to discharge the whole jury. The Attorney-General sought to commit Fraill for contempt of court and the Divisional Court convicted her, sentencing her to eight months' imprisonment.[86]

---

83. Ministry of Justice, *Consolidated Practice Direction* (Ministry of Justice, 2013) IV, 42.7.
84. See *R v Thompson* [2010] EWCA Crim 1623, [2011] 1 WLR 200, 205 (Lord Judge LCJ).
85. This offence has now been repealed and replaced with offences in the *Juries Act 1974*, ss 20A–20D.
86. *Attorney-General v Fraill* [2011] 2 Cr App R 21.

14.2.2.6 **Discharging a juror**

The final aspect to discuss concerning the empanelment of a jury is that of their discharge. Of course this is unlikely to take place immediately after their empanelment but it is discussed here for convenience. This section will examine the discharge of the entire jury (which if it takes place before the jury retire to consider their verdict would normally be as a result of an irregularity in the trial) or the discharge of an individual juror.

In respect of discharging the entire jury, it is always a matter for the trial judge to decide when this is necessary although he should discuss this with counsel and not infrequently the decision will be made after a submission from (defence) counsel to invite the discharge of the jury. The normal reason for this is if significant inadmissible evidence is given to the jury but it could also be as a result of an external factor and, in the past, cases have arisen where the jury has been discharged because of media comments. Where the latter occurs it has normally resulted in contempt proceedings being instigated.

III\ Case Box *R v McCann*

R v McCann[87] is an interesting example of this. This case concerned a terrorist case and in the middle of the trial the Home Secretary announced the end of the automatic right to silence, something widely reported. Commentators in the media noted that this could have a particular impact on terrorism cases. The Court of Appeal ruled that the jury should have been discharged when it was apparent that the suspects would not be testifying. This is an example of an innocent external factor that still necessitated the discharge of a jury in order to ensure that the defendant received a fair trial.

It is not always necessary to discharge the whole jury but it is sometimes necessary to discharge a single juror. This is permissible under s 16 JA 1974 and the provision states that when this occurs it need not lead to the discharge of the whole jury, although this is something that a judge will have to take into account. The discharge need not arise as a result of misconduct and could, for example, be as a result of personal circumstances (eg illness) but misconduct is certainly a significant factor in discharges.

The key test in all of this is whether the juror is biased. What does bias mean, however? Traditionally it was thought that it meant bias from a subjective point of view, ie was the juror biased, but in *Sanders v United Kingdom*[88] the ECtHR said that bias had to be looked at objectively not just subjectively, that is to say whether a reasonable person would believe that the juror is biased. Arguably this is a wider test and could lead to more jurors being discharged. This test also has a wider implication in that it may lead to the discharge of the entire jury. If there is a risk that the bias of one juror has contaminated the others in the jury then the whole jury should be discharged. Ultimately it is for the judge to decide whether this has happened, although his ruling would almost certainly provide a ground of appeal.

87.   (1991) 92 Cr App R 239.
88.   (2001) 31 EHRR 44.

Where the entire jury is discharged for whatever reason then the defendant is not acquitted and is liable to a retrial. Two possible impediments stand in the way of a retrial. First, the prosecution must choose to bring a retrial. The circumstances that led to the original discharge will be considered, as this could affect the evidential or public-interest test which could mean that the decision to prosecute will change and the prosecution could decide not to progress a retrial. The second possible impediment is the judge. It is possible that the judge may decide that it is not possible to have a fair retrial and he has an inherent power to order that proceedings are stayed. In *R v Taylor*[89] the Court of Appeal adopted this discretion after they quashed the conviction of two teenage sisters accused of murder, in part because of pre-trial publicity. The court stated that the publicity was so prejudicial that a retrial would not be possible.

14.2.3 Lawyers

Unlike in the magistrates' court, matters dealt with in the Crown Court are normally dealt with by professional lawyers. The use of associate prosecutors, permitted in summary matters (see 14.1.3.2), is not permitted in the Crown Court; the prosecution must *always* be represented by a professional lawyer. No such rule applies to the defendant but because of the seriousness of the charges normally heard in the Crown Court it is most common for the defendant to be represented.

The Crown Court is part of the Senior Courts of England and Wales and, accordingly, the rights of audience differ from those in the magistrates' court and county court. Solicitors do not have any automatic right to appear in the Crown Court, but barristers do. The distinction in the rights of audience is discussed elsewhere (Chapter 10) but historically the Bar had the exclusive rights to advocating in the higher courts. The *Courts and Legal Services Act 1990*, as is well known, extended the rights of audience in the higher courts to solicitors on completion of an additional course. Accordingly, solicitor–advocates can appear in the Crown Court although solicitors by themselves cannot.

14.2.3.1 Prosecuting counsel

Counsel for the prosecution has a specific role in these cases. Whilst they do represent the Crown in order to try and achieve a conviction, the overarching position is contained in an often cited statement that prosecutors are 'to regard [themselves] as ministers of justice'.[90] This means that prosecuting counsel is not to consider his duty as having the responsibility of securing a prosecution at all costs but of presenting an impartial view of the prosecution case. This, it has been argued, extends to how counsel should present his argument:

> It is important that a prosecution advocate avoids the use of emotive language or any words which will inflame an already tense situation.[91]

Viewing prosecution counsel in this way can be contrasted with other jurisdictions, most notably America, where prosecutors frequently deal with the victim on a one-to-one basis and can be seen in front of the media holding hands with the victim or,

---

89. (1994) 98 Cr App R 361.
90. See *R v Paddick* (1865).
91. Stephen Solley, 'The Role of the Advocate' in Mike McConville and Geoffrey Wilson (eds), *The Handbook of the Criminal Justice Process* (OUP 2002) 317.

in homicide cases, the victim's family. This is, in part, because, it will be remembered from Chapter 12, that in England and Wales prosecutions are not brought on behalf of the victim but of society as a whole.

An important part of the 'ministers of justice' role is that prosecuting counsel has a particular duty to the court. It has previously been noted that all advocates have a duty not to mislead a court (see 10.9), but prosecuting counsel has a duty actively to assist the court in the application of the law, even when this may mean a ruling prejudicial to the prosecution case. The other implication of this role is to be found in the duties of disclosure, including potentially any adverse issues in respect of the witnesses they are calling (eg any previous convictions of their witnesses etc).

14.2.3.2 **Defence counsel**

Counsel for the defence does not operate any function equivalent to that of the 'ministers of justice' expected of prosecuting counsel. However, it is important to note that they are bound, like all advocates, by the general rules of conduct and, in particular, the duty not to mislead the court. Bearing that in mind, however, defence counsel does have a much wider scope to advocate the matter and this may mean not always bringing legal technicalities harmful to their case to the attention of the court, unless not to do so would mislead the court,[92] but the Court of Appeal has, subsequently, decided that counsel do have a duty to bring obvious errors to the attention of the judge at trial and not reserve them for a decision to terminate the case or even as a ground of appeal after conviction.[93] The scope of the freedom is even more obvious when one looks at errors of law where, as Blake and Ashworth note, there is no duty to bring factual errors to the attention of the court even though the corresponding duty exists for prosecutors.[94]

14.2.4 **Court clerk**

Each court centre has a court clerk but their role is one of administration rather than legal advice since judges are professionally legally qualified. The clerk has no statutory qualification and assists the resident (or senior resident) judge and the senior administrative grade in the smooth operation of the courts.

14.2.5 **Stenographer**

The Crown Court, as a superior court of record, has all its proceedings recorded. Historically this was completed by a stenographer who used to type out the proceedings using a shorthand-enabled typewriter but in more modern times they have been recorded using either tape recorders or solid-state recording equipment. The stenographer need not now appear in court at all times but, rather, is responsible for ensuring that the recording equipment is working. In many Crown Court trials the stenographer is absent except for the beginning and end of each session.

---

92. Meredith Blake and Andrew Ashworth, 'Some Ethical Issues in Prosecuting and Defending Criminal Cases' [1998] *Criminal Law Review* 16, 23–4.
93. *R v Gleeson* [2003] EWCA Crim 3357.
94. Meredith Blake and Andrew Ashworth, 'Some Ethical Issues in Prosecuting and Defending Criminal Cases' [1998] *Criminal Law Review* 16, 24–5.

14.2.6 **Usher**

The usher is a visible symbol of the court and yet has no statutory or formal authority except when a jury retires; however, he is present throughout the trial. The usher assists the clerk in the smooth running of a trial and normally identifies which witnesses are within the court building. The primary purpose of the usher, to assist the jury, will be discussed later (see 15.6.2.2).

14.2.7 **The defendant**

Unlike the position in a summary trial (14.1.4.1) it is not possible to plead guilty by post during a trial on indictment. The defendant is summoned to appear and he must appear in person. If a defendant fails to attend then the judge will almost certainly issue a warrant for his arrest, requiring the police to identify the offender and bring him before the courts.

Unlike the position in the magistrates' court where it will be remembered there is now a statutory presumption that a trial in the absence of the defendant will now occur (14.1.4.3) the same is not true on a trial on indictment. In *R v Jones*[95] the House of Lords held that a judge does have the discretion to try an offender in his absence but that this discretion should be exercised sparingly. That said, their Lordships noted that where a defendant voluntarily absented himself, particularly after the trial had started, then it is quite possible that it would be appropriate to continue the trial. This is an obvious protection and is designed to prevent, for example, a trial being adjourned because a defendant refused to attend court or appear in court.[96] 'Voluntary' has been taken to include situations where a person takes intoxicating substances, rendering them incapable of following or attending the trial.[97]

487

 Summary

This chapter has introduced the people that will be involved in a trial. In particular it has:

- Shown that whilst many of the same people appear in the magistrates' court and Crown Court they may fulfil different functions.

- Identified that there is considerable difference in the role of a judge and magistrate. In the magistrates' court the magistrates are the tribunal of both fact and law whereas a judge in the Crown Court is only the tribunal of law and the tribunal of fact is the jury.

- Noted that it is possible to hold a hearing in the magistrates' court without any lawyer appearing either for the prosecution or defence.

- Shown that jurors are randomly selected from the locality and a wider body of people are now entitled to sit on the jury.

- Demonstrated that jurors must serve and employers must release employees to serve. If they do not then they commit a criminal offence.

95.   [2003] 1 AC 1.
96.   See generally, *R v O'Hare* [2006] EWCA Crim 471.
97.   See, for example, *R v Simms* [2016] EWCA Crim 9 and *R v Ehi-Palmer* [2016] EWCA Crim 1844.

End-of-chapter questions

1. Do you think it is right that in summary trials the magistrates are both the tribunal of law and fact? Is there any danger in trusting magistrates to ignore evidence that they have already heard? Is it possible to put out of mind something that has been heard?

2. Have a look at the provisions in Part 3 of the *Criminal Justice and Courts Act 2015*. Do you think that the introduction of 'trial by single justices on paper' is a good idea? Why or why not?

3. Re-read Chapter 11 on the funding of legal services. Do you think that the recent changes to funding have led to the position whereby criminal justice may be denied to some offenders? If so, why? Can there be any objection to unqualified persons dealing with uncontested charges?

4. Is it right that juries can be vetted by the police and Security Services? Does this not lead to the situation whereby it looks as though the prosecution are 'picking' the jury to hear a particular case? Would it be better to ask jurors questions in the way that they do in the US so that we can identify anyone who has pre-judged the matter or who has particular prejudices (both pro- or anti-prosecution)? Is that feasible?

 # Further reading

Darbyshire P, *Sitting in Judgment: The Working Lives of Judges* (Hart Publishing 2011) ch 9.
   This shows how judges are perceived in their role during a trial.
Grove T, *A Juryman's Tale* (Bloomsbury 2000).
   This is an excellent read on the experiences of the author sitting as a jury. It provides useful information on how people in court are perceived.
Solley S, 'The Role of the Advocate' in Mike McConville and Geoffrey Wilson (eds), *The Handbook of The Criminal Justice Process* (Oxford University Press, 2002) 311–22.
   An interesting chapter that examines what the role of the advocate is during a Crown Court trial.

For multiple-choice questions, updates to this chapter, and links to useful websites, please visit the **Online Resource Centre** at: **www.oxfordtextbooks.co.uk/orc/gillespie_els6e/**

15

The Trials

By the end of this chapter you will be able to:

- Understand how a summary trial and trial on indictment progress.
- Identify the differences between a summary trial and trial on indictment.
- Understand how the prosecution proves its case.
- Identify the order that witnesses provide testimony.
- Understand how a verdict is reached.

Introduction

Chapter 14 has presented the pre-trial procedures for both summary trials (those trials that take place in the magistrates' courts) and trials on indictment (those trials that take place in the Crown Court), including presenting how the decision is taken as to which trial mode will be chosen.

Previous chapters also presented the difference between a judge, jury, and lay magistrates. It will be remembered that magistrates have the power to hear two types of cases; summary-only matters and matters that are triable either-way. Similarly the Crown Court may hear two types of cases; either-way offences and those that are triable only on indictment. In both types of case the matter is heard by a judge and jury.

This chapter will present the course of a trial to you. Both the summary trial and trial on indictment will be presented which will allow you to compare the differences between them. The chapter will detail who is in court, what their role should be, and how they reach their various decisions.

15.1 The prosecution case

The prosecution will always go first. This is because of the presumption of innocence. Probably the most important rule in the criminal justice process within England and Wales is the presumption of innocence, ie a person is innocent until found guilty. This rule means that it is not for a person to prove his innocence, it is for the prosecution to prove his guilt. Accordingly, the prosecution must establish a case to answer, ie they adduce sufficient evidence to show, to the required standard, that the defendant could be guilty. If they establish this then the defence must adduce their evidence to convince the tribunal of fact that he is not guilty.

15.1.1 The opening speech

The prosecution always have the right to make an opening speech and this is true of both summary trials and trials on indictment. In a summary trial the speech will be made to the justices and it will ordinarily be brief because the magistrates are familiar with the type of cases that they deal with. It is likely that the speech will simply refer to the alleged facts and how the prosecution intend to prove the matter. In the Crown Court the position is slightly different. Here, the speech is to the jury—as the tribunal of fact—and not to the judge. The speech is likely to be longer and will ordinarily include a reference to the burden of proof and a summary of the legal issues that will ordinarily be raised.[1] The prosecution will then outline how they intend to prove their case, ie giving a summary of the prosecution case. By convention the prosecution does not talk about contested evidence in the prosecution case (ie evidence that the defence do not agree with) but this is often not possible, for example, in respect of a confession. The position is often easier in modern trials because most of the issues relating to the admissibility of evidence (see 15.1.2) will be dealt with at the plea and case management hearing(s) and so the prosecution should know what evidence they will be allowed to adduce. Where, however, the matter has not yet been decided (because sometimes a judge will adjourn an issue of admissibility until other consequential evidence has been heard) then the prosecution should never mention this to the jury.

15.1.1.1 Defence opening speech

Where the defence intend to call a witness other than the defendant himself then they too have the right to make an opening speech. Sometimes this will take place at the opening of their case (15.3) but in longer or more complicated cases it is not unusual for the judge to ask for the speeches to be heard at the same time.

15.1.2 Calling the evidence

This book does not address the issue of evidence and reference should be made to other texts that cover this topic or to the substantive module *Law of Evidence* that many universities provide as an optional subject. However, it is necessary to understand that there are different types of evidence that can be adduced to help prove a case.

If someone was to ask 'what type of evidence is adduced in a criminal trial?' the first answer would probably be 'witnesses' and certainly this is perhaps the form of evidence that will be used in almost every case. That said, it is recognized that witness testimony is sometimes flawed[2] and that will be discussed if you study evidence. Despite this they remain an important form of evidence and are discussed later.

There is lots of other evidence that can be adduced. 'Real' evidence is often used to describe physical evidence so as to distinguish it from witness testimony. This could include, for example, objects found at a crime scene or photographs of a scene or incident, including CCTV evidence.[3] This can be very important evidence, not least

1. Iain Morley, *The Devil's Advocate* (3rd edn, Sweet & Maxwell 2015) 110.
2. Andrew Choo, *Evidence* (3rd edn, OUP 2012) 360ff.
3. See, for example, *Attorney-General's Reference (No 2 of 2002)* [2002] EWCA Crim 2373 discussed in Andrew Choo, *Evidence* (3rd edn, OUP 2012) 10.

because it is something that the tribunal of fact (be that a jury or magistrates) can touch, look at, and reach their own conclusions on. Sometimes real evidence will be accompanied by witness testimony and this is particularly true where, for example, the real evidence is scientific evidence where the tribunal of fact requires assistance to understand the evidence being put forward.

A branch of real evidence is documentary evidence. In many trials there can be a variety of documents that would help a jury in understanding whether a defendant committed a crime. Documentary evidence has proven to be one of the more controversial types of evidence, with the rules governing its admissibility having changed over the years.[4] At one point documents had to be the 'best available' or the original which sometimes caused difficulties but s 133 *Criminal Justice Act 2003* (CJA 2003) provides that a document can be proved either by adducing the original or a certified copy.

15.1.2.1 Witnesses

Perhaps the type of evidence that people are most familiar with are witnesses. This is where a person provides testimony in court by being asked a series of questions on what they have seen or done. Nearly every case will involve at least one witness although sometimes there may only be one (for example where a person contests a speeding offence it is likely that the only evidence will be the police officer who operated the device that measured the speed) and complex cases may have multiple witnesses of various descriptions.

Again, for our purposes it is not necessary to consider all the evidential rules that relate to witnesses but instead we should focus on key aspects. The evidence of witnesses in England and Wales is taken usually by means of questioning, with each type of question being referred to by a specific name and it alternating between sides. In a prosecution the order of witnesses is given in Table 15.1.

Where there is more than one defendant then each defendant is allowed to cross-examine the witness for the prosecution although there is no obligation to do so and in long trials it is not unusual for minor witnesses to be asked questions on behalf of only one defendant and for the other lawyers to 'adopt' those answers in support of their own case.

The order does not change between trials in the magistrates' court or Crown Court. Where it does differ is in respect of questions from the bench. In the magistrates' court it will be remembered that the magistrates are the tribunal of both fact and law and so they can ask whatever questions they wish. Questions are fed through the chair of the

Table 15.1 Order of witness testimony

Examination-in-chief	Prosecution lawyer asks the questions
Cross-examination	Defence lawyer asks the questions
Re-examination	Prosecution ask questions but only to clarify points already adduced from the witness
Questions from the bench	Judge or magistrates ask questions

4. Andrew Choo, *Evidence* (3rd edn, OUP 2012) 8.

bench, the wingers putting their questions through the chair. It will be remembered from Chapter 13 that district judges (magistrates' court) (DJMCs) will sit by themselves and are also the tribunal of fact and law. There is some evidence to suggest that district judges are more likely to be proactive in a trial and ask questions of witnesses.[5] It is believed that this is because district judges are better able to understand the legal and evidential issues arising from the case and will therefore seek direct answers to questions that relate to those issues.

The position in the Crown Court is more complicated. The judge is the tribunal of law and the jury are the tribunal of fact. A judge can ask questions of the witnesses although he will ordinarily only do this where he thinks it is necessary to assist the jury in clarifying some of the issues. Judges will ordinarily be slow to ask questions because it can be seen as interfering in the role of the lawyers and could lead to an appeal where, for example, there is an appearance of bias.

Theoretically the jury can also ask questions although it is a cumbersome procedure. The juror who wishes to ask a question passes a note to the judge. The judge then reads the note and decides whether the question can be put to the witness. If the answer to that is 'yes' then the judge will put the question direct to the witness. It has been noted that the courts try so far as possible to deter notes being passed[6] and this creates, in the words of one observer, the rather strange position whereby the tribunal of fact takes a 'very passive role in the course of the trial'[7] which, of course, can be contrasted with the position in the magistrates' court where they may take a more active part. Of course it is difficult to see how an alternative arrangement could exist. There are twelve persons on a jury and if each were permitted to ask questions then it could become extremely complicated very quickly.

Witnesses not present

Sometimes a witness will exist but not attend court. There may be any number of reasons why this is the case, including the fact that the defence may not contest the evidence given of a minor witness. In those circumstances it is usual for the witness statement to be read out aloud to either the magistrates or jury and they treat this as though it was (uncontested) evidence from the person himself.

There are other reasons why a witness may not turn up, including fear or unavailability. Rules do exist for whether the statement of the witness can be read in court.[8] It is not necessary to discuss these in depth here but it is worth noting that allowing the evidence of an unavailable witness to be given where it is contested is extremely controversial. Article 6(3)(d) of the ECHR provides that everyone has the right to examine witnesses, ie that they should be able to test the truthfulness of the witness or put alternative questions to that witness. Where the witness is not present then this is not possible and so it could be said that a breach of Article 6 may be found. In practice the right to examine witnesses is not absolute, in part because of the fact that there may be legitimate reasons why a witness is not available to testify. Again, it is not necessary to summarize these rules here as they are best left to a study on the law of evidence.

5. Rod Morgan and Neil Russell, *The Judiciary in the Magistrates' Courts* (Home Office 2000) 46.
6. Sean Doran, 'Trial by Jury' in Mike McConville and Geoffrey Wilson (eds), *The Handbook of The Criminal Justice Process* (OUP 2002) 395.
7. Sean Doran, 'Trial by Jury' in Mike McConville and Geoffrey Wilson (eds), *The Handbook of The Criminal Justice Process* (OUP 2002) 394.
8. See, for example, *Criminal Justice Act 2003*, s 116.

The unrepresented defendant

There is no obligation for a defendant to be represented although in contested matters funding will ordinarily be available for a lawyer, particularly in the Crown Court (Chapter 11 discusses the funding of legal services).

In summary trials the clerk to the court (or the justices' legal adviser) will ordinarily assist the defendant by asking questions of witnesses where it is helpful to do so although the defendant may demand the right to ask questions himself. In trials on indictment the judge does not act as a surrogate lawyer for the defendant although he does have an obligation to ensure a fair trial and this will sometimes require him to ask certain questions of witnesses so that the jury are aware of the theory of the defence but he must not put forward the case for the defence, that is a matter for the defendant.

Where matters become complicated is where the defendant wishes to personally examine vulnerable witnesses. Historically, sexual offence cases and those committed against children were considered to be the same as any other case, and therefore a defendant could personally cross-examine the complainant regardless of what effect this could have on the victim.

Example Ralston Edwards

Ralston Edwards had been charged with the rape of Julia Mason (Julia bravely waived her right to anonymity to highlight her case) and he represented himself. His defence was not clear but he made her describe the attack and his genitalia in detail. He also went through her entire sexual history, ie asking questions about every sexual partner she had ever had. The cross-examination lasted for six days and Ms Mason said it felt as if she had been raped again. The judge felt unable to end the ordeal although this is perhaps highly questionable since controlling cross-examination and the protection of witnesses is undoubtedly a role of the judge.[9]

The criticism of Ms Mason's treatment was immense and the government eventually acted by restricting the right of a defendant in person to conduct cross-examination of a victim when charged with a sexual offence.[10] Where a person is restrained from personally cross-examining a witness, how will the defendant's case be put to him? There had been a ban on the cross-examination of child witnesses that pre-dated the 1999 Act and under those circumstances the judge would cross-examine the child[11] but this was unsatisfactory, not least because it is the classic example of a judge assuming the 'robes of an advocate', to borrow Lord Denning's phrase (see 14.2.1.2). The 1999 Act created a more acceptable system when it decided that the court, when denying the opportunity to a defendant to cross-examine, could appoint counsel to conduct the cross-examination even if the defendant did not request one.[12]

9. Philip Otton, 'The Role of the Judge in Criminal Cases' in Mike McConville and Geoffrey Wilson (eds), *The Handbook of The Criminal Justice Process* (OUP, 2002) 327.
10. *Youth Justice and Criminal Evidence Act 1999*, s 34.
11. Jenny McEwan, 'Special Measures for Witnesses and Victims' in Mike McConville and Geoffrey Wilson (eds), *The Handbook of The Criminal Justice Process* (OUP 2002) 247.
12. *Youth Justice and Criminal Evidence Act 1999*, s 38.

This provision is undoubtedly controversial for a number of reasons. First, it can be argued that it could place the defendant at a disadvantage since, in effect, any counsel will be appointed late in the day and the person appointed will not necessarily be counsel for the defence, meaning that issues arise as to cooperation and indeed privilege.[13] Second, it could be argued it is contrary to Article 6 of the ECHR. Article 6(3)(c) states that everyone has the right to:

> defend himself in person or through legal assistance of his own choosing or, if he has not sufficient means to pay for legal assistance, to be given it free when the interests of justice so require.

It could be argued that preventing personal cross-examination is not allowing the defendant to defend himself in person but the syntax of Article 6(3)(c) does not appear to require that absolutely and does provide for the right of assistance. Admittedly it does appear to suggest that ordinarily the defendant should be able to choose his own counsel but this is then qualified by the final sentence which implies that it may be possible to provide alternative counsel. Similarly, any challenge under Article 6(3)(d), which provides the right to examine or have witnesses examined, would fail since the court-appointed lawyer can examine witnesses. It should also be noted that the ECtHR has on occasions said that Article 6 is not an absolute right and it needs to be placed into context. In this situation, other Convention rights are in play because the victim almost certainly has rights under either Article 3 (prohibition of, inter alia, degrading treatment) and Article 8 (right to respect for private life).

15.2 No case to answer

It will be remembered from the beginning of the previous section that the burden of proof is on the prosecution to prove their case. At the conclusion of the prosecution case the defence may seek to argue that the prosecution have not discharged that burden, ie they have not proven to the required standard that the evidence shows the defendant is guilty. This is known as a submission of no case to answer although it is colloquially known as a 'half-time submission'.

Whilst the test is the same for both summary trials and trials on indictment the process of making the submission differs. As the tribunal of fact and law are the same in the magistrates' court then the submission is made to either the lay justices or the DJMC, whereas in the Crown Court it is made only to the judge and the jury are not present when the judge makes the decision. The principal reason the jury are not present is so that they are not prejudiced by hearing the judge rule that a defendant is prima facie guilty and so they may feel less persuaded to acquit the defendant after hearing his evidence. That said, it does raise an interesting issue in respect of summary trials where, of course, the magistrates or district judge will continue to hear all the evidence and must somehow put out of their mind the legal ruling they have made that the defendant has a case to answer.

The principle behind the submission was set out by the Court of Appeal in *R v Galbraith*.[14] The essence of the test is:

---

13. Jenny McEwan, 'Special Measures for Witnesses and Victims' in Mike McConville and Geoffrey Wilson (eds), *The Handbook of The Criminal Justice Process* (OUP 2002) 248.
14. (1981) 73 Cr App R 124.

[I]f the judge comes to the conclusion that the prosecution evidence, if taken at its highest, is such that a jury properly directed could not properly convict upon it, it is his duty ... to stop the case.[15]

The test is the same in a summary trial save that it is formulated that the justices must consider whether any reasonable tribunal could convict the defendant on the evidence heard.[16] The difference in the tribunal of fact between summary trials and trials on indictment does raise an issue in terms of what can be taken into account when deciding the submission. The judge in the Crown Court should not usurp the role of the jury and the Court of Appeal in *Galbraith* continued by noting that where the decision involves making an assessment of the reliability or credibility of the witness then the case should ordinarily continue, as the judge should not try to become the arbitrator of facts. That said, where a witness has obviously no credibility then this must be something the judge will take into account. In summary trials, however, the magistrates or district judge are also the tribunal of fact and therefore they can take into account their findings on the credibility or reliability of a witness as it is their job to make these findings. This potentially means that the same trial could lead to two different decisions depending on where the submission was made.

Where the trial takes place in the Crown Court then it is important to note that this is not an 'all or nothing' submission. Whilst a judge may reject an initial submission of no case to answer he must continually have the test in his mind and if, following evidence from the defence, he concludes that the *Galbraith* test is satisfied then he must stop the case.

At both summary trials and trials on indictment it is perfectly possible for a judge or the magistrates to decide that a submission succeeds in part. In other words they may conclude that the evidence adduced does not show a case to be answered by the defendant in respect of some charges. In those situations the correct decision is to direct an acquittal in respect of those charges where the defendant has no case to answer but to allow the trials to proceed in respect of the others.

The latest figures available show that in 683 cases in 2015–16 a judge directed the acquittal of the defendant which, in essence, must encapsulate this submission.[17] The CPS states that this amounts to only 0.7 per cent of all cases heard in the Crown Court.[18] It would seem therefore that whilst the submission is an important part of the trial process, it leads to very few cases being stopped.

15.3 Defence case

If a submission of no case to answer is not made, or if it is rejected, then the trial proceeds on to the case for the defence. In the Crown Court it will be remembered that so long as a witness other than the defendant himself will be called to give evidence then the defence are entitled to make an opening speech. Traditionally this will take place at the opening of the defence case but increasingly it is taking place immediately after the prosecution opening speech.

The order of testimony for defence witnesses is the same as for prosecution witnesses but obviously the nature of the questioning changes, as presented in Table 15.2.

---

15. *R v Galbraith* (1981) 73 Cr App R 124, 127.
16. *Practice Note* [1962] 1 All ER 448.
17. Crown Prosecution Service, *Annual Report and Accounts 2015–16* (CPS 2016) 61.
18. Crown Prosecution Service, *Annual Report and Accounts 2015–16* (CPS 2016) 61.

Table 15.2 Order of witness testimony

Examination-in-chief	Defence lawyer asks the questions
Cross-examination	Prosecution lawyer asks the questions
Re-examination	Defence ask questions but only to clarify points already adduced from the witness
Questions from the bench	Judge or magistrates ask questions

Where there is more than one defendant then each defendant can ask questions to the witness in cross-examination. Note that their questions are classed as cross-examination rather than examination-in-chief because the witness was not called on their behalf.

15.3.1 Defendant testifying

The defendant himself is competent to give evidence (ie he may be legally heard) but he is not compellable (ie he cannot be forced to testify). While this continues to be true, if a defendant does not give evidence in court, the justices or jury can draw an adverse inference against the defendant.[19] In both summary trials and trials on indictment the lawyer for the defence will ordinarily be asked whether he has warned the defendant about the consequences of not testifying, this question taking place in open court.[20] Precisely what constitutes an adverse inference is a matter of some debate[21] but it is clear that an inference by itself cannot be the sole or main reason for a conviction.[22]

If the defendant does intend to testify then ordinarily he should give evidence first although the judge (trial on indictment) or justices (summary trial) do have discretion to allow other witnesses to be heard first;[23] however, it is likely that this discretion would be exercised only in exceptional circumstances. The reason for the defendant going first is that, unlike all the other witnesses, he will be present in court throughout the whole trial. By going first there is no danger that he tries to 'adapt' his answers so as to be compatible with the comments of other witnesses, potentially making the answers seem more credible.

15.4 Closing speeches

After the evidence is complete there is an opportunity for closing speeches.

15.4.1 Summary trials

The defence always have the right to make a closing speech and they will ordinarily take the opportunity to highlight evidence that they believe supports their case theory. Where the trial is heard by a district judge the speech is likely to be shorter because it

---

19. *Criminal Justice and Public Order Act 1994*, s 35.
20. See *R v Cowan* [1996] QB 373.
21. Andrew Choo, *Evidence* (3rd edn, OUP 2012) 127–42.
22. *Criminal Justice and Public Order Act 1994*, s 35(3) and see *Murray v United Kingdom* (1996) 22 EHRR 29.
23. *Police and Criminal Evidence Act 1984*, s 79.

is unlikely that the district judge would welcome being told the law or the implications of various factual findings. Where the case is heard by lay justices then it is likely the speech will be longer and it could involve inviting the justices to consider certain legal proceedings and also inviting them to make findings in respect of the credibility of witnesses etc.

Traditionally the prosecution did not have the right to give a closing speech although the latest version of the *Criminal Procedure Rules* now make clear that the prosecution can give a statement in two instances: where the defendant is represented by a lawyer and irrespective of whether the defendant is represented, if he introduced witnesses other than himself.[24] It is not immediately clear why the fact that a lawyer represents the defendant should be a ground for the prosecution making a closing speech, it would seem more sensible to limit it to situations where more than one defence witness gave evidence. At least in that situation there is an argument for the prosecution reminding the justices, as the tribunal of fact, of their evidence whereas where only the defendant testifies it is likely that this evidence will remain.

15.4.2 Trials on indictment

The general rule is that both the prosecution and defence have the right to make a closing speech. Of course just because a person has the right to make a speech does not mean that they always will and in some simple trials it is possible that at least one counsel may decide not to give a closing speech.

Assuming that both sides do intend to make a closing speech then the prosecution goes first. The principle of counsel for the prosecution acting as a 'minister of justice' still applies and accordingly counsel should give a fair speech. It is likely that the prosecution will remind the jury of the standard and burden of proof and then highlight key issues that the jury have heard. The defence go last and they will ordinarily remind the jury of issues that they believe help support their case.

An important restriction on closing speeches is that counsel can only comment on evidence that has been seen or heard and this includes questions put to witnesses. Therefore if counsel did not put a point to a witness then they are not able to adduce it during the closing speech; they must only remind the jury of what they have seen or heard. This can be problematic where counsel forgot to put a point to a witness during cross-examination but it is an important rule: counsel are not supposed to speculate about what a witness may have said and must restrict themselves to what they did say.

Even if the defendant is not legally represented he is entitled to make a closing speech to the jury.

15.5 Judicial summing up

In other jurisdictions the closing speech of counsel for the defence is the last word in a trial but in trials on indictment in England and Wales the judge speaks last, his speech being known as the 'summing up'. There are two primary functions of the summing up; first to direct the jury as to the law; and second to remind the jury of the facts and evidence of the case.

24. *Criminal Procedure Rules* (as amended April 2016), r 24.3(3)(h).

Guidance on summing up and directing juries is provided in the new *Crown Court Compendium*,[25] which has replaced all previous guidance issued by the Judicial College. The Compendium, issued in 2016, provides checklists of points that may need to be covered by judges when summing up particular cases, as well as example directions. The aim is to 'provide a useful starting point for framing legal and evidential directions', but it is explicitly noted that judges must tailor the guidance given in relation to each particular case.[26]

Some question why a judge should sum up, given that, in essence, the summing up not infrequently leads to a ground of appeal.[27] However, others believe that reminding the jury of the evidence they have heard and possible links between the issues is helpful. They do not, however, explain why it is that Scotland, for example, manages to do well without a full summing up (the judge merely provides legal directions to a jury) and so does America where, in effect, they do not allow the judge to sum up.[28]

Another problem with the English summing up is that it is often far too long and it has been suggested that it could either be summarized or even handed to the jury in written form.[29] While this has not yet been accepted in practice, the Court of Appeal in *R v Sanghera*[30] stated that a short summing up was possible and that it was not necessary to go through each evidential point but merely to provide a summary of the points for and against the defence although it is imperative that important points favourable to the defence are included.

15.6 Reaching the verdict

The final stage of the trial (ie the proceedings that lead to a determination of whether a person is guilty or innocent) is the verdict. The procedure for reaching the verdict differs between summary trials and trials on indictment.

15.6.1 Summary trials

Where lay justices preside it is likely that they will retire, ie leave the courtroom, to consider their verdict. It is not unusual for a district judge to give judgment straight away.

15.6.1.1 Legal adviser retiring with the justices

The position of the clerk/legal adviser was discussed at the beginning of this chapter ('The unrepresented defendant') and it was noted that his principal responsibility is to advise the lay justices on legal issues arising from the case. In the past it was not uncommon for a clerk to retire with the justices to their deliberation room and, in essence, advise them in secret. Recently this practice has altered because there is the belief that it looks wrong even if the advice itself is appropriate.

25. Judicial College, *The Crown Court Compendium. Part I: Jury and Trial Management and Summing Up* (Judicial College 2016) <https://www.judiciary.gov.uk/wp-content/uploads/2016/05/crown-court-compendium-part-i-jury-and-trial-management-and-summing-up.pdf>.
26. Judicial College, *The Crown Court Compendium. Part I: Jury and Trial Management and Summing Up* (Judicial College 2016) <https://www.judiciary.gov.uk/wp-content/uploads/2016/05/crown-court-compendium-part-i-jury-and-trial-management-and-summing-up.pdf> 1–4.
27. Philip Otton, 'The Role of the Judge in Criminal Cases' in Mike McConville and Geoffrey Wilson (eds), *The Handbook of The Criminal Justice Process* (OUP 2002) 328.
28. Andrew Sanders, Richard Young, and Mandy Burton, *Criminal Justice* (4th edn, OUP 2010).
29. Lord Justice Auld, *A Review of the Criminal Courts of England and Wales* (HMSO 2001) 534–5.
30. [2005] EWCA Crim 1248.

The *Criminal Practice Directions* make it clear that advice should ordinarily be given in open court[31] and in *R v Birmingham Magistrates' Court, ex p Ahmed*[32] the Divisional Court heavily criticized the practice of one chairman who would always invite the clerk into the retiring room so that he knew the verdict before it was returned in open court. This practice could inevitably raise concerns that if the clerk disagreed with the justices he might try to persuade them to reconsider the matter. In *R v Eccles Justices, ex p Fitzpatrick*[33] the Divisional Court was clear that the clerk should not retire with the justices unless clearly asked to do so. However, despite these cases some clerks have continued to retire with the justices, and as has been noted the *Criminal Practice Directions* merely states that advice *should* ordinarily be given in open court and expressly states that justices can request a legal adviser to join them in the retiring room.[34] That said, a crucial difference now is that where legal advice is given in the retiring room it should be considered provisional and it must be repeated in open court, providing an opportunity to the legal representatives for the prosecution and defence to comment on the advice.[35]

Given this, and because it is submitted that Article 6 of the *European Convention on Human Rights* requires any advice to be given in open court, it must be questioned whether there is any purpose in allowing a clerk or legal adviser to enter the retiring room. If the justices wish for legal advice there is no reason why they cannot return to open court in the way that a jury asking the judge a question of law does so. In this way any advice will be transparent.

QUESTION FOR REFLECTION

Is there any real difficulty in the justices retiring with the clerk? Clerks and justices are required to take oaths of office and have clearly defined roles and responsibilities. Is it not a little simplistic to suggest that a clerk will, when retiring with justices, decide to go beyond his powers and influence the decision? Or is there a real danger of bias when a clerk retires? Read *R v Eccles Justices, ex p Fitzpatrick*[36] and see what the Divisional Court thought.

15.6.1.2 Pronouncement

The verdict of the court will always be given in open court. The justices are allowed to decide by majority but in open court there will never be an indication as to how justices voted—the decision is a collective one and ordinarily a magistrate should not state that he disagreed with the others. Only the chairman will speak and he will state the verdict in respect of all the charges. Where there were alternative charges a verdict on the lesser charge will not be returned if the more serious charge was proven.

In the magistrates' court the usual way of pronouncing guilt or innocence is to say whether the case has been 'proved' (ie guilty) or 'not proved' (ie not guilty). The justices must follow the same rules as a jury in the Crown Court, ie if there is any doubt as to the guilt of an offender they must acquit.

---

31. *Criminal Practice Directions* (as amended April 2016), CPD VI Trial 25A.15.
32. [1994] COD 461.
33. (1989) 89 Cr App R 324.
34. *Criminal Practice Directions* (as amended April 2016), CPD VI Trial 25A.15.
35. *Criminal Practice Directions* (as amended April 2016), CPD VI Trial 25A.15.
36. (1989) 89 Cr App R 324.

If the defendant is acquitted then he is free to go. If he is convicted then the court will proceed to the sentencing stage.

15.6.2 Trials on indictment

In the Crown Court the verdict on guilt or innocence is in the hands of the jury and there are a number of procedural steps that arise in how this verdict is ascertained and reported to the court.

15.6.2.1 Immediate steps

The first step is that the judge directs the jury that they should elect a foreperson of the jury. The person who is elected becomes, in effect, the chair of the jury and will help structure their deliberations. The foreperson is the only member of the jury who will speak in court.

The second step is that the jury are told to ignore anything that they have heard about majority verdicts. A judge much explain that at least initially a unanimous verdict must be reached, this being to comply with the requirements of s 17 *Juries Act 1974*. The judge will explain when a majority verdict is appropriate (see 'Majority verdict').

15.6.2.2 Jury bailiff

The jury is placed in the charge of a jury bailiff who is an usher and who swears an oath to keep the jury in their charge, not to discuss the case with them, or to allow anyone to talk to the jury. The oath is not mere words and the bailiff is the only person who can speak to the jury outside of the courtroom while they are considering their verdict. This means that he should be in a position to stop anyone speaking to the jury, ie he should stay outside and guard the jury room.

The bailiff is, in essence, the conduit between the jury and the judge and if questions arise (see 15.6.2.3) it is the bailiff who alerts the judge and carries the question from the jury to the judge. In *R v Anderson and Mason*[37] the Court of Appeal stated that the jury bailiff must pass on all communications to the judge and not screen them, a point that has been restated by the Court of Appeal.[38] Interestingly in *Finlayson* the court held that if a single juror asked to write a note to the judge then the jury bailiff could direct that should not happen (as notes should come from the jury as a whole) but it implied, albeit *in obiter*, that if the note was actually passed to the bailiff then it would need to be passed on.

Whilst the bailiff is not entitled to be inside the room, he does have responsibility for ensuring that the deliberations occur at the correct time. In *R v Hastings*[39] a juror was always late to court after retirement. The Court of Appeal stated that the bailiff should have reminded the jury not to deliberate until all twelve members were present although they also noted that the ultimate responsibility for this lay with the judge.

15.6.2.3 Questions

The jury are not cut off from all contact and they have the right to ask questions if they wish clarification of either the law or evidence, or if they want to be reminded of

---

37. 1990, unreported.
38. See *R v Finlayson* [2012] EWCA Crim 1139.
39. [2003] EWCA Crim 3730.

evidence. The jury (normally the foreperson) will write the question and hand it to the bailiff. The bailiff will then pass the note to the judge who will normally convene the court and ask both counsel for their opinion on how to answer the question although the decision on how to answer is ultimately one for the judge. The jury will then be brought into court and the answer given to them. No discourse is entered into and if this does not answer their question then the process is repeated.

15.6.2.4 Improper considerations

A problem that has become increasingly prominent in recent years is what to do where there is the suspicion that the jury have considered something improperly. It should be understood that the jury does not necessarily hear all the evidence in a case. The judge may rule that some facts are not admissible and cannot be put before the jury. Perhaps one of the most common facts withheld is whether the defendant has previous convictions. In these modern times it is increasingly easy to find out information that has not been presented to the jury.

A difficulty where there are allegations of improper deliberations is the secrecy of jury deliberations. This area was previously governed by the *Contempt of Court Act 1981*, but new offences were introduced in 2015. Section 74 *Criminal Justice and Courts Act 2015* amended the *Juries Act 1974* to create the offence of disclosing jury deliberations, thus making it a criminal offence to solicit, obtain, or disclose information about the deliberations of the jury.[40] This will be considered in more detail in Chapter 16. The general rule is that a court can inquire about potential improper deliberations before the verdict has been reached,[41] although it is conceded that it will be comparatively rare for the court to discover this before the verdicts are returned and the majority of reported situations have been considered on appeal.

It is also an offence for jurors to research the case or information relevant to the case during the trial period[42] and for jurors to share research with other members of the jury.[43] The consequences of failing to follow the judicial direction on behaviour and to introduce improper material can be serious. In *Attorney-General v Dallas*[44] the Attorney-General sought to commit the defendant, a juror, for contempt of court[45] as she had introduced inappropriate material into the jury deliberations. The defendant had been empanelled as a member of a jury who were called upon to try a person for grievous bodily harm with intent contrary to s 18 *Offences Against the Person Act 1861*. During the trial the defendant looked at the Internet, ostensibly because she did not understand the meaning of the word 'grievous' and then to conduct research on dangerous crime in Luton.[46] After the jury were sent out one of the jurors approached the jury usher and complained that the defendant had sought to tell them about the information she found on the Internet.[47] The defendant was kept separate and the foreperson of the jury was asked about the incident in open court and confirmed it.

501

40. *Juries Act 1974*, s 20D.
41. See *R v Mirza* [2004] 1 AC 1118 and *Juries Act 1974*, s 20E. This remains the case even after the introduction of the 2015 reforms.
42. *Juries Act 1974*, s 20A.
43. *Juries Act 1974*, s 20B.
44. [2012] 1 WLR 991.
45. This was an offence under the *Contempt of Court Act 1981* before the Act was repealed by the *Criminal Justice and Courts Act 2015* and new offences introduced under the *Juries Act 1974*, s 20.
46. *Attorney-General v Dallas* [2012] 1 WLR 991, 996.
47. *Attorney-General v Dallas* [2012] 1 WLR 991, 997.

The jury were then discharged. The Divisional Court found that contempt of court was proven and the Lord Chief Justice, presiding, stated: 'misuse of the Internet by a juror is always a most serious irregularity and an effective custodial sentence is virtually inevitable. The objective of such a sentence is to ensure that the integrity of the process of trial by jury is sustained.'[48] The court sentenced the defendant to six months' imprisonment.[49]

⟳ QUESTION FOR REFLECTION

Is it realistic to expect members of the jury not to use the Internet and related resources to consider issues relating to the case? Given that witnesses give their name out in court, is there a danger that the jury could try to look up the witnesses and defendant on the Internet or social networking sites (eg Facebook)? Can this be avoided? Do you agree with the Lord Chief Justice that looking at the Internet undermines the 'integrity of the process of trial by jury'?

The Internet has led the courts to reconsider the warnings they issue to the jury. There is now a specific jury direction that must be given to the jury about attempting to conduct research on the Internet.[50] This has been reinforced by the fact that courts will now include notices specifically informing jurors that they are not to conduct their own research in the jury rooms, including the deliberation room.[51]

Continuing issues of juror misconduct has meant that judges now have the power to order that electronic communication devices are surrendered at court[52] as well as being able to order court staff to search jurors in order to find electronic devices.[53] These powers were introduced under the *Criminal Justice and Courts Act 2015*, following recommendations made by the Law Commission on dealing with juror misconduct.[54]

It can be seen therefore that improper deliberations by a jury are considered serious by the criminal justice system and it will be interesting to see whether the offences and procedures outlined above mean that fewer jurors try to break the rules.

15.6.2.5 Deliberating for more than a day

Until 1994 a jury, once sent out to begin its deliberation, had to be kept together until they reached their verdict. In cases where the jury could not arrive at a decision on the first day they would be sequestered and taken to a hotel overnight. Section 43 *Criminal Justice and Public Order Act 1994* (CJPOA 1994) abolished the automatic application of this rule although it is important to note that a judge still has the discretion to order a jury to stay in a hotel overnight. Where the jury are permitted to disperse and go home for the night, the judge must warn them not to talk to anyone about the case.

One point to note about this direction is the swearing of the jury bailiff. The bailiff must be sworn each day because in order to permit the jury to be dispersed then the

---

48. *Attorney-General v Dallas* [2012] 1 WLR 991, 1001.
49. Dallas complained to the European Court of Human Rights, alleging that her rights under Article 7 had been breached in relation to her conviction for contempt of court. Her complaint was dismissed by the Court (*Dallas v United Kingdom* (2016) 63 EHRR 13).
50. Discussed in *R v Thompson* [2011] 1 WLR 200, 205.
51. *Attorney-General v Dallas* [2012] 1 WLR 991, 995.
52. *Juries Act 1974*, s 15A.
53. *Courts Act 2003*, s 54A.
54. Law Commission, *Law Commission Report No 340: Contempt of Court (1): Juror Misconduct and Internet Publications* (HMSO 2013).

usher must be released from his oath, and accordingly each new day involves the usher being sworn in as jury bailiff in open court.

 QUESTION FOR REFLECTION

Reconsider the earlier issue about the use of the Internet. If juries are now allowed to go home does this make it more or less likely that they could access the Internet for issues relating to the case? Also, is there a danger that the jury could talk about the case on, for example, Facebook or instant-messenger services?

15.6.2.6 Returning the verdict

The verdict will ultimately be for the jury to decide. Whilst it has been noted that a judge has the right to order the acquittal of a person the converse is not true and it is never permissible for a judge to direct a jury to convict.[55]

Unanimous verdict

Ideally the jury will return with a unanimous verdict. If they do then the clerk of the court asks the foreperson to stand and asks them whether they have reached a verdict upon which they all agree. Assuming that the answer is 'yes' then the clerk reads each count aloud and asks whether the jury finds the defendant guilty or not guilty. The verdict is then recorded.

Majority verdict

It was noted earlier that when a jury is first asked to retire to consider their verdict they are told that only a unanimous verdict will be permitted. However, it is also known that this is not always true and s 17 JA 1974 permits a majority verdict to be reached. Majority verdicts are controversial because some argue that it contradicts the burden of proof—if some of the jury cannot agree the guilt of the defendant then surely there must be some doubt and yet the standard of proof is 'beyond all reasonable doubt'.[56] The counter-argument, however, is that it is an insurance policy against intransigent jurors or 'nobbling' a jury by bribing a single juror.[57]

It is for the judge to decide when a majority verdict should be permitted but s 17 states that the minimum period of deliberation is two hours since they originally retired. The *Criminal Practice Directions* repeats previous practice directions, which add ten minutes to this time to ensure there is no doubt as to compliance with the statute.[58] The argument is that the deliberation does not start until they reach the jury room and not as soon as they leave the court; the extra ten minutes is supposed to account for the time it will take to walk to and from the courtroom etc. However, it is important to note that this is merely a *minimum* time and in complicated cases this period of time may not be sufficient and in very serious cases judges have been known to continue with the requirement of a unanimous verdict for two or three days. Indeed

---

55. *R v Wang* [2005] UKHL 9.
56. Sean Doran, 'Trial by Jury' in Mike McConville and Geoffrey Wilson (eds), *The Handbook of The Criminal Justice Process* (OUP 2002) 396.
57. Sean Doran, 'Trial by Jury' in Mike McConville and Geoffrey Wilson (eds), *The Handbook of The Criminal Justice Process* (OUP 2002) 396.
58. *Criminal Practice Directions* (as amended April 2016) CPD VI Trial 26Q.2.

nothing in the statute requires a judge to permit majority verdicts and the judge could, theoretically, decide that a case was not suited to one.

Section 17 states that the permissible majority depends on the size of the jury (bearing in mind that jurors can be discharged). The rules are set out in Table 13.3.

Receiving a majority verdict is quite complicated and it is set out in the *Criminal Practice Directions*.[59] The process can be summarized as follows. If the jury return before two hours and 10 minutes have elapsed:

- the foreperson stands
- the clerk of the court asks, 'Have you reached a verdict upon which you are all agreed? Please answer "Yes" or "No"'
- if the answer is 'No' then the judge sends them out again (or considers discharging them) for them to consider a majority verdict if they cannot arrive at a unanimous one.

When the jury finally return:

- the foreperson stands
- the clerk of the court asks, 'Have at least ten (or nine if appropriate) of you agreed on a verdict?'
- if the answer is 'Yes' then the clerk says: 'What is your verdict?' Where there is more than one count on the indictment this process is repeated for each count
- if the foreperson says 'Not guilty' then the verdict is so recorded
- if the foreperson says 'Guilty' then the clerk asks: 'Is that a verdict of you all or by a majority?'
- the foreperson will (presumably) reply 'Majority'
- the clerk then asks: 'How many of you agreed to the verdict and how many dissented?'
- the foreperson provides the numbers but not the names.

This convoluted process is designed to ensure that if an acquittal is reached nobody knows whether it was a majority verdict or not,[60] whereas if it is a guilty verdict a check is built in to ensure that it is a valid majority verdict (and not, for example 7–5). The importance of this was reiterated by the Court of Appeal in *R v Turner*[61] where the clerk to the court asked the judge whether the acquittal was by majority, something the Court of Appeal said should not have happened.

Table 15.3 Permissible majority

Twelve jurors	11–1; 10–2
Eleven jurors	10–1
Ten jurors	9–1
Nine jurors	Must be unanimous

59. *Criminal Practice Directions* (as amended April 2016) CPD VI Trial 26Q: Majority Verdicts.
60. *Criminal Practice Directions* (as amended April 2016) CPD VI Trial 26Q.6.
61. [2011] EWCA Crim 604.

QUESTION FOR REFLECTION

Not every jurisdiction permits a majority verdict, perhaps the most obvious example being America. Is it right to allow for a majority verdict? The argument against such a verdict is that the prosecution must prove guilt beyond all reasonable doubt. If one or two jurors do not believe that he is guilty how can it be said that there is no reasonable doubt since at least two members of the jury obviously doubted the evidence?

Are there any consequences to only allowing a unanimous verdict?

15.6.2.7 Failure to reach a verdict

It is quite possible that a jury will not be able to reach a verdict no matter how long they are given. The judge should give them as much time as possible to reach a decision but eventually there may come a time when the judge needs to ask whether, even if more time was given to the jury, they would be capable of reaching a verdict. At this time the judge will give what is known as a *Watson direction*[62] which states that part of the jury oath is that if they are not able to reach a verdict they should say so. If the foreperson of the jury states that the jury is deadlocked then the jury can be discharged and a retrial is considered.

15.6.2.8 Perverse verdicts

It has been noted that each juror must swear 'to faithfully try the defendant and give a true verdict according to the evidence' (see 14.2.2.4). In the review of the criminal justice system, Auld LJ believed this did not always happen and that jurors would return what he categorized as 'perverse verdicts'.[63]

Auld admits that:

> ... there are many, in particular the Bar, who fervently support what they regard as the right of the jury to ignore their duty to return a verdict according to the evidence and to acquit when they disapprove of the law or the prosecution in seeking to enforce it ...[64]

This is an interesting dimension of a jury trial. Nobody can order a jury to convict[65] and thus a jury could, if they so wished, decide to ignore the law and bring in a verdict for whatever reason they wish. Indeed the fact that juries do not have to give reasons for their verdict (something Auld noted was in itself extremely controversial)[66] means that it is sometimes impossible to decide why a jury reached a particular verdict. When the defendant is convicted this is something that can be corrected on appeal, especially where the verdict is inconsistent or clearly against the evidence (see Chapter 16 for further details on this) but what troubled Auld more was where the perverse verdict was an acquittal.

Auld noted that 'although juries may have the ability to dispense with or nullify the law, they have no right to do so',[67] and suggested that it was 'an affront to the legal

---

62. *R v Watson* [1988] QB 690.
63. Lord Justice Auld, *A Review of the Criminal Courts of England and Wales* (HMSO 2001) 173ff.
64. Lord Justice Auld, *A Review of the Criminal Courts of England and Wales* (HMSO 2001) 173.
65. A principle forcibly restated in *R v Wang* [2005] UKHL 9.
66. Lord Justice Auld, *A Review of the Criminal Courts of England and Wales* (HMSO 2001) 168–73.
67. Lord Justice Auld, *A Review of the Criminal Courts of England and Wales* (HMSO 2001) 174.

process'.[68] One reason for this statement was that since only 1 per cent of crime was heard by a jury, why should it be entitled to disapply the law when those subject to summary trial will not receive such favour?[69] On the other hand, this ability of the jury has long been considered a notable feature of the system and has attracted the label 'jury equity'.[70]

⚡ CLIVE PONTING

Perhaps one of the most famous examples of 'jury equity' is the case of Clive Ponting who was charged with breaching the *Official Secrets Act 1911*. Ponting was a senior civil servant in the Ministry of Defence and came across material that related to the sinking of the *General Belgrano*, an Argentine cruiser which was sunk during the 'Falklands War'.[a] The official version of events was that the *Belgrano* was a threat to the Royal Navy Task Force and was sunk near an exclusion zone. The documents that Ponting identified demonstrated that it had been sighted a day earlier and was steaming away from the Task Force.[b] Ponting passed these papers to a Labour MP who had been critical of the execution of the campaign.

As a matter of law this was a simple breach of the *Official Secrets Act 1911* yet the jury acquitted him. The defence was, in essence, that it was in the public interest and yet this would not afford any defence in law. However, this did not stop a jury from acquitting him.

a   The campaign colloquially known as the 'Falklands War' took place in 1982 when Argentinian military forces invaded the disputed Falkland Islands, a British colony. In fact although known as the 'Falklands War' this is not strictly accurate since war was not declared by either the United Kingdom or Argentina. Instead the military action took place under the auspices of the United Nations Convention.

b   Not that this would mean that it could not be counted as a threat to the Task Force. Whilst the sinking of the *Belgrano* remains controversial most military observers believe it was a legitimate military tactic but politically the sinking was handled badly.[71]

The difficulty with this 'jury equity' power is that in effect it means that the law laid down by Parliament is circumvented and observers have even suggested it 'sabotages crime control'[72] and others agree that it does have serious implications for the administration of justice.[73] Alternatively it can be argued that this is society deciding whether it wishes its laws (for laws are made on behalf of society) to be enforced in circumstances where they believe the 'greater good' should prevail. Mischievously a comparison to the public interest prosecution test (see Chapter 12, 'Public-interest test') could be drawn. At the pre-trial procedure the prosecution may halt some crimes stating it is not 'in the public interest' for them to be prosecuted. One way of looking at 'jury equity' is to suggest that it is the jury saying that it is not 'in the public interest' for a person to be convicted. If the prosecution can decide it is not in the public's interest not to prosecute, why can't the public decide that it is not in the public interest to convict?

---

68.   Lord Justice Auld, *A Review of the Criminal Courts of England and Wales* (HMSO 2001) 175.
69.   Lord Justice Auld, *A Review of the Criminal Courts of England and Wales* (HMSO 2001) 174.
70.   Andrew Ashworth and Mike Redmayne, *The Criminal Process* (4th edn, OUP 2010) 301.
71.   The definitive statement of the sinking is given in Lawrence Freedman, *The Official History of the Falklands Campaign: Volume 2* (Routledge 2005).
72.   Andrew Sanders, Richard Young, and Mandy Burton, *Criminal Justice* (4th edn, OUP 2010).
73.   Sean Doran, 'Trial by Jury' in Mike McConville and Geoffrey Wilson (eds), *The Handbook of The Criminal Justice Process* (OUP 2002) 399.

It should be noted, finally, that the government did not act upon Auld's recommendation and thus the principle of 'jury equity' is alive and well although its controversiality remains untouched.

15.7 Youth trials

What has been discussed so far in this chapter is how trials take place for adults. However, a different system exists for youths (ie those who have not yet reached their eighteenth birthday) and it is necessary to briefly summarize this.

15.7.1 The need for a separate system

Why is it that youths should be treated differently from adults? This is not a particularly new concept, with youth courts first being created as a separate branch of the court system in 1908 (originally this was for those under the age of 16 but this was later extended to include those under 18). From the very beginning the youth courts sat at different times, and in different locations from the magistrates' court[74] in an attempt to ensure that young defendants did not mix with adult offenders.

Whilst youth courts are undoubtedly criminal in nature s 44 *Children and Young Persons Act 1933* states that the courts must 'have regard to the welfare of the child or young person'.[75] This is in line with the (later) requirements under the UN Convention on the Rights of the Child (see, for example, Article 40) but there is some doubt as to the extent to which this influences youth justice policy in reality.[76] This is perhaps particularly true in respect of the age of criminal responsibility which is set at ten in England and Wales, an age that many find unreasonably low.[77]

The 1980s and 1990s led to a system whereby the serious and persistent offenders were treated more seriously but the so-called 'nuisance' offenders were dealt with in a less serious way.[78] The election of the New Labour government in 1997 led to significant changes to youth justice and, in particular, a more formalized approach. Whilst the welfare principle included within the 1933 Act was never repealed, the *Crime and Disorder Act 1998* stated that the 'principal aim' of the youth justice system should be to prevent offending by children and young persons.[79] It was suggested that this perhaps meant a more punitive approach should be adopted. This was combined with more formalized approaches to non-court disposals. Instead of police cautioning there was a defined system that incrementally responded to actions, with an informal warning only being permitted once, before more formal responses and ultimately the matter having to be referred to a court.[80]

Although the process has become more formalized, what has not changed is the belief that the systems should be separated and, as will be seen, the actual trial should

507

74. Nicola Padfield and Jonathan Bild, *Text and Materials on the Criminal Justice Process* (4th edn, Routledge 2008) 404.
75. *Children and Young Persons Act 1933*, s 44(1).
76. Jane Fortin, *Children's Rights and the Developing Law* (3rd edn, OUP 2009) 710.
77. The competing issues in respect of this are discussed in Jane Fortin, *Children's Rights and the Developing Law* (3rd edn, OUP 2009) 684–93.
78. Nicola Padfield and Jonathan Bild, *Text and Materials on the Criminal Justice Process* (4th edn, Routledge 2008) 405.
79. *Crime and Disorder Act 1998*, s 37.
80. Jane Fortin, *Children's Rights and the Developing Law* (3rd edn, OUP 2009) 707.

not be as formalistic as an adult trial. The judgment of the ECtHR in *T and V v United Kingdom*,[81] which will be discussed later, has arguably strengthened this distinction and the clear presumption is that those under 18 should ordinarily be tried in the youth court.

15.7.2 **The youth court**

The 'default' court for dealing with youth crime is the youth court. This is a branch of the magistrates' court but, as will be seen, it has much greater powers. It also differs in a number of crucial ways from the traditional magistrates' court.

The key difference between the youth court and the magistrates' court is its informality. Whilst it is a formal trial, the courtroom is usually set out differently and the procedure will ordinarily involve more explanation so that the defendant can follow proceedings. The first point to note is that a youth court must have its own separate entrance. Whilst the youth court will, more often than not, be located inside an ordinary magistrates' court building, there should be a separate entrance that can be used to access the building together with separate waiting areas.[82] The idea behind this is to ensure that children are not forced to wait with adult offenders.

The youth court is not a public court and so ordinary members of the public cannot attend (unlike the magistrates' court and the Crown Court). That said, the parents (or persons with responsibility for the child) will be permitted to attend and indeed where the defendant is under the age of 16 the parent must be present.[83] Whilst the media are able to attend proceedings of the youth court[84] they may not report the names and address of any offender without leave of the court,[85] and leave may only be given once an offender has been convicted; even then it will be only given rarely.

The layout of the youth court will often be more informal than a traditional court. The youth defendant will not appear in a dock but rather the offender will sit with his lawyer and, where appropriate, his parents or other supporters. This allows the young offender to follow proceedings more closely and is also supposed to ensure that the child is not objectified by sitting in a dock. It is usual in youth courts for everyone to sit on the same level, ie there is no raised dais upon which the bench would sit. The furniture is usually less formal too.

As with the magistrates' court, a youth court will ordinarily be presided over by three lay magistrates (known as a panel in the youth court rather than a bench) or by a single DJMC. Where the matter is presided over by lay magistrates the panel must contain at least one male magistrate and at least one female magistrate. Lay magistrates are given special training before they are permitted to sit on youth courts and they will normally be experienced magistrates before sitting. It is not uncommon for DJMCs to now sit and again these will ordinarily be specially trained. It is the responsibility of the judge or panel to ensure that the young defendant is able to follow the proceedings and this will include avoiding using legal language where possible and explaining the relevant terms and procedure.

---

81. (2000) 30 EHRR 121.
82. *Children and Young Persons Act 1933*, s 31.
83. *Children and Young Persons Act 1933*, s 34A(1).
84. *Children and Young Persons Act 1933*, s 47.
85. *Children and Young Persons Act 1933*, s 49.

15.7.2.1 **Jurisdiction**

It will be remembered from Chapter 12 that the magistrates' court may only hear cases that are classified either as summary only or triable either-way (with the consent of the defendant). The youth court, however, has much wider jurisdiction and can hear matters that include indictable-only offences[86] although it has no jurisdiction where a juvenile is charged with homicide, in which case the matter must be heard in the Crown Court.

Where a child is charged alone or with another juvenile then the clear presumption is that they should be tried in a youth court and may only be sent to the Crown Court where it involves homicide or certain firearms offences.[87] The senior courts have been very clear that it should be rare for a trial not to proceed in the youth court. In *R (On the application of W) v Southampton Youth Court*[88] Lord Woolf CJ stated:

> There is no doubt that the general policy of the legislature is that young offenders should where possible be tried by a youth court. That is a policy which the courts should promote. It is obviously desirable that, where appropriate, young offenders should not be tried before the Crown Court unless this is clearly necessary.[89]

Lord Woolf continued by noting that where a child is particularly young then it may be more appropriate for the trial to proceed in the youth court irrespective of sentencing powers because of human rights considerations, particularly whether it will be possible to achieve a fair trial.[90]

15.7.2.2 **Procedure**

The procedure in the youth court is the same as that would occur in a summary trial and thus the steps presented in this chapter continue to be followed. That said, there are a couple of relatively crucial differences. The charges are still read to the defendant but they must be explained in language that the child understands. Similarly, the nature of the proceedings and what the process is going to be should also be explained to the defendant even when he is represented by a lawyer. This is to ensure that the court is satisfied that the child understands what is happening.

Where the young defendant is under the age of 14 then, if they testify, they will not testify under oath.[91] Even though the evidence is unsworn this does not prevent a person who lies while giving unsworn testimony from being charged with perjury although it would be somewhat rare for this to ever happen to a juvenile defendant.

The final subtle change between a trial in the magistrates' court and trial in the youth court is in respect of the decision. By statute, the term 'conviction' is not permitted[92] and instead the term 'guilty' is used, presumably because it is thought that children will understand what that means. Of course, in the adult magistrates' court it is more common to say the case is 'proved' or 'not proved' but in the youth court clarity and understanding is paramount and therefore guilty and not guilty should be used.

---

86. *Magistrates' Courts Act 1980*, s 24(1).
87. *Magistrates' Courts Act 1980*, s 24(1B).
88. [2002] EWCA Civ 1640.
89. *R (On the application of W) v Southampton Youth Court* [2002] EWCA Civ 1640 [11].
90. *R (On the application of W) v Southampton Youth Court* [2002] EWCA Civ 1640 [16].
91. *Youth Justice and Criminal Evidence Act 1999*, s 55.
92. *Children and Young Persons Act 1933*, s 59.

15.7.3 **The Crown Court**

As identified earlier, exceptionally youths can be sent to the Crown Court for trial. Unlike the youth court, where special processes and procedures are in place, there tend to be far less amendments to the Crown Court process although following the ruling in *T and V v United Kingdom*[93] there are more adaptions then there were before.

III\\ Case Box *T and V v United Kingdom*

One of the most important and controversial cases in this area was the decision of the ECtHR in *T and V v United Kingdom*.[94] This was a case that concerned Robert Thompson and Jon Venables, two ten-year-old boys who abducted and murdered a two-year-old boy, Jamie Bulger.

The case provoked uproar in the general population and they were put on trial in the Crown Court at Preston. The ordinary rules of the Crown Court were followed in that it took place in open court and the defendants sat in a dock. The dock had been specially raised— so that the defendants could follow the proceedings—but this had the effect of making the defendants more visible and able to see the (hostile) public watching the trial.

The judge did make some concessions in an attempt to minimize the effect on the children. The trial followed school-day times (which the children would be familiar with) and a ten-minute break was taken every hour to allow a rest from the proceedings.

The ECtHR rejected the argument that it would always be unfair to subject ten-year-olds to a trial but they did state that Article 6(1) means that 'a child charged with an offence is dealt with in a manner which takes full account of his age, level of maturity, and intellectual and emotional capacities, and that steps are taken to promote his ability to understand and participate in the proceedings'.

The court continued: 'in respect of a young child charged with a grave offence attracting high levels of media and public interest, it would be necessary to conduct the hearing in such a way as to reduce as far as possible his or her feelings of intimidation and inhibition.'[95]

The court found that the raised dock, whilst done for the right reason, almost certainly raised the fears of the defendant and many of the arcane proceedings of the Crown Court would look strange and mean it was unlikely that eleven-year-olds (the age the defendants were when the trial started) could follow the trial. Accordingly, they held that there had been a breach of Article 6.

Whilst the ruling of the ECtHR provoked a political and popular storm of criticism, the courts took on board many of the comments and the then Lord Chief Justice, Lord Bingham, issued a practice direction specifically targeted at such trials.[96]

The Practice Direction includes a number of statements that demonstrate the willingness of the English courts to react to the decision in *T and V*:

> The trial process should not itself expose the young defendant to avoidable intimidation, humiliation or distress. All possible steps should be taken to assist the young

---

93. (2000) 30 EHRR 121.
94. (2000) 30 EHRR 121.
95. (2000) 30 EHRR 121 [87].
96. *Practice Direction (Crown Court: Young Defendants)* [2000] 1 WLR 659.

defendant to understand and participate in the proceedings. The ordinary trial process should so far as necessary be adapted to meet those ends.[97]

The Direction then lists a number of factors that should ordinarily occur, including the fact that pre-trial visits should occur so that the child is aware of the court, the police should attempt to bring the child to court in such a way as to minimize potential disruption, the trial should take place in a courtroom where everyone is on the same, or almost the same, level (as occurs in the youth court), the child should ordinarily not be in the dock, and the proceedings should be explained in a language that he is used to. Robes and wigs should ordinarily not be used unless the young defendant wishes them (which mirrors the position that occurs with child witnesses) and the court should consider limiting the number and types of people allowed into the public gallery.

To an extent these would seem obvious steps but they were a major shift from how Crown Court proceedings ordinarily proceeded. That said, whilst it is clear that the Practice Direction sets out a number of steps that should ordinarily be followed, breach of this will not necessarily be fatal to a case unless the reviewing court believes that the omissions are such that it causes the fairness of the trial to be brought into question.[98]

Auld LJ, in his report, had recommended that young defendants should no longer find themselves in the Crown Court. Auld believed that it would be preferable for a specially created youth court to be empanelled, it being presided over by a judge and specially trained magistrates.[99] This was rejected, in part because the three-tier court structure proposed by Auld was also rejected, but it must be questioned whether a distinction could have been drawn for young defendants. It has already been noted that the youth court has jurisdiction to hear matters that ordinarily would be heard by a jury. It is only a small step to state that any crime committed by a young defendant should be heard in the absence of a jury and, if there are concerns about the training of those in the youth court to deal with grave crimes, the solution, as Auld proposed, would be to introduce a senior judge into the process. Sadly there appears little likelihood of such proposals being introduced but it must be seriously questioned whether subjecting young defendants to a Crown Court trial, even when it is adapted along the lines of the Practice Direction, would be considered fair.[100]

⟳ QUESTION FOR REFLECTION

Auld LJ reported that in 2000 some 4,718 young defendants were sent to the Crown Court. Are you surprised that so many young people found themselves in the Crown Court? What is the justification for allowing offenders to appear in the Crown Court rather than a specially formed youth court?

15.7.4 Young defendants in the adult courts

For completeness it should also be noted that some young defendants will be tried in the adult courts. Of course technically the Crown Court, even when specially adapted,

---

97. *Practice Direction (Crown Court: Young Defendants)* [2000] 1 WLR 659 [31].
98. See, for example, *R v H* [2006] EWCA Crim 853.
99. Lord Justice Auld, *A Review of the Criminal Courts of England and Wales* (HMSO 2001) 215.
100. See, for example, *SC v United Kingdom* (2005) 40 EHRR 10.

is an adult court but this part of the book addresses the fact that a child can find themselves in an ordinary adult court.

The youth court has jurisdiction to deal with youths. It therefore has no jurisdiction to deal with adults (although where it proceeds on the basis that D is a youth but later discovers that he is an adult they can decide to continue hearing the matter).[101] What is the position where a child is charged with a person who is obviously an adult?

Example

Michael, aged 13, is charged with Alfred, aged 32, of theft. The particulars are that Michael caused a diversion in a supermarket, allowing Alfred to place a bottle of whisky in his coat.

In this example both Robert and Alfred would appear prima facie to be guilty of an offence under the *Theft Act 1968*. As Alfred is an adult he cannot be tried in the youth court. Theft is an either-way offence and assuming that both plead not guilty then it would seem likely that both Michael and Alfred will appear in either the (adult) magistrates' court (if both elect this) or the Crown Court.[102] If Michael pleaded guilty and Alfred not guilty (or vice versa for that matter) then the trials may be separated and Michael's could be heard in the youth court but where they both plead not guilty then they will appear together.

There is discretion where the defendants are not charged together but are charged as a result of the same circumstances.

Example

Rebecca, aged 14, is charged with causing criminal damage. Sarah and Tina, both aged 32, are charged with being drunk and disorderly, affray, and assault occasioning Actual Bodily Harm. The particulars are that Rebecca meets up with Sarah and Tina, who she knows, and who have been drinking. Sarah and Tina start a fight with another girl and as they are being arrested Rebecca, who dislikes police officers, thinks it would be funny to throw a brick through the police car's window.

In this example Rebecca's liability is not dependent on the liability of Sarah and Tina. Whilst it all arguably comes from the same incident, it is possible to separate the liability of Rebecca and statute provides the court with discretion to either hear the matter in the (adult) court (alongside the adult defendants) or to send the young defendant to the youth court for trial.[103]

---

101. *Children and Young Persons Act 1933*, s 48.
102. *Children and Young Persons Act 1933*, s 46.
103. *Children and Young Persons Act 1963*, s 18.

QUESTION FOR REFLECTION

Is it not unfair for a young defendant to be tried in an adult court in circumstances where, if they committed the crime alone, they would be tried in a youth court? What reasons do you think there are for not having two trials (one in the adult court and one in the youth court)?

Summary

In this chapter we have examined the trial process and identified the differences between summary trials and trials on indictment. In particular we have noted that:

- In the magistrates' court the tribunal of fact and law are the same—either the lay justices or the DJMC—whereas in the Crown Court the tribunal of law is the judge and the tribunal of fact is the jury.

- The prosecution always tenders its evidence first as this is an important part of the presumption of innocence. The defendant should only be required to call evidence when the prosecution have proved that there is a case to answer.

- Each witness that is called by a party will then be asked questions by the opposing side(s). This is known as cross-examination. There then follows a short period of re-examination by the side calling the witness but that is subject to rules restricting what can be asked.

- In a trial on indictment the jury will sum up the evidence to the jury, ie produce a summary of the evidence and direct them as to the type of questions they should ask. There is no equivalent in a summary trial.

- In a Crown Court trial the jury will retire, ie leave the court, to consider their verdict. In a summary trial it is likely that lay justices will retire but a DJMC is likely to give an immediate answer.

- It is not always necessary to reach a unanimous decision. In the magistrates' court the decision can be by majority (although no one will know) and in the Crown Court a majority verdict is also permitted but not when the jury first starts to deliberate.

End-of-chapter questions

1. It has been seen that the primary role of the judge is to ensure that there is a fair trial and that the judge should not adopt the mantle of an advocate. However, an important aspect of that role is to allow advocates to put forward their case. Read *R v Lashley*[104] which is an extraordinary case where a judge becomes hostile to counsel. What do you think the jury and defendant would have made of this? Is it possible for it to be a fair trial in such instances?

---

104.   [2005] EWCA Crim 2016.

2. Read Sean Doran, 'Trial by Jury' in Mike McConville and Geoffrey Wilson (eds), *The Handbook of The Criminal Justice Process* (OUP 2002) 398–9. Do you think it is right that a jury should be able to dis-apply the law, or is Auld LJ correct to say that it is 'an affront to justice'?

3. Is it realistic to expect jurors not to check the Internet when deciding a case? How will removing telephones etc from the jurors combat jurors looking at inappropriate material?

4. Read Jane Fortin, *Children's Rights and the Developing Law* (3rd edn, OUP 2009) 709–15. Can it ever be justified to try children in the adult Crown Court?

 Further reading

Darbyshire P, 'Raising Concerns about Justices' Clerks' in Sean Doran and John Jackson (eds), *The Judicial Role in Criminal Proceedings* (Hart Publishing 2000).

This is one of the few commentaries that examines the issue of justices' clerks. It raises some interesting points about their role within the summary system.

Darbyshire P, *Sitting in Judgment: The Working Lives of Judges* (Hart Publishing 2011) ch 8.

This considers the experiences of district judges (magistrates' court) while hearing matters in both the adult magistrates' court and also the youth court.

Doran S, 'Trial by Jury' in Mike McConville and Geoffrey Wilson, *The Handbook of The Criminal Justice Process* (OUP 2002).

This is an intelligent essay that highlights some of the controversial aspects of a trial on indictment.

Fortin J, *Children's Rights and the Developing Law* (3rd edn, OUP 2009) ch 18.

This chapter considers the treatment of young offenders and, in particular, how their rights under the UN Convention on the Rights of the Child are upheld (or not).

Thornton P, 'Trial by Jury: 50 Years of Change' [2004] *Criminal Law Review* 683–701.

This is an interesting piece that demonstrates how far trial by jury has altered in fifty years, particularly in respect of those who are entitled to sit on a jury.

For multiple-choice questions, updates to this chapter, and links to useful websites, please visit the **Online Resource Centre** at: **www.oxfordtextbooks.co.uk/orc/gillespie_els6e/**

16

Criminal Appeals

By the end of this chapter you will be able to:

- Identify where appeals following summary trials and trials on indictment are heard.
- Distinguish between interlocutory and final appeals.
- Discuss the circumstances in which the prosecution may make an appeal.
- Explain how appeals are heard.
- Identify the powers an appellate court has.

Introduction

The previous chapters have identified how criminal trials take place. We have noted that there are two forms of trial: the summary trial which takes place in the magistrates' court and the trial on indictment which takes place in the Crown Court. However, the trial does not necessarily end the matter since in certain circumstances it is possible for either the defendant or prosecution to appeal against rulings of the judge.

This chapter will examine under what circumstances someone is entitled to appeal and how that appeal is heard. It completes our examination of criminal trials and will help place the duties and responsibilities of the appellate courts into context.

16.1 Summary trials or trials on indictment

It has been seen from the previous chapters that the law differentiates between summary trials and trials on indictment and this distinction continues with appeals. It will be seen that there are completely separate ways of dealing with appeals depending on the mode of trial, this distinction including even whether it is possible to appeal against matters of fact.

Figure 16.1 demonstrates the different paths that can be taken depending on the type of trial and these will be explored in the remainder of this chapter. The dotted line demonstrates the path an appeal from a summary trial takes and the solid line demonstrates the path an appeal following a trial on indictment takes. It can be

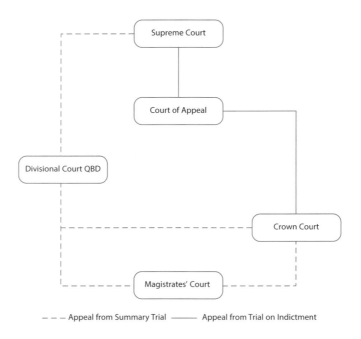

Figure 16.1 Appellate structure of the Criminal Justice System

seen that although some courts share jurisdiction the processes are quite distinct and accordingly will be discussed separately.

16.2 Appeals from a summary trial

Figure 16.1 presents the appellate structure for summary trials and it can be seen that there are two possible avenues for an appeal from the magistrates' court: either to the Crown Court or to the Divisional Court. A third possibility also exists, that of judicial review, since the magistrates' court is an inferior body but the courts prefer the matter to proceed on the basis of appeal by way of case stated as they argue that this is the more appropriate avenue.[1] That said, it remains an important method of appeal and the decision over which method to adopt is not always easy.[2]

16.2.1 Appeal to the Crown Court

The first appeal route is an appeal to the Crown Court. This is an opportunity that is restricted to the convicted defendant and is unique within the appellate system in that its form is not that of a legal argument but rather a complete rehearing. The appeal can be against sentence or conviction.

---

1. *R (on behalf of Stace) v Milton Keynes Magistrates' Court* [2006] EWHC 1049 [13].
2. *R (on behalf of Stace) v Milton Keynes Magistrates' Court* [2006] EWHC 1049 [15].

The appeal is permitted under s 108 *Magistrates' Courts Act 1980* (MCA 1980) and does not require leave (permission) to be granted; the appeal exists as a matter of right. The composition of the court when hearing the appeal is that a Crown Court judge (normally a circuit judge or recorder but theoretically a puisne judge could sit) presides with usually two lay justices. The judge is the tribunal of law and accordingly the lay justices must take the law as directed by the judge. However, the judge has no veto in respect of decisions of fact where only a simple majority is required.

As noted earlier, the appeal takes the form of a complete rehearing, with all evidence being reheard (including the witnesses) and the decision made at the end of the trial. Theoretically the Crown Court could decide to remit the matter back to the magistrates' court for another hearing or for disposal regarding sentence but usually the matter is dealt with by the Crown Court with the proviso that the powers of the Crown Court are the same as in the magistrates' court. However, that does not mean that a sentence cannot be increased: since it is a rehearing a person challenging his conviction could find that his appeal is dismissed and his sentence is actually increased. Ashworth and Redmayne argue that the ability to increase the sentence is unfair[3] and certainly it is not comparable to the position that exists in respect of appeals from trials on indictment where the Court of Appeal has no such power (discussed later). Sprack argues that the provision is probably a tool by which appeals are discouraged[4] but it is submitted that this is an inappropriate way of doing it: a person should not feel unable to challenge a conviction because they are afraid their sentence could be increased. A better approach would be to impose a leave requirement (16.3.1) whereby someone must convince a judicial officer that there is merit in an appeal.

Auld disagreed with this right of appeal to the Crown Court. He argued that it historically arose because there was suspicion about the competency of the magistracy[5] but he argued that this was no longer true, although it was seen in Chapter 13 that the position is arguably not so straightforward. A further argument advanced is that ordinarily the magistrates will provide reasons for their decision and thus if there is a perception that they have acted in a way contrary to the law then an appeal by way of case stated could be brought.[6] This last point does have some weight to it. The existence of the right to a complete rehearing purely on the basis that the defendant disagrees with the decision of the magistrates is not replicated in respect of any other type of appeal which is based purely on an issue of law. It does have the appearance of being anomalous and can only be based on the premise of a lack of trust in the decision of magistrates. However, this is perhaps undermined by the fact that the right of appeal applies to any summary trial and thus includes trials conducted by a district judge (magistrates' court).

Auld suggested restricting appeals to matters of law and before a single judge[7] which would have been controversial and somewhat unprecedented; appeals normally take place in respect of at least two judges and this should (except for issues of leave) be retained for confidence. In any event the government rejected this proposal, or at the very least did not act upon it, and thus the current position is that the appeal to the Crown Court continues in the way that it always has. It is also undoubtedly the most

517

3. Andrew Ashworth and Mike Redmayne, *The Criminal Process* (4th edn, OUP 2010) 340.
4. John Sprack, *A Practical Approach to Criminal Procedure* (15th edn, OUP 2015) 457, 27.13.
5. Lord Justice Auld, *A Review of the Criminal Courts of England and Wales* (HMSO 2001) 617.
6. Lord Justice Auld, *A Review of the Criminal Courts of England and Wales* (HMSO 2001) 620.
7. Lord Justice Auld, *A Review of the Criminal Courts of England and Wales* (HMSO 2001) 621–2.

popular method of appeal. The 2015–2016 CPS Annual Report notes that 16,930 appeals were heard in the Crown Court.[8]

16.2.1.1 Subsequent appeals

For sake of completeness it should be noted that for matters of fact there is no appeal from the Crown Court when sitting in its appellate capacity but where either the prosecution or defence wish to argue that it has made an error of law when determining the appeal then they can currently appeal by way of case stated.[9] The matter would be heard in the same way as though it was being stated by the magistrates' court, discussed later.

The Law Commission has argued that the right to appeal by way of case stated from the Crown Court should be removed.[10] The Law Commission argued that removing this appeal would simplify criminal procedure although they noted that it is relatively rare for such appeals to be made. They also noted that even if it were abolished then judicial review of the decision of the court (when acting in its appellate capacity) would still exist. The government has never accepted this proposal, presumably in part because it is used so rarely. That said it must be questioned whether there is a need for this 'additional bite of the cherry' and it would be preferable for offenders wishing to appeal against a decision of the magistrates to decide at the outset whether they wished the appeal to be premised on law (appeal by way of case stated) or fact (appeal to the Crown Court).

16.2.2 Appeal by way of case stated

The second form of appeal is to appeal to the High Court by way of case stated. This, as it will be seen, is a different species of appeal from appeal to the Crown Court and has more in common with other appeals. The first point to note is that both the prosecution and the defence can appeal by way of case stated[11] and accordingly an acquitted person can find himself the subject of an appeal. This is an important distinction and it can be contrasted with appeals following a trial on indictment, where even with recent changes set out in the *Criminal Justice Act 2003* (CJA 2003) (see 16.4), it remains relatively rare for an acquittal to be reversed.

An appeal by way of case stated is where either party is arguing that the magistrates have made an error of law and requires the magistrates to identify the case upon which they based their decision, ie the reasons for their finding. It is for this reason that it is known as 'case stated'. Along with this, they will identify a series of questions that they want the High Court to answer. Since the appeal arises out of a matter of law it is unusual for an appeal to relate to a sentence passed, as it would be rare for a court to pass an illegal sentence, but in exceptional cases such appeals have been brought, most notably in driving cases where the prosecution have sought to overturn a decision not to disqualify a driver.[12]

---

8. Crown Prosecution Service, *Annual Report and Accounts 2015–16* (CPS 2016) <https://www.cps.gov.uk/publications/docs/annual_report_2015_16.pdf> 59.
9. *Senior Courts Act 1981*, s 28.
10. Law Commission, *The High Court's Jurisdiction in Relation to Criminal Proceedings* (Law Comm Report No 324).
11. *Magistrates' Courts Act 1980*, s 111(1).
12. See, for example, *Haime v Walkett* (1983) 5 Cr App R(S) 165.

Any appeal must be lodged within twenty-one days of the determination by the magistrates and should initially be made by requesting the justices to state a case.[13] The magistrates can refuse to state a case although they should only do so where they believe it to be frivolous.[14] In *R (on behalf of Miller) v Redbridge Justices*[15] the Divisional Court held that frivolous meant 'futile, misconceived, hopeless or academic'.[16] Where the justices do refuse to state a case, a right of appeal exists from this refusal, again to the High Court.[17] Technically that appeal is a judicial review[18] not least because the remedy of the appeal is a compelling order, which is a traditional administrative law remedy (discussed more fully in Chapter 18).

Where a case is prepared it will initially be done in draft and this draft sent to both the appellant and respondent[19] for comment and, ideally, an agreement as to the nature of the case (ie what questions of law are raised) is made and then this case proceeds to the High Court for hearing.[20] The hearing is heard in the Administrative Court and normally takes place before at least two judges, making it a Divisional Court.[21] It is usual for at least one judge to be a Lord Justice of Appeal but it has become increasingly common for two puisne judges to sit and there does not appear to be any requirement for a Lord Justice to sit. It is not unusual in these cases for the judgment to be handed down immediately after the hearing although the court does have discretion to give judgment later. There are three options open to the court:

- dismiss the appeal
- allow the appeal and direct that the magistrates should convict or acquit the defendant[22]
- allow the appeal and remit it back to the magistrates' court for a rehearing before either the same or a new bench.[23]

A peculiar difficulty with an appeal by way of case stated is that as the constitution is ordinarily a Divisional Court of two members it is quite possible that the judges could be divided. Technically in these circumstances the rule is that the appeal fails.[24] There are circumstances when this could be considered unduly harsh and in *Associated Lead Mills Ltd* Kennedy LJ stated that they considered relisting the matter for the consideration of a three-judge panel but decided not to do so in that particular case as they thought the point in principle was not sufficiently serious.[25] In 2012, however, the Divisional Court did just that. The Divisional Court was hearing an appeal by way of case stated by Paul Chambers who had been convicted under s 127 *Communications*

---

13.   *Magistrates' Courts Act 1980*, s 111(2).
14.   *Magistrates' Courts Act 1980*, s 111(5).
15.   [2002] EWHC Admin 1579.
16.   [2002] EWHC Admin 1579 [14].
17.   *Magistrates' Courts Act 1980*, s 111(6).
18.   See *R (on behalf of Miller) v Redbridge Justices* [2002] EWHC Admin 1579.
19.   The term 'respondent' continues to be used to indicate the party in the original proceedings (eg where the prosecution are appealing the defendant and vice versa) whereas technically, of course, it is the justices themselves who are responding to the appeal. However, the term probably continues out of ease of use and certainly both the original parties are represented at court whereas the justices ordinarily are not.
20.   See, *Criminal Procedure Rules* (as amended October 2016), r 35.3.
21.   Technically, following the *Access to Justice Act 1999* any appeal by way of case stated does not have to go to a Divisional Court because the statute simply refers the matter to the High Court. However, as a matter of custom it will normally proceed before a Divisional Court and thus be heard by more than one judge.
22.   This can be a partial appeal, ie the court could decide to vary the order of the magistrates.
23.   See *Griffith v Jenkins* [1992] 2 AC 76.
24.   *Cambridgeshire County Council v Associated Lead Mills Ltd* [2005] EWHC Admin 1627 [14].
25.   *Cambridgeshire County Council v Associated Lead Mills Ltd* [2005] EWHC Admin 1627 [14].

Act 2003 for sending a message that was grossly offensive, indecent, obscene, or of a menacing character by a public telecommunications network. Chambers had used Twitter to tweet a 'joke threat' to blow the airport up as he was upset that it had closed due to snow. His appeal to the Crown Court was rejected and he appealed by way of case stated but in February it was reported that the two judges hearing the matter were divided and Gross LJ had ordered the matter to be relisted before three judges. The three-judge court ultimately decided that the conviction should be quashed.[26]

A further right of appeal exists from a decision of the High Court by way of case stated but only to the Supreme Court and only when it involves a point of public importance.[27] It is extremely rare for such appeals to be brought and in essence therefore the appeal by way of case stated will usually be the last stage of any appeal.

Unfortunately the courts no longer publish detailed statistics of the number of appeals by way of case stated but the *Judicial and Court Statistics 2011* state that there were seventy-nine appeals by way of case stated, seventy-three of which were from the magistrates' court (the remaining six would be from the Crown Court). Of those appeals that were dealt with only 37 per cent were successful. It demonstrates that the number of appeals by way of case stated is small in comparison with the number of appeals brought before the Crown Court.

16.2.3 Judicial review

The third appellate route from the magistrates' court is to petition the High Court for a judicial review of the decision of the justices. This route arises because magistrates' courts are inferior bodies and thus subject to the supervisory function of the High Court[28] although, as will be seen, the courts prefer the matter to be heard by one of the other routes. This is perhaps set out most notably in *R (on the application of Clark-Darby) v Highbury Magistrates' Court*[29] where the court held that unless the matter was one where an allegation of natural justice was raised (eg a magistrate was biased and should have excused himself) then the normal recourse should be to appeal by way of case stated since that allowed the full reasoning of the magistrates to be set out before the appellate court for examination.

16.3 Appeal from a trial on indictment

Perhaps the appeals that are more readily visible are those that arise from a trial on indictment as these invariably concern the more serious offences. Apart from matters that do not relate to a trial on indictment, which will be discussed later, all appeals from the Crown Court proceed to the Court of Appeal (Criminal Division). This was created in 1966 and is a creature of statute[30] although it recognizes a progression from the original Court of Criminal Appeals.

The Lord Chief Justice is the President of the Criminal Division and this has remained true even after the reorganization of the judiciary.[31] In 1997 an honorary

---

26. *Chambers v DPP* [2012] EWHC 2157 (Admin).
27. *Administration of Justice Act 1960*, s 1.
28. See, for example, *R (on behalf of Stace) v Milton Keynes Magistrates' Court* [2006] EWHC 1049.
29. [2001] EWHC Admin 959.
30. *Senior Courts Act 1981*, ss 2 and 3.
31. *Constitutional Reform Act 2005*, s 7.

title of Vice-President of the Criminal Division was created, with Rose LJ being the first appointee. The *Courts Act 2003* (CA 2003) formalized this arrangement, albeit implicitly, by recognizing the term 'Vice-President' of either Division[32] but it remains, in effect, an honorary title and the holder is still formally styled a Lord (or Lady) Justice of Appeal[33] and does not receive any additional pay for the duties he discharges, nor is he classed as a 'Head of Division' (see 8.1.1.4). The current Vice-President is Lady Justice Hallett. That said, the Vice-President has important delegated authority given to her and is in de facto day-to-day charge of the Court of Appeal (Criminal Division). Apart from the Lord Chief Justice and Vice-President, the court is staffed by Lords Justices of Appeal and puisne judges asked by the Lord Chief Justice to sit (normally these will be judges of the Queen's Bench Division but they need not be and where the matter raises welfare issues it is possible a Family Division judge will be appointed). Since 1995 certain circuit judges have also been eligible to sit in the Criminal Division.[34] Previously they were restricted to sitting on appeals that were not heard at first instance by a puisne judge but this was abolished by the CA 2003. Also in any bench of the Court of Appeal only one circuit judge may sit[35] although there is no restriction on the number of puisne judges who may sit.[36]

The Court of Appeal will normally sit in panels of three but they can sit in panels of five (known as a 'full court') for significant matters (normally reserved for the issuing of practice directions or where they seek to depart from precedent—see *R v Simpson*[37]) and they may also sit in panels of two although not where this involves the determination of an appeal against, inter alia, a conviction or unduly lenient sentence.[38] Auld argued that extending the power of a panel of two judges to include the determination of appeals against convictions could lead to greater efficiency in the court[39] but this was rejected in part because of the dangers of a two-judge panel being divided. Whilst, as a matter of statutory law, such a split decision would lead to the rehearing before a three-judge court[40] this would lead to problems of delay, costs, and indeed added stress to a convicted appellant, especially where he is held in gaol.

16.3.1 Leave

There is no automatic right to an appeal to the Court of Appeal, one must get permission first. Two routes exist for the granting of leave to a convicted defendant who wishes to appeal against his conviction. The first is to seek permission from the trial judge and the second is to seek permission from the Court of Appeal itself.[41] It must be noted at the outset that the first course of action is extremely unusual and indeed the Court of Appeal itself has stated that it should only be in the most exceptional circumstances that a judge certifies a case as fit for appeal, arguing that it should normally be for the judges of the Court of Appeal to grant leave.[42]

32. *Courts Act 2003*, s 64.
33. *Courts Act 2003*, s 63.
34. *Senior Courts Act 1981*, s 9 and *Criminal Justice and Public Order Act 1994*, s 52.
35. *Senior Courts Act 1981*, s 55(6).
36. In other words, theoretically at least a Division of the Court of Appeal could be constituted solely with puisne judges.
37. [2004] QB 118.
38. *Senior Courts Act 1981*, s 55(4).
39. Lord Justice Auld, *A Review of the Criminal Courts of England and Wales* (HMSO 2001) 646–7.
40. *Senior Courts Act 1981*, s 55(5).
41. *Criminal Appeal Act 1968*, s 1.
42. See, for example, *R v Bansal* [1999] Crim LR 484.

The most usual route is to ask the Court of Appeal for permission. The first stage in this process is deciding whether it is possible to appeal. Section 1 CAA 1968 makes clear that a right exists against a conviction and this has led to the question over in what circumstances, if any, an appeal may be brought when a person has pleaded guilty, and thus has not been *convicted* per se. The Court of Appeal has adopted the approach of permitting an appeal to be brought where the plea of guilty was equivocal, ie where the defendant thought there was no other option but to plead guilty. This can arise from two principal reasons; the first is where the plea was made under duress[43] and the second is where a judge has made a ruling in law which leaves the defendant with no other option but to plead guilty.[44]

Petitioning the Court of Appeal will normally lead to a 'single judge' considering whether to give leave. The single judge is a puisne judge and ordinarily each judge of the Queen's Bench Division will serve. All of the applications are on paper without any hearing. Auld noted that whilst some applications may be easy to dispose of, others will take a considerable period of reflection[45] and yet no time is specifically allocated to the judges to undertake this task, with the vast majority of the applications being undertaken in the evenings or at weekends, particularly when the judge is sitting on circuit.[46] This has led some to question the consistency of single-judge decisions with the implication that pressure could lead to a cursory inspection.[47] That said, however, a right of appeal does exist from the refusal by the single judge and this is to the Court of Appeal itself although only a minority of applications will be accepted.[48] The same position appears to occur now. In 2014/15 there was a total of 1,518 applications for leave to appeal against conviction.[49] Of those, 299 (19.6 per cent) were heard. Of those appeals against conviction brought, 40.5 per cent of appeals against conviction were successful.

16.3.2 **The hearing**

Assuming that leave is granted then the matter will proceed to a full hearing (although in some cases the leave and substantive issues will be rolled into a single hearing). Before arriving at the court a lot of procedural issues will have occurred, most notably counsel will be required to prepare 'skeleton arguments'. Despite their name, skeleton arguments are comprehensive documents that set out the arguments of both the appellant and respondents. The appellant will prepare their skeleton argument first and this will be served upon the respondents who will then have the opportunity to comment on it. This therefore forms the basis of the arguments although Auld found that it was not unusual for skeleton arguments to be sent in late or amended[50] and there is some evidence to suggest this continues today.[51] Counsel are able to depart from their skeleton argument and indeed may do so at the request of the judges.

---

43.   *R v Turner* [1970] 2 QB 321.
44.   *R v Clarke* [1972] 1 All ER 219.
45.   Lord Justice Auld, *A Review of the Criminal Courts of England and Wales* (HMSO 2001) 639.
46.   Penny Darbyshire, *Sitting in Judgment: The Working Lives of Judges* (Hart Publishing 2011) 294.
47.   Andrew Ashworth and Mike Redmayne, *The Criminal Process* (4th edn, OUP 2010) 342–3.
48.   Andrew Ashworth and Mike Redmayne, *The Criminal Process* (4th edn, OUP 2010) 343.
49.   Court of Appeal, *In the Court of Appeal Criminal Division* (Court of Appeal 2015) <https://www.judiciary.gov.uk/wp-content/uploads/2015/12/coa-criminal-division-annual-report-2014-15.pdf> 25.
50.   Lord Justice Auld, *A Review of the Criminal Courts of England and Wales* (HMSO 2001) 643.
51.   Penny Darbyshire, *Sitting in Judgment: The Working Lives of Judges* (Hart Publishing 2011) 332–3.

It is often said that the basis of an appeal remains the oral argument but even this has changed. Dunn, himself a former Lord Justice, comments that the traditional practice propagated by a senior Court of Appeal judge was:

> I like to come with an open mind to each case. So I never read anything about it, except glance at the judgment and the notice of appeal, before I go into court.[52]

The modern court will not adopt this approach. The judges will have read the papers in advance and one judge will ordinarily be tasked to write the judgment of the court. Interestingly Darbyshire sheds some light on how this decision is reached. Where the trial judge was a puisne judge then the Lord Justice will ordinarily give judgment otherwise the Criminal Appeals Office proposes who gives it.[53] The judge who is to give judgment will take the lead on the questioning of counsel. The amount of work is increased where the judgment of the court is reserved (that is to say, instead of judgment being handed down immediately at the end of the case the judges adjourn for a period of weeks to allow them to conduct research and produce a written judgment that is then handed down).

Unlike an appeal by way of case stated, which is purely an argument as to law, the Court of Appeal has discretion to hear evidence although it is rarely exercised.[54] The principal reason why evidence is rarely heard is that the role of the Court of Appeal is not to conduct a trial but rather to review the trial at first instance and this should not require them to hear much evidence. Indeed their power to hear evidence is effectively restricted to 'fresh evidence' which is defined as evidence that could not have been adduced at the original trial.[55] Where evidence is heard then the courts have to be careful as to what the purpose of the evidence is; it is not to assist the court in determining whether the appellant is guilty or not but rather whether his conviction is safe. It will be seen later that it does not necessarily follow that someone whose conviction is quashed did not necessarily commit the crime for that is a matter that only a trial at first instance, usually through the provision of a jury, can decide. Instead the purpose of the appellate court is to decide whether the conviction is safe or whether there is any doubt as to the guilt of a person; this will usually be found where the court finds that some evidential or legal rule would have affected the jury's deliberations, as at that point it cannot be predicted what the jury may have done.

⚡ WITNESS TESTIMONY

One interesting issue of distinction in the Court of Appeal is that where it decides to hear witness testimony it is quite possible that the court rather than any party will call the witness. In this case a member of the court will examine the witness (although this will not adhere to the principles of examination-in-chief) and then the person will be tendered for cross-examination. If the court decides that it does not want to call the witness but permits a party to adduce the evidence then the traditional pattern arises.

---

52. Robin Dunn, *Sword and Wig: Memoirs of a Lord Justice* (Quiller Press 1993) 234.
53. Penny Darbyshire, *Sitting in Judgment: The Working Lives of Judges* (Hart Publishing, 2011) 336.
54. Andrew Ashworth and Mike Redmayne, *The Criminal Process* (4th edn, OUP 2010) 347.
55. *Criminal Appeal Act 1968*, s 23.

16.3.2.1 Improper deliberations by the jury

It will be remembered from Chapter 15 that there has been concern that some jurors use inappropriate material in their deliberations (15.6.2.4). This is a good example of when the Court of Appeal may need to receive evidence. Where the potential evidence of improper deliberation arises after the verdict has been given then it will be for the Court of Appeal to decide what, if anything, can be done. Sometimes it will be possible to ascertain whether there has been improper deliberation without looking at the deliberations of the jury. This could be because the deliberation took place where it should not (perhaps the most notable example of this being *R v Young*[56]) or because the material shows a real risk of prejudice without needing to enquire into the deliberations of the jury. An example of this is *R v Karakaya*[57] where after the jury had returned a verdict in a rape trial, the jury usher found material that had been printed off the Internet and which must have been brought in by a juror. The material included inaccurate and controversial statements about how rape was treated within the legal system and thus the Court of Appeal ruled that it was not necessary to consider how the material had been used, its very presence in the jury room showed that there was a real risk of prejudice which raised an issue as to the safety of the conviction.

> **II\ Case Box** *R v Young*
>
> *R v Young*[58] was one of the more unusual examples of improper deliberations. In the days when a jury was sent to a hotel overnight, the Court of Appeal accepted evidence that certain members of the jury had used a Ouija board to 'contact' one of the murder victims. The Court of Appeal quashed the conviction on the basis that the jury should not have been deliberating outside of the jury room.

The leading decision on whether a court can consider suspected improper deliberations is that of the House of Lords in *R v Mirza*.[59] *Mirza* was heard at the same time as another case—*Rollock*—and both related to letters received from jurors. Mirza did not speak English and instead relied on an interpreter. Despite being warned not to take this into account a juror complained that a number of jurors had convicted the defendant on racist grounds. In *Rollock* a juror complained that the majority had considered him and a co-defendant at the same time, and not, as instructed, separately. Again a letter was written to that effect.

The House of Lords had the thorny issue of considering how these appeals should be disposed of without prejudicing the secrecy of jury deliberations. The House held there remained a rule that the courts will not receive evidence as to the deliberations of the jury, fearing that to do so would undermine the principle that a verdict ought to be final but also as to do otherwise could interfere with the full and frank discussions that are essential in a jury trial. In both instances the House held that there was no evidence to show a lack of impartiality on behalf of the jury and so they dismissed the

56. [1995] QB 324.
57. [2005] EWCA Crim 346.
58. [1995] QB 324.
59. [2004] 1 AC 1118.

appeal, stating that the letters from the individual jurors were no more than an explanation of how the verdicts were reached and accordingly inadmissible.

Potentially this seems harsh, at least in *Mirza*'s case where, if the juror was correct, there was real bias on behalf of the jury and this would seem to be an abrogation of the jury oath to try matters fairly. This was picked up by the Court of Appeal in *R v Adams* [2007] 1 Cr App R 34 where they ordered an inquiry—and indeed then received witness evidence from the jury—in circumstances where there were allegations of bias. The Court of Appeal was clear *Mirza* did not prevent them from doing so (at p 460), partly because bias is a breach of the jury oath. This decision is to be welcomed and perhaps the better way of looking at the decision in *Mirza* was that the House of Lords was not convinced that there was sufficient evidence to show potential bias.

The House in *Mirza* acknowledged that there are exceptions to the exclusionary rule but that these are premised on the basis that the jurors acted on extraneous influences (see, most notably, the opinion of Lord Hope at p 1158). The question is how would this be proven? Obviously in the examples presented earlier—*Young* and *Karakaya*—there was clear evidence that external influences were applied and so this could be admitted without it breaching the exclusionary rule relating to jury deliberations. This will not always be possible, however. The other crucial point arising from *Mirza* was that the court itself does not breach s 8 by inquiring into the circumstances of how a jury deliberates. Thus the court can hear evidence, including from jurors themselves, if they believe that there are reasons to do so. In most cases this is impractical and where it is thought that there does need to be an investigation into the circumstances of the jury verdict—not what was said but how it was reached, ie whether there were any external influences—then the Court of Appeal relies on the *Criminal Cases Review Commission* (CCRC) to undertake this role.

Section 15 *Criminal Appeal Act 1995* authorizes the Court of Appeal to require the CCRC to make an investigation into any matter directed to it by the court. However, in doing so the CCRC acknowledges that it is treading a fine line because of s 8 *Contempt of Court Act 1981*.[60] The CCRC cannot ask how the jury reached its verdict but can instead ask questions about the circumstances in which that decision was reached, including, for example, whether additional material had been brought in or whether a juror did something that contradicted the good behaviour direction of the judge or their jury oath. The advantage of the CCRC doing this is that they are a statutory, independent body and are thus completely impartial from the case. There is therefore little risk that pressure may be placed on jurors or their answers interpreted in a partisan way. It is obviously a sensitive matter to make these enquiries and the Court of Appeal is slow to direct the CCRC to do so. In 2014–15 four requests were made of the CCRC. This represents an increase on the two requests made in 2013–14, but is still significantly lower than the nine requests made in 2012–13 and the thirteen made in 2010–11.[61] It is not known why there has been an overall reduction although it could partly be as a result of jurors alleging impropriety at an earlier stage (during the initial trial) and trial judges dealing with alleged impropriety promptly.

In considering potential improper deliberations, the courts place considerable faith in the collective responsibility of jurors. In *R v Thompson*[62] the Lord Chief Justice

---

60. 'Interviewing Jurors' presented on the CCRC website.
61. Criminal Cases Review Commission, *Annual Report and Accounts 2014/15* (CCRC 2015) <http://www.ccrc.gov.uk/wp-content/uploads/2015/07/CCRC-Annual-Report-and-Accounts-2014-15.pdf> 17.
62. [2011] 1 WLR 200.

stated that where a juror did something outside of his oath—for example, stated expressly that he was going to decide the case on the basis of racial bias—then the other jurors should report that matter to the judge according to the directions given to them.[63] It can be questioned whether this is necessarily appropriate. The jury experience can be unusual and indeed unsettling for people, especially the formality of proceedings. Relying on jurors to go against one of their own and make a formal report to a judge may be placing too much reliance on the individual resilience of jurors. That said, it is difficult to see an alternative. In *Mirza* the House of Lords was concerned that investigating each allegation of impropriety could be unduly complicated, expensive, and potentially undermine the integrity of the jury. Certainly to do so would place considerable power in the hands of a single juror who could, for whatever reason, cast doubt on a conviction after a trial simply by writing a letter.

QUESTION FOR REFLECTION

How should the courts react when a juror suggests that the verdict may have been reached by improper processes? Are there dangers in investigating whenever a single juror does allege misbehaviour? If allegations are not examined, however, is there a danger that an injustice has happened but that the courts will allow it to pass in order to protect the 'greater good' of the jury trial?

16.3.3 Decision

It has been noted already that the purpose of the appellate court is *not* to decide the guilt or innocence of the appellant although that is how it may be interpreted by some. The basis upon which the court should exercise its powers is to be found in s 2 CAA 1968 which states that the court shall:

> allow an appeal against conviction if they think the conviction is unsafe ... and shall dismiss such appeal in any other case.

This simplified test was introduced in 1995 to replace a previous test that permitted a conviction to be quashed when the conviction was unsafe, unsatisfactory, based on an error of law, or where there was a material irregularity. Whether the change in test means anything substantively different or whether it was simply codifying the original tests into one overarching test has been the subject of debate since it was introduced. At the heart of the discussion is whether the Court of Appeal is able to act as suitable guarantor to prevent miscarriages of justice. In the 1970s to 1990s it would appear the answer was 'no' and some argue that the court was too ready to accept police evidence and too slow to accept allegations of corruption,[64] something that other authors have previously commented upon.[65]

At its most basic, the new test shares with the old test the notion of the safety of the conviction and the Court of Appeal in *R v Graham*[66] stated:

---

63. *R v Thompson* [2011] 1 WLR 200, 203.
64. Andrew Ashworth and Mike Redmayne, *The Criminal Process* (4th edn, OUP 2010) 353.
65. For an illuminating potted history of how the miscarriages of justice in the 1980s led to a 'crisis' for the criminal justice system, read Richard Nobles and David Schiff, *Understanding Miscarriages of Justice: Law, Media and the Inevitability of a Crisis* (OUP 2000) 117–49, esp 124–8.
66. [1997] 1 Cr App R 302, 308 (Lord Bingham CJ).

[The test] is plainly intended to concentrate attention on one question: whether, in light of any arguments raised or evidence adduced on appeal, the Court of Appeal considers a conviction unsafe. If the Court is satisfied that, despite any misdirection of law or irregularity in the conduct of the trial or any fresh evidence, that the conviction is safe, the Court will dismiss the appeal.[67]

Notwithstanding this, it is apparent that the conduct of the trial will be a central feature in any appeal and in *R v Togher*[68] the Court of Appeal decided that the new test effectively encapsulated the old tests and that where there was a material irregularity this may lead to the safety of the conviction being undermined and requiring the appeal to be allowed. This case was distinguished in *R v Llewellyn*[69] although only to the extent that it was said that if the procedural error forming the basis of the appeal was known at the time of trial but not the subject of any objection then it should not normally form the basis of an appeal. To an extent this is an application of the usual rule that the Court of Appeal will not revisit issues that *should* have been addressed at first instance but it can be argued that this is slightly harsh as there may be tactical reasons why counsel does not raise an objection at first instance.

In 2006 the government consulted on changing s 2 to prevent it quashing a conviction where the evidence suggested that the defendant was guilty despite any errors of law that had been made by judges.[70] The proposals were not welcomed but the government sought to introduce the change in the (then) *Criminal Justice and Immigration Bill*. The proposed clauses would have prevented the Court of Appeal from quashing a conviction where there was no reasonable doubt as to guilt. The clauses were not, however, supported in Parliament and they were withdrawn before the Act received Royal Assent.

527

16.3.3.1 European Convention on Human Rights

In Chapter 5 it was noted that the courts are expressly considered public authorities within the meaning of s 6 *Human Rights Act 1998* (HRA 1998) and accordingly this means they must give effect to the convention rights of an individual. Article 6 of the *European Convention on Human Rights* (ECHR) provides that everyone has the right to a fair trial. Whilst it was noted that Article 34 does not expressly form part of the 1998 Act[71] this is, in part, because HRA 1998 is considered to be the practical application of Article 34 and s 8 states that a court may provide 'such relief or remedy ... within its powers as it considers just and reasonable' for a breach of the Convention. What should the remedy be for someone who has suffered an unfair trial? Should it quash the conviction even if the court considers that the person was, in fact, guilty? In other words, should a finding of a contravention of Article 6 automatically lead to a finding that a person's conviction is unsafe?

The answer appears to be a qualified 'yes'. In *Togher* the Court of Appeal considered the impact of HRA 1998 and were clear that unfairness could undermine the safety of a conviction, something that the court had earlier stated in *R v Rowe, Davis*

67. [1997] 1 Cr App R 302.
68. [2001] 1 Cr App R 33.
69. [2001] EWCA Crim 1555.
70. Home Office, *Quashing Convictions—Report of a review by the Home Secretary, Lord Chancellor and Attorney-General: A Consultation Paper* (Home Office 2006).
71. Jason Coppel, and Michael Supperstone, 'Judicial Review after the Human Rights Act 1998' [1999] 3 *European Human Rights Law Review* 301, 307.

and Johnson[72] which was an appeal that considered the safety of a conviction after the European Court of Human Rights (ECtHR) had considered that their Article 6 rights had been infringed.[73] However, Ashworth and Redmayne note that the position cannot be that simple and cite the example of Robert Thompson and Jon Venables, two schoolboys who were convicted for the murder of a toddler known as Jamie Bulger.[74] They note that the ECtHR had held that there had been a breach of Article 6 in respect of their trial[75] but that it had never been seriously argued that they were *not* the killers or that the breach of Article 6 cast doubt on the safety of their conviction. They argue, therefore, that quashing a conviction need not be the appropriate remedy[76] and the courts have accepted this logic and in *R v Williams*[77] the Court of Appeal accepted this logic when they held that a breach of Article 6(2), breach of the presumption of innocence, would not automatically undermine the safety of a conviction. The submission of Ashworth and Redmayne together with the decisions of the Court of Appeal must be correct and are probably compatible with s 8 HRA 1998 which states that a court must provide the most effective remedy. Not every breach of Article 6 may necessarily require a conviction to be quashed in that this may not be the effective remedy where the safety of the conviction is not compromised; alternative remedies (eg financial compensation or a declaration that a person's rights have been infringed) may be more appropriate and in line with s 8. However, a finding of a breach of Article 6 (the right to a fair trial) must at least lead to the investigation of whether an appeal should be allowed given that the procedural process would appear relevant to the safety of any conviction.

16.3.3.2 'Lurking doubt'

It would be thought that s 2 CAA 1968 was quite specific and that given that the Court of Appeal is a statutory body it should not be able to go beyond the remit of its statutory jurisdiction. However, recently the court has begun to accept that it does have residual power and brought into effect a remedy previously used by the court for Criminal Appeals, that of quashing a conviction as a result of a 'lurking doubt'. In *R v B*[78] the court explained it thus:

> [T]here remains in this Court a residual discretion to set aside a conviction if we feel that it is unsafe or unfair to allow it to stand. This is so even when the trial process itself cannot be faulted.[79]

Thus the court is stating that even though statute sets out its jurisdiction it can continue to access the inherent jurisdictions of the court, in part because of its role as a senior court. This was not always the view it took and in *R v F*[80] a different constitution of the court held that the concept of 'lurking doubt' was no longer applicable following the change to the single test for appeals. Smith, in an insightful commentary, questions the decision in *F* arguing that the single appellate test was simply codifying

---

72. [2001] 1 Cr App R 115.
73. See *Rowe and Davis v United Kingdom* (2000) 30 EHRR 1.
74. Andrew Ashworth and Mike Redmayne, *The Criminal Process* (4th edn, OUP 2010) 356.
75. See *T v UK; V v UK* (2000) 30 EHRR 121.
76. Andrew Ashworth and Mike Redmayne, *The Criminal Process* (4th edn, OUP 2010) 356–7.
77. [2001] EWCA Crim 932.
78. [2003] 2 Cr App R 13.
79. [2003] 2 Cr App R 13, 204 (Lord Woolf CJ).
80. The Times, 20 October 1999.

existing legislation and accordingly the 'lurking doubt' concept remained.[81] Certainly there is no reason why the single test should have abolished the 'lurking doubt' concept as the argument is that if the court have a doubt as to whether a person is guilty then his conviction cannot be safe. In *R v B*[82] and the Court Martial Appeals Court[83] it was stated:

> There can be no doubt that the lurking doubt notion ... continues to be a tool available to this Court. It is plainly an application of the test of unsafety of a conviction, as it is now expressed in splendid isolation in section 2 of the Criminal Appeal Act 1968 as amended.[84]

This is the most accurate position and accordingly a court, even when faced with no apparent procedural impropriety, can set aside a conviction where it believes that it is in the interests of justice to do so.

16.3.4 Frivolous appeals

It was noted earlier that at Crown Court a person who appeals against either his conviction or sentence can have his original sentence increased (see 16.2.1). The Court of Appeal does not have this power as the ability to increase a sentence was abolished in 1966 with the formation of the Court of Appeal (Criminal Division). However, the court can order that time spent in gaol pending an appeal can be disregarded for the purposes of early release, in other words ensuring that a sentence is de facto increased as a result of appealing. This process is known as the 'loss of time' provisions.[85]

Zander notes that these provisions were used in the 1970s by the Lord Chief Justice to ensure that frivolous appeals were not brought.[86] There was an impression that the appellate rules were so relaxed that nothing was to be lost by appealing against a conviction, especially where the defendant had been imprisoned. If the gamble paid off the person would be released, whereas if it did not the person continued his or her sentence in prison. The use of the 'loss of time' provisions ensured that those in prison were more careful in bringing hopeless appeals as their sentence was, in effect, frozen during the appellate process even though they continued to be incarcerated. In the immediate years following the *Practice Note* the number of appeals almost halved[87] but some question whether it is appropriate to use this power. Ashworth and Redmayne argue that the provisions serve as a de facto deterrent to an individual exercising their legal right[88] although the court would almost certainly contest this allegation noting that, in effect, no loss of time would be ordered where an appeal was brought on the advice of counsel,[89] the argument being that such appeals are not frivolous.

In recent times it has been suggested that the courts were reluctant to order loss of time. In *R v K*[90] the Court of Appeal noted, however, that the provisions are actually

81. John Smith, 'Commentary on *R v F*' [1999] *Criminal Law Review* 306, 307.
82. [2005] EWCA Crim 63.
83. In effect the Court of Appeal sitting under another name: the Court Martial Appeal Court hears appeals from courts martial, ie courts that try members of HM Forces for breaching laws while in service.
84. [2005] EWCA Crim 63 [19] (Auld LJ).
85. *Criminal Appeal Act 1968*, s 29.
86. Michael Zander, *Cases and Materials on the English Legal System* (10th edn, OUP 2007).
87. Michael Zander, *Cases and Materials on the English Legal System* (10th edn, OUP 2007).
88. Andrew Ashworth and Mike Redmayne, *The Criminal Process* (4th edn, OUP 2010) 341.
89. See *Practice Direction (Crime: Sentence: Loss of Time)* [1980] 1 WLR 270.
90. [2005] EWCA Crim 955.

rarely invoked, with only four orders being made in 1998, two in 1999, none in 2000, and two in 2001.[91] It was not known why so few orders were given, whether it was the judges simply not using their power or whether it was concerns that the provisions could cause prisoners to be reluctant to risk an appeal.[92]

The Court of Appeal appears to have had a change of heart, however, and in 2014 quite publicly and forcefully stated that it would use its powers. In *R v Gray and others*[93] the Court of Appeal, presided over by the Vice-President, Hallett LJ, decided to remind everyone that the loss of time provisions applied. Hallett LJ stated: 'unmeritorious renewal applications take up a wholly disproportionate amount of staff and judicial resources in preparation and hearing time. They also waste significant sums of public money.'[94] Her Ladyship noted that whilst the court had the power to make an order for costs this was usually not effective[95] and that the more appropriate remedy is to order the loss of time served.

Hallett LJ was clear that 'in every case where the court is presented with an unmeritorious application, consideration should be given to exercising these powers'[96] and promptly did so in the series of cases that were presented. It is obviously an example of the courts losing their patience with offenders who simply try their luck with appeals.

It will be remembered that Ashworth and Redmayne disapprove of the loss of time rules and believe it is inappropriate but it is worth noting that the ECtHR has held that the 'loss of time' provisions do not breach either Articles 5 or 6,[97] although it should also be noted that the ECtHR accepted that Article 6 was engaged and, accordingly, representation as to the loss of time should be permitted. Ashworth and Redmayne disapprove of this decision[98] but the decision appears to be a common-sense approach to the issue and recognizes that the courts should have the right to impose a 'sanction' on those who try to abuse the provisions.

16.3.5 **The judgment**

One point of note about judgments of the Court of Appeal is that, unlike civil appeals or civil or criminal appeals in the Supreme Court, only a single judgment is ordinarily given in the Criminal Division, particularly where the conviction is to be quashed. It has been reported that the reason for this is that the public should not be left in doubt as to whether the defendant is, in fact, guilty which may arise if it were a majority decision and the public were aware of the number of judges who believed the offender remained guilty.[99] It is also notable that most judgments are given *ex tempore* (that is to say orally immediately after the hearing rather than it being reserved) and this appears to be a deliberate policy so as to avoid further delays.[100]

91. [2005] EWCA Crim 955 [18].
92. See Andrew Ashworth and Mike Redmayne, *The Criminal Process* (4th edn, OUP 2010).
93. [2014] EWCA Crim 2372.
94. [2014] EWCA Crim 2372 [2].
95. [2014] EWCA Crim 2372 [7].
96. [2014] EWCA Crim 2372 [10].
97. *Monell v United Kingdom* (1988) 10 EHRR 205.
98. Andrew Ashworth and Mike Redmayne, *The Criminal Process* (4th edn, OUP 2010) 342.
99. Penny Darbyshire, *Sitting in Judgment: The Working Lives of Judges* (Hart Publishing 2011) 339.
100. Penny Darbyshire, *Sitting in Judgment: The Working Lives of Judges* (Hart Publishing 2011) 339.

16.4 Appeal following an acquittal

Until recently the prosecution had extremely limited options open to them when faced with an acquittal at the Crown Court. To an extent it was thought that this was less problematic because of the usual rule of criminal justice that it is better for a guilty man to be acquitted than for an innocent man to be convicted and gaoled. There was also the additional issue that the vast majority of acquittals arise not from any error of law but as a result of a jury acquitting the defendant and it was thought that the jury had the right to acquit even when they thought, in law, a person was guilty because society has the right to decide when acts should be punished.

However, some trials will lead to an acquittal not because the jury have acquitted the defendant but because the trial judge has made a ruling of law that has the effect of terminating the case. It will be seen that there are two types of rulings: first, when a judge decides that the trial should be halted (eg upon a submission of no case to answer: see 15.2) and the second when a ruling by the judge as to the admissibility of evidence is such that the prosecution decides that it is no longer able to continue with the prosecution (and the prosecution are under a legal duty to continue to review the decision to prosecute during the course of the trial). It will be remembered that although the Crown Court does not create precedent, where a High Court judge sits his rulings of law can form persuasive precedent (see 3.4.1.5) and clearly there is a danger that if such a judge does make an error of law and this is cited to other Crown Court judges then a series of acquittals will arise with little opportunity for the appellate courts to correct this error of law.

Eventually, therefore, it was decided that there should exist a system of referring matters to the Court of Appeal and in 1972 the system of Attorney-General's References was created.[101] However, pressure grew for the system to be extended and the *MacPherson Report* into the tragic death and subsequent investigation of the murder of Stephen Lawrence recommended that consideration should be given to whether prosecutions should be permitted after appeal and identified two distinct areas: the first is the notion of 'double jeopardy' which prohibits a defendant from being retried for the offence he is acquitted of even if fresh evidence of his guilt comes to light. The second, and for our immediate purpose more relevant, was the notion of an appeal which could take place immediately after the acquittal in the same way as with appeals from conviction, a successful application for which would lead to an immediate retrial. The government asked the Law Commission to consider this and in a report[102] they recommended there should be a partial relaxation of both rules. Auld LJ, in his report, followed this up by suggesting that the rules should be relaxed but he went further since here the Law Commission thought the rule should be restricted to murder alone. Auld argued for a more widespread relaxation.[103]

Eventually the government legislated to introduce a (limited) right of appeal through the CJA 2003. However, the right of appeal has not interfered with the right of the Attorney-General to bring a reference to the Court of Appeal and thus both will be considered.

---

101. *Criminal Justice Act 1972*, s 36.
102. Law Commission, *Law Commission Report No 267: Double Jeopardy and Prosecution Appeals* (HMSO 2001).
103. Lord Justice Auld, *A Review of the Criminal Courts of England and Wales* (HMSO 2001) 633–4.

16.4.1 Reference to the Court of Appeal

As noted earlier, the Attorney-General has had the right to refer a matter to the Court of Appeal since 1972. This type of reference differs quite radically from the sentencing reference in that although both require a specified offence and the personal approval of a Law Officer, the reference following acquittal takes the form of a de facto hypothetical appeal.

The outcome of the reference will make no difference to the acquittal of the defendant; even if the Court of Appeal agrees that the judge made an error of law and that he should never have been acquitted, the person will remain acquitted and protected from any subsequent trial for the same offence. Although the statute does not expressly say so, it is submitted that where the prosecution refers a matter to the court rather than use its new powers under the CJA 2003 it would be unjust to allow the prosecution subsequently to use its powers to apply for the removal of the restriction of double jeopardy (see 16.4.3) unless new issues are raised that could not have been considered at the time of trial because to do so would be unjust since the prosecution could have appealed instead of referring the matter to the court.

What is the point of a referral to the Court of Appeal if it does not lead to any change in the status of the acquittal? The simple answer is one of precedent: whilst the ruling of a High Court judge may be persuasive for other judges, a ruling of the Court of Appeal is binding on the trial courts and it can thus ensure that any error of law can be corrected. This is, therefore, an important way of correcting the law following a dubious decision of first instance. It is important to note that the problem must be real, ie arising from a case, and it has been held that there is no power for the Attorney-General to refer a purely hypothetical point of law.[104]

Auld believed that even the extension of prosecution rights of appeal would not remove the justification for Attorney-General's References[105] and this must be correct. There will be any number of reasons why an appeal from an acquittal may not be possible, not least the safeguards built into the system (see 16.4.3) and the impact it could have on an *individual* defendant and the Attorney-General's Reference system continues to be the most appropriate system for dealing with such matters. That said, only one reference has been made under s 36 since 2010[106] which may call into question the necessity of retaining the power. However, they were never common and allowing the power to remain is probably prudent in case a situation does arise which requires a Reference rather than formal appeal (for example the Crown may decide that it is not in the public interest to appeal a decision to terminate a case but does wish the point of law to be clarified).

16.4.2 Prosecution rights of appeal

Granting prosecution rights of appeal has been somewhat controversial even though it has long been accepted for those tried summarily. One objection to the granting of such a right is because of the distress that could be caused to a person acquitted to then have the possibility of a conviction held over him, but this is to an extent a false argument. Notwithstanding the point about magistrates' courts it completely ignores the

---

104.   *Attorney-General's Reference (No 4 of 1979)* (1980) 71 Cr App R 341.
105.   Lord Justice Auld, *A Review of the Criminal Courts of England and Wales* (HMSO 2001) 637.
106.   *Attorney General's Reference (No. 94 of 2014)* [2014] EWCA Crim 2752.

reality of the pre-CJA 2003 appellate system. If a person had been convicted at the end of his trial and imprisoned but successfully appealed to the Court of Appeal he would have his conviction quashed and be released from prison. If, however, the prosecution appealed to the (then) House of Lords (something they were entitled to do; they were simply not permitted to appeal to the Court of Appeal) and the House overturned the acquittal then the defendant was obliged to surrender himself to custody and serve his sentence. For completeness it should be noted that this remains the case today—the prosecution are able to appeal to the Supreme Court where they believe that the Court of Appeal has erred in law when quashing a conviction.

The scheme contained within Part 9 CJA 2003 marks a radical departure from the historical position although not as radical as had been suggested. Auld was concerned with the issue of 'perverse acquittals' which he took to mean those where a defendant was acquitted in circumstances that were clearly contrary to the evidence presented.[107] However, this was denounced by many groups, not least because juries represent society and have the right to decide whether people deserve punishment[108] and the government rejected this proposal. Part 9 contains two distinct appeals: appeals against terminal rulings and appeals against evidential rulings. The Act also expressly states that no appeal can be brought against a decision of the judge to discharge a jury or against any ruling where a right of appeal exercisable by the prosecution already exists.[109]

16.4.2.1 Terminal rulings

The first, and perhaps most controversial, change is that the prosecution can appeal against certain terminal rulings. Dennis notes that the term 'terminal ruling' has always been used when describing this provision even though CJA 2003 does not itself use this specific term.[110] However, it is a good summary of what the position is as s 58 permits an appeal to be brought against a decision to accept a submission of no case to answer or a ruling that would inevitably lead to the acquittal of a person. That it will lead to an acquittal is implicit within s 58(8)–(9) which states that if leave to appeal is refused or the appeal is abandoned or unsuccessful then the defendant will be formally acquitted. The essence of this condition (discussed later) is that the prosecution would only appeal a ruling that leaves them in the position of offering no evidence against the defendant (which will lead to his acquittal) as to do otherwise risks the offender being acquitted in any event.

The prosecution must at the time of the ruling they believe will be terminal, either indicate that they are going to appeal or request an adjournment so as to consider an appeal.[111] In *CPS v C*[112] the Court of Appeal held that the requirements under s 58 were mandatory and thus if the prosecution are denied an adjournment to consider their options they must *immediately* indicate to the judge that they intend to appeal *and* must provide the assurance under s 58(8) that they agree that if the appeal is unsuccessful then the defendants are to be acquitted. If either of these steps does not

---

107.   Lord Justice Auld, *A Review of the Criminal Courts of England and Wales* (HMSO 2001) 636.
108.   Liberty, *Liberty's Briefing on the Criminal Justice Bill for the House of Lords* (Liberty 2003) <http://www.liberty-human-rights.org.uk/pdfs/policy03/crim-jus-lords-june-2003.pdf> 94.
109.   *Criminal Justice Act 2003*, s 57.
110.   Ian Dennis, 'Prosecution Appeals and Retrial for Serious Offences' [2004] *Criminal Law Review* 619, 624.
111.   *Criminal Justice Act 2003*, s 58(4).
112.   [2009] EWCA Crim 2614.

occur then there is no jurisdiction to hear the appeal.[113] In *R v M*[114] the necessity of strictly adhering to these steps was reinforced by the Court of Appeal. In this case a judge acceded to a submission of no case to answer. Counsel for the prosecution asked whether the judge had borne in mind a particular statutory provision and the judge replied 'yes' and then immediately indicated to the defendant that he was to be discharged. There then followed an adjournment of ten minutes after which the prosecution stated they wished to appeal against the terminatory ruling. The Court of Appeal held that the procedure within s 58 had not been satisfied and that immediately meant just that: counsel for the prosecution should have immediately asked for an adjournment to consider the possibility of an appeal or instantly complied with the requirements of s 58, the ten minutes that elapsed were fatal to any possible appeal.[115] One possible reason for this decision is that the judge had adjourned adjudicating on the submission of no case to answer overnight and so counsel for the prosecution could have anticipated losing the submission and potentially on what grounds.[116] *M* reinforces the decision of *C* that prosecuting counsel must be aware of the need for speed in deciding whether they can appeal and that the procedural requirements must be complied with precisely.

If an appeal is to be brought then it is possible that the appeal could be expedited.[117] The Act suggests that only when an appeal is not to be expedited can a jury be discharged[118] but it is submitted that this must be read in the context of the general powers of trial judges which include the dismissal of a jury when it is not possible for a person to gain a fair trial. The purpose behind this is no doubt to ensure that lengthy trials are not started again if the prosecution appeal succeeds (if the appeal fails then, of course, no jury will be required as the defendant is acquitted) but it must be seriously questioned whether a jury could continue. Whilst they cannot, presumably, be told that an appeal has been lodged (as that would appear to be highly prejudicial) the Act does not make clear what an 'expedited' appeal is. If the expedited appeal takes longer than a few days then it is submitted that a jury will inevitably speculate as to why the trial has been adjourned for a period of several days or weeks. It has been speculated that one reason for this power is that the ruling may be in relation to only certain counts on the indictment and, therefore, the trial could take place on counts not related to the appeal.[119] This would only partially solve the problem as there would no doubt be speculation, but judges are used to telling juries that a count has been withdrawn from them. The difficulty is, however, that this would ordinarily lead to a formal acquittal and thus a knowledgeable jury would be able to identify why a count has been withdrawn rather than the defendant being formally acquitted of it. It would seem more straightforward to discharge the jury pending any appeal and this would be the more likely scenario.

The Court of Appeal has three options open to it when determining an appeal:[120]

---

113. See also *R v LSA* [2009] EWCA Crim 1034.
114. [2012] EWCA Crim 792.
115. [2012] EWCA Crim 792 [28].
116. [2012] EWCA Crim 792 [29].
117. *Criminal Justice Act 2003*, s 59.
118. *Criminal Justice Act 2003*, s 59(3).
119. Richard Taylor, Martin Wasik, and Roger Leng, *Blackstone's Guide to the Criminal Justice Act 2003* (OUP 2004) 88.
120. *Criminal Justice Act 2003*, s 61.

- **Uphold the ruling.** This will lead to the acquittal of the defendant on those counts that are affected by the ruling.

- **Reverse the ruling.** If the court does this then it may order that the trial is resumed or started afresh with a new jury.

- **Vary the ruling.** It may be that the prosecution are only partially successful. When this happens the Court of Appeal has the right to decide whether to acquit the defendant or to order the trial to continue/begin again.

Unlike in respect of appeals by defendants, the Court of Appeal has a much more limited discretion in deciding whether to overturn a ruling; it may only do so when it is wrong in law, involved an error of law, or was irrational[121] and this draws an immediate comparison to judicial review[122] and this will certainly restrict the use of the power as irrational is a high threshold; merely disagreeing with the decision or preferring an alternative decision will not suffice.

The Court of Appeal was only permitted to order the resumption of a trial or order a fresh trial when it considered that it was in the interests of justice to do so. The *Criminal Justice and Immigration Act 2008* (CJIA 2008) amended this provision and now requires the Court of Appeal to only acquit the defendant when it is satisfied that an offender could not receive a fair trial if the matter was resumed or a new trial resumed.[123] However, the Court of Appeal, albeit *in dicta*, has suggested that the interests of justice remain valid. In *R v A*[124] the court ruled that whilst Parliament has altered s 61(5), it is notable that the Court of Appeal must grant leave (permission) before an appeal may be brought. The court suggested that the wider interests of justice must be considered when deciding whether to permit leave to be granted.[125] Their Lordships suggest that if it would never be in the interests of justice for a new trial to take place then leave will simply not be granted. On a semantic level the decision is correct in that leave is required and this is frequently granted or denied after a full hearing, but it would also seem that this is an attempt by the Court of Appeal to circumvent the intentions of Parliament. Such an approach could not be taken if, as with most defence cases, the issue of leave was dealt with separately to the determination of the appeal.

Perhaps surprisingly no statistics are published on the use of the power under s 58 and so it is not possible to state how many applications for leave are made and how many applications are successful. It would obviously be of interest to those within the justice system if such statistics were published and there would seem no reason why the CPS or the *Court Statistics (Quarterly)* could not make this available.

16.4.2.2 Evidentiary rulings

The second type of appeal is that which relates to evidentiary rulings. It should be noted here that the sections relevant to evidentiary rulings in the Criminal Justice Act 2003 are not yet in force, however, we will still consider these provisions. This type of appeal owes its background more to Auld as the Law Commission had rejected the

---

121. *Criminal Justice Act 2003*, s 67.
122. Ian Dennis, 'Prosecution Appeals and Retrial for Serious Offences' [2004] *Criminal Law Review* 619, 624.
123. *Criminal Justice Act 2003*, s 61(5).
124. [2008] EWCA Crim 2186.
125. [2008] EWCA Crim 2186 [9].

idea of an appeal against anything other than a terminatory ruling.[126] However, s 62 permits evidentiary rulings to be appealed in certain circumstances. There are a number of differences between s 58 and s 62 appeals. The first is that the range of offences is more limited. Section 58 appeals can be brought in any case tried on indictment whereas s 62 appeals can only be brought in those cases that have been prescribed.[127] The second is that the appeal can only be brought in respect of a ruling that takes place before the opening of the defence case[128] and this, in effect, limits the matter to rulings on prosecution applications although the vast majority are likely to be dealt with at the Plea and Directions Hearing stage. The third, and perhaps most significant, is that there is no requirement that the evidential ruling would be a terminal ruling: indeed if the result of the evidential ruling was to cause the acquittal of the person then it is more likely that s 62 would be the more appropriate appeal. That said, an appeal is only possible where it significantly weakens the prosecution case[129] although quite what this means in practice is open to interpretation.[130]

The final difference between the sections is that an unsuccessful appeal will not automatically lead to the acquittal of the defendant. The Court of Appeal has the right to uphold, vary, or reverse the ruling made by the trial judge, and can decide whether to allow the trial to continue or start again.[131] It may only acquit the defendant where the prosecution state that they do not wish the prosecution to continue,[132] presumably in circumstances where the Court of Appeal either upholds or varies the ruling.

Areas of similarity between ss 58 and 62 are that appeals may be expedited[133] and the grounds upon which the Court of Appeal can determine the appeal remain the same.[134]

It has been suggested that the case for the prosecution rights of appeal is strong[135] and, since they are restricted solely to decisions of the law by the judge, this is probably true. Trial judges are not immune from mistakes and if, as has been suggested, the purpose of the criminal justice system is to enforce the criminal law[136] then the public have the right to expect that mistakes that occur before the final determination of an appeal can be put right. The prosecution are sometimes thwarted by perverse or incorrect rulings and until now had no avenue available to them: the defendant would be acquitted. It was difficult to identify how that necessarily served the best interests of the criminal justice system.

16.4.3 Double jeopardy

It was noted in Chapter 12 (12.7.1) that at the time of plea, a person can enter two special pleas known as *autrefois convict* and *autrefois acquit*, that being the person

126. Ian Dennis, 'Prosecution Appeals and Retrial for Serious Offences' [2004] *Criminal Law Review* 619, 624–5.
127. *Criminal Justice Act 2003*, sch 4.
128. *Criminal Justice Act 2003*, s 62(2).
129. *Criminal Justice Act 2003*, s 63(2).
130. Ian Dennis, 'Prosecution Appeals and Retrial for Serious Offences' [2004] *Criminal Law Review* 619, 622.
131. *Criminal Justice Act 2003*, s 66.
132. *Criminal Justice Act 2003*, s 66(2)(c).
133. *Criminal Justice Act 2003*, s 64.
134. *Criminal Justice Act 2003*, s 67.
135. Ian Dennis, 'Prosecution Appeals and Retrial for Serious Offences' [2004] *Criminal Law Review* 619, 626.
136. Ian Dennis, 'Rethinking Double Jeopardy: Justice and Finality in Criminal Process' [2000] *Criminal Law Review* 933, 945.

has previously been tried and either convicted or acquitted. Traditionally this was a barrier to any subsequent proceedings but CJA 2003 has altered this position and it is now possible for a person who has previously been acquitted to be retried for the offence. This differs from a prosecution appeal in two ways. The first is that it is not an immediate remedy in the way that an appeal is. Where the prosecution believe that a judge has erred in law and that this resulted in the termination of proceedings prior to the jury retiring, then the more appropriate response will be to use the powers under Part 9 CJA 2003 (see 16.4.2). The second is that a person can be retried even if it was the decision of a jury to acquit the defendant whereas an appeal is only possible from decisions by the judge.

It has to be recognized that the proposals to modify double jeopardy were, and are, extremely controversial as it was considered to be a long-standing freedom,[137] although, interestingly, it is not an absolute right in terms of either the ECHR or the EU *Charter of Fundamental Rights*.[138] The pressure for reform of the rule appears to stem from the *Macpherson Report* into the death of Stephen Lawrence.[139] Stephen Lawrence was a black teenager who was murdered in an unprovoked racist killing. The subsequent investigation by the police was flawed and led to the acquittal of those who were accused of his murder. The Macpherson Inquiry examined all issues surrounding the case, including allegations that the police themselves were racist in the handling of the investigation, and also the conduct of the prosecution. Recommendation 38 of the *Macpherson Report* suggested that the protection of double jeopardy should be removed. This was followed by a Law Commission report which held that there was an arguable case for the restriction of the right of double jeopardy but only to murder. This, in turn, was examined by Auld in his review of the criminal justice system and he ultimately questioned why the power should be restricted to murder and argued for a wider restriction.[140] Ultimately this led to the introduction of the power contained in Part 10 CJA 2003.

It is important to note that the double jeopardy rule is not totally abrogated as it applies only to specified offences (although the number of offences is extremely wide and can be added to without the need for primary legislation).[141] Also, it is not just for the prosecuting authorities to decide to bring a new prosecution; they must first seek permission to do so and for the acquittal to be, in effect, quashed.[142] The application must be brought with the personal consent of the DPP[143] and is heard by the Court of Appeal (Criminal Division).

The language of the statute appears to suggest that the Court of Appeal has little say in whether the acquittal should be quashed, with s 77(1)(a) stating that if the conditions are met, then the court 'must make the order applied for'. However, it is not necessarily so straightforward since the second of the two conditions is that it is

---

137. See, for example, Liberty, *Liberty's Briefing on the Criminal Justice Bill for the House of Lords* (Liberty 2003) <http://www.liberty-human-rights.org.uk/pdfs/policy03/crim-jus-lords-june-2003.pdf> 15–16, and Ian Dennis, 'Prosecution Appeals and Retrial for Serious Offences' [2004] *Criminal Law Review* 619, 619.

138. Ian Dennis, 'Prosecution Appeals and Retrial for Serious Offences' [2004] *Criminal Law Review* 619, 636–7.

139. Richard Taylor, Martin Wasik, and Roger Leng, *Blackstone's Guide to the Criminal Justice Act 2003* (OUP 2004) 96–7.

140. Lord Justice Auld, *A Review of the Criminal Courts of England and Wales* (HMSO 2001) 631–4.

141. Richard Taylor, Martin Wasik, and Roger Leng, *Blackstone's Guide to the Criminal Justice Act* 2003 (OUP 2004) 100–2.

142. *Criminal Justice Act 2003*, s 76.

143. Ian Dennis, 'Prosecution Appeals and Retrial for Serious Offences' [2004] *Criminal Law Review* 619, 626.

in the interests of justice for the acquittal to be quashed.[144] This quite clearly provides the court with discretion as they can take almost any matter into consideration when deciding what is in the interests of justice. In tandem with this is the first condition which is that an acquittal can be quashed only where there is 'new and compelling' evidence to suggest that the acquittal should be set aside.[145]

It has been suggested that the need for compelling new evidence is directly linked to the justification for permitting an exception to the double jeopardy rule in that new evidence may cast doubt on the efficiency of the criminal justice system.[146] In other words, new evidence (for example, DNA evidence which was perhaps unavailable at the time of the trial)[147] may demonstrate that the criminal justice system has failed a victim and society, and that if the purpose of the criminal justice system is to enforce the criminal law then perhaps such a tainted acquittal should be quashed in the same way that a tainted conviction is.[148] Setting aside the objections to any interference with double jeopardy this point is well made. Whilst there are many reasons why the quashing of a conviction will be preferable to the quashing of an acquittal, it cannot be doubted that there have been some acquittals that, for any number of reasons, are extremely dubious and where the criminal justice system appears to be as faulty as it did at the height of the miscarriages of justice era. The more salient question, however, is whether this justification can permit a draconian change to a fundamental right to the finality of a trial.

It is clear from the wording of the statute that the procedure is considered to be exceptional, and the fact that there are so many stages to any retrial perhaps demonstrates this. In terms of new evidence, it has been noted that although this takes the form of evidence that was not *used* at trial, the suggestion is that the mere oversight or negligence of a prosecutor in not using the evidence at the trial would not be sufficient to justify quashing an appeal.[149] The Act does not, however, require the court to consider whether this would have an impact on the acquittal[150] and to this extent it may be contrasted with, for example, appeals against conviction by a convicted person where the court must consider the safety of the conviction. However, it is submitted that the court will undoubtedly consider this issue when considering the 'interests of justice' as the potential impact of the evidence must, it is submitted, be a factor.

A criticism of the proposal to relax the rule of double jeopardy was that it could undermine the finality of decisions, leaving those acquitted with the constant nagging worry that they would never be left in peace by the authorities[151] but the Act includes two quite significant safeguards (independent of those discussed earlier) against repeated investigations. The first is that the timing of any application to quash an acquittal is crucial since, by statute, the prosecution may only make an application

144. *Criminal Justice Act 2003*, s 79.
145. *Criminal Justice Act 2003*, s 78.
146. Ian Dennis, 'Rethinking Double Jeopardy: Justice and Finality in Criminal Process' [2000] *Criminal Law Review* 933, 945, and Ian Dennis, 'Prosecution Appeals and Retrial for Serious Offences' [2004] *Criminal Law Review* 619, 631.
147. Richard Taylor, Martin Wasik, and Roger Leng, *Blackstone's Guide to the Criminal Justice Act 2003* (OUP 2004) 105.
148. Ian Dennis, 'Rethinking Double Jeopardy: Justice and Finality in Criminal Process' [2000] *Criminal Law Review* 933, 945.
149. Ian Dennis, 'Prosecution Appeals and Retrial for Serious Offences' [2004] *Criminal Law Review* 619, 633.
150. Ian Dennis, 'Prosecution Appeals and Retrial for Serious Offences' [2004] *Criminal Law Review* 619, 634.
151. Liberty, *Liberty's Briefing on the Criminal Justice Bill for the House of Lords* (Liberty 2003) <http://www.liberty-human-rights.org.uk/pdfs/policy03/crim-jus-lords-june-2003.pdf> 16.

against an acquittal once.[152] It is important to note that the statute expressly states only one *application* and not one order quashing the conviction. Accordingly, if the application is rejected then that is the end of the matter even if, in future years, further compelling evidence is adduced. Similarly, if the retrial ends in a further acquittal (other than in circumstances whereby a prosecution appeal under Part 9 of the Act can be brought) then no further applications can be brought. The second is that investigations into the acquitted persons are constrained by the Act.[153] The Act restricts the power of arrest, search, and seizure in connection with an acquitted person, permitting it only with the written application of the DPP. Further, the application can only be made by someone of chief-officer rank[154] which ensures that only the most significant cases are likely ever to be the subject of any application.

‖\ Case Box William Dunlop

The first application under Part 10 CJA 2003 was made in November 2005 when the DPP gave personal consent to apply to the Court of Appeal for an order quashing the acquittal of William Dunlop for the murder of Julie Hogg.[155] The murder of Julie Hogg had been a cause célèbre in the North-East of England and, to an extent, the wider United Kingdom for many years. Dunlop had been accused of the murder and had stood trial twice, testifying each time (denying the allegation), but the juries could not reach a conclusion and he was formally acquitted.

In 2000 he was charged, and convicted, of perjury following a confession he made to a prisoner that he did, in fact, kill Hogg. In 2005 the DPP applied to the Court of Appeal presumably, in part, on the basis that the 'confession' was new and compelling evidence (it has been suggested that admissions by defendants are likely to be fruitful forms of new evidence).[156]

The application was granted and in 2006 Dunlop pleaded guilty to murder and became the first person to be convicted of an offence having previously been acquitted. In October 2006 he was sentenced to life imprisonment.

One issue that will need to be raised in any subsequent trial will be, what will the jury be told? In simple (immediate) retrials it is not uncommon for the jury not to be told anything about the original trial. Where there has been a significant gap (eg the Court of Appeal has quashed a conviction and ordered a retrial) then it is often the case that juries are directed as to the fact that there was an original trial but not to take this into account. What will the position be here? Berlins argues that a difficulty here is that if the jury are aware of the test for quashing an acquittal (new and compelling evidence) then they may question how they could ignore this evidence and not consider it so compelling as to convict, but does that not turn the jury into a rubber-stamp?[157]

---

152. *Criminal Justice Act 2003*, s 76(5).
153. *Criminal Justice Act 2003*, s 85.
154. *Criminal Justice Act 2003*, s 85(4).
155. CPS, *DPP Refers William Dunlop Case to Court of Appeal as First under Double Jeopardy Law*, CPS Press Release, 10 November 2005.
156. Ian Dennis, 'Prosecution Appeals and Retrial for Serious Offences' [2004] *Criminal Law Review* 619, 633.
157. Marcel Berlins, 'Clarify Jury's Role Under Double Jeopardy Law' *The Guardian* (2005) <https://www.theguardian.com/society/2005/nov/14/penal.law>.

It could be argued that the jury will not know that this is the test but given that juries may now include members of the criminal justice system in their ranks this cannot be guaranteed so how should a jury be directed? As yet there is no guidance on this point. In reality, however, it may well be that it is academic because the quashing of an acquittal will lead to a guilty plea on the basis that the defence will realize that it has no answer to the 'compelling' evidence.

16.4.3.1 **Retrospectivity**

It has been noted that the first case to be referred to the Court of Appeal seeking the quashing of an acquittal is that which relates to a murder committed in 1989 and this demonstrates an important aspect of the provisions, that being that they are retrospective. To an extent it is easy to see why this is the case: the very nature of the pressure leading to the interference with double jeopardy would imply retrospectivity but this is a significant departure from the usual rule that criminal laws cannot be retrospective.

It has been noted that the argument against retrospectivity is, in effect, the same as the arguments against the provision itself[158] and that the approach is likely to be compliant with the ECHR because the issue is whether the person knew *at the time of the conduct* that it was illegal[159] which they would. Part 10 CJA 2003 does not render conduct that was lawful in the past unlawful under new laws but rather applies only when a person was acquitted of committing a crime then. On that basis it can be argued not to be an interference with Article 7. Any conviction will be based upon the substantive law then (although evidential changes since the trial will be implemented) and any punishment will be based on the maximum sentence at the time the offence was committed and not based on any changes that have been brought about since the acquittal.

The powers under Part 10 CJA 2003 have been rarely exercised. There have, at the time of writing, been less than a dozen applications but the care that is taken in choosing the cases perhaps explains why in a clear majority of the cases the application has been granted. Their rarity demonstrates that the courts and the CPS are reluctant to step beyond double jeopardy and that an acquittal will ordinarily be the end of the matter, save where there are strong public interest considerations that the acquittal amounts in itself to a miscarriage of justice.

16.5 **Appeal against sentence**

It is not just a conviction that will give rise to an appeal: the sentence imposed by a court can also be the subject of review. Sentencing is perhaps one of the most crucial aspects of a criminal trial as it is gives rise to emotions surrounding the proper disposition of a convicted person. Sentencing has usually marked one of the principal battlegrounds between politicians and the judiciary and is certainly an area where the legislature has increasingly become involved. This was perhaps best demonstrated in mid-2006 when a furore erupted over the sentencing of sex offenders (see, for

---

158. Richard Taylor, Martin Wasik, and Roger Leng, *Blackstone's Guide to the Criminal Justice Act 2003* (OUP 2004) 105.
159. Richard Taylor, Martin Wasik, and Roger Leng, *Blackstone's Guide to the Criminal Justice Act 2003* (OUP 2004) 106.

example, the case of 'Sweeney'[160] and *Attorney-General's Reference (Nos 14 and 15 of 2006))*.[161] Over the past decade there has been an increase in 'mandatory' sentences where Parliament has sought to limit the discretion of judges, although these have been robustly contested by the courts who have normally found reasons justifying an exception where they believe the interests of justice so require.[162] Against this background it is not surprising that sentences give rise to appeals and it is also notable that since 1988 the prosecution has a limited right to appeal against sentences, this being perhaps indicative of the political reality of sentencing.

16.5.1 Appeal by convicted person

The more usual appeal is that which is brought by the defendant. The defendant, when considering an appeal, is perfectly entitled to bring an appeal against both conviction *and* sentence even though this is the equivalent of saying, 'I did not do it, but if I did do it, I was sentenced too harshly!' Leave is required to appeal against sentence in the same way as with an appeal against conviction. In 2014–15 4,518 applications for leave to appeal against sentence were received of which 997 (22 per cent) were allowed.[163]

Whereas appeals against conviction will normally be dealt with by a panel of three judges, the same is not true of appeals against sentence and indeed it is more common for an appeal to be heard by two judges. This increases the number of potential panels of the Court of Appeal (Criminal Division) that can sit on these matters.

In the same way that an appeal against conviction is not an exercise of the appellate court deciding whether they would have reached a different conclusion, an appeal against sentence is examining whether a sentence was imposed correctly. Sentencing is perhaps more difficult in that in connection to a conviction it is possible to decide factors that may undermine the safety of a conviction whereas a sentence must reflect the individual characteristics of an offender. Sentencing is often said to be more of an art rather than a science[164] meaning that it is not possible to produce a mathematical formula to decide what an appropriate sentence must be. Accordingly, unless the sentence is illegal or procedurally flawed then the court must decide whether the judge could properly have reached his decision.

The two particular areas that the court concentrates on are the factual basis upon which a sentence was imposed and whether it is manifestly excessive.

16.5.1.1 Factual basis

A particular problem with convictions in the Crown Court is that it is not always clear what the factual basis is upon which a person is convicted. The reason for this is that sometimes a person will, as a matter of law, have committed an offence but the manner in which a person has committed the offence will make a significant difference to the sentence.

---

160. Alisdair Gillespie, 'Reviewing Unduly Lenient Sentences' (2005) 10 *Archbold News* 5.
161. [2006] EWCA Crim 1335.
162. See, for example, *R v Blackall* [2005] EWCA Crim 1128.
163. Court of Appeal, *In the Court of Appeal Criminal Division 2014/15* (Court of Appeal 2015) <https://www.judiciary.gov.uk/wp-content/uploads/2015/12/coa-criminal-division-annual-report-2014-15.pdf> 23.
164. See, for example, *Attorney-General's Reference (No 77 of 1999)* [2000] 2 Cr App R(S) 250, 252 (Rose LJ).

Example Grievous bodily harm

Causing grievous bodily harm is an offence contrary to ss 18 or 20 of the *Offences Against the Person Act 1861* (depending on the *mens rea*) and is committed by the infliction of grievous (meaning 'really serious') bodily harm.

Let us take an example. Derek is accused of causing grievous bodily harm to Paul after they had been fighting. The prosecution case is that Derek attacked Paul in an unprovoked manner and stamped on Paul's head. Derek denies this and says that he attacked Paul after he had called him names, and that he had hit and kicked him.

Derek cannot deny that he is guilty of grievous bodily harm but, since stamping is an aggravating factor[165] and provocation may be a mitigating factor, if he were to be sentenced on the basis of the prosecution case he could expect a more severe penalty than if he were sentenced on the basis of the facts put forward by the defence.

How should a court resolve the matter? It was seen in an earlier chapter that where the matter is by plea then the court has a number of options open to it. The most appropriate is that a written basis of plea is tendered (if the prosecution disagree with this basis then they could seek to try the defendant) and this, therefore, sets the factual background upon which a judge should sentence.[166] The other alternative is that where a jury returns a verdict of guilty the judge can, after hearing all the evidence, decide what the likely facts accepted by the jury are.[167] This is the more complicated scenario, however, and the judge must make clear that not only is his assessment consistent with the jury's verdict, but also that he expressly states the factual basis of the sentence.[168]

In these situations the Court of Appeal will simply examine whether the judge was entitled to assume the factual basis upon which he acted and whether the sentence was accurate in light of those facts.

16.5.1.2 Manifestly excessive

The most usual ground cited by appellants is that the sentence imposed by the judge is 'manifestly excessive' and should be reduced on appeal. 'Manifestly excessive' is not contained within statute but has been the traditional approach by the Court of Appeal to reviewing sentences on appeal and continues, in part, because of the doctrine of precedent. It is also a useful mechanism by which to ensure that too many appeals are not sent to the court and reinforces the point that sentencing is an art not a science.

The general basis upon which the court will act is to decide upon a range of sentences for which a person convicted of a crime is subject to and normally to interfere only when the matter is outside of this range. A classic example of this can be provided by the *dicta* of Ackner LJ (as he then was) in *R v Waddingham*[169] when he differentiates between an excessive sentence and a severe sentence,[170] the point being

---

165.   See *Attorney-General's Reference (No 59 of 1996)* [1997] 2 Cr App R (S) 250.
166.   *R v Kesler* [2001] 2 Cr App R(S) 126.
167.   *R v Solomon and Triumph* [1984] 6 Cr App R(S) 120.
168.   See, for example, *R v Ibrahima* [2005] EWCA Crim 1436.
169.   (1983) 5 Cr App R(S) 66.
170.   (1983) 5 Cr App R(S) 66, 69.

that a tough sentence within the range of discretion by the sentencing judge cannot be interfered with. In *R v Bibi*[171] the Court of Appeal argued that they tried to achieve a consistency of approach rather than of precise mathematical comparisons and that accordingly the starting point is to identify the range and then to examine the aggravating and mitigating features.

Mitigation is the usual way in which the Court of Appeal will alter a sentence, usually arguing that a judge has not given sufficient credit for a particular factor. However, the Court of Appeal is entitled to take account of information that the sentencing judge did not have available to him, and it is not unusual for it to refer to how the person has behaved in prison pending his appeal (although this was strongly disapproved of in *Waddingham*[172]).

16.5.2 Unduly lenient sentence

Prior to the system of prosecution appeals the only substantive appeal the prosecution had was in connection with unduly lenient sentences. The right of the senior appellate courts to increase sentences upon appeal was removed in 1966 with the establishment of the Court of Appeal (Criminal Division) (now incorporated in s 11(3) CAA 1968) but this was soon regretted and in 1972 Dr David Thomas, perhaps the leading authority in the field of sentencing, called for a power to review lenient sentences.[173] During the 1980s there was increased concern over the consistency of sentencing.[174] In fact the issue of sentencing has perhaps been the most controversial topic, in part because it demonstrates the tension that will invariably exist between the elected politicians and the judiciary, especially when media attention focuses on individual cases. Eventually the pressure led to the government introducing a scheme whereby the prosecution could refer certain offences to the Court of Appeal for re-sentencing where it was thought that the sentence was 'unduly lenient'.

The statutory power for this provision is contained within ss 35 and 36 of the *Criminal Justice Act 1988* and it provides a power for the Attorney-General to refer an unduly lenient sentence to the Court of Appeal but only if it is a qualifying sentence, meaning an offence that is triable only on indictment or is prescribed by statutory instrument for this purpose.[175] The latter has proved quite controversial in part because the list of prescribed offences has not kept pace with statutory reform; for example none of the either-way offences contained in the *Sexual Offences Act 2003* was prescribed until two years after the Act came into force.[176]

The Attorney-General or his deputy, the Solicitor-General, must examine each complaint personally,[177] even though members of their legal secretariat (qualified lawyers) will have reviewed the cases and provided a summary. It must be seriously doubted whether this is actually necessary. Given that the DPP has been given the authority to seek the leave of the Court of Appeal to appeal against an acquittal (see 16.4) it seems an absurd waste of time to demand that the law officers give personal consent and the jurisdiction could easily be exercised by the Crown Prosecution Service.

171. [1980] 2 Cr App R(S) 177.
172. (1983) 5 Cr App R(S) 66, 69.
173. DA Thomas, 'Increasing Sentences on Appeal: A Re-examination' [1972] *Criminal Law Review* 288.
174. Stephen Shute, 'Prosecution Appeals against Sentence: The First Five Years' (1994) 54 *Modern Law Review* 745, 746.
175. *Criminal Justice Act 1988*, s 35(3).
176. See *Criminal Justice Act 1988 (Reviews of Sentencing) Order 2006*, SI 2006/1116.
177. *Hansard*, HL Deb, vol 653, col 882 (14 October 2003) (Lord Goldsmith).

⚡ THE LAW OFFICERS

The Attorney-General (A-G) and his deputy, the Solicitor-General (S-G), are known as the 'Law Officers'. The S-G is by virtue of s 1 *Law Officers Act 1997* the formal deputy of the A-G and can perform any of his functions.

The A-G and S-G are political appointments and are members of one of the Houses of Parliament. The current A-G and S-G are members of the House of Commons (Rt Hon Jeremy Wright QC and Robert Buckland QC MP respectively) but in the last Labour government, Lord Goldsmith was A-G while a member of the House of Lords.

Traditionally if the A-G or S-G are not already Queen's Counsel upon appointment this distinction will be given to them. Although the term Solicitor-General implies otherwise, the first solicitor to hold the post of S-G was the Rt Hon Harriet Harman QC who was appointed in 2001 (and was appointed QC at the same time). Prior to that time all holders of the post were barristers.

As political appointees the Law Officers must resign when asked by the prime minister to do so and/or when the government falls. Neither is of cabinet rank although the A-G will attend cabinet when required. Although political, the primary role of the A-G and S-G is to be the principal legal advisers of the government and they act apolitically when performing their legal functions.

It is important to note that even if the matter is a qualifying offence it is not certain that an offence will be altered; the sentence must be 'unduly lenient'. Theoretically leave is required from the Court of Appeal to bring such an appeal but in *Attorney-General's Reference (No 24 of 1991)*[178] the Court of Appeal indicated that it was administratively preferable for the substance of the matter and the leave to be heard at the same time.[179] This, however, confuses the substantive challenge and the requirement for leave and undoubtedly causes delay and wasted court time.[180]

An illustration of the meaning of 'unduly lenient' can be found in *Attorney-General's Reference (No 4 of 1989)*[181] where the Court of Appeal stated that they would not interfere with a sentence merely because they would have imposed a different penalty, saying:

> A sentence is unduly lenient ... where it falls outside the range of sentences which the judge, applying his mind to all the relevant factors, could reasonably consider appropriate.[182]

The requirement to have regard to the range of sentences undoubtedly sets the threshold reasonably high: the sentence must be outside the normal range of sentences. This can be contrasted with the appeal against sentence by the defendant where the court is prepared to interfere at a much lower range. Even if the court does decide that a sentence is unduly lenient any alteration of the sentence is discretionary.[183] Accordingly the Court of Appeal could decide that it is not going to interfere with a sentence irrespective of the fact that it is unduly lenient.[184]

178. (1992) 13 Cr App R(S) 724.
179. (1992) 13 Cr App R(S) 724, 725–6.
180. Alisdair Gillespie, 'Reviewing Unduly Lenient Sentences' (2005) 10 *Archbold News* 5, 8.
181. (1990) 90 Cr App R 366.
182. (1990) 90 Cr App R 366, 371 (Lord Lane CJ).
183. Alisdair Gillespie, 'Reviewing Unduly Lenient Sentences' (2005) 10 *Archbold News* 5, 9.
184. See, for example, *Attorney-General's Reference (No 1 of 2003)* [2003] EWCA Crim 1051.

Controversially, the Court of Appeal argued that there was an element of 'double jeopardy' involved in a prosecutorial appeal in that a prisoner faces the trauma of being re-sentenced. This invariably led to a discount being awarded and the courts stated that this was especially relevant where a person is to be imprisoned after initially been handed a non-custodial sentence. It is possible to see the justification for a discount under these circumstances but it is less easy to justify the discretion when an offender is already incarcerated, where all that is being discussed is the length of incarceration and not the possibility of being deprived of liberty once again.[185] Persons subject to an unduly lenient sentence have been convicted of a specified offence and the sentence imposed was one that was outside the usual range of sentences, ie almost certainly less than that which the person had expected to receive. Is any trauma caused in such circumstances?

The government believed that giving a discount for 'double jeopardy' was wrong, especially in the most serious offences. The CJIA 2008 amended the law so as to preclude a discount for 'double jeopardy' being given where the sentence imposed is a discretionary life sentence (mandatory life sentences were already exempt from this principle by the CJA 2003) or certain other sentences, most notably imprisonment for public protection. Where a determinate sentence is being reviewed, however, the principle still exists and the court continues to give a discount.[186]

16.6 Appeals to the Supreme Court

It is possible to appeal a decision from the Court of Appeal to the Supreme Court.[187] Either party can appeal the matter irrespective of who brought the matter to the Court of Appeal (ie if the defendant appealed against conviction to the Court of Appeal the prosecution can appeal to the Supreme Court). For the matter to be heard by the Supreme Court it is necessary for the Court of Appeal to certify a point of general public importance is raised in the case[188] and leave must be sought either from the Court of Appeal or the Supreme Court directly. An interesting issue arose in *R v Dunn*[189] where the Court of Appeal refused to certify a point of public importance. The appellant sought to argue that this was a breach of Article 6 ECHR because the Court of Appeal was, in essence, sitting in judgment on its own decision and was biased. The appellant sought to argue that since the Court of Appeal would not wish to be reversed by the Supreme Court it could, by declining to certify a point, prevent a case from reaching the Supreme Court. Perhaps unsurprisingly the Court of Appeal ruled against the submission noting that the certification point was separate from the merits and that an impartial observer would not consider themselves to be biased when making the decision. The requirement for points of law to be certified exists in both the civil and criminal jurisdictions and is seen by the courts as a method of ensuring that only the most important cases appear before the Supreme Court. As was seen in Chapter 6 the Supreme Court has the capacity to only hear a limited number of cases and the certification process is a part of the filter mechanism.

185. Alisdair Gillespie, 'Reviewing Unduly Lenient Sentences' (2005) 10 *Archbold News* 5, 9.
186. See, for example, *Attorney-General's Reference (No 105 of 2011)* [2012] EWCA Crim 257 [14].
187. *Criminal Appeal Act 1968*, s 33.
188. *Criminal Appeal Act 1968*, s 33(2).
189. [2010] EWCA Crim 1823.

16.7 Miscarriages of justice: The Criminal Cases Review Commission

It has been noted already that there was, during the 1970s and 1980s, a series of miscarriages of justice that began to undermine public confidence in the criminal justice system. Part of the difficulty with the miscarriages was that they centred on terrorism trials and the person with responsibility for deciding whether to refer a matter back to the Court of Appeal, following an unsuccessful appeal after trial, was the Home Secretary and there was at the very least the appearance of bias in terms of whether to refer a matter to the court, particularly as Home Secretaries became increasingly combative with the judiciary. Whilst a politician was responsible for decisions to refer matters to the Court of Appeal, ie considering whether the criminal justice system had made a terrible mistake, there was concern that politics might interfere.

The *Criminal Appeal Act 1995* (CAA 1995) removed the political aspect of the decision from the Home Secretary through the establishment of the *Criminal Cases Review Commission* (CCRC) which from 1997 replaced the Home Secretary as the referring body for fresh appeals.[190] There are two principal methods by which the Commission can become involved. The first (and more usual) is that a convicted person will make an application to the Commission for a matter to be referred. There were early fears that the Commission would be overwhelmed by applications[191] and whilst there have been backlogs at times, most of the time they have managed to cope.[192] However, recent budget cuts (discussed later) have led to an increase in cases that are not dealt with immediately, creating a growing backlog. Indeed, the situation is such that the House of Commons Justice Committee called for an additional £1 million of funding to be allocated to the CCRC. However, this call was rejected by the government.[193]

The second way that the Commission may become involved is that the Court of Appeal can direct that the Commission investigate a matter and report to it.[194] This power was traditionally rarely exercised[195] but in recent years the numbers have increased[196] in part because of the increase in possible cases of jury misconduct (discussed earlier). The power is undoubtedly useful and the Court of Appeal has vocally supported the CCRC in conducting its role.[197]

Although the Commission is undoubtedly independent, it is interesting to note that not everyone necessarily believes that this is preferable. Some suggest that a difficulty with the Commission is that it is not directly accountable to Parliament in the way that the Home Office, through the Home Secretary, was.[198] That is not

---

190. *Criminal Appeal Act 1995*, s 9.
191. Michael Zander, *Cases and Materials on the English Legal System* (10th edn, OUP 2007).
192. CCRC, *Annual Report 2004–05* (Criminal Cases Review Commission, 2005) 25, and Kevin Kerrigan, 'Miscarriages of Justice in the Magistrates' Court: The Forgotten Power of the Criminal Cases Review Commission' [2006] *Criminal Law Review* 124, 126–7.
193. Terry McGuiness, *Criminal Cases Review Commission* (House of Commons, Briefing Paper Number 7448, 2016) 3.
194. *Criminal Appeal Act 1995*, s 15.
195. CCRC, *Annual Report 2004–05* (Criminal Cases Review Commission, 2005) 32.
196. CCRC, *Annual Report 2004–05* (Criminal Cases Review Commission, 2005) 13.
197. *R v Spicer* [2011] EWCA Crim 3247.
198. Richard Nobles and David Schiff, *Understanding Miscarriages of Justice: Law, Media and the Inevitability of a Crisis* (OUP 2000) 224.

to say, however, that there is no accountability and the Commission must issue an annual report to the Justice Secretary[199] and they can be, and indeed have in the past been, called before Parliamentary Select Committees to discuss their work. Aside from accountability others argue that there is less freedom to refer matters since political pressure could sometimes have persuaded the Home Secretary to refer cases where there was little prospect of success whereas the Commission can only refer where there is a 'real possibility' of success.[200] The issue of 'real possibility', however, can cause problems with some suggestions that this means that the 'lurking doubt' cases will never be referred since the Commission needs to identify some tangible ground.[201] It has been suggested that as an abstract term it is relatively meaningless[202] and that this means that the Commission must take notice of the working practice of the Court of Appeal[203] and that, in essence, this means that something 'new' (not necessarily evidence) is required before a matter could be referred. Where the 'new' matter is evidence there would appear to be an additional hurdle because not only should the Commission ask itself whether this would affect the safety of the conviction, it must also consider whether the evidence would, in fact, be admissible within the Court of Appeal.[204] Where the matter is one of due process it is perhaps easier to deal with since the court has identified that human rights requirements will usually mean that the safety of such convictions will be questioned, and accordingly the discovery of due process arguments may assist the Commission but only where they were not known at the time of the trial.

The CJIA 2008 has also resolved one question about 'old' appeals. The CCRC had begun to send cases to the Court of Appeal where the sole ground of appeal was that statutory law had overridden the previous common-law rules under which the person had been convicted, ie the law had changed. The Court of Appeal itself would ordinarily refuse to allow leave to appeal to defendants in such cases but this was not possible when the matter was referred by the CCRC since leave is not required. The CJIA 2008 amendment allows for the Court of Appeal to dismiss the appeal where the only ground for the appeal is that there has been a new development in the law and where, had the appellant himself petitioned the court, leave would not have been granted.[205]

Whether the CCRC refers enough cases has long been controversial. Ashworth and Redmayne argue that the Commission largely get the balance right[206] although they concede that it can be difficult to identify what is the appropriate rate. Other commentators have been less charitable, however. It has been noted that some miscarriage of justice campaigners believe the CCRC is too cautious.[207] In 19 years 626 cases have been referred and Cooper argues that this low number shows that 'something is not working'[208] and this is supported by others who believe that the fact that their success

199. *Criminal Appeal Act 1995*, sch 1.
200. Richard Nobles and David Schiff, *Understanding Miscarriages of Justice: Law, Media and the Inevitability of a Crisis* (OUP 2000) 224.
201. Richard Nobles and David Schiff, *Understanding Miscarriages of Justice: Law, Media and the Inevitability of a Crisis* (OUP, 2000) 221.
202. Kevin Kerrigan, 'Miscarriages of Justice in the Magistrates' Court: The Forgotten Power of the Criminal Cases Review Commission' [2006] *Criminal Law Review* 124, 133.
203. Andrew Ashworth and Mike Redmayne, *The Criminal Process* (4th edn, OUP 2010) 359.
204. Andrew Ashworth and Mike Redmayne, *The Criminal Process* (4th edn, OUP 2010) 359.
205. *Criminal Justice and Immigration Act 2008*, s 43.
206. Andrew Ashworth and Mike Redmayne, *The Criminal Process* (4th edn, OUP 2010) 360.
207. Jon Robins, 'The Case for the Defence' *Law Society Gazette* (9 October 2008) 12.
208. John Cooper, 'CCRC and Court of Appeal' (2011) 175 *Criminal Law & Justice Weekly* 298.

rate is around 70 per cent shows that there is an 'in-built conservatism'.[209] Zellick, a former chairman of the Commission, disagrees and believes that the rate is 'about right',[210] arguing that the CCRC should not be trying to clog up the Court of Appeal, a court that already suffers from chronic delays.

The resources of the Commission must, however, have an impact on the work of the body. In the 2014–15 annual report, it was noted that 'the main source of risk and uncertainty faced by the Commission … relates to the level of funding it receives … The continuing need for budgetary savings to be made across government is particularly difficult for the Commission as the majority of its expenditure relates to staff costs. This makes it difficult to plan ahead with any confidence.'[211] The budget cuts made to the CCRC have coincided with a 60 per cent increase in applications, resulting in a current backlog of over 350 cases awaiting review.

Prior to 2013–14 there was also concern about the number of Commissioners. The *Criminal Appeal Act 1995* states that the Commission must have no fewer than eleven Commissioners[212] and yet during 2011–12 there were only nine.[213] The statute makes clear that the fact that it is 'below strength' does not affect the validity of its activities[214] but it is more likely that it was intended to cover short-term vacancies and not a determined plan to be under-strength. The CCRC make clear that the Ministry of Justice deliberately intended the number to fall below eleven[215] even though this is clearly breaching the statute. By 2014–15 the number had risen again to the full complement of twelve commissioners although not all are full-time and thus the Full Time Equivalent (FTE) is 8.41[216] although this is still a substantial increase from previous years where the FTE had fallen to 7.7.

 Summary

This chapter has examined how an appeal from a decision of a first instance criminal court is dealt with. In particular, it has shown that:

- The paths of appeals differ depending on the mode of trial of the original criminal hearing.

- There are two potential criminal appeal avenues from a summary trial: either to the Divisional Court (by way of case stated or (exceptionally) judicial review) or to the Crown Court.

- Appeal from the Crown Court is to the Court of Appeal (Criminal Division).

- An appeal ordinarily requires leave (permission) but appealing to the Crown Court from the magistrates' court does not require leave.

---

209.   Jon Robins, 'Wrongly Accused' (2011) 175 *Criminal Law & Justice Weekly* 675.
210.   Jon Robins, 'Wrongly Accused' (2011) 175 *Criminal Law & Justice Weekly* 675.
211.   CCRC, *Annual Report and Accounts 2014–15* (Criminal Cases Review Commission 2015) 29.
212.   *Criminal Appeal Act 1995*, s 8(3).
213.   CCRC, *Annual Report and Accounts 2011–12* (Criminal Cases Review Commission 2012) 9.
214.   *Criminal Appeal Act 1995*, sch 1, para 6(4).
215.   CCRC, *Annual Report and Accounts 2011–12* (Criminal Cases Review Commission 2012) 9.
216.   CCRC, *Annual Report and Accounts 2014–15* (Criminal Cases Review Commission 2015) 28. A Full Time Equivalent is where the head-count is converted into the number of staff that would exist if each had a full-time contract.

❓ End-of-chapter questions

1. In *R v Hanratty*[217] the Lord Chief Justice said: 'We do however emphasise that there have to be exceptional circumstances to justify incurring the expenditure of resources ... including those of this Court, on a case of this age.' This was in connection with a murder case that took place in 1962 and for which the offender was executed later that year. The judgment in this case alone consisted of 215 paragraphs spread over eighteen pages in the law reports. In *R v Nicholson*[218] the Court of Appeal quashed a conviction for theft that dated back to 1957. The court stated that it did not condone the referral of historic cases but accepted that an error had been made in this case. Should the Commission refer historic cases or do you think that its time and money would be better spent in referring cases where the applicant is still in, or has been recently released from, prison?

2. Kevin Kerrigan ('Miscarriages of Justice in the Magistrates' Court: The Forgotten Power of the Criminal Cases Review Commission' [2006] *Criminal Law Review* 124) argues that the Commission is not using its powers correctly in referring miscarriages of justice that occur in summary trials. Should the CCRC deal with summary matters or is it designed to protect public confidence through examining only serious cases that are heard in the Crown Court?

3. Read pp 364–9 of Andrew Ashworth and Mike Redmayne, *The Criminal Process* (4th edn, OUP 2010). Was it right to abolish the rule of double jeopardy? Can the powers be abused by the police or are there sufficient safeguards built into the legislation?

≣ Further reading

Kerrigan K, 'Miscarriages of Justice in the Magistrates' Court: The Forgotten Power of the Criminal Cases Review Commission' [2006] *Criminal Law Review* 124–9.

This is a fascinating article that considers the power of the CCRC to appeal decisions within a summary trial. It raises important issues about the status of convictions (ie whether a summary conviction is as important as a conviction by the Crown Court).

Leigh LH, 'Lurking Doubt and the Safety of Convictions' [2006] *Criminal Law Review* 809–16.

This is an interesting article which examines how appeals are determined by the Court of Appeal, including where there is no flaw in the trial process.

Roberts S and Malleson K, 'Streamlining and Clarifying the Appellate Process' [2002] *Criminal Law Review* 272–82.

This is an interesting critique of the Auld proposals in respect of criminal appeals, particularly the prosecution right of appeal.

Spencer JR, 'Does Our Present Criminal Appeal System Make Sense?' [2006] *Criminal Law Review* 677–94.

This is a comprehensive article which examines the history of criminal appeals and discusses, in particular, the absurdity of two appeal mechanisms from a summary trial.

For multiple-choice questions, updates to this chapter, and links to useful websites, please visit the **Online Resource Centre** at: **www.oxfordtextbooks.co.uk/orc/gillespie_els6e/**

---

217.   [2002] 3 All ER 534.
218.   [2004] EWCA Crim 2840.

PART IV

THE CIVIL JUSTICE SYSTEM

17

Civil Litigation

By the end of this chapter you will be able to:

- Understand the basic elements of civil litigation.
- Identify the key principles adopted by the civil courts.
- Understand how three different types of civil litigation progress through the courts.

Introduction

It is now time to turn our attention away from the criminal justice system to civil litigation. Although the criminal justice system is probably responsible for the majority of the headlines and stories within the media, the civil justice system is used more frequently. The civil system straddles numerous different types of cases from public child-law cases (where the courts have to decide whether a child should be removed from its parents) through divorces to high-value litigation (eg the dispute over the building of the Wembley stadium where the parties sued for a combined total of £66,000,0000) and then through to public remedies such as judicial review.

This chapter will take a slightly different approach to the issue of litigation. Whilst the initial section will discuss certain common concepts of civil litigation, the main part of the chapter will look at three examples of civil litigation. Each type of litigation will involve the presentation of a case study and the section will then identify how this matter will be litigated. This will allow you to understand how some forms of civil litigation occur in real life.

17.1 Civil litigation

The civil justice system partners the criminal justice system in providing a forum through which disputes of law can be resolved. The disputes, however, can be quite varied. It is often said that the English Legal System does not operate a separate court system for 'public law' in that there are no separate courts that deal with matters relating to the resolution of disputes between the state and the citizen. However, this is not strictly true since, as you will see from related modules, there is now a distinct body of law known either as *Administrative Law* or *Public Law* which details how citizens can hold the government to account for their actions. Indeed, arguably, there is now a de facto separate court in that there is now a court known as the Administrative Court where such matters are heard. However, technically this is just part of the High Court of Justice and so the convention may still hold.

Setting aside public-law matters the civil justice system predominantly concerns disputes between citizens. This chapter discusses some of the ways that these disputes are resolved and the next chapter will then discuss what remedies can be sought from the civil courts and how an appeal is made against a decision. Chapter 19 details methods of resolving civil disputes without recourse to formal litigation, a topic known as 'Alternative Dispute Resolution' (ADR). Given the reduction in legal aid (discussed in Chapter 11) it is likely that ADR will become increasingly common. Finally, Chapter 7 discusses alternative bodies that have been created to resolve certain specialist disputes, those known as tribunals.

17.1.1 Procedural rules

As with criminal litigation, the courts have developed a series of rules that govern the way in which litigation takes place. There are two sets of rules; the *Civil Procedure Rules*, which govern the rules in most civil litigation, and the *Family Procedure Rules* which govern litigation in the Family Court. The CPR was the first set of rules to be established and they were introduced in response to the Woolf Reforms. They are publicly available[1] and are updated as and when necessary by the *Civil Procedure Rules Committee*.[2]

⚡ CIVIL PROCEDURE RULES COMMITTEE

This is a non-departmental body (ie it is independent of government although it is sponsored, and paid for, by the Ministry of Justice. It consists of:

- Master of the Rolls (as Head of Civil Justice)
- Deputy Head of Civil Justice
- Two puisne judges
- A circuit judge
- A Master of the High Court
- Two district judges
- Three barrister members
- Three solicitor members
- Two lay members.

---

1. <https://www.justice.gov.uk/courts/procedure-rules/civil>.
2. Established by *Civil Procedure Act 1997*, s 2.

The *Civil Procedure Rules* (CPR) and *Family Procedure Rules* (FPR) apply on a jurisdictional rather than a court-based basis. In other words, the CPR applies to all civil litigation other than family proceedings[3] and it does not matter whether the proceedings are in the county court or the High Court. Prior to the establishment of the CPR, the rules differed between courts. Lord Woolf, in his review of civil justice, recommended that the rules were the same across jurisdictions and this led to the establishment of the CPR as it simplifies the procedure.

⚡ REFERRING TO THE CPR

In order to refer to the CPR and accompanying practice direction in an understandable way, we will be referring to them in the following manner:

- **Rules**. The CPR consists of 89 parts, each with individual rules. The convention CPR Part. Rule will be adopted: CPR 31.2 means rule number 2 in Part 31 of the CPR.

- **Sub-rules**. These will follow the usual convention of brackets, eg 31.2(1).

- **Practice directions**. Whilst it is technically one practice direction, in essence each Part has its own practice direction relating to it. The convention PD Part.paragraph will be adopted: PD 31.7.6 means the practice direction relating to Part 31, paragraph 7.6.

The same approach will also be made in respect of the FPR.

17.1.1.1 Overriding objective

The first rule is known as the 'overriding objective' and is, in essence, a statement of intent as to how civil litigation should be conducted. Rule 1 states:

(1) These rules are a new procedural code with the overriding objective of enabling the court to deal with cases justly and at proportionate cost.

(2) Dealing with a case justly includes, so far as is practicable–

    (a) ensuring that the parties are on an equal footing;

    (b) saving expense;

    (c) dealing with the case in ways which are proportionate–

        (i) to the amount of money involved;

        (ii) to the importance of the case;

        (iii) to the complexity of the issues; and

        (iv) to the financial position of each party;

    (d) ensuring that it is dealt with expeditiously and fairly; and

    (e) allotting it an appropriate share of the court's resources, while taking into account the need to allot resources to other cases.

    (f) enforcing compliance with rules, practice directions and orders.

The overriding objective could be criticized as being more of a mission statement than a plan on how this will happen but, as will be seen, the courts take the overriding

---

3. The Court of Protection also has its own rules but these are set by Statutory Instrument: see *Court of Protection Rules 2007*, SI 2007/1744.

objective very seriously. The rest of the CPR sets out requirements but also provides powers to the court. The court considers the exercise of their discretionary powers in such a way as to ensure the overriding objective is met. This can include, for example, refusing adjournments where it is thought that a case is taking too long, refusing evidence where it would lead to disproportionate cost, and ensuring the right type of judge hears the appropriate case.

Rule 1.2(f) was inserted comparatively recently (2013) and was designed as a culture shift: to send a signal that the courts will be proactive in terms of managing litigation and holding parties to account for their actions. It may seem a strange thing to say, because should courts not ordinarily be in charge of litigation? Traditionally, however, they were not. The nature of the adversarial system and the neutrality of the 'umpire' meant that the courts were somewhat reticent to intervene in a case, lest it generate an appeal.[4] Those days are now long gone and, as will be seen, the courts are very willing to intervene where necessary.

17.1.1.2 Case Management

Case management is more than just ensuring that the proceedings in the courtroom are running smoothly, and that relevant issues are being discussed. Case management means that judges are at the heart of many of the procedural issues that occur in a case. This means not leaving matters to the parties, but questioning and deciding matters. Common issues of case management would include:

- Deciding which court should hear the matter. Whilst the parties may apply to a particular court, it does not follow that the courts will consider themselves bound by this, and they could transfer it to another court.

- Allocate the appropriate judge to hear the case. Civil litigation is heard by a variety of judges and the case management process will ensure that the right judge is allocated for the type of case, and its seriousness.

- The court will allocate a case to a particular track (see 17.2.3). This ensures that there is greatest control and also flexibility in those situations where litigation is likely to be complicated or lengthy. Conversely, it also ensures that minor cases are dealt with swiftly.

- The courts will ensure that Alternative Dispute Resolution (ADR) is at least actively considered (discussed in Chapter 19).

- The court will usually decide the evidence it wants to hear. Unlike in criminal cases where, if it is relevant, the judge will usually be required to let the tribunal of fact (the jury) hear it, a judge in civil proceedings has much more discretion. A judge can decide that he will only listen to certain evidence. The judge could decide that certain evidence need only be provided in writing or limit the number of issues that are to be litigated.

- The court will ensure its orders and directions are dealt with. As will be seen, a failure to comply with the directions of the court can be financially significant.

---

4. Stuart Sime, *A Practical Approach to Civil Procedure* (19th edn, OUP 2016).

17.1.2 Actions before litigating

The courts are now clear that litigation should only be commenced as a final resort and to ensure this, they have established a series of pre-trial protocols. The *Practice Direction on Pre-action Conduct and Protocols*[5] states that the protocols have the force of the CPR, being appended to them.[6] There are a number of pre-action protocols that cover different types of litigation that can be heard by the courts but if no protocol exists then the Practice Direction must be followed.

Perhaps the most important rule is that contained within paragraph 3:

Before commencing proceedings, the court will expect the parties to have exchanged sufficient information to—

(a) understand each other's position;

(b) make decisions about how to proceed;

(c) try to settle the issues without proceedings;

(d) consider a form of ADR to assist with the settlement;

(e) support the efficient management of these proceedings, and

(f) reduce the costs of resolving the dispute.

This applies to even the most minor litigation and therefore someone who hopes to use the small claims track (see 17.2) would still be expected to have tried to settle this dispute. The usual means of doing so is to send a letter to the would-be respondent stating what the dispute is about, what remedy is sought, and indicating that if they do not respond then the matter will be referred to the courts.

Realistically the pre-action procedure cannot be said to be onerous. It is designed to do four key things:

1. Test whether it is really necessary to go to court (including, by considering whether ADR is possible).

2. Identify what the issues in dispute are.

3. Identify what remedy the claimant is seeking.

4. Minimize costs by focusing only on what is in dispute.

17.1.3 Issuing proceedings

Assuming that the pre-trial approach did not work, then the beginning of the process is the issuing of proceedings.

For most forms of litigation, the general form is used. This is form N1 (Figure 17.1). The key features of this are:

Court. At the top right, the words 'In the' and a blank box appears. This is because N1 is used by most courts and therefore the claimant will indicate which court (High Court (including Division), county court (stating where it is sitting)) etc.

---

5. Available online at <http://www.justice.gov.uk/courts/procedure-rules/civil/rules/pd_pre-action_conduct>.
6. PD, para 1.

Personal details. The addresses for the claimant and defendant are included.

Brief details of the claim. Whilst this looks to be a relatively lengthy space to write in, it is traditionally used to provide only the most basic of details. A very concise summary of the key information is provided and a description of the remedy sought. The Online Resource Centre that accompanies this book has examples of N1 forms completed for the examples that are contained in this chapter.

Value. Assuming that the claim is for money, the value of the claim is placed here. There are rules on how the claim is calculated, including claiming for interest, and this will be discussed later. It is important to note, however, that if those details are not included on form N1 then the claimant will not be entitled to them. Given that litigation is extremely lengthy, omitting a claim for interest could be extremely costly.

Human Rights Act 1998 statement. This is a simple yes/no question but it is designed to help the courts identify those cases where there is a potential action under the *Human Rights Act 1998*. This is important because in those cases the court will normally ensure that a professional judge sits (as distinct from an acting judge) and where the matter relates to a potential declaration of incompatibility, this will normally mean that a puisne judge will be assigned.[7]

Particulars of claim. These can either be set out here or they can be attached as a separate, and more formal, document. Where they are set out on form N1 itself then it is more common for them to be slightly more informally set out. That said, it is important that the key facts and issues in dispute are set out here, so that the defendant can respond.[8]

One of the peculiarities of the English Legal System is that alternatives are permitted even though they may contradict each other. So, for example, it is perfectly reasonable to say, 'I had a contract with X, but if I did not have a contract with him, I allege that he was negligent in his actions towards me.' This seems to contain two contradictory pleadings—that there was a contract or there was not a contract—but it does not matter so long as the claimant believes that they are valid claims. That said, it should be noted that a party cannot contradict facts, because they could not otherwise attest to the truth of the claim (below).[9] An alternative claim above would not fall foul of this rule because a contract may not exist because of a legal, rather than factual, dispute.

Statement of Truth. Proceedings before the courts are formal and the claimant must attest that it is true to the best of their knowledge. A deliberate lie can be construed as a criminal offence.

17.1.3.1 Money claims online

HMCTS has established a system whereby disputes under £100,000 not relating to a child or protected party can begin online. Indeed to facilitate this, the fee for issuing service (see later) is discounted.

---

7. PD 2B, para 7A.
8. Stuart Sime, *A Practical Approach to Civil Procedure* (19th edn, OUP 2016) 148.
9. Stuart Sime, *A Practical Approach to Civil Procedure* (19th edn, OUP 2016) 150 and see *Clarke v Marlborough Fine Art (London) Ltd* [2002] 1 WLR 1731.

Claim Form

In the	
Fee Account no.	
Help with Fees - Ref no. (if applicable)	H W F – ☐☐☐ – ☐☐☐

You may be able to issue your claim online which may save time and money. Go to www.moneyclaim.gov.uk to find out more.

	For court use only
Claim no.	
Issue date	

Claimant(s) name(s) and address(es) including postcode

SEAL

Defendant(s) name and address(es) including postcode

Brief details of claim

Value

You must indicate your preferred County Court Hearing Centre for hearings here *(see notes for guidance)*

Defendant's name and address for service including postcode

	£
Amount claimed	
Court fee	
Legal representative's costs	
Total amount	

For further details of the courts www.gov.uk/find-court-tribunal.
When corresponding with the Court, please address forms or letters to the Manager and always quote the claim number.

N1 Claim form (CPR Part 7) (06.16)   © Crown Copyright 2016

Figure 17.1 Form N1: the form used for most types of civil litigation
Reproduced with permission from HM Courts and Tribunals Service

	Claim No.	

Does, or will, your claim include any issues under the Human Rights Act 1998? ☐ Yes ☐ No

Particulars of Claim (attached)(to follow)

Statement of Truth
*(I believe)(The Claimant believes) that the facts stated in these particulars of claim are true.
* I am duly authorised by the claimant to sign this statement

Full name _____

Name of claimant's legal representative's firm _____

signed _____ position or office held _____
  *(Claimant)(Litigation friend)   (if signing on behalf of firm or company)
  (Claimant's legal representative)   *delete as appropriate

Claimant's or claimant's legal representative's address to which documents or payments should be sent if different from overleaf including (if appropriate) details of DX, fax or e-mail.

Figure 17.1 (Continued)

Exactly the same issues are completed online but in a more intuitive way. You are provided with a series of text boxes and these are then completed and the form is created automatically. When the form is submitted (with the relevant fee) it passes to the central registry (based in Northampton) who issue the proceedings. A paper copy of the claim form is sent to the claimant who can either respond online or on paper. If the proceedings go ahead to trial, the matter is transferred to the nearest relevant court to the claimant. If, however, the proceedings do not continue because, for example, the defendant admits liability or refuses to acknowledge service, the matter can be dealt with online.

17.1.3.2 **Identifying the correct court**

It was noted above that form N1 applies to all civil courts, so how does one identify the appropriate court to bring the action in? The rules governing where litigation starts are set out in *The High Court and County Court Jurisdictions Order*[10] and are also subject to Practice Direction 7A which states:

2.1 Proceedings (whether for damages or for a specified sum) may not be started in the High Court unless the value of the claim is more than £100,000.

2.2 Proceedings which include a claim for damages in respect of personal injuries must not be started in the High Court unless the value of the claim is £50,000 or more (paragraph 9 of the High Court and County Courts Jurisdiction Order 1991 (S.I. 1991/724 as amended) describes how the value of a claim is to be determined).

2.3 A claim must be issued in the High Court or the County Court if an enactment so requires.

2.4 Subject to paragraphs 2.1 and 2.2 above, a claim should be started in the High Court if by reason of:

(1) the financial value of the claim and the amount in dispute, and/or

(2) the complexity of the facts, legal issues, remedies or procedures involved, and/or

(3) the importance of the outcome of the claim to the public in general,

the claimant believes that the claim ought to be dealt with by a High Court judge.

Some types of dispute have to begin in the High Court, most notably claims for judicial review. However, for the vast majority of business, the county court has jurisdiction. The jurisdiction of the county court has grown in recent years, partly to encourage more work to be dealt with in the county court. Given that, outside of London, most High Court business is dealt with by circuit judges acting as High Court judges, there is little point in starting in the High Court unnecessarily.

What happens when a case is begun at the wrong level? Theoretically where the claim has been lodged for an inappropriate reason the matter could be struck out as an abuse of process[11] but this will be comparatively rare. The more likely sanction is that the matter will be moved to the correct court and the claimant will bear the costs involved in the transfer irrespective of whether they succeed in the ultimate claim.

---

10. SI 1991/724.
11. *Restick v Crickmore* [1994] 2 All ER 112.

Where the error was to begin in the High Court when the matter should have been brought in the county court the judge has power not only to order that the costs of the transfer are paid but also could reduce the overall costs bill by up to 25 per cent.[12] Where it was a bona fide mistake to start the proceedings in the wrong court then it is unlikely that a sanction would be imposed although it would seem inevitable that the party will be liable for the costs of the transfer.

17.1.4 Allocating a track

Assuming that a defendant announces that he is going to contest the action—explored later—then the next principal decision that has to be taken is to allocate the matter to a relevant track. The CPR ushered in a new system of trying to manage civil litigation and it introduced three 'tracks' which govern how cases will proceed.

The initial decision is taken by an administrative officer of HMCTS[13] but this will be notified to the parties who will have the right to make representations. At the same time, a questionnaire will be sent to both parties which seeks to encourage settlement (including through ADR), identify the key issues of the case, including whether expert testimony is to be required, and which witnesses and documents they are seeking to rely upon.[14]

Once the questionnaires are received, a judge will then allocate the case to an appropriate track. The three tracks are:

Small claims track. This encompasses what was, and indeed still is, colloquially known as the 'small claims court' although it was never a separate court (it is part of the county court) and it is not necessarily that small a claim any more.

The general rule is that claims under £10,000 will ordinarily be considered suitable for the small claims track, save that the following cases will not ordinarily be so assigned:

(a) Personal injury cases, where the value of the claim for pain, suffering, and loss of amenity exceeds £1,000.

(b) Claims by tenants of residential premises seeking orders that their landlords should carry out repairs or other works to the premises where the value of the claim exceeds £1,000.

(c) Claims by residential tenants seeking damages against their landlords for harassment or unlawful eviction.

(d) Claims involving a disputed allegation of dishonesty.[15]

It should be noted that the £10,000 is not an absolute ceiling. There may be reasons why a larger sum could be considered suitable for the small claims court. As will be seen, one advantage of the small claims track is its costs regime and its informality. It is rare for lawyers to be involved in cases in the small claims track and so litigants in person may prefer larger claims to be heard under this track.

---

12. *Senior Courts Act 1981*, s 51(8).
13. *Civil Procedure Rules*, r 26.3(1).
14. Stuart Sime, *A Practical Approach to Civil Procedure* (19th edn, OUP 2016) 164ff.
15. *Civil Procedure Rules*, r 26.

Bernard asked Wreckers Ltd to install a swimming pool in his house. He claims that the pool is not fit for purpose as it leaks, meaning the water level is unsafe. It cost £21,000 to install and Bernard has been told it will cost £11,000 to repair.

Realistically Bernard's claim will be for £11,000 (the cost of the repair) but this is over £10,000. However, if both Bernard and Wreckers Ltd agree that the issue is relatively simple then they may both seek to keep the matter in the small claims track as it will limit the potential for costs.

Fast track. The fast track is designed to be the 'normal' track for cases with a value of between £10,000 and £25,000.[16] They will also ordinarily include those cases above that were deemed not suitable for the small claims track even though the value was under £10,000. However, the financial threshold is subject to one important exception. Cases in the fast track should normally be capable of being heard within one day and will not involve more than two expert witnesses.[17] Whilst the CPR does not require longer cases to be heard in the multi-track, as it states 'normally', it has been noted that the default position is normally that they will be sent to the multi-track.[18]

As will be seen, it is in the parties' best interests to try and ensure that the dispute is limited to issues that could be dealt with in under one day, because the costs implications between the fast track and multi-track can be significant.

Multi-track. The multi-track is, in essence, the track that is to be used for cases that do not fall within either the small claims track or fast track. It is perhaps the widest track and it demonstrates that the other two tracks are really filters to try and deal with less complicated cases quickly.

17.1.5 Costs of litigation

Litigation is expensive. There can be no denial of that fact and it is one of the reasons why the courts have been so keen to try and ensure that litigants consider alternative forms of dispute resolution. In some instances the costs can far exceed what the claim is about, meaning that litigation can be potentially ruinous.

≣ **Example** Warring Couples and Costs

In September 2012 it was reported that a judge had criticized two solicitors who squandered £1.7 million in litigation costs while fighting various issues in respect of their divorce. The media reported that the litigants were left with joint assets of just over £90,000 after years of litigation. This perhaps demonstrates the challenges of the overriding objective and the fact that sometimes litigation is pursued when it is arguably unreasonable to do so.

---

16. Stuart Sime, *A Practical Approach to Civil Procedure* (19th edn, OUP 2016) 175.
17. *Civil Procedure Rules*, r 26.6(5).
18. Stuart Sime, *A Practical Approach to Civil Procedure* (19th edn, OUP 2016) 176.

Costs have become an extremely complicated area of law and realistically we cannot do justice to the topic in a book like this. It is too complex and complicated and probably far outside the scope of what you will need for a course such as *English Legal System*. Reference on specific points of costs management should be made to key texts in the field.[19]

In this section, what will be considered are the different costs regimes between the tracks and then how the courts use costs to control litigant behaviour.

17.1.5.1 Costs: The general rule

The general rule in civil litigation is that the loser pays the costs.[20] Whilst a court has general discretion as to costs, a judge departing from this general rule must give clear reasons for doing so.[21] Of course, what is meant by 'the losing side' is open to question since in some forms of litigation, deciding who wins and who loses is not always easy. There are also rules that relate to how costs will be apportioned where a party seeks to settle a case, and this is one of things that will be discussed later. But this, again, remains an exemption from the general rule which is that the losing side pays the costs of both parties.

17.1.5.2 Costs for each track

One of the reasons for differentiating between the tracks is that the costs regime is different across them all. This section will provide a summary of the costs regime, which will help illustrate the importance of a case being assigned to the appropriate track.

Small claims track

Cases in the small claims track are the most restrictive when it comes to costs. This is considered a key advantage of the small claims track and means that, in many instances, litigation is affordable and proportionate. As will be seen (at 17.2.3), the small claims track is designed to be used by litigants in person and therefore legal fees will not ordinarily be permitted.

The CPR sets out the position as regards costs:

The court shall not order a party to pay a sum to another party in respect of that other party's costs, fees and expenses, including those relating to an appeal, except—

(a) The fixed costs attributable to issuing the claim which—

    i.   Are payable under Part 45, or

    ii. Would be payable under Part 45 if that Part applied to the claim;

(b) In proceedings which included a claim for an injunction or an order for specific performance a sum not exceeding £260[22] for legal advice and assistance relating to that claim;

(c) Any court fees paid by that party;

(d) Expenses which a party or witness has reasonably incurred travelling to and from a hearing or in staying away from home for the purposes of attending the hearing;

---

19. See, for example, Stuart Sime, *A Practical Approach to Civil Procedure* (19th edn, OUP 2016) (which is arguably the pre-eminent academic text on civil litigation) and also the *White Book*.
20. *Civil Procedure Rules*, r 42.2.
21. *Aspin v Metric Group Ltd* (2007) LTL 25/9/07; and see Stuart Sime, *A Practical Approach to Civil Procedure* (19th edn, OUP 2016) 517.
22. PD 27, para 7.2.

(e) A sum not exceeding £95[23] for any loss of earnings or loss of leave by a party or witness due to a hearing.

(f) A sum not exceeding £750[24] for an expert's fees;

(g) [Certain costs relating to personal injury claims].

This is restrictive and there are a number of points to note here. The first is that legal advice is only permitted as a cost if the remedy sought is for an injunction or an order of specific performance. In all other types of cases, it is not possible to claim for legal advice, including the initial advice that may have said that a person has a legitimate legal claim and that they should use the small claims track. Even in cases with injunctions, the cost is for legal advice and not representation. Whilst there is a right to bring a lawyer to a small claims track case, the costs of doing so are not recoverable, even if a party wins.

An additional point of interest is the amount of expenses that can be claimed for loss of earnings. Assuming that most people would need to take a day's leave to attend the court hearing, as either a party or witness, the costs do seem remarkably scant. The maximum amount payable is £95 per day. To put that into context, that would equate to a salary of £24,700 per annum. Many people are on significantly more than this. If a person is self-employed, it is more likely that it would equate to £22,800.[25] This means that a person who needs to attend court, and take a day's holiday, is likely to lose money. Whilst it could be argued this is not unreasonable for the claimant, who has decided to initiate the litigation, it would seem less appropriate for a (successful) defendant or a witness, neither of whom will necessarily have chosen to appear. To incur a loss on behalf of someone else seems somewhat harsh. Of course there is nothing to stop the relevant party paying more money to the witness but this is the maximum that could be reclaimed from the losing party.

The fee for an expert would seem high—£750—but it will be comparatively rare for experts to be used in the small claims track, particularly where there is a dispute between experts. Such disputes are likely to be too lengthy and complicated for a hearing in the small claims track and is more likely to see a dispute shifting to the fast or multi-track. That said, it is quite possible that there may be some disputes that call for a (shared) expert opinion. Whether a maximum of £750 is appropriate for all experts is perhaps another matter though: many will charge much more, meaning that the party commissioning the expert will need to pick up the extra.

565

☰ **Example** Experts in the Small Claims Track

Deborah buys a second-hand car from 'Dodgy Dave Motors Ltd' for £21,500. It was described as having one owner who looked after it immaculately, with a full service history. The car starts to develop faults and Dodgy Dave Motors Ltd say that it is just bad luck and the fact that the car is three years old. Deborah commissions a mechanic, who reports that the engine does not look original and it looks as though other parts of the car have not been maintained properly. He quotes the costs of repair at £7,500.

Deborah may wish to rely upon this report to justify her claim against Dodgy Dave Motors.

---

23. PD 27, para 7.3.
24. PD 27, para 7.3.
25. Five days a week for forty-eight weeks per year (allowing four weeks' holiday).

17.1.5.3 Costs on the Fast Track.

It will be remembered that the second track is the fast track and one of the perceived advantages of this track (over the multi-track) is that costs are, to a large extent, fixed. This means that a litigant will know approximately what level of costs they may be eligible for.

The cost regime is now contained within the *Civil Procedure Rules*[26] and is somewhat complicated, so an example only will be provided here. Let us take the following example:

> Saanvi was out running one day. At a pelican crossing, she started to cross when the 'green man' came on but Aanya, who was distracted, did not stop her car in time, causing a glancing collision with Saanvi. Whilst there were only bruises, Saanvi could not work for four days and suffered pain and discomfort for a number of weeks. She required treatment for grazes and some physiotherapy to minimize the discomfort in her leg.
>
> Saanvi is suing Aanya for personal injury damages. It is estimated that these damages will be less than £25,000 and the case is relatively simple and so has been allocated to the fast track.

Protocols exist for personal injury cases now, and these would apply to Saanvi's case. What costs would the losing party be liable for?

Parties agree damages before proceedings are issued

Agreed damages	At least £1,000 but not more than £5,000.	More than £5,000 but not more than £10,000	More than £10,000 but not more than £25,000

Fixed costs.	The greater of–
	(a) £550, or
	(b) the total of–
	  (i) £100; and
	  (ii) 20% of the damages.
		The total of–
		(a) £1,100 and
		(b) £15% of damages over £5,000.
			The total of–
			(a) £1,930; and
			(b) 10% of damages over £10,000

Parties agree a settlement after the issuing of proceedings but before trial

Stage at which it is settled.	On or after the date of issue, but prior to allocation of track.	On or after the date of allocation of track, but prior to the date of listing.	On or after the date of listing, but prior to the date of trial.
Fixed costs.	The total of– (a) £1,160, and (b) 20% of the damages.	The total of– (a) £1,880 and (b) 20% of damages over £5,000.	The total of– (a) £2,655; and (b) 20% of damages over £10,000

The claim is disposed of at trial

Fixed costs.	The total of– (a) £2,655, and (b) 20% of the damages; and (c) the relevant trial advocacy fee.

26. *Civil Procedure Rules*, pt 45.

The relevant advocacy fee, depends on the award.

Agreed or awarded damages	Not more than £3,000	More than £3,000 but not more than £10,000	More than £10,000 but not more than £15,000	More than £15,000
Advocacy Fee	£500	£710	£1,070	£1,705

Let us return to our example of Saanvi, and let us take three possible ways that the action is resolved. What would be the total costs recoverable?

Disposition	Costs
Agree damages of £8,000 after issuing a claim but before the allocation of track.	£1,550[27]
Agree damages of £12,000 the day before the case is due to be listed.	£3,055[28]
After a (contested) trial, the judge awards damages of £14,000.	£6,525[29]

In addition to this, the following additional costs can be claimed:

- Cost of obtaining medical records and expert medical reports as permitted under the Protocol
- The cost of any non-medical expert reports as permitted under the Protocol
- Court fees
- Any expert's fee for attendance where the court granted permission for the expert to attend
- Expenses which any party or witness has reasonably incurred in travelling to or from the hearing
- A sum not exceeding £90 (where the damages are less than £10,000) or £135 (where the damages are for £10,000 or more) for the loss of earnings for a party or witness.

Of course, the costs are, in effect, doubled since both sides will have similar costs incurred amongst them. Even without this, however, it can be seen that the costs of a fast-track case are not unreasonable for relatively low amounts. It also demonstrates one of the challenges for legal professionals, however, since these are the maximum costs that can be claimed for.

17.1.5.4 **Multi-track**

The costs for multi-track cases are too complicated for a book of this nature. Even though it is worth noting that costs are becoming increasingly fixed for some forms of work,[30] the costs of multi-track cases can be enormous. Multi-track cases have far fewer limitations on them, and whilst the courts will use their case-management powers to try and keep costs proportionate, the reality is that some multi-track cases can

27. £1,100 plus 15 per cent of £3,000 (ie the damages above £5,000).
28. £2,655 plus 20 per cent of £2,000 (ie the damages above £10,000).
29. £2,655 plus 20 per cent of £14,000 plus advocacy fee of £1,070.
30. Discussed in chapter 45 of Stuart Sime, *A Practical Approach to Civil Procedure* (19th edn, OUP 2016).

incur costs of several million pounds. Indeed, costs can be so significant that it is not unusual for there to be satellite litigation after the final disposition of the hearing, with this litigation concerning who should pay what, and for how much.

17.1.5.5 Using costs to control litigation

It has been noted on a number of occasions now that the courts see their role as managing cases, and ensuring that time and resources are not wasted. Whilst the CPR states that costs will normally follow the decision, (ie 'loser pays')[31] the broad discretion the courts have in respect of costs means that they can use costs decisions to control how parties litigate. Under the rules, this specifically includes:

(a) A proportion of the other party's costs.

(b) A stated amount in respect of another party's costs.

(c) Costs from or until a certain day only.

(d) Costs incurred before proceedings have begun.

(e) Costs relating to particular steps taken in proceedings.

(f) Costs relating only to distinct parts of the proceedings, and

(g) Interest on costs from or until a certain date, including a date before judgment.[32]

As will be seen, the courts will use some of these powers when they formally try to encourage settlement, but they can also use them informally. For example, a judge may make clear that he sees no reason why a particular issue should be gone into, or advises that they concentrate on only points x, y, and z. If a party chooses to also look at points a, b, and c, it is quite possible that the judge will consider that those costs should not be paid for.

Where a party breaches the orders of a court, a practice direction within the CPR, or the CPR themselves, it is highly likely that discretionary costs will be incurred. For example, if party X was told to submit some documents by a particular date so that they could be considered at a hearing, but they were instead submitted at, or the day before, the hearing requiring an adjournment, then it is quite likely that the party who failed to submit the paperwork in time would bear the costs for that wasted hearing, even if they deserved the costs of litigation for winning.

17.1.5.6 Wasted costs order

Perhaps one of the most significant powers a court has at its disposal is the wasted costs order. This is an order that is used to signal extreme judicial displeasure at a course of action, and is notable because it is a position whereby a lawyer can be ordered to be personally liable for the costs of the action.[33]

The wasted costs order is a creature of statute:

> In any proceedings ... the court may disallow, or (as the case may be) order the legal or other representative concerned to meet, the whole of any wasted costs or such part of them as may be determined in accordance with rules of court.[34]

---

31. *Civil Procedure Rules*, r 42.2.
32. *Civil Procedure Rules*, r 44.2(6).
33. Theoretically, a third party could also be personally liable for costs if they did something that warranted it, but it is more common for lawyers to be the subject of such an order.
34. *Senior Courts Act 1981*, s 51(6).

It is used to mark judicial disapproval of the conduct of litigation or advocacy where it has led to costs (including the costs of the court) being wasted. In respect of advocates, this can include not only their work in court but also their preparation of advice, drafting, or applications.[35] It can also be used against lawyers for action before the trial takes place.

Wasted costs orders are draconian, and indeed designed to be, and so there is a relatively high threshold for an order to be made.

'Wasted costs' means any costs incurred by a party—

(a) As a result of any improper, unreasonable or negligent act or omission on the part of any legal or other representative or an employee of such a representative; or

(b) Which, in the light of any such act or omission occurring after they were incurred, the court considers it unreasonable to expect that party to pay.[36]

The test is extremely high—improper, unreasonable, or negligent—and where a court imposes a wasted costs order on a lawyer, they must now inform the relevant regulator[37] that they have done so. The regulator will then consider whether their actions amount to unprofessional conduct and the lawyer may therefore face further sanction.

⫼ Case Box: Wasted Costs *Thompson v Go North East Ltd*

The claimant had pursued a claim of damages in respect of a bus accident. After issuing the proceedings, he discontinued them. The respondents, the bus company, sought damages from the claimant but also from the solicitors as it became evident that the whole claim was fraudulent. The CCTV footage had been viewed by the solicitors and it was clear from the footage that the claimant's case was inconsistent with what the evidence showed. Nonetheless they issued proceedings and began the pre-trial protocols.

The judge held that wasted costs were appropriate in this case. Whilst solicitors had to act on the basis of instructions, once they had viewed the CCTV evidence they should have realized that the case was flawed and it was inconsistent with their instructions.

17.1.6 Allocating the judge

It has already been noted that a case will be allocated to a specific track, but how is the judge allocated to the case? Civil law arguably has the widest range of judges employed to adjudicate matters, ranging from a deputy district judge to a Lord Justice of Appeal sitting on a judicial review. How is a judge allocated?

The general rule is that unless a practice direction or other rule says otherwise, any judge, deputy judge, or Master shall have the right to conduct the business of the court.[38] The principal practice direction that seeks to limit jurisdiction is the one that deals with the allocation of the judiciary.[39] Reference should be made to full details of this list, with this section merely providing an overview.

---

35. *Brown v Bennett* (Wasted Costs Order) [2002] 1 WLR 713.
36. *Senior Courts Act 1981*, s 51(7).
37. eg Solicitors Regulation Authority, Bar Standards Board, and CILEX.
38. *Civil Procedure Rules*, r 2.4.
39. PD 2B—Allocation of Cases to Levels of Judiciary.

17.1.6.1 **High Court**

The principal rules of the High Court state when proceedings cannot be heard by someone other than a judge (including a circuit judge or deputy judge acting as a High Court judge[40]). The following proceedings cannot be heard by a Master or district judge:

- Search orders, freezing orders, and an ancillary order under rule 25
- Orders, including interim remedies, relating to the liberty of the public, relating to criminal proceedings, claims for judicial review, appeals from Masters or district judges, appeals against costs, vexatious litigants, and certain mental health problems.[41]

Where a claim under the *Human Rights Act 1998* raises either a claim in respect of a judicial act or is a claim for a declaration of incompatibility, then a deputy judge, Master, or district judge may not try this case.[42] A circuit judge sitting as a High Court judge is not classed as a 'deputy judge' and so would be entitled to sit on such cases, although it is more common for a puisne judge or Lord Justice of Appeal to sit on these matters.

Additional rules apply to Chancery business and the specialist courts, but there is no need to rehearse these here.

17.1.6.2 **County court**

The county court is slightly easier. Small claims track cases will usually be heard by a district judge rather than a circuit judge, although the latter is able to do so.[43] Realistically it will always be a district (or deputy) district judge that sits on such matters as the pressure for judicial time is so great, particularly as many circuit judges will be undertaking High Court business on circuit.

District judges will ordinarily also deal with fast-track cases,[44] partly because these are considered to be relatively straightforward cases (as they must be capable of being heard within a day). Most preliminary matters will also be listed before a district judge[45] and this demonstrates that district judges are the mainstay of the county court. This is partly because circuit judges will primarily sit on criminal matters (in the Crown Court) and therefore when they do sit on civil cases, they tend to be the more complicated cases. Ordinarily cases in the multi-track above £25,000 will be heard by a circuit judge (including a recorder) as will certain hearings for technical matters.[46] Applications relating to liberty, including the committal of a person to prison, must be made to a circuit judge.

17.1.7 **Juries in the civil courts**

Unlike in the Crown Court, the tribunal of fact in the court is usually the judge alone. It is extremely rare for juries to be used in civil cases, partly as a response to the demands of costs and timeliness of trials.

---

40. *Senior Courts Act 1981*, s 9(1).
41. PD 2B, paras 2 and 3.
42. PD 2B, para 7A.
43. PD 27, para 1.
44. PD 2B, para 11.1.
45. PD 2B, para 8.
46. PD 2B, para 12.

One of the few remaining classes of action where a jury could be used was defamation. However, the *Defamation Act 2013* created a statutory presumption against the use of a jury.[47] Notably, the Act does not say under what circumstances the court should allow a jury to be used but it is clear that it is designed to be exceptional. In *Yeo v Times Newspaper Ltd*[48] the High Court implied that it would only be cases where there is a need to counter any allegations of involuntary bias on the part of a judge that would warrant trial by jury.[49] Warby J gave the example of a judge suing someone. In such instances, it would be difficult for a judge alone to be trusted to make this decision because there may be the perception that a judge has ruled a particular way to advantage their brethren. However, such examples demonstrate the fact that the courts believe that it should be truly exceptional.

In *Elliott v Rufus*[50] Sharp LJ made an interesting point about how the 2013 Act may have a tangential but important role. Prior to the 2013 Act, a judge could not make a preliminary judgment about what a potentially defamatory statement meant as to do so could pre-empt what a jury (if it were to be empanelled) would decide. This has serious implications for costs where this is the only issue that the parties dispute, because it would necessitate a full trial. However, since juries will not normally be empanelled, it is now possible for a judge to make a preliminary ruling as to meaning, particularly if that means one side would settle if they believed that the statement had a particular meaning.[51]

So when will a jury be used? In the High Court, the rule is:

Where ... the court is satisfied that there is in issue—

(a) A charge of fraud against that party; or

(b) A claim in respect of malicious prosecution or false imprisonment; or

(c) Any question or issue of a kind prescribed for the purposes of this issue.

The action shall be tried with a jury, unless the court is of opinion that the trial requires prolonged examination of documents or accounts or any scientific or local investigation which cannot conveniently be made with a jury.[52]

Matters in the Patent Court, Admiralty Court, and Commercial Court are not permitted to be heard by a jury.[53]

If a jury is to be sought, the party seeking the use of the jury must make an application to the court within 28 days of the service of the defence.[54] This ensures that the issue can be decided early on and that all the parties understand how the case is to be prepared.

The same wording is found within the *County Court Act 1984*,[55] meaning that trials by jury are similarly restricted in the county court. The 1984 Act includes additional proceedings that may not be heard by a jury[56] but these are not mentioned here as the clear presumption against jury trial remains.

---

47.   *Defamation Act 2013*, s 11.
48.   [2014] EWHC 2853 (QB).
49.   [2014] EWHC 2853 [80].
50.   [2015] EWCA Civ 121.
51.   [2015] EWCA Civ 121 [28]. Indeed this happened in *Hiranandani-Vandrevala v Times Newspapers Ltd* [2016] EWHC 250 (QB).
52.   *Senior Courts Act 1981*, s 69(1).
53.   *Senior Courts Act 1981*, s 69(1) when read in conjunction with s 6.
54.   *Civil Procedure Rules*, r 26.11.
55.   *County Court Act 1984*, s 66(3).
56.   *County Court Act 1984*, s 66(1).

If a jury trial does take place, then a jury of eight is empanelled in the county court but a jury of twelve in the High Court. As with criminal cases, verdicts should usually be unanimous, but in the county court, a verdict of 7–1 is permissible, and in the High Court, verdicts of 11–1, 10–2, 10–1, and 9–1 are permissible.[57]

17.1.8 Encouraging settlement

The courts now see it as their duty to encourage cases to settle. Indeed, the *Civil Procedure Rules* require the court to help the parties 'settle the whole or part of the case'.[58] Chapter 19 will discuss how the courts are prepared to assist the parties to use Alternative Dispute Resolution (ADR) to settle their differences. However, the courts will also facilitate settlement and the costs regime is designed to do this.

Perhaps the most notable process for encouraging settlement is known as Part 36 offers. This is a system, now contained within the *Civil Procedure Rules* (in Part 36, hence its name!), that allows either party to make an offer to settle the litigation, with significant cost implications if a side does not do so.

17.1.8.1 *Calderbank* offers

Prior to Part 36 offers, the usual approach was one of *Calderbank* offers. This is named after the landmark case of *Calderbank v Calderbank*.[59] This was a divorce case where there was a dispute as to the financial settlement. The wife offered the husband property worth a certain amount of money in a letter entitled 'without prejudice'. She then followed this up with an affidavit, undertaking to transfer the property. The husband rejected this, believing it was not sufficient. The judge at trial ordered the transfer of less money than the wife offered, but ordered that each party bear their own costs.[60] The wife appealed, suggesting the husband should pay more costs because she attempted to settle the case.

The Court of Appeal allowed the appeal. They stated that whilst she could not rely on the letter (for reasons set out shortly), she could rely on the affidavit. The husband should have accepted this (generous) offer and because he did not, he was liable for the costs of both parties from the time he should have accepted this.

Out of this case come the general rules for *Calderbank* offers. The first is that an offer must be made in writing and state on it, 'without prejudice save for costs'. This wording has two implications:

1. 'Without prejudice' means that it cannot be used in court to show, for example, a party is admitting liability or is prepared to pay *x* in damages etc.

2. 'Save for costs' means that the letter *is* relevant and admissible after the final disposition of the case, as it should be taken into account when deciding costs.

The offer must be clear as to the circumstances, the period by which the offer will be paid, and also the length of time the other party has to settle the dispute. Either side may make a *Calderbank* offer (ie 'I will give you *x*' or 'I will accept *x*'). If the opposing side does not accept the offer then no mention is made of it during proceedings.

---

57. Stuart Sime, *A Practical Approach to Civil Procedure* (19th edn, OUP 2016) 448.
58. *Civil Procedure Rules*, r 1.4(2)(f).
59. [1976] Fam 93.
60. In family proceedings it is more common for each party to pay their own costs of litigation rather than apply the 'loser pays' principle of civil litigation (see *Family Procedure Rules*, r 28.3).

At the end of proceedings, a decision is made whether the order of the court is at least as good as the offer made. If it is, then the opposing side will (usually) be required to pay the costs of both sides from the date that the offer expired. That said, the courts retain discretion as to costs and so they can depart from this general rule if they so wish.

Calderbank offers still exist although using Part 36 is more common. This is partly because Part 36 is governed by a set of rules and therefore there is greater certainty as to what the outcome of the process will be in terms of costs. However, some of the flexibility that arises in *Calderbank* is lost, because Part 36 is very clear as to how the settlement will be executed etc.

17.1.8.2 Making a Part 36 offer

Part 36 was developed from the *Calderbank* principles. In other words, many of its features are the same. According to rule 36.5 of the *Civil Procedure Rules*, the following must be complied with to make a Part 36 offer; it must:

(a) be made in writing. Although it is not mandatory to use it, a form has been designed to facilitate this.[61]

(b) make clear that the offer is being made pursuant to Part 36.

(c) specify a period of not less than twenty-one days, during which the offeror will be responsible for the costs.

(d) state whether it applies to the whole, or part, of a claim.

(e) state whether it takes account of counterclaims.

573

The period of twenty-one days mentioned in (c) is the time which a person has to accept the offer. In other words, during those twenty-one days, the usual rule as to costs applies. At the end of that twenty-one-day period, this will be considered the time at which a person could have accepted the offer. The offer can be made at any time in proceedings, but where it is made less than twenty-one days before the hearing, the twenty-one-day rule does not apply and it must be accepted before the end of the trial.

Where the offer is to pay money, it must be paid in a single lump sum and an offer to pay more than fourteen days after the date of acceptance will not be considered a Part 36 offer unless the other party accepts the offer.[62] This latter sentence means that the costs advantage that would ordinarily come with a Part 36 offer will not apply unless the claimant accepts it. The rule about a single payment within fourteen days is one reason why *Calderbank* offers remain live. There is no such restriction with a *Calderbank* offer.

⬚ Example *Calderbank* vs Part 36

Susan is suing Edward for £45,000, which she claims she is entitled to due to Edward selling an asset without permission. Edward believes the loss is more like £30,000. He is prepared to settle for that amount but wishes to pay the sum in three tranches of £10,000 due to his cash-flow situation.

---

61. Form N242A and see PD 36A.
62. *Civil Procedure Rules*, r 36.6.

> In this situation, Edward could not use Part 36 because the settlement is not to be paid in a lump sum and (some of) it will be paid more than fourteen days after the offer has been accepted. Edward could, however, use a *Calderbank* offer.

17.1.8.3 **Withdrawing an offer**

It is possible to withdraw a Part 36 offer but only in certain circumstances. The first, and perhaps most important, is that it cannot be withdrawn after the other party has accepted it. If the party accepts the offer then it becomes a binding agreement.[63] However, if the other side has not yet accepted the offer, then it can be withdrawn if notice is given to the other side to that effect, but it requires the permission of the court to do so if the applicant purports to accept the offer before the expiry of the period.[64]

A Part 36 offer does not automatically lapse[65] and therefore if the offeror wishes to withdraw the offer then they must do so expressly, even after the twenty-one-day period has elapsed.

17.1.8.4 **Accepting an offer**

There is no prescribed manner in which an offer is accepted, but it must be done in writing and a party must inform the court that they have done so.[66]

The general rule is that where a party accepts the offer, the defendant will pay the costs of both parties up to the point at which the offer was accepted.[67] There is no discretion to award partial costs, and so the position is somewhat simpler as regards the costs regime, in that certainty is shown.

It was noted that a party could accept the offer after the expiry of the twenty-one-day period. If they do so, however, then the costs position shifts. The general rule is:

- The defendant pays the costs of the claimant up until the date of the expiry period.
- The claimant pays the costs from the date of the expiry date until the date of acceptance.[68]

The parties could choose to sort costs out as part of the Part 36 offer, although that would be somewhat unusual. The slightly more complicated rule as to costs for late acceptance is to mark the court's disapproval of not accepting the offer when it should have been accepted, ie the end of the expiry period.

17.1.8.5 **Failing to better an offer**

As with *Calderbank* offers, the main issue of relevance to Part 36 offers is what happens if a person does not 'match' an offer. The principal issue is one of costs.

---

63. *Civil Procedure Rules*, r 36.9(1).
64. *Civil Procedure Rules*, r 36.9 when read in conjunction with r 36.10.
65. See *C v D* [2011] EWCA Civ 646.
66. *Civil Procedure Rules*, r 36.11.
67. *Civil Procedure Rules*, r 36.13.
68. *Civil Procedure Rules*, r 36.13(4).

Offers made by defendants

Where a claimant does not obtain a judgment more advantageous than a Part 36 offer, the costs position is as follows:

1. The defendant will be liable for the costs of the claimant up until the date of expiry of the Part 36 offer. This is, in essence, an application of the usual rule that 'costs follow the event', ie because judgment was still entered against the defendant, they will be liable for the costs.

2. The claimant will be required to pay the costs of the defendant from the date of the expiry of the Part 36 offer until the date of judgment.

3. The claimant will be required to pay interest on the costs of the defendant.[69]

Thus it is in the interests of a defendant who believes that he is likely to be held liable, to make an early offer to settle. Of course, the offer needs to be sensible because it must take into account the likely judgment that is to be awarded at trial, but if he does so, he could be protected from significant costs if the judge does not better the offer.

> **≡ Example** Defendant making an offer
>
> An accident involving Tom's water storage caused considerable damage to Amelia's property. It is estimated that the damage will cost £30,000–£40,000 to put right but Amelia is claiming £75,000.
>
> After acknowledging the service, Tom makes a Part 36 offer to settle the dispute for £42,000, giving twenty-one days to accept the offer. Amelia does not accept the offer.
>
> At trial, the judge awards damages of £37,000 to Amelia. Amelia's costs until the date the offer expired came to £2,100. Her remaining costs were £8,000. Tom's costs were £500 until the date of the expiry of the Part 36 offer and £7,500 from that date.
>
> As Amelia has not bettered the offer, she will be awarded the £37,000 by the judge, but will only receive £2,100 in costs. She will then have to pay £7,500 of Tom's costs, plus her own costs of £8,000. She will also need to pay interest on the £7,500 costs from the date the offer expired.
>
> Had she accepted Tom's offer, she would have received £42,000 plus £2,100 in costs.

Offers made by claimants

Where the offer was made by a claimant, then so long as the judge makes an award that is *at least as advantageous* as the one the claimant made, then the following will be the position in respect of costs:

1. Interest on the judgment at a rate not exceeding 10 per cent above base rate, for some or all of the period since the expiry of the offer period.

2. The defendant to pay the claimant's costs after the relevant expiry period on the indemnity basis.

3. Interest on those indemnity costs at a rate not exceeding 10 per cent above base rate.

4. An additional amount, as calculated below.

69. *Civil Procedure Rules*, r 36.17(3).

⚡ INDEMNITY COSTS

There are two ways of calculating costs. The first is the 'standard basis' and the second is the 'indemnity basis'. The difference is really in whose favour doubt is resolved. On the standard basis, where there is doubt as to whether the costs are recoverable or reasonable, the benefit goes to the person paying. On the indemnity basis, it is the reverse. So, where there is any doubt as to whether the costs are payable or reasonable, the benefit goes to the person receiving the money. This potentially means costs could be significantly higher on the indemnity basis than the standard basis.

The additional amount referred to in #4 was introduced as a result of the *Legal Aid, Sentencing and Punishment of Offenders Act 2012* which sought to introduce some of the changes brought about by the *Jackson Review* into the costs of litigation.[70] The 2012 Act permits the Lord Chancellor to make regulations concerning the settlement of cases[71] and this has occurred.[72] The effect of these rules is to introduce the new 'additional amount' that is to be paid where a defendant rejects an offer from a claimant, and then subsequently does not achieve a more favourable result from court.

Where the claim is for money, the additional amount is calculated as shown in Table 17.1.[73]

Where the claim involves a non-monetary claim, the additional amount is 10 per cent of awarded costs up to the value of £500,000 and for costs awarded up to £1,000,000 the additional amount is 10 per cent of the first £500,000 and 5 per cent of any costs above that figure.[74] Where costs are above £1,000,000 the award would not be increased because the order makes clear that the maximum amount *for such claims* is to be £75,000,[75] which is the amount that would be paid for £1,000,000 worth of costs.

Where a claim involves both monetary and non-monetary value, then the maximum award should be calculated for both monetary and non-monetary claims using the 10 per cent/5 per cent methodology above,[76] again with a maximum payment of £75,000.

Table 17.1 Additional amount calculation

Award	Additional Amount
Up to £500,000	10% of the amount awarded
Above £500,000 but less than £1,000,000	10% of the first £500,000 and 5% of the amount awarded above that figure.
Above £1,000,000	7.5% of the first £1,000,000 and 0.001% of the amount awarded over that figure.

70. Lord Justice Jackson, *Review of Civil Litigation Costs* (Judiciary of England and Wales, London 2010).
71. *Legal Aid, Sentencing and Punishment of Offenders Act 2012*, s 55.
72. *Offers to Settle in Civil Proceedings Order 2013*, SI 2013/93.
73. SI 2013/93, art 2.
74. SI 2013/93, art 3(4)(b).
75. SI 2013/93, art 3(5).
76. SI 2013/93, art 3(4)(a).

> ### ☰ Example Claimant making an offer
>
> Charles was suing Esther for negligence in respect of some investments she was managing for him. His statement of claim states the damages sought are £750,000. However, shortly after receiving the defence statement, Charles enters a Part 36 offer whereby he agrees to settle for £600,000 payable immediately. Esther rejects this offer. It goes to trial eight months later and the judge awards £650,000 to Charles.
>
> Charles' costs were £13,000 up until the point the Part 36 offer expired and £700,000 from that point, although Esther's lawyers believe that a more reasonable figure would be £625,000. Esther's costs are £800,000.
>
> Esther will be liable for:
>
> - £650,000 damages awarded by the court
> - £13,000 costs for the period up to the expiry of the Part 36 offer
> - Interest on the £650,000 damages at a rate no more than 10 per cent above base rate for the eight months since the Part 36 offer (the interest continuing until the amount is paid)
> - £700,000[77] plus interest on this in the same way above
> - An additional amount of £62,500 calculated as above
> - Her costs of £800,000.

The implications for a defendant when a claimant makes an offer are therefore significant. The new regime is designed to ensure that defendants think very carefully about refusing offers to settle, particularly where they believe that they are, or could be, held liable. In the example above, had Esther accepted the offer, she would be in a very different position. If we assume her costs were similar to Charles' at the time the Part 36 offer was made, then she would have had to pay a total of £626,000. Instead she would be looking at paying a sum in excess of £2,000,000 assuming an interest rate of 8 per cent.

The consequences of Part 36 mean that lawyers have to be very clear with clients when advising them whether to accept a Part 36 offer or not. This is particularly true when the litigation is being funded in alternative ways. Insurance companies and solicitors employing contingency fee arrangements are likely to be highly cautious about rejecting a Part 36 offer. However, even private clients would need to think extremely carefully given the potential differences.

17.1.8.6 Judge not to be told

The last point to note on Part 36 is the fact that a judge should not be told that a Part 36 offer has been made until either (a) it is accepted, or (b) the court has made its determination as to the award. The reason for this is to ensure that there is no possibility that the judge is influenced by knowledge of the Part 36 offer. Let us return to our earlier example of Charles and Esther. If the judge realized an offer had been made for £600,000 and he was minded to award £610,000, could he be influenced by that if he knew that the consequences of that additional £10,000 were that Esther

---

77.   As it is on the indemnity basis, where there is doubt as to whether the reasonable figure is £700,000 or £625,000, the benefit will be given to Charles.

could pay hundreds of thousands of pounds more? Similarly, if he had been minded to award £590,000, would he be influenced knowing that by not awarding £600,000 the consequences would be that the fees would almost certainly dwarf the award, meaning Charles would actually lose money rather than gain any?

Where a judge believes that no prejudice would be caused by his continuing to sit with the knowledge, then the case can proceed.[78] At least one commentator has stated that judges should not be too quick to stand down[79] although where either party objects, it is quite likely that it would be difficult to continue (save where the difference in costs is likely to be relatively modest) because the appearance that a determination has been influenced must be relatively strong.

17.2 Case study: The small claims track

The remainder of this chapter will look at three hypothetical case studies. The point of these is to try and show you how litigation can work and the steps that are taken during proceedings.

The first form of litigation to consider is that of the small claims track. This was presented earlier, but this section will provide a walk-through of how a case would be heard.

> ### ▤ Example A faulty television
>
> Amy Daventry is a resident of Northampton. She buys a television costing £250 from Screens 'R' Us Ltd a national company with a branch in Northampton (their head office is in Carlisle). After six weeks Amy's television blows up. She contacts Screens 'R' Us who say that 'it is nothing to do with us, that is what they do'. They offer to put her in contact with a repair service who will fix it for £150. She declines the offer.

If you consult your *Contract Law* textbook you will see that this scenario is a very simple contract matter. Since this is a private transaction between a shop and a consumer, the *Consumer Rights Act 2015* covers this purchase. Section 9 of that Act states that goods must be of satisfactory quality, and s 10 requires goods to be fit for a particular purpose. A television blowing up for no reason within six weeks of purchase would not meet either test. The 2015 Act provides a short-term right to reject goods[80] but this only lasts thirty days. However, a longer period of rejection is also contained within the Act and, for a faulty television set, this would be within six months of purchase.[81] How does Amy secure her right to a refund?

17.2.1 Pre-action procedure

The first thing that Amy must do is to complain to the shop. She has done this verbally, but it would be prudent for her to write to them, explaining she wishes a refund.

---

78. *Garratt v Saxby* [2004] 1 WLR 2152.
79. Stuart Sime, *A Practical Approach to Civil Procedure* (19th edn, OUP 2016) 417.
80. *Consumer Rights Act 2015*, s 20.
81. *Consumer Rights Act 2015*, s 24.

Table 17.2 Fees payable when the N1 form is served

Amount claim(£)	Paper Fee(£)	Online Fee(£)
Up to 300	35	25
300.01–500	50	35
500.01–1,000	70	60
1,000.01–1,500	80	70
1,500.01–3,000	115	105
3,000.01–5,000	205	185
5,000.01–10,000	455	410

Assuming she does not do this, then her next port of call could either be litigation or the *Consumer Ombudsman*.

The *Consumer Ombudsman* is a form of Alternative Dispute Resolution that was created under secondary legislation.[82] It provides a 'single point of contact' for consumers who believe that their rights have been breached. It is free to use for consumers (it is funded by charging a fee for organizations that sign up to it). However, as with other forms of ADR (discussed in Chapter 19), it is reliant on the organization cooperating with the dispute.

Let us assume that Amy did contact the *Consumer Ombudsman* but the shop refuses to cooperate with the Ombudsman, saying 'it's not our problem'. The only solution left is to litigate. As noted earlier, an attempt at resolving the dispute must be made before commencing litigation. Clearly this has happened. If, however, Amy had not gone to the Ombudsman then she would have needed to write a letter saying why she was rejecting the goods and wishes a refund.

The first action is to complete the claim form (N1), presented earlier in this chapter. The Online Resource Centre includes a completed form N1 in respect of Amy's claim so that you can see what needs to be included. Reference should be made to 17.1.3 for an explanation of what to complete in respect of this claim. It will be remembered that the claim can begin online. If this option is chosen then Amy need only complete the details there. If she chooses to lodge the case at court, then she will need to photocopy the form twice so that there are three copies (one for her, one for the defendant, and one for the court). All three copies are lodged with the court.[83]

A fee is payable when the form is served. The fee depends on the sum of the claim and whether it is started online or at court. The current fees are set out in Table 17.2.

17.2.2 Defendant's response

The defendant will receive a copy of the N1 claim form and the appropriate notes for completion. A 'response pack' will also be sent. A copy of the forms and response pack

82.   See *Alternative Dispute Resolution for Consumer Disputes (Competent Authorities and Information) Regulations 2015* (SI 2015/542).
83.   For online claims, the system prints out three copies automatically.

is included online—it is not replicated here as it can be a lengthy form. However, in essence, the defendant has four options open to him:

- admit the whole of the claim
- admit *some* of the claim but deny the rest
- deny the whole of the claim
- counterclaim.

In fact the options are slightly increased since a counterclaim can be combined with an admission and partial admission of the claim. A counterclaim is where the defendant argues that the claimant owes money. It is not necessary to discuss in detail the process of counterclaiming but in essence the defendant becomes the 'claimant' for that part of the claim and the claimant becomes the 'defendant'. To avoid doubt and ensure consistency, however, the claimant and defendant continue to be so labelled for the duration of the proceedings. We will not cover counterclaims in this section as to do so could only confuse matters and this 'walkthrough' is simply an illustration of how civil litigation can occur and is not designed to be a comprehensive analysis of all aspects of the civil litigation system.

17.2.2.1 Admission of the claim

The most straightforward situation is that the defendant admits the claim and decides to settle. No money is paid to the court but instead the defendant tells the court he admits the claim and will pay the money to the claimant. When the claimant receives the money he will notify the court that the matter is settled. An advantage of the small claims track is that this can occur relatively quickly, especially where a major business is the defendant. The consequences for a business of losing a judgment can be significant as it will be entered onto a register to which credit agencies have access. Whilst a prompt settlement will lead to the entry being withdrawn the initial damage occurs. Also, where there is an arguable case many businesses will simply pay the money owed in a small claims case as it would cost more for them to fight it (as no legal costs can be paid the 'costs' of their in-house or contracted legal department who would inevitably deal with such matters would probably be more than the amount claimed).

It is for this reason that the small claims track is particularly useful for consumers. As there is no liability for costs, the 'threat' of a court summons (which, as seen from the costs stated earlier, will not cost much money to issue) can often settle customer-relations disputes. It has been questioned whether this was an appropriate use of the court's time, and whether a better approach for consumer disputes would be by way of ADR. Obviously, it was noted above that the *Ombudsman Scheme* is now operational but it is not mandatory. For relatively simple claims under a certain threshold, it could legitimately be questioned whether mandating some form of adjudicative ADR would not be more appropriate. It would free up judicial time that could be used for other cases.

17.2.2.2 Admission of part of the claim

One possibility is that the defendant admits part of the claim but not all of it. In these circumstances the defendant explains to the court what part of the claim he admits and what part he is contesting and why. The defendant would normally pay the amount admitted although this need not be done at once. The claimant will then be asked whether he accepts the partial admission as full settlement or whether he wishes to pursue the matter for the remainder.

> **☰ Example** Smoke in the kitchen
>
> Susan purchases a new saucepan but when it is first used it burns badly causing intense smoke damage to the wall by the cooker. Susan believes that the whole kitchen should be repainted because painting only one wall would not look right. The sellers of the saucepan believe it is possible to paint one wall.

Here, the seller may well admit liability but contest the damages that are being asked for. In this case, a partial admission will be made whereby the seller accepts to refund the cost of the saucepan and for the work involved in painting one wall. They deny that it is necessary to pay for full redecoration.

Susan would have to decide whether to accept this partial admission or seek a hearing to decide whether her full claim would succeed.

17.2.2.3 Denying the claim

Where the defendant contests the entire claim then he must tender a defence which is a formal statement saying *why* he contests the claim. This is also part of the response form. In the small claims court it is usual for the defence to be supplied at the time of acknowledging the service of the claim but this need not occur and it is possible to acknowledge receipt of the claim within fourteen days and serve a defence within twenty-eight days.[84]

581

17.2.2.4 Defendant does not respond

It is possible that the defendant will simply fail to respond. Although the claim form is a formal document issued by the county court it is surprising how many people, firms, and companies will simply ignore the form hoping that 'it will go away'. In fact it rarely does and refusing to respond to a claim can cause significant complications, allowing the claimant to seek 'judgment by default'.[85]

A judgment by default is where a court rules on the matter without considering any evidence. Indeed, it has been noted that it is a purely administrative exercise that takes place when no defence is filed.[86] In straightforward cases such as the one in Amy's example, the matter would not be put before a judge. The court staff would check that the procedural steps have been completed appropriately and would then simply enter judgment on behalf of the court.

There is the power to set aside a judgment in default. Where the judgment was entered incorrectly (eg because the claim was not served in time etc) then the court *must* set aside the judgment.[87] These situations are, however, comparatively rare because most people take care to ensure that claims and documents are served appropriately.

---

84. *Civil Procedure Rules*, r 15.4.
85. *Civil Procedure Rules*, r 15.3 when read in conjunction with pt 12.
86. Stuart Sime, *A Practical Approach to Civil Procedure* (19th edn, OUP 2016) 137.
87. *Civil Procedure Rules*, r 13.2.

The court has discretion to set a judgment aside if:

(a) the defendant has a real prospect of successfully defending the claim; or

(b) it appears to the court there is some other good reason why—

  (i) the judgment should be set aside; or

  (ii) the defendant should be allowed to defend the claim.[88]

Paragraph (a) is considered the issue that the courts will focus most directly upon; they will require considerable persuasion to allow a case to be reopened where judgment is likely to be given against the defendant thereafter.[89] Examples could include situations where a defendant did not receive the claim forms. Service can be to the last-known address of an individual[90] but if no forwarding address or service was active, it is quite possible the defendant did not know about the proceedings. It is notable that this is *discretionary* rather than mandatory. As service can be to the last-known address, a court could decide that the proceedings took place appropriately. However, it is more common for them to set aside a judgment in this instance.[91]

Judgments are public documents and a county court judgment can cause significant problems to a credit rating of either an individual or company. It has been suggested therefore that where an unaware defendant applies for a judgment to be set aside because he would have otherwise settled the case without the need for a judgment, this could be a reason for setting the judgment aside.[92] It is to be hoped that such applications are tested, however. A person should not be allowed to set aside the judgment to save embarrassment save where he was not aware of the claim, since otherwise the person is being rewarded for his lax conduct.

A fee is payable by the defendant to set the judgment aside (currently £255) and if there are costs incurred by the claimant (unlikely in the small claims track) then these would be payable by the defendant.

17.2.3 Track allocation, management, and mediation

When the defence is received, a court officer will make a preliminary assessment of the track that the case should be assigned to. In a case such as Amy's, there is no doubt that it would be the small claims track. It was noted earlier (17.1.4) that for non-personal injury cases under £10,000 there is a clear presumption that the small claims track will be used.

The court will send a directions questionnaire to both the claimant and defendant. A copy of the questionnaire for the small claims track can be found on the Online Resource Centre. The questionnaire asks to confirm the personal details of the parties, the proposed court centre that the matter will be heard at, whether experts are to be present, and the number of witnesses to be heard.

Perhaps one of the more important questions is whether the parties are prepared to consider mediation. This is part of a recent trend to encourage alternative forms of dispute resolution (discussed further in Chapter 19). If both parties consent, then the case

---

88. *Civil Procedure Rules*, r 13.3.
89. Stuart Sime, *A Practical Approach to Civil Procedure* (19th edn, OUP 2016) 144.
90. *Civil Procedure Rules*, r 6.9.
91. See, for example, *Akram v Adam* [2004] EWCA Civ 1601.
92. Stuart Sime, *A Practical Approach to Civil Procedure* (19th edn, OUP 2016) 144.

will be stayed and sent to the small claims mediation service.[93] This is a service that is operated by HM Courts and Tribunal Service where court staff act as mediators to try and settle the dispute. The mediation usually takes place via a teleconference. If mediation fails, then the stay is lifted.

Before the hearing takes place, a further fee has to be paid. This is known as the 'hearing fee' and the current level is set as in Table 17.3:

Table 17.3 The current fee to be paid for a hearing

Claim value(£)	Fee(£)
Up to 300	25
300.01–500	55
500.01–1,000	80
1,000.01–1,500	115
1,500.01–3,000	170
3,000 or more	335

It should be noted that whilst these costs are relatively modest, it does mean that even a small claims track case can cost a relatively significant amount of money. Amy will now have had to pay £50 or £60 in court fees to recover £150, although this will of course be reimbursed if she is successful.

Whilst the hearing will usually be in public,[94] it will generally take place not in a courtroom but in a judge's room. Whether this is truly 'in public' is therefore open to question. Theoretically, there is nothing to stop someone going to the court and saying that they would like to watch proceedings, but how many people will know this and/ or want to do so?

Whilst the small claims track is civil litigation, the hearing will usually differ from the formality inherent in other forms of civil litigation:

1. The court may adopt any method of proceeding at a hearing that it considers to be fair.
2. Hearings will be informal.
3. The strict rules of evidence do not apply.
4. The court need not take evidence on oath.
5. The court may limit cross-examination.
6. The court must give reasons for its decision.[95]

The judge will normally take the lead in small claims track cases and it will usually have the feel of an inquisitorial approach or even be more akin to adjudication, where the judge will ask questions of the parties to understand what is at the heart of this dispute. This is partly because lawyers within the small claims track are relatively

93. *Civil Procedure Rules*, r 26.4A.
94. PD 27, para 4.1.
95. *Civil Procedure Rules*, r 27.8.

unusual, not least because the costs of representation are not normally recoverable in the small claims track.

The attendance of the parties is usually necessary but it is possible to provide written notice to the court and other party at least seven days in advance that they will not be present.[96] If this is done and all other documents are submitted in the usual way, the court will take account of those documents (eg the statement of claim or the statement of defence). If they do not provide the relevant notice and submit the appropriate documents and do not attend, then summary action can be taken. This means that where it is the claimant who does not turn up, the case can be struck out (meaning the action fails).[97] Where it is the defendant who does not turn up then the case will be decided solely on the claimant's evidence (if the claimant appears or has given the necessary notice not to attend),[98] meaning in all likelihood that the action will succeed.

The judge will normally pronounce judgment immediately after the conclusion of the hearing. This will not be in the form of a usual judgment and will instead be a simple explanation of his decision.[99] Ordinarily the judgment will be given verbally rather than in writing. However, hearings are recorded and therefore if a transcription is required then this can be arranged.

17.2.4 Remedies and appeal

Obtaining a judgment by itself is not sufficient, a remedy must be sought. The remedies and avenues of appeal will be considered in Chapter 18.

17.3 Judicial review

The second form of litigation to consider is judicial review. This is an area of civil litigation that is very different from the previous example. Instead of two sides arguing over money or some other form of dispute, judicial review is about holding the state to account. It is arguing that a decision that has been, or will be, made is legally impermissible (whether through illegality, irrationality, or procedural impropriety[100]). Many challenges under the *Human Rights Act 1998* are judicial reviews, in part because the 1998 Act states that a public body acts unlawfully if it acts contrary to a Convention right,[101] which is a ground for judicial review.

This section will not consider the substantive law relating to judicial review as that is a matter for other texts and modules.[102] Instead, this section will be similar to the previous section in that it will take a hypothetical case study and walk through the stages of the hearing. Judicial review has increased significantly in recent years and this has proven a thorn in the government's side. The government sought to make changes to judicial review, although in the end relatively modest changes were introduced by legislation.[103]

---

96.   *Civil Procedure Rules*, r 27.9(1).
97.   *Civil Procedure Rules*, r 27.9(2).
98.   *Civil Procedure Rules*, r 27.9(3).
99.   PD 27, para 5.3(1).
100. *Council for Civil Service Unions v Minister for the Civil Service* [1995] AC 374.
101. *Human Rights Act 1998*, s 6(1).
102. You are likely to cover this in your Public Law module.
103. *Criminal Justice and Courts Act 2015*, pt 4.

Unlike the previous example, we have shifted from the Crown Court to the High Court of Justice. Save for a few issues that are not relevant to us, claims for judicial review are brought in the Administrative Court,[104] which forms part of the Queen's Bench Division of the High Court. Traditionally, claims for judicial review took place in a Divisional Court (ie two or more judges, usually presided over by a Lord Justice of Appeal) but recently there has been an increase in single-judge hearings.

Let us now consider our hypothetical example.

> ### ☰ Example A mother's march
>
> Matilda wishes to campaign against the decision of the (fictional) Rutland County Council to close a nursery she uses in Smallville. She has organized a number of parents and they wish to march two miles down the centre of Smallville to the offices of Rutland County Council where they will make speeches and wave placards. The protest is planned to take place the day a Home Office minister is due to visit Smallville and so the Chief Constable of the (fictional) Rutland Police has decided to ban the march because he doesn't want the town to look unruly. Matilda wishes to challenge this decision. She visits the Chief Constable but he refuses to back down and thus she wishes to take action in court.

17.3.1 Pre-action protocols

As with other types of civil litigation there are procedural steps that must be considered before a claim for judicial review can proceed.

17.3.1.1 A public function?

The first point to note is that a judicial review can only be brought against a public body. The rules state that 'judicial review' means:

> ... a claim to review the lawfulness of—
>   i.   an enactment; or
>   ii. a decision, action or failure to act in relation to the exercise of a public function.

Thus judicial review is an action against an organ of the state. Whilst it is traditionally said that the English Legal System differs from certain continental jurisdictions (most notably France) in not having a separate court system for public matters, this is arguably no longer true with the advancement of judicial review and the creation of the Administrative Court.

Quite what is a public function is the subject of some debate and it is outside the scope of this book. It can be summarized as a function that the public would ordinarily be expected to be delivered by the state, even if it is not actually doing so. For example, the incarceration of prisoners would be a function of the state even if they are being incarcerated in a private prison. However, for more detailed reference it is necessary to refer to texts that consider this in more depth.[105]

---

104.   PD 54A, para 1.1.
105.   See, for example, Hilaire Barnett, *Constitutional & Administrative Law* (9th edn, OUP 2016) Part IV.

17.3.1.2 *Locus standi*

The first issue that must be considered is whether the claimant has the right to issue judicial review proceedings. There is not an absolute right to begin proceedings, and only persons with 'standing' (the anglicized meaning of *locus standi*) can bring proceedings. The test for this is set out in statute:

> No application for judicial review shall be made unless the leave of the High Court has been obtained in accordance with rules of court; and the court shall not grant leave to make such an application unless it considers that the applicant has a sufficient interest in the matter to which the application relates.[106]

Two issues arise from this. The first is that there is not an automatic right to judicial review, permission must be sought (discussed later at 17.3.4) and the second is the test of standing, that is 'sufficient interest'. Rather unhelpfully neither the Act nor the CPR define what 'sufficient interest' means but it has been considered to mean that a person has a genuine interest in seeking a remedy and can show they are, or are likely to be, affected by the issue to be reviewed.[107] The essence of the test is to prevent purely theoretical disputes from arising or to prevent people who will not be affected by the decision challenging it for non-legal reasons.

Example More about the march

If we refer back to our example of Matilda, it would be extremely difficult to argue that Matilda does not have standing in this matter since she uses the nursery the protest relates to. If, however, Hazel, who lives 200 miles away, wishes to challenge the decision because she objects to 'police suppression of the right to march' then it is unlikely that she would have standing because she cannot show a link to the action.

That said, it has been suggested that some abuses of power are so widespread that any citizen would have the right to intervene.[108]

Arguably standing can be dealt with at one of two stages; either the permission stage or at the actual hearing. The general rule is that it will be dealt with at the permission stage although in exceptional cases the courts have said that the decision can be postponed so that they can reflect on standing in light of the evidence adduced.[109] However, arguably this does not breach the general rule since such instances are known as 'rolled up' hearings, ie ones where the permission and merits are dealt with at the same time. Section 31 is clear that permission is required in order to bring a review and that permission can only be given if the person has standing. In a rolled-up hearing a court will consider all the evidence and either allow the application and grant relief (subject to their discretion) or, instead of rejecting the case, often state that permission was refused even though the effect is the same.

---

106.   *Senior Courts Act 1981*, s 31(3).
107.   See *Halsbury's Laws*, vol 61, 656.
108.   See, by way of discussion, *R v Somerset County Council and ARC Southern Ltd, ex parte Dixon* [1997] COD 323.
109.   *R v Inland Revenue Commissioners, ex parte National Federation of Self-Employed and Small Businesses Ltd* [1982] AC 617.

Human rights

A slight issue arises in respect of applications under the HRA 1998. Section 7(7) HRA 1998 expressly states that when deciding whether to permit someone to bring an action under s 7 of the Act (which permits someone to bring proceedings claiming a breach, or future breach, of their rights) the court must make reference to Article 34 of the ECHR. Article 34 defines a 'victim' and it has been suggested that the definition of victim under the ECHR is more restrictive than the test ordinarily adopted by the courts when making decisions under Part 54. However, it is not necessarily easy to identify any practical issue because many issues raised as human rights issues would also be relevant under the grounds of judicial review.

> **Example** Matilda and her human rights
>
> If we refer back to our example Matilda's application may, or may not, raise human rights issues. On the one hand she could use s 7 HRA 1998 because the right to protest is contained within Articles 10 (freedom of expression) and 11 (right of assembly) of the ECHR. However, she could also complain about the decision using only domestic law (that it was irrational).
>
> In fact, in this scenario it would make no substantive difference since Matilda would be considered a victim under Article 34 as well as having ordinary standing under s 31.

Exhaustion of alternative remedies

As part of the decision about whether a person has standing to bring an action in judicial review the courts will consider whether all alternative remedies have been exhausted. Judicial review is considered to be an action of last resort and therefore where there is, for example, an internal complaints or review system by a public body this should be exhausted before judicial review proceedings are brought. That said, the courts are willing to relax this where alternative proceedings would not be 'so convenient, beneficial and effectual' or where the alternative will not provide an effective remedy.[110]

In our example, it is unlikely that this would cause any real difficulty. There is no statutory or alternative appeals process where a chief constable decides to ban a march.

17.3.1.3 Timing

Judicial review actions are supposed to be timely: they are designed to review either decisions made recently or decisions that are about to be made. Save for planning and procurement cases, which were the subject of control as part of the 'reforms' to judicial review,[111] a claim for judicial review must be lodged 'promptly' and, in any event, not less than three months from the date of the decision to be challenged.[112] It should be noted that 'promptly' and 'three months' are not part of the same test: it is quite

587

110. *Halsbury's Laws*, vol 61, 657.
111. See *Civil Procedure Rules* and *Public Contracts Regulations 2015*, SI 2015/102, reg 54.4(5).
112. *Civil Procedure Rules*, r 54.4(1).

possible that waiting three months to judicially review a decision is considered not to be prompt, meaning that the application is dismissed.[113]

Example Returning to the march

Let us assume that the march was organized two months before it is due to commence. The Chief Constable within the first three days said that he would ban the march. If Matilda left it until the week before the march then the court may decline to give permission.

What if Matilda had actually been in discussion with the Chief Constable for four weeks in an attempt to reach a conclusion? If, after these talks, the final 'no' arrives then there would be little difficulty in showing the timeliness of the action because any delay was incurred by trying to resolve the dispute.

17.3.1.4 Exchange of letters

Save where time prevents it, a potential claimant should ordinarily send a letter to the defendant, stating why they are seeking to challenge the claim and asking for it to be resolved. The defendant should ordinarily acknowledge this letter and state a brief summary of why they contest the issue.[114]

17.3.2 Applying for permission

Unlike most forms of civil litigation, pursuing judicial review is not a matter of right. An applicant must first seek the permission of the High Court to do so.

A specific form exists to begin a claim for judicial review (N461 which can be found on the Online Resource Centre) and this must be used. Along with the personal details of the claimant, proposed defendant, and any interested parties, it includes a request for details of the decision that is to be judicially reviewed and also the date the decision was made. Details of the proposed remedy sought must also be included, together with details of any other decisions that are to be made.

The form must also be accompanied with the relevant documentary evidence that is to be relied upon to justify the decision. This is because the initial application for permission will ordinarily be done on papers, and therefore sufficient evidence must be submitted to show that there is a case to answer. In Matilda's case, it is quite likely that the chief constable will have written to her, explaining why he will not permit a march. This, together with the letters she sent requesting permission etc, would form part of the documentary evidence. A fee is to be paid when the form is lodged (currently £154).

Once the form is served (and unlike the county court proceedings discussed before, the claimant will be responsible for service rather than the court), all parties must acknowledge service, using the appropriate form. This must take place within twenty-one days of service[115] and should include a summary of his grounds for contesting the claim or indeed contesting that permission should be given.[116]

---

113.   See, *Senior Courts Act 1981*, s 31(7).
114.   Stuart Sime, *A Practical Approach to Civil Procedure* (19th edn, OUP 2016) 556.
115.   *Civil Procedure Rules*, r 54.8(2).
116.   *Civil Procedure Rules*, r 54.8(4)(a).

The matter then proceeds before a 'single judge' (who is a puisne judge). This judge will consider the evidence placed before him and decide whether to give permission for a judicial review to proceed. The test for whether judicial review should proceed was summarized as raising 'an arguable ground ... having a reasonable prospect of success'.[117] Where it is thought that a successful claim would have no practical effect, permission can also be refused.[118] As part of the 'reforms' to judicial review, an additional threshold was introduced that may be considered by a court on its own motion or must be considered if the defendant so requests.[119] This additional threshold is that the court must refuse leave if 'it appears to the High Court to be highly likely that the outcome for the applicant would not have been substantially different'.[120] This is a higher threshold than the 'no practical difference' adopted by the Supreme Court, but it is designed to ensure that the cost of judicial review is avoided where the proceedings would, in essence, be theoretical.

17.3.2.1 Challenging a refusal

If the single judge refuses to grant leave, a person can seek to renew permission before a hearing.[121] This allows them an opportunity to persuade the judge that there is an arguable case or that the outcome would be 'substantially different' where the s 31(3C) test is considered. A fee of £385 must be paid to renew permission.

If permission is again refused, the only opportunity is to appeal to the Court of Appeal (Civil Division).[122]

Where the single judge decides that an application is 'without merit'[123] then it is not possible to seek a hearing to renew permission,[124] and instead the only avenue will be an appeal to the Court of Appeal (Civil Division). That said, such a challenge is unlikely to succeed.

17.3.2.2 Success rate

Although it was said earlier that the threshold for permission would seem relatively low (an arguable case) it is clear that a substantial number of cases fail to gain permission. The latest statistics show that of 4,680 applications received in the Administrative Court, only 765 cases received permission to proceed,[125] approximately 16 per cent. Of those, 621 were given permission by the single judge, and 144 had their permission granted after seeking a hearing to review the denial of permission.[126] Four hundred and seventy claimants had sought an oral hearing, meaning that the success rate for a review of permission being denied is approximately 30 per cent.

The relatively low success rate is one reason why governments have sought to restrict judicial review. The 4,680 applications lodged require a public authority to respond in some way to the application, incurring cost and effort. However, as problematic as the government may view judicial review to be, it is now clearly considered an important constitutional safeguard that allows the state to be held to account.

117. *Sharma v Brown-Antoine* [2007] 1 WLR 780, 787.
118. *R (on behalf of O) v Secretary of State for the Home Department* [2016] UKSC 19.
119. *Senior Courts Act 1981*, s 31(3C).
120. *Senior Courts Act 1981* as inserted by the *Criminal Justice and Courts Act 2015*, s 31(3D).
121. *Civil Procedure Rules*, r 54.12(3).
122. *Civil Procedure Rules*, r 52.15.
123. *Civil Procedure Rules*, r 23.13.
124. *Civil Procedure Rules*, r 54.12(7).
125. 'A Guide to Civil and Administrative Justice Statistics' (Ministry of Justice 2016) 15.
126. 'A Guide to Civil and Administrative Justice Statistics' (Ministry of Justice 2016) 15.

17.3.3 The hearing

Assuming that permission is granted then the matter will begin to proceed towards a hearing. A fee of £770 must be paid at this stage, although this is halved to £385 if the claimant required a hearing to gain permission.

17.3.3.1 Courts hearing judicial review claims

As already noted, it is the Administrative Court that hears applications for judicial review, but that does not mean it sits in one place. The majority of judicial review proceedings continue to be heard in London but they are increasingly being heard in the regions too, either by puisne judges or acting judges of the High Court.[127] The principal courts where it sits include Cardiff, Bristol, Birmingham, Leeds, and Manchester. That said, as it is part of the High Court of Justice, it can sit anywhere and can certainly sit in any other court if it is convenient for the parties and/or judiciary to do so.

17.3.3.2 Pre-hearing matters

Once permission has been granted, the court will issue directions that will set out the timescale of proceedings and indicate who is going to hear the case (including whether it is necessary for the matter to be heard by a Divisional Court).

Theoretically judicial review cases could be decided without a hearing[128] but this is likely to be extremely rare and would be where the dispute is minor. Such cases are now more likely to be resolved through the use of ADR and therefore a hearing is more likely.

The claimant must submit, at least twenty-one days before the hearing, a skeleton argument outlining their case.[129] This must be served on all parties and include:

(a) a time estimate for the complete hearing.

(b) a list of issues.

(c) a list of the legal points to be taken (together with any relevant authorities with page references to the passages relied on).

(d) a chronology of events.

(e) a list of essential documents for the advance reading of the court.

(f) a list of persons referred to.[130]

'Skeleton arguments' are a misleading term as they can be extremely comprehensive. In judicial review hearings (and indeed in appeals), they are a written explanation (fully referenced) of the submissions of the individual. Whilst they will be expanded upon during the hearing, they are also used by the court to identify what issues they do not want to discuss in the hearing.

The other parties must file and serve a skeleton argument no less than fourteen days before the hearing, ie they will have sight of the claimant's skeleton argument for seven days and they should ordinarily address area of the skeleton argument that they disagree with in their own skeleton argument.

---

127.   *Senior Courts Act 1981*, s 9 permits a circuit judge or recorder to sit as a judge of the High Court for a particular case.
128.   *Civil Procedure Rules*, r 54.18.
129.   PD 54, para 15.
130.   PD 54, para 15.3.

17.3.3.3 Oral hearing

The hearing itself will take place in open court and it will, unlike the small claims track cases which were discussed in the previous section, take place in a courtroom. The court itself can decide on the format of the hearing but ordinarily the claimant will open proceedings, followed by the defendant and then any interested parties.

Hearings on judicial review do not generally involve hearing testimony from witnesses, although the court does have a discretion to hear witnesses if they believe it would be helpful.[131] In practice, it is generally rare for witnesses to be heard as judicial review is rarely about the facts, it is normally a question of law, ie whether the decision complained of is illegal, irrational, or one that was reached in a procedurally improper way. The documentation that is submitted to the court is normally sufficient to reach the decision.

17.3.4 Decision and remedy

The verdict will either be given at the conclusion of the hearing or may well be reserved. Where it is given at the conclusion of the hearing it will be given *ex tempore* but where it is reserved then ordinarily a full judgment will be prepared, that will then be handed down later. Where it is a Divisional Court (two or more judges) then a single judgment may be given or all judges may speak. Where a two-judge court is divided then technically the case is resolved against the defendant.[132] That said, the court does have discretion to re-list the matter before a three-judge panel before judgment is given, although it is likely that this will only be considered in exceptional circumstances.

The remedies available for a successful claim for judicial review will be considered in the next chapter.

591

17.4 The Family Court

The third, and final, example of civil litigation looks at a completely different issue, that of family law. As was discussed at 6.2.4, this is now the province of the Family Court and the court has its own procedure rules (*Family Procedure Rules*).

Family justice is a very broad type of civil activity that encompasses numerous different types of litigation. Some are akin to ordinary litigation (for example, partners seeking to dispose of property) whereas others are more specialist. Public childcare proceedings involve the state seeking to exercise its powers to protect children and can include, for example, decisions whether to remove a child from its parents.

As with the other two types of litigation we will start with an example.

Example Increased contact

Deborah and Joshua were married for eleven years and had one child, Sarah, who is aged six. When they divorced, Deborah obtained a residence order for Sarah meaning that she stays with her. Joshua was granted a contact order that says that Sarah will see her father on

---

131. *Civil Procedure Rules*, r 54.17.
132. See *Cambridgeshire CC v Associated Lead Mills Ltd* [2005] EWHC 1627 (Admin) [14].

certain days. During school term-time the contact is Tuesday evenings and all-day Saturday. During school holidays he can see her on Tuesday afternoons and all-day Saturday.

Joshua wishes to increase the amount of time he spends with Sarah as she grows up. He requests overnight contact on Friday evenings (so that she would stay with him on Friday evening through to Saturday evening) and the right to take her on holiday for one week a year.

Deborah is happy to allow for the holiday but she thinks Sarah is too young for overnight contact away from her at the moment.

This is what is known as a private child-law dispute. It is characterized as a private dispute because, by itself, it does not involve the state. It is for Joshua and Deborah to settle the matter although, as will be seen, this is not strictly true as the interests of Sarah are directly relevant to this dispute. In terms of law, contact arrangements are dealt with under s 8 *Children Act 1989* and it is under this section that Joshua will apply to the court.

17.4.1 Beginning the claim

As with other forms of litigation, there are procedures that must take place before proceedings can commence. The main issue is the desire to avoid litigation. It was seen earlier (and will be seen more clearly in Chapter 19) that the courts seek to avoid litigation more generally, but this is certainly the case in respect of family disputes, particularly those involving a child. Litigation is undoubtedly disruptive to family life, particularly when it is seen as a 'battle' over the upbringing of children which has the danger of spilling into the child's consciousness.

Part 3 of the *Family Procedure Rules* refers to non-court dispute resolutions. The rule is clear:

> The court must consider, at every stage in proceedings, whether non-court dispute resolution is appropriate.[133]

This rule is followed by a requirement that, for certain applications, non-court disposals must be considered. The detail of these rules will be considered in Chapter 19 but we can note at this point that private-law proceedings relating to children are one of these cases. Therefore, before Joshua can apply for a court order, he will first need to either attempt mediation or be given a waiver.

For our purposes, let us assume that Joshua and Sarah try mediation but it becomes clear that neither side is willing to 'budge' in terms of what they wish. Therefore, mediation has been tried but ultimately fails and only a court will be able to settle the dispute.

17.4.1.1 Claim form

As with other forms of litigation, the first step to litigation is to complete the claim form. The Family Courts have their own forms, and the relevant form to be used in this instance is form C100. A copy of this form can be found on the Online Resource Centre. The form is more detailed than the other claim forms that have been examined.

---

133. *Family Procedure Rules*, r 3.3(1).

However, the form is also accessible, with the sections being phrased as questions, generally without the use of legalese. This is a reflection of the fact that legal aid is not normally available for private family-law disputes, and therefore there is an increase in litigants in person who are pursuing applications themselves. A dispute such as the one in our example between Deborah and Joshua could easily be completed without the need for a lawyer.

The form asks the claimant to say what the application is about. Section 8 of the *Children Act 1989* permits the making of various orders in respect of the upbringing of a child, but the one that we are concerned with is a 'child arrangements order' which deals with who has residence of the child, and at what point in time etc. The claimant is also to indicate whether there are any potential risks of harm (so that these can be investigated by the appropriate authorities), including issues relating to the history of the case and whether the court is being invited to ratify a consent order. Full details of the child must be given and information provided about whether they are known to the local authority social services department.

Section 2 of the form requires details about the mediation attempted. The most common answers here are that either the parties have attended mediation (as in our example), or that they have a mediation exemption. This is where the mediator accepts that mediation would not be appropriate (and they must sign the relevant part of C100 to indicate that). As will be seen from Chapter 19, there is some concern that mediators are allowing too many people to escape the requirement to attend a mediation hearing. There is some anecdotal evidence that the courts are beginning to take a harder line and are not accepting a wish not to pursue mediation. However, practice is not consistent as some courts do allow this.

Later sections of the form require details of the claim and details of the remedy sought (ie if the object is to settle the arrangements for access to the children, what pattern of contact will be used etc).

As with the other forms, there is a requirement that the claimant signs a statement of truth, with the usual consequences for any misleading statements.

A fee is payable at the time the application is lodged. This fee is currently £215 which is a not insignificant fee to be paid. There are real concerns about the costs of family law cases,[134] and whether this puts people off going to court. Where there is a disparity between incomes, it can also mean that a party could misuse the cost of litigation to benefit themselves unreasonably.

17.4.2 Allocating the judge

Whilst the Family Court is one joined-up court, it encompasses three levels of existing courts; the magistrates' court (where it used to be known as the *Family Proceedings Court*), the county court, and the High Court. It would not be appropriate to talk about where the case goes in terms of these courts because the Family Court is truly a joined-up court. However, this also means that cases are heard by magistrates, district judges (including deputy district judges), circuit judges (including recorders), and puisne judges. The judge should be allocated for the right seriousness of case. The Family Court is under considerable pressure in terms of the amount of people seeking to use its services, so it is important that circuit and puisne judges are only used where

---

134. 'Dramatic Increase in Court Fees Causing Deep Concern, Say Senior Judges' *The Guardian* (19 January 2015) News.

their judicial experience truly warrants it. As with other forms of civil litigation, the 'workhorses' of the court are district judges, but with magistrates playing a surprisingly intensive role within the Family Court.

Upon receipt of the claim form, it shall be sent to a 'gatekeeper'. This is a nominated legal advisor or district judge[135] whose job it is to make an initial allocation to an appropriate judge of the Family Court. Guidance has been issued by the President of the Family Court[136] to determine the allocation but this must also be read in conjunction with the allocation order.[137] There appears a presumption that private family-law matters such as the one that Joshua wishes to initiate should be heard by lay justices,[138] and certainly this seems to be the default these days. The exceptions are where it is considered too complex or it is likely to take more than three days.

For our purposes, however, we will assume that the case will proceed as normal and will therefore be allocated to magistrates sitting in the Family Court. Ordinarily this should mean a bench of two or three magistrates, ordinarily including both a man and woman.[139] The magistrates are all specially trained and the chairman of that bench must be someone who has been approved to chair family proceedings.

17.4.3 **The hearing**

Hearings of family matters, including private family-law disputes, are ordinarily held in private, even if the courtroom is being used. Thus the general public will not be entitled to attend the court, although the parties will normally be allowed to bring a person to accompany them for moral support.

As a hearing in the magistrates' court, only the chair or the legal advisor will speak. The chair will usually be addressed as 'Sir' or 'Madam'. Much of the formality of court proceedings is abandoned because the intention is to get to the truth of the matter. Known as the 'welfare principle', the overriding concern of a court when dealing with matters relating to children, is to do what is in the best interests of the welfare of the child.[140]

It is unlikely that the strict rules of adversarial trial will be adopted and instead it will be more quasi-inquisitorial. The justices (or their legal advisor) are likely to ask questions of each party, to try and understand their position. In many instances they will try to get both sides to agree a way forward, as this is preferable to a court-ordered settlement, since both parties consider themselves to have a 'stake' in what has been agreed.

In matters such as the example involving Joshua, it is likely that judgment will be given on the day of the hearing. The justices, or their legal advisor, will summarize what the court has decided and why. Ultimately an order of the court will be produced, but this may not follow for a few days. The judgment, however, is usually in force from the time that it has been pronounced in court.

The remedies and avenues for appeal are considered in the next chapter.

---

135.   PD 12B, para 9.2.
136.   'President's Guidance on Allocation and Gatekeeping for Proceedings under Part II of the Children Act 1989' (22 April 2014). Available online at: <https://www.justice.gov.uk/downloads/family-justice-reform/allocation-and-gatekeeping-guidance.pdf>.
137.   *The Family Court (Composition and Distribution of Business) Rules 2014*, SI 2014/840.
138.   *Presidents Guidance*, para 23.
139.   *Family Court (Composition and Distribution of Business) Rules 2014*, SI 2014/840, r 3(2).
140.   *Children Act 1989*, s 1.

Summary

This chapter has introduced some of the concepts of civil litigation and, in particular, how a case proceeds through the small claims court, Administrative Court, and the Family Court. It has also:

- Identified that a single set of rules now govern most civil litigation (the *Civil Procedure Rules*).
- Identified that the family system has its own set of rules known as the *Family Proceedings Rules*.
- Noted that the judge has specific responsibility for ensuring the case management of trials within the civil justice system.
- Noted that a wide variety of judges can sit on civil matters and their powers differ.
- Identified that there are three 'tracks' through which civil litigation ordinarily proceeds. These are the 'small claims track', 'fast track', and 'multi-track'.
- Demonstrated how a case would proceed through the fast track and noted that the procedure is more informal than in many other proceedings.
- Noted that costs can be used as a negotiating tool to allow cases to be settled.
- Demonstrated how a judicial review case would begin and proceed through the Administrative Court.
- Demonstrated how a private child-law matter is heard in the Family Court.
- Identified that family proceedings are often more inquisitorial than adversarial.

595

(?) End-of-chapter questions

1. Read Hazel Genn, 'Do-it-yourself Law: Access to Justice and the Challenge of Self-representation' (2013) 32 *Civil Justice Quarterly* 411–14. Is it right that decisions about the welfare of a child, albeit in a private-law context, are left to litigants in person? Is there not a danger that emotion means that disputes are litigated beyond their limit?

2. Read Pablo Cortes, 'The Online Court: Filling the Gaps of the Civil Justice System?' (2017) 36 *Civil Justice Quarterly* 109–26. To what extent do you think it is possible to look at alternative forms of litigation in order to ease the pressure from the courts?

 Further reading

Koo AKC, 'Ten Years after Halsey' (2015) 34 *Civil Justice Quarterly* 77–95.
This looks at how the decision in *Halsey v Milton Keynes NHS Trust*[141] has influenced the conduct of litigation and, in particular, the use of Alternative Dispute Resolution.

141. [2004] EWCA Civ 576.

Lightman G, 'The Civil Justice System and Legal Profession' (2003) 22 *Civil Justice Quarterly* 235–47.

The (then) Lightman J discusses civil litigation and he suggests that much of the blame for the systemic delays in litigation can be laid at the door of lawyers.

Sorabji J, 'Part 36: A Rule in Need of Reform' (2015) 34 *Civil Justice Quarterly* 11–28.

This is an interesting article that suggests that Part 36, which was designed as a simple procedure to help encourage disputes to be settled quickly, has become overly technical and now instead leads to satellite litigation, meaning that litigation is an even longer process.

For multiple-choice questions, updates to this chapter, and links to useful websites, please visit the **Online Resource Centre** at: **www.oxfordtextbooks.co.uk/orc/gillespie_els6e/**

18

Remedies and Appeals

By the end of this chapter you will be able to:

- Understand what the key remedies available in civil litigation are.
- Identify the key differences between pecuniary and non-pecuniary damages.
- Understand when equitable remedies may be used.
- Identify the correct route for a civil appeal.
- Understand the circumstances under which leave for appeal will be given.
- Identify the correct tests for granting leave and allowing or refusing an appeal.

Introduction

Chapter 17 presented how civil cases progress through the courts and focused on three different examples of civil action. Where it ended was the trial but what was not discussed, except in the context of costs, was what happens if the claimant succeeds. This is known as remedies and it is the order of the court as to what the losing side should do in respect of the claim. As will be seen there are different types of remedies that can be ordered and all are subject to certain rules and discretion. This chapter will also discuss what happens when a party disagrees with the ruling of the judge, ie appeals. The issue of criminal appeals was discussed in Chapter 16 and this, the second chapter on appeals in this book allows you to compare civil and criminal appeals.

This chapter will follow the same structure as Chapter 17, ie at the beginning some brief general comments will be made but it will then return to the three case studies that were presented in Chapter 17. It will be remembered that this consisted of:

- Amy Daventry's faulty television where action was brought in the small claims court (technically the small claims track of the county court)
- Matilda's proposed march against the closure of a nursery, where the action was for judicial review before the Administrative Court of the High Court
- Joshua's application for extra contact with Sarah, his child, where the action was brought in the county court under the *Children Act 1989*.

For each of these examples a discussion will be made of the potential remedies and what the rules governing the remedies are. In the second half of the chapter the same studies will be used to understand how an appeal would be brought against the decision.

18.1 Civil remedies

The first issue to examine therefore is civil remedies. A difficulty with discussing remedies is that there are so many different types and that they are contingent on what the type of case is. Generally the claimant will indicate what remedy they wish but the court is able to grant such remedy as it considers appropriate. This section will consider some of the key types of remedies and, in essence, this will be under three broad headings:

- damages (ie financial compensation to remedy a wrong)
- equitable remedies (including specific performance in contractual disputes and injunctions)
- public law remedies (ie that which can be expected from a judicial review).

Each of these types of remedy will be discussed briefly although after the general issues have been discussed we will return to the case studies presented in Chapter 17 and discuss what remedy each claimant can expect.

18.1.1 Interim remedies

Whilst we tend to think of remedies as being something that occurs at the end of proceedings this is not always the case and sometimes a remedy will be sought at the beginning of, or during, proceedings. This is known as an interim remedy. In essence an interim remedy is supposed to secure the position so as to ensure that the full matters can be heard.

18.1.1.1 Identifying the defendant

One of the more unusual interim remedies is an action to identify the actual defendants. Whilst it may be thought that the identity of a defendant is always known this is not necessarily correct. One of the most important remedies here is the *Norwich Pharmacal* order.[1] This is a remedy that is designed to discover the identity of the defendant since in some instances the true identity may not be known. Where a third party is aware of the identity of the defendant and has in some way facilitated the wrong that the claimant is seeking to remedy then they are able to bring an action to discover the identity of the true person although it must only be done where it is contemplated that judicial or other proceedings will be instigated,[2] the latter potentially including employee misconduct proceedings.[3]

---

1. This is named after the resolution of the case *Norwich Pharmacal Co v Customs and Excise Commissioners* [1974] AC 133.
2. *British Steel Corporation v Granada Television Ltd* [1981] AC 1096.
3. *Ashworth Hospital Authority v MGN Ltd* [2002] 1 WLR 2033.

18.1.1.2 Interim injunction

Perhaps the most common type of interim remedy is that known as an interim injunction. The essence of an interim injunction is that it allows for the status quo to be maintained pending the full proceedings being heard. In some instances the fact that an interim injunction is made may suffice to resolve the whole proceedings but generally it will simply be a way of ensuring that the state of affairs continues pending litigation.

599

Rules exist over when interim injunctions can be made[6] but also which judges are able to make injunctions (ordinarily only circuit judges and puisne judges). Also, it is likely that as injunctions are complicated (in that breach of an injunction can have significant consequences as it may be viewed as contempt of court and so breach could lead to detention) it is probable that they will lead to a matter being listed on the multi-track meaning that there are costs implications. One important aspect of an interim injunction is that ordinarily there will be an undertaking by the applicant to pay damages to the defendant if the case is ultimately resolved against them.[7] The reasoning behind this is that an interim injunction is ordinarily preventing a person from doing something and this may incur a cost. Where it was shown that there is no cause of

---

4. [2008] EWHC 1781 (QB).
5. [2012] EWHC 92 (QB).
6. *Civil Procedure Rules*, pt 25.
7. Stuart Sime, *A Practical Approach to Civil Litigation* (19th edn, OUP 2016) 469.

action then that cost was, in effect, accrued inappropriately and the respondent should not have to pay for trying to do something they were entitled to.

> **Example** Undertaking as to damages
>
> Let us return to the position earlier in respect of Rebecca and Peter. Let us assume that Peter had arranged for contractors to begin blocking the path. Rebecca's interim injunction will almost certainly cost Peter money since he may have to pay the contractors during the period the litigation is ongoing or pay a penalty fee to defer the work. If it turns out that Rebecca is wrong and that Peter was entitled to block the path then Rebecca will probably have to pay these extra costs that were incurred by Peter.

18.1.2 Final remedies: damages

The more traditional forms of remedies are those that are made after the conclusion of successful litigation and it is to this that we now turn.

Perhaps the most obvious form of remedy is that of damages. This is the collective term that is given to financial compensation to remedy a wrong. It may be a contractual dispute where party X claims that they have suffered financial loss from party Y, or it may be a tort claim where X is claiming that he has been injured by Y (the tort of trespass to the person) or that X has invaded his property and caused damage (the tort of trespass to land).

Damages vary widely and in this section it will only be possible to describe some of the key rules in respect of their award. The first issue to note is that there are some differences in the way that damages can be awarded. So, for example, damages in contract are ordinarily assessed on the basis of the actual loss suffered[8] and it will be for the claimant to prove (to the civil standard) that these losses have been incurred. Damages for tort, however, may include general damages based on suffering, and this may be particularly true in personal injury claims.

If we look at damages for tort (and for these purposes we will consider a personal injury claim as being typical) then it is possible to distinguish between 'pecuniary' and 'non-pecuniary' damages. Pecuniary damages relate to identifiable sums of money that can be quantified as an actual loss. The general rule of pecuniary damages is that a person should be placed in the position that they would have been had the injury or loss not occurred.[9] How this is done will be discussed later but it will mean that all direct losses will ordinarily be covered, including expenses, loss of earnings etc. However, in line with this principle deductions will be made for any benefit that is received because of the injury (eg disabled living allowance) since to do otherwise may mean that the victim benefits from the injury.

Non-pecuniary damages are those that cannot be quantified as a direct loss but instead attract compensatory awards. Classic examples of this include damages for pain and suffering, loss of amenity, psychological distress etc. Both pecuniary and non-pecuniary damages are divided into past and prospective damages. Past damages

---

8. *Slater v Hoyle & Smith* [1920] 2 KB 11.
9. *Livingstone v Raywards Coal Co* (1880) 5 AC 25.

relate to the loss of suffering that a person has suffered already and prospective damages involve that which will occur in the future, including any future pain and suffering.

☰ Example An injured pedestrian

Robert is an employee of a leading supermarket chain. Robert is employed as a store assistant. Whilst Robert is crossing a road (on a pelican crossing) he is struck by Wayne, who was driving negligently. Robert suffers a broken back and is hospitalized for four months. It is thought that when he recovers he will only be able to stand for no more than twenty-five minutes at any one time.

Robert will be entitled to various types of compensation. The first is pecuniary damages. This will, for example, include his loss of earnings. This would include any loss of salary he has suffered as a result of being in hospital for four months. It will also include any loss of salary that he will accrue if he is not able to return to his job because of his reduced mobility. If he is required to pay for ongoing medical treatment (either for a determinate or indeterminate period of time) then this will also be classed as pecuniary damages since its cost can be calculated or estimated.

Robert will also be eligible to receive non-pecuniary damages. In this example the most obvious reason for receiving non-pecuniary damages will be as a result of pain and suffering. How these are calculated will be discussed later but it is clear that he is eligible to receive this category of damages.

601

The primary test for deciding what should be recovered in tort is that of foreseeability[10] meaning that a person is liable to pay damages for loss or injury that is foreseeable by his actions that caused the harm. Perhaps the key example of this is a personal injury case. Let us assume that D injures V in a car accident. It is foreseeable that claims could arise for pain and suffering, expenses incurred, damage to property, loss of earnings etc.

Damages for claims arising out of an incident should ordinarily be dealt with by one action. All forms of awards (eg loss of earnings, future loss of earnings, pain and suffering, medical expenses etc) should be calculated at the one time and a person will not be able to reopen the litigation even where further loss was unexpected.

18.1.2.1 Pecuniary damages

As noted earlier pecuniary damages will include quantifiable damage. In a road traffic accident this would include damage to the car and any other property (including clothing if this is damaged by blood or because it had to be cut open), other expenses (including medical expenses (eg prescription charges, physiotherapy costs etc)), and loss of earnings.

Perhaps the classic example of pecuniary damages is loss of earnings but this is not always easy to quantify. Courts do not order periodic payments (ie a sum to be paid as an annuity) but rather order a lump sum. However, it is too simplistic to say that if it could be proven that X could lose £10,000 per year for the next ten years then he should be awarded a lump sum of £100,000. This is because compensation is

---

10. *Halsbury's Laws*, vol 29 (Damages) 408ff.

supposed to leave you in the position you would have been in. If X is given £100,000 but invests that money then after ten years he will have received more than £100,000 because of interest etc. Therefore the courts adopt a discounted multiplier to take into account the investments that a person can be expected to make. Traditionally it was thought that a claimant would invest any compensation in the equity markets but the volatile nature of the stock market in recent years led to a re-think and it is now decided to use a safer investment multiplier.

Even if the multiplier is resolved there are still difficulties in identifying loss of earnings. For example, how does one deal with the issue of possible promotion. For example, if V is a lecturer in a higher-education establishment when he is struck down by a motor vehicle and left with cognitive injuries that make it difficult to work as a full-time academic should he be compensated on the basis of his salary as a lecturer or the fact that he may become a professor at some point in his academic career? How does one decide the probability (or otherwise) of that? Where it is possible to assess the chances of a promotion then the courts will take this into account[11] but where it is not then they will consider a lump sum.

A particularly difficult issue, however, is where it involves a child who has never worked. How can one estimate what the loss of earnings for that child is? The starting point appears to be to use a sum that equated to the national average earnings in early working life[12] but this will change where a child is particularly intelligent[13] or there is other evidence to suggest that the child would be otherwise very successful.[14]

18.1.2.2 **Non-pecuniary damages**

Alongside pecuniary damages there will sometimes be non-pecuniary damages, particularly where it is a personal injury case. Perhaps the classic example of this will be compensation for pain and suffering. This is a compensatory award that is not based on actual losses but rather is designed to provide an award that reflects the pain and suffering a person will suffer. It is separate from the amount of award that will be paid to reflect ongoing medical bills since this is quantifiable and is therefore a pecuniary, rather than non-pecuniary award. Pain and suffering will also include any emotional harm that is caused either by the illness itself or by awareness of the harm, for example, where a young person suffers significant facial scarring, the award should not only be for the pain involved in the actual injuries but also include a factor for the emotional distress that may be caused by a realization that his face is permanently scarred and he may therefore attract unwelcome attention from members of society.[15] Where the injuries reduce the life expectancy of the victim the courts must also take this into account.

Identifying the level of compensation for pain and suffering is not easy. The usual approach is to look at past awards and try to find a comparable case, adjusting it for inflation etc. One of the more interesting legal texts that is available is *Kemp & Kemp: Quantum of Damages* (published by Sweet & Maxwell). This an updatable reference work that lists previous cases and awards given for damages. Each case will discuss the injuries that were received, the compensation awarded, and a brief

---

11. *Doyle v Wallace* The Times, 22 July 1998 (CA).
12. *Croke v Wiseman* [1982] 1 WLR 71.
13. *Almond v Leeds Health Authority* [1990] 1 Med LR 370.
14. For a discussion see *Halsbury's Laws*, vol 29 (Damages) 445.
15. See *Dimmock v Miles* (1969, unreported) cited in *Halsbury's Laws*, vol 12(1) 883.

summary of how that award was reached. A judge will consider these previous awards in deciding at what level to set the compensation for this aspect.

Separate to any amount of compensation for pain and suffering, a person who receives a loss of amenity (eg a sense, or a limb, or the ability to walk etc) can expect to receive a compensatory award for this. As with compensation for pain and suffering this is a non-pecuniary award that is designed to reflect the additional suffering involved in this. This loss of amenity can also be extended to other forms of foreseeable yet unquantifiable situations such as the loss of marriage prospects etc.[16] As with pain and suffering assessing the quantum of such damage is difficult and it is often said that the starting point is to look at previous cases to identify the likely award and to update this for inflation where appropriate.

18.1.3 Final remedies: equitable remedies

After damages, equitable remedies are perhaps the most common. There are a variety of different types of equitable remedies but two are of particular importance here. The first is specific performance, a particular equitable remedy in respect of contract disputes, and the second is injunctions. Injunctions were mentioned briefly earlier in the context of interim remedies but they can also feature in the Family Court. These are the two remedies that will be discussed briefly in this section.

18.1.3.1 Specific performance

Perhaps one of the better-known equitable defences is that known as specific performance, which applies to relationships bound by a contract. The essence of the defence is that the court will 'enforce against a defendant the duty of doing what he agreed by contract to do'.[17] The remedy differs from damages in that the latter will compensate a person for not fulfilling their contract whereas specific performance requires that the contract *will* be performed. It is possible that damages can also be awarded where, for example, the delay in fulfilling the contract has led to pecuniary losses being incurred.

▤ Example Selling on products

Arnold has an agreement with Peter to purchase four miles of cabling for £2,500. Arnold has a separate agreement with Telly Communications Ltd to supply them with three miles of cables for £4,500. The agreement with Peter is that the cable will be delivered to Arnold by 3 February 2016 and the agreement with Telly Communications Ltd is that Arnold will supply them the cable by 5 February 2016. The contract with Telly Communications Ltd states that Arnold will be liable to pay £50 per day that the contract is unfilled because this offsets additional charges that Telly Communications Ltd will occur in their building project.

On 3 February Peter contacts Arnold and says that he is not going to supply any cable because he can sell the cable to a building developer for £1,000 more. He says it will be at least four weeks before he gets any more cable. Arnold immediately tells Peter that he will instigate legal proceedings. The matter is heard on 8 February.

---

16.   See *Halsbury's Laws*, vol 12(1) 884.
17.   *Halsbury's Laws*, vol 95 (Specific Performance) para 301.

> The judge hearing the case identifies that Peter has not yet sold on the cable. He makes an order of specific performance which will require Peter to supply Arnold with the cable. He separately makes an order for damages to cover, in part, the late penalty charges.

As an equitable remedy it is discretionary, ie the court does not *have* to make the order but the fact that it is discretionary should not be taken to mean that the circumstances when it could be used are vague as it is subject to precise rules and regulations and it has been suggested that 'if the contract is within the category of contacts of which specific performance will be granted, is valid in form, has been made between competent parties and is unobjectionable in its nature and circumstances, specific performance will be granted as a matter of course'.[18] There are some equitable defences that can be pleaded but the action has, over the years, been refined until the point when it has become a standard remedy in breach of contract cases.

The relationship between equitable remedies should be understood. Where a person is aware that a contract is likely to be breached in the future (eg in the example earlier relating to Arnold and Peter, Peter tells Arnold on 1 February that he is not going to adhere to the contract) then the correct remedy is probably an injunction rather than specific performance,[19] the injunction restraining a person from breaching the contract. An advantage that this would bring of course is that it is possible to gain an interim injunction and so when the possibility of breach is first raised it may be possible to prevent that breach at the earliest opportunity.

As an equitable remedy it would ordinarily be used where common-law remedies, ie damages, will not suffice. There will be occasions where the breach of a contract does not require the specific performance of a contract (because, for example, goods can readily be obtained in another way) but rather the award of compensation. Where the court decides that a monetary payment will suffice then the courts will ordinarily decline to order specific performance.[20] It does not seem to matter whether the contract stipulates the quantum of damages in breach or whether damages are liquidated or unliquidated.[21] Some contracts will make clear that the remedy for breach is financial compensation and whilst this may lead the court to decide that it will not enforce specific performance it would seem that the court is more concerned with the intentions of the parties. Where the items which are the subject of the contract are hard to obtain or are of particular significance then it is likely that damages would not be appropriate and specific performance would be exercised.

≔ Example The rare vase

Veronica agrees to purchase a rare, twelfth-century vase from Dianne for £25,000 and transfers the money to her. When she goes to collect the vase Dianne refuses to hand it over and says that she is going to sell it to another person who has offered her £10,000 more.

---

18. *Halsbury's Laws*, vol 95 (Specific Performance) para 301.
19. See *James Jones & Sons Ltd v Earl of Tankerville* [1909] 2 Ch 440.
20. *Adderley v Dixon* (1824) 1 Sim & St 607.
21. *Halsbury's Laws*, vol 95 (Specific Performance) para 313.

> Veronica had also ordered a set of china plates from Edwina. These plates are sold in lots of shops but Edwina sold them to Veronica for £100 whereas the next cheapest seller sold them for £225. When Veronica goes to collect them Edwina refuses to hand them over, and says she is going to sell the plates to another customer who wants to order a lot more china at the same time. Edwina says she can't get any more of the plates because she has decided not to sell that range anymore.
>
> If Veronica was to bring an action against Dianne it is likely that the courts would order specific performance as the vase is very particular and can, in essence, only be obtained from Dianne. In respect of the plates, however, the courts may well take the approach that specific performance is not required. Veronica could buy the plates from another seller and if, as seems likely, she pays more than she paid Edwina then she can simply claim that additional sum as damages.

The most obvious example when specific performance will not be ordered is where it is no longer possible to do so.[22] There may be a number of reasons why this is the case, including the possibility that factual circumstances have changed or even that the property is no longer available. For example, in the earlier example of the vase, if Dianne had accidentally dropped the vase and destroyed it then there can be no specific performance—which would, in essence, require Dianne to somehow procure another vase (which may be impossible)—and instead the dispute would be settled with damages. The same could be true of the example of cabling presented earlier. If Peter has no cable because, for example, his supplier has none or it is stolen then it would not be possible for the court to order specific performance. That is not to say there is no breach in the contract because clearly there is but it is an example that would be best resolved by damages and not specific performance.

18.1.3.2 Injunctions

The other classic equitable remedy is that of an injunction. The issue of interim injunctions was considered earlier but they can also be a final remedy, either as an alternative to or in combination with damages. It should be noted that whilst there are some statutory provisions that allow a county court to make an injunction, the vast majority of injunctions are part of the inherent jurisdiction of the court and thus only actionable by the High Court. Only High Court injunctions will be considered in this section.

An injunction is normally used in contractual disputes where the breach, or anticipated breach, is negative in character (in *Evening Standard Co Ltd v Henderson*[23] an injunction was used to restrain an employee from working for a competitor in circumstances where their employment contract indicated that they could not do so). An injunction is also common in tort claims, for example, where a person is illegally trespassing on land they may ask a court to issue an injunction requiring that person to leave the land.

There are two types of injunction; an order that prohibits someone from doing something (a prohibitory injunction) and an injunction that requires a person to do something (a mandatory injunction). These are in essence two sides of the same coin

22. *Watts v Spence* [1976] Ch 165.
23. [1987] ICR 588.

and there is no real difference in how they are granted or what their effect is. The prohibitory injunction is the more usual, in part because the nature of many types of civil litigation is such that what is feared is somebody doing something that they should not do which causes harm or loss.

As with specific performance, the injunction is an equitable remedy and therefore it is used where damages by themselves would not suffice.[24] There will be circumstances where financial compensation suffices and in those cases the court will decline to act although where it believes that there is the potential for future damage then this may provide a reason to use its equitable powers to grant an injunction.

The consequences of breaching an order can be severe and accordingly it has been said that the wording of an injunction must be very clear so that the person it is served upon knows exactly what he is expected not to do (or to do, depending on the type of injunction).[25] Where a mandatory injunction is used then the injunction will ordinarily include a time by which it must be complied with. Prohibitory injunctions ordinarily come into force immediately but do not need to and the court may give the defendant(s) time to comply with the order.

Breach of an injunction is a serious matter; it amounts to contempt of court, something that is stated on the face of the injunction. There are two types of contempt: criminal contempt and civil contempt. Refusing to obey an injunction is civil contempt but the consequences can be just as serious, and may even lead to imprisonment. The burden is on the person served to understand the means by which they can obey the order[26] (although, as noted earlier, the actual injunction should be written in a manner that makes it readily understood). The responsibility for showing contempt is the plaintiff's, and they would return to the court to allege that the side who has breached the injunction has done so and seek an order for committal for contempt.[27]

Whilst it is possible to imprison for civil contempt it has been stated that this power should only be exercised with great care.[28] The maximum term for which a person can be committed to prison (technically it is not imprisonment which is a criminal sanction) is two years.[29] The actual term should depend on how serious the breach is; the more blatant the breach, and the greater the challenge to the court's authority, the longer the committal. There is no power to commit a person to prison pending the determination of sentence meaning that a person will either be committed immediately or will be at liberty while the court investigates the breach and considers sentence. If the court decides not to commit a person to prison it could issue a fine. Technically there is no upper limit to any fine[30] although realistically the court will take account of factors such as the gravity of the breach, previous instances, and the particular circumstances of the person.

Section 13 *Administration of Justice Act 1960* permits an appeal against a decision that a person is in contempt of court and any sentence imposed. Appeal from contempt in the High Court is to the Court of Appeal and, as it is civil contempt, it will be heard in the Civil Division even where a person has been committed to prison.[31]

---

24. *Attorney-General v Sheffield Gas Consumers Co* (1853) 3 De G M & G 304.
25. *Attorney-General v Staffordshire County Council* [1905] 1 Ch 336.
26. *Attorney-General (at the relation of Leyton Essex Urban District Council) v Walthamstow Urban District Council* (1895) 11 TLR 533.
27. See *Halsbury's Laws*, vol 22 (Contempt of Court) 98 for a discussion of the procedure.
28. *Halsbury's Laws*, vol 22 (Contempt of Court) 112.
29. *Contempt of Court Act 1981*, s 14(1).
30. *Halsbury's Laws*, vol 22 (Contempt of Court) 114.
31. For an example of this, albeit an unusual one, see *Slade v Slade* [2009] EWCA Civ 748.

18.1.4 Final remedies: public law remedies

Public law remedies are those that can be awarded after a claim for judicial review. Whilst it is possible that damages will be awarded it is more likely that a public law remedy will be made. It is important to note that in public law the court has complete discretion as to whether to grant a remedy.[32] This means that even if the court decides that a judicial review should succeed it may decline to grant any relief because it believes it is not in the interests of justice to do so. Indeed some applicants may not even seek a remedy but instead just want a ruling that a public authority has acted in an inappropriate manner.

> **Example** Use of a leisure centre
>
> Let us assume that Peabody District Council operate a leisure centre and they wish to restrict the opening hours. In order to do this, they need to seek permission from (a) the Council Leader, (b) the Mayor, (c) the Leader of the Council of the neighbouring district council, and (d) the (fictional) Department for Administrative Affairs.
>
> For some reason, although all bodies were contacted, the Department for Administrative Affairs' reply was not received. A judicial review is brought by Jim Naseum, who uses the leisure centre after work. The court finds that the Department's permission was not granted because it was not received (and to that extent the decision to restrict opening hours was procedurally flawed) but this was simply because the letter was lost in the post. The Department had intended to grant permission.
>
> In this example the court may well deny relief even though Jim Naseum will succeed in his application for judicial review. The court may well consider that there is little point in granting relief because the Department intended to give permission and when a copy of the letter is sent to the Council the decision can then be retaken lawfully.

There are four principal remedies that are available in judicial review proceedings:

- quashing orders
- mandatory (and prohibiting) orders
- injunctions, and
- declarations.

It is quite possible that there will be a combination of two or more remedies. So, for example, it is quite possible that a court may declare that there has been a breach of the law and quash the decision. Alternatively, it may quash a decision but then mandate that an authority acts in a particular way. In this section the four orders will be briefly discussed.

18.1.4.1 Quashing orders

Perhaps the most common public law remedy is that of the quashing order. Until the *Woolf Reforms* and advent of the Civil Procedure Rules banished Latin from civil proceedings this was also known as a *writ of certiorari*. The effect of the remedy is that

---

32. See *Glynn v Keele University* [1971] 1 WLR 487.

it quashes whatever decision has been made and returns the position legally to what it was before the order was made.

> ### :≡ **Example** Quashing a decision to refuse bail
>
> A slightly unusual, but certainly illustrative, example of a quashing order can be found in *R (on the application of S) v Newcastle Crown Court*.[33] S had been charged with a series of rapes relating to a complainant that he had purported to marry. S was a final year student and had been denied bail by a circuit judge sitting at the Crown Court at Newcastle-upon-Tyne. The ruling by the judge denying bail had the appearance of the judge adopting the wrong test for bail and Foskett J, whilst believing that an experienced judge was unlikely to have made such an error (as he will deal with bail decisions daily) decided that the appearance of the wrong test justified the use of a public law remedy. He therefore directed that the decision was quashed and remitted the matter back to the Crown Court for a new decision but before a different judge.

The effect of a quashing order will depend on the circumstances of the case. Elliott and Thomas distinguish between two types of situations: those where the decision was made in an inappropriate way and those where the decision itself was inappropriate.[34] Where the decision was reached in an inappropriate way then the quashing order will quash that decision but there is nothing to stop the authority from reaching the same decision again, albeit by adopting the correct process. Where the decision itself is wrong then the quashing order will mean that the authority must reconsider the matter and identify a different decision.

A quashing order is most effective when it is prospective action, ie the alleged illegal act is to occur in the future. In these cases the quashing order will almost certainly be the sole remedy as by quashing the order the status quo returns meaning the illegal act should not occur. Where it is in respect of a past matter it can be more complicated as the court may need to consider whether it is necessary to award compensation for the consequences of that unlawful decision etc.

18.1.4.2 **Mandatory and prohibiting orders**

Technically these are two distinct types of remedies but they are, in essence, two sides of the same coin. Before the abolition of Latin they were known as a *writ of mandamus* and a *writ of prohibition*. As with a quashing order, the name of the order accurately describes what the consequences of the action are. Given the nature of these orders they can only be used in respect of prospective decisions (since if it has already happened there is nothing to mandate or prohibit).

A mandatory order simply requires an authority to do a particular act. They therefore have no option but to do what is ordered by the High Court. If they do not do this then they are not only acting unlawfully but are arguably in contempt of court because they have failed to follow an order. A mandatory order will require a body to do something that they have legal power to do but that does not mean that it is restricted

---

33. [2012] EWHC 1453 (Admin).
34. Mark Elliott and Robert Thomas, *Public Law* (OUP 2011) 555–6.

to situations where an authority *has* to do something, it is simply that an order will require them to do something that is lawful.

≡ **Example** Holding an inquest

In *R (on the application of Medihani) v HM Coroner for Inner South District of London*[35] the High Court was asked to rule on the issue of whether an inquest into the death of a fifteen-year-old girl should resume. A person was charged with the murder of the girl but he attempted to commit suicide while in detention and suffered brain damage as a result of hanging himself. At a pre-trial hearing a judge held that he was unfit to tender a plea in respect of the charge of murder and a jury was then empanelled to decide whether he had, in fact, committed the *actus reus* of the crime.[36] They decided that he had committed the act of killing and he was detained in a secure institution.

The Administrative Court considered that Article 2 of the ECHR required an inquest to be held in these circumstances and therefore they made a mandatory order requiring (a) that an inquest be held, and (b) that the inquest be held before a different coroner than the one who declined to reopen the inquest.

A prohibiting order is the exact opposite. Instead of requiring a person to do something it prohibits them from doing it. The principal use of these orders is where an authority intends to do something and a claimant believes that this would be illegal. By seeking a prohibiting order (rather than a quashing order) it makes clear that the authority *cannot* do as it intended (whereas a quashing order may mean that the authority considers the matter again, reaches the same conclusion, and therefore further judicial review proceedings are required).

18.1.4.3 **Injunctions**

Injunctions have already been discussed in the context of private law remedies (in that they are an equitable remedy considered in 18.1.3.2). Elliott and Thomas believe that it may be advisable in some instances to seek an injunction rather than seek, for example, a prohibiting order. That said, at least part of the logic is that injunctions can be obtained in ordinary litigation[37] which, whilst correct, means that the litigant would not engage in a public law action but instead ordinary principles of litigation.

An advantage of injunction is that, as seen earlier, it is possible to receive an interim injunction. Therefore where time is of the essence it is possible to obtain an interim injunction while the arguments are decided by the courts whereas public law remedies can only be granted at the end of proceedings. Whilst this is true, it should be noted that the courts are able to expedite matters, including hearing proceedings and applications by telephone (something quite common in the Family Division of the High Court). There may be some logic to the argument of Elliott and Thomas, however, especially, as they note, it is now clear that a public body, including a minister of the

---

35.   [2012] EWHC 1104 (Admin).

36.   See *Criminal Procedure (Insanity) Act 1964* and David Ormerod, *Smith & Hogan's Criminal Law* (13th edn, OUP 2011) 288–93 for a discussion on how this operates.

37.   Mark Elliott and Robert Thomas, *Public Law* (OUP 2011) 558.

Crown, can commit contempt of court[38] meaning they will almost certainly obey an injunction.

18.1.4.4 Declarations

The final remedy is arguably not a remedy at all, it is merely a statement of the court as to what the legal position is. They do not carry any requirement or sanction but instead it is just a judicial statement about the legality, or otherwise, of a proposed decision. It was noted earlier that sometimes a claimant themselves may decide that they do not wish to seek a remedy because the mere statement of illegality will suffice.

One point to note is that even though there is no remedy attached to a declaration, a court will not use this to permit purely hypothetical cases to be raised.[39] The courts are clear that they are there to resolve disputes between parties and, in public law, to ensure that actions that have, or potentially have, an impact on individuals are reviewed. Where there is no impact or real dispute then the courts are reluctant to become involved, in part as a matter of public policy since there are already significant delays in the court system, a problem which could be exacerbated by permitting hypothetical questions to be raised.

Sometimes the courts will use a declaration as part of their discretion over remedies. For example, they may believe that a mandatory order is not required because a public body (particularly a court) would simply follow the logic of the declaration made and does not require the compulsion inherent in an order.

18.1.5 Applying the remedies

The preceding section has explained many of the basic principles of remedies but it is necessary very briefly to look at what remedies would be likely in the examples first introduced in Chapter 17. These case studies will then be carried forward to the second part of the chapter which discusses appeals.

18.1.5.1 Small claims track

The first example that we considered was that of Amy who purchased a television set that proved to be faulty. This is therefore a contract claim and it is arguably one of the easiest to consider.

It will be remembered that Amy purchased the television for £250 and only six weeks later it blew up and the retailer simply offered to put her in contact with a repairer who will charge her £150. This will be a contractual dispute so that we will be considering the issue of damages. As noted earlier, there are some restrictions on what can be claimed in contract but realistically in a claim as small as this it is unlikely this is going to be problematic.

Amy has two options; the first is to sue initially for £150 (the cost of the repair) but, more probably given the fact that the television is only one month old, the request would be for £250, the cost of the television itself. This is obviously known as pecuniary damages.

In addition to this Amy will be able to claim for other pecuniary losses. This will include the cost of the litigation, any expenses incurred in the court proceedings (for

---

38. *Re M* [1994] 1 AC 377.
39. See, for example, the comments of Lord Hutton in *R (on the application of Rushbridge) v Attorney-General* [2004] 1 AC 357, 371.

example, travel to court), any costs incurred in attempting to resolve the dispute (telephone calls etc), or other identifiable and foreseeable losses (eg if she hired a television set while this matter was in dispute). Amy will also be able to claim interest as identified earlier.

18.1.5.2 Judicial review

The second example was that of Matilda who was challenging the decision of the Chief Constable to ban her march. It will be remembered that this action was brought by way of judicial review and so the issue is one of public law remedies.

As Matilda wishes the march to go ahead there are, in essence, two options open to her. The first is a quashing order which would quash the decision of the Chief Constable to ban the march. The second option is to seek a mandatory order—requiring the Chief Constable to allow the march—but this would need to be in combination with a quashing order as this will always be required since to do otherwise would leave the Chief Constable's decision to ban the march in force.

The question is whether the High Court is likely to issue a mandatory order. Realistically there are a number of arguments to suggest that they would not. First, it could be argued that if the High Court declares that Matilda has the right to hold a protest, the police, as a public authority bound by s 6 *Human Rights Act 1998*, would recognize this and allow the protest. However, the stronger argument is that the High Court may not wish to rule on whether Matilda has the right to hold a protest. It is more likely that they would simply restrict their review to the question of whether it should be banned because the Home Secretary is also visiting the county at the same time. It is difficult to see how the court would construe this as anything other than an irrational decision. However, there may be other reasons for restricting a march, including the route of any march, and the court is not the best place to consider these issues: that is something that, under statute and common law, is the role of the Chief Constable. Accordingly, it is more likely that the Administrative Court will exercise their discretion to quash the decision of the Chief Constable but make no further order. This would mean that the Chief Constable would have to consider the issue again with the benefit of the decision of the judge in terms of understanding the importance of the right to protest.

18.1.5.3 Children's contact

Our final example was that of Joshua who wishes to see his child Sarah. Family remedies have not been considered before now because there are so many different examples of remedies within family law, partly due to the wide range of proceedings that exist within this area. As was noted in Chapter 15 the application Joshua made was under s 8 *Children Act 1989* (CA 1989) and the Act itself makes clear what remedies are available.

Section 10 CA 1989 permits the Family Court to make a s 8 order when certain persons apply for it. Obviously here Joshua has made an application and it was seen in Chapter 17 that he is permitted to apply for an order. A consequence of s 10 is that the court can make *any* order under s 8 once an application has been made for *any* s 8 order although in a matter such as the one presented in Chapter 17 it is highly unlikely the court will consider making any other form of s 8 order (eg revisiting who has residence ('custody') of the child). Section 11 permits the court to make directions on how any order is to be implemented and to impose conditions on any order. This could, for example, be used to phase in any change in contact regimes etc.

In essence the judge has three options open to him:

- allow the application by Joshua and alter the s 8 contact arrangements
- reject the application by Joshua meaning that the arrangements remain the same
- partly allow the application by making an order different to that sought by Joshua.

The third option shows the flexibility of CA 1989 proceedings. Just because Joshua has requested a particular contact pattern does not mean that the judge should approve it. Indeed the judge should only accede to the application if he decides that it is in the child's best interests to do so.[40] It will be remembered from Chapter 17 that Joshua wished not only weekly overnight contact but also a one-week holiday. Deborah, his wife, did not object to the holiday and it is likely that the judge would be influenced by that and place this within the order, almost certainly stating that the parties are to agree a suitable week between them (so that the court is not involved in comparing diaries). What was contested was the overnight contact. One possibility is that the judge may decide, rather than ordering weekly overnight contact immediately, to phase it in. This could be done through the powers within s 11 or, perhaps more likely, he may decide to make a s 8 order that allows for overnight contact once a month and then adjourn the application for six months. After six months the judge (through CAFCASS) would have more information about how Sarah has reacted to overnight contact and this is likely to influence his decision as to increased contact.

18.2 Appeals

As in criminal cases, not everyone will consider that the tribunal of fact (usually a judge sitting alone) will make the correct decision and thus it is also necessary to consider appeals. Unlike in criminal appeals where, it will be remembered, there are limitations regarding when one party (the Crown) may appeal, the same is not true in civil litigation and the general rule is that either party may appeal.

Civil appeals differ slightly from criminal appeals in that the avenues of appeal are slightly more complicated, partly because it is less clear where an appeal is heard.

18.2.1 Route of appeals

In civil cases it is necessary to distinguish between first appeals and second appeals. To an extent this is quite an easy distinction since it operates in the same way that it sounds. That is to say, in some matters it may be possible to appeal a matter more than once. The route that this takes will differ, as will be seen later.

As a general rule, with the exception of final decisions made in multi-track cases (which will be discussed later), in civil cases an appeal is made to the next most senior level of judge. So unlike in criminal appeals where the matter will ordinarily proceed to the next highest court (an appeal from the magistrates' court will proceed to the Crown Court or High Court; an appeal from the Crown Court will go to the Court

---

40. *Children Act 1989*, s 1.

of Appeal (Criminal Division)) an appeal in civil matters tends to be in respect of the judge. Table 18.1 presents the general rule.

Where the matter relates to the final decision of a multi-track case then the rule is more simple, it reverts to the court-type route. Thus the final decision of a judge sitting in the county court (including a circuit judge) will *always* go to the Court of Appeal (Civil Division) as will a final decision on a multi-track case within the High Court. The rationale behind this is that the multi-track cases are the more serious and complicated cases and therefore appeals should ordinarily proceed to the principal appellate court.

The position in respect of second appeals adopts the same pattern. Instead of following the route already discussed it will return to the court-based system. If the route adopted in Table 18.1 was adopted then an appeal from a district judge sitting in the county court would go to a circuit judge within the county court and from there to a puisne judge. However, the rule states that this second appeal would actually go to the Court of Appeal (Civil Division). Again the logic behind this is that a second appeal is no longer just about whether a matter was wrongly decided but should be based on the ordinary principles of review that one would expect in the Court of Appeal (Civil Division).

18.2.2 **Leave**

The general rule of civil cases is that there is ordinarily a requirement that a person requires permission (leave) before bringing an appeal.[41] There are some exceptions to this rule but ordinarily it applies to all proceedings, including an appeal against interim matters and not just final decisions.

The general rule is that permission can be sought either from the judge that has made the ruling to be appealed (and it is more common for leave to be granted in this way in civil cases whereas it was seen in Chapter 16 that this was highly exceptional in criminal cases) or from the judge where the appeal will be heard.[42] So, for example, a circuit judge makes a ruling in a fixed-track case. The first appeal will be heard by a puisne judge (see Table 18.1). The person appealing can either ask the circuit judge who made the judgment for permission to appeal or he can petition the High Court for permission. The exception to this rule is where it relates to a second appeal. It will be remembered that second appeals go to the Court of Appeal and because there has already been an appeal then the rule is that leave must be sought from the Court of Appeal itself,[43] in part to ensure that it hears only those matters that it thinks are most relevant.

Table 18.1 Appeals: the general rule

District judge (county court)	Circuit judge (county court)
Master of the High Court	Pusine judge
Circuit judge (inc deputy)	Puisne judge
Puisne judge (inc deputy)	Court of Appeal (Civil Division)

41. *Civil Procedure Rules*, r 52.3.
42. *Civil Procedure Rules*, r 52.3(2).
43. *Civil Procedure Rules*, r 52.3(3).

18.2.2.1 **Test**

The test for granting leave for first appeals (irrespective of who grants it) is:

(a) the court considers that the appeal would have a real prospect of success; or

(b) there is some other compelling reason why the appeal should be heard.[44]

Ground (a) is the more usual one and it will be difficult to persuade a judge that ground (b) is satisfied, in part because that will ordinarily mean that the judge has decided that there is not a real prospect of success. Of course an example of where it may be used is where precedent is against an individual but it is widely accepted that the precedent is wrong. There would not be an arguable prospect of success in that the court will be obliged to follow the precedent but by granting leave it may be that the case proceeds to a sufficiently high court that can remedy the breach of precedent.

> **Example** Bad precedent
>
> A wishes to appeal against the final decision of a district judge in a fixed-track case. The district judge felt obliged to follow a precedent of the High Court although practitioners and academics have suggested that it was wrongly decided. The avenue for this appeal will be to a circuit judge sitting in the county court. That judge will similarly be bound by the High Court precedent and so it cannot be said that there is 'a real prospect of success' but the district judge believes that, once that appeal has been disposed of, the matter is likely to proceed to the Court of Appeal (Civil Division) who will not be bound by the High Court precedent and could, if it chose, overrule it.

The test of 'real prospect' is not supposed to be a statistical test but is simply supposed to weed out those cases where the prospects are fanciful.[45] Where there has been a material irregularity leave should ordinarily be given even if there is doubt as to whether the decision itself is wrong[46] which accords to the usual issue about justice being seen to be done.

The test for second appeals is more restrictive and is:

(a) the appeal would—

   (i) have a real prospect of success, and

   (ii) raise an important point of principle or practice; or

(b) there is some other compelling reason for the Court of Appeal to hear it.[47]

The rationale behind this tighter restriction is that the first appeal should have resolved most irregularities. It is notable that both of these grounds would deal with the issue of bad precedent discussed later.

18.2.2.2 **Reconsidering permission**

It is not unusual for leave to appeal to be dealt with purely on papers, especially where it is a petition to the next most senior court (rather than judge) or to the Court of

---

44. *Civil Procedure Rules*, r 52.3(6).
45. *Swain v Hillman* [2001] 1 All ER 91.
46. *Re W (Children)(Permission to Appeal)* [2007] Fam Law 897.
47. *Civil Procedure Rules*, r 52.7.

Appeal itself. Where the decision to deny leave is granted on an appeal then an appellant may request that a hearing takes place to determine leave.[48] Strictly speaking this is not an appeal since it will ordinarily be considered by a judge of the same level. Where, on papers, a judge decides that the appeal is 'without merit' then they can order that an appellant is not permitted to request a hearing.

18.2.3 The hearing

A civil appeal will ordinarily involve decisions of law and will not therefore amount to a rehearing. When granting leave it is open to the court granting leave to restrict leave to certain grounds[49] in which case only those matters should be raised with the court unless (exceptionally) the court hearing the appeal grants permission to go beyond those grounds.

Skeleton arguments are widely used in civil cases and counsel will be expected to file these in appropriate time. They will be read by the judge and the appeal will tend to be more inquisitorial than adversarial, in that the judge will almost certainly restrict himself to those aspects that he believes have some merit and may question counsel on the legal submissions that he has put forward. Although the term 'skeleton' is used they are not merely bullet-point summaries but are instead complex legal arguments. Within the Court of Appeal a skeleton argument should 'normally' be no more than twenty-five pages in length[50] which shows how long they can be. They summarize the key points that are to be argued but must show why a party is referring the court to a particular authority and what the effect of that authority is.

Where legal authorities are to be cited then ordinarily in the county courts and the Court of Appeal it will be for the appellant to file a bundle that contains photocopies of the authorities that *both sides* will rely upon. The Practice Direction makes quite clear that both sides are supposed to communicate about the authorities that they wish to rely upon and these will then be filed in the same bundle. The advantage of this system is that it ensures that it is easy to access the various authorities and to ensure that each person is looking at the same thing. In the High Court it is not usually necessary to provide photocopies of the legal authorities but it is necessary to list what the authorities are so that they can be laid before the judge before the hearing.

18.2.3.1 Composition of the courts

For first appeals that take place before a puisne judge or below (see Table 18.1) then ordinarily the court will consist of a single judge of the rank identified within that table. Where the appeal is to the Court of Appeal (because, for example, the matter is against a ruling of a puisne judge or because it was against a final ruling in a multi-track case) then ordinarily a two-judge panel will sit. It is comparatively rare (although not unheard of) for puisne judges to sit in the Court of Appeal (Civil Division) and accordingly the court will consist of two Lord Justices of Appeal. If a two-judge bench is equally divided then the matter should ordinarily be re-listed before a three-judge bench.

Where the matter is an appeal from a decision of the High Court, particularly where it entails a multi-track case, or where it is a second appeal from the High Court

---

48. *Civil Procedure Rules*, r 52.3(4).
49. *Civil Procedure* Rules, r 52.3(7).
50. PD 52C, para 31.1.

(ie a decision of a circuit judge was appealed to a puisne judge and from there to the Court of Appeal) then it will ordinarily be a three-judge panel.

18.2.3.2 Powers of the appellate court

The general powers of an appellate are the power to:

(a) affirm, set aside or vary any order or judgment;

(b) refer any claim or issue for determination by the lower court;

(c) order a new trial or hearing;

(d) make orders for the payment of interest; and

(e) make a costs order.[51]

Ordinarily the appellate court will not refer matters back to the lower court save where it believes that a matter of fact needs to be resolved (including through the hearing of witness testimony). Usually (and certainly where it is a first appeal before a judge not in the Court of Appeal) the court will deal with the matter itself.

> **Example** Appeals varying an order
>
> Thomas appealed the decision of a circuit judge in a fast-track case. He complains that whilst the judge gave judgment in his claim for damage to property and awarded £14,000 he wrongly excluded loss of earnings of £5,000. The puisne judge hearing the matter agrees. Rather than returning the matter to the circuit court and requiring the judge to alter the judgment the puisne judge hearing the matter will simply alter the judgment and order to state that the damages are now £19,000.

18.2.4 Appeals to the Supreme Court

As with criminal law there is an appeal from the Court of Appeal (Civil Division) which will lie to the Supreme Court. These will be exceptional cases—although the majority of appeals the Supreme Court hears are civil rather than criminal, they still account for a miniscule proportion of all the appeals heard by the Court of Appeal. Permission to appeal to the Supreme Court should initially be made to the Court of Appeal that determined the original appeal although it is not unusual for that court to deny permission. Irrespective of this it is possible to seek leave from the Supreme Court itself (which will be determined by three justices) and whilst it is not necessary to certify a point of public importance (as occurs in criminal cases) it is likely to be only those types of cases that would be selected by the Supreme Court to be heard.

18.2.5 Examples of appeals

The final section of this chapter will return to the case studies that were first presented in Chapter 17. In each of the examples a brief synopsis will be presented which demonstrates how the appeal will take place, where, and how it will be resolved.

51. *Civil Procedure Rules*, r 52.10.

18.2.5.1 **Small claims track**

The first case study involved Amy, who purchased a faulty television. The small claims track is, as identified in Chapter 17, simply one of the three tracks that civil litigation is ordinarily assigned to. Accordingly, the general rules of appeals contained within CPR 52 apply. This means that Table 18.1 applies and since a small claims hearing is ordinarily heard by a district judge (see 17.1.6.2) this means that any appeal will be made to a circuit judge sitting in the county court. This is one of the reasons why it would be extremely rare for a circuit judge to sit on a small claims track hearing since then an appeal would be to a puisne judge and, given the delays that exist within civil litigation, there are better things for a puisne judge to sit on than a small claims hearing (although, in reality, such an appeal would almost certainly be heard by a deputy judge).

Leave

As noted already, it is necessary to seek leave to appeal. Given that lawyers rarely appear in the small claims court it is quite likely that leave will not be sought from the district judge that made the ruling. That said, after the district judge has explained the reasoning of his judgment it is quite possible that a litigant may ask how they appeal. In those circumstances it is possible that a district judge may allow for the request to be made at that time but it is more likely that he would recommend that the party goes away and considers it.

A special form exists for appeals in respect of small claims appeals (N164 available on the Online Resource Centre) and this includes a section that allows a person to apply for permission to appeal at the same time as initiating the appeal. The form then asks the appellant to explain why they are appealing against the decision of the judge. This should allow the judge to decide whether to grant leave on papers but if there is insufficient detail then a judge may call the appellant into court so that a hearing can be held and the reasons better articulated.

Pre-trial matters

The process for small claims appeals is simplified in much the same way as the hearing itself is. Ordinarily a series of documents are required to be filed for appeals, but this does not apply to appeals on the small claims track. Indeed, a standard document that should automatically be submitted is a transcript of the judgment or hearing. However, a transcript is not required for a small claims hearing.[52] Similarly, more formal documents such as skeleton arguments are not required, with section 5 of Form N164 taking its place.

A fee is payable (currently £120) and the court will serve all the various papers on the respondent and if the respondent seeks to contest the appeal then they will serve the papers on the appellant.

Hearing

As with the small claims the key presumption is that the hearing of the appeal will take place without the use of lawyers. The case will probably still be heard in chambers and the judge is likely to take a proactive stance in identifying what the key issues are and identifying what, if any, grounds there are for the appeal to succeed. As litigants in person are common, part of the difficulty with the hearing will be ensuring that the appeal

---

52. PD 52B, para 6.2.

is restricted to legal issues rather than a person simply arguing that he did not like the result. An appeal is based on the argument that a judge made an error of law in reaching the decision that they did. Laypersons are unlikely to have researched the law making the position more difficult for the judge who will not be an expert in each area of the law.[53]

The test that the judge must use to decide whether to grant the appeal is the same as discussed earlier, ie whether the judge at first instance was wrong or whether there was a procedural flaw that renders the case an injustice. Judgment will almost certainly be given immediately and it is highly unlikely that the judge would ever refer the matter back to a district judge and would instead simply exercise his powers to vary an order.

Costs

Until comparatively recently the small claims track contained a potentially disadvantageous system in respect of appeals. Whilst, as noted in Chapter 17, the small claims track limited the costs of litigation there was no cap in respect of appeals. Accordingly, in our example, if Amy had succeeded in her claim, Screens 'R' Us could have threatened to appeal and state that they would engage a barrister to represent them at the hearing. The potential costs for this are such that Amy might decide not to contest any appeal.

That is no longer the case, however, and small claims track appeals are dealt with in a very similar way. Indeed, the rules governing costs for the small claims track expressly include 'costs relating to an appeal'[54] and thus the same costs as identified in 17.2 can be claimed, with the court fee of £120 being one of these. No costs for legal representation will ordinarily be payable.

There is (theoretically) the right to appeal against the decision of the appeal, this lying to the Court of Appeal (Civil Division) as it is a second appeal. It would be extremely rare for an appeal to be granted leave, however. A rare case where a small claims track issue did arrive at the Court of Appeal was *Akhtar v Boland*[55] and to the surprise of even the court itself, it would seem that the costs protection applies to those proceedings too.[56]

18.2.5.2 Judicial review

The second case study was in respect of Matilda's claim for judicial review. It will be remembered from Chapter 17 that this is a matter that takes place before the Administrative Court in the High Court. Therefore any appeal will be direct to the Court of Appeal (Civil Division) even for a 'first' appeal.

Where the judicial review was heard by two judges in the Administrative Court (ie a Divisional Court) then the matter will be heard before a three-judge panel of the Court of Appeal but where it was heard only by a single judge then it is possible that it will be heard by a two-judge panel.

Leave

As noted earlier the first issue is that the losing party must seek leave to appeal. Let us assume that Matilda was successful and she received an order quashing the decision of the Chief Constable to ban the march. The Chief Constable believes that the judge did

---

53. For an interesting discussion on this see Penny Darbyshire, *Sitting in Judgment: The Working Lives of Judges* (Hart Publishing 2011) 245.
54. *Civil Procedure Rules* r 27.14(2).
55. [2014] EWCA Civ 943.
56. See [2014] EWCA Civ 943 [7].

not take account of the cost involved in providing security for two high-profile events (the march and the visit of the Home Secretary) and that the decision is irrational.

Here the Chief Constable will be the appellant and Matilda will be the respondent. The Chief Constable must seek leave to appeal. As identified earlier, this can be sought from the court of first instance (the Administrative Court) or, if this is refused, from the Court of Appeal itself. As with the small claims track there is a form (form N161 available on the Online Resource Centre) and there is a section of this form that allows the applicant to seek the leave of the court. However, rather than just complete the form the person must file the appropriate documents that identify what the decision is and what grounds are relied upon for the appeal,[57] including identifying the grounds of appeal.

The respondent has the right to make representations to the court on why permission should not be allowed, although these will normally be confined to paper submission.[58] The statement should not be more than three pages long and ordinarily no costs can be claimed for doing so;[59] this is partly because the respondent does not *have* to answer the appeal at permissions stage: it is for the claimant to persuade the court that they should have the right to appeal so silence from the respondent would not realistically change their success.

The clear presumption is for leave to be considered on the papers (by a single (puisne) judge) but if leave is refused then the appellant has the right to ask for a hearing in respect of seeking permission unless the judge, who considers the papers, refuses a hearing. Such an appeal will take place in open court and will be before a normal bench of the Court of Appeal, ie two (or more likely three) Lord Justices of Appeal.

Regardless of whether permission is sought by papers or by hearing, the test remains the same. Leave shall only be granted if:

(a) the court considers that the appeal would have a real prospect of success; or

(b) there is some other compelling reason why the appeal should be heard.[60]

'Real' prospect means that the appeal must have a realistic chance of success and is not merely fanciful.[61] In essence this means that the threshold is higher than prima facie, but it will obviously not be so high as to amount to the hearing of the appeal. Only the judge(s) can predict how the court will act, but there must be sufficient reason to believe that the grounds of appeal could be successful.

 APPEAL AGAINST PERMISSION FOR JUDICIAL REVIEW

It was noted at 17.3.2 that permission was required before a judicial review could proceed. If permission is refused (even after a renewed hearing) then this can be appealed to the Court of Appeal (Civil Division) but only on the ordinary grounds of appeal. An appeal must be made within seven days of permission being refused, and where the Court of Appeal allows the appeal they have the power to grant permission for judicial review rather than remit the matter back for reconsideration.[62]

The fee for seeking permission to appeal is currently £528.

---

57. PD 52C, para 3.
58. PD 52C, para 19.
59. PD 52C, para 20.
60. *Civil Procedure Rules*, r 52.3(6).
61. *Swain v Hillman* [2001] 1 All ER 91.
62. *Civil Procedure Rules*, r 52.8.

Pre-trial matters

Assuming that leave has been granted then there are a number of matters that must be adhered to. As with the High Court, the Court of Appeal will not serve papers on any party and will expect the parties to use the usual rules of service, so that the court and all parties receive everything.

The appellant must complete the 'appeal questionnaire' that will be distributed by the court.[63] This will ask a series of case-management questions, including providing a time estimate. If the respondent disagrees with this time estimate, they must notify the court within seven days of this decision. Providing an unrealistic time estimate can disrupt the listing of the appeal but also lead to costs sanctions.

A core bundle must be compiled. This should include:

- The notice and grounds of appeal sealed by the court
- Skeleton argument
- Chronology of relevant issues
- Transcript of the first-instance judgment
- Written permission from first-instance decision (if applicable)
- The original claim form for judicial review
- The (original) acknowledgment of service and defence.

Details of any other information or evidence that is to be relied upon should be included as a 'supplementary bundle'.

It has been suggested that there are three types of respondent:

i. Those who are seeking to uphold the first-instance decision for the reasons set out in the judgment.

ii. Those who are seeking to uphold the first-instance decision but for reasons that differ from the judgment.

iii. Those who are seeking a variation of the first-instance decision.[64]

The most common respondent is #1 but then probably #3. An example of #3 may be where, for example, a judge made a finding of contributory negligence against the respondent, or where they believe the damages should have been greater or, perhaps more commonly, where they disagree with a costs order.

A respondent in position #3 is cross-appealing and therefore must submit a notice of appeal in the same way as an appellant, albeit after the appeal has been lodged. A respondent in #2 is not cross-appealing but he must issue a respondent's notice.[65] A respondent's notice is similar to an appellant's notice of appeal and sets out the reasons why the respondent is disagreeing with the reasons at first instance. A respondent in position #1 does not need to file a respondent's notice.

Where a respondent wishes to make representations to the court then they must submit a skeleton argument, which should also be filed on the appellant.

A fee (currently £1,199) must be paid before the hearing can take place.

63. *Civil Procedure Rules*, PD 52C, para 23.
64. Stuart Sime, *A Practical Approach to Civil Litigation* (19th edn, OUP 2016) 571.
65. *Civil Procedure Rules*, r 52.5(2).

Hearing

Usually an appeal from the Administrative Court will take place before three judges and ordinarily these will be Lord Justices of Appeal rather than including puisne judges. For judicial review cases, it is usual for an appeal to be heard by a three-judge panel, but this has to occur when the first-instance decision was a Divisional Court (ie two or more judges sitting together).

Where the bench consists of Lord Justices of Appeal then the administrative head of civil appeals will ordinarily not only decide the constitution of the panel but also decide who will be the 'lead' judge, ie the one who is identified as probably giving the judgment of the court.[66] This will not necessarily be the judge who presides over the court as that is decided purely by seniority (ie date of appointment). Where the Lord Chief Justice, Master of the Rolls, or Head of Division sits then they would ordinarily preside (again, in seniority, so where exceptionally both the Lord Chief Justice and Master of the Rolls sit, the Lord Chief Justice would preside as he is President of the Courts of England and Wales which trumps the Master of the Rolls even though the latter is head of civil justice). Where the Lord Chief Justice, Master of the Rolls, or Head of Division sits, they would ordinarily decide who will give the lead judgment. Increasingly the Court of Appeal (Civil Division) has attempted to move towards single judgments;[67] although a number of cases will still involve different judgments, especially where the bench is divided, unlike the position in the Criminal Division, there is no custom that prohibits the issuing of minority judgments.

Whoever is the 'lead' judge will ordinarily take the lead on asking the questions of counsel although the other judges can contribute as they wish. As the skeleton arguments will have been read and digested by the court the judges will ordinarily focus only on those aspects that they believe have merit. For example, it will not be unusual for counsel to be told that of three grounds of appeal they are only interested in hearing ground 2. It would be a very brave (and in legalese 'brave' means 'stupid') counsel who would ignore such statements and seek to go beyond that ground.

One interesting practical point to note for the law student is the fact that counsel for the appellant is rarely asked to open the appeal. When a student moots, they are invariably told that they must introduce everyone, provide a summary of the first-instance decision and the grounds for appeal. Whilst this may have been common practice in the appellant courts some time ago, it is not the practice now. The judges will have read the skeleton arguments and digested the bundle, and so they do not want the court's time wasted by telling them things that they already know. To that extent, whilst it remains adversarial in that there are two sides trying to persuade neutral umpires of their case, it is perhaps more inquisitorial in terms of judicial control and interaction.

Judgment will either be given *ex tempore* (ie immediately and without being typed up verbatim) or will be reserved. Sometimes the reservation may only be for a short period of time, including overnight. All judgments, even *ex tempore* ones, are recorded and may therefore be transcribed or reported for the law reports. The Court of Appeal has the same powers as identified earlier. This can include, for example, remitting the matter back to the court of first instance. In judicial review cases it is unlikely that they will do this, not least because there may be questions of timing, save where it is necessary to hear factual evidence. It is more likely that the Court of Appeal will adopt its powers of endorsing, varying, or quashing the order.

621

66. Penny Darbyshire, *Sitting in Judgment: The Working Lives of Judges* (Hart Publishing 2011) 245.
67. Penny Darbyshire, *Sitting in Judgment: The Working Lives of Judges* (Hart Publishing 2011) 343.

Subsequent appeals

As noted earlier there is technically a further appeal but only to the Supreme Court. This is exceptional. Whilst the Court of Appeal can give permission to appeal, in civil matters it usually leaves the issue of leave to the Supreme Court itself.

18.2.5.3 Children's contact

The third example was Joshua's application under the *Children Act 1989* to see Sarah, his child. It will be remembered from Chapter 17 that specific rules exist for family proceedings—the *Family Procedure Rules* (FPR)—and these apply also to (some) appeals. Appeals within the Family Court are dealt with by the FPR but appeals to the Court of Appeal (Civil Division) are dealt with under the CPR as the Court of Appeal is not part of the Family Court.[68] Thus the procedure discussed earlier would apply to family appeals. Appeals within the Family Court ordinarily take the approach of escalating an appeal to the next level of judge. This is set out in Table 18.2.

Separate to this, however, both the Family Court and the High Court have discretion to decide that the matter should instead be dealt with by the Court of Appeal (Civil Division) but they should do so only when:

(a) it raises an important point of principle of practice; or

(b) there is some other compelling reason for the Court of Appeal to hear it.[69]

The position of a circuit judge is slightly complicated as it depends on the matter they ruled. The general rule is that an appeal from a circuit judge is to a puisne judge, even where it is a final decision (cf the position for general civil litigation discussed earlier). However, for certain categories of appeal, an appeal goes to the Court of Appeal (Civil Division). These include:

- Decisions relating to public childcare proceedings, orders relating to the protection of children or children abroad.

- Decisions relating to adoption.

Table 18.2 Route of appeals

Justices of the Peace sitting in the Family Court	Circuit judge
District judge of the county court sitting in the Family Court	Circuit judge
District judge of the High Court sitting in the Family Court	Puisne judge
District judge of the principal registry of the Family Division	Puisne judge
Costs judge	Puisne judge
Circuit judge or recorder sitting in the Family Court	Puisne judge or Court of Appeal (see below).
Puisne judge (inc deputy) sitting in either the Family Court or the High Court of Justice	Court of Appeal

68. *Family Procedure Rules*, r 30.1 makes clear the extent of the rules.
69. *Family Procedure Rules*, r 30.13.

- A decision to hold a party in Contempt of Court, or an order following the finding for contempt.
- A decision that was made on appeal.[70]

This is a relatively restricted list and it means that for most private-law proceedings, a decision of a circuit judge will go to a puisne judge.

If we refer back to our example of Joshua, it will be remembered that the decision was heard by justices of the peace, and therefore the appeal will go to a circuit judge (or a recorder).

Leave

As with the ordinary civil rules, there is not ordinarily an absolute right. That said, the FPR make clear that no permission is required to appeal a decision of lay magistrates to circuit level.[71] Presumably the logic of this is similar to the logic for appeal in criminal cases, ie that the magistrates are not legally trained and that justice requires the right of access to a legally qualified judge. However, given that a legal advisor will always be present in the Family Court and the justices are given specialist training, it must be questioned whether this is overly generous and that leave should be required for all cases.

For our example, if we assume that Joshua does not agree with the decision of the justices not to increase contact with the child, then it would seem that he can take this to a circuit judge without permission. That said, unlike a Crown Court appeal, the matter will not be a rehearing, it is an appeal and the same test will be adopted (see later).

Pre-trial matters

Joshua has submitted his appeal. He must now adhere to several pre-trial matters before his appeal can be heard, the most notable being the preparation of an appeal bundle.[72] As with other appeals, a skeleton argument is usually required. Where it is 'an appellant who is not represented [they] need not file a skeleton argument but [are] encouraged to do so since this will be helpful to the court'.[73] Even if a skeleton argument by a litigant in person is not as detailed or polished as one prepared by an advocate, the reason for requesting one is that it will help the judge in the pre-reading. An appeal is a review of a decision, not a rehearing, and thus the judge hearing the appeal will wish to concentrate on the key issues, and a skeleton argument can assist with this.

In many family matters there will not have been a written judgment per se. In the original hearing of Joshua's application it is likely that the district judge will simply have stated why it was that he refused to make the order that he did. It is quite possible, and indeed likely, that he would do this verbally. How can this be adduced before the circuit judge for consideration on appeal? The Practice Direction states that the parties should attempt to agree a version of the ruling and to submit that before the judge who made the decision.[74] Interestingly where an advocate was used in the proceedings then the Practice Direction *expressly states* that their fee for appearing in the original matter includes remuneration for taking a note of the judgment, transcribing

---

70. PD 30A, para 2.1.
71. *Family Procedure Rules*, r 30.3(a). The rule is by omission: the rule states that permission is required to appeal a circuit judge, recorder, district judge, or costs judge. Thus a decision by justices of the appeal must not require permission.
72. PD 30A, para 5.8 sets out what is required.
73. PD 30A, para 5.15.
74. PD 30A, para 5.23.

it, attempting to reach an agreed version, submitting it to the judge, and making any amendments required by the judge.[75] Where, therefore, a different barrister is engaged for the appeal or the litigant decides to represent himself, the original advocate is under a duty to supply their note of the judgment.

Once these documents are prepared they must be served on all other parties[76] and ultimately a date will be set for the appeal, including any procedural hearings that may be required (although in a matter as simple as this one it is likely that the only hearing will be the appeal itself). The court will request a time estimate for the appeal (which is easier to gauge when professional advocates are used but even litigants in person will be required to give an estimate) as this will assist the court in listing the appeal.

The respondent(s) to the appeal will also be required to prepare a bundle and skeleton argument and this will then be served on the court and the appellant.

Hearing

As this appeal will be to a circuit judge, the Designated Family Judge[77] will assign a judge to the appeal at a relevant and convenient court.

The actual hearing is a 'review of the decision';[78] in other words it is not a rehearing but an appeal. It will concentrate on whether the first-instance decision was (legally) wrong. The fact that it is a review and not a rehearing is emphasized by the fact that ordinarily evidence (including witness testimony) will not be adduced[79] and this is because it is not its decision to reach matters of fact but rather to conclude whether the judge of first instance erred in reaching his judgment.

The test for allowing the appeal is if the court believes the decision was:

(a) wrong; or

(b) unjust because of a serious procedural or other irregularity.[80]

Most appeals will be decided on ground (a) and it is notable that the test is that it is *wrong*. It is not enough that a judge may have decided differently, it must decide that the decision was wrong meaning, in essence, that it should not have been reached. As with main civil litigation appeals the appellate judge has the same powers as the original judge[81] and has the power to affirm, set aside, or vary an order or alternatively order a new hearing etc.[82] In the example of Joshua the circuit judge would decide what to do. It is highly unlikely that he would refer it back for a rehearing and would instead just make a revised order if he believes it appropriate to do so. Alternatively, he would dismiss the appeal.

Subsequent appeals

As the decision was in respect of an appeal, any subsequent appeal would go to the Court of Appeal (Civil Division) rather than to a puisne judge. The permission of the Court of Appeal would be required to do this and it would only succeed if the grounds set out earlier (at 18.2.2.1) were to be met.

---

75.   PD 30A, para 5.25.
76.   PD 30A, para 6.2.
77.   A senior circuit judge who has judicial management control for family proceedings in their area.
78.   *Family Procedure Rules*, r 30.12.
79.   *Family Procedure Rules*, r 30.12(2).
80.   *Family Procedure Rules*, r 30.12(3).
81.   *Family Procedure Rules*, r 30.11(1).
82.   *Family Procedure Rules*, r 30.11(2).

Summary

This chapter has introduced the concept of civil remedies and then presented the different methods of appeals from decisions of the civil courts. This allows you to draw comparisons to the avenue of criminal appeals in Chapter 16. It has also:

- Identified that there are many different types of remedies that a court can award to a successful litigant.

- Demonstrated that the most common form of remedy is that which is known as 'damages' and that there are various heads of damage that can be claimed for, but that the main distinction is that between 'pecuniary' and 'non-pecuniary'.

- Equity has a number of remedies and these will only ordinarily be used where damages by themselves will not suffice but they can be combined with damages.

- It is possible to obtain remedies before the conclusion of a trial and these are known as interim remedies. Perhaps the most notable of these is the interim injunction but for this to be granted a claimant must give an undertaking to compensate the defendant if the claim is resolved against him.

- Appeals in the civil courts follow a slightly more complicated structure than in criminal cases.

- Save where it is a final decision in a multi-track case, the usual rule is that the appeal will be heard by the next most senior judge.

- It is possible to have a second appeal but the courts are reluctant to allow this except in the most serious cases.

- In order to appeal in civil cases it is usually necessary to seek permission before proceeding with a civil appeal.

625

❓ End-of-chapter questions

1. Should a court discount an award to take account of the fact that damages can be invested? What kind of investment should they base their decision on? Is this not risky given that even bank interest rates have been stagnant for the past few years?

2. Read Penny Darbyshire, *Sitting in Judgment: The Working Lives of Judges* (Hart Publishing 2011) 251 where she states that circuit judges do not like sitting on the appeals of district judges who sit in the same building as them. Is there not a danger of apparent bias (even if there is no actual bias) that a judge who works with the judge whose decision he is reviewing will uphold the ruling 'for a quiet life'? How does this differ, however, from puisne judges sitting in the Court of Appeal (Criminal Division)?

3. Is it fair that the costs for small claims track appeals are restricted? If an appeal concerns points of law should it not be appropriate that lawyers are allowed to be used?

For multiple-choice questions, updates to this chapter, and links to useful websites, please visit the **Online Resource Centre** at: **www.oxfordtextbooks.co.uk/orc/gillespie_els6e/**

19

Alternative Dispute Resolution

By the end of this chapter you will be able to:

- Understand why the pressure for ADR arose.
- Define ADR and explain the three principal forms of ADR.
- Identify how the courts are able to persuade litigants to use ADR.
- Appreciate some of the advantages and disadvantages of ADR.

Introduction

It has been seen in the previous chapters that there are several different ways in which disputes can be resolved formally through the invocation of the judicial or tribunal system. However, court proceedings are not the only ways in which disputes can be resolved and in recent times there has been a push towards Alternative Dispute Resolution (ADR). As has been seen, the courts are expensive and therefore there is an argument for suggesting that disputes should only reach the courts or tribunals if there is no other alternative. Certainly, as will be seen, the courts are increasingly adopting this approach and are using their powers to encourage attempts at settling the dispute before a formal judicial resolution is sought.

This chapter will examine how ADR has grown and consider its application and some difficulties that may arise through its use.

19.1 What is Alternative Dispute Resolution?

There is no single definition of Alternative Dispute Resolution (ADR). Whilst there are agreed types of ADR, the term just realistically means a way of resolving a dispute without formally invoking the courts or tribunals. Thus ADR could range from an agreement by the parties (for example, party A deciding to forgo $x\%$ of a disputed bill because they accept that they did not perform the contract adequately) to a third party intervening in the dispute to make findings of fact, in which case it may look not dissimilar to a court case.

It is widely accepted that ADR involves two distinct types of resolution. These are known as adjudicative options and non-adjudicative options.[1] 'Adjudicative' means that a person sits as an adjudicator, ie a person independent of the parties will hear from the other parties and reach a conclusion on the dispute and, in most instances, decide upon the remedy. To that extent, as has been noted already, it could be questioned what the difference is between an adjudicative resolution and litigation. The answer lies primarily in the lack of formality, speed, and cost.[2] The legal process is complicated. As was seen in Chapters 17 and 18, there are rules governing how litigation is conducted within the courts. Alongside these procedural rules are rules of evidence. They will limit the types of evidence, or the circumstances in which the evidence can be presented to the courts. However, ADR operates outside of the legal system and therefore the parties themselves can decide what the rules are, without being bound by traditional understandings of the law and process.

Non-adjudicative forms are much broader. They tend to rely on facilitating an agreement. A third party may still be present, but their role is not to be determinative, but rather to try and bring the two sides together, to understand the point of view of the others, and to work towards a settlement that both are happy with. Non-adjudicative forms can therefore sometimes create situations where a party does not think that they have 'won' or 'lost' because it is about identifying a compromise that both are happy about and which avoids the requirement to spend considerable sums of money on litigation.

At the outset, it is important to understand the scale of ADR. It is tempting to think of ADR as being 'local' resolution of small-scale disputes. Whilst undoubtedly this will sometimes be the case, ADR can involve vast sums of money. For the reasons that are set out more fully later, it is increasingly common for commercial cases to be settled via ADR. This means that it is not uncommon for multi-million pound disputes to be settled through adjudicative ADR. Indeed the popularity of ADR, particularly arbitration, has caused the current Lord Chief Justice to speculate whether there is a danger that it will stifle the development of the common law since disputes that would otherwise be adjudicated by the courts, allowing precedent to develop, are now being dealt with outside of the judicial process.[3]

It is equally important to recognize a second truth of ADR. That it is not new. By bringing together all the forms of dispute resolution under the title of 'ADR' it is sometimes possible to believe that ADR is a modern concept. Indeed, it was realistically not until the twentieth century that 'ADR' became a popular concept, it largely centring on the work of Frank Sander, a professor of law at Harvard University.[4] However, some forms of ADR are much older. Arbitration, a form of arbitrative justice, has been in existence for hundreds of years, having existed in (English) ecclesiastical law since the seventh century.[5] In the 1920s, English commercial arbitration was lauded as being the exemplar that other countries, most notably the USA, should follow.[6] There is no doubt,

---

1. See, for example, Susan Blake, Julie Browne, and Stuart Sime, *The Jackson ADR Handbook* (2nd edn, OUP 2016) 13, 16.
2. Susan Blake, Julie Browne, and Stuart Sime, *The Jackson ADR Handbook* (2nd edn, OUP 2016) 13.
3. Lord Thomas of Cwmgiedd, 'Developing Commercial Law through the Courts: Rebalancing the Relationship between the Courts and Arbitration' 2016 BAILII lecture. Available online at: <https://www.judiciary.gov.uk/wp-content/uploads/2016/03/lcj-speech-bailli-lecture-20160309.pdf>.
4. An illuminating history of the development of ADR and the place of Frank Sander can be found in Michael L Moffitt, 'Frank Sander and His Legacy as an ADR Pioneer' (2006) 22 *Negotiation Journal* 437–45.
5. Paul L Sayre, 'Development of Commercial Arbitration Law' (1928) 37 *Yale Law Journal* 595, 597.
6. Paul L Sayre, 'Development of Commercial Arbitration Law' (1928) 37 *Yale Law Journal* 595.

however, that in recent years ADR has enjoyed a renaissance where its popularity has increased and where the judiciary encourage it to be tried as an alternative to litigation.

19.2 Why use ADR?

Some of the reasoning behind this has already been discussed: it can be a cheaper, less formal, and quicker way to resolve disputes. It can operate in a more flexible way than the law, particularly the English law.

19.2.1 A shift away from combat?

It has been noted numerous times in this book that the English Legal System is based on the adversarial system of litigation. In essence this means that both sides separately prepare their respective submissions and then they arrive in court and participate in a quasi-gladiatorial contest until the tribunal of fact (in civil trials this usually being a judge) pronounces the winner. The manner in which this contest occurs was seen in Chapter 17 and even in tribunals, a system of justice that is usually considered to be more informal, the adversarial system remains intact with both sides still competing against each other (discussed in Chapter 7).

Yet in recent times there has been an increasing debate as to whether the adversarial system is the appropriate way of resolving all disputes. To an extent this was realized in specialist proceedings, perhaps most notably in proceedings relating to the welfare of a child. The *Children Act 1989* makes clear that the best interests of the child must be the court's paramount consideration[7] and this has led to the conclusion that in certain proceedings, most notably child protection proceedings, the full adversarial system is unhelpful and that making the proceedings more inquisitorial can be of assistance (see the discussion on family litigation at 17.4).

Even within ordinary litigation it is now becoming increasingly accepted that the adversarial system is not always of assistance and that it inherently involves both extensive cost and delay.[8] It has also been suggested that it involves two further disadvantages: an imbalance of power (which could be likened to the 'equality of arms' principle contained within Article 6 of the *European Convention on Human Rights* (ECHR) (see 5.4.5.4)) and the restriction of civil legal aid (see Chapter 11) means that the adversarial system allows the rich to exploit the law.[9] It is difficult to argue against these and although Article 6 will try to level the 'battleground' so far as possible, eg through exchange of documents (although this is not an automatic right: see for example *Secretary of State for the Home Department v MB*[10]) or the provision of legal assistance (see, for example, *Steel and Morris v United Kingdom*[11]) it is simply a fundamental part of the legal system.

Wider concerns exist over the adversarial system, not least being whether it encourages the resolution of disputes and the discovery of the facts or merely seeks to identify

---

7. *Children Act 1989*, s 1(1).

8. Geoff Davies, 'Civil Justice Reform: Why We Need to Question Some Basic Assumptions' (2006) 25 *Civil Justice Quarterly* 32.

9. Geoff Davies, 'Civil Justice Reform: Why We Need to Question Some Basic Assumptions' (2006) 25 *Civil Justice Quarterly* 32.

10. [2006] EWCA Civ 1140.

11. (2005) 41 EHRR 22.

who has the better advocate. The advocate in adversarial systems, while being under a professional duty not to mislead the court, owes a duty to his client and will act in a partisan way before the neutral umpire, seeking to exploit the weaknesses of the opposing side while at the same time trying to hide their own weaknesses. Not only are the lawyers inherently partisan but most witnesses almost certainly will be, not least by the labelling of witnesses as being 'for' or 'against' a side. A witness will not be called unless it is thought that they would assist the argument being put forward by the party, regardless of whether or not the person has anything to contribute to the finding of fact.

The adversarial system ensures that lawyers are central to the process. Since the analysis and presentation of evidence is key to the adversarial approach, one requires a lawyer who is able to assimilate the facts quickly and apply them with an appropriate knowledge of law. This by itself is not sufficient, however, since a lawyer must also advocate the points, ie use persuasion to encourage the tribunal of fact to make the appropriate rulings. In a market society such as England and Wales, this means that the best lawyers will always be in demand and can therefore charge significant fees. This not only makes litigation expensive but also creates a power imbalance between those who can afford these fees and those who cannot.[12]

19.2.2 Advantages of ADR

The shift away from the adversarial system must undoubtedly be considered a key advantage of ADR. However, there are more tangible advantages in its use.

As was noted in Chapter 17 the courts are beset by delays. Whilst procedure rules seek to try and improve the situation, it must be accepted that litigation can take a considerable length of time. This is particularly true of complicated cases. For the quarter January to March 2016, it was reported that the average length of time between claim and hearing in fast- or multi-track claims was 51.9 weeks.[13] This is the *average* length of time, meaning that for many cases it took considerably longer. Even simpler cases took time. The average length of time between claim and hearing was 32.2 weeks for small claims actions, yet these are supposed to be the simplest of cases. In both instances it should be noted that this is the time between claim and the *main* hearing. There will then be a further hearing before the judgment is given.

In many instances, waiting over a year for a resolution to a dispute is simply not possible. For example, if the dispute is over a crucial factory part or the performance of a contract, considerable losses could be incurred if the status quo continues for the year it takes for the matter to proceed before the courts. ADR can be much quicker as it is, in essence, a case of ensuring that the parties agree and that a suitable time can be found with the person who facilitates ADR. As there are a considerable number of these, it is possible to move very quickly. Indeed, some forms of ADR now take place online, meaning that the process is even quicker.[14]

It is not just about speed, however. The costs of ADR are usually much cheaper than litigation. While this year-long trial process has been going on, there will have

---

12. Geoff Davies, 'Civil Justice Reform: Why We Need to Question Some Basic Assumptions' (2006) 25 *Civil Justice Quarterly* 32, 37.

13. 'Civil Justice Statistics Quarterly, England & Wales: January to March 2016' (Ministry of Justice) 5.

14. Julia Hörnle, 'Online Dispute Resolution: The Emperor's New Clothes?' (2003) 17 *International Review of Law, Computers & Technology* 27, 28.

been considerable work undertaken by barristers and solicitors. Indeed, even prior to the court action being commenced there will have been considerable legal costs incurred. Where a dispute is over not very much money, it is quite possible that the costs of litigation will take up most of, or indeed exceed, the money being disputed. The *Money Advice Service*, a governmental website that helps provide financial advice, notes that a *negotiated* financial settlement in a divorce could cost upwards of £3,000.[15] That is where there is agreement. Where the divorce is contested, it states that costs of £36,000 are not unusual. In many instances it will be more. The average family will probably not have much more than that in savings or indeed equity, and what equity there is in property should ideally be used to allow both parties to gain alternative property rather than paying for lawyers. Mediation, a form of ADR, however, may only cost £100 per hour, and if the parties are capable of being sensible and compromising, it is possible that agreement on the way forward could take place in 4–6 sessions.[16]

The informality of ADR also means that it is sometimes possible to go to the heart of the dispute, whereas the adversarial nature of litigation requires each side to establish their case. Indeed, adversarial systems tend to encourage so-called 'satellite litigation' where minor disputes start off and encircle the principal dispute, causing additional costs and delays. ADR can puncture this by encouraging people to concentrate on what is important to both parties.

A final and yet very important advantage, in some cases, is that ADR is generally confidential. As it is, in essence, an agreement between parties, both can assist on confidentiality. This can be important where the dispute is sensitive or where the issue at the heart of the dispute may cause reputational damage to one or other of the parties. Whilst it is possible in some cases to have confidentiality within litigation, the clear presumption is that litigation is public.[17] This may be uncomfortable for either or both parties, meaning that ADR becomes attractive.

19.2.3 Disadvantages of ADR

It is easy to get caught up in the enthusiasm of ADR but there are disadvantages too. ADR requires a degree of consent. In the absence of any law or rule to the contrary, both parties must agree to use ADR rather than litigate.[18] This is not always possible, particularly where disputes seem personal. In the raw emotion of feeling 'wronged', people do not often want to think rationally and instead prefer the idea of 'vengeance', even when the courts are not interested in that as a concept. A good example of this is divorce. As will be seen later, ADR is strongly recommended in family matters, but when a marriage has broken down it is not uncommon for the parties to want a fight rather than a compromise. Where, for example, adultery is admitted, the courts do not care about the circumstances of the adultery and the hurt that this may have caused a

---

15. <https://www.moneyadviceservice.org.uk/en/articles/how-much-does-divorce-or-dissolution-cost>.
16. Of course, there would be the formal costs of applying to the court for a divorce. A petition for divorce costs £550 to file and an application for a financial order costs £255. Applications in respect of children will be in addition to this (if required).
17. See *Civil Procedure Rules*, r 39.2.
18. An example of where a law may provide a requirement would be a clause within a contract that required disputes to be settled by way of arbitration. The *Arbitration Act 1996* will enforce this as a contractual term and a court, faced with an attempt to litigate the dispute, will stay proceedings in the courts until the adjudication has happened.

party. Legally it is irrelevant once admitted[19] and it is not relevant to the dispersal of assets. Yet the 'wronged' party is likely to believe it is material and therefore may be less willing to compromise in ADR.

There is also the disadvantage that it might end up in court in any event. Whilst it will be seen that some forms of ADR are protected by the courts, in that they will not readily interfere with the ultimate decision, that is not the case with all forms. It is quite possible that in non-adjudicative forms of ADR, time and expense are incurred trying to identify a solution, only for it to collapse at the last minute or be rejected. It will be seen that the courts may take notice of this (when, for example, determining costs: see 17.1.5.5), but ultimately they are unlikely to reject litigation on this basis alone.

One of the advantages of ADR—informality—can also be a disadvantage. Whilst the legal system can be overly prescriptive and traditional, it does have the advantage that there is an established set of rules (both procedural and evidential) that neither side can influence. With ADR, the rules are generally agreed between the parties and thus if there is any power imbalance, it is possible that they may become skewed. Also, as ADR sits outside of the legal system, it is not affected by precedent. Therefore, the mere fact that a similar case had resolution x before does not necessarily mean that the second case will have the same resolution. Therefore, there is perhaps a degree of uncertainty with ADR.

Finally, some of the advantages are arguably over-stated. Whilst it is said that ADR is quick and cheap, it need not be. For example, for relatively minor disputes, the costs of ADR are likely to be more than the costs incurred under the small claims track in the county court (where costs are fixed: see 17.2). Also, ADR usually involves more work than for minor disputes. The small claims procedure requires the filing of the claim form, acknowledgement of service (and submission of defence, where appropriate, although that tends to be on the same form), and then the hearing. Some forms of ADR will require several steps, meaning that even if the process is quicker, it may seem more protracted.

That said, it should be recognized that in many cases, ADR is likely to be an appropriate alternative to litigation, particularly where disputes are greater than the small claims track. The courts welcome ADR as the civil courts are overwhelmed with work and struggle to process the volume of cases that come before them. If they can encourage ADR, then this lightens the load before the courts. Where the dispute is either minor or simple, the courts will often view this as a more preferable outcome.

19.3 Types of ADR

It has been noted that there are two broad classifications of ADR; adjudicative and non-adjudicative, but what are the common forms of ADR? Table 19.1 summarizes the most common forms that are found within the UK.[20]

---

19. It would be relevant if not admitted because adultery is one of the grounds for divorce (*Matrimonial Causes Act 1973*, s 1(2)(a)) and therefore a party seeking to prove adultery would need to be able to prove it happened.

20. Table 19.1 is based on chapter 2 of Susan Blake, Julie Browne, and Stuart Sime, *The Jackson ADR Handbook* (2nd edn, OUP 2016) which is published on behalf of the *Judicial College, Civil Justice Council*, and the *Civil Mediation Council* and which is widely considered to be the most authoritative statement of ADR in England and Wales.

Table 19.1 Types of ADR in the UK

Adjudicative	Non-adjudicative
Arbitration	Offer and Acceptance
Adjudication	Negotiation
Expert determination	Mediation
	Neutral/Expert Evaluation
	Conciliation

19.3.1 **Adjudicative forms**

Adjudicative forms of ADR are those where the process does not lead to an agreement but instead somebody makes a decision as to the dispute.

19.3.1.1 **Arbitration**

Perhaps the most common form of adjudicative ADR is arbitration. As noted earlier, this is one of the oldest forms of resolving disputes, and it remains one of the most common forms of ADR. It is also the most formal of the forms, being very similar to a court process.

Arbitration is one form of ADR that is expressly recognized by the law. The *Arbitration Act 1996* sets out the three principles under which arbitration must take place:

1. The object of arbitration is to obtain the fair resolution of disputes by an impartial tribunal without unnecessary delay or expense.

2. The parties should be free to agree how their disputes are resolved, subject only to such safeguards as are necessary in the public interest.

3. The courts should not intervene save where prescribed by the *Arbitration Act 1996*.[21]

These principles encapsulate what arbitration is about. It is about the resolution of a dispute and it must be done fairly. As an adjudicative form of ADR, a person (or persons) is appointed to be the arbitrator and they must decide what the outcome of the dispute is. To that extent, they are analogous to a judge. The second principle demonstrates the flexibility of the arbitration, in that the parties can form their own rules on how the arbitration will take place (including ascertaining what is, or is not, part of the dispute) or they could delegate this to the arbitrator to decide.

The final point is an important one. The *Arbitration Act 1996* is very clear that the courts will be very slow to interfere with arbitration. Where a contract stipulates that disputes will be resolved through arbitration, or where the parties have reached an agreement to arbitrate, the courts will stay any proceedings brought before the courts that seek to litigate the dispute which is supposed to be the subject of arbitration.[22] Similarly,

---

21. *Arbitration Act 1996*, s 1.
22. *Arbitration Act 1996*, s 9.

it is only possible to appeal a decision of an arbitrator under exceptional circumstances, usually a serious irregularity[23] or where there has been a material breach of law.[24] The courts are very slow to entertain any appeal because they fear that to do so would lead to the re-litigation of the dispute and would undermine the principle of arbitration.

Arbitration has also been used as a form of permitting religious tribunals to adjudicate on trials. In recent years there has been much media attention paid to the growth of so-called 'Sharia courts' where disputes are resolved under the principles of Islamic law. Other religions also have religious tribunals, including the Beth Din for Judaism. Do they have any legal force? The answer would seem to be both 'yes' and 'no'. Formally, religious tribunals do not form part of the English Legal System (save for the ecclesiastical courts of the Church of England (known as consistory courts) which do form part of the legal system due to the establishment of the Church of England[25]), however, there is no reason why they cannot act as a form of ADR. In *Al v MT (Alternative Dispute Resolution)*[26] the High Court stayed private family law proceedings to allow the matter to be the subject of arbitration in the Beth Din. The court ultimately upheld the ruling of that tribunal, although it noted that family law matters are not covered by the *Arbitration Act 1996* and thus the court could refuse to implement a decision. However, it demonstrated that the courts are willing to allow Alternative Dispute Resolution by religious arbitration, and this is one manner in which religious tribunals can be used to settle some forms of dispute.

QUESTION FOR REFLECTION

Should the English Legal System recognize the resolution of a dispute by a religious tribunal? Is this not permitting religious law to enter into the English Legal System via the 'back door'? However, if arbitration—and indeed most ADR—is about encouraging people to resolve their disputes on their own terms, why should it be any different if the parties wish to resolve their dispute according to the religious principles they believe in?

19.3.1.2 Adjudication

Adjudication is very similar to arbitration, in that it involves a specialist person adjudicating on a dispute.[27] It is arguably more specialist than arbitration in that it is often used to resolve very technical disputes rather than a wider dispute. It is often to be found in contracts where questions as to performance will be determined by an adjudicator. A failure to use the adjudicator would be considered a breach of contract and thus could be litigated in the courts.

19.3.1.3 Expert determination

In some disputes, the dispute will be about something extremely technical, and which can realistically only be resolved by an expert. Litigation involving expert witnesses

23. *Arbitration Act 1996*, s 68, although it is possible to exclude this right of appeal under the arbitration agreement or contract.
24. *Arbitration Act 1996*, s 69.
25. See the *Ecclesiastical Jurisdiction Measure 1963* which reformed the ecclesiastical courts and the work before them.
26. [2013] EWHC 100 (Fam).
27. Susan Blake, Julie Browne, and Stuart Sime, *The Jackson ADR Handbook* (2nd edn, OUP 2016) 14.

can be particularly expensive and therefore where the sole dispute concerns something resolvable by an independent expert, it is sometimes preferable to refer the matter to an expert to resolve the factual circumstances. The parties would need to agree to be bound by the decision of the expert and also agree what the consequences of that expert determination are. It differs from arbitration and adjudication, in that the expert is not resolving a dispute per se, but rather providing an independent (binding) opinion of a fact.

19.3.2 Non-adjudicative forms

Offer and acceptance and negotiation have, to an extent, already been covered as these are traditional forms of resolving a dispute. Technically neither require any sort of third-party intervention and it can be done by the parties themselves through the exchange of communications.

19.3.2.1 Mediation

Mediation is arguably a form of facilitated negotiation. A third party acts as a facilitator but, unlike arbitration, the third party has no role in determining issues and they instead simply try to encourage the parties to see things from the other's point of view. Mediation, as will be seen, is strongly encouraged within the family arena (where the justice system has a vested opinion in trying to ensure that disputes, particularly relating to children, are resolved in as amicable a manner as possible) and a number of not-for-profit bodies exist to facilitate family mediation.[28]

Mediation will frequently not involve both parties being in the same room at the same time initially. A typical mediation process may involve pre-sessional contact, so that the mediator understands the respective positions of the parties. The parties will then be placed in different rooms and the mediator will discuss matters with the parties and then start to shuttle between the two locations. In fact, in some instances the parties may never be in the same room: the mediator simply relays positions to each party until agreement is reached. In other situations, once the positions have been narrowed, the two parties will be brought together to try and resolve the dispute.

As with other non-adjudicative forms, it is relatively high-risk in that an uncooperative party is unlikely to engage with the process and therefore mediation could be considered a waste of time. A party that refuses to budge from their position is likely to mean that mediation collapses. Indeed, there is a danger that it does more harm than good, as the other party entrenches their position in response and because they feel that they 'did their bit' by trying to engage in mediation.

19.3.2.2 Neutral/expert evaluation

This is similar to expert adjudication (see 19.3.1.3) but is non-adjudicative. It is quite possible that the dispute is based on the opinions of the parties in respect of a factual circumstance. That being the case, sometimes bringing in a neutral expert to evaluate that issue can help resolve it. Unlike adjudicative expert evaluations, the parties will not be bound to accept the view of the expert, but instead it is used to encourage the parties to negotiate an appropriate settlement based on the viewpoint of the third party.[29]

28. Susan Blake, Julie Browne, and Stuart Sime, *The Jackson ADR Handbook* (2nd edn, OUP 2016) 17.
29. Susan Blake, Julie Browne, and Stuart Sime, *The Jackson ADR Handbook* (2nd edn, OUP 2016) 19.

19.3.2.3 **Conciliation**

Identifying what conciliation is, and how it differs from mediation, is extremely difficult.[30] It realistically must be considered a branch of mediation and so may not exist in its own right. Conciliation is sometimes referred to as the 'shuttle' form of mediation presented above, with 'mediation' being restricted to those situations where both sides are together. However, in many other contexts, this is called 'mediation'.

One potential difference is that in conciliation, the mediator might propose a solution independent of the parties.[31] This would differ from arbitration in that it is non-binding. Realistically, it is more that the third party is putting forward a suggestion to try and break an impasse between the parties. This is not uncommon in mediation either but, admittedly, some mediators see their role as being completely neutral and simply convey positions rather than put forward their own, so perhaps this is where conciliation may differ.

 CONCILIATION

Conciliation is often used in industrial disputes. A good example would be where trade unions and employers disagree over work conditions, health and safety, etc. It is often used to try to settle disputes before strike action takes place. The alternative is either lengthy industrial disputes or litigation being brought where an employer seeks to interfere with strike action or where the trade union seeks declarations regarding health and safety legislation. By using conciliation, however, both sides can understand what the other's position is and try to reach a compromise that is suitable to both sides. A key to the success of conciliation is that the conciliator must be completely impartial. ACAS is often used in this role because of the reputation it has accrued over the years.

635

19.4 **ADR and the courts**

It may seem strange to think of the courts as wishing ADR to be used, but this must be placed into the context of extreme pressure being placed on the courts. Also, judges are realistic about litigation and the policy of the courts is that litigation is a measure of last resort.[32] How is this approval of ADR shown? The most notable shift in recent years is that the courts are using their powers to ensure that ADR is, at the very least, considered as part of the process of litigation.

19.4.1 **Family law**

Perhaps one of the best-known examples of how the courts encourage ADR is in respect of private family law, ie divorce and issues relating to the upbringing of children.[33] The

---

30. Susan Blake, Julie Browne, and Stuart Sime, *The Jackson ADR Handbook* (2nd edn, OUP 2016) 20.

31. Susan Blake, Julie Browne, and Stuart Sime, *The Jackson ADR Handbook* (2nd edn, OUP 2016) 20.

32. See the speech by Lord Justice Jackson 'Civil Justice Reform and Alternative Dispute Resolution' (20 September 2016). Available online at: <https://www.judiciary.gov.uk/wp-content/uploads/2013/03/lj-jackson-cjre-form-adr.pdf>.

33. Public family law is primarily focused on situations where the state is trying to intervene. So, for example, a local authority trying to take a child under supervision or into care, decisions as to the welfare and upbringing of vulnerable members of society.

Family Procedure Rules place a positive duty on both the courts and the parties to consider the applicability of ADR. Rule 3.3 requires '[t]he court [to] consider, at every stage in proceedings, whether non-court dispute resolution is appropriate'. Where a court considers that ADR is appropriate, the court can order the adjournment of proceedings or a hearing in order to facilitate these approaches.[34]

More than this, however, the courts require parties to, at the very least, consider ADR before commencing litigation in respect of private family disputes. Rule 3.7 of the *Family Procedure Rules* requires an application for a private family law matter to enclose a form that says a person has attended a MIAM (Mediation Information & Assessment Meeting[35]) or that one of the exemptions for attending a MIAM applies. Rule 3.7 is an important provision but it could be suggested that it is too tame. Whilst Rule 3.8 appears to limit the circumstances under which mediation need not be sought, the reality is perhaps different. One of the grounds for not requiring mediation is that the proceedings would be for a financial remedy,[36] which is a very broad exemption. Given that ADR is perhaps most commonly used in respect of financial disputes—particularly commercial litigation—it is perhaps surprising that a financial remedy should be exempting proceedings.

However, the more significant failing is in respect of mediators themselves. A mediator is entitled to certify that 'mediation is not … suitable as a means of resolving the dispute'[37] and many mediators will sign the waiver form if the claimant turns up and says that he will not participate in mediation. Whilst this probably does meet the threshold—in that mediation is required to be consensual—it does give people a 'cop out'. Perhaps a better position would be to require at least one round of mediation (in that if people are required to attend, a mediator may be able to engage with them in order to persuade them that ADR is the best solution for everyone) or indeed to require other forms of ADR. For example, should an adjudicative form of ADR be required for some forms of private family law? Whilst it would not be suitable for all forms of disputes, it is not necessarily clear that the courts are the best location for all disputes. For example, under the *Children Act 1989*, if a parent wishes to take their child outside of the United Kingdom, they need the consent of the other parent or a court. Parents can often abuse this to cause difficulties for a parent who wishes to take the children abroad with a new partner. Does this really require the time of a court, or could this be dealt with by arbitration? The fact parents do not like the idea of a child having a foreign holiday is not a reason to prevent it or a reason for occupying the time of a salaried judge.

Rules 3.7 and 3.8 should be placed in the context of rule 3.3 discussed earlier. So, for example, the mere fact that an individual has sought to circumvent mediation does not mean that it cannot happen. If one party says they wish to participate in mediation and the other party does not, the judge would have the right under rule 3.3 to adjourn proceedings to give the parties time to think whether ADR is appropriate. In these situations they also have the power to take cooperation into account when determining costs (discussed later).[38]

---

34. *Family Procedure Rules*, r 3.4(1).
35. In essence, MIAM is a session with a mediator that is authorized to provide private family mediation services (see *Family Procedure Rules*, r 3.9).
36. *Family Procedure Rules*, r 3.8(h)(ii).
37. *Family Procedure Rules*, 3.8(2)(c).
38. *Family Procedure Rules*, r 28.1 states that 'the court may at any time make such order as to costs as it thinks just'. Where a party has deliberately tried to circumvent ADR then the principles identified by the civil courts could easily be applied within the Family Court.

19.4.1.1 Civil disputes

ADR is designed to facilitate the resolution of civil disputes. Historically it was thought that this meant private disputes, but in 2001 the government conceded that ADR could have a role in public-law matters too.[39] The courts enthusiastically supported this. In *Cowl v Plymouth City Council*[40] the then Lord Chief Justice (Lord Woolf) stated that:

> ... even in disputes between public authorities and the members of the public for whom they are responsible, insufficient attention is paid to the paramount importance of avoiding litigation whenever this is possible.[41]

The case concerned residential care for the elderly and the decision of Plymouth City Council to close two care homes. There existed a complaints process, by which grievances could be submitted that demonstrated that a decision would be reconsidered if considerable hardship was shown. The Court of Appeal believed that judicial review was inappropriate until the complaints procedure had been exhausted, partly because they believed that this provided a cheaper, faster, and more appropriate disposal than litigation.

Since that time, the courts have readily applied this principle to other forms of judicial review[42] and so it would seem that ADR is not restricted to private disputes, although it would be fair to say that this is the most common position. However, the commitment to allowing ADR to be used in public disputes demonstrates that they are committed to ensuring that it is used to encourage the settling of disputes.

In terms of wider civil litigation, the *Civil Procedure Rules* mirror the *Family Procedure Rules* in ensuring that ADR is actively considered. However, as will be seen, the civil courts are perhaps more robust than the family court, partly to take account of the fact that the disputes in the civil courts rarely involve matters concerning the welfare of a vulnerable person where other interests must take precedence.

Initially the rules are somewhat obscure about the place of ADR, with a reference to the court having the power to 'take any other step or make any other order for the purpose of managing the case and furthering the overriding objective, including hearing an Early Neutral Evaluation with the aim of helping the parties settle the case'.[43] Whilst express reference is made to Early Neutral Evaluation, a form of non-adjudicative resolution identified at 19.3.2.2, this rule gives wider authority to the courts to make orders to facilitate the early disposition of the case. Indeed, in determining the compliance of the overriding objective, the rules state that the court has a duty to encourage the parties to use ADR where the court believes this is appropriate.[44]

Perhaps the strongest, and clearest, encouragement comes from a Practice Direction that accompanies the rules. The *Pre-Action Protocols* apply to all civil litigation and 'explain the conduct and set out the steps the court would normally expect

---

39. See the speech by Lord Justice Jackson 'Civil Justice Reform and Alternative Dispute Resolution' (20 September 2016). Available online at: <https://www.judiciary.gov.uk/wp-content/uploads/2013/03/lj-jackson-cjreform-adr.pdf> 2.
40. [2001] EWCA Civ 1935.
41. [2001] EWCA Civ 1935 [1].
42. See, for example, *R (on the application of Crawford) v Newcastle-upon-Tyne University* [2014] EWHC 1197 (Admin).
43. *Civil Procedure Rules*, r 3.1(2)(m).
44. *Civil Procedure Rules*, r 1.4(2)(e).

parties to take before commencing proceedings for particular types of civil claims'.[45] Importantly, it includes specific reference to ADR:

> Litigation should be a last resort. As part of a relevant pre-action protocol or this Practice Direction, the parties should consider whether negotiation or some form of ADR might enable them to settle their disputes without commencing proceedings.
>
> If proceedings are issues, the parties may be required by the court to provide evidence that ADR has been considered. A party's silence in response to an invitation to participate or a refusal to participate in ADR might be considered unreasonable by the court and could lead to the court ordering that party to pay additional court costs.[46]

These are powerful statements and show that the courts are prepared to treat ADR seriously. Along with the general powers of the court to adjourn a matter, the CPR specifically provides that a party may seek a stay of proceedings while ADR is attempted.[47] If both parties agree to this request, then the stay is automatic, but the court retains discretion to stay proceedings if it 'otherwise considers that a stay would be appropriate' to permit ADR.[48] This provides the court with the power to put pressure on the parties to consider ADR. The courts can go further, however, including through the use of the so-called 'Ungley Order'. This is an order named after QBD Master Ungley who pioneered its use.[49] The order, in essence, requires the parties to meet to discuss whether mediation (or other ADR) could solve their dispute. It does not require them to use ADR, it requires them to meet to discuss whether ADR is appropriate. This can be particularly useful where a party is equivocal about using ADR.

Can the courts go further and mandate that ADR takes place? In *Halsey v Milton Keynes General NHS Trust*,[50] the (then) Dyson LJ held that it would not be compatible with Article 6 ECHR to compel a party to undertake ADR.[51] The logic is that Article 6 safeguards the right to a fair and public hearing by an independent and impartial tribunal, which is considered to mean a court. However, not everyone agrees with this premise. It has been noted that other signatories to the ECHR have compulsory ADR and they have not attracted criticism for this.[52] It is also notable that in certain other common-law jurisdictions, where the right to justice is considered equally important, compulsory ADR can be found. A good example of this is Canada, where in Saskatchewan, litigants must attend a mediation session immediately after the initial papers have been filed.[53] This can be contrasted with the position in England which requires the parties to *consider* mediation, but it does not compel attendance. Perhaps the English position is based on the premise that non-adjudicative forms of ADR (which is what the courts appear to prefer in terms of encouraging ADR) can only work if both parties wish to cooperate, meaning mandating ADR would not work.

Whilst the English courts cannot mandate ADR, it is clear that by using their discretion over costs they can do the next best thing. It was seen from Chapter 17 that costs are now increasingly used by the courts in civil proceedings as a tool to persuade parties

---

45. *Practice Direction: Pre-Action Conduct and Protocols*, para 1.
46. *Practice Direction: Pre-Action Conduct and Protocols*, paras 9 and 11.
47. *Civil Procedure Rules*, r 26.4.
48. *Civil Procedure Rules*, r 26.4(2A).
49. Susan Blake, Julie Browne, and Stuart Sime, *The Jackson ADR Handbook* (2nd edn, OUP 2016) 96.
50. [2004] EWCA Civ 576.
51. [2004] EWCA Civ 576 [9].
52. Susan Blake, Julie Browne, and Stuart Sime, *The Jackson ADR Handbook* (2nd edn, OUP 2016) 96.
53. Barbara Billingsley and Masood Ahmed, 'Evolution, Revolution and Culture Shift: A Critical Analysis of Compulsory ADR in England and Canada' (2016) 45 *Common Law World Review* 186, 192.

to do something. This is particularly true of ADR. The *Civil Procedure Rules* provide considerable flexibility in respect of costs[54] and in recent years, they have been prepared to use these.

One of the key landmarks was the decision in *Halsey v Milton Keynes General NHS Trust*[55] where the Court of Appeal held that unreasonable refusal to engage in ADR could be dealt with by a costs order. The court did note that the parties were free to engage with ADR in the manner that they wished, and thus the court will not look at the strategy they adopted.[56] In deciding whether there has been an unreasonable refusal, the court said that factors would include, but were not limited to:

(a) the nature of the dispute;

(b) the merits of the case;

(c) the extent to which other settlement methods have been attempted;

(d) whether the costs of the ADR would be disproportionately high;

(e) whether any delay in setting up and attending the ADR would have been prejudicial; and

(f) whether the ADR had a reasonable prospect of success.[57]

Perhaps predictably, a solution to *Halsey* was for a party to maintain silence upon a request. If an unreasonable refusal could limit costs, then one strategy for parties was to neither accept nor refuse ADR. In *PGF II SA v OMFS Company 1 Ltd*[58] the Court of Appeal held that silence in the face of a request to engage in ADR was *by itself* unreasonable. Briggs LJ stated:

> In my judgment, the time has now come for this court to endorse the advice given in Chapter 11.56 of the ADR Handbook,[[59]] that silence in the face of the invitation to participate in ADR is, as a general rule, of itself unreasonable, regardless whether an outright refusal, or a refusal to engage in the type of ADR requested, or to do so at the time requested, might have been justified by the identification of reasonable grounds.[60]

This is tough language from the Court of Appeal and it is notable that Briggs LJ states that it should be regarded as unreasonable even if a refusal would not have been. The logic of this is undoubtedly that a party has the right to know whether their offer of ADR is to be accepted and, if not, why not. This is partly to ensure there is no loss of time, but also so that the case can be prepared in an appropriate way. The court believed that silence is not an option in civil litigation and there is an expectation that both sides will try to avoid litigation and ensure that any differences they may have are narrowed.[61]

Whilst *PGF* could be taken to be a sensible step forward from *Halsey*, it is notable that it is now recognized as a 'landmark' judgment.[62] It demonstrates, quite clearly,

639

54.   *Civil Procedure Rules*, pt 44.
55.   [2004] EWCA Civ 576.
56.   [2004] EWCA Civ 576 [14].
57.   [2004] EWCA Civ 576 [16].
58.   [2013] EWCA Civ 1288.
59.   This being Susan Blake, Julie Browne, and Stuart Sime, *The Jackson ADR Handbook* (2nd edn, OUP 2016) (note this footnote does not appear in the judgment).
60.   [2013] EWCA Civ 1288 [34].
61.   [2013] EWCA Civ 1288 [37].
62.   See the speech by Lord Justice Jackson 'Civil Justice Reform and Alternative Dispute Resolution' (20 September 2016). Available online at <https://www.judiciary.gov.uk/wp-content/uploads/2013/03/lj-jackson-cjreform-adr.pdf> 5.

the importance that the courts place on ADR and they will not allow 'gameplay' to try and skew the results of ADR. In other contexts this can be seen where the courts have reacted to cases where a person seeks to litigate midway through an (unfinished) ADR process.[63] This is undoubtedly an attempt to frustrate the process of ADR and the courts are, quite correctly, likely to consider such activities unreasonable.

Costs orders are sufficiently flexible to ensure that either party can bear the costs irrespective of the general principle that the losing party bears the costs of the winning party. As litigation, particularly in multi-track cases, can be extremely expensive, the ability to order costs should focus the minds of the parties.

║\ Case Box *Laporte & Christian v Commissioner of Police for the Metropolis*

Two claimants had sought to argue that their arrest had been unlawful.[64] Whilst commencing their action, they indicated that they would be prepared to participate in ADR. The Metropolitan Police did not answer many of their queries and was equivocal as to whether they would participate in ADR.

During the substantive hearing, the Metropolitan Police Commissioner won on all grounds. He sought costs from the claimants and asked for them to be on the indemnity basis.[65] Turner J refused to do this and applied *Halsey v Milton Keynes General NHS Trust*.[66] His Lordship held that the Metropolitan Police had been unreasonable in not participating in ADR. On that basis, he ordered that only two-thirds of the costs claimed by the Metropolitan Police should be payable by the claimant. The costs were in excess of £200,000 so the one-third loss demonstrates how seriously the courts take these issues, even against public authorities.

19.5 Online court

A recent innovation has seen the judiciary once more seeking to invoke ADR in place of litigation. Lord Justice Briggs was asked by the Lord Chief Justice to examine the structure of the civil courts. In his final report,[67] he recommended the creation of an 'online court'.[68] Whilst called 'a court', it is clear that Lord Justice Briggs intended that it would primarily be a dispute resolution service.

The online court (which is a name that Lord Justice Briggs wishes changed although there is no consensus to what[69]) would differ from the traditional courts in that, as its name suggests, it would take place entirely virtually. It is envisaged that there will be three stages to any dispute.

---

63. Susan Blake, Julie Browne, and Stuart Sime, *The Jackson ADR Handbook* (2nd edn, OUP 2016) 134.
64. [2015] EWHC 371 (QB).
65. Indemnity costs are, in essence, more severe than normal costs and mean that where there is a dispute as to costs, the party gaining indemnity costs gets the benefit of the doubt, meaning that their claimed costs are payable. In standard costs situations, it is not unusual for a judge to summarily assess costs, ie decide himself how much should be payable for certain actions.
66. [2004] EWCA Civ 576.
67. Lord Justice Briggs, *Civil Courts Structure Review: Final Report* (Judiciary of England & Wales 2016).
68. Lord Justice Briggs, *Civil Courts Structure Review: Final Report* (Judiciary of England & Wales 2016) ch 6.
69. Lord Justice Briggs, *Civil Courts Structure Review: Final Report* (Judiciary of England & Wales 2016) 61.

Stage 1.   This would be the lodging of the claim. An online portal would facilitate this. Unlike traditional claim forms (which provide very generic questions), this portal would ask targeted questions so that the issues at the heart of any dispute would be identified. Where a matter is not disputed, it would be identified at any early stage and sent down a different path (ie to enforcement rather than adjudication). A degree of ODR (online dispute resolution) would be used at this stage.[70] This is where electronic communication is used to try and resolve the dispute. This would, in essence, be very similar to the position used by Amazon, eBay, and PayPal where there is a dispute. The various positions and offers would be put to the parties by an online facilitator (with parts of it potentially being automated) to see whether this could be resolved. In essence, this is not dissimilar to the offer/agreement or negotiation forms of non-adjudicative ADR identified earlier.

Stage 2.   This would be a compulsory form of ADR, probably conciliation. The online court is designed to simplify procedures and try to avoid cases proceeding to court. As part of this, there would be a requirement that the parties try to identify a solution. It has been suggested that the conciliation is likely to take place by telephone, but it could also conceivably be dealt with via VoIP services (eg Skype, Facetime etc) or even chat-based services.

Stage 3.   Assuming that the dispute has still not been settled, the matter would proceed to trial. Depending on the issue, this would either be a decision on the papers, with both sides providing their written arguments, or alternatively an online trial, where the parties would participate. It could also be a hybrid, where a judge considers the papers but if he has any questions, he telephones either party to ask for further information or clarity.

The proposal seems quite radical although, as Lord Justice Briggs himself notes, such courts are commonplace elsewhere in the world. Perhaps predictably the reaction of the legal profession was somewhat mixed. The chairman of the Bar Council was particularly lukewarm, suggesting that it would create a 'two-tier' justice system, arguing that those who can afford lawyers will continue to litigate whilst others will need to go through this process.[71] However, that rather neglects the point that if this is how two-tier justice is defined, that is already the position: cuts in legal aid have meant that those who cannot afford to litigate are arguably in a much poorer position. Indeed, it could be argued that if this online court is accessible for litigants in person, then a person seeking compensation would be better off using this than pursuing a conditional fee arrangement, as they are likely to lose less money.[72]

A more pertinent criticism was that if the costs of legal advice and limited representation were not included, that could mean that people rely on non-legal experts to decide the merits of their claim.[73] The judiciary have previously shown concern at so-called 'McKenzie friends' who charge payment for their services and are, in essence, becoming

---

70.   See <https://www.judiciary.gov.uk/reviews/online-dispute-resolution/> for the website of the 'Online Dispute Resolution' Advisory Group, set up by the Master of the Rolls. This website provides comprehensive information about ODR and how it works.

71.   Chantal-Aimée Doerries, 'Too Much, Too Soon' (2016) 166 *New Law Journal* 7692.

72.   As fees would be recoverable and the matter may be solved quicker through the compulsory conciliation. In many personal injury cases, it is the damages that are being contested, not liability. A conciliator could suggest an appropriate award and see what both parties make of that.

73.   Chantal-Aimée Doerries, 'Too Much, Too Soon' (2016) 166 *New Law Journal* 7692.

faux-lawyers.[74] If legal advice or legal representation is not permitted for claims of up to £25,000,[75] then such services may become more prominent. Lord Justice Briggs conceded that this could be right and there may be an argument for recovering some types of legal advice and services, although in a fixed way.[76] That has to be right: £25,000 is a serious amount of money and the suggestion that, for example, personal injury litigation could be pursued without any recourse to lawyers is perhaps unlikely. The online court should allow for the cost of initial legal advice to be provided and some form of representation at stage 3. That said, as with fast-track cases, these costs should be fixed to encourage settlement and proportionality of litigation.

Summary

This chapter has examined the use of ADR within the civil justice system. In particular it has:

- Identified that there has been a shift away from the 'pure' form of an adversarial trial, although not to a full inquisitorial system.
- Noted that ADR is often cheaper and more informal than civil litigation, meaning disputes can sometimes be resolved more quickly and more amicably than through litigation.
- Discussed the three principal forms of ADR: arbitration, mediation, and conciliation.
- Noted that some contracts will now include an arbitration clause within them, meaning that disputes must proceed through arbitration first.
- Discussed the merits of the ACAS employment arbitration scheme, including noting that it potentially reduces the legal avenues open to someone claiming a breach in employment rights.
- Noted the finality of arbitration where courts are reluctant to interfere with the decision of an arbitrator.

End-of-chapter questions

1. Read Geoff Davies, 'Civil Justice Reform: Why We Need to Question Some Basic Assumptions' (2006) 25 *Civil Justice Quarterly* 32–51. Is there a case for moving away from the adversarial system of justice? What would the difficulties be with such an approach?

2. Read Roberts 'Family Mediation After the Act' (2001) 13 *Child and Family Law Quarterly* 265–73. Why were the mediation proposals in the 1996 Act dropped? With many divorces is there not a danger that clients are arguing over relatively small assets, leading to acrimony and high legal bills? Would mediation not ensure a smoother transition through divorce?

---

74. See 'Reforming the Courts' Approach to McKenzie Friends: A Consultation' (Lord Chief Justice of England & Wales 2016).
75. The level proposed for the online court.
76. 'Reforming the Courts' Approach to McKenzie Friends: A Consultation' (Lord Chief Justice of England & Wales 2016) 43.

3. Why do you think there is no right of appeal against the decision of an arbitrator? Is there a danger that by allowing an appeal to take place it would detract from the whole point of arbitration? It could allow an unhappy side simply to engage in expensive litigation after deciding that they did not like the decision of the arbitrator. Could an appeal be restricted to errors of law? One difficulty with this presumably must be the fact that arbitrators are not legally qualified so would they understand the legal principles they would then have to uphold? If only legally qualified arbitrators were used, how would this differ from a tribunal?

Further reading

Davies G, 'Civil Justice Reform: Why We Need to Question Some Basic Assumptions' (2006) 25 *Civil Justice Quarterly* 32–51.

This an excellent article by a former Australian judge that questions many of the basic premises over the place of ADR in civil litigation.

Genn H, *Court-based ADR Initiatives for Non-Family Civil Disputes* (HMSO: London 2002).

This presents the report of Professor Genn who was examining the use of ADR in non-family civil disputes. It makes some interesting points about the perceptions of counsel and the judiciary over the use of ADR in complex commercial cases.

Koo, AKC 'Ten Years after Halsey' (2015) 34 *Civil Justice Quarterly* 77–95.

This looks at how the decision in *Halsey v Milton Keynes NHS Trust*[77] has influenced the conduct of litigation and, in particular, the use of Alternative Dispute Resolution.

643

For multiple-choice questions, updates to this chapter, and links to useful websites, please visit the **Online Resource Centre** at: **www.oxfordtextbooks.co.uk/orc/gillespie_els6e/**

---

77. [2004] EWCA Civ 576.

THE FUTURE

20

The Future

Since the first edition of this book, it has been traditional in the final chapter to try and glimpse into the future and see what future changes are likely to be brought to the ELS. In some editions, the issues discussed have been significant—for example, the Supreme Court, Alternative Business Structures, and the *Courts and Crime Act 2013*—and in others the predicted changes have been relatively minor. However, this edition discusses the most significant change to the English Legal System in recent years.

By the time the eighth edition of this book is out in four years' time, the English Legal System will look very different from how it does now. It is possible that some of these changes will be in effect by the time of the seventh edition, although that seems unlikely. The key issue is, of course, the withdrawal from the EU. At the time we are writing this chapter, we are waiting for the judgment of the Supreme Court in *R (on the application of Miller) v Secretary of State for Exiting the European Union*.[1] Whilst an important constitutional case, it will not, unlike what most of the press have suggested, make any real difference to the result of the referendum. It would be a brave Member of Parliament who voted to defy the wishes of the British public, in particular the views of their own constituents.[2] Therefore, at some point during 2017—very probably the end of March/beginning of April—the United Kingdom will trigger Article 50 of the *Treaty of the European Union* and this will put in place a mechanism that will lead to the repealing of the *European Communities Act 1972*.

Whilst this is undoubtedly important, there are other probable changes that need to be considered. These include:

- Continued membership of the Council of Europe
- Devolution or federalization
- Legal education
- Transformation of the justice system
- Leaving the EU.

Legal aid funding should probably also be included within the chapter but, perhaps for the first time since the first edition, it will not. That is not because we do not believe that legal aid will be controversial in the future, or that questions will be asked about how litigation should be funded. We believe that these questions will continue to be asked. But realistically little more can be said than that which is contained in Chapter 11. Legal aid will continue to be squeezed, it will be politically controversial, and there

---

1. [2017] UKSC 5.
2. Whilst it is difficult to show exactly how people voted in each constituency, it is widely believed that most parliamentary constituencies voted to leave.

will be pressure for alternative sources of funding. Insurance products are likely to increase as people realize the risk of them being involved in litigation grows. It is conceivable that insurance policies to cover criminal litigation may be developed and that litigation insurance becomes as common as house and car insurance. ADR is likely to grow too but the fact will remain that litigation is expensive and no government appears to believe that expanding legal aid is an option, even in circumstances where there is a proven need for it to exist.

20.1 Council of Europe

As was noted in Chapter 4, the current Prime Minister, Theresa May, is not a fan of the *European Convention on Human Rights*. She believes that it curtails parliamentary sovereignty and prevents the government from fulfilling its primary duty of protecting the public. Of course, this is an extremely controversial belief and a number of people disagree with this position, including many in her own party. The decision to withdraw from the EU has meant that any discussion on what to do about the ECHR has been placed on the back-burner.

The previous Conservative Prime Minister, David Cameron, had argued that there was a need to repeal the *Human Rights Act 1998* and introduce a 'British Bill of Rights'. Little was said about how the latter would differ from the former. There was a persistent comment that it would free the courts from being bound by the ECtHR but, as was noted in Chapter 5, the *Human Rights Act 1998* does not require them to be bound. Whilst there has been judicial disagreement as to how closely the domestic courts should follow the ECtHR—including by the current Lord Chief Justice who believes that we should be willing to depart—it is clear that it is the courts that are choosing to align themselves to the ECtHR, not Parliament. Thus it can be legitimately questioned whether a British Bill of Rights would do anything different. It is unlikely that the Bill of Rights would contain anything significantly different from the rights contained within the ECHR as they are a relatively uncontroversial statement of rights. It is how they have been interpreted that has proven to be controversial. Whilst Parliament could choose to put some restrictions within it, the reality is that the courts are quite adept at interpreting legislation the way that they choose.

Theresa May understands this. She believes that so long as the UK is a signatory of the ECHR, the courts will interpret the laws in a way that respects the opinions of the ECtHR. There is also the problem, from her viewpoint, that as a signatory, we are subject to the ECtHR in direct cases. As was noted in Chapter 3 there is theoretically no precedent emanating from the ECtHR, although it obviously provides a steer on how they will rule in later cases. However, the United Kingdom has always obeyed the rulings of that court. That said, this is a matter of choice and a number of countries have decided not to follow the rulings, but the UK always has. To that extent, Theresa May believes that we need to withdraw from the ECHR.

In principle, it should be less problematic to withdraw from the ECHR than the EU, although not in the context of Northern Ireland; however, this is outside the scope of this book.[3] The ECHR has never had the same status as EU legislation and it is not

---

3. The *Northern Ireland Act 1998* placed human rights at the forefront of devolution in Northern Ireland, in part because of the distrust that exists between the different communities in Northern Ireland. It would be difficult (although not impossible) to disentangle the ECHR from Northern Ireland devolution.

directly effective. It is unlikely that the government would admit to wanting to 'water down' human rights and thus the withdrawal would be accompanied by a domestic piece of legislation that would put forward a statement of rights. An example of this could be the *Canadian Charter of Rights and Freedoms*. Whilst this now forms part of Canada's (written) constitution, there is no reason why such an instrument could not be enacted as a stand-alone piece of legislation. Parliament could provide the 'fig-leaf' of entrenchment by stating that it can only be repealed or amended by a certain majority. It did this in the *Fixed-term Parliaments Act 2011*[4] but the reality of parliamentary sovereignty is that this is of no legal force. As Parliament cannot bind its successors, a subsequent piece of legislation that abolished the required majority would take precedence. Politically it would look good though.

Would this make any difference? The primary difference it would make is that the final decision on any matter would rest with the Supreme Court and not with any international court. Thus, the government could be assured that the final adjudicator is at least familiar with the laws of the United Kingdom. Whether that would lead to a different result is perhaps more moot. The courts already look towards the law in other countries and the laws of international agreements. It is unlikely that they would cease to pay any attention to what is happening in the ECtHR, although it is likely that they would be more cautious about altering domestic law on the basis of their rulings. It would almost certainly make the Supreme Court a more political court (with a small 'p'). There are already calls by the press for the Justices of the Supreme Court to be appointed in a different way, although no one has yet shown that requiring the approval of Parliament would in any way improve the quality of the court. Indeed, the current impotence of the Supreme Court of the United States of America,[5] and the narrow focus on specific issues when confirming justices, suggests the latter.

Can the UK withdraw from the ECHR but not the (wider) Council of Europe? It would seem unlikely. The *Statute of the Council of Europe*[6] requires member states to 'accept the principles of the rule of law and of the enjoyment by all persons within its jurisdiction of human rights and fundamental freedoms',[7] which is taken to mean the ECHR.

Would leaving the Council of Europe matter? Probably. Whilst it is of lesser constitutional significance, it is important for many aspects of how the law operates. Alongside the ECHR, the Council of Europe has numerous other conventions, including ones that protect against cybercrime, the sexual abuse of children, human trafficking, and domestic violence. These treaties provide a common framework and require countries to assist each other, and facilitate extradition and mutual legal assistance. Without this, there would be a number of cross-jurisdictional crimes that would be very difficult to prosecute.

It is too early to say what will happen because the Conservative party is divided on this issue, in a way more significant than it was over the EU. However, if Euroscepticism continues to rise, it is quite possible that it will feature in a manifesto in 2020. The extent to which there is credible opposition at that general election could prove crucial in terms of whether we stay within the Council of Europe or not.

---

4. Section 1(1) requires a two-thirds majority of the House of Commons to trigger an early election.
5. At the time of writing, there are only eight justices as Congress has refused to proceed with the nomination of President Obama (arguably contrary to the principles of the US Constitution). Where the court is divided, then an appeal falls and so some controversial appeals have simply fallen away.
6. CETS No 1. This is, in essence, the constitution of the Council of Europe.
7. CETS No 1, Article 3.

20.2 Devolution or federalization?

As was noted in Chapter 1, the result of the Scottish referendum in 2014 was a request for further devolution which was later fulfilled by the *Scotland Act 2016*. The withdrawal from the EU has raised tensions again. Whilst the population of England and Wales voted to leave the EU, a majority of people in Northern Ireland and Scotland voted to stay. As a UK-wide vote, the vote to remain by Scotland and Northern Ireland is (legally) irrelevant but politically it is likely to lead to renewed calls for further devolution, particularly over powers that were vested within the EU. The argument of many (including in Wales) is that powers need not return to Westminster, they could go to the devolved institutions.

The future shape of the United Kingdom is probably open for debate. It was noted in Chapter 1 that there is talk of a second Scottish independence referendum, although currently this seems unlikely as there is no evidence that the answer of the electorate would be different. However, there is likely to be continued pressure. Northern Ireland and Wales look enviously at the powers enjoyed by the Scottish Parliament, which are considerably more than afforded to either of the other two devolved institutions. There is pressure for 'English Votes on English Matters', meaning that Scottish, Welsh, and Northern Ireland MPs should not get a vote on matters that purely affect England. There have been isolated calls for an English Parliament but others have suggested that Parliament should continue to decide English laws, but with only English MPs voting on them. Of course, this would mean that English legislation would be sovereign legislation (unlike legislation from the delegated legislatures which could technically be overruled by Westminster) but whether, in practice, this means anything is perhaps open to debate.

What should the role of the United Kingdom be? The *Constitution Reform Group*, an all-party Parliamentary group, has suggested that the EU provides an opportunity to create a federal structure.[8] They suggest that the four constituent countries should be given full sovereignty over all issues, save for a small number of matters that would remain a UK function. These would include the monarch, foreign affairs, defence, national security, international treaties, and a single currency. They also propose that the Supreme Court would retain its position as the pre-eminent court, allowing a degree of consistency across the four countries.

Adopting a federal structure would be extremely radical but it is perhaps one way of ensuring that the Union could survive. Each country would have the same powers and thus would be accountable for the decisions that they take. However, it is unlikely that this will occur in the short term. The Westminster Parliament and UK government would lose most of its power and influence, meaning that they are likely to be slow to adopt such an approach. Federalization without changing the constitutional construction of the executive and legislature would also be problematic. More likely is greater push towards delegation although that path will eventually lead to questions being asked about the extent to which some form of federalization is required, particularly where the devolved institutions start to compete with each other over, for example, corporation tax.

---

8. See <http://www.constitutionreformgroup.co.uk>.

20.3 Legal education

Chapter 19 of the fifth edition of this book noted that there were proposed changes to the way that legal education operated. It was thought that by the time of the sixth edition, these changes would be known, but if anything they are even less certain.

Until 2014, the two principal professions operated an agreed framework for legal education. As noted in Chapter 10 this was abolished and the *Solicitors Regulation Authority* and *Bar Standards Board* have now decided to go off and 'do their own things', much to the disquiet of universities who would prefer a single regulator to deal with. The SRA and BSB have very different views on how members should be recruited. The BSB has continued to believe that the Bar should be a graduate profession, i.e. that a person seeking admission to the Bar should first hold a degree.[9] This does not need to be a law degree, but the BSB is clear that in the absence of a law degree, some form of conversion programme should be required[10] as they believe that graduate-level knowledge of the law is an important part of the training programme.

The SRA appear to believe that solicitors need not be graduates. They suggest that a person should have a degree, apprenticeship, 'or equivalent'.[11] Quite what is equivalent to a degree is not made clear. This does seem somewhat odd when, for example, nursing and the police, which were traditionally considered to be vocational professions, have chosen to become graduate professions. The SRA believe that this could make it more accessible to a broader range of persons and, admittedly, this could be true of an apprenticeship degree, but it neglects the existence of CILEX. Someone without a degree is already able to access the legal professions through CILEX. Whilst many may be happy to remain as a Fellow, particularly as judicial appointments and equity partnerships are now available, some will wish to progress to becoming a solicitor. Thus the existing pathways already permit this.

The SRA also suggests abolishing the QLD, GDL, and LPC. Instead will come a 'solicitors qualification examination' (SQE).[12] There would be two parts to this; the first would be on legal knowledge and the second would be on legal practice. The tests would be computer-based examinations rather than any form of traditional examination. There would be no requirement that a person has done a law degree or GDL before attempting to do so. Could this mean that training providers will create 'crammer courses' that try to ensure the requisite knowledge is developed in a short time? Perhaps, but it would probably be challenging to do this. Instead, it is more likely that a law degree or GDL-type course would provide the best chance of success. Indeed, the SRA acknowledges this by suggesting that law degrees are likely to integrate the preparation of the SQE 1 into the curriculum.[13] If this goes ahead, that is likely to be true. Not all students will be prepared for the SQE, but those who choose to do so are likely to have modules that are designed towards those elements of the SQE that are

9.   'Future Bar Training: Consultation on the Future of Training for the Bar: Future Routes to Authorisation' (Bar Standards Board, London 2016).
10.   'Future Bar Training: Consultation on the Future of Training for the Bar: Future Routes to Authorisation' (Bar Standards Board, London 2016).
11.   'A New Route to Qualification: The Solicitors Qualifying Examination' (Solicitors Regulation Authority, London 2016).
12.   'A New Route to Qualification: The Solicitors Qualifying Examination' (Solicitors Regulation Authority, London 2016).
13.   'A New Route to Qualification: The Solicitors Qualifying Examination' (Solicitors Regulation Authority, London 2016) 9.

not included within an LL.B. (eg wills, professional practice, and certain procedural rules). The question is whether this will be at the expense of studying other types of law that could, for example, broaden the educational view of a student and/or assist them in identifying the area of law that they wish to practise in? It would seem relatively inevitable.

The LPC would be abolished and replaced by SQE 2 that would cover more practical skills. This would be taken alongside work-based learning, ie the training contract, although conceivably some or all of these skills could also be developed in the undergraduate curriculum (eg working with the *Citizens Advice Bureau*, a law clinic, or a 4-year placement degree). There is perhaps greater legitimacy in this proposal in that the usefulness of a vocational academic qualification by itself could be questioned. It would make more sense for the LPC (and BPTC for that matter) to be studied alongside real-life work, so that theory and practice are integrated from the start.

It is not known what the SRA will do. The initial consultation was received negatively but the SRA are continuing to press ahead. They believe that the SQE is the only way of guaranteeing standards, although why they believe that (a) external quality assurance regulators such as the *Quality Assurance Agency* cannot do so, and (b) computer-based exercises are hallmarks of standards, is less clear. It is likely that the law degree will continue for some time yet. As has been noted, the easiest way of getting the knowledge required for the SQE is likely to be by studying law as an undergraduate or postgraduate degree. Firms are also likely to continue to desire students who have degrees rather than other forms of qualifications, due to the conservative nature of the profession. However, the LPC is in a more precarious situation and it is almost certain to be replaced.

20.4 Transforming the justice system

In September 2016 the Lord Chancellor, the Lord Chief Justice, and the Senior President of the Tribunals published a joint paper on radical reforms that will be made to the courts, tribunals, and justice system. Underlying the proposed reforms is a desire to ensure that the justice system works as efficiently and effectively as possible for everyone who comes into contact with it, while simultaneously modernizing the system to update and speed up processes which often delay or inhibit the delivery of justice. In short, they want to ensure that the 'courts and tribunals always deliver swift and certain justice for everyone'.[14]

Central to the proposed reforms is the digitization of the courts and tribunals systems and the use of new technology. A single online system for cases across the criminal, civil, family, and tribunal jurisdictions will be introduced. Underlying this is the aim that all cases will at least be started online, with others being dealt with entirely online. The digitization of the court system is expected to have the consequence that fewer buildings are needed as more cases are dealt with online, and the buildings that are used being modernized to reflect the increased use of technology.

In relation to the criminal courts, pre-trial cross-examination will be introduced nationally from 2017. This will allow 'vulnerable witnesses to pre-record their

14. Lord Chancellor, Lord Chief Justice, and Senior President of Tribunals, *Transforming our Justice System* (Ministry of Justice 2016) 5.

evidence ahead of the trial taking place',[15] to make giving evidence a less stressful and distressing experience. The criminal courts will also be unified under a single leadership structure to ensure that cases are heard in the appropriate court as quickly as possible. Finally, consideration will be given to the introduction of 'problem-solving' courts, designed to 'change offender behaviour by tackling underlying problems, such as drug and alcohol addiction or mental illness'.[16]

In the civil courts the reforms aim to reduce costs for those involved in litigation, as well as making the recovery of costs and debts easier. In the family courts, uncontested divorce and probate cases will have their processes simplified and as much as possible put online. Finally, the tribunals will be 'part of a single justice system with a single judiciary'[17] by 2020. This finalizes the merging of the courts and tribunals, which initially began with the merger and creation of *HM Courts and Tribunals Service*.

It is clear that the proposed reform programme is ambitious. However, its success is clearly a priority with commitments to embrace reform from the judiciary, and significant additional investment from the government to modernize the courts and tribunals and invest in the criminal justice system.

20.4.1 **Combined judiciary?**

In Chapter 8 it was noted that the Lord Chief Justice and Senior President of Tribunals have begun to integrate the tribunal and courts judiciary. One of the aims of the modernization programme is to consider ways in which we can think of a combined judiciary. That is to say, there is no differential between judges and tribunal judges. This could take some time to achieve, but it is an interesting aim.

Part of the argument is that if judges are now deployable in either the tribunals or the courts, does it matter what we call them? Instead of having titles such as 'District Judge', 'Circuit Judge' and 'Puisne Judge' should we just have grades? The titles are arguably meaningless now, with district judges and circuit judges sitting in the same location: it merely describes their work and pay-grade. It was noted that First-Tier Tribunal judges rank alongside district judges. Should these be referred to as 'Grade 7 judges'? Similarly judges of the Upper Tribunal are Grade 6.1 judges, the equivalent of a circuit judge. Should we refer to them that way? That would seem a radical step, but what if we went the other way? Instead of a judge being a judge of the First-Tier Tribunal, could they not be known as district judges and judges of the Upper Tribunal be known as circuit judges? This may bring formality into the tribunal system but this has begun in any event, partly because of the increasingly judicial nature of tribunal work, particularly in the Upper Tribunal.

The Employment Appeal Tribunal (EAT) suffers from staffing problems. It deals with some extremely complicated and sensitive cases that deserve to be dealt with by a puisne judge. However, the High Court of Justice also suffers from delays and too much work. Does it help either the courts or tribunals if a person is appointed puisne judge and then immediately lent to the EAT? Similarly, a judge assigned to the EAT will only sit for a finite period of time, but is there not an argument for having a

---

15. Lord Chancellor, Lord Chief Justice, and Senior President of Tribunals, *Transforming our Justice System* (Ministry of Justice 2016) 8.
16. Lord Chancellor, Lord Chief Justice, and Senior President of Tribunals, *Transforming our Justice System* (Ministry of Justice 2016) 10.
17. Lord Chancellor, Lord Chief Justice, and Senior President of Tribunals, *Transforming our Justice System* (Ministry of Justice 2016) 15.

permanent puisne judge dealing with complicated employment matters? Rather than create a puisne judge for these purposes, would it not be better to create a Grade 4 judge to be located within the EAT?

This all seems quite radical at present. However, if there is to be a unified judiciary then it is likely that consideration will need to be given as to the titles that judges are assigned. Otherwise there is the danger that judges will be perceived in a particular way, partly because of the title that they are given. 'Her Honour Judge X' sounds more grand than 'Judge X' and yet both could be Grade 6.1 judges. Assumptions may be made about their respective positions given their titles. Could we look forward to a position where, as in the USA, most judges are just called 'Justice X' or 'Judge X'? It would be one way to simplify a unified judiciary, but it is likely that many judges and lawyers would prefer the etiquette to continue.

20.4.2 Judicial promotion

Whilst a truly unified judiciary is some way off, it is perhaps easier to see how a career judiciary could be developed. It was noted in Chapter 8 that tribunal judges come from a variety of professions and not just the Bar. This is to be welcomed and it is possible that the grading of judges makes it easier to identify how promotion may be sought.

Whilst it is unlikely that promotion at the senior levels will change any time soon (although it should be noted that the Ministry of Justice is, at the time of writing, consulting on whether leadership positions, including Heads of Division, should be for a fixed period of time[18]), how a person reaches certain positions could easily be changed. It is conceivable to identify a position whereby X starts their career as a First-Tier Tribunal judge and then progresses to a circuit judge or an Upper Tribunal judge. Or an Upper Tribunal judge becomes a puisne judge. If more appointments were by promotion, with the applicant using their judicial experience to demonstrate their competence, then it may also mean that the Bar's grip on the judiciary will be relaxed.

The Judicial Appointments Commission is starting to look at this. For example, at the time of writing there is a competition for puisne judges. There are two 'tracks'. The first is for existing judges and practitioners who meet the eligibility criteria, but the second track is for section 9 judges only, ie existing judges who have been vetted by the JAC to be eligible to sit as a puisne judge when requested by the Lord Chief Justice. Part of the application process is to 'provide up to 3 judgments, or notes of judgments or determinations', which clearly demonstrates that the JAC will take judicial experience into account. It was noted in Chapter 8 that relatively few circuit judges have become puisne judges (and, to the best of our knowledge, no tribunal judge has been appointed direct[19]) and it is to be hoped that this approach may lead to other exercises (eg for the circuit bench) adopting a similar approach (for example, specifically targeting those who are already district judges or tribunal judges).

---

18.   'Modernising Judicial Terms and Conditions: Consultation on Proposals to Introduce a New Tenure for Fee Paid Office Holders, Provide for Fixed Term Leadership Positions and Modernise Judicial Terms and Conditions' (Ministry of Justice, London 2016).

19.   Mr Justice Hickinbottom (soon to be Hickinbottom LJ) served as a tribunal judge but he then became a circuit judge before returning to the tribunals but as a circuit judge. He was then elevated to the puisne bench but this would be from the circuit bench not the tribunal bench.

20.5 Leaving the EU

The final element to discuss returns us to the introductory comments within this chapter. The biggest change in the future will be withdrawal from the EU. Regardless of what some may hope, it is beyond doubt that the UK will now withdraw. The only issue is how and what the consequences of this will be. Many of the issues that relate to withdrawal from the EU are outside the scope of this book because they relate either to constitutional law or EU law. However, some aspects do relate directly to the English Legal System.

The UK will formally leave the EU when two things happen. The first is that Article 50 is satisfied. This means either reaching an agreement with the twenty-seven remaining Member States or leaving without a deal. The second step is that the *European Communities Act 1972* is repealed. At the time of writing, the government has refused to discuss in detail how they plan to withdraw from the EU, arguing that to do so would jeopardize the Article 50 negotiations. To others, the delay is to provide time to establish a position for the Article 50 negotiations. Whichever is true, the *European Communities Act 1972* will need to be repealed.

With the repeal of the 1972 Act, EU legislation will cease to become *directly applicable* to UK law. No more will regulations form part of domestic law. No more will there be a requirement to give effect to EU directives. It will be for domestic law to decide what the position is. Or will it? Advocates of those who sought to remain within the EU point out that the UK will still need to comply with many of the laws. Product safety is a good example. If a UK company wishes to sell products to the EU then the product will need to comply with EU law. Whilst products sold in the UK would not, it is unlikely that a company would want two production lines or to publicly suggest that there were 'safe' and 'almost safe' products.

Whilst some believe that Article 50 will lead to the end of the influence of EU law, this is not true. What is known of the government's position is that they wish to put forward a 'great repeal Bill'.[20] The idea behind this is that at the time the 1972 Act is repealed, all existing EU law is made part of domestic law. From that point on, Parliament can choose whether to accept, amend, or repeal the law. However, that will take a considerable amount of time. Nobody knows how much time is required, but both sides agree that a considerable amount of legislation came from Europe. If all of this law is to automatically become part of UK law then realistically we are talking decades before all of this law is analysed and considered.

Therefore EU law is going to remain 'in force' for some time. Advocates of withdrawal can argue that Parliament is ultimately in control and therefore is invoking sovereignty to *choose* to accept EU law in this manner and that is true. However, as pointed out before, whatever MPs and media outlets say, Parliament chose in 1972 to make EU law automatically part of domestic law so is there a difference? Ultimately the answer must be 'yes' because Parliament could choose to amend the law, something that it would not be entitled to do if the UK remained in the EU.

By leaving the EU, however, certain aspects of the law change. Whilst EU law will operate under the 'guise' of being domestic law, there will be no steer from the EU as to what the purpose of the law was. Whilst in the EU, domestic courts can—and in

---

20.   See 'Legislating for Brexit: The Great Repeal Bill' available at <http://researchbriefings.parliament.uk/ResearchBriefing/Summary/CBP-7793>.

some instances must—refer a matter to the Court of Justice of the EU for a decision on what the law means. To Eurosceptics, this is an example of the EU's failings: why should a European court tell the UK what the law says? However, to others, it allows a European court to identify a consensus position. Referrals to the EU have been used by the UK government, not just used against them, but they will now go. Whilst we will be bound by the law (in the sense that it becomes part of UK law), we will not be able to ask Europe what they meant by this provision. Of course the courts could, and in all likelihood will, look to how the Court of Justice has ruled, but they need not follow that decision.

Depending on the deal that is struck with the EU, indeed *if* a deal is struck with Europe, it is quite possible that some parts of EU law will remain part of UK law. It is quite possible that, for example, to stay within the customs union we may accept that we are bound by some laws. As already noted, we will need to comply with standards for goods and services, but this is less about the manner in which law is made than about ensuring that the end result complies with the legislative requirements of Europe. Legislation will be required to implement any such deal and that will mean clarifying the role EU law has within the English Legal System.

What of law students? Both the BSB and SRA have been clear that EU law remains one of the 'qualifying' subjects and this is unlikely to change. Even if we are not subject to EU law, we need to understand the rules of Europe so we can make deals with them. Europe is likely to remain one of the most important trading partners for the UK and thus a knowledge of EU law is going to be as important as contract law, tort law etc. It is likely that you, and those students who follow you, will need to study EU law for some time yet. Indeed, if we're right that it will take decades to 'unpick' EU law from UK law, an understanding of EU law could become quite lucrative for a fledgling lawyer …

Index

661

665

G

H

685

Aim High!
Concentrate

Concentrate Revision & Study Guides
Concentrate Questions & Answers
Both series available in your campus bookstore
or buy online at **www.oup.com/lawrevision**